D1096216

THE COMPLETE BOOK OF LIGHT OPERA

Mander & Mitchenson

Evelyn Laye as "Sarah" in *Bitter Sweet*

THE COMPLETE BOOK OF LIGHT OPERA

by

MARK LUBBOCK

with an American section

by

DAVID EWEN

APPLETON-CENTURY-CROFTS

NEW YORK

First Published in Great Britain in 1962 by
PUTNAM & COMPANY LIMITED
42 Great Russell Street · London WC1
and Printed by
Richard Clay & Co Ltd
Bungay · Suffolk

For Bea

Preface

The Complete Book of Light Opera is intended to serve as a companion volume to *Kobbé's Complete Opera Book.* Although by reason of the immeasurably slighter content of the material there is inevitably less historical detail worth recording, each section of the present volume contains an introduction in which the development of the school of Light Opera of the appropriate country is discussed.

Lord Harewood's comments in his preface to *The Complete Opera Book* on selectivity apply equally to *The Complete Book of Light Opera.* It is obviously impossible, if the book is to be kept within manageable proportions, to include *all* operettas that people might see or hear, indeed might have seen or heard, for some of the appeal of the present volume, to the older generation of theatre-goers at any rate, will be bound up with nostalgia. My selection is limited to the lightest genre of Light Opera. I have deliberately excluded *Opéra Comique* (Delibes, Adam, Auber), *Singspiel* (Mozart, Lortzing, Nicolai) and such light operas as Vaughan Williams' *The Poisoned Kiss*, Arthur Benjamin's *The Prima Donna*, Ethel Smyth's *The Boatswain's Mate*, and Ballad Opera. Nor does my American colleague, David Ewen, include such operas as Menotti's *The Telephone* and *Amelia Goes to the Ball*, or earlier operas by composers like Walter Damrosch, Charles Wakefield, Cadman and Deems Taylor.

Our selection is intended to feature "Musicals" which the traveller is likely to encounter. Visitors to the Vienna Musical Festival of 1962, for instance, will have had an opportunity of hearing at the Volksoper: Gilbert and Sullivan's *The Mikado*, Von Suppé's *Boccaccio*, Johann Strauss's *Die Fledermaus* (also given at the Staatsoper), *The Gipsy Baron*, *A Night in Venice*, Oscar Straus's *A Waltz Dream*, Leo Fall's *Rose of Stamboul* and *Madame Pompadour*, Offenbach's *La Vie Parisienne*, Franz Lehár's *The Merry Widow* and *The Land of Smiles* and Emmerich Kálmán's *Countess Maritza*, and *The Circus Princess*, and, at the Raimundtheater, his *Lady Aus U.S.A.* (*Arizona Lady*). Also in the 1962 season, at Munich, the Theater am Gartnerplatz has in its repertoire: Johann Strauss's *Die Fledermaus*, *The Gipsy Baron*, *Die Tänzerin Fanny Elssler* (a pasticcio), Carl Zeller's *The Bird Seller*, Franz Lehár's *Land of Smiles*, Kálmán's *The Gipsy Princess*, and Offenbach's *Orpheus in the Underworld*, while Das Theater "Die Kleine Freiheit" offers *Irma La Douce*, and the Münchener Theater in Der Brienner Strasse gives *Lilac Time* and Ralph Benatzky's *Meine Schwester und ich* (*My Sister and I*).

In addition to the above, there can be seen in Germany revivals of Lincke's *Frau Luna* (Aachen and Giessen), Lehar's *The Count of Luxemburg*, Benatzky's *White Horse Inn* (Dortmund), Offenbach's *Madame Favart* (Flensburg and Karlsruhe), *La Périchole* (Heidelberg), Richard Heuherger's *The Opera Ball* (Darmstadt), Millöcker's *The Beggar Student* (Düsseldorf/Duisburg),

Millöcker-Mackeben's *The Dubarry* (Giessen), Lehár's *The Czarevitch* (Karlsruhe), to mention only a few. The Berlin Festival is giving a new production of *My Fair Lady*, while Cologne has enjoyed recent productions of *The Pajama Game*, *Can-Can*, *Bells Are Ringing*, *The Crooked Mile*, *Irma La Douce*, *Kiss Me Kate* and *West Side Story*.

Paris has a revival of Oscar Straus's *Rêve De Valse* (*A Waltz Dream*) at the Mogador, and has also seen recent revivals of Hervé's *Mam'selle Nitouche*, Offenbach's *Mesdames de La Halle* and *La Vie Parisienne* (given by the Jean Louis Barrault players) and Reynaldo Hahn's *Ciboulette* (at the Opéra Comique).

In London we have had revivals by the Sadlers Wells Company of *The Merry Widow*, *The Land of Smiles*, *Die Fledermaus*, *Orpheus in the Underworld*, *La Vie Parisienne* and *Merrie England*. The D'Oyly Carte Opera Company is always with us, and since the expiry of copyright on the works of Gilbert and Sullivan, Sadlers Wells have presented *Iolanthe* and *The Mikado*, and Sir Tyrone Guthrie *HMS Pinafore* and *The Pirates of Penzance*. Amateur talent still turns to old musical comedy. Recently I was present at a performance of *The Geisha* in Hammersmith and on my week-end drive from London to Essex I pass theatrical bills announcing productions of *The Gipsy Baron* and *The Dubarry*.

Commercial success has inevitably influenced my choice, but many shows—such as Walter Leigh's *The Pride of the Regiment* and *Jolly Roger*, and Alfred Reynolds' *Derby Day*—find their place because I admire their quality.

MARK LUBBOCK

London
Easter 1962

CONTENTS

PARIS

BERLIN

LONDON

LIST OF ILLUSTRATIONS

PARIS

PARIS

French *Opérette* and *Opéra bouffe* as we know it today began in Paris in the Second Empire. The inventor was an eccentric but highly gifted individual, who called himself Hervé. His real name was Florimond Ronger and he was always known by the nickname "Le Compositeur Tocqué" ("The Crazy Composer"), the title of one of his shows. As a young man Hervé was appointed organist to a lunatic asylum in Paris called the Bicêtre Hospital, where his mother had charge of the wardrobe. He worked hard to inculcate the principles of music into the minds of the poor mad inmates and was in the habit of organising concerts and dramatic performances for their benefit. The latter consisted of little musical plays which he wrote himself, and in which the lunatics acted, his idea being to keep their minds off their morbid obsessions. The fame of these performances soon spread abroad and enterprising theatrical managers came to see them. As a result Hervé was offered the post of conductor at the Théâtre du Palais-Royal, where he rapidly established himself as a successful composer of the genre which he had created in the *Opérette*. But it was the genius of Offenbach which consolidated and developed what Hervé had invented. In collaboration with two brilliant librettists, Henri Meilhac and Ludovic Halévy, Offenbach gave Paris a series of satirical operettas, which enchanted and convulsed his audiences: satires on Court and society, such as *La Vie Parisienne*, *La Belle Hélène*, *Orphée aux Enfers*, *Barbe-Bleu*; satires on big business in *Les Brigands* (with much appreciated *bon mots* like "One must steal according to the position one occupies in society"), and on the army in *La Grande Duchesse de Gérolstein*. Offenbach's satirical operettas were designed specifically for the pleasure-loving public of the Second Empire. But with the coming of the Franco-Prussian War and the fall of the Emperor Napoleon III the mood of Paris changed. People who had starved in the siege were no longer in the mood for frivolity. The Republicans, especially, associated Offenbach with the Imperial regime and regarded his ribaldry as immoral and his satire as merely idle jesting. It was on the crest of this Republican wave that Charles Lecocq sailed into prominence, supplanted Offenbach in public favour and changed the face of operetta. Lecocq's attitude to the theatre differed fundamentally from that of Offenbach. He regarded it as the home of escapism, and operettas like *La Fille de Madame Angot* and *Le Petit Duc* are devoid of any direct and critical bearing on real life. They incline more towards the form of *Opéra comique* made popular by Auber and Scribe. Lecocq set a fashion, which was followed by subsequent theatre-composers: by Planquette with *Les*

Cloches de Corneville and Audran with *La Poupée*, *La Cigale et la Fourmi* and *La Mascotte*; by Messager with *Les P'tites Michu* and *Véronique* and by Reynaldo Hahn with *Ciboulette*. Other composers worthy of mention are Louis Varney, Louis Ganne, Claude Terrasse and Henri Christiné (who both attempted to revive the Offenbachiade, with *Monsieur de la Palisse* and *Phi-Phi* respectively), Maurice Yvain, José Padilla and Francis Lopez.

Mam'zelle Nitocheu

Comedy-Operetta in Three Acts

By HENRI MEILHAC *and* ALBERT MILLAUD

Music by HERVÉ

First produced on the 26th January, 1883, at the Théâtre des Variétés, Paris, with Madame Judic as "Denise".

CHARACTERS

CÉLESTIN *alias* FLORIDOR, *a composer*
MAJOR CHATEAU-GIBUS
VICOMTE DE CHAMPLATREUX
CORINNE, *an actress*
THE MOTHER SUPERIOR, *of a Convent School*
DENISE DE FLAVIGNY (*"Mam'zelle Nitouche"*)
CHORUS OF PUPILS, OFFICERS, DRAGOONS AND ACTORS, ETC.

The action takes place in a Convent School, a Paris Theatre, and a military barracks in the year 1883.

ACT I

In a convent school, Le Couvent des Hirondelles, conducted with extreme piety by the Mother Superior, the appointment of organist is held by a young man called Célestin. In the presence of the nuns and their pupils he poses as a solemn, earnest and deeply religious character. He leads, however, a double life as Floridor, composer of hilarious operettas, and he has a raffish mistress, Corinne, a star of the musical stage. His latest opus, *Babet et Cadet*, is nearing production and he is already a prey to first-night nerves. Among the pupils of the convent is a young girl, Denise, who is in many ways parallel in character to Célestin. She feigns an apparent piety so successfully that she is the apple of the Mother Superior's eye, but under this cloak of holiness she is, in fact, entirely worldly and longs for a gay life of parties, dancing and theatres. She has discovered Célestin's score of *Babet et Cadet* and has already committed to memory the leading part, including one of the "hit" numbers about a toy soldier:

On the day the curtain rises the Mother Superior's brother, Major Chateau-Gibus, arrives with important news. Denise's parents have decided to marry her off to a brother officer of his, Lieutenant le Vicomte de Champlatreux, and she is to return home that very day. Denise puts on a convincing act of grief and unwillingness to leave the convent, but she is secretly delighted, especially at the prospect of being able to attend the first night of *Babet et Cadet*. As the curtain falls the Mother Superior, the nuns and her fellow pupils wave good-bye to Denise, who drives away to this gay ensemble:

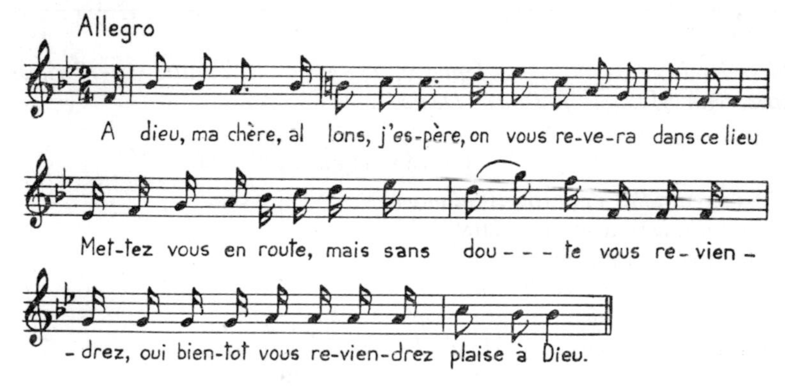

ACT II

The scene is the foyer of the Théâtre de Pontaroy. It is the premiere of Célestin's operetta *Babet et Cadet* and the first act has just come to a triumphant end. In the audience are Major Chateau-Gibus and Lieutenant le Vicomte de Champlatreux, and during the interval the Lieutenant makes the acquaintance of Denise. He is quite unaware that he is talking to his prospective fiancée, for Denise is visiting the theatre incognito and calls herself Mam'zelle Nitouche. The two get on famously and de Champlatreux learns in the course of conversation that the young girl happens to be word and note perfect in the leading part. Through an unlucky mischance Corinne, Célestin's mistress, sees him in intimate conversation with Denise, and being of a temperamental and violently jealous nature she creates an appalling scene. Working herself up into an uncontrollable rage, she takes off her make-up and sweeps out of the theatre, leaving *Babet et Cadet* with two acts to go and no leading lady. This is Denise's big chance. She jumps into the breach and triumphantly finishes the show, and the Vicomte de Champlatreux, carried away by her courage, talent and beauty, makes her a fervent declaration of love. But the troubles of this stormy first night are not yet over. It so happens that Major Chateau-Gibus is also one of Corinne's lovers, and as Célestin is being fêted by the public as the successful composer, the Major suddenly recognises him as his rival for Corinne's favours. With cries of jealous rage he advances on the unfortunate Célestin, who in terror seizes Denise by the hand and manages to reach the safety of a dressing-room, barricading the door against the Major's noisy assaults. With dismay they listen to his threats to remain outside the door all night if need be.

ACT III

SCENE 1. During the night, in order to evade the clutches of the furious Major, Célestin and Denise escape from the theatre dressing-room by a window. Unfortunately they fall into the hands of a military patrol, who, suspecting them of criminal intentions, arrest them and march them back to barracks. Here they find the Vicomte de Champlatreux, who is delighted to see them and immediately orders their release. He opens a bottle of wine, and Denise joins the officers in singing some suitably military airs. This jolly party is broken up by the arrival of Major Chateau-Gibus, who has discovered that Célestin and Denise have eluded him, and with difficulty the two of them escape again, on horseback.

SCENE 2. The last scene takes place at the convent on the following morning. Denise has returned to the fold, piously confessing to the Mother Superior that mundane pleasures and the call of marriage hold no attractions for anyone so spiritually inclined as herself. The Mother Superior is deeply touched by such lofty ideals in one so young. Later Major Chateau-Gibus arrives with a message from the Vicomte de Champlatreux to the effect that now that he has met Mam'zelle Nitouche he no longer wants to marry Denise. On receiving the message Denise obtains permission from the Mother Superior to talk to the erring suitor. "Maybe I can turn his soul to righteousness," she urges. The Mother Superior consents and leaves the couple alone. Returning shortly afterwards she is startled to find them in each other's arms, but she accepts Denise's explanation that she is prepared to sacrifice herself by marrying the Vicomte to save him from future temptation. Fervently the Mother Superior calls Heaven to witness the virtues of Denise, her good angel, while the Major and Célestin, now reconciled to sharing Corinne, cynically raise their eyebrows and murmur, "Angel?" They know better.

Le Mariage aux Lanternes

Operetta in One Act

By JULES DUBOIS (M. CARRÉ *and* L. BATTU)

Music by JACQUES OFFENBACH

First produced on 10th October, 1857, at the Théâtre des Bouffes-Parisiens, Paris. London production on 11th May, 1860, at the Lyceum Theatre (in French), with Monsieur Geoffroy as "Guillot".

CHARACTERS

GUILLOT, *a farmer*
DENISE, *his cousin*
FANCHETTE } *two widows*
CATHERINE }
A NIGHT-WATCHMAN

A little one-act pastoral, originally presented under the title *Le Trésor à Mathurin* at a concert in 1853. The libretto was by Offenbach's friend Léon Battu, and its ingredients included the chiming of bells, lights in the darkness and love. Offenbach's intention was to impress the *Opéra comique*, but in this direction the results were quite negative. Four years later, however, he had the satisfaction of seeing this despised piece leap to world fame as *Le Mariage aux Lanternes.*

The action takes place outside a country farm-house, and a prominent feature of the set is a large barn standing in the shade of a lime-tree. Guillot, the farmer, has fallen in love with his cousin, Denise, a young girl, who keeps house for him. Though she returns his love, Denise's life is plagued by Guillot's jealousy. In addition she has to stand patiently by, watching the amorous approaches of two widows, Fanchette and Catherine, both of whom are anxious to marry Guillot. Their quarrelling duet ("Ah! la fine, fine mouche, la sainte ni touche"), which ends in a free fight in which each throws her shoes at the other's head, is one of the gems of a score which Offenbach seldom equalled and which belongs to the style of *The Tales of Hoffman.* Denise, despairing of ever being able to come to terms with Guillot, writes to their

Uncle Mathurin, begging for his advice. Guillot has also written to Uncle Mathurin, announcing that he wants to get married and asking for money. In time Denise and Guillot both receive answers to their letters. Denise's reply reads: "I know the cure for your unhappiness, my dear niece. You need a good husband, and I will provide him. Seat yourself under the lime-tree by the barn this evening and at the first stroke of the angelus bell he will appear." To Guillot his uncle writes, informing him that under the lime-tree by the barn he will find hidden treasure. That evening at the hour of the angelus Denise is waiting under the lime-tree, when Guillot appears with a spade. Fanchette and Catherine are also at hand, as their presence is needed for an attractive quartette ("Voici l'angelus qui sonne"). Guillot's energetic digging is quite without reward and he has given up all hope of finding the treasure when he notices Denise asleep under the lime-tree, Uncle Mathurin's letter in her hand. Taking the letter gently from her, Guillot reads it and realises that in Denise he has found his hidden treasure; and by the light of the villagers' lanterns the two celebrate their betrothal.

Un Mari à la Porte

(A Husband on the Mat)

Operetta in One Act

By ALFRED DELACOURT (ALFRED CHARLEMAGNE LARTIQUE) *and* L. MORAND

Music by JACQUES OFFENBACH

First produced in Paris on 22nd June, 1859, at the Théâtre des Bouffes-Parisiens. First London production by the London Opera Club on 21st February, 1950, at the Fortune Theatre, translated by Geoffrey Dunn, with Max Worthley, Maureen Springer and Rose Hill.

CHARACTERS

MARTIN, *a dun*
SUZANNE, *his newly married wife*
ROSINE, *her friend*
FLORESTAN DUCROQUET, *a composer*

The scene is a sitting-room in an apartment on the third floor of a house in Paris. It is well furnished and the table is laid for supper for two. Other features of the room are two windows, one looking out on to the street, the other over the garden, and a built-in cupboard.

When the curtain rises the room is in darkness, lighted only by the moon, shining in through a window. In the distance an orchestra is playing a waltz and obviously the owners of the apartment are giving a dance. Suddenly in the darkened room there is a violent clatter of fire-irons in the grate and down the chimney slides a young man, distraught and covered with soot. Looking round for cover he spies the cupboard. He takes refuge in it and closes the door as Suzanne and Rosine enter the room. They are attractive young women in full evening dress and are arguing energetically. Suzanne is reviling her newly-married husband and Rosine is endeavouring to defend his behaviour. At the same time she seeks to soothe Suzanne, who is threatening to bar her bedroom door against her erring spouse.

The row between Suzanne and her husband is a storm in a teacup and has arisen over a letter which he refused to show her, declaring it to be a business letter which would not interest Suzanne. Rosine advises her to make peace with her husband and Suzanne calms down and promises to follow Rosine back to the ballroom after bathing her eyes, which are red from crying. Standing before a mirror, Rosine sings to the accompaniment of the distant orchestra:

After her song Rosine goes back to the ballroom, leaving Suzanne in a much mellower mood and quite determined to be reconciled to her husband. As she is making-up her face before the mirror, Suzanne becomes aware of sounds in the cupboard, where, to her amazement, she discovers a young man in the last stages of suffocation. She demands to know how he got in, and he answers: "Down the chimney." "Then you must depart the way you came," she insists. But the young man refuses, declaring that he is no chimney-sweep. Eventually Suzanne persuades him to attempt a descent through the window into the garden, where the lawn is soft and a convenient vine climbs up the wall of the house. He has just disappeared out of the window when Rosine returns from the ballroom in search of Suzanne. She exclaims at Suzanne's foolhardiness in exposing herself to the night air, and is about to close the window when a loud cracking of branches is heard. The vine has given way under the young man's weight and with difficulty he crawls to safety back through the window. They demand his name and into the startled ears of the two ladies Florestan Ducroquet pours his doleful story. He is a composer of works for the stage and at the moment is seeking production of his opera *The Midnight Corpse*. A mutual interest in music has brought him into contact with the pretty wife of a tailor called Murner, a man of an Othello-like jealousy. Tonight he believed that this tailor would be absent from home and took the opportunity to visit his wife, but their cosy tête-à-tête was rudely interrupted by the premature return of the furious husband. Having beaten poor Florestan black and blue he locked him into the kitchen, vowing in the morning to have him arrested for debt; for, as Florestan admits, he is heavily in debt and the tailor is one of his principal creditors. Looking around for some means of escape, Florestan discovered a ladder leading up on to the roof. Scaling it, he crossed the roofs of several houses and, coming to a likely-looking chimney, climbed down it—and here he is. This adventure, he finishes, is the climax to a week of misery spent dodging a dun, a monster by the name of Martin. "Good heavens!" exclaims Suzanne. "My husband!" "Oh no!" wails Florestan in despair. "So I have walked straight into the lion's den! At all costs I must escape." At this moment Martin's voice is heard, calling to Suzanne to let him in, for she has taken the precaution of locking the door. The ladies call to Martin to go away and return later, and he retires. For the moment the situation is saved. But Rosine and Suzanne are adamant that Florestan must leave, and they try to persuade him to give himself up and face a debtor's prison. Florestan in a panic snatches the key from the door, and Rosine wrestles with him to recover it. Florestan has his back to the open window and inadvertently drops the key into the garden. At this moment Martin returns and demands to be admitted, but the ladies refuse to open the door and Suzanne tells him cheerfully that they are perfectly happy and have for company a handsome young man. Florestan, forgetting himself, bursts out with: "Madame, are you mad?" Rosine whispers to him to shut up, but Martin merely congratulates Suzanne on her gift for mimicry and refuses to be jealous. They sing a quartette, with Martin still outside the door, in which they taunt him, repeating a popular tag applicable to a jealous husband:

Martin now stages a dramatic act, threatening suicide if Suzanne does not open the door. He even goes to the length of firing off a pistol, and Suzanne, frightened, confesses that the key of the door has fallen into the garden. Martin hurries down to find it and the ladies threaten Florestan with what Martin will do to him when he discovers him in their company. Florestan resigns himself to a death-leap into the street and is about to hurl himself down, when as though by a miracle a house-painter's cradle appears outside the window. It is unoccupied, and lying on it is a workman's smock. In a moment the ladies have helped him into the smock and he has climbed out and on to the cradle. With a shout Martin tells them that he has found the key, and as he unlocks the door, to be ecstatically embraced by Suzanne, Rosine at the window watches Florestan, precariously dangling, lower himself out of sight.

Orphée aux Enfers
(Orpheus in The Underworld)

Opéra-Féerie in Four Acts (twelve scenes)

Taken from a German scenario By KARL CRAMER

By HECTOR CRÉMIEUX

Music by JACQUES OFFENBACH

First production in two acts (four scenes) on 21st October, 1858, at the Théâtre des Bouffes-Parisiens, Paris, with Mademoiselle Lise Tautin and Messieurs Desiré, Leonce and Bache. The revival, which the present synopsis follows, took place on 7th February, 1874, at the Théâtre de la Gaieté with Mademoiselle Marie Cico and Messieurs Christian, Montaubry and Alexandre. London production on 26th December 1865 at the Haymarket Theatre (in English), adapted by J. R. Planché as Orpheus in the Haymarket, *with Louise Keeley, David Fisher and Mr. Burtleman.*

CHARACTERS

ARISTAEUS (*Pluto in disguise*)
JUPITER, *father of the Gods*
ORPHEUS, *Director of the Academy of Music, Thebes*
JOHN STYX, *ex-King of Boeotia and Pluto's servant*
EURYDICE, *married to Orpheus*
PUBLIC OPINION, *rôle de travestie*
JUNO
CUPID
DIANA
CHORUS OF GODS AND GODDESSES, NYMPHS, USHERS, ETC.

The action takes place in mythological times in the countryside near Thebes, on Mount Olympus and in the Underworld.

ACT I

The scene is the countryside adjacent to Thebes. In the distance can be seen the houses on the outskirts of the city. To left and right of the stage are two huts.

Over the door of one is the notice: "Aristaeus, Manufacturer of Honey: Wholesale and Retail. Warehouse on Mount Hymethus." The other hut exhibits a placard which reads: "Orpheus, Principal of the Academy of Music, Thebes. Violin lessons given." Stage centre at the back stands a temple, its colonnade bearing the inscription "ΕΥΔΟΕΙΑ". As the curtain rises a procession of municipal councillors passes by, accompanied by Public Opinion, a character resembling the Chorus of Greek Drama. After being introduced by a lictor he explains in a monologue his duties as Protector of Public Morals. He then indicates to the audience the approach of Eurydice and withdraws to wait in the wings, whence he proposes to act as *Deus Ex Machina*. Eurydice enters, gathering flowers, which she weaves into a garland to hang on the door of her lover, Aristaeus. As she picks the flowers she sings a gay little song ("La Femme dont le cœur rêve n'a pas de sommeil"). At the end of her song her husband Orpheus appears, his violin in his hand. Orpheus' and Eurydice's marriage is on the rocks. They have come to the parting of the ways and find one another unspeakably boring. In a duet Orpheus threatens her with his concerto, which he tells her plays for an hour and a quarter, and Eurydice inveighs to heaven against her husband in a famous tune:

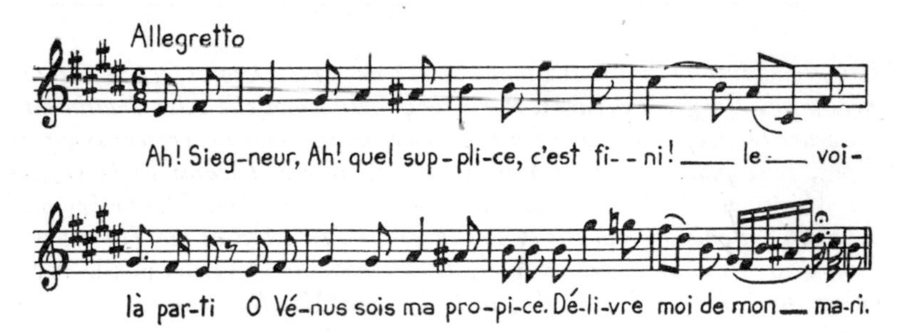

They both desire a separation, but Orpheus tells Eurydice that in his position he dare not offend Public Opinion and must take a strong line about her lovers, and he hints darkly that he has already taken reprisals against Aristaeus. He then goes off to his daily duties at the Academy, and Eurydice departs to try and discover the nature of his reprisals. Her exit is followed by a pastoral ballet danced by shepherds, shepherdesses and fauns. As the ballet finishes a plaintive oboe heralds the arrival of Aristaeus. After his recit. and song ("Je suis Aristée, berger d'Arcadie") he is joined by Eurydice. She warns him that Orpheus has discovered their affair and has filled the ground round his hut with poisonous serpents. Aristaeus pooh-poohs the idea of danger and walks straight home, while Eurydice, with courage born of love, follows him. Suddenly with a cry she stops with one foot in the air. She has been bitten by a snake. Aristaeus lays her down gently on a bench and turns to the audience. There is a clap of thunder and a flash of lightning, and in place of Aristaeus stands a figure in dark robes holding a trident, who announces that he is Pluto, King of the Underworld. Aristaeus was merely a disguise. He tells Eurydice that she is dying and she sings a beautiful "Invocation to death":

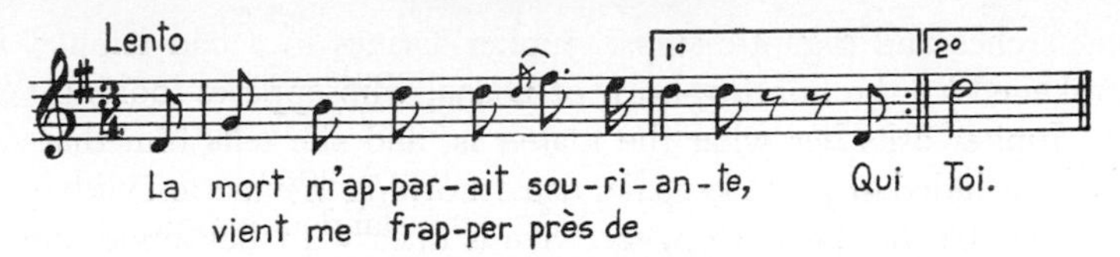

Pluto hands her his trident, and with it she writes a farewell message to Orpheus on his front door in letters of fire:

"Je quitte la maison
Parce que je suis morte.
Aristée et Pluton,
Et le diable m'emporte."

With a disparaging comment on her poetic gifts, Pluto takes Eurydice's hand, and sinking through the ground he carries her off to the Underworld. When Orpheus returns home, reads her message and realises he is rid of Eurydice, he is delighted. He rushes straight off to break the glad news to his mistress, the nymph Maquilla. But every path he tries to take is barred by Furies, who threaten him ("Anathème sur celui qui, sans pitié, refuse une larme même à sa moitié"). Public Opinion now appears. He reads Orpheus a moral lecture on his attitude to the loss of his wife and insists that he accompany him to Olympus to demand from Jupiter that Pluto return Eurydice. Orpheus is anything but willing, but Public Opinion is adamant. Orpheus insists on first making arrangements for his pupils, and going to his hut he opens the front door. Out come twenty small children, each armed with a violin. They bid Orpheus a fond farewell:

"N'allez pas là-haut
Oublier Toto
Lolo ni Coco
Partez donc presto
O grand Maëstro."

Then, encouraged on his way by the returning Municipal Councillors, who assure him that honour demands his journey, Orpheus departs reluctantly with Public Opinion in the direction of Mount Olympus.

ACT II

The curtain rises on an expanse of darkened sky above Mount Olympus. It is the early hours of morning before the dawn, and on the clouds which float in the sky Gods and Goddesses are sleeping. Venus, Mars and Cupid separately return from amorous, nocturnal assignations and seek their beds. Morpheus appears, followed by Night, who stands on a blue globe—the clock of Heaven—swinging a pendulum. As the clock strikes, the Hours appear one by one, and in a ballet proceed to chase away Night and various Dreams, coloured black, pink, gold and silver. Eventually Dawn is ushered in. The clouds turn pink and slowly vanish, revealing the marble hemisphere of Olympus, with gleaming arches and gigantic steps. Jupiter arrives in a bad temper, having been awakened by the hunting-horn of Diana, who appears looking very depressed. Jupiter asks her what the matter is, and she tells him that she had arrived at a secluded grove to keep her usual morning assignation with her lover, Actaeon, but that he did not appear. She is uneasy in her mind about him. Jupiter then tells Diana that their affair was becoming the subject of gossip among mortals and that, not wanting her to compromise herself further, he has changed Actaeon into a stag. Diana is furious, and the other Gods side with her in criticising Jupiter's high-handed action. With his dubious record he is the last person to comment on or interfere with other people's love affairs. What with Jupiter's tyranny and the boredom of Olympus, with its monotonous diet of nectar and ambrosia, life is not worth living. The Gods retire grumbling and Juno joins Jupiter. She reports the rape of Eurydice by Pluto, and Jupiter sends Mercury off to inquire into the situation. On his return he reports that Pluto absented himself from the Underworld for six weeks and then came back, bringing with him a lady called Eurydice. Pluto is sent for, and on arrival denies that he carried off Eurydice. The other Gods side with Pluto and remind Jupiter in the gayest of songs of his own infidelities, of how he made love to Danae in a shower of gold, to Europa in the form of a bull and to Leda as a swan.

Mercury announces the arrival of two strangers, and Public Opinion enters, dragging with him the unwilling Orpheus. Asked what they require, Orpheus, under the threatening eye of Public Opinion, replies, to Gluck's famous air from his *Orfeo*, that he has been robbed of his Eurydice. The Gods are obviously already aware of his troubles, as they insist on finishing the song. Jupiter orders Pluto to restore Eurydice to her husband, and Pluto's dismay at the prospect of losing her is almost as great as Orpheus' dismay at the prospect of her return. Jupiter further announces that he will visit Hades in person to see that his orders are carried out. "Take us all with you," beg the Gods and Goddesses, and when he grants their request they join in a hymn of praise. The departure is organised to a gay galop tune to which all the Gods and Goddesses of classical mythology parade round, and the older Gods are driven away in an omnibus labelled "Ligne P.Y. Champs-Elysées–Barrière des Enfers", with Mercury acting as conductor. Finally the heavens open and Apollo's chariot drawn by white horses slowly descends, and all the young Gods and Goddesses pile into it as the curtain falls.

ACT III

The first scene is Pluto's study in his palace in the Underworld. Here Eurydice is imprisoned with John Styx, an elderly eccentric, as her gaoler. She detests him and suspects that he drinks, although he swears he never touches anything stronger than the waters of Lethe, which do make him very forgetful. He tries to entertain Eurydice with reminiscences of his earthly existence as King of Boeotia. (Song: "Quand j'étais roi de Béotie".)

After his song, sounds of the arrival of Jupiter, Pluto and all the other Gods and Goddesses are heard. Acting under his master's instructions, John Styx bundles the protesting Eurydice into the next room and turns the key on her.

Jupiter and Pluto enter the study and Jupiter calls on Pluto to produce Eurydice. As Pluto still denies carrying her off, Jupiter asks him if he is prepared to stand trial, and Pluto declares he is most anxious to clear his good name. "That is a good thing," says Jupiter, "as I have already arranged with Themis to have you tried before the Judges of the Underworld." An usher now announces that the court is sitting and the scene changes to the court-room. Minos, Eacus and Rhadamanthus are the judges. Two of them, Jupiter's sons by Europa, greet their father respectfully. Pluto is cross-examined. He calls, as supporting witness, the savage dog Cerberus, and a scene follows which is reminiscent of Scribe and Offenbach's comic opera *Barkouf*. Cerberus is brought into court and takes the stand. He barks loudly in reply to questions from the judges, and Pluto surreptitiously feeds him. The judges interpret Cerberus' evidence as testifying that Pluto returned to Hades alone: he brought no lady with him. But Jupiter declares the evidence to be biased, that Pluto curried favour with the witness by feeding him. He forces Cerberus' jaws open to prove his point and the ferocious dog seizes him by the arm. This leads to an uproar which ends by Jupiter producing an electric gadget he carries around with him and launching a thunderbolt. The court, judges, Cerberus, Pluto and John Styx disappear into the nether regions, and Cupid appears at Jupiter's side and perches on the arm of a chair. The scene has changed back to the study, where Cupid proceeds to rebuke his master for involving himself with these underworld officials, and promises to trace the whereabouts of Eurydice. He summons aid, and some twenty little "agents de Police de l'Amour" appear, wearing Phrygian helmets and carrying truncheons, who join Cupid in a song in which they imitate the sounds of kissing. In a pause in the song answering sounds of kissing are heard, coming from next-door, and one of the policemen says: "She's in there." They wish to break down the door, but Jupiter won't hear of it. Instead, he proceeds to change himself into a fly and creeps through the key-hole, which grows larger and larger till the whole of the adjoining room becomes visible and moves forward on a truck. Eurydice is lying on a couch, and Jupiter, in the guise of a fly, buzzes round her, enchanted by her beauty. Eurydice is greatly taken with the elegant fly ("Belle insecte à l'aile dorée") and they sing and buzz a duet together, at the end of which he assumes his own voice and reveals his identity. Eurydice is enchanted to have made a conquest of the Father of the Gods and begs him to carry her off. "There will be an opportunity during the dancing after supper," he tells her, and they just manage to get out of the room before Pluto, now wise to Jupiter's pursuit of Eurydice, hurries in. John Styx, who had caught sight of them as they were leaving, is no help, as he has been at the waters of Lethe and has forgotten all about it; and Cupid finally confuses the issue by filling the stage with flies. Pluto gives up in despair, and the act finishes with a grand ballet of insects.

ACT IV

In an enormous hall in Hades a bacchanalian revel, in which all the Gods and Goddesses take part, is in progress. Eurydice has by now been turned into a Bacchante by Jupiter, who hopes that Pluto may not recognise her in this guise.

Cupid persuades her to sing a Bacchic hymn, and she obliges with "Evohé, Bacchus m'inspire". After this, the dancing starts. Jupiter dances a minuet, and then follows the famous can-can tune with its abandoned refrain.

During the dancing Jupiter and Eurydice attempt to escape, but are stopped by Pluto, who tells Jupiter he is not such a fool as Jupiter supposes, and that he was never for a moment deceived by Eurydice's appearance. He reminds Jupiter of his promise to restore her to her husband. "Goodness!" each exclaims, "I had forgotten all about him." "That is not an uncommon experience with lovers," says Pluto cynically. Now the sound of a distant violin is heard, and in comes Orpheus, still reluctantly accompanying Public Opinion. He renews his request for the return of Eurydice, and Jupiter tells him she will be restored to him on one condition. On their return to Earth, Orpheus is to walk in front of Eurydice and in no circumstances must he look back at her until they have passed the barriers of Hades, on pain of losing her forever. Orpheus agrees and sets off, followed by Eurydice, but they have not gone far before Jupiter, producing his electric gadget, discharges a thunderbolt. With an involuntary movement Orpheus turns, and Eurydice is lost to him for ever. He is of course overwhelmed with joy, and so is Eurydice, for now that she is a Bacchante she is at liberty to divide her favours between both her lovers, Jupiter and Pluto.

La Belle Hélène

Operetta in Three Acts

By HENRI MEILHAC *and* LUDOVIC HALÉVY

Music by JACQUES OFFENBACH

First produced on 17th December, 1864, at the Théâtre des Variétés, Paris, with Hortense Schneider, Mademoiselle Silly and Monsieur Dupuis. London production on 30th June, 1866, at the Adelphi Theatre (in English) as Helen or Taken from the Greek, *adapted by F. C. Burnand, with Miss Furtardo, Miss E. Woolgar, Mrs. A. Mellon and J. L. Toole.*

CHARACTERS

PARIS, *son of King Priam*
MENELAUS, *King of Sparta*
HELEN, *his consort*
AGAMEMNON, *King of Kings*
ORESTES, *his son*
CALCHAS, *High Priest*
ACHILLES, *King of Phtiolides*
AJAX I, *King of Salamis*
AJAX II, *King of Locris*
CHORUS OF COURTIERS, SLAVES, SOLDIERS AND TOWNSFOLK

ACT I

In a public square in Sparta, before the Temple of Jupiter, a crowd of worshippers are presenting offerings such as flowers, fruits, cheese and cages containing doves. The flowers predominate, to the evident disgust of the High Priest, Calchas, who observes in the words of an English adaptor, Charles Lamb Kenney:

"Time was when to the Temple gates were driven
Whole herds and flocks to buy the smiles of Heaven.
We now for pay must sorry stuff like this count.
The Gods, alas! The Gods are at a discount."

It is the Feast of Adonis, a day of sacrifice, and Helen arrives with her Ladies-in-Waiting, pausing outside the Temple to sing the well-known song:

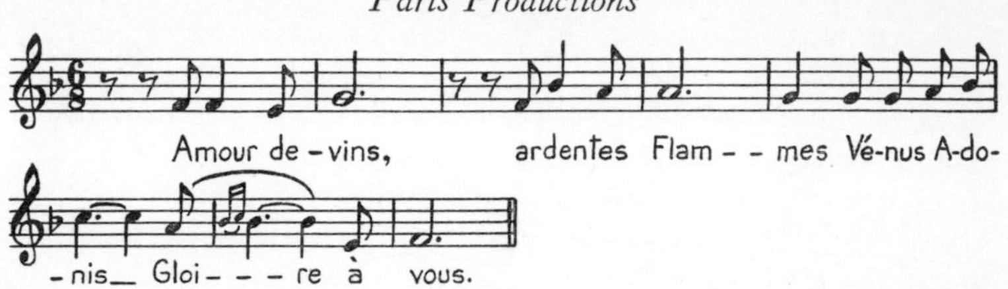

The song over, Helen inquires of Calchas whether he has any fresh news of "the business on Mount Ida". It appears that at a Beauty Contest, at which the three contestants were the Goddesses Juno, Minerva and Venus, Prince Paris, son of Priam, King of Troy, was the adjudicator. He awarded the prize to Venus, and in return she has promised him the favours of the most beautiful woman in the world, Helen, consort of Menelaus, King of Sparta. On his arrival in Sparta, disguised as a shepherd, ostensibly to take part in a World Competition of Wit and Intellect, Paris seeks out the High Priest and tells his story in one of the hit numbers of the operetta:

Calchas arranges a meeting of Paris with Helen and it is a case of love at first sight on both sides. The Kings of Greece now appear: the two Ajaxes, Kings of Salamis and Locris; Achilles, King of Phtiolides; Agamemnon, King of Kings, and Menelaus, King of Sparta—but in the Competition of Wit and Intellect which follows none of the Kings can compete with the Shepherd in the intelligence tests. On being proclaimed the victor, the Shepherd discloses his identity and receives from Helen's hands the prize. To the High Priest's inquiry if he is now content, Paris answers that he would be still more so were Menelaus absent. So Calchas announces to the populace that the oracle is about to speak. There is a roll of thunder and Calchas declares that Jupiter has commanded King Menelaus to depart for a month to the mountains of Crete. Loudly protesting, Menelaus sails away and there is now no obstacle to the love of Helen and Paris.

ACT II

Act Two takes place in Helen's bed-chamber. Since the departure of her husband, Menelaus, she has had a bad attack of conscience and is keeping Paris at a distance, to his discomfiture. With her eyes on a picture of her mother, Leda, and her father, Jupiter, in the form of a swan, Helen sings her famous invocation to Venus:

Presently there is a sound of music without, and Bacchis, a maid, reminds Helen that she has invited the Kings of Greece, Calchas, and Orestes to supper and a game of cards. In the game which follows, Calchas wins large sums from all the players in turn, but is finally detected in cheating and the party breaks up in disorder, with four furious Kings pursuing the High Priest out of the room. Paris, having failed to make any headway in his advances to Helen, now solicits the aid of Calchas. Promising to do his best, the High Priest visits Helen late at night and at her request prays to the Gods to send her a dream in which Paris shall appear to her. No sooner is she asleep than Paris, disguised as a slave, slips into the room and, falling on his knees by the bed, takes Helen in his arms. When she awakens, Calchas comforts her with the assurance that she is really dreaming. The lovers, alone at last, sing the enchanting duet:

As the duet finishes with the lovers in each other's arms, the curtains are roughly pulled apart and Menelaus enters. His cries of rage and dismay summon the Court, who all turn on Paris. Helen is quite impenitent, however, and declares that any husband who returns home unexpectedly late at night is a fool. Paris, secure in the love of Helen and with Venus' backing, retreats, defying the Kings and promising to return.

ACT III

It is a week since Menelaus' ill-timed return from Crete, and the whole Court is enjoying a summer holiday on the beach at Nauplia. Menelaus is still bitterly taxing Helen with her infidelity, and is puzzled and irritated by her repeated assertion that he is talking nonsense and that: "It was all a dream." In Sparta everything is at sixes and sevens, and an epidemic of divorce has broken out. Husbands are leaving their wives and wives their husbands wholesale. Calchas declares this to be the scourge of Venus. After all, when Paris awarded her first place in the Beauty Competition she promised him the most beautiful woman in the world, and Menelaus had therefore no right to drive away Paris from Helen's side. The Kings back up the High Priest; Menelaus must give up his wife for the good of the country and sink the husband in the King. Menelaus is indignant and informs them all that he has already written to Venus requesting her to send her Grand Augur to settle the matter. At this moment a magnificent galley is seen approaching the shore. At the prow stands the Grand Augur himself, surrounded by Cupids, who form the crew. The Grand Augur disembarks and, addressing the populace, delivers a message from Venus. With a little co-operation from King Menelaus, he says, the matter of Paris and Helen can be satisfactorily settled. Helen is to return to Cythera with the Grand Augur, sacrifice a hundred white heifers to the Goddess and that will settle the whole affair. It now only needs Helen's consent —but the Queen is reluctant to go, until the Grand Augur is seen to whisper in her ear. She then hastily embarks and the galley puts out to sea. And now, to the consternation of the spectators on shore, the Grand Augur throws off his disguise. He is Paris. With a shout of triumph he bids Menelaus say farewell to Helen for ever; their destination is Troy. Menelaus, crying with rage, throws himself into the sea in an effort to follow the galley, and is saved from drowning by Calchas; while Agamemnon hurries away to mobilise an army and launch the Trojan War.

Barbe-Bleu

(Bluebeard)

Opéra bouffe in Three Acts

By HENRI MEILHAC *and* LUDOVIC HALÉVY

Music by JACQUES OFFENBACH

First produced on 5th February, 1866, at the Théâtre des Variétés, Paris, with Hortense Schneider and Monsieur Dupuis. London production on 2nd June, 1866, at the Olympic Theatre (in English) as Bluebeard Repaired, *with Miss Galton and Mr. W. M. Terrott.*

CHARACTERS

BOBÈCHE, *King of Brittany*
CLÉMENTINE, *his consort*
HERMIA, *their daughter*
BLUEBEARD, *a Knight*
BOULOTTE, *a peasant girl*
POPOLANI, *an alchemist*
COUNT OSCAR, *Court Chamberlain*
PRINCE SAPPHIR
BLUEBEARD'S *ex-wives*
CLÉMENTINE'S *ex-lovers*
CHORUS OF PEASANTS AND COURTIERS

The action takes place in the fifteenth century.

ACT I

The scene is a village square in the neighbourhood of Nantes in Brittany. The landscape is dominated by a mighty castle, perched on a rocky mountain height, seat of the nobleman known as Bluebeard. Bluebeard, a powerful vassal of Bobèche, King of Brittany, suffers from a constitutional disability—a wife is a positive necessity to him on the one hand; but, on the other, no sooner has he married than he wearies of her company and summons his private alchemist, Popolani, to poison her.

When the opera begins Bluebeard has already disposed of five wives in this arbitrary fashion, and Popolani now has instructions to find him a sixth. Popolani's method of setting about his task is to summon the girls of the village to a lottery. Their names are thrown into a basket and a draw is made, the winner to be Bluebeard's sixth wife. The winning girl on this occasion is Boulotte, a regular country wench, strong and lusty, gauche and clumsy, with no airs and graces to recommend her. Boulotte is thrilled at the prospect of becoming the bride of the much-married Bluebeard, roundly declaring that she is not afraid of any man.

While the village awaits the arrival of Bluebeard to inspect his new bride, Popolani meets an old acquaintance, Count Oscar, Chamberlain of King Bobèche's Court. Count Oscar is in search of His Majesty's long-lost daughter, Princess Hermia, abandoned in babyhood in favour of her younger brother, whose succession the King preferred. Count Oscar by tactful questioning identifies the Princess as a village girl calling herself Fleurette, and is about to remove her to the royal palace when Bluebeard arrives on the scene and catches sight of her. He is overcome by admiration and secretly determines that she shall become his seventh wife. For the moment he is all agog to inspect his village bride, and this scene contains his well-known song on the joys of wedded bliss:

Bluebeard is enchanted with the appearance of Boulotte, whom he compares to a portrait by Rubens, and the act finishes with the return of the whole entourage to his castle to prepare for the wedding.

ACT II

SCENE I. The first scene takes place in the throne-room of King Bobèche's palace. The King is announced, and when he is seated on his throne Count Oscar, Court Chamberlain, reads out the royal agenda for the day. This includes the betrothal ceremony of the long-lost Princess Hermia to Prince Sapphir. But not even the prospect of this joyful occasion is able to raise His Majesty's spirits. Brooding and heavy-eyed, he maliciously eyes young Alvarez, whom he suspects of being the lover of his consort, Queen Clémentine. In the past he has given orders for four of her suspected lovers to be liquidated, and he now instructs Count Oscar to have Alvarez tactfully put to death. But Count Oscar, like Bluebeard's alchemist, has a rooted objection to murder and has kept Queen Clémentine's lovers alive, but carefully concealed in the palace; and Alvarez now joins them in hiding. The next item on the royal agenda is the ceremonial visit of the nobleman Bluebeard to present his sixth wife. On hearing this the King flies into a great rage. He declares that he will not receive in audience a man who has already liquidated five women. Count Oscar mildly observes that His Majesty himself has already liquidated five men, but he is severely snubbed. No! Bluebeard must be punished. "But that, Your Majesty, is not possible," points out Count Oscar. "Bluebeard is well equipped with artillery, but Your Majesty has not a single cannon; they all went last year to pay for your equestrian statue." The King on hearing this is very cast down. "And what does my Master of Artillery do with the money I pay him, now he has no artillery?" he asks. "He spends it on parties for his women," replies Count Oscar. "Then he might at least invite me to one occasionally," comments the King sadly.

Bluebeard now arrives to present his sixth wife, but the first person he sets eyes on is Princess Hermia, and the sight of her beauty reinforces his determination to make her his seventh. Meanwhile the state visit is a fiasco. Boulotte, a simple village girl, is ignorant of all Court etiquette and makes one stupid *faux-pas* after another. The climax is reached when she is instructed to kiss the King's hand. Mounting the throne, she throws her arms round his neck and kisses His Majesty on both cheeks. In the uproar which follows Boulotte is forcibly ejected from the palace, and Bluebeard, mortified and ashamed, escorts her home.

Scene 2. The second scene of Act Two is set in the Alchemist's Laboratory in Bluebeard's castle, to which Bluebeard brings Boulotte at dead of night. He coldly tells her that she is to die, like his five other wives, to make way for a seventh, and though she pleads piteously for her life he cynically insists on a change of love in this enchanting duet:

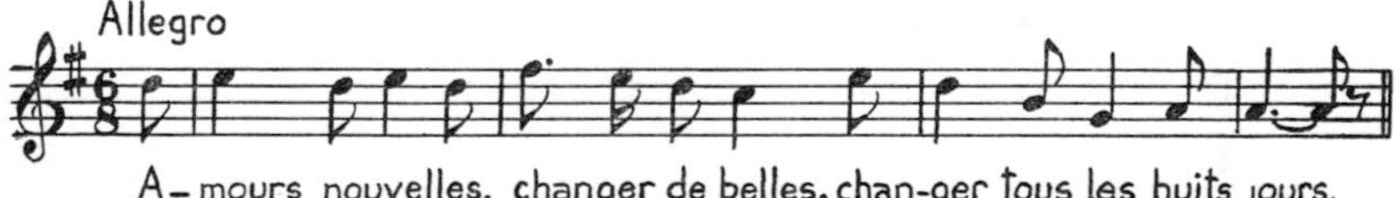

Bluebeard finally leaves Boulotte to the tender mercies of Popolani with instructions that she is to be immediately poisoned. Protesting that she does not want to die, Boulotte swallows the fatal draught and falls unconscious. When Bluebeard returns to confirm that she is really dead, Popolani proudly points to the corpse, and Bluebeard, after removing Boulotte's wedding ring, goes out gaily singing. Then Popolani, alone with the corpse, applies to it an electric current from a galvanic battery and after a short time Boulotte opens her eyes and sits up, restored to health and vigour. Popolani has merely administered a drug to Boulotte, as he has done to the other wives in the past, who, unknown to Bluebeard, are all alive and well. The crafty alchemist has agreed to spare their lives on condition that they all become his mistresses. Boulotte is now introduced to her five fellow-wives, and Popolani judges the moment ripe to confront Bluebeard with all his wives and teach him a lesson. So, led by Popolani, the ladies leave the comfortably furnished tomb where they have been living.

ACT III

The last Act takes place in a state room of King Bobèche's palace. It is midnight and the marriage of Princess Hermia to Prince Sapphir is about to be solemnised, when suddenly Bluebeard appears. He interrupts the ceremony to inform the King that his sixth wife has expired, and coolly demands the hand of Princess Hermia as his seventh. When King Bobèche indignantly refuses, Bluebeard insolently threatens to blow them all sky-high with his heavy guns. As a last resort to keep his bride, Prince Sapphir challenges Bluebeard to a duel. In the fight he falls wounded and unconscious, and Bluebeard leads the Princess unresisting to the altar. During the wedding ceremony Popolani arrives at the palace with Bluebeard's six wives. They are joined by Queen Clémentine's five lovers and Prince Sapphir, recovered from his duel. After the wedding Count Oscar announces an entertainment by a troupe of Bohemians. They are of course the wives and lovers, suitably masked, and as a finale to their entertainment they remove their masks, to the horror of both Bluebeard and King Bobèche. As the curtain falls the five wives pair off with Queen Clémentine's lovers, Princess Hermia is restored to Prince Sapphir, and the ebullient Boulotte decides to take on Bluebeard and make herself responsible for his future behaviour.

La Grande Duchesse de Gérolstein

Opéra Bouffe in Three Acts

By Henri Meilhac *and* Ludovic Halévy

Music by Jacques Offenbach

First produced on 12th April, 1867, at the Théâtre des Variétés, Paris, with Hortense Schneider and Monsieur Dupuis. London production on 18th November, 1867, at the Royal Opera House, Covent Garden, (in English) with Julia Mathews, Augusta Thomson, W. Harrison, Frank Mathews, Fred Payne and Aynsley Cook.

Characters

THE GRAND DUCHESS	BARON PUCK
WANDA	GENERAL BOUM
FRITZ	BARON GROG
PRINCE PAUL	CHORUS OF COURTIERS, PAGES, SOLDIERS, ETC.

ACT I

The scene is a military encampment in the countryside of Gérolstein. The troops are under canvas and are commanded by an old fire-eater, General Boum. War has been declared against a neighbouring state and the army are only waiting to be inspected by their hereditary ruler, the Grand Duchess, before marching into battle. The young Grand Duchess is conspicuous for wanting—and getting—her own way. She also has an enthusiastic eye for a soldier:

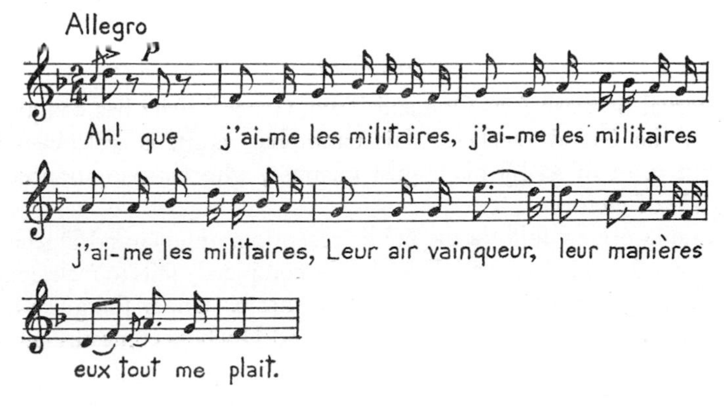

In the ranks is a certain Private Fritz, who is detested by the Commander-in-Chief because he has gained the affections of a peasant girl, Wanda, in whose direction General Boum has cast a roving eye. But the General dislikes Private Fritz even more when, on the arrival of the Grand Duchess, his good looks attract her notice. She calls him out of the ranks to converse with her, and he presently finds himself promoted from private to corporal—and a few minutes later, when she hears he has a sweetheart, to the rank of lieutenant. The Grand Duchess greatly enhances her popularity with her soldiers by singing them the Song of the Regiment.

In the highest spirits after the army's tumultuous applause for her song, the Grand Duchess further promotes Lieutenant Fritz to the rank of captain. Prince Paul of Steis-Stein-Steis-Laper-Bottmoll-Schorstenburg now arrives. The Chamberlain of the Court, Baron Puck, is trying to arrange a marriage between the Grand Duchess and this Princeling. But she despises his effeminacy, and for the moment has eyes for no one but handsome Captain Fritz. General Boum, Prince Paul and Baron Puck sit down with the Grand Duchess to consider General Boum's plan of campaign. The General's plan as unfolded by him strikes Fritz as so incompetent that he bursts into the conversation, ridiculing Boum's proposed form of attack, whereupon the Grand Duchess invites Fritz to sit down at the conference table and elaborate his views. When Boum protests that no one who is not an officer of superior rank and also noble is entitled to take part in a council of war, the Grand Duchess announces that she will promote Fritz to the rank of General, create him Baron de Vermont-von-bock-bier and make him Commander-in-Chief of the army. To his skill and valour the conduct of the campaign is now committed and as a crowning proof of her confidence she entrusts to Fritz the sacred broadsword which her late father wielded in battle:

To the strains of this martial air the curtain falls on the departure of Fritz at the head of the Grand Duchess's army.

ACT II

In the interval between Acts One and Two, General Fritz has conquered the enemies of the Grand Duchess. His triumphal return is welcomed by the people, but most of all by his august mistress, who listens entranced to his exciting tale of victory.

A private interview follows the public reception. The Grand Duchess is by now head over heels in love with Fritz, but he completely fails to realise the other great victory he has won in conquering her heart. Under the guise of intercession for a lady of her own Court, the Grand Duchess confesses her passion for Fritz in this tender song:

Mortified by Fritz's indifference to her charms and angered by a request he later sends her, to be allowed to marry Wanda that night, the Grand Duchess resolves to revenge herself. Learning of a conspiracy between Puck, Boum and Prince Paul to assassinate Fritz, she bursts in upon the conspirators and offers to join them. Her proposal is joyfully accepted. As the curtain falls the four conspirators plan to strike down Fritz that very night as he enters the bridal suite.

ACT III

Scene 1. The first scene of Act Three takes place in the Crimson Suite, the scene of the projected murder of Fritz. A new character has joined the conspirators in the person of Baron Grog, Emissary of the Elector of Steis-Stein-Steis-Laper-Bottmoll-Schorstenburg, who has been fruitlessly attempting to obtain audience of the Grand Duchess in order to persuade her to marry Prince Paul. Baron Grog is exceptionally good-looking, and her resentment against Fritz entirely vanishes, extinguished by her new interest in the fascinating stranger. She accordingly cancels the assassination, and when General Boum blusters about his honour and his right to slay Fritz, the Grand Duchess proposes that the General meet Fritz in single combat. The General's consternation is great, but he cannot well refuse. When Fritz and Wanda enter on their way to the cathedral to get married, Puck explains to Fritz that he must fight with Boum before he can wed, and hurries him away. Fritz is reluctantly compelled to postpone the wedding for an hour or two and the disgruntled guests in the cathedral await the arrival of Wanda and her bridegroom.

Scene 2. The last scene takes place in the market-place of Gérolstein, dominated by the cathedral. General Boum has failed to turn up to fight with Fritz, and this has given Puck an idea for a plan by which not only may Fritz be discredited in the eyes of the Grand Duchess but Prince Paul be made to appear a hero. Puck strikes a bargain with Fritz, who somewhat unwillingly agrees. Fritz shall (at a price) appear in the guise of one who has been ignominiously defeated in a duel. He is to tell the tale that he has met a mysterious, masked adversary. Puck, knowing the romantic temperament of the Grand Duchess, foresees that she will feel sentimentally drawn towards the unknown hero who can defeat so distinguished a fighter as General Fritz. At the proper moment the masked adversary will appear and turn out to be none other than Prince Paul. The bargain struck, Fritz goes off to dishevel himself and Prince Paul to assume his disguise. The wedding guests, tired of waiting, appear from the cathedral, and the Grand Duchess enters, eager for news of the duel. Presently General Boum makes a rather shame-faced appearance and is obliged to admit that he has failed to meet his antagonist. Next comes Fritz, cut about and battered, and tells the tale of the masked warrior. The Grand Duchess, to the delight of Puck and Boum, deprives Fritz of all his honours and decorations, but to their disgust bestows them on Baron Grog. Grog gratefully thanks the Grand Duchess in the name of himself and his wife, and she learns that he is a proud father of six. He is immediately stripped of his new honours and General Boum is reinstated as Commander-in-Chief of the army. Puck now gives the signal for the *dénouement*. Shouts are heard, and, to the acclamations of the crowd, there enters the victor in the supposed fight, masked and cloaked. In her enthusiasm the Grand Duchess promises him her hand as a reward for his chivalry. He throws off his disguise and Prince Paul is revealed. Resignedly she agrees to keep her promise. She forgives Fritz and consents to his marriage with Wanda, and as the curtain falls the two couples proceed to the cathedral accompanied by the cheers and good wishes of the populace.

La Vie Parisienne

Opéra Bouffe in Four Acts

By HENRI MEILHAC *and* LUDOVIC HALÉVY

Music by JACQUES OFFENBACH

First produced on 31st October, 1866, at the Théâtre du Palais Royal, Paris, with Mademoiselle Zulma Bouffar and Monsieur Léonce. London production on 30th March, 1872, at the Holborn Theatre, with Claire Shelley, Lionel Brough, Lottie Venn and Frederick Mervin.

CHARACTERS

BARON DE GONDREMARCK *from Sweden*
BARONESS DE GONDREMARCK
RAOUL DE GARDEFEU, *a boulvadier*
BOBINET, *his friend*
JOSEPH, *a courier*
METELLA, *a demi-mondaine*
POMPA DI MATADORES, *a wealthy Brazilian*
FRICK, *a shoe-maker*
GABRIELLE, *a glove-maker*
ALFRED, *a head waiter*
CHORUS OF RAILWAY OFFICIALS, SHOP ASSISTANTS, TOWNSFOLK, SERVANTS AND RESTAURANT GUESTS

The action takes place in Paris during the Second Empire.

ACT I

The scene is a Paris railway station, la Gare du l'Ouest. On a platform awaiting the arrival of the train from Trouville are two young men, Bobinet and Raoul de Gardefeu. As the time for the train's arrival approaches they eye each other jealously, for each knows that the other, like himself, has come to meet a young woman called Metella. But when the train arrives Metella alights from it with a new young man and cuts both Bobinet and Gardefeu dead. Resignedly Bobinet decides to return to the salons of the Faubourg St. Germain and recoup his sunken fortunes by falling in love with an heiress.

Gardefeu is about to follow him when he runs into his late valet, Joseph. Joseph, no longer in domestic service, is now a guide, attached to the "Grand Hotel", his job being to introduce tourists to the delights of Paris. He has come to the station to meet Baron and Baroness Gondremarck, a wealthy couple from Sweden, and Gardefeu bribes Joseph to allow him to take his place. He has decided to set his cap at the Baroness. So, when the Swedish couple arrive, Gardefeu presents himself as an envoy sent by the "Grand Hotel" especially to meet them and he takes the couple to his house, which he passes off as an annexe of the hotel. This promising beginning results in the most comic situations. A conspicuous passenger on the platform is a Brazilian followed by two little negroes carrying his luggage. In this infectious song he describes how he has come to Paris from his native Rio de Janeiro determined to plunge into the vortex and squander his substance on the ladies of the town.

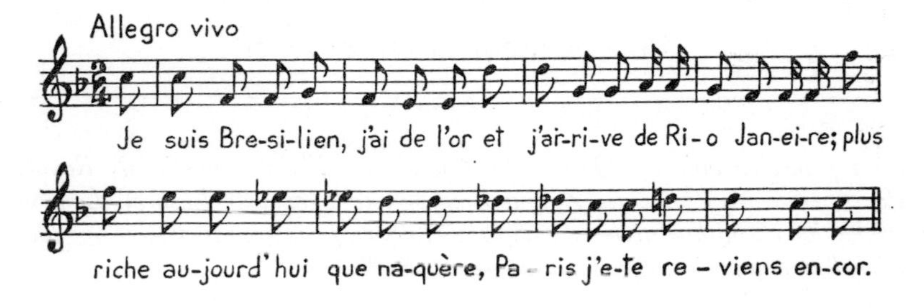

ACT II

Gardefeu now arrives at his apartment, bringing with him the Baron and Baroness Gondremarck. They accept his story that the "Grand Hotel" is full and that they have in consequence been put up in the annexe, and though they complain that the place is a bit on the small side, are tolerably content with their rooms. The Baron asks what time dinner will be and is much put out to be told that it will be served at his convenience. "But is there no table d'hôte?" he asks. "I certainly have no intention of dining alone with the Baroness. I have come to Paris for gaiety, for laughter, for company, to see life, for a bit of fun. If there is no table d'hôte I shall certainly change my hotel." To pacify the Baron, Gardefeu assures him that there will be a table d'hôte served at seven o'clock, and is faced with the problem of raising a sufficient crowd to impersonate hotel guests at the table d'hôte. He is fortunate enough to encounter his shoe-maker, Herr Frick, a German, and a most attractive little glove-maker, Gabrielle, who promise to present themselves at seven with a host of their colleagues and friends to play the part of hotel guests.

Bobinet now appears. He has heard of the arrival of the Swedish couple and wishes to know if he can be of any help. He suggests a grand reception for the following evening. His aunt, the Dowager Countess of Quimper-Karadec, is away from home and her flat will be at his disposal. The flat is large and luxurious and he will play host in the rôle of Admiral Walter of the Swiss Navy. As guests he can provide the Countess's butler, her footman, her parlourmaid and the porter's six nieces. The Swedes are bound to be most impressed.

Gardefeu delightedly accepts the offer and hurries Bobinet away before the Baron becomes too familiar with his appearance. Shortly before dinner the Baron takes Gardefeu aside. He has a letter of introduction from a Swedish friend, Baron de Frascata, to a certain Mademoiselle Metella. Does Gardefeu know the young lady and will he have the letter delivered? The Baron is obviously hopeful of seeing a bit of life in Metella's company. Gardefeu promises to see that the letter is delivered, and later Metella herself arrives and is introduced to the Baron. As dinner-time approaches Frick and Gabrielle appear with news that their colleagues are on their way. Frick is dressed as the sort of army major to be seen at any table d'hôte in any hotel and Gabrielle, as a colonel's widow, sings this charming song:

Frick and Gabrielle are followed by a noisy throng of glove- and shoemakers with the minimum of social graces, all shouting for their food. The Baron remarks on the lack of distinction of the guests but, as he has been rather mean about the *en pension* terms, Gardefeu tells him that he cannot expect a better class of guest for the money he is paying. All are in high spirits at the thought of a free meal and Gabrielle, at the top of her form, leads the way into the dining-room carolling a gay Tyrolean air.

ACT III

La Vie Parisienne is first and foremost a glittering vision of Paris life and a picture of the modern, democratic society of the 1860s, by which time the dictatorship had already been undermined. Act Three especially emphasises this, showing domestic servants who have no difficulty in aping the manners and behaviour of high society, and presenting the whole thing in a manner which certainly does not give the disadvantage to the lower classes. The scene is the flat of Bobinet's aunt, the Dowager Countess of Quimper-Karadec, and the servants, under the supervision of Bobinet, are decorating the apartment in preparation for Baron Gondremarck's reception. The butler, the footman, the parlourmaid and the porter's six nieces are all dressed up to represent the guests, and Gabrielle, the little glove-maker, is also present. When the Baron arrives they are presented to him as various princes, generals, viscomtesses, marquises, etc., and the Baron is enchanted. This is really seeing life! On Gardefeu's advice he has come without his wife, for Gardefeu is hopeful of getting the Baroness to himself for the evening. The Baron is particularly attracted to his hostess, Pauline, the parlourmaid, in the role of Admiral Walter's wife. There is much disappointment when she announces that the Admiral will be unable to come, as he is so fat that he can no longer get into his uniform. A moment later, however, there is a ring at the front door and in comes Bobinet in his role of Admiral Walter of the Swiss Navy. He receives a hilarious welcome as host, and much amusement is caused at the sight of a gaping split in the back of his Admiral's jacket.

The climax of the act is reached with the serving of supper, and the champagne produces an atmosphere of sheer delirium. Jules Claretie, who was at the first night, declared that *La Vie Parisienne* made him laugh so much that somebody might have been tickling the soles of his feet, and added that the effect of this scene was as if the whole house had been taking hashish. And what could be more rapturous than Offenbach's tune from the Finale, "Tout tourne, tout danse"?

ACT IV

The last act takes place in a Parisian restaurant. Alfred, the head-waiter, who knows all there is to be known about his patrons, is preparing for a terrific party to be given that night by the Brazilian visitor, whom we met on the platform at the Gare du l'Ouest in Act One. Baron Gondremarck arrives to have supper tête-à-tête with Metella. But when she appears she tells him that she has decided to go back to her former lover, Raoul de Gardefeu. She has, however, brought with her a charming girl-friend, who will be delighted to sup with him in her stead. The girl-friend is so closely veiled that the Baron fails to recognise his wife and rather sourly agrees to give her supper. He is furious with Metella, as he has discovered the trick Gardefeu played upon him and he has now moved to the genuine "Grand Hotel". Incidentally this scene contains one of the most atmospheric songs in the score, in which Metella describes the parties at the Café Anglais and the "hangover" which generally followed:

Such is the Baron's rage that he forces his way into the Brazilian's party at which Gardefeu is a guest and challenges him to a duel. However, the Brazilian calms him down, and when his complaints are investigated the Baron has difficulty in substantiating them. Was he not comfortable in Gardefeu's rooms? Yes, very. Was he over-charged? No, it was much more reasonable than the real "Grand Hotel". Did he not enjoy Admiral Walter's reception? Enormously. Was the champagne bad? No, excellent. Then, what is all the fuss about? The Baron and Gardefeu make it up, the Baron and his wife are reconciled, the party is resumed and the curtain falls on a scene of rapturous hilarity.

La Périchole

Opéra Bouffe in Three Acts

By HENRI MEILHAC *and* LUDOVIC HALÉVY

Music by JACQUES OFFENBACH

The plot suggested by Prosper Merimée's one-act play La Carosse du Saint Sacrement. *Original version in two acts produced on 6th October, 1868, at the Théâtre des Variétés, Paris, and subsequently in an extended version on 25th April, 1874, at the same theatre with Hortense Schneider and Monsieur Dupuis on both occasions. London productions on 27th June, 1870, at the Princess's Theatre (in French), with Hortense Schneider, and on 30th January, 1875, at the Royalty Theatre (in English), with Selina Dolaro, Walter Fisher and F. Sullivan.*

CHARACTERS

PIQUILLO, LA PÉRICHOLE — *street singers*
DON ANDRÈS DE RIBIERA, *Viceroy of Peru*
DON PEDRO, *Governor of Lima*
THE MARQUIS DE SANTAREM
MANUELITA, GUADALENA, BUGINELLA — *proprietors of the inn, "The Three Cousins"*
CHORUS OF COURTIERS, SERVANTS, GUARDS, TOWNSFOLK AND CIRCUS ARTISTES

ACT I

The scene is a public square in the city of Lima, the capital of Peru. A prominent feature of the set is the tavern of "The Three Cousins", and as the curtain rises a colourful crowd are promenading, drinking at the tables or playing cards, while the three cousins hurry to and fro, serving drinks and pouring out wine. A public holiday has been announced in celebration of the Viceroy of Peru's birthday, and Don Andrès de Ribiera, a gay and somewhat irresponsible ruler, is spending his birthday roaming the streets of his capital, incognito, in search of adventure and information.

To the square come two down-at-heel street singers, Piquillo and La Périchole. They are deeply in love, eager to get married and anxious to earn the wedding fees. Full of optimism, they give their entertainment to the clientele of "The Three Cousins". But La Périchole and Piquillo meet with little response from the public and are about to try another number when a troupe of gaily coloured acrobats clatter by, drawing a cart full of performing dogs. In a moment the square is empty. The crowds have followed the acrobats, and Piquillo and Périchole find themselves quite alone. Périchole, exhausted, declares she can go no farther, so Piquillo goes off alone to try his luck elsewhere, leaving his beloved Périchole asleep in the sunshine. Here she is found by the Viceroy, who, struck by her beauty, is immediately attracted and invites the hungry girl to dinner. He later reveals himself as Viceroy and offers her a position among the ladies of his Court. As Piquillo shows no sign of returning and she feels that she can no longer face a life of poverty and hunger, La Périchole reluctantly consents; and while the Viceroy gives instructions to his First Gentleman-in-Waiting to prepare for her reception, La Périchole sits down to write a letter of farewell to Piquillo. Among all the gems of melody which Offenbach contributed to Light Opera, this letter song is one of the brightest jewels:

While La Périchole is writing her letter, the First Gentleman-in-Waiting and the Governor of Lima remind the Viceroy of a certain rule imposed on the Viceregal Court, which reads that "none but married ladies living under the protection of their husbands are allowed to reside in the precincts of the Palace, by Royal Decree". Refusing to be baulked, the Viceroy orders them to procure a husband and a notary so that La Périchole may be married to some man or other immediately. Piquillo, who has by now received La Périchole's farewell letter, is the husband selected by the First-Gentleman-in-Waiting, quite unaware that he has chosen La Périchole's lover. However, the Governor's notaries produce legal impediments to the proposed marriage, while the Viceroy has considerable difficulty in persuading La Périchole to marry a stranger. But alcohol proves to be the solution to all these problems. The Governor entertains the notaries lavishly at their offices, Périchole is generously treated to champagne by the Viceroy, while the First Gentleman-in-Waiting busily plies Piquillo with brandy in the tavern. Directly La Périchole realises that Piquillo has been chosen as her husband, she agrees to the marriage: Piquillo is, however, in no condition to recognise his sweetheart with or without her wedding-veil. In these circumstances the ceremony takes place, and after its conclusion bride and bridegroom are immediately parted and separately conducted to their respective apartments in the Palace.

ACT II

Act Two takes place the following morning. Piquillo has been attired in Court dress and informed that he has been created Count de Tobago and Marquis du Mançanarès. Such is his "hangover" that only with difficulty can he recollect any of the incidents of the previous evening. From conversations he has with the courtiers, and from their attitude, he gathers that he has married a lady whose arrival at Court is not welcomed by the officers and ladies of the Viceroy's suite. But one factor *does* stand out clearly in his memory, and he reminds the First Gentleman-in-Waiting of his promise that once Piquillo is safely married to the lady he will be paid a large sum of money and be free to leave the Court and return, as he thinks, to La Périchole. The First Gentleman-in-Waiting and the Governor of Lima agree that this is so. But before his departure there is one formality with which Piquillo must comply. He is in duty bound to present his wife upon her marriage, to the Viceroy. Piquillo agrees, but when he discovers who his wife is, he becomes violently jealous of the Viceroy and turning on La Périchole denounces her furiously. La Périchole tries her best to calm him but, finally exasperated by her hysterical husband, she delivers herself of a devastating homily on the stupidity of men. And what capital Hortense Schneider made out of this refrain!

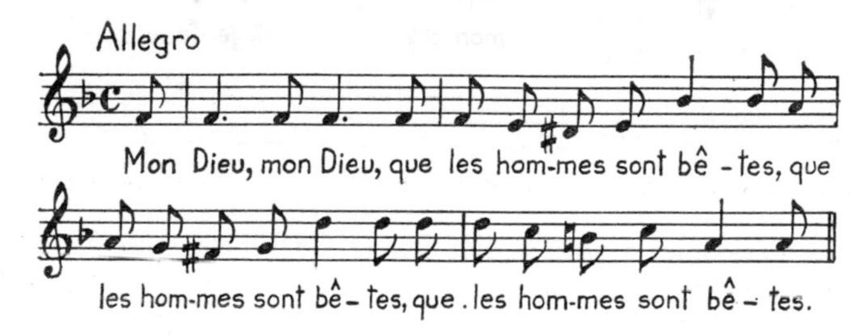

Exasperated beyond endurance by this treatment, Piquillo, seizing her hand, advances to the throne and venomously presents La Périchole to the Viceroy as "the fairest woman in creation with the falsest heart on earth". Pandemonium ensues, and at the Viceroy's command Piquillo is arrested and dragged away, protesting, to prison.

ACT III

Scene i. The first scene of Act Three takes place in Lima Gaol, where Piquillo, in solitary confinement, is brooding over his misfortunes. To his cell comes La Périchole, who has obtained the Viceroy's permission to visit him. Piquillo is at first furiously angry with her, but his resentment quickly vanishes under the influence of La Périchole's tender affection and her assurance that she has resisted the Viceroy's advances. The lovers, reconciled, determine to try to bribe the gaoler, with jewels Périchole has appropriated, to help them to escape together. But the gaoler turns out to be the Viceroy in disguise, and his reply to Périchole's appeal is an order that she and her husband shall spend their honeymoon in prison, chained to opposite walls of the cell. Before leaving them the Viceroy whispers to her that he will wait outside for any signal of her repentance. Left to their fate, despair descends on the lovers, when suddenly, to their amazement, they see a slab of stone in the prison wall dislodge itself and a figure emerge. It is an old prisoner, the Marquis de Santarem, who during a sentence of twelve years has contrived to effect a communication between his own cell and theirs. The Marquis instantly frees them both from their shackles and the three concoct a plan. La Périchole gives a signal and the Viceroy, entering, is seized and bound to a pillar. His keys are then appropriated and the three prisoners make their escape.

SCENE 2. The second scene of Act Three is once more the public square of Lima, outside the tavern of "The Three Cousins". Making their way through an excited crowd come La Périchole, Piquillo and the old Marquis de Santarem. They appeal to the three cousins for shelter and hide in the tavern, while the Governor of Lima and the First Gentleman-in-Waiting, who have been vainly scouring the countryside in search of the fugitives, are roundly abused by the angry Viceroy for their lack of success. But when he turns on the three cousins, accusing them of sheltering the prisoners and threatening to have them stripped to the skin and publicly flogged, La Périchole and Piquillo come out from the tavern with the Marquis and appeal to the Viceroy for pardon. Touched by the lovers' constancy, he releases them with his blessing, even allowing La Périchole to retain her jewellery. And so, with a happy ending to all their troubles and money in their pockets, the curtain falls on a brighter future for Piquillo and La Périchole.

Les Brigands

Opéra Bouffe in Three Acts

By HENRI MEILHAC *and* LUDOVIC HALÉVY

Music by JACQUES OFFENBACH

First produced on 10th December, 1869, at the Théâtre des Variétés, Paris, with Mademoiselle Zulma Bouffar, Monsieur Dupuis and Monsieur Léonce. London productions on 22nd April, 1871, at the Globe Theatre as Falsacappa *(in English), with Cornelie D'Anka, Annetta Scasi, Dan Leeson, and on 16th September, 1889, at the Avenue Theatre, translated by W. S. Gilbert as* The Brigands.

CHARACTERS

FALSACAPPA, *a brigand chief*
FIORELLA, *his daughter*
PIETRO, *his Lieutenant*
FRAGOLETTO, *a young farmer*
THE DUKE OF MANTUA
THE BARON DE CAMPOTASSO, *his equerry*
ANTONIO, *his treasurer*
THE PRINCESS OF GRANADA
THE COUNT GLORIA-CASSIS, *her chamberlain*
ADOLPHE DE VALADOLID, *her page*
PIPO, *an innkeeper*
A COURIER
THE MARCHIONESS
THE DUCHESS
COMMANDER OF THE CARBINIERS
CHORUS OF BRIGANDS, CARBINIERS, PEASANTS, NOBLES, LADIES AND SERVANTS OF THE COURTS OF MANTUA AND GRANADA

ACT I

The scene is a rugged mountain pass up which there winds a pathway leading past the entrance to a cavern; the headquarters of a band of brigands. When the curtain rises three brigands on sentry duty are watching the approach of a little procession ascending the mountain, consisting of a venerable Hermit, followed by eight young peasant girls. The girls, weary and footsore, keep asking where they are going, to which the Hermit's only answer is: "This is the road to Wisdom true." As they arrive at the cavern the Hermit throws off his beard and gown, appearing as Falsacappa, chief of the banditti. The terrified girls are seized by the brigands and Falsacappa delivers a breezy song, descriptive of a bandit's life. When the song is over the girls are removed to the cave and Falsacappa settles down to a tête-à-tête with his elderly Chief-of-Staff, Pietro. It seems there is trouble brewing, and a deputation waits on the Captain with a grievance. Business, they say, is bad. "Last week," states the deputation, "we marched ninety miles to steal seventeen francs, which had to be divided among sixty-three. And you," they accuse Falsacappa, "took ten francs of it for yourself. It is our unanimous opinion that something must be done." Falsacappa promises them that something shall be done forthwith—"upon my honour". Complaining that they do not trust such security, the deputation withdraws.

Falsacappa's daughter, Fiorella, now appears to wish her father many happy returns of his birthday. As they are talking, some bandits enter, escorting a prisoner, who proves to be a local farmer whose property the brigands recently pillaged. During the operation this young farmer, by name Fragoletto, saw and fell in love with Fiorella and he has called to ask for her hand in marriage. But there is a stumbling-block. In the words of Falsacappa: "Marry my daughter to an honest man! Never! Family traditions must be observed." So Fragoletto volunteers to join the brigands and is hurried away on a short excursion into the mountains to give a proof of his courage. Fiorella and old Pietro are now left alone, and to their surprise they see a young man descending the mountain path, elegantly attired in riding dress. Though neither of them is aware of it, he is the Duke of Mantua. As he approaches, Pietro tells Fiorella to detain the young man in conversation, while he fetches Falsacappa, who will certainly want to pluck such a prosperous-looking pigeon. But the young man is handsome and Fiorella tender-hearted—so tender-hearted that she confesses that her father is a brigand-chief and will shortly return with his band—sixty-six of them. Then the young man thinks he had better go. In this attractive patter song Fiorella describes the way back to Mantua and speeds the young man on his way.

When Falsacappa returns with Pietro and finds the bird has flown he is furious with Fiorella. But his good humour is restored when the brigands return with a prisoner, whom Fragoletto has captured. The prisoner, it appears, is a diplomatic courier from Granada, and the papers he carries in his dispatch-case refer to the projected marriage of the Princess of Granada to the Duke of Mantua. The important passage which Falsacappa reads aloud to the assembled bandits runs: "Deducting the two millions, which represent the Princess's dowry, the sum due to the Court of Granada from the Court of Mantua is reduced to three millions. These three millions will be paid over to the officer who escorts the Princess." In addition to the papers a portrait of the Princess is enclosed for the purpose of identification, as the Duke has never set eyes on her. Examining the portrait and comparing it to one of Fiorella, Falsacappa decides to substitute Fiorella's likeness for the portrait of the Princess. He then orders the courier to take his dispatch-case, his horse and to ride off. In spite of angry protests from the brigands, the courier is allowed to depart and Falsacappa addresses them in these words: "Gentlemen, you desired that something should be done. Very good! Tomorrow we put into execution the most magnificent project that brigand-chief ever conceived. Send for the ladies. Tonight we hold revel to celebrate Fragoletto's accession to our band." And Offenbach launches into one of his splendid extended Finales. When the fun is at its height the distant tramp of marching feet is heard and the bandits hide as a patrol of carbiniers approach. They all wear boots of exaggerated size and announce in song that unfortunately they always arrive too late. The effect is extremely comic. From their hiding-place the brigands watch and sing this catchy refrain, one of the hits of the score.

When the carbiniers have departed, the brigands resume their interrupted party and the curtain descends on a veritable orgy of wine, women and song.

ACT II

In the garden of a large country inn the Landlord and his staff are busy laying tables and preparing a magnificent meal. For it is here that the escort sent by the Duke of Mantua is to meet his bride, the Princess of Granada, and accompany her to the ducal palace. To the Landlord's annoyance the inn is invaded by a company of itinerant beggars, who sing a mournful "Facitote caritem, Date panem, Date panem". Gradually more and more beggars arrive and their singing takes on a menacing tone, till Falsacappa, throwing off his beggar's dress, orders the brigands to seize the Landlord and his staff, remove their clothes and lock them in the cellar. He then explains to the brigands the details of his plan. "First," he says, "we must assume the character of these hotel people, in order to receive the escort from Mantua. Having effected this, we must overpower them and incarcerate them in the tavern, and then, assuming their characters, we will receive the Princess and her party from Granada. Lastly, we will imprison the Princess and her party and in their place we will make our way to Mantua and collect the three millions. Simplest thing in the world!"

The first part of the plan goes without a hitch. The escort from Mantua, headed by Baron Campotasso, equerry to the Duke, and a captain of carbiniers with his men, duly arrives. They eye the staff dubiously, and the Baron remarks to Falsacappa, who is impersonating the Landlord: "These are queer-looking cooks," and then, pointing to daggers and pistols in their belts, he asks: "Are those culinary implements?" "Yes," answers Falsacappa; "we use them when cooking geese." And the Mantuans are seized and hurried into the inn. The brigands have barely time to assume the clothes and characters of the Mantuan escort when there is heard the distant sound of gay, Spanish music and there arrive the Princess of Granada, her preceptor, her page, Count Gloria-Cassis, four lords, four ladies and four pages. All have tambourines and castanets with which they accompany themselves as they sing and dance a jolly Bolero. As the brigands are busy hastily donning the uniforms and clothes of the Mantuan escort, no one is present to receive the Princess, and she is greatly offended. Eventually Falsacappa appears. He is now impersonating the Captain of carbiniers—at least to the waist. Below he remains a brigand. His cuirass is back to front and he has only one epaulette. The brigands are grotesquely dressed as carbiniers, and old Pietro, who is supposed to be Baron Campotasso, gets confused and keeps reverting to his original characterisation of a waiter, shouting: "Coming, sir, coming! Soup, fish, steaks, filet de bœuf." The Spaniards are beginning to realise that something is wrong, when the real Baron Campotasso and the Landlord, who have managed to free themselves, appear on the balcony of the inn and shout to the Spaniards that they are in the hands of Falsacappa and his bandits but to be of good heart as help is coming. They will release the real carbiniers, who are locked into the cellar. Presently the Baron appears from the inn with the carbiniers. They are armed with bottles, are quite drunk and quickly fraternise with the brigands. All that remains now is for the brigands to dress up in the Spaniards' clothes, with Fiorella as the Princess, imprison the Spaniards, the Mantuans, the Landlord and his staff, and make their way to the ducal palace at Mantua to this infectious tune:

ACT III

The last act takes place in a salon in the Duke of Mantua's palace. When the curtain rises the Duke is taking official farewell of his bachelorhood while awaiting the arrival of his bride. He sends for his Treasurer and commands him for the last time to pay the Marchioness's rent and the Duchess's milliner's bill. He also reminds the Treasurer that three million francs are due to be paid over to the Spanish Embassy that very day. This is terrible news for the Treasurer, who for years has been helping himself liberally to the treasury funds to pay for his own mistresses. At the moment the Royal Exchequer is reduced to the insignificant sum of twelve hundred and eighty-three francs, twenty-five centimes. "I couldn't help it," laments the Treasurer to himself: "I'm a creature of impulse, and when a woman asks me for money I can't refuse it."

His gloomy meditations are interrupted by the sound of gay Spanish music, and the brigands enter dressed as the members of the Granada Embassy, with Falsacappa as Gloria-Cassis, Pietro as the Preceptor, Fiorella as the Princess and Fragoletto as her page. After ceremonial greetings are over Falsacappa, in his role of Count Gloria-Cassis, Minister of Finance to the Court of Spain, broaches the subject of the three million francs and the Duke orders his Treasurer to pay the money. After a great deal of equivocation, including an attempt at bribery, the Treasurer is compelled to admit that he cannot produce the money. With a furious cry of "He's in the same line of business", Falsacappa is about to hurl himself upon the unfortunate Treasurer when there is an interruption. The members of the Spanish Court and Mantuan escort have managed to free themselves and now enter the salon. Things look black for the brigands, and they are only saved by the presence of mind of Fiorella. Throwing herself on the mercy of the Duke, she reminds him of the day she saved his life on the mountain by preventing him from being captured by the brigands. Magnanimously the Duke pardons Falsacappa and his bandits, and all ends happily with Falscappa declaring that he will turn respectable and then he need never more tremble "when we hear the tramp of the royal carbiniers".

Vert-Vert

(The Green Parrot)

Opéra Comique in Three Acts

By HENRI MEILHAC *and* CHARLES NUITTER

Music by JACQUES OFFENBACH

First produced on 10th March, 1869, at the Théâtre de l'Opéra-Comique, Paris, with Monsieur Capoul as "Valentin" ("Vert-Vert"), Madame Girard as "La Corilla" and Madame Cico as "Mimi". Produced in London (in English) (translated by H. Herman and R. Mansell) on 2nd May, 1874, at the St. James's Theatre, with Mademoiselle Manetti, Elisa Savelli and Mrs. Buckingham White.

CHARACTERS

VALENTIN (*nick-named* VERT-VERT)
BALADON, *a dancing master*
BINET, *Head Gardener*
BELLECOUR, *a tenor*
COUNT D'ARLANGE, THE CHEVALIER DE BERGERAC — *Officers of Dragoons*
FRIQUET, *a dragoon*
MANIQUET, *Theatrical Impresario*
LA CORILLA, *a singer*
MIMI, BATHILDE, EMMA — *Head girls of the convent school of Saint-Rémy*
MADEMOISELLE PATURELLE, *Deputy Headmistress*
PACOT, *Deputy Gardener*
CHORUS OF SCHOOL-GIRLS, DRAGOONS AND ACTORS.

ACT I

In the garden of the convent school of Saint-Rémy a solemn ceremony is in progress. When the curtain rises the gardener, Binet, has just finished digging a tiny grave, as down the garden path advances a procession of pupils, led by three Head girls—Bathilde, Emma and Mimi. Mimi is carrying a cushion on which reposes the corpse of Vert-Vert, the school parrot, who that morning has been discovered lifeless in his cage. At the graveside Monsieur Valentin, the young nephew of the Headmistress, speaks the funeral oration, recalling the beauty and virtue of the dead bird and bidding him farewell. After the funeral the three head girls remain behind to thank Monsieur Valentin for his splendid oration. "You must have loved Vert-Vert very dearly to have spoken so movingly," they tell him, and are startled when he replies that, for his part, he never could stand the bird. "All your attention, all your affection," he complains, "was lavished on Vert-Vert. No one has ever given a thought to me, and I am just as fond of bon-bons as was Vert-Vert." The girls explain that, as nephew of the Headmistress, they have always accepted him as part of the furniture, as it were, and taken him for granted. They now for the first time become aware of him as a man and Mimi, especially, takes a violent fancy to him. Accordingly they decide to offer him the vacant position of Vert-Vert and promote him to the status of School Pet. Valentin, greatly flattered, accepts the honour and assumes the name of Vert-Vert.

Among the pupils of the Convent of Saint-Rémy are two young married women, the sisters Bathilde and Emma de Brimonet, who married secretly two officers of Dragoons, the Count D'Arlange and the Chevalier de Bergerac. But their parents heard of the marriages and they were met at the church door, torn from their husbands' sides and escorted back to the convent, there to remain until the time was judged ripe for them to assume the responsibilities of married life. Today Bathilde's husband, the handsome Count D'Arlange, pays a clandestine visit to his wife. He enters the convent garden by climbing a wall, accompanied by a fellow officer, Count Roger de Sameuse, nick-named Friquet. Count D'Arlange compels the gardener, Binet, by threats of violence to bring Bathilde to him, and he then tells her that he and de Bergerac have decided to kidnap herself and Emma the following week. After a romantic duet, throughout which they are obstinately chaperoned by the offended gardener, the Count D'Arlange departs. Friquet, a gay spark with an eye for the girls, is enchanted to find himself so well situated and is in no hurry to leave. By good fortune he encounters Pacot, a jobbing gardener, who is to take Binet's place for a fortnight while he is absent accompanying Vert-Vert (Valentin) on a trip to Nevers to visit a relative. Friquet, by generous financial inducement, succeeds in persuading Pacot to allow him to take his job. Discarding his uniform in a summer-house, he appears in Pacot's fustian, presents his references to Mademoiselle Paturelle, the deputy headmistress, and is engaged to take Binet's place for a fortnight.

Mademoiselle Paturelle, outwardly a pillar of impregnable respectability, is secretly married to the school's dancing master, Monsieur Baladon. He cannot afford to support her and she fears that, should their marriage become known, she would lose her job. So they meet secretly. But of late Monsieur Baladon has been becoming more importunate and she has had to agree to give him a key to the convent garden and to meet him there after dark. They are surprised, with Monsieur Baladon's arm round Mademoiselle Paturelle's waist, by the girls

Bathilde, Emma and Mimi, who make some very caustic remarks at their expense. Mimi, who has developed a school-girl passion for Vert-Vert (Valentin), now learns of his projected departure for Nevers and is desolated. With the courage born of love she determines to pursue him unseen. Pondering on how best to achieve this, she encounters Friquet, whom her eagle eye detects as no gardener. He confesses that he arrived with Bathilde's husband, has taken the gardener's job and discarded his Dragoon's uniform in the summer-house. Here is the perfect disguise for Mimi, and she makes tracks for the summer-house. Later, in the guise of a slim Dragoon, she slips out of the garden gate and conceals herself in the coach which is to transport Vert-Vert and Binet to Nevers. The whole school turns out to speed the travellers on their way, lamenting Vert-Vert's departure, to one of Offenbach's characteristically bustling tunes:

ACT II

In the hall of the inn, "The Golden Lion" at Nevers, a company of officers of Dragoons, which includes Count D'Arlange and the Chevalier de Bergerac, is entertaining an operatic diva, La Corilla, who is due to appear at the theatre that week. They invite her to dine and promise her their warmest support. "Anybody failing to show the wildest enthusiasm for your performance shall be instantly put to the sword," swears de Bergerac. The Impresario of the company, Monsieur Maniquet, appears and asks obsequiously whether La Corilla would favour him by consenting to rehearse. "To go as far as the theatre would fatigue me, but I am prepared to rehearse here in the hotel," she tells him graciously. "But where is the tenor?" At last he enters. But alas! the distinguished tenor, Monsieur Bellecour, has contracted a cold and is voiceless.

He has had a terrible experience. Travelling to Nevers on the top of a coach and surrounded by acquaintances, he was holding forth on the subject of singing. Next to him was sitting a young man accompanied by a vulgar but voluble valet. This servant insisted on taking part in the conversation, declaring that no one had an organ comparable to his master's voice. "Sing, sir," he begged. "The young man burst into song and I burst into laughter," continues Bellecour. "Immediately the valet seized me and the next moment had thrown me bodily off the top of the coach into the Loire. Rescuers came to my assistance. My life was saved, but *not* my top C." Obviously he will be in no condition to sing at tomorrow's performance and, as it is to be a benefit for La Corilla, not only Monsieur Maniquet but La Diva is in despair. "If only I could lay my hands on that villain——" Monsieur Maniquet is fulminating, when into the hall come Vert-Vert and Binet. "That's him," declares Bellecour, pointing to Binet. "And you dared——" the Impresario is beginning when Binet interrupts with: "Yes, and I'll serve anyone who laughs at my master the same way." La Corilla has said nothing, but she has taken a fancy to Vert-Vert. She welcomes him with kind words, declaring an interest in his singing and begging him to give her the pleasure of hearing his voice. Reluctantly Vert-Vert obliges, while Bellecour says rudely: "This'll make you laugh." "Faulty production and no tone," is Bellecour's comment when Vert-Vert has finished his song, but La Corilla is ravished. "Now, sir," says the Impresario to Vert-Vert, "I should be obliged if you would kindly pay me the sum of 3,482 pounds, 12 sous, which will be the approximate loss resulting from your valet's action in throwing my tenor into the Loire." Vert-Vert is in despair at the turn affairs have taken and cannot, of course, produce the money. But La Corilla has a solution. Taking him aside, she proposes in her silkiest tones that Vert-Vert take over Bellecour's role the following night. Vert-Vert is reluctant but desperate. "When you look at me like that," he admits, "I don't know if I am coming or going. Peculiar things have been happening to me all day," he continues. "On the ship, crossing over, for instance." And in a romantic song he describes a lovely girl who caught his fancy:

Convinced by Vert-Vert's expressive performance that he is talented, La Corilla drags him off to rehearse, and much to the annoyance of the Dragoons she arbitrarily informs them that dinner, as far as she is concerned, is off. "The show must go on."

Now, during Vert-Vert's interview with La Corilla, Mimi, who in Friquet's Dragoon's uniform has travelled with him unseen all the way to Nevers, has stolen into the room and from a place of concealment has witnessed the whole scene. She now joins the Dragoons, confesses to them her identity and asks their help. Will they assist her to rescue Vert-Vert from the clutches of the designing La Corilla? In the course of conversation Mimi divulges that Friquet is at the Convent of Saint-Rémy, masquerading as the gardener. Immediately Count D'Arlange and de Bergerac declare it to be an urgent necessity to remove their wives from the proximity of this notorious lady-killer. They strike a bargain with Mimi. If she will admit them to the convent they, for their part, will undertake to get Vert-Vert away from La Corilla:

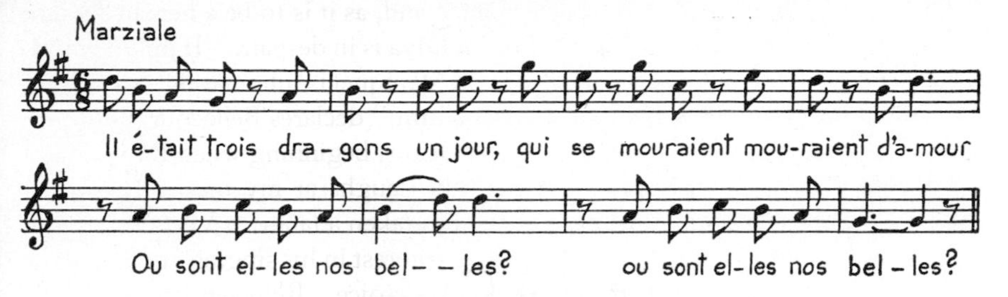

The Dragoons' plan to effect Vert-Vert's removal is simplicity itself. They invite the whole theatrical company, headed by La Corilla, to supper. A wild party ensues during which champagne flows and Vert-Vert's glass is never for a moment allowed to remain empty. As the curtain falls he is in such a parlous condition that the Dragoons will obviously encounter no opposition when they decide to remove him.

ACT III

Back in the convent garden at night, Mimi is reunited to Vert-Vert, but when she scolds him for his outrageous flirtation with La Corilla he is quite impenitent. He tells Mimi that it was La Corilla who taught him that he had a heart and that, having discovered that he had a heart, he realised that it belonged to Mimi. Count D'Arlange and de Bergerac are reunited to their wives, Bathilde and Emma, and D'Arlange dispatches Friquet to admit the other Dragoons, who are stationed outside the garden gate. Then through the darkness appear Mademoiselle Paturelle from the house and Monsieur Baladon through the garden gate to keep their assignation. "Psst, psst," they call to each other in the darkness, and "Psst, psst," call Mimi and Vert-Vert to confuse them. A scene reminiscent of Act IV of Mozart's *Le Nozze di Figaro* follows, with Monsieur Baladon's arm round Mimi's waist under the impression that he is caressing Mademoiselle Paturelle, and Mademoiselle Paturelle snuggling up to Vert-Vert, mistaking his manly chest for that of Monsieur Baladon. This scene is rudely interrupted by the sound of the bell of the garden gate, and in comes Binet, very mellow and quite undeterred by Mademoiselle Paturelle's haughty reception of him. She demands to know what he wants, and he replies that he has come, not to garden, but to intercede for Count D'Arlange to be officially reunited to Bathilde, the Chevalier Bergerac to Emma and for permission for Vert-Vert and Mimi to get married. Mademoiselle is adamant in her refusal. "What about permission for us to be reunited?" says Monsieur Baladon slyly, and Mademoiselle hisses back at him, "Be quiet!" "It would be a good idea, Madame Baladon," says Vert-Vert, giving the game away. Even then the haughty schoolmistress refuses, until Count D'Arlange beckons to Friquet and into the garden pour all the Dragoons. They immediately pair off with the school-girls, who have all appeared in their nightgowns, each carrying a lighted candle. Nothing is left for Mademoiselle Paturelle to do but to capitulate, and the curtain falls to a reprise of "Il était cent dragons".

Le Roi Carotte

(King Carotte)

A Spectacular Opéra Bouffe-Féerie in Four Acts (seventeen scenes)

Based on E. T. A. HOFFMANN'S *tale* Kleinzackes Genannt Zinnober

By VICTORIEN SARDOU

Music by JACQUES OFFENBACH

First produced on 15th January, 1872, at the Théâtre de la Gaieté, Paris, with Mademoiselle Zulma Bouffar, Madame Judic, Monsieur Masset and Monsieur Vicini. London production on 3rd June, 1872, at the Alhambra Theatre, with Elisa Savelli, Cornelie D'Anka, F. H. Celli, Annetta Scasi and Harry Paulton.

CHARACTERS

ROBIN-LOURON, *a wizard*
FRIDOLIN XXIV, *Hereditary Prince of Krokodyne*
KING CAROTTE
TRUCK, *Court Necromancer*
PIPERTRUNCK, *Chief of Police*
QUIRIBIBI, *a sorcerer*
BARON KOFFRE, *Chancellor of the Exchequer*
FIELD-MARSHAL TRAC, *Minister of War*
COUNT SCHOPP, *Privy Councillor*
ROSÉE-DU-SOIR
PRINCESS CUNEGONDE
COLOQUINTE, *a witch*
CHORUS OF STUDENTS, CITIZENS, SOLDIERS, PRIESTS, BRIDESMAIDS, INSECTS, MONKEYS, VEGETABLES, ETC.

Sardou's play is a satire on the Second Empire and his intention was to show the dangers resulting from Louis Napoleon's policy. Prince Fridolin, the hero of the play, whom he made very like the Emperor in some respects, tries to extricate himself from his very grave difficulties by favouring the Radicals instead of the bourgeoisie. But no sooner are the Radicals in power than they chase him from the throne and usurp the power themselves under the leadership of their Red King Carotte, and of course lead the country to disaster.

ACT I

The first scene is the garden of an inn, "The Lion of Hungary", situated at the gates of the capital city of Krokodyne. The garden is full of promenaders enjoying the evening air and a noisy element is provided by a crowd of students, calling loudly for beer. At a table apart sit Prince Fridolin XXIV, the ruler of Krokodyne, and four of his Cabinet Ministers. All are disguised as students. The reason for his appearance incognito is that the Prince, who is to marry Princess Cunegonde, daughter of the neighbouring King of Krackhausen, is anxious to catch a glimpse of the Princess on her arrival without himself being seen. Her father is ill with gout and cannot escort her, so Prince Fridolin is determined, if he does not like the look of her, to pack the Princess home to her papa. While they are waiting they are joined by a young student, Robin-Louron, an extremely affable and talkative young man. In conversation he expresses some very critical views on the reigning Prince, and when Fridolin asks him if he knows to whom he is talking, Robin promptly replies, "To His Royal Highness and his Cabinet."

Now Robin is a professional wizard, and he goes on to tell Prince Fridolin that he knows he is short of money to pay for his wedding to Princess Cunegonde, and that he has a plan to provide him with the necessary funds. In the Old Palace is an armoury full of the suits of armour worn by his ancestors in battle. Robin undertakes to find a buyer who will give Prince Fridolin a hundred thousand florins for them, and Fridolin agrees to sell provided he decides to marry. Robin then points out a pretty girl who has just arrived on horseback and tells him she is Princess Cunegonde, who is travelling incognito for exactly the same reason as himself. Fridolin at once gets into conversation with her and finds her attractive and excellent company. She accepts a cigarette, tells Fridolin that she is scheduled to marry the reigning Prince and asks what he is like. Fridolin assures her he is young, handsome and fond of pleasure and gaiety. He makes up his mind then and there to marry her, and they part the best of friends. When Princess Cunegonde has left, Robin and the Cabinet Ministers return and depart with Prince Fridolin towards the armoury.

SCENE 2. High up in an attic in the Old Palace, derelict and deserted except by rats, lives an old witch, Coloquinte. With her lives Rosée-du-Soir, a King's daughter. Coloquinte stole her out of her cradle and has kept her a prisoner ever since. Rosée's only diversion has been an occasional glimpse of Prince Fridolin when he takes a walk in the palace garden, and she has fallen in love with him. As she is working at her tambour-frame by moonlight, into the room walks a young man. It is Robin-Louron, before whose wizardry all locks fly open. He knows Rosée's story and has come to rescue her. First of all he finishes her embroidery work for her by magic and then gives her a ball of silk, telling her to repeat certain magic words and when the ball rolls away to follow wherever it may lead her, for all bolts and bars will open before it. He tells her all this to one of Offenbach's most captivating tunes:

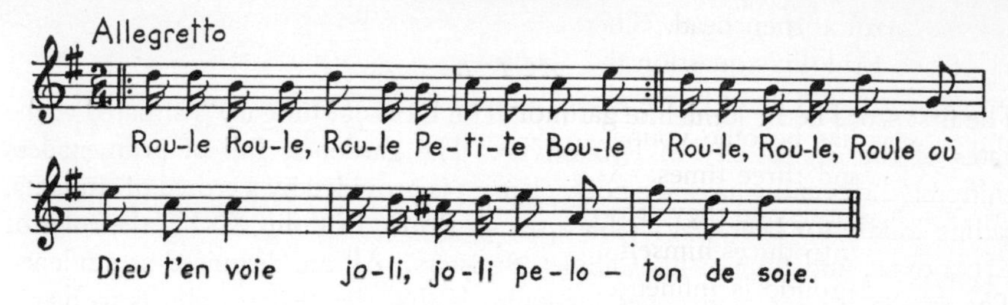

Presently the old witch enters. She greets Robin with respect as a professional colleague, for it was owing to Robin's influence that Coloquinte has been deprived of her powers for ten years, which expire tonight. He tells her that he intends to give Prince Fridolin a little education and training in conduct and deportment and that two or three weeks of exile will give him the best lesson. Coloquinte by the aid of her magic wand is to start a revolution, cause Fridolin to be deposed and produce a King to succeed him. Coloquinte agrees to help and Robin departs. Scolding poor Rosée for entertaining young men instead of working, the witch tells her she can go to bed without her supper and goes out, double-locking the door. Immediately Rosée tries out the power of her magic charm. She places the ball of silk on the ground and away it rolls towards the window, which changes into a doorway leading to a stairway, down which Rosée makes her escape.

SCENE 3. In the armoury of the Old Palace, Fridolin, accompanied by his Cabinet Ministers, Robin, and a party of students, is carousing surrounded by ancestral suits of mail which survey the debauch with evident disapproval. As the party gets wilder all start drinking out of helmets and impudently sticking lighted pipes in vizors, mockingly addressing the armour-suited forms as "Grandpapa". Suddenly, to the terror of everybody, there is a shuddering sound of metal clanking and the mailed figures speak, threatening Fridolin with the punishment his frivolity deserves and declaring their intention to follow him to his palace to wreak their vengeance. All fly in terror.

SCENE 4. In the kitchen garden of the royal palace Coloquinte is performing a magic incantation by moonlight. "Carrots, radishes, turnips, cauliflowers and cabbages, come forth at my command and follow me," she orders. And out of the earth the vegetables mount and, assuming a semblance of human form, obediently follow her.

SCENE 5. In the formal gardens of the royal palace Prince Fridolin is giving a party in honour of his forthcoming marriage to Princess Cunegonde. The gardens are brilliantly illuminated and on a raised platform an orchestra is playing for dancing. When Fridolin and Cunegonde meet she is delighted to recognize in him the gay student she encountered at the city gate, and they are about to open the ball with a waltz when grotesque-sounding music is heard. Then, to everyone's amazement, a procession of vegetables appears, with a swollen-looking carrot at their head. There is a burst of laughter from the guests, and in reply to Fridolin's question the carrot declares that he is a King—the great King Carotte. "The ugly wretch; what a hideous fright," all exclaim. Coloquinte, who has become young and beautiful, then appears unobserved and waves her wand three times. As she does so a kind of electric shock passes through the guests and they crowd with admiring words and looks round King Carotte who introduces himself in a high falsetto voice.

Even Cunegonde is influenced by Coloquinte's witchcraft, and she turns from Fridolin and makes shameless advances to King Carotte. Worse still, Coloquinte by her magic makes all King Carotte's loutish behaviour appear to emanate from Fridolin. Thus, when a waiter carrying a salver with glasses of punch is stopped by King Carotte, who swallows the lot, it is Prince Fridolin who is accused of being drunk. When dancing is resumed and King Carotte, partnering Madame Pipertrunck, falls down, it is Fridolin who is commiserated with, to his annoyance. Furiously Fridolin demands "Am I to abandon the crown and the palace of my forbears to this grotesque vegetable?" when a sound of grim, metallic tramping is heard and on to the scene marches a slow procession of the mailed suits of armour. They stand threateningly before the Prince with cries of "Death to Fridolin". The cry is taken up by the Court as Fridolin flies in terror, pursued by Robin and the Court Necromancer, Truck. As the curtain falls the Court and the soldiery all pay homage to King Carotte.

ACT II

SCENE I. In the courtyard of a country inn a fête is in progress when a herald interrupts the proceedings with a proclamation: "In the name of His Majesty King Carotte the First, this is to make known to all whom it may concern that a reward of one thousand ducats is hereby offered for the body of the banished Prince Fridolin the Twenty-fourth, dead or alive." As the herald leaves with his trumpeters, the crowd go off to prepare to dance the farandole, and into the courtyard come Fridolin, Robin and Truck. Sitting down at a table they order wine and are drinking it when a page approaches, following a ball of silk which rolls to Fridolin's feet. The page is, of course, Rosée-du-Soir. Without divulging her identity she greets Fridolin and begs to offer him her service as page, which he gratefully accepts. Soon after this Pipertrunck, Koffre and Trac appear with a detachment of soldiers in pursuit of Fridolin. They suddenly see Robin, and Pipertrunck is setting the soldiers on to them when into the courtyard dance all the farandole participants to a jolly rustic tune:

So greatly do the dancers hamper the soldiers in their efforts that Fridolin, Rosée, Robin and Truck escape with ease.

SCENE 2. The next port of call of the fugitives is the study of the sorcerer, Quiribibi. A large room, part library, part laboratory, it is filled with globes, crucibles, retorts, alembics and appliances pertaining to the magical arts. While they are waiting for Quiribibi to appear, Pipertrunck, Chief of the Krokodyne Police, arrives and begs Prince Fridolin to let him follow him once more. He is taken back into favour, and after this episode Quiribibi arrives; a very old man with a white beard, dressed in a long robe. He greets Robin affectionately and Truck, a former pupil, coldly. In reply to Robin's questions as to the source of Fridolin's misfortunes, Quiribibi declares that he is himself the cause of their origin. Had Fridolin been less lazy, less frivolous and less extravagant he might still have been upon the throne of his fathers. But he has one powerful enemy beside himself: the witch, Coloquinte, who discovered his contemptible successor, King Carotte. Producing a magic mirror he causes to appear in it a picture of Carotte and Cunegonde, affectionately posed. From the picture Quiribibi can tell that Carotte belongs to a species of subterranean dwarf over which he has no control. There is only one charm that can help them—the talisman of talismans, the ring of Solomon, which lies buried in the ruins of Pompeii. Quiribibi promises to help them find it provided they agree to help terminate his existence. They are to cut him limb from limb and cast him bit by bit into a furnace. Unwillingly they set to work. Off come his arms, off come his legs. His head is unscrewed and placed on the table, where it instructs them to "throw my body after the rest". Finally, as the head is thrown in, the furnace blows up with a violent explosion and out of it darts Quiribibi as a young man. His final injunction to them is to find in Pompeii a certain soldier who obtained possession of the ring of Solomon after the siege of Jerusalem, and as a parting present he gives them a magic lamp. A relic of Pompeii, it will show them the way there and back again. "Only light it and breathe your wishes. They will be obeyed. Farewell." And the rejuvenated Quiribibi hurries away in pursuit of two pretty girls who have caught his eye. Lighting the lamp, Fridolin exclaims, "Lamp, do your duty. To Pompeii," and Fridolin, Rosée-du-Soir, Robin, Truck and Pipertrunck sink through the ground on the first stage of their journey to Pompeii.

SCENE 3. The ruins of Pompeii by moonlight present a magnificent but awe-inspiring spectacle. Duly impressed, Fridolin, Rosée, Robin and Pipertrunck sing a quartette:

"But this," Fridolin says, "brings us little nearer to the charmed ring. Where is the soldier who perished Anno Domini 79? We want the old city with its temples, its market-place, its populace. Lamp, do your duty. To the Pompeii of the ancients."

Scene 4. As Fridolin finishes, the scene changes to the bustling market-place of Pompeii in the days before its destruction in the eruption of Vesuvius. Stall-holders are crying their wares, selling fruit, wine and bread. Fridolin and his companions stand, unobserved, watching a wedding procession approaching. As it halts by them Rosée whispers to Robin: "The lamp has disappeared", and Robin replies: "Then the ring is here." They are now questioned as to their identities, where they have come from and how they have come. By the railway, they reply, and explain exactly what a railway is.

"And, pray, what brings such powerful magicians to our poor little city?" they are asked, and they explain that they seek the ring of King Solomon. "Why," says Pyrgopolinice, a soldier, "it came into my possession after the siege of Jerusalem, and I presented it to Corinna." It seems that after passing through many hands it has come to rest as a wedding ring on the hand of today's bride, Lepida. "After being hawked all over Pompeii," she exclaims furiously to her husband. "There's your wedding ring," and she throws it on the ground. Robin picks it up and hands it to Fridolin, and to the accompaniment of angry cries of "Down with the strangers who sow discord between husband and wife," Fridolin lifts up the ring and cries: "Djinn of Solomon, to the rescue." An enormous green figure with a camel's head rises out of the ground and asks, "Master, what would you?" "We would instantly to Krokodyne," Fridolin tells it. "Mount upon my shoulders and I obey." They climb up and the djinn ascends into the air. Thunder rumbles, lightning flashes and the sky is illuminated by the red fire of Vesuvius.

ACT III

Scene 1. In a salon in the palace King Carotte welcomes back Baron Koffre and Field-Marshal Trac. He inquires whether they have captured the late Prince Fridolin. Learning that he has escaped them, King Carotte flies into a rage and orders the Cabinet to be arrested. They are, however, released again when Baron Koffre explains that by "escaped" he meant that Fridolin's death has prevented his capture. Travelling merchants are now announced, who have come to Court, attracted by the forthcoming wedding of King Carotte and Princess Cunegonde. They are Robin, Rosée, Truck and Pipertrunck disguised in Persian costumes, and they proceed to cry their wares. But Fridolin has slipped away without anyone noticing and they search for him in vain. King Carotte refuses to buy the "merchants'" wares and is flirting with Cunegonde, when the witch, Coloquinte, arrives to warn him that Fridolin is in the palace. "But he is dead," argues Carotte. "Unfortunately he is alive and has returned with a power greater than my own," she tells him. The foolish Fridolin is as much in love with Cunegonde as ever in spite of her behaviour, and now, falling for her wiles, is silly enough to allow her to steal the ring of Solomon. At the last moment, however, he is rescued by Robin, to Coloquinte's fury.

SCENE 2. Following her silken ball Rosée arrives in the Kingdom of Ants, and here she encounters Robin. He inveighs against the blind, infatuated Fridolin, but Rosée defends him and begs Robin not to abandon him. She is willing to pay any price to save him. "Listen, then, my brave Rosée. In this forest, and here only, grows a magic flower, the four-leaved shamrock," he tells her. "Armed with this talisman you can challenge the witch Coloquinte to do her worst. Each time you pluck a leaf your wish will be granted. Even a fifth wish will be granted, but this one will be at the expense of your life." Without a moment's hesitation Rosée picks the shamrock and, tearing off a leaf, cries: "Where is my Prince? Take me to him, I command you." At this moment a procession of ants approaches under the command of a Brigadier. Robin greets him as an old friend. He asks to see the prisoners whom the ants have taken, and Fridolin and Truck are both produced. They have been put to work as gardeners, and Fridolin is very contrite about his lapse with Cunegonde. "Tell me, Brigadier," says Robin, "is Coloquinte still at war with the Queen of the Bees?" "At daggers drawn," the Brigadier tells him. "The wicked witch has destroyed all the hives in the country. The bees will fight for you to the last sting."

SCENE 3. A procession of bees now approaches, escorting the Queen Bee, and their arrival is followed by a grand ballet. At the end of the ballet a huge hive rises and the bees group round it. Suddenly thunder is heard and Coloquinte arrives in a dragon car. "Merry-making—and I not invited!" she cries. "We must put a stop to this." "Not yet," Rosée tells her, and plucks a leaf from the shamrock. The hive opens and Coloquinte falls backwards into it, while wasps surround it and menace her with their stings. "Fly, my friends," urges the Queen Bee. "We will keep her prisoner as long as possible." "One hour will be enough to enable us to reach the Island of Monkeys," Robin tells her. Then, climbing into Coloquinte's dragon car, they drive away.

ACT IV

SCENE 1. En route to the Island of Monkeys a terrible storm—raised by Coloquinte's witchcraft—wrecks the travellers' boat near to shore and they are parted. Fridolin saves Rosée's life and in the process discovers that she is a woman. The scene ends with them both blissfully in love with each other, and Robin, watching them, declares: "Everything goes as I wish. Little did Coloquinte imagine that by raising that tempest she was helping me to carry out my plans." Robin's purpose in visiting the island is to kidnap the King of the Monkeys, who is destined to deliver Fridolin from his enemy, Carotte. By a trick he lures the Monkey King to his side, seizes him and binds him. Throwing a handful of sweets to the other monkeys, who scramble for them, the party escape, bearing with them the King of the Monkeys.

SCENE 2. In a room in the palace a Cabinet meeting is being held. Things in Krokodyne have come to a serious pass. King Carotte has lost all his following and is now prostrate with terror. Only Cunegonde can do anything with him and, half dragging him along, she persuades him to show himself to his angry subjects.

SCENE 3. To the market-place come Fridolin, Rosée, Robin and Truck with the monkey, who, to the children's delight, is made to dance. Truck has managed to retain a packet of Zizanie magic powder, given him by Quiribibi, and Robin orders him to scatter it on the ground and await results. Almost immediately a revolt breaks out, citizens complaining of prices, abusing the Government, grumbling at taxes, insulting King Carotte.

Into the middle of this ugly scene comes the trembling Carotte with Cunegonde and his followers. Vainly Coloquinte tries to rally his failing courage, telling him that Rosée's fifth wish on the four-leaved shamrock is Fridolin's last hope and that it will cost the life of his beloved. "No matter, I will use it," cries Rosée, and Robin is just in time to stop her as the monkey rushes forward, seizes the green tuft from Carotte's head and eats it. Carotte sinks into the earth and his followers flee. With a cry of "All is lost", Coloquinte, too, sinks into the ground.

SCENE 4. Robin addresses the populace with the words "People, behold your true Sovereign and his Princess." With cries of "Long life to Fridolin and his bride", the people pay their homage as the curtain falls.

La Fille du Tambour Major

(The Drum-Major's Daughter)

Opéra Comique in Three Acts and Four Scenes

By ALFRED DURU *and* HENRI CHIVOT

Music by JACQUES OFFENBACH

First produced on the 13th December, 1879, at the Théâtre des Folies-Dramatiques, Paris, with Mademoiselle Simon-Gerard, Monsieur Leper and Monsieur Luco. London Production on 19th April, 1880, at the Alhambra Theatre (in English), with Constance Loseby, Fred Leslie, W. Carleton and Frederick Mervin.

Note. The story of La Fille de Tambour Major *is a thinly veiled adaptation of the plot of Donizetti's opera* The Daughter of the Regiment. *It was one of Offenbach's major successes, being produced two years before* The Tales of Hoffmann. *It was the last work to be produced during his life.*

CHARACTERS

MONTHABOR, *Drum-Major*
ROBERT, *Lieutenant*
THE DUKE OF DELLA VOLTA
THE MARCHESE BAMBINI
GRIOLET, *Regimental Drummer*
CLAMPAS, *innkeeper*
THE MOTHER PRIORESS
STELLA
THE DUCHESS OF DELLA VOLTA
CHORUS OF SOLDIERS, SCHOOL-GIRLS, COURTIERS AND TOWNSFOLK

The action takes place in Lombardy in 1806.

ACT I

The scene is the garden of a convent school for girls. In the wall surrounding it is a door and among the trees stands a small pavilion. In a niche in the pavilion is a statue of the Madonna, and the curtain rises to disclose the pupils on their knees in prayer to the Madonna, while the Mother Prioress dozes placidly in a garden chair in the morning sunshine. This peaceful scene is interrupted by the arrival of Stella, a high-spirited girl, who is always in trouble with authority. Her entrance awakens the Mother Prioress, who tells the girls that in honour of the Saint's day they may have a holiday. She urges Stella to remember that she is the daughter of a Duke and to behave with decorum, and then she withdraws. Stella repeats to the girls a political rumour she has heard at the house of her father, the Duke of Della Volta. Napoleon's troops are reported to have crossed the Alps and invaded Italy, and it is rumoured that a strong underground movement among the Italians is ready to welcome the French army as deliverers who will liberate them from the yoke of Austrian domination. This underground movement has adopted a patriotic song of which Stella has obtained a copy. With great éclat she proceeds to sing it to her schoolmates:

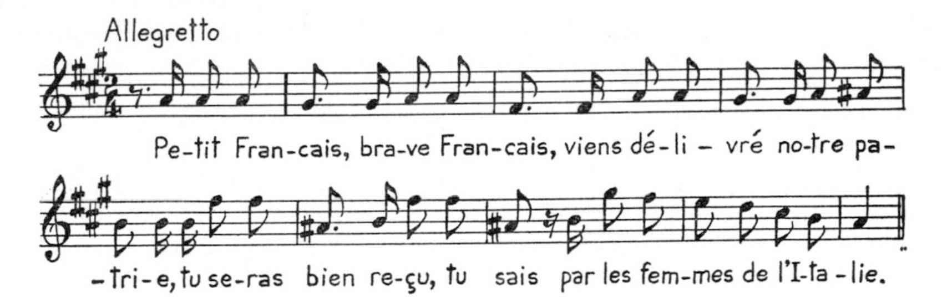

As Stella is singing this revolutionary song, the Mother Prioress returns and is horrified at what she hears. For her disloyalty, Stella is ordered solitary confinement in the school and a diet of bread and water. As she departs, defiantly, the girls whisper that they will see to it that she doesn't starve. After Stella has left, the Mother Prioress lectures the girls on the advantages of obedience. As she is doing so a gardener rushes in in a state of terror, to announce that a detachment of French troops is approaching the convent. Sounds of distant drums can now be heard, of men's voices shouting military orders and the tramp of marching feet. The Mother Prioress orders her girls to form themselves into a "crocodile" and marches them off to seek refuge in the neighbouring convent of Santa Maria, a league distant. As they vanish there comes a loud knocking on the garden door and cries of "Open". As there is no response, one of the soldiers, Griolet, a drummer, scales the convent wall and, opening the garden door, admits his colleagues. They are headed by young Lieutenant Robert and an elderly Drum-Major, Monthabor, and followed by the Regimental Vivandière, Claudine, mounted on a neat cart drawn by a donkey. As Claudine has run out of provisions, a sergeant and some men are sent off to the house to forage. They return with Stella, who had remained in solitary confinement in the house and whose existence the Mother Prioress had completely forgotten in the frenzy of escape. She is at first scared stiff, but soon conquers her fears and is delighted to find herself surrounded by so many handsome soldiers. Lieutenant Robert is greatly attracted towards Stella, to the jealous annoyance of Claudine, who is in love with him and who pays no attention to the poor Drummer, Griolet, who adores her. After a meal the soldiers, escorted by Stella, repair to the house to arrange sleeping accommodation.

When the garden is empty two elderly gentlemen arrive, the Duke of Della Volta and the Marchese Bambini. It is the Duke's intention to marry his daughter, Stella, to the old Marchese as the only means of ending a law-suit of many years' standing between their two families, which has become a crippling financial burden. He has brought the Marchese to the convent to introduce him to Stella and he is horrified to find the place in the possession of French troops. As the two old men are standing about in a bewildered fashion, the Mother Prioress at the head of her girls rushes in, pursued by the military and begging for mercy. With the soldiers is Stella, and the Duke is furious to find her on the best of terms with the Frenchmen. He tries to drag her away, but Stella stays to bid the troops an affectionate farewell and promises to remember them in her prayers. Finally she bursts into a defiant rendering of the Revolutionary song and, as the scandalised Duke drags her away, she blows kisses to Lieutenant Robert.

ACT II

Back home at the Duke's château, Stella refuses even to consider marrying the old Marchese Bambini. As she is arguing with her parents three French soldiers are observed approaching the house. They are Lieutenant Robert, Drum-Major Monthabor and the Drummer, Griolet. They present a billeting order and demand accommodation at the château, which the Duke against his will has to provide. It is late evening and guests are arriving for a ball. The servants turn the three soldiers out of the reception-rooms and as they go off to inspect their accommodation the dance band strikes up a waltz to which the guests are soon revolving.

Meanwhile Monthabor has inspected their quarters and, finding them to be draughty attics, hurries downstairs and strides into the ballroom, fuming. He asks a footman where the hosts are, and the footman points out the Duchess. The Drum-Major advances to make his complaint. As the Duchess turns, he exclaims: "My God, Margot!" and she cries: "Bernard!" She almost faints and has to be revived. Later in a scene between the Duchess and Monthabor it emerges that they were formerly married to one another in the days when Monthabor was a dyer and the Duchess a washer-woman. Monthabor asks what has happened to their daughter, and the Duchess, not wishing to prejudice her chances of marrying the Marchese, does not divulge the fact that Stella is their daughter. She lies to Monthabor, pretending that Stella is the Duke's child and that their daughter is at school in Paris. The Duchess swears him to silence as to their former relationship and Monthabor promises to be discreet.

After this Stella and Robert meet, and are overjoyed to see each other. He is madly in love with her and, when she hears that his regiment is moving away the next day, she does not attempt to hide her love for him:

Later Monthabor waylays Stella and questions her about her childhood. Did she always live in these luxurious surroundings? Stella tells him she vaguely remembers a small cottage, poorly furnished, and she remembers vividly a man who used to play with her, whose hands were never the same colour two days running. This is proof that Stella remembers him when he was a dyer, and Monthabor breaks the news to her that he is her father. She embraces him warmly and begs him to take her with him when the regiment marches. Father and daughter then withdraw to find Stella a Vivandière's uniform. The lawyer now arrives with the marriage contract. The guests all assemble to watch the signing; the Marchese, the Duke and the Duchess are waiting, but there is no sign of Stella. A search is made, Stella's name is called and in she comes in her smart Vivandière's uniform. "What are you doing in that get-up, my daughter?" asks the Duke, and Stella tells him firmly in front of everybody that she is not his daughter. "This is my father," she says, pointing to Monthabor, "and I am the Drum-Major's daughter."

"And now," cries Monthabor, "come, my daughter, we must take the road." As they are about to move off a sergeant dashes in with news that the house is surrounded by Austrian troops, and the curtain falls on a thrilling scene in which the Duke and his guests all draw their swords in an endeavour to prevent the Frenchmen leaving. But the superior skill of the professional wins the day and, taking Stella and Claudine under their wing, the French fight their way triumphantly out of the Château.

ACT III

Scene i. The scene is set in the interior of an inn in Milan. The landlord, Clampas, is a pillar of the Italian underground movement, favouring the French, and when the curtain rises, he is sheltering Lieutenant Robert and Claudine, who after the escape from the château have become separated from Monthabor, Stella and Griolet. They are anxious to rejoin the regiment, but Clampas tells them that to leave Milan it is necessary to procure a safe-conduct pass. He suggests they go and stay with a friend of his, Signor Palamos, who lives at 27 Via Bonafacio. The house is situated next to a gate of the city and if they bide their time they may be able to slip through it unobserved. Claudine, disguised as an old woman with red umbrella and basket, a long cloak covering her Vivandière's dress, is sent off to interview Signor Palamos.

The Duke and Duchess now arrive at the inn, and Robert hides himself. They have an assignation with Marchese Bambini, who has gone to procure from the Governor of Milan a safe-conduct pass to give the Duke freedom of movement in his search for Stella. The Marquis returns with four Austrian soldiers, whom the Governor is placing at the Duke's disposal. He mentions that the Governor is greatly worried at the absence of his son, who is missing, and will send round the safe-conduct pass later. Monthabor, Griolet and Stella now arrive at the inn. They have encountered the Governor's son on the road, travelling with a monk, and have overpowered him and taken his and his companion's clothes and his carriage. Griolet is impersonating the Governor's son, Monthabor the monk, and Stella is dressed in an elegant coachman's outfit. During a conversation with them the Duke mentions his missing daughter, and Stella boldly invents a colourful story of finding a pretty girl in a Vivandière's dress crying by the roadside and of driving her to Milan. "And to what address?" asks the Duke eagerly. At a loss for a moment, Stella's eyes fall on a piece of paper on the table, bearing Signor Palamos' address. "Twenty-seven Via Bonifacio," she tells the Duke, and he hurries away to dispatch his soldiers thither to bring Stella back. Meanwhile the Governor has sent round the safe-conduct pass and, in the Duke's absence, Clampas has given it to the Duchess.

Monthabor, in his monk's habit, makes himself known to her and persuades her to give him the safe-conduct pass. Then he calls Griolet and Robert. They bid Clampas farewell, but unfortunately the Duke returns with his soldiers just as Clampas is saying: "Good-bye, Lieutenant Robert." "Arrest that man," cries the Duke, pointing to Robert, and poor Robert is seized. The Duke, full of glee, informs the Duchess that the soldiers report that there *was* a young woman in Vivandière's uniform at 27 Via Bonifacio and that she has been removed to the Governor's house. He also boasts that he has thought of a way of compelling Stella to marry the Marchese Bambini.

SCENE 2. The last scene takes place in a public square outside the inn. On the right stands a church and at the back of the stage a bridge crosses the river. A marriage is obviously about to take place. The Duke and the Marchese Bambini arrive at the church, and the Duke tells the Marchese that he has put it to Stella via her mother, that, if she will consent to marry the Marchese, Lieutenant Robert will be released. Robert is now marched in by the Austrian soldiers. He tells Clampas that he has been granted his freedom but has no idea why. As they are talking, bells start ringing and the bride arrives at the church. "Here is Stella," cries the Duchess, and Robert overhears her. Putting two and two together, he decides that Stella has been blackmailed to marry the Marchese with his liberty as the bribe. He strides over to the bride and snatches off her veil, to disclose Claudine. For Claudine, in league with the Duchess, was prepared to go through with the mock marriage up to the words "I will", to outwit the Duke. The Duke is livid at being deceived and orders the soldiers to re-arrest Robert and remove him to gaol. But at the eleventh hour fate steps in. There is a sound of distant military music and the tramp of marching feet. Napoleon's victorious army enters Milan across the bridge. With banners waving and crowds cheering, the French troops are acclaimed as the liberators of Italy. And now there is no barrier to the happiness of Robert and Stella, the Drum-Major's daughter.

Le Docteur Miracle

Operetta in One Act

By LÉON BATTU *and* LUDOVIC HALÉVY

English version by DAVID HARRIS

Music by GEORGES BIZET

First produced on 9th April, 1857, at the Théâtre des Bouffes-Parisiens, Paris.

Note. In 1856 Offenbach announced a prize to be awarded by the Bouffes to the composer of a suitable operetta. After a weeding-out process the six surviving candidates were provided with a libretto written by Léon Battu and Ludovic Halévy. The winners were Georges Bizet and Charles Lecocq and in April 1857 both works, which were total failures, were produced at the Bouffes.

CHARACTERS

THE MAYOR OF PADUA
LAURETTA, *his daughter*
VÉRONIQUE, *his wife and Lauretta's stepmother*
CAPTAIN SILVIO, *Lauretta's lover*

The action takes place in the living-room of the Mayor of Padua's house in the Middle Ages.

When the curtain rises on the living-room of the Mayor of Padua's house it is early morning. Despite the early hour, leaning out of the window in a mixture of irritation and curiosity are the Mayor, his wife, Véronique, and his daughter, Lauretta. From the neighbouring square come the sour and raucous sounds of trumpet, trombone and drum. Who, they wonder, dares to disturb the town at such an hour with such a din? The Mayor, prompted by seeing his daughter out of bed at such an hour, hazards the belief that Lauretta's undesirable follower, Captain Silvio, is serenading her. But he is proved wrong when the author of the hullabaloo turns out to be a travelling quack doctor, advertising his nostrums. The Mayor promptly leaves the house to quell the noise and warns the women that a new servant may arrive while he is out, and that if he does arrive he is to await the Mayor's return. "Yes, young lady," he tells Lauretta, "he is to replace that scalliwag who used to bring you letters from Captain Silvio." When the Mayor has left, Véronique scolds Lauretta for falling in love with a soldier—"here today and gone tomorrow" is her description of soldiers. But Lauretta is hopelessly in love and admits it:

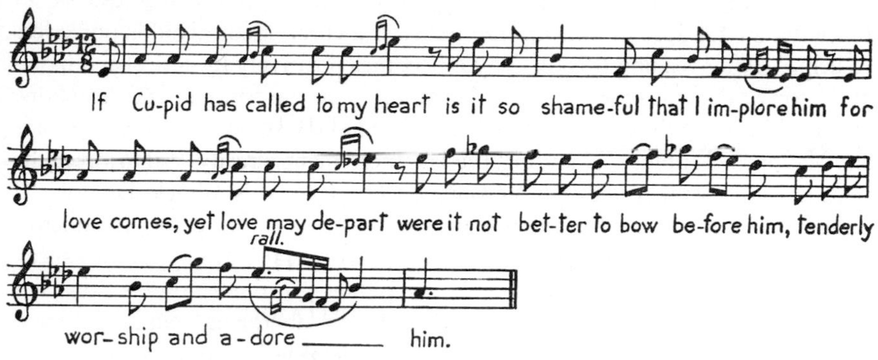

They are arguing the merits of soldiers as husbands when the Mayor returns with the new servant, Pasquin. With the two women arguing, the Mayor cannot get a word in edgeways, and turns them out of the room. He then interviews Pasquin, a hideous-looking lout with a patch over one eye. He endears himself to the Mayor by his declared dislike of soldiers, and, when the ladies return, to Véronique by taking her for the Mayor's daughter. Lauretta, however, is disgusted with him. Pasquin is told to prepare breakfast and lay the table and starts by dropping a pile of plates and breaking them. He then sets about preparing and serving an omelette *à la Française*. There is much discussion over the recipe. But though Pasquin talks learnedly about cooking, the omelette in practice tastes revolting and the Mayor spits it out. After breakfast, feeling that a walk is necessary to restore his digestion, the Mayor takes Véronique out with him. Lauretta is not allowed to accompany them, for fear she might encounter the undesirable Captain Silvio, so she is left behind with Pasquin. They sing a duet which starts with Lauretta making offensive comments on Pasquin's appearance. But he tells her to look again, and she suddenly realises that he is her lover, Silvio, disguised under a masterly make-up. They fall into each other's arms with passionate joy:

As the duet finishes with the lovers in each other's arms, the Mayor surprises them. He soon discovers that Pasquin is the detested Captain Silvio and throws him out neck and crop. Then he turns on the weeping Lauretta and upbraids her for her treachery. Véronique enters with a letter for him, and he tells her testily to open it. But she has read only a few lines when she cries out in dismay. For the letter reads: "To the Mayor of Padua. Revenge is sweet. Frustrated in my intentions with regard to your daughter, this morning I had the honour and enormous pleasuring of administering to you through the medium of an omelette, a fatal dose of poison. Do not seek a cure. Medical aid is powerless to help." After reading this the Mayor becomes positively hysterical and bawls at the top of his voice for a doctor. At this moment the trumpet and trombone music advertising the quack doctor bursts forth in the square. "What?" groans the Mayor. "Trumpets sounding the last judgement already?" However, he pulls himself together and tells Véronique to send for this Miracle-Doctor. "I will give him my entire fortune if I survive this horror." In comes the doctor, takes one look at his patient and remarks: "Pisonatus!" He appears to speak only Latin, but Véronique fortunately understands it, due to the fact that her fourth husband was a chemist. She translates for the doctor and tells her husband that though he is suffering from a violent attack of poisoning, the doctor can cure him, but it will cost five thousand ducats. All this time the doctor has been eyeing Lauretta in an admiring fashion. When the Mayor tries to beat him down in price Doctor Miracle tells him he will cure him if he can marry his daughter. The Mayor immediately consents and Lauretta, surprisingly, agrees with perfect equanimity to sacrificing herself. The doctor demands the Mayor's consent in writing, and while he is setting it down on paper, Doctor Miracle writes out the prescription of his infallible cure. But when he reads it Lauretta's father flies into a great rage. The prescription runs: "Mayor, as you read this prescription you are completely cured by your future son-in-law, Silvio, army Captain, who never had any intention of shortening your days." For the second time Silvio has got the better of Lauretta's father. The Mayor has to put the best face he can on the situation and he gives the lovers his blessing.

Le Docteur Miracle

Opéra Comique in One Act

By LÉON BATTU *and* LUDOVIC HALÉVY

Music by CHARLES LECOCQ

First produced on the 8th April, 1857, at the Théâtre des Bouffes-Parisiens, Paris.
See also Le Docteur Miracle, *music by Bizet.*

CHARACTERS

THE MAYOR OF PADUA
LAURETTA, *his daughter*
VÉRONIQUE, *his wife and Lauretta's stepmother*
CAPTAIN SILVIO, *Lauretta's lover*

The action takes place in the living-room of the Mayor of Padua's house in the Middle Ages.

Note. For synopsis of the plot see Bizet's Le Docteur Miracle (p. 62).

The two extracts from Lecocq's score given below are taken from the same numbers quoted from Bizet's setting.

1. Lauretta defends her action in getting engaged to a soldier:

2. Lauretta joyfully recognises Captain Silvio's features under Pasquin's make-up:

Les Cents Vierges
(The Hundred Virgins)

Opéra Bouffe in Three Acts

By Messieurs CLAIREVILLE, CHIVOT *and* DURU

Music by CHARLES LECOCQ

First produced on 16th March, 1872, at the Théâtre des Fantaisies-Parisiennes, Brussels, with Mario Widmer and Mademoiselle Gentien. Modern version by André Mouëzy-Éon and Albert Willemetz produced on 15th September, 1942, at the Théâtre de l'Apollo, Paris.
London productions on 21st June, 1873, at the St. James's Theatre (in French), and on 14th September, 1874, as The Island of Bachelors *at the Gaiety Theatre (in English), with Constance Loseby, Arthur Cecil and Ellen Farren.*

CHARACTERS

LE DUC ANATOLE DE QUILLEMOIS
MARCEL, *a young painter*
POULARDOT, *a grocer*
CAPTAIN BORDENAVE, *Captain of a man-of-war*
BAPTISTIN, *innkeeper*
GABRIELLE, *engaged to Anatole*
OPPORTUNE, *married to Poulardot*
IRMA, *a lady of the town*
DUFLAGNARD, *Governor of the Île Verte*
CLOPINETTE, *his secretary*
BOUFFIGUE } *Colonists*
POUPETTE }
CHORUS OF DEMI-MONDAINES, SAILORS, EMIGRÉS, COLONISTS, TOWNSFOLK.

The action takes place in 1872, in Paris, Marseilles and on the Île Verte. This synopsis follows the Paris version of 1942, which is in two acts (seven scenes).

ACT I

SCENE I. The first scene is a dance-hall in Paris, "Le Bal Mabille", a meeting-place of wealthy young men-about-town and ladies of the demi-monde. Several of these ladies are discussing what is to become of them in the future when one of them, Irma, produces a cutting from a newspaper, headed "The Colonists of the Île Verte". The Île Verte is a newly acquired French possession situated between the Antipodes and the Equator. It has recently been colonised and the Government are advertising for "a hundred virgins" to volunteer to go out to the island as prospective wives for the colonists. The ladies are most excited and withdraw to discuss the project.

A young girl, pursued by an importunate young man, then enters the hall. He tries to kiss her and she smacks his face. Startled and somewhat aggrieved, he apologises and retires, while the young girl turns to a friendly looking middle-aged woman seated at a nearby table. The young woman, Gabrielle, who is of a very different class from the habitués of "Le Bal Mabille", is engaged and is to be married on the morrow to the Duc de Quillemois. Having heard him say he was going to celebrate his farewell to bachelorhood at "Le Bal Mabille", Gabrielle has pursued him there from curiosity. Gabrielle's friendly acquaintance is a certain Opportune Poulardot. Married to a wealthy grocer, she and her husband are on a tour of France to see the sights. The two women are soon on the best of terms. They order a bottle of champagne and both become very gay—so much so that when the importunate young man who had his face smacked returns, Gabrielle is delighted to see him. He showers her with compliments and endearments and she is enchanted. He tells her his name is Marcel Davray and that he is a painter. He asks her to dance and they waltz away together.

Gabrielle's fiancé, Anatole, Duc de Quillemois, now arrives and is warmly welcomed by all the ladies of the town. He is greatly dismayed to find Gabrielle in "Le Bal Mabille" and proposes to take her home immediately. She introduces him to her new friend Opportune Poulardot and to her husband, the grocer, Monsieur Poulardot, who is thrilled to meet a Duke, though Anatole rebuffs his advances. But Gabrielle has taken a fancy to the Poulardots and confides to them that she and Anatole are to spend their honeymoon in the South of France, Marseilles, Nice, Monte Carlo; and Poulardot secretly makes up his mind to follow the same itinerary. Presently Anatole tells Gabrielle he is taking her home. She begs for one more dance, which Anatole stipulates must be with him. But he has drunk far too much champagne to be able to partner her, so Gabrielle goes off happily with Marcel. Marcel is by now desperately in love with Gabrielle, although she insists that she is marrying the Duc de Quillemois. He tells her significantly that she may marry the Duke but he will see to it that she does not become his wife. As they dance he sings to her:

SCENES 2, 3 AND 4. The rest of Act One takes place outside Baptistin's inn on the quay at Marseilles. Captain Bordenave, who commands the man-of-war "La Belle Marseillaise", tells Baptistin of his commission to deliver a hundred virgins at the Île Verte. They will later be assembling at the inn. Anatole and Gabrielle arrive at the inn on their honeymoon. Anatole is very disgruntled. Why, he complains, when he can afford to stay at the best hotel in Marseilles, does Gabrielle insist on putting up at an obscure inn? From Anatole's point of view the honeymoon so far has proved a dismal failure. Owing to the importunity of the Poulardots, who have stuck to them like leeches, they have hardly had a moment to themselves by day and a series of misadventures has ruined their nights. Anatole complains he has not even had an opportunity to consummate the marriage. At Lyon, owing to a misunderstanding, a commissionaire took Gabrielle and their luggage to one hotel, while Anatole waited up all night in a freezing room in another hotel. At Valence, just as they were going to bed, a police official knocked on their bedroom door, demanded Anatole's passport and insisted that he should accompany him to the police station. There he was locked up for the night and released next morning with apologies. The police had mistaken him for a dangerous anarchist called Billembois. At Avignon, having a headache, he asked the floor-waiter in the hotel for a cachet fèvre and the waiter gave him a veronal cachet, as a result of which he slept for twenty-four hours. All this may have been sheer bad luck, but Anatole recalls a strange resemblance between the commissionaire at Lyon, the policeman at Valence and the floor-waiter at Avignon. All he now wants is Gabrielle to himself and he believes they have really shaken off the Poulardots by pretending they were going to Aix-les-bains.

And now, to Anatole's fury, the familiar voices of the detested Poulardots are heard and they appear with cries of delight at the reunion. They clamour for a room at the inn, and though none is vacant the landlord is prepared to let the Poulardots have the housekeeper's room. As it is not very comfortable, Poulardot suggests to Anatole that their wives occupy his and Gabrielle's room and that the two men share the housekeeper's room. Anatole rages, but is compelled out of politeness to acquiesce. A postman now approaches and delivers a letter to Gabrielle. Anatole remarks that the postman bears a marked resemblance to the commissionaire at Lyon, the police officer at Valence and the floor-waiter at Avignon. He observes that the handwriting of the letter is that of a man, but Gabrielle declares that the letter is from her aunt, the Marquise. Anatole, faintly suspicious, goes off to see about visas for Italy, and Poulardot, to his annoyance, accompanies him. Opportune joins Gabrielle and declares that she wishes to visit one of the big ships moored in the harbour. Ships are so romantic! Gabrielle too is keen. They consult the innkeeper, who tells them that many other ladies are going on board a man-of-war and that he will speak to the Captain. While they are waiting Marcel approaches and renews his impassioned love declarations to Gabrielle. She tells him that in spite of his series of disguises, as commissionaire, as policeman, as floor-waiter and postman, her husband has recognised him. Marcel refuses to be downcast, vows Gabrielle shall be his and goes off to disguise himself as a sailor.

A number of ladies, who include Irma and all the habitués of "Le Bal Mabille", now arrive at the inn. They are signing on to sail for the Île Verte as prospective wives for the colonists. Captain Bordenave reads the assembed ladies the terms of agreement. They are:

1. To take a husband on arrival at the Île Verte.
2. To be faithful and dutiful wives.
3. To become mothers in the shortest time possible.

All sign the declaration, and the Captain is just saying, "Now, ladies, you may go on board", when Gabrielle and Opportune appear. They tell the Captain that they too wish to go on board, and as the Captain needs just two more to make up his complement of a hundred virgins, he welcomes them. The inn-keeper gets them to sign a paper of whose implication they are completely unaware—he is in Marcel's pay—and Gabrielle and Opportune go on board the man-of-war, whose crew includes Marcel. As Anatole and Poulardot return, the harbour cannon is fired and the battleship sets sail. Anatole is watching its departure through a spy-glass when to his horror he sees Gabrielle and Opportune on deck. He and Poulardot learn with dismay that the ship is carrying a cargo of virgins ("Virgins—Opportune!!" exclaims Poulardot) to the Île Verte. The two distracted husbands hurry off to seek transport and follow their erring wives.

ACT II

SCENE 5. On the Île Verte the atmosphere is tense. The colonists become daily more disgruntled as the expected ship, laden with wives for them, fails to put in an appearance. The Governor, Monsieur Duflacnard, and his secretary, Clopinette, try to pacify them by telling them that the first vessel with its precious cargo is feared lost at sea and that now a man-of-war, "La Belle Marseillaise", with a second hundred of virgins is on its way. As he is talking, news is brought that "La Belle Marsellaise" is sailing into harbour. With cries of joy the colonists run off to the harbour to greet their prospective wives, and the seashore, where they were assembled, is deserted. Now round a rocky headland floats a barrel containing two men. They are Anatole and Poulardot. Shipwrecked en route from Marseilles, they contrived to climb aboard a convenient barrel and complete their voyage. They manage to jump ashore, and when the islanders return they hide behind some rocks. From their hiding-place they overhear a conversation between their wives and the Governor. Gabrielle and Opportune explain that they are not available as wives for the colonists because they are already married. The Governor asks for proof of their statement. Anatole and Poulardot are about to emerge to claim their wives when the Governor adds: "Even if your husbands did appear, I should have them sewn into sacks and thrown into the sea." In this dilemma their only chance of safety is to disguise themselves as two women, which they do by making contact with Gabrielle and Opportune, who provide them with female attire. They then appear as mother and daughter. Poulardot calls himself "Arsinoë Petrowskott" and Anatole "Léocardie Barbarina Barbarini". They tell the Governor an elaborate story of being captured by pirates, sold to agents of the white-slave traffic and escaping en route for Buenos Aires. The Governor welcomes them as additional wives for the colonists, for it is discovered on arrival that "La Belle Marseillaise's" cargo of virgins, instead of numbering one hundred, is reduced to only nineteen. Captain Bordenave regrets that at Madeira thirty-four virgins deserted the ship and another forty-seven at Madagascar. The Governor's solution to the question of apportioning the wives fairly is to draw lots. Now Marcel, who has managed to get himself accepted as a colonist, has bribed the secretary, Clopinette, to fix matters so that Gabrielle shall be assigned to him as wife. But the Governor's lottery frustrates Marcel's scheming, and Gabrielle, who no longer attempts to hide her love for him, is desolated. The lots are now drawn. For the name of each colonist which Clopinette draws out of a blue basket the Governor draws the name of a virgin out of a pink one. Gabrielle is given to a hideous bearded colonist called Bouffigue. Opportune is drawn by a handsome type, Poupette. The Governor draws Léocadie (Anatole) and Clopinette draws Arsinoë (Poulardot).

Scene 6. Later Marcel and Gabrielle manage to meet in a secluded grove. They bewail the miscarriage of their plans, but Marcel puts new heart into Gabrielle by assuring her that love such as theirs is capable of moving mountains.

Scene 7. In the Governor's palace Monsieur Duflacnard with Léocadie (Anatole) and Clopinette with Arsinoë (Poulardot) sit down to their wedding breakfast. The Governor's amorous advances to Léocadie (Anatole) are primly repelled with "Please, *not* before my mother," while Arsinoë (Poulardot) is archly coy with Clopinette. After a glass or two of wine Léocadie (Anatole) is prevailed on to sing while the others join in the chorus.

This domestic scene is interrupted by the sudden arrival of Bouffigue and Poupette, the colonial husbands of Gabrielle and Opportune respectively. They complain that on attempting to make love to their "wives" each of them received a black eye, and that later in Gabrielle's and Opportune's rooms they found two complete outfits of male attire and in addition two razors. The Governor immediately assumes that Gabrielle and Opportune are men impersonating women. He sends for them, and Anatole and Poulardot seize the opportunity to slip away. When Gabrielle and Opportune arrive, the Governor greets them with "Come in, gentlemen", and to prove their sex they are reduced to staging a faint. The Governor and Clopinette hurry to loosen their clothing and their contours reveal them, without shadow of doubt, as two shapely women.

The situation is further complicated by the Governor's amorous pursuit of Gabrielle. A revolt of dissatisfied colonists who have failed to draw wives, encouraged by Marcel, brings about the *dénouement.* The army has joined the revolt and Marcel is elected Governor of the island in place of Monsieur Duflacnard. Marcel appeals to Anatole to release Gabrielle to marry him and when Anatole realises that she truly loves Marcel he agrees to an annulment of a marriage that has never been consummated. Great excitement now greets the arrival of the original vessel which sailed, with its cargo of one hundred virgins intact. Every colonist is provided with a wife and all the Parisians, including the ladies from "Le Bal Mabille", decide to sail for home.

La Fille de Madame Angot

Opéra Comique in Three Acts

Book and Lyrics by MESSIEURS CLAIRVILLE, GIRAUDIN *and* KONIG

Music by CHARLES LECOCQ

First produced on 4th December, 1872, at the Théâtre des Fantaisies Parisiennes (Alcazar Royal), Brussels, with Pauline Luigini, Alfred Jolly and Mario Widmer. London productions 17th May, 1873, at the St. James's Theatre (in French), and 4th October, 1873 (in English, translated by H. J. Byron), at the Philharmonic Theatre, Islington, with Selina Dolaro, Julie Mathews, Mr. Nordblom and John Murray.

CHARACTERS

CLAIRETTE ANGOT, *a florist*
POMPONNET, *a hairdresser*
ANGE PITOU, *a revolutionary poet*
MADEMOISELLE LANGE, *a famous actress*
LARIVAUDIÈRE, *her secret lover*
CHORUS OF TRADESMEN, HUSSARS, TOWNSFOLK, ETC.

ACT I

The scene is a market square in Paris, and prominent features of the set are two shops, one with the sign "Pomponnet, Hairdresser–Barber" and the other "Clairette, Florist". A placard on both shop doors reads "Closed on account of marriage". The action of the operetta takes place during the Directorate which followed the French Revolution of 1793. Barras is at the head of the Government and Mademoiselle Lange, a famous actress, is his reigning mistress. In the market lives Clairette Angot, a young orphan. She has been adopted as child of the market and given a good education and upbringing by the tradesmen who work there. She has grown into a clever, modest and charming girl, very different from her mother, the famous Madame Angot, a Parisian fishwife. One of the women of the market gives a lively account of how Madame Angot crossed the seas in a balloon, was nearly eaten by cannibals in Malabar, and captured the heart of the Grand Turk in competition with his five hundred wives. This is sung to Lecocq's sparkling tune:

On the day the curtain rises Clairette Angot is to be married to a well-to-do barber called Pomponnet, but just as the wedding party is setting off for the ceremony news comes of a hitch. Clairette, it appears, was born in the harem at Constantinople and there is some doubt as to paternity. She is delighted at the delay, as she is really in love with Ange Pitou, a satirist and writer of political songs against the Government, who cannot afford to marry. Ange Pitou has been directing his lampoons against the wealthy Larivaudière, the secret lover of Mademoiselle Lange. Larivaudière, fearing discovery of his liaison with Mademoiselle Lange by Barras, bribes Ange Pitou with thirty thousand crowns to direct his satire elsewhere. Ange Pitou, rich at last, runs to the market declaring his intention to marry Clairette— but her adopted parents are determined that Clairette shall marry Pomponnet. Ange Pitou has announced that he will appear in the market square to sing his new song at eleven o'clock, and an expectant crowd is gathered to hear him. But having accepted Larivaudière's money, Ange Pitou cannot very well present a lampoon directed against his patron's mistress, Mademoiselle Lange. Now, whenever Ange Pitou sings one of his anti-Government songs he is always arrested but invariably released the following day with a caution. Clairette remembers this, and desiring at all costs to delay her marriage to Pomponnet, sees in arrest a perfect solution to her problem. She has memorised Ange Pitou's new song directed against Mademoiselle Lange and now, standing up in the market square, she tells the crowd that she knows the song and proceeds to sing it:

Clairette is promptly arrested by the military and, despite the protests of the market people, is dragged away to gaol.

ACT II

When Mademoiselle Lange hears of the public singing of a lampoon directed against herself by a young girl in the market, she arranges with Barras to have her brought from prison to her house to discover the reason for the attack. Pomponnet, who is Mademoiselle Lange's hairdresser, confesses that his bride-to-be, Clairette Angot, was the singer, but he assures Mademoiselle Lange that she is innocent and that Ange Pitou, the author of the song, alone is guilty. Mademoiselle Lange sends Pomponnet away to fetch the offending song, and later Clairette arrives. As soon as they meet, Lange and Clairette recognise each other as old school friends. While they are talking over the old days and Clairette is explaining that her singing in the street was to make sure that by being arrested she could avoid marrying Pomponnet, Ange Pitou arrives at the house. He has also been sent for by Mademoiselle Lange to explain the reasons for his attacks on her. She sees him alone and there springs up between them an instant tenderness and sympathy. But their intimate scene is interrupted by the arrival of the jealous Larivaudière. Mademoiselle Lange, in answer to his reproaches, assures him that Ange Pitou has come to the house to see not her but Clairette, whom he loves and by whom he is equally adored. Mademoiselle Lange has no idea that she is telling the truth about the attachment between Clairette and Ange Pitou, for she is unaware of it; but Larivaudière is convinced. Lange goes on to tell him that it is important to win the Royalist poet over to their side—and it now becomes clear that Lange, Barras and Larivaudière, while posing as Republicans, are really working for the Royalist cause and that that very evening Royalist conspirators are to meet at Mademoiselle Lange's house at midnight. They duly enter wearing their badge of recognition, a black collar and white wig, to this conspiratorial tune:

and all are conspiring happily when the alarm is given. The house is surrounded by Hussars, sent to arrest the conspirators. By her quick wits, however, Mademoiselle Lange saves the situation. Lights are brought, music strikes up and the appearance of a ball is improvised. The Hussars are invited to join the dance and soon all are revolving to an infectious waltz.

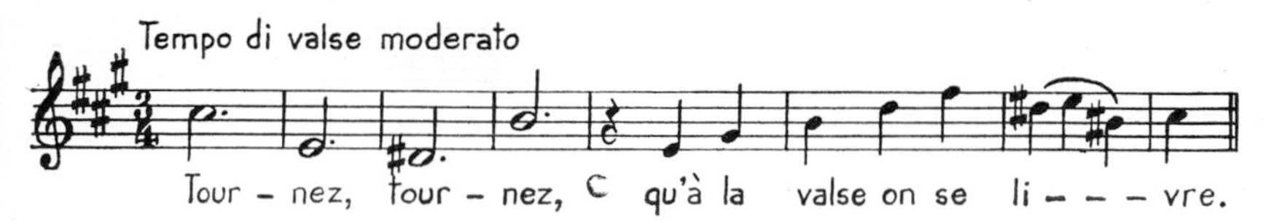

The only cloud on the horizon is the discovery, during the dance, by Clairette and Lange that they are mutually attached to Ange Pitou.

ACT III

The last act is played outside a dance-hall in the gardens of Belleville. Determined to find out if Mademoiselle Lange means to rob her of Ange Pitou, Clairette writes a letter to each of them, as though from the other, making a rendezvous in the gardens. She also summons Larivaudière and all her foster-parents from the market. The lovers are surprised, and there is a lively squabble between Lange and Clairette. Finally differences are happily settled. Clairette tells Lange that in giving Ange Pitou to her for nothing she gives him for exactly what he is worth, and she marries Pomponnet after all.

Giroflé-Girofla

Operetta in Three Acts

By Albert van Loo *and* Eugène Letterrier

Music by Charles Lecocq

First produced on 21st March, 1874, at the Alcazar Royal, Brussels, with Paula Luigini, Mario Widmer and Paul Ginet. London production on 6th June, 1874, at the Opera-Comique (in French), with the Brussels cast.

Characters

DON BOLÉRO D'ALCARAZAS, *Governor of an African Colony*
AURORE, *his wife*
GIROFLÉ, GIROFLA } *their twin daughters*
PEDRO, *butler in the service of Don Boléro*
MARASQUIN, *a banker*
MOURZOUK, *Chief of an Arab tribe*
ADMIRAL MATAMOROS *of the French Navy*
CHORUS OF SERVANTS, WEDDING GUESTS, PIRATES, AND ARABS IN MOURZOUK'S SERVICE

ACT I

The scene is a hall in the house of the Governor of an African colony, Don Boléro d'Alcarazas. On this happy day his twin daughters, Giroflé and Girofla, are getting married. The twins resemble each other so closely that it is virtually impossible to tell them apart. (In performance the twins are played by the same actress.) Giroflé is marrying Monsieur Marasquin, the son of a wealthy banker to whom her father is heavily in debt, and Girofla is promised to Mourzouk, the chief of an Arab tribe which has often threatened the security of Don Boléro's colony. Marasquin duly appears and is impatient to get married without delay. As it seems unlikely that Mourzouk will show up until the following day, Giroflé with her parents and bridegroom departs for the church, leaving Girofla alone at home in case Mourzouk should appear unexpectedly early. Soon after the wedding party have left, to Girofla's terror and dismay the house is invaded by a band of pirates. They have been for some time the scourge of the neighbourhood and are reputed to be particularly partial to kidnapping young girls. In vain she pleads for mercy. In company with the butler, Pedro, she is taken captive and removed. Meantime Giroflé and Marasquin have married and the wedding party returns from church to discover the terrible events that have taken place during their absence. Don Boléro immediately applies to Admiral Matamoros, begging him to trace the pirates and rescue Girofla. If only she can be retrieved safe and sound before the arrival of the wild Arab, Mourzouk! But, as ill-luck will have it, Mourzouk arrives earlier than expected. No one has the courage to break the news of Girofla's fate to him and various delaying tactics are attempted. But the violent Arab insists on marrying Girofla at once. In desperation Madame Boléro thinks up a solution, making capital out of the girls' resemblence to each other. Giroflé is persuaded to exchange her blue wedding veil for Girafla's pink one and to impersonate her sister at the altar. She is duly married to the Arab chief and for the moment the two bridegrooms are satisfied.

ACT II

The action takes place in the dining-room of the Governor's house, where the bridegrooms have been inveigled into taking their places at the wedding breakfast on the promise that they will shortly be joined by their respective brides. Meantime Giroflé has been imprisoned in her bedroom on the hopeful assumption that Girofla's return cannot long be delayed. But alas! it is not Girofla but Pedro who is the first to reappear. He has succeeded in making his escape and his news is far from encouraging. The Governor, when he commissioned Admiral Matamoros to pursue the pirates, promised him a handsome reward to rescue his daughter. It now transpires that the mercenary Admiral refuses to set sail until the reward is paid in advance. Grinding his teeth in rage and mortification, Don Boléro is compelled to pay up. Giroflé, meanwhile, has no intention of spending her wedding day in solitary confinement. She manages to escape from her room and runs into several of the wedding guests, young cousins of hers, who ply her assiduously with champagne. Then, full to the brim with Bollinger and bonhomie, Giroflé presents herself before the two bridegrooms. An altercation ensues; Marasquin claiming her, correctly, as his Giroflé in the face of Mourzouk's equally energetic assertion that she is Girofla. Even at this critical stage the harassed parents (and the librettists) manage to escape a *dénouement* and persuade the bridegrooms to retire to their respective bridal chambers on the assurance that they will shortly be joined by their wives. Giroflé is happily enfolded in her husband's embrace with no further delay, while Don Boléro takes the precaution of locking the door on the temperamental Mourzouk. But any hopes of Girofla's speedy return are dashed when news comes that Admiral Matamoros has been captured by the pirates.

ACT III

The last act takes place the next day in the hall of Don Boléro's house. While Giroflé and Marasquin are blissfully happy in a paradise of love, it is not to be expected that the wild Mourzouk would accept the frustrating circumstances of a solitary wedding night, so to speak, lying down. He has, in fact, broken out of his bedroom and left the house in high dudgeon. But in the morning he is observed from a distance to be returning, and the desperate parents resort to further extremes of improvisation to placate the wild Arab. They decide to take Marasquin into their confidence and make a clean breast of all the circumstances of the marriage, including the part which Giroflé has played, of which, unaccountably, he is quite unaware. They then throw themselves on his mercy and beg him to give permission for Giroflé once again to impersonate her sister in order that Mourzouk's anger may be appeased. They assure the couple that no risk attaches to the venture, as Mourzouk is due to return that day to his tribe and had not intended taking his wife with him. Reluctantly Marasquin and Giroflé consent and presently Mourzouk arrives. He is perfectly prepared to be placated, but so obvious are the attempts to speed the parting guest and hurry him on his way that his suspicions are aroused. He demands to be left alone with "his wife". This causes consternation, especially on the part of Marasquin, who resorts to desperate measures to interrupt the tête-à-tête, while Giroflé takes refuge in fainting. Finally there is nothing for it but to own up and Mourzouk is told the truth. A fearful fracas follows and a lively altercation as to whom Giroflé really belongs—for she is in point of fact married to both men. Things are beginning to look really ugly when there is heard the sound of distant cheering and the arrival of a carriage. The front door is opened and there stands Admiral Matamoros. He has turned the tables on the pirates and rescued the happy, delighted girl who stands at his side. The proud parents present Girofla to her bridegroom. Tempers are restored. Honour and both couples are satisfied and so is everyone else, except, presumably, the pirates.

Le Petit Duc

(The Little Duke)

Opéra Comique in Three Acts

By Henri Meilhac *and* Ludovic Halévy

Music by Charles Lecocq

First produced on 25th January, 1878, at the Théâtre de la Renaissance, Paris, with Jeanne Granier and Monsieur Berthelier. London production on 27th April, 1878, at the Philharmonic Theatre, Islington, (in English) with Alice May, Alice Burville, Emma Chambers and Harry Paulton.

Characters

THE DUKE DE PARTHENAY

MONTLANDRY

FRIMOUSSE

THE DUCHESS DE PARTHENAY

DIANE DE CHÂTEAU-LAUSAE, *Headmistress of a girls' school*

CHORUS OF COURTIERS, SCHOOL-GIRLS, OFFICERS, SOLDIERS, VIVANDIÈRES. CAMP FOLLOWERS, ETC.

ACT I

The scene is a stateroom in the Palace of Versailles and the time is the beginning of the eighteenth century. It is midnight and a crowd of courtiers are awaiting the arrival of the youthful Duke de Parthenay and his bride, who are that very moment being married in the chapel nearby. The bride and bridegroom are only fifteen years old. Heavy politics lie behind the marriage, which is one of convenience, for the bride, neé Blanche de Cambry, is an heiress. Presently the courtiers are joined by the singularly hideous Maître Frimousse, tutor to the little Duke, and the good-looking Monsieur Montlandry, his preceptor in military matters. Montlandry is just warning Maître Frimousse that with his marriage the little Duke will cease his intellectual education and concentrate on his military studies, when the wedding procession enters. After the little Duke and his little Duchess have received the guests, they are invited to open the ball and lead off in a gavotte. The dance over, the compelling clink of coin from an adjoining room announces that gambling has begun and in a moment the apartment is cleared and the Duke is alone with his Duchess. There follows a charming and delicately written love-scene between the two young people. Though their marriage may be one of convenience, and though they are only fifteen years old, there is no doubt of their ardent love and devotion. His tender gallantry and her eager affection are most touching and find expression in a duet:

At the end of the duet they are in each other's arms, when there enter two ladies-in-waiting, sent by her grandparents to fetch the Duchess. The young people part quite happily, for both believe that the bride is being taken away to be prepared for bed and that the young bridegroom will later be joining her. Neither is aware that their respective guardians consider them too young to set up as man and wife and that they are to be separated for two years. And indeed when the little Duke arrives at the nuptial chamber, the door is locked; the little Duchess is being driven through the night to the security of an Academy for Young Ladies at Lunéville. The poor Duke is beside himself and throws all the blame for the separation on his ill-favoured tutor, Maître Frimousse. Frimousse, exerting his authority, has just punished his royal pupil by setting him five hundred lines when Monsieur Montlandry enters with an order from the King. Maître Frimousse is to proceed at once to the Young Ladies' Academy at Lunéville. It appears that the Headmistress needs a Professor of Etymology whose appearance is sufficiently ugly to guarantee that he will not inspire feelings of love in the breasts of the young ladies. Maître Frimousse is obviously an ideal choice. Very disgruntled he retires, and Montlandry gives the little Duke the welcome news that he has been promoted Commander-in-Chief of his family regiment, the de Parthenay Dragoons. The Duke is thrilled. "What!" he exclaims. "My very own regiment with soldiers and trumpets and drums and a real Drum Major, that I can march wherever I want to?" Montlandry assures him that it is all true, and the little Duke summons his officers. After they have sworn oaths of allegiance, he warns them to prepare for the regiment to march that very night on a specific manœuvre, though he refuses to divulge its purpose or direction. In spite of the protests of the Ladies of the Court that they are losing their dancing partners, the curtain falls on the officers' departure to this rousing tune:

ACT II

The second act takes place in the music-room of the Academy for Young Ladies of noble birth at Lunéville. The little Duchess has arrived and has just been presented to her fellow pupils by the Headmistress. This Headmistress is a splendid creation by Meilhac and Halévy; a veritable dragon with character, personality and a wealth of ironical humour. A singing lesson is in progress and woe betide the unfortunate girl whose vocal performance falls below the required standard. This very effective scene ends with a small chorus; one of Lecocq's happiest inspirations:

But the principal target for the Headmistress's satire is the new Professor of Etymology, Maître Frimousse. The little Duchess has confided to the girls the story of her marriage and enforced separation, and when they hear that Frimousse is responsible, they all band against him. Frimousse—in the face of devastating comments from the Headmistress—is delivering a lecture on the origin of speech, when a junior-mistress rushes in and breathlessly announces that the school is surrounded by Dragoons and an officer desires to parley with the Headmistress. The regiment is of course the Duke's, and he has marched them to the rescue of his bride. Montlandry is now admitted and declares the terms of his ultimatum. The Headmistress's retort to this ultimatum is a threat to have the emissary thrown out of the window. When Montlandry protests that it is against all the canons of international law to throw emissaries out of windows and wonders how she is to carry out her threat, the Headmistress without more ado instructs Frimousse to execute her order. But he cravenly protests that he has been sent there to teach etymology to young ladies, and declines. The scene ends with Montlandry's withdrawal to parley further with his Colonel.

The next incident is the arrival of a distraught peasant girl, flying from the pursuit of the licentious soldiery. She is of course given sanctuary, and her vivid accounts of the officers' good looks soon have the staff and all the young ladies hanging out of the windows. Immediately she is alone the peasant girl picks up her skirts, and a pair of military boots with spurs reveal the little Duke in disguise. There follows a comedy scene between the Duke in his role of peasant girl and Frimousse. Determined to gain possession of the house-keys held by Frimousse, the Duke makes amorous approaches to him and, having purloined the keys during a burlesque duet, chases him out of the room at the point of a pistol. He next discovers the Duchess. They throw the keys out of the window and in a moment the house is in possession of the Dragoons. Montlandry and the little Duke call on the Headmistress to surrender, but with her back to the wall the old Dragon cries shame on them. Have the Duke's Dragoons no worthier work than to break into schools and make war on little girls? Such conduct will hardly add to their regimental laurels! Such is the effect of her eloquence that she completely wins the day. The regiment is about to withdraw, when two Dragoons appear dragging a miserable figure they have found hiding in the cellar. It is the cowardly Frimousse. To teach him a lesson and in the hope of instilling into him some courage, he is enlisted in the regiment, and as the curtain falls they march away, mocking him to a military air:

ACT III

The last act takes place in a military camp two years later. It is army Headquarters, and Montlandry arrives to report that the de Parthenay Dragoons are on their way and should arrive on the morrow. His news is received with black looks, as the army expect to be attacked at any moment and reinforcements are badly needed. The troops are passing the time drinking and carousing with their girl-friends, vivandières and camp followers. Suddenly the alarm is raised and the army turn out to the attack, leaving the camp deserted except for the terrified women, who huddle together, while the noise of battle continues in the background. Just as they have given up all hope, news comes of victory. It seems that at a critical moment of the battle the de Parthenay Dragoons under the command of their eighteen-year-old Colonel, the Duke, arrived in the nick of time and saved the day. He is the hero of the hour and is summoned to headquarters to receive the personal congratulations of the General. When he returns from his interview he passes on the official compliments to officers and men—but there is one fly in the ointment. The General has taken exception to the presence of women in the camp and in future any soldier caught with a woman in camp will be severely punished. To drive home his point, the little Duke announces the pass-word for the coming twenty-four hours—"*No Women*".

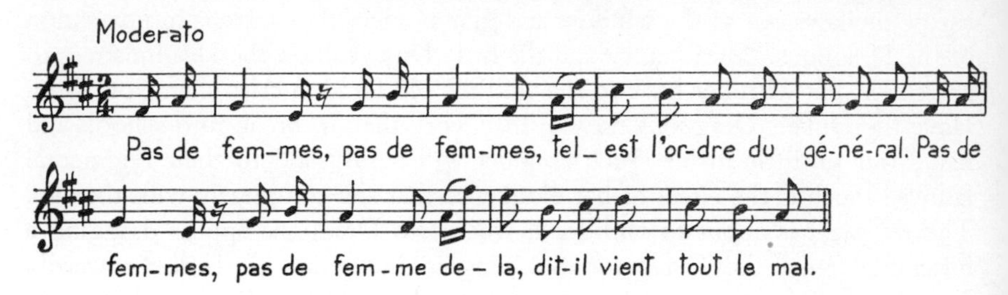

Bidding the troops good night, the Duke retires to his tent and is soon fast asleep, dreaming of his little Duchess. Suddenly he is awakened by the sound of a shot and confused shouting. He turns out, and as he leaves his tent the slight figure of a young girl slips in unperceived and closes the flap. The Duke enquires as to the cause of the alarm and is told that a shadowy figure has been seen creeping into camp. Someone humorously suggests it is a woman and that she is hidden in the Colonel's tent. When order is restored the Duke returns to his tent. To his astonishment and with mixed feelings of ecstasy and embarrassment he discovers his Duchess. She has escaped from the Academy at Lunéville and found her way to the camp. They are rapturously kissing and embracing, when a patrol passes the tent and the Duchess hears the pass-word "No Women". When the Duke explains the origin of the pass-word, she roars with laughter and kisses him with even greater abandon. But the sounds of their affectionate reunion have been noticed and reported and Montlandry descends upon them and, calling out the little Duke, informs him in a "This-hurts-me-more-than-it-hurts-you" voice that he has disobeyed his General's order and in punishment is required to surrender his sword. But his valour on the battlefield is held to mitigate the little Duke's offence. His sword is restored to him and he is officially despatched to report the victory to Versailles. With the news that his term of separation is ended his cup is full and the curtain falls on an ecstasy of happiness for the little Duchess and her Duke.

Le Cœur et la Main
(With Heart and Hand)

Opéra Comique in Three Acts

By CHARLES NUITTER *and* ALEXANDRE BEAUMONT

Music by CHARLES LECOCQ

First produced on the 19th October, 1882, at the Théâtre des Nouveautés, Paris, with Mademoiselle Vaillant-Couturier as "Micaela", Monsieur Vautier as "Don Gaeton" and Monsieur Berthelier as "The King". London production on 6th October, 1892, at the Lyric Theatre with Sedohr Rhodes as "Micaela" and W. Brownlow as "Don Gaeton".

CHARACTERS

DON GAETON, *Duke of Madeira*
THE KING OF ARAGON
PRINCESS MICAELA, *his daughter*
JOSEFA, *a gardener at the palace*
DONA SCHOLASTICA, *Lady-in-waiting to Princess Micaela*
MORALES, *a servant, betrothed to Josefa*
CHORUS OF PEASANTS, COURTIERS, PAGES AND SOLDIERS

The action takes place in and around the Royal Palace of Aragon and in a military camp nearby.

ACT I

In an orange grove in the Royal Park girls are picking orange blossom for the wedding bouquet of the Infanta, Micaela, who is marrying Don Gaeton, Duke of Madeira. One of their number, Josefa, reads out a decree of the King of Aragon, declaring that in honour of the wedding of his royal daughter all girls being married on the same day shall be married at the Crown's expense and that the brides shall be honoured by serving as Ladies-in-Waiting to the Infanta during the festivities. Josefa tells the girls the tradition that the orange blossom for the royal bouquet must be picked by virgins. In the hands of any girl who is not one, the orange blossom will wither and turn black:

In former days it was traditional to present the brides who shared their wedding day with the Infanta with a dowry. But this custom has now been discontinued, and the girls decide to compose a petition to the Infanta begging for a revival of the custom. They hide the petition in a basket full of orange blossom.

The King now appears in a very bad temper. The bridegroom has disappeared! The King turned out to meet him by appointment on his arrival, escorted by the Royal Bombadiers, but the Duke of Madeira suddenly set spurs to his horse and disappeared into the forest. His Majesty gives instructions to the military to find the Duke and bring him back, and to the Infanta's Duenna to see that his daughter spends the next two hours at her devotions in chapel, until such time as her bridegroom has been recovered. Josefa, gardener to the Royal Household, is engaged to Sergeant Morales. They are anxious to get married but must wait until the Sergeant receives promotion. Josefa is just picking a rose to give him when, concealed in the rose-bush, she finds a ruby. This is a pre-arranged signal that the Infanta is coming to visit her. The two girls are great friends, and the Infanta often disguises herself in one of Josefa's dresses and escapes from the palace for an hour or so's freedom. Josefa gets rid of Morales, and the Infanta Micaela arrives. Josefa tells her about Morales and how they must wait to get married until his promotion, and Micaela promises to see that he gets it. Josefa gives her a letter from Morales to herself with details of his regiment, etc., and she also gives Micaela an account of her bridegroom, the Duke of Madeira, whom Micaela has never seen. According to Josefa he is gay and handsome—a man any woman would be proud to marry. The girls now return and tell Josefa that they presented the petition requesting the granting of their marriage dowries, but it was returned to them with the information that the Infanta was in retreat in the chapel. Micaela, whom the girls do not recognise in Josefa's dress, asks to see the petition and, while they are talking, surreptitiously signs it. She then tells them they must be mistaken, for the Infanta has endorsed the petition with her signature. The girls are delighted at the prospect of receiving their dowries and insist on celebrating the occasion with a song. So Micaela sings them a song about a young girl who eloped with the man she loved:

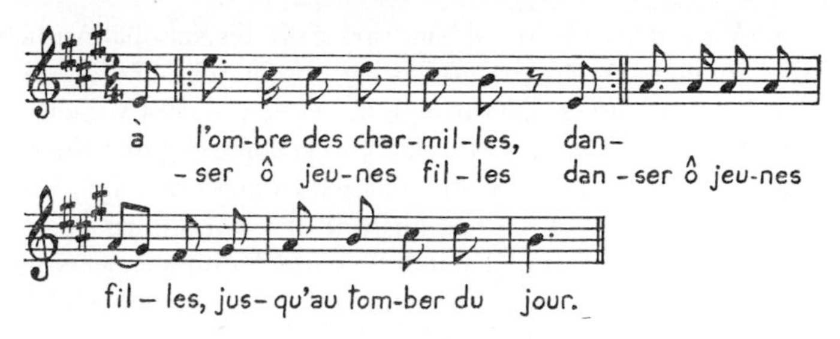

The song finishes with a round dance, and as it ceases with the girls exhausted and laughing, a male voice shouts, "Bravo." Seated on top of a wall, a smiling young man is watching them. Josefa whispers to Micaela: "That is your bridegroom, the Duke." "Leave us alone together," Micaela whispers back. The Duke jumps down off the wall and when they are alone they are soon on terms of easy familiarity. Micaela is enchanted with her handsome husband-to-be and the Duke tells her frankly that he is already half in love with her. He pours out the story of his marriage of convenience and how he escaped from his future father-in-law and his escort of Bombadiers. "Of course they'll get me, but one thing I swear: I'll never speak one word of love to the Infanta Micaela or even look at her," he finishes. He notices Morales' letter to Josefa stuck in the bodice of Micaela's dress. He snatches it and reads "My Dearest", signed "Morales" and addressed to "Senora Josefa, Gardener to the Royal Household". "So, Josefa, you spend your life close to the Infanta and I shall often see you and I shall tell you all the loving things I ought to tell my wife, for I adore you," he tells her ardently. "But I'm going to be married," she protests, "and besides I'm a virtuous girl." As they are talking voices are heard. Micaela vanishes and the Bombadiers appear. They have found the Duke. They escort him to the King, who rebukes him stiffly for his conduct and tells him that he expects him to mend his ways in the future. The Duke is quite impenitent, but he does follow the King to meet his bride as the curtain falls.

ACT II

It is some days later, and the wedding night of the royal couple. The Infanta is being waited on by the brides, who have shared her wedding day and who include Josefa. For Micaela, true to her promise, has arranged for Morales to receive promotion and he is now an officer. The King is very dissatisfied at his son-in-law's attitude to his bride. So eccentric and unreliable has been his behaviour that the King is nervous that he might even decamp during the night, and he has ordered all the palace doors to be locked. The royal band has been posted in a strategic position with instructions to play the National Anthem immediately anybody attempts to leave the palace. Morales, as junior officer, is detailed to be on duty all night in the palace, and Josefa, who hangs about till the last moment before going home in the hope of getting a moment alone with him, leaves her departure so late that she finds all the palace doors locked and herself unable to leave. When the Duke believes that everybody has retired to bed, he attempts to escape from the palace. But every time he opens a door or a window the royal band strike up the National Anthem and he has to retire, fuming. At last he notices an obscure exit and as this time no music is heard he hopes to escape through it. As he vanishes Micaela comes out of the bridal suite and encounters Josefa. Josefa confesses that she is shut into the palace and bewails the fact that she is parted from Morales on their wedding night. Micaela tells her that, as her husband has not shown up, Josefa and Morales are welcome to the bridal suite. So when Morales appears Josefa lures her willing bridegroom into the bedroom and shuts the door, while Micaela goes in search of her missing husband.

The King now appears on a journey of reconnaissance and listens at the door of the bridal suite. Hearing sounds of kissing and of passionate love-making, and being quite unaware that they emanate from Morales and Josefa, he assumes that all goes well with the royal pair. At this moment the Duke is making an exhaustive tour of the palace in search of an exit but, failing to make his escape, returns to his original point of departure. Observing a commodious sofa outside the door of the royal suite, he makes himself comfortable on it for the night. Presently down the darkened corridor a figure approaches carrying a lighted candle. It is Micaela. Determined to find her husband, she has changed into Josefa's dress—the dress she was wearing when he first saw her and fell in love with her. The Duke is enchanted to see his beloved "Josefa" and takes her tenderly in his arms. Micaela is thrilled and, after a token resistance, surrenders herself happily to him. So while Josefa and Morales pass their wedding night in luxury in the royal suite, the royal couple spend their's less luxuriously but just as ecstatically, on a sofa in the palace corridor.

ACT III

Some days later the Duke has placed his wife in a convent and marched the army on manœuvres. The scene is a camp, and the act opens with several officers chaffing Morales about his rapid promotion—for the Duke has now promoted him to 1st Lieutenant. They also discuss the mysterious visits to the Duke of a messenger boy. There is a rumour that this boy is a woman in disguise and furthermore that she is Morales' wife. Hence his rapid promotion. The Duke is in a fretful mood. It is two days since his "Josefa" last visited him and he is missing her. When she does appear he upbraids her for her long absence. She pleads that it is not always easy to get away from her mistress, the Infanta, and leave the convent. Anyhow, things cannot go on like this for ever. The Infanta is not a fool and will soon weary of her husband's continued absence. But the Duke is so busy holding her hand and kissing her that he doesn't listen to a word she is saying. They are interrupted by the arrival of the real Josefa. She brings news that the King is approaching the camp in company with the Infanta. She has come to warn "her little cousin". Micaela hastily disappears and Josefa goes in search of Morales. When she finds him he asks coldly where she has come from. "From the Duke," she tells him. A scene of frantic jealousy follows. Morales has heard the officers' gossip and accuses Josefa of carrying on a liaison with the Duke, refusing to accept her vigorous denials.

The King then arrives in a jovial mood, having heard some welcome news from the Court Physician. "He tells me that in the near future I shall be a grandfather," he announces. He congratulates his son-in-law on doing his duty as a husband and ensuring the continuation of the dynasty. The Duke is completely mystified. Later this mystification turns to alarm. Morales asks to see the Duke confidentially, and tells him something is weighing on his conscience and confesses that he spent his wedding night in the royal suite. The Duke is appalled. If the Duke and "Josefa" were on the sofa in the corridor and Morales was in the royal suite, Morales must have spent the night with the Infanta. Nothing could be clearer. Morales must be the father of his wife's child.

With the arrival of Micaela these nightmare thoughts are dispersed. For the first time the Duke really looks at his wife and realises that his beloved "Josefa" and the Infanta Micaela are one and the same person. There is no longer any barrier to their love and Micaela can acknowledge fully and freely that he is hers with heart and hand.

Les Cloches de Corneville

(The Chimes of Normandy)

Opéra Comique in Three Acts

By Messieurs CLAIRETVILLE *and* CH. GABET

Music by ROBERT PLANQUETTE

First produced on 19th April, 1877, at the Théâtre des Folies-Dramatiques, Paris, with Mademoiselles Gélabert and Girard and Messieurs Milher and E. Vois. London production on 23rd November, 1878, at the Folly Theatre (in English), with Cora Stuart, Emma Chambers, Shiel Barry, Frederick Mervin and Harry Paulton.

CHARACTERS

HENRI, *Marquis of Corneville*
GRENICHEUX, *a fisherman*
SERPOLETTE, *a country girl*
GASPARD, *a miser*
THE BAILLIE
CHORUS OF VILLAGERS, FISHERFOLK, SAILORS, SERVANTS, ETC.
GERMAINE, *daughter of Comte de Lucenay*

The action takes place in the village of Corneville, Normandy, during the reign of Louis XV.

ACT I

In the village of Corneville in Normandy stands a dilapidated castle belonging to the Marquis de Corneville, a political exile. It has stood empty for twenty years, but there is a legend in the village that the long-expected heir will one day return to claim his own and that the ghostly bells of Corneville will signal his return. "The Legend of the Bells" is one of the most popular numbers in the score and is sung by the heroine, Germaine:

The caretaker of the castle is old Gaspard, formerly in the employ of the Comte de Lucenay. When the Comte was banished on political grounds, he left his daughter and his fortune in Gaspard's charge. Gaspard, a crafty, avaricious old miser, has hidden the treasure in the castle and introduced the girl as his niece, Germaine. To safeguard the treasure he deceives the superstitious villagers into the belief that the castle is haunted, frequently visiting it himself to gloat over his money-bags. Germaine is in a difficult position. Gaspard is trying to force her to marry the pompous old village Baillie, while she has betrothed herself to Grenicheux, a ne'er-do-well young fisherman, whom she believes once saved her life.

Though Germaine believes Grenicheux saved her life, her real rescuer was Henri, the young Marquis de Corneville. Paying a secret visit to Corneville a year before, he saw from his boat a young girl fall from the rocks into the water. He dived into the sea, rescued the girl and, handing over her unconscious form to a nearby fisherman, hurried back to save his boat from being dashed to pieces on the rocks. Grenicheux has dishonestly allowed Germaine to continue in the belief that he was her rescuer. As for the Marquis, the incident has made a deep impression upon him. "I only had her a moment in my arms. I never saw her face, but of all my adventures by sea and land that one moment still haunts me," he says:

Today the young Marquis returns to Corneville to claim his estate. He ridicules all idea of ghosts, and having engaged Germaine, Grenicheux and a village girl called Serpolette as staff, he announces his intention of setting up house in the castle.

ACT II

The scene is the ancestral hall of the Château de Corneville, furnished in medieval style. All around is dust and decay. Standing prominently near a window is a suit of armour mounted on a truck. As the curtain rises a distant chorus echoes eerily through the castle, and as the sound increases there enter a company of sailors bearing torches and escorting the Marquis. He is accompanied by Germaine, Serpolette, Grenicheux and the Baillie. At first all except the Marquis are overcome by fear, but by degrees their courage returns and Serpolette declares that as no real man holds any terrors for her, why should a ghost?

The Marquis first searches the castle, and one of his finds is a portfolio full of documents. One of them is the birth certificate of Clemence Lucienne, Viscountess de Lucenay, born at Bourges in 1667. This is the year of Serpolette's birth, and as she started life as a foundling, she now convinces herself that she must be the missing Viscountess. Another document is a letter from the Comte de Lucenay to Gaspard entrusting him with the care of his daughter and declaring his intention of one day returning to Corneville.

The Marquis, who has noticed traces of various activities and occupation, such as the suit of armour standing on the truck, is convinced that there is human agency behind the hauntings. He is determined to solve the mystery and resolves to hide and surprise the intruder. Grenicheux is concealed in the suit of armour on the truck; the Marquis and the rest of the party hide themselves behind a tapestry-hanging, and the vigil begins. Presently a watching sailor reports that someone has entered the castle by the postern gate. Shortly afterwards there enters old Gaspard carrying a dark lantern and three money-bags. Going to the window, he draws back the tapestry curtains and, wrapping a sheet around himself, gesticulates wildly, muttering "Now, ghosts, arise and phantoms, come." Finally he works the remainder of his ghostly spectres, pushing the truck with the suit of armour, containing the terrified Grenicheux, backwards and forwards before the window to frighten away inquisitive trespassers. Watching all this from his hiding-place, the Marquis determines to punish the old miser and teach him a lesson, and when Gaspard is greedily gloating over his money-bags, he is horrified to hear the chiming of the ghostly bells, to see the room illuminated by a flood of light, and to witness grim, mail-clad warriors start from the shadowy gloom of ages and point to him threateningly with their gauntleted hands as they sing:

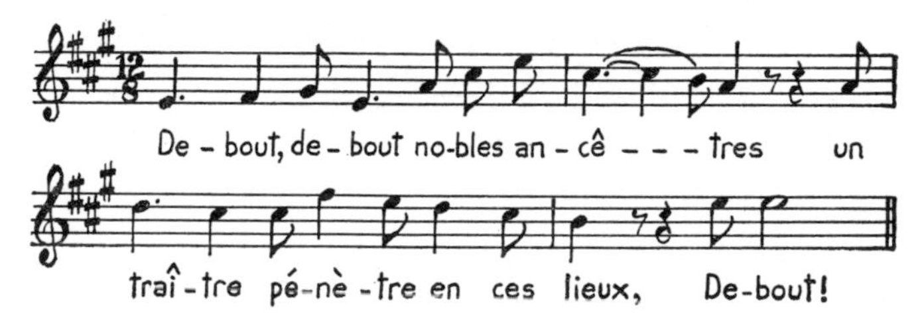

Under the influence of terror and a guilty conscience, the old man goes out of his mind and the Marquis is more than ever determined to solve the mystery regarding the Comte de Lucenay and the identity of his missing daughter.

ACT III

The last act takes place in late summer in an orchard in Corneville Park. Peasants are in holiday attire and girls on ladders are picking and shaking down apples.

The identity of the Comte de Lucenay's daughter is still unknown and Serpolette is still convinced that she is the noble child. One thing the Marquis does manage to straighten out, however, is that it was he and not Grenicheux who saved Germaine from drowning. Finally, the identity of the Comte de Lucenay's daughter is brought to light through the half-crazy mutterings of old Gaspard. He eventually recovers his reason, begs forgiveness and establishes that Germaine and not Serpolette is the heir to the de Lucenay fortune. She becomes the bride of the Marquis de Corneville, who so romantically rescued her from the sea, and the bells of Corneville ring out their wedding chimes

Henri Meilhac in his study

Jacques Offenbach

Ludovic Halévy with Madame Simon-Gérard in her dressing-room at the Théatre des Varietés, during a performance of the 1900 revival of *La Belle Hélène*

La Belle Hélène. The gambling scene as performed in the 1900 revival at the Théatre des Varietés

Hortense Schneider in her dressing-room at the Théatre des Varietés during a performance of *The Grand Duchess of Gerolstein*

Mander & Mitchenson

Lawrence Rea as "Florestan" and Ruth Vincent as "Hélène de Solanges" in the Donkey duet, in the London production of *Véronique*

Austrian National Library

A page of Offenbach's manuscript full score of the "Chanson de Fortunio", composed for Alfred de Musset's play *Le Chandelier*

Les Mousquetaires au Couvent

(Musketeers in a Convent)

Opéra Comique in Three Acts

By Paul Ferrier *and* Jules Préval

Music by Louis Varney

Act III composed by M. Mansour

First produced on the 16th March, 1880, at the Théâtre des Bouffes-Parisiens, Paris, with Mademoiselle Rouvroy as "Marie", Monsieur Marcelin as "Gontran", Monsieur Achard as "Brissac", and Monsieur Hittemans as "L'Abbé Bridaine". London productions at the Globe Theatre on 31st October, 1880 (in English), and at the Coronet Theatre, Notting Hill, on 10th April, 1907 (in French). The English cast included Mademoiselle Sylvia, Elsie Moore, F. H. Celli, Henry Bracey and Harry Paulton.

Characters

NARCISSE DE BRISSAC, GONTRAN DE SOLANGES } *officers of Musketeers*
L'ABBÉ BRIDAINE
COMTE DE PONTCOURLAY, *Governor of Touraine*
MARIE, *niece of the Governor*
LOUISE, *her sister*
SIMONE, *maid at the inn*
RIGOBERT, *Sergeant-Major of Musketeers*
MOTHER SUPERIOR, *head of an Ursuline convent*
OPPORTUNE, *Sister of the Convent*
CHORUS OF VILLAGERS, MUSKETEERS, SCHOOL-GIRLS

The action takes place in Touraine during the reign of Louis XIII.

ACT I

The scene is the courtyard of "Au Mousquetaire Gris", an inn at Vouvray. The Comte de Pontcourlay, Governor of Touraine, has two nieces, Marie and

Louise, pupils at an Ursuline convent school. Marie has fallen in love with a young Captain of Musketeers, Gontran de Solanges, and her love is returned. This love affair was born in a singular fashion. The Abbé Bridaine, a household friend of the Governor and formerly Gontran's tutor, is entirely responsible for it, for he has consistently spoken so warmly to the young girl of the young man and vice versa that the two have fallen in love, although they have scarcely met. The Governor is a close friend of the Cardinal of Touraine, and the Cardinal has expressed a wish that the Governor's nieces should take the veil. The Cardinal's word is law as far as the Governor is concerned, and he desires his old friend, the Abbé, to break the news to the girls. This puts the Abbé in a very awkward position, for he has just promised Gontran to deliver a love-letter of his to Marie at the convent. Poor Abbé Bridaine has one of those expansive natures. He is always over-anxious to help everybody, too ready with his tongue and consequently prone to get embarrassingly involved in other people's affairs.

As the Governor and Abbé Bridaine are talking, seated outside the inn, two mendicant monks approach and attempt to obtain a free meal from the landlord. He is just sending them away when the Governor intervenes and instructs the landlord to give the monks the best room in the inn: he will pay for their board and lodging. In return he asks the monks to visit the Ursuline convent and preach a sermon to the girls in praise of renouncing the world for the benefits of Mother Church. This he hopes will incline Marie and Louise towards taking the veil. The monks gratefully promise to carry out the Governor's assignment and pass into the inn, while the Governor takes his leave. The Abbé is joined by Gontran and his brother-officer, Captain de Brissac. As they are talking Simone, the pretty maid of the inn, appears with a tray of food and drink for the monks. As she passes de Brissac he puts an arm round her waist and gives her a resounding kiss. Simone, secretly delighted, pretends to be affronted and moves on to the monks' room. In a moment she is back in a state of shock and fluster. It seems that the monks have removed their habits and all the rest of their clothing and, in the heat of the day, have fallen fast asleep. The sight of them has been a shock to Simone's maidenly modesty, and the two Musketeers tease her unmercifully. When she has departed the Abbé tells Gontran the Governor's decision that Marie and Louise must take the veil. Gontran is appalled at the news and decides that the girls must be removed from the convent at once: de Brissac promises to help. But how are they to arrange matters so that they will be received at the convent? Suddenly they have a bright idea and disappear into the inn.

The villagers now assemble in the inn courtyard. The Governor has been distributing largesse and everyone is in a good mood. They join Simone in a song and dance. As the dancing is in full swing de Brissac and Gontran reappear from the inn, clad in the sleeping monks' habits. The singing and dancing stop forthwith and the crowd kneel and ask a blessing. De Brissac in an undertone orders Sergeant-Major Rigobert to put a guard of four musketeers on the door of the monks' room and to allow no one to enter or leave it till further orders. He and Gontran then leave for the convent, bent on getting there before the Abbé.

ACT II

The scene is the school-room of the convent. As the girls are taking dictation from Sister Opportune, the Mother Superior arrives to announce that two Reverend Fathers have called at the convent at the instigation of the Governor of Touraine. The Mother Superior thinks it would benefit the girls to seize the opportunity of a confessional. The girls are then left to themselves for some moments of meditation and, at Louise's suggestion, they write out a list of sins common to them all which they can safely confess to the Reverend Fathers. For this situation Varney has composed a musical scene of great charm:

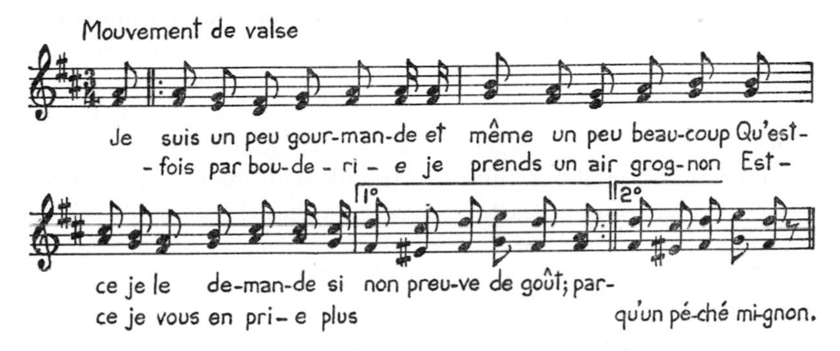

Marie's own confession, which she, too, commits to paper, is much more romantic and reads:

> When I pray
> My lips say
> "Mary",
> But my heart repeats
> "Gontran".

All her thoughts are of the handsome Captain, and she prays to God to further their love:

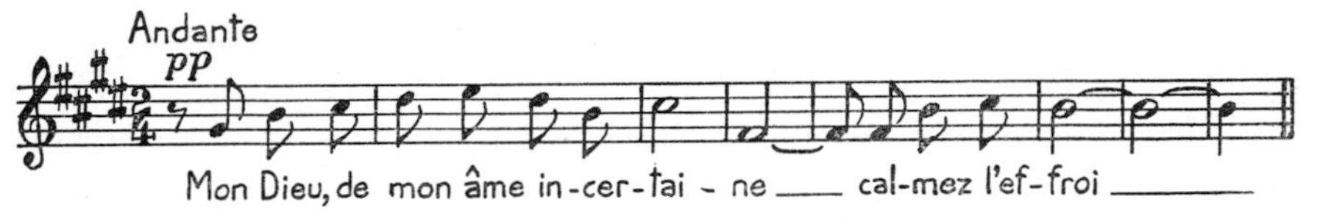

On the return of the Mother Superior all the girls hide their confessions in their desks. The two "Reverend Fathers" are now introduced. Gontran and de Brissac cut curious figures as monks and de Brissac is continually interspersing his conversation with military metaphors which strike the Mother Superior as singularly out of place. Gontran makes himself known to Marie, while de Brissac is enchanted with Louise, who is not yet in the secret but who has noticed that there is something between Marie and one of the Reverend Fathers, and whose curiosity is thoroughly roused. When the girls withdraw for supper, to de Brissac's disgust he and Gontran are not invited. Left alone in the school-room he rummages in the girls' desks in the hope of finding food and happens upon Marie's avowal of her love for Gontran. This places Gontran in the seventh heaven of happiness. Presently the Mother Superior returns. She tells them that she had considered preparing a generous feast but remembered in time that it was Lent and realised that the Reverend Fathers would be fasting. She is therefore providing them with bread and water. But this is more than de Brissac can stand and he tells the Mother Superior that, much as it goes against the grain, whenever he has to preach, as he proposes to do this evening, in the interest of his sermon he gives up fasting in favour of a square meal. He is then escorted by the Mother Superior into the refectory, where he is served with a Lucullan feast.

Abbé Bridaine now arrives. He seeks out Marie and tells her of her uncle's decision, at the Cardinal's instigation, that she and Louise shall take the veil. He also demands that Marie write a letter to Gontran telling him that she no longer loves him and bidding him good-bye. "But such a letter would be a lie," Marie protests. "It will be a safeguard against Gontran committing any impulsive action which might get him into trouble with the Cardinal," Bridaine tells her gently, and with a heavy heart Marie writes the letter. While she is writing Gontran enters, and the Abbé is appalled to find the Musketeer Captain masquerading as a monk in a convent. When Marie has withdrawn he gives Gontran her letter, but after her avowal of her love for him Gontran cannot believe that this letter expresses Marie's true sentiments. As he is arguing with the Abbé sounds of raucous singing are heard and de Brissac lurches into the school-room, clasping a bottle of brandy. He is quite drunk. In spite of all the efforts of the Abbé and Gontran to dissuade him, he declares that he is going to address the school, and when the Mother Superior appears with the girls he scandalises everybody by preaching a most unsuitable sermon, glorifying love:

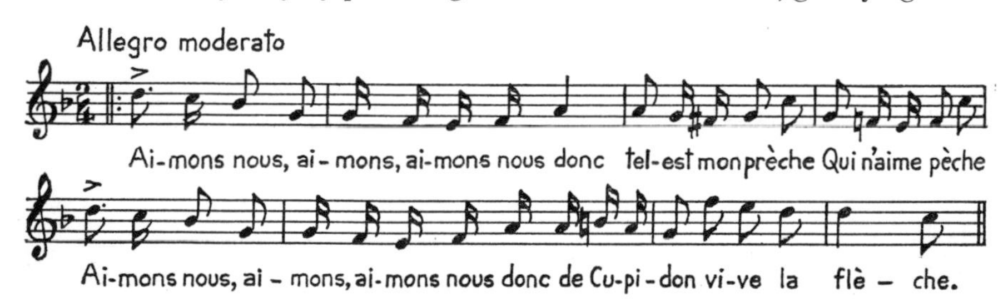

The Mother Superior and Sister Opportune are affronted, but the girls, enchanted by the gaiety of the sermon and the preacher, leap to their feet and dance hilariously round de Brissac, and the curtain falls on a scene of pandemonium.

ACT III

The last act takes place in a courtyard of the convent. To excuse the scandalous behaviour of the "Reverend Father" on the preceding evening, Abbé Bridaine resorts to further white lies. He tells the Mother Superior, who had, quite correctly, assumed that it was a case of drunkenness, that the "Reverend" was suffering from the after-effects of sunstroke contracted during a pilgrimage to Palestine. The Mother Superior accepts this explanation and no more is said, though the fact remains that a bottle of brandy has disappeared from the cellar. Meanwhile Gontran and de Brissac are planning the abduction of Marie and Louise, and a detachment of Musketeers under Sergeant-Major Rigobert is waiting outside the walls to lend a hand. Simone now arrives with a message from the landlord of the inn, begging that the Guard placed on the monks may be relieved and that they be allowed to depart as there are ceaseless rows and friction. Has the Abbé seen Captain de Solanges or Captain de Brissac? The Abbé tries to prevent Simone from discovering the Musketeers, but she does find them and Gontran entrusts her with a letter to Marie begging her to join him. When Simone has departed the Mother Superior appears and invites the "Reverend Fathers" to stay for the arrival of the Cardinal on the morrow. De Brissac tactfully manœuvres the Mother Superior into the convent to discuss plans for the Cardinal's welcome, leaving the coast clear for Gontran and Marie.

Gontran now urges Marie to come away with him, Louise, and de Brissac, as the Cardinal's imminent arrival makes immediate escape necessary, and Marie agrees. Simone produces a ladder and Gontran, Marie, Louise and de Brissac escape down it, when they are surprised by the Abbé, who is about to follow them, having climbed out of a window on to the roof. Simone, however, removes the ladder, leaving him marooned astride a gable. At this moment the Cardinal and the Governor arrive unexpectedly and the fugitives and the Abbé are trapped. Things are looking black for all concerned when the Governor informs them of a dastardly plot against the Cardinal's life that has been discovered: the assassins are masquerading as travelling monks and have been traced to Vouvray. Triumphantly Gontran and de Brissac declare that they have the assassins under lock and key in the inn. After that, no reward could be too great for having saved His Eminence's life, and the Governor gladly gives his nieces' hands in marriage to the two Musketeers.

Le Grand Mogul
(The Grand Mogul)

Opéra-Comique in Four Acts
originally in three acts

By HENRI CHIVOT *and* ALFRED DURU

Music by EDMOND AUDRAN

First produced on 24th February, 1877, at Marseilles. London production on 17th November, 1884, (in English) at the Comedy Theatre, with Florence St. John, Henry Bracey, Fred Leslie and Arthur Roberts.

CHARACTERS

PRINCE MIGNAPOUR
NICOBAR, *Grand Vizier*
JOQUELET, *a dentist*
IRMA, *his sister, a snake-charmer*
CAPTAIN CRAKSON, *an Englishman*
PRINCESS BENGALINE
CHORUS OF COURTIERS, SLAVE-GIRLS, GUARDS, RAJAHS AND MERCHANTS

The action takes place in and around Delhi, the seat of the Grand Moguls, in the year 1750.

ACT I

The scene is the market square in Almora, a small town near Delhi. When the curtain rises merchants are crying their wares, and in a prominent position on the square stands a caravan, bearing a notice which reads: "Joquelet, Parisian Dentist". Joquelet, a quack dentist, and his sister, Irma, have had to leave Paris hurriedly to dodge their creditors. They have come to India in the hope of making their fortunes, but so far the Hindus have not proved particularly profitable customers and there is more enthusiasm for Irma's snake-charming than there is for Joquelet's dentistry. Before the market closes, Joquelet announces that Irma will be giving an exhibition of snake-charming in an hour's time. As he is making the announcement, a long, lanky individual approaches the caravan. He is an Englishman, late of the British Army, Captain Crakson. He is out in India as a British agent, endeavouring to arrange a trade agreement to import cheap jewellery, pocket-knives, Benares brass ware made in Birmingham, and opium. He is in love with Irma. But she has no use for the Captain and sends him about his business. Her thoughts are all of a handsome young Indian who came to watch her performance in Benares and never took his eyes off her.

The young man in question is Prince Mignapour. He is the future Grand Mogul and will inherit the title on attaining his majority, provided, according to tradition, that his virginity is intact. The Grand Moguls possess a collar of white pearls which is worn by each heir-apparent until he comes of age—it is an heirloom descended from Buddha, founder of the dynasty. Should the heir-apparent sacrifice his virginity prematurely, the collar of pearls will turn black, and he is then no longer eligible to become Grand Mogul. Princess Bengaline, a beautiful young widow of twenty-three, also has her eye on Prince Mignapour and is anxious to share his throne. As Joquelet and Irma are talking, Princess Bengaline passes by, reclining in a litter, carried by four slaves and attended by her Ladies-in-waiting. Assisted by the Rajahs of Tangore she alights from her palanquin, and is accorded a welcome by the populace. As she is about to pass on to her palace, which overlooks the market square, Princess Bengaline is stopped by Nicobar, Grand Vizier and Regent. He speaks to her of his charge, Prince Mignapour, who is suffering from acute depression. He is obviously in love and his condition dates from the time that Princess Bengaline left Delhi. Nicobar believes that the Prince is in love with her, and the Princess is thrilled at the prospect of marrying the future Grand Mogul, and she promises Nicobar that the day she shares the throne, his position at Court is assured. But when Prince Mignapour joins her, Bengaline finds that Nicobar's information is quite false. The Prince's attitude to her is lukewarm and she retires in a rage to her palace. Prince Mignapour's thoughts are all of the attractive snake-charmer whom he saw at Benares. He cannot get her out of his head and he is amazed to meet her again on the market square of Almora. Irma is overwhelmed by the young man's ardour, tells him it is time for her performance, but promises to meet him later. Mignapour departs and Irma begins her snake-charming performance, watched by Princess Bengaline and a party of her guests from the Terrace of her palace. As she charms her snakes, Irma sings:

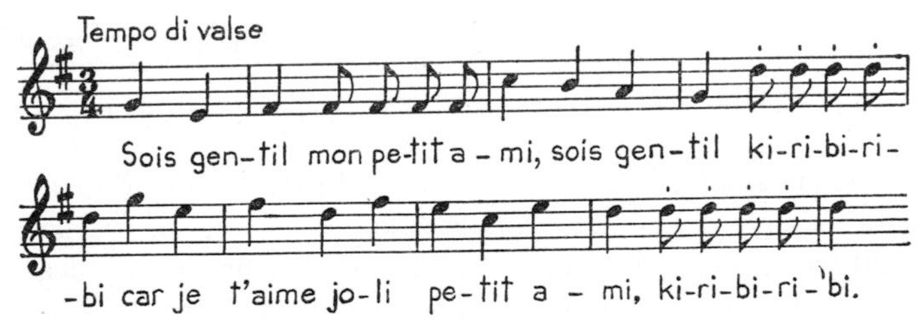

Irma is just finishing her performance when there is a flourish of trumpets and on to the square in royal regalia rides Prince Mignapour on horseback, accompanied by the Grand Vizier and his whole suite. He receives a royal welcome from the populace, while the Grand Vizier whispers to Bengaline, who has descended from the terrace, that he is sure Prince Mignapour has come to ask for her hand in marriage. But Bengaline suffers a bitter blow when the Prince halts before Joquelet's caravan and formally asks for Irma's hand. Bengaline, the Grand Vizier and Captain Crakson boil with rage, while from every pagoda bells ring and the crowds cheer and throw their hats in the air as the curtain falls.

ACT II

The scene is the garden of the palace of the Grand Mogul in Delhi. On the right of the set is an oriental pavilion in front of which is a formal bench, and at the back of the stage, centre, a summer-house covered with roses. The curtain rises on a conversation between Bengaline, the Grand Vizier and Captain Crakson. All three are determined to prevent Prince Mignapour from marrying Irma, and they are discussing ways and means of achieving their object when the Grand Vizier has an idea. His plan is to hire a troupe of Bayaderes or dancing-girls, well versed in the arts of ensnaring men by their voluptuous beauty and erotic dances. It will be their task to seduce Prince Mignapour, and once he has lost his innocence he will no longer be eligible to reign as Grand Mogul and will have to leave the country. This plan is enthusiastically adopted and the three withdraw to put it into action. Joquelet and Irma now arrive at the palace to take up their quarters there and prepare for the wedding. Prince Mignapour gives Irma some female slaves to serve her and particularly recommends to her notice Kioumi, a deaf mute. Irma and Joquelet, accompanied by the slaves, then withdraw to their apartments. Mignapour, left alone, sits down on the bench and dreams of his future with Irma, of her beauty and her sweetness, of the ecstasy of loving her. In a romantic reverie he closes his eyes as out of the pavilion behind him tiptoe the Bayaderes and surround him in a seductive dance. Mignapour watches as though in a dream as Bengaline appears as Queen of the Houris and sings an exotic air:

As the song ends Bengaline leans over him seductively, and Mignapour seizes her in his arms and is about to embrace her, when out of the palace come Joquelet and Irma. Bengaline, foiled and furious, disappears, and Irma, jealous and piqued at Mignapour's lapse on the eve of his wedding, bursts into tears. Mignapour is so obviously sincerely penitent that she forgives him, and summoning the whole Court, he presents to them his future wife. After the presentation Irma and Mignapour are left alone, and Mignapour, already roused by the Bayaderes, becomes very ardent. He begs Irma to let him make love to her—tomorrow and marriage seem such a long way off. But Irma won't hear of it. She tells him that a friend of hers in Paris allowed a man to make love to her before they were married and when they'd finished he said he was going out to buy a tie and never came back! Mignapour won't take no for an answer and begs Irma to meet him after dark in the summer-house of roses. But Irma is adamant and leaves him with a firm refusal.

This conversation has been secretly overheard by Bengaline and Crakson, both in hiding, and Bengaline determines to turn the situation to her advantage. She accordingly writes a note to Mignapour, signing it "Irma", and sends it by the slave Kioumi, who was formerly in her employ and who is her creature. The letter reads: "I shall be in the summer-house of roses at midnight. Irma." So great is Mignapour's joy that he confides his good news to Crakson and begs him to take the Palace Guard out for a drink that night and surreptitiously dope their liquor. But Crakson, who has a store of opium, decides to put it to quite another purpose.

ACT III

The scene is the throne-room of the palace. Today Prince Mignapour attains his majority and is to be crowned Grand Mogul, but although the morning is well advanced the Prince is, unaccountably, not yet awake. The Grand Vizier confides to the Head Brahmin that the Guard reported seeing Mignapour in amorous conversation with a woman near the summer-house of roses, near midnight. And now he is still asleep—strange, very strange. At mid-day the whole Court is assembled for the Coronation. But when Prince Mignapour enters the throne-room, to the horror of everyone it is seen that the pearls forming the collar round his neck have turned black. The Grand Brahmin—the High Priest—steps forward, and in the name of Brahma, Mignapour is deprived of his throne and ordered to leave the land in ignominy.

ACT IV

The scene is the lounge of a luxury hotel in Delhi. Here Irma and Joquelet are staying. Irma is in despair at losing her Prince and Joquelet does his best to console her. Who knows? Some day everything may come right. Joquelet and Irma are without money, and the proprietor of the hotel hints broadly that they must either pay their bill or find accommodation elsewhere. But now they have a stroke of luck. On the banks of a river they pick up a casket containing a scroll of parchment. The scroll is addressed to the Grand Mogul, and the writing on it reads: "My son, now that you occupy the throne of your ancestors by the exercise of your virtue and self-discipline, learn the truth concerning the collar of pearls. There is nothing magical about them, nor are they capable of changing colour. The legend was invented to keep the line of heirs-apparent on the royal road of virtue. Pass on the legend to your son, if you have one, that he too may walk in paths of virtue and the tradition be perpetuated. Signed, Baldur."

It is quite obvious from this document that Mignapour is innocent, and the details of a wicked intrigue, the joint work of Bengaline and Crakson, are now exposed. It seems that on the night before the projected marriage of Mignapour and Irma, Crakson, who had learned from the Prince that Irma had promised to meet him in the summer-house of roses at midnight, decided to drug Mignapour with opium and, disguised in his robes, keep the rendezvous with Irma himself. He is quite unaware that the lady in the dark was not Irma, but Bengaline. Later Bengaline, finding Mignapour in a drugged sleep, exchanged his collar of white pearls for another collar of discoloured ones. So the trick was played. Finally everything is straightened out. Mignapour is crowned Grand Mogul and the only revenge he takes is to compel Crakson to marry Bengaline as *amende honorable* for the night he spent with her in the summer-house of roses. Joquelet is appointed Grand Vizier in place of the treacherous Nicobar, and the curtain comes down with wedding bells for Mignapour and Irma.

Les Noces de Olivette

(Olivette)

Opéra Comique in Three Acts

By HENRI CHIVOT *and* ALFRED DURU

Music by EDMOND AUDRAN

First produced on 13th November, 1879, at the Théâtre des Bouffes-Parisiens, Paris. Produced in London on 18th November, 1880, at the Strand Theatre (in English), with Florence St. John, Violet Cameron, Knight Ashton, Henry Ashley and J. C. Mather.

CHARACTERS

MONSIEUR MARVEJOL, *Mayor of Perpignan*
OLIVETTE, *his daughter*
CAPTAIN DE MERIMAC, *a Sea Captain*
VALENTIN, *his nephew*
COUNTESS DE ROUSSILLON
THE DUC DES IFS, *her cousin*
VELOUTINE, *Olivette's maid*

The action takes place on the shores of the Mediterranean at Perpignan in the earldom of Rousillon, in the reign of Louis XIII.

ACT I

The scene is the house of Monsieur Marvejol, Seneschal to the Countess of Roussillon and Mayor of Perpignan. Monsieur Marvejol has a daughter, Olivette, who has recently returned home from a convent to marry, at her father's wish, an elderly Sea Captain, de Merimac, of the Corvette "Cormorant". While at the convent Olivette has made the conquest of a young man, Valentin, a handsome officer in the Rousillon Guards, and she is not indifferent to his good looks. Valentin, who is the nephew of Captain de Merimac, has also caught the eye of the young Countess Bathilde de Roussillon. She has fallen in love with him and has come over to Perpignan to stay with her Seneschal especially to see him. During the night the repose of the Countess is disturbed by a lover's serenade sung by a familiar voice under her window. The singer is Valentin.

At the end of his song Valentin invades the solitude of the Countess, fondly believing that he is climbing the balcony of Olivette's room, but he is caught red-handed by the Duc des Ifs, an impecunious cousin of the Countess, who calls the Watch. Valentin is arrested and questioned by the Mayor but, fearing to implicate Olivette and betray their love, he does not attempt to defend his action and is hauled off to prison.

Meanwhile the romance between Olivette and the old Sea Captain is not prospering and Olivette finds him extremely tedious. Captain de Merimac is in the Countess's good graces, and before leaving for a cruise in the "Cormorant" he writes her a letter, begging her to use her influence to speed his marriage plans. After the Captain has sailed, Valentin succeeds in escaping from the tumble-down roundhouse in which he is imprisoned and embarks on a daring deception. He acquires a duplicate uniform of his uncle's and, being thoroughly conversant with his physical peculiarities, contrives to pass himself off as old Captain de Merimac. The Countess graciously presents him, thus disguised, with the hand of Olivette, who is, of course, secretly delighted, although she puts on a pretence of the utmost reluctance and appeals to her father not to force her into marriage, which the nuns in her convent always told her was a dreadful state. As Florence St. John sang in her well-known sob song:

The first act ends with wedding bells for the marriage of Olivette to Valentin, though everybody but the bride is convinced that she is the wife of old Captain de Merimac.

ACT II

A midnight fête is given by the Countess to celebrate the wedding. She has forgiven Valentin for his escapade and has approved his release from gaol.

This makes the night a hectic one for Valentin, who finds that he has to appear not only as himself but also in the guise of his uncle by constant change of dress. In the midst of the wedding festivities the real Captain de Merimac appears, having been forced back by contrary winds, and is greeted by everybody as the happy bridegroom. His perplexity is resolved when Valentin appears in his "old-man" disguise. The old Captain learns the truth about the wedding and is determined to take the bride that Valentin has married in his name. A violent argument follows.

In this dilemma Olivette intervenes. She has overheard the details of a plot which the Duc des Ifs is hatching to acquire the estates of the Countess de Roussillon. The Duc is anxious to get the co-operation of Captain de Merimac in connection with a *coup d'état* which he is planning, for which his ship would come in handy. Olivette introduces Valentin disguised as his uncle to the Duc, and the Duc delightedly accepts "Captain de Merimac's" co-operation. The conspiracy thus established, Olivette's next step is to denounce the Duc and the real de Merimac, who are arrested by order of the Countess. Olivette has thus for the moment got rid of her elderly bridegroom, who is completely mystified by the charge of treason brought against him. But Olivette has not reckoned with the Countess's love for Valentin, and all her calculations are upset when the Sovereign Lady of Roussillon announces her intention of marrying the loyal soldier who has quelled the conspiracy. In desperation Valentin, at Olivette's instigation, joins the plot himself and sets the Duc des Ifs free. The Countess is made prisoner and is to be exiled. Finally the curtain falls on a gay Farandole.

ACT III

Pursuing his plot, the Duc leads his cousin the Countess, closely veiled, down to Captain de Merimac's ship "Cormorant". The Captain is now also free but as puzzled as ever as to what is going on all round him. When he learns the true state of affairs he agrees to deport the Countess and then return to find Olivette. Olivette, however, has taken flight, and with her maid and Valentin, disguised as sailors, comes to seek a vessel to take them off. In this scene Florence St. John had a very popular song, "The Torpedo and the Whale", with a ridiculous refrain:

Unfortunately Valentin is recognised by the Duc des Ifs, who distrusts him and has him apprehended. The light-hearted Duc now sets his cap at Olivette. To avoid him Olivette manages to set the Countess free and assumes her dress,

Veloutine, Olivette's maid, takes her place and the Duc, who is very short-sighted, does not notice the change and continues his ardent love-making. By and by de Merimac returns. He is horrified to hear the Duc des Ifs boasting to Valentin of his success with Olivette, and both Valentin and his uncle turn against the bride they had so eagerly claimed at the palace. The return of the Countess with her guards and the unveiling of Olivette clear up the complications. The *coup d'état* is reversed. Valentin and Olivette are united. The Countess, to guard against future plots, accepts the Duc, and old Captain de Merimac is advised to follow the example of the Doge of Venice and "Marry the Sea".

La Mascotte

Opéra Comique in Three Acts

By Alfred Duru *and* Henri Chivot

Music by Edmond Audran

First produced on 29th December, 1880, at the Théâtre des Bouffes-Parisiens, Paris, with Monsieur Morley as "Pippo" and Mademoiselle Montbazon as "Bettina". London production on 15th October, 1881, at the Royal Comedy Theatre (in English), with Violet Cameron, M. Gaillard and Lionel Brough.

Characters

LAURENT XVII, *Prince of Piombino*
PIPPO, *a shepherd*
PRINCE FRITELLINI, *Crown Prince of Pisa*
ROCCO, *a farmer*
BETTINA, LA ROUGEANDE, *a country girl (La Mascotte)*
FIAMETTA, *Prince Laurent's daughter*
CHORUS OF COURTIERS, SOLDIERS, PEASANTS AND ACTORS

The action takes place in the principality of Piombino in the seventeenth century, and in Pisa.

ACT I

The scene is a farmyard. On the right stands the farm-house and on the left a barn. At the rise of the curtain farm labourers are celebrating the end of the wine harvest, and with their wives and sweethearts they drink the new wine as they sing the opening chorus. All are gay, in contrast to Rocco, the farmer, who is in the depths of gloom. He is the victim of bad luck which pursues him persistently. One of his barns has been burned down, his sheep have developed foot-rot, he is involved in a law-suit over some property which looks as if it were going against him, the tailor refuses to deliver his new suit till he gets the money and, finally, today one of his cows is lost. As Rocco is moodily pacing the farm, his shepherd, Pippo, delivers a letter and a box of eggs from the farmer's brother. In the letter Antonio informs him he is sending him Bettina, a goose-girl, and a bringer of good luck. Rocco grumbles at having an extra mouth to feed, but his brother has actually done him a very good turn in sending him Bettina, as a mascot. Pippo, who is in love with Bettina, knows all about her powers of bringing good-fortune and tells Rocco and his colleagues all about mascots. Sure enough, Bettina has been with Rocco but a very short time when news comes that he has won the law-suit, his sheep are miraculously cured, his cow is found and the tailor makes no more trouble about credit.

During the afternoon hunting horns are heard in the neighbourhood and the Royal Hunt, led by Prince Laurent XVII of Piombino, stops at the farm for rest and refreshment. The party includes Prince Laurent's daughter, the Princess Fiametta, and her fiancé, Prince Fritellini. In conversation with Rocco the old Prince Laurent complains about his ill-fortune. Whenever he goes to war he loses his battles, everything he invests in loses its value, and if he aims at a stag he hits a rabbit. Rocco unwisely boasts about his mascot, and Prince Laurent immediately declares his intention of taking Bettina back with him to Court. Meanwhile Princess Fiametta, who has lost all interest in her fiancé Prince Fritellini, is casting amorous glances in Pippo's direction. Bettina is furiously jealous, for she adores Pippo as much as he does her. In fact she tells him that she loves him even more than her geese:

After this Prince Laurent sends for Bettina. He pretends to her that she is no country peasant girl but is descended from the ancient family of Panada, and that her place is not on a farm, but at Court. Bettina, in spite of the fact that it means leaving Pippo, is thrilled at the prospect of playing a Countess at a royal Court. Rocco is to come too, as compensation for losing his mascot, and, leaving the disconsolate Pippo behind at the farm, Prince Laurent with Rocco, Bettina and all his Court departs to this gay tune:

ACT II

The scene is a grand salon in Prince Laurent's palace. Bettina has exchanged her country clothes for a Court dress and is much admired by the courtiers, but she feels embarrassed and out of her element in such grand surroundings and she misses Pippo. Bettina has been deliberately parted from Pippo by Prince Laurent for a specific reason. Rocco has shown him the letter he received from his brother, Antonio. The letter arrived with Bettina, and in it Antonio sets out the rules which govern mascots. So long as a mascot remains a virgin, her powers of luck-bringing are effective. Should she lose her virginity, her powers wane. It is therefore vital that Pippo be kept well away from Bettina, and to assure this, old Prince Laurent proposes formally marrying her himself. But Pippo is a young man of enterprise and is determined to rescue Bettina and marry her without delay. To achieve this he joins, as a dancer, a troupe of entertainers who are visiting the Court of Piombino to give their performance. Pippo's contribution to the programme is a lively Saltarello:

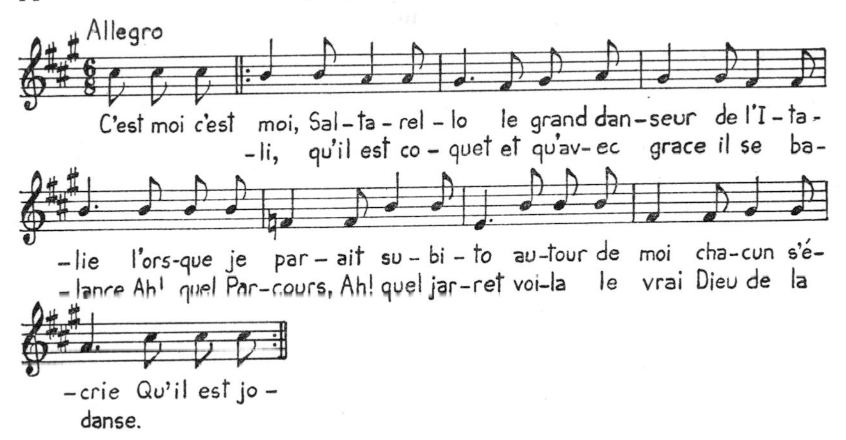

Pippo finds Bettina and manages to get a few moments alone with her—long enough to work out a plan of escape. Bettina then retires to her room to change into her country clothes and she and Pippo arrange to escape from the palace. Left alone, Pippo runs into Prince Fritellini, who recognises him and asks him what he is doing in the palace. Pippo tells him he has come to remove Bettina, and the Prince advises him not to tamper with "the Royal Favourite". Pippo asks him what he means, and Prince Fritellini passes on the palace gossip that Bettina is Prince Laurent's mistress and is shortly to marry him. Pippo is shattered at this news, and as the two men are talking Prince Laurent appears with the palace guards. He orders them to keep Pippo under observation and to prevent him leaving the palace. Laurent and Fritellini both depart and, as Pippo is brooding over Bettina's fickleness, Princess Fiametta enters. Fiametta has always had a soft spot for Pippo, and when she sees him again, his splendid physique rouses all her amorous desires. She tells him how unfair it is that girls must always wait for the man to propose, blurts out that she loves him and asks him to marry her. Pippo, stung by Bettina's behaviour, accepts her on the rebound and old Prince Laurent is delighted to give his consent, reflecting that, married to Fiametta, Pippo will be permanently removed from Bettina. So furious is Bettina when she hears that Pippo is to wed Fiametta, that she promptly agrees to marry Prince Laurent, and the double wedding is arranged to take place that afternoon.

In the Grand Salon the sun is shining in through the open windows, below which flows a broad river, dividing Piombino from the neighbouring Principality of Pisa. At the appointed hour Bettina enters on the arm of Laurent and Fiametta on that of Pippo. As the two couples are advancing towards the improvised altar, by a spontaneous movement Bettina leaves Laurent and Pippo Fiametta. They meet in the middle of the room, all resentment forgotten in the love which wells up at sight of each other. "Can you swim?" whispers Bettina. "Like a fish," answers Pippo. "Then we'll make a dash for it," she tells him. Before anybody can divine their intention, they have flung themselves through the open windows into the river and are swimming for dear life towards Pisa and sanctuary.

ACT III

The scene of the last act is army headquarters in Pisa. Having been jilted by Princess Fiametta, Prince Fritellini has returned home. His father, the Prince of Pisa, has declared war on Piombino, and Fritellini is in command of the army. Bettina, disguised as a boy, in company with Pippo, has joined the Pisan army. With his mascot at his side Pippo has covered himself with glory on the battlefield by his skill and valour and has reached the rank of Major. Prince Fritellini, too, with a mascot in his ranks, has won every battle he has fought, while Laurent, deprived of Bettina's services, is out of luck and has lost all along the line. His disgruntled subjects have revolted, deposed him and turned him out of the country, and in company with Rocco and Fiametta, disguised as itinerant musicians, he is wandering disconsolately in Pisa. Laurent has one idea in his head: to regain the services of Bettina, recoup his fortunes and rehabilitate himself. Arriving at the Pisan Army Headquarters, they find to their dismay that Pippo and Bettina are about to be married. Laurent does his best to dissuade Pippo, but this time to no avail. Prince Fritellini, however, in victory proves a magnanimous conqueror. He has never ceased loving Fiametta, and adversity has given her a true set of values and she is now ready to make him a good wife. So the opera ends with a double wedding with a change of bridegrooms. Pippo comforts Prince Laurent with the reflection that a mascot's powers are hereditary. Bettina is sure to have a daughter. "Make it twins," urges Laurent, and Bettina promises to do her best.

La Cigale et La Fourmi
(La Cigale)

Opéra-Comique originally in Three Acts and Six Scenes

Based on the idea of LA FONTAINE'S *fable* La Cigale et La Fourmi (The Grasshopper and The Ant)

By HENRI CHIVOT *and* ALFRED DURU

Music by EDMOND AUDRAN

First produced on 30th October, 1886, at the Théâtre de la Gaieté, Paris. London production on 9th October, 1890, at the Lyric Theatre. English adaptation in three acts by F. C. Burnand with additional lyrics by Gilbert à Becket and additional music by Ivan Caryll, with Geraldine Ulmar, Effie Clements and Chevalier Scovell.

CHARACTERS

CHEVALIER FRANZ DE BERNHEIM
MATHEW VANDERKOOPEN, *uncle to Marton and Charlotte*
WILLIAM
VINCENT KNAPPS
THE DUKE OF FAYENSBERG
THE DUCHESS OF FAYENSBERG
MARTON
CHARLOTTE, *her sister*
LA FRIVOLINI, *a dancer*
CHORUS OF COURTIERS, PEASANTS, TOWNSFOLK, ETC.

ACT I

The scene is the exterior of a Flemish farm-house: the time is the middle of the seventeenth century. The farm-house is the home of two orphan sisters. Charlotte, from her industrious nature and steady character, is nicknamed "La Fourmi" ("The Ant"). Her sister, Marton, "The Grasshopper", gifted with a beautiful voice, is of an entirely different nature. She longs for the city, bright lights, music and gaiety, and her ambition is to go on the operatic stage. In his music Audran has skilfully characterised the natures of these two girls.

The curtain rises on Charlotte's wedding day. The ceremony is over, the wedding guests have returned from church and the wedding breakfast has been served under the trees outside the farm-house. Prominent among the guests is Mathew, uncle to the two girls and a wealthy innkeeper from Bruges. It was, indeed, while staying with Uncle Mathew that Marton acquired her taste for opera and the city lights after which her soul now hankers. When the guests have dispersed to the orchard, where the bridegroom William has fixed up a swing, Vincent, a devoted young admirer, waylays Marton. Charlotte's wedding has turned his thoughts to love and he now proposes to Marton. Much as she likes him, with kindly words she rejects him, telling him that for the moment her only concern is her career. Dogged and devoted, he tells her he can wait. The chatter of voices now attracts their attention and in a field nearby they see a picnic party preparing an alfresco meal. The Duke of Fayensberg, an irresponsible and flirtatious nobleman who is in the throes of an affair with La Frivolini, Prima Ballerina of the opera company appearing at Bruges, is the host of the picnic. In self-defence and to revenge his neglect, the Duchess has embarked on a flirtation with the handsome Chevalier Franz de Bernheim, several years her junior. These two have also made a country assignation and by an unlucky coincidence have picked on exactly the same locality as the Duke. In fact, hidden in an arbour, she is nearly discovered by her husband when he comes to the farm-house to borrow a corkscrew. The Duke is greatly surprised to find the Chevalier there. He guesses that the Chevalier is with a girl-friend and is all agog to learn her identity, and he is just going to explore the arbour when La Frivolini calls from the field that she has found a corkscrew. The Duke returns to the picnic, telling the Chevalier as he goes: "I shall find out. My Secret Police will soon be on the scent and in less than twenty-four hours I shall know her name." Hearing these words the Duchess is greatly perturbed. There is only one solution: the Chevalier must pretend to fall in love with someone else, to divert the Duke's suspicions. Then if anyone starts a scandal her husband will believe the evidence of his own eyes. Reluctantly Franz agrees and goes off in search of a likely girl. But those who play with fire are liable to be burned, and the Chevalier runs straight into Marton, with her arms full of flowers and looking ravishingly pretty. He promptly falls head over heels in love and Marton is obviously attracted to the handsome young aristocrat. But her ambitions are centred on an operatic career. When La Frivolini hears that the girl has ambitions as a singer (and *not* as a dancer), she introduces her to the Duke and suggests that he use his influence to get her an engagement with the opera at Bruges. The Duke, to try out her voice, asks her for a song, and Marton renders a rustic ditty about poor Margot who had the misfortune to fall into the river and three young men who ungallantly bargain with her for a kiss each as the price of rescue. As the girl is rapidly drowning, she agrees. But when the young men fish her out Margot gives one of them a perfunctory kiss and tells them to divide it among three. Marton's performance is a great success, and the Duke guarantees her a year's training and then an engagement at the opera. Franz suggests as her stage-name La Gloria, and the combined wedding guests and picnic party give her a send-off as Marton, escorted by Uncle Mathew, leaves for Bruges and operatic fame.

ACT II

Act Two takes place a year later in the Place des Echevins, Bruges. It is Kermesse time and the whole city is en fête. The carnival spirit is especially enjoyed by Charlotte and William, who are on a visit to Uncle Mathew to see Marton and are staying at his inn, "The Golden Rain". Marton has profited greatly by her training, and for some months now she has been queen of opera as "La Gloria" and the toast of Bruges, with Uncle Mathew as her manager, Vincent as prompter and the Chevalier Franz as her ardent and devoted lover. But the Chevalier's attentions to La Gloria do not find favour with the Duchess de Fayensberg. She waylays Franz outside the "The Golden Rain" and orders him to give up La Gloria. "But," objects Franz, "in paying court to La Gloria I am only carrying out your orders. Did you not command me to make love to her in order to distract attention from ourselves and put the Duke on a false scent?" Unfortunately this conversation is overheard through an open window by Charlotte, William and Vincent, who are in the inn. They assume that Franz is trifling with Marton's affections and decide to expose him.

Marton now appears in the streets as the glamorous La Gloria and is ecstatically greeted by the crowd. She notices an old street singer trying to make himself heard. But his voice is old and feeble and everybody is ignoring him. Filled with compassion for a fellow artiste, Marton addresses the crowd and announces that La Gloria will give them a song for the old man's benefit and urges them to give generously. She then sings one of the hit tunes of the opera in Gavotte tempo:

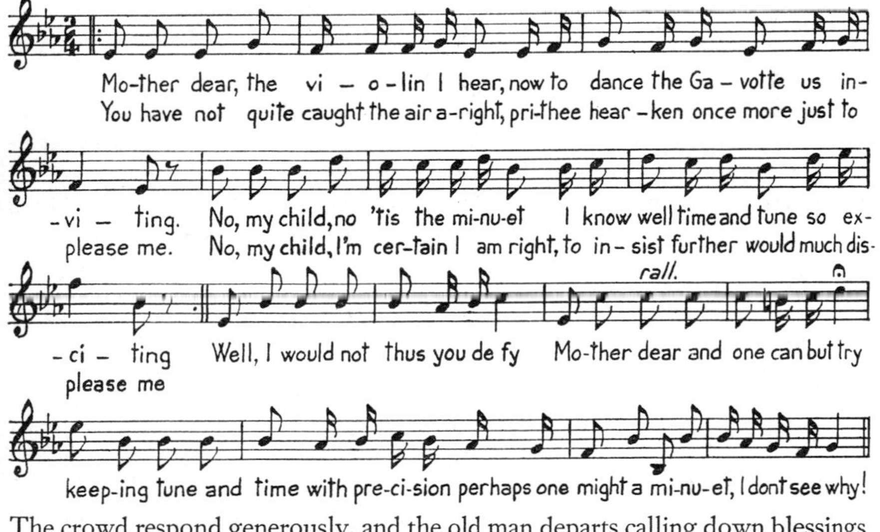

The crowd respond generously, and the old man departs calling down blessings on La Gloria's head.

Shortly after this episode, Marton is told by Charlotte, William and Vincent of the conversation they have overheard. She refuses to doubt Franz's integrity, however, and when he denies utterly that there is anyone but her in his life she is joyfully convinced. As they are talking the Duke appears with a letter for Franz and asks Marton to leave them. He tells Franz that his association with La Gloria is assuming the proportions of a scandal and must stop, and giving him the letter from the Duchess advises Franz to go to her and make his peace with her. When Marton returns the Duke tells her the letter is from the Colonel of Franz's regiment recalling him. But Marton has seen the superscription on the envelope and realises that the letter is from the Duchess. She is now convinced of Franz's treachery and is determined to attend the Duke's ball that night and denounce the Duchess as Franz's mistress before the whole Court. The curtain falls on her departure for the ball in a sedan chair and disguised in a domino.

ACT III

Act Three is the scene of a ball in the palace of the Duke of Fayensberg. During the dancing Franz summons all his courage and tells the Duchess that his love for her was only make-believe and that his heart belongs to Marton. "And who is Marton?" asks the Duchess. When she learns that Marton is La Gloria she turns on Franz in a jealous fury, but while she is hesitating as to her next move, La Gloria sweeps into the ballroom. There, under the pretence of giving a dramatic scena, she denounces the Duchess and her lover, Franz. Franz in consternation rushes forward with a cry of "Marton!" But she rounds on him with the words "Farewell! you will never see my face again" and, stumbling towards the door, falls fainting to the floor. In a trance, as she lies unconscious, she sees a vision of her old home in winter. She sees Mathew outside the farm-house and watches Charlotte admit him to its warmth and comfort. Then, as the music changes, she sees herself as a street-singer, worn and poorly clad, timidly approaching the farm-house and falling exhausted in the snow. Thus is realised Lafontaine's fable of *La Cigale et La Fourmi.* When she regains consciousness all the spectators are wildly applauding what they believe to be an exceptional piece of acting—all, that is, except her relations, Franz, and the Duchess, who whispers to her that her lover, Franz, has never wavered in his loyalty to his precious Marton. And when the Duke declares to the Duchess: "The acting was so real, that I very nearly said to you, 'Madam, what is the meaning of this most serious accusation?'", the Duchess answers: "Had you done so, I should have said, 'Sir, hadn't you better ask Signora Frivolini?'" Finally all the necessary explanations are made and accepted, and Marton gives her hand to the happy Chevalier.

Miss Hellyett

(Miss Decima)

Operetta in Three Acts

By MAXIME BOUCHERON

Music by EDMOND AUDRAN

First produced on 12th November, 1890, at the Théâtre des Bouffes-Parisiens, Paris, with Mademoiselle Biana-Duhamel as "Miss Hellyett" and Monsieur Piccaluga as "Paul Landrin". London production on 23rd July, 1891, at the Criterion Theatre entitled "Miss Decima", *adapted by F. C. Burnand, with Mademoiselle Nesville, David James and Charles Conyers.*

Note. The name "Hellyett" is probably a French phonetical version of the American "Eliot".

CHARACTERS

PAUL LANDRIN, *a painter*
THE REV. SMITHSON, *an American clergyman*
PUYCARDAS, *a Gascon toreador*
JAMES RICHTER, *a Chicago business-man*
BACAREL, *a friend of Paul Landrin*
MISS HELLYETT, *the Rev. Smithson's daughter*
MANUELA FERNANDEZ, *a young Spanish girl*
SENORA FERNANDEZ, *her mother*
CHORUS OF HOTEL GUESTS, PAINTERS, SERVANTS

The action takes place at Bagnères in the Pyrenees in 1890.

ACT I

The scene is the lounge of the Casino Hotel de Val-Montois. The hotel is situated at the foot of a mountain and commands a magnificent view of snow-capped peaks. Although it is eleven o'clock in the morning the hotel orchestra is already playing and dancers are vigorously performing a quadrille, the men cavorting energetically and excited girls lifting up their skirts to kick their legs in the air. As the dance is in progress Miss Hellyett, a strong-minded young woman of sixteen-and-three-quarters, enters the lounge. Brought up in a narrow-minded, puritanical atmosphere by her father, an American Nonconformist clergyman, Hellyett Smithson is shocked by the abandon of the dancing and the girls' immodest display of their legs. She interrupts the dance and quotes to the startled company one of her father's maxims, to the effect that "no woman should allow any part of her anatomy, with the exception of her lips, her forehead, her hair, her chin, her eyes, her nose and her ears, to be seen by any man except her husband". She is laughed to scorn by the dancers, who resume their quadrille.

A popular guest now arrives, Paul Landrin, a painter. He is warmly welcomed as future leader of all the hotel social life. But Paul assures his friends that he has come to the Pyrenees to do some serious painting. Later he runs into Hellyett, whom he had not seen for two years. Although he finds her changed, Paul cannot bring himself to treat her otherwise than as the child he met in New Orleans. But poor Hellyett is piqued by his fatherly approach to her. The Rev. Smithson, whose other nine daughters are all settled, has taken Hellyett on the Grand Tour in the hope of finding her a rich husband. One of her admirers, James Richter, has pursued her from Chicago, but although he follows her about like a faithful spaniel, Hellyett does not find him very exciting. She does, however, tell him after yet another proposal that she will marry him in three months' time if she is still heart-whole. After all, James does treat her as a grown-up person, which is more than Paul does, though she finds Paul attractive.

Hellyett announces her intention of climbing the mountain. James, as her fiancé, claims the right to accompany her, but she points out to him that they are not *actually* engaged, only *possibly*, and she goes off for her walk alone. Paul Landrin now appears with his friend, Bacarel, and suggests a climb to the Chamois Peak. But Bacarel has an assignation and Paul goes off alone. As the Rev. Smithson is reading the newspaper, Hellyett returns to the hotel, breathless and distraught, her hair and dress in disorder. It seems that having climbed to the top of one of the crags, she became faint or giddy, lost her footing and rolled down the mountain-side until her fall was arrested by a convenient bush which hitched on to her skirt and held her hanging head-downward over a precipice with her legs in the air. She had hung there for some time, when she heard a masculine shout. The next instant she felt herself lifted by two strong arms and carried to a place of safety. But not until she was sure that her rescuer had departed did she open the hood which covered her face, for she recalled her father's maxim that "no woman should allow any part of her anatomy, with the exception of her lips, her forehead, her hair, her chin, her eyes, her nose and her ears to be seen by any man except her husband". Goodness knows, she reflects, how much of *her* the man on the mountain must have seen! They must trace him and silence him by insisting that, having compromised Hellyett, he must marry her. Hellyett and her father swear an oath that they will not cease in their endeavours until they have identified "The Man of the Mountain".

ACT II

On the terrace outside the hotel the guests are congregated after lunch and guides are organising excursions into the mountains. In his efforts to trace "The Man of the Mountain", the Rev. Smithson is making a perfect nuisance of himself, butting into some conversations and eavesdropping on others. Discouraged by his failure to make any headway in his search, he begins to lose heart and, waylaying James Richter, asks him if he is really serious in wanting to marry his daughter. James assures him he is. "Very well, then," says the Rev. Smithson, "walk up to her, look her straight in the eye and say, 'I am the man of the mountain'." He refuses to give James any explanation of the mystery, however. James, clutching at a straw, duly carries out his instructions, and Hellyett promptly accepts him. After all, she reflects, it is more than likely that after she left him James *did* follow her up the mountain-side and *did* rescue her. Unfortunately in the course of conversation it becomes clear that at the time of her accident James was in the hotel writing letters and could not possibly have been her rescuer. So the search continues.

In the hotel are staying two Spaniards, Manuela Fernandez and her mother. Manuela is engaged to a Gascon toreador called Puycardas, a boaster and a coward. Manuela adores him, but her mother detests and despises him and reluctantly accepts him as a son-in-law. She is particularly resentful at Puycardas' refusal to escort them on an excursion into the mountains. The truth is he suffers from vertigo and is afraid of heights. But when Senora Fernandez accuses him of cowardice, he pretends that he rescued a young girl on the mountain only the day before. Hellyett happens to overhear this conversation and is convinced that Puycardas must be "The Man of the Mountain". The pill is a bitter one to swallow, for the swarthy Puycardas is to her quite repulsive. Getting him alone, she cross-questions Puycardas on his rescue story, but to conceal his ignorance he adopts the expedient of echoing Hellyett's words. She, in her anxiety to learn the truth, rehearses the whole story in an interrogative manner, he assenting. Finally she asks him how he came to leave the lady alone on the mountain-side, and he airily replies that she wasn't much to look at—a scraggy piece. Furiously Hellyett boxes his ears and goes off to find her father. Nevertheless she steels herself to become Puycardas' bride, however unpalatable her duty. That evening Senora Fernandez presents her future son-in-law to the guests. Congratulations are being showered on Manuela and Puycardas when the Rev. Smithson and Hellyett interrupt the proceedings and "forbid the banns". To Manuela's and the Senora's fury, Hellyett declares that *she* is going to marry Puycardas, and the curtain descends on an unseemly brawl.

ACT III

In the lounge of the hotel next morning the guests are all discussing the scandal of the previous night. Some hard comments are passed on Hellyett, and Paul is vigorous in her defence, while poor Hellyett resigns herself to a living death in marrying Puycardas. She is by now deeply in love with Paul and only thinks of making herself attractive to please him. Paul, too, is revolted at the prospect of Hellyett marrying Puycardas. But when Puycardas tries to get out of marrying Hellyett the Rev. Smithson produces a revolver, and at the point of a gun Puycardas changes his mind. When Paul comes to say good-bye he begs Hellyett to allow him to draw her so as to have a souvenir of her beauty to take away with him. As he sketches her, their conversation becomes more and more affectionate. At last he finishes his drawing and hands Hellyett his sketch-book. As she takes it, she drops the book and it falls open at another page on which Paul has sketched her accident on the mountain-side. In a flash she realises that Paul is "The Man of the Mountain", and with joy in her heart she flings herself into his arms.

La Poupée

Operetta in a Prologue and Three Acts

By MAURICE ORDONNEAU

Music by EDMOND AUDRAN

First produced on the 21st October, 1896, at the Théâtre de la Gaieté, Paris. First London production (translation by Arthur Sturgess) on 24th February, 1897, at the Prince of Wales Theatre, with Courtice Pounds as "Lancelot", Alice Fayer as "Alesia" and Willie Edouin as "Hilarius".

CHARACTERS

FATHER MAXIME, *Superior of a monastery*
LANCELOT, *a monk*
BARON CHANTARELLE, *his uncle*
LOREMOIS, *Chantarelle's friend*
HILARIUS, *a toymaker*
MADAME HILARIUS, *his wife*
ALESIA, *their daughter*
HENRI, *an apprentice*
CHORUS OF MONKS, WORK-PEOPLE AND WEDDING GUESTS

PROLOGUE

The scene of the Prologue is a monastery. The monks have fallen on evil times, the building is going to rack and ruin, and their income is so reduced that they can scarcely afford to buy food for themselves, let alone supply alms to the poor and needy who come to the door. Attached to the order is a shy young monk called Lancelot. He is a nephew of the wealthy Baron Chanterelle and is serving his novitiate. Baron Chanterelle has made it clear to Lancelot that if he decides to take his final vows he will be disinherited, but that if on the other hand he is willing to get married his uncle will make him a present of a hundred thousand francs. In a local newspaper, which comes into Lancelot's hands as wrapping-paper, there is an advertisement which reads: "Splendid offer to Bachelors, Misanthropes and Widowers. Female automatons, absolutely life-like, to order. Blonde or Brunette, guaranteed free of tantrums. Any age supplied.

HILARIUS, Manufacturer of Dolls." This advertisement suggests to Father Maxime, Superior of the monastery, a way to save the monks from ruin. By purchasing one of Hilarius' dolls and introducing it to his uncle as his intended, Lancelot, without being involved in a real marriage, can acquire his uncle's money and save the monastery, and still remain a monk. So Lancelot discards his monkish robe and, dressed in civilian clothes, makes his way to Hilarius' doll shop in the local town.

ACT I

In his workshop Hilarius has just completed a masterpiece, a life-size automaton which is an exact reproduction of his daughter Alesia. By operating a switch, mechanism is set in action which causes the automaton to speak, sing and dance exactly like a living girl. This masterpiece claims all Hilarius' love and skill, and as a result he has neglected his daughter Alesia. She is furiously jealous of her father's preoccupation with the automaton and in a fit of temper damages it, wrenching off an arm. Horrified at what she has done and fearful of her father's anger, she begs his apprentice, Henri, to mend the doll. But before Henri has time to complete his work Lancelot arrives from the monastery, entrusted with the slender savings of the brothers to purchase a life-sized doll. He explains to Hilarius what he wants and Hilarius suggests his latest masterpiece. Henri then appears leading Alesia, who, to save the situation, is impersonating the doll. Neither Lancelot nor Hilarius (whose spectacles Alesia has wisely removed) notices the substitution. Alesia plays her part to perfection and she is delighted to recognise in Lancelot a young man she has often noticed with favour in church. As for Lancelot, he admits to himself that he wishes that the attractive form which stands before him were flesh and blood—especially when she dances and sings so charmingly:

Having made his purchase, the "doll" is carefully packed in a shock-resisting box, and Lancelot sets off with it for his uncle and Chanterelle, taking with him Hilarius and his wife, who is also a party to the deception, as "in-laws".

ACT II

In a salon in Baron Chanterelle's villa guests are assembled for Lancelot's wedding. Alesia, who in the presence of Lancelot and her father continues to play the automaton, is her own charming, natural self with Baron Chanterelle and his friend, Loremois. They are enchanted with her and greatly puzzled by the conceited Hilarius, who nearly wrecks everything by launching into a highly technical description of the bolts, screws and cog-wheels which go to make up the mechanism by which Alesia works. She promises the Baron to do all in her power to make his nephew a good wife.

At the wedding the guests are puzzled by the rigid demeanour of the bride and her curiously stiff walk. However, the marriage contract is signed without a hitch and Baron Chanterelle pays over the hundred thousand francs to his nephew. Lancelot and his bride depart, and then too late Hilarius, blinded by his self-conceit as an inventor, learns from his wife the true facts of his daughter's marriage. He starts in pursuit of Lancelot, followed by the wedding guests.

ACT III

Back at the monastery the monks are anxiously awaiting Lancelot's return and by now are beginning to doubt his intention of honouring his pledge. To calm their fears Father Maxime reads them a lecture in philosophy:

(Audran wrote that song, "A Jovial Monk Am I", especially for the London production to words by Clifton Bingham.) Presently Lancelot arrives and duly hands over the money. He has brought the "doll" with him, and the monks are amazed at Alesia's life-like appearance. Lancelot is, however, allowed to keep the doll in his cell, and she is not put in the cellar, as was originally intended. In the night Alesia wakes the sleeping Lancelot with a kiss. He is overjoyed when he realises that she is no automaton, but a woman of flesh and blood, and rapturously he sings:

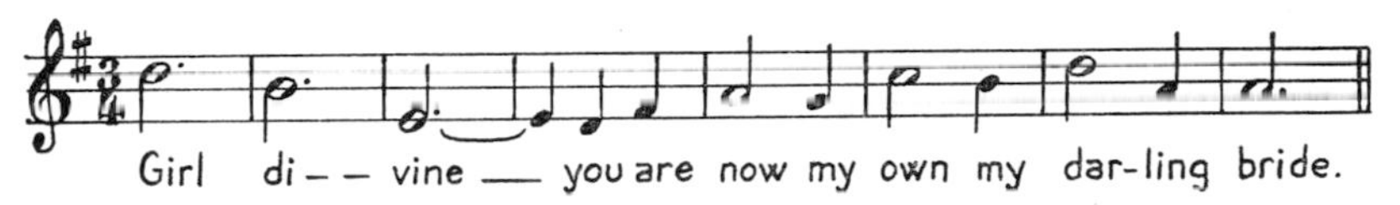

In the morning Hilarius arrives with all the wedding guests to find a blissful pair. He can no longer withhold his blessing, and as Lancelot is already married there is no question of his remaining a monk. Free of his vows he walks out of the monastery to a new life of love and happiness with his bride.

Ma Mie Rosette

A Romantic Opera in Two Acts

By JULES PRÉVEL *and* ARMAND LIORAT (GEORGES DEGAS)

English version by GEORGE DANCE

Music by PAUL LACOME

Additional music by IVAN CARYLL

First produced on 4th February, 1890, at the Théâtre des Folies Dramatiques, Paris, with M. Huguet as "Henri IV", M. Gobin as "Vincent", and Mlle. Nesville as "Rosette". London production on the 17th November, 1892, at the Globe Theatre, with Eugène Oudin, Mademoiselle Nesville and Frank Wyatt.

CHARACTERS

HENRI IV, *King of France*
COLONEL COGNAC
BOUILLON
SÉGUR
MOUSTAJON
VINCENT
CORISANDRE
MARTHA
ROSETTE
CHORUS OF PEASANTS, HUNTSMEN, COURTIERS, ETC.

ACT I

On the farm of Monsieur Moustajon labourers are hard at work harvesting. From the farmyard there is a picturesque view, and on a hill-top in the distance stands the Château de Nerac, the palace of King Henri IV of France—Henry of Navarre. Moustajon has a pretty daughter called Rosette, and she is to be married on the morrow to her rustic sweetheart, Vincent, a simple labourer. They are a devoted couple and look forward to their future together.

While work is in progress on the farm, the King arrives on a hunting expedition. Now, when he was a small boy, Henri and Rosette had been playmates. They had often played at being sweethearts, and when he asks for refreshments and receives a glass of milk from the hands of Rosette, the King is charmed by her looks and moved by the memories that she revives. The King's favourite, Corisandre, is filled with jealousy at his attentiveness to Rosette, and is angry at being relegated to the company of Colonel Cognac, an old warrior who has one eye, one arm, and who is deaf in one ear. The King has a valet called Bouillon, who fancies himself as a lady-killer. Bouillon is unwise enough to make advances to Rosette's aunt Martha, who is thrice widowed and eagerly on the look-out for a fourth husband. When the valet declares himself to be the Duc de Bouillon and boasts that he has several castles, Martha determines to marry him, and Bouillon, entirely taken in by her accommodating tenderness, proposes and is promptly accepted, only to find later that he has married a virago.

Meanwhile Henri with flattering words of love—for he is an incorrigible flirt—has completely turned Rosette's head:

Though she knows in her heart of hearts that she is being disloyal to Vincent by listening to her royal lover, Rosette is carried away by his words, and when Vincent appears she boasts to him of the King's homage to her beauty. "He told me I was born to be clad in robes of silk and that diamonds should sparkle on my breast so that my eyes might outshine them. And then in the softest of whispers he told me of the love that was burning in his heart." Vincent is greatly troubled, but his love is true, and he tells her that he will set off for the Spanish wars, win fame and fortune and "When I am in a position to offer you all that will gratify your heart, I will ask you to marry me, but not before." Too late Rosette realises the folly of her behaviour. The King, of course, only too anxious to get rid of Vincent, accepts the offer of his services as a soldier, and even gives him his own sword to carry on the battlefield. As Vincent bids Rosette a tender farewell, she falls fainting in his arms.

ACT II

After Vincent has departed to the war, Henri, determined in his pursuit of the innocent Rosette, persuades her to come to the Château de Nerac every night with a jug of milk. She tries to get out of it by promising to send her father instead, but the King tells her, "You do not understand. Its charm would be gone served by other hands than yours." So Rosette consents and appears at the château every evening. But Henri is playing a waiting game to gain the confidence of the unsuspecting girl, and one evening about a month later when Rosette has duly delivered her jug of milk the King requests her to remain at the château. He tells her he is giving a ball that night in her honour. Much against her will Rosette remains and, dressed in a ravishing dress and wearing some beautiful jewellery, takes her place at the King's side, in spite of Corisandre's jealous protests at his entertaining "this new protégée of yours—this daughter of a common gardener". But Henri gaily replies that Corisandre need not worry: his heart is large enough to love a hundred women. During the ball a courier from the Spanish war-front is announced. It is Vincent who is the dispatch-rider. He has won promotion and distinction with his sword, and his pay is now more than sufficient to support Rosette in comfort. Vincent's return is not at all welcome to the King. He interviews him and learns that he has proved himself a hero on the battlefield and led a victorious charge—all to win a woman's love. At this moment Vincent hears Rosette's voice singing outside, but Henri declares that it is one of the maids singing at her work, and Vincent thinks no more of it. The King now writes a dispatch to General Duclos, Commander-in-Chief, and orders Vincent to return with it to the front immediately. The dispatch reads: "Keep this man with you. Do not let him ever return here. You understand." Vincent begs to be allowed to see his sweetheart, Rosette, if only for a moment, but the King haughtily orders him to leave immediately and Vincent departs. Corisandre, however, has read the King's dispatch, and her scheming mind evolves a plan to recover Henri's attention by arranging matters so that Vincent will return and take Rosette away. She accordingly sends old Colonel Cognac after Vincent to bring him back with a message that Rosette is at the château and needs him, and that he is to wait outside on the balcony until he is admitted. Vincent duly returns and is waiting on the balcony when Corisandre beckons him in. She tells him that Rosette is in the next room with the King and shows him the text of the King's dispatch. Vincent is now convinced that Rosette has deceived him, and watching through a secret door he sees Henri put his arm tenderly round Rosette's waist while they sing:

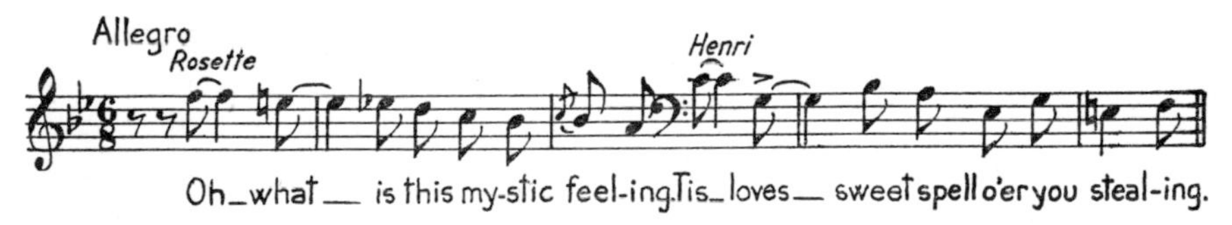

With a furious cry of "Villain, is this how King Henry of Navarre rewards those who fight his enemies?", Vincent bursts into the room. Swords are drawn, a commotion ensues, the courtiers rush in and Vincent is arrested. Then, turning on Rosette, the King orders her out. She appeals to Vincent, who waves her angrily away, and on this picture the lights dim. When they are raised again we are once more in the farmyard of Act One. Vincent wears the King's sword and Rosette is asleep on a sheaf of corn and moves uneasily, as though dreaming. Vincent, watching her tenderly, muses: "Poor Rosette! She fell into a swoon half an hour ago and has been tossing about ever since as though stirred by some inward emotion. Today's excitement has been too much for her. Ah! She is waking." The whole thing has been a dream, and Rosette awakes to find her lover still true to her and she to him.

La Basoche

(King of the Students)

Opéra Comique in Three Acts

By ALBERT CARRÉ

Music by ANDRÉ MESSAGER

First produced on 30th May, 1890, at the Théâtre de l'Opéra-Comique, Paris. Produced in London on 3rd November, 1891, at the Royal English Opera House (now the Palace Theatre), the second and last production there after Sullivan's Ivanhoe. *English dialogue by Sir Augustus Harris; English lyrics by Eugene Oudin; with Ben Davies as "Clément", David Bispham as "Le Duc de Longeville", Esther Palliser as "Marie", and Lucile Hill as "Colette".*

CHARACTERS

ROLAND, *a student of law*
CLÉMENT MAROT, *a poet*
COLETTE, *his wife*
PRINCESS MARIE OF ENGLAND
THE DUC DE LONGEVILLE
L'EVEILLÉ, *Clément's friend*
LOUIS XII, *King of France*
CHORUS OF STUDENTS, TOWNSFOLK, COURTIERS, ROYAL RETAINERS

In 1303 A.D. Philippe le Bel authorised the students of Paris to form themselves into a guild called "La Basoche". He granted them a charter giving them privileges, which they maintained intact for nearly five hundred years. The head of "La Basoche" was authorised to assume the title of King and enjoyed the privilege of wearing the royal crown and mantle. The King was elected annually, and his Supreme Court consisted of a Chancellor, a Vice-Chancellor, a Master of Petitions, a Grand Usher, an Attorney-General, etc. The plot of the opera hinges on the student, Clément Marot, elected King of the Basoche, being mistaken for Louis XII, King of France.

ACT I

The scene is a public square in Paris not far from the Grand Châtelet. The year is 1514. On the left is the hostelry of "The Pewter Platter" and in the centre a fountain. It is the day of the annual election of the King of the Basoche, and there are two candidates: Roland, a student of law, and Clément Marot, a poet. There is noisy support for each candidate from their partisans. Roland advertises his claims for election on the grounds of his legal address and intelligence, and Clément gives a taste of his creative ability in a charming romance:

Their speechifying is interrupted by the entry of the Grand Provost with his suite. Unrolling a long scroll he reads: "Louis, by the Grace of God, King of France and of the Kingdom of Naples, to all present and to come, hail! Desirous of giving to our loyal and beloved subjects a good Queen and of securing prolonged peace to the Kingdoms of France and England, we have chosen as Royal Consort the Most Noble Lady, Marie, sister to our great and powerful cousin, Henry VIII of England. (*Trumpets.*) And know all men that our beloved spouse will make her public entry into our good city of Paris tomorrow at mid-day and we command that it be kept as a day of public feasting and rejoicing. Signed, Louis." The Grand Provost passes on, followed by his suite, and the students withdraw to elect the King of the Basoche.

Now Clément Marot sought election under false pretences. One of the rules of the Basoche is that the King must be a bachelor, and Clément has a wife, a little peasant girl, Colette, whom he keeps in Chevreuse. He is therefore greatly embarrassed when Colette appears and claims him as her husband. He whispers to her to pretend that she does not know him, and Colette, puzzled but loyal and obedient, declares that she is mistaken. Truly Clément strongly resembles her husband, but it is only a resemblance. But Roland is not deceived and determines to catch out Clément and succeed him as King of the Basoche. Clément's friend, L'Eveillé, arranges for Colette to get employment at "The Pewter Platter" and promises that Clément will come to her there. Colette, slightly comforted, enters "The Pewter Platter" with the Landlord.

Into the square now comes Princess Marie of England, accompanied by the Duc de Longeville. The Duke has been to England, has married the Princess by proxy in the name of his royal master, King Louis XII, and has escorted Her Royal Highness to France. But the high-spirited Princess has given her entourage the slip at Pontoise and, pursued by the Duke, is going about the streets of Paris without an escort, for King Henry VIII, anxious to get his sister safely married, has told her that King Louis of France is "a charming young man", and she has anticipated her public entry into Paris in the hope of a chance of catching a glimpse of her royal husband. To the Duke's dismay she announces her intention of staying the night at "The Pewter Platter". She engages two rooms, while the Duke, unwilling to take the responsibility for what this madcap Princess may do next, hurries to the palace to tell the King what is going on.

Now, to the ringing of bells, the sound of trumpets and cries from the crowd of "Long Live the King", Clément makes his triumphal entry into the square as King of the Basoche. Riding on a horse, he wears the crown on his head, the mantle on his shoulders and holds the sceptre in his hands. Hearing cries of "Long Live the King", the Princess, watching him from her window in "The Pewter Platter", naturally assumes that Clément is King Louis of France and is enchanted with her royal husband's good looks. She instructs the hotel maid (Colette) to hand a bouquet, which she gives her, to the King with the words: "Sire, a lady unknown craves a few words alone and lays these flowers at your feet." Colette takes the bouquet and, descending to the square, timidly inquires which is the King and, when Clément is pointed out to her, is so shocked and surprised to learn that her husband is, as she also believes, King of France, that she drops the bouquet. Princess Marie comes quickly forward and explains that the girl's awkwardness is due to her awe of His Majesty. "I'm but a man; so why this terror?" asks Clément innocently, and the Princess replies:

Clément, puzzled but gallant, gives her a flower from his bouquet and tells her, "Whatever I am, thou art a Queen", while Roland tries, by prompting Colette's jealousy, to trap her into an admission that Clément is her husband. But Colette is obstinately loyal. "Tomorrow," says the Princess to Clément as he gallantly kisses her hand and, wondering at her meaning, he repeats "Tomorrow".

ACT II

When the curtain rises it is closing time the same night in the public room of "The Pewter Platter". As the students leave, Roland, with an eye on Colette, says meaningly that he intends to return later and hopes to catch her with Clément. After closing time the Landlord orders Colette to lay the table for supper for their two guests—i.e. Princess Marie and the Duke. But Colette's head is in a whirl and dreamily she sings to herself:

"That legend is like my story," she tells herself. "The shepherdess—that is I; the young handsome King—that is Clément, or rather His Majesty Louis XII, King of France. That is the reason that obliges him to keep our marriage a secret. I will hold my tongue as I have promised and we shall continue to meet in secret—like tonight. How shall I ever dare to kiss him again, kiss him, a King?" But when Clément does arrive, Colette has no cause to complain of his lack of ardour, and they sing a love duet:

When the Duke returns to "The Pewter Platter" from the palace, having failed to see the King, Princess Marie sends him straight back there with instructions to invite the King in her name to have supper with her at the inn. "He would never do such a thing," declares the Duke. "Give him this flower from me," says the Princess, taking Clément's flower from her dress, "and I'll answer for his coming." So when she comes into the public room and sees Clément with Colette, Marie naturally assumes that the King has accepted her invitation. Supper follows with Colette as waitress. Princess Marie is very affectionate, and Clément is convinced she is a creature of Roland's sent to spy on him and Colette. During supper Colette rushes in to say that Madame's husband has returned, and is puzzled that Marie is not put out at the prospect of being discovered tête-à-tête with the King. When Marie goes to open the door to the Duke, Clément slips out of the room. The Duke is amazed to hear that His Majesty did turn up for supper. He declares that the Princess's conduct is no longer his responsibility, it is the King's business now and he's going to bed. Colette is shocked at his callous cynicism. Especially when the Duke tells her: "You had better go too and be out of their way." "How shocking! Just because it's the King he shuts his eyes," thinks Colette. As she is leaving the room Clément's friend L'Eveillé steals in. He has come to warn Colette that Roland is on the alert, hoping to take her by surprise with Clément. But when Roland and the other students arrive, it is not with Colette but with Marie that they find Clément. Clément tells her not to be alarmed. "These are members of my Parliament," he says. "Come to pay homage to their King?" she asks. Roland says sneeringly to the students, "The King has good taste, although he is not married." "Not married!" says Marie, flaring up. "What do you mean? I am his wife!" "His wife! Then I am right," declares Roland, and calls on the Chancellor of the Basoche to pass judgement on Clément. Just as Clément is about to be officially deposed, the Duke appears on the staircase. "What are you doing here, Madame?" he asks the Princess. "Who is this man and by what right do you question the lady?" asks the Chancellor of the Basoche. Choking with anger, the Duke declares, "She is my wife." Amid general amazement Clément adds, "And so, you see, she's certainly not mine," and he slips out of the room. The Duke leads Princess Marie up the stairs and the Chancellor of the Basoche gives judgement on the incident. Roland is fined ten écus and flounces out furiously. Clément, returning, has his crown restored to him and is carried shoulder high out of the room by cheering students. When all but Colette have departed there is the sound of trumpets without, and the excited Landlord ushers in the King's Equerry, followed by his archers. He announces that he has been sent by his royal master to find his fair and gentle spouse, who, disguised in humble dress, is hiding in the inn. Colette steps forward. "I am she whom you seek," she tells him. "I am the Queen." Taking her hand, the Equerry leads her out amid the acclamations of the crowd and shouts of "Long Live the Queen".

ACT III

The scene is the Grand Hall of Louis XII's palace of the Tournelles, with high windows overlooking the Rue St. Antoine. The King appears, old and careworn. He is dismayed to find how young his Queen is, as Colette enters in royal robes, the crown upon her head, followed by her Ladies-in-Waiting. The King advances to greet her with the words: "The King of France could not suffer his noble spouse to remain longer at an inn." Gaily Colette replies, "I am so glad he sent for me. Shall I see him soon?" Nothing will induce her to believe that she is in the presence of the King, and Louis assumes that she does not understand that she was married by proxy, and that she is speaking of the Duc de Longeville. "Did he not explain to you?" he asks Colette. "What did he tell you?" "Tell me? He told me he loved me, of course. He kissed me." The King is livid at the Duke's flagrant betrayal of his trust, and tells him furiously to escort the Princess back to her royal brother in England. "I leave it to him to punish you and to annul this marriage. In an hour you must be gone," he commands, and leaves the room. Princess Marie now arrives and is shattered at the Duke's news that she is to return to England. She declares that she now understands the King's coldness and embarrassment at supper last night. He regrets the marriage. He does not love her.

The complications are finally cleared up when the students pass the palace singing the song of the Basoche. Colette and Marie at the windows pointing at Clément, cry: "The King, the King! There he is, that young man on the horse. Don't you hear them shouting 'Long Live the King'?" "But that is the King of the Basoche, the King of the students, a Carnival King," exclaims the Duke. "Was it he you took to be your husband?" "Yes," answers the disconcerted Marie. The Duke orders Clément to be brought in to the palace under escort, and he takes Princess Marie off with him to explain everything to the King. When His Majesty returns all is straightened out. Roland succeeds Clément as King of the Basoche. Clément and Colette are reunited, and the happy couple set off on a second honeymoon, for the King commands them to travel for a while. Looking at Marie he comments: "Yes, I think it would be prudent."

Les P'tites Michu

(The Little Michus)

Opéra Comique in Three Acts

By Albert van Loo *and* Georges Duval

Music by André Messager

First produced on 16th November, 1897, at the Théâtre des Bouffes-Parisiens, Paris, with Alice Bonheur as "Marie-Blanche", Odette Dulac as "Blanche-Marie", Monsieur Maurice Lamy as "Aristide", and Monsieur Manson as "Gaston Rigaud". London production 29th April, 1905, at Daly's Theatre, with Mabel Green, Adrienne Augarde, Robert Evett and Willie Edouin.

Characters

GENERAL THE MARQUIS DES IFS
MICHU, *a pastry-cook*
MADAME MICHU, *his wife*
ARISTIDE, *his shop assistant*
GASTON RIGAUD, *a Captain of Hussars*
MARIE-BLANCHE
BLANCHE-MARIE
MADEMOISELLE HERPIN, *Headmistress of a girls' school*
BAGNOLET, *an Army batman*
CHORUS OF GUESTS, SCHOOL-GIRLS AND MARKETEERS

The action takes place in Paris in 1810.

ACT I

Some seventeen years before the curtain rises, the Revolutionary Tribunal of France had ordered the arrest of the Marquis des Ifs, but when they came to take him they found he had fled. The night before his escape the Marquise had died, giving birth to a baby girl. Distraught and helpless, the Marquis entrusted the child, along with a generous sum of money to pay for its upbringing and education, to a peasant couple called Michu, who lived on his estate. Then, telling them that he would send for his daughter when times were more settled, he rode away to join the Royalist army. By a coincidence Madame Michu had also given birth to a baby girl on the same day as the Marquise, and the Michus decide to bring up the two little girls as twin sisters. But now fate steps in and plays them an ironic trick. Commanded by Madame Michu to give the babies their bath, Michu undresses them and incautiously seats them side by side in the same bath. The result of this manoeuvre is that when he comes to take them out he is unable to tell which is his own daughter and which the Marquis'. The implications of this contretemps hang over the Michus like the sword of Damocles, but as the years pass and the Marquis does not claim his daughter their fears are lulled.

With the Marquis' money Michu has moved to Paris and is now a prosperous pastry-cook with a shop in the food market and an assistant. The two girls, aged seventeen and christened Blanche-Marie and Marie-Blanche, are finishing their education at a boarding school. They are inseparable companions, dress alike and do everything together as though they were in fact the twins they believe themselves to be.

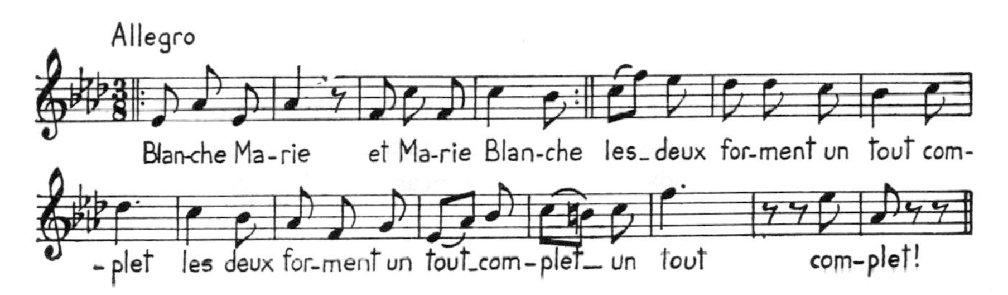

The scene of Act One is the garden of a girls' school conducted on strictly military lines by Mademoiselle Herpin, a soldier's daughter. Soon after the curtain rises the girls are given a recreation break and occupy the time with a game of blind-man's buff. During the game Blanche-Marie incurs a forfeit and as a penalty the girls decide that she must kiss the first person to enter the garden. Hardly are the words out of their lips when into the garden strides a handsome Captain of Hussars, Gaston Rigaud. He has overheard the whole conversation and, to save Blanche-Marie embarrassment, it is he who does the kissing. Then, so as not to be accused of favouritism, he kisses Marie-Blanche. He has just finished when Mademoiselle Herpin enters. She is Gaston's aunt and is delighted to see her nephew. She notices his Captain's stars, and he tells her proudly that he was fortunate enough to save his General's life on the battlefield of Saragossa and as a reward his General, the Marquis des Ifs, has promoted him to the rank of Captain and has promised him the hand of his daughter in marriage. Monsieur and Madame Michu now arrive to visit Blanche-Marie and Marie-Blanche. They are accompanied by Aristide, the shop assistant, bearing a box full of the finest examples of the pastry-cook's art, which the girls share generously with their schoolmates. Aristide has known the girls all their lives, and Marie-Blanche cherishes a school-girl passion for him. Presently Mademoiselle Herpin announces a visitor for the Michus and

Private Bagnolet arrives. He has been detailed by the Marquis to discover the whereabouts of the Michus, recover his daughter from them and escort her home to him. But Michu's explanation, or rather lack of explanation of why he cannot identify the Marquis' daughter, so confuses Bagnolet that he insists that the Michus, accompanied by their daughters, return with him to interview the Marquis. Seen off by Mademoiselle Herpin and the whole school, the Michus and Bagnolet depart to this rousing tune:

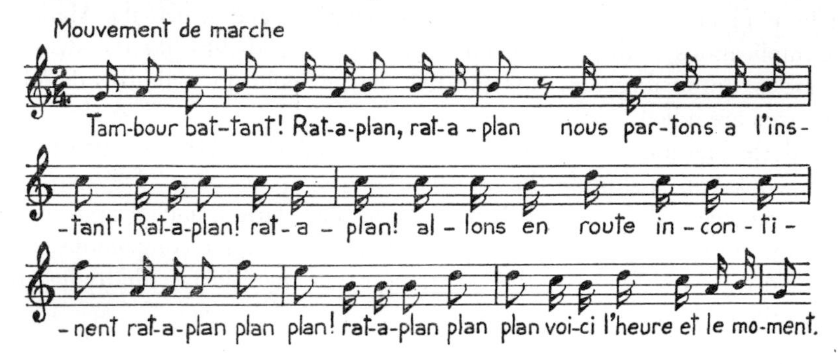

ACT II

At his town house in Paris, General the Marquis des Ifs is entertaining his prospective son-in-law, Captain Gaston Rigaud, while waiting the arrival of the daughter whom for nearly eighteen years he has not set eyes on. The Marquis is greatly put out when Bagnolet eventually arrives with Monsieur and Madame Michu, Blanche-Marie and Marie-Blanche, but the Captain is enchanted to meet again the little Michus, whose acquaintance he made and whom he kissed in the garden of his aunt's girls' school. After greetings are over the Marquis commands Michu to present to him his daughter. But Michu, now the terrible moment has come, completely loses his nerve, stutters and stammers, equivocates and gives so confused an explanation as to why he cannot produce the Marquis' daughter, that the Marquis angrily brushes him aside and turns to Madame Michu. Eventually from her he extracts the painful story of the babies, the bath and the lost identities. Blanche-Marie and Marie-Blanche are at first shattered at the thought of being parted and each prays to St. Nicholas, patron saint of children, that she may not turn out to be the Marquis' daughter. But after renewing acquaintance with Captain Gaston Rigaud both are enchanted with him and radically revise their prayer to St. Nicholas, while Gaston, unaware that one of the Michus is the Marquis' daughter, asks them if they know anything about her. Both the girls tell him that she resembles themselves in every detail:

After this the Marquis orders Michu to produce his daughter within the next half-hour. If he does not do so the Marquis will take the matter into his own hands. The problem is a knotty one and involves much scratching of heads. The Marquis, however, solves the problem *à la militaire* by arbitrarily deciding that Marie-Blanche is his daughter. So Act Two ends with Marie-Blanche, re-christened Irene des Ifs and officially betrothed to Gaston, remaining in the Marquis' household, while Blanche-Marie returns with the Michus to confectionary and Aristide.

ACT III

The scene is Michu's confectionary shop in the food market of Paris. Ever since the little Michus were so cruelly separated everything for them has been at sixes and sevens. The stiff, conventional atmosphere at the Marquis' household is irksome to a girl of Marie-Blanche's expansive temperament and she is constantly in trouble with her chaperone for some breach of etiquette. Also, now that she is betrothed to Gaston she finds that they have little in common, and she realises that her heart belongs to Aristide. She spends every spare minute she can in the confectioner's shop. Commerce she feels is her true background: Marie-Blanche is a born saleswoman. Blanche-Marie, on the other hand, rather envies Marie-Blanche the calm, well-ordered dignity of the aristocrat's life. She is not the least in love with Aristide, but her heart yearns after Gaston. This unhappy situation is brought to a head by drastic action on the part of Marie-Blanche. In her bedroom in the Marquis' house hangs a portrait of his late wife, and Marie-Blanche has discovered in a drawer the identical dress that the Marquise is wearing in the picture. Smuggling Blanche-Marie into the house, she dresses her in the Marquise's gown and does her hair exactly as the Marquise wore it in the picture. She then leads Blanche-Marie to the Marquis. Blanche-Marie's resemblance to his late wife is so striking that the Marquis is convinced without doubt or further argument that she is his daughter. So it becomes a case of change of partners. Blanche-Marie is betrothed to Gaston, while Marie-Blanche throws herself ecstatically into Aristide's arms. The Marquis is satisfied, the Michus relieved, and the happy ending features the double wedding of the Little Michus.

Véronique

Operetta in Three Acts

Book and Lyrics by ALBERT VAN LOO *and* GEORGES DUVAL

Music by ANDRÉ MESSAGER

First produced on 10th December, 1898, at the Théâtre des Bouffes-Parisiens, with Jean Perrier as "Florestan" and Mademoiselle Mariette-Sully as "Hélène". First London production (in French) at the Coronet Theatre, Notting Hill, 5th May, 1903; and in English at the Apollo Theatre 18th May, 1904, with Ruth Vincent.

CHARACTERS

COQUENARD, *a florist*
AGATHA, *his wife*
ERMERANCE DE CHAMP-D'AZUR
HÉLÈNE DE SOLANGES (VÉRONIQUE)
FLORESTAN DE VALAINCOURT, *betrothed to Hélène*
LOUSTOT, *a bailiff*
AUNT BENOIT
DENISE, *her niece*
SÉRAPHIN, *a groom, betrothed to Denise*
CHORUS OF FLOWER-GIRLS, CUSTOMERS, MEMBERS OF THE NATIONAL GUARD, WEDDING GUESTS, ETC.

ACT I

The scene is Monsieur Coquenard's flower-shop in the Paris of 1840. All is bustle on a fine summer's morning; flower-girls serving customers, making up buttonholes, assembling bouquets. The proprietor, Monsieur Coquenard, is in a state of high excitement, for he is expecting to hear at any moment that he has been gazetted a captain in the National Guard. But Madame Coquenard is dreadfully cast down. Her lover, Comte Florestan de Valaincourt, has decided to get married to a Mademoiselle Hélène de Solanges, and the marriage contract is to be signed that very evening in the Tuileries in the presence of Their Majesties the King and Queen of France. At eleven o'clock Madame Coquenard announces a break for coffee and the girls go off chattering to their refreshment, leaving a deserted shop.

Hélène de Solanges now arrives with her Aunt Ermerance to buy flowers for the marriage ceremony that night. The ladies are attended by a groom, Séraphin. He is very impatient at being kept hanging about on this day of all days, as in two hours' time he himself is to be married and he is longing to get back to his bride. Hélène, noticing Séraphin's impatience, remarks to her aunt that she only wishes that her own fiancé, Florestan, was as impatient to be with her. She complains of the unromantic circumstances of her engagement. "What happened?" she exclaims. "Her Majesty sent for me and said, 'Child, as a proof of our royal favour, the King and I have arranged a marriage for you with Monsieur le Comte Florestan de Valaincourt.' But I want to be wooed before I'm won. I know he's young and presentable, for I've seen him, which is more than he has me." At this moment one of the flower-girls, Sophie, appears to serve the ladies and bears them away to the conservatory to select bouquets for their visit that night to the Tuileries. Having bought their flowers, Hélène and Ermerance are about to depart, when Hélène sees Florestan approaching the shop. She determines to remain and spy on his movements; and in spite of Ermerance's warning, "My dear, I shouldn't, you'll only learn things", Hélène persuades Sophie to hide her and her protesting aunt in the gallery running round the shop, where they can watch events without being seen. Florestan has come to the flower-shop with two objects in view: to terminate a tepid but protracted affair of the heart with Madame Coquenard and, secondly, to invite all the flower-girls to a party to celebrate the end of his bachelorhood. He explains to Madame Coquenard that he is compelled to marry money to pay his debts or be committed to prison. His guardian is adamant and has employed a bailiff—Monsieur Loustot—whose business it is to dog his footsteps until he is safely married. Madame Coquenard asks Florestan what his future bride is like, and Florestan confesses that he has never seen her, but pictures her as "a dowdy little frump with white eyelashes and two sandy pigtails down her back". This is too much for Hélène, who is fuming with rage in her concealment. She tells her aunt that they will both attend the farewell party and that she is determined to get Florestan away from Madame Coquenard. She has seen a notice in the shop window advertising for two flower-girls. "We shall apply for the jobs," she tells her startled aunt and adds, "unless you say 'yes' to everything I propose, I'll say 'no' to Monsieur de Valaincourt tonight before the King, the Queen and the whole Court." The obliging Sophie provides two spare dresses, and Hélène and Ermerance retire to the back of the shop to disguise themselves as flower-girls.

Soon after this the music to the Finale of Act One begins and heralds Florestan's announcement that the carriages are waiting to transport the whole company to the Restaurant Tournebride at Romanville. This news produces a burst of excited chatter from the flower-girls, during which Monsieur Coquenard can be observed trying to say something. When he can make himself heard he announces with pride and satisfaction that he has received his commission and is now Captain Coquenard of the National Guard. All gather round him with congratulations and Florestan celebrates the occasion with a suitably military compliment:

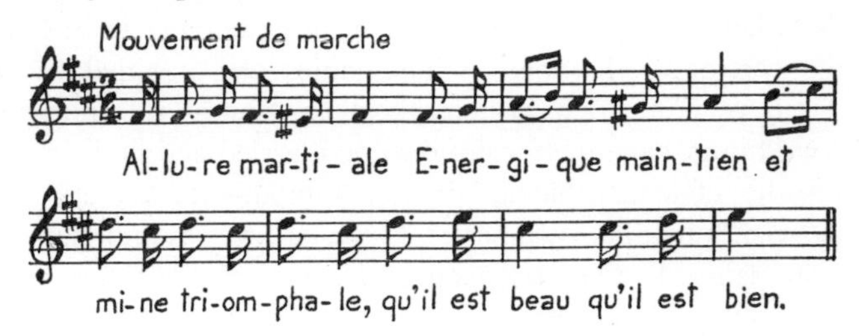

After this song Hélène and Ermerance enter disguised as flower-girls, calling themselves Véronique and Estelle. They shyly ask for the proprietor, and Florestan is bowled over by Hélène's beauty as Monsieur Coquenard asks them what they want. Hélène explains that they have seen the advertisement in the window and want to apply for the jobs. Both are promptly engaged by Monsieur Coquenard, who is greatly taken with Estelle (Ermerance), and Florestan, with his eye on Véronique (Hélène), invites them both to join his picnic party at Romanville. The company depart to this breathless tune as the curtain falls:

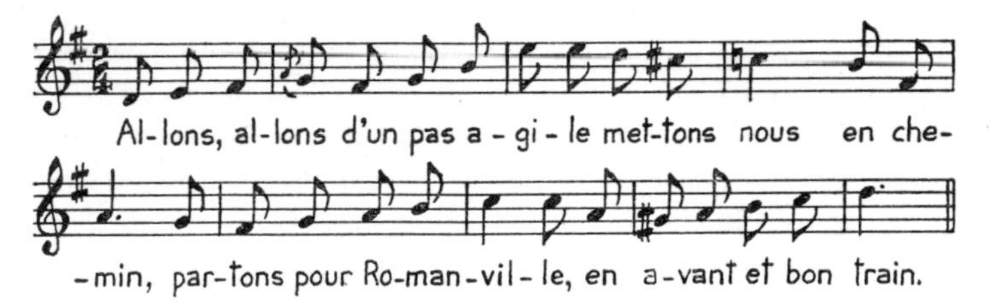

ACT II

In the open air "Restaurant Tournebride" in the middle of the woods at Romanville, Séraphin's wedding party have just finished luncheon. The bride and bridegroom are toasted and the usual speeches are in progress, punctuated by protests from the blushing bride. Florestan's party have finished lunch and are strolling about the forest. Coquenard has invited a detachment of the National Guard to celebrate his commission, so the flower-girls are well supplied with male escorts. Monsieur Coquenard is very attentive to Estelle (Ermerance), and Florestan has eyes for no one except Véronique (Hélène). To divert her he hires a donkey and gives her a donkey ride. This episode provides one of Messager's best-known numbers: "Trot here, trot there":

Ermerance (Estelle) has less luck when Coquenard gives *her* a donkey ride, for the donkey bolts and deposits her in a ditch, fortunately a dry one. The attraction between Florestan and Hélène is entirely mutual, and Hélène confides to her aunt that her fiancé is charming. "I think he has forgotten Madame Coquenard, Hélène de Solanges, everyone but Véronique the florist's assistant. I want to hear him say, 'My dearest Véronique.' I'll teach him to say 'Hélène' later." Florestan makes his declaration of love in a scene which contains the famous "Swing Song":

As Florestan is helping Véronique down from the swing, he kisses her, but she reminds him that he is to marry Mademoiselle de Solanges and gives him the slip. Monsieur Loustot, the bailiff, is greatly disquieted at Florestan's pursuit of Véronique. He reminds Florestan of his appointment at the Tuileries and tells him that the carriages for the return journey to Paris will be round in half an hour. "Not if I know it," says Florestan to himself, and goes off to dismiss the drivers. His action is the cause of great inconvenience to Hélène and Ermerance, who are thus left with no transport to convey them back to Paris. But Hélène is not to be daunted. She seeks out Madame Séraphin. With a bribe of sixty louis she persuades the bride to lend her her veil and the bride's aunt to lend Ermerance her bonnet and cloak. Her plan is to take the bride's place in Séraphin's carriage and with Ermerance disguised as the aunt to be driven back to Paris by Séraphin. This plan works perfectly, and after the unsuspecting Séraphin has driven Hélène and Ermerance away in his carriage, Madame Séraphin delivers a farewell note from Véronique to Florestan, urging him to forget her and to "fly to the bride, who will adore you".

Florestan is shattered by the loss of Véronique and declares his firm intention to go to a debtor's prison rather than marry the dowdy little frump he has pictured, especially while the chance remains of winning the charming Véronique. He turns a deaf ear to the urging of his friends to forget her and get married.

ACT III

The scene is a salon in the Tuileries off the main suite of state apartments. Ermerance is discovered lost in a reverie. She is recalling the fun she enjoyed as Estelle and thinks sentimentally of handsome Monsieur Coquenard. Various

Ladies-in-Waiting stand near by. Afraid to disturb her, they sing an enchanting whispering chorus, a characteristic example of Messager's delicate art:

After the chorus Hélène enters, looking irresistible, and shortly after, Florestan arrives. Monsieur Loustot, the bailiff, has persuaded him to listen to reason, to return to Paris, put on Court dress and he is now waiting to meet his fiancée. When they meet, Florestan is amazed to discover that Véronique and Hélène de Solanges are one and the same person, but he is at the same time slightly piqued to remember that while he spent the whole afternoon making love to the guileless Véronique, Mademoiselle de Solanges was laughing up her sleeve at him. So he tells Hélène that she has rendered their marriage impossible, and he pretends to write to this effect to his guardian. But when he sees Hélène's distraught expression he repents and hands the letter to her. Opening it she reads: "My Dear Uncle, you have made me the happiest man in the world. Hélène is as sweet as she is lovely. I ask nothing better of life than to pass it with her. Your devoted nephew, Florestan." And taking her in his arms he murmurs: "Hélène, my dearest Véronique."

Les Saltimbanques
(The Acrobats)

Opéra Comique in Three Acts and Four Scenes

By Maurice Ordonneau

Music by Louis Ganne

First produced at the Théâtre de la Gaieté, Paris, on 30th December, 1899, with Jeanne Saulier, Lise Berty and Monsieur E. Perrin.

Characters

MALICORNE, *Circus Director*
MADAME MALICORNE, *his wife*
PAILLASSE, *a clown*
GRAND PINGOUIN, *a strong man*
ANDRÉ DE LANGÉAC, RIGOBIN, CORADET — *Officers*
LE COMTE DES ÉTIQUETTES
SUZANNE, *a singer*
MARION, *Comedienne*
MADAME BERNADIN
MARQUIS DU LIBAN, *André's uncle*
BARON DE VALENGOUJON
CHORUS OF CIRCUS FOLK, SOLDIERS, VILLAGERS AND GUESTS, ETC.

ACT I

Scene I. *Les Saltimbanques* is a story of circus life and circus folk; their laughter and tears, their triumphs and heart-aches. The opening scene is a field near Versailles where the troupe of the Circus Malicorne have pitched their tents. The principals of the troupe include the Director, Malicorne, and his wife; Paillasse, a clown; Grand Pingouin, the strong man; Marion, his sweetheart; and Suzanne, singer and tightrope-walker. Suzanne is seventeen and there is some mystery regarding her origin. Her mother, also a tightrope-walker, left her as a baby to the tender mercy of the Circus Director, Malicorne. His bullying treatment and exploitation of Suzanne are an ever-present source of disgust to the old clown, Paillasse, who worships her. Marion is in love with her partner, Grand Pingouin, and pesters him to marry her, but, as he points out, the circus never remains long enough in one place for them to comply with the registration requirements necessary for marriage.

Soon after the rise of the curtain the box office opens and a crowd collects. Marion, before she became an acrobat, was in domestic service as housemaid to the Baron de Valengoujon, and she now sees her late employer in the crowd. The Baron, an amorous old fool, accosts her and is trying to make love to her when the voice of Grand Pingouin is heard off-stage. She hurriedly tells the Baron to say that it is Mademoiselle Suzanne whom he has come to see, but unfortunately it is Paillasse who enters. Calling the Baron a dirty old satyr for running after young girls, Paillasse kicks him across the stage. At the exit the Baron meets Grand Pingouin, who asks what he wants. This time the Baron tells the truth, and hearing that it is Marion he is after, Grand Pingouin kicks the unfortunate man back to the turnstile where he came in. But Marion thinks Grand Pingouin has been unnecessarily brutal to the Baron and turns on him, at which the mighty Hercules cowers before her, causing her to remark that she ought to have been a lion-tamer. Suzanne has been sent off to buy tobacco for Malicorne and now returns, greatly agitated. It seems she has been accosted by three young officers, who have followed her into the circus and tried to kiss her. She defends herself, and one of them, Lieutenant André de Langéac, is sensitive enough to realise the poor girl's genuine terror. He calls the other two off, and when they have gone he apologises to her and they sing a charming duet:

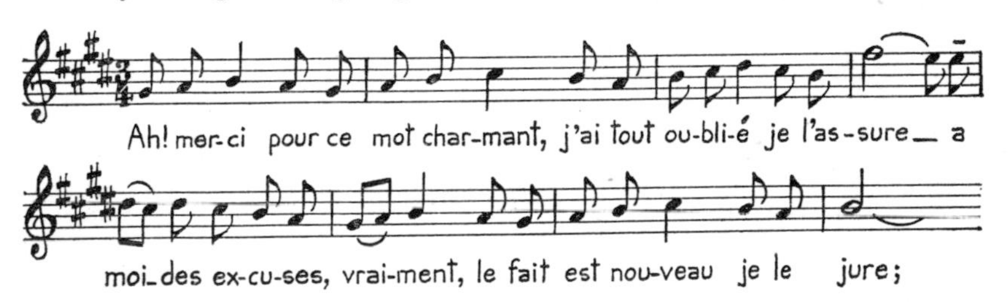

SCENE 2. In front of the box office an apron-stage has been erected, and on this the artistes are presented to the public by the Director Malicorne. The Baron, still infatuated by Marion in spite of former discouragements, is well to the fore, and offers to buy a season ticket for the stay of the circus. But the crowd hold back, and so, to stimulate their appetite, Suzanne appears and sings them a song about the shepherdess, Colinette, and her encounter with the Big Bad Wolf. After her song Suzanne goes among the crowd to collect money for her performance and once again she meets the three officers who tried to kiss her. This time they are charming, and two of them present her each with a bunch of violets, and Lieutenant André wants her to accept a present of money. This Suzanne refuses. Malicorne, overhearing the conversation, is furious with Suzanne for refusing the money, but she is adamant. When they say good-bye, Suzanne, obviously greatly attracted by André, gives him a bunch of violets as

a keepsake. He goes and, turning away, she encounters Baron de Voulengoujon. He has had no success with Marion, and now tries with Suzanne. He attempts to kiss her and she boxes his ears. Malicorne happens to be passing, and is affronted. Not only does Suzanne refuse money but she assaults the clients of his circus. An angry scene develops in which the crowd takes sides. But when Malicorne threatens Suzanne with violence, Paillasse, Grand Pingouin and Marion go to her defence. Flexing his brawny biceps, Grand Pingouin forces the bully to his knees and informs him that the three of them are leaving the circus and taking Suzanne with them. Fortunately they remain long enough to render the hit tune of the score before the curtain falls:

ACT II

Act Two takes place in the square of Bécanville, a village in Normandy. It is decorated with poles and bunting as if for a fête, for today the finals of a choral competition are to be held. At mid-day outside the inn the villagers are drinking, and an interesting conversation ensues between the *patron* and the steward to the Comte des Étiquettes, Lord of the Manor. It seems that the Count and Madame Bernardin, wife of the chairman of the competition, are lovers, and that before her marriage they are rumoured to have had a love-child. The affair has continued, and that very day they have a rendezvous for which the Count will communicate the time to her by means of his choir. If they sing in $\frac{2}{4}$ time, the rendezvous is for 2 p.m.; if in $\frac{3}{4}$ time at 3 p.m., and if in common time at 4 p.m. When the villagers have dispersed to the choral competition, four familiar figures arrive. They are Paillasse, now a clipper of dogs and veterinerary surgeon to cats; Grand Pingouin, a mender of chairs; Marion, a fortune-teller; and Suzanne, a street-singer. They go in fear of losing their liberty, for they have broken their contracts and Malicorne has set the police on them. Finding the village deserted, Paillasse and Grand Pingouin, disguised as Ratapoil Frères, go off in search of chairs to mend, poodles to clip and cats to neuter, and Marion and Suzanne depart to cope with the housekeeping.

A bugle then sounds and a company of soldiers march on under the command of Lieutenant André de Langéac. They are followed by villagers, peasants and members of various choral societies, and André sings the Chanson Militaire:

The song concluded, André orders the soldiers to fall out and goes in search of his old friend, the Comte des Étiquettes, but before leaving he orders a glass of beer at the inn. The village bunting reminds him of Versailles and the circus, and as he drinks his beer he wonders what has become of Suzanne. At that moment she enters, and they are delighted to see each other. She tells him frankly that he has been always in her thoughts, for he is the only person beside Paillasse who has ever been especially good to her. She asks if he remembers her giving him the bunch of violets and is deeply touched when he produces them. André tells Suzanne that he loves her and asks her to marry him, but he confesses that his guardian is a martinet who would disinherit him at any suggestion of his marrying an acrobat. Meanwhile he suggests that she and her companions stay with his friend the Comte des Étiquettes, who loves artistes and would willingly entertain them at his castle. But Suzanne tells him it is all a beautiful dream and they part with an affectionate kiss of the hand.

The familiar blare of music now announces that the circus is in the neighbourhood. A crowd collects and Malicorne and his wife announce a special performance at three o'clock. He then enters the inn, where he is to meet a troupe of new acrobats, "The Gigolettis". Marion now appears, dressed as a fortune-teller, and sets up a little table. Malicorne, returning, decides to have his fortune told. He does not recognise her and requests Marion to concentrate on his past, which, of course, suits her. She tells him that he is the Director of a circus, that his high-handed methods have got him into trouble and that four of his artistes have recently left him. When he asks if they are in the neighbourhood, she tells him that they are far away by the sea, about to embark on a ship. He hurries away to warn the police to arrest them, leaving Marion a free pass for the circus. The other three now return in a state of agitation, for they have seen Madame Malicorne and fear she may have recognised them. They learn from the innkeeper of the projected arrival of "The Gigolettis", for their luggage is blocking up a passage of the inn and he would like it removed. This is a heaven-sent opportunity for disguise. The four friends claim to be part of the Gigoletti troupe, and, dressed in Gigoletti costumes, false moustaches, masks, etc., they present themselves to Malicorne and are promptly engaged for the circus. Hardly has the parade begun when the genuine Gigolettis arrive and are outraged at seeing four strangers in their costumes. But as they can only speak Italian, they cannot converse with Malicorne, and so for the moment the four acrobats are safe. But something about them has struck Malicorne as familiar. Biding his time he at last snatches off Grand Pingouin's false moustache and the identity of the four acrobats stands revealed. Furiously Malicorne calls the police. But he has chosen an inconvenient moment. The Inspector is assisting at the confinement of his wife, who is busy producing a fine pair of twins. Thwarted in his intentions, the angry Malicorne is about to lay hands on the absconding artistes himself, when they are saved by the arrival of André and his soldiers and the Comte des Étiquettes. At André's request the Comte des Étiquettes indemnifies Malicorne for the broken contracts. He then invites the four acrobats, André and the soldiers to visit the Château des Étiquettes as his guests, and the curtain falls on a splendid spectacle: the simultaneous departure of the circus and the military.

ACT III

For the last act the scene is the grounds of the Château des Étiquettes, where the guests include André's guardian, a Marquis, the Baron de Valengoujon, and Monsieur and Madame Bernardin. Suzanne arrives with her arms full of flowers and is tenderly greeted by André. He begs the Count to intercede with his guardian to allow him to marry Suzanne, and the Count promises to do his best. Meanwhile Paillasse has been made Bailiff of the castle and is convinced that Suzanne will now consent to marry him because of his grand position. But Grand Pingouin and Marion tactfully point out that Suzanne does not belong to their class and is destined to marry above them. They believe that her heart belongs to Lieutenant André. The poor old clown is hard hit, but they finally convince him, and the three decide to take the road so as not to prove an embarrassment to Suzanne. Hardly have they departed when there is a familiar blare of brassy music and the circus appears, summoned by the Count, who proceeds to cross-question Malicorne as to Suzanne's antecedents. Malicorne is about to reply when, with a cry of surprise, he recognises in Madame Bernardin his past tightrope-walker. He then divulges that she is Suzanne's mother and that the father is—the Comte des Étiquettes. After this proof of her aristocratic parentage André's guardian waives all objections to his marrying Suzanne, and the opera ends with the Count buying the circus and presenting it as a gift to Grand Pingouin, Marion and Paillasse.

Phi-Phi

Operetta in Three Acts

By Albert Wïllemetz *and* F. Sollar

Music by Henri Christiné

After a preliminary run at the miniature Théâtre "L'Abri", it was produced at the Théâtre des Bouffes-Parisiens, Paris, on 12th November, 1918, with Monsieur Urban as "Phidias", Monsieur Dréan as "Le Pirée", Monsieur Ferréal as "Archimédon", Pierrette Mad as "Madame Phidias" and Alice Cocéa as "Aspasie". London production on 16th August, 1922, at the London Pavilion, with Evelyn Laye, Stanley Lupino and Jay Laurier.

Characters

PHIDIAS (PHI-PHI), *a sculptor*
LE PIRÉE, *his servant*
PERICLES, *a statesman*
ARCHIMÉDON, *a stranger Prince*
MADAME PHIDIAS
ASPASIE
CHORUS OF MODELS AND DANCERS

The action takes place in the studio of Phidias in 600 B.C.

ACT I

The scene is the studio of the sculptor Phidias and is set supposedly in 600 B.C. in Greece. But in atmosphere, except for the décor and costumes, it resembles the Paris of the 1920s. Phidias, the sculptor of the "Venus de Milo" and "Winged Victory", has been commissioned by the wealthy Pericles to sculpt a group to be entitled "Love and Virtue are the Foundations of Domestic Bliss". A diligent search is being made to discover a model for "Virtue", but it seems that a virtuous woman is not to be found in this Parisian Athens. The models who have applied for the job sing a virtuous opening chorus:

Phidias now arrives in a state of great excitement. He has met on the street a most enchanting young woman called Aspasie. She will make an ideal model for "Virtue", and now it is vital that Le Pirée find him a suitable model for "Love" so that work may begin on Pericles' commission. Aspasie then enters and explains to the audience that an innocent girl must beware of "wolves in sheeps' clothing". Phidias is delighted to see her and preliminary work on the statue begins. But just as Phidias is about to take liberties with the model, his wife appears. An argument follows as to the "virtuous" qualities of Aspasie. Madame Phidias, determined to prove how virtuous *she* is, tells how an attractive young man has followed her all day long, but *she* has resisted all his advances and remained a faithful wife. No sooner is she left alone than the young man arrives. He is Prince Archimédon, and declares himself to be madly in love with Madame Phidias. Le Pirée, eavesdropping, as is the duty of any faithful servant, proposes to the enamoured Prince that he offer his services as the male model for "Love" so as to be near the sculptor's wife. The models are delighted with their good-looking colleague and Archimédon assures them that he is made for love. The curtain descends on the models singing a paean in his praise.

ACT II

Act Two also takes place in the studio, some time later. Le Pirée has sold all Phidias' statues to back a favourite horse, Ptolemy II, but his luck is out and the steed finishes last. However, the models, for a modest fee, consent to pose on the pedestals until the statues can be recovered. Pericles now visits the studio to buy some works for his collection. But the first time he examines its contours, the "statue" screams and runs off, pursued by its would-be purchaser. Aspasie then enters and sings a brilliant parody of the aria from Massenet's *Manon*—"Je suis encore tout étourdie"—protesting her innocence and lack of experience. She has been to a fortune-teller, who has predicted that she will be happily married to a rich, dark man. Pericles returns and is fascinated by Aspasie. But she is coyly elusive, for he has red hair, and therefore cannot be the man she is destined to marry. As they are talking, Madame Phidias enters. She informs Aspasie that her services as a model are no longer required: she herself is in every way more suited to pose as "Virtue". When Aspasie has left on the arm of Pericles, Madame Phidias, by nature a prude, expresses her doubts as to the wisdom of posing in close proximity to such an unrestrained lover as Archimédon. When he joins her they sing a waltz duet, the best-known number in the score, and by the end of the duet Madame Phidias has, rather hesitantly, agreed to accept him as her lover.

As their duet ends they retire to the next room and shut the door. In a flash Le Pirée has his eye to the key-hole. But the models drag him away and, taking his place, embark on a running commentary on what they see happening on the other side of the door.

ACT III

Next morning Le Pirée is discovered sleepily dusting the studio and waking the models who have fallen asleep "on the watch". Madame Phidias and Archimédon then emerge, enchanted with each other and with the prospect of future dalliance. Phidias discovers them in a fond embrace, which he tells them is the perfect pose for his work, but he remarks that they both look exhausted and had better rest before the sitting begins. Aspasie returns, dressed to kill, and sings a song about how important things like clothes, shoes, make-up are to the modern "Grecian" woman. She explains to Phidias that she has married Pericles so that she can take Phidias as a lover and at the same time afford to keep herself attractive for him at Pericles' expense. Pericles has of course had his hair dyed black, and Phidias cannot resist commenting on how easily these politicians change their colour. Overjoyed at Aspasie's news he sings a gay song in praise of feminine delights:

After the song they retire to Phidias' room. Le Pirée then comes in carrying a balance, and Archimédon asks him what he is weighing. He explains that it is the "pros" and "cons" which are being balanced and that he is afraid he will have to inform his master of Madame Phidias' illicit relationship; the blackmail is successful. Archimédon then returns to Madame Phidias. Le Pirée tries the same trick on Phidias and is again successful, for Phidias greatly fears the jealous anger of his strait-laced wife. However, returning to join Aspasie, he opens the wrong door and discovers his wife in the arms of Archimédon. At the same moment Pericles enters as Aspasie emerges from Phidias' bedroom. The only solution to this tangle, they all agree, as in every operetta in the great French tradition, is a final quintette à la Audran or Planquette. So husband, wife, mistress, lover and patron join in a grand ensemble about domestic bliss. Prince Archimédon produces the money for Le Pirée to buy back the statues, and it is decided that the group commissioned by Pericles will NOT be done. So the private lives of the "ménage" will never be revealed to posterity.

Ciboulette

Operetta in Three Acts and Four Scenes

By ROBERT DE FLERS *and* FRANCIS DE CROISSET

Music by REYNALDO HAHN

First produced in Paris on 7th April, 1923, at the Théâtre des Variétés and revived at the Théâtre Marigny on 2nd October, 1926, with Edmée Favart as "Ciboulette" and Henry Defreyn as "Antonin" in both productions.

CHARACTERS

DUPARQUET, *Manager of Les Halles*
ANTONIN DE MOURMELON, *an aristocrat*
ROGER, *an officer*
ZÉNOBIE, *Antonin's ex-mistress*
MADAME PINGRET, *flower-seller*
CIBOULETTE, *a country girl*
PÈRE GRENU, *her uncle*
OLIVIER MÉTRA, *an impresario*
CHORUS OF MARKET WORKERS, SOLDIERS, COUNTRYFOLK AND PARISIAN SOCIALITES

The action takes place in and around Paris in 1867.

ACT I

SCENE 1. The story of *Ciboulette* has a Second Empire setting and the first act takes place in a night club-cum-café, "Le Chien qui Fume", adjoining les Halles, the market of Paris. It is 4 a.m., and the night club is gradually emptying. When the curtain rises there remain six Lieutenants of Hussars with their girl-friends and their handsome Captain, Roger de Lansequet. They are drinking and teasing the Captain about the absence of his sweetheart, Zénobie de Guernsey. He tells them philosophically that it is Monday. Monday, Tuesday, Wednesday and Friday she dedicates to the young Viscount Antonin de

Mourmelon, and Thursday and Saturday to himself. By courtesy of her mother he also has her on Sundays. But is he not jealous? ask the Hussars. "No," says the Captain; "for when one has twenty million one is never loved for oneself alone."

When the Hussars and their girl-friends have departed to a private room for supper, Viscount Antonin de Mourmelon arrives with Zénobie. Antonin is thankful to sit down. Zénobie has dragged him half round Paris from one night club to another. Hearing her poodle sneeze, she discovers that the dog's coat is missing and must have been left at one of the night clubs they have visited. Poor Antonin is sent off, protesting, to recover it. Directly he has gone, Zénobie asks the *patron* to inform Captain Roger de Lansequet of her presence. Roger appears and they greet each other ecstatically. All sense of time is forgotten in each other's company, until the *patron* warns them of Antonin's return. "Give me time to get rid of him and I will come to you," says Zénobie, and Roger goes off. Zénobie artfully picks a quarrel with Antonin, who has returned without the poodle's coat, and flounces out. Antonin, much perturbed, is about to pursue her, but refrains on the advice of the elderly Monsieur Duparquet, Manager and Chief Accountant of the fruit market, who is seated at a nearby table. Duparquet is something of a philosopher. He describes to Antonin the scene between Roger and Zénobie, and when Antonin bursts out with "When are women ever sincere?" he answers: "Only when they are deceiving us."

The scene finishes with the formal handing over of Zénobie by Antonin to Roger with a legacy of bills for jewellery, dresses, furs, hats, shoes, etc., amounting to five hundred and sixty thousand francs. On this dramatic note the curtain falls.

SCENE 2. This scene takes place in the market itself. It is 5.30 a.m. A furious merchant is stamping up and down complaining that a market gardener from Aubervilliers is half an hour late with her delivery of vegetables. A moment later a cart drives up, and from it alights the defaulting market gardener. She is Ciboulette, a twenty-one-year-old country girl, good-looking with lots of character. She apologises for her tardiness, but is rudely told by her customer that, as she is half an hour late, the deal is off. Ciboulette appeals for arbitration to Duparquet, official arbiter of the market, but he tells her, reluctantly, that the merchant is within his rights and Ciboulette must resign herself to the loss of some five hundred francs. Bitter as is the blow, Ciboulette finds it hard to be cast down for long this morning, as she has just had her fortune told by an old market women, Mère Pingret, and it appears that fate has astonishing things in store. According to the prediction Ciboulette will find her future husband underneath a cabbage, a young woman who tries to take him away from her will go pale in a moment, and she will receive a proposal of marriage in a tambourine. Antonin, wandering about the market in despair at the loss of Zénobie, runs into Ciboulette, who is deploring the loss of her five hundred francs, and when he hears of her loss he generously insists on reimbursing her and the two strike up a friendship:

This duet cements their friendship and they are mutually attracted. But it is time for Ciboulette to return to Aubervilliers and she says good-bye to Antonin and goes off to "clock out" of the market. Antonin, left alone, is suddenly overcome by fatigue. He can no longer keep his eyes open and, climbing into a handy farm-cart, falls fast asleep. Ciboulette, having signed out, gets two of the porters to re-load her cart with her unsold vegetables. Nobody notices Antonin peacefully asleep, and the vegetables are piled on top of him. Ciboulette and Duparquet, who is returning with Ciboulette to lunch, mount the box and away they drive to Aubervilliers.

ACT II

The scene is a farm-house at Aubervilliers, where Ciboulette lives with her uncle and aunt. It is lunch-time and Ciboulette and Monsieur Duparquet are late. Her uncle and aunt are speculating as to the cause, when there is a knock at the door and a soldier stands there. He is orderly in charge of picnicking arrangements for the officers' mess of his regiment of hussars. Can the farmer offer facilities for a picnic? Père Grenu assures him that all will be in readiness, and with a parting injunction to put flowers on the table, as there will be ladies present, the orderly departs. Ciboulette has still not turned up, and her uncle begins to grumble at his niece's unsatisfactory behaviour. Here she is twenty-one today and not even engaged. "I tell you," he says to her aunt, "on the day Ciboulette produces a fiancé I will give you a hundred francs." "In that case," says the aunt, "you owe me eight hundred francs—for Ciboulette has eight young men." "Eight!" exclaims her uncle, affronted at such prodigality. "Eight in one village! That is positively a 'Call-up'. I shall have to have a few words with my niece." At that moment a familiar cart drives up to the door. Ciboulette and Duparquet descend from it and launch into a duet which is the high-spot of the score with its bustling tune and clever lyric describing the beauties of the countryside and all the people and things they have encountered en route:

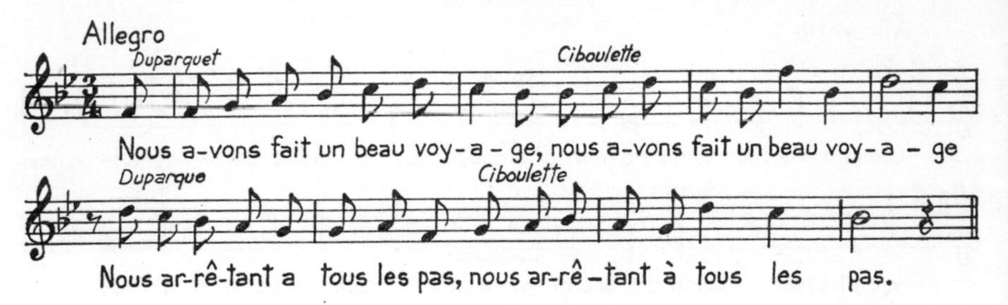

At the end of the duet Monsieur Duparquet remarks that the village square is black with people. "Yes," says Père Grenu, "with Ciboulette's young men." He embarks on a tirade accusing his niece of disgracing the family with her eight young men and ending with an ultimatum that unless she becomes engaged to a genuine fiancé within the hour, she can pack her bags and go. Ciboulette is shattered by her uncle's fury and begs Duparquet to help her. She is just telling him of Mère Pingret's prediction that she will find her future husband under a cabbage, when she stops short open-mouthed. The vegetables in her cart are stirring into movement and a moment later the figure of a young man rises out of them. It is Antonin, half asleep and entirely puzzled as to his whereabouts. He is delighted to see Ciboulette and Duparquet and they are soon telling him of Ciboulette's dilemma. Will he agree to impersonate the necessary fiancé? He is too kind-hearted to refuse. At that moment the servant enters with a telegram. It is from the new farm bailiff, due to arrive that day, postponing his arrival for a fortnight. So Antonin assumes the identity of the absent bailiff, Nicholas Chanson, and Ciboulette is provided with a fiancé. Père Grenu is delighted with his niece's fiancé, but it is time for the officers' picnic, and Antonin is sent off to the cellar to fetch wine and cider. While he is in the cellar the officers arrive with their ladies, among whom Ciboulette sees Zénobie. During the celebrations Zénobie is invited to sing the song of the Regiment, and directly she begins Ciboulette bursts into laughter at her feeble efforts. Zénobie tartly challenges her to sing it better, and Ciboulette responds with a colourful performance in suitable military style. Ciboulette's performance is rapturously applauded by the officers, and this leads to a quarrel between her and the slighted Zénobie, culminating in an unladylike scene in which Ciboulette hits her rival. Zénobie's reaction to the blow vividly recalls the second part of Mère Pingret's prophecy, and Ciboulette exclaims in a startled voice: "She went pale in a moment." Vowing vengeance, Zénobie and Captain Roger depart.

In the meantime, Ciboulette has artfully locked Antonin into the cellar to prevent him meeting Zénobie. When the latter has gone, she lets him out, but Antonin, already vexed at being locked in the dark, is furious when he hears he has missed Zénobie. He declares that Zénobie's return is a proof of her love for him and that he will go back to her. Ciboulette is greatly distressed. Apart from the fact that Antonin has shown obvious signs of affection for her, she is by now in love with him. Furiously jealous, she turns on him and the two part on a high note. In her despair, Ciboulette once again turns to Monsieur Duparquet. He comforts her with the reflection that true love never did run smoothly and quotes a tragic little love affair of his own:

He bids her be of good cheer. To win back Antonin's love there are two essentials: to get away at once from Aubervilliers and to make a name for herself. He knows Antonin well enough to realise that this once accomplished, he will be at Ciboulette's feet. Duparquet was formerly in the theatrical profession, and from Ciboulette's performance of the Regimental song he can tell she has great histrionic talent. He promises to introduce her to an impressario friend of his, Olivier Métra, who will launch her as the famous revue star Conchita Ciboulero. And so with the good wishes of her family and the whole village, Ciboulette and Duparquet leave for Paris on the first stage of her journey to stardom.

ACT III

The last act takes place in the studio of the impressario, Olivier Métra. To a select audience, which includes the Viscount Antonin de Mourmelon, the new star, Conchita Ciboulero, dressed *à l'Espagnol* and wearing a mask, is introduced. Her vibrant personality makes an immediate impression and she brings the house down with a haunting waltz-song:

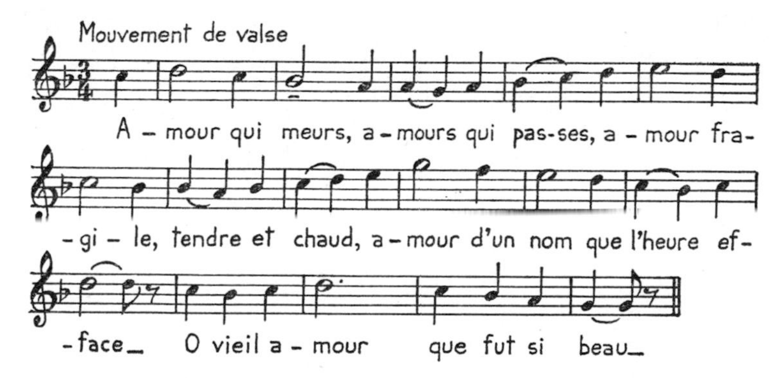

Antonin is soon at the new star's feet, but when he declares his love, Conchita only laughs at him and tells him that his trouble is that he isn't very bright. Puzzled, he tells her that another girl once told him the same thing. "Who was she?" she asks. "A little girl called Ciboulette," he tells her. "Then," says Ciboulero, "before you ask for my love, write on this programme: 'I no longer love Ciboulette.' " "No! That I cannot do," says Antonin—and in that instant realises that Conchita Ciboulero and Ciboulette are one and the same woman. As they fall into each other's arms, a note is delivered to Ciboulette by Olivier Métra in a tambourine made of flowers. It is a love-letter which Antonin wrote to her earlier in the evening. And so the third part of Mère Pingret's prophecy is fulfilled.

Irma-la-Douce

Comedy with music in Twenty-two Scenes

By Alexandre Breffort

English Book and Lyrics by Julian More, David Henneker *and* Monty Norman

Music by Marguerite Monnot

First produced on 12th November, 1956, at the Théâtre Gramont, Paris. London production on 17th July, 1958, at the Lyric Theatre, with Elizabeth Seal and Keith Michell.

Characters

BOB-LE-HOTU
ROBERTO-LES-DIAMS
JO-JO-LES-YEUX-SALES
BÉBERT-LA-MÉTHODE
IRMA-LA-DOUCE
NESTOR-LE-FRIPÉ
POLYTE-LE-MOU
DUDU-LE-SYNTAX
CLIENTS OF IRMA-LA-DOUCE, POLICE, LEGAL REPRESENTATIVES, INHABITANTS OF DEVIL'S ISLAND, ETC.

The action takes place in Paris and on Devil's Island. The time is the present.

The story opens in the back streets of Pigalle. Near the bridge of Caulaincourt is the "Bar des Inquiets", the resort of members of a gang greatly concerned to escape the vigilance of the police. A frequenter of the bar is Irma-la-Douce. She is a *poule* and she has fallen in love with a penniless law student called Nestor-le-Fripé. Irma-la-Douce and Nestor-le-Fripé are naïve enough to imagine that a girl and her boy-friend have only to be sufficiently in love for everything in life to fall into place. They set up house together in Irma's apartment and are blissfully happy:

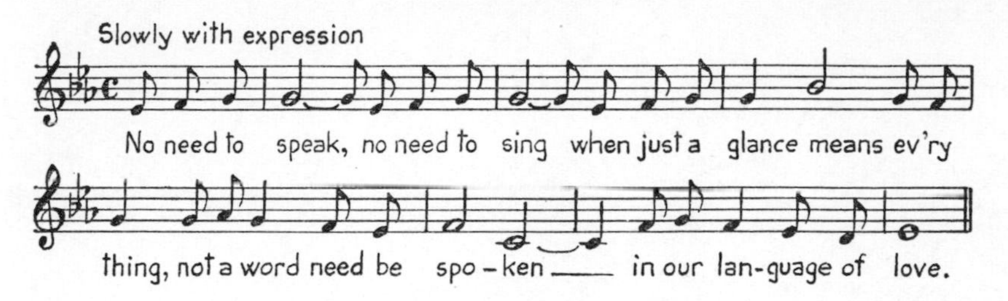

Irma goes out to work for Nestor so that he can continue his studies. Her clients are plentiful and enthusiastic. "She's got the lot," they sing:

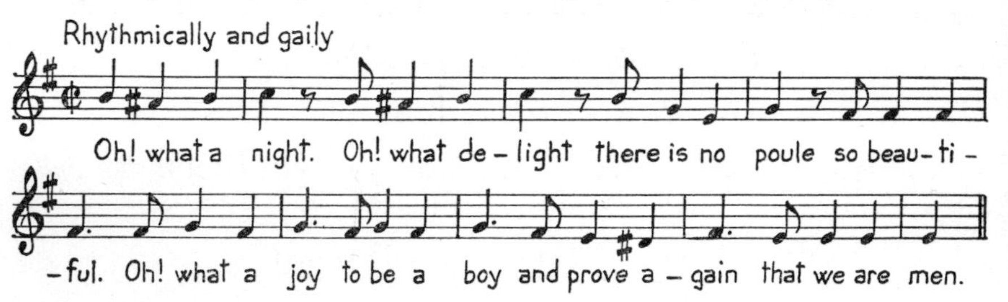

But Nestor is furiously jealous of Irma's other lovers, so he puts on a false beard and a bowler hat and himself becomes her exclusive client, Monsieur Oscar. Irma is in a seventh heaven:

Nestor, however, soon wearies of his double life as client and Mec (Pimp). Furthermore, as time passes he becomes resentful of his *alter ego* and decides to destroy Monsieur Oscar. The gang warn him that murder is a crime, but without effect. Following the disappearance of Monsieur Oscar, Nestor is arrested, tried and found guilty and sentenced to imprisonment on Devil's Island. Here in solitary confinement he pines for Irma and Paris.

Back in Paris, Irma has given up her work, and when Nestor hears that he is to be the father of her child he determines to escape. With the rest of the gang he returns to Paris by raft, and after various adventures proves his innocence to the police. He is just in time for the birth of Irma's twins and the lovers are reunited.

VIENNA

VIENNA

Viennese Operetta started as a direct result of Offenbach's international popularity. In the 1860s his Parisian operettas were having a tremendous vogue in Vienna. In fact, Offenbach became a positive cult there. As his operettas became more and more successful, Offenbach demanded higher and higher terms, until the Viennese theatre managers groaned under the tyranny of his rule and thought it high time this invading Napoleon of operetta was dethroned. But who was the man to do it? Franz von Suppé was the first composer to make the attempt with an operetta *Das Pensionat.* But he failed to dislodge Offenbach. The man who succeeded was Johann Strauss, the composer of the popular *Blue Danube* waltz. At the age of forty-five, under pressure from a Viennese manager, Maximilian Steiner, and his own wife, the singer Jenny Treffz, he gave up an enormously successful career as dance-band conductor and composer to compose his first operetta *Indigo, or The Forty Thieves*, produced in 1870.

Even Offenbach had seldom scored such a triumph. There followed fifteen Johann Strauss operettas which included the incomparable *Die Fledermaus.* Johann Strauss' association with the dance band naturally resulted in his exploiting in his operettas the rhythms of the dance. And so it was that the waltz became the staple ingredient not only of Johann Strauss' operettas, but also of those of his followers. Viennese Operetta is divided into two periods: the "Classical", which includes the works of Johann Strauss, Franz von Suppé, Karl Millöcker, Karl Zeller and Richard Heuberger; and the "Modern", which includes Franz Lehár, Leo Fall, Oscar Straus and Emmerich Kálmán.

Die Schöne Galatea

(The Beautiful Galatea)

Operetta in One Act

By POLY HENRION (LEOPOLD K. DITTMAR *and* KOHL VON KOHLENEGG)

Music by FRANZ VON SUPPÉ

First produced on 30th June, 1865, at Meysel's Theater, Berlin. London production as Ganymede and Galatea *on 20th January, 1872, at the Gaiety Theatre with Ellen Farren, Constance Loseby, F. Sullivan and J. L. Toole. Last revived in London on 18th September, 1936, at the Victoria Palace.*

Note. Modern version with revised book by Aldo von Pinelli and free musical adaptation by Theo Mackeben.
Note: This synopsis follows the modern version.

CHARACTERS

PROFESSOR AGYRIS, *an archaeologist*
PYGMALION, *a young sculptor*
GANYMEDE, *his servant*
MIDAS, *an art dealer*
GELONIDA, *his assistant*
GALATEA, *a statue*

After the overture the curtain rises on a scene set in a typical landscape in modern Greece. There are unmistakable signs of extensive archaeological diggings in the neighbourhood and on account of these excavations the road has been closed. When the curtain rises Professor Agyris, in charge of the excavations, is directing the operations of two of his staff, who are carrying a magnificent statue of a female figure to a pedestal. All the workmen gather round to admire the effigy of the beautiful Galatea. One of them remarks: "To think it has taken us nine months to bring her into the world," and another adds: "Two months earlier and she would have been in time for the Munich Art exhibition." As they are talking and admiring, agitated voices are heard and three travellers appear, a young married couple and their chauffeur. They are vexed to find the road closed to traffic, but when the Professor informs them of the discovery of the studio of the ancient Greek sculptor Pygmalion and the finding of Galatea's statue, the husband, himself a sculptor, is greatly interested. The Professor allows them to view the statue. As they are advancing towards the plinth, the wife drops her handbag. In a flash the young, good-looking chauffeur retrieves it and, in returning it, kisses his mistress's hand. The husband angrily orders him to confine his attentions to the bare necessities of politeness, and the chauffeur remarks in an injured tone: "After all, I was at a public school and a university." "A pity," says the husband coldly, "that they never taught you how to change a wheel." All now admire the statue. "How superbly rounded off the figure is," comments the husband. "Too true, too true," adds the chauffeur, voluptuously caressing Galatea's thighs. The wife asks Professor Agyris to tell them the legend of Pygmalion and Galatea, and the Professor begins: "Over two thousand years ago in a town in ancient Greece there lived a rich and covetous art-dealer called Midas."

As he speaks, the Professor's voice fades away and the lights dim; and the stage revolves to the scene of Midas' art gallery in ancient Greece. A crowd of angry customers is clamouring to view the famous statue of Galatea which Midas has promised to put on exhibition but which he cannot now produce. With difficulty Midas gets rid of his pertinacious customers and settles down to discuss with his assistant, Gelonida, how they can acquire the statue from Pygmalion, who is positively in love with his beautiful creation and guards it jealously. They decide to enlist the help of Pygmalion's man-servant, Ganymede, with a bribe of five thousand drachmas. He happens to be Gelonida's boy-friend, and Midas is full of hope. As they leave the gallery Ganymede arrives. He is the chauffeur of the Prologue, but is now dressed in slightly eccentric, ancient Grecian style. He comes on gaily and launches into his entrance song:

After the song Gelonida joins him and puts the proposition to Ganymede that he use his influence to persuade Pygmalion to sell Galatea's statue to Midas. "Think what you could do with five thousand drachmas," she tells him. "You could marry me, buy a cottage in the country and a new donkey-cart of at least four m.p.h. We should be the perfect modern couple." They are then joined by Midas, anxious to discover Ganymede's reaction to the bribe of five thousand drachmas. Ganymede, after a token refusal, pushes him up to five thousand five hundred drachmas and promises to do his best. "And when may I inspect the beautiful Galatea?" asks Midas, and Ganymede answers that as his master is at the club there is no time like the present. He goes on ahead to spy out the land, and Midas promises to follow.

In Pygmalion's studio three hefty young women are working on the statues of three virile nudes. Nuthea is at work on "Apollo at the Baths", another is chiselling away at "A Discus-thrower" and a third at "A Marathon Runner". All three bewail the fact that their only male associates are blocks of stone. They are interrupted at their work by Ganymede, and shortly afterwards Midas arrives and the ladies retire. Midas is immediately shown the statue of the beautiful Galatea and is enthusiastic. "What a noble forehead!" he exclaims. "This alabaster neck, those classical breasts, those superbly modelled thighs——" "Stop," protests Ganymede; "if you go any further you'll lower the tone of the conversation." They are interrupted by a cry of anger, and Pygmalion enters the studio. "Get out, you crook!" he orders Midas. "And you, Ganymede, how dared you let him in!" Ganymede, always the opportunist and never at a loss, turns on Midas. "I had only just turned my back for a moment when the villain slipped in," he assures Pygmalion, and Midas is duly thrown out. No sooner has he gone than Ganymede is given notice to quit and leaves in high dudgeon. Left alone with Galatea, Pygmalion stands before her admiringly. It is now apparent that Pygmalion and Galatea are the young married couple of the prologue. From the neighbouring Temple of Venus sound the voices of the priestesses and, perhaps inspired by their prayer, Pygmalion prays to Venus to endow Galatea with the flesh and blood of life. Even as he prays, the statue is suffused with light and the marble effigy assumes the form of a living woman glowing with life and love:

Galatea, now warmed into life, steps down off her pedestal. "I never realised how lovely it would be to be alive," she murmurs. "The light, the warmth, the flowers. But those blocks of stone must be removed, for they remind me of my past and no woman cares to be reminded of her past." Pygmalion clasps her in his arms with a burning kiss and Galatea asks innocently if all men are equally passionate. "What was your reaction when you felt my kiss?" asks Pygmalion; and "A sensation of gnawing hunger," is Galatea's rather crushing reply. Pygmalion hurries off to prepare two Athenian frankfurters with mustard, and Galatea breaks into her famous waltz song:

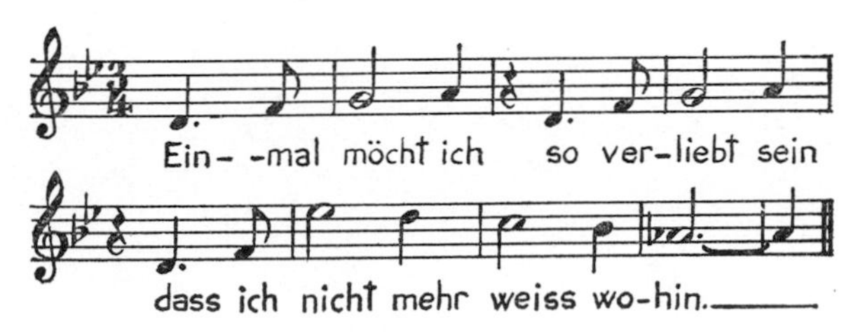

The next scene is in Gelonida's bed-sitting-room. Ganymede is telling her that Pygmalion has dismissed him and that he is now prepared to assist Midas in purloining the statue. Ganymede is, of course, unaware that Galatea has come to life. He returns to the studio to pack his belongings and comes face to face with the living statue. Galatea is enchanted with Ganymede and makes immediate advances to him, and Ganymede is greatly attracted to her. Midas, who arrives next, is also greatly charmed by Galatea. As a bid for her favours, Midas presents her with a valuable bracelet, and altogether Galatea is thoroughly enjoying herself with her two admirers when Pygmalion returns. Midas hides, standing on the pedestal where Galatea's statue stood behind the curtain. Pygmalion, finding Ganymede present, grudgingly takes him back into service, and Galatea insists that Ganymede join them for supper. During the meal Pygmalion is called away on business and Galatea sets out to seduce Ganymede, insisting that they elope together that very night. When Ganymede protests that he could not afford to do it, Galatea assures him that Midas' bracelet will more than finance them. At this Midas dashes out of his hiding-place to rescue his bracelet, just as Pygmalion returns. An angry argument follows. Midas clamours for his bracelet, and reveals that he has paid Ganymede five thousand five hundred drachmas for the purpose of purchasing the statue of Galatea. "But I am not for sale," she tells him. "What!" exclaims Midas, "you are the beautiful Galatea? I shall never be able to persuade my customers to believe that." Finally Galatea informs Pygmalion of her intention to elope with Ganymede. Exasperated, the disillusioned Pygmalion offers up a final prayer to Venus. "Venus," he prays, "you gave me a woman with all her beauty, but also with all her frailty. Restore her to what she was. Turn her once more to stone." Before their gaze the miracle occurs, and the frantic Midas has to watch his valuable bracelet also turned to stone.

In the epilogue, back in modern Greece, Professor Agyris has just concluded his story when the husband turns to the chauffeur. "You'd better look out for another job," he tells him. "But what has the poor man done?" protests the wife. "He's too much like that damned Ganymede," he replies. However, the chauffeur is reprieved, and the curtain falls to a reprise of Ganymede's song claiming that to conquer a pretty woman is the best sport in the world.

Fatinitza

Operetta in Three Acts

By F. Zell (Camillo Walzell) *and* Richard Genée

Founded on Scribe's La Circassienne

Music by Franz von Suppé

First produced on 5th January, 1876, at the Carl Theater, Vienna, with Antonie Link, Hermine Meyerhoff, William Knaak and Josef Matras. New version with book by Eduard Rogati, lyrics by Herbert Witt and Eduard Rogati and additional music by Bruno Uher produced in 1950 at the Bayrische Staatsoperette (Theater Am Gärtnerplatz), Munich. London production on 20th June, 1876, at the Alhambra Theatre.

Characters

COUNT TIMOFAY GABRILOVITSCH KANTSCHAKOFF, *a Russian General*
PRINCESS LYDIA USANOVA, *his niece*
IZZET PASCHA, *Governor of the Turkish Fortress of Ipsala*
VLADIMIR MICHAILOFF, *Lieutenant*
JULIAN GOLZ, *war-correspondent of a German newspaper*
SERGEANT STEIPAN
MANJA, *a gipsy girl*
A PEDLAR
IZZET PASCHA'S FOUR WIVES
CHORUS OF RUSSIAN SOLDIERS, TURKS, CIRCASSIANS, ETC.

ACT I

The scene is a Bulgarian military outpost facing the Turkish fortress of Ipsala, under the governorship of Izzet Pascha, Commander-in-Chief of the regiment of Baschi-Bozuks. The time is 1877 and the Russo-Turkish War is in full swing. The Bulgarian force, awaiting orders to attack the Turks, is in a state of low morale. They have been hanging about doing nothing for months, and inaction has made them low-spirited, impatient and introspective. This affects the personnel in different ways: Sergeant Steipan is suffering from an inferiority complex and in consequence is unmercifully teased by the cadet section, and

Lieutenant Vladimir Michailoff is pining for his sweetheart, Lydia Usanova, of whom he sings in a waltz-song after dreaming about her:

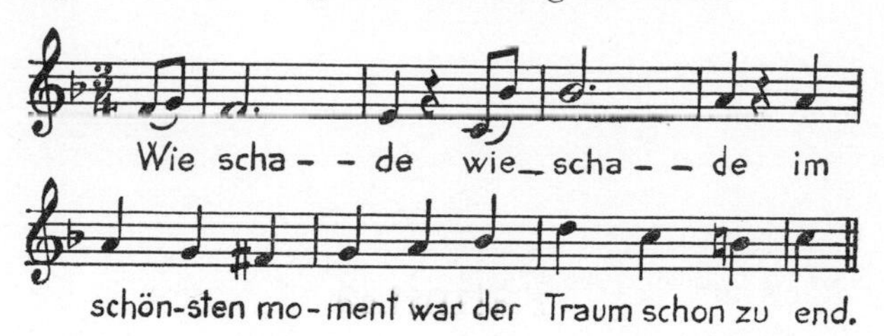

Like a breath of fresh air there arrives a distraction at the camp in the shape of Julian Golz, a young German war-correspondent. He greets Lieutenant Vladimir Michailoff as an old friend, and has not been long in camp before he realises that what is needed here is some form of mental stimulus. So he suggests, to wile away the time, that they take part in amateur theatricals. He tells the officers the story of Lieutenant Vladimir's adventure when he embarked on a spying expedition; how he disguised himself as a Turkish girl, Fatinitza, and succeeded in stealing the Turkish marching orders. Vladimir admits that on yet another occasion he adopted the disguise of "Fatinitza". This was when he was denied access to his sweeheart, Lydia, by her odious guardian, an old bear by the name of General Kantschakoff. On this occasion he applied for and got the post of lady companion to Lydia. But it turned out badly, for General Kantschakoff fell in love with him in his disguise as "Fatinitza", and he had to give notice. Vladimir's story is greeted with loud laughter, interrupted by the entrance of Sergeant Steipan, who announces the arrival of a pedlar selling vodka. With the pedlar is a gipsy girl, Manja, who proceeds to tell the officers' fortunes. The pedlar is in reality a Turkish spy, seeking information of the Bulgarian garrison strength. Through an indiscretion of one of the cadets, he gets the necessary information and shortly after withdraws.

After the pedlar's departure, the conversation reverts to Lieutenant Vladimir's adventure in his disguise as the Turkish girl "Fatinitza". Julian Golz informs the company that he has immortalised Vladimir's adventures in the form of a play and suggests that this is the ideal time to produce it, with Vladimir himself as "Fatinitza". His suggestion is enthusiastically adopted; the roles are distributed among the company and Sergeant Steipan is cast as General Kantschakoff with his famous expletive "By pistol-slugs, cannon-balls and thunder-bombs". All disappear to hunt for suitable theatrical costumes, and Sergeant Steipan is left alone to study his part of the General. Suddenly to his astonishment he hears outside a furious shout of "By pistol-slugs, cannon-balls and thunder-bombs", and in storms the real General Kantschakoff, who has arrived on a surprise visit of inspection. Finding nobody on duty, he is in a furious rage, shouting violently and threatening everyone with the knout. The last straw is the presence of Julian Golz, a civilian. But in the end it is Julian who succeeds in pacifying the General, when in his capacity of journalist he flatters the General's vanity by asking his permission to write an article on his career. Among the questions he puts to the General is: "Have you ever been in love?" upon which he is immediately treated to a panegyric of the General's only love, "Fatinitza". Unfortunately at this moment Lieutenant Vladimir enters, made up as "Fatinitza", and with a cry of "My darling, I've found you at last" the General starts to his feet. Vladimir manages with gestures of maidenly modesty to keep him at bay, while Julian explains to the General that "Fatinitza" is in search of her brother Lieutenant Vladimir Michailoff, who has been captured by the Turks. On hearing this the General swears "By pistol-slugs, cannon-balls and thunder-bombs" that her brother shall be rescued. The General is by now in a mellow mood. He closes his eyes to the lack of discipline he has detected and then, with the intention of getting "Fatinitza" to himself, orders two hours' drill-parade for all ranks. A very funny scene follows, with Vladimir desperately trying to ward off the General's efforts to make love to him, punctuated by interruptions from Julian. As the General is on his knees proposing marriage and Vladimir is in fits of laughter, Julian rushes in to announce the arrival of a lady in a sleigh. To Vladimir's mixed joy and embarrassment it is Lydia, the General's ward and the girl he adores. On her entrance Lydia sings this attractive refrain:

The General is not at all pleased to see his ward and tells her that the battle-front is no place for women. She must leave immediately for a convent and "Fatinitza" shall go with her. Lydia is greatly puzzled by the resemblance "Fatinitza" bears to her sweetheart Vladimir Michailoff, but she says nothing, and the two girls are shown to a hut to wait with Julian while the General inspects the parade before escorting them to the convent. The officers' mess is now completely empty, when through the door creeps the pedlar. Seeing that the coast is clear he beckons in a wild horde of unkempt Turkish soldiers, for, acting on the information of their spy, the Baschi-Bozuks have succeeded in penetrating the Bulgarian outpost. Lydia and "Fatinitza" are quickly seized and bound, and Julian is tied to a pillar. He is commanded to present himself at Izzet Pascha's headquarters on the following day with ten thousand Turkish pounds of ransom money. Then, bidding him an ironic farewell, the soldiers carry off the female captives to Izzet Pascha's harem. After the Turks have departed General Kantschakoff enters rubbing his hands and very pleased with life. "Now I've turned them into soldiers," he chortles. "The Turks can come." "They've already been and gone," replies a voice, and the General suddenly notices Julian bound to his pillar. He realizes that the women have been carried off and shouts to the soldiers to fall in. With a cry of "Fatinitza, I fly to your rescue", and waving the Bulgarian flag, he rushes out as the curtain falls.

ACT II

Act Two takes place on the following day in Izzet Pascha's harem—a scene straight out of the Arabian Nights. Izzet Pascha is on his throne, and on either side of him, reclining on cushioned divans, are his four favourite wives. Manja, the pedlar's companion in Act One, is called upon to read the horoscope for the day and prophesies that Izzet Pascha will that day acquire two new wives. Hardly are the words out of her mouth when Mustapha, the harem eunuch, ushers in the pedlar who has arrived with Lydia and "Fatinitza". Izzet Pascha is ravished by Lydia's beauty and tells her she shall be his favourite wife, to the fury of the four existing wives and he sends her away with "Fatinitza" to make herself beautiful for his pleasure. Vladimir now reveals his identity to Lydia, and while they are discussing their next move Manja joins them. She makes a pact with Vladimir, of whose identity she was never in a moment's doubt, that she will arrange his escape, providing that he return with Julian Golz, to whom she has taken a violent fancy. She has managed to obtain the key of the harem from Mustapha on the promise of a supply of "Schnapps". Four furious wives now storm in, threatening Lydia with jealous violence. But Manja calms their rage, assuring them that Lydia is no real rival, and the wives, who are thrilled to discover that "Fatinitza" is a man, all promise to assist in the escape. An enchanting septette follows in which details of the plan are formulated:

Julian and Sergeant Steipan now arrive to parley with Izzet Pascha for the return of Lydia and "Fatinitza". Julian and Manja are delighted to see each other and celebrate their reunion with the hit number of the 1950 revival:

But Izzet Pascha is not nearly so co-operative. While he evinces no interest whatever in "Fatinitza", he firmly refuses to release Lydia, and in fact utterly declines even to discuss the question. He does, however, put on an entertainment for his guests. This entertainment takes the form of the traditional Moslem shadow pantomime concerning the Princess Sulima, who lowered herself by falling in love with a commoner, Ben Omar, and in revenge was thrown by her father to the wild beasts. This is mimed in silhouette to a running commentary. But when the climax is reached, instead of wild beasts appearing on the screen, the shadows of Vladimir and Steipan are seen. They tear their way through the sheet, followed by the Bulgarian troops with whom Vladimir has returned. The Turks are overpowered and Izzet Pascha is taken prisoner. The only malcontent amid all the rejoicing is General Kantschakoff. Since Vladimir has resumed his uniform, "Fatinitza" has, of course, disappeared, and the curtain falls on the General's noisy grief.

ACT III

Act Three takes place in a room in Lydia's house in Sofia. The General is trying to force his ward to marry old Prince Swertikoff, who, the General declares, once saved his life by dragging him out of a burning powder magazine. Lydia complains that this must have been many years ago, as the Prince is now lame, partially blind and deaf in the right ear—and anyhow she is in love with Vladimir and wants to marry him. The General, however, is adamant and tells her that in life one cannot always have what one wants. He wants "Fatinitza" but he cannot have her because he cannot find her. This gives Vladimir an idea, and he makes the General a proposal. If he can produce "Fatinitza", may he marry Lydia? The General readily agrees, and so for the last time "Fatinitza" is revived. But the General's joy at seeing her once again is cut short when Vladimir, stepping out of "Fatinitza's" dress, admits the deception. The General at first is, of course, furiously angry, but eventually he has to acknowledge that the episode has its funny side and laughingly tells Lydia that as he himself fell in love with Vladimir he cannot very well stop her doing the same thing, and the operetta ends with the union of two pairs, Vladimir and Lydia and Julian and Manja.

Boccaccio

Operetta in Three Acts

By F. Zell (Camillo Walzell) *and* Richard Genée

Music by Franz von Suppé

First produced on 1st February, 1879, at the Carl Theater, Vienna, with Antonie Link, Karl Blasel and Rosa Streitmann. Modern version with new Libretto by Alfred Rott and Friederich Schreyvogel, and musical adaptation by Anton Paulig and Rudolf Kattnigg produced in 1951 at the Volksoper, Vienna. London production on 22nd April, 1882, at the Comedy Theatre, with Violet Cameron, Lionel Brough and Alice Burville.

Characters

GIOVANNI BOCCACCIO
PIETRO, PRINCE OF PALERMO
SCALZA, *a barber*
BEATRICE, *his wife*
LEONETTO, *her lover*
LOTTERINGHI, *a cooper*
ISABELLA, *his wife*
LAMBERTUCCIO, *a grocer*
PETRONELLA, *his wife*
FIAMETTA, *their adopted daughter*
THE DUKE OF TUSCANY
CHORUS OF STUDENTS, TOWNSFOLK, BEGGARS, ETC.

ACT I

The scene is laid in Florence and its environs in the year 1331. Act One opens in a piazza where a collection of beggars are discussing how to profit by the Patron Saint's day, when they know that purse-strings will be loosened and charity readier. A peddling bookseller passes by with his cart, selling the latest novels, prominent among which are the works of Boccaccio. His novels are adored by the women and detested by their husbands, at whom Boccaccio is always poking fun. The men decide to apply to the magistrate to have him banished and the crowd disperses, leaving Scalza, a barber, Lotteringhi, a cooper, and Lambertuccio, a grocer, in conversation. They move off towards the house of Scalza, whose wife, Beatrice, observes her husband's approach. As she is receiving her lover, Leonetto, at the moment, she decides to create a diversion to distract her husband's attention. She therefore begins to scream and rushes out of the house, crying for help. She tells her husband that a fine cavalier entered the house, imploring her aid and that he was followed by another man, threatening his life. Scalza is a terrible coward, and when two men duly appear from his house and begin to fight he hides behind his wife's petticoats. The two men are Leonetto and Boccaccio, and Beatrice is relieved and delighted to see that her husband, Scalza, is entirely taken in by the diversion. Soon a crowd of students collect and a sham fight ensues in which no one is hurt and under cover of which Scalza and Beatrice retire. When order is restored, Boccaccio gaily tells the students that that is how he gets the material for his novels. They can hardly be called fiction, for he lives his plots.

As the time for service approaches, worshippers move towards the church. Among them are Petronella, wife of the grocer, Lambertuccio, and their adopted daughter, Fiametta. Fiametta, though she is quite unaware of it, is the illegitimate daughter of the Duke of Tuscany, who has boarded her out with the worthy grocer and his wife. Petronella tells her foster daughter that if she offers up a special prayer to the Saint today her prayer will be answered, and urges her to pray for a rich husband. But Fiametta's thoughts are full of a young man of whom she has lately become aware, and she sings:

As Fiametta is singing, Boccaccio approaches, disguised as a beggar. Fiametta recognises him and drops her handkerchief. He picks it up, and in returning it kisses her hand. Happy at heart, she then follows Petronella into church. The citizens of Florence, who in the opening scene departed to persuade the magistrate to issue a decree banishing Boccaccio from the city, now return in a rage, having got no satisfaction. They decide therefore to take the matter into their own hands and, seeing a young man resembling Boccaccio in size and appearance, they seize him and administer a sound flogging. But Scalza, the barber, is horrified to recognise in the victim Pietro, Prince of Palermo. The young Prince has been sent to Florence to find the bride intended for him. He is to marry Fiametta, the Duke of Tuscany's daughter, but he is determined to enjoy himself in Florence for a while before seeking her out. He good-naturedly pardons the floggers. When the bookseller returns with his cart, the citizens fall upon it and destroy Boccaccio's volumes, while the author in his beggar's gown placidly watches the scene. He knows that nothing can destroy the genius which created them.

ACT II

Act Two is reminiscent of *The Tales of Hoffmann* in construction, for, in a similar manner, the authors of *Boccaccio* have made their hero the principal protagonist in his own tales. In Act Two we find him still in search of material for a novel as he and Pietro decide to serenade their lady-loves, Fiametta and Isabella, the cooper's beautiful wife. They take with them Leonetto, whose task it is to attract Petronella and thus divert her attention from Fiametta and leave the coast clear for Boccaccio. The houses of the two ladies are side by side, and outside his house the cooper and his workmen are making barrels. It is thirsty work, and Isabella is forever nagging her husband about the amount of alcohol consumed. To drown her complaints the cooper and his men sing a rousing refrain, beating time on the barrels:

After the first barrel is finished the coopers go off to have a drink and Fiametta, Isabella and Petronella come out of their houses. Each has a love-letter, and reads with delight that her lover will be visiting her in disguise. Two of the lovers now arrive, and while Leonetto occupies the attention of Petronella, Pietro makes love to Isabella. They are interrupted by the return of the cooper, and Pietro hides in the barrel. Isabella, noticing that her husband has been drinking, receives him ungraciously. To soothe her, the cooper shows her two ducats for which he has sold the new barrel, but, annoyed at the low price, she replies that she has already sold it for five, which Pietro surreptitiously hands her out of the barrel. Then, crawling from his hiding-place, he presents himself as the purchaser of the barrel. He explains his presence in this unusual situation by informing the cooper that the barrel is not water-tight. So the cooper fetches some pitch and crawls into the barrel, while Pietro and Isabella continue their love-making outside.

Boccaccio now appears next door disguised as a peasant. He tells Lambertuccio, the grocer, that he has been sent by his master, a rich farmer, to collect some olives which have been ordered from the grocer. As the olives are not yet gathered, he has been told to pick them himself and he begins to climb a tree.

But he soon cries out that the tree is bewitched. Scrambling down, he tells Lambertuccio that he has just seen him in passionate embrace with his foster-daughter, Fiametta. Lambertuccio indignantly denies that he did anything of the sort. But he is a superstitious and timid man, a believer in ghosts and witchcraft and continually afraid of bad omens. He regards the tree with awe and climbs it in order to see for himself. Looking down, he is amazed to observe Fiametta being passionately embraced by the peasant (Boccaccio), and his own wife, Petronella, in the arms of a student (Leonetto), while a third couple (Isabella and Pietro) are similarly occupied in his neighbour's garden. Of course by the time he has descended from his tree and Lotteringhi has crawled out of the barrel the three women and their lovers have disappeared. Scalza now arrives in a state of great excitement. He has been listening to some students conversing and has learnt that Boccaccio must be hidden in one of their houses. Lambertuccio and Lotteringhi are wondering whether it was the peasant or one of the two other visitors who has fooled them when a stranger appears and tries vainly to make himself heard. He is immediately taken to be Boccaccio and soundly beaten. But the poor man is really the Duke of Tuscany, disguised as his own envoy. He has come to take Fiametta away, having decided to acknowledge his child and marry her to Pietro, Prince of Palermo. Fiametta, however, refuses to leave her present home, until she suddenly hears Boccaccio's voice comforting her and promising to follow her wherever she goes. Then she promises to go with the stranger. They are about to depart when Boccaccio appears made up as Satan, brandishing two huge torches. All believe him to be the Devil, and while they fall to their knees and pray for grace, Satan paves the way for himself and his friends to escape unmolested.

ACT III

Act Three is laid in the palace and gardens of the Duke of Tuscany. The Duke is giving a grand reception to celebrate the forthcoming marriage of his daughter, Princess Fiametta, to Pietro, Prince of Palermo. In addition to the assembly of distinguished guests, Fiametta's old friends have been invited. Lambertuccio is summoned to appear before the Duke and is in great trepidation, remembering that the stranger of Act Two, who was beaten in mistake for Boccaccio, was the Duke himself. However, he returns radiant, having received in full the favours of the Duke. After his departure, Pietro seeks out Boccaccio. He is aware of Boccaccio's love for Fiametta and is quite ready to resign his claim to her. When she appears Pietro tactfully leaves the lovers alone and they sing a charming duet.

But Boccaccio's presence in the palace angers the citizens of Florence. They complain to the Duke, pressing for a decree of banishment, while their wives defend him and plead for him to be allowed to remain. The Duke decides to postpone a settlement of the issues until after the performance of the comedy with which Boccaccio is to entertain the guests. With his ever-ready wit, Boccaccio's comedy is concerned with Columbine's suitor, who has to yield his bride to a lover who claims older rights. The significance of the plot is not lost upon the Duke when he comes to pass judgement on Boccaccio, and his judgement is that Boccaccio be sentenced to life imprisonment as Fiametta's husband. He is furthermore appointed Poet Laureate to the Court and commanded to be married to Fiametta on the morrow, and the curtain falls on general rejoicing.

Der Karneval in Rom

(Carnival in Rome)

Comic Operetta in Three Acts

Based on SARDOU'S *comedy* Piccolino

By JOSEF BRAUN

Music by JOHANN STRAUSS

First produced on 1st March, 1873, at the Theater an der Wien, Vienna, with Albin Swoboda as "Arthur Bryk" and Marie Geistinger as "Marie".

CHARACTERS

COUNT FALKONI
COUNTESS FALKONI
ARTHUR BRYK } *artists*
BENVENUTO RAFAELI } *artists*
ROBERT HESSE } *artists*
MARIE, *a peasant girl*
DONNA SOFRONIA, *Principal of a home for ladies*
CHORUS OF PEASANTS, MODELS, CARNIVAL REVELLERS, TOWNSFOLK

The action takes place in the year 1873.

ACT I

On his student travels through Italy, Arthur Bryk, a painter, has taken up his quarters in a picturesque village. Here he has met and made love to a peasant girl called Marie. Although it was only a light-hearted flirtation on his part, Marie has fallen seriously in love with the handsome artist and fondly believes he means to marry her, but when he announces his departure, her joy is turned to sorrow. He leaves her, as a souvenir of their association, a portrait of her that he has painted. After Bryk's departure there arrive at the village two other painters, Robert Hesse and Benvenuto Rafaeli. Rafaeli, the son of a wealthy father, has no need to work for a living. He is lazy and unscrupulous by nature and, desiring to make his name as a painter without exerting himself, he makes a practice of buying the paintings of young unknown artists and offering them for sale as his own work. He now offers Marie a thousand lira for Arthur Bryk's portrait of herself, and Marie joyfully accepts the money, for with her new-found wealth she proposes to set off in search of her lover, who, Rafaeli tells her, is in Rome. Hesse and Rafaeli have made the acquaintance on their travels of Count and Countess Falkoni. The Countess, a woman of the world, gay, light-hearted and an arrant flirt, carries on so blatantly with the two painters that Count Falkoni's jealousy is aroused and it takes all the Countess's tact and persuasion to smooth ruffled feelings and avoid bloodshed in a duel.

ACT II

Scene 1. The first scene is a square in Rome. Marie, pursuing her determination to find Arthur Bryk, has dressed herself in the suit of a peasant boy from Savoy. It is carnival time in Rome and the streets are so crowded that she despairs of ever tracing her beloved. At last, however, her persistence is rewarded and she finds him in company with Hesse, Rafaeli and the Falkonis, with whom Rafaeli has made him acquainted. But the reunion is no happy one for Marie. Arthur Bryk does not recognise her in her boy's clothes and she has to look on while Countess Falkoni flirts with him to which he obviously takes no exception. But the Countess's behaviour with Arthur Bryk again rouses her husband's jealousy, and this time he arranges to have her taken care of in a Home for Ladies, under the eagle eye of the Principal, Donna Sofronia. This, however, is in no way to prove a discouragement to Arthur's intentions. When his friends have left him and he is alone, Marie, still disguised as a boy, approaches him and asks to be taken on as his pupil. Bryk still does not recognise her, but agrees to accept her in that capacity.

Scene 2. The grounds of the Ladies' home, where Countess Falkoni is in residence, happen to be just over the wall from the café where all the artists of Rome forgather with their models. It is therefore an easy task for Arthur Bryk to persuade several of the girl models to distract Count Falkoni's attention while he climbs the dividing wall to spend an hour of love with the Countess. But his intentions are foiled by the jealous Marie in her disguise as Beppino. She raises the alarm and rouses Donna Sofronia and all her ladies, who rush out into the garden in tumult while the lovers retire discomfited.

ACT III

Scene 1 takes place in Bryk's studio. Once again he has arranged a rendezvous with Countess Falkoni and once again it is Marie who prevents it taking place. Looking very handsome in her Savoyard boy's costume, Marie as Beppino makes passionate love to the Countess and, in a charming duet, robs her of a kiss. Arthur Bryk and Count Falkoni are both witnesses of this episode, which finally removes any illusions which may have remained to Bryk as to the Countess's constancy. In the scene which follows—the most effective, dramatically, in the piece—Beppino reproaches Bryk with the fact that all his lady-loves have deceived him. In a musical number she sketches the portraits of all these faithless loves and adds as a final portrait the likeness of the only girl who has remained faithful to him—Marie. The memory of his lost love stirs him and full of emotion he rushes out into the city streets to search for Marie.

SCENE 2. The scene is a square in Rome. After an endless search through the carnival in the streets of the city, Arthur Bryk succeeds in finding Marie, who has reverted to her woman's clothes. Their passionate embrace is witnessed by Count Falkoni, who realises there is now no further cause for jealousy and tenderly forgives his Countess.

Carnival in Rome was Johann Strauss' second work for the stage. After the first performance a Viennese paper, *Das Fremdenblatt*, drew attention to the remarkable development of his music since his first operetta *Indigo*. The music, declared the critic, was no longer in a purely popular vein but divided itself into two styles—a light rhythmic style for the comedy numbers and a lyrical, operatic style for the romantic numbers. Some he picked out for special mention were:

1. A coloratura aria for Countess Falkoni in Act I, "Kann er nicht liebenswürd'ger sein".

2. Marie's pathetic love song from the same act, "Nur in liebe kann ich leben".

3. Tarantella from act Two.

4. One of Strauss' most enchanting melodies which occurs in Act Three when Marie is sketching the features of the only girl who has remained faithful to Arthur Bryk—herself.

Die Fledermaus
(The Bat)

Operetta in Three Acts

By CARL HAFFNER *and* RICHARD GENÉE

Based on a comedy Das Gefängnis (The Prison) *by* R. BENDIX *and the Vaudeville* Le Réveillon (The Midnight Supper) *by* HENRI MEILHAC *and* LUDOVIC HALÉVY

Music by JOHANN STRAUSS

First produced on 5th April, 1874, at the Theater an der Wien, Vienna, with Jani Szika, Marie Geistinger and Karoline Charles-Hirsch. London production on 18th December, 1876, at the Alhambra Theatre (in English), with Kate Munroe, Miss Beaumont and Miss Robson.

CHARACTERS

GABRIEL VON EISENSTEIN
ROSALINDA, *his wife*
FRANK, *Governor of a prison*
PRINCE ORLOFSKY
ALFRED, *a teacher of singing*
DR. FALKE, *a notary*
DR. BLIND, *an advocate*
ADELE, *a lady's maid*
FROSCH, *a gaoler*
CHORUS OF PRINCE ORLOFSKY'S GUESTS

ACT I

In a fashionable watering-place, described as "near a big city", lives Gabriel von Eisenstein, a wealthy man of independent means, with his attractive wife Rosalinda, and their maid Adele. The light-hearted story of *Die Fledermaus* tells of the revenge taken by a certain Dr. Falke on this Gabriel von Eisenstein for playing a practical joke on him. When the story opens von Eisenstein is in trouble with the law and has been sentenced to prison for eight days for using abusive language to a policeman. Despite all the efforts of Blind, his advocate, to get him off, von Eisenstein is due to start his sentence by midnight and is spending the day preparing for prison, while his wife, Rosalinda, packs all his oldest clothes to wear in gaol. While she is away Dr. Falke, a notary and von Eisenstein's closest friend, arrives. He bears an invitation for von Eisenstein to a party to be given that night by Prince Orlofsky. "All the ladies from the ballet will be there," he tells von Eisenstein, and he suggests that he should postpone his surrender to the prison authorities till the following day and enjoy a last night of glorious revelry, wine, women and song. Von Eisenstein eagerly accepts Prince Orlofsky's invitation, little suspecting that it is the first move in Dr. Falke's plan of revenge. Adele, the maid, has a sister among the dancers who are invited, and she herself receives a letter suggesting that she borrow one of her mistress's evening dresses and impersonate a dancer for the occasion. After some difficulty she obtains permission to have the evening off. Von Eisenstein then bids Rosalinda a tearful farewell and departs, ostensibly to prison, in full evening dress, much to her amazement. Johann Strauss' music to this farewell scene is a masterpiece of comic irony:

No sooner are Rosalinda's husband and maid out of the house than the inevitable lover appears. In this case it is Alfred, a bumptious tenor. Rosalinda entertains him to a cosy supper with champagne and they toast each other:

But an embarrassing situation arises. Rosalinda and Alfred are supping tête-à-tête when the Governor of the prison, Herr Frank, arrives on the scene. He has come to arrest von Eisenstein in person. Alfred attempts to deny that he is the man, but Rosalinda assures the Governor that that is only Herr von Eisenstein's fun. Careful of her reputation, she presses home the point. She is von Eisenstein's wife, that is her husband's dressing-gown: how can its occupant not be her husband? There is no escape for Alfred, and his only consolation is a series of farewell kisses before being led away to prison.

ACT II

At Prince Orlofsky's ball the fun is fast and furious. As the "Marquis Renard" von Eisenstein has been presented by Dr. Falke to a young woman in whom he detects a likeness to his wife's maid, Adele; who indeed she is. In a charming little song she asks the Marquis what lady's-maid ever had a hand or foot like hers, to say nothing of her Grecian profile, her figure and her frock (which is, of course, Rosalinda's):

Later in the evening Prince Orlofsky introduces the guest of honour, a Hungarian Countess wearing a mask. Von Eisenstein is greatly attracted by the Countess, little suspecting that the mask conceals the features of his own wife. Rosalinda's appearance at the party has been stage-managed by Dr. Falke as the final move in his revenge. Von Eisenstein flirts outrageously with the Countess and, as a result of his advances, she sinks down on a sofa, pressing her hand to her heart. She pretends that her heart has always been her weakness and she asks von Eisenstein to take her pulse. During the operation she manages to annexe his repeater watch, and thus holds a valuable piece of evidence of her husband's misdemeanours. This enchanting tik-tak duet is one of the highlights of Johann Strauss' score:

At supper the conversation turns on the practical joke that was played on Dr. Falke by von Eisenstein, who, forgetting that he is temporarily masquerading as Marquis Renard, regales Prince Orlofsky and his guests with the story. It appears that in their youth von Eisenstein and Dr. Falke both attended a fancy-dress ball in a country house two miles from town. Von Eisenstein went as a butterfly and Dr. Falke as a bat (Fledermaus), tightly sewn up in a brown skin, with long claws, broad wings and a yellow beak. When morning came Dr. Falke had drunk more than was good for him, and on the way home through the woods von Eisenstein, assisted by the coachman, lifted him out of the carriage and placed him under a tree and left him sleeping, unconscious of his fate. When he woke, the poor man had to walk home, still in fancy dress, through the town in broad daylight, to the joy of all the street arabs, and after that he was always known in the district as "Dr. Bat". This story is greatly enjoyed, particularly by a certain M. le Chevalier Chagrin, whose adopted name conceals the identity of Herr Frank, Governor of the prison. Without either of them having any idea of their respective identities, he and von Eisenstein strike up the warmest friendship. By now the champagne has had effect and everyone is feeling mellow. All join in a chorus in praise of champagne, the king of wines, and, at Falke's suggestion the whole company, glass in hand, swear eternal brotherhood and sisterhood:

Finally, as 6 a.m. strikes, von Eisenstein and Herr Frank both hurry off on their independent ways to prison.

ACT III

Act Three takes place in the prison, and here misunderstandings are cleared up. Rosalinda's possession of von Eisenstein's watch is compensated for by the presence in prison of Rosalinda's lover, Alfred, arrested while masquerading as her husband. As von Eisenstein philosophically declares, it's best to blame it all on the champagne.

Cagliostro in Wien
(Cagliostro in Vienna)

Comic Operetta in Three Acts

By GUSTAVE QUEDENFELDT

New version from the original of
F. ZELL (CAMILLO WALZELL) *and* RICHARD GENÉE

Music by JOHANN STRAUSS

Arranged by KARL TUTEIN

First produced on 27th February, 1875, at the Theater an der Wien, Vienna, with Carl Adolf Friese as "Cagliostro", Marie Geistinger as "Lorenza" and Alexander Girardi as "Blasoni". New version produced on 18th May, 1941, in Danzig.

CHARACTERS

THE EMPRESS MARIA THERESA
MARIE LUISE, *Infanta of Spain*
BARON SEBASTIAN SCHNUCKI, *Royal Commissioner of Public Morals*
COUNT CAGLIOSTRO
LORENZA, *an Italian street-singer*
FERI VON LIEVEN, *Lieutenant*
FRAU ADAMI
ANNEMARIE, *her niece*
TEIGLEIN, *confectioner and Annemarie's guardian*
BLASONI, *Count Cagliostro's assistant*
CHORUS OF COURTIERS, TOWNSFOLK, SOLDIERS AND POLICE

The action takes place in Vienna in 1765.

ACT I

The scene takes place outside the inn "Türkenschanze". The presence in Vienna of the celebrated magician, Cagliostro, has created interest and curiosity among the townsfolk. The wonders of his magic art are admirably publicised by his assistants, notably by his mistress, Lorenza. Lorenza, as singer and dancer, is appearing in a booth set up outside the "Türkenschanze". Her purpose is to attract Baron Schnucki, Commissioner of Public Morals, and gain his goodwill, as he is known to disapprove of Cagliostro's magic arts and has threatened to have him arrested. Thanks to her beauty and her skill Lorenza soon has the Baron fast in her toils. She sends him a love-letter (which he carries in his breast-pocket, close to his heart) and at the same time gives Cagliostro an exact transcript of it. By means of this he is able to astonish Baron Schnucki and convince him of his supernatural powers by reciting to him the exact wording of Lorenza's love-letter, although it is still concealed in the Baron's breast-pocket. Cagliostro takes advantage of this success to advertise his patent rejuvenating draught, and this arouses enthusiastic interest among the ladies.

Cagliostro's principal objective in Vienna is to gain an audience with the Empress. He is anxious to bring off in secret a diplomatic coup in the interests of France by preventing the forthcoming betrothal of the Archduke Leopold to the Spanish Infanta, Marie Luise. Cagliostro's original intention was to use Lorenza to persuade Schnucki to arrange the audience. Eventually, however, he himself extracts the promise of an audience from the Baron, provided he is able by his magic powers to restore to health a rider who has just been thrown from his horse and lies on the ground apparently mortally hurt. The Baron confidently wagers that he will fail. But Baron Schnucki loses his bet, for the "mortally injured" horseman is no other than Blasoni, Cagliostro's principal assistant and arch-swindler. Among the customers of the "Türkenschanze" who have witnessed these marvels, are Frau Adami; her niece, Annemarie; Annemarie's guardian, the confectioner, Teiglein; and Lieutenant Feri von Lieven. Annemarie is hoping to marry the Lieutenant, but her aunt is looking for a better match and refuses to put up the necessary security to enable the young people to marry. She herself also has matrimonial ambitions. Years earlier Baron Schnucki proposed to her in writing, and she is determined by hook or by crook to force him to honour his promise.

ACT II

Scene I takes place in an audience-room in the palace of Schönbrunn. On his arrival at the palace Cagliostro is greeted by the excited and admiring Infanta, Marie Luise. She is thrilled to make his acquaintance and little suspects his hidden purpose. Cagliostro succeeds in hypnotising her and forces her, while under his influence, to write a letter to the Empress declaring her wish to withdraw from her betrothal to the Archduke, as she does not love him. This letter, however, never reaches the Empress, but falls by a lucky chance into the hands of Baron Schnucki and Lieutenant Feri. Its contents create the greatest consternation and the Lieutenant is determined to investigate the affair. Suspicion falls on Cagliostro, and a warrant is sought for his arrest. For the moment he manages to keep his head, but fresh dangers threaten from the actions of Lorenza, whom he discovers preparing to expose his diplomatic secrets. However, by his magic powers and renewed protestations of love he regains his power over her. Trusting to his luck, Cagliostro then appears in audience before the Empress, Maria Theresa. He claims that by means of the Philosopher's Stone he can transmute base metals into gold, and he so excites the Empress' curiosity that she determines to visit his laboratory.

Scene 2 is set in Cagliostro's laboratory. The patent rejuvenation draught is selling well. Elderly women queue up to purchase the mixture and Frau Adami in her enthusiasm to get rid of her lines and wrinkles pays out five hundred golden ducats. This gold could not have come at a more convenient moment, for it will be useful for the "experiment" which Cagliostro is to make before the Empress. When she appears with her escort, Cagliostro, to the accompaniment of much impressive mumbo-jumbo, "transmutes" copper and silver coins in his furnace into ducats of pure gold. The Empress is tremendously impressed with Cagliostro's powers, and when Lieutenant Feri arrives with the police to accuse him of political intrigue and of obtaining money under false pretences, she will not hear a word against him. Nothing will make her believe that the dignified alchemist could have had anything to do with Marie-Luise's hysterical letter, and Cagliostro triumphs accordingly.

ACT III

The last scene takes place outside Teiglein's confectionary shop. Lorenza warns Cagliostro of fresh dangers. His assistant, Blasoni, has deserted him and has gone off with Cagliostro's secret documents relating to the royal betrothal, and Cagliostro must rely on the favour of the Empress to protect him. But this time he is out of luck. Blasoni has disposed of the documents to Lieutenant Feri, who delivers them to the Empress as she is visiting Teiglein's shop with the Infanta. The documents provide indisputable proof of Cagliostro's connection with the attempt to prevent the royal betrothal, and the Empress signs a warrant for his arrest. The police and the military search vainly for the missing magician, hindered by two of his assistants, who put them on a false scent. Eventually Cagliostro appears in person before the Empress. She demands that he release the Infanta from the hypnotic influence by which he can still control her mind. He does so and is granted his freedom, and to the cheers of the populace Cagliostro and Lorenza sail away in a balloon. The Empress then turns to Baron Schnucki and discusses the question of his marriage to Frau Adami, who has sought royal grace and favour to assist her in persuading the Baron to marry her. It turns out, however, that Frau Adami has received a more recent proposal of marriage from the confectioner Teiglein and has accepted him. Melted by her own happiness, she smiles on the romance of Annemarie and Lieutenant Feri and gives them her blessing and the necessary money to get married, .

Ludwig Speidel, a Viennese music critic, wrote of *Cagliostro in Vienna* that Johann Strauss's music rose and fell with the interest of the situations. Among the numbers he picked out for special praise were:

1. A sextette of old women, all clamouring for Cagliostro's rejuvenation mixture, which came from Act Two.

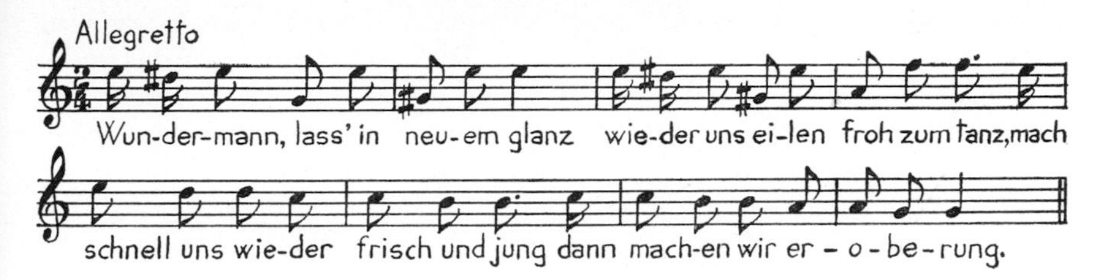

2. A waltz-duet between Frau Adami and Blasoni, also from Act Two:

Prinz Methusalem

Operetta in Three Acts

By KARL TREUMANN

Book translated from the French of VICTOR WILDER *and* DELACOUR

Music by JOHANN STRAUSS

First produced on 3rd January, 1877, at the Carl Theater, Vienna, with Antonie Link as "Prince Methusalem", Karoline Finaly as "Pulcinella" and Josef Matras as "Sigismund, Prince of Trocadero". London production on the 19th May, 1883, at Folies Dramatiques Theatre with Camille Clemont, Camille Dubois, W. S. Rising, Philip Day and Ethel Pierson.

CHARACTERS

SIGISMUND, *Prince of Trocadero*
PULCINELLA, *his daughter*
CYPRIAN, *Duke of Riccarac*
SOPHISTIKA, *his wife*
PRINCE METHUSALEM, *their son*
TROMBONIUS, *a composer*
COUNT VULCANIO, *Lord Chamberlain at the Court of Trocadero*
CHORUS OF SOLDIERS, TOWNSFOLK, BANDITS, SOLDIERS AND COURT PAGES

ACT I

In the palace of the Prince of Trocadero the wedding of Princess Pulcinella, his daughter, to young Prince Methusalem of Riccarac is being celebrated. Everyone at Court is in the highest spirits, and the father of the bridegroom, Cyprian, Duke of Riccarac, after a glass or two of wine has even forgotten to complain of his gout. There is much applause for the Festival Cantata by the composer, Trombonius. A military treaty is in process of negotiation between the two neighbouring countries, when Prince Sigismund receives confidential information that during the Duke's absence from Riccarac, Cyprian's subjects have started a revolution and have deposed him. In these circumstances Prince Sigismund greatly regrets that he ever allowed his daughter to marry into such a wretched family and determines to have nothing more to do with them. The treaty negotiations are called off and Pulcinella, in spite of the fact that she is already married to Prince Methusalem, is locked up in a room in a distant wing of the palace and abandoned there in solitary confinement. Prince Sigismund is determined to allow Methusalem no further contact with his bride. But Methusalem is equally determined to circumvent these measures and, being by nature resourceful, manages to identify the room in which Pulcinella is imprisoned and climb in through the window.

ACT II

Scene 1 is set in a street in Trocadero. Four bandits, lurking on a corner of the street, are discussing an underground plot to overthrow Prince Sigismund. A courtier passes by and is seized by the bandits. He proves to be the Court composer, Trombonius, an enemy of the Prince, who has already proved himself a good friend to the Revolutionaries, and he is allowed to go free.

Scene 2 is set in a salon in the royal palace. Sigismund has not passed on his confidential information of the events in Riccarac to Duke Cyprian, and the Duke now receives a letter from home giving him good tidings, from which Sigismund gathers that the revolution in Riccarac has been put down. Cyprian and his wife Sophistika are promptly restored to favour and even bidden to breakfast with their host. But the exhausted postman delivers yet another missive from Riccarac. This brings official confirmation that the revolution is entirely successful and Duke Cyprian must consider himself dethroned. The earlier communication was sheer wishful thinking on the part of the correspondent. Cyprian is shattered at the news, but a worse blow is to follow. Two envoys arrive from Riccarac to offer the throne to Prince Sigismund. He accepts the Crown of the neighbouring kingdom, and Cyprian is now completely abandoned.

ACT III

The scene of the last act is a square in Trocadero. Cyprian and Sophistika disguise themselves as street-singers and travel around stirring up the inhabitants of Trocadero to revolt against Sigismund. The underground movement, too, is rapidly gaining adherents, for its leaders have not been idle. Pulcinella, who is deeply in love with her husband, rebels against her parents and presents Prince Methusalem with the baton of a Field-Marshal—to which rank he had been gazetted before all the trouble started. The army rally to him to a man, and Sigismund, unable any longer to command the loyalty of his own troops, is forced to conclude a peace treaty by which Prince Methusalem is crowned ruler of both Trocadero and Riccarac.

The libretto of *Prinz Methusalem* came in for some hard words from the critics after the first performance. They declared it could have played no part in inspiring the uniformly excellent score provided by Johann Strauss. Among the outstanding numbers were:

1. The song of the Lord Chamberlain, Vulcanio, from Act One, in which he recalls his days as a Court page, when all the pretty women made a fuss of him.

2. The entrance number of the happy pair, Prince Methusalem and Pulcinella, "O ihr glücklichen Alpenrosen".

3. The most popular number, Sigismund's comic song with its catchy refrain:

Das Spitzentuch der Königin
(The Queen's Lace Handkerchief)

Operetta in Three Acts

By Heinrich Bohrmann-Riegen *and* Richard Genée

Music by Johann Strauss

First produced on the 1st October, 1880, at the Theater an der Wien, Vienna, with Eugenie Erdösy as "The King", Karoline Tellheim as "The Queen", Alexander Girardi as "Don Sancho" and Felix Schweighofer as "Count Villalobos".

Note. The famous waltz Rosen aus dem Süden (Roses from the South), *consists of tunes from this operetta.*
Note. This is the original version of the operetta.

CHARACTERS

THE KING
THE QUEEN
DONNA IRENES, *Lady-in-Waiting*
MIGUEL DE CERVANTES
COUNT VILLALOBOS, *Prime Minister and Regent*
DON SANCHO D'AVALLANEDA Y VILLAPINQUEDONES
ANTONIO, *a Landlord*
CHORUS OF ARTISTS, PAGES, SENTRIES AND PEASANTS

ACT I

The scene is the garden of the royal palace at Lisbon in the year 1580. In the early morning hours the poet, Miguel de Cervantes, arrives with a company of artist friends to sing a mocking serenade beneath the window of the detested Prime Minister, Count Villalobos. In addition to being Prime Minister, Count Villalobos is also Regent, the King being a minor. He makes it his business to keep the young monarch as far away as possible from any State business, and the King is virtually his pawn. The Prime Minister, angered by the jeering singing, calls in vain for the Watch. Don Sancho d'Avellaneda y Villapinquedones, who is in the King's confidence, has, however, temporarily dismissed the Watch while the King is keeping an assignation with a pretty young woman. And, although the Prime Minister does not know it, the pretty young woman is his own wife. He almost runs into the King as he is leaving the Count's house, and might have recognised him were it not for Cervantes' forethought in providing His Majesty with a mask. As soon as the King has made his get-away the Watch returns and Cervantes and his serenaders are arrested as disturbers of the peace. The King, however, orders his release, and Cervantes is appointed to the post of Royal Reader to Her Majesty the Queen. This mark of royal favour towards Cervantes does not suit the Prime Minister at all. As Regent his policy is to crush the masses, and he is planning a coup, to be put into action at the psychological moment, which is to depose the King and unite Portugal with Spain. In Cervantes he recognises an enemy and he determines to engineer his downfall. The famous poet, however, enjoys the full confidence of the Queen. She is perfectly aware of her neglectful consort's infidelities, and she longs for a little tenderness and affection. Cervantes is a man after her own heart, with whom she feels she could be happy. After he has finished reading to her, she writes on a lace handkerchief the words: "A Queen is in love with you. But you are not a King!" She conceals the handkerchief in Cervantes's book and anxiously awaits his answer.

ACT II

The scene of Act Two is the throne-room of the royal palace. Cervantes has duly discovered the Queen's lace handkerchief in his book but believes it is intended for the King and that the words refer to his "unkingly" behaviour. He himself has been offended by the Monarch's neglect of his young Queen. He broaches the subject to the Queen and promises to use such influence as he possesses over the King to persuade him to mend his ways, and he begs her as a special favour to be allowed to retain the lace handkerchief. Cervantes now makes it his business to acquire an influence over the Monarch, who has just come of age. He persuades the King to take over the reins of government himself and to dismiss the Prime Minister, who is now more determined than ever to injure Cervantes and to prejudice him in the eyes of the King. Under the kindly influence of Cervantes, the King is a changed character, an attentive, faithful husband and a tender and affectionate lover to his Queen. As ill luck has it, Cervantes loses the Queen's lace handkerchief and it comes into the possession of the ex-Prime Minister. He takes it straight to the King and the fat is in the fire. The King immediately assumes that there is an understanding between the Queen and Cervantes and that he has been cuckolded. Cervantes is banished from Court and the Queen is sent away to a distant convent.

ACT III

The last act takes place in the countryside of the Sierra de Suazzo near to the convent where the Queen has been imprisoned. Cervantes is posing as an innkeeper and has rented a country inn. His one ambition is to bring the royal pair together again. To this end he collects a party of friends and dresses them up as brigands. Biding their time, they hold up the carriage in which the Queen and her ladies are taking the air. Cervantes tells her that ever since her departure the King has been melancholy and unhappy; that he has recalled the Prime Minister and virtually handed over the government of the country to him. He also tells her that the King and the Court are expected to come hunting in the district that day, and in due course the hunt arrives. The King decides to take some refreshment at the inn, and the Queen, dressed as a waitress, serves him with a particular truffle pasty which he had eaten and enjoyed on their wedding night. He recognises the Queen and there is a grand *rapprochement*. Cervantes gives the King his interpretation of the words on the lace handkerchief and His Majesty accepts the implied rebuke of his "unkingly" behaviour with good humour. As for Cervantes, he is rewarded for all his troubles with the love of the beautiful Donna Irenes, Lady-in-Waiting to the Queen.

Das Spitzentuch der Königin

(The Queen's Lace Handkerchief)

Operetta in Three Acts

New Book and Lyrics by RUDOLF OESTERRICHER *and* JULIUS WILHELM

Music by JOHANN STRAUSS, *adapted by* KARL PAUSPERTL

Note. This is an entirely new version of the original operetta and the plot bears no relation whatsoever to the original.

CHARACTERS

THE ARCHDUKE
LIEUTENANT TOMBA
BARON ENZIAN
LORI, *proprietress of "The Golden Goose"*
ROSETTA FALCARI, *a Prima Donna*
CHIEF OF THE SALZBURG POLICE
A CAPTAIN OF INFANTRY
THE PRINCESS MARGUERITE
THE PRINCE, *her fiancé*
CHORUS OF THEATRE PATRONS, SOLDIERS AND PARTY GUESTS

PROLOGUE

When the curtain rises the Archduke is discovered in the act of finishing a letter. When it is sealed he sends for Lieutenant Tomba. The Lieutenant duly arrives, and the Archduke takes from a casket a small lace handkerchief and, handing it and the letter to the Lieutenant, bids him ride to the Court at Munich on a delicate mission. It is vital that the letter and the lace handkerchief should be in the hands of the Princess Marguerite in three days' time. "Remember," says the Archduke, "that the honour, the happiness and the whole future of a woman may hang on the success of your mission. Let nothing delay you, but ride through storm and rain, by day, by night." And in ten minutes the Lieutenant has mounted his horse and is galloping away from Vienna.

ACT I

The scene is a square in Salzburg. On the left is the theatre, with the stage door opening on to the square, and on the right is an inn called "The Golden Goose". When the curtain rises Baron Enzian, a resident, is seated at a table outside the inn demolishing a hearty meal, while through the stage door, where the evening performance is in progress, float sounds of music. While the Baron is consuming his meal, Lori, the proprietress of the inn, comes out to inquire how he is enjoying his food, and the Baron, who fancies himself as a gourmet, is pedantically critical of her cuisine. This irritates Lori, who reminds him that he owes her four months' board and lodging amounting to three hundred guilders for himself, his horse and his dog, and she suggests that he pay her. The Baron declares he will do more than that, and then and there he offers Lori his heart, his hand and his name. But Lori replies that, although she is only twenty-three, she has been married three times already and that is enough.

At this moment members of the audience stroll out of the theatre during the interval. Presently the Prima Donna, Rosetta Falcari, comes out of the stage door for a breath of air. It is a warm summer's night and she looks very attractive, a wrap thrown over her boy's costume—for she is playing a role—*de travestie*. She is greeted enthusiastically by her public and replies to them in waltz time:

When the interval is over and the audience has re-entered the theatre, the Chief of Salzburg Police arrives and orders a drink at the inn. He complains to Lori of the dullness of his job. "No crime, no crime at all," he grumbles, but cheers up when he reads in the newspaper of spying activity on the German frontier. He voices his determination to capture the spy, and while he is talking a horseman clatters up to the inn and dismounts, with instructions to the groom to stable his horse, feed it and rub it down. The rider is Lieutenant Tomba, on the first stage of his journey to Munich. He has been in the saddle for twelve hours and is exhausted—but not too exhausted to render a waltz song, an avowal of his determination not to fail Princess Marguerite, but to arrive in Munich on time:

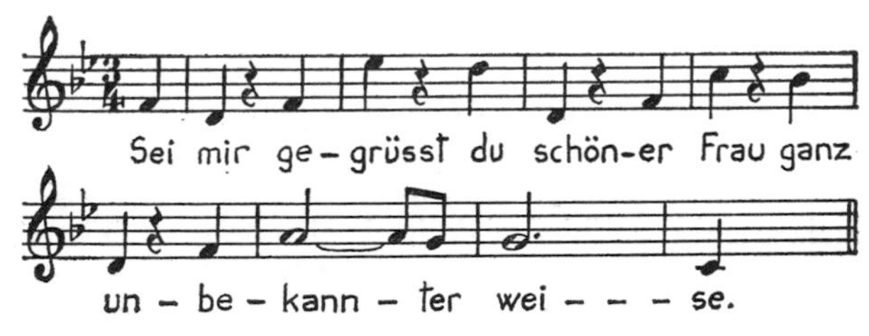

Tomba is immediately a source of suspicion to the Chief of Police, whose head is still full of spies, and he is determined to find out what the Lieutenant is carrying in his dispatch-case. However, he has to bide his time, as Tomba is for the moment otherwise engaged.

The performance at the theatre is concluded, and from the stage door emerges Rosetta Falcari, who seats herself on a bench and calls over to the inn, asking them to bring her a glass of wine. Tomba, who is sitting at a table in the open air, gallantly hurries over to her with the wine. He introduces himself, and the mention of his name produces a marked reaction from Rosetta. Observing her more closely, Tomba suddenly recognises her and exclaims: "Is it possible?" "Yes," Rosetta assures him. "The young Countess Rosy Falkenberg you used to know is now the singer Rosetta Falcari." She goes on to tell him that in those early days she was madly in love with him and refused to marry the man of her parents' choice. Eventually she ran away from home and went on the stage. Looking at the beautiful woman he says sadly: "To think that happiness was so close to me and I passed it by." Then, plucking a rose from a nearby bush, she tells him to cheer up and take the rose as a keepsake, and they sing:

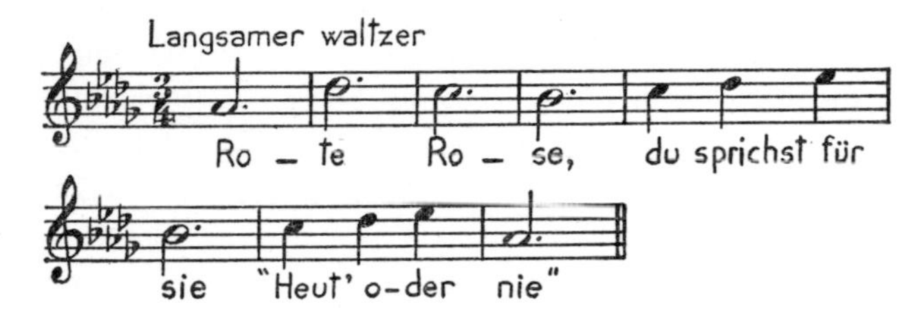

Lori now encounters Baron Enzian carrying a bouquet of flowers and looking very depressed. To raise his spirits she tells him she has changed her mind and is now ready to marry him, and she thanks him for having brought her such lovely flowers. But when she learns that he has brought the flowers for his horse, Babette, who has died, she hurls them angrily into a tree. However, she is still prepared to marry him, and fancies the prospect of becoming a Baroness. Tomba now decides to continue his ride to Munich and says good-bye to Rosetta. But she will not hear of his departure. She is giving a party and invites Tomba to come to it. However, he is insistent that he must leave. He is already mounted once more on his horse, and is about to gallop out of the inn yard, when he catches sight of Rosetta. Her eyes are full of love for him and the sight of her beauty tugs at his heart. His mission is forgotten, discretion is thrown to the winds. Leaping off his horse, he goes in pursuit of Rosetta.

ACT II

In her apartment Rosetta's party is in full swing. Among the guests are Lori and Baron Enzian, and the Chief of Police is also present. Then, to Rosetta's joy, Tomba arrives. He tells her he could not leave without seeing her once more and asks permission to visit her on his way back from Munich. She does not attempt to hide her feelings from him and the two join in a passionate duet:

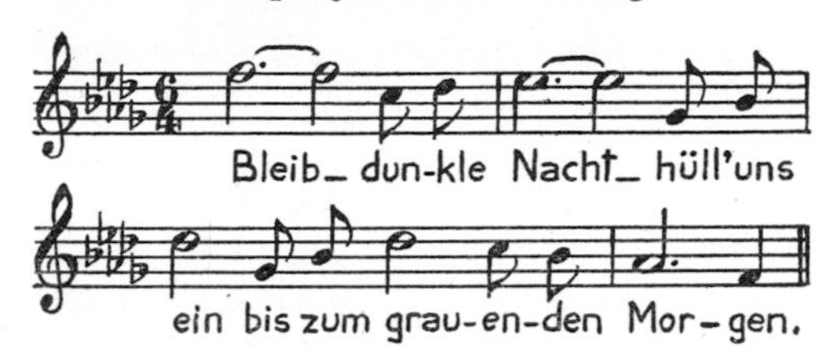

The Chief of Police is becoming more and more convinced that Tomba must be a spy, and his suspicions are increased by Lori's report that Tomba is never parted for a moment from his dispatch-case—not even when he is taking a bath! The Chief of Police voices his suspicions to Rosetta, who refuses to take them seriously and asks why Tomba should take to spying. "Oh, men often take to spying for the sake of a pretty woman," he replies—and a pang of jealousy stabs Rosetta. However, Tomba sets her mind at rest by telling her, in confidence, that his Colonel, the Archduke, has dispatched him on a mission to Munich to return a lace handkerchief to Princess Marguerite. Some years ago they fell in love but had to part and the Princess gave him as keepsake the Queen's Lace Handkerchief, a family heirloom. Now she is to be married and must have the lace handkerchief, as it is a custom in her family for the daughter of the house to present it to her bridegroom. It is vital that he reach Munich by tomorrow afternoon at the latest. Rosetta, realising the importance of his mission, is speeding Tomba on his way when the door is flung open and a section of soldiers marches in. The officer in charge tells Lieutenant Tomba he is under arrest and orders him to surrender his sword. This is, of course, the work of the Chief of Police. Protests and pleas are of no avail, and Tomba sees himself disgraced and degraded, the trust of the Archduke forfeited. One concession the Captain allows him—a quarter of an hour's grace to say good-bye to Rosetta. When the quarter of an hour is up the Captain returns and Tomba is marched away under escort.

ACT III

At the Court of Munich, Princess Marguerite is having a difficult interview with her domineering mother. "The Queen's Lace Handkerchief" is missing and the whole story of its presentation to the Archduke has come out. The old lady is furious and declares that the only way out of the difficulty is to borrow the copy of the original lace handkerchief which is on exhibition in the Royal Museum. While she hurries off to arrange this with the director the Major-domo confidentially tells Princess Marguerite that a man is waiting outside who claims that he has been sent by a Colonel in Vienna with instructions to deliver in person a parcel to the Princess Marguerite. "Show him in," she orders excitedly—and in comes Baron Enzian. "You have come from Vienna, from the Archduke?" she asks hopefully, and is puzzled by his reply that he has come from Salzburg with Lori. He goes on to explain that he was about to set off with his fiancée, Lori, on an unofficial honeymoon by carriage, when a distraught woman rushed out and stopped them. "Where are you off to?" she cried, and they answered: "Into the wide world." "Then take me with you as far as Munich," she begged.

"The happiness of a woman and the honour of a man may depend upon it." So the three of them have arrived in Munich. "And I see it is not too late," says the Baron kindly. The Princess insists on thanking Lori and Rosetta personally for their services on her behalf, and they then retire. When they have gone, Princess Marguerite's fiancé arrives. Charmingly she tells him the story of the family tradition of "The Queen's Lace Handkerchief", and presents the Prince with the handkerchief she received from Baron Enzian. But hardly has she made the presentation when her mother appears with a second "Queen's Lace Handkerchief"—the one from the museum. The Prince at first looks puzzled and then annoyed. However, he passes off the contretemps lightly. When the Princess' mother has retired, however, he gently accuses her of having given the handkerchief to a former lover and having failed to get it back in time—hence the necessity of providing a duplicate. The Princess wisely admits the truth of his words and is fully forgiven and the royal pair make their way to the chapel for the wedding. Finally Tomba arrives to find everything satisfactorily arranged, owing to the courage and enterprise of his beloved Rosetta. So in addition to wedding bells for the royal couple, they will soon be ringing also for Tomba and Rosetta and Lori and Enzian—all because of "The Queen's Lace Handkerchief".

Der Lustige Krieg

(The Merry War)

Operetta in Three Acts

By F. ZELL (CAMILLO WALZELL) *and* RICHARD GENÉE

Music by JOHANN STRAUSS

First produced on 25th November, 1881, at the Theater an der Wien, Vienna, with Karoline Finaly as "Violetta, Countess Lomellini", Alexander Girardi as "Marchese Sebastiani" and Felix Schweighofer as "Balthasar Groot". London production on the 15th October, 1882, at the Alhambra Theatre with Constance Laseby, Madame Amadi, Henry Walsham, Allen Thomas and Albert Lefevre.

ARTEMISIA, PRINCESS MALAPINA, *Consort of the reigning Prince of Massa-Carrara*
VIOLETTA, WIDOWED COUNTESS OF LOMELLINI, *her cousin*
UMBERTO SPINOLA, *Colonel of the Genoese Army*
VON SCHEELEN, *Colonel, seconded to service in the Duke of Limburg's household*
BALTHASAR GROOT, *tulip-grower from Haarlem, Holland*
ELSE, *his wife*
MARCHESE FILLIPI SEBASTIANI, *nephew of the reigning Prince of Massa-Carrara*

The action takes place in and around the Italian town of Massa on the Mediterranean in the early eighteenth century.

ACT I

The scene is the Genoese war encampment before Massa. There are some remarkable features about this merry war which is being waged between the Prince of Massa-Carrara and the Doge of Genoa. The initial *causa belli* is a dispute over a prima ballerina. The Prince of Massa-Carrara's army is entirely officered by ladies of his Court and the Commander-in-Chief is Countess Violetta Lomellini. So far the only casualties reported are Genoese soldiers who have lost their hearts to enemy officers. At the moment the battle is going badly for the Massa-Carraran army, for the Genoese, by an encircling movement, have hemmed them in to the fortress of Malapina, which is their headquarters. From the captured Marchese Sebastiani, the Genoese Colonel Spinola learns that Countess Lomellini is intending to marry the Duke of Limburg, whom she has never seen, in the expectation of his supplying her with reinforcements and money. The Marchese, an incorrigible chatterbox, also gives away that an official representative of the Duke of Limburg is on his way to Massa to marry Countess Lomellini by proxy. Consequently, when this official representative, Colonel von Scheelen, appears, the Genoese are waiting for him and he is caught sneaking through their lines.

Another character who is taken prisoner by the Genoese is Balthasar Groot, a Dutch tulip-grower, who has come to Italy on business. He loudly laments the loss of his wife, Else, and the fact that the ignorant soldiers have eaten all his sample tulips. Later Countess Lomellini appears, disguised as a peasant girl, and boldly asks for a pass to enable her to reach the Massa-Carrara headquarters. Colonel Spinola, enchanted by her beauty, falls head over ears in love with her and boldly gives himself out to be the representative of the Duke of Limburg—exhibiting Colonel von Scheelen's papers to prove his assertion. So he and Violetta set off together on their way to get married.

ACT II

The scene is a salon in the castle of Malapina, headquarters of the Prince of Massa-Carrara's army. The marriage between Countess Violetta and Colonel Spinola (in the role of representative of the Duke of Limburg) has taken place and the royal pair are being received with appropriate pomp by Princess Artemisia. Colonel Spinola has seen to it that his entourage includes several disguised Genoese officers. The Colonel now introduces Balthasar Groot, whom he forces to play the part of the Duke of Limburg, and, to the Dutchman's acute embarrassment, he is received with festive ceremony. The Court, it is true, is somewhat astonished at Violetta's obvious antipathy to her husband, and Balthasar is appalled at the situation in which he finds himself. His embarrassment becomes even more acute when the Marchese Sebastiani arrives at the castle with Else, his wife. The Marchese has been released from captivity by the Genoese, who regard him as a harmless lunatic, and on his way home he has fallen in with Else Groot in search of her husband. The Groots are amazed to meet under such peculiar circumstances, but the situation makes it impossible for them to recognise each other openly. Marchese Sebastiani soon observes the presence of the disguised Genoese officers and calls out a detachment of troops to arrest them. But Violetta, as Commander-in-Chief, orders their release and invites them to her wedding festivities.

ACT III

The last act also takes place in the castle of Malapina. Else Groot is getting tired of her husband's protracted impersonation of the Duke of Limburg and her jealousy of Violetta is making his life a hell upon earth. Vainly he tells her that there cannot be any harm in kisses that are given and received with aversion. But Else tells Balthasar tartly that the comedy must end. This conversation is overheard by the garrulous Sebastiani, who immediately reveals all. Colonel Spinola is called to account for his presence in the castle, and he answers quite simply that his marriage to Violetta is a legal one and he regards her as his wife. News comes now of a truce between the two opposing forces. Now that the merry war is over there is no obstacle to the happiness of Violetta, who has come to love Spinola dearly, and the curtain falls on the official recognition of their marriage.

In spite of its triviality, the libretto of *The Merry War* offered plenty of opportunities to Johann Strauss to develop the many facets of his musical style. Musically perhaps the high spot is the quintette—"Kommen und gehen".

The most popular number was the waltz song "Nur für Natur" specially composed for Alexander Girardi, who threatened to throw up the part of Marchese Sebastiani unless Strauss provided him with a hit number:

Eine Nacht in Venedig

(A Night in Venice)

Operetta in Three Acts

By F. ZELL (CAMILLO WALZELL) *and* RICHARD GENÉE

Music by JOHANN STRAUSS

Written for the new Friederich-Wilhelm Städtisches Theater, Berlin, and produced there on the 3rd October, 1883, with Herr Josessy as "The Duke of Urbino", Karolin Finaly as "Annina", Alexander Girardi as "Caramello", Rosa Streitmann as "Ciboletta" and Felix Schweighofer as "Pappacoda". New version by Hubert Marischka and Erich Wolfgang Korngold produced at the Vienna State Opera on 23rd June, 1923. London production on 25th May, 1944, at the Cambridge Theatre, with Henry Wendon, Daria Bayan, Dennis Noble and Jerry Verno.

CHARACTERS

GUIDO, *Duke of Urbino*
BARTOLOMEO DELACQUA, STEFANO BARBARUCCIO, GIORGIO TESTACCIO — *Venetian senators*
BARBARA DELACQUA, AGRICOLA BARBARUCCIO, CONSTANTIA TESTACCIO — *their wives*
ANNINA, *a fisher-girl*
CARAMELLO, *the Duke's confidant and barber*
PAPPACODA, *a macaroni-seller*
CIBOLETTA, *a cook*
ENRICO PISELLI, *a naval officer*
CHORUS OF TOWNSFOLK, SERVANTS AND CARNIVAL CROWDS

Time: The 18th century.

ACT I

The scene is a small square in Venice on the Grand Canal overlooking the Doge's Palace and San Giorgio. It is carnival time and Guido, Duke of Urbino, the presiding Royalty, is to give a magnificent reception to which the Senators of the city with their wives have been invited. The Duke is a notorious Don Juan, and the Senators are dubious as to the wisdom of taking their wives with them. Senator Delacqua is particularly worried, as he is elderly and has a young wife of great beauty called Barbara. The Duke has heard of her loveliness and is particularly anxious to meet her. But Delacqua, determined to safeguard his wife's virtue, makes arrangements to send her away for the night by gondola to her aunt at Murano. As the Duke does not know Barbara by sight, Delacqua plans to take his cook, Ciboletta, to the reception and present her as his wife. This plan, however, is overheard by Caramello, the Duke's confidant and barber, and in his master's interest he bribes the gondolier deputed to ferry Barbara to Murano to allow him to take his place, his purpose being to deliver Barbara at the Ducal palace. But in all this intrigue no one has reckoned with the beautiful Barbara herself. She is in the throes of a passionate love-affair with a handsome young naval officer, Enrico Piselli, her husband's nephew. Carnival time, when everyone is masked and disguised in dominoes, is ideal for lovers' meetings, and Barbara is determined to avoid going to Murano. She therefore persuades her friend Annina, a fisher-girl, to take her place in the gondola, suitably disguised. Ciboletta the cook and her fiancé, a macaroni seller, Pappacoda, are also in the secret. Barbara's plan works to perfection. Old Delacqua solicitously helps the disguised Annina into the gondola, somewhat puzzled at his wife's reticence, and bids her "bon voyage" to Murano; while Caramello, convinced that his passenger is Barbara, propels his gondola towards the Ducal palace, his gondolier's song echoing along the canal. As the gondola

disappears, Ciboletta and Pappacoda hurry Delacqua up to the balcony of his house to acknowledge a serenade sung officially in his honour (but with a decidely ironical undertone) by a crowd of sailors and their sweethearts. They are led by Enrico, who is on his way to keep his assignation with Barbara. The sailors' voices form a rhythmical counterpoint to Caramello's romantic gondolier's song, and as the moon shines down on the canal the curtain falls:

ACT II

Act Two takes place in a salon in the Duke of Urbino's palace, where, in spite of their husbands' attitude, the Senators' wives have arrived in full force for the Duke's reception. The Duke, however, is interested only in Barbara and impatiently awaits her arrival. While he is waiting he sings a song in which he admits his inability to remain faithful to any one woman for long:

After this song, Caramello's arrival with a masked lady is announced. The Duke is delighted, but Caramello is greatly upset when the masked lady turns out to be Annina. For Annina and Caramello are sweethearts, and Caramello is mortified when he finds that he has, all unsuspecting, led his own girl into the presence of the notorious Duke. He endeavours to persuade Annina to come away before it is too late, but Annina is determined to enjoy herself. Naturally Caramello is unable to divulge Annina's true identity to the Duke and is forced to look on jealously while she is affectionately greeted by the amorous Duke and invited to supper. Later Signor Delacqua arrives with Ciboletta, whom he presents to the Duke as his wife, Barbara. The Duke is greatly puzzled at the advent of a second Barbara and amused when Annina whispers to him that Delacqua is presenting his cook, Ciboletta. However, he preserves his countenance and greets Ciboletta courteously. Delacqua has instructed her to influence the Duke to give him the appointment of Steward of his Estates, but Ciboletta takes advantage of the situation to lobby for the Duke's patronage of her sweetheart, Pappacoda, who wishes to be taken on as Royal Chef. Supper is now served, and Caramello and Pappacoda have to act as waiters and watch jealously while the Duke gaily flirts with their girls, who enjoy the situation hugely. They do, however, manage to spin out the meal interminably, thereby ensuring that the Duke is never left alone for any length of time with either Annina or Ciboletta, for they know that when midnight strikes he must make his traditional appearance in St. Mark's Square to lead the Carnival procession. As the act ends the guests set off from the palace in high spirits to the tune of an infectious polka:

ACT III

Act Three is played in the square of St. Mark's in front of the cathedral. It opens with a production number which created a sensation at the première: "The Pigeons of St. Mark's." While the Duke is thoroughly enjoying himself with Annina, Ciboletta slips away to find Pappacoda and gives him the joyful news that he has been appointed Royal Chef. Caramello, however, is in the depths of despair at the thought of his beloved Annina being a willing victim to the vicious Duke. Sadly he bewails the falseness of all women, in this enchanting waltz:

Senator Delacqua, too, is terribly agitated. He has been to Murano and discovered that his wife never arrived, and he has learned from the gondolier that his Barbara was ferried away to some unknown destination by the rascally Caramello. Finally he identifies her in the crowd, and she manages to pacify him with a very unconvincing story of how she was kidnapped by an unknown gondolier and taken to the Lido, where she was rescued by Enrico. Annina is restored to Caramello's arms by the Duke on the understanding that Caramello marries her and becomes his steward—thereby ensuring that his delicious Annina will never be far away. And so everybody is satisfied and the curtain falls on an atmosphere of carnival gaiety on a night in Venice.

Der Zigeunerbaron
(The Gipsy Baron)

Operetta in Three Acts

By J. Schnitzer

Adapted from a libretto based on his story Saffi *by* Moriz Jókai

Music by Johann Strauss

First produced on 24th October, 1885, at the Theater an der Wien, Vienna, with Alexander Girardi as "Kolman Zsupan", Karl Streitmann as "Sandor Barinkay" and Ottilie Collin as "Saffi". According to Alfred Loewenberg's Annals of Opera, *it was first produced in London (in English) by amateurs at the Rudolf Steiner Hall in 1935.*

Characters

COUNT PETER HOMONAY, *Governor of the Temesvar Province*
COUNT CARNERO, *Royal Commissioner*
SANDOR BARINKAY, *a young exile*
KOLMAN ZSUPAN, *a wealthy pig-breeder*
ARSENA, *his daughter*
MIRABELLA, *her governess*
OTTOKAR, *Mirabella's son*
CZIPRA, *an old gipsy*
SAFFI, *a gipsy girl*
CHORUS OF BOATMEN, GIPSIES, SOLDIERS, ETC.

ACT I

The scene of Act One is a river-side swamp near the village of Banat in the province of Temesvar, Hungary, in the middle of the eighteenth century. In the background is a ruined castle with water reaching to the threshold; to the right is a gipsy cabin with a smoking chimney; and in the immediate foreground stands a large house—the only prosperous-looking building of a deserted village which is slowly sinking into the morass. The hero is a young man called Sandor Barinkay. In his youth during the Turko-Hungarian War he was sent into banishment with his father and their estates were confiscated. When the curtain rises there has been a general amnesty. Sandor Barinkay has returned home, and now arrives with the Royal Commissioner, Count Carnero, to reclaim his ancestral dwelling. During his exile he has earned his living in various ways. He has been snake-charmer, lion-tamer, sword-swallower and conjurer, and he regales the Royal Commissioner with a description:

Sandor is horrified at the desolation into which his property has fallen. It is now nothing more than a derelict camping ground for gipsies. The only respectable neighbour is a wealthy pig-breeder, Kolman Zsupan. He is quite illiterate and explains: "I've got no time for reading for the pigs will keep on breeding." Zsupan has an extremely pretty daughter called Arsena, and Sandor reflects that if he is going to settle down to life in a castle in the country he might do worse than marry her, for a castle should have a chatelaine. Zsupan welcomes the proposed alliance but, unfortunately, Arsena is already in love with a young man called Ottokar and haughtily tells Sandor that she would not consider marrying anybody below the rank of Baron.

The gipsies now arrive on the scene. One of them, an old hag called Czipra, recognises Sandor as his father's son and their overlord, and the gipsies give him an ovation and swear allegiance to him. Quite by chance Sandor is witness to a love-scene between Arsena and Ottokar, and abandons all further thought of marrying her, especially as he now meets and falls in love with Saffi, a beautiful girl who is Czipra's ward. Her gipsy song is one of the high-lights of the score:

Determined to be revenged on Arsena for her deceitful behaviour to him, Sandor calls out Zsupan and informs him that as Arsena desired to marry a baron he can now offer himself as a gipsy baron. Then, in reply to the sneers of Arsena and Zsupan, who ridicule his title, Sandor announces his intention of marrying the gipsy girl, Saffi. Zsupan is furious at what he considers a slight upon his daughter and would attack Sandor, but the gipsies protect him and bear him away on their shoulders towards his castle as the curtain falls.

ACT II

The scene is a gipsy encampment in the neighbourhood of Sandor Barinkay's castle. He and Saffi are by now deeply in love and Czipra is delighted that the first part of a prophecy she made to Sandor has come true—that he would find a bride. The second part of her prophecy was that he would find a treasure. Now there is a belief that before Sandor's father was exiled he buried a very considerable treasure within the precincts of the castle, and both Zsupan and Ottokar have been observed from time to time engaged in digging operations. On Czipra's advice Sandor begins excavations on his own account, and eventually, dislodging some bricks in the castle wall, he discloses the treasure. The joy and excitement of his discovery are expressed by Johann Strauss in a Waltz-Trio:

Some gipsies now arrive to report that a coach has broken down nearby, and soon after Zsupan, Arsena and Ottokar appear in search of help to get their wagon out of the ditch. Some young gipsy lads dextrously steal Zsupan's watch and money and he complains of this to Count Carnero, who, as Guardian of Public Morals, arrives on Sandor's track. He sternly inquires of Sandor and Saffi who married them, and receives the reply in a duet: "Cock Robin, he married us two."

The Guardian of Public Morals is duly shocked and is making himself extremely unpleasant when he is interrupted by the arrival of Count Homonay, who comes recruiting with his hussars. Hungary is on the brink of war with Spain and needs every able-bodied man's service as a soldier. The recruiting procedure is that whoever accepts a glass of recruiting wine is automatically enrolled as a soldier. Zsupan and Ottokar, unaware of this, accept glass after glass of wine, only to discover to their horror that they are in the army. Count Carnero now complains to Count Homonay, the Governor of Temesvar, of Sandor Barinkay's immoral conduct. But the Governor only laughs and congratulates Sandor on his good taste in choosing such a pretty wife. This enrages Carnero, Zsupan, Arsena and Ottokar to such a degree that they turn on Saffi with jeers and insults. But old Czipra comes to her defence with documentary evidence to prove that Saffi is of noble birth, the daughter of the last Pasha in Hungary. The crowd is astonished and delighted, while the gipsies humbly kiss their companion's garment. Sandor, however, is in despair. The disclosure of her noble birth puts Saffi out of his reach for ever, and in spite of her tears, he declares his intention of joining the hussars to march against the enemy. He hands over the whole of his father's treasure to Count Homonay for his country's benefit and joins the marching soldiery.

ACT III

The last act takes place in Vienna at the Glacis before the Kärtner Tor. A crowd has collected at the city gate to welcome the Austrian army, on its victorious return from the war in Spain. Ottokar and Zsupan are among the soldiers and Zsupan gaily relates his war-time adventures, which apparently consisted mainly of acquiring loot and dodging any form of danger. He declares that Sandor Barinkay saved his life, and when Sandor arrives he is hailed as a hero and saluted by Count Homonay as the officer whose courage won so many battles. Count Homonay returns his father's treasure to him and honours him by conferring on him the title of Baron. "Since I owe all to the heroism of my brave gipsies," declares Sandor amid cheers, "I claim the title of Gipsy Baron." And now, as Saffi's equal in station, he can clasp her in his arms, and with general rejoicings, to the strains of the inevitable waltz, the curtain falls.

Simplicius

Operetta in a Prologue and Two Acts

Based on HANS JACOB GRIMMELSHAUSEN'S *Romance*
Simplicius Simplicissimus

By VIKTOR LÉON

Music by JOHANN STRAUSS

First produced on 17th December, 1887, at the Theater an der Wien, Vienna, with Alexander Girardi as "Simplicius", Antonie Hartmann as "Hildegard", Karl Streitmann as "Armin" and Ottilie Collin as "Tilly".

CHARACTERS

SIMPLICIUS
THE PILGRIM
COUNT VON BLIESSEN-WELLAU
HILDEGARD, *his daughter*
ARMIN, *a law student*
TILLY
SCHNAPPSLOTTE, *her mother*
BARON VON GRÜBBEN
CHORUS OF SOLDIERS, SWEDISH TUMBLERS

The time is the seventeenth century.

PROLOGUE

The scene of the Prologue is a clearing in a dense forest in the Sudeten Land. Before a wayside cross the Pilgrim is kneeling. Suddenly the silence is shattered by the ringing sound of bugle-calls and into the clearing dashes a terrified figure. Simplicius, a young peasant, babbles an incoherent story of being pursued by Iron Men. They prove to be a troop of soldiers, armed and in battle-dress, who have lost their way in the forest. In spite of the Pilgrim's protests, the soldiers seize Simplicius and take him along to guide them out of the forest.

ACT I

The scene is a military camp near Olmütz in the year 1644. The troops are under the command of General Count von Bliessen-Wellau. Today the arrival is expected from Vienna of Baron Melchior von Grübben, who is to celebrate his engagement to Hildegard, the General's daughter. Neither the General nor his daughter is acquainted with the Baron, for the marriage is one of convenience, arranged by the heads of their respective families to preserve intact two adjoining estates. As the former heir, Bruno von Grübben, is dead, or at any rate has disappeared, Melchior has taken his place. Melchior, whose two enthusiasms in life are astrology and a Swedish ballet dancer, arrives at dawn in the camp and, being tired and travel-stained, retires to his tent without reporting to his host.

Later, the troop of soldiers encountered in the Prologue arrive with Simplicius. The peasant boy is terrified and is convinced that he has arrived in the nether regions. He is, however, treated kindly by the General, who takes him into his service, and hands him over to the good offices of an old woman, Schnappslotte, who supplies the Commissariat with alcohol, to be cleaned up and made presentable. Another recent recruit is a young law student, Armin. He has joined the army to forget a girl with whom he fell in love in Prague and who suddenly vanished from the city. To his amazement, in the camp he meets this girl in the person of Hildegard. He is just pouring out to her the tale of his love, when they are surprised by the General, who asks him his name. Without hesitation he answers: "Baron von Grübben." The General, delighted, congratulates Hildegard on acquiring such a charming fiancé.

Camp is now struck and the troops line up to march away. Simplicius has been keeping a watchful eye on Melchior von Grübben, who has been behaving in such a peculiar manner that he takes him for an enemy. He marches him in front of the General, who is greatly confused to be confronted with two Barons von Grübben, two suitors for the hand of Hildegard. Before the question can be settled, however, there come from army headquarters orders to arrest Baron von Grübben, at present resident in camp at Olmütz, on a charge under the Official Secrets Act of corresponding with Sweden. Melchior remembers with dismay that at home are all his letters from his lady love, the Swedish dancer. But he can only trust to his fate, and until the General is able to decide which is the genuine Baron von Grübben, Melchior and Armin are both put under arrest.

ACT II

The scene is the castle of Hanau in the province of Hess. Two years have elapsed since Act One, and Simplicius has developed into a gay dragoon with a penchant for practical jokes and a fearless nature. The only person with whom he is shy and gentle is little Tilly, the daughter of old Schnappslotte who befriended him on his first appearance in camp. Tilly can do what she likes with him. One day there arrives at the castle the Pilgrim who was kneeling before the cross in the Prologue and simultaneously there comes a dispatch from the Emperor commanding General Count von Bliessen-Wellau to treat the young trooper Simplicius, serving under his command, with special consideration, as he is in reality the son of Baron Bruno von Grübben. Simplicius is now promoted to the rank of lieutenant and the General informs him that as heir to his father it is his duty to marry Hildegard to save the family estates. Simplicius agrees, but poor little Tilly is shattered by the turn of events. She adores Simplicius and now tells him of her love for him. But Simplicius, still the simple peasant boy, has no idea of the significance of love and hardly reacts to Tilly's declaration.

Armin and Hildegard now plan to elope, disguised as Swedish tumblers. A troupe of them has appeared at Hanau, headed by Melchior von Grübben's girl-friend, the Swedish ballet-dancer, Ebba. Melchior is not *au fait* with the change of circumstances following the disclosure of Simplicius' identity, and is still under the impression that he is going to marry Hildegard and that Ebba, for whom he has lost enthusiasm, stands in his way. He decides to offer her money to retire from the scene. Now the Swedish tumblers are not as innocent as they appear. Two members of the troupe are secret agents, whose purpose it is to murder the General. His plumed hat is to be the target for their bullet. Simplicius discovers the plot, steals the General's feathered headgear and, appearing in it, is duly shot at. In this moment of life and death the thought flashes through his mind—from whom would he most dread being parted? To his surprise, his answer is "Tilly". His wound is only a slight one, and during his convalescence he decides to give up all claim to the family estates and marry Tilly. Suspicion has fallen on the Pilgrim of being the dread assassin, but Simplicius recognises in him his long-lost father, Bruno von Grübben, who, when his wife died in giving birth to Simplicius, decided in his grief to give up the world and dedicate himself to the service of God. The happy ending sees the marriage of Simplicius to Tilly, while Armin is united with Hildegard.

Once again a Johann Strauss operetta suffered from the shortcomings of its libretto, for Viktor Léon was unable to get much fun or interest out of Grimmelhausen's story of the Thirty Years War. The most admired number, musically, was Simplicius' and Tilly's love-duet from the third act—"Dummer Bub' ".

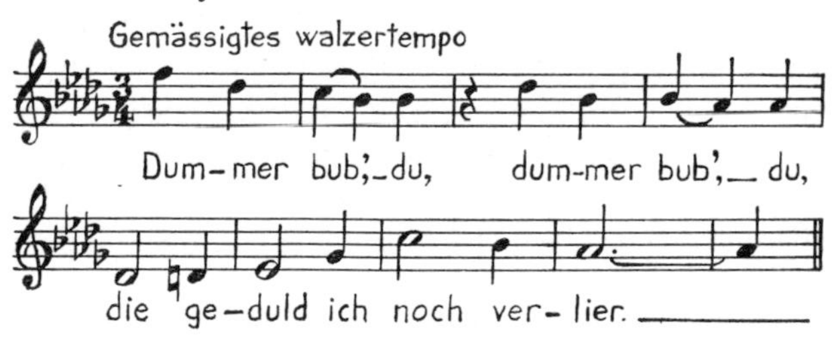

Another popular favourite was the Pilgrim's song from Act Two:

Wiener Blut

Operetta in Three Acts

By VIKTOR LÉON *and* LEO STEIN

Music by JOHANN STRAUSS

Arranged under his personal supervision for the stage by ADOLF MÜLLER *Jr.*

First produced on 26th October, 1899, at the Carl Theater, Vienna, four months after Johann Strauss' death.

CHARACTERS

PRINCE YPSHEIM-GINDELBACH, *Prime Minister of Reuss-Schleiz-Greiz*
BALDUIN, COUNT ZEDLAU, *Ambassador of Reuss-Schleiz-Greiz to Vienna*
GABRIELE, *his wife*
COUNT BITOWSKI
FRANZISKA CAGLIARI, *dancer from the Kärtnertor Theatre*
KAGLER, *her father, fairground proprietor*
PEPI PLEININGER, *a mannequin*
JOSEF, *valet to Count Zedlau*
CHORUS OF MUSICIANS, SERVANTS, LAUNDRY-MAIDS AND SOLDIERS

The action takes place in Vienna during the Congress of Vienna in 1815.

ACT I

The scene is a room in Count Zedlau's villa in Döbling, a surburb of Vienna. In this villa he keeps his reigning mistress, Franziska Cagliari, a well-known dancer. Although he has only recently married, the Count is parted from his wife. Soon after their wedding the gay Viennese girl returned to her parents, bored stiff by her husband, at that time a narrow-minded provincial from the small state of Reuss-Schleiz-Greiz. Since they parted, however, the Count has developed into a sophisticated man of the world who has once again fallen in love—this time with an enchantingly pretty model. He dictates a letter to his valet, Joseph, inviting his new love to meet him for supper that night in Hietzing—and Joseph little suspects that the invitation is intended for his own fiancée, Pepi. Count Zedlau is slightly worried. His wife is in Vienna, and he must at all costs find means to prevent her from visiting his villa in Döbling. He bids Franziska a fond farewell and explains the purpose of his visit to Vienna. After his departure Pepi arrives with a new dress for the famous dancer, whose real name is the good old bourgeois one of Franzi Kagler. Pepi greets her fiancé, Joseph, and they arrange to meet that night at Hietzing.

There now arrives unexpectedly on a visit to the villa Prince Ypsheim, Prime Minister of Reuss-Schleiz-Greiz and Count Zedlau's boss. He is greatly puzzled at meeting Franzi's father, Kagler, the fairground proprietor and clarinet player. Kagler, who fondly believes that the Count intends to marry Franzi, behaves as the prospective father-in-law he believes himself to be and Prince Ypsheim does not know what to make of his Viennese dialect. When Franzi appears the Prince assumes that *she* must be Countess Zedlau, and during their conversation refers to rumours which have reached him of her husband's affair with a dancer. Franzi, incensed, flounces out of the room. Hardly has she done so, when in comes the real Countess Zedlau. Prince Ypsheim is convinced that here is the erring dancer, and starts reproving her for daring, as the Count's mistress, to force her way into his home. At this moment the Count returns to find himself in a very tricky situation. Taking the Prince aside, he begs him to save his face by introducing Franzi as his wife, and is appalled when the old man, willing to oblige, innocently presents Countess Zedlau as the Princess Ypsheim.

ACT II

In the ballroom of his palace in Vienna Count Bitowski is giving a dance. Count Zedlau is having a difficult time pacifying both his wife and his mistress, for his wife, Gabriele, is showing distinct signs of a possessive, wifely interest in him, while Franzi has not the slightest intention of giving him up to a rival, as she supposes Gabriele to be. But for the moment the Count's head is full of his rendezvous at Hietzing with Pepi, who is also at the ball as one of a troupe of girls providing the cabaret. To his dismay, however, first Gabriele and then Franzi beg him to take *them* to supper at Hietzing, and only with great difficulty does he avoid the dilemma. During the evening Pepi quarrels with Joseph, and this makes her doubly determined to keep her date with the Count. Old Prince Ypsheim adds to the complications of the evening. Still under the impression that Franzi is Countess Zedlau, he lectures Herr Kagler, telling him that, as a father-in-law, it is his duty to reason with his son-in-law's mistress, whereupon Kagler proceeds to lecture Gabriele on her behaviour. The situation becomes increasingly tangled as the evening advances. Gabriele takes Pepi for Franziska Cagliari, while Franzi believes Gabriele to be the Count's latest girl-friend and Pepi believes Gabriele to be the dancer. At the height of the evening identities are proved when Bitowski in a speech presents Gabriele as his guest of honour, Countess Zedlau. The whole episode is an embarrassing one, particularly to the Count and Prince Ypsheim, and it takes the heady strains of a vintage Viennese waltz to restore the party spirit.

ACT III

Act Three is set in the Casino garden at Hietzing, Count Zedlau's rendezvous with Pepi. They meet, but no sooner are they cosily esconced in an arbour than there is an interruption. Gabriele arrives, escorted by Prince Ypsheim, and then Franzi escorted by Joseph. It was the loyal Joseph's purpose to warn his master of approaching danger, but when he finds him in tender dalliance with his own Pepi there is trouble, with noisy accusations of faithless treachery. In the meantime, Franzi has decided that she has had enough of the Count and now does everything she can to help Gabriele to win back her husband. The dizzy experiences of the last forty-eight hours have also convinced the Count what a mistake it is to take on too many love affairs and that it is far wiser for a man to live contentedly with his own wife, especially when she is as attractive as Gabriele. So while Gabriele is cunningly rousing her husband's jealousy by letting him find her in another man's company, Franzi joins Prince Ypsheim in an arbour—to find the old gentleman fast asleep. The Count, thoroughly ashamed of his behaviour, swears eternal fidelity to Gabriele, and Joseph and Pepi make it up when the Count assures Joseph that he never so much as kissed Pepi in the arbour. The final scene is of old Prince Ypsheim on his knees in the arbour, covering Franzi's hands with kisses. As all agree, it's in the blood—Viennese blood—*Wiener Blut!*

In spite of the fact that *Wiener Blut* is a posthumous work, Adolf Müller's skilful adaptation of Johann Strauss' music, combined with the hilarious comedy of mistaken identities and general confusion, combine to make it one of the most successful Strauss operettas. It still holds the stage in Germany and Austria. Among the most admired numbers are the sparkling polka "In Hietzing":

(2) "Du Süsses Zuckertäuberl Mein":

(3) "Grüss dich Gott, du liebes Nester!"

(4) "Wiener Blut."

Gräfin Dubarry

Operetta in Three Acts

By F. ZELL (CAMILLO WALZEL) *and* RICHARD GENÉE

Music by KARL MILLÖCKER

First produced on 31st October, 1879, at the Theater an der Wien, Vienna. A new version, Die Dubarry, *in nine scenes, by Paul Knepler, J. M. Welleminsky and Hans Martin Cremer, with music by Millöcker, adapted and added to by Theo Mackeben, was produced in 1931 at the Admiralspalast, Berlin, with Gitta Alpar. London production on 14th April, 1932, at His Majesty's Theatre, with Anny Ahlers.*

Note. This synopsis follows the new version.

CHARACTERS

LOUIS XV, *King of France*
DUC DE CHOISEUL, *Prime Minister*
MARQUIS DE BRISSAC
PRINCESS DE LUXEMBOURG
COMTE DUBARRY
DUC DE LAUZIM
MADAME LABILLE, *milliner*
MARGOT, MARIE JEANNE BEÇU, LUCILLE — *her assistants*
RENÉ LAVALLERY, *a painter*
LES SŒURS VERRIÈRES, *night-club proprietors*
CHORUS OF COURTIERS, SERVANTS, MODISTES, CITIZENS OF PARIS

The action takes place in Paris during the reign of Louis XV.

SCENE 1. In the millinery establishment of Madame Labille works little Margot. She has had the good fortune to capture the interest of a wealthy protector, the Marquis de Brissac, who invites her out with all her fellow midinettes. Marie Jeanne Beçu, who also works in the hat shop, returns very late from an errand.

During her absence she has been picked up by a handsome young painter called René Lavallery, and is so absorbed in him that she never notices the theft of two hats she is supposed to deliver at customers' houses. On her return she is punished for her carelessness by Madame Labille, who insists on her staying on after hours to work in the shop; but Jeanne has a rendezvous with René which nothing will induce her to break, and so when the shop is deserted she departs via the window.

SCENE 2. In a Parisian pleasure garden the Comte Dubarry is discussing with the Duc de Lauzim the question of a successor to the ageing Pompadour as the King's mistress. The Count is very emphatic that the sister of the Prime Minister, the Duc de Choiseul, will not be the lucky lady, whatever her brother may suppose. There are political reasons that militate against such a choice. Quite near to where the two noblemen are talking Jeanne meets René Lavallery. They are already in love and have eyes only for one another. Watching the two lovers Comte Dubarry is greatly attracted to the girl and makes a mental note, for future reference, of her personality and charm.

SCENE 3. In his studio René and Jeanne are living together, and both are convinced that their love will last for ever. But Jeanne's extravagance soon lands them in financial difficulties, for Jeanne cannot resist new clothes. Then Margot visits them. She is now prosperously situated and lavishly kept by her wealthy protector, the Marquis de Brissac. While René is out shopping, Comte Dubarry calls at the studio. He is anxious to buy a painting of Jeanne which René has just completed. With calculated intent he stresses the good things in life that Jeanne is missing through lack of money, and is making more concrete suggestions when Jeanne abruptly rejects his offers, and he leaves. Secretly tempted and unsure of herself, Jeanne conceals Comte Dubarry's visit from René. But through the inquisitiveness of a neighbour he comes to know of it and later discovers a purse of money which the Comte has left behind in the studio to tempt Jeanne. Furious to find that she is, as he believes, deceiving him, René throws her out of the studio without further ceremony.

SCENE 4. At Comte Dubarry's palace, a stag party is in progress. At it the Marquis de Brissac reports the advent of an attractive new cabaret artiste called Manon Rançons, who sings and dances at the night club, "Chez Les Sœurs Verrières". All the gentlemen determine to visit the establishment.

SCENE 5. "Chez Les Sœurs Verrières." Here Jeanne, calling herself Manon Rançon, has made a hit with her dancing and her risqué songs. Dubarry recognises her at once. All the men are round her like flies, but Jeanne never drops her calculated reserve with any of them. She is gambling at the tables, but her luck is out and she loses a fortune provided by one of her rich admirers. When he protests at her reckless play she only laughs at him, and he then abuses her with insulting epithets. But Dubarry is at her elbow. He pays her gambling debt and, playing the part of her ostensible lover, leads her out of the room.

SCENE 6. A room in Comte Dubarry's palace. Dubarry intends to use Jeanne as a pawn to further his political ambitions. To this end and to satisfy convention he has married her off to his brother. She is now living in Dubarry's house, where she is being trained to take her place as a lady in Court circles. Jeanne waxes cynically sarcastic over his vaunted ambitions. An invitation for them both to a soirée at the Princess of Luxembourg's is to prove the next stage in her destiny.

SCENE 7. In her salon the Princess of Luxembourg is giving a brilliant soirée. Among the guests is the Prime Minister, the Duc de Choiseul. He is convinced that his sister is destined to succeed the Pompadour as the King's mistress, although he is aware of an attempt on the part of his enemies to influence the King in favour of Jeanne by showing him her portrait, painted by René Lavallery. But this evening he receives evidence that his hopes in this direction are doomed to disappointment, and he leaves the party greatly cast down. The Princess of Luxembourg, who favours Dubarry's faction and is opposed to Choiseul, now breaks the news to Jeanne that a gentleman-in-waiting of the royal household will be coming to escort her to the palace to sup with the King. In a panic she realises that she is being used as a pawn in some political intrigue. At this disturbing moment she meets René Lavallery, also a guest of the Princess. Their love for each other is re-awakened when they meet, and Jeanne would willingly run away with him and finish with this life of political intrigue and double dealing. But by chance she learns that the King's interest in her has been aroused by René's portrait. She assumes that René must have presented it to His Majesty and, turning her back on him, she departs to the palace.

SCENE 8. In a salon at Versailles, Monsieur Lebell, First Gentleman-in-Waiting, coaches Jeanne for her first audience with Louis XV. When they meet, the King is greatly attracted by her charm of personality and her looks and is altogether gracious. At the close of the evening he commands the Duc de Choiseul to escort Jeanne home to her new apartments in the Petit Trianon, and the Duke realises bitterly that Jeanne and not his sister is destined to succeed La Pompadour.

SCENE 9. The last scene is a Fête Champêtre in the park of the Trianon. Jeanne, as Countess Dubarry, is now royal favourite, reigning supreme in the King's affections. But the Duc de Choiseul obstinately intrigues against her, seeking to prejudice her in the eyes of the King, hoping against hope to establish his sister, the Countess de Grammont, as royal favourite in her place. He has discovered that Jeanne has a rendezvous with René. Choiseul informs the King of this meeting and arranges that he shall be a witness of it from a hiding-place close at hand. From here the King hears Jeanne rebuke René for his importunities, and tell him unequivocally that her feeling for him is dead and that her heart now beats for no one but the King, who occupies her every waking thought. The King, enchanted at what he has heard, turns on Choiseul and dismisses him from Court. Jeanne manages to shake off the importunate Count Dubarry and proudly listens to the King as he announces to the Court: "From now on Countess Dubarry is next in precedence to the throne."

Der Bettelstudent

(The Beggar Student)

Operetta in Three Acts

By F. ZELL (CAMILLO WALZELL) *and* RICHARD GENÉE

Music by KARL MILLÖCKER

First produced on 6th December, 1882, at the Theater an der Wien, Vienna, with Karolin Finaly as "Laura", Felix Schweighofer as "Colonel Ollendorf" and Alexander Girardi as "Symon". Revised in 1942 with new libretto by Gustav Quedenfeldt and Richard Bärs and musical adaptation by Oskar Stalla. London production on 12th April, 1884, at the Alhambra Theatre, with Fanny Leslie as "Laura", Frederick Mervin as "Colonel Ollendorf" and Marion Hood as "Symon".

CHARACTERS

PALMATICA, *Countess Nowalska*

LAURA, BRONISLAWA — *her daughters*

COLONEL OLLENDORF, *Governor of Cracow*

JAN JANICKI, SYMON SYMANOWICZ — *two students, committed to prison*

ENTERICH, *a gaoler*

LIEUTENANT VON SCHWEINITZ

CHORUS OF TOWNSFOLK, SOLDIERS, WEDDING GUESTS, GAOLBIRDS, ETC.

ACT I

SCENE I. It is the year 1704, and Cracow, the ancient capital of Poland, is occupied by the troops of Saxony. Outside the gates of the citadel a number of Polish women are anxiously waiting for a brief reunion with their loved ones, who are imprisoned within. The soft-hearted gaoler permits a meeting in the prison courtyard between the prisoners and their women-folk, but a visit from some German officers brings this to an abrupt termination. The prisoners are hustled back to their cells and the women are dismissed. The officers have been summoned to the prison to meet the Governor of the city, Colonel Ollendorf. While they are waiting they discuss a rebellion scare, and Major von Wangenheim tells them that the Polish patriot, Stanislaus Lechinski, heads a party that grows stronger every day. Is this, they wonder, what is worrying the Governor? According to one of the younger officers, the Governor is worrying about something quite different. It seems that Colonel Ollendorf has been paying marked attention to a beautiful Polish girl, Countess Laura Nowalska. After dinner the previous night at Count Felinski's, the Governor, in a mellow mood, got so carried away while he was dancing with the Countess that he kissed her on the shoulder—in public! Lieutenant von Schweinitz is just asking: "And what did the Countess do about it?" when there is a cry of "Look out! the Colonel." And there stands Colonel Ollendorf in a towering rage at finding his officers discussing his private affairs. However, he goes on to tell them that his chaste salute—purely paternal, of course—was rewarded by a slap in the face. Fancy striking a German officer! He must be revenged. The Countess must be punished.

Since the incident at the dance the Colonel has intercepted a letter from Laura's mother to a sister in Warsaw. "Listen to this," he says: " 'My dear Anuschka, your inquiry as to whether Colonel Ollendorf would be a suitable match for my daughter Laura amuses me greatly. You cannot seriously imagine that I would give Laura away to that coarse, purple-faced old Turkey-cock. My Laura shall marry a Pole and anyone beneath the rank of Count need not apply.' " This letter has given the Colonel an idea for accomplishing his revenge. He inquires of the gaoler whether among the prisoners there are any good-looking young men. There are, says the gaoler, and produces two handsome young students, Symon Symanowicz and Jan Janicki. A gayer, more care-free couple would be hard to find:

The Colonel's plan for revenge is to release one of the young men, dress him up as a prince, lend him some money and turn him loose on society. The Countess wants a Polish noble for her daughter, and he will supply one. The proposition is put to Symon. He will receive his freedom and a sum of ten thousand crowns provided he will, under the guise of Prince Wybitzky, a Polish millionaire, consent to marry a certain young lady. Symon, a political prisoner with an adventurous spirit and nothing to lose, immediately accepts, on condition that Jan accompanies him as his secretary. The two students are marched away to be groomed for their respective roles, while Colonel Ollendorf chuckles to think of the scandal there will be when the noble Countess Laura discovers she is married to a penniless student.

SCENE 2. Scene Two takes place at the annual fair at Cracow. Among those present are Countess Nowalska and her two daughters Laura and Bronislawa. They are very hard up and can only afford a lunch of potatoes and cold water. They are much embarrassed to be discovered at this humble meal by Colonel Ollendorf, who greets the ladies and begs leave to present Prince Wybitzky, the Polish millionaire, who has come to Cracow in search of a wife. Symon is now presented in his disguise, and a mutual attraction between himself and Laura is immediately established. It is love at first sight, and it is not long before he has proposed and been accepted—much to the delight of Laura's mother and, of course, Colonel Ollendorf. Symon tenderly sings to Laura:

and Laura replies with all the joy in her heart:

The act ends with rejoicing and congratulations and the curtain falls on a rousing march song accompanied by the Cracow Town Band.

ACT II

One week has elapsed—a week during which all Cracow society has been agog with excitement at the prospect of Laura's marriage to the wealthy Prince Wybitzky. Today is the wedding day and Countess Nowalska and Laura are at home awaiting the arrival of the bridegroom. A tenderness has also sprung up between Bronislawa and Jan. Symon now arrives for his wedding in an agitated state. He has fallen genuinely in love with Laura and feels that he cannot bring himself to marry her under false pretences. He confides in Jan, but Jan is too full of his own news to listen. He tells Symon that he is not the student Symon imagines him to be, but aide-de-camp to the King of Poland. The King's nephew, Duke Casimir, is in Cracow and the rebellion against the Saxons may break out at any moment. All the Duke is waiting for is two hundred thousand crowns from the King with which to bribe the commander of the garrison and then the fun will really begin. When Jan has left, Laura arrives and the lovers join in a duet:

Symon cannot bring himself to confess to Laura his true circumstances and decides to write her a letter. But Colonel Ollendorf hears of Symon's intentions. He tries to reason with Symon and to intercept the fatal letter, but Symon gives it to Laura's mother with the request that Laura read it before the wedding. Ollendorf craftily takes the Countess aside and tells her that the letter concerns Laura's dress allowance. Surely it is a little tactless of the young millionaire to discuss money matters with his bride on their wedding day, he says: it would be more fitting for her to receive it after the ceremony. Laura's mother agrees with the Colonel and eventually entrusts the letter to his safe keeping. There follows a conversation between the Colonel and Jan. The Colonel tells him that he has received a dispatch from Warsaw informing him that Jan is in fact Count Opalinski, aide-de-camp to King Stanislaus. "The Minister of War," he continues, "says that you know the present whereabouts of Duke Adam Casimir. Tell me where he is and you shall have fifty thousand crowns." They eventually come to terms, and Jan agrees to betray his country for two hundred thousand crowns cash down as soon as the wedding ceremony is over. By the time Colonel Ollendorf and Jan arrive at the wedding, Symon and Laura are man and wife. The wedding breakfast is followed by a dance, and a mazurka is in full swing when there is an interruption. Led by their gaoler, a mob of convicts storms into the room, half drunk and singing tipsily. Colonel Ollendorf announces that they are friends of the bridegroom, and while the gaoler ostentatiously presents Laura with a bouquet, the convicts swarm round Symon with noisy congratulations. Colonel Ollendorf cynically tells Laura that "His Highness Prince Wybitzky" was just a little joke. The bridegroom is nothing more nor less than a beggar student let out of prison and provided by the Colonel with money and clothes. "But why have you done all this?" asks Laura, and the Colonel replies:

And poor Laura realises that, as the victim of a cruel vengeance, she is now married to a beggar, and a criminal.

ACT III

The last act takes place in the garden of the Nowalska Palace. Symon, in despair over the loss of Laura, is found by Jan, who is full of news. He tells Symon how he has extracted two hundred thousand crowns from Colonel Ollendorf ostensibly to betray the whereabouts of Duke Adam Casimir. The money is really going to be used to buy off the commander of the garrison, and all Duke Casimir will have to do is to march into Cracow. But Colonel Ollendorf must be provided with a dummy. "That is where you come in," Jan tells him. "You mean I'm to pretend to be the Duke?" asks Symon. "Exactly," says Jan. "Will you do it, Symon, for Poland?" And of course Symon consents. At this moment Colonel Ollendorf is seen approaching. "I've told him you're the Duke," whispers Jan. "Now act for your life." Ollendorf is about to arrest "the Duke" when Laura's mother appears. Seeing Symon, she vents her wrath upon him, calling him "reptile, wastrel, crook and gaolbird". When she pauses for breath, Ollendorf blandly announces that Symon is in fact Duke Adam Casimir, now in German custody. Immediately the Countess' abuse becomes a paean of praise to the "Champion, Defender, Guardian and Patron", and in a gleeful aside to her daughter she says: "You're a Duchess, Laura dear." This scene is interrupted by a sudden burst of gun-fire from the citadel, and Jan rushes in to announce that Duke Adam Casimir has captured the city. The operetta ends with the surrender of Colonel Ollendorf as Governor while Bronislawa surrenders to her Jan—Count Opalinski—and Laura to her beggar student.

Das Theater-an-der-Wien in which were given the first performances of Mozart's *The Magic Flute*, Beethoven's *Fidelio*, Johann Strauss's *Die Fledermaus*, and Lehár's *The Merry Widow*

Franz von Suppé

Austrian National Library

Johann Strauss (son)

K. k. priv. Theater  an der Wien.

Unter der Direktion Geistinger & Steiner.

Sonntag den 5. April 1874.

Die Fledermaus.

Komische Operette in 3 Akten nach Meilhac und Halevy's *„Reveillon"*, bearbeitet von C. Haffner und Richard Genée. **Musik von Johann Strauss.**

Tänze arrangirt von der Balletmeisterin Frau Therese v Kilany.

Die neuen Dekorationen des ersten und zweiten Aktes von Herrn Alfred Moser. — Die neuen Kostüme angefertigt vom Obergarderobier Herrn Schulze.

Möbel von Aug. Kitschelt's Erben (Rudolf Kitschelt), k. k. Hoflieferant.

Gabriel von Eisenstein, Rentier	Hr. Szika.
Rosalinde, seine Frau	Marie Geistinger.
Frank, Gefängniß-Direktor	Hr. Friese.
Prinz Orlofski	Frl Nittinger.
Alfred, sein Gesanglehrer	Hr. Rüdinger.
Dr. Falke, Notar	Hr. Lebrecht.
Dr. Blind, Advokat	Hr. Rott.
Adele, Stubenmädchen Rosalindens	Fr. Charles Hirsch a. G.
Ali-Bey, ein Egypter	Hr. Romani.
Ramusin, Gesandschafts-Attaché	Hr. Jäger.
Murray, Amerikaner	Hr. Liebold.
Carikoni, ein Marquis	Hr. Thalboth.
Lord Middleton	Hr Fink.
Baron Oskar	Hr. Mellin.
Frosch, Gerichtsdiener	Hr. Schreiber.
Yvan, Kammerdiener des Prinzen	Hr. Gärtner.
Ida, (Gäste des Prinzen Orlofski)	Frl. Jules.
Melanie, (Gäste des Prinzen Orlofski)	Frl. Kopf.
Felicita, (Gäste des Prinzen Orlofski)	Frl. Schindler.
Sidi, (Gäste des Prinzen Orlofski)	Frl Treuge.
Minni, (Gäste des Prinzen Orlofski)	Frl. R. Grünfeld.
Faustine, (Gäste des Prinzen Orlofski)	Frl. A. Grünfeld.
Silvia, (Gäste des Prinzen Orlofski)	Frl. Künzler.
Sabine, (Gäste des Prinzen Orlofski)	Frl. Stubel.
Bertha, (Gäste des Prinzen Orlofski)	Frl. Steinburg.
Lori, (Gäste des Prinzen Orlofski)	Frl Tonner.
Paula, (Gäste des Prinzen Orlofski)	Fr. Romani.
Erster (Diener des Prinzen)	Hr. Buchner.
Zweiter (Diener des Prinzen)	Hr. Kaschke.
Ein Amtsdiener	Hr. Schwellak.

Herren und Damen. Masken. Bediente.

Die Handlung spielt in einem Badeorte, in der Nähe einer großen Stadt.

Vorkommende Tänze:

1. **Spanisch**, ausgeführt von Frl. Grillich und 8 Damen vom Ballet.
2. **Schottisch**, Frl. Geraldini, Fechtner, Wollschack, Meier und Wiest.
3. **Russisch**, Frl. Angelina Bonesi, Frl. Stuvenvou, Nagelschmidt, Gwetkofsky, Guhr, Schmidt und Graßeli.
4. **Polka**, Frl. Walter, Frl. Raab und Anna Thorn.
5. **Ungarisch**, ausgeführt von Frl Benda und Herrn Couqui.

Anfang 7 Uhr.

K. k. Hoftheater-Druckerei. (B. R. St B.)

Playbill of the first performance of *Die Fledermaus*

Page of Johann Strauss's manuscript full score of Barinkay's entrance song from *Der Zigeunerbaron* (*The Gipsy Baron*)

Austrian National Library

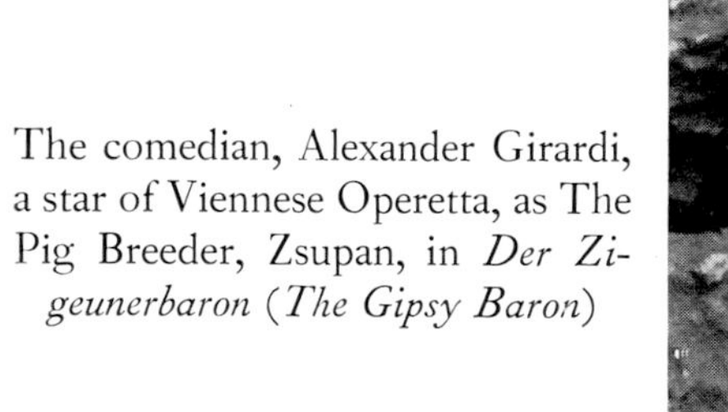

The comedian, Alexander Girardi, a star of Viennese Operetta, as The Pig Breeder, Zsupan, in *Der Zigeunerbaron* (*The Gipsy Baron*)

Carl Millöcker

Karl Felix Schweighofer as "Colonel Ollendorf" in Millöcker's *Der Bettelstudent* (*The Beggar Student*)

Gasparone

Operetta in Three Acts

By F. ZELL (CAMILLO WALZEL) *and* RICHARD GENÉE

Music by KARL MILLÖCKER

First produced on 26th January, 1884, at the Theater an der Wien, Vienna, with Maria Theresa Massa as "Carlotta" and Josef Joseffy as "Erminio". Revised by Eduard Rogati and Paul Burkhardt in 1938.

Note. This synopsis follows the revised version.

CHARACTERS

THE GOVERNOR OF SICILY
CARLOTTA, *widowed Countess of Santa Croce*
CABOLENO NASONI, *Chief of Police*
SINDULFO, *his son*
COUNT ERMINIO, *a mystery man*
BENOZZO, *a landlord*
SORA, *his wife*
LUIGI, TONIO } *smugglers*
CHORUS OF LADIES AND GENTLEMEN, TOWNSFOLK, PEASANTS AND FISHERMEN, CARABINIERI, DANCERS

The action takes place in and around Syracuse at the beginning of the nineteenth century.

ACT I

The scene is set outside Benozzo's inn on the sea-coast near Syracuse on the island of Sicily in the year 1820. The inn is the headquarters of a band of smugglers, and to distract the attention of the police and thus leave themselves free to carry out their "runs" of contraband, the smugglers have invented a brigand, "Gasparone", to whom they attribute all the crimes of the neighbourhood. To add conviction to their legend of Gasparone, the smugglers are delighted to accede to the request of Count Erminio, a rather mysterious character, to waylay the Countess Carlotta Santa Croce during a drive through the forest, and abduct her old dragon of a companion. Erminio, who is anxious to get to know Countess Carlotta, proposes to play the part of her intrepid protector. Everything goes according to plan, and Carlotta is obviously attracted to Erminio, while he kisses her hand in fervent admiration. Signor Nasoni, Chief of Police, who is always being called out to catch Gasparone—and always fails to do so—considers Count Erminio's presence at the attack on Carlotta highly suspicious. He suspects that the Count is Gasparone, and does not share Carlotta's admiration for her rescuer. Nasoni is bent on bringing about a marriage between Carlotta and his son, the ne'er-do-well Sindulfo, for Carlotta, a widow, is involved in an action over her late husband's will, which if she wins will make her enormously wealthy. Nasoni is determined to secure a daughter-in-law rich enough to be able to pay his considerable debts, and he therefore persuades Carlotta that only through his personal influence can she hope to win the action—although he has private information that the Court of Naples has already decided the case in her favour. Nasoni also impresses on his worthless son the importance of attracting Carlotta. Anxious as Sindulfo is to get rid of Erminio, however, he spends most of his time hanging about Sora, the pretty young wife of the innkeeper-cum-smuggler, Benozzo. News now comes from Naples that Carlotta has won her case and, convinced that she owes the victory to Nasoni, she engages herself to Sindulfo. In vain Erminio warns her against both Nasoni and Sindulfo: she feels it her duty to be a daughter to the man who has earned her gratitude. Carlotta receives the congratulations of all the peasantry and calls for music and dancing, while Sora, supported by a lusty chorus, strikes up a gay Tarantella:

The curtain comes down on a scene of colour, movement and swirling skirts.

ACT II

Scene i. As Carlotta sits alone in the boudoir in her castle, her thoughts are far more of Erminio than they are of her fiancé, Sindulfo. But when Erminio for the second time warns her against Nasoni and his machinations, the idea flashes through her mind that Erminio himself might be Gasparone. Nasoni's suspicions of a similar nature are strengthened by a passage in a letter from the Governor of the Province, who, in announcing his prospective visit, instructs Nasoni to "Keep a watchful eye on a certain Count Erminio". Erminio and Carlotta are sitting together in tender tête-à-tête. Erminio has brought her flowers and sings her a song of love:

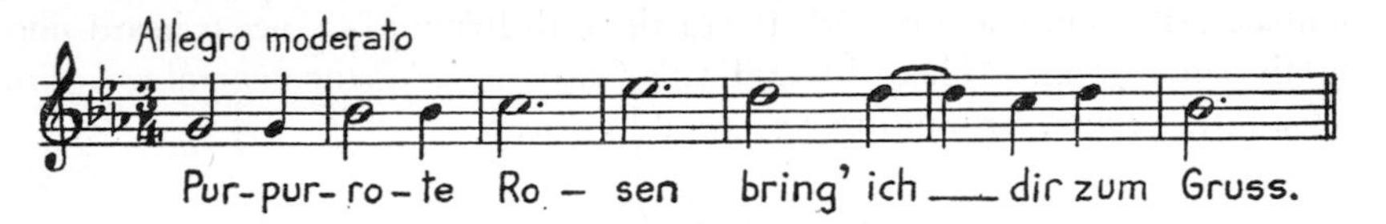

Their tête-à-tête is interrupted by the entrance of Nasoni. Finding the suspect closeted with Carlotta, he is about to have him arrested when Erminio leaps agilely through the window and escapes. Meanwhile Sindulfo has been taken prisoner by Benozzo and the other smugglers and is being held in a cave. Benozzo, pretending concern, bursts in on Carlotta and Nasoni to give the alarm that Sindulfo has been captured by Gasparone. He hands Nasoni a note, demanding ten thousand ceccini ransom money. Of course Carlotta immediately puts the money at Nasoni's disposal and, although the avaricious Nasoni would prefer to pocket the money himself, he is forced to hand it over to Benozzo in order to procure Sindulfo's liberty. Nasoni has been in a state of perturbation ever since he received warning of the Governor's prospective visit, for he has been helping himself liberally to Government funds and there is a serious deficiency in monies under his charge, which he fears the Governor is bound to detect. Nasoni confides his awkward predicament to Carlotta. and again she generously agrees to help him, but gradually doubts as to his honesty begin to assail her. As she is pondering the matter alone, Erminio appears through the window and coolly demands at the point of a pistol her entire fortune. He accompanies his demand with a gay bandit's song:

Then, as Erminio vanishes through the window with Carlotta's fortune, there is no longer any doubt in her mind as to Gasparone's identity.

Scene 2. The scene is a salon in the castle. News of the dastardly robbery has spread abroad, but Carlotta keeps silent as to the thief's identity. The police are also hot on the scent of the criminal who captured Sindulfo. In the excitement they make several false arrests. First, Benozzo and a fellow smuggler are brought in, only to be released again, for Benozzo declares that when he went to hand over the money he was set upon by Gasparone and the money was forcibly taken from him without Sindulfo being released. The third prisoner to be brought in by the police turns out to be Sindulfo. He describes his imprisonment in a cave that smelt strongly of coffee and sugar (some of the smugglers' contraband) and how in the darkness he heard a voice that seemed familiar. At this moment outside the castle walls Erminio's voice is heard singing his bandit song. "That's him. That's Gasparone," is the general cry. But, to Carlotta's relief, Erminio makes good his escape.

ACT III

Sindulfo, on whom imprisonment has had a sobering effect, is now willing to settle down to a steady life and marry Carlotta. But now that she has lost her fortune Nasoni will not hear of the match. At last Carlotta realises Erminio's reason for staging his "robbery" of her fortune, though he is still wanted by the police, and when he manages to visit her, she no longer attempts to hide her love for him. When Nasoni and the police come to arrest Gasparone, Erminio follows them willingly to prison. In due course the Governor arrives on his visit and demands that Gasparone be led before him. But the prison cell, instead of containing Erminio, is occupied by his servant, Luigi, for Carlotta has had her lover secretly brought to the castle. Erminio turns out to be the Governor's son and he now takes Carlotta as his bride. As for Gasparone, Carlotta declares that he is a reformed character and has returned her fortune. So all ends happily.

Der Vogelhändler
(The Bird-seller)

Operetta in Three Acts

By MORITZ WEST *and* LUDWIG HELD

Based on an idea by BIÉVILLE

Music by KARL ZELLER

First produced on 10th January, 1891, at the Theater an der Wien, Vienna, with Alexander Girardi as "Adam", Ilka Palmay as "Christel" and Ottilie Collin as "Princess Marie". First London production (in German) on 17th June, 1895, at the Theatre Royal, Drury Lane. Revived on 29th May, 1947, at the Palace Theatre (in English), with Adele Dixon as "Princess Marie", Irene Ambrus as "Christel" and James Etherington as "Adam". The conductor was Richard Tauber.

CHARACTERS

BARON WEPS, *Master of the Royal Hunt*
COUNT STANISLAUS, *his nephew*
HERR SCHNECK, *Burgomaster*
ADAM, *the Bird-seller*
CHRISTEL, *his fiancée*
PRINCESS MARIE
ADELAIDE, COUNTESS MINNE, *her lady-in-waiting*
SÜFFLE } *two professors*
WÜRMCHEN }
CHORUS OF TYROLEAN VILLAGERS AND COURTIERS

The action takes place in the Rheinpfalz in the eighteenth century.

ACT I

The first act takes place in a village in the valley of the Rhine at the beginning of the eighteenth century. The reigning Prince of the Province has announced his intention of coming to hunt wild boar in the district, and has sent on his

Master of the Royal Hunt, Baron Weps, in advance to organise the hunt. To his dismay the Baron discovers that over a period of years the peasants have indulged in poaching to such an extent that there are now no wild boar left. In a somewhat embarrassing conversation, the Burgomaster, Herr Schneck, proposes to provide some tame sows as substitutes for the wild boar and silences Baron Weps with a considerable financial *douceur*. Baron Weps badly needs this money to pay the debts of his nephew, Count Stanislaus, a handsome but flighty Guards officer. No sooner is this financial transaction concluded than an order reaches the Baron from his royal master to cancel the hunt. Now the Baron has not the slightest intention of foregoing his convenient "hush-money". So he arranges with Stanislaus to impersonate the Prince, whose appearance is unfamiliar to the peasants.

There now arrives on the scene a cheerful young man, who hails from the Tyrol. He is a bird-catcher by profession and his name is Adam. He receives a rousing welcome from the villagers to this jolly tune:

Adam has come to pay a visit to his fiancée, Christel, the attractive young village post-mistress. He is an ebullient character, and the fact that he is engaged does nothing to prevent him flirting outrageously with a pretty peasant girl called Marie whom he meets in the village. He does not know that the pretty peasant girl is really Princess Marie, the Prince's consort, who is travelling in disguise with her Lady-in-Waiting, Adelaide, Countess Minne, hoping to keep an eye on her royal husband. When Adam meets his Christel she tells him with shining eyes of her intention to seize the opportunity of the Prince's visit to apply to him on Adam's behalf for the job of Director of the Royal Menagerie. Adam is opposed to her plan. The Prince has a bad reputation with women and he is filled with jealousy and foreboding at the thought of Christel visiting him. But Christel is a determined young woman and not to be diverted from her intention. She visits a small pavilion which the Prince is occupying and returns smiling. Stanislaus in his role of "The Prince" has graciously granted her request. Adam, furiously jealous, has unworthy suspicions as to the nature of the price which Christel paid to achieve her purpose. Angrily he turns his back on her and renews his attentions to the peasant girl, Marie. The Princess, who believes that her husband is in fact occupying the pavilion, is aware of the anger of both Adam and the peasants and their suspicions of the Prince's behaviour to Christel. So to distract their attention from the Prince and to focus it on herself, she presents Adam with a bouquet of roses from the Tyrol, which he accepts believing it to be a token of her love:

The curtain falls on a situation of grief and jealousy between Christel and Adam.

ACT II

Under the patronage of the Princess, Adam is called to the palace to be interviewed for the job of Director of the Royal Menagerie by an appointments board consisting of two elderly professors, Süffle and Würmchen. Adam does not want the job, for nothing will persuade him to accept a post from the Prince whom he believes to be Christel's seducer, and he tries to fail by giving every stupid answer to their questions that he can think of. However, he passes and is appointed. The Princess is convinced from Christel's account of her experience in the pavilion that it must really have been her husband who tried to kiss the girl, but to make absolutely sure of the facts and to expose the guilty party, the Princess and Christel arrange that Christel shall watch for his arrival at the palace and announce it by ringing a bell.

Meanwhile Baron Weps is in a state bordering on despair. His nephew's debts are by now so enormous as to be quite beyond his control. So he has compelled Stanislaus to propose to the wealthy but elderly Countess Adelaide. He is joyfully accepted and Baron Weps proceeds to present the newly engaged pair to the Princess. As they enter the throne room for the formal presentation, Christel's bell rings and Stanislaus is revealed as the impersonator of the Prince. As it is he who has jeopardised Adam's honour, Adam is given the task of passing judgement on Stanislaus. The new Menagerie Director decides to offer Stanislaus the choice of being cashiered from the Guards or of marrying Christel. In vain Christel protests her innocence and Adelaide bewails the loss of her bridegroom: Stanislaus has to make up his mind and he decides to marry Christel.

ACT III

The last act takes place in the palace park and contains an enchanting solo in the manner of a folk-song for the Princess:

Since Adam has discovered that his little peasant girl, Marie, and the Princess are one and the same person, and so quite beyond his reach, his thoughts of love have returned to his beloved Christel. Christel herself is heart-broken by Adam's desertion. Quite by chance Adam overhears in conversation Christel telling Stanislaus that she cannot possibly marry him, and he also learns from their talk that the episode in which Christel petitioned "The Prince" on his behalf was a perfectly innocent affair. So Adam and Christel are reconciled and decide to leave the palace and seek their fortune in the Tyrol, while old Adelaide is reunited to her handsome Stanislaus.

Der Opernball
(The Opera Ball)

Operetta in Three Acts

By VIKTOR LÉON *and* H. VON WALDBERG

Adapted from the farce Les Dominos Roses
by DELACOURS *and* HENNEQUIN

Music by RICHARD HEUBERGER

First produced on 5th January, 1898, at the Theater an der Wien, Vienna, with Anna Dirkens as "Hortense".

CHARACTERS

BEAUBISSON
MADAME BEAUBISSON, *his wife*
HENRI, *a sea-cadet, their nephew*
PAUL AUBIER
ANGÈLE, *his wife*
GEORGES DUMÉNIL
MARGUÉRITE, *his wife*
HORTENSE, *their maid*
FÉODORA, *a dancer*
PHILIPPE, *a head waiter*

ACT I

The first act takes place in the apartment of Georges and Marguérite Duménil, a young married couple. It is carnival time in Paris and the Duménils have staying with them another married couple, Paul and Angèle Aubier. They come from Orléans, where Paul is in business. Angèle has an old aunt and uncle, Monsieur and Madame Beaubisson, living in Paris, who come to call on her. Madame Beaubisson is a regular old dragon with a sadly hen-pecked husband, and she disapproves of the Duménils, whom she considers "fast". She asks Angèle how she is enjoying her visit to Paris. Angèle is enthusiastic: "The world is a beautiful place, but Paris is like the most beautiful rose in a beautiful bouquet":

The two husbands are extremely gay dogs in perpetual pursuit of pretty women. Their motto is "Live for today and the more the merrier". Their wives differ greatly in character. While Marguérite has her eyes wide open and has no illusions as to Georges's "goings on", Angèle is under the delusion that Paul is the perfect husband and is deeply sympathetic about his constant absences "on business" (for Paul has a well-trained secretary, prepared at any moment to dispatch a telegram summoning him to a "conference"). The two wives happen to be discussing their husbands when Marguérite calmly volunteers the fact that she would not trust hers farther than she could see him and she expects that Paul is much the same. Angèle is indignant, and when Marguérite proposes a plan to put his constancy to the test, Angèle agrees without a qualm. Marguérite's plan is to send two anonymous letters on scented note-paper to George and Paul, making appointments to meet the writer that night at the Opera Ball at midnight under the clock. The fair anonymous will be masked and will wear a pink domino. Angèle is not quite happy about the joke. Is she, she wonders, behaving quite fairly to her husband? But Marguérite is a determined woman. She summons her maid, Hortense, sits her down at the writing-table and dictates the two letters:

When the letters are written, Hortense is instructed to deliver them to Messieurs Duménil and Aubier. It now only remains to buy Angèle a pink domino. Marguérite already has one, but Hortense protests that it is too shabby and faded to wear to the Opera Ball, and so Marguérite decides to join Angèle in buying a new one. This suits Hortense admirably. Now she can go to the Opera Ball in her mistress's discarded domino. But who can she get as partner? She decides on Henri, a young Marine cadet who is just at the age when a young man falls in love with every girl he meets, and she sends him a third anonymous note. When the two husbands receive their anonymous invitations they both fall delightedly head first into the trap. Paul arranges for the usual telegram to be sent, summoning him to Orleans "on business", and Hortense gleefully tells Angèle that Monsieur Aubier's packing for his "business trip" includes a tail-coat and white waistcoat. During dinner the telegram is duly delivered and Paul puts on a fine acting performance of dismay and disappointment, cursing the Post Office and all its works.

ACT II

Act Two takes place in the foyer of the Opera House, Paris, on the night of the annual Opera Ball. On the right is the entrance to the ballroom, and at the back of the set can be seen the doors of four boxes, numbered 1, 2, 3 and 4 respectively. These boxes have been fitted out as private rooms or *chambres-separées* for the occasion. In addition to Marguérite, Angèle, Hortense, George, Paul and Henri, old Monsieur Beaubisson has decided to attend the Opera

Ball. He is a grass widower for the night and has picked up a promising-looking cocotte, Fédora, and is looking forward to enjoying himself with her. But Fédora, after engaging a *chambre-separée* (number one) and ordering an expensive supper, gets bored with the old man and tells him that she is going dancing and disappears for the rest of the evening. The next arrivals are Henri and Hortense, Hortense is masked and wearing her mistress' pink domino. Young Henri, out with a girl for the first time, is shy of his fair, anonymous partner, but Hortense soon puts him at his ease, luring him into a *chambre-separée* in this well-known duet:

They disappear into number three and shut the door. Hot on their heels follow Georges with Angèle and Paul with Marguérite. The ladies are masked and are wearing pink dominoes. Both couples are duly accommodated in *chambre-separées*, numbers two and four. Marguérite and Angèle, independently, take the precaution to warn the head waiter that if they should ring in an agitated manner, he is to knock on the door of the appropriate *chambre-separée* and announce that Monsieur Paul and/or Monsieur Georges is wanted urgently. Obviously neither wife has any confidence in the capacity of her friend's husband to behave himself. Paul, a country cousin from Orleans, is concerned to know whether his "fair anonymous" is a genuine Parisienne. Marguérite pretends to be insulted by his doubts and is at pains to prove her authenticity in this duet:

Presently the bells in numbers two and four both ring in agitation. Evidently the gentlemen are becoming very ardent. The head waiter, true to his promise, bangs on both doors, paging Messieurs Georges and Paul. Both men dash out and laughingly recognise each other, but finding no one there, they go off in different directions in search of the head waiter. Hortense now appears from number three, where Henri, exhausted in the lists of love, has dropped off to sleep. She is alone in the foyer when George returns. He naturally mistakes Hortense for his "fair anonymous", for, like Angèle and Marguérite, she is masked and wears a pink domino. Georges, who has drunk a lot of champagne, makes ardent love to Hortense, watched with amusement by his wife, Marguérite, who of course imagines he is kissing Angèle. No sooner has Georges returned to his *chambre-separée* than Paul arrives. He also mistakes Hortense for his girl-friend and covers her with kisses, to the horror of Angèle, who is affronted to behold her model husband abandoning himself, as she believes, to the charms of Marguérite. Hortense is thankful to see the back of both of them. Apart from not relishing their kisses, Georges has burnt a hole in her domino with a cigarette and Paul has torn the shoulder. As for the two wives, they have had quite enough of the Opera Ball and call for their wraps. But by now dancing in the ballroom has got quite out of hand. Overflowing from the dance-floor into the foyer a crocodile of riotous revellers engulfs and separates Marguérite, Angèle and Hortense from Georges, Paul and Henri. And the curtain falls on a mad confusion in Galop tempo.

ACT III

The scene is the same as that of Act One—the living-room in Georges and Marguérite Duménil's apartment in Paris. It is the morning following the Opera Ball, and an exhausted Hortense is attempting to cope with household chores. The opening scene—a musical monologue, in which she reviews the events of the ball—is a palpable copy of the famous return to the prison of the Governor, Herr Frank, after Prince Orlovsky's Ball in the third act of Johann Strauss' operetta *Die Fledermaus*. The day begins by Georges discovering in a drawer some writing-paper identical with that on which his anonymous invitation to the Opera Ball was written. Putting two and two together he realises that the invitations to himself and Paul were sent by their respective wives, and he is able to warn Paul to this effect on his "return" from his "business trip". The two men go in immediately to the attack, informing their wives that they are aware of their presence at the Opera Ball, which greatly disconcerts the ladies. Each husband, however, is under the impression that he was in the *chambre-separée* with his own wife, and when it comes out in the post mortem argument that each was apparently making love to the other's wife, there is a row royal which almost leads to a duel. The truth comes to light when Georges apologises for burning his partner's domino and Paul for tearing the shoulder of his. Both wives deny any knowledge of such incidents and exhibit their dominoes as proof. Finally, Henri produces his anonymous invitation in the same handwriting as the other two, and Hortense's share in the proceedings is exposed, to the acute embarrassment of both husbands. Paul is particularly concerned, and voices a final appeal to Hortense to assure him that she is, at least, a Parisienne. But when she informs him that she is no Parisienne but, like himself, a native of Orleans, his cup is full.

Das Süsse Mädel
(The Sweet Girl)

Operetta in Three Acts

By ALEXANDER LANDESBERG *and* LEO STEIN

Music by HEINRICH RHEINHARDT

First produced on 5th October, 1901, at the Carl Theater, Vienna. London production, with English adaptation by E. Demain Grange and additional music by Ernest Irving, on 26th July, 1902, at the Princess of Wales' Theatre, Kennington, with Claudia Lasell.

CHARACTERS

COUNT BALDUIN VON LIEBENBURG
LIZZI, *his niece*
COUNT HANS VON LIEBENBURG, *his nephew*
LOLA WINTER, *a cabaret star*
FLORIAN LIEBLICH, *a painter*
FRITZI WEYRINGER, *his fiancée, a masseuse*
PROSPER PLEVNY, *a secretary*
CHORUS OF ARTISTS, MODELS, GUESTS AND SERVANTS, ETC.

ACT I

The scene is the elegant living-room of a well-to-do bachelor, Count Hans von Liebenburg. Statues, busts and easels, scattered about the room, reveal it as the home of an artist. A party is in progress and the guests, consisting of painters and their pretty models, are in good form, for their host has seen to it that there is plenty of champagne. There is loud applause for the cabaret star, Lola Winter, who is persuaded to sing the song that has brought her fame:

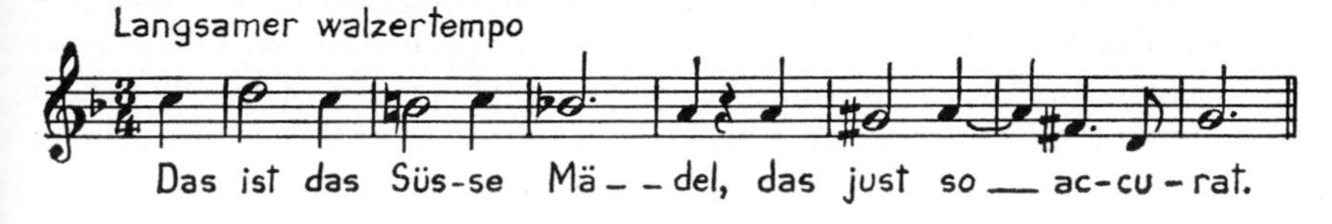

Lola is anxious to marry Hans von Liebenburg, but Hans holds back, afraid to face the effect upon his family of such a misalliance. Like a bolt from the blue there now arrives at the party Hans' uncle, Count Balduin von Liebenburg. He has come to urge his nephew to accompany him back to his country house. It is time Hans got married, and his uncle is anxious for him to get engaged to his cousin Lizzi. Hans is not at all taken with this idea, but he dare not make public his affection for Lola. He introduces her to his uncle as Baroness Ebenstreit, and a friend, the painter Florian Lieblich, poses as her husband. The elderly Count Balduin von Liebenburg takes a violent fancy to Lola and invites her and her "husband" to visit him for the celebration of Hans' engagement. Lola accepts, though Florian is nervous of the reaction to all this of his own girl-friend, an energetic masseuse called Fritzi Weyringer. The old Count tells Hans that he knows of his affair with the famous cabaret star, Lola Winter, but that it is nothing to worry about. He himself in his youth got involved with such a woman and had had to drop her owing to their difference of birth. However, an illegitimate child was the result of the affair. He has lost track of the mother and does not even know whether the child was a girl or a boy. Lola now tells the old Count that on second thoughts she and her "husband" have decided to rent a villa in the neighbourhood of his house. She is determined to be on hand to prevent at any cost her beloved Hans from marrying Lizzi. The curtain falls on a song describing "The Villa by the Lake":

ACT II

The scene of Act Two is another party. This time it takes place in the drawing-room of Count Balduin von Liebenburg's castle. The party has been organised by the Count's secretary, Prosper Plevny. He is secretly in love with Lizzi, and she is determined to marry him, and not Hans, her uncle's choice for a husband. The old Count is anxious for Hans to announce his engagement to Lizzi, but no proposal occurs, for Lola, who is close at hand, never allows Hans to get near enough to Lizzi to propose. During the party Fritzi Weyringer arrives at the castle in a jealous mood to discover what her boy-friend, Florian, is up to, and she is shattered to find him posing as the husband of Lola. But she is disturbed during her investigation and takes refuge in a closet. As ill luck will have it, this closet is Count Balduin von Liebenburg's secret cellar. Officially he poses as a teetotaller, but in reality he enjoys a nip in private. The only person who knows the Count's secret is his secretary, Prosper, and he is just helping himself to a drink when he is caught by the Count and is promptly dismissed.

Fritzi is also discovered in the closet. The Count questions her about her family and origins, and from her conversation believes that in her he has found his illegitimate child. Another conclusion to which the old Count comes from his conversation with Fritzi is that she is none other than Lola Winter, the famous cabaret star and his nephew's mistress. He tenderly invites his "long-lost daughter" to remain with him, and as the party fun becomes livelier he begs "the famous cabaret star" to sing her well-known song. Fritzi makes a feeble attempt, but breaks down, and Lola, unable to bear competition of any kind, launches into the song to tumultuous applause. The old Count, who has visited his secret cellar several times during the party, is now terribly confused. Lola is obviously no dilettante, while the other girl is no professional singer. He shakes his head in perplexity as the curtain falls on all the guests singing Lola's rousing song.

ACT III

Act Three takes place in the villa which Lola has rented. Hans, who is weary of all the excitements and efforts to make him marry Lizzi, has proposed to Lola and she is ecstatically happy. Fritzi has forgiven Florian for his desertion and the four friends are blissful. But the old Count has still not given up hope of seeing Hans married to Lizzi, and he still believes Fritzi to be Lola Winter, his nephew's mistress. Accordingly he seeks Fritzi out to enlist her aid, and offers her twenty thousand Austrian shillings to give up Hans. Fritzi manages to push the price up to one hundred thousand cash down, and the Count is quite happy to hand over this sum to the girl he believes to be his own daughter. In fact, he had already deposited such a sum with his solicitor, Dr. Müller, in case his child should ever reappear. Fritzi in return for the money signs a paper undertaking to give up all claim to Hans. Finally, Prosper, the lately dismissed secretary, reappears and asks for Lizzi's hand in marriage. The old Count is furious and calls him a good-for-nothing pauper. "But I'm not," protests Prosper. "I've received a hundred thousand shillings from a solicitor, Dr. Müller, who tells me that they are from my father." "And who *is* your father?" asks the Count. "That is the trouble," Prosper tells him. "I don't know." Then it dawns on the Count that Prosper is his long-lost child. He resigns himself to the loss of the hundred thousand shillings to Fritzi, and the curtain falls on the union of three happy pairs.

Wiener Frauen

(The Girls of Vienna)

Operetta in Three Acts

By OTTOKAR TANN-BERGLER *and* EMIL NORINI

Music by FRANZ LEHÁR

First produced on 25th November, 1902, at the Theater an der Wien, Vienna, with Alexander Girardi as "Nechledil" and Hansi Niese as "Claire". This was the first of Lehár's long and successful series of operettas.

CHARACTERS

PHILIP ROSNER
CLAIRE SCHROTT, *his bride*
GEORGE, *his valet*
JOHANN NEPOMUK NECHLEDIL, *proprietor of an Academy of Music*
FINI, *his daughter*
WILLIBALD BRANDL, *a piano-tuner*
FRAU SCHROTT, *Claire's mother*
DR. WINTERSTEIN, *a lawyer*
CHORUS OF WEDDING GUESTS, MUSIC PUPILS AND GARDEN-PARTY GUESTS

ACT I

Wiener Frauen tells a story of the matrimonial complications of a piano-tuner, and this prompted Lehár to incorporate in the overture a piano solo imitating the effect of a piano-tuner at work—a device both charming and original. Act One takes place in the living-room of the apartment of a certain Philip Rosner. Philip has been married that very morning to Fräulein Claire Schrott, and the guests are partaking of the wedding breakfast in the adjacent dining-room. During the meal the bridegroom slips away to assure himself that the apartment is in perfect readiness for his bride. To his annoyance, however, he discovers that his man-servant, George, has forgotten to have the piano tuned. It is essential that this be done, as Claire is extremely musical. So George goes off to procure a piano-tuner without delay. There now enters a tall, eccentric gentleman of military appearance, accompanied by his eldest daughter. He is the proprietor of an Academy of Music, Johann Nepomuk Nechledil by name. He is slightly and cheerfully drunk, and during the wedding breakfast a waiter has upset a coffee-pot all over him and ruined his shirt. He asks Philip to lend him a clean shirt, and then goes off to change, leaving his daughter, Fini, with Philip. The girl confesses that the atmosphere of the wedding has made her long to get married herself. Philip promises to find her a young man, and the two return to the wedding breakfast.

The piano-tuner now arrives. He is Willibald Brandl, a down-at-heel musician, who went to America to make his fortune, has returned without a penny and now ekes out a precarious living playing the piano by night in a low-class "dive" and tuning pianos by day. Urged on by George, he settles down to tune the piano in a neighbouring room. Frau Schrott, the bride's mother, comes in and opens the door of the nuptial bedroom, but with a scream hurriedly shuts it, exclaiming angrily: "It is usual to lock the door when taking a shower." For she has intruded on Herr Nechledil, sobering up under the cold shower. Frau Schrott is joined by her daughter Claire, whom Lehár has provided with a charming entrance song:

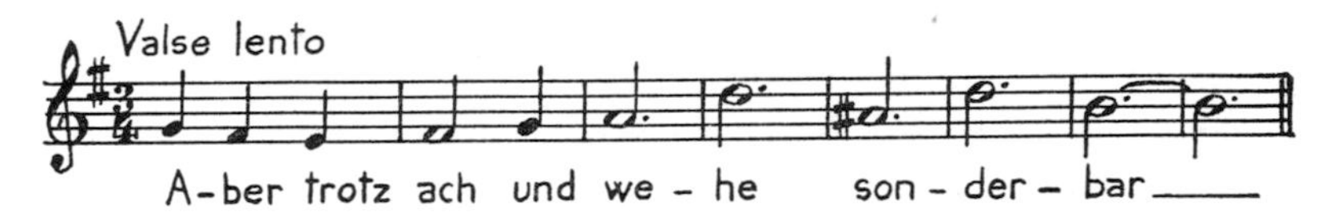

Claire is singularly cast down for a bride on her wedding day, and she confesses to her mother that she is haunted by memories of her childhood—particularly by the memory of the pact she swore with her youthful lover—her piano-teacher—to remain faithful till death. "But I told you he was drowned en route for America," says her mother impatiently. "I cannot forget him or that charming song of his he dedicated to me: 'Lovely Roses'." "Well, anyhow, he's dead now," says her mother, and proceeds to lecture her daughter on how to manage a husband:

After his shower, Herr Nechledil, now quite sober, encounters the piano-tuner, and in the course of conversation he engages him to play dance music on the following day at a party at his Academy of Music to celebrate his fiftieth birthday. The bridal party then enter and after a formal "good-night", the happy pair are left alone. Philip becomes very ardent:

But Claire is still obsessed by the memory of her youthful lover's pact. Suddenly through the wall float the strains of the very song he dedicated to her, sung by his voice:

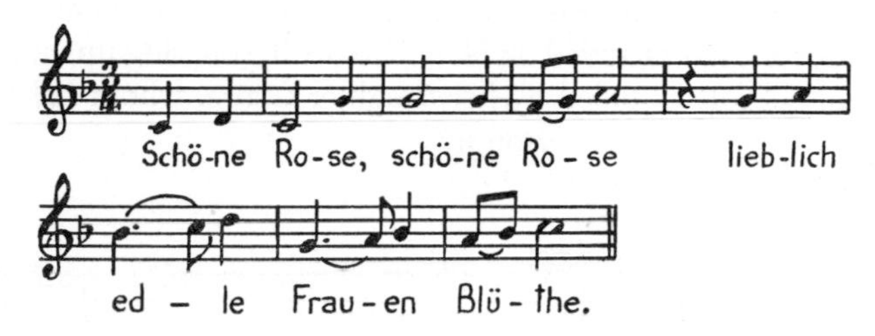

With a cry to Philip "You lied to me, he is alive", she rushes away. Willibald Brandl, the piano-tuner, entering at that moment to announce that his job is done, is set upon by a furious husband and, to his surprise and discomfort, is forcibly ejected.

ACT II

Act Two takes place next evening in the garden of Nechledil's Academy of Music. His fiftieth birthday party is in full swing and the guests include Philip and Frau Schrott. Philip asks his mother-in-law to explain why the playing of a particular song by an unknown piano-tuner should be the cause of her daughter's desertion of her husband on their wedding night. Frau Schrott tells him of Claire's youthful infatuation and how she invented the story that her lover had been drowned en route for America. "Claire was very upset and has never eaten fish since," adds Frau Schrott. "And I must say that shows great delicacy of feeling," is Herr Nechledil's comment. "When I catch that dirty dog, I shall cut off his ears," says Philip belligerently. "But I don't think he is the kind of dog that wears its ears clipped," declares Nechledil.

Willibald Brandl now appears to fulfil his engagement to play dance music at Nechledil's party. He is accompanied by Claire's maid, Jeanette, an attractive Viennese girl, and the two are obviously delighted with each other. But the luckless piano-tuner is swiftly spotted by the outraged Philip who waylays him, and a conversation takes place conducted at the point of a pistol. The result is that poor Brandl, who is convinced that he has to do with a madman, finds himself promising to marry Fini, Herr Nechledil's eldest daughter, the girl for whom Philip in Act One promised to provide a young man. When Philip has finished with him, the piano-tuner is caught by Frau Schrott. Frau Schrott has decided that the only way to effect a reconciliation between her daughter and Philip is for Claire to be convinced that her youthful lover, though he may still be alive, is faithless. So she has decided that Brandl must marry at once, and she has selected Herr Nechledil's second daughter, Lini, as his bride. Under a threat of slow poisoning by vitriol, the piano-tuner consents, still convinced that he has strayed into a lunatic asylum.

Chinese lanterns illuminate the garden for the climax of the party—a production number staged by Herr Nechledil with his academy pupils. Dressed in the uniform of a regimental drum-major, he marches on a platoon of pretty girls to a stirring march refrain, which, after the first night, all Vienna was soon humming:

After prolonged applause for the number has died down, Herr Nechledil goes in search of the piano-tuner and invites him to marry his youngest daughter, Tini. "Everybody in this house seems mad to get married," complains poor Brandl as he refuses. "If you refuse——" threatens Herr Nechledil. "I know," interrupts Brandl. "I shall be shot or poisoned with vitriol." "No," says Nechledil, "made mincemeat of." "But I particularly dislike mincemeat," argues the unhappy piano-tuner. But there is no repeal and the finale of Act Two finds poor Brandl being vilified by Philip, Frau Schrott and Herr Nechledil and pulled in different directions by four women (for Jeanette has also laid claim to his hand). "I'll see you all at the solicitor's," he calls to them as he manages to escape, while the curtain falls on a reprise, fortissimo, of the Nechledil march.

ACT III

The last act is set in the office of Dr. Winterstein, a celebrated divorce lawyer. Hither come the four female claimants to the piano-tuner's hand, with their various supporters. Twist and turn as he may, the unfortunate Brandl cannot escape from the advances of the rapacious women. But when they finally insist that he make up his mind which of the four he proposes to marry, he startles them all by declaring that he can marry none of them. For when he was in America he contracted a marriage with a wealthy negress from the Congo. At this the lawyer pricks up his ears. "What?" he asks. "Are you Willibald Brandl from America?" "I am," he replies. "Then I have news for you," says Dr. Winterstein. "Your wife has obtained a divorce for desertion and you are free to marry again." So Brandl chooses Jeannette. Philip and Claire are reconciled, as everyone assures the disappointed Herr Nechledil that he will soon find husbands for three such pretty daughters, and the curtain comes down on a song in praise of lovely women.

Die Lustige Witwe
(The Merry Widow)

Operetta in Three Acts

By VIKTOR LÉON *and* LEO STEIN

After HENRI MEILHAC'S *comedy* L'Attaché

Music by FRANZ LEHÁR

First produced on 30th December, 1905, at the Theater an der Wien, Vienna, with Mizzi Guenther as "Hanna Glawari" and Louis Treumann as "Danilo". First London production on 8th June, 1907, at Daly's Theatre, with Lily Elsie as "Sonia" ("Hanna Glawari") and Joseph Coyne as "Danilo".

CHARACTERS

BARON MERKO ZETA, *Pontevidrinian Ambassador in Paris*
VALENCIENNE, *his wife*
COUNT DANILO DANILOWITSCH, *Secretary to the Legation*
HANNA GLAWARI, *the Merry Widow*
CAMILLE DE ROSILLON
VICOMTE CASCADA
KROMOW, *Counsellor at the Legation*
OLGA, *his wife*
NJEGUS, *Messenger to the Legation*
CHORUS OF GUESTS, GRISETTES, MUSICIANS AND SERVANTS

The action of *The Merry Widow* takes place in Paris, and the first act is set in the ballroom of the Pontevidrinian Embassy. The problem facing the Pontevidrinian Ambassador, Baron Zeta, is how to save his country from bankruptcy. One solution is to ensure that the beautiful young heiress, Hanna Glawari, does not marry a foreigner. Hanna's husband has recently died, leaving her a fortune of twenty millions, and the Ambassador is determined that the Merry Widow shall marry a Pontevidrinian husband and that her money shall remain in the country. He has decided that young Count Danilo Danilowitsch, one of the Embassy attachés, would be the ideal bridegroom, and the purpose of the reception he is giving that evening is to bring the two together. But the Ambassador is worried. Handsome Danilo, an irresponsible and light-hearted character, has not yet put in an appearance at the party. Owing to his worries, Baron Zeta has failed to observe that his attractive young wife, Valencienne, is in the throes of a violent flirtation with a French officer, Camille de Rosillon. However, Valencienne is only prepared to go so far and no further, and makes this quite clear to Camille.

Soon after this the word goes round that Hanna Glawari has arrived, and the Merry Widow, escorted by a galaxy of hopeful suitors, sweeps into the ballroom. For her entrance Lehar has written an effective waltz refrain in which she ironically tells her escort of gallants that it does occasionally cross her mind that she might be loved more for her millions than for herself:

After her song, the Ambassador escorts Hanna Glawari to supper, and shortly after Count Danilo arrives. He has been traced to his favourite resort "Chez Maxim", where, surrounded by Lolo, Dodo, Jou-Jou, Clo-Clo, Margot, Frou-Frou he has been in his element:

The Ambassador's message which has brought Danilo to the Embassy was an urgent one, but he has not been to bed for four nights and feels he must have a short nap before reporting to the Ambassador. So he lies down on a sofa and is soon fast asleep. Into the deserted ballroom now come Valencienne and Camille, considerably perturbed. As Valencienne has forbidden him to declare his love, Camille has written upon her fan the words "I love you", and now she has lost the fan and it cannot be found anywhere. The search, however, has to be postponed, for Hanna Glawari appears on the scene and Danilo wakes up and greets her. The two are old friends; in fact, Danilo had wanted to marry her, but his uncle threatened to disinherit him and Hanna had married instead the old banker, Glawari, and has now become the Merry Widow, courted by all men. She reminds him of their old affair, but Danilo tells her quite frankly that he will never marry her now because of her millions. Meanwhile Valencienne's fan has been found by a member of the Embassy staff, Counsellor Kromow. He is furiously jealous by nature and, reading the words "I love you" written upon it, assumes that it belongs to his wife, Olga. In order to calm him, the Ambassador begs Valencienne to acknowledge the fan as hers and to tell Kromow that himself. After these complications the Ambassador confides to Danilo that his country requires him to marry Hanna Glawari in order that her millions may not go abroad. Danilo replies that he would marry any other woman, but not Hanna. He promises, however, to save her millions by driving off all other suitors. When "Lady's choice" is announced, Hanna chooses Danilo as her dancing partner. In doing so she realises that her affection for him is still alive in her heart, and to a whirling waltz the curtain falls:

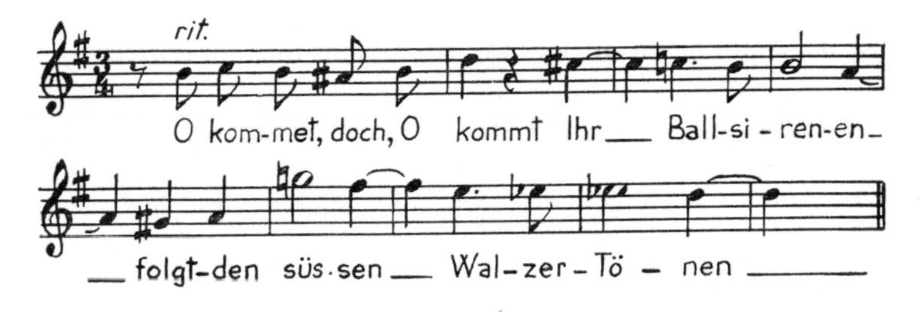

ACT II

Act Two opens at another party; this time in the garden of Hanna Glawari's house. All the Pontevidrinians are in national dress, and Hanna obliges with a national folk-song. This is "Vilia", one of Lehár's greatest successes:

Baron Zeta confides to Danilo the story of the fan, and when Danilo sees the writing on it, he immediately recognises it as Camille's and is all agog to discover who the lady in the case can be. He then runs into Hanna, who is vexed with him for avoiding her. She is now definitely in love with Danilo, and so is he with her, and it is only her wretched millions and his pride that prevent him proposing. In this situation they sing a teasing duet:

But try as she may Hanna cannot extract a declaration from Danilo, and he continues his search of the owner of the fan. In this connection, however, his efforts are of no avail and he has to confess: "You may study her ways as you can, but a woman's too much for a man":

The fan now comes into Hanna's possession, and when she reads on it the inscription "I love you", her wish for it to be true convinces her that the declaration is Danilo's. They meet and dance together to one of the most famous waltz tunes in the world:

But still Danilo is silent.

When the coast is clear, Valencienne and Camille appear. Camille's ardour and the beauty of the garden and the moonlight make it hard for Valencienne to resist the passionate Frenchman, and they disappear into a little summer-house after a romantic duet:

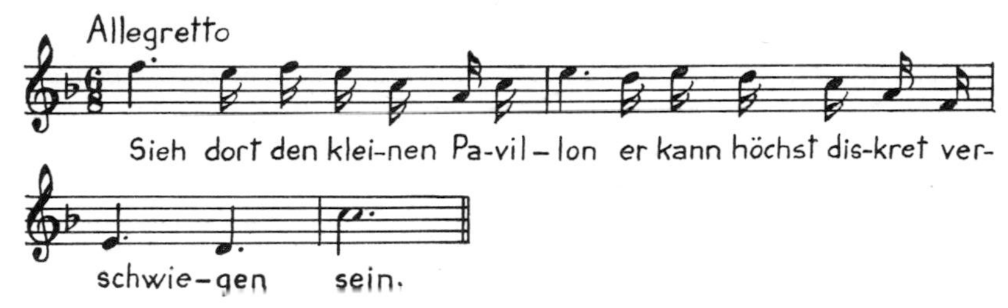

Now, as ill luck has it, the Ambassador has summoned his staff to meet him for an emergency conference in this very summer-house. Finding the door locked, he looks through the keyhole and believes that he recognises his wife with a man whom he can clearly see is Camille. Furiously he tries to force an entry, while Valencienne escapes by another door and Hanna, in order to shield her, takes her place. Both the Ambassador and Danilo are amazed when Hanna and Camille come out of the summer-house and announce their engagement. Hanna is jubilant, for she realises from Danilo's reception of her news that he is furiously jealous—a sure sign that he is still in love with her.

ACT III

Act Three takes place in a salon in Hanna's house. It has been cleverly decorated to represent "Chez Maxim", and all the grisettes from the night club have been invited. Danilo is delighted to learn from Hanna herself the truth of the episode in the summer-house; namely, that she was shielding a married woman who had the rendezvous with Camille. But owing to the wretched millions and his pride he still does not declare himself. Only when she tells him that, by the will of her late husband, she loses all her money if she marries again, does he throw his arms round her and ask her to marry him. She accepts him and then explains that in losing the money it goes to her next husband; and the curtain falls to a reprise of the song declaring that "A woman's too much for a man".

Der Graf von Luxemburg
(The Count of Luxembourg)

Operetta in Three Acts

By A. M. WILLNER *and* ROBERT BODANSKY

Music by FRANZ LEHÁR

Originally produced in Vienna on 12th November, 1909, at the Theater an der Wien, Vienna, with Fräulein von Ligety (whose debut and farewell this was) as "Angèle", Otto Storm as "René" and Louise Kartousch as "Juliette". New version by Wolf Völker produced in Berlin in 1937, with Hans Heinz Bollmann as "René" and Elisa Illiard as "Angèle". London production on 20th May, 1911, at Daly's Theatre with Lily Elsie and Bertram Wallis.

CHARACTERS

RENÉ, COUNT OF LUXEMBOURG
PRINCE BASIL BASILOVITCH, *a Russian Prince*
COUNTESS STASA KOKOZOFF, *a Russian Countess*
ARMAND BRISSARD, *painter*
ANGÈLE DIDIER, *an Opera Diva*
JULIETTE VERMONT, *Brissard's girl-friend*
MENTSCHIKOFF, *notary*
PAVLOVITSCH, *Russian courier*
PÉLÉGRIN, *civil servant*
CHORUS OF PAINTERS, ARTISTS' MODELS AND WAITERS

The action takes place in Paris before the 1914 war.

ACT I

The first act opens in a Paris street. It is carnival time and a festive crowd is making merry. Here young René, Count of Luxembourg, having run through a considerable fortune, now manages to scrape together a living as a struggling artist. In a sparkling song René voices his bohemian philosophy:

The crowd takes up the chorus and the scene changes to the studio of a Parisian artist, Armand Brissard. Brissard is trying to persuade his girl-friend, Juliette Vermont, to pose for him as Venus, but Juliette tells him firmly that she will do nothing of that sort until she is safely married to him. The conversation touches on René, Count of Luxembourg, and Brissard tells Juliette that he will always stand by the young man, whose father, the old Count, once paid Brissard's art-school fees. As they are talking a noisy crowd of painters with their models burst into the studio. They are laden with food, and soon all are enjoying a delicious meal *al fresco*. They are shortly joined by the Count of Luxembourg with a party of girls, all in carnival dress, and the fun is fast and furious. René, though down to his last two sous, is undismayed, and he is at the top of his form when the party is interrupted by three masked figures in black dominoes who ask to speak with the Count of Luxembourg in private. Mysteriously they infer that the matter involves a considerable sum of money which could be his. René begs the carnival party to depart and he is soon left alone with the three masked men, who turn out to be emissaries from Prince Basil Basilovitch, a Russian aristocrat. Presently the Prince himself, an elderly man well on in his sixties, joins them.

It appears that Prince Basil is in love with the famous Parisian singer, Angèle Didier, and wants to marry her. The trouble is one of class, it being impossible for a Prince to marry a commoner. Prince Basil's proposal is that in return for payment of half a million francs, René shall marry her, thus making her Countess of Luxembourg. After three months of marriage he is to agree to a divorce. Other conditions of the pact are that he is not to set eyes on the bride during the marriage service, that during the three months he is not to appear in Paris under his own name, and that he is to make no attempt to enforce his marriage rights. René, who has a distinct streak of irresponsibility, at once enters into the spirit of the masquerade and agrees. Prince Basil is delighted, as no possible objection could be raised to his marrying the ex-Countess of Luxembourg.

By this time Angèle Didier has arrived at the studio. She has consented to marry the old Prince partly from ambition, partly from gratitude for the help he has given her in her career. An outsize painter's easel is now set up to act as a dividing screen between René and Angèle. The marriage service is conducted by one of the three masked men who is a notary, and when it comes to the exchange of rings a hole is made in the easel and their two hands meet. Immediately to each of them is communicated a peculiarly intimate sense of sympathy, in spite of the fact that neither of them has set eyes on the other, and they give expression to this in a charming duet:

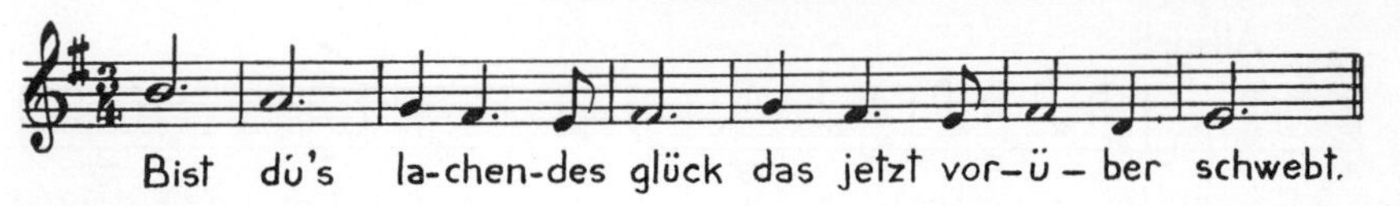

The wedding over and a cheque for five hundred thousand francs having been handed to René, the Prince removes Angèle. René, left alone in the studio, stares as in a dream before him and feels himself deeply in love with an unknown woman. The dream is shattered by the return of the carnival crowd, who, bursting into the studio, bring down the curtain to a reprise of the opening carnival music.

ACT II

The scene is the ballroom of Angèle Didier's house. Three months have elapsed since Act One, and Angèle is giving a party—a double celebration of her retirement from the operatic stage and of her coming divorce from the Count of Luxembourg. During the past three months Juliette, who has tired of waiting for Brissard to marry her, has become companion to Angèle, and Brissard and René have been travelling abroad. They have recently returned to Paris, and René has that evening attended Angèle's farewell performance. Enchanted with her beauty and talent, he has fallen desperately in love with her, quite unaware, of course, that he has fallen in love with his own lawful wife. He has followed her back to her house, and now appears at the party, calling himself "Baron Revel". He dances with Angèle and makes open love to her, and though they both confess that they are married, the attraction is obviously mutual. However, Angèle does put up a token resistance. Meanwhile Brissard, who has also come to the party, has sought out Juliette, but Juliette, still smarting at his delay in leading her to the altar, receives him coolly. However, she eventually succumbs in this well-known duet:

René's appearance at the party and Angèle's obvious interest in him greatly disturb old Prince Basil. He is fearful lest she discover the fact that she is lawfully married to René, and having failed to persuade René to leave the party, the old Prince announces to the guests his forthcoming marriage to Angèle. Then, to everyone's surprise, Brissard protests that Angèle is not free to marry anyone, for she is already married. This forces the Prince and Angèle to make public the facts of the marriage of convenience, and Angèle openly declares her contempt for the man who has thus, by marrying her, sold his name for money. Immediately René steps forward and admits that he is the Count of Luxembourg, the bridegroom she so despises, reminding her that he was also helping her on her way to becoming a Princess. "Farewell, Angèle," he says. "Forget me. For you I sold much more than my name, I sold my chance of happiness." But Angèle cannot bear to see him go. Realising the depth of her love for him, she takes her place at his side and they leave the ballroom together.

ACT III

The last act takes place in the lounge of the Grand Hotel some hours after Angèle and René have left the party. René has taken her to the Grand Hotel, where he is staying, and they are discussing the difficulties of their situation. Technically, under the agreement he made with old Prince Basil, René is supposed to have no contact with Angèle until after the divorce is made absolute. But their mutual passion for each other, excited still further by the champagne René orders, causes them to fall into each other's arms and thus they are surprised by one of the hotel guests—an elderly woman of eccentric appearance and mannish demeanour. She turns out to be a Princess Stasa Kokozoff, recently arrived from Russia, and she triumphantly tells them that she has obtained from the Tsar an order commanding her marriage to Prince Basil Basilovitch. Of course Angèle and René are overjoyed at her news. Shortly after, the Prince arrives at the hotel and is frozen with horror at the sight of Princess Kokozoff. There is no other course open to him but to release René from his obligation. René pays back the half a million francs, which he is able to do, as he has had his confiscated property conveniently restored to him and poverty is a thing of the past; and the operetta ends in weddings for three couples: Prince Basil and Princess Kokozoff, Brissard and Juliette, and René and Angèle.

Zigeunerliebe
(Gipsy Love)

Romantic Operetta in Three Acts

By A. M. WILLNER *and* ROBERT BODANZKY

Music by FRANZ LEHÁR

First produced on 8th January, 1910, at the Carl Theater, Vienna, with Mitzi Zwerenz, revised in 1938 and finally adapted as an opera in three acts and presented under the title Garaboncias *at the State Opera, Budapest, on 20th February, 1943, with Libretto by Innocent-Vincze Erzö. London production on 1st June, 1912, at Daly's Theatre with Sari Petras, Robert Michaelis, Gertie Millar and Harry Dearth.*

CHARACTERS

PETER DRAGOTIN, *a landed proprietor*
JONEL BOLESCU, *engaged to Zorika*
JOZSI, *a gipsy fiddler*
ZORIKA, *Dragotin's daughter*
JOLAN, *his niece*
DIMITREANU, *Burgomaster*
KAJETAN, *his son*
ILONA VON KÖRÖSHÁZA, *a lady of property*
MIHÁLY, *innkeeper*
CHORUS OF BOYARS, OFFICERS, ROUMANIAN AND HUNGARIAN BOYS AND GIRLS, CZARDAS MUSICIANS, WAITERS

ACT I

The scene is the garden of a hunting lodge on the banks of the river Czerna in a mountainous district on the borders of Hungary and Roumania. It is the property of a wealthy Roumanian landowner, Peter Dragotin, an elderly widower with a young daughter called Zorika and a niece, Jolan. When the curtain rises a party is in progress to celebrate Zorika's engagement to a well-to-do young man, Jonel Bolescu. The match is an eminently suitable one, and perhaps for this very reason the romantic Zorika turns coldly from her lover. Her head is full of fanciful ideas about love and, chafing under the restrictions of the formal occasion, she escapes from the party into the garden. Here she encounters the gipsy fiddler, Jozsi. The strains of his violin arouse in her romantic yearnings and she is carried away by his tales of gipsy love, which he describes as "wild as fiery wine and strong as deadly hatred". As the sun is going down they sing this duet:

Jozsi is Jonel's illegitimate half-brother, but he detests Jonel and grudges him his beautiful fiancée. Later, the guests assemble for the traditional betrothal ceremony, and when the bride and groom exchange bunches of roses the strains of Jozsi's distant violin so play on Zorika's emotions that in a moment of passion she hurls Jonel's roses into the river. Zorika also refuses to give Jonel the traditional betrothal kiss, but the general embarrassment which follows is banished by the arrival of Ilona von Körösháza, a wealthy neighbour. She has witnessed Zorika's action and tells Jonel not to take it too seriously. "Women often do things for effect," she tells him. "I do myself."

The guests withdraw into the house for refreshments, leaving Jolan in the garden alone with the burgomaster's shy young son, Kajetan. Dragotin's niece is what would have been known in 1910 as a "flapper", and she is as anxious to get married as her cousin, Zorika, is reluctant. She is trying to get the bashful Kajetan to kiss her when they are surprised by the highly amused Ilona, who volunteers to give Kajetan a kissing lesson in this gay trio:

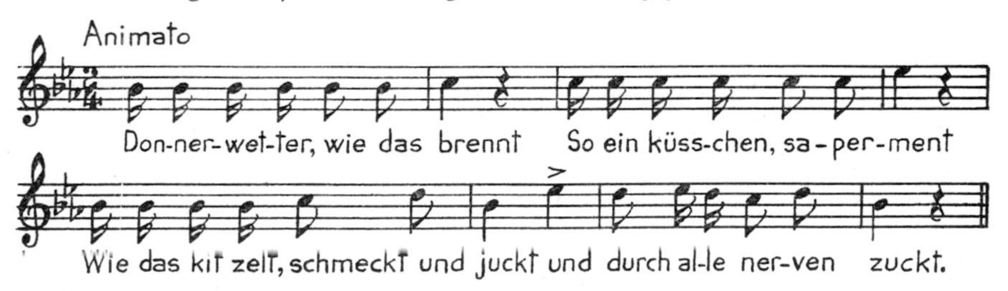

After the trio Jozsi arrives to play to the guests, and Ilona is much attracted by the handsome gipsy and his song:

While he is playing, Zorika steals out into the garden. She has remembered the superstition that a girl who drinks the waters of the Czerna on her betrothal night will have her future revealed. She drinks and, her head full of romantic thoughts of the handsome gipsy, sinks down on a moss-covered rock on the river bank. The moon is shining and, to the sound of the lapping water and the song of nymphs and water-sprites, she falls asleep and dreams.

ACT II

NOTE. In the original version the events of Act Two are supposed to take place in Zorika's dream. For the London production, however, Act Two was presented as reality. The present description follows the original.

The scene is a country inn on the estate of Ilona von Körösháza. When the curtain rises the landlord, Mihály, is welcoming Jozsi and Zorika, for Zorika has eloped on her betrothal night with the gipsy. The landlord is delighted to see them, as Ilona is giving a party to her guests at his inn and he suggests, as part of the entertainment, a gipsy wedding, with Zorika and Jozsi as bride and bridegroom. Zorika, believing that Jozsi really intends to marry her, is overjoyed and pours out her heart in the refrain:

Ilona arrives with Dragotin to see to the arrangements for her party. Old Dragotin is extremely attentive and gallant, but he is jealous of Jozsi, to whom Ilona is obviously attracted. She pacifies the old man by promising to reveal to him the secret of perpetual youth:

Two other arrivals are Jolan and Kajetan. They have been married for three years, and poor Kajetan pushes two children in a pram. He fills the dual role of husband and nursery-maid and is obviously thoroughly henpecked. For them Lehár wrote this graceful tune:

Ilona manages to give Dragotin the slip and finds Jozsi. She is jealous of his love for Zorika and does her best to poison his mind against her, and succeeds well enough to bring home to Zorika the realisation that Jozsi will never marry her; that she is only a plaything to him. The climax of the act is the gipsy wedding, and Zorika is confronted with Ilona's guests, which include her father, Jonel, Jolan and Kajetan. She rushes to greet her father, only to be coldly told that he has no gipsy daughter and there is no longer a home for her under his roof. Distraught, she turns to Jozsi, only to have it confirmed from his own lips that he merely intended to go through the ceremony of a gipsy wedding, as an empty form. Unable to bear the shame of her situation, the poor girl rushes out of the inn and the curtain falls with Ilona standing, triumphant and possessive, at Jozsi's side.

ACT III

In Dragotin's hunting-lodge the party of Act One is still in progress and it is getting late. From the windows of the drawing-room Jonel watches Zorika lying still fast asleep on the moss-covered rock by the river Czerna, and thinks how lovely she looks in the moonlight and how much he loves her in spite of all her romantic obsessions and false ideas of glamour. Love seems to be very much in the air, in fact, for Jolan, after a good deal of hard work, has extracted a proposal from Kajetan and has persuaded her uncle Dragotin to give them his blessing. Ilona, excited by the champagne, is holding court, surrounded by an admiring crowd of men, with Dragotin well to the fore. Glass in hand, she sings a fiery czardas song:

The men all declare their undying devotion and demand to know on whom she intends to bestow her love. "Supposing it were an outsider," she tells them. "You know whom I mean," she adds, with a meaning look at Jozsi, who has come into the room. But the gipsies are moving camp, and Jozsi goes with them. "I'm a gipsy vagabond, free the wide world over; hating, loving, fierce and fond, evermore a rover" is his farewell:

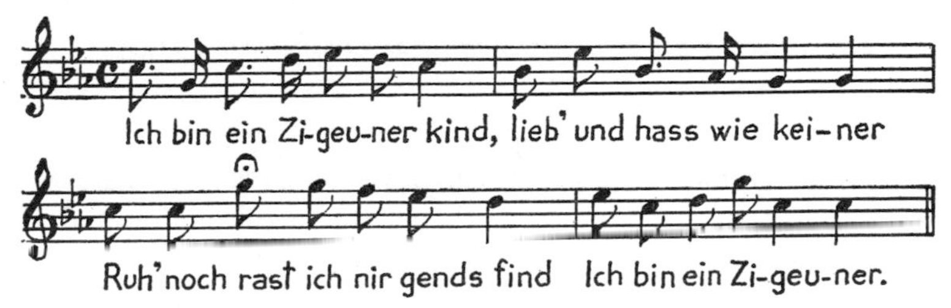

With the rising of the sun, Zorika awakes to find that all the nightmare events of her elopement with Jozsi and the gipsy wedding were only a dream. Gratefully she clings to her faithful Jonel, and when he sings to her as "his own", she answers:

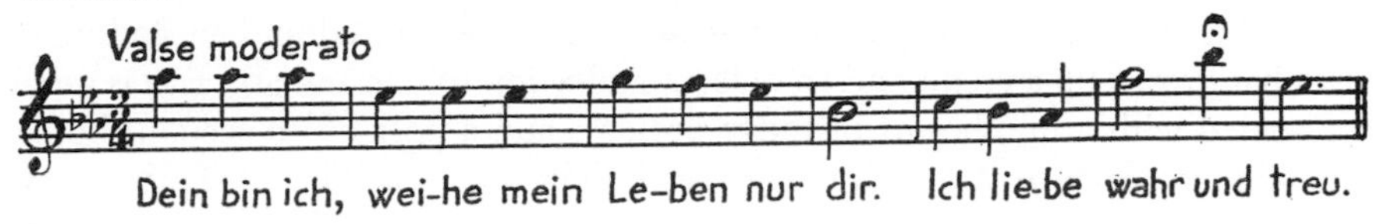

Eva

(Das Fabriksmädel)

Operetta in Three Acts

By A. M. WILLNER *and* ROBERT BODANZKY

Music by FRANZ LEHÁR

First produced on 24th November, 1911, at the Theater an der Wien, Vienna, with Mizzi Guenther as "Eva", Louise Kartousch as "Pipsi", Louis Treumann as "Octave" and Ernst Tautenhayn as "Dagobert". So far Eva *has never been presented in London.*

CHARACTERS

OCTAVE FLAUBERT, *industrialist*
DAGOBERT MILLEFLEURS, *his friend*
PEPITA DESIRÉE PAQUERETTE, *known as Pipsi*
BERNARD LAROUSSE, *a factory worker*
EVA, *an orphan*
PRUNELLES, *a clerk*

The action takes place in Brussels and Paris in the year 1912.

ACT I

The scene is a large ante-room to the main plant of the Flaubert Glass Works at Brussels. The room is decorated as though for a celebration and various placards bear the inscription " Many happy returns of the day to Eva". As the curtain rises the workers assemble and are joined by Bernard Larousse, the most senior worker, accompanied by a girl of about twenty years of age. In a speech Larousse reminds the older workers of how some fifteen years ago he arrived at the factory with a child of five, who had been left in his care; how he had suggested to them that the orphan should become their ward and responsibility, under his charge; how they had enthusiastically agreed to adopt her, and how Eva has grown up a credit and an object of affection to one and all. Eva is now presented with a number of birthday presents and a post-office account book containing a balance of one thousand two hundred francs. The chief clerk then announces the projected arrival that day of the new Managing Director of the firm, and the workers disperse, leaving Larousse and Eva alone. In a conversation between the two, Eva confesses her discontent with the present drabness of her life and her longing for pretty dresses, luxury and bright lights, which, something tells her, are her natural birthright. She begs Larousse to tell her the true facts of her origin, and Larousse tells her how he had always worshipped her mother from afar, how a lover had seduced her and how she had come to him in poverty and in rags and with her dying breath had entrusted him with her child, Eva, and how he has always tried to do his best for her. But Eva tells him that she has always imagined her mother quite differently, and as though in a trance sings a romantic song with the refrain:

When Eva has finished her song and left the stage, the new boss, Octave Flaubert, is announced. He proves to be a sophisticated young man-about-town who knows nothing about the business and whose interests are obviously social rather than industrial. While he is becoming acquainted with his chief clerk and book-keeper, a young man arrives, vague and rather naïve, by name Dagobert Millefleurs. Dagobert is considerably upset, and embarks on an incoherent story of how he was dining alone in a restaurant, sitting discreetly in an alcove, when a distracted young woman rushed in, turned out the light in his alcove and implored his protection. Apparently her husband had been pursuing her with threats of ill-treatment and she was terrified. Dagobert's sense of chivalry was, of course, thoroughly aroused and he is now in love. He brings in his girl-friend, Pepita Paquerette, known as Pipsi, and they sing a duet:

After their duet, Dagobert goes off in search of Octave Flaubert, and Pipsi is joined by the book-keeper, Prunelles. It soon becomes apparent that these two are old friends and we learn that Pipsi on a former occasion worked the old gag of the brutal husband on Prunelles. It appears that she always does this just before her holiday is due in the hope of annexing a wealthy protector to provide her "keep", trusting to the "brutal husband" in the background to defend her virtue. Prunelles promises not to give her away and shortly afterwards Pipsi is introduced to Octave. He immediately takes to Pipsi and she is not averse to him, and they plan a future night out in Paris:

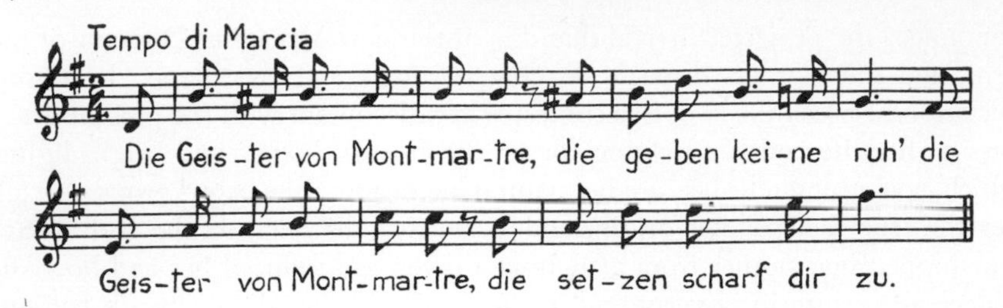

Meanwhile Octave promises to put up both Pipsi and Dagobert in his flat and she goes away to unpack. Prunelles now hands Octave a telegram. It is from fourteen of his Parisian friends announcing that as he will not come to Paris, Paris is coming to him; they will arrive the following day. Octave decides to give a party in their honour and Prunelles is entrusted with the arrangements.

Meanwhile, Octave has made the acquaintance of Eva. Her beauty, her simplicity and her lack of sophistication have won his heart, and he feels himself greatly attracted to her. Eva, too, is not unaware of him. With her new-found longing for glamour, Octave with his good looks and sophistication stands for romance. Old Larousse is worried as he notices the growing attraction between the two. But Eva will not heed his advice to come away, and by the time the curtain falls the flame of love has already been fanned.

ACT II

Act Two takes place at Octave Flaubert's party. His Parisian friends are all present and Pipsi, and Dagobert are in particularly good form. Lehár has caught the party spirit to perfection with this infectious ensemble:

But Octave, for all his care-free behaviour, is haunted by the memory of Eva and he longs to see the little factory girl once again. Suddenly, to his amazement, he catches sight of her face pressed against the french windows and a moment later she is in the room. She and Octave are delighted to see each other and Eva is enchanted by the beauty of the ballroom, the lights, the lovely dresses and the luxury. As in a dream she joins Octave in this romantic duet:

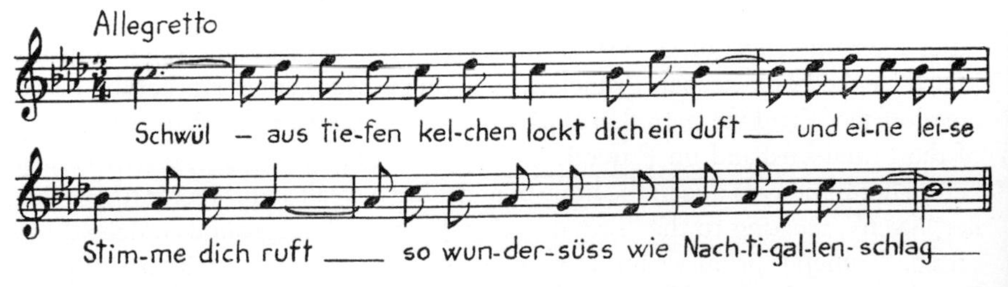

At the end of the duet they are in each other's arms and Eva no longer attempts to hide her love for Octave. She is easily prevailed upon to return home and put on an evening dress which Octave procures for her, and later she returns wide-eyed, in love, a young girl at her first party. Octave is greatly moved by her beauty and likens her to Cinderella in her ball-dress. He presents her to the company, the band strikes up a waltz and all is gaiety, colour and movement. At midnight champagne is served and Dagobert proposes a toast to Octave and Eva, which is drunk with musical honours.

At this moment of rapturous gaiety there is an interruption. Angry voices are heard approaching and the ballroom is invaded by a group of factory workers, led by a furious Larousse. He has missed Eva, has traced her to the party and has come with his mates to take her home and away from Octave Flaubert's pernicious influence. When Larousse threatens his employer, Eva throws herself between the two men, protecting Octave with her body. Octave gets rid of the workmen by assuring Larousse that he and Eva are engaged and that he intends to marry her. Crestfallen and embarrassed, Larousse and the workmen withdraw. Lightheartedly Octave turns to Eva. "There, you see," he tells her. "Just one little white lie and the whole matter is settled." Horrified, she realises the significance of his words; he does not intend to marry her; he only wants a mistress. With a gesture of revulsion, Eva rushes out of the house and Octave murmurs brokenly, "What have I done?"

ACT III

In Act Three Eva is installed as the guest of Pipsi and is enjoying the luxury of her attractive summer home in the Bois de Boulogne. Eva is no longer the simple factory girl but, under Pipsi's tuition, has blossomed out into a sophisticated society woman with half Paris, including an archduke, at her feet. By plunging into the social round she hopes to forget Octave and her humiliation. Then one summer's afternoon he appears, having tracked her down through the good offices of one of his friends. But Eva receives him coldly. She reminds him of his treatment of her, casting his very words in his teeth, and tells him that she has no time for him now; an archduke seeks her hand. Then coldly she leaves him, and Octave realises at last the depth of his love for her. But as night falls and moonlight casts its spell over the garden the two lovers are reunited. Eva, too, realises that Octave is her world. The past is forgotten, the archduke is forgotten and, wrapped in each other's arms, they sing as the curtain falls:

Wo Die Lerche Singt

(Where the Lark Sings)

Operetta in Three Acts

Based on an idea of DR. FRANZ MARTOS

By A. M. WILLNER *and* HEINZ REICHERT

Music by FRANZ LEHÁR

First production on 1st February, 1918, at the Königstheater, Budapest.

CHARACTERS

TÖRÖK PAL, *an old peasant*
MARGIT, *his grand-daughter*
ZÁNDOR ZAPOLJA, *a painter*
VILMA GARAMY, *a singer*
BARON ÁRPÁD FERENCZY
BODROGHY PISTA, *a peasant*
BORCSA, *a maid*
KOVACS LAJOS, *innkeeper*
CHORUS OF PAINTERS AND PEASANTS

The action takes place in the year 1918.

ACT I

The first act takes place in a Hungarian village. It is a favourite resort of artists on account of the beauty of its countryside and the paintability of its landscapes. The curtain rises on an afternoon in autumn. Members of the artists' colony are leaving to return to Budapest and are bidding the villagers good-bye till next year. The only artist to remain behind is Zándor Zapolja, a young and talented painter. He is at work on the portrait of a village girl, Margit, and has fallen in love with her pretty face, her freshness and lack of sophistication. His friend Baron Árpád Ferenczy has observed the flowering of this love with dismay, and warns Margit's grandfather, the old peasant Török

Pal, of the dangers of leaving the young painter and his model so much alone. For Zándor is obviously completely under her spell and is trying hard to persuade her to leave the village and share his life in the big city:

But Margit justifies her grandfather's confidence in her by resisting all Zándor's blandishments. She has no hankering after city life and is blissfully happy in the countryside, "where the lark sings". Besides, she is engaged to be married to a young peasant boy, Bodroghy Pista, who at present is away bringing in the harvest at Banat.

During the afternoon a large car arrives from Budapest and out of it steps a beautiful woman, sophisticated and dressed in the height of fashion. Her name is Vilma Garamy and she is a famous singer. She is greatly attracted to Zándor, has heard tell of his pursuit of the country girl and has come to see for herself what he is up to. Making inquiries at Török Pal's cottage she is entertained by the old man and Margit to a cup of coffee. Vilma exerts all her feminine charm to persuade Zándor to return with her to Budapest, but he is adamant, and even resists the persuasiveness of her waltz song:

Seeing that for the moment she is wasting her time, Vilma, determined to play a waiting game, returns in her car to Budapest. And now Margit's young man, Pista, comes back from the harvest at Banat. He and his fellow peasants receive a warm welcome from the village, and Pista is delighted to see his Margit. However, he is greatly incensed by the presence of Zándor, and when he finds out that he is painting Margit's portrait Pista is furiously jealous. He repairs to the inn to drown his sorrows in wine, and on emerging encounters Zándor. A quarrel develops and the two men begin fighting each other. At one point in the quarrel, when Zándor has pinned his opponent down, Pista draws a knife, which old Török just manages to snatch from his grasp. Margit is horrified at Pista's murderous behaviour, and although he blames it on the wine, she throws herself into Zándor's arms and promises to follow him to the city.

ACT II

Act Two takes place in Zándor's studio in Budapest. Margit has been in residence for some months now, chaperoned by her old grandfather. She is eagerly waiting for Zándor to finish her portrait, and when it is completed they are to be married. Excitedly they look forward to the day when the portrait has brought him fame and all the world will be asking: "Who is the man with the lovely wife?" But with all her happiness Margit has her share of pain. Vilma is there, biding her time, determined to win Zándor back to her side. To accomplish this she determines to make a fool of the little country girl in front of him. She arrives at the studio one afternoon with a crowd of cynical companions and, under the guise of friendship, tells Margit that if she wants to hold Zándor's love she ought to improve her appearance and substitute for her peasant dress something more glamorous. While she takes Margit off to effect a transformation, her girl-friends collect round Török Pal, flattering the old peasant and telling him how handsome and attractive he is. "Well," says the old man, "I don't know about now, but when I was a young man in Temesvàr all the girls were after me":

After the song Vilma returns with Margit, whom she has dressed in a fashionable and rather spectacular frock. The little country girl looks quite out of place in such clothes, and Vilma's friends, while appearing to be superficially friendly, enjoy a laugh at her expense. Zándor is extremely embarrassed and uncomfortable and Margit is becoming more and more unhappy when the maid whispers to her: "Don't you see? they're all laughing at you." At last Margit realises Vilma's intention, and turning on the company she tells them to get out. Then, railing at Vilma for her treachery and at Zándor for his disloyalty and lack of protection, she runs sobbing out of the room. Vilma, left alone with Zándor, now deliberately sets out to seduce him, and gradually Zándor feels himself falling more and more under her spell as they sing this duet:

They arrange to meet that evening at the artists' club, and Zándor goes to see Vilma off. When they have gone, the maid, Borcsa, appears and, calling Margit, ushers in a visitor. It is Pista who, finding the village intolerably lonely without Margit, has taken an office job in Budapest. In spite of the past they are delighted to see each other and Pista is quite resigned to Margit's engagement to Zándor. As they are drinking a friendly glass of wine together, Zándor returns. The old antagonism between the two men is aroused by Zándor's contemptuous attitude, and he finally orders Pista out of the studio. Margit is affronted at Zándor's rudeness and asks why he threw Pista out. "And why did you throw my friends out?" he retorts. The argument develops into a violent quarrel, at the climax of which Margit attacks Zándor with clenched fist, her eyes blazing. In a moment Zándor is at his easel. He has seen an expression in her eyes for which he has been searching and which he needs to finish her portrait and bring it to life. In the moment of triumph the quarrel is forgotten. The portrait is finished, and Zándor and Margit dance for joy. Margit looks forward to a celebration together, but to her chagrin Zándor tells her he is due at the club and, with a light kiss on the brow, leaves her. Alone with her grandfather, Margit asks him what a club is, and he tells her that to the best of his knowledge it is a meeting place for men, where no women are admitted and where they smoke, drink and play cards. Margit is partially convinced, but her heart is heavy at Zándor's neglect, and her grandfather is still trying to comfort her as the curtain falls.

ACT III

The last act also takes place in Zándor's studio. Margit's portrait has won him the big prize at the Academy of Art and he is a famous man. But in his hour of triumph he has deserted Margit for Vilma. Margit was his artistic inspiration, but Vilma is the woman of his dreams. Zándor has not even thanked Margit for her share in bringing him fame. With disillusionment comes a longing for home, and she realises that true happiness for her lies in the countryside. The faithful Pista has also bided his time, and one morning very early he, Margit and Török Pal slip out of the studio and make their way back to the village. Zándor, returning home, finds the birds flown. For a moment he feels a pang of sorrow and remorse, but on reflection he knows that it is better so, and he bids Margit a tender farewell.

Die Blaue Mazur

(The Blue Mazurka)

Operetta in Two Acts and Three Scenes

By LEO STEIN *and* BELA JENBACH

Music by FRANZ LEHÁR

First production on 28th May, 1920, at the Theater an der Wien, Vienna, with Hubert Marischka as "Julian", Betty Fischer as "Blanka", Ernst Tautenhayn as "Adolar" and Louise Kartousch as "Gretel Aigner". London production on 19th February, 1927, at Daly's Theatre with José Collins.

CHARACTERS

JULIAN, COUNT OLINSKI, *a Polish aristocrat*
BLANKA VON LOSSIN, *a Viennese girl, his bride*
KLEMENS, BARON FREIHERR VON REIGNER, *an elderly aristocrat*
ADOLAR (ENGELBERT) VON SPRINTZ, *his nephew*
ALOIS, *his butler*
GRETEL AIGNER, *a dancer and Julian's ex-mistress*
HERR VON PLANTING
HERR KLAMMDATSCH
CHORUS OF WEDDING GUESTS, SOCIALITES AND PEASANTS

The action takes place at a castle near Vienna and in the city itself in 1920.

ACT I

SCENE 1. In the private chapel of the Palais Olinski, near the city of Vienna, the marriage has just been celebrated between two young people: Count Julian Olinski, a Polish aristocrat, and an Austrian girl, Blanka von Lossin. As the curtain rises the wedding party are leaving the chapel, outside which the bridegroom addresses his Polish relations and Viennese friends and the bridal pair receive their congratulations and good wishes. After the guests have entered the palais to partake of the wedding breakfast the happy pair manage to snatch a moment alone. They first met dancing the "Blue Mazurka"—traditionally the last dance at every ball in Poland and only danced by any self-respecting Pole with the woman whose heart he desires to win. Julian is Blanka's first love, and as she is an orphan he is doubly dear to her. She shyly tells him she believes utterly in his love and loyalty and is confident that she will never need to investigate the contents of her mother's silver medallion. Julian asks her curiously what she means, and Blanka tells him that her late mother gave her the medallion, telling her if ever her marriage went wrong to open it and follow the instructions it contained. But, alas! the hour is close at hand when fate is to step in and force her to change her mind. Before his marriage Julian had led a life of wild extravagance and bohemian gaiety with his friend, Adolar von Sprintz, and his mistress, Gretel Aigner, a Viennese ballet dancer. Since the night he met and fell in love with Blanka, however, Julian has not set eyes on either of them. He has in fact dropped them without a word of farewell, and, wishing to break completely with the past, he has not even asked Adolar to his wedding. But Adolar turns up with very disquieting news. Gretel Aigner has discovered that Julian is to be married that day, and she intends to force her way into the wedding reception and create a scandal. During their conversation Blanka has wandered out on to a balcony above them and has heard every word. With her romantic notions of true love and exaggerated ideals of moral purity, her faith in Julian is shattered, and when Gretel Aigner duly forces her way in and Blanka is face to face with her husband's ex-mistress, she makes up her mind to leave Julian. Before leaving, however, she receives a deputation of peasants who arrive with good wishes, and replies to them in waltz time:

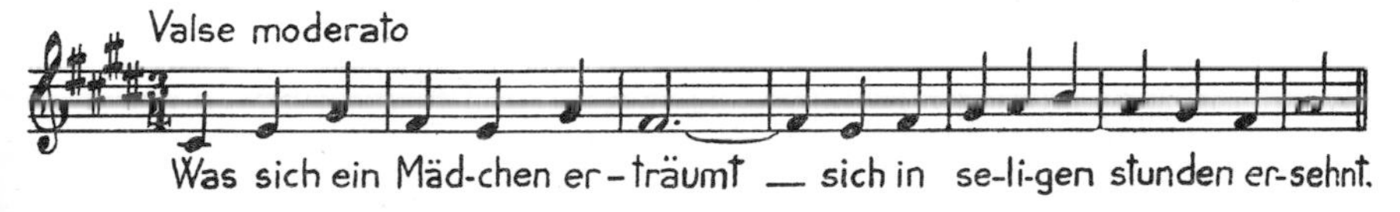

Then, biding her time, Blanka slips away and in a quiet corner opens the medallion. It contains the name and address of an old friend of her mother's youth, Baron von Reigner, with a promise in her mother's writing that if he is still alive he will offer Blanka shelter and protection. Taking a car that is waiting in the drive, she tells the startled chauffeur to drive her to the Baron's address in Vienna and vanishes into the night.

Scene 2. Scene 2 is set in a well-appointed smoking-room in Baron von Reigner's house in Vienna. When the curtain rises the Baron is enjoying the company of two old friends, Herr von Planting and Herr Klammdatsch. The three habitually meet to play poker, but tonight Baron von Reigner is restless and uneasy. It is eleven o'clock and his nephew Engelbert is not yet home. This is most unusual, for Engelbert is a model character—punctual, sober, regular in his habits and certainly not given to staying out till all hours. Herr von Planting is of the opinion that Engelbert is out with a girl, but the Baron cannot imagine such behaviour in connection with Engelbert and is supported by his butler Alois, who tells them confidentially that Engelbert is secretly taking a course in Greek at a night school, which accounts for his absence. The Baron is delighted at this proof of his nephew's industry. When Engelbert appears he apologises for his late arrival and, in spite of violent gesticulations from the butler which he does not see, embarks on a long and complicated story in explanation. He claims to have rescued a child from being run down by a horse, but the tale gets very confused in the telling, for, having declared the child to be an orphan, he ends up by taking it home to its grateful parents by tram. The old gentlemen roar with laughter and the butler wrings his hands. Engelbert is embarrassed by this reception of his story, which is, of course, pure fiction to disguise his real goings-on. For underneath the make-up of a pious bookworm Engelbert hides the identity of the dissipated Adolar, who appeared as Julian's friend in the first scene. Nightly he bids the Baron good night and retires to his room, ostensibly to study. Then, donning evening dress, aided and abetted by the butler, he creeps away to the night life of Vienna, to be the life and soul of the wildest parties. Tonight his departure has to be delayed, for the Baron insists on a game of dominoes. As they are playing, the front door bell rings, and a moment later Blanka, nervous and distraught, is shown in. She tells the Baron the circumstances of her disastrous wedding night and shows him her mother's message in the silver medallion. The Baron welcomes her kindly and promises her shelter and protection. His two old friends retire in the face of this family drama, and when the Baron goes off to see about her room she is left alone with Adolar. She accuses him of having an evil influence on her husband and being the ultimate cause of the breaking up of her marriage. Adolar denies his identity and claims to be Adolar's brother, Engelbert, but Blanka is unconvinced. The Baron now returns with the news that her room is nearly ready. He sends Engelbert to bed and leaves, and Blanka finds herself alone. Unhappy and depressed, she sings a little song to cheer herself up:

Then, exhausted, she falls asleep on a sofa, and when the Baron returns he tucks her up for the night with a rug and turns out the light. Later the door opens and a slim figure tip-toes through the room in the moonlight. It is Adolar, stealing out of the house to begin his night life. His exit is accompanied by the melody of his theme song as a man-about-town:

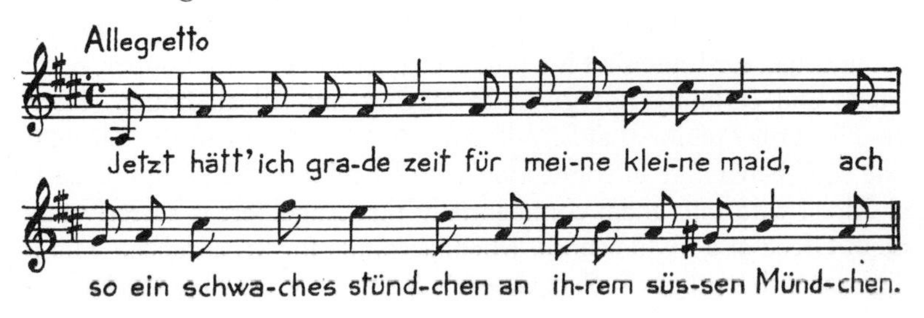

But Blanka sleeps on, and in a dream Julian comes to her with a song of love which comforts her.

ACT II

The last act takes place in Baron Reigner's country house, where Blanka is still his guest. Julian has come to realise during the weeks of his wife's absence how devotedly he loves her, and he at last tracks her down, and turns up unexpectedly. Blanka receives him coldly, and the Baron stands protectingly behind her. But he is quite friendly to Julian, who declares he has only come to offer his wife her freedom. Blanka asks to speak to him alone, and there follows a conversation of lunge and parry during which jealousy is apparent in both of them and it is quite obvious that they still love each other. When Adolar appears, Julian attacks him for not telling his old friend of Blanka's whereabouts, and Blanka uses this to hint at an imaginary engagement between herself and Adolar. They are still at loggerheads when Gretel Aigner turns up. Gretel is basically a good-hearted girl, and her share in the breaking up of Julian and Blanka's marriage has preyed on her mind. She has come to try and undo the damage she has caused, and to achieve this she tells Adolar that he must marry her at once: only in this way can she prove to Blanka that she has abandoned all claim to Julian. Adolar pretends to be comically resigned, but he is in reality delighted. Finally, Julian tells Blanka he has decided to return to his own land and is prepared before leaving to give her a divorce: she has only to sign a document and the law will be set in motion. However, faced with the moment of parting, all Blanka's love for Julian wells up, and to the strains of the "Blue Mazurka" the two of them are whirled into happiness together for life:

Frasquita

Operetta in Three Acts

By A. M. Willner *and* Heinz Reichert

Music by Franz Lehár

First production on 12th May, 1922, at the Theater an der Wien, Vienna, with Betty Fischer as "Frasquita". London production on 23rd April, 1925, at the Princes Theatre with José Collins, Thorpe Bates and Edmund Gwenn.

Characters

ARISTIDE GIROT, *industrialist*
DOLLY, *his daughter*
ARMAND MIRBEAU, *his nephew*
HIPPOLYT GALLIPOT, *anthropologist*
FRASQUITA, SEBASTIANO, } *gipsies*
JUAN, *innkeeper*
INEZ, LOLA } *singers*
CHORUS OF PEASANTS, SAILORS, NIGHT-CLUB VISITORS, TOWNSFOLK

ACT I

The operetta is set in the present day, and the first act takes place in the square of a port in southern Spain. On the left of the stage is a picturesque inn, and on the right a garden door in a wall surrounding a private house. Through the cyprus and olive-trees can be seen glimpses of the open sea. It is mid-day at high summer. After the opening chorus there enters a rich business-man, Aristide Girot, and his daughter Dolly. He buys some Marsala from the innkeeper and it becomes apparent that he is expecting a visit from his nephew, Armand, who is coming from Paris to marry Dolly, though the two have never met. Armand arrives unexpectedly early with his friend Hippolyt Gallipot, a student of anthropology. Armand is warmly greeted by his uncle and goes off to see about the luggage. When Dolly appears she mistakes Hippolyt for her cousin and gives him a resounding kiss. On Armand's return, however, identities are established. Dolly and Armand then go into lunch, and a company of gipsies arrives at the inn. Prominent among them is Frasquita, young, beautiful and passionate. In answer to calls for a song she sings to the customers:

During the song Girot, Dolly, Armand and Hippolyt come out of the house, and Hippolyt is delighted at the chance of studying the Spanish female of the race at close quarters. He has plenty of opportunity for this, for a blazing quarrel breaks out between Frasquita and another girl. Frasquita draws a knife from her stocking, and Armand is only just in time to prevent her stabbing her opponent. Dolly is terribly upset by the scene and to soothe her nerves Armand offers her a cigarette, only to find that his golden cigarette case has been stolen. Unwisely, for he has no proof, Armand accuses Frasquita of the theft. His accusation is proved to be groundless when the cigarette case is returned to him by an old gipsy crone who has stolen it, but the beautiful gipsy girl's pride is wounded by Armand's unjust suspicion and, with hatred in her heart, she is determined to be revenged. She plans to make him fall in love with her and, once in her toils, to make a fool of him. So when Armand comes to apologise she deliberately sets out to seduce him, and her burning kisses stir up all his passion:

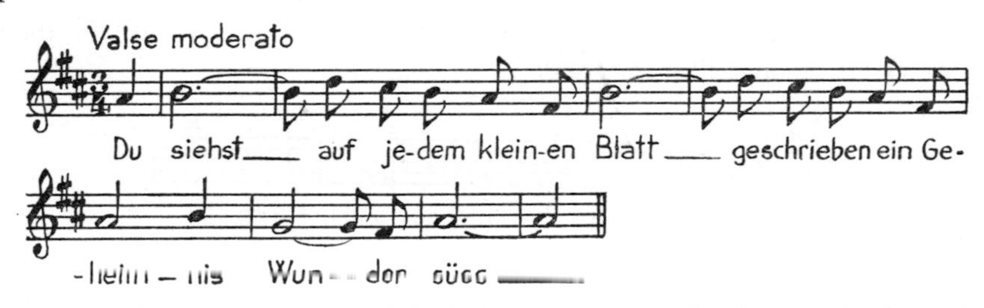

She leaves him a victim of unfulfilled desire, and in the distance he hears her mocking song as the curtain falls.

ACT II

Act Two is set in a fashionable night club, decorated in Moorish style. A crowd of elegant guests in evening dress are present, among them Girot, Hippolyt, Dolly and Armand. Hippolyt, surrounded by "lovelies" and encouraged by Girot, an incorrigible old flirt, decides that this is an ideal spot to pursue his anthropological studies. It is obvious that he is greatly attracted to Dolly, whom Armand is neglecting shamefully. The reason for this neglect is the presence of Frasquita. The beautiful gipsy girl has been engaged as a cabaret attraction and appears on the stage to sing an Andalusian song. At the sight of Frasquita, all Armand's passion for her is reawakened. He manages to get a few moments alone with her, but she plays the heartless coquette, teasing him, tantalising him, still bent on her revenge; she is nevertheless beginning to feel the stirring of love for Armand which expresses itself in a duet:

After the duet Armand tells Frasquita that he cannot live without her love and begs her for a kiss. Frasquita tells him that love and kisses cannot be given in cold blood. They require "atmosphere". If he will come to her later with his arms full of red roses she will think about it. And it is when he has acquired the roses that Armand sings one of Lehár's most enchanting melodies; the well-known serenade:

Old Girot also has designs on Frasquita's virtue. Inspired by champagne, he feels the promptings of his long-lost youth, and having managed to steal Armand's roses, he is advancing to the fray when he is set upon by a horde of flower-hungry ballet girls. They divide the roses among them and with their assistance Girot sings this gay song:

Having lost his red roses to old Girot, Armand has acquired a fresh bunch and is in search of Frasquita, when he runs into Dolly. Having been neglected the whole evening by her fiancé, Dolly is naturally vexed with Armand, but is mollified by the sight of the roses, which she assumes are for her. She is quite prepared to forgive him, but unfortunately at this moment Frasquita appears with an escort of young men. Seeing the roses she takes them from Armand with a pretty speech of thanks. Dolly is dismayed and urges Armand to recover her roses. Armand hovers between the two women till Dolly advances to Frasquita and demands their return. Ironically handing back the roses, Frasquita urges Armand to be more attentive to his fiancée, until, unable to bear her mockery, he escorts Dolly out of the room. But Armand is still obsessed by Frasquita and returns to her side, after refusing to accompany Dolly home, although Girot expostulates at his conduct. Frasquita, in reply to his insistent pleading, agrees to meet him in half an hour's time. She has had an offer of a princely salary to repeat her cabaret act at a party in a private room given by some young men. During the party there is an interrruption, and Armand forces his way into the room. He is affronted at the idea that Frasquita should expose herself to the gaze of these young men while he is kept waiting outside. Realising from his demeanour that he is prepared to make an ugly scene, Frasquita persuades the young men to depart. Alone with her, Armand again declares his love, whereupon Frasquita, turning on him, reminds him of the day that he accused her of stealing, and tells him that far from loving him, she hates him. She shows him the door, and, completely shattered, he leaves her. Then, with the waywardness of women, she breaks down, sobbing to herself: "I love him, I love him", as the curtain falls.

ACT III

The last act takes place in Armand's flat in Paris. It is carnival time, but the season awakes no carnival spirit in Armand, who is eating his heart out for Frasquita. Dolly has married Hippolyt, and in her new-found happiness has quite forgiven Armand his shortcomings as a lover. The newly-weds express their happiness in a charming duet: "Du, Küss' mich immerzu". When they have departed, Uncle Girot arrives. He tells Armand that the father in him is still vexed at his daughter's treatment, but the uncle in him is prepared to forgive his nephew. He then asks if he may have the use of Armand's flat for the evening. He has found the most wonderful girl and proposes to spend the evening with her tête-à-tête. Armand laughingly agrees, promises to leave a bottle of champagne in a cooler, and even writes the invitation to the girl, though Girot insists on addressing the note himself. The old man then departs, chuckling. Later, just as Armand is about to vacate the flat in favour of his uncle, he hears a key turn in the lock and in the doorway stands Frasquita. In a moment they are in each other's arms, and as the curtain falls to the melody of their love duet, old Girot stands in the doorway with his arms raised in a silent blessing on the happy lovers.

Clo-clo

Operetta in Three Acts

By Bela Jenbach

Adapted from the farce Der Schrei nach dem Kinde (The Urge for a Child)

by Julius Horst *and* Alexander Engel

Music by Franz Lehár

First production on 8th March, 1924, at the Bürgertheater, Vienna, with Louise Kartousch as "Clo-clo" and Ernst Tautenhayn as "Severin". London production on 6th June, 1925, at the Shaftesbury Theatre, with Cicely Debenham, A. W. Bascomb and Paul England.

CLO-CLO MUSTACHE, *revue star*
SEVERIN CORNICHON, *Mayor of Perpignan*
MELUSINE, *his wife*
MAXIME DE LA VALLÉ
MARAMBOT, *minister*
CHABLIS, *a piano teacher*
A POLICE COMMISSIONER
CHORUS OF DANCERS, GUESTS, POLICEMEN AND SERVANTS

The action takes place in 1924.

ACT I

The first act takes place in Paris and the scene is the apartment of the revue star, Clo-clo Mustache. Clo-clo is giving a party, and the guests are privileged to witness a pre-view of a new number she is in process of rehearsing for the "Folies Bergère".

Clo-clo, young, attractive and predominantly extrovert, has collected a bodyguard of admirers who escort her everywhere and on whom she has bestowed honorary titles of Marquis, Count, Prince, etc. This bodyguard includes the elderly Severin Cornichon, Mayor of Perpignan, who periodically escapes from his respectable background, and his dragon of a wife, Melusine, to the delights of Paris and Clo-clo, though Clo-clo always calls him "Papa" and he has never achieved closer contact with her than the kiss of her hand. Her favourite is young Maxime de la Vallé. Unfortunately he is extremely poor and money plays an important part in Clo-clo's calculations—hence her toleration of her "Sugar Daddy", Severin, of whom Maxime is furiously jealous. Still, in her heart of hearts, Clo-clo has a tenderness for Maxime.

During Clo-clo's party Severin arrives from Perpignan. Clo-clo is hardly overjoyed to see him, for although she had written to him: "Darling Papa, I am in urgent need of quite a lot of cash", and addressed it to "The Mayor of Perpignan" at his private address, Severin has left home before the arrival of her letter and has not brought the money. Worse, his wife may have opened the letter. We soon learn that his wife *has* indeed opened the letter, for Melusine arrives in person at Clo-clo's apartment. She assumes that the writer is her husband's illegitimate daughter and, being a childless wife, her maternal instinct has been aroused by the letter. She is determined to make a home for the poor, abandoned waif and proposes to take Clo-clo back with her to Perpignan. As it happens, the proposal suits Clo-clo admirably. She has recently been in trouble with the police for striking an officer, and a policeman now arrives to arrest her. But Clo-clo, by pretending to be a manicure girl, so arranges matters that one of Maxime's girl-friends whom she detests is arrested in her place. Then, the coast now clear, she goes off happily to Perpignan with her adopted mother, Melusine.

ACT II

In Severin Cornichon's house in Perpignan, the Mayor is celebrating his sixtieth birthday. But his wife's birthday surprise proves to be a mixed blessing when he is faced with Clo-clo's presence in his house and gathers that she is believed to be his illegitimate daughter. Melusine takes Clo-clo's education firmly in hand, and she begins with piano lessons from Monsieur Chablis. But he falls in love with her, and progress on the pianoforte is slow. Clo-clo also spends much of her time in fending off Severin's advances. But being continually on her best behaviour proves a considerable strain on Clo-clo (re-christened Babette, as being a more respectable name) and at moments she finds herself missing Maxime unbearably:

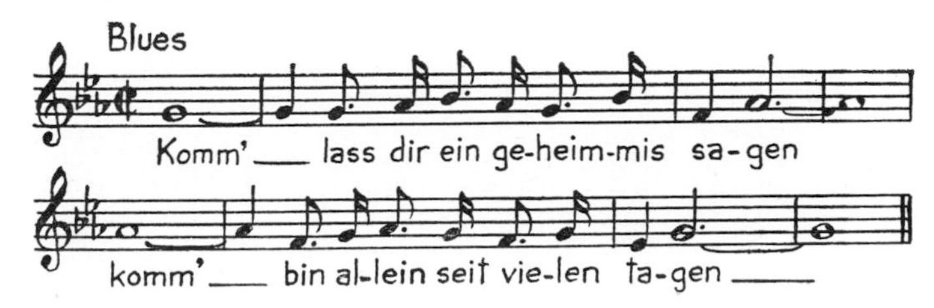

However, Maxime duly turns up, and Clo-clo is overjoyed to see him. She asks, maliciously, after a specific girl-friend, and is delighted to hear that she really did have a bad time with the police and that she has now quarrelled with Maxime.

The high light of Severin's birthday celebrations is a deputation conveying good wishes from the citizens of Perpignan, and a visit from a Cabinet Minister who happens to be passing through the town and calls upon the Mayor to congratulate him and decorate him with an order. But the festive proceedings are interrupted by the arrival of the police. They have tracked down Clo-clo, and the very policeman whom she assaulted is present to identify her. Nothing can save her now, and she is arrested and removed to prison. The only bright spot is the unanimous determination of all her admiring males to mitigate the rigours of her sentence.

ACT III

In the last act Clo-clo has been sentenced to fourteen days for striking a policeman and is sitting miserably in her prison cell. In the depths of despair, she is convinced that she has been deserted by all her friends, when a warder announces visitors. In come the Clo-clo bodyguard at full strength, led by old Severin. With the influence of the Cabinet Minister behind him, Severin has obtained permission to soften the rigours of Clo-clo's imprisonment, and the bodyguard now appear with a load of carpets, arm-chairs, sofas, bed-linen, loose covers, flowers, etc., and succeed in transforming the gloomy prison cell into a tolerable reproduction of Clo-clo's own apartment. Surrounded by her bodyguard and colleagues from the theatre, it is quite obvious that Clo-clo's fourteen days' sentence will develop into one long party with champagne flowing. Her cup is full when her faithful Maxime appears. Severin is reconciled to his Melusine, who had threatened to divorce him after the scandal in Perpignan, and the curtain falls on a joyful celebration.

Paganini

Operetta in Three Acts

By PAUL KNEPLER *and* BELA JENBACH

Music by FRANZ LEHÁR

First produced on 30th October, 1925, at the Johann Strauss Theater, Vienna, with Richard Tauber as "Paganini" and Vera Schwarz as "Anna Elisa". Produced in London on 30th May, 1937, at the Lyceum Theatre, with Richard Tauber as "Paganini" and Evelyn Laye as "Anna Elisa".

CHARACTERS

MARIA ANNA ELISA, *Princess of Lucca and Piombino*
PRINCE FELICE BACCIOCCI, *her consort*
NICCOLÓ PAGANINI
BARTUCCI, *his manager*
COUNT HÉDOUVILLE, *General on Napoleon's staff*
MARCHESE GIACOMO PIMPINELLI, *Chamberlain to the Princess*
BELLA GIRETTI, *Prima Donna of the Court Opera at Lucca*
CHORUS OF COURTIERS, DANCERS, PEASANTS, SOLDIERS, SMUGGLERS, PROSTITUTES

ACT I

The first act takes place outside a small Italian inn at the village of Campanari near the town of Lucca. The inn garden is full of customers enjoying a mid-day glass of wine. When the curtain rises absolute silence reigns, for all the customers are listening intently to the distant sounds of a violin superbly played. It is the great Paganini, now a young man on the threshold of fame, practising in a small pavilion adjoining the inn. He is en route for Lucca, where he is to give a concert, and his manager, Bartucci, is not slow in publicising the fact. While Bartucci is addressing the customers there arrives at the inn Maria Anna Elisa, Princess of Lucca and Piombino, and sister to Napoleon the First. She has been out hunting and has called at the inn with her Chamberlain, Marchese Pimpinelli, and her Ladies-in-Waiting. Presently she hears the sound of the violin and watches fascinated when Paganini, young, attractive and devastatingly good-looking, emerges from the pavilion. He receives an ovation from the crowd and breaks into a lively song in Tarantella rhythm:

Anna Elisa is greatly attracted to the fascinating violinist and is determined to delay his departure. "I welcome sensation at my Court," she declares. Paganini, who is able to hypnotise audiences with his playing, has already mesmerised the Princess by his personality and good looks and she is more than half in love with him. Her husband, however, Prince Felice Bacciocci, is not so well disposed towards Paganini. Tired of the hunt, he arrives at the inn in company with Bella Giretti, Prima Donna of the Court Opera, Lucca. Bella, with her blonde beauty, is used to having men at her feet and one of her most fervent admirers is the susceptible Chamberlain, Pimpinelli. Prince Felice has forbidden Paganini to give performances in any town under his rule, to the violinist's rage and consternation, and to the horror and fury of his manager, for the hall is already sold out. Paganini is about to leave for Florence in high dudgeon when Anna Elisa intervenes. She begs him to stay and promises to persuade the Prince to raise the ban on his performance.

Anna Elisa is able to arrange the matter of the concert to Paganini's advantage by the timely discovery of a flirtation between Prince Felice and Bella Giretti. Paganini is filled with gratitude, and as the curtain falls he confesses to himself that his whole heart is hers.

ACT II

Act Two takes place at the Court of Lucca. Paganini has remained there for six months, deeply in love, a slave to Anna Elisa's beauty. He is also a slave to gambling, and on one occasion even manages to stake and lose his most precious possession, his violin. The Chamberlain of the Court, Marchese Pimpinelli, is the fortunate winner, and returns the violin to Paganini in exchange for a lesson on how to win a woman's love. Part of the lesson is expressed in the following song:

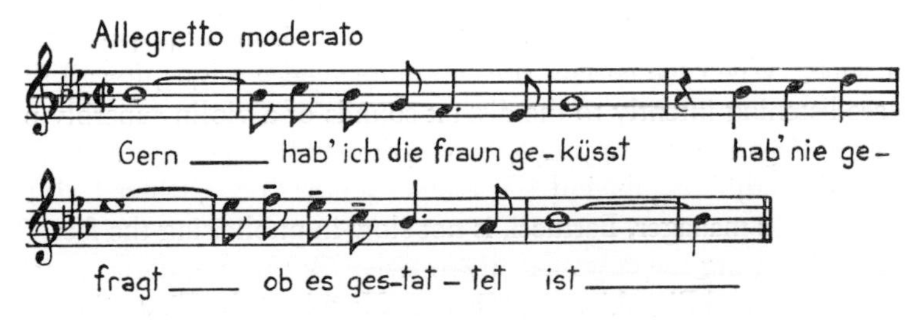

But it is his love affair with the Princess which keeps Paganini immobilised at Court and causes him to refuse all Bartucci's pleas to resume his concert tours. Tenderly he pours out his love for her in this romantic song:

Then one day there arrives at Court a certain General Hédouville from the Court of Napoleon. News has reached the Emperor's ears of his sister's liaison with the famous violinist, and General Hédouville's orders are to accompany Paganini over the frontiers of Lucca or, alternatively, to arrest him. Anna Elisa is shattered. How can she be parted from her beloved Paganini, to whom she has given her whole heart and to whom she has said repeatedly: "No one loves you just as I do."

Anna Elisa attempts to carry through the situation with a high hand, but General Hédouville declares that her affair with Paganini is common gossip in Paris. "And what do I care about Parisian gossip?" she proudly retorts. The General assures her that the Emperor is implacable, and unless Paganini leaves the Court immediately he will obey orders and have him arrested. He leaves Anna Elisa to think matters over, and she realises that Fate is too strong. Her prayer of "Love, life's beginning and ending, stay with me always," will remain unanswered:

A complication now arises. For some months the Prima Donna of the Court opera, Bella Giretti, has been pursuing Paganini, and in a weak moment he has dedicated to Bella a love-song he composed for Anna Elisa. Of course Bella brandishes the song delightedly before the eyes of the Princess, and in an agony of wounded jealousy Anna Elisa orders Paganini's arrest. That evening for the last time Paganini plays at Court, and he plays as he has never played before. As his performance finishes he receives an ovation and, as he is acknowledging the deafening applause, Anna Elisa sees General Hédouville advancing down the room and realises that he is going to arrest Paganini. Rising to her feet, she crosses to the violinist, saying: "Give me your arm, Paganini; I have never heard you play as you played tonight." She leads him from the room, and a moment later Paganini is in a carriage en route for the frontier, safe for the time being from all fear of arrest.

ACT III

The scene of the last act is an inn called "The Rusty Horseshoe", situated on the frontier of the province of Lucca. It is patronised by all manner of dubious characters—smugglers, thieves, tramps, ladies of the town—and prominent among its habitués are Anita, a fortune-teller, and Beppo, a hunchback. It is night time and all are herded together in a frowsty cellar, and the curtain rises on a scene of riotous gaiety. Paganini now arrives at the inn. In order to escape arrest he bargains with two smugglers to guide him over the frontier, but they tell him that he must wait until the frontier patrol has passed by. While he is waiting with his manager, Bartucci, the Prima Donna, Bella Giretti, arrives at the inn. She begs Paganini to take her with him, but Paganini tells her that he intends to devote himself entirely to his art and that there is no place for her in his new life. Bella thereupon decides to accept the Marchese Pimpinelli's proposal of marriage and returns happily to Court. A street-singer now arrives at the inn and entertains the customers with a song. Paganini, seeing through the street-singer's disguise, recognises Anna Elisa. She has come to bid him a final farewell, realising that the great artist in him belongs to the world and that she has no right, despite her deep love, to keep him for herself. Paganini watches her walk slowly through the inn and out of his life and turning to Bartucci cries: "Now, out into the world!"

Der Zarewitsch

(The Czarevich)

Operetta in Three Acts

By BELA JENBACH *and* HEINZ REICHERT

Based on the play of the same name by the Polish author GABRYELA ZAPOLSKA

Music by FRANZ LEHÁR

First produced on 21st February, 1927, at the Deutsches Künstler Theater, Berlin, with Richard Tauber as "The Czarevich" and Rita Georg as "Sonja".

CHARACTERS

THE CZAREVICH
THE GRAND DUKE, *his uncle*
THE MINISTER PRESIDENT
THE LORD CHAMBERLAIN
SONJA, *a dancer*
IVAN, *a valet*
MASCHA, *his wife*
CHORUS OF COURTIERS, OFFICERS, DANCERS, SENTRIES AND LACKEYS

The action takes place in St. Petersburg and in Naples at the end of the nineteenth century.

ACT I

The first act is set in the palace of the Czar in St. Petersburg towards the end of the nineteenth century. The apartments of the heir to the throne do not suggest a palace and are of remarkable austerity in their furnishings—for the eighteen-year-old Czarevich makes a fetish of physical fitness. This attitude includes an avoidance of society and a distrust of women. Even his man-servant Ivan has to hide the fact that he is married—a somewhat difficult task with a jealous wife like Mascha, who forces her way into the Czarevich's apartments to see what her husband is up to. Only after this charming duet can Ivan get rid of her:

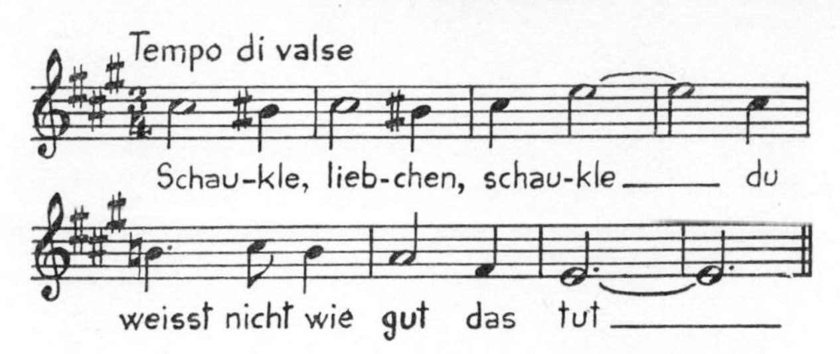

The time is rapidly approaching when, for political reasons, the Czarevich will have to marry. His attitude to the female sex, however, is likely to prove a difficulty. To help him to get acclimatised to the society of women, his uncle, the Grand Duke, arranges for a young dancer, Sonja, to be introduced to the Czarevich disguised as a man. Sonja, slim and young, with a dancer's boyish figure, arrives at the Czarevich's apartments in the uniform of a Circassian officer and makes a most presentable young man. The Grand Duke's plan is that Sonja, when the Czarevich discovers her sex, shall make him fall in love with her. While she is waiting for the Czarevich's arrival, Sonja wonders what he will be like and whether her mission will be successful:

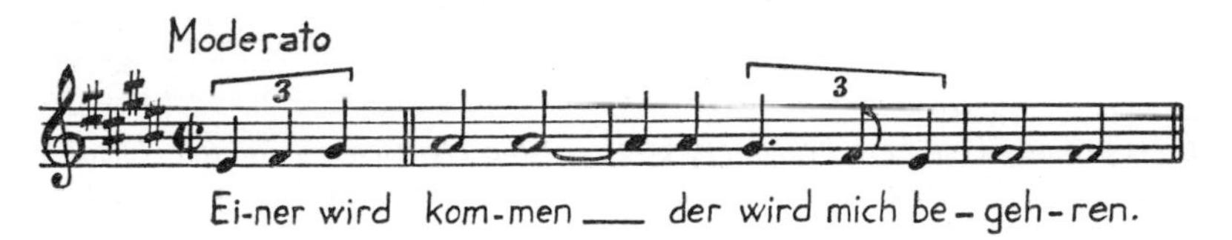

When the Czarevich does arrive, he immediately takes to the "young man" and a sympathy is established between them. It is the Czarevich's craze for physical fitness which proves to be Sonja's undoing. He proposes a bout of gymnastics, and Sonja is compelled to remove her officer's tunic. Immediately the contours of her figure reveal her sex and the Czarevich, is, understandably, annoyed at the deception. But Sonja explains the circumstances which led to her presence and begs him to let her remain, explaining that if she is known to have failed in her mission it may go hard with her. So ardent is her pleading that the Czarevich has not the heart to refuse. Already he feels a sympathy towards this attractive girl, and in order that the Grand Duke may think that his plan has succeeded, they arrange that Sonja may come and go exactly as she pleases. They drink a toast to their better acquaintance and Sonja departs. Alone, the Czarevich silently ponders the situation, and the curtain falls on a reprise of the popular hit of the show, the Czarevich's "Volga Song":

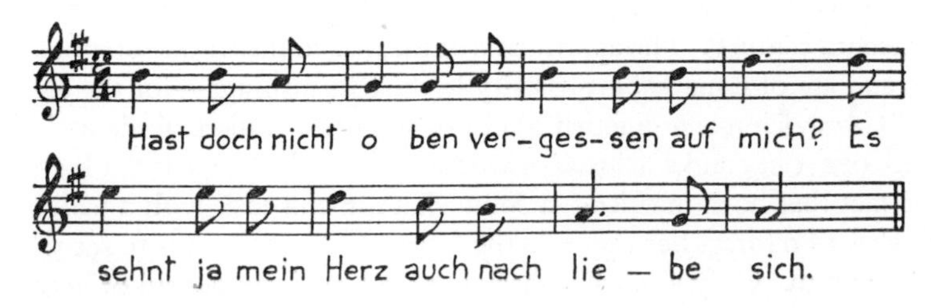

ACT II

Act Two takes place in the Czarevich's palace. To the Grand Duke's delight, Sonja's mission seems to be working out well, for she and the Czarevich have played the comedy with skill and conviction. But as time goes on the two find themselves really in love and give expression to their feelings in the duet:

As the time appointed for the Czarevich's marriage approaches, the Grand Duke decides that Sonja's continued presence in the palace is no longer necessary, or indeed desirable, and that her mission is at an end. He tells her that she is to say good-bye to the Czarevich and that she is to pretend that she has no regrets; that, as far as she is concerned, he is just one more lover. Sonja at first indignantly refuses, but soon realises the danger of resisting protocol, and with a heavy heart she signifies her obedience. But when she meets her lover she cannot bring herself to speak the words of farewell and the only words they speak are words of love:

After this duet the Lord Chamberlain is announced. He brings a command from the Czar that the Czarevich attend the Court that evening to welcome his fiancée, Princess Militza. Angrily the Czarevich informs the Lord Chamberlain that he can tell the Czar that he will not be in attendance, and the Lord Chamberlain has no option but to withdraw. That evening the Czarevich gives a party for Sonja's friends and colleagues from the Ballet. When the fun is at its height the Grand Duke walks in. The music breaks off and there is an awkward silence. The Grand Duke repeats the Czar's command, but the Czarevich, unabashed, declares that he has no intention of marrying Princess Militza. Sonja is the woman he loves. Then the Grand Duke plays his trump card. "So," he says, "you have given your heart to a lady of many loves, to a prostitute." Furiously the Czarevich defends Sonja's reputation and is told to question her himself. To his horror, Sonja does not attempt to deny the accusation, and brokenly he turns to the Grand Duke with the words: "Tell my father, the

Czar, that I will obey." When the Grand Duke and his retinue have departed and they are alone, the Czarevich turns on Sonja savagely and she, unable to go through with her part, confesses to him that she was only obeying the orders of the Grand Duke. He is her first and only love and will always remain so, and the curtain falls on their passionate embrace.

ACT III

The scene of the last act is the garden of a villa near Naples, where the Czarevich has brought his beloved Sonja. The two have fled from the wrath of the Czar, and in this idyllic spot, overlooking the blue Mediterranean, the world seems well lost for love. But even in the midst of all this enchantment he is haunted by the fear of a power that may prove strong enough to wreck his happiness:

With the Czarevich is his faithful servant Ivan, and Mascha, the wife who formerly pursued her husband with her jealous suspicions. But now the boot is on the other foot, and Ivan is driven to the extremity of jealousy by Mascha's behaviour with the fiery Neapolitan men. Desperately he promises to mend his ways and remain the world's most faithful husband.

One day the lovers' idyll is rudely interrupted. The Grand Duke has discovered their retreat and comes with an urgent plea to the Czarevich to return home. The Czar is ill and his successor must hold himself in readiness. But the Czarevich is adamant in his refusal, saying that his future is at Sonja's side and that he will renounce his right to the throne. The Grand Duke in despair turns to Sonja. His country needs the Czarevich: will she intervene and use her influence to persuade him, even though it means sacrificing their love? After a moment's inward struggle, she promises to try, and the Grand Duke withdraws. Fervently Sonja pleads with the Czarevich, urging him to renounce their personal happiness and follow the path of duty for Russia. The Czarevich is still refusing when the Grand Duke returns, bearing a telegram. The Czar is dead. The officers salute the new Czar. And it is then that he leaves Sonja to follow his destiny.

Friederike

Singspiel in Three Acts

By LUDWIG HERZER *and* FRITZ LÖHNER

Music by FRANZ LEHÁR

First produced on 4th October, 1928, at the Metropol Theater, Berlin, with Richard Tauber as "Goethe" and Käthe Dorsch as "Friederike". London production on 9th September, 1930, at the Palace Theatre, with Lea Seidl and Joseph Hislop.

CHARACTERS

KARL AUGUST, *Grand Duke of Saxony and Weimar*
JOHANN JAKOB BRION, *Pastor of Sesenheim*
MAGDELENA, *his wife*
SALOMEA } *his daughters*
FRIEDERIKE }
JOHANN WOLFGANG GOETHE, *law student*
FRIEDERICH LEOPOLD WEYLANDT, *medical student*
JAKOB MICHAEL REINHOLD LENZ, *theological student*
MAJOR KARL LUDWIG VON KNEBEL, *tutor at the Court of Weimar*
MADAME SCHÖLL
HORTENSE, *her daughter*
A POSTILLION
CHORUS OF GUESTS, PEASANTS, FRIENDS OF FRIEDERIKE'S AND GOETHE'S, CHILDREN

The action takes place in Sesenheim and Strasburg in the years 1771 and 1779.

ACT I

The first act takes place in the garden of the rectory of the small town of Sesenheim, in Alsace-Lorraine, on Whit Sunday in 1771. To the strains of the organ Pastor Brion and his wife come out of church and settle down in an arbour in the garden to drink a well-earned cup of coffee after matins. They are joined by their younger daughter, Salomea, and soon a crowd of peasants arrive carrying baskets with Whitsun gifts for the rector. When the peasants have presented their offerings and withdrawn, and the garden is empty, Friederike, the rector's elder daughter, enters. Unlike her flighty, younger sister Salomea, Friederike is a quiet, serious, romantic girl. She is fond of children, and at the moment she is accompanied by six. She sings them a song and they help themselves to the remains of the rector's meal. Then the postillion of the post chaise arrives and hands her a packet, telling her that Monsieur Goethe commanded him to deliver it to her. Having dismissed the children, she opens the packet. It contains, done up with pink ribbon, a poem. She is reading it ecstatically when her sister runs in to say that the Strasburg students are arriving. There is a sound of distant singing and in they march to a rousing students' song, in which Salomea energetically joins. Among the students is her faithful admirer, Friederich Weylandt, a medical student, whom she teases unmercifully. When she hears that another student, Jakob Lenz, is on his way after stopping to buy her a ribbon similar to the one Goethe bought for Friederike, Salomea insists on leading the students away to meet him. As soon as the garden is empty young Goethe enters carrying a bouquet for Friederike, who has retired to her room. Underneath her window, he sings:

Friederike now joins him, wearing the pink ribbon he sent her. They are deeply in love, and sing a romantically emotional duet. The next arrival is the student Lenz. He is loaded with parcels and leads a lamb by a rope. He has missed the colleagues who went to meet him and explains that the peasants of neighbouring Drusenheim have persuaded him to transport their Whitsun presents for the rector. Friederike and her mother accompany him into the house for refreshment, and Goethe, left alone, sits down to compose a lyric, singing as he writes:

When Friederike returns she has good news for Goethe: she and her sister have been invited to stay with their aunt and uncle, the lawyer Schöll, in Strasburg, and they will often be able to meet. The students now return and dancing on the lawn begins. During the dance Lenz takes the opportunity to warn Friederike kindly not to take Goethe's love-making too seriously. His heart is too susceptible to make a faithful husband and she will only get hurt. But she is all unheeding, and the curtain falls with the lovers in each other's arms.

ACT II

In the drawing-room of her house in Strasburg, Madame Schöll is giving a party in honour of the young poet, Goethe. While the guests dance a minuet, the hostess sits talking to her friend, Madame Hahn. They discuss Salomea's engagement to Weylandt and the prospect of Friederike becoming engaged to Goethe. Both girls are visiting their aunt and are present at the party. Goethe is the last to arrive, with many apologies, and is immediately surrounded by a crowd of girls, each clamouring for him to write a verse in her album. At last he can turn his attention to his beloved Friederike. They are delighted to see each other and express their love in duet:

At the end of the duet they are in each other's arms, when Weylandt, Salomea's fiancé, enters and sees them. As Friederike's future brother-in-law he rebukes Goethe for flirting with her, and when Goethe retorts that his intentions are serious, Weylandt protests that he is in no condition, financially, to support a wife. But he has nothing to say when Goethe pulls out of his pocket a letter from the Archduke of Saxe-Weimar offering him the post of Poet Laureate to the Court. The letter also informs him that Captain Knebel, tutor to the Archduke, will shortly be waiting on him to accompany him to Weimar. Weylandt wishes him good luck and leaves him, and Goethe, alone, sings an ecstatic song, expressing his happiness and his love for Friederike:

Shortly after this Captain Knebel arrives at the party and asks to see Dr. Goethe. The Captain has already been to Goethe's lodging and has followed him to the party. They are to leave immediately for Weimar. Goethe expresses his appreciation of the appointment and his misgivings at following so distinguished a poet as the famous Wieland. He asks the reason for his resignation, and learns that the Archduke considered that Wieland's wife and six children were a drag upon his artistic creativity, and desires a Laureate unencumbered with a wife and family. Goethe is horrified at this news and will not for a moment consider giving up his beloved Friederike at any cost. In vain the Captain reasons with him, pointing out the splendid chances he is sacrificing by his refusal. Goethe is adamant. But Weylandt has heard the whole conversation, and goes straight to Friederike. He explains to her the situation and insists that it is her duty to arrange matters so that Goethe accepts the Court appointment. Weylandt warns her that if she keeps the poet at her side it will only create frustration for him and misery for them both. So Friederike makes the big decision and with sorrow in her heart she sings:

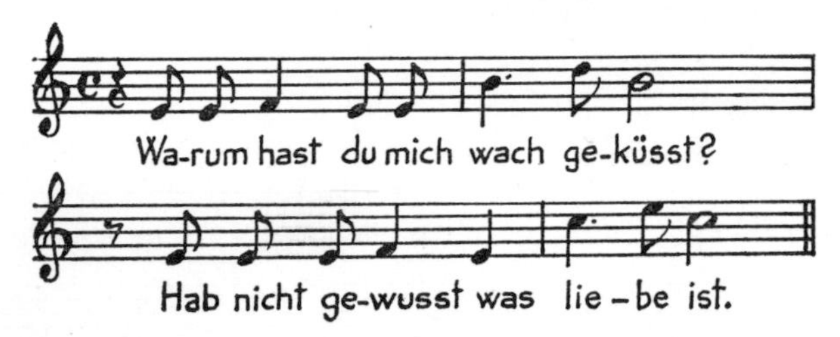

In the scene with Goethe which follows, Friederike reasons with him and tells him that it is both his duty and her wish that he should go to Weimar. She will not stand in his way and he is to forget her. Goethe obstinately refuses to give her up, and as a last resort to make him change his mind she goes off dancing with Lenz, playing the part of a gay, care-free girl to whom love is only an incidental attraction. Stabbed by jealousy and disappointment at her apparent coolness, Goethe informs Captain Knebel that he has changed his mind: he will accept the Archduke's offer; they can start at once. He bids Freiderike a cold farewell and with a breaking heart she watches him walk out of her life to find fame and fortune.

ACT III

The last act is in the rectory garden at Sesenheim. It is 1779, and eight years have passed since Friederike's love idyll ended so sadly. Nothing remains but the memory of her lost love and she has never married, though her sister Salomea has found happiness as the wife of Friederich Weylandt. One September afternoon the Archduke, attended by Goethe, calls on the Rector. They happen to be in the neighbourhood, and the Archduke is anxious to see with his own eyes the scene of his poet's youth and happiness. Goethe presents Friederike to the Archduke, and now learns for the first time from her lips the full story of how she sacrificed her love to his future. Once again it is farewell, and once again Friederike watches Goethe walk out of her life; this time for ever.

Das Land Des Lächelns

(The Land Of Smiles)

A Romantic Operetta in Three Acts

By LUDWIG HERZER *and* FRITZ LÖHNER

Based on an earlier operetta Die Gelbe Jacke (The Yellow Jacket)

Music by FRANZ LEHÁR

First production on 10th October, 1929, at the Metropol Theater, Berlin, with Richard Tauber as "Souchong". Revived at the Vienna State Opera in January, 1938. London production on 8th May, 1931, at the Theatre Royal, Drury Lane, with Richard Tauber, Hella Kurty and Renée Bullard.

CHARACTERS

COUNT FERDINAND LICHTENFELS
LISA, *his daughter*
COUNT GUSTAV VON POTTENSTEIN (GUSTL), *Lieutenant of Hussars*
PRINCE SOUCHONG
MI, *his sister*
TSCHANG, *his uncle*
CHORUS OF MEMBERS OF SOCIETY, YOUNG GIRLS, MANDERINS, SERVANTS

The action takes place in Vienna and Pekin in 1912.

ACT I

The first act takes place in the drawing-room of Count Lichtenfels's villa in Vienna. It is an evening in 1912 and the Count is giving a party to celebrate the equestrian success of his daughter, Lisa, at an important horse show. Lisa is a popular girl with many admirers, prominent among whom is Count Gustav von Pottenstein, nicknamed Gustl. Young Gustl is desperately in love with Lisa but has not yet plucked up sufficient courage to tell her so. Today he means to propose, for he has managed to save the necessary twenty thousand Kronen, which in those days the army insisted an officer must deposit with the War Office before he could be permitted to marry. But Gustl's luck is out, and Lisa tells him kindly but firmly that they can only be friends. Lisa has another warm admirer: the Chinese diplomat, Prince Souchong. He has sent her a beautiful ivory statuette of Buddha and now arrives in person. It is clear from his entrance song that behind an enigmatic Chinese smile there smoulders a passion for Lisa:

Lisa receives the Prince and thanks him prettily for his costly present—much too valuable to give away. He tells her that it is a family heirloom, adding tenderly that nothing could be good enough to give her. Immensely attracted to the exotic foreigner, Lisa offers the Prince some refreshment and they sit down to tea.

During the evening Prince Souchong receives news from an agitated secretary of his Embassy that he has been appointed Minister-President of his country, which means an immediate return to China. As Lisa hears the news she realises its significance to her, and for the first time she owns to herself that her heart belongs to Souchong. Shall she accompany him to his own country as his wife? Her father is bitterly opposed to the idea and tries to hold her back, assuring her that Gustl, who belongs to her background, would make her an infinitely better partner for life. But love will not be denied, and as she confesses her love for him, Souchong pours out all his love and gratitude in this romantic song:

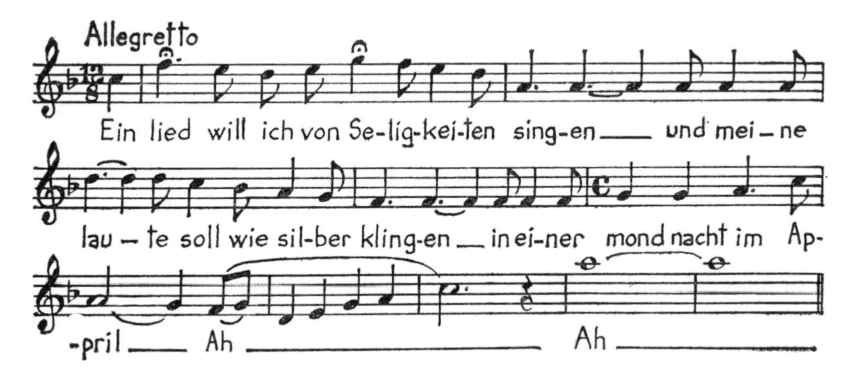

ACT II

In Act Two Lisa is living in Pekin as wife of the Minister-President. She is blissfully happy in the early days of her marriage to Prince Souchong. In spite of their different backgrounds, a warm affection unites the two:

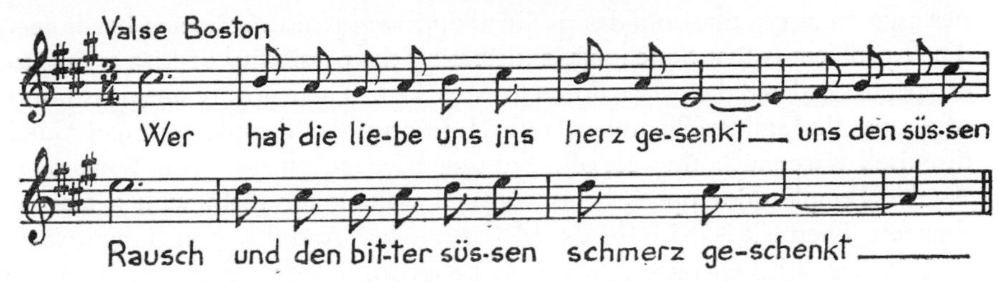

Souchong has a sister, an enchanting little Chinese girl, Mi. Mi is an enthusiastic follower of European customs and fashions, but her uncle, the Mandarin Tschang, a fanatical supporter of Chinese tradition, is appalled at her free-and-easy manners. The Mandarin is particularly affronted at Mi's appearance in shorts. She has been playing tennis with Gustl, who, to keep an eye on Lisa, has got himself appointed Austrian Military Attaché to Pekin. Finding Lisa blissfully happy with her husband, however, Gustl is consoling himself with Mi and a mutual attraction has drawn them to each other:

Gustl's arrival and his news of her family and Vienna have aroused a wave of homesickness in Lisa, and she begs her husband to allow her to visit her father. Terrified of losing her to her homeland, he refuses. This is Lisa's first grievance. The second is Souchong's confession that according to the custom of his country he is compelled to take four Chinese wives. It is only a formality, he promises, and has no significance. All his heart belongs to Lisa alone:

Lisa is shattered both by her husband's refusal to let her go home and by the prospect of sharing him with four wives. She tries to reason with him, but he tells her bluntly that he is master and reminds her of Confucius' words to the effect that a woman may not exercise a will of her own. The argument boils up into a quarrel and Lisa, at the end of her tether, lashes out at him with the words "I hate you". Souchong recoils as though from a blow. His dream of happiness is shattered.

ACT III

The last act takes place in the women's quarters of Prince Souchong's palace. After much heart searching Lisa has decided to leave her husband and return to her own country. She confides in Gustl and he promises to escort her home. Their problem is that Souchong, anticipating the possibility of Lisa trying to escape, has ordered the palace doors to be locked. There is only one possibility of escape: through the Temple. With Mi to open the Temple door and Gustl disguised as a eunuch, they set off. But they have reckoned without Souchong. As the Temple door opens he is revealed waiting for them with a face of thunder. Their fate is in his hands: what is it to be? And then Souchong reveals the nobility of his character. Tenderly he tells Lisa that she may go, and entrusts to Gustl's care his most precious possession. For a moment the two, who once were everything to each other, take one last look before they part for ever. When Lisa has gone, Souchong comforts his sister, who weeps bitter tears for Gustl, but he hides his own sorrow behind an enigmatic Chinese smile.

Schön ist die Welt

(So Fair the World)

Operetta in Three Acts

By Ludwig Herzer *and* Fritz Löhner

A revised version of an earlier operetta Endlich Allein

Music by Franz Lehár

First produced on 21st December, 1931, at the Theater an der Wien, Vienna, with Hans Heinz Bollmann as "The Crown Prince" and Adele Kern as "Princess Elizabeth".

Characters

THE KING
CROWN PRINCE GEORGE
THE DUCHESS MARIA BRANCKENHORST
ELIZABETH, PRINCESS ZU UND VON LICHTENBERG
COUNT SASCHA KARLOVITZ, *Lord Chamberlain*
MERCEDES DEL ROSSA, *ballerina*
MANAGER, *of the "Hotel des Alpes"*
CHORUS OF HOTEL GUESTS AND STAFF

ACT I

The scene is the lounge of the "Hotel des Alpes" in a Swiss spa surrounded by mountains. It is tea-time on a sunny afternoon, the band is playing and guests are dancing. In a corner a distinguished-looking man is conversing with the manager. Royalty is expected in the person of the reigning King of an European country with his son, the Crown Prince George. At the hotel they are to meet the young Princess Elizabeth of Lichtenberg, who is travelling with her aunt, the Duchess of Branckenhorst. A marriage has been arranged between the Crown Prince and Princess Elizabeth and the two young people will be meeting for the first time. The Lord Chamberlain is impressing upon the manager the importance of the occasion and the vital necessity of preserving the incognito of the King. Both parties duly arrive, and Prince George to his delight discovers in the hotel an exceedingly pretty girl, whom he recently helped to mend a puncture by the roadside when her car broke down. He has no idea who she is. Princess Elizabeth is also delighted to see her good Samaritan of the break-down incident, and is also unaware of his identity. It is vital that the Crown Prince's marriage to Princess Elizabeth take place at the earliest opportunity, for his country is in desperate financial straits, a situation which the Princess' dowry will conveniently relieve. The King is consequently shattered when the Crown Prince calmly announces that he has changed his mind and has no intention of going through with the marriage. The world is so wonderful a place that he wants to enjoy it free of encumbrances for a little while longer:

The Lord Chamberlain, Count Sascha Karlovitz, is an unhappy man. In addition to the complications caused by the Crown Prince's refusal to marry, he has troubles of his own. He has been secretly married to a Prima Ballerina, a South American beauty, Mercedes del Rossa, full of fire and temperament. Sascha dare not inform the King of his marriage for fear of losing his post, and on the other hand Mercedes is for ever prodding him to approach His Majesty. Sascha has on several occasions timidly asked for "permission" to marry Signorina del Rossa and been roundly told that it was out of the question. At this juncture the King is introduced to Mercedes. His Majesty has an appreciative eye for a pretty woman and he is enchanted with Mercedes' dark beauty and with her performance of the Tango:

Meanwhile, Prince George and Princess Elizabeth, each still unaware of the other's identity, have met again and discovered a mutual interest in mountaineering. Prince George invites her to accompany him on an alpine climb the following day: she eagerly accepts and they make their plans. It will necessitate a start at 4 a.m. and a rendezvous is arranged for the next morning. Then, their two heads full of thoughts of each other, they retire to bed.

ACT II

When the curtain rises on Act Two the two mountaineers have reached the summit of a peak and are resting on a plateau surrounded by giant rocks. The whole of the act consists of a long lyrical duet between Prince George and Princess Elizabeth, each still unaware of the other's identity. On the mountain top stands a hut, and Elizabeth is soon in possession, promising Prince George that she will produce a tasty picnic meal. While she is busy cooking it, George has leisure to ponder, and he now decides in his mind, irrevocably, that she is the only girl for him:

After the song Elizabeth appears and, true to her promise, serves a delicious meal of scrambled eggs, ham, bread and fruit, washed down with ice-cold water from a mountain spring. Every comfort is to hand in the hut, including a radio, which when switched on broadcasts dance music. Quietly happy, the two are dancing together when the music is interrupted. They stop dancing to listen to the announcement of an S.O.S. to the effect that Princess Elizabeth zu und von Lichtenberg has been missing since daybreak. The Princess is reported as wearing a brown skirt and a green blouse, and as having been seen in the company of a young man dressed in climbing kit. A check-up of all professional guides in the canton has been made, and as none are missing it is suspected that the Princess' companion may well be a member of an international gang of crooks, known to have been lately in Switzerland. As the S.O.S. finishes George stares silently at Elizabeth. "Brown skirt, green blouse," he says. "So you are the Princess zu und von Lichtenberg." She does not attempt to deny it, and at that moment both of them realise for the first time the lateness of the hour. Worse, there are signs of a storm gathering. George, an experienced mountaineer, tells her candidly that in such conditions to attempt the descent would be to endanger their lives, but the desperate girl tells him that if he prefers to remain behind she will make the descent alone. At this moment the storm breaks and at the same time they hear an earth-shuddering roar. Elizabeth in terror throws herself into George's arms and he calms her fears, telling her that the noise was caused by an avalanche and that, though there is now no immediate danger, they must resign themselves to a night on the mountain. Their common danger has brought the two of them very close, and neither of them any longer attempts to conceal their mutual love:

The storm has abated, the moon has risen and the sky is full of stars as George, his arm around Elizabeth, walks with her to the hut. He opens the door and she goes in. George settles down for the night on a bench on the veranda, and the last thing we see as the curtain falls is his cigarette smouldering in the darkness.

ACT III

Down in the valley the "Hotel des Alpes" is in a turmoil over the disappearance of the Princess. An airman has reported seeing a man and woman on the mountain-side, but otherwise there has been no news. Elizabeth's aunt is in a state of terrible anxiety, and the King wonders, if Princess Elizabeth does materialise, how he is to break the news to her aunt that George refuses to get married. Then out of the blue the young lovers suddenly appear. Elizabeth, the picture of happiness, tells her aunt airily that there is now no question of *her* marrying Prince George. She has no idea who her climbing companion is, but she loves him to distraction and he is the only husband for her. The waltz-song which Lehár has written to express her emotions is alive with joy and excitement:

Finally it is Elizabeth's aunt who plucks up courage to tell the King of her niece's decision, and the King counters with the information that George too is a defaulter. Princess Elizabeth is now presented to the King, and at this moment George enters in formal dress and is about to address his father when he and Elizabeth catch sight of each other. Before either of them can speak the aunt addresses George: "Tell me, Prince, did you make an expedition to the mountains yesterday?" "I did," replies George, and then to Elizabeth: "I climbed the mountain to avoid the Princess zu und von Lichtenberg and at the top I found you." Smilingly the King turns to Elizabeth's aunt. "Yes! I think we managed that very well," he says.

Giuditta

A Musical Comedy in Five Scenes

By PAUL KNEPLER *and* FRITZ LÖHNER

Music by FRANZ LEHÁR

First produced on 20th January, 1934, at the Vienna State Opera, with Jarmila Nowotna as "Giuditta" and Richard Tauber as "Octavio".

Note. The generic term "musical comedy" used in this context has no affinity with its usual English connotation.

CHARACTERS

MANUEL BIFFI, *a labourer*
GIUDITTA, *his wife*
OCTAVIO, *Army Captain*
LORD BARRYMORE
A DUKE
IBRAHIM, *proprietor of the night club "The Alcazar"*
PROFESSOR MARTINI
PIERRINO, *fruit-seller*
ANITA, *a fisher-girl*
A WAITER
ANTONIO, *Army Lieutenant*
CHORUS OF OFFICERS, SOLDIERS, TOWNSFOLK, DANCERS, GUESTS, MUSICIANS, ETC.

SCENE I. The first scene is the market-place of a Mediterranean port. On the left of the set is an inn with chairs and tables in the open air, the table-cloths contributing a splash of colour to the scene. Opposite the inn is a picturesque house with a large balcony. In the distance, shimmering in the sunlight, is the sea. It is an afternoon in late summer and the market-place is full of colour and activity: the voices of itinerant singers with their mandolines mingle with the hammering of a shoe-maker; a barber is busily shaving a customer; while peasant women are doing the weekly washing. Into the market-place drives Pierrino, a young fruit-seller, in a trim little cart drawn by a donkey, and in a short time Pierrino by skilful salesmanship has disposed of his entire stock, his cart and even his donkey. He has decided to turn his back on poverty and fruit-selling and to chance his luck in a fresh country, and he and his sweetheart intend to elope to the coast of North Africa. Anita declares philosophically that she is one of a family of fifteen and will not be missed for two or three days, and that her departure will mean one less mouth to feed. The lovers adore each other and are excited, happy and optimistic.

A contrast to this happy pair is Manuel, a working man, disgruntled and old before his time. He is constantly complaining of poverty and hardship and he lives for one thing alone, his most precious possession, his beautiful wife, Giuditta. With every means in his power he works to keep Giuditta's love. He has just completed an ornamental bird-cage for the wealthy Count Orsini, purely to be able to spend the money on finery for her. But the bird-cage is symbolical of Manuel's attitude to his love: he keeps her caged up, and she on her part has long since ceased to care for him and yearns for freedom, romance and affection.

This afternoon two army officers, Octavio and Antonio, visit the inn. Their regiment is under orders to sail for North Africa to put down an Arab rising and they drink a farewell toast to Home and Beauty. When Antonio has departed on embarkation duty, Octavio, sitting alone, hears a woman's voice singing in the house with the balcony:

As she is singing, Giuditta comes out on to the balcony. Her breath-taking beauty has a devastating effect on the susceptible Octavio, and his good looks are not lost on Giuditta. She descends the balcony steps and joins Octavio in a duet which develops into a passionate love-song in which Giuditta tells him of her longing for love and affection:

Octavio replies with a paean in praise of her beauty:

By the end of the duet the two are passionately in love, and when the ship carrying Octavio and his regiment sails for North Africa, Giuditta is on board.

SCENE 2. Set in the garden of a villa which Octavio has taken for himself and Giuditta and which is situated on the outskirts of a small garrison town on the coast of North Africa. For fourteen blissful days the lovers have lived in Paradise—"The world forgetting by the world forgot".

Octavio's one dread is that there may be renewed Arab unrest, which would mean marching orders for his regiment and separation from Giuditta. One afternoon two visitors call on Giuditta. They are Pierrino, ex-fruit vendor, and his sweetheart, Anita. They have had no luck, having joined a theatrical touring company which has done no business and has finally closed down. They are unemployed and destitute, but just as much in love. Pierrino is determined to return home and resume his fruit business, and Giuditta promises to look after Anita until such time as he can establish himself sufficiently to be able to support her. Giuditta invites them to stay the night, and is proposing to put them both in one room when Anita makes a horrified protest. Speaking of her parents, she assures Giuditta that before there was anything of that sort her father came to fetch her mother in frock-coat, top hat and white gloves. So Pierrino is relegated to an attic, which he has to share with the coloured house-boy. Late that night, when everyone is in bed, Pierrino steals out into the garden. From somewhere he has managed to acquire a frock-coat, a top hat and white gloves. Nothing fits and he cuts a ridiculous but rather touching figure. He finds a ladder and rests it against the side of the house near Anita's bedroom window. Looking out, she sees him in the moonlight and her heart melts, and she beckons to him. In a flash he is up the ladder and through her window. A moment later the light is out and all is still.

SCENE 3. A desert camp. The regiment is under canvas and awaiting orders to advance and attack the Arabs. Octavio is in despair at the thought of leaving Giuditta now the moment has come, for he is convinced that she will never remain faithful to him. Did she not desert her husband, Manuel, for him? She comes of a hot-blooded race—the daughter of a Spaniard and a North African dancer. Giuditta is his life, his everything. How can he tear himself away from the one thing he holds dear?

While Octavio is fighting the urge within himself to flout the call to duty and remain with Giuditta, she appears at the camp. With every means in her power she tries to make him promise not to march with his regiment but stay behind in her arms. "I will give you love such as you have never known," she promises. Even as the bugle is sounding the signal to march, Octavio tells Lieutenant Antonio that he is remaining behind. He is deaf to protests and pleading until Antonio, rounding on him, hurls at him the contemptible epithet "Deserter". Only then is Octavio recalled to a sense of duty. He bids Giuditta a brief farewell and walks out of the tent with Antonio.

SCENE 4. In a luxurious night club, "The Alcazar", in a North African city, Giuditta is the star. She appears there nightly with her company and is an enormous draw. Anita is still her companion. One evening, out of the blue, Pierrino appears: he has managed to buy back his donkey and cart, business has been good and he is now in a position to support Anita. The young pair are ecstatically happy, and Giuditta, touched and envious of their joy in each other, insists on putting up the capital to enable Pierrino to open a shop. Happily they say good-bye and start for home. Now there is a stir of excitement in the night club and Ibrahim, the proprietor, ushers in Lord Barrymore, a wealthy English peer, who is Giuditta's favoured lover at the moment. This is the signal for Giuditta's stage appearance, and she makes her entrance to sing:

After her number Giuditta is invited to sup with Lord Barrymore in a private room. While they are at supper, Octavio enters the night club. Since his parting from Giuditta he is a broken man; with his peace of mind destroyed, he is a shadow of his former self. He has left the army and is now a homeless wanderer. As he is sitting in gloomy solitude, he hears an order given to call "Lord Barrymore's car" and out of a private room comes the peer with Giuditta on his arm. Octavio watches as he fastens a priceless pearl necklace round the throat of his beloved, and then, with difficulty restraining himself, he sees Giuditta drive away in Lord Barrymore's car. In an agony of mind he cries out: "My life, my happiness, destroyed!"

SCENE 5. The last scene takes place in a private room in a luxury hotel in a European capital. Octavio is now earning his living as a cabaret pianist. This evening he has been put on to a special job, and once again and for the last time Fate throws him in Giuditta's path. She is supping tête-à-tête with an elderly Duke, and Octavio has been engaged to play "soft music without". He watches Giuditta arrive, and when she is left alone for a moment he softly plays the melody associated with their love-idyll in the villa in North Africa:

In a moment she is at his side and with one glance she realises the depth of his misery and all that he has gone through. Her old passion for Octavio awakens and she begs him to come back to her. But he cannot bring himself to do so. Life has destroyed all his illusions: Giuditta's love has proved his curse. And Giuditta realises that what he says is true. The old Duke returns, but Giuditta begs him to excuse her. She does not feel well—another time—she wants to go home. And, to the weary sound of Octavio's piano, Giuditta leaves the restaurant on the Duke's arm. Octavio, lost in his tragic thoughts, plays on till the waiter touches his arm and tells him the customers have gone. He gets up and shuts the piano and, as the curtain falls, in his mind's eye he sees a picture of Giuditta's fatal beauty and he sings:

Der Fidele Bauer

(The Merry Peasant)

Operetta in a Prologue and Two Acts

By VIKTOR LÉON

Music by LEO FALL

First produced on 27 July, 1907, at an Operetta Festival in Mannheim. London production on 23rd October, 1909, at the Strand Theatre, with Courtice Pounds and Florence St. John.

CHARACTERS

LINDOBERER, *a peasant*
VINZENZ, *his son*
MATTHÄUS SCHEICHELROITHER, *a peasant*
STEFAN, *his son*
ANNAMIRL, *his daughter*
ZOPF, *village constable*
"RED LIZZY", *a cowherd*
HEINERLE, *her little boy*
COUNSELLOR VON GRÜMOW, *of Berlin*
VICTORIA, *his wife*
HORST, *their son, a Lieutenant of Hussars*
FRIEDERIKE, *their daughter*
CHORUS OF PEASANTS, SERVANTS, FAIRGROUND BUSKERS, MERCHANTS AND STUDENTS

The action takes place in the village of Oberwang in Upper Austria and in Vienna in 1896 and 1907.

PROLOGUE

The Student

The scene of the Prologue is the main street of the village of Oberwang, in a remote province of Austria. The most notable character in the village is Matthäus Scheichelroither. He is a peasant of an old-fashioned, traditional type, who has never in his life left the village and never wants to. Perfectly contented with his lot he struts about wearing his comically pointed peasant cap, and if people want to laugh at him, so far as he is concerned they are perfectly at liberty to do so.

Though the old peasant has no personal ambitions he is tremendously ambitious for his son, Stefan, the pride and joy of his heart, and he wants him to enter the Church in accordance with his late wife's dearest wish. Stefan is able to adopt a professional career by the generosity of his well-to-do godfather, the peasant Lindoberer. He has already graduated from Grammar School ("Gymnasium") and today he is to leave for Vienna to continue his studies. Stefan is heavy in heart, for he is greatly attached to his sister, Annamirl, and each of them will miss the other:

Stefan is showered with gifts by his family and is given a rousing send-off by the whole village. With the posthorn blowing a fanfare, he drives away in a coach towards the university life of Vienna.

ACT I

The Doctor

The scene is the village square in Oberwang. It is the anniversary of the dedication of the church and the day of the annual fair. It is also recruiting day, and several of the lads of the village have to join up and do their National Service, among them Vinzenz, son of the well-to-to peasant, Lindoberer. "Red Lizzy", the local cowherd, visits the fairground with her little boy, Heinerle. He begs her to buy him sweets and a toy, but she has no money and none of the better-off peasants seem willing to adopt him.

Matthäus Scheichelroither is expecting a visit from his son, Stefan. Eleven years have passed since he last saw him, on the day Stefan left Oberwang for the University of Vienna. Stefan meanwhile has not entered the Church but has become a Doctor of Medicine. Matthäus is mightily proud of his son, and as for Annamirl, her brother's success has so gone to her head that she refuses to dance with any of the lads of the village, not even with Vinzenz Lindoberer, who adores her and with whom she used to be so friendly. He is just off to do his National Service, and when he begs her to wait for him, she only makes fun of the poor boy.

At long last the eagerly awaited Stefan arrives. He excuses his long absence and dearth of letters, blaming everything on to his studies, his practice and the fact that he is writing a medical text-book. The villagers are aware of the change that has come over Stefan and feel ill at ease in his society, but his father is overcome by pride in his son and will not hear a word against him. But when Stefan announces that his visit is only a fleeting one and tells his father casually that he is off to Berlin to marry the daughter of the wealthy Counsellor von Grümow, the old peasant is bitterly hurt. It soon becomes obvious that Stefan is ashamed of his relations and of his peasant background. With every sign of embarrassment he does his best to discourage his father and sister from coming to his wedding, telling them that the journey would tire his father and that they would feel uncomfortable among the fine folk in Berlin society. Then he departs. Matthäus is shattered. Seeking comfort, he crosses over to the fairground, where a "Punch and Judy" show is being given. Among the wide-eyed children watching it is little Heinerle. Taking him by the hand, Matthäus tells him: "You shall be my son."

ACT II

The Professor

The scene is the drawing-room of Stefan's house in Vienna. Here he is living, happily married to Friederike von Grümow, and he has just been appointed to a professorship at his old University. Today he is expecting a visit from his parents-in-law and his brother-in-law, Horst von Grümow, a Lieutenant of Hussars. Stefan has never confessed to his wife the fact that he comes of peasant stock. In some things he considers silence to be golden. But Nemesis is at hand, and Stefan's lowly origin is made clear to his wife when a surprise visit from Matthäus, Annamirl, Vinzenz and his godfather Lindoberer coincides with the arrival of the von Grümows. Matters of business have brought Lindoberer to Vienna and he it is who has suggested taking Matthäus and Annamirl along with him to visit Stefan. Stefan is acutely embarrassed by this contretemps and turns helplessly to his wife, who shows her good manners and breeding by according her relations-in-law a friendly welcome. But the von Grümows turn up their noses at the simple peasants and do not attempt to conceal their dislike and contempt for them. Friederike's father is appalled and her mother urges her to leave her husband, arguing that his concealment of his low-class origin amounts to deceit. At this Stefan sides with his father, but old Matthäus has realised the situation that he has precipitated by his unwelcome appearance, and pathetically declares that in the future he will remain in his own little corner:

The admirable behaviour of the peasants and their dignified bearing in adversity, and Matthäus' readiness to sacrifice his own happiness as a father to save the children's marriage are not lost upon Friederike's parents, and there is a reconciliation. Annamirl, too, is made aware to what lengths false pride may lead and happily gives her heart to Vinzenz. The final curtain comes down to a spanking march tune, glorifying the Merry Peasant.

Die Dollar Princessin

(The Dollar Princess)

Operetta in Three Acts

By A. M. WILLNER *and* FRITZ GRÜNBAUM

Based on a comedy by GATTI-TROTHA

Music by LEO FALL

First produced on 2nd November, 1907, at the Carl Theatre, Vienna, with Mizzi Guenther, Luise Kartousch and Louis Treumann. London production on 25th September, 1909, at Daly's Theatre, with Lily Elsie, Gabrielle Ray, Joseph Coyne, Basil Foster and W. H. Berry.

CHARACTERS

JOHN COUDER, *President of a Coal Trust*
ALICE, *his daughter*
DAISY GRAY, *his niece*
DICK, *his son*
TOM, *his brother*
FREDDY WEHRBURG } *natives of Berlin*
HANS FREIHERR VON SCHLICK } *natives of Berlin*
OLGA LIBINSKI, *a cabaret singer*
CHORUS OF STENOGRAPHERS, CABARET GIRLS, GUESTS, SERVANTS AND PORTERS

The action takes place in New York and Aliceville, Canada, in 1907.

ACT I

The scene is the business office of John Couder, a millionaire. His daughter, Alice, is in charge of the office staff, and when the curtain rises she is rebuking the stenographers for arriving late at the office. "Always running after men," she tells them and goes on to declare that for her part she would not waste any time on them. "If I should ever want a man, I'd buy one—you might have to pay a bit more for a Baron or an Earl. I regard a man as much a plaything as a monkey on a stick."

John Couder has a peculiar passion for engaging employees who are Europeans of good family. Among those working for him at the moment is Hans Freiherr von Schlick, a German aristocrat, whose financial adversity has driven him abroad. He is now in charge of John Couder's racing stables. Hans has fallen in love with the millionaire's niece, Daisy, whom he is teaching to ride, but Daisy, though she likes him well enough, treats him merely as a good companion. Another of Couder's employees is Freddy Wehrburg. He is greatly attracted to his employer's daughter, Alice. He is no more to her than a reasonably efficient secretary in her father's business, but she is quite ready to flirt with him and does so in this waltz:

John Couder, who is a widower, has decided to engage an unattached European aristocratic lady to act for him in the capacity of hostess. His brother, Tom, and his son, Dick, have been dispatched to Europe to bring back a suitable candidate, and they return with a lady who calls herself the Countess Przibiczevska. She relates colourful stories of life in her native Russia, of her remarkable father who terrorised his dependants with the knout, and of her own achievements and conquests. Couder accepts all these tales with open-mouthed amazement, but Alice and Daisy do not believe a word the Countess says. When she is introduced to Hans and Freddy, the three of them recognise each other as old friends. The two men recall that the Countess was formally Olga Libinski, a Berlin cabaret singer and once a mistress of Freddy's, but in response to her whispered injunctions of "Don't give me away", they pretend to Couder that the Countess was a well-known figure in Berlin society and Hans recalls frequently dancing with her at Court balls. So the first act ends with Olga mistress of the situation, to the disgust of Alice and Daisy.

ACT II

The scene is the winter garden in John Couder's mansion in New York. Alice and Freddy Wehrburg are immensely attracted to each other, but the spoilt, imperious American girl considers that any man worthy of her love should be her helpless slave, to be ordered about from pillar to post. Freddy, however, has far too much pride to submit to any position so humiliating, so at the moment their love for each other has no opportunity to develop. John Couder, on the other hand, is head over heels in love with Olga, and in spite of his daughter's and his niece's warnings is determined to make her his wife. He is anxious to see Alice safely married, and she confidently tells him that she has only to whistle up Freddy for him to come to her call, for she has not the slightest doubt that the prospect of marrying a millionaire's daughter will prove irresistible. Daisy and Hans are also in love and anxious to get married, though Daisy, teasingly, insists that for them married love must be entirely platonic and as innocent as Hansel's love for Gretel in the fairy tale:

But John Couder will not hear of a marriage between Daisy and Hans, and so the two of them decide the matter arbitrarily by eloping. That night at a reception John Couder announces his engagement and presents his bride, Countess Przibiczevska. He also tells his guests that his daughter has decided to get married and calls upon Alice to name the man of her choice. "What a nerve the girl must have!" murmurs Freddy to himself. Full of confidence, she chooses Freddy, only to hear him, to her amazement, brusquely decline the honour. Her father, appalled at the situation, offers to settle an enormous sum of money on his daughter as an incentive to Freddy to marry her, but Freddy only expresses his pity and contempt for girls like Alice who have sacrificed all feelings of love on the altar of Mammon and believe that money will buy them anything they want. Thus pride succeeds in separating two hearts which in reality beat warmly for each other. Freddy walks proudly out of John Couder's house and employment and Alice is left, deserted and abandoned, a lonely Dollar Princess:

ACT III

The scene of the last act is Freddy Wehrburg's country house in Canada. A year has passed since he left John Couder's employ, and here in Canada by dint of hard work and good management he has bought and rehabilitated a failing business and developed some oil-wells whose yield promises much for the future. But he has not been able to forget Alice and, bent upon seeing her again, has written to her father in the former name of his firm, offering to sell him the business at a knock-down price. In this way he hopes to renew relations with Alice. Daisy and Hans, who after their elopement had emigrated to Canada, are also anxious to make it up with Couder. There is now no question of the platonic in their relationship and the young couple are deeply in love. Couder duly arrives accompanied by his wife, Olga, and his daughter, Alice, and he soon realises that the firm he has come to inspect is no bankrupt business but, under

Freddy's efficient direction, a profitable and going concern. Couder revises his opinion of Freddy, and Alice, though she makes a pathetically gallant effort to play the proud heiress and pretends not to care, eventually breaks down and throws herself into Freddy's arms. Hans is reconciled to Daisy's uncle by diplomatically persuading Olga, for a financial consideration, to agree to a divorce from John Couder. The marriage has been a complete failure, and Couder is thankful to settle a generous sum upon her, and so regain his freedom. And so the story ends happily for him as well as for the Dollar Princesses and their husbands, and Freddy and Alice tie up the story with an affectionate waltz duet:

Die Geschiedene Frau

(The Girl in the Train)

Operetta in Three Acts

By VIKTOR LÉON

Music by LEO FALL

First produced on 23rd December, 1908, at the Carl Theater, Vienna, with Anny Dirkens, Mizzi Zwerenz and Hubert Marischka. London production on 4th June, 1910, at the Vaudeville Theatre, with Phyllis Dare, Clara Evelyn, Robert Evett, Rutland Barrington and Huntley Wright.

CHARACTERS

KAREL VAN LYSSWEGHE, *Civil Servant*
JANA, *his wife*
PIETER TE BAKKENSKIJL, *her father*
GONDA VAN DER LOO, *actress*
LUCAS VAN DEESTELDONCK, *Judge in the Divorce Court*
SCROP, *sleeping-car attendant*
WILLEM KROUVEVLIET, *a fisherman*
MARTJE, *his wife*
CHORUS OF JOURNALISTS, MEMBERS OF THE PUBLIC AND COURT OFFICIALS

The action takes place in Amsterdam and in Makkum in Holland in 1908.

ACT I

The scene is a divorce court in Amsterdam. Jana van Lyssweghe is suing her husband Karel for a divorce. It appears that they were both at Nice on holiday when he was recalled to Amsterdam on business. Karel booked a sleeping-compartment for the two of them, but shortly before their departure, hearing that Arctic conditions prevailed in Amsterdam, he persuaded Jana to remain in Nice. At the station Karel ran into a young musical-comedy actress, Gonda van der Loo, who was trying vainly to book a sleeper for Amsterdam. He gallantly offered his sleeping compartment and helped her into it. But when he wanted to leave the compartment and find himself a seat on the train, to his dismay the lock of the door jammed. Unable to get out, Karel had been compelled to spend the night with Gonda in the sleeper. The story came to Jana's ears, and she started the divorce proceedings. Karel maintains his innocence. In offering the lady his sleeper he only did what any other gentleman would have done in similar circumstances. It was not his fault that the door stuck. The fisherman, Willem Krouvevliet, and his wife, Martje, who work for the Lyssweghes, give evidence in support of Karel's character, declaring that to their knowledge he has always been a model husband. Their broad dialect creates much amusement in court.

The other witnesses, including the sleeping-car attendant, Scrop, do not favour Karel. As for Gonda van der Loo, she declares in the witness-box that she believes in the doctrine of free love, and this prejudices Karel sadly. Gonda creates a sensation in court and fascinates everybody, especially the Judge, with her song "O sleeping-car":

The court grants Jana her divorce, and all Karel's efforts towards reconciliation fail. In a pique he asks Gonda to marry him, but she maintains that in her view marriage is slavery. If Karel likes to live with her in free love, well and good. Karel accepts Gonda's conditions, while the Divorce Court Judge marks her down as the girl for him.

ACT II

Act Two takes place in the Lyssweghe villa in Amsterdam, where Karel is giving a party for Gonda. She still refuses to marry him, although he has asked her repeatedly.

At the party there appears, out of the blue, Jana. She has had a telegram from her father that he is arriving, totally unexpectedly, from abroad. She dreads telling him of her divorce, and though there is no question of reconciliation, she begs Karel to pretend for the evening that they are still married. Karel is overjoyed to see Jana again and eagerly agrees to pretend to be her husband. It is at the start difficult to maintain the deception, and when Pieter te Bakkenskijl first arrives he keeps on observing that they do not seem to be as much in love as formerly. But soon their pretence becomes reality.

During the course of the evening there appears Scrop, the sleeping-car attendant who was on duty the night of Karel and Gonda's journey from Nice to Amsterdam. He has come with the intention of telling the truth about the whole affair, and it is from him that Jana's father learns of her divorce. The effect of the story on him is to awaken his guilty conscience, for he had also once figured in an incident in a sleeping-car, with very much less innocence than in poor Karel's case. Another guest at the party is the Judge who granted Jana her divorce. Ever since the case he has pursued Gonda without success, and tonight he proposes marriage to Jana in the hopes of rousing Gonda's jealousy. Karel, who assumes that Jana is going to accept the Judge, is shattered, and on the rebound he again proposes to Gonda. In front of Jana he invites her to "Dance with me, child, as though you're my wife," and Gonda mockingly answers: "All our lives through now, I'll be your wife."

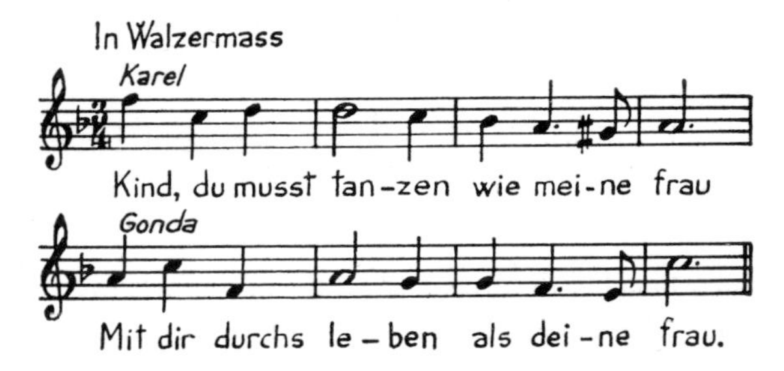

ACT III

The last act takes place next day during kirmess, or carnival time, in Makkum. Thanks to the efforts of the Judge, Karel's innocence has been proved and he is exonerated, while his father-in-law's episode in the sleeping-car comes in for some very unwelcome publicity. The sleeping-car attendant, Scrop, comes out of the whole business with a somewhat tarnished reputation, though his gay duet with Gonda, "Mann steigt nach", restores everyone's good humour.

Karel and Jana are reconciled and remarried, and Gonda decides to give up her ideas of free love to become a Judge's wife.

Der Liebe Augustin

(Princess Caprice)

Operetta in Three Acts

By RUDOLF BERNAUER *and* ERNST WELISCH

Music by LEO FALL

First produced on 3rd February, 1912, in Berlin. This was a revised version of Der Rebell *produced in 1905 in Vienna. London Production on 11th May, 1913, at the Shaftesbury Theatre, with Courtice Pounds, Harry Welchman, Cicely Courtneidge and Clara Evelyn.*

CHARACTERS

PRINCE BOGUMIL, *Regent of Thessaly*
PRINCESS HÉLÈNE, *his niece*
PRINCE NICOLA OF MIKOLICS
JASOMIRGOTT, *Major-domo*
ANNA, *his daughter*
SIGILOFF, *a bailiff*
AUGUSTIN HOFER, *a piano teacher*
MATTHAEUS, *porter at the Monastery*
CHORUS OF LADIES AND GENTLEMEN OF THE COURT, SOLDIERS, OFFICIALS, SERVANTS AND BRIDESMAIDS

The action takes place in Thessaly in the year 1905.

ACT I

The scene is Princess Hélène's boudoir at the Court of Thessaly. Extravagant living has landed her uncle the Regent, Prince Bogumil, in financial difficulties and his principal creditors are the Income Tax authorities. They have applied for and obtained a court order authorising them to distrain on the Regent's possessions. As the curtain rises the bailiffs are demanding admittance and are soon busily assembling an inventory of the palace effects. The Major-Domo, Jasomirgott, is greatly distressed at his master's humiliation, and his daughter,

Anna, a snobbish young woman who is immensely proud of her Court connection, is indignant. The coolest person at the palace is the Regent. His solution to his difficulties is a marriage between his niece, Hélène, and the wealthy Prince Nicola of Mikolics. It is true that the two men are deadly enemies, for eighteen years before Prince Nicola had headed an unsuccessful rising against Bogumil and had taken refuge in flight. This all happened on the night before Hélène and Anna were born, and the two girls, as well as sharing a birthday, as babies shared the same foster-mother. Prince Nicola has now returned to Thessaly a very wealthy man, and Bogumil's plan is to offer, for a financial consideration, to abdicate in Nicola's favour on his wedding to Hélène. The fly in the ointment is Hélène herself, who has far too much temperament to submit tamely to a marriage of convenience. She detests the formality and etiquette of life at Court and she has a tenderness for her piano teacher, Augustin Hofer. Augustin is an engaging, easy-going Viennese, who subscribes to a philosophy of *laisser aller*:

Augustin is officially engaged to Anna, but Anna, a confirmed social climber, considers herself far too good for Augustin, whose easy-going temperament she despises. He confides to Hélène, his beloved "Princess Caprice", his concern that Anna and he have so little in common and he also remarks that she herself does not seem cut out for Court life. But she tells him that she has decided to sacrifice herself to politics, fall in with her uncle's wishes, marry Prince Nicola and share his throne. "I shall have so few friends and am so alone," she tells him, and begs him pathetically to "always be my comrade".

As she finishes Jasomirgott appears with a candle to light her to bed. As Hélène bids Augustin good night she drops a rose, which he picks up and rapturously kisses, while Jasomirgott, affectionately threatening, orders him to bed.

ACT II

A salon in the palace is the scene of Act Two. Prince Nicola has arrived for the wedding ceremony. He is a formal, cold and calculating character, who has no thought in his head beyond the throne which his money has enabled him to buy. Hélène takes a dislike to him on sight, and Nicola makes no especial effort to be polite to her. Jasomirgott, who is aware of Augustin's love for Princess Hélène, warns him to put all such foolish dreams out of his head and advises him to take Anna away with him to Vienna, where he is negotiating to buy an inn which he proposes to run with Anna when they are married. But to Augustin's and to her father's surprise Anna refuses to leave Court, and Augustin asks her for her reasons:

The truth is that Anna is the only person at Court of whom Prince Nicola has taken notice. He has in fact been making up to her and has promised her the post of Lady-in-Waiting to his future wife. But the more Hélène sees of Nicola the more she dislikes him, and she confesses to Augustin that she only wishes she could go with him to Vienna and lead the simple life. They discuss it in a duet:

Hélène is under no illusions as to the direction in which her future husband's amorous interests lie, and her reply to Nicola's appointment of Anna to be her Lady-in-Waiting is to appoint Augustin to be her Gentleman-in-Waiting.

ACT III

The last act is set in a castle which was formerly the country seat of Prince Bogumil's family and is now a monastery. Here the wedding between Prince Nicola and Princess Hélène is to be celebrated. Bogumil and the Major-Domo, Jasomirgott, are exchanging reminiscences with one of the monks concerning the night, seventeen years earlier, on which Hélène and Anna both came into the world. Father Matthaeus remembers it well and recalls that on the baby

Princess's shoulder he had noticed a birth-mark in the likeness of a champagne cork—a hereditary birth-mark in Prince Bogumil's family. It now becomes clear that at their christening the two babies must have got mixed up, for it is Anna on whose shoulder the birth-mark appears, and Hélène is therefore Jasomirgott's daughter. Bogumil is anxious to keep this discovery secret, for fear of jeopardising the marriage. Meanwhile, Augustin has broken off his engagement to Anna, disgusted by her amorous attitude to Nicola, Anna is longing desperately to be Nicola's wife, and Hélène is equally anxious to marry Augustin. To put the two girls out of their misery, Jasomirgott tells them the true facts of their origins. Hélène leads the delighted Anna to Prince Nicola and then teasingly tells Augustin that he must marry Jasomirgott's daughter. But Augustin, too, has heard the glad news, and finally clasps Hélène in his arms.

Die Rose von Stambul

(The Rose of Stamboul)

Operetta in Three Acts

By JULIUS BRAMMER *and* ALFRED GRÜNWALD

Music by LEO FALL

First produced on 2nd December, 1916, in Vienna, at the Theater an der Wien, with Betty Fischer, Louise Kartousch, Ernst Tautenhayn and Hubert Marischka.

CHARACTERS

HIS EXCELLENCY KAMEK PASHA
KONDJA GUEL, *his daughter*
ACHMED BEY
HERR FRIDOLIN MÜLLER, *from Hamburg*
FRIDOLIN, *his son*
MIDILI HANUM, SÜZELA, FATIMA, DURTANE, EMINE, SOBEIDE — *Kondja's girl-friends*
LYDIA KOOKS, *Kondja's companion*
BLACK, *an American journalist*
SADI, *Major-domo to Kamek Pasha*
CHORUS OF SOCIALITES, HOTEL GUESTS AND STAFF

ACT I

The first act is set in the harem of Kamek Pasha in Stamboul. Kondja Guel, the beautiful daughter of Kamek Pasha, is to be married to Achmed Bey, the son of an influential minister. But the idea of this marriage does not appeal to her, and she recalls sadly the days of her childhood when she had freedom and was allowed plenty of licence. Now that she is grown up, however, her whole life is governed by restrictions and she must go everywhere veiled. So heavily-veiled is she, in fact, that she has never set eyes on her fiancé—nor has she ever set eyes on the popular novelist, André Lery, with whom she has been conducting a fervent correspondence and with whom she firmly believes herself to be deeply in love. Now it so happens that Achmed Bey writes novels and that André Lery is his pen name. He is anxious that Kondja Guel shall love him for himself alone, and has therefore concealed from her the fact that he is also André Lery. He is deeply in love with the beautiful Turkish girl and describes his passion for her in an ardent song:

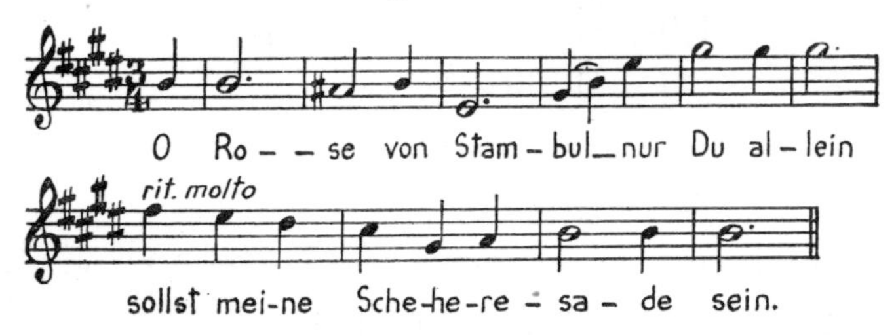

But Kondja Guel treats him with far less warmth and affection than her friend Midili Hanum treats her boy-friend, Fridolin Müller, son of a wealthy Hamburg business-man. Fridolin is a much craftier lover than Achmed Bey and has persuaded Midili Hanum to remove her veil and reveal to him all the charm of her beauty. He is consequently madly in love with her, and when she has misgivings over her sin against her religion committed by unveiling, he comforts her with the thought that all life is governed by Destiny and that the path of life is either one of roses or of thorns.

Coolly as Kondja Guel treats Achmed Bey, she is curious enough to be interested in his appearance, and as he is leaving the house she removes her veil and out of an upper window has an unimpeded view of him. To her surprise she has to admit that he is far better-looking than she had imagined—slim, elegant and handsome. She had written in her diary: "In the fifth month of Moharram, Kondja Guel was betrothed against her will to a man whom she had never seen." But now, opening her diary once again, she amends her entry, altering it to: "Kondja Guel was betrothed to a man with a pair of the most attractive but at the same time the boldest and most impertinent eyes."

ACT II

A few days later, in Achmed Bey's villa in Stamboul, he and Kondja Guel are married, and at last she removes her veil, for him to bask in the light of her beauty. Ardently he advances to take her in his arms, but she eludes him, coolly telling him that the mere signing of a marriage contract is not sufficient to inspire the flame of love within her. Before he can possess her he must woo her in the same way as women in the western cities—Vienna, for instance—are wooed by their lovers. Even when she is in his arms dancing a waltz on their wedding night he cannot really get any nearer to her. She is still hankering after André Lery. Although she has received a letter from the novelist (duly penned by Achmed Bey) telling her that he is so broken-hearted at the thought of her marriage to another man that he has left Stamboul and proposes to settle in

Switzerland, her thoughts are firmly with her dream-lover, and vainly does Achmed Bey try to woo her with the spell of a waltz:

Finally Achmed Bey loses patience with the capricious girl and threatens to use force to conquer her resistance. But Kondja Guel escapes through the bedroom door, locking it behind her, and appears in hat and fur coat on the veranda. She tells Achmed Bey that she is leaving him for André Lery and is on her way to Switzerland. Then it is that Achmed Bey tells her triumphantly that he has conquered her resistance, for *he* is André Lery. Kondja Guel laughs this ridiculous statement to scorn. "You, the genius who wrote those wonderful books? Never!" she declares, and telling him that the modern way with marriage is to make a trial and if that is a failure to admit defeat and say good-bye, she disappears into the night.

ACT III

The last act takes place some weeks later in "The Honeymoon Hotel" in a Swiss spa. Midili and Fridolin, who eloped during Act Two, are here happily married and blissfully in love.

Kondja Guel arrives, elegantly dressed in European clothes. She has written to inform André Lery of her arrival, and is shattered to learn from a lift-boy that the novelist has not yet arrived, but has ordered a room to be reserved for himself and his wife. This is a death-blow to her romantic dream of love, and she now greatly regrets that she so hastily brushed aside the love of her elegant, charming husband. Of course Achmed Bey arrives, and Kondja Guel learns that he is in truth André Lery, and nothing remains to interrupt the happiness of their stay at "The Honeymoon Hotel".

Madame Pompadour

Operetta in Three Acts

By Rudolph Schanzer *and* Ernst Welisch

Music by Leo Fall

First produced on 2nd March, 1922, at the Carl Theater, Vienna. London production on 20th December, 1933, at Daly's Theatre, with Evelyn Laye, Derek Oldham, Bertram Wallis and Huntley Wright.

Characters

MARQUISE DE POMPADOUR
KING LOUIS XV OF FRANCE
RENÉ D'ESTRADES
MADELEINE, *his wife*
BELOTTE, *lady's-maid to the Marquise*
JOSEPH CALICOT, *a poet*
MAURÈPAS, *Chief of Police*
CHORUS OF GRISETTES, BOHEMIANS, COURTIERS AND SOLDIERS

The action takes place in Paris in the middle of the eighteenth century.

ACT I

Act One takes place in a Paris tavern. It is Carnival time, and on the evening when the curtain rises a noisy crowd is enjoying itself listening to the revolutionary poet, Calicot, whose satirical songs are directed against King Louis, and especially against his reigning favourite, the Marquise de Pompadour. But the singing of revolutionary songs in public places is, traditionally, a dangerous game. Tonight, for instance, concealed among the crowd is the Chief of Police, Maurèpas. A bitter enemy of the Pompadour, he is always hoping to catch her out in some discreditable adventure or situation so that he may report her to the King and jeopardise her position as Court favourite. Tonight he has noticed her steal away from the Court Ball in company with her maid, Belotte, and has followed them to the tavern. The Pompadour is masked and all set for a romantic adventure, as she confesses to Belotte:

Soon after her arrival at the tavern the Pompadour is picked up by a handsome young man, Count René d'Estrades, who, bored by his wife and by life in the country, has come to Paris, *en garçon*, to enjoy the Carnival. René is a friend of Calicot's and has been one of the principal instigators in encouraging him to sing his political songs. He is enchanted by the beautiful unknown in the mask and asks her name. She tells him it is Jeanne. The Pompadour also is greatly attracted to René. While she is talking to him she spots the Chief of Police among the crowd. Taking the bull by the horns, she marches straight up to him and urges him to lay the revolutionary element by the heels: she has had her suspicions that this sort of thing was going on and has come out to see for herself. After accosting Maurèpas, the Pompadour endeavours to persuade René to leave the tavern, but before he has time to get away Maurèpas enters with a detachment of soldiers, and both René and Calicot are arrested. To their dismay, the Pompadour, declaring that midnight has chimed and that Carnival is therefore at an end, removes her mask and declares herself. Calicot is seized with terror and René with rage. He turns on the Pompadour, accusing her of leading him on with words of love and affection only to land him in a trap, and bursts into Calicot's insulting song. Maurèpas is about to remove his prisoners to the Bastille when the Pompadour stops him. She sentences Calicot to an appointment as Court Poet and appoints René a member of her personal bodyguard.

ACT II

The scene is the boudoir of the Marquise de Pompadour. From her attitude to René it is quite obvious why she has had him seconded to her personal bodyguard, and they are now on the most intimate terms. René is passionately in love and full of hope:

Meanwhile René's wife, Madeleine, agitated at her husband's long absence and complete silence, has come to Paris in search of him. Seeking help, she presents a letter of introduction to the Marquise de Pompadour from her late father. From the letter the Pompadour realises that Madeleine must be her half-sister, but she has no inkling of the fact that René and Madeleine are husband and wife. She receives Madeleine kindly and generously, and tells her maids to provide her with a new dress more in keeping with the fashion at Court than the one she is wearing.

Meanwhile, Calicot has been struggling to compose a Court Masque. At first he finds the change-over from revolutionary satires disconcerting. But a tenderness between him and Belotte has sprung up and he finds her company most inspiring. Maurèpas has by no means given up hope of embarrassing the Pompadour and is perpetually on the *qui vive*, hoping to trap her *en tête-à-tête* with her lover in the presence of the King. But he has wrongly assumed that her lover of the moment is Calicot. When Calicot hears of the fact that he is suspected of being the Pompadour's lover, he works himself up into a terrible state. He begs her to leave him in peace, and not to demand his love, as Potiphar's wife did Joseph's:

The Pompadour, however, is delighted that Maurèpas' suspicions are directed against the wrong man and, lulled into a sense of false security, she smuggles the ecstatic René into her bedroom, promising to come to him before midnight. René is in the seventh heaven and sings:

But before she can join René the Pompadour meets Madeleine, and during their conversation Madeleine shows her a portrait of René. Soberly the Pompadour realises the impossibility of conducting a love affair with her sister's husband, and she promises Madeleine to find René and to restore him to her. Then, with totally unexpected suddeness, the King appears. Maurèpas has informed him that the Pompadour is betraying him with Calicot and that he can catch them *in flagrante delicto*. Actually poor, innocent Calicot *is* in the room when the King enters, but he has just time to conceal himself in a cabinet containing State papers concerning matters whose control the King has delegated to the Pompadour. Highly suspicious from what Maurèpas has told him, the King forces his way into the Pompadour's bedroom and René is discovered and is led away under arrest. The Pompadour refuses to be intimidated by the King's threats, however, and tells him boldly that in future he can conduct all matters of State without her assistance and she orders the servants to remove the cabinet containing the State papers—and Calicot—to the King's apartments. She has only one thought in her mind: to save René from disgrace and death.

ACT III

The last act takes place in the King's study. He has already signed the warrant for the prisoner's execution. The warrant is made out in the name of Calicot, for his was the name reported by Maurèpas to the King as the Pompadour's lover, but when Calicot is discovered in the cabinet it becomes immediately apparent that the suspicions levelled against him are unfounded. The Pompadour, too, is able to claim her innocence when she proves that the man in her bedroom was, in fact, her sister's husband. The King forgives her and delegates a handsome young officer to escort her back to her apartments. From the way the Pompadour looks at him as they leave the room, the young officer is obviously destined to be René's successor. Calicot, to his delight, receives from His Majesty a life pension—officially intended for Voltaire—and is able to marry Belotte. And René returns to the arms of his faithful Madeleine.

Hugdietrichs Brautfahrt

(Hugdietrich in Search of a Wife)

Comedy Fairy-Operetta in Three Acts

By RIDEAMUS (FRITZ OLIVEN)

Music by OSCAR STRAUS

First produced on 10th March, 1906, at the Carl Theater, Vienna.

CHARACTERS

HUGDIETRICH, *Ruler of Byzantium*
THE FAIRY BELLADONNA
LADISLAUS, *King of Salonica*
PRINCESS MIKI, *his daughter*
PRINCE KAKERLAK, *her fiancé*
SCHNIDIBUMPFEL, *a Dragon*
CHORUS OF COURTIERS, VARLETS AND MEMBERS OF THE LEAGUE OF VIRTUE

The action takes place in Byzantium and Salonica in mythical times.

ACT I

In the throne-room of the palace at the Court of Byzantium the courtiers are assembled to wish their ruler, Hugdietrich, many happy returns of his birthday. A slight effeminate-looking figure seated on the throne, he returns thanks to his courtiers for their good wishes, singling out for especial mention the lady dancers of the Royal Ballet. The only clouds which darken the horizon on this happy day are the adverse reports from several Ministers of State. The Chancellor of the Exchequer reports that the country is bankrupt, largely due to the expense of keeping up the Court—an especially heavy item being the cost of the royal mistresses. Then the Home Secretary reports very adversely on the moral standards of the people. It seems the country faces both financial and moral bankruptcy. The King cheers up when the return of the Royal Marriage Commission is announced, and he wonders whether its members have come from abroad with news of a wealthy bride for him to marry. They do report that they found one eminently suitable candidate, wealthy, beautiful, of impeccable lineage—but one of the Commission, Alcibiades, has married her himself. The King is livid at his disloyalty, but Alcibiades calms him down by telling the King that he is well out of the match, for she turned out to be such a termagant that she and Alcibiades have already parted. Very cast down, the King dismisses the Court and, closing his eyes, drops off to sleep.

As he sleeps, out of the shadows steal a company of elves and fairies who dance around the throne, and presently there enters the Fairy Belladonna, a character corresponding to the Fairy Queen of Pantomime. Standing over the sleeping monarch she conjures up a dream and sings to him:

When he awakes, she tells him the reason for her visit. She believes that she and the King may be able to assist each other mutually. She has offended her father and been banished from Fairyland, and her only hope of redeeming her fault is to help a sinner to find once more the path to virtue. Here she believes King Hugdietrich can help her. Apparently, after her fall from grace, Fairy Belladonna took the post of Lady-in-Waiting at the Court of Ladislaus, King of Salonica. But the King tried to assail her virtue, and when she demanded marriage as the price of her favours, he gave her the Order of Virtue, a small letter of credit, and the Order of the Boot. In her fury she swore an oath that she would serve King Ladislaus' daughter as he served her, and knowing that Hugdietrich is seeking a wealthy bride she suggests that Princess Miki would fill the bill. There is only one snag. Fearing Fairy Belladonna's revenge, King Ladislaus has imprisoned his daughter in a tower and she is guarded by a ferocious Dragon, who has instructions to devour any man who approaches. Hugdietrich makes it quite clear that he has no intention of taking on a Dragon. But the Fairy Belladonna assures him that that will not be necessary. She will change the King by her magic arts into a beautiful girl, and then he can safely enter the tower. The King is all agog, and a long and amusing production number follows in which Hugdietrich is dressed up as a girl and coached by the Fairy in the arts of deportment and love-making:

Finally, seen off by the whole Court, King Hugdietrich sets off on his journey to seek his fortune in Salonica.

ACT II

In Salonica, Princess Miki, young, golden-haired, wealthy and beautiful, is sitting, bored and gloomy, on the balcony of her tower prison, guarded by an equally bored and depressed Dragon called Schnidibumpfel. The Dragon complains that no knight has shown up for a fortnight and in lieu of meat his diet has been grass and he has, in consequence, acute indigestion. The Princess is visited by her fiancé, Prince Kakerlak, whom she detests. He is President of the League of Virtue, and a moralising pedant. She makes open fun of his vaunted moral principles and when he asks her how she spends all her time, she answers that she spends it playing tunes on her comb.

King Ladislaus visits his daughter, and the Princess protests at her continued captivity. The King assures her that she needs protection against the threatened revenge of Fairy Belladonna. "What did you do to her to earn such undying hatred?" asks the Princess. "What did *I* do?" replies the King. "She tried to seduce *me* and I sacked her." At this a disembodied voice comments:

"Ladislaus, it's no good trying
To get out of it by lying."

Prince Kakerlak rebukes the King in his best moralising manner, giving his opinion that His Majesty's conduct must have been particularly abominable to conjure up such spirit voices.

The arrival of a lady is now announced, and in comes Hugdietrich in the form of a beautiful girl, wringing her hands and begging for shelter and protection from the amorous advances of the dissolute King Hugdietrich. Ladislaus immediately tries to make love to the new arrival, and a ridiculous scene follows with him chasing Hugdietrich, shouting for help, round a tree. His cries summon the League of Virtue. Prince Kakerlak is affronted at Ladislaus' behaviour, but Ladislaus declares he was testing the girl's moral defences and, finding them impregnable, now intends to appoint her Lady-in-Waiting to Princess Miki. This is of course playing straight into Hugdietrich's hands, and the act finishes with the ceremonial installing of Huglinde (as Hugdietrich has named himself) in the tower, with the Princess standing on her balcony in the moonlight offering up a prayer for a knight to come to her rescue. Down below the Dragon offers up a similar prayer: a well-covered knight would make a nice change of diet from grass.

ACT III

In a room in the tower Princess Miki is chatting to her new Lady-in-Waiting, Huglinde. The two girls have become great friends and both are enjoying a cigarette. But Hugdietrich nearly gives himself away by forgetting his adopted role and declaring that he does not approve of women smoking. "And what about yourself?" asks Princess Miki. "Are you a woman or aren't you?" She goes on to tell Huglinde of her longing for love and romance, especially now that spring has come:

Eventually Hugdietrich discloses his sex to the Princess, steps out of his dress and appears before her in doublet and hose, at which she bursts into a joyous melody:

Princess Miki and Hugdietrich retire, and as soon as the room in the tower is empty, a secret door opens and in come the members of the League of Virtue. They are sick and tired of their virtuous lives and to assert their independence they propose to slay the Dragon and try their luck with the girls. But Schnidibumpfel is not to be so easily caught, and he is about to devour the members of the League of Virtue when the Fairy Belladonna appears. She tells the Dragon he is welcome to devour the male members of the League, but he is not to touch the women. Schnidibumpfel has not much time for women, and embarks on an account of how his girl-friend played him false. Fairy Belladonna succeeds in soothing him, and the members of the League of Virtue are safe for the moment. They ask the Fairy who she is, and she tells them how she was Lady-in-Waiting at this very Court and how King Ladislaus tried to force his way into her bedroom. At that moment footsteps are heard approaching and all hide, as into the room in the tower tip-toes the King. He obviously has amorous designs on Huglinde. But in his path stands a figure of Nemesis, and Ladislaus, to his horror, recognises Belladonna. She tells him that her revenge is complete. She is responsible for the Princess's new Lady-in-Waiting, and Huglinde is a man. However, in come Princess Miki and Hugdietrich, very pleased with life and with themselves, to ask for Ladislaus' blessing. "But what about Prince Kakerlak?" he asks. "I have devoured him," answers the Dragon, and the Princess' cup of happiness is full.

Ein Walzertraum

(A Waltz Dream)

Operetta in Three Acts

By FELIX DÖRMANN *and* L. JACOBSON

Based on a short story from Buch der Abenteuer *by* HANS MÜLLER

Music by OSCAR STRAUS

First produced on 2nd March, 1907, at the Carl Theater, Vienna. First London production in 1908 at Hicks' Theatre, with Robert Michaelis, W. H. Berry and Lily Elsie. Modern version, with revised Libretto by Armin Robinson and Eduard Rogati and musical adaptation by Bruno Uher, produced in 1957 at the Volksoper, Vienna.

CHARACTERS

JOACHIM XIII, *Prince of Flausenthurm*
PRINCESS HÉLÈNE, *his daughter*
COUNT LOTHAR, *his cousin*
LIEUTENANT NIKI
LIEUTENANT MONTSCHI
FRIEDERIKE VON INSTERBURG, *Lady-in-Waiting to Princess Hélène*
FRANZI STEINGRUBER, *Conductor of a ladies' orchestra*
TSCHINELLENFIFI, ANNERL } *members of the orchestra*
CHORUS OF COURTIERS, OFFICERS, TOWNSFOLK, MEMBERS OF A LADIES' ORCHESTRA

ACT I

The first act is set in the throne-room of the castle of Prince Joachim XIII in Flausenthurm. It is the wedding day of his daughter, Princess Hélène, who marries handsome young Niki, Lieutenant of Hussars. Now, Niki ought by all natural laws to consider himself a very lucky young man, for, during a visit to Vienna, Princess Hélène met and fell in love with him and insisted on marrying the man of her choice. Not that Lieutenant Niki was averse to the match: he also fell genuinely in love with his beautiful Princess. But ever since his arrival in Flausenthurm, the combination of Court etiquette and the hostility of Count Lothar, the Prince's cousin, who had himself hoped to marry Princess Hélène, have conspired to turn love's young dream into a nightmare. This has had a palpable effect on the young couple, and their relation to each other has changed from affectionate intimacy to cold formality. Beneath the surface, however, there still glows the flame of an abiding love in both of them. Princess Hélène is continually being urged by her Lady-in-Waiting, Friederike von Insterburg, to show more restraint in her attitude to her husband; after all, he is only Prince Consort. "He is my husband *before* all," says the Princess angrily. "But, remember, a little indifference will make him love you more," advises Friederike. "I hope so," sighs the Princess. "But it is very difficult."

Niki's only solace is his friend, Lieutenant Montschi, whom he has been allowed to retain as his personal Aide-de-Camp. He confides to Montschi his realisation that he is only a pawn in a political game, otherwise of no importance. "But," he adds significantly, "a pawn may call checkmate sometimes, and I've a good mind to show them I'm a man of flesh and blood, and not a mere puppet." In this belligerent mood he stands up to the critical attitude of both his father- and cousin-in-law, and finally asks the Prince straight out why he has been chosen to marry the Princess. "To be the male parent of my grandchildren," is the reply. "So, you expect me to be a puppet, a lay figure to dance at the end of a dozen apron-strings," says Niki angrily. "Well, then, good-bye. I don't know much about marriage in general, but this one's a failure and it's not my fault." Prince Joachim and Count Lothar depart, fuming, and Montschi re-appears. He has great news. In the public gardens near the castle a Viennese orchestra—all girls—is playing. A longing comes over the two young men to hear Viennese music and dream themselves back in Vienna, and they sing nostalgically:

That evening, as soon as it is dark, Niki and Montschi creep out of the palace en route for the public gardens. Montschi feels himself in duty bound to remind Niki that it is his wedding night, but Niki is in a devil-may-care mood and quite oblivious of other considerations. Their departure, however, has not gone entirely unnoticed; and Count Lothar shakes his fist at their retreating backs.

ACT II

Act Two takes place in the public gardens near the castle of Flausenthurm. On the right is an open-air restaurant and on the left a band-stand. As the curtain rises an all-ladies Viennese orchestra is just finishing a rousing march. The lively applause calls for an encore, and this is a "speciality" for the Conductor, an attractive girl called Franzi. By this time Niki and Montschi have arrived on the scene. Niki is enchanted with Franzi and just in the mood to be consoled by a pretty girl. Franzi too is greatly attracted to the handsome young Viennese officer, without suspecting for a moment that he is the Prince Consort. The two are soon on terms of affection and sing a tender duet:

But trouble is on the way in the form of Count Lothar, who turns up in pursuit of Niki, accompanied by Prince Joachim. He is very hopeful of catching Niki *in flagrante delicto* with one of the Viennese girls and thus accomplishing his downfall and possible banishment (in which case Lothar would be heir-apparent to the throne). The trouble is that in their search Lothar and Joachim are deflected and both fall victims to members of the ladies' orchestra. Prince Joachim, thoroughly enjoying himself with Fifi, who plays the Big Drum, tells Lothar that he has come to the conclusion that Princes do not mix sufficiently with their subjects. Count Lothar also takes one look at Franzi and immediately forgets the purpose of his visit. But Franzi refuses to take him seriously, and makes fun of him in this amusing duet:

Princess Hélène and her Lady-in-Waiting now appear in search of the fugitive Niki. She happens to ask Franzi if she has seen a friend of theirs who comes from Vienna—a Lieutenant. Franzi soon realises that they are talking about Niki. "Oh!" she says, "I've been having supper with him during the interval and now he's wandering about the garden, I suppose, flirting with some girl. But I know how to get him back. He loves our Viennese music. He'll come back to me when I play my Dream Waltz." And sure enough Niki returns to the music. He sees Hélène and, taking her hand, begins to dance with her. But Franzi from her position on the band-stand has seen the two of them, and is furious with the strange girl for taking away her boy-friend. She leaves the orchestra and, pushing her way through the dancers, drags Niki away from Hélène, exclaiming angrily: "He's my boy." Franzi starts to dance with Niki, but he gently releases her and returns to Hélène. By now the crowd have recognised Princess Hélène and her Consort and give them a rousing welcome, waving hats and handkerchiefs, and Franzi suddenly realises who Niki must be. With a cry of "The Prince Consort!", she sinks down on the steps of the bandstand. Then, recovering herself, she resumes the conducting of her orchestra, while Niki, offering his arm to Hélène, returns with her to the castle.

ACT III

In the throne-room at Castle Flausenthurm some days later, the courtiers are discussing the scandal caused by the Prince Consort's disgraceful desertion of Princess Hélène on their wedding night. The Princess, however, is determined to win back her husband's love, and to this end she enters into a conspiracy with Franzi. She has Franzi come to the castle daily to teach her the words and music of "The Dream Waltz", which has such a fascinating effect on Niki. Franzi also reads her a lecture on life, based on her own experience of men. "Women are queer creatures," she tells the Princess. "So are men. A woman wants to be made love to, that's her nature—and a man wants to make love, that's his nature. And when the right woman won't let the right man make love to her it's against nature, and then there's trouble. Your husband is in love with you, and it is because he *is* in love with you that he felt desperate and made a little love to me. Pretended to make love. He is not in love with me. He is in love with you. Show him you want his love and he won't take it elsewhere." And so, thanks to Franzi's philosophy, all ends happily. For Niki hears Hélène singing "The Dream Waltz" and rushing to her clasps her in his arms; while Hélène murmurs happily: "We must thank Franzi, Niki."

Der Tapfere Soldat

(The Chocolate Soldier)

Operetta in Three Acts

By RUDOLF BERNAUER *and* LEOPOLD JACOBSON

English version by STANISLAUS STANGE

Music by OSCAR STRAUS

Book and Lyrics based on G. B. SHAW'S Arms and the Man

First production on 14th November, 1908, at the Theater an der Wien, Vienna. First London production at the Lyceum Theatre on 10th October, 1910, with C. H. Workman as "Lieutenant Bumerli" and Constance Drever as "Nadina".

CHARACTERS

COLONEL POPOFF, *of the Bulgarian army*
AURELIA, *his wife*
NADINA, *their daughter*
MASCHA, *Nadina's cousin*
MAJOR ALEXIUS SPIRIDOFF, *Nadina's fiancé*
SERGEANT MASSAKROFF, *of the Bulgarian army*
LIEUTENANT BUMERLI, *of the Serbian army*
CHORUS OF SOLDIERS, COUNTRYFOLK, ETC.

ACT I

The scene is a bedroom in the house of Colonel Popoff of the Bulgarian army, situated near the Dragoman Pass in Bulgaria. The year is 1885, and the Serbo-Bulgarian war is in full swing. Colonel Popoff has gone to the war, leaving his family, which consists of his daughter Nadina, her cousin, Mascha, and her mother, Aurelia, at home. Terrified, the three women listen in the darkness to the sound of distant cannon and rifle-shooting as the battle draws nearer, and deplore the absence of their menfolk—especially Nadina, who sings of her absent fiancé, Major Alexius Spiridoff. Since his brilliant cavalry charge against the Serbians he is idolised by Nadina for his heroism.

As she finishes her song, in through the window climbs a young officer in Serbian uniform. He is Lieutenant Bumerli, a Swiss officer attached to the commissary department of the Serbian forces. He has been attacked by a Bulgarian patrol, but has eluded them by climbing into Nadina's bedroom. By the exercise of charm, skilful argument, quick wits and his good looks, Bumerli persuades Nadina, half against her will, to conceal him. She mocks at him for greedily devouring chocolate drops, and disparagingly nicknames him "The Chocolate Soldier". During their conversation Bumerli explodes the myth of Alexius' much-vaunted courage by telling Nadina that he never intended to lead the famous cavalry charge at the Battle of Slivinski. In fact, he was pulling in his horse as hard as he could, but it ran away with him. "When he found he couldn't stop," continues Bumerli, "he yelled for the others to join him. On they came, riding to certain death, for one discharge of our guns would have blown them to pieces. How we laughed until we discovered that we had the wrong ammunition and couldn't fire a shot. Then they cut us to bits." Nadina is furious to hear her fiancé thus disparaged and orders Bumerli to leave; but she is already beginning to fall for the smiling Lieutenant, and they sing a duet:

The military patrol are on Bumerli's track and now arrive to search Colonel Popoff's house for the supposed spy. Nadina hides him behind a portière and pretends to be innocently asleep in bed when the soldiers enter. Their search is fruitless and they withdraw. After they have gone, loud snoring from behind the portière betrays Lieutenant Bumerli's hiding-place, and Nadina introduces him to her mother and her cousin. The three women, who are longing for the sight of a man, are enchanted by Bumerli's good looks. They ply him with food and champagne, and when he explains that he cannot leave the house in Serbian uniform, for fear of being shot, they give him Colonel Popoff's house-coat and trousers and each of the women slips, unobserved, a signed photograph of herself into the pocket. Then the exhausted Bumerli is put to bed. He immediately falls fast asleep, and the three women watch over him in turn to a tender lullaby.

ACT II

Act Two takes place in the courtyard and gardens outside Colonel Popoff's house six months later. It is a May morning, and the household are welcoming home the heroes from the war to a rousing tune, while the heroes are equally glad to be back:

Thrilled as Nadina was at the idea of welcoming home her fiancé, Alexius, reality brings disillusion. He strikes her as pompous and conceited, especially when he tells her: "Any girl should consider herself most lucky to be my future wife." He tries to boast about his prowess in the cavalry charge at the Battle of Slivinski, but Nadina quickly shows that she knows the truth of that story, and Alexius is puzzled and annoyed. Colonel Popoff now tells the ladies about the funny Swiss called Bumerli, who escaped capture by climbing into a young lady's bedroom—only to have three women fall in love with him. The ladies are greatly embarrassed, especially as Bumerli has never returned Colonel Popoff's house-coat, which they lent him for his escape. Aurelia is wondering what to do if her husband demands the missing house-coat, when Lieutenant Bumerli walks in to return it, and he has just handed it over when Colonel Popoff enters. He is amazed to see Bumerli, but greets him warmly and invites him to stay for Nadina's marriage to Alexius. Colonel Popoff now asks for his house-coat, which is handed over to him by Aurelia. Too late the three ladies discover that their signed photographs are still in the pockets, and they are in a fever lest Colonel Popoff discover them. Eventually, after several abortive attempts, the ladies do recover the photographs, but two of them get the wrong one. Thus Mascha gets possession of Nadina's signed, "From Nadina to her Chocolate Soldier", while Nadina gets Mascha's likeness inscribed, "Mascha to the Swiss, who could go for once without". Bumerli is sincerely in love with Nadina, and she indicates to him that she also is by no means indifferent to his charms. But they say a sad farewell, and Nadina is presenting him with her photograph as a parting present when she happens to look at it and reads: "Mascha to the Swiss who could go for once without." "Without what?" she asks, and Bumerli points to his trousers. "Mascha gave this to you?" she asks furiously. "Let me explain," he begs, but she answers inexorably: "There is nothing to explain," and rushes away.

The guests now enter for Nadina's wedding to Alexius, and among them is Sergeant Massakroff, who was in command of the patrol of men who were pursuing Bumerli on the night he climbed through Nadina's window. Massakroff immediately identifies Bumerli, and the whole story of his sojourn in Nadina's bedroom is revealed. To make matters worse, Mascha, who is in love with Alexius and wants to marry him, produces the photograph inscribed "Nadina to her Chocolate Soldier" and triumphantly shows it to Alexius. He turns from Nadina with a cry of "Betrayed!" while she retorts that he can consider himself free from his engagement to marry her, and the curtain falls on her question: Where is my hero? Where's my ideal?

ACT III

The last act takes place in the same setting that afternoon and is concerned with the sorting out of the tangled love affairs of Nadina, Bumerli, Mascha and

Alexius. Nadina sits down and writes a tart letter of farewell to Bumerli. But Bumerli is a pertinacious character and is not so easily put off. He is even undismayed by a prospect of a duel with the hero Alexius. This is, however, avoided, and Nadina finally capitulates to his persistence—only to find that Bumerli is a wealthy man with a castle in Spain, a palace in Italy, a ducal estate in Germany and several Swiss chalets, and, in fact, the senior partner of the firm of Bumerli and Co., the largest universal providers of the Continent. Mascha surrenders herself to Alexius, and so the curtain falls on the happiest of endings.

Der Letzte Walzer

(The Last Waltz)

Operetta in Three Acts

By JULIUS BRAMMER *and* ALFRED GRÜNEWALD

Music by OSCAR STRAUS

First produced in 1920 at the Berliner Theater, Berlin, with Fritzi Massary and Otto Storm. London production on 7th December, 1922, at the Gaiety Theatre, with José Collins.

CHARACTERS

GENERAL MIECU KRASINSKI
BARON IPPOLITH MRKOVICH BASCHMATSCHKIN, *his nephew*
ALEXANDROVNA NATASIA OPALINSKI, *a General's widow*
VERA LISAVETA, ANNUSCHKA, HANNUSCHKA, PETRUSHKA — *her daughters*
PRINCE PAUL
COUNT DIMITRI VLADIMIR SARRASOV
CAPTAIN KAMINSKI, *Officer of the Guard*
OFFICERS, GUESTS, DANCERS, SERVANTS

The action takes place one winter's night in 1910 in General Krasinski's castle near Warsaw and in Prince Paul's palace in Warsaw.

ACT I

The scene is an ante-room off the ballroom in General Krasinski's castle in the countryside near Warsaw. The General is giving a celebration ball and dancing has just begun. The situation when the curtain rises is an unusual one. In the custody of General Krasinski is Count Dimitri Vladimir Sarrasov, who lately had occasion to rescue two ladies from the drunken importunities of the dissolute Prince Paul during a Court ball in the royal palace in Warsaw. The Prince immediately ordered his arrest and a court-martial has condemned him to death. The interval between the sentence and the execution Dimitri is passing in the custody of General Krasinski. Both the General's and his fellow-officers' sympathies are with Dimitri, and the General treats him more as an honoured guest than as a prisoner. One of the ladies whom he so gallantly rescued, Vera Lisaveta, is staying at the castle with her mother and her three sisters. Prince Paul has commanded a marriage between Vera Lisaveta and General Krasinski (who is years older than his fiancé) to hush up the recent scandal and to stop wagging tongues. Tonight's ball is to celebrate the engagement of the ill-matched pair. During the ball Vera Lisaveta catches sight of her gallant rescuer, for Dimitri is allowed the run of the house and is watching the dancing from the ante-room. Vera Lisaveta's heart beats disturbingly at sight of the man who sacrificed his life for her sake. He has stirred up forgotten feelings, which she likens to words unspoken, kisses untasted, red roses that have never bloomed:

Seeing Dimitri watching the dancing, the General invites him to put on full evening dress and attend the ball. Captain Kaminski, who is directly responsible for the prisoner, protests at this unorthodox procedure, but relents on condition that Dimitri gives his word of honour not to attempt to escape. During the evening Dimitri dances with Vera Lisaveta, to whom he is as greatly attracted as she is to him, and as they dance together they think sadly of the cruel fate destined to separate them. This is the last waltz that they will ever dance together:

ACT II

The scene is the ballroom in General Krasinski's castle an hour or so later. Vera Lisaveta is racking her brains to find some means to effect Dimitri's escape from the castle and execution. At last she manages to organise a plan to smuggle him over the frontier to safety. But Dimitri at first refuses point-blank to seize the opportunity of escape. He has given his word and cannot break it. Passionately Vera Lisaveta argues and pleads with him. "Think of my situation," she begs him. "How shall I feel when I stand at the altar tomorrow as General Krasinski's bride in the knowledge that another man has sacrificed his life for me? For my sake you *must* live," she tells him. "But what about my word of honour?"

he argues. "There is something of even greater importance than the honour of a man," she tells him. "It is the honour of a woman. Listen," she continues. "I have made up my mind to save your life, and nothing is going to stand in my way. If you refuse to fall in with my plans and escape immediately, the General and all his guests shall be summoned to discover us in each other's arms. Now choose between your honour and mine. If you love me you will go." Unable to resist her appeal he kisses her, and she helps him into a fur coat, then, opening a garden door, she lets him out and from a window watches his figure vanish into the night.

Now, Dimitri's execution is fixed for the following morning, and it is Captain Kaminski's responsibility to deliver his prisoner at the barracks in Warsaw this evening. In view of the ball and his regard for Dimitri he has delayed departure till the last possible moment. But now he is anxious to be off and sends several junior officers to collect the prisoner. Standing at the window from which she watched Dimitri's escape, Vera Lisaveta remarks on the beauty of a Polish winter night: the moon on the snow, the stars in the sky, the distant lights of the city. She calls Captain Kaminski over to the window and points out to him a thin, moving pencil of light in the distance. "The Nice express," she tells him, "bound for sunshine and the blue Mediterranean." "But, wait," breaks in the General, who is also watching. "Why is it stopping at the local station?" He is interrupted by the entrance of the officers to report that Dimitri is nowhere to be found. At that moment the whistle of a railway engine is heard and as Captain Kaminski orders the officers to resume their search, Vera Lisaveta tells him triumphantly that it is useless. Dimitri has escaped, and is in the Nice express and beyond their reach. "I can't understand it," protests the troubled Kaminski. "To think that Dimitri should so far forget his duty as to break his word of honour!" "You are mistaken. *That* I would never do," declares a voice in ringing tones. All turn and there stands Dimitri. "Dimitri, why have you done this to me?" wails Vera Lisaveta, and Dimitri confesses that when he got out into the beauty of the starlit night, sanity returned. He realised that he could not break his word of honour and let down the friends who had stood sponsor for him during his last hours. Captain Kaminski steps forward. "Your hand, Count Sarrasov," he says. "I knew I could trust you." And as Dimitri is led away to Warsaw and execution, Vera Lisaveta breaks down at the thought of what might have been, and sadly sings:

ACT III

The last act takes place in a salon in the royal palace at Warsaw. The dissolute Prince Paul has had Vera Lisaveta brought secretly to the palace. He lusts after her, and this time there is no gallant cavalier to frustrate his desires and rescue the lady, for Dimitri is in a prison cell awaiting a summons to die. But the Prince has underestimated his adversary in Vera Lisaveta. Using all her woman's wiles and her whole battery of charms, she soon has him at her mercy, promising to give her anything she asks him. He even agrees to give her absolute jurisdiction over the palace for the next twenty-four hours. And the first order that she gives is for Dimitri to be released and brought before her. Realising that Vera Lisaveta has got the better of him, Prince Paul makes the best of a bad job. He pardons Dimitri, agrees to their marriage and gives them both his blessing.

Drei Walzer

(Three Waltzes)

Operetta in Three Parts (Twelve Scenes)

By PAUL KNEPLER *and* ARMIN ROBINSON

Music by OSCAR STRAUS

First produced on 5th October, 1935, in Zürich. London production on 1st March, 1945, at Princes Theatre, with Evelyn Laye and Esmond Knight.

PART I

CHARACTERS

FANNY PICHLER, *a dancer*
BELTRAMINI, *Ballet Master*
JOSEF BRUNNER, *theatrical agent*
JOHANN BRUNNER, *his son*
FRAU ZORNGRÜBER, *a landlady*
COUNT RUDOLF SCHWARZENEGG, *an officer*
COUNTESS KATHERINA, *his aunt*
OTHER PARTS INCLUDE VARIOUS MEMBERS OF THE SCHWARZENEGG FAMILY, CHORUS OF BALLET-GIRLS AND SERVANTS

The action takes place in Vienna in 1865.
The music of Part I is based on themes by Johann Strauss, the elder.

SCENE I. The curtain rises on a rehearsal in the ballet room of the Kärtnerthortheater. The rehearsal is an important one, as the ballet is about to fulfil an engagement in Paris. The Ballet Master, Herr Beltramini, complains that his most talented dancer, Fanny Pichler, is late, and the giggling ballet-girls tell him that Fanny has a rendezvous with Count Rudolf Schwarzenegg. Herr Beltramini is very vexed with her when she *does* appear, full of apologies, but nobody can be angry with Fanny for long and her charm and gaiety soon restore his good humour. Fanny, however, will not consider the engagement in Paris, although her agents, Josef Brunner and his son, urge her to sign the contract. With all the intense passion of a nineteen-year-old girl she loves Rudolf Schwarzenegg and looks forward to a future as his wife.

SCENE 2. In the house of Count Rudolf Schwarzenegg's aunt, Katherina, a family council is being held. The family is shocked to learn that Rudolf's latest affair with the ballet-girl, Fanny Pichler, is no light-hearted flirtation but that he is seriously in love. It is their intention to read the riot act. But, to his Aunt Katherina's secret admiration, Rudolf holds his own and tells his grim old uncles that he has a right to lead his own life and to marry whom he chooses, even though it should necessitate resigning his commission. With that he makes his escape, leaving his elders sadly vexed and troubled.

SCENE 3. In her lodgings Fanny is awaiting her lover. Her kind-hearted landlady, Frau Zorngrüber, gives her a friendly warning about the dangers of marrying above her station. But the love-sick girl is deaf to her well-meant advice. Her agents arrive to renew their attempts to persuade her to sign the Paris contract. But Fanny begs Herr Brunner to give her time to think it over. She tells him frankly that though dancing has always been her life, her love for Rudolf is something bigger and for it she would not hesitate to give up her career. Shaking their heads sadly, the two agents depart. Any doubts which might have assailed Fanny, however, disappear when Rudolf arrives and she is folded in his arms. She is even proof against his Aunt Katherina's warning, when she calls on Fanny. The Countess Katherina in impressed by Fanny's charm and intelligence and can quite understand her nephew's feelings. She tells Fanny that she hopes he will never regret having to give up his commission and the Emperor's uniform, of which he has always been so proud. But Fanny comforts herself with the reflection that if she and Rudi were very poor, she could always support them by dancing. As the lovers are conversing, a regiment marches down the street—his Lancer regiment. He dashes to the window, and she notices with pain his care to conceal himself so that he should not be seen at her window; she notices, too, in his expression the eagerness, the dedication of the born soldier watching his regiment on the march. And suddenly she realises how heavy a sacrifice it would be for her lover to give up his career. Rather than make him unhappy she will renounce her love. She signs the contract for the Paris engagement, and when Rudolf kisses her good night that evening and makes his way back to barracks he little knows that he has said good-bye to his beloved for the last time.

PART II

Characters

CHARLOTTE PICHLER, *operetta star*
ALEXANDER JENSEN, *actor*
JOHANN BRUNNER, *theatrical agent (now aged about fifty)*
COUNT OTTO SCHWARZENEGG, *son of Rudolf*
FRITZ VON BODENHEIM, *his friend*
BARON LIEBINGER, *wealthy backer of theatrical productions*
HELENE, *his wife*
FRANZ, *a head-waiter*
OTHER PARTS INCLUDE PARTY GUESTS, THEATRE PEOPLE

The action moves to Vienna in 1900.
The music of Part II is based on themes by Johann Strauss the younger.

Scene 4. The cast are acknowledging the applause of an enthusiastic audience after the first performance of a new operetta, and in the wings a group wait to congratulate the star of the show, Charlotte Pichler. The congratulations of her colleague, Alexander Jensen, and her manager, Johann Brunner, mean more to her than anyone's, and Brunner tells her that her singing is just as beautiful as was her mother's dancing. Charlotte is very thrilled to meet Otto Schwarzenegg, the son of Rudolf of that name, of whom her mother often used to speak. Wanting to learn more about him, she accepts Baron Liebinger's invitation to a first-night supper-party at his house, though Brunner tells her she must be tired and should go home. But Charlotte already feels drawn to the young man and insists on going.

Scene 5. On the way to the party Otto Schwarzenegg confides to his friend, Fritz von Bodenheim, that his family are urging him to get married and that he has promised to wed the girl of their choice. This will mean the end of his affair with Baroness Liebinger—but how many such "affairs" has he already had without yet finding real love!

Scene 6. At Baron Liebinger's house the first-night party is in full swing, and Charlotte Pichler, as star of the show, is naturally the centre of attention. Baroness Liebinger manages to get Otto Schwarzenegg to herself. She is angry and unhappy at the termination of their affair. She does not for a moment believe that his forthcoming marriage is the true reason that he is giving her up and she jealously watches him in conversation with Charlotte. Later she realises that the two of them have left the party without Otto even saying good night to her. Swept off her feet, Charlotte has allowed him to take her to supper in a private room at Sacher's Hotel.

Scene 7. In a private room in Sacher's Hotel, Charlotte and Otto are supping. Otto is a regular client of Sacher's and well known to the head-waiter, Franz, who is quite accustomed to his frequent love affairs. For the first quarter of an hour Charlotte is on her best behaviour, but as Otto grows more and more ardent she finds herself responding to his passion and soon they are in each other's arms. A knock on the door warns them of the presence of Johann Brunner, who has called to take Charlotte home. Otto is walking on air. At last he believes he has found his true love. But the head-waiter smiles cynically: how often has he heard those same words from Otto's lips?

SCENE 8. Scene Eight is set in Charlotte's dressing-roon at the theatre. Both Brunner and Alexander Jensen are worried about her. Ever since she met Otto Schwarzenegg at Baron Liebinger's party she seems to have been under a spell. Brunner, now in his fifties and still a good-looking man, takes it upon himself to warn Charlotte. Having acted as impresario to her mother and having loved her, he has known that story before—the story of a Count Schwarzenegg and a simple Pichler. Charlotte remembers Brunner's warning when she receives a visit from Baroness Liebinger and the jealous woman proceeds to blacken Otto's character, declaring him to be a heartless flirt, content to lead a woman on by telling her she is "the only one" and then breaking her heart. This painful conversation is interrupted by the entrance of Otto. He quickly realises the trend of their talk and confesses frankly and freely to Charlotte his weaknesses and shortcomings. He swears to her that she is "the only one", and the phrase stabs her heart. Is he just playing with her and is she just one of a crowd, as Baroness Liebinger said? Coldly she bids Otto good-bye, and before he leaves she introduces Alexander Jensen to him as the man she is going to marry.

SCENE 9. The scene is the stage of the Theater an der Wien, Vienna's leading operetta theatre. The second act finale is in progress, and Charlotte has just reached an emotional climax in the music:

Suddenly she falls to the ground in a dead faint, a victim of unfulfilled love, and the curtain is lowered. For the second time the meeting of a Pichler and a Schwarzenegg has ended in sorrow.

PART III

CHARACTERS

FRANZI JENSEN-PICHLER, *a film actress*
COUNT FERDINAND SCHWARZENEGG
HERR LINDHEIM, *film producer of the Vienna Film A.G.*
JOHANN BRUNNER, *now in his eighties, but hale and hearty*
OTHER PARTS INCLUDE FILM TECHNICIANS, ACTORS, AN INNKEEPER, FILM EXTRAS, ETC.

The action takes place in Vienna in 1935.
The music of Part III is by Oscar Straus.

SCENE 10. The Vienna Film A.G. are making a picture to be entitled *Fanny Pichler's First Love*, depicting the romance of the famous dancer and Count Rudolf Schwarzenegg. Johann Brunner, now a hale and hearty eighty-year-old, is the author of the scenario. He was, of course, well acquainted with the protagonists of the story and is familiar with the details of their romance. The film company congratulate themselves on casting in the leading role Franzi Jensen-Pichler, daughter of Charlotte, the singer, and grand-daughter of the famous dancer. This is the work of Johann Brunner. He made her grandmother an international dancer, her mother a famous operetta singer, and now he wants to make Franzi a film star. Shooting is held up at the moment by the loss of the juvenile lead cast for the part of Count Rudolf Schwarzenegg, and the producer is in a quandary. At this juncture there calls at the studio a Count Ferdinand Schwarzenegg, who asks to see the scenario. He maintains that his family, though impoverished, is a distinguished one and he claims the right to censor any passages in the script of which he disapproves. Impressed with the young man's handsome appearance and aristocratic bearing, the producer agrees to his demands and ends up by offering him the chance to play the role of his ancestor. Ferdinand, at first nonplussed by the offer, finally accepts and is introduced to Franzi. He takes to her immediately, though Franzi is shaken to meet a descendant of the family whose men brought such unhappiness to her mother and grandmother. However, she pulls herself together, and the first day's work goes very amicably.

SCENE 11. At the inn, "Der Grüne Hirsch", Franzi and Ferdinand find old Johann Brunner and tell him of Ferdinand's film engagement. At first, remembering all the sadness of the past, he doesn't want to hear the name of Schwarzenegg. But when Ferdinand stands before him and he realizes his uncanny likeness to Rudolf, he has to admit that he is perfectly cast. Alone with Franzi, Ferdinand then tells her that he loves her. But all the bitterness and unhappiness of the past rise before her and in a panic she runs away from him.

SCENE 12. On the floor of the film studio the final scene of the film is to be shot today. Franzi and Ferdinand have worked well together and have become close friends. Johann Brunner, watching the shooting, complains of several liberties which have been taken with his scenario, protesting that was not at all what really happened; but even he has to admit that things have altered in seventy years when he sees Franzi and Ferdinand, after the final shot, locked in a lovers' embrace.

In one of the most charming of all his later operettas, Oscar Straus has succeeded admirably in characterising in his music the three contrasted periods. Following the title he has featured a waltz in each of the three parts: in Part I the flowing "Wien ist ein Liebeslied" for Fanny and Rudolf:

in Part II the emotional "Ich liebe das Leben" for Charlotte and Otto:

and in Part III Oscar Straus' own charming "Man sagt sich beim Abschied Adieu" for Franzi and Ferdinand:

Bozena

Operetta in Three Acts (Four Scenes)

By Julius Brammer *and* Alfred Grünwald

Music by Oscar Straus

First produced on 16th May, 1952, at the Theater am Gärtnerplatz, Munich, with Nora Jungwirt as "Bozena" and Bruno Manazza as "Karel".

Characters

BOZENA
KAREL
KOUDJELA, *a rich peasant*
NEPOMUK } *his sons*
SVATOPLUK }
THE STRANGER (BORISLAV)
KLOPOTKA, *innkeeper*
CILKA, *his daughter*
JAN BURRIAN, *a forester*
LIDUSCHKA, *Bozena's maid*
VACLAV PLEVNY, *a marriage broker*
THE BURGOMASTER
CHORUS OF PEASANTS, DANCERS, MUSICIANS, TOWNSFOLK, STALL-HOLDERS

ACT I

The scene is a village in Slovakia and the time the eighteen-eighties, when Bohemia was still a part of the Austro-Hungarian Empire. In the background stands the church and to the left an inn, "The Red Cat". The whole village square is gaily decorated with bunting, for today is a holiday. When the curtain rises dancing is in progress in the open air and the scene is a colourful one, with boys and girls in their national peasant dresses revolving to the music of a loud and cheerful band:

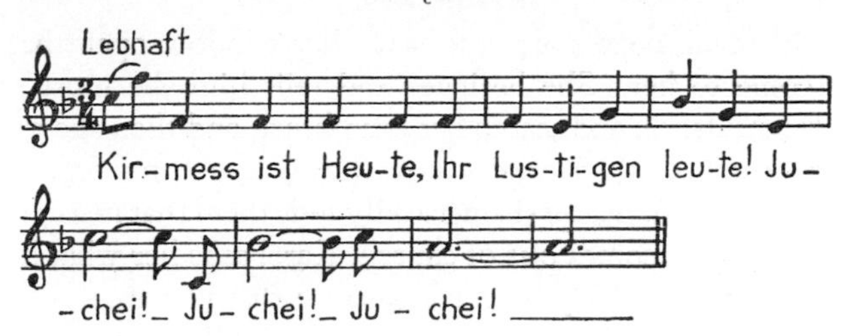

The inn is doing brisk business, all the tables in the open air are taken and there are continual shouts from the peasant boys for the landlord's pretty daughter, Cilka. She is jealously watched by Jan Burrian, a young forester, who is in love with her and wants to marry her. Formerly she had seemed to like him, but lately she has been avoiding him, and his heart is sore. The marriage broker—that familiar character in every Bohemian village—urges the landlord to marry off Cilka to one of the sons of the rich brewer, Koudjela. This brewer now arrives in the village in a great rage. He has been to visit Bozena, a wealthy but unattached young woman, who lives with her maid and farms in the neighbourhood. Koudjela's intention was to arrange a marriage between Bozena and one of his two sons, Nepomuk and Svatopluk. But Bozena, beautiful, proud and dignified, has peremptorily turned down both Koudjela's sons. He is smarting at her treatment and is determined to have his revenge.

To the delight of everyone today also marks the return of a handsome and popular young man called Karel. He has just completed three years' military service and receives a great ovation from the village, and especially from Cilka. He had promised to marry her before he went away and he is now prepared to fulfil that promise. In the meantime, Koudjela has been inflaming popular opinion in the village against Bozena as part of his plan of revenge. His idea is to persuade one of the good-looking peasant boys to win her love and, having done so, to turn her down. And who would fill the role more ideally than the handsome Karel? Karel is quite prepared to enter into the joke, and so the plot is laid. Later, Bozena with her little maid, Liduschka, appears in the village, where, instead of the usual black looks and cold reception—for the village regard Bozena as stand-offish and a snob—she is welcomed with smiles and the friendliest greetings. Karel approaches her, and she consents to dance with him, but she will not listen to any of his compliments when he tries to flatter her. When a service begins in the church, all becomes quiet on the village square, and Karel and Bozena are left alone together. Then, completely forgetting his self-imposed task, Karel falls genuinely under the spell of the beautiful woman, and she, too, is attracted to him. Passionately they sing:

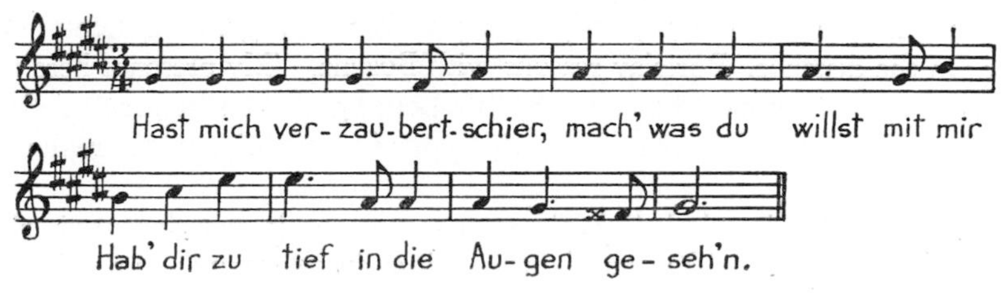

Karel, afire with love, begs Bozena to leave her window open that night and promises to come to her. She hesitates and tells him she must pray to her patron saint for guidance, and search her own heart, and then she goes into the church. The peasants ask excitedly how Karel is getting on, and whether Bozena is falling for him. Karel shamefacedly tells them that he is pretty sure of success. When Bozena comes out of church, Karel asks her what her heart has told her, and she answers: "My heart has told me that you are a cruel scoundrel who would disgrace me and bring about my downfall." She leaves him, but her words have greatly impressed him, and when Cilka tells him: "Karel, don't mind about a girl like Bozena," he pushes her furiously aside with: "No, I should not have done what I did."

ACT II

Scene 1. Next evening in a room in her farm-house Bozena bids the servants good night and then settles down to a chat with her maid, Liduschka. They discuss Bozena's brother, who years before deserted from the army and disappeared. As Bozena is saying her prayers there is a knock at the door and on the threshold stands a stranger. He tells her he brings news of her brother, Borislav. Something about him strikes her as familiar and she suddenly realises that the stranger himself is her long-lost brother and she embraces him warmly. He tells her how he came to desert. He was a young soldier in Prague, engaged to a girl whom he loved more than anything in the world. His Lieutenant seduced her and one day he caught them in each other's arms. He struck his superior officer in the face and then there was nothing for it but flight. He went to America, and now has an American passport and calls himself Andreas Smith. As they are talking there is a sound of distant music approaching and laughter and chatter. It is Karel with some of the lads of the village come to serenade Bozena and ask her forgiveness for his behaviour to her yesterday. Bozena, anxious for them to leave, is perfectly prepared to let bygones be bygones, but Karel is not to be got rid of so easily. He has brought the band and wants Bozena to dance with him to show that she really has forgiven him. He asks her to come out and join them in the garden. "Not now," says Bozena, thinking nervously of her brother. "I can't come out now. Please go." "You haven't by any chance got company?" asks Karel suspiciously and he springs lightly through the window into the room and discovers Borislav. "And that is the cold and haughty Bozena who never wanted to have anything to do with men," says Karel bitterly. "She has a lover, after all!" Bozena is furiously angry, but she will not give her brother away, and must therefore suffer the cynical sneers of Karel and his companions. They are all agog to spread the scandal of Bozena's behaviour round the village, and depart, their music growing fainter and fainter in the distance. Borislav reasons with Bozena. "My presence here will only land you in trouble," he tells her. "I'd better go." But Bozena is defiant. "I live my own life and am answerable to no one for my doings," she replies.

Scene 2. A musical interlude links these two scenes, and when the curtain rises it discloses the garden of Bozena's house. It is early morning in summer. The beds are gay with flowers and across the fields is a distant view of the church tower. Children are passing by on their way to school, and stop as usual to receive the little gifts of sweets and flowers that Bozena always gives them. But today they are reluctant to linger, for owing to village gossip their parents have forbidden them to speak to Bozena.

After the children have gone on their way to school, Bozena receives a visit from the Burgomaster of the village and his wife, and Koudjela. They have come to threaten her with summary justice at the hands of the "Village Court" for harbouring a lover in her house. (The Village Court was a court of morals which operated in Bohemia in the nineteenth century. The sentence of the court on guilty parties was the removal of the roof of their house so that their forebears in Heaven should see the wickedness of their ways.) Karel has heard of the villagers' intentions and hurries to Bozena's house to warn her of her danger. He is greatly concerned for her safety, and now knows that it is she whom he loves, and he longs to tell her so.

But Bozena will have nothing to do with Karel, nor will she confide to him the identity of the stranger in her house, so he is powerless to prevent the proceedings of the Village Court, which is now set up in the garden. Koudjela acts as judge, in a red cloak, with sceptre and a crown of golden paper. Half threatening, half joking, he requires Bozena to submit to the judgement of the "Court of the People", and Nepomuk and Svatopluk read the indictment against her. But Bozena tells them all to clear off her land. "I am in no mood for Kermesse—for fun," she shouts. "We'll see about that," says Koudjela. "We've tried to deal reasonably with you, but you are determined on defiance, and now we mean business. You have brought disgrace on the village by living openly with a man without the blessing of the Church. You know the consequences. The roof will be pulled off your house, so that your parents in Heaven may see that their daughter has turned her home into a brothel." Ladders are put up against the house and men prepare to demolish the roof. In an agony of shame and desperation Bozena screams, and Karel can bear no more. "Stop!" he cries out. "If anyone dares to touch that roof I will break every bone in his body." In the row which follows Karel's word prevails. He frightens Koudjela by reminding him that the law condemns the "Jury of the People" as mob violence. Bozena gratefully takes Karel's hand. "How can I thank you?" she asks. "By telling me the name of the man who is living with you," he answers. But Bozena still witholds his name, and Karel resents her proud defiance. He turns to Cilka. "Come on, darling," he says. "I'll marry you next week." Bozena is stricken to the heart, but she tells them scornfully: "I'll dance at your wedding."

ACT III

The scene of Act Three is again the village square. It is Karel and Cilka's wedding day, yet neither of them is in that state of ecstasy normal to lovers on their nuptial day. Karel's thoughts are all with Bozena, and Cilka is worried about Jan Burrian, who sits moodily outside the inn drinking and fingering his rifle. She tries to cheer him up, but he tells her that if he sees her married to another man he will move right away from the district, and her conscience pricks her. Then to the wedding comes Bozena, bold as brass, with her stranger. The villagers are scandalised at her effrontery, and the Burgomaster tells her that if she proposes to remain all the village will retire, and leave the wedding ceremony. But at last Borislav takes matters in hand. He tells the village that he is Bozena's brother, who for years has been under a cloud for desertion from the army. At last, however, his name has been cleared, for on application from the village priest to the Court at Vienna his case has been examined and he has received the Emperor's pardon. Karel begs Bozena to forgive him for his suspicions, and the two of them look lovingly at each other. Cilka observes their affection and she approaches Bozena. "We were never friends," she says, "and we have quarrelled a lot: but I realise that marriage between Karel and me would be a failure. He doesn't love me—he loves you. Take him and be happy." Then Cilka herself takes the jubilant Jan Burrian. The church door opens, the organ plays, the bells peal and the curtain descends on two happy pairs approaching the altar.

Bruder Straubinger

(Brother Straubinger)

Operetta in Three Acts

By M. West *and* J. Schnitzer

Music by Edmund Eysler

First produced on 20th February, 1903, at the Theater an der Wien, Vienna, with Alexander Girardi as "Straubinger".

Characters

LANDGRAVE PHILIP
LOLA, *his wife*
BROTHER STRAUBINGER
OCCULI, *a child of Nature*
SCHWUDLER, *a showman*
LIUDUSCHKA, *his wife*
BONIFACE, *a deserter*
BARON NAUPP, *Director of the Court Theatre*
CHORUS OF LADIES AND GENTLEMEN OF THE COURT, OFFICERS, APPRENTICES, TOWNSFOLK, SERVANTS

ACT I

The time is the eighteenth century, and the scene is a square before the gates of a city in the Rhineland of Germany. A large crowd is collected to welcome back the Landgrave, who is returning at the head of his army from the wars. Prominent in the crowd is the booth of the showman Schwudler and his wife Liuduschka, with his special attraction "Occuli, the child of Nature", whom he advertises to the customers with much shouting and trumpeting. Baron Naupp, the Director of the Court Theatre, passes by in search of Counsellor Ruckemich to instruct him to engage a gardener for the royal rose-gardens. His search leads him past Schwudler's booth, and the showman draws the Baron's attention to Occuli's beauty. It is part of the Baron's duty to procure pretty girls for the Landgrave's delectation and entertainment, and he instructs Schwudler to bring Occuli to the palace gardens in an hour's time for the approval of the

Landgrave. Schwudler promises to do so. The way in which her husband "carries on" with young girls is a cause of constant irritation to the Countess Lola. Her usual method of dealing with the situation is to have the girl arbitrarily married off to some convenient peasant. Today, however, she is allowing no cloud to dim the warmth of her welcome and, to add a festive touch to her reception, she and all her Ladies-in-Waiting have dressed themselves in a smart uniform and march up and down singing:

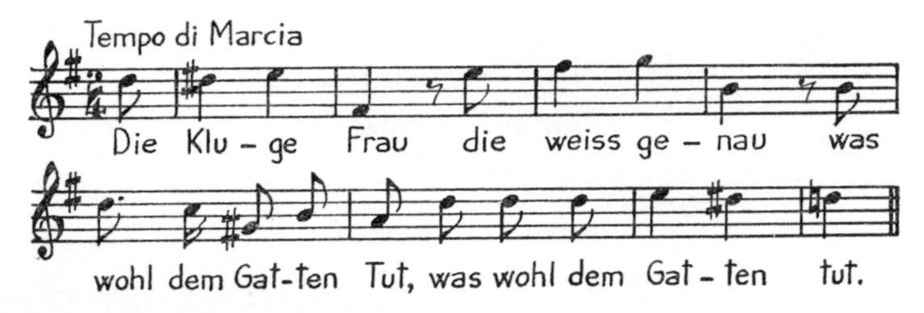

Among the crowd are two young men who have just arrived in town. One is Straubinger, a rose-gardener by profession, and the other, Boniface, has deserted from the army, and in consequence is without passport and identification papers. Straubinger is weary with much journeying, and finding a convenient grassy bank he settles down to sleep and dream of his lost love, Marie. While he is asleep Boniface passes by and, determined at any cost to procure for himself a passport, steals Straubinger's papers from a folder by the side of the sleeping man. Boniface is then able to apply successfully for the post of gardener to the royal rose-garden. When Straubinger wakes and discovers the theft of his passport, he is greatly put out and, despairing of getting better employment, joins Schwudler's show.

Schwudler now has a brilliant idea. Straubinger is in possession of the passport of his grandfather, who, were he still alive, would have been one hundred and fourteen years old. Schwudler's idea is to dress Straubinger up in military uniform and exhibit him, suitably made up, as the oldest surviving soldier in Germany. Occuli is appointed his attendant and Straubinger is struck by her likeness to his lost love, Marie. The hoax is entirely successful. Countess Lola awards a pension of one thousand gulden to the veteran warrior, and the Landgrave, who is enchanted by Occuli's looks, responds by awarding her a similar pension, while Schwudler is appointed Organiser of Court Entertainments.

ACT II

The scene is the palace garden. Schwudler does not see much prospect of making a profitable livelihood in this small, down-at-heel principality. But he has had one stroke of luck. His wife, whom he detested, has gone off with one of the attendants at the Town Hall. From Schwudler, Countess Lola now learns that her husband is paying court to Occuli and, following her normal practice, she arranges to have Occuli compulsorily married to Boniface, who, with the help of the stolen passport, has obtained the job of royal rose-gardener and is now masquerading as Straubinger. Occuli, however, strenuously resists all attempts to force her into marriage, especially when she knows that her intended is impersonating the real Straubinger, a good, honest man and her best friend, with whom she was formerly in love. Occuli is, of course, unaware that standing at her elbow, concealed behind the make-up of a centenarian, is her faithful lover himself, while Straubinger is overjoyed to hear her ardent words, which prove to him that she is his lost love, Marie. He at once proposes himself to Occuli as a husband. For an instant she looks at him blankly, but a moment later he sings her this song:

Immediately Occuli recognises the song as one which Straubinger used to sing to her in the days when they were lovers. She knows that the voice must be his and she accepts his proposal of marriage—in spite of the cynical laughter of others at the prospect of May marrying December.

ACT III

Occuli and Straubinger have set up house in a summer cottage in the royal park. It is the morning following their wedding night. Countess Lola is still concerned at the possibility of her husband's interest in Occuli persisting; for, she argues, marriage to a man of one hundred and fourteen will never prove sufficient hindrance. Therefore, with the assistance of her Ladies-in-Waiting, she prepares to keep a close watch on her husband's movements. The married couple are having a honeymoon breakfast on their veranda to the accompaniment of much affectionate by-play. Straubinger is in favour of continuing to impersonate the veteran, for without his passport he might encounter difficulties if he tried living under his own name. However, Occuli finds his passport on the veranda, which Boniface, stricken by his conscience, has returned, and Straubinger is able to throw off his disguise for ever. Countess Lola now tracks her husband to the summer-house, where he has gone in the hope of a rendezvous alone with Occuli. Surprised by his wife and all her Ladies-in-Waiting, the Landgrave decides to pardon the young couple for their hoax; and Straubinger, wisely, removes his wife out of harm's way.

Die Goldene Meisterin

(The Lady Goldsmith)

Operetta in Three Acts

By JULIUS BRAMMER *and* ALFRED GRÜNWALD

From the comedy Die Goldene Eva *by* VON SCHÖNTAN *and* KOPPEL-ELLFELD

Music by EDMUND EYSLER

First produced on 13th September, 1927, at the Theater an der Wien, Vienna, with Betty Fischer, Mizzi Zwerenz, Gretl Natzler, Hubert Marischka, Franz Glawatsch and Fritz Steiner.

CHARACTERS

MARGARET, *proprietress of a wealthy goldsmith's business*
COUNTESS GIULIETTA
CHRISTIAN, *goldsmith's apprentice*
FRIDOLIN VON GUMPERTSDORF
COUNT JAROMIR VON GREIFENSTEIN
PORTSCHUNKULA, *housekeeper*
BROTHER IGNATIUS
BROTHER SEVERINIUS } *three monks*
BROTHER PEREGRINI
CHORUS OF TOWNSFOLK, VISITORS, APPRENTICES, ETC.

The action takes place in Vienna and in Klosterneuburg in the sixteenth century.

ACT I

The scene is the interior of a goldsmith's shop in sixteenth-century Vienna. The proprietor is Margaret, the widow of a wealthy goldsmith and herself a Master Goldsmith. A woman of brains and character, Margaret has one amiable weakness: she cannot resist a title. She recalls how, at an aristocratic masked ball the previous day, one of her dancing partners mistook her for a Princess; and how at a festival banquet of all the Guilds the Emperor actually kissed her. But great as is the pleasure she derives from such experiences in her leisure time, in business hours she is tireless in her attention to the job in hand. Countess Giulietta, one of her customers, desires a specially chastened golden platter, and Margaret decides that the job shall be done by the excellent new apprentice, Christian. When the Countess visits the shop to discuss in detail the design of her golden platter, she recognises in Christian an acquaintance from Rome, for Christian had been a sculptor in Rome until hard times drove him to take up the more profitable profession of goldsmith. Margaret finds the efficient, self-reliant apprentice most sympathetic, until a chance turn in the conversation divulges that he was the masked dancing partner who, for a joke, pretended to mistake her for a Princess. For a while she feels she would prefer to dismiss him, but the Countess' platter has got to be finished—and after all, she realises, she does enjoy discussing the fun at the ball with him.

That evening Margaret is giving a small dance at her house. During the afternoon a well-to-do (and of course well-born) customer, Fridolin von Gumpertsdorf, whom she has invited to the dance, visits the shop to ask if he may bring his friend, Count Jaromir von Greifenstein, with him to the dance. This impoverished and down-at-heel Count is anxious to recoup his family fortunes by a wealthy marriage, and he regards the rich Lady Goldsmith as the perfect solution to his troubles. But Christian has known Count von Greifenstein from his boyhood days in Nürnberg, where the Count had an unsavoury reputation, and he begs Margaret not to have anything to do with such a dissolute and undesirable character. Margaret, however, is smitten by the prospect of entertaining a title and refuses to heed Christian's urgent warning.

ACT II

The scene is the courtyard of Margaret's house. Ever since the night of Margaret's dance her housekeeper, Portschunkula, has become as arrant a snob as her mistress—for at the dance Herr von Gumpertsdorf got rather drunk and proposed to her. Unfortunately, however, the gentleman seems to have forgotten about it and has done nothing since but support his friend Count von Greifenstein's suit with the Lady Goldsmith. Margaret is in the seventh heaven at the prospect of being wooed by an aristocrat. She cannot really credit the fact that at one time she actually thought of Christian as a wooer, although she still considers him a charming young man and talented at his job; indeed, one whom the apprentices are already beginning to regard as their master. "But I am the real boss, and the boss I intend to remain," she tells herself. Christian, however, has no intention of allowing Margaret to throw herself away on this effete and dissipated nobleman. In order to provide proof of his bad character Christian writes to an old friend of his in Nürnberg, an official in the Post Office who is the grandfather of a girl to whom Count von Greifenstein was engaged and whom he deserted. Christian asks him to come to Vienna and testify to the bad character of the Count. But before the old man has time to arrive, the Count proposes. Desperate situations call for desperate measures, and Christian makes-up as the old Post Office official and enters the room just as Margaret is about to accept the Count. He testifies to the Count's desertion of his former fiancée, and the embarrassed nobleman beats a hasty retreat. After his departure Christian makes himself known to Margaret. She realises that he was in the right and is full of gratitude and anxious to make up to him for all her unfriendliness. But Christian is determined to leave Vienna, so, sad at heart, Margaret resigns herself to the painful separation.

ACT III

The scene is the garden of the restaurant adjoining the monastery of Klosterneuburg, in the vicinity of Vienna. Apprentices and pupils of Margaret's goldsmith's business are celebrating the promotion of one of their number, Friedel, from apprentice to journeyman. But a pall is cast over the happy occasion by the absence of Christian. Everyone misses the firm but tactful guidance of his master hand. As they are talking affectionately of him, Christian arrives at the monastery restaurant for a short rest and some refreshment on his journey away from Vienna. Shortly afterwards Margaret and Portschunkula appear. Finally, Herr von Gumpertsdorf and the Count turn up, both of them hungry and footsore. An atmosphere of deepest gloom pervades the company, but Brother Ignatius, the monk in charge of the restaurant, a philosopher and psychologist well-versed in the ways of the human heart, realises what is wrong with these unhappy people. He produces "St. Bonifacius' Stool", a seat which exerts a soothing influence and compels whoever sits on it to tell the truth. And so Christian is moved to declare his love for Margaret, Herr von Gumpertsdorf honours his proposal of marriage to Portschunkula, and Count von Greifenstein is all agog to hurry back to Nürnberg and marry the fiancée whom he deserted.

Das Dreimäderlhaus

(Lilac Time)

Singspiel in Three Acts

Book (adapted from the novel Schwammerl *by* DR. R. H. BARTSCH)

and Lyrics by A. M. WILLNER *and* HEINZ REICHERT

Score adapted from FRANZ SCHUBERT'S *music by* HEINRICH BERTÉ

First produced on the 15th January, 1916, at the Raimund Theater, Vienna, with Fritz Schrödter as "Schubert" and Anny Rainer as "Hannerl". London production, with further musical adaptation and additional music by G. H. Clutsam, on 22nd December, 1922, at the Lyric Theatre, with Courtice Pounds, Clara Butterworth, Percy Heming and Edmund Gwenn.

CHARACTERS

CHRISTIAN TSCHOELL, *a glazier*
MARIA, *his wife*
HANNERL, HEDERL, HAIDERL — *their daughters*
FRANZ SCHUBERT
BARON SCHOBER
DEMOISELLE LUCIA GRISI, *a Prima Donna*
ANDREAS BRUNEDER, *a saddler*
FERDINAND BINDER, *a postman*
CHORUS OF PARTY GUESTS, SERVANTS, MUSICIANS, CHILDREN, ETC.

ACT I

On a sunny afternoon in 1826 Franz Schubert is entertaining a party of men friends in the courtyard of his home in Vienna. The wine is circulating freely and all are in good spirits, especially Baron Franz Schober, who enlivens the company with a diverting account of his amorous experiences with the beautiful opera star, Lucia Grisi. The friends then join in singing the quintette "Underneath the Lilac-tree", with its refrain:

To the courtyard come three young girls, Hederl, Haiderl and Hannerl, daughters of the glazier Herr Tschoell. Hederl and Haiderl have a secret rendezvous with two young men, Andreas Bruneder, a saddler, and Ferdinand Binder, a postman. The three girls enter to a well-known Schubert melody:

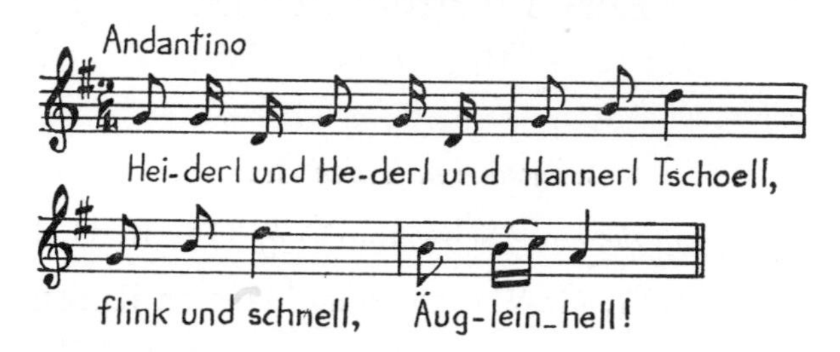

Hannerl, the youngest, has been brought along as chaperone. But the young people's love-making is rudely interrupted by the arrival of the glazier in pursuit of his daughters. The young men manage to hide, while Baron Schober, who has realised the situation, rescues the girls by telling their father that Hannerl, accompanied by her sisters, has come to Schubert for a singing lesson. Herr Tschoell's paternal pride in his talented daughter is immediately awakened and he is easily persuaded to take a glass of wine. Under its influence he mellows to such an extent that Haiderl and Hederl introduce their young men and he benevolently gives his blessing to their matrimonial ambitions. Hannerl thanks Schubert prettily for his help in extricating them from their dilemma, and Schubert, who is enchanted by her beauty, tells her ardently that he will be only too happy to give her real singing lessons in the future. The curtain comes down on their duet:

ACT II

Act Two takes place in the living-room of Herr Tschoell's house, where the marriage of his two daughters, Hederl and Haiderl, is being celebrated. At the reception Schubert is persuaded to sing one of his songs to an appreciative audience. It is a love-song, and no one suspects that all his songs are secretly dedicated to Hannerl, with whom he is now deeply in love. He has not the courage to declare himself, however, although Hannerl is only waiting for him to speak. As ill luck will have it, the opera star, Lucia Grisi, appears at the reception. The beautiful singer is desperately jealous of Baron Schober, and because of this she warns Hannerl to be wary in her dealings with "Franz", who, she declares, is a heartless deceiver. Hannerl assumes that "Franz" refers to Schubert, not realising that he and Baron Schober share the same christian name. This sidelight on his character, she decides, explains his reluctance to propose. When the party breaks up she bids Schubert a cold "good night" and he is greatly puzzled by her change of face. After the guests have all departed and the parents are left alone, Frau Tschoell becomes sentimentally tearful, and to comfort her Herr Tschoell sings this affectionate little song:

After the song Schubert and Schober return. They do not feel like going to bed and the old people welcome them delightedly. The composer, unable to understand Hannerl's sudden coldness, is determined to make a supreme effort to win his beloved's heart, and begs his friend Schober to woo Hannerl on his behalf with this love-song:

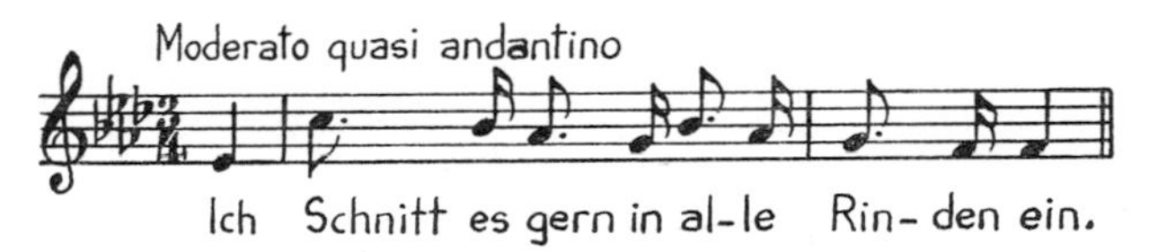

Schober, although he himself is greatly attracted to Hannerl, consents; but the effect of the love-song is totally unexpected. As Schober finishes singing, Hannerl throws herself passionately into his arms, and they are still in a loving embrace when Schubert enters the room. Haltingly, Schober explains that he did not intend to betray his friend, it just happened. Schubert generously tells him not to worry, for he bears him no ill will; but when Schober has departed the broken-hearted composer reflects that perhaps after all he would do better to eschew the joys of matrimony and give himself to his music alone. Sadly he sings to himself the refrain of his love-song that became the bridal song of another:

ACT III

The last act takes place on a square in Hietzing, where Schober comes to ask a favour of the composer. He begs Schubert to break the news of his engagement to Lucia Grisi and make clear to her that all must be at an end between them.

Before Schubert has time to deliver this message, however, the singer herself appears. She makes a noisy scene, and from her conversation Hannerl learns that her suspicions of Schubert have been groundless, and that it was against Schober that Grisi was warning her. However, Hannerl's love is proof against everything and she is determined to marry Schober and reform his character—though she gives him full warning that in future he must behave himself. Schubert now realises that he must put out of his mind all thought of winning Hannerl's love. But his art, his music, will lend him strength to triumph over his sorrow.

Tártájárás (Ein Herbstmanöver)

(Autumn Manœuvres)

Operetta in Three Acts

By KARL VON BAKYONYI

Lyrics by ANDOR GABOR

Music by EMMERICH KÁLMÁN

First produced on 22nd February, 1908, at the Vigszinhaz Theater, Budapest. Produced on 1st January, 1909, at the Theater an der Wien, Vienna, with Louise Kartousch, Otto Storm and Max Pallenberg. London production on 25th May, 1912, at the Royal Adelphi Theatre, with Robert Evett, Gracie Leigh, Phyllis Legnand and Huntley Wright.

CHARACTERS

LIEUTENANT-COLONEL LÖRENTHY
BARONESS RISA VON MARBACH
VOLUNTEER MAROSI
FIELD-MARSHAL LOHONAY
TRESZKA, *his daughter*
COLONEL VON EMMERICH
CADET WALLERSTEIN
LAJOS, *an old retainer*
CHORUS OF COUNTRY-HOUSE GUESTS, SOLDIERS AND SERVANTS

The action takes place in the park and in the drawing-room of a country house in Hungary in 1908.

ACT I

The scene is the park of a country house in Hungary, the seat of a titled widow, Baroness Risa von Marbach. By her permission the army are camping in the park for their autumn manœuvres, and the Commander-in-Chief, Field-Marshal Baron von Lohonay, his daughter Treszka, and four officers are to be her guests for the duration of the military exercise. From the conversation of two old servants we learn that the estate formerly belonged to the Lörenthy family, that the family became impoverished, and that the late owner, Lieutenant-Colonel Lörenthy, was forced to sell. The purchaser was a certain Baron von Marbach, who, not content with buying his house, had married the Colonel's fiancée, Risa, and had finally died a week after his marriage, leaving the estate and all he possessed to his widow. While the two servants are talking Baroness Risa von Marbach passes by on a walk with some of her lady guests. They are discussing the officers who are to be billeted in the house, and the others ask Risa whether she is acquainted with a Lieutenant-Colonel Lörenthy. Her evident embarrassment reveals that she is emotionally disturbed at the mention of his name, and she hastily remarks that the first to arrive is sure to be Treszka's young Volunteer Marosi. And Volunteer Marosi duly comes on to sing his entrance song:

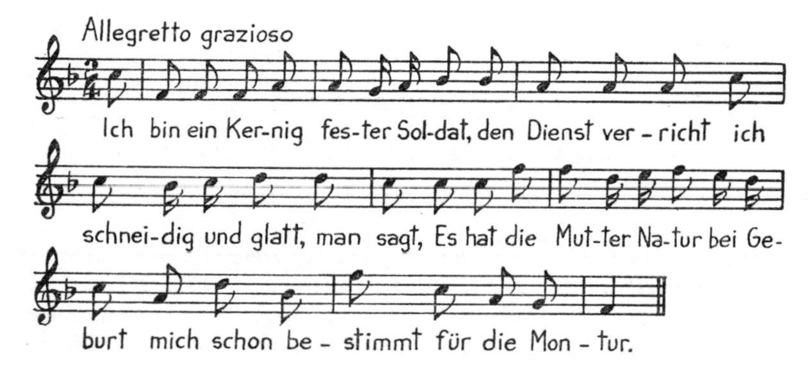

After the song Lieutenant-Colonel Lörenthy arrives and meets one of his old servants, Lajos, who is still working on the estate and who greets him affectionately. Lörenthy is pursued by little Treszka, his commanding officer's daughter, who, much to Volunteer Marosi's jealous disapproval, has a passion for him. He tells her he has long ago put all thoughts of love behind him. Ever since one magical summer night under the moon. And he sings:

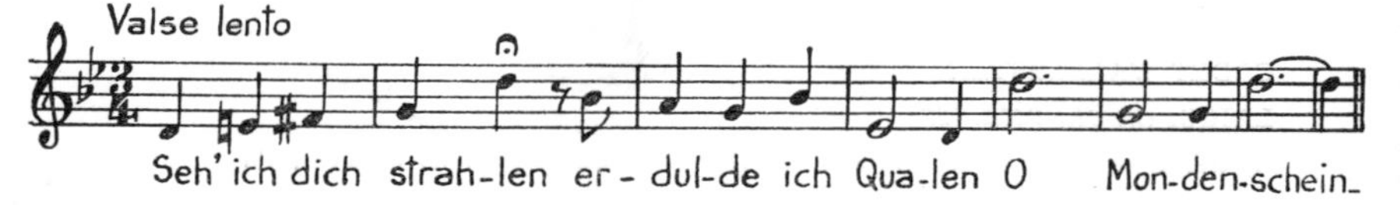

A platoon of infantry now marches on, with a fantastic character, Cadet Wallerstein, in charge. (This part was played in the Viennese production as a comic Jewish type by the famous comedian, Max Pallenberg, and he used to bring the house down nightly.) Cadet Wallerstein is quite inexperienced in army drill, marches his platoon straight into a stone wall, completely loses his head and has to be extricated from his difficulties. Cadet Wallerstein then has a conversation with Colonel Lörenthy and tells him that he is very keen to see the inside of the house. "But there!" he sighs, "I have strict orders to stay on duty all night and guard something. What was it? Our right flank, I think. I suppose you are billeted in the house?" Lörenthy, however, tells him that he will not be visiting the house. "You go along in," he tells Cadet Wallerstein. "I'll do guard duty for you."

Lörenthy, after Cadet Wallerstein has left, is now visited in the darkness by Risa, who begs him to come to the house. All his comrades are there and the guests will think his absence strange, she tells him. She asks his forgiveness for the unhappiness she has brought him in the past. Her marriage was a tragic mistake into which she was forced, and she has never ceased to love him. But Lörenthy is adamant. "You must know I never could or would cross the threshold of your house," he tells her. "And supposing, in spite of all your protests, you did enter my house?" she asks. "What then?" The suggestion strikes him as so ridiculous that he answers with a laugh: "In that case I should stay till daybreak, dance like a dervish, make love to all the women and drink myself silly." "Have I your word on that?" she counters, smiling. "My word," he assures her, and Risa leaves him. One by one the lights in the camp go out and Lörenthy listens alone in the darkness to a bugler sounding the Last Post.

ACT II

In the house that night all is light and laughter. The drawing-room presents a brilliant scene. Ladies in full evening dress, partnered by officers in their colourful uniforms, are dancing a quadrille. After the dance Volunteer Marosi is called on for a song, and sings the hit number of the show:

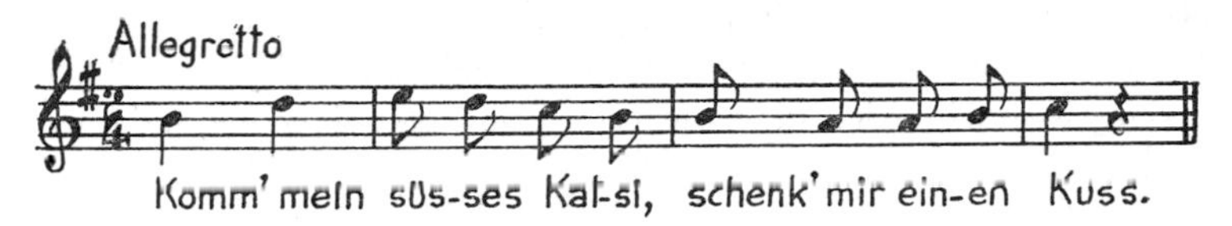

After this Cadet Wallerstein appears. He has had considerable difficulty in getting into the house, for his eccentric personality has aroused the servants' suspicions. Moreover, once in he behaves in such a pretentious and conceited manner that the officers all make fun of him. Marosi manages to get a word alone with Treszka. Her thoughts, however, are all of Lörenthy, the only officer who has not accepted Risa's invitation. In vain Marosi reminds her that "A Volunteer in the hand is worth two Colonels in the park".

Risa now proposes that all the lights be turned out and that a serenade be sung to the starry night. "And to whom is this serenade to be dedicated?" asks Treszka. "Who else but the stars?" replies Risa. "Oh! I thought you meant two specific stars," comments Treszka, pointing significantly to her shoulders, where a Lieutenant-Colonel's stars would normally be placed. "Who will sing the serenade?" asks Colonel von Emmerich. "Risa, of course," says jealous Treszka. Risa then breaks into a reprise of her duet with Lörenthy, but her strategem is in vain. "The desired reaction is missing," comments Treszka sarcastically. "What a waste of a pretty serenade."

Risa then calls for lights and dancing is resumed, when suddenly there is an interruption. An orderly brings a report from Colonel Lörenthy that an enemy patrol is lurking in the vicinity of the park and is bringing up guns. All officers are to return to their posts. Risa turns to the officers. "It is quite obvious that we have disturbed Colonel Lörenthy's repose, and this is his way of taking his revenge. Don't fall into the trap, gentlemen. On with the dance!" The music strikes up, and all are dancing merrily when Lörenthy storms in through the french windows. "Are you all mad?" he asks, and reminds them brusquely that they are soldiers, not dancers. Shamefacedly they leave the house, and Lörenthy is about to follow them when Risa stops him. "You must stay here," she tells him. "You gave your word that if you entered my house you would stay till daybreak." In vain he pleads that his place is on the battlefield. But Risa is adamant. "After all, it's only manœuvres—imaginary warfare," she tells him, and holds him to his word. "Now," she orders: "let me see you dance like a dervish, make love to the women and drink yourself silly." "I feel ashamed of myself for still loving you," he groans. At this moment Treszka enters and Lörenthy has a sudden inspiration as to how he can punish Risa. He makes violent love to Treszka in front of Risa and ends up by proposing marriage. Treszka, nonplussed but thrilled, tells him he shall have her answer tomorrow. Lörenthy then calls for champagne and music, and his old servant Lajos produces both. The gipsy band strikes up and Lörenthy dances a wild Czardas with Treszka, emptying champagne glasses and hurling them to the ground. As he is dancing several officers return, having been unable to find their horses, but Lörenthy pays no attention to them till Colonel von Emmerich, in a rage, orders him as his superior officer to return to duty. Risa pleads with him to go, but Lörenthy rounds on her. "You compelled me to stay here, and before your eyes I shall be marched away to a court-martial. I loved you, and you have returned my love with trick and treachery. You have ruined me, and now I hope you are happy."

A burst of cannon-fire is now heard and in through the windows crowd a troop of soldiers wearing white cap-bands, the ensignia of the enemy, with hot on their heels a furious Field-Marshal Lohonay, Treszka's father. With a fine flow of language he abuses the Colonel and the whole squadron, finally ordering Lörenthy to be placed under close arrest. Risa in tears throws herself into Lörenthy's arms just as Treszka enters, and seeing their embrace Treszka utters a cry of jealous rage as the curtain falls.

ACT III

The next morning Risa's drawing-room shows every trace of the morning after the night before. There is open war between Risa and Treszka: each is determined to have Lörenthy for her own. When he enters, Treszka tries to lure him out for a walk in the park. He tells her to go on ahead, and promises to follow. Then Risa, when they are alone together, reminds him of his proposal of marriage to Treszka, which he has since forgotten. They then discuss his coming interview with Field-Marshal Lohonay. Risa insists that he must put the blame for his conduct entirely on her: it is the only way she can make up to him for the harm she has done. When he refuses, Risa bursts into tears and he takes her in his arms. At this moment Treszka returns, sees them and hurries away, also in tears. Risa and Lörenthy are then interrupted by Cadet Wallerstein, and they retire. Cadet Wallerstein has lost his sword and dare not go on parade without it. "Oh dear," he murmurs, "the army's no place for the likes of us—me and my friend Löbl". And he sings a pointed number with which Pallenberg nightly brought down the house:

When Field-Marshal Lohonay discovers that Treszka intends to marry Lörenthy, he is determined that every excuse must be found to justify his wild conduct of the night before and his absence from manœuvres. He conducts a ridiculously biased court-martial, prompting Lörenthy to all the right answers, and eventually sentences him to twenty-four hours' house arrest. Proudly he tells Treszka that he gives them both his blessing, when she astonishes everybody by declaring that she has come to realise that she is too young for Lörenthy and that Risa is the wife for him. "Damned fellow!" says the smiling Field-Marshal. "If I'd known *that*, he'd have got thirty days!"

Der Zigeunerprimas

(Sari)

Operetta in Three Acts

By JULIUS WILHELM *and* FRITZ GRÜNBAUM

Music by EMMERICH KÁLMÁN

First produced on 10th October, 1912, at the Johann Strauss Theater, Vienna, with Alexander Girardi, Grete Holm, Willy Strehl and Max Brod.

CHARACTERS

RÁCZ PALI, *a retired musician*
SARI, *his daughter*
JULISKA, *his secretary*
LACZI, *his eldest son*
COUNT GASTON IRINI
CADEAU, *his guardian*
THE KING OF MASSILLIA
THE COUNTESS IRINI
CHORUS OF COUNTRYFOLK, SOCIALITES, CHILDREN, ETC.

ACT I

It is the year 1912, and the scene is the living-room of a typical Hungarian peasant house in the village of Lörinczfalva. Here lives an elderly, retired musician, Rácz Pali, a widower with sixteen children ranging from the ages of three to twenty. Rácz, for many years leader of a gipsy orchestra with an international reputation, is living in retirement, a martyr to gout, and is looked after by his eldest daughter, Sari, who keeps house for him. He supports his family by running an agency which supplies instrumentalists to gipsy orchestras in all the capitals of the world, and Rácz's niece, Juliska, acts as his secretary. Soon after the rise of the curtain Juliska arrives with the morning post. In addition to routine applications for a double-bass player from Stockholm and a clarinet player from Paris, there is a letter from a Count Gaston Irini, announcing his intention to visit Rácz. The old man is delighted at the prospect of welcoming a long-time, favourite friend. During the conversation between Rácz and Juliska, Rácz's eldest son, Laczi, enters, who like his father is a violinist. The two are forever arguing and quarrelling about music, for while the old father is quite uneducated and unacquainted with any music except old Hungarian folk-songs and czardas melodies, the son has been to concerts in Budapest and has become acquainted with the classics, Bach and Handel, and the music of Wagner. Father and son, as usual, start an argument which ends in a quarrel, and are duly scolded by Sari.

Shortly after this young Count Gaston Irini arrives, accompanied by his guardian, Cadeau. Sari is bending over the cot of the youngest child when they enter and does not hear them, and the high-spirited Gaston, stealing up to her from behind, snatches a kiss. Sari is indignant with the young man for taking such a liberty and threatens to tell her father. Rácz now arrives, is delighted to see his old friend and asks the reason for his visit. Gaston tells him that the King of Massillia is to visit him in Paris, and his idea is that Rácz shall come to Paris with his orchestra to entertain the King. Rácz declares that were it anywhere but Paris he might consider it, but Paris is sacred in memory to him. In explanation he tells Gaston how as a boy of seventeen he was playing in an orchestra at a ball in London when he got to know a young Parisian girl, a Baroness, who was there as a guest. They sat out the supper interval together while he told her of his home and the gipsies and forests, and then they spoke of love and kissed and kissed each other till her father caught them and dragged her away. And he has never since found it in his heart to visit Paris. Gaston tells Rácz to think the matter over and they go out talking.

A scene follows between Laczi and Juliska. Juliska is attracted to the young man and rather piqued at his lack of interest in her, but she joins him enthusiastically in this duet:

Gaston is spending his time between flirting with Sari, who has forgiven him for the stolen kiss, and trying to persuade old Rácz to come to Paris. "Don't tell me I've come all the way to Lörinczfalva for nothing," he says. "For nothing?" expostulates Cadeau. "The journey cost five hundred francs." Rácz turns to his son Laczi; "Count Irini wants me to appear in Paris and I don't want to go. What solution do you suggest, which will also save Monsieur Cadeau's money?" "Quite simple," says Laczi. "Someone else must go." "And who?" asks Rácz. "Why, me," replies Laczi. "That settles the matter." The old man is up in arms at the impertinence of the young upstart. "Give me my fiddle," he demands and, seizing the bow, he starts to play an old and well-remembered czardas. "I can still play," he cries delightedly, and his family and members of his gipsy orchestra all join in as the curtain falls.

ACT II

Act Two takes place in the Grand Salon of the Palais Irini in Paris, where Gaston is giving a reception in honour of the King of Massillia. His Majesty is present, incognito, calling himself Count Estragon. As the curtain rises guests are dancing to the music of an orchestra conducted by Laczi. Unable to bear any more of his father's hostility and criticism, he left home at the end of Act One and has been engaged by Gaston, who took a liking to the boy, as conductor of his house orchestra. Rácz now arrives, for tonight is the night when he is due to appear before the King of Massillia. An amazing change has taken place in the old man. He has been to the spa of Pistyan and been cured of his gout; he has shaved off his beard and grown a neat moustache and dyed his hair jet black, and he is wearing a fashionably cut morning-coat. He is altogether elegant and looks half his age. Gaston introduces Rácz to the King and much by-play is made of the uneducated old man's familiar behaviour to His Majesty, and his failure to observe his incognito. Rácz refuses point blank to be parted from his violin, his precious Stradivarius, and sings this charmingly tender song in praise of it:

In the meantime, Gaston has sent old Cadeau to fetch Sari and Juliska to Paris, and they now arrive. Gaston is in love with Sari but, partly to tease her and partly to watch her reaction, he pretends to be more pleased to see Juliska. Sari, who worships Gaston, is very cast down. Laczi is delighted to see Juliska, for since he left home she has occupied all his thoughts, but Juliska is piqued with him for leaving her so casually. She pretends that she is engaged to someone else, and they sing a plaintive duet of disappointed love:

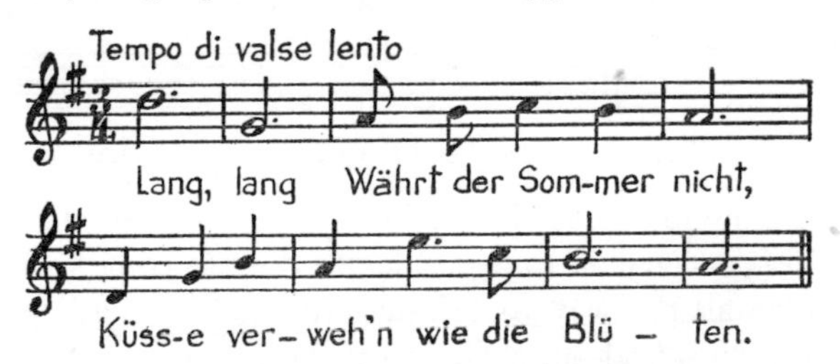

Rácz and Laczi meet and the old man is delighted to see his son and begs him to come home, but the old rivalry reappears when he hears that Laczi is in charge of the house orchestra. "So that's what you've come down to," he sneers. "Playing music as an accompaniment to eating or for young misses to dance to!"

Poor Sari is in the depths of despair at Gaston's apparent neglect and she is pouring out her heart to his guardian Cadeau, when Gaston tiptoes into the room. He motions Cadeau to withdraw and, without Sari noticing, takes his place. Sari continues her confidences and exclaims: "What have I done to

Gaston that he should treat me like this—I, who adore him?" In a moment Gaston has her in his arms. They shower kisses on each other and break into one of the most joyous of Kálmán's waltz songs:

After this the King tells Gaston that he desires to hear the famous gipsy fiddler, but Rácz cannot be found. So as not to keep His Majesty waiting, Laczi then steps into the breach, and his beautiful phrasing and sweetness of tone make a tremendous impression. While he is playing Rácz enters the salon and witnesses his son's success. He is now asked to play and at first refuses. "Typical artistic jealousy," declares one of the guests. "Or envy," says another. This rouses old Rácz. Tuning up his fiddle, he launches into one of his old czardas pieces, full of trills, octave passages and various gipsy effects. But the King is frankly bored. "Old-fashioned gipsy-scraping" is his judgement on Rácz's playing. "Not to be compared with the son." He walks out of the room, and the guests, following his lead, also disperse. Rácz, absorbed in his playing, at first notices nothing, but suddenly he turns, sees a practically empty room and realises the situation. Then sadly he owns to his family and friends that his old Stradivarius has given him the proof that he is past his prime.

ACT III

The scene of the last act is the boudoir of Countess Irini, Gaston's grandmother. She is playing piquet with three elderly men and discussing her grandson. The Countess is a strong-minded old lady and the short last act is concerned with her successful efforts to sort out the matrimonial affairs of the various members of the cast. In the case of Gaston and Sari she hides Sari behind a curtain in her boudoir, sends for Gaston and tells him she has found the right girl for him and that she is hidden in the room. He searches the room, encouraged by the Countess' comments of "You're getting warmer", till he finally discovers Sari and they fall delightedly into each other's arms. The Countess has also learned from Sari that old Rácz is seriously thinking of marrying Juliska, though Juliska is madly in love with Laczi. So she sends for Rácz and tells him that he is far too old for Juliska. Rácz disputes this and in the course of conversation it comes out that Countess Irini and the little Parisian Baroness at the ball in London are one and the same person. Of course Laczi get his Juliska and Rácz formerly acknowledges him as his successor and presents him ceremonially with his precious Stradivarius. Finally, with a mischievous look at the Countess, he says: "You may call me an old donkey, but I still have luck with lovely women."

Die Czardasfürstin

(The Gipsy Princess)

Operetta in Three Acts

By LEO STEIN *and* BELA JENBACH

Music by EMMERICH KÁLMÁN

First produced on 17th November, 1915, at the Johann Strauss Theater, Vienna, with Mizzi Guenther, Susanne Bachrich, Karl Bachmann, Josef König and Max Brod. London production on 20th May, 1921, at the Prince of Wales Theatre, with Sari Petras.

CHARACTERS

LEOPOLD MARIA, PRINCE OF LIPPERT-WEYLERSHEIM
ANHILTE, *his consort*
EDWIN RONALD, *their son*
COUNTESS STASI, *their niece*
COUNT BONI KANCSIANU
SYLVA VARESCU, *an actress*
EUGEN VON ROHNSDORFF, *an officer*
COUNT FERI VON KEREKES
A NOTARY
CHORUS OF ACTRESSES AND YOUNG MEN-ABOUT-TOWN

ACT I

The first act takes place in a café-chantant in Budapest. When the curtain rises the last performance is just finishing and there is tumultuous applause for Sylva Varescu, the star singer, known as "The Gipsy Princess", who is making her farewell appearance before leaving to fulfil an engagement in New York. When the auditorium has been cleared, waiters begin to lay a table for a farewell supper party which Count Boni Kancsianu is giving in Sylva's honour. Boni confides to his friend, Feri von Kerekes, his surprise at the absence of young Prince Edwin Lippert-Weylersheim, Sylva's ardent admirer. It is common knowledge that his father, the old Prince, has been trying for some time to persuade Edwin to give up Sylva and return home, but so far without success.

Boni has a telegram in his pocket for Edwin and assumes it is yet another parental summons home. "Well," says Feri, "it wouldn't be the first time the aristocracy and the stage had united." It was Boni who discovered Sylva and gave her her first chance. He is devoted to her, but Sylva's heart belongs to her Prince Edwin. Later Edwin arrives and Boni gives him his telegram and counsels him to obey his father and return home. Edwin, however, laughs it off and joins Sylva. He is greatly distressed at the prospect of her departure, though she tells him he will soon forget her and find another girl, far more beautiful. But Edwin tells her seriously that his love for her is no light emotion: it is deep and lasting. They sing this duet:

Boni now busies himself with seating his guests, mostly Sylva's colleagues and members of the theatrical profession. He is a very popular person, and all protest against his departure for America. It is bad enough losing Sylva, but why one earth must Boni go with her? they ask. Humorously he tells them he is getting old and cannot stand Budapest night life any longer.

With the arrival of Sylva supper is served and the fun becomes fast and furious, when suddenly there is an interruption and into the room walks Edwin's cousin, Lieutenant Eugen von Rohnsdorff. He hands Edwin an order to report immediately to the headquarters of his regiment in Vienna. "This is my father's doing," says Edwin bitterly. "If it is," replies Rohnsdorff, "he is in the right, Edwin. You are disgracing the family with this actress. Remember your engagement to Countess Stasi." "That was just a childish betrothal and meant nothing," argues Edwin, but Rohnsdorff tells him that Stasi is very much in earnest and that his parents are anxious to hurry on the marriage. Edwin realises he must go to Vienna, but he begs Rohnsdorff for half an hour's grace before their departure. Rohnsdorff agrees and leaves him, promising to return in half an hour.

Directly he has gone, Edwin works fast. He sends for a notary and summons all the guests—all, that is, except Boni, who is packing for America. He tells them that it is his firm intention to marry Sylva then and there and that nothing will alter his decision. Sylva vainly attempts to reason with him, pointing out what an impossible situation he is creating, but Edwin silences her with the question "Do you love me?" and this she cannot deny. A marriage contract is then drawn up which reads: "I, Edwin Ronald Karl Maria, Prince of Lippert-Weylersheim, hereby declare that I take Sylva Varescu to be my lawful wedded wife and that I will, within two calendar months, fulfil this contract before the law, the State and in the eyes of Heaven." Edwin and Sylva sign the contract, and the health of the happy pair is drunk to the strains of Mendelssohn, and there is general rejoicing that in view of her marriage Sylva will not be leaving for America. When Edwin has left for Vienna with von Rohnsdorff, Boni returns. He knows nothing of the hastily improvised marriage and he is horrified when he reads the marriage contract. "But Edwin cannot marry you," he tells Sylva: "he is engaged to Countess Stasi. Rohnsdorff gave me this announcement of his engagement." And he shows Sylva a card which the old Prince of Lippert-Weylersheim has had printed. Sylva is shattered, but she is forced to believe the evidence of her eyes and, with a breaking heart, she turns her eyes towards America.

ACT II

Two months have passed since Sylva's unhappy departure for America, and during her absence Edwin has not so strenuously opposed the idea of his marriage to Stasi. Tonight, in the palace of the Lippert-Weylersheims in Vienna, Edwin's father is giving a party, and he and Edwin's mother are delighted to see how well the young couple seem to be getting on. Stasi is hoping that their engagement will be announced during the evening, but Edwin will not hear of this. He is mysterious about his reason for the delay and will only say that he is waiting for a specific piece of news. He asks Stasi if she loves him, and she answers: "Just about enough to marry you," and they sing a duet.

Now, unexpectedly, Sylva and Boni arrive. Sylva is back from New York and, overcome by a longing to see Edwin again, has persuaded Boni to introduce her to the old Lippert-Weylersheims as his wife, just for the evening. The Old Prince is delighted to welcome the son of his best friend, Count Kancsianu, and his beautiful new wife. When Edwin and Sylva meet, Sylva is at first very bitter, but she gradually softens, and they agree to be friends.

Meanwhile, Boni has fallen head over heels in love with Stasi and she is also attracted to the gay little man. He quite forgets that he is pretending to be Sylva's husband and proposes to Stasi, who accuses him of being a faithless Don Juan. Boni whispers to her mysteriously that his wife is no wife, but he refuses to say more at the moment, telling her that his lips are sealed until the morrow. Edwin and Sylva, who have spent the whole evening together, now admit that they are both more in love than ever, and they are clasped in each other's arms when Boni comes into the room. After pretending to be horrified, Boni tells Edwin that his own marriage to Sylva has only been arranged for the evening and gives them both his blessing. Delighted, the lovers sing the hit number of the show:

But the path of true love is not yet destined to run smoothly. Edwin is delighted to be able to present Sylva to his father as Countess Kancsianu, for he realises that though his father would not welcome as his daughter-in-law Sylva

Varescu, "The Gipsy Princess", he would have no objection to his marrying the divorced Countess Kancsianu. Sylva, however, takes this to mean that Edwin is ashamed to marry a girl from the theatre, and before everybody she gives herself out to be Sylva Varescu, the actress. Then, after showing the old Prince their marriage contract, she tears it in pieces and sweeps out of the palace.

ACT III

The last act takes place in a hotel in Vienna. Sylva and Boni have come here after the scene in the Palais Lippert-Weylersheim and are shortly followed by Edwin in pursuit of Sylva and the old Prince in pursuit of Edwin, who, he fears, might resort to desperate measures in his grief and despair. The old Prince is very vexed with Boni, and tells him that had he not introduced Sylva at the party as his wife, Edwin and Stasi would now be engaged. As it is there is no engagement and Stasi is compromised. "But Stasi is not compromised, for I ask you officially for her hand here and now, sir," says Boni. "But Stasi loves Edwin, not you," argues the Prince. "Does she?" says Boni. "Let's see." He puts through a telephone call then and there, with the Prince at his elbow, and Edwin's father hears Stasi promise to be Boni's wife. The old Prince then gives them both his blessing, but he is still adamant in refusing to look with favour on the union of Edwin and Sylva. This, however, is eventually brought about by the chance arrival of the elderly Count Feri von Kerekes, who pleads with the Prince to allow the marriage. The old man proudly tells him that no one in his family has ever married an actress, a singing girl, and Feri then discloses that the Princess of Lippert-Weylersheim, whom the Prince has married *en deuxième noce*, was, before her first marriage, on the stage of the very same theatre as Sylva. After this disclosure the Prince can say no more, and the curtain falls on a double wedding for Stasi and Boni, Sylva and Edwin.

Die Faschingsfee

(Carnival Fairy)

Operetta in Three Acts

By A. M. WILLNER *and* RUDOLF OESTERREICHER

Music by EMMERICH KÁLMÁN

First produced on 21st September, 1917, at the Johann Strauss Theater, Vienna, with Mizzi Guenther and Karl Bachmann.

CHARACTERS

PRINCESS ALEXANDRA MARIA
OTTOKAR, DUKE OF GREVLINGEN
HUBERT VON MÜTZELBERG
COUNT LOTHAR MEREDIT
VICTOR RONAI, *a painter*
LORI ASCHENBACH, *a chorus-girl*
CHORUS OF ARTISTS, MODELS AND MEMBERS OF BOHEMIAN SOCIETY

ACT I

In a café in Munich much frequented by artists, Carnival is being celebrated with a great deal of noise and gaiety. Worries and cares are drowned in wine and beer and laughter is the order of the day. A cheer from the crowd greets the announcement that a hitherto unknown young painter has won a much-sought-after prize of fifty thousand marks offered by Count Lothar Meredit, and everyone drinks the health of the lucky young man, Victor Ronai. He in turn invites them all to a celebration party in his studio on the following day. Among the frequenters of the café is an elegant young man-about-town, Hubert von Mützelberg. He is in white tie and tails and is on his way to a ball at one of the Embassies. But his departure does not suit his girl-friend, Lori Aschenbach, from the musical-comedy chorus, who makes a noisy scene of disapproval before poor Hubert can make his escape.

During the evening a beautiful young woman comes into the café and sits down alone at a table. She is quite unknown to the habitués, and there is much speculation as to her identity. As she is sitting alone, two impudent young men approach her table and attempt to force their company upon her. She makes it perfectly clear that she does not welcome their attentions, but they persist in annoying her until Victor Ronai realises the situation and intervenes. The elder of the two men is extremely offensive, and Victor offers to fight him and hands him his visiting-card. "Oho!" says his opponent. "So you are Victor Ronai, the painter! Then you may be interested to learn my name." Glancing at the visiting-card handed to him, Victor is horrified to read the name "Count Lothar Meredit". Before him stands his benefactor. Sneeringly the Count tells Victor that his conduct has cost him the fifty thousand marks of prize money. "I do not habitually help young men who associate with ladies of the town," he adds, and walks out of the café. Victor, shattered and disappointed, puts a good face on his misfortune, but the unknown woman whom he championed is very distressed at the trouble she has caused him. He makes light of the situation and tells her he has only one wish—to see her again. "Perhaps you will," she tells him and walks towards the door. Suddenly she turns and comes back to him and, taking his head in her hands, kisses him full on the lips and runs out of the café into the night.

ACT II

Act Two takes place in Victor Ronai's studio. His celebration party is in full swing, for, to his surprise, the fifty thousand marks has arrived. He imagines that Count Lothar Meredit must have changed his mind. Victor cannot get the memory of his beautiful unknown out of his mind, and he has painted a portrait of her from memory as "The Spirit of Carnival", clad in very diaphanous and revealing draperies. The portrait is displayed on an easel and is much admired. During the evening, to Victor's delighted surprise, Hubert von Mützelberg arrives with the unknown beauty, who turns out to be Hubert's cousin, Princess Alexandra Maria. It is the eve of her marriage to the elderly Duke of Grevlingen. and she is enjoying a final fling. Enchanted by her portrait, and seeing the costume draped upon the artist's dummy, she retires to put it on and returns wearing it, to receive a rousing reception from the guests. Kálmán has given Alexandra a particularly attractive song in which she expresses her enjoyment of carnival time:

Later, Count Lothar Meredit arrives. Victor has invited him to the party, and now thanks him for his generosity in paying him the fifty thousand marks. But Count Lothar Meredit looks blank. He does not know what Victor is talking about, and tells him he has never paid over the money. Now, Hubert von Mützelberg knows very well that it is Princess Alexandra who has sent Victor the fifty thousand marks, and when Count Lothar disclaims the payment of the money, Hubert is at pains to conceal the truth from him. So confused, however, is his explanation that the Count is led to believe that Hubert himself has paid it. In order not to appear mean and a defaulter, Count Lothar pays over the fifty thousand marks to Hubert, who in his turn attempts to present it to Princess Alexandra. When she refuses to take it, Hubert stuffs the money into her handbag. Unfortunately this action is seen by Lori Aschenbach, his girl-friend. In her jealousy Lori puts a totally false construction on Hubert's action, and, worse still, runs to Victor and blurts out the whole story. The canker of jealousy and suspicion now attacks Victor and he demands an explanation of the incident from Alexandra, who, shocked and distressed by his unworthy suspicions, refuses to answer him. The scene is now interrupted by the arrival of her fiancé, the elderly Duke of Grevlingen, whom Hubert has brought to the studio to take Alexandra away and thus end the unpleasant atmosphere. The Duke is shocked and surprised to find Alexandra in her scanty carnival dress and in such Bohemian society. She calms him by assuring him that she has come to Victor Ronai's studio to sit for her portrait, which she intended to give her future husband as a wedding present. The Duke makes no secret of the fact that he would have preferred a more dignified portrait, but nevertheless offers Victor a hundred thousand marks for the painting. But Victor, who has by now worked himself into an emotional state over his disappointment at Alexandra's apparent fickleness and the Duke's criticism of his picture, bluntly refuses to sell and taking the canvas off the easel, throws it into the fire "What have you done?" cries Alexandra. "I've put an end to a poor sort of carnival joke," he replies. Without further comment Alexandra and the Duke leave the studio as the curtain falls.

ACT III

The last act takes place in the lounge of the Hotel Regina. Hubert has explained the whole business of the money to Victor, who is very upset and ashamed of his unworthy suspicions. Meanwhile, the scene in Victor's studio has made the old Duke gradually realise that the young artist means everything to Alexandra. True, when he offers to retire from their engagement she declares with great energy that any feelings she may have had for Victor have been killed by the wavering and unstable quality of his so-called "love"; but the Duke is unconvinced. "Youth calls to youth," he tells himself, and sacrificing himself for Alexandra's happiness, he brings Victor to her. And all is forgiven and forgotten as the two are clasped in each other's arms to the echoes of the Carnival Theme:

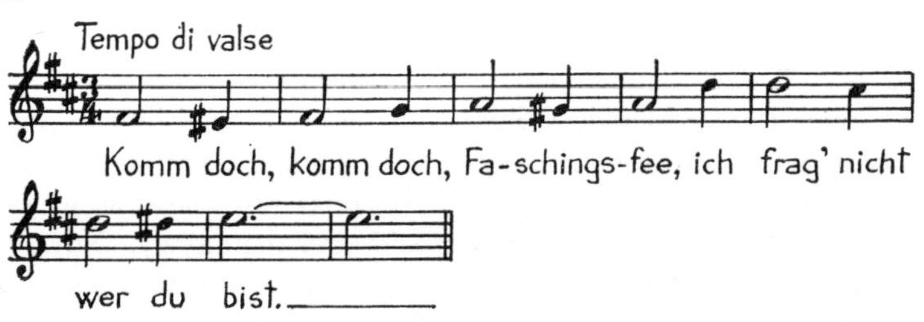

Das Hollandweibchen
(The Little Dutch Girl)

Operetta in Three Acts

By LEO STEIN *and* BELA JENBACH

Music by EMMERICH KÁLMÁN

First produced on 30th January, 1920, at the Johann Strauss Theater, Vienna, with Ida Russka as "Princess Jutta", Karl Bachmann as "Prince Paul" and Fritz Werner as "Udo von Sterzel". London production on 1st December, 1920, at the Lyric Theatre, with Maggie Teyte, Cicely Debenham and Jack Hulbert.

CHARACTERS

PRINCESS JUTTA
ELLY VON DER WEYDE, *Lady-in-Waiting*
PAUL RODERICH, *Prince of Usingen*
DR. UDO VON STERZEL, *equerry and private secretary to Prince Paul*
VON STOPP, *Prime Minister*
BARON SEEBORG
KLAAS, *an innkeeper*
CHORUS OF COURTIERS, SERVANTS, MEMBERS OF THE WYK YACHT CLUB, TOWNSFOLK, ETC.

ACT I

The first act takes place in the throne-room of the palace at the little German Court of Sonneburg-Glücksburg. Princess Jutta, and Prince Paul of Usingen were betrothed as children and the time has now come for their marriage. The curtain rises on their wedding day, and Princess Jutta and the whole Court are on tenterhooks of expectation at the prospect of Prince Paul's arrival, for he and the Princess have never set eyes on each other. Princess Jutta has, however, created in her mind a romantic picture of Prince Paul, based on his portrait and his ardent letters. "Every girl dreams of a man to whom she would mean everything," she sings:

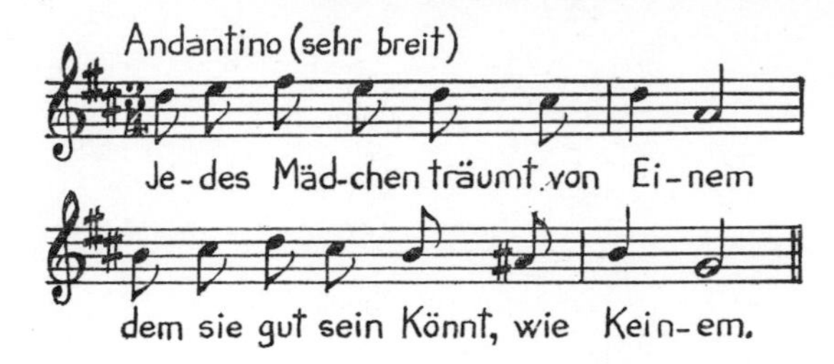

After an eve-of-wedding reception the Princess retires to dress for the royal wedding and a deputation leaves for the railway station to welcome the Prince on his arrival. He is escorted through cheering crowds who line the route to the palace, but on arriving there the recipient of this magnificent welcome calmly announces that he is not Prince Paul, and furthermore that Prince Paul has revolted against the idea of being compelled to marry for reasons of state. He is yachting at Wyk-on-Sea in Holland and has sent his personal equerry, Udo von Sterzel, to make excuses for his non-appearance. This causes consternation at Court. At all costs the dreadful news must be kept from the Princess. A Cabinet meeting is hastily called, and at first it is decided to break off diplomatic relations with Usingen. But the Prime Minister, Obersthofmeister von Stopp, remembers an Act of Parliament to the effect that "When a royal bridegroom is prevented through unavoidable circumstances from appearing for the marriage service, this can take place legally by proxy". Accordingly Princess Jutta is told that her bridegroom, Prince Paul, has been taken ill, and in his place Udo von Sterzel leads the Princess to the altar and signs the contract. But the Princess Jutta is naturally resentful at the affront offered her by her royal bridegroom's default, and she soon succeeds in discovering the true state of affairs by forcing an admission from von Sterzel, who is also the author of all Prince Paul's ardent love-letters. The Princess is determined to be revenged upon her elusive bridegroom and decides to track him down on his yacht at Wyk-on-Sea.

ACT II

Act Two takes place on the quay outside the yacht club-house at Wyk-on-Sea in Holland. Here the defaulting bridegroom, Prince Paul of Usingen, is enjoying a sailing holiday, free from the cares of the world and, to the best of his belief, from the importunities of the Princess he should have married. But Princess Jutta has tracked him down and arrives incognito with her Lady-in-Waiting, the young Baroness Elly von der Weyde. Elly is hopeful of renewing acquaintance with Udo von Sterzel, to whom she took a great fancy on his visit to Sonneburg-Glücksburg. Both the Princess and Elly are girls of spirit and, hearing that two expected waitresses have not turned up at the Yacht Club, they apply for and get the jobs under the names of Bella and Kaatje.

Paul is about to go sailing with his friend, Baron Seeborg, when he hears a girl singing in the hotel opposite the Yacht Club. She has a beautiful voice and is singing a song about a faithless lover. As she is singing, Princess Jutta appears at her window, and Prince Paul, enchanted by her beauty and her voice, abandons the idea of a sail and remains on shore to listen to her song.

That night at the Festival of Tulips their acquaintance ripens into closer friendship, and soon Prince Paul's heart is filled with thoughts of love for the little Dutch girl Bella (as he supposes her to be).

Elly renews acquaintanceship with Udo von Sterzel. They are both delighted to see one another and Kálmán has given them a particularly "catchy" duet:

But that evening during the Tulip Festival a big yacht ties up at Wyk-on-Sea, carrying on board the Ministers of State from Sonneburg-Glücksburg who are to ratify Prince Paul's marriage to Princess Jutta. The Prince, however, his head completely turned by the beauty of Bella, is adamant. "Whatever you may tell me of its legality I do not recognise this marriage by proxy. I am not afraid of this Princess and I would tell her so to her face." At this moment through the door of the Yacht Club comes Bella and faces him with the words: "Very well, then, tell her. Here she is." Prince Paul is shattered at the realisation that Bella and Princess Jutta are one and the same person and humbly begs her pardon. But the Princess tells him coldly that she has no time for a Prince or a man who does not keep his word. She adds that their marriage is at an end and, boarding the royal yacht, sails away, leaving Prince Paul a sadder and a wiser man.

ACT III

Two days later, back at the palace of Sonneburg-Glücksburg, which should have been the scene of her honeymoon, Princess Jutta is missing Paul's company and regretting her arbitrary dismissal of such an attractive husband. But in due course he appears, determined to persuade his enchanting wife to change her mind, and Jutta thoroughly enjoys herself by teasing and tormenting the lovesick Paul. Eventually she sends for the contract of their marriage by proxy and, to his despair, proceeds to tear it up. But his sadness is turned to joy when she reminds him: "You swore you wouldn't marry a Princess, but you did not say you wouldn't marry a little Dutch girl." And, throwing off her cloak, she reveals herself dressed in Bella's peasant dress as they fall happily into each other's arms.

Die Bajadere

Operetta in Three Acts

By Julius Brammer *and* Alfred Grünwald

Music by Emmerich Kálmán

First produced on 23rd December, 1921, at the Carl Theater, Vienna, with Louis Treumann as "Prince Radjami", Christl Mardayn as "Odette Darimonde", Louise Kartousch as "Marietta" and Ernst Tautenhayn as "Napoleon".

Characters

MARIETTA LA TOURETTE
LOUIS PHILIP, *her husband*
MARQUIS NAPOLEON ST. CLOCHE
ODETTE DARIMONDE, *an actress*
PRINCE RADJAMI, *of Lahore*
COLONEL PARKER
PIMPRINETTE, *of the Théâtre Chatelet*
CHORUS OF THEATRE PATRONS, PARTY GUESTS, HOTEL VISITORS, ETC.

ACT I

The scene is the foyer of the Théâtre Chatelet, Paris, during the interval. The first act of the première of the operetta *La Bayadère* is just over and an elegant audience is promenading the foyer, excitedly discussing the production. Glamour is added to the occasion by the presence of Prince Radjami, the heir to the throne of Lahore, a handsome and distinguished Indian perfectly dressed in "tails" and wearing on his head a jewelled turban. He is the centre of attraction, especially for the women, and Marietta la Tourette is particularly anxious to make his acquaintance. She is a young married woman, rather bored with her husband, Louis Philip, a worthy chocolate manufacturer, and is attracted to the young Marquis Napoleon St. Cloche, who is longing to be her lover. Napoleon, to gain her good opinion, pretends to have visited India and to be on intimate terms with the Prince and is considerably embarrassed by Marietta's request to be presented. His efforts to scrape acquaintance with the Prince are not very successful and for the moment he manages to put off Marietta.

Prince Radjami, on his part, is greatly attracted to the star of the show, Odette Darimonde, and begs the impresario to present him. Odette receives him graciously and the Prince gives her a bouquet of magnificent roses. He tells her they are from the gardens of the Taj Mahal in Agra and were first grown by the Emperor Akbar for his bride twelve hundred years ago. They are called "Lovers' roses" and whoever breathes in their perfume is sure to fall in love. Odette playfully tells the Prince that her love is not to be won by the magic of flowers. Though on the stage she may play a Bayadère, a slave-girl and dancer who must follow her Prince, in real life she is quite a different person. He retorts by asking her to supper with him after the show, and when she declines he warns her that it is in his power to compel her to come. "When the show is over," he tells her, "I shall stand here and I shall will you to come to me and you will come. You will take my arm, you will get into my car and be a guest in my house." Odette laughs at his fantastic claims, but the Prince warns her not to be too sure of herself.

Shortly after this Colonel Parker, an officer of the British Raj attached to the Prince's suite, craves audience of His Highness. He apologises for bothering His Highness at the theatre but his business is urgent and the Prince has been deliberately avoiding him, both at his palace and at the Embassy. Colonel Parker reminds the Prince that in three days he celebrates his thirtieth birthday, and that by the law of his country he technically forfeits his right to the throne of Lahore unless he is married by that date. The Colonel then hands him a communication which has just arrived from Lahore. It is from the reigning Prince, Radjami's uncle, and informs him that as he shows no signs of returning home to choose a consort a bride has been selected for him, and the note concludes with a command that he return to Lahore to celebrate his marriage. Colonel Parker tells the Prince that a battleship is waiting at Bordeaux to take him to Bombay and there is a train at 10.30 p.m. But the Prince is adamant in his refusal to go, and Colonel Parker rightly suspects that a woman is at the bottom of it, as His Highness sings the hit tune from *La Bayadère*:

The Prince now summons his equerry and tells him to organise a supper party at his palace after the show. It is to be impromptu and, needing guests, the Prince accosts Napoleon, whom he vaguely remembers, inviting him and any friends he likes to bring to the party. Napoleon delightedly tells Marietta and her husband that they are to be the Prince's guests, and Marietta is very impressed at Napoleon's influence with His Highness. Colonel Parker makes one more attempt to persuade the Prince to leave for Bordeaux and not to flout his Government's wishes, but to no effect. The Prince is at the top of his form and bursts into a song in praise of champagne. As he finishes Odette enters in a beautiful evening cloak and carrying her bouquet of "Lovers' roses". Walking as in a dream, she goes straight up to the Prince, and, taking him by the arm, she leads him to the waiting car as the curtain falls.

ACT II

In the drawing-room of his palace Prince Radjami's guests are assembled. Elegant members of Parisian society rub shoulders with dark-skinned Indians from the Prince's entourage. The party is in full swing. Presently the Prince arrives with Odette on his arm. She still behaves as though she were living in a dream, and the Prince, escorting her to a chair, sings her a tender love-song:

At the end of the song he touches her forehead and she "comes to" like one awakening from an hypnotic trance. For a moment she does not know where she is, but she soon recovers herself and tells the Prince that she remembers standing before the mirror in her dressing-room at the theatre with every intention of going home and being suddenly overcome by an irresistible desire to accept his invitation. "The magic of the 'Lovers' roses' is working," he tells her. "Today you will come to me and tell me that you love me. If I will you to, you will even tell me in writing that your heart belongs to me." "If ever I get so far as to put that down in writing," she challenges, "I shall admit defeat." "Is that a promise?" he asks. "It is," she assures him, and they move to the ballroom.

Meanwhile, Marietta and Napoleon are becoming more affectionate every moment, and Marietta keeps telling him how much she admires a brave, strong man like himself who has been to India and hunted tigers and elephants with Prince Radjami—never dreaming that Napoleon's stories are a figment of his imagination and that he has never travelled farther than Chablis. Kálmán has written a charming duet for these two, describing a cosy little bar where two lovers could conveniently snuggle up to one another with a drink to keep out the cold:

Eventually Marietta decides that Napoleon would suit her better as a husband than her present one, and, calling for Louis Philip, she informs him that Napoleon wishes to ask him for her hand in marriage. Louis Philip magnanimously agrees to give her up and gratuitously hands Napoleon an enormous bill which Marietta is owing to a jeweller. The scene ends with a cynical trio describing a wife's methods of extracting fur coats, jewellery, expensive cars, etc., from her long-suffering husband:

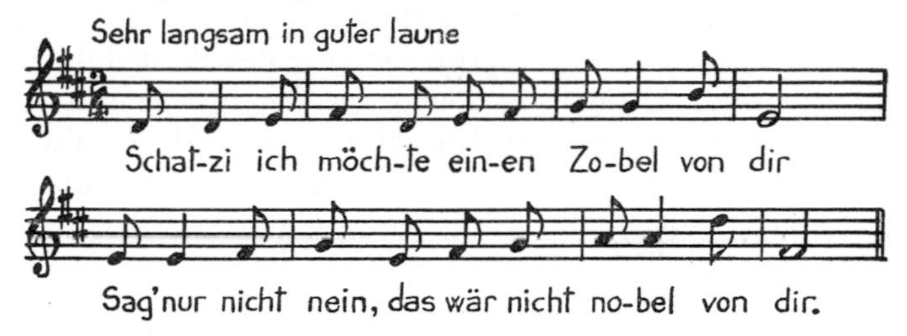

At the party Colonel Parker makes one last despairing effort to persuade the Prince to return to Lahore to be married. "Listen," says His Highness. "The law of my country and my uncle require me to get married." "So does my Government," adds the Colonel. "Very well," says the Prince. "I will oblige them all. Tonight I will get married, and my bride will be Odette Darimonde." The Colonel is amazed, especially when he learns that Odette is unware of the honour in store for her. "You will need two witnesses as to your identity—as a foreigner," he tells the Prince. "I shall be happy to act as one myself." The Prince persuades Napoleon, who is greatly flattered, to act as the other witness and the drawing-room is prepared for the marriage ceremony. Odette now joins the Prince to say good night and to thank him for the party, but he tells her that when she reaches the door she will stop and bury her face in his roses, and that then a great love for him will well up in her heart and she will stay with him. Everything that he has predicted happens, and Odette finds herself unable to leave, and then and there, at his command, she sits down at a table to confess her love in writing. Then, throwing off her cloak, she appears in the Bayadère costume that she wears on the stage as the slave-girl, Leilo Rahi.

When the Prince's entourage are all assembled the marriage service begins. The scene is a magnificent one, with the Prince in his full regalia of Indian royalty and Odette in her barbaric slave-girl's costume, richly jewelled. Part of the ceremony is the binding together of wrists, and this is followed by the ceremonial kiss of love. The Prince is just repeating the response "White Flower of love, offer me the red of your lips to kiss", when Odette, suddenly snatching away her hand, severs the band of love. Then, turning on Prince Radjami, she tells him cruelly that things have gone far enough and that as far as she was concerned the whole thing was play-acting. She was never for a moment under his hypnotic influence but has made a fool of him to teach him a lesson in how to treat a European woman. The Prince is overcome. "But you have confessed your love for me in writing," he protests. "Read what I have written," is her reply, and he reads: "Odette Darimonde will never be conquered by the methods you adopt. You believe yourself the victor, but the whiplash of a woman's fury will be your punishment." Then, snatching up her cloak, Odette sweeps out of the room. Gaining control of his emotions, the Prince calls after Odette: "In spite of everything you will love me. Our fates are linked together."

Then, calling for champagne, he orders the party to be resumed, and the curtain falls on a scene of hectic gaiety.

ACT III

The last act takes place in the bar of a smart Parisian hotel. Marietta and Napoleon enter. They have been married for some months and things are not going at all smoothly. Marietta has found out that Napoleon was never in India and never hunted a tiger or an elephant in his life. He has also begun to put on weight. The last straw is the arrival of her first husband, looking slim and elegant and at the top of his form with two pretty girls. Marietta, a girl of character, succeeds as usual in getting what she wants, and this time it is Napoleon who magnanimously gives her back to Louis Philip. Finally, Odette and her Prince come together through the good offices of an old official of the Théâtre Chatelet, Pimprinette. He tells the Prince that he knows all the tricks of the theatre and he persuades him to write Odette a letter which he promises to deliver. The letter is one of farewell, telling her that he is returning to Lahore to marry an Indian girl and regretting the unhappy end to their love. Directly she knows that she has lost him Odette's heart is afire with love for her Prince, and bitter regrets assail her as she sits in the bar with Pimprinette reading and re-reading his letter. Then suddenly the door opens and her Prince is there and she is in his arms, while old Pimprinette murmurs: "Sardou always said 'a letter is the simplest solution' in the theatre, and there [pointing to the lovers] you have the final curtain to *La Bayadère*."

Die Gräfin Mariza
(The Countess Mariza)

Operetta in Three Acts

By JULIUS BRAMMER *and* ALFRED GRÜNWALD

Music by EMMERICH KÁLMÁN

First produced on 28th February, 1924, at the Theater an der Wien, Vienna, with Betty Fischer as "Countess Mariza" and Hubert Marischka as "Tassilo". London production on 6th July, 1938, at the Palace Theatre, with Marie Lossef as "Countess Mariza" and John Garrick as "Tassilo".

CHARACTERS

COUNTESS MARIZA
PRINCE POPULESCU
BARON KOLOMAN ZSUPAN, *a wealthy landowner of Varasdin*
COUNT TASSILO ENDRÖDY-WITTEMBURG
LISA, *his sister*
PRINCESS BOZENA GUDDENSTEIN ZU CHLUMETZ
PENIZEK, *her butler*
TSCEKKO, *an old servant of Mariza's*
BERKO, *a gipsy*
MANJA, *a young gipsy fortune-teller*
CHORUS OF GUESTS, GIPSIES, CHILDREN, PEASANTS, ETC.

ACT I

The scene is the terrace of a country house in Hungary near the Bulgarian border. Rolling parkland stretches far into the distance, and the estate is the property of Countess Mariza, an heiress, young, lively and attractive. She rarely visits her country seat, preferring a social life in the city, and the estate is managed for her by a bailiff, Bela Török. Bela Török is really Count Tassilo Endrödy-Wittemburg, but his father's disastrous speculations have reduced the family fortunes to such an extent that everything has been sold up to meet pressing creditors and Tassilo has taken a bailiff's job under an assumed name. His one aim is to spare his young sister, Lisa, the pain and disgrace of family misfortune and to save enough money to provide her with a suitable dowry when the time comes for her to marry. Tassilo likes his country life and his job, which is very well paid, but moments come, inevitably, when he misses his old life, his friends and Vienna:

On the day the curtain rises Countess Mariza announces her intention of visiting her country house, and Tassilo has orders to prepare supper for thirty guests. She duly arrives and is rapturously received by her tenants, who include a colony of gipsies, complete with zigeuner orchestra. The Countess is an unconventional, independent, strong-minded young woman, accustomed to getting her own way and demanding instant obedience. The object of her visit is to celebrate her engagement to "Baron Koloman Zsupan". Actually there is no such person (she has borrowed the name of a character in Johann Strauss' operetta *The Gipsy Baron*), and she has announced her engagement purely to discourage the multitude of suitors who want to marry her for her money. The guests, who are unaware of the circumstances, are astonished but amused at this strange celebration of an engagement minus fiancé. They put it down to an eccentric whim of the Countess—"typical Mariza," says old Prince Populescu. But to Mariza's amazement and embarrassment a visitor turns up at the house whose name really is Baron Koloman Zsupan. He was greatly surprised to read in the newspaper the announcement of his engagement to Countess Mariza, whom he has never seen, but he is quite prepared to marry her and invites her to visit him at his home in Varasdin. The Countess has to put the best face she can on the situation and introduces Baron Zsupan as her fiancé to the guests.

Among the guests is Tassilo's sister, Lisa, who is very surprised to find her brother masquerading, as she supposes, as a bailiff. She assumes there is a lady in the case in the vicinity. She promises to keep his secret and they sing an affectionate duet:

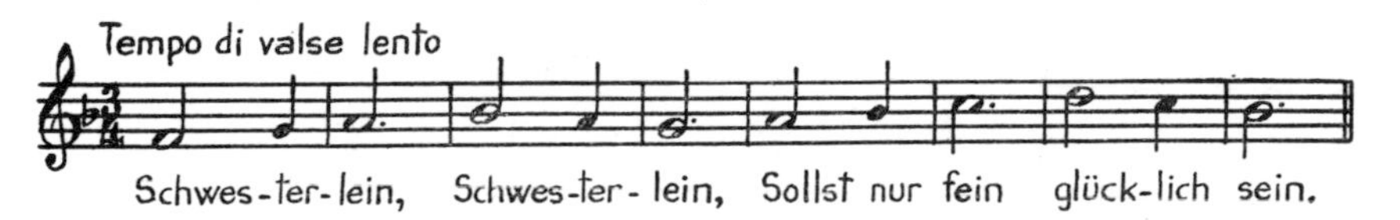

The guests now sit down to supper. Tassilo, as bailiff, is of course not invited and remains on the terrace, feeling rather out of it. His employer, Countess Mariza, has behaved to him in a very high-handed and unfriendly manner which has upset him and fuel is fed to the flame when she sends him out, via the butler, a bottle of wine with a patronising message. Swallowing his pride and several glasses of wine, he breaks into a song, urging the gipsies to cheer him with their music:

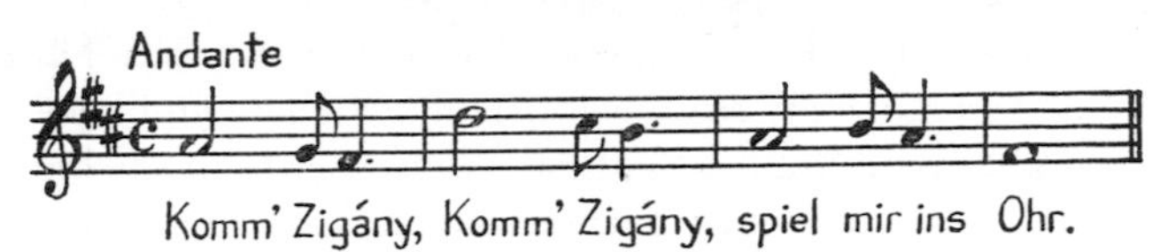

At the end of the song the gipsies strike up a rousing czardas to which Tassilo executes a lively dance. His whole performance has been watched, unknown to him, by Mariza, who has wandered out on to the terrace in search of fresh air. She now commands him to repeat his performance for the entertainment of her guests. Tassilo bluntly refuses. "I am employed by you as bailiff, not as entertainer. If you want entertainment, there are the gipsies," he tells her. Irritated by his refusal, Mariza sacks him on the spot.

To cover the tension and restore a happy atmosphere, Baron Zsupan and Prince Populescu suggest a visit to a night club in the nearby town. As the party are setting off they are stopped by a gipsy girl who offers to read Mariza's hand. Examining the lines on her palm, the girl tells the Countess: "Before the rise of the next new moon your proud heart will glow with love for a man, well-born and handsome." Mariza is strangely moved by the prophecy. She packs her party off to the night club and remains behind alone. "Here," she tells herself, "I am, at any rate, unlikely to meet any man who is handsome and well-born." At this moment Tassilo appears to take his leave. Eyeing his good looks, Mariza regrets his summary dismissal and asks him to stay. "Let us be friends and try again," she says, and Tassilo agrees to stay. Mariza now retires, and Tassilo remains alone on the terrace in the moonlight. The gipsies softly repeat his song, and he is singing quietly to himself when he hears Mariza's voice joining in. Looking up he sees her at her bedroom window, and she throws him a rose, which he presses to his lips as the curtain falls.

ACT II

Act Two takes place two weeks later in the same country house, and Mariza is waiting for the end of the period during which the gipsy prophesied that she would fall in love. Baron Zsupan has made no headway with the Countess and has turned his attention to Lisa, who is much more forthcoming. Mariza is being urged by her bailiff to interest herself in the profit and loss and other details of the home farm. She does her best to comply, but finally tells Tassilo that business bores her and that she would much prefer him to entertain her socially. A charming scene follows in which Tassilo plays the part of a young society man making up to a pretty girl, and Mariza is greatly diverted. But Tassilo gets caught up in his own play-acting and he ends by making her a sincere declaration of love:

The course of true love, however, is not destined to run smoothly for Mariza and Tassilo. Unlucky coincidences conspire to stir up trouble. For one thing, Tassilo leaves lying about a letter he has written to a friend in Budapest. In it he writes: "You know my reasons for staying on here till I have made sure of her money and a secure future." These words refer to his determination to secure his sister Lisa's future—but Mariza, who finds and reads the letter, interprets it to mean that he intends to marry her for her money just like all the others. Then she hears from Prince Populescu that he has witnessed a tender scene between Tassilo and Lisa in the park. He also tells Mariza that he does not for a moment believe that Tassilo is a genuine bailiff: he is no commoner, but a man of breeding. Mariza is beside herself with rage and jealousy and determines to be revenged. In front of everybody she deliberately picks a quarrel with Tassilo, accuses him of playing the bailiff in order to further his plan of marrying her for her money, and flourishes his letter in front of him as evidence. Finally, she humiliates him by throwing down bank-notes for eighty, ninety, hundred and thousand crowns at his feet and tells him to get out. After a struggle with himself, he picks up the money for Lisa's sake. At that moment Lisa enters, and he takes her in his arms with a cry of "My darling little sister". Mariza is amazed to hear that they are brother and sister, and as she watches Tassilo walk out of the room with Lisa, she knows in her heart that he is the man she really loves, and is determined that he shall return to her.

ACT III

The last act takes place next morning, and the scene is the same. Tassilo presents himself before Mariza to give an account of his stewardship as bailiff and to say good-bye. In spite of all their quarrels and Mariza's outrageous behaviour, the two of them are obviously deeply in love. The trouble is that neither of them will take the first step towards a reconciliation. As Mariza murmurs angrily to herself: "I can't very well throw myself into his arms." However, she does write him a reference and says good-bye.

Tassilo and Lisa are just leaving when an elderly lady is announced. It is the Princess Bozena Guddenstein zu Chlumetz, Tassilo's aunt, accompanied by her old retainer, Penizek. The Princess has only just heard of Tassilo's family misfortunes and is determined to help her nephew. She is the proprietor of several porcelain and china factories and is enormously wealthy. She has even got a wealthy bride for Tassilo in mind, but when she meets Mariza the Princess can well understand Tassilo's devotion. No word of reconciliation has been spoken, however, and finally Mariza asks Tassilo if he has read the reference she gave him to help him get his next job. Tassilo opens the envelope, takes out the reference and reads:

"Though as bailiff you won't do
As husband I would welcome you."

And they fall into each other's arms, while Zsupan consoles himself with Lisa.

Die Zirkusprinzessin
(The Circus Princess)

Operetta in Three Acts

By Julius Brammer *and* Alfred Grünwald

Music by Emmerich Kálmán

First produced on 26th March, 1926, at the Theater an der Wien, Vienna, with Hubert Marischka as "Mister X" and Betty Fischer as "Princess Fedora Palinska".

Characters

PRINCESS FEDORA PALINSKA
PRINCE SERGIUS VLADIMIR
STANASLAVSKY, *director of a circus*
MISTER X
MABEL GIBSON, *a bareback rider*
CARLA SCHLUMBERGER, *proprietress of "The Archduke Carl Hotel," Vienna*
TONI, *her son*
PELIKAN, *an old waiter*
CHORUS OF MEMBERS OF SOCIETY, GUESTS, OFFICERS, COSSACKS, CLOWNS AND OTHER CIRCUS FOLK, SERVANTS, WAITERS, ETC.

ACT I

Act One takes place in the foyer behind the scenes in the permanent home of the Stanaslavsky Circus in St. Petersburg. A passage-way leads into the ring and to reach it all the animal acts have to cross the foyer as they leave their stables. On the right a broad staircase leads to a gallery, which crosses the foyer and is used by the public as a promenade. At the foot of the steps is a bar at which a barman and barmaid are serving drinks. The first part of the programme has just finished and it is the interval. The scene is a colourful one—clowns, riders, ringmaster in hunting pink and white breeches, all mingling with members of the general public. Many of the ladies are in full evening dress, and their escorts are in tail-coats and white ties. Stanaslavsky, the Director, is surrounded by an enthusiastic group of patrons, who congratulate him on the performance. They are particularly interested in the latest star performer, "Mister X", whose sensational act, "The Devil's Leap", is the talk of the town. He is due to appear in the second half of the programme. As they are talking, down the staircase comes a beautiful woman, dressed in the height of fashion and escorted by several men. She is Princess Fedora Palinska, a wealthy widow, who is thrilled to be visiting the circus and greatly intrigued at the prospect of seeing Mister X. She is telling her companions that she was recently sent for by the Czar and told that it was his wish that she should marry again in the near future and that she should marry a man of Russian nationality. It was, said the Czar, vital that the revenue accruing from the Palinska property and mines should remain in the country. She promised the Czar that she would search for a husband. "And have you found one?" ask her companions. "No," she replies. "All men talk about love —but is it really so amusing?"

The party then go to their box to watch the performance, and Prince Sergius Vladimir enters with his aide-de-camp. The Prince, a man of about forty, is conceited and pompous and at the moment is in a very bad temper. It appears that he has proposed to Princess Fedora and she has had the impertinence to turn him down. He now demands a box for the circus. As there is not one available, he sends his aide-de-camp to tell a young man who is occupying a box alone that he must give it up to Prince Sergius. The young man, an amiable Viennese called Toni Schlumberger, is quite unabashed by the Prince and tells him he can have the box for a while as he wants to try and make the acquaintance of one of the artistes, an equestrienne called Mabel Gibson, with whom he has fallen in love. He does make her acquaintance and is delighted to find that she is no foreigner but, like himself, a Viennese, and that Mabel Gibson is only her stage name. He tries to flirt with her and invites her out to supper after the show, but Mabel warns him not to try to get round her with champagne. She remembers her mother's motto: "No funny business until after marriage."

The star of the circus, Mister X, now arrives. He is a mysterious character and is never seen without his black silken mask. He orders a glass of champagne before he goes to do his act and, sitting at the bar, sings the big number of the score:

After the song Mister X is sitting at the bar, awaiting his call to go into the ring, when down the staircase come Princess Fedora and her male escort. She is talking loudly about Mister X and giving her opinion that his wearing of a mask is just a cheap form of publicity. "Why, there he is," says one of the young men. "We'll soon find out." They cross over to the bar and accost Mister X, telling him that the Princess requests him to remove his mask. When he refuses to do so they inform him that in Russia a lady's slightest wish is law, and they are about to use force when Fedora calls them off and tells them to leave her alone with Mister X. He thanks her charmingly for her intervention and begs leave to kiss her hand in gratitude. This, however, she haughtily refuses. "So," says Mister X, "a circus artist, a made-up clown, is not worthy to kiss your noble hand? Who knows? One day such a one may be your Fate. Destiny plays funny tricks." In spite of herself Fedora feels strangely drawn to this mysterious man, and they sing a romantic duet:

After the song they part; Fedora to her box and Mister X to prepare for his entrance.

Toni now reappears. He has picked up six pretty girls from the circus ballet troupe and with their assistance he sings this "catchy" number:

After this song Prince Sergius comes on in a very bad humour. He has proposed again and this time Fedora has told him that rather than wed him she would marry a circus rider. This has given him an idea. Mister X now enters the ring, mounted on an Arab horse, and goes through his act watched by Prince Sergius and Director Stanaslavsky from the foyer. As the Arab gallops alone round the ring Mister X climbs to the roof of the circus, and above the heads of the audience, out on the high wire, plays a violin solo. Then, to the accompaniment of a drum-roll, he leaps from the wire and with precision timing lands on the back of the galloping horse, to thunderous applause. After his exit Mister X encounters the Prince, who congratulates him and asks him his reason for wearing his mask. Mister X confesses that he leads a double life. In real life he calls himself Baron Korosow and enjoys a normal social life, but every evening he dons his mask and becomes Mister X the circus artiste. Before they part Mister X has accepted an invitation to supper with Prince Sergius at the circus at midnight—not as Mister X but, at the Prince's suggestion, as Baron Korosow. Sergius promises to introduce him to Princess Fedora. At the mention of her name an enigmatic look comes over Mister X's face and he murmurs: "So, I am to make *her* acquaintance." However, he accepts the invitation and promises to be there at midnight. True to his word, he arrives punctually, and is duly introduced to Princess Fedora and gallantly kisses her hand. During the party, to the Prince's amazement, "Mister X" is carried in shoulder high by a mob of circus enthusiasts and he asks "Baron Korosow" for an explanation. "Oh! that is my valet," he says. "He often takes my place on such occasions." As the champagne circulates the party gets livelier. Princess Fedora is obviously greatly taken with the handsome Baron Korosow, and the curtain comes down to a rousing ensemble, suggestive of the party spirit:

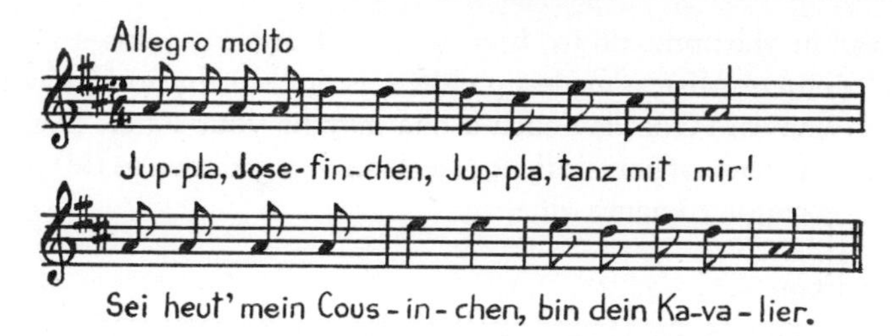

ACT II

The scene is a salon in the palace of Prince Sergius in St. Petersburg six weeks later. It is an eighteenth-century room and a feature of it is a small chapel built into the far end. Prince Sergius is giving a ball and Princess Fedora is present. The Prince asks her casually if she has given any more thought to the Czar's command that she shall find a husband, and she tells him that she believes she has found the right man. When Mister X as "Baron Korosow" arrives at the party it is quite obvious who the "right man" is. But behind Prince Sergius' apparent concern for Fedora's matrimonial welfare is dark intrigue, and it's mainspring is revenge for Fedora's treatment of him. The Prince's plan is, in fact, to manage matters so that Fedora and Baron Korosow fall in love and marry, and then to shame Fedora by exposing her as the wife of a circus performer. The curious feature of the whole thing, however, is the apparent willingness of Mister X to participate in the plan. Actually he has fallen sincerely in love, and though he despises himself for the part he is playing, for the moment he is letting things drift and is basking in the sunshine of Fedora's love. Happily they sing of their love:

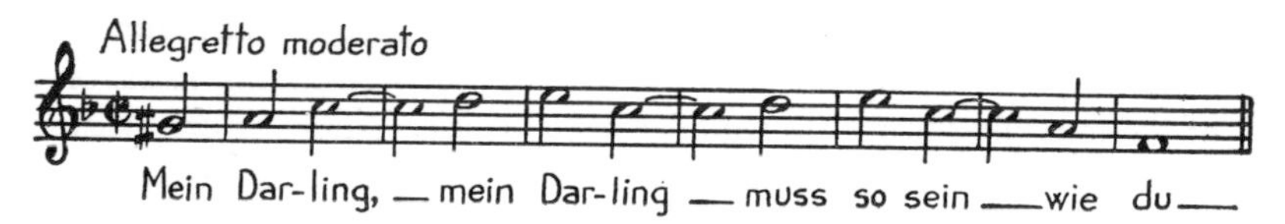

Toni and Mabel, who are now very much in love, are also at the ball. Prince Sergius, who greatly appreciated Toni's good-nature in giving up his box at the circus, has, owing to a complete misunderstanding, made great friends with him. Toni is the son of the proprietor of a Viennese hotel, "The Archduke Karl", but his explanation of this to Prince Sergius is so confused that the Prince jumps to the conclusion that he is the son of his old friend the Archduke Karl of Austria. And that is how Toni and Mabel come to be at the ball.

As midnight approaches Prince Sergius puts his plan of revenge into action. He has forged a letter purporting to be from the Czar, telling Fedora that as she has taken no notice of his command to find a husband he has himself found one for her, and insisting that she marry without delay. The Prince has this letter delivered to Fedora, pretending that it has been brought by special messenger. Fedora is in despair at this development and is only too eager to fall in with the Prince's proposal that the only way to escape the consequences of the Czar's action is to marry Baron Korosow, the man of her choice, this very night in the palace chapel, and then pretend to the Czar that his letter arrived too late. The plan is jeopardised by Mister X's last-minute attack of conscience. However, he pulls himself together, the Prince's Chaplain is sent for, and not only Fedora and Mister X but, at their urgent request, Toni and Mabel too are married. No sooner is the ceremony concluded than a blare of music is heard outside and into the salon march the entire company of the Stanaslavsky Circus. Fedora sees by Prince Sergius' expression that this is his doing and asks the meaning of the joke, only to be told that her bridegroom and Mister X, the circus performer, are one and the same person and that by her marriage she is raised to the rank of Circus Princess. Bitterly ashamed, she turns on Mister X, and begs the Prince to protect her from "any future annoyance on the part of this clown". Now, however, it is Mister X's turn. "Look at me," he tells Fedora. "I am Fedja Palinska." Then, before everybody, he discloses the fact that, as a young hussar officer, he had fallen in love with Fedora, but that she had preferred to marry his rich old uncle. In consequence he had found himself disinherited and his career ruined, and finally he had started a new life in the circus. Fedora is shattered by his news. "Fedja, can you ever forgive me?" she begs him. But slowly turning his back on her, he walks out of the room.

ACT III

Act Three is set in the dining-room of the hotel "The Archduke Karl" in Vienna two months later. Like most last acts in operetta, its purpose is to bring about the conventional "happy ending" for the hero and heroine. It is also remarkable for two excellent character parts of an old waiter, Pelikan, and the elderly Frau Schlumberger, mother of Toni and wife of the proprietor of "The Archduke Karl". These parts were beautifully played in the production in Vienna in 1926 by Hans Moser and Mizzi Zwerenz, respectively, for whom they were written.

Some comedy is derived here from Toni's terrified reluctance to tell his mother of his marriage to Mabel, who is heartily sick of being merely "The lady in room 16". Frau Schlumberger eventually learns from Mabel's lips of their marriage. She is at first horrified to hear that Mabel comes from the circus, but her disapproval turns to joy when she learns that she is the daughter of Baron Burgstaller, with whom she herself was madly in love as a young girl, and she gives their marriage her blessing. Finally, it is entirely through the old waiter, Pelikan, that Fedora and Mister X are reunited. Fedora is dining with Prince Sergius, who keeps complaining of a draught. At another table sits Mister X. Of course he and Fedora are still as much in love as ever, and Mister X calls Pelikan over to his table and asks him if he can think of a way of getting rid of the Prince for a few minutes. The old waiter is quite equal to the occasion. He turns on an electric fan just behind the Prince's chair, and the Prince, starting up, apologises to Fedora and leaves the restaurant to fetch a scarf. In a moment Mister X is at Fedora's side and all differences are settled. "Fedja, darling, promise me that now you'll give up the circus," she begs him. "Oh! does it embarrass your Highness to read my name on the bills?" he asks, offended. But she tells him tenderly that she is terrified some accident might happen to him. Then at last he gives her his promise, and their happiness is complete.

Die Herzogin von Chicago

(The Duchess of Chicago)

Operetta in a Prologue, Two Acts and an Epilogue

By JULIUS BRAMMER *and* ALFRED GRÜNWALD

Music by EMMERICH KÁLMÁN

First produced on 5th April, 1928, at the Theater an der Wien, Vienna, with Rita Georg as "Miss Mary Lloyd" and Hubert Marischka as "Crown Prince Sandor Boris".

CHARACTERS

SANDOR BORIS, *Crown Prince of Sylvarien*
PRINCESS ROSE-MARIE, *his cousin*
COUNT BOJATZOVITCH, *Minister of Finance*
MARQUIS PEROLON, *Lord Chamberlain*
BENJAMIN LLOYD, *the Sausage King of Chicago*
MARY, *his daughter*
JOHNNY BONDY, *her secretary*
CHARLES FOX, *of Fox Films*
KING PANKRAZ XXVII
CHORUS OF OFFICERS, NIGHT-CLUB PATRONS, COURTIERS, PARTY GUESTS, ETC.

PROLOGUE

"How Mary Lloyd wanted to dance the Charleston"

The scene of the prologue is a fashionable night club in Budapest. Formerly a typical café, complete with gipsy orchestra, it has been re-decorated and modernised. The gipsy orchestra has become an up-to-date dance band specialising in Charlestons and Black Bottoms, and the place functions under the name of the "Grill Americain". Tonight the proprietor is in a state of high excitement, for Miss Mary Lloyd, American millionairess and daughter of the Sausage King of Chicago, has booked a table and is bringing a party. Soon after the rise of the curtain a party of men enter and sit down at a table. The party consists of the Crown Prince of Sylvarien, Sandor Boris, and his entourage. Now Prince Sandor is allergic to all things American, especially jazz, and he asks the orchestra for some Viennese music, adding his fine tenor voice to their melody.

At this moment Mary Lloyd, accompanied by the American Ambassador, her secretary Johnny Bondy, and a large party sweeps into the room. She receives a rousing welcome from the guests and replies with a few well-chosen words on America with especial emphasis on American ladies. The Ambassador inquires the purpose of Mary's trip to Europe, and she tells him that she is out to win a prize of a million dollars offered by the Young Ladies' Eccentric Club of New York. The prize is for the member who succeeds in acquiring that which is most difficult to purchase for money. During the meal the Crown Prince of Sylvarien is pointed out to Mary. "Sylvarien," she remarks. "That is the state from which Papa's Trust acquired the oil concessions. Go over to his table," she orders her secretary, "and tell the Crown Prince I should be pleased to partner him in a Charleston." Sandor listens amusedly to the "invitation", but shakes his head. "Tell the lady that the Crown Prince of Sylvarien dislikes American music and American dances, but that he would be honoured to partner her in a waltz or Hungarian czardas." Mary is furious at her rebuff and orders the band to play a Charleston. The Crown Prince, not to be outdone, clamours for a waltz, but when Mary sweetens her demand with a tip of five thousand dollars, the band leader breaks into a lively Charleston. A wild dance ensues, and as it finishes Mary returns exhausted to her table. Sandor now returns to the attack, and so fervently does he plead with the band leader that the gipsy in him is aroused and he becomes once again the Primas (gipsy leader). All the Hungarians side with the Prince. The coloured saxophone player is ceremonially carried out of the room shoulder high, and the musicians take their violins and begin a nostalgic gipsy melody. Gradually the tempo quickens, and the curtain falls on a lively czardas sung by Sandor and all the Hungarians:

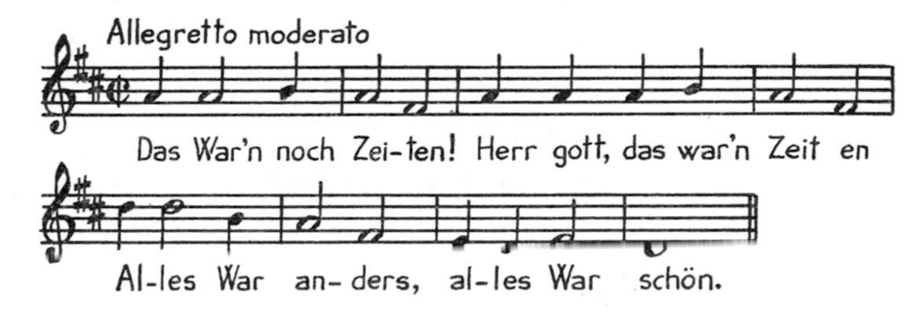

ACT I

"Crown Prince Sandor Boris"

The scene is the audience-chamber in the castle of Graditza, Prince Sandor's palace. In spite of her rebuff Mary Lloyd is greatly attracted to the Crown Prince, and the idea comes into her head to win the Young Ladies' Eccentric Club prize by buying the castle of Graditza. She sounds out two Ministers of the Crown, Count Bojatzovitch, Minister of Finance, and the Marquis Perolon,

Lord Chamberlain, as to her chances. She is prepared to offer six million dollars for the castle and all its contents. The Finance Minister is enthusiastic at the prospect of so much money, but the Lord Chamberlain is affronted at the idea; and Mary leaves them to broach the subject and convey her offer to the Prince.

Sandor's cousin, Princess Rose-Marie of Morenia, now pays him a visit. She is in low spirits, for on account of her lack of dowry, she has been turned down by six princes in succession whom her parents hoped might marry her. What with this and her congenital lisp, which embarrasses her, she is very much cast down. She has heard that the latest plan is for her to marry Sandor, and she has come to beg him to refuse, for she does not want to marry Royalty, but to find her happiness with a commoner. When later she meets Johnny Bondy she is enchanted with his American humour and gaiety and he with her attractive lisp, and they sing:

When Mary's offer is conveyed to him, Sandor tells her that he would not consider for a moment selling Graditza, which is bound up with all his memories and is the home of his ancestors. Mary laughs at his sentimental attitude and tells him that old castles and European royalty are out of date—a Prince, she says, is only a puppet. Later, to Mary's amazement, Sandor changes his mind and tells her that he is prepared to sell. He will not accept a cent of the six million dollars for himself; everything is for his country, and if there is a little over he begs that it be used to build a home for fatherless children. The two Ministers of State and Johnny Bondy then draw up an agreement of sale, which is signed by both Sandor and Mary, and Sandor, mounting the throne for the last time, takes emotional leave of his palace home.

Sandor then makes his adieux. The only thing he desires to take with him is a bunch of red roses, a present from his cousin, Princess Rose-Marie. As he is walking out of the room strains of military music are heard. His regiment of Guards has come to escort His Majesty; and Mary out of the window watches Sandor march away at the head of his regiment. "There is only one thing lacking now," remarks Bondy to Mary. "To get even with the Prince who refuses to Charleston." With a smile Mary sends a cable to her father: "Have just bought a marvellous Prince's castle and now propose to buy the Prince to go with it."

ACT II

"The Duchess of Chicago"

The scene is once again the audience-chamber in the castle of Graditza. It has been entirely refurnished, and over the throne, in place of Sandor's ancestor, hangs a portrait of Mary's grandfather—a blacksmith standing with his hammer at an anvil. The only piece of furniture that remains unaltered is the throne, and on it, as the curtain rises, Mary is seated. She is giving a house-warming party, and Marquis Perolon and Count Bojatzovitch are among her guests. Bondy arrives with the newspapers full of the Crown Prince and his doings. "You wait," murmurs Mary. "You'll dance with me before I've finished."

Sandor now arrives to pay his respects and is startled at the changes to his audience-chamber, which he hardly recognises. Mary asks him what he thinks of the improvements, and he says he thinks them superb, but that it is the end of tradition. "Oh! I prefer central heating to tradition," says Mary with characteristic sentiment. "I hear that for the last few weeks you have been having my Court Fiddler here," says Sandor. "Why, yes. He has been teaching me that dance you love so—the Viennese Waltz. And I hear," she goes on, "that you have been taking lessons from my band leader in the Charleston." Sandor admits to it. "But I thought you had banned the Charleston throughout the land?" "True, but one must be familiar with what one bans, and now I find the Charleston is practically an American czardas. But whereas you dance the Charleston using only your feet, you dance the waltz with your whole soul and body:

To Mary's delight, her father, Benjamin Lloyd, now arrives from Chicago. He has received her telegram and is rather concerned at her news, for though he takes kindly to Sandor as an individual and realises that he is a humane and conscientious ruler, he does not consider the Crown Prince of a small state a good enough match for the daughter of the Sausage King of Chicago. But by this time Sandor and Mary are beginning to fall in love, and Mary is determined to marry him if he will have her. Unfortunately, Sandor happens to meet in the palace eight young women, daughters of the richest men in America and Mary's fellow members of the Young Ladies' Eccentric Club of New York. From their gossip he learns all about the competition and that he himself is Mary's purchase, and he is devastated by the information. The guests are now assembled to hear an important item of news. King Pankraz XXVII of Sylvarien has telegraphed from Monte Carlo, creating Mary "Duchess of Chicago", so that the question of birth is now no hindrance to her marrying Sandor. As Mary's health is being drunk, Sandor enters and announces in a speech that his people have long desired him to choose a bride and he will postpone doing so no longer. Mary whispers to her girl-friends: "This is my big moment"—but to her grief and fury Sandor crosses over to Princess Rose-Marie and, leading her forward, presents her as his chosen bride. Mary, affronted, bursts into a diatribe against Europe, princes, crowns and waltzes. Calling for her dance band and tap dancers, she orders them to give her American dance music, and the curtain falls on an orgy of Charleston and Black Bottom.

EPILOGUE

"Happy End"

The Epilogue takes place in the Grill Americain. Here old King Pankraz XXVII of Sylvarien, back from Monte Carlo, is enjoying himself with some girls. Despite his age and deafness he is a real *bon viveur* and full of gaiety. Sandor enters alone and rather sad. In a conversation with the Primas he learns that Mary visits the night club every evening with an unknown young man. They order champagne and call for waltzes and czardas music till Sandor, in a fit of jealousy, calls for an American number. As the band is playing, Mary enters with the stranger. Old King Pankraz, who has an eye for a pretty girl, is very much taken with Mary and even offers her his throne, but she laughingly manages to evade him. A newspaper boy now appears with the late-night final edition and Sandor reads that Princess Rose-Marie has eloped with Johnny Bondy. "Rose-Marie was always a sensible little thing," says Sandor. "Now I must celebrate my freedom." And he orders more champagne. Presently Sandor tells his adjutant that the stranger sitting with Mary Lloyd is staring at him in an insulting way, and he calls the stranger over to his table. The stranger admits that he was staring. "I did so on purpose to provoke you." He adds: "I wanted you to betray to Miss Lloyd how much in love with her you are and to inform you that Miss Lloyd is so much in love also that she cannot live without you." "And what concern is this of yours and who are you?" demands Sandor. "I am Charles Fox, general manager of Fox Films, New York. Our latest novelty is 'Films from Life'. The Young Ladies' Eccentric Club competition was the start of our film, and your meeting with Miss Lloyd here was the second instalment. Her elevation to the aristocracy as 'Duchess of Chicago' gave us our title. Now we only need the Happy Ending. All America is waiting. And to achieve it Miss Lloyd wishes you to know that she loves you." "Is it true, Mary?" "Yes, my darling, and now will you dance a Charleston with me?" "Not a Charleston," says Sandor, "but what about:

Kaiserin Josephine

(The Empress Josephine)

Operetta in Eight Scenes

By PAUL KNEPLER *and* GÉZA HERCZEG

Music by EMMERICH KÁLMÁN

First produced on 18th January, 1936, at the Stadt Theater, Zürich, with Paula Brosig and Karl Pistorius.

CHARACTERS

NAPOLEON BUONAPARTE
JOSEPHINE BEAUHARNAIS
MARION, *a negress*
THE DUCHESS DE AIGUILLON
THÉRÈSE TALLIEN
PAUL BARRAS
CAPTAIN CALEMET
EUGÈNE BEAUHARNAIS, *Josephine's son*
GENERAL BERTHIER
JULIETTE, *Josephine's maid*
CORPORAL BERNARD, *Napoleon's batman*
LIEUTENANT BOURRIENNE, *a cousin*
CHORUS OF GUESTS, SOLDIERS AND WEDDING GUESTS

SCENE 1. The living-room of Josephine Beauharnais' house in the rue Chanteraine, Paris, in September 1795. The room is poorly furnished. A series of shopkeepers—dress-makers, furriers, shoe-makers, greengrocers—are arriving with goods that have been ordered, only to refuse delivery without payment. In the middle of the mêlé Josephine Beauharnais appears. She has been to an art dealer to try to raise money on a picture, but he has refused to buy and she has returned empty-handed. She tells the tradespeople to keep their goods, for she has no money to pay them. Grumbling they retire, leaving Josephine alone with an old negress, Marion, who recalls to her a prophecy she made when Josephine was Josephine Tascher de la Pagerie, the daughter of a harbour-master in Martinique. "I repeat that prophecy to you now," says the old negress. "Josephine, Marquise Beauharnais, will one day be queen of France." Sadly Josephine shakes her head. How could that happen to anyone as poor and friendless as herself?

At that moment a carriage drives up to the door and deposits two ladies who have come to call. One is the Duchess de Aiguillon, with whom Josephine had made friends when they were both prisoners of the Revolution in the Maison des Carmes. The Duchess has brought the light-hearted Madame Tallien to call. Thérèse Tallien, gay, amorous leader of Parisian society, is determined to reintroduce the beautiful widowed Marquise Beauharnais to fashionable Paris. Josephine is hesitant, but before her two guests leave she has promised to attend a party that night at Madame Tallien's. After the two ladies have departed Josephine begs old Marion to lay the cards. The seven of hearts lies next to the king of clubs. "Tonight a man of destiny will cross your path," Marion tells her. "You must go to Madame Tallien's."

Scene 2. In the salon of Madame Tallien's house "La Chaumière" in the Champs-Élysées the scene is a brilliant one. An elegant, fashionable crowd includes women in daring creations, officers in colourful uniforms and young men in full evening dress. Among the guests is Paul Barras, the head of the Government (the Directory). General Berthier presents his colleague, General Buonaparte, a young Corsican, to Madame Tallien. Buonaparte's uniform is shabby and he is feeling thoroughly out of place in this glamorous assembly when Josephine Beauharnais is announced. Buonaparte is bowled over by the beauty of the young woman and looks on enviously as she goes off to dance on the arm of an elegant young man, Charles Calemet. For Buonaparte it is love at first sight:

Madame Tallien has noticed that young General Buonaparte is rather out of it and takes him under her wing, and, encouraged by her friendliness, he confides in her that he is temporarily out of commission and money is tight. Generously she promises to help him, and then and there writes a note which she gives him. It reads: "To Monsieur Lefeuvre, Paymaster of the 17th Military Division. You would earn my warmest thanks if you could see your way to issuing General Buonaparte with a new uniform—Thérèse Tallien." Buonaparte is delighted. "I feel this may be a turning point in my career," he tells Charles Calemet. "People set great store by appearances—especially women." At that moment Josephine passes by on Barras' arm. "Who is that comic-looking little officer?" she asks, pointing at Buonaparte. "Oh, he's a Corsican called Buonaparte," answers Barras. "Buonaparte! what a funny name," is her comment. "He looks like 'Puss-in-Boots'."

SCENE 3. A small room in barracks. Buonaparte is now General commanding the Paris Division. On the table lies a sword, and there is some talk between two warrant officers of a house-to-house search for weapons (it is soon after the Revolution) and of the arrest of a boy of fourteen who had refused to give up his sword, claiming that his late father had left it to him. When General Buonaparte enters he is informed of the incident and asks the boy's name. It is Eugène Beauharnais, son of the widowed Marquise Beauharnais. Buonaparte orders that Madame Beauharnais be brought before him. Thrilled at the prospect of seeing Josephine again, he bursts into lyrical song:

When Josephine appears to plead for her son, Buonaparte pretends to take a serious view of his offence before finally releasing him. He is delighted that Josephine remembers him from Madame Tallien's and eagerly accepts when she invites him to visit her.

SCENE 7. A room in Josephine's house on the evening of her marriage to Buonaparte. After the ceremony champagne is served and the guests, who include Barras and Charles Calemet, drink the health of the happy pair. Buonaparte has just declared to Josephine: "Now, nothing can tear me from your side," when General Berthier is announced. He brings an important dispatch from the War Office. General Buonaparte has been appointed Commander-in-Chief of the forces now fighting in Italy, and must leave forthwith to take up his post at the seat of war. Momentarily weakening, Buonaparte tells Berthier that he cannot go: someone else can have the job. But Josephine tells him it is his destiny, the start of his rise to fame. Seizing her in his arms, he embraces her and then leads her out of the room. Tonight at least is theirs.

SCENE 5. In camp at High Command Headquarters in Italy. It is night time, and on a table outside Buonaparte's tent are lighted lanterns and ordnance maps. After a preliminary greeting from his officers they withdraw, and Buonaparte is left alone. He seats himself at the table and writes a letter brimful of love to Josephine. As he finishes the letter the lights dim and the scene dissolves into Josephine's bedroom in the rue Chanteraine, Paris. Although it is already evening Josephine is still asleep, for she did not get home from a party until the early hours of the morning. Her whole life, in fact, is one long round of parties and social gaieties. Juliette, the maid, wakens Josephine with the post, which includes a letter from Buonaparte which has just arrived by courier from Italy. Josephine cannot be bothered to read all the four closely written sheets of notepaper, but she does gather that Buonaparte is asking her to come to him in Italy. Juliette urges her mistress to go, for Juliette is engaged to Corporal Bernard, Buonaparte's batman. Josephine examines her engagement book, but what with parties, routs and race-meetings she does not seem to have a day free to start for Italy. So Buonaparte must wait. Meanwhile, she is conducting a promising flirtation with Charles Calemet. Juliette reminds Josephine several times that the courier is waiting for a reply to take back to Buonaparte and wants to be off. Finally, exasperated at the delay, the courier, a Lieutenant Bourrienne, forces his way into Josephine's room and angrily demands her letter. But the sight of her beauty *en negligée* softens his anger and he agrees to wait. He is about to withdraw when the door opens and Charles Calemet enters. Even the least observant of couriers could hardly fail to realise the significance of Charles' presence, and when they are alone Josephine scolds Charles for his lack of forethought. It is now almost time for the guests to arrive for a party Josephine is giving that evening, and as she starts to dress the lights fade and we are in the salon downstairs. The party is in full swing when the dancing is interrupted by the entry of Lieutenant Bourrienne, the courier, booted and spurred for his return to Italy and Buonaparte. He coldly demands the letter he is to carry back. Josephine callously tells her guests that she has got to write a letter to her husband and asks if they will help her. With their assistance she manages to put down four sentences on paper and seals the envelope, which Lieutenant Bourrienne bears away. Dancing is resumed, and on a lively Can-Can the lights dim and we are back at Buonaparte's headquarters. Buonaparte is waiting eagerly for the courier's return with Josephine's letter, but when Lieutenant Bourrienne hands him her laconic reply and he learns that she has no intention of visiting him, he is bitterly disappointed. He cross-questions Lieutenant Bourrienne on the reasons for his tardy return, and in the course of the conversation learns of the presence of Charles Calemet in Josephine's bedroom. Distressed by this news, he is hardly aware of General Berthier's announcement of victory at Millesimo, and brokenly murmurs: "I have conquered at Millesimo, but in Paris I have suffered defeat."

SCENE 6. Buonaparte's headquarters in a castle near Verona. Josephine has changed her mind and decided to visit Buonaparte, after all, and she is expected at any moment. The first to arrive is Juliette with the luggage, and she and Corporal Bernard are blissfully reunited:

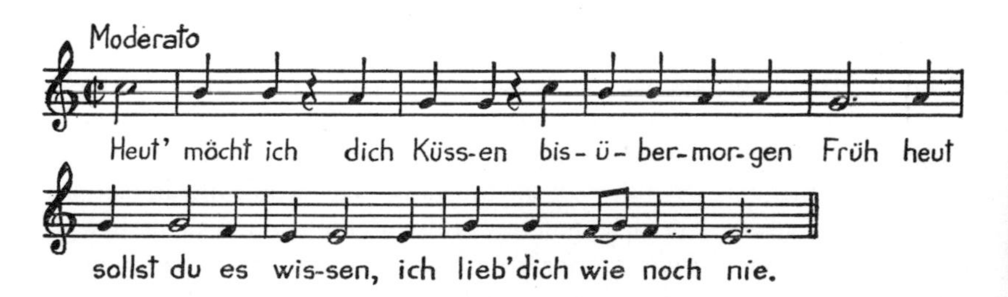

Buonaparte in spite of everything is longing for Josephine's arrival and releases his pent-up yearning, while he waits, in one of Kálmán's most effective songs:

Eventually Josephine arrives, and husband and wife embrace. But Buonaparte's joy is short-lived when Josephine announces that she has brought a volunteer who is anxious to serve under him as Ordnance Officer. It is Charles. Now it so happens that a highly dangerous manœuvre is scheduled for that very day; an attack on a bridge at Arcole. To Josephine's dismay she hears Buonaparte giving orders that two battalions are to proceed to the attack under the command of Captain Charles Calemet. She protests that Charles has come from the salons of Paris and is not experienced in active warfare; so Buonaparte tells Charles sarcastically that, as a result of such ardent pleading on his behalf, and in view of the softening effect of dalliance in Paris salons, he will be sent to the Army Service Corps at Brescia. Buonaparte now himself takes command of the expedition against the bridge of Arcole. In view of this the whole army, officers and men, volunteer for the dangerous mission. And in the hour of deadly peril Josephine at last realises her love for her gallant husband.

Scene 7. A room in the Tuileries in the year 1803. Buonaparte, now first Consul, is shortly to be crowned Emperor of France. There is a movement afoot to have his marriage to Josephine annulled, for she has given him no son, and for her place to be taken by the Infanta of Spain. But Buonaparte hesitates. In his heart of hearts, despite all her short-comings, he sincerely loves Josephine. It is their wedding anniversary and he has had his portrait painted in miniature as a present. But he is troubled by a report that Josephine daily leaves the palace in a carriage and visits a house in the rue Marcel, and he becomes highly suspicious of the reason for these visits. Bernard and Juliette, however, clear up the mystery. Josephine has had the same idea as Buonaparte for their wedding anniversary. The house in rue Marcel is the home of the painter, Isabey, and he has been painting her miniature for Buonaparte, and joyful are their wedding anniversary celebrations.

Scene 8. It is the 2nd of December, 1804. In the cathedral of Notre Dame the Emperor Napoleon Buonaparte and his consort Josephine are crowned amid the plaudits of the multitude.

Arizona Lady

Operetta in Two Acts (Seven Scenes)

By Alfred Grünwald *and* Gustave Beer

Music by Emmerich Kálmán

First public performance on 1st January, 1954, on radio (Bayrische Rundfunk, Munich). First theatrical production on 14th February, 1954, at the Stadttheater, Berne, Switzerland, with Hansy von Krauss, Walter Lederer, Lia Held and Peter Garden.

Characters

LONA FARRELL, *owner of Sunshine Ranch in Arizona*
ROY DEXTER, *a cowboy*
SHERIFF SULLIVAN
LOPEZ IBANEZ
NELLY NETTLETON, *proprietress of a mobile store*
CHESTER KINGSBURY, *apprentice-pupil at Sunshine Ranch*
SLAUGHTER, *ex-ranch manager*
UNCLE CAVARELLI, *a magician*
BENCHLEY, *a hobo*
MAGNOLIA, *Nelly's sister*
CHARLIE, *her fiancé*
CHORUS OF COWBOYS, RANCH HANDS, RACE-COURSE PATRONS, ETC.

ACT I

Arizona Lady, Emmerich Kálmán's last operetta, takes place in the year 1920, when prohibition is in force in the United States of America. Its setting is a ranch in Arizona, close to the Mexican border. In this district emigrants from Hungary have settled, and by years of unremitting toil have acquired a number of farms, and this has stirred up against them considerable envy and ill-will.

Scene 1. *The Garden of Sunshine Ranch.* Lona Farrell, the owner of Sunshine Ranch, which she has inherited from her father, is a Hungarian. By the exercise of enormous energy and iron discipline the attractive young woman has earned and retained the respect and obedience of her ranch employees. It is a condition of employment on her ranch that an employee shall confine his dealings with the boss to matters of business only, but recently her ranch manager, Slaughter, tried to kiss her and has been fired. The cowboys on the ranch are very much cast down at Slaughter's departure, and Lona was also reluctant to let him go, for the annual rodeo and race meeting to be held at Tucson County Fair is close at hand. Lona has entered her mare, Arizona Lady, and so far Slaughter has proved the only rider capable of handling this temperamental mount.

One morning there arrives at Sunshine Ranch a singing cowboy, by the name of Roy Dexter. Dismounting from his horse he takes his guitar and sings:

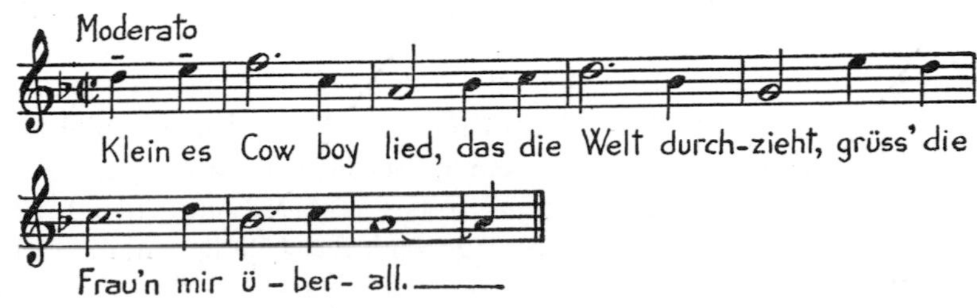

Dexter's good looks and sympathetic personality recommend him at once to Lona, and without admitting it even to herself she falls in love. Dexter is well aware of Lona's feelings towards him, and so is Sheriff Sullivan, who hopes one day to marry her. The Sheriff warns Lona against Dexter, telling her that he believes him to be a horse-stealer called Burt Morton who is wanted in Colorado. His suspicion is strengthened by the fact that Roy Dexter has actually just left Colorado. Later a rich neighbour, Lopez Ibanez, of Mexican origin and a friend of Lona's late father, arrives. He is anxious to buy Arizona Lady, and Lona is inclined to sell, for now that Slaughter has departed there is no one to ride the mare. She had hoped that Dexter would have ridden her. She has offered him the post of ranch manager, but he has refused, telling her that "The boss is much too pretty". However, when Dexter hears that Lona is considering selling Arizona Lady, he tells her he has changed his mind and that he will take the job of ranch manager and ride the horse. So Lona accepts his service, subject to the usual conditions of keeping his distance.

Side by side with the main plot runs the sub-plot which chronicles the doings of Nelly Nettleton and Chester Kingsbury. Nelly drives a mobile store about the countryside, selling everything from babies' nappies to tiles for the roof, and Chester is apprentice-pupil at Sunshine Ranch. The two of them sing affectionately:

SCENE 2. *Loose-box in the stable of Sunshine Farm.* The second scene is a romantic one with a good deal of comedy between Lona and Dexter. He assures her that he will abide literally by his promise not to speak one word of love to her, but at the same time he persists in telling her how beautiful she is and how he adores her. When Lona rebukes him, Dexter declares he is talking about Arizona Lady and asks innocently: "Whom did you think I meant?" while Lona stamps her foot in pique and frustration.

SCENE 3. *County Fair, Tucson.* The scene is the annual rodeo and cowboys' race-meeting. Nelly Nettleton's travelling store is in evidence and her Uncle Cavarelli is running a Magic and Fortune-telling Booth. Nelly has received a letter from her sister Magnolia—she writes that she is engaged to be married, but greatly fears that if her fiancé, Charlie, finds out that she has an illegitimate child he will not marry her. She has therefore told him that the child is her sister Nelly's, and he is willing to adopt it, but demands a payment of two thousand dollars for doing so, as he wants to buy a café in Louiseville. If Nelly cannot send the money, Magnolia does not think that Charlie will marry her. Nelly is anxious to help her sister, but has only five hundred dollars. She therefore seeks out Chester Kingsbury, gives him the five hundred dollars and begs him to put it on the winner of the big race. Chester promises to do so.

Also on the course are Lopez Ibanez and Slaughter. From their conversation it is clear that they are a couple of crooks and are prepared to go to any lengths to eliminate Arizona Lady from the race, for the mare is the only serious competition to Lopez' horse, Mexican Cavalier. Slaughter tells Lopez not to worry; that he will take care of Arizona Lady. Lona, to her annoyance, now learns that Sheriff Sullivan is going to back Mexican Cavalier, and she tells him that she will take any bet that Arizona Lady will win. So the Sheriff makes a bet with Lona that if Arizona Lady loses she will engage herself to marry him. But the race brings disaster. Arizona Lady, who is leading the whole way, suddenly falls just before the winning-post and Mexican Cavalier wins the race. Arizona Lady's saddle-girth has been severed by the knife of an unknown villain. Lona has to consent to be engaged to the Sheriff, but Nelly receives her two thousand dollars. For Chester (only son of a wealthy meat-packer) backed every horse in the race out of love for Nelly.

ACT II

SCENE 4. *The living-room in Sunshine Farm.* It is a fortnight later and Lona is giving a party to celebrate her engagement to Sheriff Sullivan. Lopez and Slaughter are present and so are Nelly and her Uncle Cavarelli. Lopez and Slaughter are planning fresh villainy against Roy Dexter, for Arizona Lady will soon be running against Mexican Cavalier again in the Kentucky Derby, and Dexter will be in the saddle. After the incident of the severed saddle-girth Dexter trusts no one and never leaves Arizona Lady unguarded night or day. He refuses to attend the party and declares his intention of remaining in Arizona Lady's stable. Later that night he will leave with the horse for Kentucky. But this does not suit Lona. She orders him—especially as the Sheriff is absent on sudden professional business—to come to the party and dance with her. In Dexter's place, Chester is put on stable duty, and Lona and her cowboy enjoy themselves hugely together.

Nelly hears that Dexter is travelling to Kentucky and asks him to take the two thousand dollars to her sister, and Dexter promises to deliver the money. The Sheriff's professional business is the result of a communication from Lopez. According to Lopez he will find a certain Bonita, a Mexican dancer, in "The Paradise Bar" at Nogales, and she is in possession of curious and remarkable information which Lopez knows will interest the Sheriff. The Sheriff has of course no idea that Bonita is in Lopez's pay and is his mouthpiece. At "The Paradise Bar" she tells the Sheriff that a notorious horse-stealer calling himself "Roy Dexter" is in the district. His real name is Burt Morton. On Bonita's evidence Dexter is arrested and the possession of Nelly's two thousand dollars does not suggest his innocence. At this moment a cowboy bursts open the door to report that Arizona Lady has been stolen and that the thieves have abducted Chester. The Sheriff is now convinced that Dexter's two thousand dollars is part of the proceeds from Arizona Lady's theft, and the prisoner is marched away to gaol.

Scene 5. *In the County Gaol.* Dexter is greatly touched to receive a basket of provisions and a bunch of red roses which Nelly and Uncle Cavarelli have left for him, and the red roses inspire Dexter to one of Kálmán's most melodious songs:

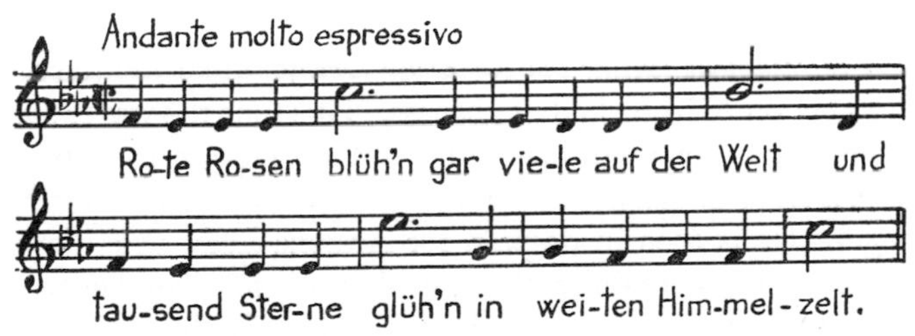

His fellow prisoner, a hobo called Benchley, has occupied the cell for some weeks, and he confides to Dexter that he has employed all his time and energy in penetrating the wall of the prison. That night under cover of darkness the two prisoners slip out of the gaol, which is situated conveniently on the Mexican border, and are soon safely over the frontier and outside American jurisdiction.

Scene 6. *"The Paradise Bar" in Nogales.* "The Paradise Bar", situated near the County Gaol, has been built literally on the frontier between the U.S.A. and Mexico, and in the bar itself a white line, running down the centre of the room, registers the line of demarcation. The bar counter on the Mexican side advertises "Vino—Cognac—Champagne—Tequilla", while, on the American side, a notice says: "Soft drinks only—Lemonade—Orangeade—Milk". In the bar on the American side is Sheriff Sullivan. He is startled to catch sight of Roy Dexter, who has come into the bar with Benchley. They are in jovial mood. The Sheriff is very anxious to tempt Dexter over to the American side of the bar and re-arrest him, but Dexter is not to be trapped. He does tell the Sheriff, however, that if he will bring Lona to the bar and allow him ten minutes' conversation with her alone, he will then give himself up. The Sheriff, who sets great store by the capture of the horse-stealer Burt Morton, goes off to fetch Lona. Chester Kingsbury, who has been in captivity ever since he was abducted from Sunshine Ranch on the night of Arizona Lady's theft, is now brought into "The Paradise Bar" by two of the thieves, who are prepared to release him for a ransom of three thousand dollars. Fortunately Nelly is in the bar with Uncle Cavarelli. She still has her two thousand dollars recovered from Dexter, and she buys Chester's liberty, after the thieves have confessed that they were prepared to take far less to be rid of him. When Lona arrives she is very terse with Dexter, but she agrees to listen to what he has to say. He then tells her how when he was a boy his father had been shot dead before his eyes by horse-thieves, and how he swore an oath that he would not rest until he had destroyed the thieves and avenged his father's memory. With the help of his fellow-prisoner, Benchley, he has now succeeded. Lopez, he tells her, is the head of the band and Slaughter is no other than Burt Morton. Both of them and the rest of the band have been arrested and Arizona Lady has been recovered safe and sound. After hearing his story Lona offers Dexter his job back, but he refuses it, even declining to accept the back-pay she owes him. But Lona, for her part, will not accept anything from Dexter, and she insists on his taking as a present Arizona Lady, the horse which has brought her so much unpleasantness. This present Dexter joyfully accepts.

SCENE 7. *A refreshment tent at the Kentucky Derby.* Lona and the Sheriff once again make a bet on Arizona Lady's chances. This time the wager stands that if Arizona Lady wins, Lona will marry the Sheriff. Dexter has entered Arizona Lady, but he is not riding her, and it is only just before the race that he learns of Lona's wager. He is then in despair, for Arizona Lady wins the race. The Sheriff, however, has come to realise Lona's great love for Dexter and magnanimously releases her to marry the man she loves. So there is a happy end for three couples—Lona, and Roy Dexter, Nelly and Chester, and for two late arrivals, Nelly's sister Magnolia and her Charlie.

Hoheit Tanzt Walzer

(Her Highness Waltzes)

Operetta in Three Acts

By Julius Brammer *and* Alfred Grünwald

Music by Leo Ascher

First produced on 24th February, 1912, at the Raimund Theater, Vienna.

Characters

DOMINIK GAUDENZDORF, *a librarian*
LIZZY, *his daughter*
PLUNDERER, *a wealthy innkeeper*
PEPERL GESCHWANDTNER, *a music teacher*
ALOISIUS STRAMPFL
PRINCESS MARIE
FRAU VON KALESCH, *Lady-in-Waiting*
PRINCE VICTOR BOGUMIL
CHORUS OF COURTIERS, GUESTS, SERVANTS, PAGES, MUSICIANS, ETC.

ACT I

The scene is the study of Dominik Gaudenzdorf, an elderly man, who today celebrates his twenty-fifth anniversary as Librarian of the University Museum in Vienna. A number of friends and colleagues are present with congratulations and good wishes. On this happy occasion there is only one cloud upon the old man's horizon. If only he could see his daughter, Lizzy, safely and happily married! The wealthy innkeeper, Plunderer, would be the ideal husband, but Lizzy unfortunately has eyes for no one but the young ne'er-do-well, Aloisius Strampfl. Herr Gaudenzdorf has forbidden him the house, but in spite of this Aloisius pays Lizzy a secret visit and tells her that he has a chance of buying an inn, "The Silver Brezn". It is going for a few hundred guilders, but, alas, the sum exceeds his savings. Lizzy's music master, Peperl Geschwandtner, now comes to their rescue. An incurable optimist, he has applied for the post of Court Conductor, and is convinced that the job is as good as his. Peperl accordingly presents Aloisius with his entire savings and Aloisius acquires "The Silver Brezn". In the meantime, Herr Plunderer calls at the house. Loud-mouthed and boastful of his wealth, he considers that he is conferring the greatest possible favour on Lizzy by consenting to marry the daughter of a mere Civil Servant. But Herr Plunderer is the recipient of a nasty shock when Lizzy informs him in front of her father's guests that she will not marry him, and he learns to his fury that the penniless Aloisius Strampfl is now an innkeeper and has filched his bride from under his nose. Lizzy and Aloisius are in the seventh heaven of happiness, but Peperl, the author of their joy, receives news that he has been turned down for the post of Court Conductor.

ACT II

Act Two is set in the garden restaurant of "The Silver Brezn". Aloisius, assisted by his wife Lizzy, has slaved to make the business a success, but Fortune has not smiled on the undertaking. Competition is fierce from "The Golden Ox" opposite, where Josef Lanner and his orchestra are a tremendous attraction. Apart from this, the landlord of "The Golden Ox" is Herr Plunderer, who is still smarting at Lizzy's refusal to marry him and is determined to ruin Aloisius. Things have also turned out badly for Peperl, who has had to give up music and take a job as waiter in "The Silver Brezn". A faithful friend, he is determined to bring prosperity to the restaurant, and to this end he inserts some attractively worded advertisements in the local newspaper. As a result the restaurant is nightly filled with a clientele of lovers and engaged couples. The crowning stroke of good fortune is the visit of Princess Marie with her Lady-in-Waiting. Weary of the rigid etiquette of life at Court, she has come to "The Silver Brezn" to enjoy herself incognito with the *hoi polloi*. Peperl, who waits on the ladies, takes them for two servant-girls out on the spree. He falls for the Princess and encourages her to sing "The Lark of Hernals". Then the Princess, at the top of her form, secretly commands Lanner and his orchestra from "The Golden Ox" opposite to come over to "The Silver Brezn" and play for her pleasure. There, blissfully revolving in Peperl's arms, she tastes all the joys of a Viennese waltz. But the time comes to end her incognito, and the Imperial coach arrives at the door of "The Silver Brezn" to take Princess Marie home. Peperl is speechless as she thanks him and Aloisius for her lovely evening. The future is a rosy one: there will no longer be any lack of customers at "The Silver Brezn".

ACT III

It is Princess Marie's wedding day and the scene is a salon in her summer palace. Sadly she thinks, on the eve of her *mariage de convenance*, how much more amusing her journey through life would have been as the companion to the simple, gay, attractive Peperl. There is of course no question of love between them, as both of them fully realise, but the Princess has done what she could to ease his material path. She has arranged his engagement as music master to her younger brothers and sisters, and on the way to her wedding she hands him an official document appointing him to the post of Court Conductor. This is the crowning achievement of his musical career, and should have brought him the happiness of fulfilment. Yet his heart is heavy within him as he accepts the document from her hands.

Liebe im Schnee

(Love Adrift)

Operetta in Three Acts

By RALPH BENATZKY *and* WILLY PRAGER

Music by RALPH BENATZKY

First produced on 2nd December, 1916, at the Ronacher Künstlerbühne, Vienna.

CHARACTERS

DAGOBERT, *reigning Prince of Landskron*
GERTRUDE, *his daughter*
FRAU GEHEIMRAT VON SIEBERT, *a widow*
HENDRIK VAN RHYN, *a tenor*
KILIAN DIETRICH, *Duke von Parthey*
BURGOMASTER VON SASSEN
HIS WIFE
CHORUS OF COURTIERS, PIERROTS, COLUMBINES, SERVANTS, CHILDREN, ETC.

ACT 1

The first act takes place in the drawing-room of Frau von Siebert's house in Sassen, a small market town in the neighbourhood of the palace of Prince Dagobert, the ruler of Landskron. The heroine of the story is his daughter, Princess Gertrude, and the plot concerns her efforts to shake off the shackles of Court etiquette and assert her right to lead her own life like any commoner. It is Christmas time, and the countryside is covered in deep snow. When the curtain rises Frau von Siebert is at the window watching with amusement some boys building a snowman and snowballing each other. Presently Gertrude arrives, excited and happy. She has been out in the forest with her secret lover, a handsome tenor from the Court Opera House, Hendrik van Rhyn. He is a strong character and a good man and the two of them are deeply in love. Later Hendrik arrives to have tea with Frau von Siebert, who is also entertaining the Burgomaster and his wife. Hendrik is asked to sing and, looking laughingly into Gertrude's eyes, sings a gay song on the theme of kissing. Later the lovers are left alone and sing a love duet, the song of the title. But its words, warning all maidens that love in the snow is only a temporary affair, promise no happy future for them.

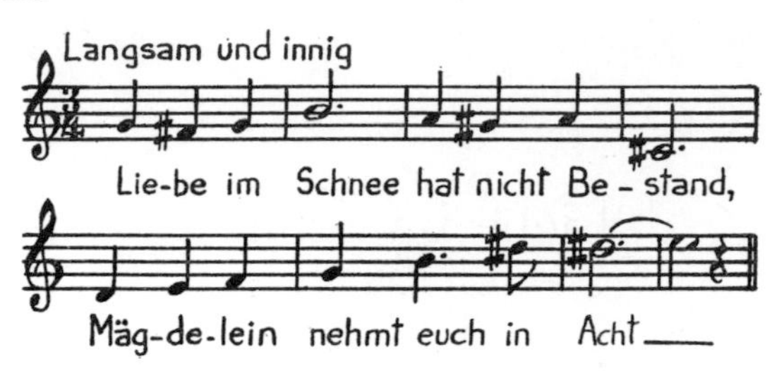

Alas! the love-story of Princess Gertrude and Hendrik is indeed fated to have no happy ending, in spite of her vehement promises to remain true to him whatever pressure is brought to bear on her to give him up. It is a case of history repeating itself for many years ago Gertrude's father, Prince Dagobert, had fallen in love with the lady who is now the widowed Frau von Siebert. He had been compelled on account of his royal rank to put her out of his life, but still every Christmas he pays her a visit. Gertrude joyfully accompanies her father, for the free-and easy atmosphere of life in a country house makes it easier for her to meet her lover while her father and his old flame are reliving happy days of the past.

The first act finishes with the departure of Prince Dagobert and his personal staff for his hunting lodge. After an entertaining and melodious ensemble descriptive of the thrill of the chase, a sleigh drawn by horses is driven round to the front door. Through the window the Prince can be seen embarking and to the jingle of sleigh-bells and cracking of whips he is driven off, waved away by Frau von Siebert and Gertrude, who is left in her charge. Night has fallen, and later at bedtime the two ladies put out the lights and retire. But when all is quiet in the house Gertrude steals down to meet her lover in the snow.

ACT II

Inevitably the day comes when at home in his palace Prince Dagobert sends for his daughter and tells her that the time has come for her to get married, and that the bridegroom, selected to be Prince Consort, is the Duke von Parthey. Her dream of love is at an end. Now that the moment has come and she faces compulsion, all Gertrude's vows of resistance are forgotten and she submits to her father's will. It is an old custom of the Court of Landskron to present, on the night of the betrothal of a Princess of the reigning house, a masque known as "The Story of the Rose". The Princess herself is to appear in it, and her partner in the production is to be Hendrik van Rhyn. The two meet again when Hendrik comes to the palace. Gertrude has written him a letter, telling him that, whatever the future may hold for them both, she will always bless the hour when he entered her life. As she is reading over her letter, Hendrik is shown in. She tries to conceal it, but in her confusion she drops the letter and he picks it up and reads:

Passionately the lovers fall into each other's arms. That night (it is New Year's Eve) they meet again in the masque. At one point in the play the dramatic action demands that they kiss. But their passions get the better of them and their stage kiss becomes reality, a kiss of farewell. The Prince is momentarily affronted, but Gertrude with an effort pulls herself together and places her hand in that of the Duke von Parthey. Turning to her father she repeats the final words of the masque: "I have made my choice", and Prince Dagobert formally announces his daughter's engagement to the Duke.

ACT III

The last act takes place in the green-room of the Court Opera House. Hendrik has given in his notice, for he feels he cannot remain any longer where everything reminds him of Gertrude and his unhappy love affair. By a coincidence his final operatic appearance is as the Duke in *Rigoletto*, singing "La donna è mobile". Gertrude, too, is sharing his unhappiness, and their farewell is full of pain. She is now the Duke von Parthey's wife. He has realised the situation between her and Hendrik and has shown tact and sympathy for her in her suffering, and this has greatly touched her and helped to lighten the sadness of parting. So with a silent handshake their romantic dream of love is ended—Love Adrift.

Der Lila Domino

(The Lilac Domino)

Operetta in Three Acts

By EMMERICH VON GATTI *and* BELA JENBACH

Music by CHARELS CUVILLIER

First production in 1912 in Vienna. London production in February, 1918, at the Empire Theatre, with Clara Butterworth as "Georgine" and Jamieson Dodds as "André" and additional music by Howard Carr. This synopsis follows the English version by Harry and Robert B. Smith.

CHARACTERS

CORNELIUS CLEVEDEN, *an American multi-millionaire*
ELLISTON DEYN, *his nephew*
GEORGINE, *his daughter*
LEONIE FORDE, *her friend*
BARONESS DE VILLIERS, *Georgine's chaperone*
HON. ANDRÉ D'AUBIGNY
PROSPER WOODHOUSE } *his friends*
NORMAN T. CALMAN }
CARABANA, *leader of a Spanish gipsy orchestra*
CHORUS OF PIERROTS, PIERRETTES, DOMINOES, GUESTS, ETC.

ACT I

In the lounge of the *Pavilion de Danse* in "The Baccarat Hotel", Palm Beach, Florida, a fancy-dress dance is in progress. Most of the guests are disguised in dominoes. When the curtain rises Colonel Cleveden, an elderly American multi-millionaire, is being mercilessly teased by a bevy of pretty girls. He has got engaged to be married, and the girls are all agog to know the name of his fiancée. She is, in fact, Leonie Forde, a friend of his daughter Georgine. The trouble is that Leonie, although she has an eye to the main chance, is not particularly attracted to the Colonel—who is twice her age. She has, however, a tenderness for his nephew, Elliston Deyn. Now the Colonel has selected Elliston as a suitable bridegroom for his daughter Georgine, recently returned home from being educated in England. Elliston is not at all keen to marry Georgine, for he is just as interested in Leonie as she is in him. Leonie, looking to a secure future and not trusting her old *roué* of a fiancé a yard, has extracted an unsigned cheque for a million dollars from the Colonel as a kind of guarantee of his fidelity. Should she catch him making love to or even flirting with another woman within the next forty-eight hours, he pledges himself to sign it.

Georgine is being chaperoned by a Baroness de Villiers. She is a high-spirited girl with a sense of adventure and of a romantic turn of mind. She tells her chaperone:

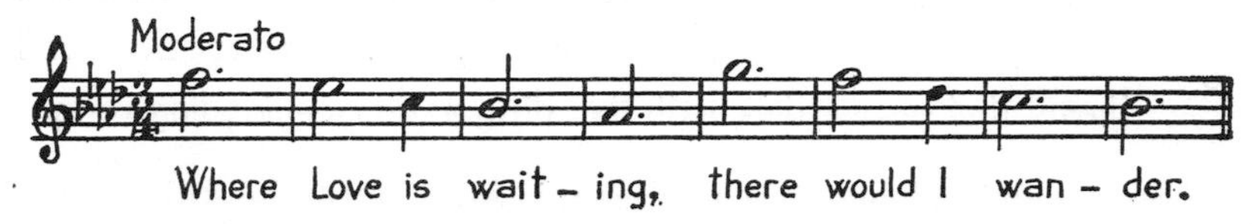

Giving the Baroness the slip, Georgine visits the fancy-dress dance, disguised in a lilac domino. Here she meets her father and her cousin (and prospective fiancé) Elliston. Neither recognises her in her domino and they ask her name. She answers that all gentlemen ask the same question in the same words:

Also at the dance are three impecunious characters: the Hon. André D'Aubigny and two friends, Prosper Woodhouse and Norman T. Calman. All three are irresponsible gamblers and have lost their money. To recoup their fallen fortunes they enter into an agreement with Carabana, the leader of a Spanish gipsy orchestra. This enterprising Latin also runs a matrimonial agency. The proposal is that one of them shall marry an heiress and thus provide financially for all three. Carabana undertakes to provide the heiress—a young girl of eighteen—just left school, beautiful, clever, of good family and fabulously wealthy. To decide on who is to embark on the matrimonial adventure the three gamblers throw dice, and André is the winner. Later he meets the Lilac Domino. She is asleep on a settee and she looks so young and sweet that he leans down and kisses her. Georgine wakens and pretends to be vexed at his presumption, but in her heart she is greatly attracted to the handsome young Englishman.

ACT II

Next day Colonel Cleveden is giving a *thé-dansant* in the garden of his house. Here André makes the acquaintance of Georgine and is puzzled by her apparent resemblance to the Lilac Domino, whom he kissed at the fancy-dress dance. Georgine tells him teasingly that she does not believe the Lilac Domino ever really existed and that the champagne he had drunk created an hallucination. But André tells her that their two voices are identical. "They are as clear as a bell in my mind," he says, and she replies tenderly: "Perhaps the nicest things are like bells in our minds." "And in our hearts," he adds, and they sing:

By now André and Georgine are deeply in love, but André still has no idea that Georgine is the heiress selected for him to marry. Georgine and Elliston have also come to a definite understanding that neither of them wants to marry the other: both are free to make their own choice. But, alas! through the indiscretion of Carabana, Georgine learns that she has been the stake for a gamble. Shattered by André's apparently cynical treatment of her, she tells her father that she is after all ready to marry Elliston, greatly to her cousin's dismay.

ACT III

The last act takes place in the Court of Palms during High Carnival. Here the complicated tangles are sorted out. Love triumphs and the heartbroken Georgine is reunited to her André, who never for a moment associated Georgine with Carabana's heiress. The susceptible Colonel is caught by Leonie proposing to another woman and so has to honour his cheque—which comes in very handy as a wedding dowry when Leonie presents it to her lover Elliston. And the curtain finally falls to the joyous echoes of wedding bells.

Der Tanz ins Glück

(Whirled into Happiness)

Operetta in Three Acts

By ROBERT BODANZKY *and* BRUNO HARDT-WARDEN

Music by ROBERT STOLZ

First produced on 23rd December, 1920, at the Raimund Theater, Vienna, with Robert Nästlberger as "Fritz Wendelin" and Christl Mardayn as "Lizzi". London production on 18th May, 1922, at the Lyric Theatre, with Lily St. John, Mai Bacon and Billy Merson.

CHARACTERS

COUNT HANS JOACHIM VON BIBERSBACH
DESIRÉE VIVERANDE, *his girl-friend*
LUTZ VON BURGEN
HERR MUTZENBECHER, *a hat manufacturer*
FRAU MUTZENBECHER, *his wife*
LIZZI, *their daughter*
FRITZ WENDELIN, *hairdresser's assistant*
SEBASTIAN PLATZER, *theatre attendant*
COUNT VON BIBERSBACH } *Hans Joachim's parents*
COUNTESS VON BIBERSBACH }
CHORUS OF THEATRE PATRONS, PARTY GUESTS, ETC.

ACT I

The first act takes place in the theatre bar of the Alhambra Variety Theatre. Along one wall is a row of doors which give access to the boxes. As the curtain rises a distraught young man, Count Hans Joachim von Bibersbach, hurries in and accosts his friend, Lutz von Burgen. Lutz tells Hans Joachim that his girl-friend Desirée is furious at being kept waiting, and Hans Joachim says, unsympathetically, that she can go on waiting for ever as far as he is concerned. He has fallen in love with someone else, and he shows Lutz a cutting which he has inserted in the personal column of a newspaper. It reads: "Young man of aristocratic extraction is particularly anxious to make the acquaintance of the beautiful young lady who occupied the carriage decorated with chrysanthemums in the procession at the recent Battle of Flowers. He will occupy the middle box in the dress circle at the Alhambra Theatre on Saturday night and will be wearing a monocle with light-blue ribbon." Unfortunately, Hans Joachim tells his friend some half-wit has booked the middle box and it is not available. "Cheer up," says Lutz, "All's well. I am the half-wit who has taken the box and you can have it with pleasure. I will tell the attendant that you will be occupying my box. He can identify you by the monocle with the light-blue ribbon." Hans Joachim thanks him warmly and goes off to buy flowers as five young girls chatter their way through the bar and enter one of the boxes. They are in a high state of excitement, for they are playing truant. One of them, Lizzi Mutzenbecher, is the "beautiful young lady who occupied the carriage decorated with chrysanthemums". She has seen the announcement in the newspaper and is all agog to have a look at the young man. However, when Hans Joachim returns with the flowers, he runs into his girl-friend Desirée Viverande, a temperamental variety star. She, too, has seen the announcement in the newspaper, and Hans Joachim's monocle with the light-blue ribbon gives him away. Desirée, beside herself with rage and jealousy, makes a physical assault upon the unfortunate young man. His tie is torn off, his collar crumpled, his hair dishevelled and his monocle thrown on the floor. After this he is in no state to occupy the middle box and he rushes out of the theatre, pursued by the avenging Desirée.

The bar is now empty, and into it steals a young man, elegant but quite unsophisticated. He has a cheerful entrance song, from which we learn that he is a barber's assistant and has no money. The young man's name is Fritz Wendelin, and it is his practice every week to buy a seat in the gallery, steal down to the dress circle and enjoy for a few stolen moments the luxury of an atmosphere of "high life". As he stands there he notices lying on the ground a monocle attached to a light-blue ribbon. He picks it up and puts it in his eye as the attendant in charge of the boxes enters. "Ah! sir, you are the gentleman who is to occupy the middle box," he exclaims, and Fritz to his surprise is ushered into a luxurious box and left alone. He soon notices that he is an object of great interest to five young women in a box opposite, and presently Lizzi, unable to resist making the acquaintance of the handsome young man, pays him a visit. They are soon on the best of terms and Lizzi confesses that it is her first rendezvous with a young man. "I suppose today is no different from any other day to a man-of-the-world like you," she says, and Fritz, who is utterly enchanted by her, says fervently: "It's a day of days for me."

Fritz has sent the attendant to buy some chocolates for Lizzi, without having the money to pay for them. However, the attendant, by name Sebastian Platzer, attaches himself to Fritz, believing him to be Count Hans Joachim von Bibersbach. As Fritz and Lizzi are leaving the theatre they run into Lizzi's father, a gay old dog, who is chasing after Desirée Viverande. He is as embarrassed to meet Lizzi as she is to meet him, and they both agree to be discreetly silent before Lizzi's Mama. Lizzi's father then invites Fritz to a party that night to celebrate the foundation of his hat factory, for which Sebastian Platzer supplies Fritz with tails and white tie out of the theatre wardrobe. He also insists on accompanying "Count von Bibersbach" to the party as his temporary valet. Fritz and Lizzi have just left the theatre when Hans Joachim returns, only to discover that "the beautiful young lady" did turn up and has gone off with a young man wearing a monocle attached to a blue ribbon.

ACT II

In the garden of the Mutzenbechers' house, Lizzi's parents are giving the party to celebrate the foundation of Herr Mutzenbecher's hat factory. Her parents are thrilled by Lizzi's friendship with "Count von Bibersbach" and enthuse over Fritz when he arrives with his valet (Sebastian Platzer). Lizzi's girl-friends, however, are well versed in society gossip and gleefully retail to her the scandals concerning the liaison of Count von Bibersbach with Desirée Viverande. Lizzi challenges Fritz as to the truth of these tales and he assures her that he loves only her and that he will break finally with Desirée. He goes so far as to put this declaration in writing and gives it to her, and Lizzi, happy in heart, joins him in a duet:

Later, Lizzi runs into Desirée and in conversation Desirée makes a point of warning Lizzi not to get involved with Count von Bibersbach, who, she declares, is an incorrigible flirt. Desirée's intention is to warn Lizzi off her own young man, and she is quite unaware of Fritz's impersonation of Hans Joachim. Lizzi triumphantly shows her Fritz's written declaration that he will have "nothing more to do with Desirée Viverande", but she is greatly perplexed when Desirée declares that the writing is not that of Count von Bibersbach, and she straightway fetches Fritz to answer Desirée, leaving the two alone together. Fritz at first tries to bluff his way through, but eventually he admits that he is not Count von Bibersbach. He is, in fact, only a hairdresser, and he reminds Desirée that he has often waved her hair at Falkmayer's. After this confession, Fritz tries to slip away from the party, but Desirée insists on his remaining to continue his impersonation and go through with his engagement to Lizzi. "That young woman needs a lesson, and I propose to keep my young man," she says. So Fritz is compelled to continue his engagement under false pretences, while Desirée rings up the real Hans Joachim at the Jockey Club, telling him all is forgiven and forgotten and he is to join her at the Mutzenbechers' party. Under pressure from Desirée, Fritz now formally asks Lizzi's father for her hand, and on the strength of this Herr Mutzenbecher rings up old Count von Bibersbach to break the news of his son's engagement. The old Count, greatly concerned at the prospect of his son marrying the daughter of a hat manufacturer, proposes to come round with his wife. Meanwhile Sebastian Platzer has learned from Desirée that Fritz is an impostor, and Fritz admits to him that he is no Count but only a hairdresser, and that he is unable to pay Sebastian for the chocolates. He promises, however, to work off the ninety-five kronen he owes in free shaves. Count and Countess von Bibersbach now arrive, and Fritz's exposure follows when they deny that he is their son. He has to admit once more that he is only a hairdresser, and Lizzi dissolves into tears of shame and mortification. Both the von Bibersbachs and the Mutzenbechers are anxious to avoid a scandal, so Lizzi is compulsorily engaged to Hans Joachim and Fritz is thrown out. But it is clear from Lizzi's farewell to him that she still loves him as much as ever.

ACT III

The happy ending takes place in Falkmayer's hairdressing establishment and is largely due to the co-operation of Sebastian Platzer. He is having the first of his free shaves from Fritz, when the voice of Lizzi's father is heard asking to be shaved. Fritz promptly disappears and Sebastian takes his place. "Haven't I seen you somewhere before?" asks Herr Mutzenbecher, when Sebastian has seated him in the chair and is soaping his face. "No," says Sebastian, "but you've probably met my twin brother, who is attendant in the dress circle at the Alhambra Theatre. He often tells stories about members of the audience. I remember one very funny one about an old fool of a hat manufacturer called Mutzenbecher who is running after Desirée Viverande and wouldn't his wife be interested to know about it?" Terrified, Lizzi's father beats a retreat, and presently Lizzi's girl-friends arrive at the shop. They have already visited fifteen hairdressers in search of Fritz and at last they have found him. They signal to Lizzi, waiting outside to enter, and then, to tease her, pretend that they have failed again. They decide, as they are in need of a rest, to have a manicure, and persuade Lizzi to go first. To her surprise she is asked to put her hand through a curtained partition and is told that this is the latest fashion in manicure. Suddenly her hand is covered with passionate kisses and a moment later she is in Fritz's arms.

Wenn die kleinen Veilchen blühen

(Wild Violets)

Singspiel

By BRUNO HARDT-WARDEN

Based on the comedy Als ich noch in Flügel Kleide
by ALBERT KEHM *and* MARTIN FREHSEE

Music by ROBERT STOLZ

First produced on 1st April, 1932, at the Princesse Schouwburg, The Hague, Holland. First London production on 21st October, 1932, at the Theatre Royal, Drury Lane, with Adele Dixon, John Garrick, Charlotte Greenwood and Jerry Verno.

CHARACTERS

HERR KATZENSTEG, *an innkeeper*
FRAU KATZENSTEG, *his wife*
GUSTL, *their daughter, a law student*
PAUL GUTBIER, *a Minister of Justice*
FRITZ GUTBIER, *his son, a law student*
HORST SÜDSTEDT } *school-friends of Paul Gutbier*
ERWIN MÜNSTER }
ISOLDE GUTBIER, *Headmistress of a girls' school*
MADEMOISELLE FAURÉ, *a teacher*
DR. FRANCK, *a professor*
HEINI, *a small boy*
LIESEL AND OTHER PUPILS OF THE GIRLS' SCHOOL
STUDENTS OF THE UNIVERSITY CORPS "RHENANIA"

SCENE I. The scene is the garden of "The Stone Jug" inn in Bacharach. Gustl (Augusta), the pretty daughter of the landlord, Hans Katzensteg, is in love with a young fellow student, Fritz Gutbier. But Fritz's father, a Minister of Justice, is against the match. He disapproves of Gustl's enthusiasm for all forms of sport and expresses an old-fashioned dislike of the type of girl he calls an "Amazon". Herr Katzensteg and his wife, however, are anxious to further the happiness of the young people, whose courtship reminds them of their own.

So the landlord makes up his mind, for the sake of his daughter's happiness, to tackle Fritz's father that very day, when the Minister of Justice will be celebrating a reunion of his Student Corps with two special friends at "The Stone Jug", and to try to influence him to agree to an engagement between the young people. As he tells Fritz and Gustl, in his youth the Minister of Justice was a gay young spark, and so were his two special friends, Horst Südstedt and Erwin Münster. "I remember in the summer of nineteen hundred and two——" he is saying when the lights fade and the story moves back in time to:

SCENE 2. The scene is a road to the Château Violette, a finishing school for girls. It is a summer day in the year nineteen hundred and two. Along the side of the road runs a wall surrounding the school, and opposite is a hedge behind which the students of the "Rhenania Corps" are wont to hide as the girls pass. When the curtain rises Paul Gutbier, Horst Südstedt, Erwin Münster and a crowd of fellow students are discovered serenading the girls:

Presently the girls in "crocodile" formation pass by, led by Mademoiselle Fauré, the French mistress. As they approach the hedge behind which the students are hiding, Liesel drops a book in the road. It is retrieved by Paul, who slips between its pages a half-folded sheet of notepaper and calls out "Heini". Immediately a small boy appears and Paul says: "Here's a penny. Take this book up to the girls' school and tell them you found it in the road" and off goes Heini, bearing with him Paul's love-letter to Liesel.

SCENE 3. In a room in the girls' school kept by Paul's aunt, Frau Isolde Gutbier, Mademoiselle returns Liesel's French grammar to her with a rebuke for "her carelessness in dropping it in the road". When she has gone, Liesel reads Paul's letter: "Sweetheart, I'm calling on my aunt this afternoon and bringing Horst and Erwin. We hope we may have a chance of seeing you." Tipped off by the maid, Augusta, the girls are ready to welcome the three young students when they arrive.

Now Paul had a plan to persuade his aunt to allow some of the elder girls to attend an evening party given by the Student Corps "Rhenania", but she has turned down the idea, and Paul is determined to have his revenge. He happens to meet Hans Katzensteg, Augusta's boy-friend and servant to the Student Corps, delivering a telegram at the school. Paul opens it and reads: "Regret missing connection. Coming by night train. Dr. Hermann Franck." Dr. Franck is the new music master, and Paul decides on the daring plan of impersonating him and thus being able to spend the evening close to his beloved Liesel. It happens to be the Headmistress's birthday, and this coincides with the arrival of a new girl, Trude, with her grandfather, to whom fall the hit number of the score: "Don't say Good-bye":

Paul now enters disguised as "Dr. Franck"—a typical Professor with a beard. He is introduced to the girls by the Headmistress, who tells them that as it is her birthday she is going out to spend the evening with friends. Dr. Franck will be in charge of the school and she hopes the girls will be on their best behaviour. She removes "Dr. Franck" for some refreshment, and the girls (quite unaware that it is Paul in disguise) excitedly discuss the handsome appearance of the new master. They finally organise a raffle for his hat, his cloak, his umbrella and, as "jackpot", the Professor himself. Liesel wins the "jackpot", and when "Dr. Franck" returns she laughingly tells him that he is hers. Paul immediately discloses his identity and receives a loving kiss. Having insinuated himself into the girls' school there is now no holding Paul. Whenever the Headmistress is within earshot he pretends to be instructing his pupils with scholarly seriousness, but as soon as her back is turned the fun is fast and furious and he is immediately at the side of his beloved Liesel.

When the Headmistress has left to spend the evening with her friends, Paul introduces the whole Student Corps "Rhenania" and there is a terrific party with singing and dancing. When the party is at its height all are startled by a ring at the front door. The Headmistress has returned unexpectedly early—and slightly tipsy. At Paul's cry of "Everybody in trousers under the table," the students and Trude's grandfather (who has been flirting outrageously with the French mistress) dive out of sight as the Headmistress enters and stands glaring balefully at the girls and "Dr. Franck", who pretends to be teaching them an innocent folk-song. She is ordering the girls to bed when once again the front-door bell rings and to Paul's dismay the real Dr. Franck is announced. A dramatic *dénouement* follows and Paul is exposed by Dr. Franck, who seizes his false beard and rips it off. At this moment Trude's grandfather, who is suffering agonies of stiffness in his constricted position, knocks over the table and the students are disclosed to the horrified gaze of the Headmistress. She faints into Dr. Franck's arms and the Doctor impatiently passes on her unconscious form to Mademoiselle, declaring that he is leaving at once and could not consider taking up his duties in such a house of ill fame. Paul and Liesel embrace rapturously and go off together as the curtain falls.

SCENE 4. This scene serves as a bridge back to contemporary times, in which the voice of Hans Katzensteg is heard finishing his story of the old days, while behind a gauze a "Wild Violets" ballet is danced by the girls.

SCENE 5. Hans Katzensteg's story finishes with the marriage of Paul and Liesel, after which Gustl, having heard the romantic details of the Minister of Justice's youthful behaviour, has no intention of allowing him to take his son, Fritz, away from her. In true Amazon fashion she challenges him to a duel, with Horst Südstedt and Erwin Münster as seconds. Paul gets the worst of the fight and has to admit defeat, but his disapproval of Gustl is changed to admiration for her skill, character and the lengths to which she has gone to win her lover. Gladly Paul and Liesel give the young people their blessing, and the curtain falls to the reprise:

BERLIN

BERLIN

Frau Luna begins the story of Berlin operetta as a separate entity, whose development is associated with the names of Viktor Holländer, R. Nelson, Eduard Künneke, Jean Gilbert, Walter Kollo, Leon Jessel, W. W. Goetze, H. Hirsch, Robert Gilbert and Walter Bromme. The genre differs from Viennese operatta in relying less on extended musical scenes than on hit numbers and spectacle. The hit number of *Frau Luna* was the waltz song "Schlosser, die im Monde liegen" (Castles in the Air):

Frau Luna
(Castles in the Air)

Operetta in Two Acts (Eleven Scenes)

By H. Bolten-Baeckers

Music by Paul Lincke

First produced on 31st December, 1899, at the Apollo Theater, Berlin, and revived in a new version in 1925 again in Berlin. London production on the 11th April, 1911, at the Scala Theatre, with Ivy Moore, Sybil Lonsdale, Frank Wood and Sybil Tancredi.

Characters

FRITZ STEPPKE, *an engineer*
LÄMMERMEIER, *a tailor*
PANNECKE, *gentleman of independent means*
FRAU PUSBACH, *a landlady*
MARIE, *her niece*
FRAU LUNA
MARS
VENUS
PRINCE STERNSCHNUPPE
STELLA, *Luna's maid*
CHORUS OF STARS AND MOON-POLICEMEN

ACT I

Scene 1. The first scene is Fritz Steppke's attic lodging in Frau Pusbach's boarding-house. Ever since he came into money Fritz Steppke, an engineer, has been engaged on the construction of a balloon, designed to make the journey to the Moon. In this project he has the enthusiastic support of his friends Lämmermeier, a tailor, and Pannecke, a gentleman of independent means. But Steppke's landlady, Frau Pusbach, who is engaged to be married to Herr Pannecke, is very hostile to Steppke's projected trip to the Moon. She has forbidden her niece, Marie, even to consider marrying him and has given him notice to quit. Marie, too, begs him to give up his mad scheme.

That night he lays himself down to a troubled sleep. Is all that follows merely a dream? His two comrades, Lämmermeier and Pannecke, enter all set for the journey, and Steppke gets up and prepares to leave with them.

SCENE 2. With horrified gaze Frau Pusbach watches the three men make their escape over the house-tops. In company with Marie she hurries in pursuit.

SCENE 3. At the airport the three aeronauts climb aboard the balloon. Vainly Frau Pusbach begs them to remain on terra firma. The balloon starts to rise and she just manages to hoist herself into the basket.

SCENE 4. To the accompaniment of the waltz "Ach Frühling, wie bist du so schön?" (What can equal the beauty of Spring?) the balloon climbs ever higher and higher on its journey to the Moon.

SCENE 5. On the outskirts of the Moon, Moon Elves are polishing the shining surface of a rocky cliff which reflects the light of the Moon. Theophilus, in charge of Moon-mechanics, recalls a piquant flirtation he had had when, during an eclipse, he paid a visit to the Berlin Zoo. Here on the Moon, however, his heart is given to Stella, personal maid to Frau Luna, Queen of the Moon. When the space travellers from Earth arrive, Theophilus does not receive them in at all a friendly spirit. "In alles stecken die Berliner ihre nasen" (Trust a fellow from Berlin to poke his nose in everything), he sings. To his dismay he recognises in Frau Pusbach his acquaintance of the Berlin Zoological Garden. Terrified of the consequences of Stella's jealous nature should she discover his lapse, Theophilus orders the Moon-police to arrest the Berliners. Frau Pusbach, however, manages to avoid arrest and threatens to make serious trouble unless he arrange transport for herself and Herr Pannecke to return to Earth. Theophilus promises to do his best to persuade Prince Sternschnuppe to give them a lift in his space automobile. The light-hearted Prince is visiting the Moon to make yet one more attempt to win the heart of Frau Luna. The travellers from Earth are now put on trial and in these unfriendly surroundings think sadly of the sights, the sounds, the smells of their native Berlin in a song: "Das macht die Berliner luft, luft, luft."

ACT II

SCENE 6. Scene Six is a magnificent salon in Frau Luna's palace. The Queen of the Moon has staying with her as guests Venus and Mars. She is delighted to hear from Stella of the arrival of the party from Berlin. The travellers are dazzled by the magnificence of the palace and amazed at being received by a woman instead of by the expected Man in the Moon. Frau Luna takes a violent fancy to Steppke. She puts on her loveliest dress and leads him out on to the dance-floor. Prince Sternschnuppe watches angrily and realises that once again his wooing of Frau Luna has failed.

SCENE 7. Prince Sternschnuppe leaves the salon and waylays Theophilus to ask his advice on the best way to approach Frau Luna.

SCENE 8. Frau Luna has tempted Steppke into her boudoir. With all her wiles she tries to seduce him, but his thoughts are all of his Fatherland and his girl-friend, Marie. Nevertheless, by her magic arts Frau Luna compels him to follow her into the Garden of Stars.

SCENE 9. In the Garden of Stars Steppke's head is turned and his senses bemused by the dances of the Rose Elves and the Ballet of the Spirits of Air.

SCENE 10. Prince Sternschnuppe decides reluctantly that his efforts to woo Frau Luna are unlikely to be successful and he resolves to take his departure. But Theophilus counsels him to fetch Steppke's fiancée, Marie, from Berlin. Frau Pusbach is affronted both with the way Steppke is carrying-on with Frau Luna and by the fact that her fiancé, Herr Pannecke, is flirting with a girl from a neighbouring star. Theophilus, too, is disquieted by the growing intimacy between his Stella and Herr Lämmermeier, and the two men almost come to blows.

SCENE 11. The last scene is on the Grand Terrace of the Moon. Frau Luna is giving a champagne party in Steppke's honour. She is convinced that he is now hers, and he has taken her in his arms and is about to kiss her passionately when Prince Sternschnuppe arrives with Marie, and Steppke hurries into the arms of his first love. Frau Luna realises where his true affections lie and decides to "make do" with Prince Sternschnuppe. He obligingly gives all the Berliners a lift home in his space-car, for their original means of transport is now *hors-de-combat*—only a pricked balloon.

Die Keusche Suzanne

(The Girl in the Taxi)

Operetta in Three Acts

By GEORG OKONKOWSKI

Based on the farce Fils à Papa *by* A. MARS *and* M. DESSULLIÈRES

Music by JEAN GILBERT (MAX WINTERFELD)

First produced on 26th February, 1910, in Magdeburg. London production 5th September, 1912, at the Lyric Theatre, Shaftesbury Avenue, with Yvonne Arnaud, Arthur Playfair, C. H. Workman and Amy Augarde.

CHARACTERS

BARON DES AUBRAIS, *scientist*
DELPHINE, *his wife*
JACQUELINE } *their children*
HUBERT }
RENÉ BOISLURETTE, *Lieutenant*
POMAREL, *scent manufacturer*
SUZANNE, *his wife*
CHARANCEY, *Professor*
ROSE, *his wife*
ALEXIS, *headwaiter at the Moulin Rouge*
POLICE INSPECTOR
CHORUS OF GUESTS, MEMBERS OF AN ACADEMY, STUDENTS

The action takes place in Paris in 1910.

ACT I

The scene is the drawing-room of Baron des Aubrais' house. "Like Father, like son" is his favourite quotation and, thanks to the success of his latest treatise on heredity, he has been newly elected to the Academy of Science. The wife of his colleague Professor Charancey, is green with envy at his success, while his own wife, Delphine, regards with admiration her brilliant, remote, ascetically virtuous husband. If only the children would take a leaf out of their father's book! Jacqueline has got herself secretly engaged to a notorious woman-hunter, Lieutenant René Boislurette, and she has succeeded in pursuading him to introduce her to the night life of Paris that very evening. Her brother Hubert, who is not nearly so innocent as his mother supposes, is also to be a member of the party. René relates an adventure he had when he got embroiled with a married woman and how, to save her face and reputation in the presence of a total stranger, he had to pose as her husband.

The des Aubrais family receive unexpected visitors from the country: Monsieur Pomarel, a manufacturer of scent, and his wife, Suzanne. On the advice of the Baron, Suzanne had entered for a competition for "Virtuous behaviour" and won the first prize. Pomarel's desire to thank Baron des Aubrais is the reason for their visit. They are both very insistent on the happiness of their marriage. Actually Suzanne has no claim whatsoever to the title of Virtue, though her innocent husband has no idea of her "goings-on" when he is absent from home on frequent business trips. Quite recently she had a most agreeable flirtation with a young Lieutenant, she muses—and then sees René standing before her in the des Aubrais' drawing-room. He it was who so gallantly saved her good name by masquerading as her husband before that total stranger. How nice to see him again! They might even be able to arrange another intimate rendezvous. But to her horror into the room comes "the total stranger" and greets Suzanne and René warmly as a married couple. He is Professor Charancey, the colleague of Baron des Aubrais. Fortunately no one else is present at the moment and they are able to pass off the incident. René is not at all pleased, however, to have caught up again with Suzanne, as he had fondly hoped that that chapter was closed; and he is delighted to observe that Hubert des Aubrais is greatly attracted to her.

The guests now depart and the household retire to bed. When all is still, there tiptoe down the darkened staircase first Jacqueline and René, then Hubert, and finally that model of propriety, Baron des Aubrais—all bent on sampling the thrills of night life in Paris.

ACT II

The Moulin Rouge presents a scene of abandoned gaiety that night. In fact, the only person out of key with the prevailing atmosphere is the headwaiter, Alexis, who has decided to exchange his post for that of butler in a fashionable house. He little suspects that the lady who interviewed and engaged him that afternoon for the job is the wife of one of his regular customers, Monsieur Boboche, the pseudonym adopted by Baron des Aubrais for his visits to the Moulin Rouge. Tonight he is entertaining—without the knowledge of his wife—Rose, the wife of his colleague, Professor Charancey. But the Baron's arrival at the night club brings a rude awakening when he discovers his son, Hubert, entertaining Suzanne Pomarel. She is obviously teaching him a thing or two:

Worse is to follow when his daughter, Jacqueline, appears in the company of that dangerous lady's man, Lieutenant René Boislurette. The Baron and his son mutually agree to preserve complete discretion at home over their meeting in the Moulin Rouge, and the poor father is compelled to sanction the public engagement of Jacqueline to marry René. In an ecstasy of romantic emotion René sings to his fiancée as they dance:

No sooner is this *dénouement* disposed of than Messieurs Pomarel and Charancey appear unexpectedly. Suzanne manages to hide from her husband in the *chambre-séparée* in which she is supping with Hubert, but Charancey is affronted to discover how the virtuous members of the des Aubrais family spend their nights. It is obviously a case of:

Charancey also discovers that Suzanne is supping with Hubert, and informs the incredulous Pomarel of his wife's presence. Pomarel, in a rage. goes off to summon the police, returning with an Inspector and two policemen. During their investigation they order one of the lady guests to remove her veil and to Charancey's fury the lady proves to be his wife, Rose. It is quite apparent to him that his wife has been supping with Baron des Aubrais and he orders the police to "arrest that Don Juan." Hubert protests that he is innocent, and Charancey retorts with: "Arrest him too." To a reprise of "When the old dog and the young dog go upon the spree" the Baron and Hubert are removed to a police cell as the curtain falls.

ACT III

The scene is once more the drawing-room in Baron des Aubrais' house. On the return of the absentees next morning they encounter an unexpected hazard at the house. It requires no particular skill to allay the Baroness Delphine's suspicions, but to their dismay father and son are faced with the presence of the new butler—Alexis, ex-headwaiter of the Moulin Rouge. A promise of higher wages, however, insures Alexis' discretion. Delphine resigns herself to Jacqueline's engagement and so, as far as the des Aubrais family are concerned, calm is restored. Suzanne alone is in a state and fearful of her husband's reaction. But Charancey comes to her rescue by persuading Pomarel to accept the story, to save his own face, that their respective wives, Suzanne and Rose, were present at the Moulin Rouge to rescue young girls from the dangers which might assail their virtue. Madame Pomarel, therefore, is able to retain her own reputation for virtue, and the curtain descends to a paean in praise of her, sung by René, Hubert and the Baron:

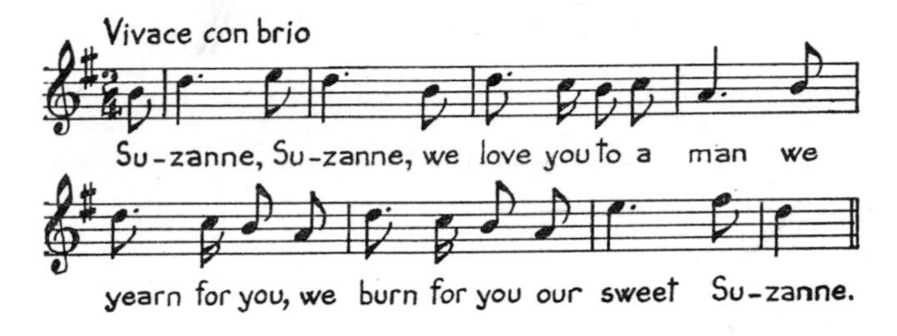

Katja, die Tänzerin
(Katja, the Dancer)

Operetta in Three Acts

By RUDOLF OESTERREICHER *and* LEO JACOBSEN

Music by JEAN GILBERT

First produced on 5th January, 1923, at the Theater an der Wien, Vienna. London production at the Gaiety Theatre (subsequently Daly's Theatre) on 21st February, 1925, with Lilian Davies, Gregory Stroud, Ivy Tresmand and Gene Gerrard.

CHARACTERS

PRINCE SASCHA KORUGA
LORD LALLAN WEBSTER, *British Ambassador*
MAUD, *his daughter*
BILL LEANDER, *his private secretary*
KATJA KARINA, *a dancer*
IVO, *her partner*
BOSCART, *Chief of the Paris police*
CHORUS OF SERVANTS, PARTY GUESTS, MEMBERS OF SOCIETY, ETC.

ACT I

In his palais in Paris the British Ambassador, Lord Lallan Webster, is giving a ball. The outstanding event of the evening is to be a cabaret entertainment, of which the star turn is a dancing act, "Katja and Partner". The arrangements for the entertainment are in the hands of young Bill Leander, private secretary to the Ambassador. But this evening his mind is not on his work, for he has fallen in love. The object of his affection is his employer's daughter, Maud. Leander, however, is out of luck, for the Ambassador is outraged by the presumption of his secretary, and the young man is peremptorily sacked. However, when the Ambassador remembers that Leander is in charge of the entertainment he is promptly re-engaged at double his former salary.

The famous dancer, Katja, and her partner now arrive, and are told by the footman to wait until the secretary can deal with them. Katja's partner, Ivo, is greatly offended at this off-hand treatment, but Katja soothes him, telling him that whatever they may have been in a former life, they are now two dancers and must accept the fact. It appears that Katja is really a Countess Ilanotch and her partner is Prince Orladin, her cousin. Their family have been the victims of political enmity and intrigue, and they have been deprived of their possessions and driven from their home. As "Katja and Partner" the two of them are earning a living as dancers, and Katja bravely faces the situation, urging Ivo to do the same:

The evening's principal guest of honour, Prince Sascha Koruga, now arrives. He asks the butler not to announce his presence immediately and sits down to a quiet cigarette and relaxation from the problems of world politics. While there he peeps through the curtains into the ballroom and watches Katja dancing. He is enchanted by her beauty and later, when he is introduced to her, he tells her quite openly that he would like to get to know her better and asks whether he might see something of her if he remained in Paris for a few days longer. Katja is immensely attracted but is non-committal in her reply, and they sing a duet:

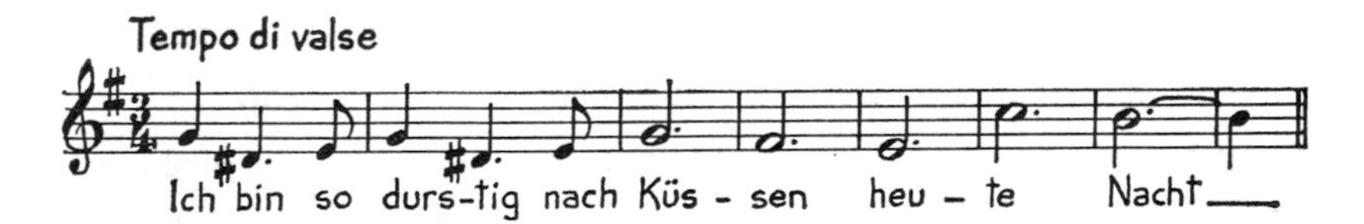

Maud and Leander are in despair at her father's opposition to their engagement, and when they are caught kissing by Prince Sascha they ask his advice as to how they can best deal with their problem. Laughingly the Prince tells them that Maud must be compromised and that then her father will be only too delighted to see her safely married to Leander. The young people accordingly go off to set their plans and the Prince goes off in search of Katja. Now, though Prince Sascha has introduced himself as Colonel Brownbury, the sharp eyes of Ivo have recognised him as the traditional enemy of their house and the head of the family who have hounded them from their home. Ivo is determined to be revenged, and to this end he influences Katja to lead the Prince on to believe that she is in love with him. When the Prince invites her to a midnight supper in his villa she therefore eagerly accepts, and all is set for an organised attack by Ivo and his comrades in which it will be Katja's part to drug Prince Sascha's wine.

ACT II

The scene is Prince Sascha Koruga's villa on the outskirts of Paris. The action takes place a few hours later, and the Prince is awaiting the arrival of Katja, who is to sup with him. He has ordered supper and a waiter to serve it to be sent in from the Ritz Hotel. As he is waiting the front-door bell rings and to his surprise and embarrassment Maud enters. She informs him that she is taking his advice and proposes to compromise herself. "But not with me?" he asks. She assures him that that is her intention and tells him she has written a note to that effect to her father, who will doubtless soon arrive. Actually it is Leander who arrives. The note has fallen into his hands and he is furiously jealous of Prince Sascha. Such is his jealousy, in fact, that without listening to any explanation he hurries away to fetch Maud's father and expose his fiancée's faithless behaviour. The Prince, who is expecting Katja's arrival at any moment, manages to persuade Maud to go home and, when Leander returns in triumph with the Ambassador, it is not Maud but Katja who is being entertained by the Prince. The Ambassador turns furiously on his secretary and tells Leander that he can only assume that he has made up the whole story. Leander is beginning to wonder whether he is suffering from hallucinations when Maud reappears and assures him that she was indeed there in person. They then decide to elope, but before doing so they sing the hit number of the score:

At last Prince Sascha manages to get rid of his unwelcome guests and alone with Katja sings a romantic waltz duet:

They sit down to supper, where in conversation Katja learns that Ivo's accusations against Prince Sascha are without foundation and she point-blank refuses to play her part in the prospective plan of revenge. Ivo, therefore, proceeds on his own. Disguised as a waiter he brings in the drugged wine, serves it and leaves the room. As the Prince is about to drink, Katja stops him and reveals the whole conspiracy, and then assists him to escape by the window, keeping up a mock conversation to cover his flight. Finally when Ivo bursts into the room it is only to find that the bird has flown.

ACT III

Later that night, at the headquarters of the police, Prince Sascha Koruga is informed that Katja, the dancer, and her partner have been arrested as they were making their get-away by train, sharing a sleeping-compartment. The fact that they were sharing a sleeping-compartment is sufficient proof to Prince Sascha that Katja and her partner must be lovers and he is bitterly disappointed, for he has fallen genuinely in love with her and after her courage in helping him to escape has been hoping to make her his wife. However, his disappointment is turned to joy when the prisoners are produced and prove to be Maud and Leander, who have been arrested in the act of eloping—a last desperate attempt to compromise Maud and thereby to compel the Ambassador to agree to their marriage. So all is finally cleared up. The Prince and Katja are happily reunited and the Prince is able to convince the police that the whole business of the attack on his person was a figment of their imagination.

Das Schwarzwaldmädel
(The Girl from the Black Forest)

Operetta in Three Acts

By AUGUST NEIDHART

Music by LEON JESSEL

First produced on 25th August, 1917, at the Komische Oper, Berlin.

CHARACTERS

BLASIUS RÖMER, *church organist*
HANNELE, *his daughter*
BÄRBELE, *his maid*
HANS } *two young travellers from Berlin*
RICHARD }
MALVINA VON HAINAU, *their girl-friend*
SCHMUSSHEIM, *a Berliner*
JÜRGEN, *landlord of "The Blue Ox" Inn*
LORLE, *his daughter*
OLD TRAUDEL, *an old village crone*
CHORUS OF VILLAGERS, MUSICIANS, SERVANTS

ACT I

The scene is the music-room of the organist and precentor of the village church of St. Christoph in the Black Forest. Blasius Römer, an elderly widower, in spite of a considerable musical reputation in the great world, prefers to live in the seclusion of a small village in the Black Forest with his daughter, Hannele, and a little maid called Bärbele. His two life interests are music and his collection of traditional peasant dresses. On the evening before the Feast of St. Cecilia, patron saint of music, two young men, Hans and Richard, are brought to the house by Hannele. They give themselves out to be two wandering musicians, and the old organist is greatly taken with their jolly marching song:

Over a glass of wine the true reason for their country ramble comes out. Hans has escaped from Berlin to avoid the enthusiastic attentions of his girl-friend, Malvina von Hainau, and Richard is keeping him company. Hans is enjoying a spell of peace and quiet and, unaware of danger just round the corner, is greatly taken with the lively, pretty maid, Bärbele. But Malvina is on his trail. She has traced him to St. Christoph and is staying at "The Blue Ox" Inn.

The landlord of the inn now appears to borrow a peasant dress from Herr Römer's collection, for one of his lady guests to wear at the St. Cecilia Festival celebration. It is for Malvina, who wants to dance with Hans. Hans, however, tells her firmly that he does not want to have anything more to do with her. They sing a duet, asking the question "Must love always end in disaster?"

During the visit of the landlord of "The Blue Ox", old Römer tells him that he is considering marrying young Bärbele. Herr Jürgen protests that the idea is ridiculous and that he is far too old to think of such a thing. Bärbele, in the meantime, is in a state of high excitement, for, thanks to Malvina's intervention on her behalf, old Römer has given her one of the peasant dresses out of his collection to wear at the Festival. In her happiness and excitement Bärbele throws her arms round the neck of the astonished old man and kisses him warmly.

ACT II

Act Two takes place in the courtyard of "The Blue Ox" Inn. The Feast of St. Cecilia begins on a cheerful note and all the peasants are in good spirits. Some of the younger ones, encouraged by a disagreeable, vulgar Berliner, called Schmussheim, think it would be a capital joke to seek out old Traudel, a village crone, and threaten her with accusations of witchcraft. Old Traudel is Bärbele's foster-mother. Ever since Bärbele's kiss, old Römer's heart is full of love for the girl and he feels twenty years younger. But is that young enough to marry her? Old Traudel tells him jokingly that it is not, but the old man refuses to accept her word and is rather distressed when Bärbele apologises for her forward behaviour in kissing him. She has fallen a little bit in love herself—not with old Römer, but with Hans, who has gone to the rescue of old Traudel and protected her from the peasants' accusations of witchcraft and threats of violence.

It is time now for the St. Cecilia Polka, the big dance of the day:

For this dance the girls are allowed to choose their partners, and Bärbele asks old Römer to dance with her. Much as he would like to he refuses, for he fears that this might cause gossip and he feels that, as an old man, his place is a seat among the old people. An unpleasant situation now occurs. With the incident of old Traudel's persecution fresh in their minds, some young peasants accuse her foster-child, Bärbele, also of being a witch, and they try to keep her off the dance-floor. Seeing that Malvina is trying by flirting with Richard to make him jealous, Hans goes to Bärbele's rescue and leads her out to dance. But the unpleasant atmosphere becomes more and more threatening, and as evening falls there is an ugly scene in which the vulgar Schmussheim is thrown out of "The Blue Ox". This precipitates a general free fight and the curtain descends on violence and tumult.

ACT III

In the bar of "The Blue Ox" both the vulgar Schmussheim and the landlord, Jürgen, are considerably bruised as a result of the night's brawl. Herr Jürgen, as Burgomaster and Chief of Police, is concerned to discover the originator of the trouble. Hans and Richard are both witnesses at the public inquiry. Richard and Malvina announce their engagement, warmly congratulated by Hans. After a sleepless night Herr Römer has decided to marry Bärbele. He has received a letter to the effect that her father, who deserted her and disappeared years ago, has died, leaving her a considerable fortune. It never occurs to the old man that Bärbele is anything but in love with him, but it does occur to him that he might be suspected of wanting to marry her for her money. He shyly puts this to her, and finds that Bärbele is amazed at the idea of marrying him. He is far too old for her, and her heart, she tells him, belongs to Hans. Herr Römer tries to persuade her that Hans' love is only the passing phase of a townee, but Bärbele assures him that she would give herself to Hans even if he were to remain with her but one short hour. Then the old man sees that it is hopeless, and sadly he takes leave of youth.

Das Dorf Ohne Glocke

(The Village without a Bell)

By Arpad Pasztor

Singspiel in Three Acts

Based on a Hungarian legend

Music by Eduard Künneke

First produced on 5th April, 1919, in Berlin.

Characters

FATHER BENEDIKT, *the priest*
SOFIE, *his housekeeper*
BARON ERWIN VON LERTINGEN
STEFFI, *his wife*
PETER, *a blacksmith's apprentice*
EVA, *his fiancée*
THE BLACKSMITH
THE SCHOOLMASTER
THE STOREKEEPER
RESI, *a waitress at the inn*
LIESCHEN, *a little girl*
THE INNKEEPER
FOUR ANGELS
CHORUS OF PEASANTS AND TOURISTS

The action takes place in a German-speaking village in the Transylvanian Alps at the end of the nineteenth century.

ACT I

The scene is the village green and standing round it are the church, the parsonage and the inn. Today there is general rejoicing among the inhabitants. Their beloved priest, Father Benedikt, is celebrating his fiftieth anniversary as their pastor, and they are determined to pay him due honour. The leading artisans of the village are in charge of the arrangements and this necessitates a consultation with Sofie, Father Benedikt's housekeeper. The blacksmith is in love with her and woos her fondly:

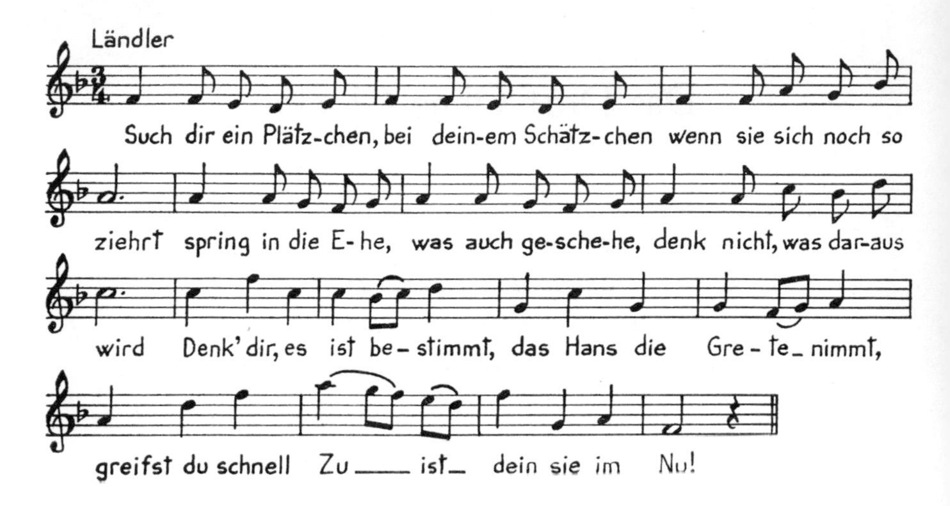

A visit is also paid to the village inn, where the pretty waitress, Resi, is a far greater attraction than the rather sour wine. Meanwhile Father Benedikt receives a wholly unexpected but welcome visit from the twenty-year-old Baron von Lertingen. He has bought back the family estate which his father had sold, and he has great schemes in mind to cultivate the land and bring life and prosperity into the poverty-stricken district. He greets the old priest joyfully and listens sympathetically to Father Benedikt's tale of woe about his church. It has no bell. In the Turko-Hungarian War the Turks attacked the village and removed the church bell. Since then the belfry has been silent. No bell rings for Angelus, no bell tolls for a passing, or chimes for a wedding. "Alas!" he finishes, "the villagers are unable to afford the necessary five hundred guilders, and a village without a bell is like a heart without love, a marriage without children." As they part Father Benedikt returns sadly to his parsonage, little dreaming that his beloved parishioners have a wonderful surprise in store for him—a surprise which is revealed when with every evidence of love and affection they present him with five hundred guilders which at long last they have managed to collect.

Later the old priest prepares to journey to the neighbouring town to order a church bell. As he is making his preparations to depart, across the village green come a tragic pair, Peter, a blacksmith's apprentice, and his fiancée, Eva. They must part, for Peter cannot manage to make a living wage sufficient to support them both and he must seek work elsewhere. Eva promises to wait for him, when Spring comes and the buds begin to blossom he will return. Hoping against hope, they sing:

Desperately Eva prays to the Virgin to provide the means whereby Peter may be able to remain with her. Father Benedikt hears her heartfelt prayer. Bending over her, he tells her the Virgin has answered her prayer. "She sends you by me five hundred guilders. Stay here, Peter," he continues. "Found a family, stay with us and work with your own people." Peter and Eva go off happily together while Father Benedikt, convinced that he has done right in the sight of God, wonders how he is going to account to his flock for the missing money.

ACT II

Act Two takes place a few days later. The villagers are puzzled at Father Benedikt's prolonged absence. They had expected him home from the town before this with news of the bell. The mean-spirited storekeeper voices unworthy suspicions against the priest and gains a hearing. Father Benedikt is in hiding in his parsonage, and the first to discover this is the blacksmith. Sofie has confessed to him that the money is missing. According to her the old priest was set upon on his way to the town by footpads and robbed. Generous in spirit and deeply in love with Sofie, the blacksmith does not repeat what he has heard, but sets about to sell his forge so that he may be able to refund to Father Benedikt the missing money. The first purchaser to make a bid for the forge is Peter. But the villagers regard Peter and Eva with suspicion and question their good faith. What do they seek in the village? Peter answers that they seek a home and a right to earn their living. Here they have found the only kindness they have ever known.

But when Peter hands over the money to pay for the forge, the notes are promptly identified as those handed to Father Benedikt to purchase the church bell, and the villagers assume Peter to be one of the footpads who robbed the priest. They set upon Peter and Eva with threats of violence and they are only saved by the appearance of Father Benedikt. He calmly tells the villagers that Peter did not steal the money. He himself gave it to him to set him up and enable him to marry Eva. The villagers are affronted. "But that was our money, handed to you to buy a bell. You had no right to give it away," they tell him angrily. "We want our bell, we want our bell." The storekeeper then repeats a scandal, that some years ago he remembers Sofie, the pastor's housekeeper, disappearing to the town and subsequently returning. He believes Eva must be the illegitimate child of Father Benedikt and that the five hundred guilders are her marriage dowry. "That'll be the truth," they cry. "If you believe that, then I have no more to say," Father Benedikt tells them. "I am sorry, Father," says the churchwarden, stepping forward, "but until your good name is cleared, I must ask you for the key of the church." In an agonised voice the priest cries: "The key of my church? After fifty years among you, you drive me away." But Baroness Lertingen intervenes. "The living is in my husband's gift. You can safely hand over the key of the church to me, Father Benedikt," she tells him kindly. At this moment a little girl comes crying to the pastor. "Father, my mummy is dying. The doctor is with her and says she will be dead before morning. She is calling for you to give her extreme unction." Father Benedikt bids the schoolmaster accompany him. "Pastor, what are you going to do?" asks the Baroness. "My duty," he answers. "I have no right to refuse a dying soul the last offices of the Church." And, taking the little girl's hand, he sets out with her across the village green.

ACT III

Midnight is past, and under the lime-tree before his house Father Benedikt has fallen asleep on a bench. In a dream he hears the singing of heavenly voices and sees four angels who bear in their arms a golden bell and carry it up to the belfry. With the coming of day the priest awakens. He makes his way into the parsonage and, after blessing his housekeeper Sofie, and the good blacksmith who have become engaged, he makes preparations for his final departure from the village. But now the church door opens and Baron von Lertingen appears with a company of workmen. He has bought a church bell and during the night has had it hung in the belfry. With the coming of morning the temper of the villagers has entirely changed. They are heartily ashamed of themselves and appear in a body at the parsonage to beg for pardon and forgiveness. While Father Benedikt is listening to them the bell suddenly rings out, and he utters a joyful cry: "See! God's Love has wrought a miracle." From the church the organ peals forth and the voices of the choir are raised in "*Gloria in excelsis Deo*". And all the villagers move towards the church to receive the blessing of their beloved pastor.

Wenn Liebe Erwacht

(Love's Awakening)

Operetta in Three Acts

By Hermann Haller *and* Rideamus (Fritz Oliven)

Book (after von Schönthan *and* Koppel-Ellfeld)

Lyrics by Rideamus

Music by Eduard Künneke

First produced on 3rd September, 1920, at the Theater am Nollendorfplatz, Berlin. London production on 19th April, 1922, at the Empire Theatre, with Juliette Autran, Edouard Leston, Harry Brindle, Betty Chester, Amy Augarde and Billy Leonard.

Characters

CONTESSA FRANCESCA DA COSTA *a widow*
TONIO, *her son*
LORENZO, *a painter*
PATER PHILIPPO, *a priest*
DR. PEDANTIUS, *Tonio's tutor*
VERONIKA, *housekeeper*
NELLA, *her niece*
MARIETTA, *an artist's model*
CHORUS OF ARTISTS, MEMBERS OF THE CASTLE STAFF, PEASANTS, ETC.

ACT I

It is the middle of the nineteenth century, and the action takes place in Italy. In a lonely castle, idyllically placed, the widowed Contessa Francesca da Costa spends her life shut off from the world, surrounded by faithful servants and retainers. She lives entirely for her religion and for the welfare of her only son, Tonio, a boy of seventeen, who has been brought up like Parsifal, "The Perfect Fool", far removed from wordly contacts. His education has been entrusted to an academic, dry-as-dust old tutor, Dr. Pedantius, but Tonio's real friend and standby is his mother's chaplain, Pater Philippo, who is continually interceding on his behalf when he is in trouble with his mother. The Contessa has commissioned Pater Philippo to find an artist to execute a painted panel for the wall of the big hall of the castle, and in the village of Trastéveré he meets a school of painters on a ramble from Rome. They are pupils of a distinguished artist, Lorenzo by name, and it is this Lorenzo whom Pater Philippo has in mind for the panel. He invites Lorenzo and his pupils to call at the castle and one morning they arrive, singing as they mount the hill:

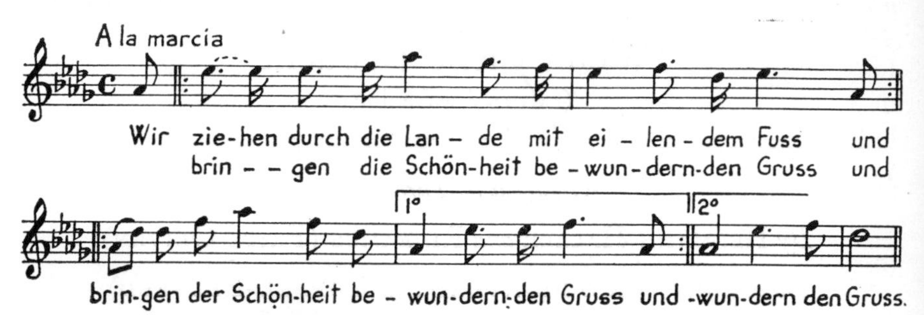

The artists are graciously received by the Contessa and she formally commissions Lorenzo to design and paint the panel. She asks him his ideas as to a subject, and he proposes "A Festival of Love" with the Goddess Venus blessing a pair of young lovers on the eve of their marriage and Bacchus tapping a cask of wine for the satisfaction of the wedding guests. The religiously-minded Contessa is shocked at this suggestion. "I had thought of a sacred subject," she tells him, "with faces full of remorse and repentance." "No," he cries, "I must paint light, joy and happiness—love that makes the world go round":

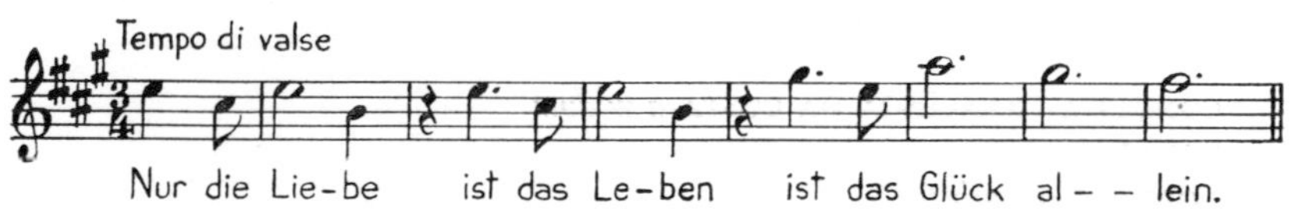

But the Contessa is far from happy about Lorenzo's proposals. Her son Tonio, Pater Philippo and all the household beg her to reconsider and give Lorenzo her consent to carry out his ideas unfettered. Lorenzo adds his personal appeal, promising her a masterpiece. Already wavering, she is about to give her consent, when from the distant chapel sound the organ and the voices of the choir, praising God. Immediately her mind revolts from their worldly thoughts and temptations. "It is the love of Heaven that redeems mankind and opens the gates of Paradise," she tells them, and withdraws her consent.

ACT II

The second act is set on the terrace of the castle overlooking the blue Mediterranean. From the moment Lorenzo set eyes on the beautiful Contessa his heart has been hers, and she also is not indifferent to his good looks, for she has changed her mind over the subject of the panel and has given him a free hand in its execution. When the curtain rises on Act Two various members of the household, including Pater Philippo, the housekeeper, Veronika, and her daughter, Nella, are taking an unofficial peep at the panel. To their rueful amusement they discover that Lorenzo has used them all as models. Pater Philippo is represented as a hump-backed publican; Veronika as the bride's mother, fat and comfortable; and Nella is depicted as a young girl feigning modest propriety while squeezing the hand of a young man under the table. However, they all take it in good part and admit that a painter is free to take his models where he can find them. Only one face is missing—that of the Goddess Venus, who is to dominate the picture. In place of any features there is a blank. Lorenzo has found no model for Venus, and in vain he endeavours to persuade the Contessa to sit to him. He still has hopes and she has promised to give him her definite decision that night at a party the artists are holding in the castle to welcome the arrival of spring. Meanwhile, Tonio is having a wonderful time with the arrival of the group of artists, who bring new life into the sleepy castle. He learns from them many things about life which have been kept from him by his mother, and one of his most successful instructors is an attractive professional model of Lorenzo's called Marietta. She is the first to initiate Tonio into the pleasures of kissing, and this delights the young man inordinately:

Tonio, with his strict upbringing, is bothered about this thing called "Love" and eagerly questions Pater Philippo as to whether or not Love is sinful. "Love is no sin," the old man tells him. "Love is a magical spell compounded of joy, of suffering, of Heaven, of Hell:

Reassured by Pater Philippo's words, there is no holding Tonio, and soon Pater Philippo catches him kissing Nella, to the old man's dismay, and the young woman's astonishment. Later, the party begins, and, caught up in the general air of abandon, the Contessa declares that Lorenzo may have his wish. She will sit to him for the portrait of the Goddess Venus, which has been his dream:

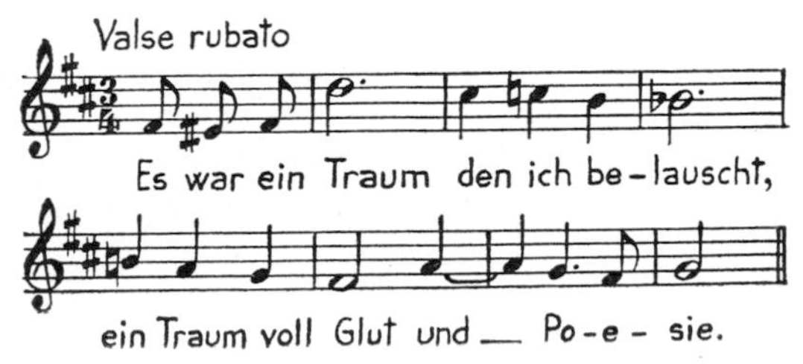

As a symbol of her surrender to his wishes, Lorenzo crowns her Queen of Love with a wreath of red roses—a symbol also of their ripening love.

ACT III

The last act takes place in a summer-house in the castle garden. Love is in the air. Even Tonio's old tutor, Dr. Pedantius, has caught the fever and has proposed to Nella, who confesses to a penchant for elderly lovers and has accepted him. To her amazed delight, the Contessa finds herself deeply in love with the handsome, romantic Lorenzo and there is no doubt as to his feelings for her. Tonio has decided to become a painter, and he departs with the school to study his adopted art, while Lorenzo remains behind as the Contessa's husband. His dream of a Goddess of Love has come true.

Franz Lehár with Mizzi Guenther as "Hanna Glarvari" and Louis Treumann as "Count Danilo" in second act costumes of *Die Lustige Witwe* (*The Merry Widow*)

Doblinger, Vienna

Lily Elsie as "Sonia" and Joseph Coyne as "Prince Danilo" in the London production of *The Merry Widow* at Daly's Theatre

Franz Lehár and Emmerich Kálmán

Oscar Straus

Doblinger

The duet "Piccolo, Piccolo" from the second act of *Ein Walzertraum* (*A Waltz Dream*)

Richard Tauber as "Schubert"
Das Dreimaedlerhaus (*Lilac T*

Fritzi Massary, a star of Berlin Operetta

Der Vetter aus Dingsda
(The Cousin from Nowhere)

Operetta in Three Acts

By HERMANN HALLER *and* RIDEAMUS (FRITZ OLIVEN)

Adapted from a comedy by MAX KEMPNER-HOCHSTÄDT

Music by EDUARD KÜNNEKE

First produced on 15th April, 1921, at the Theatre am Nollendorfplatz, Berlin. First produced in London on 24th February, 1923, at the Princes Theatre, with Helen Gilliland, Cicely Debenham and Walter Williams.

CHARACTERS

JULIA DE WEERT, *an heiress*
AUGUSTUS KUHBROT
HANNCHEN, *Julia's friend*
RODERICK DE WEERT
JOSEF KUHBROT, *Julia's uncle*
WILHELMINE, *his wife*
EGON VON WILDENHAGEN

ACT I

The scene is the garden of Julia de Weert's country house on an evening in midsummer. Julia, a young girl, orphan and heiress, is the ward of two guardians. One is her uncle, Josef Kuhbrot, and the other a certain von Wildenhagen. Both guardians are continually attempting to persuade Julia to marry their respective heirs. But Julia has no interest in either Augustus Kuhbrot or Egon von Wildenhagen, and she resents the mercenary attitude of her grasping guardians. Moreover, her romantic heart has already been given to her cousin Roderick, and when seven years ago he left to seek his fortune in Batavia she promised to be faithful to him. Though no word has come from him since, Julia firmly believes that his thoughts are still as full of love for her, as hers are for him, and she confides this to the moon:

Josef Kuhbrot is determined to get Julia safely married to her cousin Augustus before she comes of age and his guardianship lapses, and he has summoned Augustus to meet him at the village inn that evening to discuss the arrangements for the courtship of the cousin he has never met. News now comes via Egon von Wildenhagen that the Court of Chancery has declared Julia to be of age and therefore no longer under the jurisdiction of her guardians. Julia and her companion, Hannchen, feel that this news calls for a celebration. Shall they go to the cinema, without permission, to assert Julia's new independence? No it, is too late. Shall they invite Egon to stay the night? "Imagine Uncle's face when he sees him in the morning!" They shout for Egon, and an unfamiliar male voice answers from the distance. Advancing across the fields is a stranger, young but shabby and unkempt, looking like a cross between a scarecrow and a tramp. Julia has an inspiration. "Let's ask him in, pretend this is a tavern, a sort of fairy-tale tavern." Hannchen is dispatched to light a lamp, to fetch a card with "Welcome" written on it and to bring wine and cigars. When the stranger arrives he receives a royal welcome. He inquires how far it is to the village inn and, on hearing with dismay that it is another three miles, he confesses to being dead beat. Julia asks him whom he is to meet at the inn. A pretty girl? No, a fat old gentleman. He asks where he is, and Julia tells him that he is in a tavern. But it is obviously no ordinary tavern. She asks him what he particularly wants at the moment, and he tells her that what he would really enjoy would be a cigar. Hardly are the words out of his mouth when Hannchen is at his elbow with a box of cigars. He has only to express a wish for a glass of claret for a full glass to be handed to him. Duly refreshed, the stranger thanks Julia and says: "That's the end of the fairy tale, I suppose. Back to the dusty road." Then Julia tells him that all good fairies have three wishes to give away. After the cigar and the claret, what would be his third wish? The stranger tells her: "A good night's rest in a lovely four-poster bed with thick brocade curtains." And immediately Hannchen announces: "If you please, sir, your bed is ready." But the stranger is reticent as to his origins, and when Julia questions him the only answer he will give is:

So the stranger is put to bed in Julia's brother's room, while Hannchen protests: "Julia, you must be mad—putting up a tramp for the night. Apparently you've taken a great fancy to him." Julia answers: "A fancy? Oh, no—it's just the summer night, the moon maybe, or the memory of someone else."

ACT II

Next morning on the terrace Hannchen makes it her business to question the stranger as to his antecedents. But he is far cleverer than she at that game and succeeds in extracting from her the story of Julia's love for Roderick. He conceals the fact that he is in fact Augustus Kuhbrot and that he is on his way to meet Uncle Josef at the village inn. As Uncle Josef has not seen Augustus since he was a small boy, the stranger is quite safe in giving out that he is Roderick, returned from far Batavia. Julia falls on his neck, but Uncle Josef is disgusted at Roderick's reappearance. Julia is blissfully happy with her Roderick. He has remained faithful to her and all her dreams have come true. He on his part is greatly drawn to the attractive Julia, and the lovers sing romantically:

Uncle Josef is particularly irritated at the failure of his scheme for an alliance between Julia and his heir, Augustus Kuhbrot, through the young man's failure to keep the appointment at the village inn; and looks on resentfully while Roderick fascinates Julia with accounts of life in Batavia. This blissful situation, however, is brought to a bitter conclusion when Egon von Wildenhagen enters with a telegram from Batavia. Roderick de Weert has only recently sailed from Batavia, and his ship has not yet docked at Hamburg. It now becomes obvious that whoever the stranger is, he is *not* Roderick, and Julia is mortified. "I love and I always have loved only one. Are you he?" she asks. "No," answers the stranger. "Then who are you?" asks Uncle Josef, and the stranger replies:

And Julia coldly repulses the impostor.

ACT III

The last act is set in the garden of Julia's home. Uncle Josef has learned from the station-master that his nephew Augustus did arrive two days ago. What can have become of him? Has that dubious stranger attacked and murdered him by any chance? While he is discussing the matter with other members of the family, a second stranger appears, another young man, gay and sophisticated. Hannchen is the first to receive him. An immediate sympathy springs up between them and in true operetta fashion they are soon in love. It is therefore with dismay that Hannchen learns that this new stranger is the real Roderick de Weert. What will Julia say when she discovers that Roderick wants to marry not her, but Hannchen? Roderick must pretend to be Augustus Kuhbrot. In this disguise he cures Julia once and for all of her Roderick fixation by convincing her that Roderick never took their youthful promises of fidelity at all seriously. This accomplished, he admits his identity, and Julia realises that she was in love, not with an individual, but with an ideal, and she regrets her dismissal of the attractive stranger. But fortune is kind. Augustus is close at hand, and to Julia's and Uncle Josef's combined delight, he is soon safely in her arms.

Glückliche Reise
(Bon Voyage)

Operetta in Three Acts (Seven Scenes)

By MAX BERTUCH *and* KURT SCHWABACH

Music by EDUARD KÜNNEKE

First produced on 23rd November, 1932, at the Theater am Schiffbauerdamm in Berlin.

CHARACTERS

ROBERT VON HARTENAU, STEFAN SCHWARZENBERG } *two young Germans farming in Brazil*
PETER BRANGERSEN, *a ship's captain*
LONA VONDERHOFF, MONIKA BRINK } *secretaries in a tourist bureau in Berlin*
HOMANN, *manager of the tourist bureau*
COUNSELLOR WALTER HÜBNER, *his friend*
CHORUS OF POSTMEN, PASSENGERS, NATIVES, DANCING-GIRLS AND MEMBERS OF BERLIN SOCIETY

The action takes place in 1932 on a lonely farm in South America and in Berlin.

ACT I

SCENE 1. On a remotely situated farm in Brazil two young Germans, Robert von Hartenau and Stefan Schwarzenberg, are slaving to make a living. It is a hard life and they are homesick; the only gleam of sunshine in their lives is a romantic correspondence with two girls in their home town of Berlin. This interchange of letters started as the result of an advertisement which they had inserted in a Berlin newspaper. Robert's "pen friend" signs herself Lona Vonderhoff and Stefan's, Monika Brink. From her letters Stefan gathers that Monika Brink is a sophisticated, well-to-do and much-travelled young woman of society. What fun it would be, they think, to make the acquaintance of these two girls! The mailboat now arrives and the ship's captain proves to have been a fellow-officer in the war. Robert and Stefan are thrilled to see him, and his descriptions of Berlin make them more homesick than ever. They express this in a yearning tango-duet:

They confide to Captain Brangersen their longing to visit home. The trouble is that they cannot afford the fares. This difficulty is solved by their old friend, who proposes that they work their passages aboard his ship as stewards. His offer is gleefully accepted and Robert and Stefan embark on their voyage to Europe to this cheerful tune:

SCENE 2. Scene Two takes place at the office of the tourist bureau, "South American Line Co." This is Stefan's immediate objective after his arrival in Berlin, for it is to this address he has forwarded all his letters to Monika Brink. Monika is there, but not in the capacity of the well-to-do socialite she has given herself out to be in her letters, merely as a humble secretary. She is greatly startled by the sudden arrival of her "pen friend", but she pulls herself together and assumes her role of society lady with perfect aplomb, watched with amazed disapproval by her boss, Herr Homann. Stefan is enchanted with Monika and they arrange to spend the evening together. Lona Vonderhoff also works for "The South American Line Co." She is a more serious-minded girl than is the ebullient Monika Brink, and she is engaged to the middle-aged Counsellor Hübner. She is not in love with him, but she has fallen in with her mother's wish to see her "settled" and has agreed to marry him. Lona and Robert meet when he comes to the travel bureau in search of Stefan. Robert has not yet succeeded in contacting his "pen friend" to whom he has always written at a Poste Restante address. He is greatly taken with Lona and, though she is at first rather reserved, she eventually warms to him and promises to join him in an evening's excursion to Wannsee. His meeting with this charming girl has put all thoughts of his "pen friend" out of Robert's head, and their affectionate duet is proof that the attraction is mutual:

ACT II

SCENE 3. In a bar in the casino at Wannsee, Robert and Stefan meet their girls. Monika is still playing her part of a society girl and, though she is somewhat embarrassed to catch sight of her boss, Herr Homann, in the casino, she thoroughly enjoys herself with Stefan, who proves a most entertaining companion.

During the evening Robert tells Lona of his pen friendship, and when he mentions that the name of his correspondent is Lona Vonderhoff he is amazed to hear that that is her name but that she is not his "pen friend" and knows nothing of the matter. Robert and Lona's relationship is on a more serious basis than that of Monika and Stefan, and this is reflected in the music Künneke has given them:

Lona has been trying to imagine how Robert's letters from his "pen friend" could have been signed with her name. Putting two and two together, she manages to get Monika alone and tackles her. Driven into a corner, Monika owns that the letters to both young men were from her, but that whereas she signed those to Stefan with her own name, those to Robert she signed "Lona Vonderhoff". Acutely embarrassed at the situation she finds herself in, Lona declares that she can never face Robert again and rushes out of the bar, leaving Monika to give such explanations of her absence as she can. When Robert and Stefan return, Monika produces a very lame excuse for Lona's sudden departure. Robert believes that the true reason for Lona's flight is that in reality she did write the letters to him and now is embarrassed at having denied it. He presses Monika for confirmation, and suddenly Monika bursts into tears and is about to confess. But she is interrupted by Herr Homann, who greets her cheerily: "Don't be late at the office tomorrow, dear. Nine a.m., remember." And to Stefan he explains: "She's my secretary, a perfect treasure." The game is now up and Monika, shattered at being exposed, breaks down and confesses to having written all the letters. Bewildered at the turn of events, Robert and Stefan feel they would be better off among the monkeys in Brazil.

ACT III

Scene 4. Up and down the street in which Lona and Monika lodge, the two young men pace the whole night through. They know in their hearts that, in spite of all that has passed, their love for the two girls is deep and sincere, and they are determined to put matters right.

Scene 5. In Lona's bedroom are the two girls, equally miserable and just as much in love. With hearts heavy with fear but full of hope they watch their lovers in the street below.

Scene 6. Next morning, on their way to the office, the girls try their best to slip past their two young men unrecognised. Lona succeeds, but Monika is caught. A moment later she is in Stefan's arms and has promised to marry him and accompany him to Brazil.

Scene 7. Robert manages to find Lona at the office. She offers only a token resistance to his overtures, and the astonished Herr Homann is informed that he is to lose the services of his two best secretaries. He wishes them "bon voyage", but they do not even book their tickets at his travel bureau—for Robert and Lona, Stefan and Monika must work their passages to Brazil.

Die Frau Ohne Kuss
(The Woman Without a Kiss)

Comedy with Music in Three Acts

By RICHARD KESSLER

Lyrics by WILLI KOLLO

Music by WALTER KOLLO

First produced on 6th July, 1924, at the Staatliches Schillertheater, Berlin.

CHARACTERS

DR. ERNST HARTWIG, *a fashionable women's doctor*
LOTTE LENZ, *his secretary*
GEORG LANGENBACH, *an industrialist*
FRITZ SPERLING, *a portrait painter*
PRINCE HUSSEIN DSCHANGIR, *of Teheran*
OTTO, *Dr. Hartwig's butler*

ACT I

The whole play is set in the consulting-room in Dr. Hartwig's house. Dr. Ernst Hartwig is a fashionable women's doctor in Berlin. Recently he has acquired a new secretary called Lotte Lenz. His two friends, the industrialist Georg Langenbach and the painter Fritz Sperling, find her very attractive, but the Doctor, a confirmed bachelor, sees nothing more in her than an efficient piece of mechanism. He is quite unaware that he figures largely in Lotte's plans for her future as a woman and that she is not remotely interested in any other man. Dr. Hartwig is waiting to be summoned as consultant gynaecologist to a case in Teheran at the Court of a Persian prince. But when the telegram arrives, to his dismay it lays down as a condition of acceptance that the Doctor in question shall be married and shall bring his wife with him to Teheran. In this dilemma he decides to follow Lotte's advice, which is that he go through a form of marriage with her. She offers to play the part of "temporary wife" and laughingly assures him that she will not insist on her "marital rights"; they can be divorced later. A convenient friend, who works in a nearby Registry Office marries them with the minimum of formality and they leave for Teheran.

ACT II

In Act Two the unusual married couple are back from Teheran. Dr. Hartwig has had a great success professionally, but in spite of the advantage of having him all to herself on the Oriental journey, Lotte has so far failed to make the Doctor fall in love with her. In fact, not so much as a kiss has she been able to extract from this immaculately correct young man. And now she is convinced that he fully intends to go through with the agreed divorce. However, without Lotte's knowing it, the Doctor has fallen madly in love with her but cannot screw up sufficient courage to tell her so. Lotte now embarks on a deliberate course of conduct designed to rouse his jealousy. Not only does she flirt outrageously with Langenbach and Sperling but, to her delight, Prince Hussein, a Persian noble who had pursued her passionately in Teheran, turns up in Berlin especially to see and, if possible, possess her. The proximity of Prince Hussein works wonders, and Lotte, lying that night in the passionate embrace of her husband, has no longer any cause to complain of his defects as a lover.

ACT III

Next morning the lovers experience a shock. Their marriage, solemnized by their friend in the Registry Office, was conducted with such a lack of formality that it turns out to be not even legal. In order not to spoil their first day at home together, Dr. Hartwig's butler, Otto, did not hand him the official intimation to this effect. Both the Doctor and Lotte are distressed, but Lotte's dismay is turned to ecstasy by the warmth of her husband's affection. There is now no question of the Doctor abiding by his promise to Prince Hussein, made in Teheran, that Lotte should be his directly their divorce was absolute. The Prince is forced to recognise that his "Rose of Shiras" has found her happiness elsewhere, and he turns his face sadly homewards.

Im Weissen Rössl
(White Horse Inn)

Operetta in Three Acts

Freely adapted from the farce of the same name by BLUMENTHAL *and* KADELBURG

Book by HANS MUELLER *and* ERIK CHARELL

Lyrics by ROBERT GILBERT

Music by RALPH BENATZKY

Additional numbers by BRUNO GRANICHSTAEDTEN, ROBERT GILBERT, ROBERT STOLZ, *and* HANS FRANKOWSKI

First produced on 8th November, 1930, at the Grosses Schauspielhaus, Berlin. London production on 8th April, 1931, at the London Coliseum, with Lea Seidl and Clifford Mollison.

CHARACTERS

JOSEFA VOGELHUBER, *landlady of "The White Horse" inn*
LEOPOLD BRANMEYER, *headwaiter*
WILHELM GIESECKE, *manufacturer*
OTTILIE, *his daughter*
DR. ERICH SIEDLER, *solicitor*
SIGISMUND SÜLZHEIMER
PROFESSOR DR. HINZELMANN, *private tutor*
KLÄRCHEN, *his daughter*
THE EMPEROR FRANZ JOSEF

The action takes place outside "The White Horse" inn at St. Wolfgang in the Salzkammergut, Austria, before the First World War.

ACT I

The annual tourist season brings not only money and enjoyment but plenty of hard work to the famous pleasure resort on the Wolfgangsee. Leopold, the headwaiter of "The White Horse" inn, has his hands full, coping with the hordes of ravenous trippers. It is, however, not so much his job that is robbing him of his peace of mind as his passionate love for his employer and landlady, Josefa Vogelhuber. But alas! she is quite unresponsive to his devotion and expends all her love and affection on one of her regular visitors, Dr. Siedler, who is due to arrive today for his annual holiday at "The White Horse" inn. An even earlier arrival is the choleric and ridiculous manufacturer of underclothes, Wilhelm Giesecke, hot-foot from Berlin with his daughter, Ottilie. He immediately pounces on a cause for complaint. The room with a verandah, overlooking the lake, which he wanted is reserved for Dr. Siedler. To make matters worse, this Dr. Siedler is acting as solicitor to his opponent in a lawsuit, Herr Sülzheimer. Leopold, who is frantically jealous by nature, is only too delighted to do his rival in love an ill turn and he attempts, on his own authority, to assign the room with the verandah to Herr Giesecke. But all to no avail. When Dr. Siedler arrives, Josefa insists that he have the room reserved for him, and the fulminating Giesecke is compelled to move into the annexe. Leopold now tries a new tack. He engages Giesecke's daughter Ottilie in conversation and hints to her that if she were to make up to Dr. Siedler, she might be able to persuade him to influence his client, Sülzheimer, to take a more lenient view of her father's case in the law action which is pending. Leopold's machinations, however, are entirely superfluous, for Dr. Siedler has already cast an amorous glance in Ottilie's direction.

ACT II

Josefa, convinced that Dr. Siedler is fond of her, loses her temper with Leopold's jealous behaviour and gives him the sack, much to his dismay. But, as landlady of a busy inn at the height of the tourist season, Josefa has not much time to devote to her own affairs. At the moment she determines to bring the peevish Herr Giesecke into a more agreeable frame of mind by praising in song the beauties of the Salzkammergut. But he only retorts by comparing them unfavourably with such Berlin resorts as Grunewald and Ahlbeck. Soon after this Herr Giesecke has plenty to occupy his mind, for Dr. Siedler approaches him with a proposal from his opponent, Sülzheimer. This is that a marriage be arranged between his son, Sigismund Sülzheimer, and Giesecke's daughter, Ottilie. In this way, Sülzheimer suggests, they could settle their differences and bury the hatchet. Dr. Siedler offers to bring the young people together, although in his heart of hearts he has no intention of allowing Ottilie to be united to anyone except himself. But when Sigismund Sülzheimer arrives, Dr. Siedler's worries vanish, for Sigismund takes not the slightest notice of Ottilie Giesecke. He has eyes only for little Klärchen, the daughter of Professor Hinzelmann, whose lisp he finds enchanting.

Meanwhile, to the unhappily love-sick Leopold comes a glimmer of hope. He discovers that at the meeting of the Town Councillors it was announced that the Emperor Franz Josef had made known his intention to visit St. Wolfgang and furthermore to stay at "The White Horse" inn. This news, of course, reduces Josefa to a state of nervous prostration and she implores Leopold to stay with her during His Majesty's visit and lend her his support. Leopold is delighted, and he is convinced that Josefa will shortly be his. The Emperor duly arrives, and Leopold is deputed to speak the address of welcome. The hotel front is crowded with guests, staff and visitors, and Leopold is about to address His Majesty, when he catches sight of Josefa standing next to Dr. Siedler. Immediately all his lovesick emotion wells up in a flood of jealousy and, to his own and to everybody else's embarrassment, he bursts into tears.

ACT III

In Act Three everybody's difficulties are satisfactorily settled when the Emperor reads Josefa a fatherly lecture. Everybody, he tells her, must remain true to themselves. She would never be happy leading an urban life with Dr. Siedler. Indeed, in her heart she has already recognised that his love is given to Ottilie. So when Leopold comes to say good-bye and, with his bag already packed in his hand, asks her for a reference, Josefa smilingly dismisses him as waiter only to re-engage him as her husband.

Among the melodies in the score of "White Horse Inn" the following numbers are outstanding:

1. Leopold's song of love to Josefa:

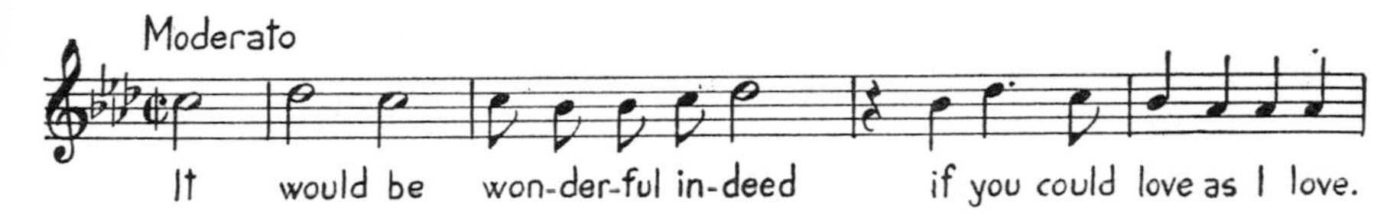

2. The title song:

3. Leopold's farewell:

Viktoria und ihr Hussar

(Viktoria and her Hussar)

Operetta in a Prologue and Three Acts

By ALFRED GRÜNEWALD *and* DR. FRITZ LÖHNER-BEDA

After the Hungarian of EMMERICH FÖLDES

Music by PAUL ABRAHAM

First produced on 23rd December, 1930, at the Theater an der Wien, Vienna. London production on 17th September, 1931, at the Palace Theatre, with Harry Welchman, Margaret Carlisle, Reginald Purdell, and Oscar Denes.

CHARACTERS

JOHN CUNLIGHT, *American Ambassador*
COUNTESS VIKTORIA, *his wife*
COUNT FERI HEGEDIIS AUF DOROSZMA, *her brother*
O LIA SAN, *Feri's bride*
RIQUETTE, *Viktoria's maid*
STEFAN KOLTAY, *Colonel of hussars*
JANCSI, *his batman*
CHORUS OF JAPANESE COOLIES, SERVANTS, GUESTS, COSSACKS AND HUSSARS

The action takes place in Siberia, Japan and Hungary shortly after the first World War.

PROLOGUE

In a prison camp on the dreary steppe of Siberia are two Hungarians; Colonel Koltay and his batman, Jancsi. It is half-past four in the morning and at five a.m. the Colonel is to face a firing-squad for suspected espionage activities. Sadly the two men remember their homeland, and Jancsi, a skilful violinist, takes his fiddle and strikes up an Hungarian love-song, in which the Colonel joins:

As they are playing and singing a sentry approaches and begs Jancsi to give him his violin. "Comrade, please," he urges. "I too was a fiddler once, leader of the Imperial Orchestra under Rimsky-Korsakoff. Let me just hold it—feel it. You don't know what it would mean to me to hold a violin in my hands again. When I play I forget everything." Jancsi gives the sentry his fiddle and soon he is oblivious to everything, lost in his music. "Now's our chance to slip away," whispers Jancsi. "Before he realises what's happened, we can be over the frontier and free." And so the two men make their escape.

ACT I

The scene is the drawing-room of the American Embassy in Tokio. John Cunlight, the American Ambassador, and his wife Viktoria, a Hungarian Countess, are giving a farewell party prior to leaving Japan. He has been posted to St. Petersburg. The party is also an excuse to celebrate the engagement of Viktoria's brother, Count Feri, to an attractive girl, O Lia San, who has a French father and a Japanese mother.

Viktoria, who is sincerely devoted to her husband, is tonight strangely disturbed. Yesterday during a trip into town she suddenly caught sight of a man whom she had believed long dead—Stefan Koltay, to whom she was formerly engaged. Colonel Koltay, who after his escape with Jancsi has made his way to Tokio, has recognised Viktoria and cannot understand why she is in Tokio. He manages to get himself invited to the Embassy party, hearing that there are Hungarians connected with the Ambassador's staff and hoping through them to trace Viktoria. Under an assumed name he is presented to Viktoria and is shattered to learn that she is the Ambassador's wife. The Ambassador is, of course, entirely unaware of Viktoria and Stefan's past association and out of the kindness of his heart is only anxious to help this Czaky, as Stefan calls himself, to get back to Hungary. He urges him to travel with them to St. Petersburg on the first stage of his homeward journey.

ACT II

Act Two takes place in the American Embassy in St. Petersburg. Ever since Stefan Koltay's return Viktoria has been in a state of emotional turmoil, though she hides her feelings from her husband. For a time she manages to avoid a meeting *tête-à-tête* with Stefan, which would inevitably involve her in a showdown. But eventually, through the good offices of her maid, Riquette, who has, incidently, started a promising flirtation with Jancsi, Stefan gets Viktoria to himself. She tells him of how news came to her that he had been killed at the front, of her grief and despair. Then she tells him of her desperate loneliness and of her decision to marry John Cunlight in gratitude for the tender, affectionate friendship he had shown her. To his plea to her to come away with him she replies: "Stefan, I must stay with him. You know I must. . . . Give me your hand and let us say good-bye—good night." Sadly they sing:

Feri and O Lia San have got married since the first act and are spending part of their honeymoon as guests of the Ambassador and Viktoria in St. Petersburg. They are blissfully happy and ecstatically in love. O Lia San is teaching Feri Japanese, and with greater enthusiasm than accuracy he declares: "Mousie, my Darling, *I li hung tschin you*," which is the cue for a duet:

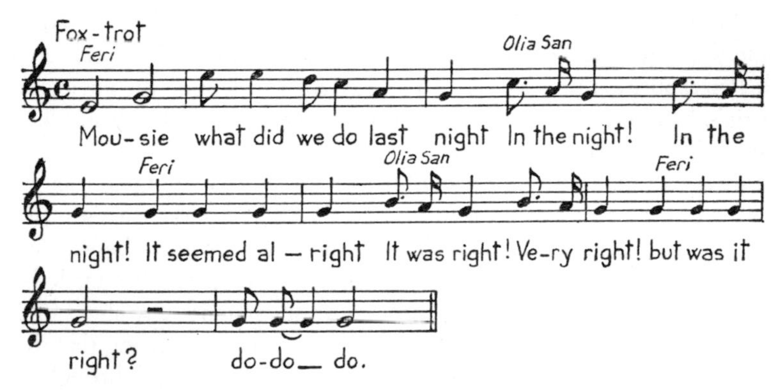

After Viktoria has made the decision to stay with her husband events move swiftly to a dramatic climax. The Russian authorities have discovered Stefan Koltay's presence in St. Petersburg and only the Ambassador's goodwill and the diplomatic immunity of the Embassy can save him. John Cunlight stands by him staunchly in spite of Feri's discovery that the man calling himself Czaky is really Stefan Koltay. One night during a party a Russian officer at the head of a platoon of soldiers presents himself at the American Embassy and asks to speak to the Ambassador. "Who are you, sir? And by what authority do you force your way in here?" asks the angry diplomat. The officer shows him a letter which reads: "I hereby authorise you to enter the American Embassy and arrest Colonel Stefan Koltay. Signed: John Cunlight." "That is Your Excellency's name?" asks the officer. "Yes," says the Ambassador, "but not my signature. Who wrote this letter? I ask again, who wrote this letter?" Stefan steps forward. "I did," he declares. "I am Stefan Koltay." "Stefan, what have you done?" wails Viktoria, and he answers: "I cannot accept my life from the man who took you from me." As the officer arrests him and he is marched away under escort, Viktoria starts after him with an involuntary cry of "Stefan, Stefan, don't leave me", and poor John Cunlight realises where her true feelings lie. "I told you long ago," he reminds her, "that if anything should come between us—if I could no longer make you happy, we would part without anger, without reproach." And he tenderly kisses her good night—good-bye.

ACT III

The last act takes place in the Hungarian village of Doroszma. A year has elapsed since Viktoria and her husband parted, and John Cunlight, solely with Viktoria's future happiness in mind, has never ceased in his efforts to obtain the release of Stefan Koltay. At last by exerting diplomatic influence he has succeeded and Stefan has been pardoned and is to return to Hungary under a prisoner-exchange scheme. Viktoria, after taking a world tour with Riquette as her sole companion, in a desperate attempt to forget the past, has now returned to Doroszma, the home of her childhood. She is living in the castle in which she was born and Feri and O Lia San are staying with her. Today is Harvest Festival, and in Hungary the end of the wine harvest is always celebrated by marrying and giving in marriage. Happily married couples, too, attend church to re-affirm their marriage vows. This year Jancsi and Riquette are getting married, and Feri and O Lia San represent the happily married. Feri is hoping that Viktoria will decide to go back to her husband and make the third bride, and he has been trying to influence her in this direction. When the villagers are all assembled on the green for the ceremonial drinking of the new wine, Viktoria sees John Cunlight walking towards her. He has been posted to Budapest. She is about to raise her glass to him, signifying her willingness to re-affirm their marriage vows, when there is a dramatic interruption. Across the village green strides a tall figure. At sight of him Viktoria drops her glass and runs to meet him with a cry of joy. And everything, everyone else is forgotten as Stefan folds her in his arms.

LONDON

LONDON

The two forms of British light opera with which this book deals are comic opera and musical comedy. Both are lineal descendants of the ballad opera, that eighteenth-century protest against the Italian conquest of the London operatic scene, which began with the arrival of Handel, who visited London and produced his opera *Rinaldo* there in 1712. Beginning with *The Beggar's Opera* in 1728, ballad operas by Arne, Dibdin, Arnold, Shield, Jackson of Exeter, Hook and others enjoyed great popularity down to the days of Bishop, Balfe and Wallace. After that no native opera enjoyed a lasting popularity until the Gilbert and Sullivan series, which belongs to that very type. The first collaboration was billed as "An entirely original grotesque opera *Thespis, or the Gods grown old*". It was presented as part of a burlesque entertainment at the old Gaiety Theatre in 1871 by John Hollingshead, who described himself as "licensed dealer in legs, short skirts, French adaptations, Shakespeare, taste and the musical glasses". It was not a great success; the public were probably not yet ready for Gilbert's wit, and found him too clever and paradoxical for their taste. Their next collaboration produced *Trial by Jury*, presented in 1875 by a popular lyric actress, Miss Selina Dolaro, at the Royalty Theatre as curtain-raiser to Offenbach's *La Périchole*. It was the success of *Trial by Jury* which decided D'Oyly Carte to embark on a policy of British comic opera, and there followed the famous series of Gilbert and Sullivan operas, beginning with *The Sorcerer* in 1877 and ending with *The Grand Duke* in 1896. The best wits and the best composers found it impossible to equal the achievements of these great collaborators, though many tried.

The nearest approach to Gilbert in wit was Basil Hood. He collaborated with Sullivan to produce *The Rose of Persia* in 1899 and the two were at work on *The Emerald Isle* when Sullivan died. Edward German was called in to complete the work, which involved harmonising and orchestrating all the numbers Sullivan had already composed in addition to completing the score. *Merrie England* by Hood and German followed in 1902, and German's other comic operas were *Tom Jones*, *A Princess of Kensington*, and *Fallen Fairies* to a libretto by Gilbert. Other notable composers of comic opera were Alfred Cellier (*Dorothy*, *Doris*), Edward Solomon (*The Nautch Girl*), G. H. Clutsam (*Young England* with Hubert Bath), H. Fraser-Simson (*The Maid of the Mountains* with James Tate), Montague Phillips (*The Rebel Maid*), Thomas Dunhill (*Tantivy Towers*), Alfred Reynolds (*Derby Day*), and Walter Leigh (*The Pride of the Regiment*, *The Jolly Roger*).

Musical comedy developed from burlesque, a form of entertainment which started with Madame Vestris' management of the Olympic Theatre in 1831, where she presented *Olympic Revels* by J. R. Planché. In the early forms of burlesque the words of the songs were fitted to popular tunes in the manner of *The Beggar's Opera.* Later, when George Edwardes became connected with this form of entertainment, composers like Meyer Lutz and Dr. Osmond Carr contributed original music. The dialogue was in the form of rhymed couplets, interspersed with excruciating puns. Here is a sample from *Faust-up-to-date*:

Mephistopheles: "Along the Riviera dudes her praises sing."
Walerlie: "Oh, did you Riviera such a thing?"

—at which the audience, understandably, groaned.

When George Edwardes saw that what John Hollingshead called "The Sacred Flame of Burlesque" was flickering, he abandoned it in favour of musical comedy, a formula of his own invention, which he established successfully with *The Shop Girl* at the Gaiety Theatre in 1894. This was the first of "The Girls", and there followed *The Circus Girl*, *A Runaway Girl*, *A Country Girl*, *The Quaker Girl* and many others. The composers of these early musical comedies were Ivan Caryll, Lionel Monckton, Paul Rubens, Sidney Jones (with his enormously successful *The Geisha* and *San Toy*), Howard Talbot and Leslie Stuart.

The lyric-writers were Adrian Ross (Arthur Reeve Ropes, a history don at King's College, Cambridge), Harry and Percy Greenbank, and Arthur Wimperis. Some of the stars were Seymour Hicks and Ellaline Terriss, Arthur Roberts, Connie Ediss, Edmund Payne, Huntley Wright, Evie Green, Marie Tempest and Gertie Millar; and later, George Grossmith, Jnr., Phyllis and Zena Dare, W. H. Berry, Evelyn Laye and Leslie Henson.

And so the story of British musical comedy continues uninterruptedly through the years. Later milestones are Noel Coward's big hit, *Bitter Sweet*; and Ivor Novello's persistently successful series of spectacular shows starting in 1935 with *Glamorous Night* and ending in 1949 with *King's Rhapsody.* Vivian Ellis has always maintained a high standard of melody in shows like *Mister Cinders*, *Jill Darling*, *Bless the Bride*, *And So To Bed* and *The Water Gipsies*, which bring us to today and two phenomenally successful shows, *The Boy Friend* by Sandy Wilson and *Salad Days* by Julian Slade.

Thespis,
or
the Gods grown old

An Entirely Original, Grotesque Opera in Two Acts

Written by W. S. GILBERT

Music by ARTHUR SULLIVAN

First produced on 26th December, 1871, at the Gaiety Theatre, London, with J. L. Toole as "Thespis" and Ellen Farren as "Mercury".

Note. This was the first association between Gilbert and Sullivan.

CHARACTERS

Gods

JUPITER
APOLLO
MARS
DIANA
MERCURY

Thespians

STUPIDUS
SILIMON
TIMIDON
TIPSICON
PRAEPOSTEROS
THESPIS

SPARKEION
NICEMIS
PRETIEIA
DAPHNE
CYMON

ACT I: Ruined temple on the summit of Olympus
ACT II: The same with Ruins restored

On the summit of Olympus the Gods are met in gloomy conclave, regretting the good old days and lamenting their loss of influence upon the world below. All the Gods and Goddesses, with the exception of Mercury, have grown deplorably old in mind and body, and, "dull, dead in look and woebegone" are experiencing a veritable "Twilight of the Gods". Into the midst of this melancholy convention stray a troupe of actors, Thespis at their head. He has given them the day off and they have climbed to the summit of Mount Olympus from the Thessalian plain with the intention of holding a picnic. A discussion between the Deities and the actors takes place and Thespis suggests that the Gods and Goddesses should travel on a visit to earth, move freely in disguise among the mortals and find out exactly in what esteem they are held in the minds of men. "But what is to become of Olympus meanwhile?" asks Jupiter. "Well, I've a very talented company," replies Thespis. "Invest us with your powers and we will fill your places till you return one year hence." Jupiter agrees, and in order that the actors be not too heavily embarrassed by their inexperience and the novelty of their roles, Mercury is left behind as Jupiter's deputy.

Directly the Gods are out of sight, however, everything is at sixes and sevens. Conditions on Olympus are chaotic and the results disastrous; and there is a confusion of love affairs that is not at all in accordance with human practice or with the *Dictionary of Classical Mythology*. The deputy Venus gives orders that all babies shall in future be born grown up. The deputy Bacchus is a confirmed teetotaller and arranges that in future the juice of the vines shall take the form, not of wine, but of ginger beer. The impersonators of the Sun and Moon insist on shining together. The deputy Diana refuses to go out alone so late at night, objecting on the grounds of both respectability and the risk of catching cold. Thespis, acting head of the Gods, boasts that during their year of government no complaints have reached him from below. But Mercury, as Jupiter's deputy, has received them all and is saving them up for the annual reckoning. This takes place on the return of the Gods—not a moment too soon. Thespis is on the mat for his administrative incompetence:

Mercury: Why, it's been a foggy Friday in November for the last six months and the Athenians are tired of it.

Thespis: There's no pleasing some people. This craving for perpetual change is the curse of the country. Friday's a very nice day.

Mercury: So it is, but a Friday six months long! It gets monotonous.

The actors beg to be allowed to stay, but Jupiter gives them short shrift:

"Enough", [he thunders]
"Your reign is ended;
Upon this sacred hill
Let him be apprehended
And learn our awful will.
Away to earth, contemptible comedians
And hear our curse, before we set you free
You shall all be eminent tragedians
Whom no one ever goes to see."

Thespis was given at the Gaiety Theatre as an after-piece to H. J. Byron's *Dearer Than Love*. It scored only a moderate success, but it looks forward frequently both to the characteristic methods and to the characters of the famous series of Gilbert and Sullivan operas. The Admiral's autobiographical song in *H.M.S. Pinafore* is clearly foreshadowed in this lyric from the first act of *Thespis*:

"I once knew a chap who discharged a function
On the North South East West Diddlesex Junction,
He was conspicuous exceeding
For his affable ways and his easy breeding.
Although a Chairman of Directors,
He was hand in glove with the ticket inspectors.
He tipped the guards with brand new fivers
And sang little songs to the engine drivers.
'Twas told to me with great compunction
By one who had discharged with unction
A Chairman of Directors Function
On the North South East West Diddlesex Junction.
Fol diddle, lol diddle, lol lol lay. . . .

He followed out his whim with vigour,
The shares went down to a nominal figure,
These are the sad results proceeding
From his affable ways and his easy breeding!
The line, with its rails and guards and peelers,
Was sold for a song to marine store dealers,
The shareholders are all in the Work'us
And he sells pipe lights in the Regent Circus.
'Twas told to me with much compunction
By one who had discharged with unction
A Chairman of Directors Function
On the North South East West Diddlesex Junction.
Fol diddle, lol diddle, lol lol lay. . . ."

In writing that lyric Gilbert had in mind a particular public figure, the Duke of Sutherland, who was fond of driving railway engines. Mercury, the factotum of the Gods, is clearly an ancestor of Pooh-Bah with his multifarious duties and propensity to patter-songs. He complains to Apollo:

"Oh, I'm the celestial drudge,
From morning to night I must stop at it,
On errands all day I must trudge
And I stick to my work till I drop at it!
In summer I get up at one
(As a good-natured donkey I'm ranked for it!)
Then I go and I light up the sun
And Phoebus Apollo gets thanked for it!
Well, well, its the way of the world
And will be through all it's futurity,
Though noodles are baroned and earled
There's nothing for clever obscurity!"

The score of *Thespis* was never published, but we can form an idea of what the music was like from two instances. The entrance chorus of General Stanley's daughters in *The Pirates of Penzance* served for the arrival on Mount Olympus of the actors in Act One of *Thespis*:

The other example of music from *Thespis* is Sparkeion's song "Little Maid of Arcadee" with its refrain:

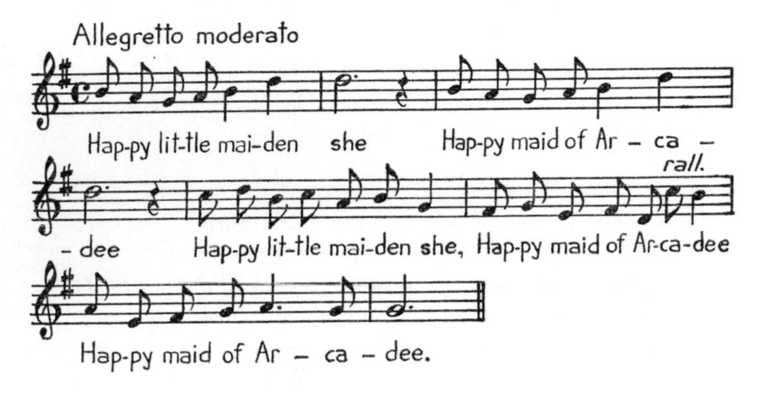

Trial by Jury

A Novel and Original Dramatic Cantata

Written by W. S. GILBERT

Music by ARTHUR SULLIVAN

First produced on 25th March, 1875, under the management of Madame Selina Dolaro at the New Royalty Theatre, London, with F. Sullivan (the composer's brother) as "The Learned Judge", Nelly Bromley as "The Plaintiff" and W. Fisher as "The Defendant".

CHARACTERS

THE LEARNED JUDGE
COUNSEL FOR PLAINTIFF
THE DEFENDANT
FOREMAN OF THE JURY
USHER
THE PLAINTIFF
CHORUS OF BRIDESMAIDS, GENTLEMEN OF THE JURY, BARRISTERS, AND ATTORNEYS

The scene is a Court of Justice. The Bench faces the audience and extends along the back of the court. The Judge's desk has a canopy overhead. On the left is the jury-box and on the right the witness-box, from which three steps lead up to the Bench. The opening chorus, sung by barristers, attorneys and jurymen, is French in flavour and construction. The orchestra has a lively, bustling tune suggesting the busy anticipation in court, and the simple, repeated chords of the singers remind one of choruses in operas of Auber and Offenbach. Sullivan's tune has tremendous verve:

After the opening chorus the Usher addresses the Jury on the conduct of the case—a breach of promise of marriage. He stresses the importance of preserving complete impartiality of outlook. In the case of the Plaintiff they must show every sympathy with the broken-hearted bride and condole with her distress of mind; "but," he goes on,

> "When amid the Plaintiff's shrieks
> The ruffianly defendant speaks
> upon the other side;
> What he may say you needn't mind.
> From bias free of every kind
> This trial must be tried."

The Defendant now arrives, and the Jury take a dislike to him on sight. Shaking their fists at him they threaten

> "We're the Jury,
> dread our Fury."

The Defendant begs them to give him fair consideration. After all, he tells them in a plaintive song, he has done no worse than many other young men in falling in love with a girl, getting bored with her and falling out of love again.

The Jurymen are quite unimpressed. They haven't a scrap of sympathy with the Defendant and jeer at him cheerfully in a legal version of "Tra-la-la": "Singing so merrily—Trial-la-law." With a stentorian shout of "Silence in court!" the Usher heralds the appearance of the learned Judge. Before getting down to the business of the court he relates in a comic song his life's history from the time when he was first called to the Bar with "an appetite fresh and hearty" till he threw over "the rich attorney's elderly daughter", who could "very well pass for forty-three in the dark with the light behind her". After the Jury have been sworn, the Plaintiff is called. She is preceded by her bevy of bridesmaids. The Judge takes a great fancy to the First Bridesmaid and sends her a note by the Usher, which she reads, kisses rapturously and places in her bosom. When the Plaintiff appears, radiantly attired in her bridal dress, she and her bridesmaids sing an enchanting little song with the tender refrain:

The Judge, having by this time transferred his admiration to the Plaintiff, directs the Usher to take the note away from the First Bridesmaid and hand it to the Plaintiff. She reads it, kisses it rapturously and places it in her bosom, while the Jurymen shake their fingers at the Judge with cries of "Sly dog, sly dog". The Counsel for the Plaintiff now addresses the court, dilating on the painful situation of his client, who, as victim of a heartless wile, has vainly attempted to persuade her fiancé to name the day. He draws a sinister picture of the Defendant equivocating, making excuses and finally backing out:

"Doubly criminal to do so
For the maid had bought her trousseau."

The Plaintiff falls sobbing first on her Counsel's breast and then on that of the Foreman of the Jury. Finally she staggers to the Bench and, sitting down by the Judge, sobs on his breast. The Defendant attempts to defend himself in the face of extreme hostility from the Jury. He suggests that, as it is a question of satisfying two young ladies, he is perfectly willing to marry this lady today and the other tomorrow. But the Counsel, consulting a law book, declares:

"In the time of James the Second,
It was generally reckoned
As a very serious crime
To marry two wives at one time."

"This," declares the Judge, "is a dilemma that calls for all our wit." The Plaintiff now makes a dead set at the Defendant, addressing him in terms of exaggerated tenderness. Cunningly she urges the Jury to notice the wealth of affection she is lavishing on him and to remember it when they come to assessing the damages he must pay. The Defendant, for his part, repels her furiously, telling the court that he is not the man to make her happy:

"I smoke like a furnace—I'm always in liquor,
a ruffian, a bully, a sot.
I'm sure I should thrash her, perhaps I should kick her
I am such a very bad lot."

The Jury find the case a most puzzling one, and they apply to the learned Judge for guidance. He counsels them as follows:

"The question, Gentlemen, is one of liquor;
You ask for guidance—this is my reply:
He says, when tipsy, he would thrash and kick her.
Let's make him tipsy, Gentlemen, and try."

Counsel for the Plaintiff: "With all respect
I do object."
Defendant: "I don't object."
All: "We do object."

Their objections infuriate the Judge, who tosses his books and papers about, and declares that no proposals seem to please the court and he is not going to hang about all day. With startling suddenness he finishes the case with the words:

"Put your briefs upon the shelf,
I will marry her myself."

He comes down from the Bench to the floor of the court and embraces the Plaintiff. And everyone joins in the gay Finale to this swinging tune:

The Sorcerer

An Original Comic Opera in Two Acts

Written by W. S. GILBERT

Music by ARTHUR SULLIVAN

First produced on 17th November, 1877, at the Opéra Comique, London, with Rutland Barrington as "Dr. Daly", George Grossmith as "John Wellington Wells" and Alice May as "Aline".

CHARACTERS

SIR MARMADUKE POINTDEXTRE, *an elderly Baronet*
ALEXIS, *of the Grenadier Guards, his son*
DR. DALY, *Vicar of Ploverleigh*
NOTARY JOHN WELLINGTON WELLS, *of J. W. Wells and Co., Family Sorcerers*
LADY SANGAZURE, *a lady of ancient lineage*
ALINE, *her daughter—betrothed to Alexis*
MRS. PARTLET, *a pew-opener*
CONSTANCE, *her daughter*

ACT I

Outside Sir Marmaduke Pointdextre's Elizabethan mansion the villagers of Ploverleigh are collected to celebrate the betrothal of Alexis Pointdextre to Aline Sangazure. All this rejoicing saddens the heart of Constance, daughter of Mrs. Partlet, pew-opener of Ploverleigh, who has lost her heart to Dr. Daly, the vicar. Mrs. Partlet promises to do all in her power to further the match, but Dr. Daly, for his part, fears he has left love behind him. Time was when he was a pale young curate!

For the moment Constance must bide her time.

Sir Marmaduke is delighted with Alexis' engagement, and he is particularly pleased at the union of the two families, as he had formerly wished to unite them by marrying Lady Sangazure himself. He and Lady Sangazure still exhibit strong emotion at sight of each other, which they endeavour to suppress, but beneath the surface both are on fire and give vent to passionate asides:

Sangazure }
Marmaduke } "Immortal!"

Sangazure }
Marmaduke } "Divine!"

"Welcome to my portal
Loved one, oh be mine."

Alexis and Aline sign their marriage contract, and Alexis, a confirmed democrat, seizes the opportunity to expatiate on his favourite doctrine. If only the world would break down the artificial barriers of rank, wealth, education, age, beauty, taste and temper and recognise the glorious principle that in marriage alone is to be found the panacea for every ill! He has preached in Mechanics' Institutes, beer-shops, work-houses and lunatic asylums and been received with enthusiasm, and has even addressed navvies on the advantages that would accrue to them if they married ladies of rank, and not a navvy dissented. Only the aristocracy hold aloof. "Ah," comments Aline, "the working man's is the true intelligence, after all." Alexis proposes to take a desperate step in support of his principles. He has engaged a sorcerer—head of the firm of J. W. Wells, Family Sorcerers, of St. Mary Axe. They have invented an infallible love-potion, and Alexis intends to distribute it through the village of Ploverleigh, steep the villagers up to their lips in love and couple them in matrimony without distinction of age, rank or fortune. John Wellington Wells, the dealer in magic and spells, duly arrives and introduces himself in a first-rate, top-speed patter song of which this is a sample:

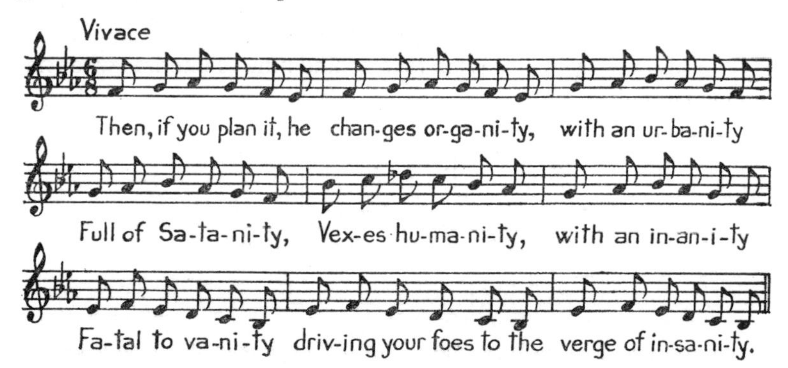

Mr. Wells confirms that his firm's love-potion is guaranteed to work within twelve hours. Whoever drinks it loses consciousness for that period and, on waking, falls in love with the first lady he meets, who, having also tasted it, then returns his affection. On married people it has no effect whatever. Aline, who is dubious as to the propriety of the experiment, is sent to fetch the tea-pot to be used for the celebration tea-party, and John Wellington Wells proceeds in an incantation to summon the aid of invisible demons, whose ghostly voices are "heard without" as he pours the contents of a magic phial into the tea-pot. After the incantation the villagers arrive for the tea-party and Mrs. Partlet and Mr. Wells distribute the cups while the villagers gaily partake of "the rollicking bun", "the gay Sally Lunn" and countless cups of tea. Presently it becomes evident by the strange conduct of everybody that the charm is working. They rub their eyes and stagger about as if under the influence of a narcotic, and at the fall of the curtain all are lying on the ground insensible.

ACT II

The scene is the same as before. It is some hours later. A moon is shining and the villagers are discovered fast asleep exactly as they were at the end of Act One. Only Sir Marmaduke, Dr. Daly, Lady Sangazure and the Notary are missing, for Mr. Wells

"Did not think it meet to see
A dame of lengthy pedigree,
A Baronet and K.C.B.,
A Doctor of Divinity
And that respectable Q.C.,
All fast asleep al-fresco-ly
And so I had them taken home
And put to bed respectably."

At this moment the villagers awaken and fall into each other's arms, while the men make wholesale proposals of marriage to the delighted girls. But already unconventional attachments are taking place. Constance has forgotten all about her affection for Dr. Daly and appears leading the Notary, who carries an ear-trumpet, by the hand.

"You very, very plain old man
I love, I love you madly,"

she tells him, to which he replies:

"I am a very deaf old man
and hear you very badly."

Alexis is thrilled with the success of his experiment. Only one thing remains to be done. He and Aline must drink the philtre themselves, that each may be assured of the other's love for ever. But to his disgust Aline, who is unhappy about the whole experiment, refuses to drink. Dr. Daly now enters. He is very puzzled. Hitherto the village of Ploverleigh has not been addicted to marrying and giving in marriage, and now the whole village has come to him in a body and implored him to join them in matrimony as soon as possible, "Even your excellent father," he tells Alexis, "has hinted that he may change his condition." But Alexis' joy at the news that his father is proposing, as he imagines, to unite himself with

Aline's mother is changed to acute embarrassment when Sir Marmaduke declares his intention of marrying Mrs. Partlet. "Though any wife of yours will be a mother of mine," Alexis tells him, "it is not quite what I could have wished." Gradually Alexis comes to realise that his experiment is not the success he hoped it to be. Lady Sangazure falls in love with Mr. Wells, to his dismay, and worst of all Aline, who on second thoughts to please Alexis has swallowed the love potion, happens to meet Dr. Daly and they, too, fall in love. Alexis is loud in his condemnation of Aline, but Dr. Daly intervenes and urges him "to be just. This poor child drank the philtre at your instance. She hurried off to meet you but, most unhappily, she met me instead. As you had administered the potion to both of us the result was inevitable. Bur fear nothing from me. I will be no man's rival. I will leave the country at once and bury my sorrow in the congenial gloom of a colonial bishopric."

Alexis now appeals to Mr. Wells for a remedy to all these difficulties. "Or you, or I, must yield up his life to Ahrimanes." "I would rather it were you," declares Mr. Wells. "I should have no hesitation in sacrificing my own life to spare yours, but we take stock next week, and it would not be fair on the Co." But Aline protests that if Alexis is sacrificed that all may be restored to their old loves, what is to become of her, with no love to be restored to? "I did not think of that," says Mr. Wells, and amid red fire he descends into the nether regions as all rejoin their former loves. Sir Marmaduke cries:

"Come to my mansion, all of you! At least
We'll crown our rapture with another feast."

And the curtain comes down with a further assault by the villagers on "the rollicking bun" and "the gay Sally Lunn".

The Pirates of Penzance

or

The Slave of Duty (*originally* Love and Duty)

Written by W. S. GILBERT

Music by ARTHUR SULLIVAN

First produced on 30th December, 1879, at the Bijou Theatre, Paignton, Devon; on 31st December, 1879, at the Fifth Avenue Theatre, New York; and in London on 3rd April, 1880, at the Opéra Comique. The cast at the Opéra Comique included George Grossmith as "Major-General Stanley", Richard Temple as "The Pirate King", Rutland Barrington as "The Sergeant of Police", and Marion Hood as "Mabel".

CHARACTERS

MAJOR-GENERAL STANLEY
THE PIRATE KING
SAMUEL, *his Lieutenant*
FREDERIC, *the pirate apprentice*
SERGEANT OF POLICE
MABEL, EDITH, KATE, ISOBEL — *General Stanley's daughters*
RUTH, *a pirate maid-of-all work*
CHORUS OF PIRATES, POLICE AND GENERAL STANLEY'S DAUGHTERS

ACT I

On a rocky seashore on the coast of Cornwall the pirates of Penzance are holding a sherry party to celebrate the apprentice Frederic's promotion to the status of full-blown pirate on the expiry of his indentures. For today is the 29th of February, 1897, and it is his twenty-first birthday. His health is duly drunk, and in a speech of thanks Frederic startles the pirates by telling them of his intention to leave them for good. It seems that he was apprenticed to them in error. Ruth, the pirates' maid-of-all-work, takes up the tale. She tells how, when she was formerly Frederic's nursery-maid, his parents instructed her to have the boy apprenticed to a pilot. Being hard of hearing she misheard, and in error Frederic was apprenticed to a pirate.

Frederic, the Slave of Duty of the sub-title, now informs the pirates that he will in future feel himself bound to devote himself to their extermination from conscientious motives. But before leaving he gives them some practical advice on how to improve their business methods. For one thing, they are too tender-hearted. They make a point of never attacking a weaker party than themselves, and consequently they invariably get thrashed; and then again they make a point of never molesting an orphan. "Of course," says one pirate, "we are orphans ourselves and know what it is." "Yes," Frederic tells them, "but it has got about, and the consequence is that everyone who is captured claims to be an orphan." Frederic now bids the pirates good-bye, making a last appeal to the Pirate King to turn respectable and accompany him back to civilisation. But the Pirate King refuses. "No, Frederic," he declares, "I shall live and die a Pirate King."

The pirates withdraw and Frederic is left alone with Ruth.

Now Ruth is determined to marry Frederic and does not scruple to take advantage of his youth and inexperience, for Frederic has spent most of his life at sea and Ruth's is the only woman's face with which he is familiar. "Compared with other women are you beautiful?" he asks her, and Ruth has just assured him that she is, when there is a burst of girlish chatter. A bevy of beautiful girls is approaching, and Frederic, smitten with their loveliness, turns on Ruth with "Oh, false one, you have deceived me."

> "You told me you were fair as gold
> And now I see you're plain and old."

He spurns her and Ruth goes off in despair, while Frederic hides in a cave as on come all General Stanley's daughters, climbing over the rocks. There are more than twenty of them, for they comprise the sopranos and contraltos of the female chorus. Seeing that they are quite alone and that the sea is as smooth as glass, the hardy maidens decide to take off their shoes and stockings and paddle. They have all taken off one shoe when Frederic emerges from the cave and, hopping on one foot, they exclaim in horror, "A man!" Frederic confesses that he is a pirate about to reform and appeals to any one of them to

> "Give up willingly
> All matrimonial ambition
> To rescue such a one as I
> From his unfortunate position."

But no girl volunteers, and Frederic cries in despair, "Not one?" In answer a female voice cries: "Yes, one; yes, 'tis Mabel," and Mabel enters and offers Frederic her heart in a florid waltz song, which is a delicious burlesque of the type of song Gounod made so popular:

After this Frederic warns the girls to depart before the pirates return. But before they can make their escape they are seized by the delighted pirates, who see in the presence of these lovelies a splendid opportunity of getting married. Mabel, however, defies them, warning the pirates that their father is a Major-General—and over the rocks comes General Stanley himself in search of his daughters, to sing his entrance song:

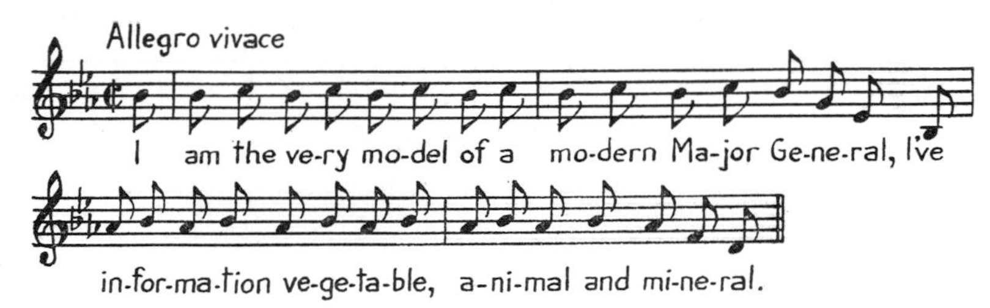

When he becomes aware of what's afoot, General Stanley will not hear of his daughters marrying buccaneers. "I object to pirates as sons-in-law," he declares, and the pirates reply that they, for their part, are not keen on Major-Generals as fathers-in-law. In this dilemma the General has a bright idea. "Do you mean to say," he demands, "that you would deliberately rob me of these, the sole remaining props of my old age, and leave me to go through the remainder of my life unfriended, unprotected and alone?" "Well, yes," says the Pirate King. "That's the idea." "Tell me," asks the General innocently, "have you ever known what it is to be an orphan?" and the pirates exclaim disgustedly: "Oh, dash it all. Here we are again." True to their creed, the pirates permit General Stanley to depart with his daughters, and Frederic accompanies them; and the curtain falls on General Stanley at the head of his company of daughters waving the Union Jack, facing the Pirate King, who, at the head of his buccaneers, hoists a black flag with skull and crossbones.

ACT II

The scene is a ruined Gothic chapel. It is night, and the curtain rises to disclose General Stanley seated pensively, surrounded by his daughters. They are vainly attempting to cheer him, but the General refuses to be comforted. He is the victim of remorse, for the story he told the pirates, that he was an orphan—the story which secured the release of himself and his daughters—was a bare-faced lie and he is haunted by the memory of his prevarication. Presently

Frederic appears. Pursuing his plan to exterminate the pirates, he has enlisted the aid of the police. The General desires to speed them on their way, and on march the policemen, led by a sergeant, to receive his blessing. Mabel and her sisters cheer them on their dangerous mission with a song:

> "Go, ye heroes, go to glory,
> Though ye die in combat gory,
> Ye shall live in song and story,
> Go to immortality!"

But the police, who are already in a highly nervous state, hardly relish such sentiments, though they are polite about it:

Sullivan develops this musical effect into an entertaining travesty of the style of an Auber-Bellini, early nineteenth-century opera, in which so often the action is held up at a moment of high tension and excitement by an extended musical ensemble. In this case the policemen keep repeating: "Forward on the foe we go, we go, we go, we go," till the Major-General, exasperated, rounds on them with: "But you *DON'T* go."

Eventually all depart, leaving Frederic alone in the chapel. He is about to leave when the Pirate King and Ruth enter, armed, and they greet Frederic affectionately at pistol point. They have come to tell him that he has been freed from his indentures in error and that he is still legally and morally apprenticed to the pirates. True, Frederic has lived twenty-one years, but the wording of his indentures reads "that his apprenticeship shall expire on his twenty-first birthday". And counting by birthdays, since Frederic was born in leap year, he is only five and a little bit over. Frederic at first does not appreciate the full significance of all this and roars with laughter at their ridiculous paradox. When, however, he realises the situation he is shattered, but his sense of duty forces him to accept it. It also forces him to disclose to the Pirate King that General Stanley—the father of his Mabel—is no orphan and escaped from them by telling a lie. The pirate's anger at this news is terrible, and he hurries away to muster his band and punish the General.

Frederic now breaks the news to Mabel that he must return to serve the pirates. His apprenticeship will expire in 1940 and he begs her to wait for him till then. "It seems so long," she sighs and begs him in this melting song not to leave her:

But Frederic insists on acting in accordance with the dictates of his conscience and leaves her. The police now return, having failed to find the pirates, and Mabel breaks the news of Frederic's change of face. All are scandalised at his defection, but Mabel claims that he has done his duty. "Go ye," she tells the police, "and do yours." And the Sergeant replies by singing his famous song: "A policeman's lot is *NOT* a happy one." Now in the distance the voices of the pirates are heard approaching, thirsting for General Stanley's blood. The police conceal themselves, and as they do so the pirates, with Ruth and Frederic, enter cautiously. Frederic whispers that the General is approaching, and in he comes in his dressing-gown, shortly followed by his daughters. The pirates spring up and seize the General, and Mabel cries distractedly: "Frederic, save us!" But poor Frederic can only answer:

> "Beautiful Mabel,
> I would if I could but I am not able."

Desperately she calls:

> "Will no one in his cause a weapon wield?"

And the police, springing up, reply:

> "Yes, we are here, though hitherto concealed."

A desperate fight follows, notable for its violence rather than for its duration, for it is decided in three bars of music. The police are overcome, and the pirates stand over them with drawn swords. But their triumph is short-lived, for the Sergeant, stepping forward, addresses the pirates:

"On your allegiance we've a nobler claim
We charge you yield in Queen Victoria's name."

Without a moment's hesitation the pirates give themselves up, and General Stanley is urging the Sergeant:

"Away with them and place them at the bar,"

when Ruth intervenes with

"One moment, let me tell you who they are.
They are no members of the common throng;
They are all noblemen, who have gone wrong."

With traditional reverence all kneel to the pirates, and General Stanley voices their thoughts:

"No Englishmen unmoved that statement hears
Because, with all our faults, we love our house of peers."

And his final bidding to them is to

"Resume your ranks and legislative duties
And take my daughters, all of whom are beauties."

H.M.S. *Pinafore*

or

The Lass that Loved a Sailor

An Entirely Original Nautical Comic Opera in Two Acts

Written by W. S. GILBERT

Music by ARTHUR SULLIVAN

First produced on 25th May, 1878, at the Opéra Comique, London, with George Grossmith as "Sir Joseph Porter, K.C.B.", Rutland Barrington as "Captain Corcoran", George Power as "Ralph Rackstraw" and Alice May as "Josephine".

CHARACTERS

SIR JOSEPH PORTER, K.C.B., *First Lord of the Admiralty*
CAPTAIN CORCORAN, *Commanding H.M.S.* Pinafore
RALPH RACKSTRAW, *able seaman*
BILL BOBSTAY, *boatswain's mate*
DICK DEADEYE, *able seaman*
JOSEPHINE, *the Captain's daughter*
LITTLE BUTTERCUP, *a Portsmouth bumboat woman*
CHORUS OF FIRST LORD'S SISTERS, HIS COUSINS, HIS AUNTS, SAILORS, MARINERS, ETC.

ACT I

On the quarter-deck of H.M.S. *Pinafore* sailors are discovered hard at work cleaning brass-work, splicing rope and singing as they work:

Presently their work is interrupted by the arrival of a Portsmouth bumboat woman, nicknamed Little Buttercup. Her basket is crammed with tempting wares—snuff, tobacco, scissors, watches, knives and ribbons and laces for wives and sweethearts. She introduces herself in a charming little ditty:

In spite of Buttercup's gay and frivolous exterior she confesses to a canker-worm of worry that is eating its way into her heart. The secret of her remorse, which provides the *dénouement* of the plot, is not unconnected with the name of Ralph Rackstraw. Young Ralph, "the smartest lad in all the Fleet", and an A.B. of H.M.S. *Pinafore*, has fallen in love with Josephine, daughter of his Captain. But Josephine is sought in marriage by no less a celebrity than Sir Joseph Porter, K.C.B., First Lord of the Admiralty. Ralph's love is returned by Josephine and to her father's dismay she confesses her love for Ralph, adding that though she can esteem, reverence and venerate Sir Joseph she cannot under any circumstances love him. "I hate myself when I think of the depth to which I have stooped in permitting myself to think tenderly of one so ignobly born—but I love him! I love him! I love him!" she cries and bursts into tears.

A barge is now seen to be approaching H.M.S. *Pinafore* and from it steps Sir Joseph Porter, accompanied by a collection of ladies, consisting of his sisters, his cousins and his aunts. Sir Joseph introduces himself in an impressive song:

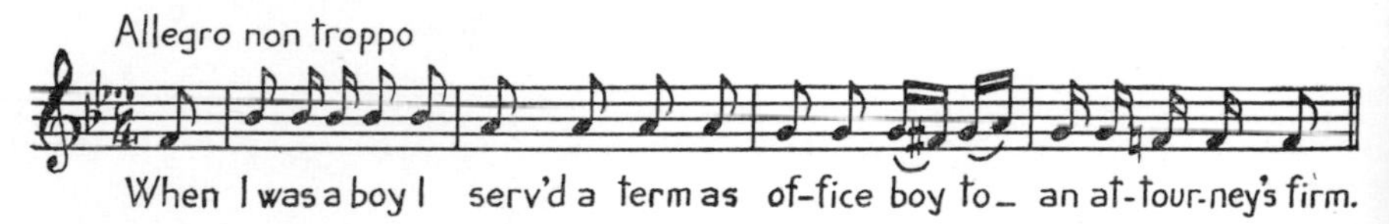

After this beginning Sir Joseph has risen to the position of First Lord of the Admiralty—a "take-off" by Gilbert of the newly-appointed First Sea Lord, William H. Smith, who, despite his lack of familiarity with the ocean, made a highly successful head of the Royal Navy. Sir Joseph inspects the crew of H.M.S. *Pinafore* and in a democratic speech declares that all men are equal. These sentiments encourage Ralph Rackstraw to propose to Josephine, who, however, temporises and rebukes him for raising his eyes to the daughter of his commanding officer: "Sir, you forget the disparity of our ranks." In despair Ralph decides to take his life, and has actually put the pistol to his head when Josephine intervenes. "Ah! stay your hand. I love you!" she tells him, making her confession before the whole ship's company. They plan to elope that very night, in spite of objections from Ralph's odious mess-mate, Dick Deadeye. Twisted in mind and body, he urges Ralph vindictively to "remember she's your gallant Captain's daughter and you the meanest slave that crawls the water". But he is howled down by the rest of the crew, who all side with Ralph and Josephine.

ACT II

That night on board H.M.S. *Pinafore* Sir Joseph expresses to Captain Corcoran his disappointment with Josephine, who has not responded favourably to his proposals of marriage. "Josephine is of course sensible of your condescension, Sir Joseph, but perhaps your exalted rank dazzles her," pleads the Captain. So Sir Joseph once again tackles Josephine, and hoping to further his own suit, he tells her that in his opinion difference of social status is no barrier to love. Little does he know how eloquently he has pleaded his rival's cause, and Josephine, who was in doubt as to the propriety of eloping with Ralph, has now no qualms. But Dick Deadeye has warned Captain Corcoran of the intended elopement and the Captain is in time to prevent it. He rebukes Josephine for the company she keeps, and Ralph Rackstraw bitterly resents the Captain's class-consciousness, telling him proudly: "I am an Englishman." The crew back him up and the boatswain sings in his support:

But Captain Corcoran is unable to repress his anger, and in front of all Sir Joseph's female relations, who have arrived on the scene, he turns on Ralph with: "Damme, it's too bad!" Sir Joseph is horrified at the Captain's bad language, and orders him to his cabin in disgrace; then, turning to Ralph Rackstraw, he inquires in fatherly fashion how Captain Corcoran came to forget himself. "I am quite sure you had given him no cause for annoyance." Ralph then admits his love for Josephine, who precipitates herself into his arms. Sir Joseph is livid with rage. "Insolent sailor, you shall repent this outrage. Seize him," he commands. And Ralph is led off in custody. "Josephine, I cannot tell you the distress I feel at this most painful revelation. You, whom I honoured by seeking in marriage—you, the daughter of a Captain in the Royal Navy," says the injured First Sea Lord.

At this point Little Buttercup intervenes with a truly remarkable story. Many years before she had been a baby-farmer and in her charge were two infants; one a well-born babe, the other of humble origin. Inadvertently she had mixed them up, and Ralph Rackstraw is really named Corcoran and the Captain is Ralph Rackstraw. On hearing this revelation Sir Joseph sends for the two affected parties, and Ralph enters dressed in Captain's uniform, and Captain Corcoran as a common sailor. Addressing Captain Corcoran, Sir Joseph says: "I need not tell you that after this change in your condition my marriage with your daughter is out of the question." The Captain protests in Sir Joseph's own words that "Love levels all ranks". "It does to a considerable extent, but it does not level them as much as that," says the First Sea Lord crushingly. Handing Josephine to Ralph, Sir Joseph admonishes him to treat her kindly, and the curtain falls on general rejoicing and a finale in which all the best tunes are repeated and which finishes on a patriotic note in praise of Englishmen.

Patience
or
Bunthorne's Bride

An Entirely New and Original Aesthetic Opera in Two Acts
Written by W. S. Gilbert
Music by Arthur Sullivan

First produced on 23rd April, 1881, at the Opéra Comique, London, with Leonora Braham as "Patience", George Grossmith as "Bunthorne" and Rutland Barrington as "Grosvenor".

Characters

REGINALD BUNTHORNE, *a fleshly poet*
ARCHIBALD GROSVENOR, *an idyllic poet*
MR. BUNTHORNE'S SOLICITOR
COLONEL CALVERLY, MAJOR MURGATROYD, LIEUT. THE DUKE OF DUNSTABLE — *officers of Dragoons*
THE LADY ANGELA, THE LADY SAPHIR, THE LADY ELLA, THE LADY JANE — *rapturous maidens*
PATIENCE, *a dairymaid*
CHORUS OF RAPTUROUS MAIDENS, OFFICERS OF DRAGOON GUARDS

ACT I

The scene is the exterior of Castle Bunthorne, approached by a drawbridge over the moat. A group of young ladies in aesthetic draperies are scattered about the stage, playing on lutes, mandolines, etc., as they sing. All are in the last stages of despair. Angela, Ella and Saphir lead their song:

The maidens are disciples of and rivals for the love of Bunthorne, a poet, aesthete and medievalist. But Lady Jane, the eldest and most drastic of the maidens, tells them that they are wasting their time: Bunthorne's fancy is for Patience, the village milkmaid. Patience, however, is unmoved. Love has never troubled her:

Bunthorne has "etherialised" the maidens and, fascinated by the new aestheticism of the fleshly poet, they have deserted their former passions, the officers of the 35th Heavy Dragoons. The Dragoons are surprised and annoyed to observe their sweethearts following the insufferable, long-haired poet, and as a counterpoint to the maidens' aesthetic melody they express their indignation at the treatment accorded to a military man. This, a favourite device of Sullivan's, is one of his happiest examples:

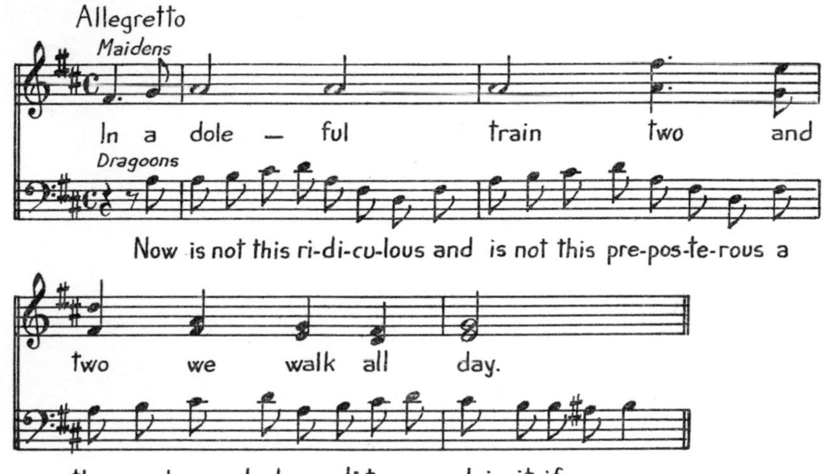

The officers try in vain to reason with the maidens. "You seem to forget that you are engaged to us," they protest. But the maidens are adamant. "It can never be. You are not Empyrean," they tell the startled officers. "You are not Della Cruscan. You are not even Early English." And Lady Jane, examining their uniforms, exclaims disgustedly: "Red and yellow! Primary colours! Oh, South Kensington!" "Gentlemen," declares the Duke, "this is an insult to the British uniform." And the Colonel goes on to say that when he first put it on it never occurred to him that the ladies would find that "the peripatetics of long-haired aesthetics are very much more to their taste."

Bunthorne tries to persuade Patience to marry him; he is even prepared to have his hair cut and become frolicsome. But all to no avail. His love-making only succeeds in alarming her, and he leaves her. Patience, puzzled, asks Lady

Angela to explain what love is, and Angela tells her that "it is the one unselfish emotion in this whirlpool of grasping greed". "Then I'll set about it at once," says Patience with determination. "I won't go to bed until I'm head over ears in love with somebody." Presently a stranger enters. Approaching Patience he sings:

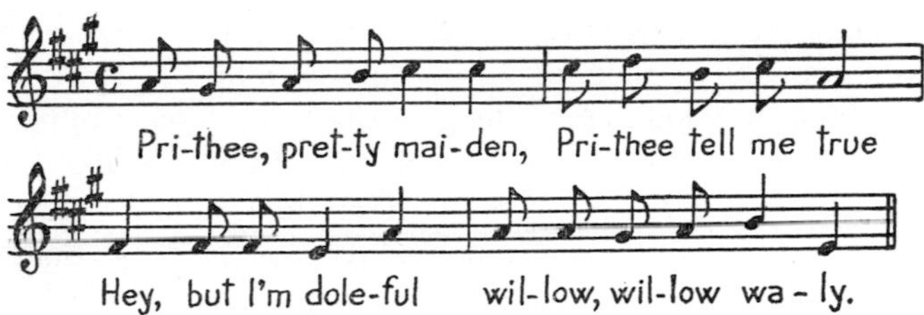

He then asks her to marry him.

The stranger turns out to be Archibald Grosvenor, an idyllic poet and Patience's childhood playmate. She is enchanted by his good looks. "Yes, Patience, I am very beautiful," he sighs. "I have loved you with a Florentine fourteenth-century frenzy for full fifteen years." They fall into each other's arms. But suddenly Patience recoils from him and Grosvenor asks what is the matter. "Why," says Patience, "you are perfection." "I know I am," he replies. "Well?" "Then, bless my heart, there can be nothing unselfish in loving you and I can never be yours," she finishes. However, as a compensation there is no selfishness in Grosvenor's continuing to love her, and this, in his idyllic way, he may do.

Bunthorne, distracted by his failure with Patience, decides to raffle himself—on the advice of his solicitor—in aid of a deserving charity. The love-sick maidens, especially the over-ripe Lady Jane, are enraptured at the prospect of drawing the winning ticket, when Patience approaches. Learning the situation, she repents and offers herself as Bunthorne's bride. With Bunthorne provided for, the maidens experience a revulsion against aestheticism. They gaze fondly at the officers, who promptly reciprocate, and mutual love is expressed in a parody of the Victorian quasi-religious part song:

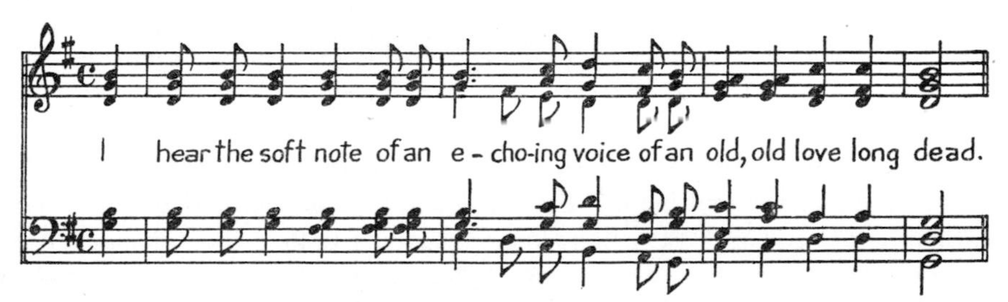

But in spite of all the promises of constancy expressed in the final lines:

> "And never, oh, never this heart will range
> from that old old love again,"

when Grosvenor appears the maidens are strangely fascinated by him and leave the Dragoons again, and the curtain falls on them grouped on their knees around Grosvenor, to the fury of Bunthorne and the Dragoons.

ACT II

The scene is a glade, with a small sheet of water in the centre. Once upon a time it was Bunthorne who hypnotised the maidens with his "O Hollow! Hollow! Hollow!", reading to them as they clung passionately to one another, thinking of faint lilies. Now it is Grosvenor with his cult of the pure and simple. "To appreciate it, it is not necessary to think of anything at all." But Grosvenor wants Patience, and has little interest in the love-sick maidens. Bunthorne and Lady Jane now get together and evolve a plot to put an end to the dominance of the idyllic poet. Grosvenor, under threat of Bunthorne's curse, will be commanded to cut his hair and become commonplace.

Meanwhile aestheticism has invaded the army. The Dragoons, determined to win back their sweethearts, abandon their scarlet uniforms, which were formerly "as successful in the Courts of Venus as on the field of Mars", and appear in aesthetic garb, walking in stiff, constrained and angular attitudes—a grotesque exaggeration of the attitudes adopted by Bunthorne. Grosvenor, wearied of his assumed affectations, is quite prepared to yield to Bunthorne's threatened demands, and they celebrate their agreement in a rollicking duet in which they give instances of the various types of commonplace young men they propose to emulate:

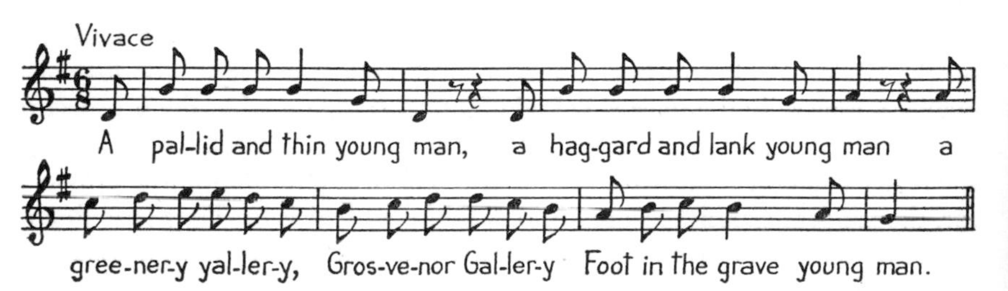

The duet ends with a lively dance and Grosvenor dances off, leaving Bunthorne cavorting alone. He is surprised by Patience, who gazes in astonishment. He then confides to her that he is a changed man. Gone is his moody, uncertain temper. "Henceforth I am mildly cheerful," he tells her. "I have modelled myself upon Mr. Grosvenor. I shall still be aesthetic, but my aestheticism will be of the most pastoral kind." Patience is entranced. "Oh, Reginald," she exclaims, "I'm so happy. It will no longer be a duty to love you, but a pleasure—a rapture—an ecstasy." But a pang of conscience assails her and she recoils. "What is the matter?" asks Bunthorne. Then she tells him that as he is absolutely reformed and henceforth a perfect being, she can never be his. For love, to be pure, must be absolutely unselfish, and there can be nothing unselfish in loving so perfect a being as he has become. So once again Patience gives herself to Archibald Grosvenor, who has now discarded aestheticism and has become such a thoroughly commonplace young man that not even Patience can find an objection to marrying him. The maidens, following Grosvenor's lead, also discard aestheticism and pair off with the military—the Duke taking Lady Jane—and all sing in Finale:

> "Greatly pleased with one another
> To get married we decide,
> Each of us will wed the other,
> NOBODY BE BUNTHORNE'S BRIDE."

Iolanthe
or
The Peer and the Peri

An Entirely New and Original Fairy Opera in Two Acts

Written by W. S. GILBERT

Music by ARTHUR SULLIVAN

First produced on 25th November, 1882, at the Savoy Theatre, London, with George Grossmith as "The Lord Chancellor", Richard Temple as "Strephon", Leonora Braham as "Phyllis" and Jessie Bond as "Iolanthe".

CHARACTERS

THE LORD CHANCELLOR
THE EARL OF MOUNTARARAT
EARL TOLOLLER
PRIVATE WILLIS, *of the Grenadier Guards*
STREPHON
QUEEN OF THE FAIRIES
IOLANTHE, *a fairy—Strephon's mother*
CELIA
LEILA
FLETA
PHYLLIS, *an Arcadian shepherdess and ward in chancery*
CHORUS OF DUKES, MARQUISES, EARLS, VISCOUNTS, BARONS AND FAIRIES

Date: between 1700 and 1882.

ACT I

The scene is an Arcadian landscape with a river, traversed by a rustic bridge, running around the stage. As the curtain rises a company of Fairies dance on to the stage to sing an enchanting, gossamer-light fairy chorus:

After the chorus the Fairies lament the absence from their revels of their sister, Iolanthe, who twenty-five years before had been banished from Fairyland for marrying a mortal. She is working out a sentence of penal servitude on her head at the bottom of the river among the frogs. It is a characteristically Gilbertian touch to make the ruler of the delicate Fairies a stolid, portly dame and give her lines to speak like: "Who taught me to curl myself inside a buttercup? Iolanthe. Who taught me to swing upon a cobweb? Iolanthe." The Fairies appeal to their Queen to pardon her and, in a musical invocation of great beauty, Iolanthe is summoned. She rises from the river covered with water-weeds and the Fairies welcome her joyfully. Iolanthe explains that she chose to work out her sentence at the bottom of the river to be near her son, Strephon, and presently he appears and his mother introduces him to his Fairy aunts. Strephon is half a Fairy down to his waist, while his legs are mortal. He is twenty-five and beside him his mother, Iolanthe, being one hundred per cent Fairy, would pass for seventeen.

Strephon is engaged to be married to Phyllis, a ward in chancery, but the Lord Chancellor refuses them permission to marry. So they decide to get married without his consent. Strephon is fearful of losing his Phyllis, for already half the House of Lords, headed by Lord Mountararat and Lord Tololler, are sighing at her feet, and the Lord Chancellor himself has cast an emphatically amorous eye in her direction. As they wander away the music of a march is heard and there enters a procession of Peers, lustily singing:

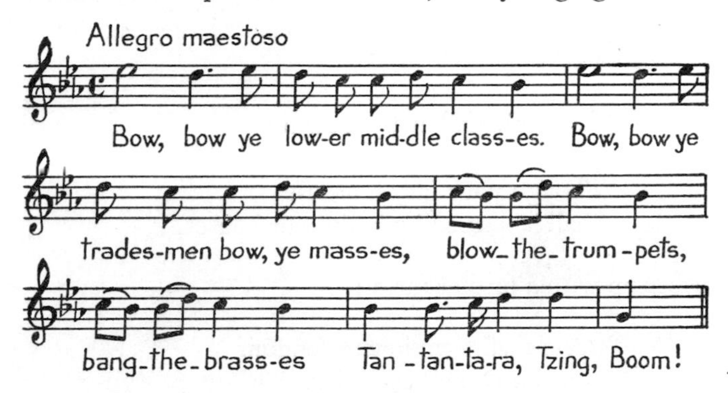

At the conclusion of the chorus the Lord Chancellor enters. The business before the House is to give Phyllis to whichever of the Peers she decides to select as a husband. But when she joins them she refuses them all on the ground of rank, telling them

"Nay, tempt me not
To rank I'll not be bound.
In lowly cot
Alone is virtue found."

Lord Tololler attempts to reason with her:

"Spare us the bitter pain
of stern denials,
Nor with low-born disdain
augment our trials.
Hearts just as pure and fair
may beat in Belgrave Square
As in the lowly air of Seven Dials."

But Phyllis is adamant in her determination to stick to Strephon. As the Lord Chancellor persists in forbidding their marriage, Strephon appeals for help to his mother and Iolanthe promises to enlist the Fairy Queen's aid.

Now Phyllis knows nothing about Strephon's fairy origin, nor has she ever met Iolanthe. So when she sees Strephon in intimate conversation with a young woman who looks about seventeen, she is seized with violent jealousy. The malicious Peers assist in estranging the pair by pointing out that the young person cannot possibly be, as she claims, Strephon's mother. Phyllis turns on Strephon, telling him that they must part for ever, and offers her hand to Lords Tololler and Mountararat, telling them to decide which of them she is to marry. At this critical juncture Fairy music is heard, as the Fairy Queen with her attendants comes to Strephon's aid. He appeals to her to set Phyllis' mind at rest by confirming that Iolanthe is his mother, and the Fairy Queen obliges.

The Lord Chancellor, however, defies Fairy authority, and the Fairy Queen in her wrath decides to revenge herself by sending Strephon into Parliament. "Backed by our supreme authority, he'll command a large majority." She tells the Lord Chancellor that

"Every bill and every measure
That may gratify his pleasure,
Though your fury it arouses
Shall be passed by both your houses,"

and she finishes up with a further threat:

"Peers shall teem in christendom
and a Duke's exalted station
be attainable by competitive examination."

The Peers cry out in horror, and they and the Fairies launch into a rousing Finale with alternative lyrics:

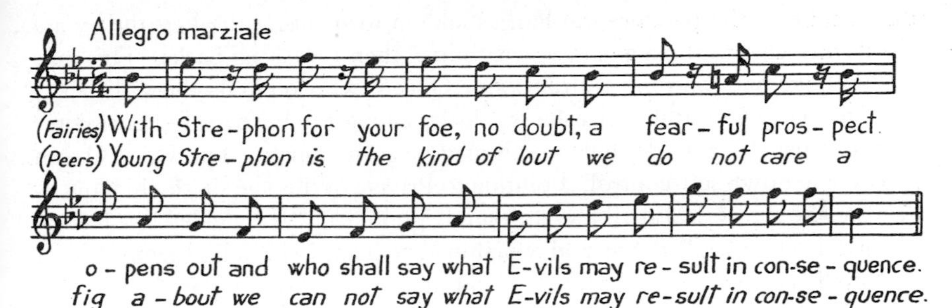

ACT II

The scene is Palace Yard, Westminster. Westminster Hall is on the left and on the right the Clock Tower. Private Willis, B Company, First Grenadier Guards, is on sentry duty beneath the full moon. Private Willis is a philosopher, and to wile away the time he ruminates on the workings of Providence which contrive

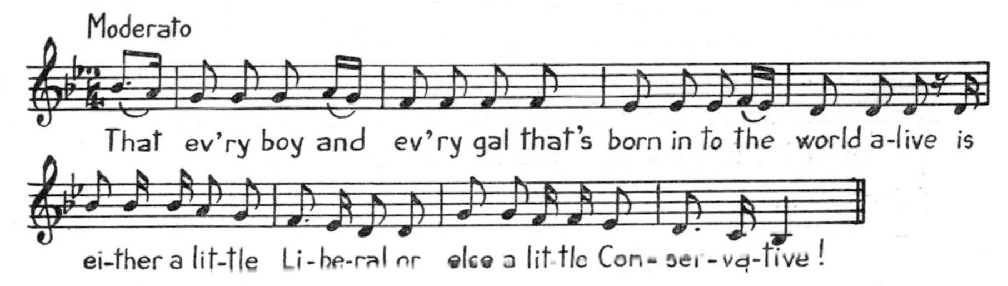

His meditations are interrupted by the entrance of the Fairies, and hard on their heels follow the Peers, who come out of Westminster Hall. The Peers are in a rage. In Parliament Strephon is playing the deuce with everything, and they are particularly vexed at his Bill to throw the Peerage open to competitive examination. The Fairies claim gleefully that they can influence members and compel them to vote just as Strephon wishes them to. "This comes of women interfering in politics," complains Lord Mountararat. "It so happens that if there is an institution in Great Britain which is not susceptible of any improvement at all, it is the House of Peers." And he sings a stirring patriotic song:

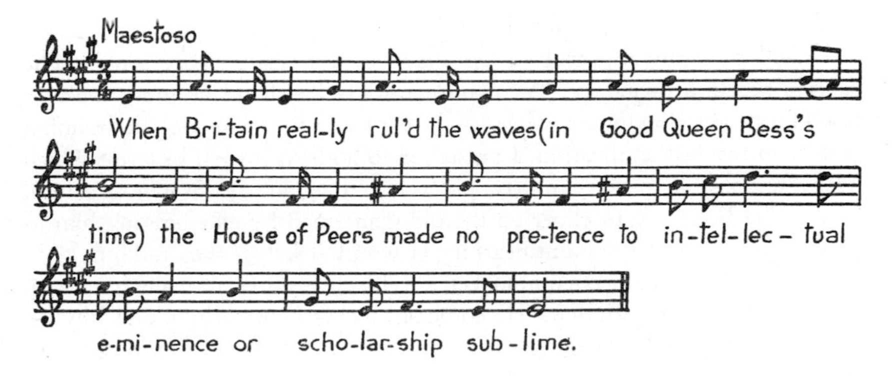

But in spite of the pleasure the Fairies take in tormenting the Peers, they are greatly attracted to them and gaze wistfully at their retreating backs. This calls forth rebuke and warning by the Fairy Queen, who reminds them that it is death to marry a mortal. Iolanthe was lucky enough to have her sentence commuted to penal servitude, but not all may be so fortunate. The Fairy Queen boasts of her own self-control. Pointing to Private Willis she singles him out as "a man whose physical attributes are simply godlike". "If I yielded to a natural impulse I should fall down and worship that man," she tells them. "But I mortify this inclination," she finishes, and sings a song boasting, in the verse, of her impregnable defences, and calling, in the refrain, on some higher power to quench the ardour of her amorous desires. (On the first night in November, 1882, Alice Barnett electrified the audience by turning directly to that part of the house where was seated Captain Eyre Shaw, Head of the London Fire Brigade, and lodging her appeal directly to him):

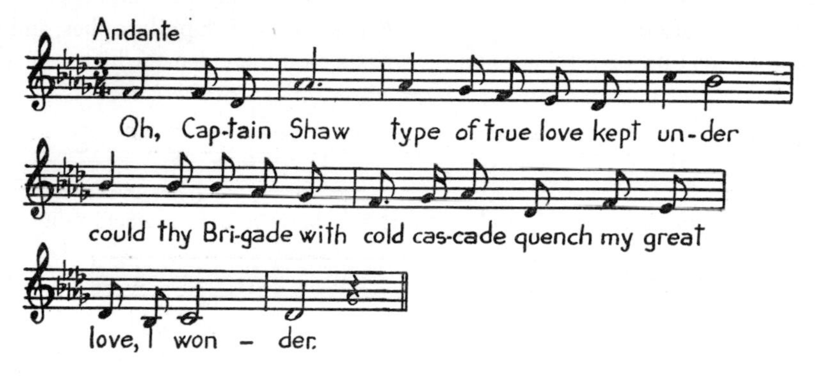

The Earls of Mountararat and Tololler now renew their efforts to persuade Phyllis to make up her mind which of them she means to marry. But Phyllis, who still hankers after Strephon, tells them to settle the question between them and that she will marry the chosen suitor. The two Earls discuss the matter but agree that the decision, whatever it be, would result in the end of a beautiful friendship. The sacred ties of friendship are paramount, and they both relinquish Phyllis. The Lord Chancellor then appears. He is desperately in love with Phyllis. "Love, unrequited, robs me of my rest," he complains. "Love, nightmare-like, lies heavy on my chest and weaves itself into my midnight slumbers." This is followed by one of Gilbert's most masterly lyrics set with vivid, imaginative skill by Sullivan—truly a nightmare of a song in every sense. The Chancellor is in a quandary. As a suitor for Phyllis' hand he must apply to himself for permission to marry her. As he confesses to the Peers, "In declining to entertain my last application, I presumed to address myself in terms which render it impossible for me ever to apply to myself again. It was a most painful scene." The Peers try to cheer up the old gentleman by encouraging him to approach himself again. "Faint heart never won fair lady," they tell him.

Free of her aristocratic encumbrances, Phyllis determines to make it up with Strephon, to his great content. He confesses to his Fairy origin, and Phyllis, while she scolds him for keeping it from her, reflects that it is better to have half a mortal you *do* love than half a dozen you don't. He introduces Phyllis to his mother, and begs Iolanthe to plead with the Lord Chancellor to allow their marriage. Iolanthe, much agitated, at first refuses. "You know not what you ask," she tells Strephon. Finally she confesses that the Lord Chancellor is her husband and Strephon's father. At that moment the Chancellor appears, jubilant. After a severe struggle he has reluctantly—most reluctantly—given himself permission to marry Phyllis. Covering her face with a veil, Iolanthe kneels at his feet and begs him to let the memory of his dead wife plead for her son. With the knowledge that she is risking death or banishment, Iolanthe then reveals her identity, and the Fairy Queen tells her that she has once again broken her vows and must die. But the Fairies intervene. "If Iolanthe must die, so must we all; for as she has sinned, so have we. We are all Fairy duchesses, marchionesses, countesses, viscountesses and baronesses." This puts the Fairy Queen in a difficulty. They have all incurred death—but she cannot slaughter the lot. To her aid comes the Lord Chancellor. As an old equity draughtsman, he proposes altering the Fairy laws to read that "Every Fairy shall die who *doesn't* marry a mortal." His proposal is adopted, and to conform to the new law the Fairy Queen, too, must marry a mortal and Private Willis obliges. Since by the introduction of Strephon's Bill all future Peers are to be recruited from persons of intelligence, all the Peers join the Fairy ranks, for "I really don't see what use WE are down here," says Lord Mountararat. And the Fairy Queen cries: "Good! then away to Fairyland."

Princess Ida
or
Castle Adamant

A Respectful Operatic Per-version of TENNYSON'S Princess
in Three Acts

Written by W. S. GILBERT

Music by ARTHUR SULLIVAN

First produced on 5th January, 1884, at the Savoy Theatre, London, with George Grossmith as "King Gama", Rutland Barrington as "King Hildebrand", Rosina Brandram as "Lady Blanche" and Leonora Braham as "Princess Ida".

CHARACTERS

KING HILDEBRAND
HILARION, *his son*
CYRIL, FLORIAN } *Hilarion's friends*
KING GAMA
GURON, ARAE, SCYTHIUS } *his sons*
PRINCESS IDA, *Gama's daughter*
LADY BLANCHE, *Professor of Abstract Science*
LADY PSYCHE, *Professor of Humanities*
MELISSA, *Lady Blanche's daughter*
SACHARISSA, CHLOE, ADA } *girl graduates*
CHORUS OF SOLDIERS, COURTIERS, GIRL GRADUATES, DAUGHTERS OF THE PLOUGH, ETC.

ACT I

The scene is a pavilion attached to King Hildebrand's palace. Armed with opera-glasses, binoculars and telescopes, soldiers and courtiers are keeping watchful eyes on the far horizon as they sing:

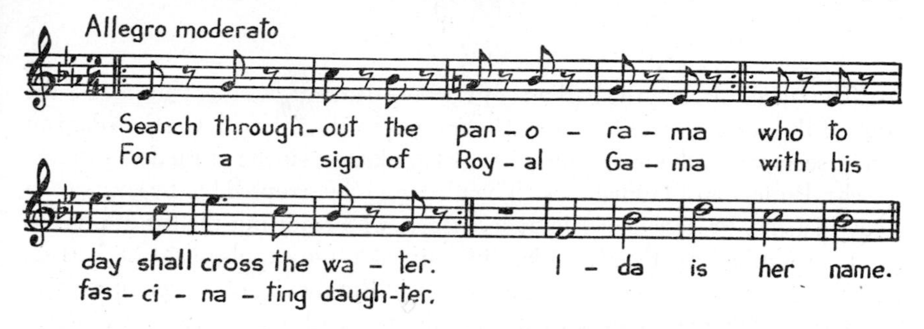

At the early age of two, Hilarion, the son of King Hildebrand, was betrothed to Ida, daughter of a rival monarch, King Gama, and on the day the curtain rises King Gama is due to bring Princess Ida to the Court of King Hildebrand for her marriage to Prince Hilarion. Hildebrand makes it quite clear that if Gama fails to appear with the Princess there will be trouble, while Hilarion speculates on his bride and wonders "what transmutations have been conjured by the silent alchemy of twenty years". King Gama arrives at Hildebrand's palace with his three sons, but without Princess Ida. He has a crafty character and is "a twisted monster—all awry—as though Dame Nature, angry with her work, had crumpled it in fitful petulance". Malicious and tactless, he considers himself a genuine philanthropist and he makes a practice of pointing out people's faults to their faces. He boasts that:

> "To everybody's prejudice I know a thing or two,
> I can tell a woman's age in half a minute and I do."

On his arrival King Gama announces that Princess Ida has decided to retire to Castle Adamant, one of her father's many country houses, and there carry on a University for Women, consisting of a hundred undergraduates. The curriculum is to be devoted to the study of Women's Rights. Princess Ida also enlarges to her girls on the enormity of Man:

> "Man is coarse and Man is plain,
> Man is more or less insane,
> Man's a ribald, Man's a rake,
> Man is Nature's sole mistake."

When Hildebrand is told that Ida has no intention of keeping her troth to marry Hilarion, he declares his determination to storm Castle Adamant and deal with the lady. Gama and his three sons will in the meantime be held as hostages in custody. Hilarion and his two friends, Cyril and Florian, are greatly excited at the prospect of making the acquaintance of a hundred girls—"a hundred ecstasies!"—and they plan to invade Castle Adamant on their own. They will use no force. "Nature has armed us for the war we wage," they declare. The curtain falls on King Gama and his sons in irons being marched off to prison to a military tune.

ACT II

Act Two takes place in the gardens of Castle Adamant. A river runs across the back of the stage, crossed by a rustic bridge. In the distance Castle Adamant can be seen and in the foreground are girl graduates, sitting at the feet of Lady Psyche, Professor of Humanities. Their lecture is interrupted by the entrance of Lady Blanche, Professor of Abstract Science, who reads out the list of punishments proscribed by Princess Ida. They include the expulsion of Sacharissa, caught in the possession of a set of chessmen. "But they're only men of wood," she pleads. "They're men with whom you give each other mate. And that's enough," is the stern retort. Another transgressor is Chloe, who has been caught making a sketch of a perambulator, shameless girl! Princess Ida then arrives to give her inaugural address to the new graduates, preceded by a prayer to the Goddess Minerva:

After the address the girl graduates withdraw for a lecture on abstract philosophy from Lady Blanche, and as soon as the stage is empty there appear, climbing over the wall and creeping cautiously among the trees and rocks, Hilarion, Cyril and Florian. Finding three sets of collegiate robes, they delightedly put them on, and mince about as "three lovely lady graduates". When Princess Ida approaches they apply to be allowed to join the University and are admitted by the unsuspecting Head. The Princess expresses the hope that they will spend a happy time in Castle Adamant, and Cyril enthusiastically tells her:

"If as you say
A hundred lovely maidens wait within
To welcome us with smiles and open arms,
I think there's very little doubt we shall."

Later, when the Princess has withdrawn, Lady Psyche appears. She is Florian's sister and, making himself known to her, he introduces Hilarion and Cyril. She and her friend Melissa are enchanted with the young men and promise not to give them away, and they also persuade Lady Blanche to befriend the young men, telling her that Hilarion is to be married to Princess Ida and that then Lady Blanche, if she plays her cards properly, will be able to succeed her as Head of the University. On the strength of it Lady Blanche and Melissa sing a graceful duet:

So the three young men are received into the University as girl graduates in all good faith. A picnic lunch is now served, and unfortunately Cyril, who partakes freely of the wine, becomes rather rowdy and obstreperous, to the manifest disapproval of Princess Ida. In spite of attempts by Hilarion and Florian to restrain him, he insists on singing a most unsuitable song about kissing, with the refrain:

Cyril's infamous behaviour provokes a quarrel among the young men and it quickly becomes apparent that these are no girls. Princess Ida runs on to the rustic bridge, calling to the girls to save themselves from the man-monsters, but, losing her balance, she falls into the stream. Hilarion dives in to rescue her and brings her safely to dry land. The girls rejoice that their chief is saved and are loud in their praises of Hilarion's courage. But Princess Ida will have no mercy on "men in women's clothes", and in punishment for their sacrilegious intrusion, Hilarion and his two friends are bound by girl attendants and led away.

Castle Adamant is now stormed by King Hildebrand and his soldiers. He demands that Princess Ida yield immediately and consent to marry Hilarion or it will be the worse for her. Her brothers, whom Hildebrand has brought with him, plead with her to yield, telling her that Hildebrand has threatened to hang them unless he gets satisfaction. Hildebrand substantiates his threat, telling her to

> "Release Hilarion then and be his bride
> or you'll incur the guilt of fratricide."

But the Princess is unyielding and the curtain falls on a picture of her standing, facing the King and his soldiers, surrounded by her kneeling girls, a symbol of defiance.

ACT III

The scene is the outer walls and courtyard of Castle Adamant. The curtain rises to disclose Melissa, Sacharissa and other ladies armed with battle-axes and swearing:

"Death to the invader!
Strike a deadly blow,
As an old crusader
Struck his Paynim foe!"

But, in spite of Princess Ida's inspiring leadership, when it comes to actual bloodshed the girls prove not to be the intrepid Amazons they believed themselves. Sacharissa, the lady surgeon, blenches at the idea of coping with the wounded; Chloe confesses that the lady Fusiliers have left their rifles in the armoury "for fear that in the heat and turmoil of the fight they might go off!" Ada, the bandmistress, reports that "the band do not feel well and can't come out today". Princess Ida angrily orders the girls to leave her, declaring: "I'll meet these men alone, since all my women have deserted me."

King Gama and Ida's three brothers now crave audience, and Gama adds his plea to his daughter to yield to Hildebrand's demands, telling her of the tortures which Hildebrand inflicts upon him. "I haven't anything to grumble at," he says pathetically. "He finds out what particular meats I love and gives me them. He suffers none to thwart my simplest plan and gives strict orders none should contradict me! He's made my life a curse." Melted by her old father's suffering, Ida yields. Hilarion, Cyril and Florian are led in, still in their ladies' academic robes. King Gama makes insulting fun of them, rouses their tempers and the scene ends with a challenge from Gama to fight his three sons, who, to a suitably Handelian air, slowly remove their suits of armour:

A desperate fight follows, which finishes with Gama's sons lying wounded on the ground and Hilarion, Cyril and Florian standing over them. Princess Ida and the maidens now formally yield to King Hildebrand. She resigns her position as Head of the University to Lady Blanche, and holds out her hand to her betrothed.

"Take me, Hilarion," [she tells him.]
"We will walk the world,
Yoked in all exercise of noble end!
And so through those dark gates across the wild
That no man knows! Indeed, I love thee. Come."

The Mikado
or
The Town of Titipu

An Entirely New and Original Japanese Opera in Two Acts

Written by W. S. GILBERT

Music by ARTHUR SULLIVAN

First production on 14th March, 1885, at the Savoy Theatre, London, with Richard Temple as "The Mikado", Rosina Brandram as "Katisha", Durward Lely as "Nanki-Poo", Leonora Braham as "Yum-Yum", George Grossmith as "Ko-Ko" and Rutland Barrington as "Pooh-Bah".

CHARACTERS

THE MIKADO OF JAPAN
NANKI-POO, *his son, disguised as a wandering minstrel and in love with Yum-Yum*
KO-KO, *Lord High Executioner of Titipu*
POOH-BAH, *Lord High Everything Else*
PISH-TUSH, *a noble Lord*
YUM-YUM, PITTI-SING, PEEP-BO — *three sisters—wards of Ko-Ko*
KATISHA, *an elderly lady in love with Nanki-Poo*
CHORUS OF SCHOOL-GIRLS, NOBLES, GUARDS AND COOLIES

ACT I

The scene is the courtyard of Ko-Ko's palace in Titipu. Nanki-Poo, son of "The great and virtuous Mikado", has fled from Court to avoid marriage with the termagant Katisha. Elderly and ugly, she describes herself as "an acquired taste", claiming that beauty resides not in the face alone. "I have a shoulder-blade that is a miracle of loveliness," she boasts. "People come miles to see it." In the disguise of a second trombone, however, Nanki-Poo has made the acquaintance of the lovely Yum-Yum and fallen in love with her, though aware that she is officially engaged to her guardian Ko-Ko, an ex-tailor. He had later heard that this Ko-Ko had been condemned to death for flirting, but now to his dismay Nanki-Poo learns that Ko-Ko has been reprieved and raised to the exalted rank of Lord High Executioner, the highest rank a citizen can attain, and that this very day Yum-Yum is returning from school to be married to her guardian. As the Nobleman Pooh-Bah tells him:

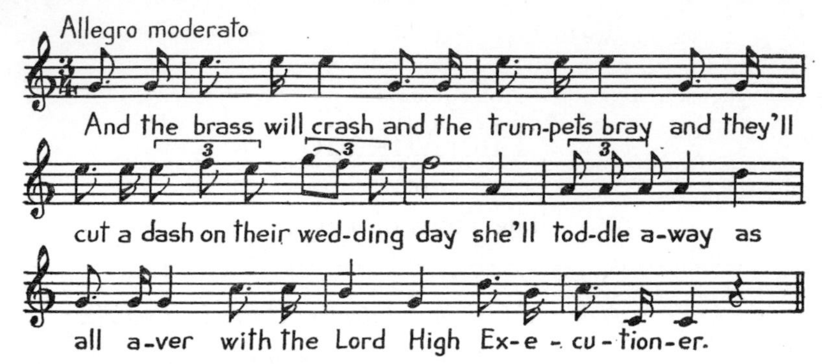

Ko-Ko duly arrives, and after being welcomed by the populace he proceeds to consult Pooh-Bah about the expense of his forthcoming wedding.

Pooh-Bah, who combines the offices of First Lord of the Treasury, Lord Chief Justice, Commander-in-Chief, Lord High Admiral, Master of the Buckhounds, Groom of the Backstairs, Archbishop of Titipu, and Lord Mayor, both acting and elect, is one of Gilbert's most effective creations, and, in the scene where Ko-Ko wishes to plan the expenses of his forthcoming marriage to Yum-Yum, the following dialogue occurs:

Pooh-Bah: Of course, as First Lord of the Treasury, I could propose a special vote that would cover all expenses, if it were not that, as leader of the Opposition, it would be my duty to resist it tooth and nail. Or, as Paymaster-General, I could so cook the accounts that, as Lord High Auditor, I should never discover the fraud. But then, as Archbishop of Titipu, it would be my duty to denounce my own dishonesty and give myself into my own custody, as First Commissioner of Police.

Ko-Ko: That's extremely awkward.

Pooh-Bah: I don't say that all these people couldn't be squared, but it is right to tell you that I shouldn't be sufficiently degraded in my own estimation unless I was insulted with a very considerable bribe.

Pooh-Bah holds Ko-Ko at his mercy and he knows it.

Yum-Yum now arrives with her school-friends, and with Pitti-Sing and Peep-Bo she sings a trio:

Nanki-Poo succeeds in getting Yum-Yum to himself, and confesses to her that he is the son of the Mikado and has fled from Court to avoid marrying Katisha and that he loves only her. Yum-Yum reminds him that flirting is now punishable by death. "If it were not for the law," they tell each other, "we should be gazing into each other's eyes (they gaze) with our arms round each other's waists" (they embrace). "But," finishes Nanki-Poo, "as you are engaged to Ko-Ko, this (kissing her) is what I'll never do." Ko-Ko now receives bad news in the form of a letter from the Mikado, which reads: "The Mikado is struck by the fact that no executions have taken place in Titipu for a year, and decrees that unless somebody is beheaded within one month, the post of Lord High Executioner shall be abolished and the city reduced to the rank of village." There is no help for it, somebody will have to be executed. The question is, who it shall be? Pooh-Bah unkindly tells Ko-Ko that as he is already under sentence of death for flirting he is the obvious choice. But Ko-Ko protests that self-decapitation is both difficult and dangerous and proposes that Pooh-Bah volunteer as substitute. But neither Ko-Ko, Pooh-Bah nor Pish-Tush relish a prospect which would condemn them to:

Coming accidentally upon Nanki-Poo, who, rope in hand, is about to commit suicide in despair at losing Yum-Yum, Ko-Ko proposes to Nanki-Poo that he shall live like a fighting-cock for a month at his expense, provided he consent at the end of the month to be beheaded by the Public Executioner. Nanki-Poo agrees to this proposal, provided he be allowed to marry Yum-Yum immediately. "How can I consent to Yum-Yum marrying you, if I am to marry her myself?" asks Ko-Ko. "My good friend, she'll be a widow in a month, and you can marry her then," is Nanki-Poo's reply. Ko-Ko finally agrees, and preparations for the wedding are in progress when the jealous Katisha appears. She does her best to get a hearing and to betray Nanki-Poo's identity, but in vain. In a rage she retires to report conditions in Titipu to the Mikado.

ACT II

In Ko-Ko's garden Yum-Yum is seated at her bridal toilet, surrounded by her maidens. Looking at herself in the glass she remarks: "Yes, I am indeed beautiful. Sometimes I sit and wonder, in my artless Japanese way, why I am so much more attractive than anybody in the world? Nature is lovely and rejoices in her loveliness," and she sings:

Nanki-Poo tenderly comforts his sorrowful bride at the prospect of losing him after one short month, but Yum-Yum is placed in a quandary when Ko-Ko discovers that, when a married man is beheaded, by the Mikado's law his wife must be buried alive. "When I agreed to marry you, my own, I had no idea, my pet, that I should have to be buried alive in a month," she tells Nanki-Poo. "It does make a difference, doesn't it?" Nanki-Poo realises that he must release Yum-Yum to marry Ko-Ko, and the three of them sing a trio:

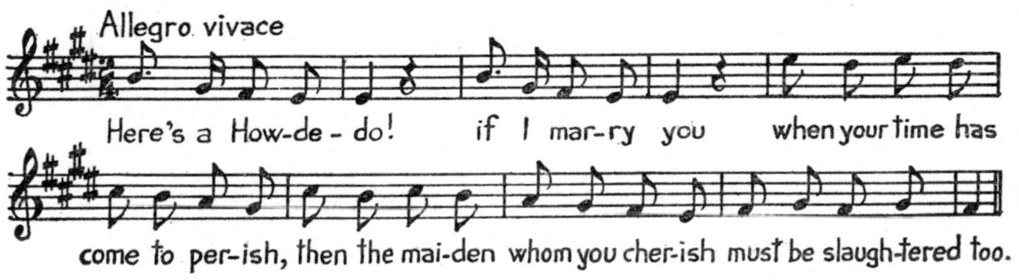

While they are arguing, the approach of the Mikado is announced, and he comes on accompanied by Katisha. The purpose of his visit is to make sure that his orders regarding an execution have been carried out. When the Mikado's arrival is observed, Ko-Ko arranges hurriedly with Pooh-Bah, in consideration of a "gross insult" in the form of a bribe to all the offices invested in Pooh-Bah's person, to draw up a false writ of the completed execution, naming Nanki-Poo as victim. What, then, is the consternation of the executioner and his allies to find that Nanki-Poo is the son of the Mikado and that according to law his death is punishable by immersion in boiling oil! It is cold comfort to the signers of Nanki-Poo's death-warrant to be told that it is really too bad that the law did not take into account the possibility of such a death occuring in ignorance of the victim's true identity. They must boil to conform to the statute, though the Mikado undertakes to have the Act altered before the next session. There is only one thing for it now. Nanki-Poo must come to life. But when Nanki-Poo hears that Katisha has arrived with his father, he informs Ko-Ko that he will only reappear if Ko-Ko undertakes to marry Katisha. Nanki-Poo and Yum-Yum are already man and wife—married by Pooh-Bah in his capacity as Archbishop of Titipu—in spite of the risk of Yum-Yum's being buried alive; but only when Katisha is safely married will existence for Nanki-Poo be as welcome as the flowers in spring. Ko-Ko, however, takes a less cheerful view as he and Nanki-Poo sing this famous duet:

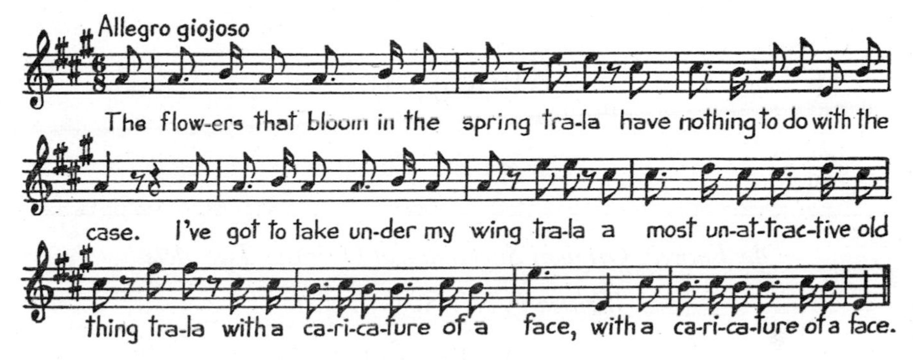

Ko-Ko is about to follow Nanki-Poo's advice when Katisha recognises in him the "miscreant who robbed her of her love". "Where shall I find another?" she asks him, and "Here! here!" answers Ko-Ko, throwing himself at her feet. "Accept my love or I perish on the spot." And he melts Katisha's heart with the sad little tale of Tit-willow who died of a broken heart:

With Katisha safely provided for, Nanki-Poo comes to life, presents Yum-Yum to the Mikado as his daughter-in-law elect, and, as the Mikado himself declares: "Nothing could possibly be more satisfactory."

Ruddigore

or

The Witch's Curse

An Entirely Original Supernatural Opera in Two Acts

Written by W. S. GILBERT

Music by ARTHUR SULLIVAN

First produced on 22nd January, 1887, at the Savoy Theatre, London, with George Grossmith as "Robin", Rutland Barrington as "Sir Despard Murgatroyd", Leonora Braham as "Rose Maybud", Jessie Bond as "Mad Margaret" and Rosina Brandram as "Dame Hannah".

CHARACTERS

Mortals

ROBIN OAKAPPLE, *a young farmer*
RICHARD DAUNTLESS, *his foster-brother, a Man-of-War's-man*
SIR DESPARD MURGATROYD, *of Ruddigore, a wicked baronet*
OLD ADAM GOODHEART, *Robin's faithful servant*
ROSE MAYBUD, *a village maiden*
MAD MARGARET
DAME HANNAH, *Rose's aunt*

Ghosts

SIR RUPERT MURGATROYD, *the first Baronet*
SIR JASPER MURGATROYD, *the third Baronet*
SIR LIONEL MURGATROYD, *the sixth Baronet*
SIR CONRAD MURGATROYD, *the twelfth Baronet*
SIR DESMOND MURGATROYD, *the sixteenth Baronet*
SIR GILBERT MURGATROYD, *the eighteenth Baronet*
SIR MERVYN MURGATROYD, *the twentieth Baronet*
SIR RODERIC MURGATROYD, *the twenty-first Baronet*
CHORUS OF OFFICERS, ANCESTORS AND PROFESSIONAL BRIDESMAIDS

ACT I

A remarkable feature of the Cornish village of Rederring is that it possesses an endowed corps of professional bridesmaids on duty every day from ten to four, ready dressed, in case their services should be needed. They complain, however, that there has been no wedding in the village for at least six months. They suggest to old Dame Hannah that she might marry, but Hannah, the victim of an unhappy girlish romance, is pledged to eternal spinsterhood. She had fallen in love with a young man who courted her under an assumed name but who, on their wedding day, she discovered to be no other than Sir Roderic Murgatroyd, one of the bad Baronets of Ruddigore and the uncle of the man who now bears that title. As a son of that accursed race, he was no husband for an honest girl, and madly as she loved him she left him there and then. The girls crowd round curiously as Dame Hannah tells them the legend of the curse.

"Sir Rupert Murgatroyd, his leisure and his riches
He ruthlessly employed in persecuting witches."

But one of his victims while being burned at the stake laid a dreadful curse upon him: that he and all his line must commit at least one deadly crime each day or perish in agony. And so it has come to pass.

As Hannah finishes her story, her niece, Rose Maybud, arrives. Rose is a foundling. She was discovered in a plated dish-cover hung on the door of the workhouse; her only possessions a change of baby-linen and a book of etiquette, to which, whenever in doubt, she refers. Rose is fond of a young farmer, and when he appears on the scene Hannah leaves the young people together. Now this young farmer, who calls himself Robin Oakapple, is in reality Ruthven Murgatroyd. In dread of the terrible curse, he fled from home, while his younger brother, Despard, believing him to be dead, succeeded to the family title and the curse. Robin is greatly attracted to Rose, but he is too shy to tell her that he loves her. So he pretends to ask her advice as to how he can bring a bashful friend of his to the point of proposing to the girl he loves, in a duet which finishes with oblique encouragement from Rose and a broad hint to her from Robin to meet him half-way.

A stir in the village heralds the arrival of Richard Dauntless, a blue-jacket, on leave. He is Robin's foster-brother and closest friend, and Robin enlists his services to propose to Rose on his behalf. In doing so, however, Richard falls in love with Rose himself, proposes on his own account and is accepted. But when Rose learns the true state of affairs she transfers her affections to the shy and modest Robin, and Richard in pique reveals the identity of Robin, who in consequence has to assume his family title with its terrible curse. Sir Despard Murgatroyd, now free, proposes to Mad Margaret, a poor, crazed creature whose brain has been turned by his previous heartless conduct; while Rose, in horror of the dreadful curse, once more bestows her affections on Richard.

ACT II

The scene is the picture-gallery in Ruddigore Castle. On the walls hang full-length family portraits of the baronets of Ruddigore since the reign of James I, the first being that of Sir Rupert of the legend, and the last that of the deceased Baronet, Sir Roderic. Robin is now in residence as Sir Ruthven Murgatroyd, with his faithful servant, old Adam Goodheart. They are discussing what the crime of today is to be. Robin asks for suggestions, and Adam proposes that, as Richard and Rose have called to ask for Robin's approval of their marriage, he might like to poison their beer. Robin will not hear of such a suggestion and counters with a proposal to tie Richard to a post and curdle his blood by making hideous faces at him, which Adam dismisses as merely rude. Alone before the portraits of his ancestors, Robin confides to them his detestation of his accursed doom and begs to be released from having to commit his daily crime. As he speaks the lights dim, the family portraits become animated and, stepping from their frames, they sing:

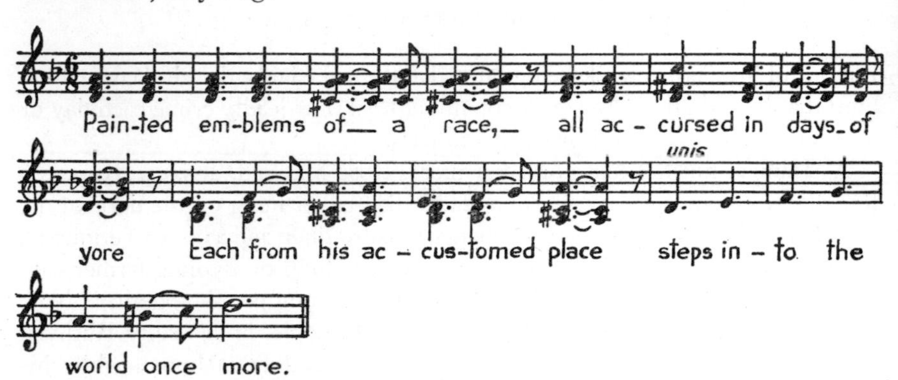

The ancestors make it clear to Robin that he has so far woefully failed to observe the terms of the curse and threaten him that unless he is prepared to set upon a course of evil he will suffer untold agonies. Robin attempts to win their sympathy by pitying their ghostly state, but Sir Roderic, in one of Sullivan's most masterly songs, assures him that the spectres are a jolly crew, especially

Robin attempts to rebel, but Sir Roderic merely exclaims: "Very good, let the agonies commence," and Robin is soon writhing in torment, shrieking for mercy. He is ordered for his next crime to carry off a lady, and after Robin has promised to be obedient in the future, the ancestors return to their frames and change once more into pictures. Adam finds poor Robin in a shattered state and, learning that he has agreed to carry off a lady as today's crime, volunteers to oblige and sets off to find the lady.

While Adam is absent Robin receives a visit from his brother Despard and Mad Margaret, who are now married and devoted to good works. Margaret is a District Visitor and she has discovered a recipe to recover her saner self. Whenever madness threatens she merely repeats the word "Basingstoke" and she is immediately in control of herself. Despard points out to Robin that he must realise that he is morally responsible for all crimes committed during Despard's occupation of his place, and Robin is more than ever determined to find some means of freeing himself from the conditions of the dreadful curse.

Old Adam, who has performed his task of carrying off a lady with more zeal then discretion, now returns to Ruddigore Castle, hustling Dame Hannah. She is in a rage at the treatment she has received and after an angry passage of words attacks Robin with a formidable dagger. Robin in alarm calls to his uncle Roderic for help, and once again Sir Roderic Murgatroyd comes to life and descends from his picture-frame. He denounces Robin for carrying off the lady who was once engaged to him, and turning tenderly to Hannah joins her in a duet about the pretty little flower and the great oak-tree.

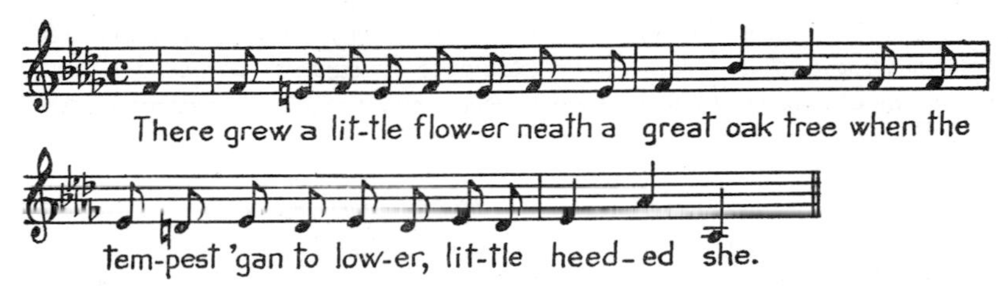

Seeing their happiness in their reunion, Robin has a brilliant idea. He puts it to Sir Roderic that a Baronet of Ruddigore can only die by refusing to commit a crime and that is tantamount to suicide. But suicide is in itself a crime. They ought therefore never to have died at all. Consequently they are all alive. It is obviously impossible to contradict this sound logic of Gilbert's and all ends on the happiest of notes with Rose united to Robin, and Richard to the prettiest of the bridesmaids, while Sir Roderic, assuming his fleshly garb, is reunited to Hannah.

The Yeomen of the Guard

or

The Merryman and His Maid

A New and Original Opera in Two Acts

Written by W. S. GILBERT

Music by ARTHUR SULLIVAN

First produced on 3rd October, 1888, at the Savoy Theatre, London, with George Grossmith as "Jack Point", Courtice Pounds as "Colonel Fairfax", Geraldine Ulmar as "Elsie Maynard", Richard Temple as "Sergeant Meryll" and Rosina Brandram as "Dame Carruthers".

CHARACTERS

SIR RICHARD CHOLMONDELEY, *Lieutenant of the Tower*
COLONEL FAIRFAX, *under sentence of death*
SERGEANT MERYLL, *of the Yeomen of the Guard*
LEONARD MERYLL, *his son*
JACK POINT, *a strolling jester.*
WILFRED SHADBOLT, *head gaoler and assistant tormentor*
THE HEADSMAN
ELSIE MAYNARD, *a strolling singer*
PHOEBE MERYLL, *Sergeant Meryll's daughter*
DAME CARRUTHERS, *Housekeeper to the Tower*
KATE, *her niece*
CHORUS OF YEOMEN OF THE GUARD, GENTLEMEN, CITIZENS, ETC.

ACT I

The scene is Tower Green in the precincts of the Tower of London, and the time is the sixteenth century. The curtain rises on young Phoebe Meryll, seated at her spinning-wheel. As she spins, she sings:

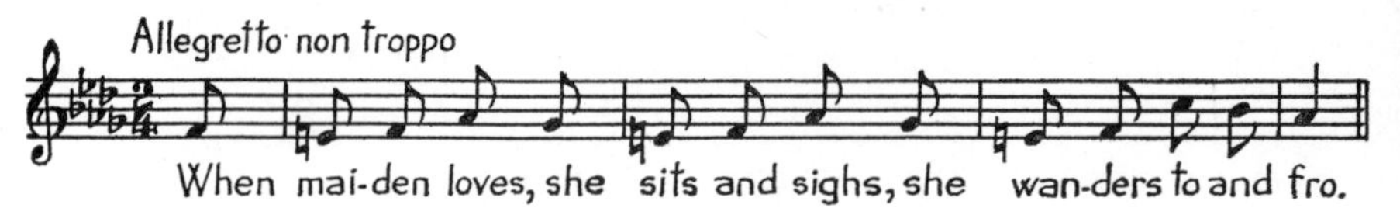

As her song finishes, Wilfred Shadbolt, the saturnine head gaoler, arrives on the scene. He loves Phoebe, though she has little time for him. Their conversation turns to Colonel Fairfax, a brave soldier who lies in the Tower under sentence of death on a baseless charge of sorcery. He is to be beheaded today, and Dame Carruthers passes by on her way to Cold-harbour Tower to prepare cell number 14, in which Colonel Fairfax is to spend his last hour alone with his confessor. Phoebe bursts out in a diatribe against "this wicked Tower, like a cruel giant in a fairy tale, that must be fed with blood, and that blood the bravest in England". Dame Carruthers silences her with a rebuke, and sings a song in praise of the Tower and all that it stands for:

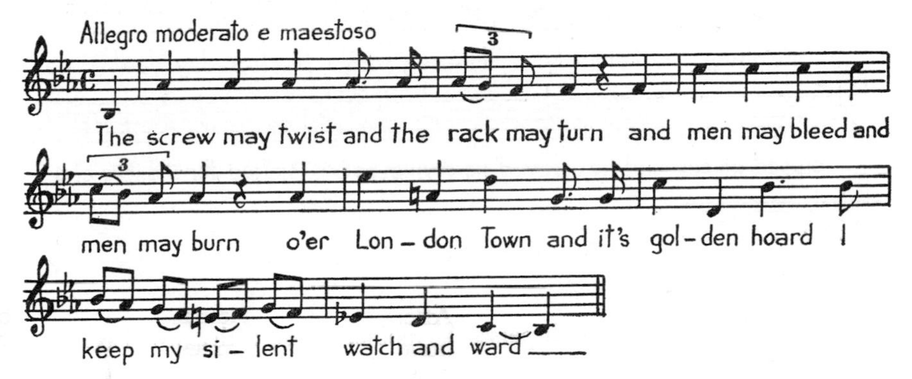

Phoebe asks her father, Sergeant Meryll, whether there is any chance of a reprieve for Colonel Fairfax, and he tells her that her brother Leonard is arriving today to take up his duties as a Yeoman of the Guard, an appointment in reward for valour on the battlefield. As he comes from Windsor, where the Court is, it may be that he will bring the reprieve with him. With Leonard's arrival hope quickly dies and Sergeant Meryll, whose life the imprisoned Colonel has twice saved, contrives a plan whereby this service may be repaid. None of the staff of the Tower knows Leonard, nor has anyone heard of his coming. Sergeant Meryll's plan is to send Leonard into hiding and to let Fairfax, disguised and shorn of his beard, take his place. So Leonard embraces his father and sister and slips away. Colonel Fairfax under escort now passes by on his way to Cold-harbour Tower and meets the Lieutenant of the Tower, an old friend. He greets his comrade in battle, Sergeant Meryll, and comforts Phoebe, who is in tears at his brave bearing in the face of death. "It is easier to die well than to live well," he tells them. "I know for I have tried both." And he sings the well-known ballad:

Fairfax is bent on thwarting his kinsman, Sir Charles Poltwhistle, one of the Secretaries of State. Sir Charles has charged him with sorcery in order that he may succeed to his estate, which he will do provided Fairfax dies unmarried. The Lieutenant of the Tower undertakes to find Fairfax a bride: her dower is to be one hundred crowns. As Fairfax reaches Cold-harbour Tower, Jack Point and Elsie Maynard, two poor strolling players, arrive on Tower Green, followed by a noisy, unruly crowd for whom they perform "The Singing Farce of the Merryman and his Maid" with its haunting refrain:

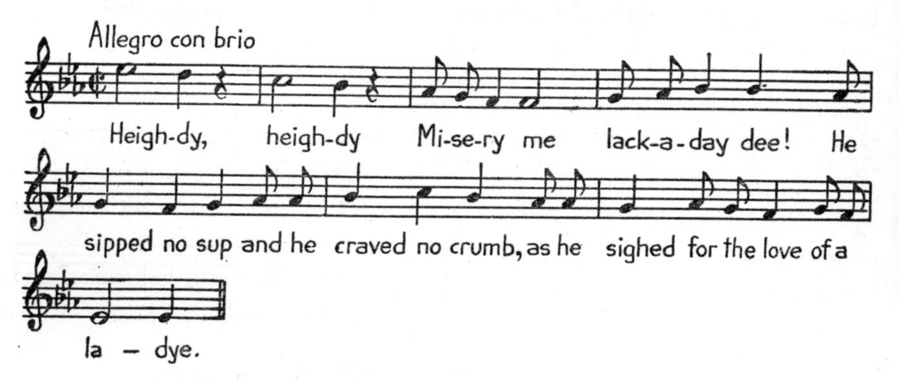

After the song the Lieutenant disperses the rabble. Then, with a promise of one hundred crowns and immediate widowhood, Elsie is easily won over to Fairfax's scheme and is led blindfold to the marriage ceremony.

It is necessary to the success of Sergeant Meryll's plot to rescue Fairfax that he should get possession of the key of his cell surreptitiously from Wilfred Shadbolt. It falls to Phoebe's lot to obtain this. She flatters the silly gaoler so that, gazing into her eyes, he never notices her slyly take the bunch of keys from his waistband and hand them to her father, who enters Cold-harbour Tower unseen by Wilfred. Soon Phoebe has completely turned the love-sick gaoler's head with her tales of how she would love him were she his bride:

During the song Sergeant Meryll returns from the Tower and hands back the keys to Phoebe, who replaces them at Wilfred's girdle entirely unnoticed by him. Presently Fairfax comes out of the Tower. He has shaved off his beard and moustache and is dressed in Yeoman's uniform. He is introduced to his fellow Yeomen by Sergeant Meryll, who simulates an aged father's pride in his gallant son, and he receives a rousing welcome from them and a hug from Phoebe.

Now it is time for the prisoner's execution, and the bell of St. Peter's begins to toll. The crowd assembles, the block is brought out and the Headsman takes his place. The Yeomen of the Guard form up. The Lieutenant enters and takes his place and orders Fairfax and two other Yeomen to bring out the prisoner to execution. As all are awaiting the prisoner's appearance, Fairfax and the other two Yeomen run out of the Tower in great excitement with tidings that he has escaped. The alarm is given, Shadbolt is arrested, Elsie faints in the arms of the supposed Leonard Meryll, and all the Yeomen and the populace rush off in different directions to hunt for the fugitive.

ACT II

The scene is Tower Green by moonlight, and the old Tower by night bears an even grimmer aspect than by day. Shadbolt has been released, but he is still under suspicion of having connived at Fairfax's escape and is determined to vindicate his character. Jack Point, too, is in low spirits, for he is in love with Elsie and it now seems that she is married to Fairfax for life, not for Death. These two now get together and evolve a plot: they pretend to shoot an imaginary Fairfax as he is attempting to swim across the Thames. A shot is fired and Shadbolt's "cock and bull" story, with Jack Point's corroboration, is accepted by the populace, who hail him as a hero and carry him off shoulder-high. Elsie Maynard meanwhile is recovering in the care of Dame Carruthers. The old lady has noticed that she has a liking for Leonard Meryll and warns the supposed Leonard (Fairfax) to beware of her, for it appears that she is a married woman. Dame Carruthers' niece, Kate, has reported that she was sitting by Elsie's bedside as she was sleeping and that in her sleep "she moaned and groaned and turned this way and that way—and 'How shall I marry one I have never seen?' quoth she—then 'Is it certain he will die in an hour?' quoth she—then 'I love him not and yet I am his wife'." Fairfax is delighted by the discovery that he is married to the winsome Elsie (for they were both married blindfolded) and when she hears of Colonel Fairfax's "death" she is quite ready to respond to the handsome "Leonard Meryll's" ardent declarations of love. But Jack Point is broken-hearted at Elsie's obvious preference, and Phoebe, who has a very soft spot for Fairfax, is consumed with jealousy. Phoebe's jealousy causes her, in an unguarded moment, to reveal to Wilfred Shadbolt that she loves the man who is to marry Elsie Maynard. In a flash Shadbolt realises that this man cannot be Phoebe's brother and must be Fairfax in disguise. Turning the situation to his advantage, he extracts a promise from Phoebe that she will marry him. Sergeant Meryll also has to promise marriage to Dame Carruthers as the price of her silence, when the real Leonard arrives with a belated reprieve for the prisoner. Fairfax is then able to reveal himself in dramatic fashion to his wife, now wooed and won, while poor Jack Point, a pathetic figure, falls insensible at the feet of his adored Elsie as the curtain falls.

The Gondoliers
or
The King of Barataria

An Entirely Original Comic Opera in Two Acts

Written by W. S. Gilbert

Music by Arthur Sullivan

First produced on 7th December, 1889, at the Savoy Theatre, London, with Frank Wyatt as "The Duke of Plaza-Toro", Courtice Pounds as "Marco", Rutland Barrington as "Giuseppe", Rosina Brandram as "The Duchess of Plaza-Toro" and Decima Moore as "Casilda".

Characters

THE DUKE OF PLAZA-TORO, *a Grandee of Spain*
LUIZ, *his attendant*
DON ALHAMBRA DEL BOLERO, *the Grand Inquisitor*
MARCO PALMIERI, GIUSEPPE PALMIERI } *Venetian gondoliers*
THE DUCHESS OF PLAZA-TORO
CASILDA, *her daughter*
GIANETTA, TESSA } *Contadine*
INEZ, *the King's foster-mother*
CHORUS OF GONDOLIERS AND CONTADINE, MEN-AT-ARMS, HERALDS AND PAGES

ACT I

In the piazetta in Venice one summer morning a group of pretty girls are busy, each tying a bouquet of roses. The flowers are for the two handsomest Gondoliers in Venice, Marco and Giuseppe Palmieri, who have declared their intention of today selecting two brides. The other Gondoliers protest at such favouritism, but though the girls insist that Marco and Giuseppe shall have first pick, they refuse to be discouraged and sing a joyous song on the pleasures of life in a gondola:

Marco and Giuseppe arrive, and their first duet, with flattering responses from the girls, is sung entirely in Italian. Sullivan's typically Southern-sounding melody gives it an air of complete reality.

Marco and Giuseppe tell the girls that all are so pretty, they really do not care to declare a preference but will capture their brides in a game of Blind-man's-buff. In an enchanting musical version of the game their eyes are bandaged, and Marco captures Gianetta and Giuseppe catches Tessa. The scene ends with the two couples dancing off to be married, followed by all the Gondoliers and Contadine.

A gondola now arrives at the steps of the piazetta and from it alight the Duke of Plaza-Toro, the Duchess, their daughter Casilda, and their royal suite of one Luiz, who carries a drum, and who follows the impecunious Duke and Duchess for love of their daughter. Casilda, however, is intended for a throne, having at the age of six months been married to the infant heir to the kingdom of Barataria. But shortly after the ceremony, the Duke tells her, the Monarch himself "abandoned the creed of his forefathers and became a Wesleyan Minister of the most bigoted and persecuting type. The Grand Inquisitor, determined that the innovation should not be perpetuated in Barataria, caused your smiling and unconscious husband to be stolen and conveyed to Venice. A fortnight since, the Monarch and all his Wesleyan Court were killed in an insurrection, and we are here to ascertain the whereabouts of your husband and to hail you, our daughter, as Her Majesty, the reigning Queen of Barataria." The penniless Duke goes off to interview the Grand Inquisitor, leaving Casilda and Luiz alone for a moment of stolen love and a beautiful duet:

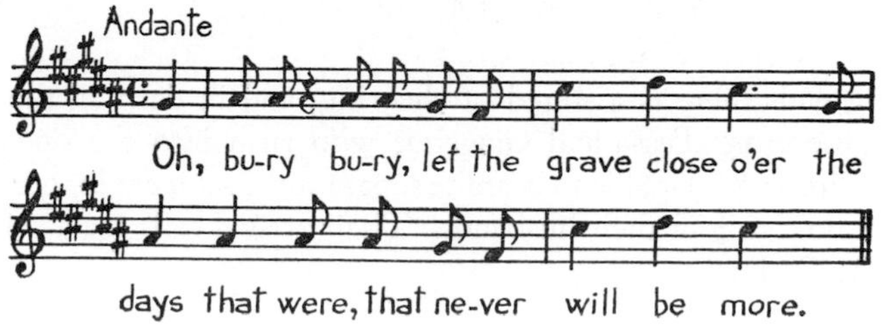

The Grand Inquisitor is unable to produce the heir to the throne, but he is convinced that he is in Venice plying the trade of a Gondolier, for as a baby he was stolen and given into the care of a certain Gondolier, Baptisto Palmieri, who in his cups had mixed up the royal babe with his own son and could not tell one from the other. The only person who should be able to solve the problem is Inez, the nurse to whom the royal child was entrusted and who is also Luiz's mother. She is now married to a brigand with an extensive practice in the hills around Cordova, and the Grand Inquisitor accordingly dispatches two emissaries to find her. The two Gondoliers who between them hide the identity of a king are, of course, Marco and Giuseppe. They now return to the piazetta, happily married to their brides and followed by their friends, but their celebrations are interrupted by the approach of the Grand Inquisitor, whose austere appearance frightens away the Gondoliers and Contadine. Marco and Giuseppe are amazed to hear that one of them is a king, but the surprise is an agreeable one. They are quite prepared to leave at once for Barataria to take up the reins of government, and the only fly in the ointment is that they may not take their wives with them. Tessa and Gianetta, however, console themselves with the knowledge that the separation will only be a short one and that then one of them will be "a regular Royal Queen". The Grand Inquisitor wisely refrains from telling their husbands that one of them is already married. So, accompanied by all their male friends and acquaintances to whom they promise the pick of the Government posts, Marco and Giuseppe set sail for Barataria.

ACT II

The scene is the throne-room in the royal palace of Barataria. As democratic kings Marco and Giuseppe are performing various menial duties, for they feel that in return for their royal prerogatives the least they can do is to make themselves useful about the place. They miss their wives unceasingly, and Marco gives expression to their yearning for them in this famous tenor song:

As the song ends there is a sound of cheering, and in dash all the Venetian Contadine, escorting Tessa and Gianetta, who rush into the open arms of Marco and Giuseppe. Unable to bear the separation a moment longer they have borrowed a boat to join their husbands. Their arrival calls for a banquet and a dance—the Cachucha:

But the joyful reunion is overshadowed by the Grand Inquisitor's arrival and his announcement that whichever of the two Gondoliers proves to be the king is married to Casilda, who will arrive in half an hour to claim him. The situation is a truly tangled one—a case not of simple bigamy but one of complicated fractions; two men wed to three women. The arrival of Inez, however, brings general happiness, for she announces that the heir to the throne is neither Marco nor Giuseppe, but Luiz. When the kidnappers came to steal the royal babe the old woman had substituted her own son and kept Luiz, giving out that he was her own child. So, with their wives restored to their arms, the Gondoliers cheerfully exchange the sceptre for the oar, while Luiz, happily united to Casilda, surrenders his drum-stick for a sceptre.

Utopia Limited

or

The Flowers of Progress

An Original Comic Opera in Two Acts

Written by W. S. GILBERT

Music by ARTHUR SULLIVAN

First produced on 7th October, 1893, at the Savoy Theatre, London, with Rutland Barrington as "King Paramount", Walter Passmore as "Tarara", Nancy McIntosh as "The Princess Zara" and Rosina Brandram as "The Lady Sophy".

CHARACTERS

KING PARAMOUNT I, *King of Utopia*

SCAPHIO, PHANTIS } *Judges of the Utopian Supreme Court (two Wise Men)*

TARARA, *the Public Exploder*

Imported Flowers of Progress:

LORD DRAMALEIGH, *a British Lord Chamberlain*

CAPTAIN FITZBATTLEAXE, *an officer of the First Life Guards*

CAPTAIN SIR EDWARD CORCORAN, K.C.B., *an officer of the Royal Navy*

MR. GOLDBURY, *a company promoter, afterwards Comptroller of the Utopian Household*

SIR BAILEY BARRE, Q.C., M.P.

MR. BLUSHINGTON, *a member of the County Council*

THE PRINCESS ZARA, *eldest daughter of King Paramount*

THE PRINCESS NEKAYA, THE PRINCESS KALYBA } *her younger sisters*

THE LADY SOPHY, *their English governess*

ACT I

In a palm-grove in the gardens of King Paramount's palace on the tropical island of Utopia in the South Pacific a group of maidens are lazily enjoying themselves in lotus-eating fashion. Life in Utopia was formerly without a care, under the rule of a fatherly Monarch, who had no other thought than to make his people contented. Then one day they heard of England; and King Paramount, eager to model his island on the principles of that great country, sent his eldest daughter Princess Zara to be educated at Girton. At home his two youngest daughters are in charge of an English governess, the Lady Sophy, a model of English propriety. The little girls are an enchanting couple—perfect specimens of English shyness and reserve, who

> "Show ourselves to loud applause
> From ten to four without a pause
> Which is an awkward time because
> It cuts into our lunch."

On the day the curtain rises Princess Zara's return after five years' absence is awaited with conflicting emotions by the community. Utopia has already adopted a number of English customs, but Princess Zara's intentions are to remodel all political and social institutions according to the British constitution. Prevailing conditions are not entirely happy from the point of view of King Paramount, who, while appearing to maintain a despotic rule, is really the helpless tool of two unscrupulous Wise Men, Scaphio and Phantis. They insist on the King carrying out all their demands and threaten, should he refuse, to hand him over to the Public Exploder, who, once having blown up His Majesty, would reign in his stead. In addition they fill the columns of the Court paper, *The Palace Peeper*, with libellous scandals about the King, which they force him—for he has a definite journalistic bent—to write himself. The King does manage to have every edition bought up by his agents, but occasional copies filter through and get into the wrong hands—Lady Sophy's, for example. Lady Sophy cherishes a Gilbertian passion for the King, but how can this paragon of propriety reconcile her moral principles with affection for a monarch who is seen dancing with the second housemaid on the oriental platform of the Tivoli Gardens?

When Princess Zara arrives she brings with her six representatives of what she describes as "the principal causes that have tended to make England the powerful, happy and blameless country which the consensus of European civilisation has declared it to be". "Place yourself," she tells her father, "unreservedly in the hands of these gentlemen and they will re-organise your country on a footing that will enable you to defy your persecutors." In the Finale to Act One "The Flowers of Progress" are introduced one by one, each with his little song. Captain Fitzbattleaxe, who on the voyage from England has fallen in love with Princess Zara, is to re-make the army of Utopia. Sir Bailey Barre, Q.C., M.P., is to administer the new legal system. Princess Zara introduces him as:

"As eminent logician, who can make it clear to you
That black is white—when looked at from the proper point of view;
A marvellous Philologist, who'll undertake to show
That 'Yes' is but another and a neater form of 'No!"

Lord Dramaleigh will clean up the stage, and, assisted by the County Councillor' Mr. Blushington, will improve the sanitation; Sir Edward Corcoran, R.N., will teach Utopia how to rule the seas; and Mr. Goldbury, as a start to reorganising the kingdom's economic fortunes, proposes to float Utopia as a Limited Company. In reply to nervous queries as to what this would involve, Mr. Goldbury airily replies in song that no risk whatever is involved:

"If you come to grief and creditors are craving,
(for nothing that is planned by mortal head
is certain in this vale of sorrow—saving
that one's liability is limited)
Do you suppose that signifies perdition?
If so you're but a monetary dunce—
You merely file a Winding-up Petition
and start another Company at once."

The King does express certain reservations:

"Well, at first sight it strikes us as dishonest,
but if it's good enough for virtuous England—
The first commercial country in the world—
it's good enough for us."

Nevertheless, Utopia is registered under the Joint Stock Company's Act of '62.

ACT II

Act Two takes place in the throne-room of the palace at night. When the curtain rises Captain Fitzbattleaxe is singing to Princess Zara. He is so madly in love with her that his top notes and cadenzas fail completely, to his great embarrassment. Zara leaves him to dress for the Court Drawing-Room, an English innovation, to be held for the first time that evening. Also for the first time a Cabinet meeting takes place. Although in theory it is held in the same form as at the Court of St. James, it is in practice much more in the style of St. James Hall—the London home of the Christy Nigger Minstrel Troupe. When the Cabinet members have ranged their chairs across the stage like Negro minstrels, each draws from the back a banjo or a pair of bones, and in the song which follows, sung by King Paramount and the Cabinet, Sullivan in his orchestration imitates the plucking of banjos and the rattle of bones and paraphrases a typical Negro Minstrel tune of that time—"Johnny get your gun":

The Cabinet meeting is followed by the Drawing-Room and at the end of the ceremony Scaphio and Phantis, the two Wise Men, manage to catch the King alone. They are furious at the innovations introduced by the Flowers of Progress: all their schemes of providing for their old age are ruined. Their Matrimonial Agency is at a standstill, their cheap sherry business is bankrupt and the company which was formed to supply the entire nation with a complete English outfit is on the rocks. "When we send in our bills," they complain, "our customers plead liability limited to a capital of eighteenpence and apply to be dealt with under the Winding-Up Act—as in England." But the King openly defies his former persecutors, and they withdraw to confer with Tarara, the Public Exploder, and concoct a plot of superhuman subtlety to overthrow the King and his English Government. This takes the form of a most effective trio in which the conspirators whisper suggestions to each other, only the comments being heard by the audience. Eventually they come to some agreement ("We won't say how and we won't say what") and depart to put their plan into action:

The reforms instituted by the Flowers of Progress have not proved any more popular with the inhabitants of Utopia, and this discontent, fanned by Scaphio, Phantis and Tarara, now flares into open revolt. The mob burst into the palace crying: "Down with the Flowers of Progress." They complain that owing to improved sanitation there is no sickness and the doctors are starving, and that the laws, remodelled by Sir Bailey Barre, have extinguished crime and litigation, and that the lawyers are starving also and all the gaols are let as model dwellings for the working classes. The King turns to Princess Zara and asks what is to be done? Sir Bailey Barre whispers to Zara, and she exclaims: "Of course, I remember." She had forgotten the most essential, the most English element of all—Government by Party. Scaphio and Phantis are banished from the realm, Lady Sophy accepts King Paramount, the little Princesses Nekaya and Kalyba marry Lord Dramaleigh and Mr. Goldbury, respectively, and of course Captain Fitzbattleaxe marries Princess Zara.

The Grand Duke

or

The Statutory Duel

A Comic Opera in Two Acts

Written by W. S. GILBERT

Music by ARTHUR SULLIVAN

This was Gilbert and Sullivan's last collaboration. First produced on the 7th March, 1896, at the Savoy Theatre, London, with Ilka von Palmay as "Julia", Walter Passmore as "The Grand Duke", Rutland Barrington as "Ludwig" and Rosina Brandram as "The Baroness von Krakenfeldt".

CHARACTERS

RUDOLPH, *Grand Duke of Pfennig Halbpfennig*
ERNEST DUMMKOPF, *a theatrical manager*
LUDWIG, *his leading comedian*
THE PRINCE OF MONTE CARLO
THE PRINCESS OF MONTE CARLO, *betrothed to Rudolph*
THE BARONESS VON KRAKENFELDT, *betrothed to Rudolph*
JULIA JELLICOE, *an English comedienne*
LISA, *a soubrette*
DR. TANNHÄUSER, *Public Notary*
PRIVATE DETECTIVE
CHORUS OF NOBLES, ACTORS, ACTRESSES, ETC.

The action takes place in the year 1750.

ACT I

Outside an inn in the market-place of the town of Speisesaal in the Grand Duchy of Pfennig Halbpfennig, members of Ernest Dummkopf's theatrical company are seated at several small tables, enjoying a repast in honour of the nuptials of Ludwig, the leading comedian, and Lisa, the soubrette. Although the wedding breakfast is being consumed, the wedding has not yet been celebrated. It appears that the Grand Duke has summoned a convocation of clergy to discuss the details of his approaching marriage to the wealthy Baroness von Krakenfeldt and there isn't a parson available for love or money. It also transpires that the present company is involved in a conspiracy to depose the Grand Duke and elect Ernest Dummkopf in his stead. In alluding to this conspiracy all members of the secret society give and receive a secret sign, which involves eating a sausage roll:

Ernest Dummkopf has promised the members of his company that if they vote for him and he is appointed Grand Duke they shall all have posts as courtiers at the royal palace. Julia Jellicoe, the leading lady, in spite of her dislike of Ernest Dummkopf is determined to play the leading part of the Grand Duchess, and resigns herself to the idea of marriage with him. Just as the election is going in Ernest Dummkopf's favour, however, Ludwig gives away the whole plot to a confiding stranger whom he discovers devouring sausage rolls and thus mistakes for a fellow conspirator, and who turns out to be Grand Duke Rudolph's private detective. Ernest Dummkopf and Julia are furious, and to settle matters the Notary Public, Dr. Tannhäuser, suggests a trial by Statutory Duel between Ludwig and Ernest.

The remainder of the plot hinges on the Statutory Duel. All laws in the State of Pfennig Halbpfennig run for a hundred years, after which they die a natural death, unless in the meantime they have been revived for another century. The Act that instituted the Statutory Duel was passed a hundred years ago and expires on the morrow, so Ernest Dummkopf and Ludwig are just in time. The Statutory Duel is fought by each contestant drawing a playing-card from the pack. Whoever draws the lowest card is doomed to die, while the winner must adopt the loser's responsibilities, discharge his debts and assume his obligations. The Statutory Duel duly takes place. Ludwig draws an ace, Ernest a King, and as Ludwig is the winner Ernest Dummkopf must retire.

The Grand Duke Rudolph now appears in the empty market-place. He is miserably dressed in old, patched clothes, though blazing with a profusion of orders and decorations; and he is weak and ill from poor living, and constantly in tears. He is joined by his betrothed, the Baroness von Krakenfeldt, who is greatly perturbed by the news she has just read in the newspaper that, although she is to marry the Grand Duke on the morrow, he was betrothed in infancy to the Princess of Monte Carlo. The Grand Duke admits the truth of this, but assures her that everything is under control, and that by the terms of the contract the betrothal is void unless the Princess marries before she comes of age, which will be at two o'clock on the morrow. Apart from this, her father, the Prince, is bankrupt and dare not leave his house for fear of arrest. At this the Baroness goes happily off, after handing the Grand Duke a letter from his private detective which gives him news of the conspiracy to dethrone him. The Grand Duke, in a frenzy of nerves, bursts into tears. Ludwig, coming into the market-place, spots the weeping Grand Duke and asks him what is the matter. The Grand Duke confides in him and then declares: "If only I could hit upon some cheap and painless method of putting an end to an existence which has become insupportable, I would unhesitatingly adopt it." To comfort him Ludwig suggests: "If you are really in earnest, why not resort to a Statutory Duel? You fight, you lose, you are dead for a day. Tomorrow, when the Act expires, you come to life again and resume your Grand Duchy as though nothing had happened. In the meantime the explosion designed to blow you up will have taken place and the survivor will have had to bear the brunt of it." "Yes," argues the Grand Duke, "that's all very well, but who'll be fool enough to BE the survivor?" Ludwig at once volunteers for the duel, and producing a pack of cards puts the Ace up his own sleeve and presents the Grand Duke with a King to put up his. They begin a bogus quarrel and a crowd collects, with the Notary Public to conduct the proceedings. Ludwig duly wins the duel with his Ace and the Grand Duke has to retire.

Ludwig, now reigning Grand Duke, promises his fellow actors that he will give out the Court appointments that afternoon "according to professional position". On the strength of this wording, Julia, as leading lady, claims the part of the Grand Duchess. Lisa protests that she is already engaged to Ludwig but Julia rebukes her:

"Now don't be foolish, dear—
You couldn't play it, darling!
Its 'leading business', pet,
And you're but a soubrette."

And so Lisa retires in tears, while preparations go forward for the wedding of Ludwig and Julia.

ACT II

Act Two takes place the following morning in the entrance hall of the Grand Ducal palace. As the curtain rises a procession of members of the theatrical company enters, all dressed in the costumes of Ernest Dummkopf's production of *Troilus and Cressida*. They carry garlands and, playing on pipes, citharae and cymbals, herald the return of Ludwig and Julia from the marriage ceremony, which has just taken place. The quasi-Greek chorus which opens Act Two is Sullivan's worthiest contribution to an otherwise sadly tired score:

Poor Lisa is intensely distressed at having to surrender Ludwig and another prospective bride who is disappointed is the Baroness von Krakenfeldt. But when she hears that Ludwig's first act as Grand Duke was to revive the Statutory Duel for another hundred years, she insists on his shouldering Rudolph's responsibilities and marrying her also. Julia is shattered, but the Baroness has the law on her side and she must submit.

No sooner has Ludwig been married to the Baroness than the Prince of Monte Carlo enters with his daughter. He has managed to pay off his debts just in time to get his daughter to Pfennig Halbpfennig to marry the Grand Duke before she comes of age at 2 p.m. Ludwig tries to get out of marrying her by explaining that he is not the Rudolph to whom the Princess was betrothed twenty years previously. "Rudolph died yesterday, quite suddenly of a cardiac affection—a pack-of-cardiac affection," he tells them, and goes on to explain about the Statutory Duel. But the Princess is not giving up. Ludwig's other wives and Lisa all protest, but the Princess tells them: "Poor ladies! I'm very sorry for you all; but, you see, I've a prior claim." Taking Ludwig's arm she is about to remove him to church when there is an interruption. Rudolph enters with the Notary and forbids the banns. The Notary explains that he has been examining the Act which regulates Statutory Duels, and finds it is expressly laid down that the Ace shall count, invariably, as the lowest card. So all the events of the past twenty-four hours are cancelled, and at long last Lisa claims her Ludwig.

Cox and Box

or

The Long-Lost Brothers

Triumviretta in One Act

Adapted from J. MADDISON MORTON'S *Farce* Box and Cox

Written by F. C. BURNAND

Music by ARTHUR SULLIVAN

First produced on 11th May, 1867, at the Adelphi Theatre, London, at a benefit performance organised by the staff of Punch, *with George du Maurier, the artist, as "Box" and Arthur Cecil as "Bouncer".*

CHARACTERS

JAMES JOHN COX, *a journeyman hatter*
JOHN JAMES BOX, *a journeyman printer*
SERGEANT BOUNCER, *late of the Dampshire Yeomanry*

The scene is a bedroom, decently furnished, containing a bed with curtains closed, a chest of drawers, and a fireplace with a few common ornaments on the chimney-piece. It is early morning when the curtain rises and Cox is dressing, preparatory to leaving for the hat shop where he works. His landlord, Sergeant Bouncer, enters and remarks that Cox has had his hair cut. "Cut!" says Cox. "I look as if I'd been cropped for the Militia." This is Sergeant Bouncer's cue for some military reminiscences:

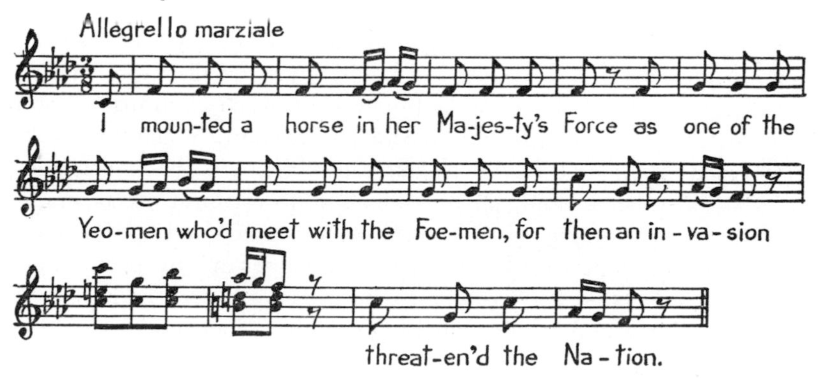

Cox then complains to Bouncer that frequently, on his return home, the room is full of smoke. Bouncer suggests that the chimney smokes, but Cox retorts that the chimney doesn't smoke tobacco. Bouncer then suggests that it must be the lodger in the attic. "Oh, the gentleman that I invariably meet coming upstairs when I am going down and going down when I am coming up," says Cox. He sarcastically points out to Bouncer that it is queer that "this gentleman's smoke instead of emulating the example of all other sorts of smoke and going up the chimney thinks proper to effect a singularity by taking the contrary direction". Bouncer tries to make his escape, but Cox has by no means finished his list of complaints. Coals, candles, tea, sugar and wood have all been disappearing. Bouncer tries his best to put the blame on the cat, and eventually Cox goes off to work without getting any satisfaction.

No sooner has he gone than Bouncer busies himself tidying the room and making the bed. "I haven't an instant to lose," he mutters. "Let me put Mr. Cox's things out of Mr. Box's way." Bouncer has artfully managed to let his room twice over, for while Cox, a hatter, works during the day, Box, a printer, is out all night. Neither is aware that the other is occupying the same room and Bouncer is receiving double rent, telling each one that the other is the lodger in the attic. When Box returns Bouncer passes on his fellow-lodger's complaint about his smoking, and Box retorts "that if he objects to the effluvia of tobacco, he had better domesticate himself in some adjoining parish". He assumes from the number and variety of the hats he has seen Cox wearing that he must be professionally associated with the hatting interest, and Bouncer replies: "Yes, sir. That's why he took the Hattics!" When Bouncer has withdrawn, Box produces a rasher of bacon. Laying a gridiron on the fire he places the rasher on it, lies down on the bed and sings himself to sleep.

But today the inevitable happens and Cox and Box meet, for Cox, on arrival at the shop where he works, is given an unexpected holiday. On his way home he purchases a mutton chop, intending to grill it at his own fireside before setting out for a day in the country. On his return he discovers a rasher of bacon sizzling on the grill and curses Bouncer for his cheek in making so free with his matches, coals and gridiron to cook his breakfast. When Box awakens, the two men meet, and a violent altercation follows. Each demands to know what the other is doing in his room and, to establish ownership, each produces a receipt for the rent. Bouncer is summoned and confesses to his deception. He manages to calm down his furious tenants by promising one of them the little back second-floor room which will shortly be available, and Cox and Box abandon their intention to fight a duel and sing a duet instead.

After their duet friendly relations are firmly established and confidences are exchanged. Cox confides to Box that he is betrothed to a proprietress of bathing-machines at Ramsgate and he asks Box if he is married. Box equivocates in answer and then, when pinned down, makes the astonishing assertion that he is defunct, having drowned himself three years previously. In an admirably composed song of Sullivan's Box proceeds to describe his suicide-of-convenience. To avoid marrying a widow, with whom he had unintentionally become entangled and who threatened him with a breach-of-promise action, he made a bundle of some of his clothes, and leaving them on the edge of a cliff, Box vanished into the blue. "So *you* are the late lamented Box," says Cox, putting two and two together in establishing that Box was the late suitor for the hand of Penelope Ann, widow of William Wiggins, to whom Cox is now betrothed. A violent argument then begins as to which of the gentlemen shall take on Penelope Ann, for both detest her. They eventually agree to dice for her. But Box detects that Cox's dice are loaded, and they decide on the spin of a coin, till Box's sixpence and Cox's shilling turn out to have two heads each and no tails. While they are hurling abuse at each other, Bouncer comes into the room with a letter. It is difficult to decipher from the writing on the envelope whether it is addressed to Cox or Box. The letter is from a solicitor at Margate, dated May the 4th, and reads: "Sir, I hasten to convey to you the intelligence of a melancholy accident, which has bereft you of your intended wife." "He means *your* intended," says Cox. "No, *yours*," says Box. "Go on." Cox resumes: "Poor Mrs. Wiggins went out for a short excursion in a sailing-boat. A sudden and violent squall took place, which, it is supposed, upset her, as she was found two days afterwards, keel upwards. As her man of business, I immediately proceeded to examine her papers, among which I soon discovered her will. The following extract from this will, I have no doubt, be satisfactory to you. 'I hearby bequeath my entire property to my intended husband.' " Each of the two men is now as anxious to appear in the role of the intended husband as he was earlier to avoid it, and they have just agreed to compromise and divide Penelope Ann's estate equally between them when Bouncer appears with a second letter. This again comes from Margate and reads: "Happy to inform you false alarm. Sudden squall, boat upset, Mrs. Wiggins picked up by a steamboat, carried into Boulogne, returned here this morning, will start by early train tomorrow and be with you by ten o'clock." "Cox, I congratulate you," says Box; and "Box I give you joy," says Cox, and both regret that important business will prevent each from witnessing the other's reunion with his intended. This conversation is interrupted by the arrival of Penelope Ann herself. She does not come in, but leaves a note, which Bouncer presents. It is addressed to Cox and reads: "Dear Mr. Cox, pardon my candour but, being convinced that our feelings, like our ages, do not reciprocate, I hasten to apprise you of my immediate union with Mr. Knox." Both men raise three cheers for their deliverance and are about to embrace when Box suddenly says to Cox: "You'll excuse the apparent insanity of the remark, but the more I gaze on your features the more I'm convinced that you're my long-lost brother. Have you a strawberry mark on your left arm?" "No," says Cox. "Then it is he," cries Box. They rush into each other's arms and swear never to be parted. As the curtain falls they join Bouncer in his theme song, a cheerful Rat-a-plan:

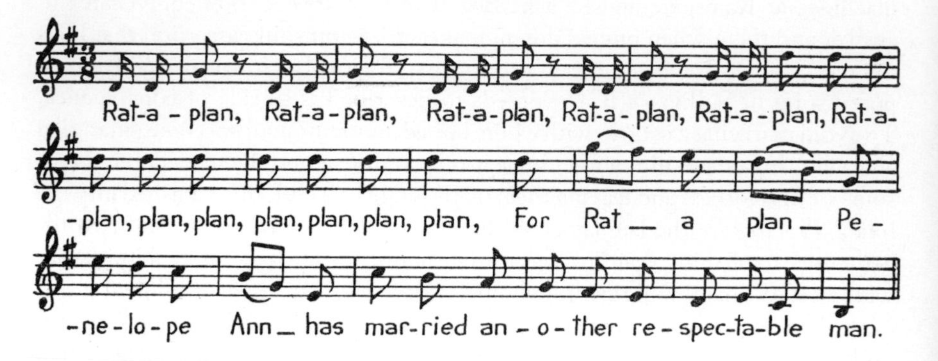

Haddon Hall

A Light Opera in Three Acts

Written by Sydney Grundy

Music by Arthur Sullivan

First produced on 24th September, 1892, at the Savoy Theatre, London, with Lucille Hill as "Dorothy Vernon", Courtice Pounds as "John Manners", Rosina Brandram as "Lady Vernon" and Rutland Barrington as "Rupert Vernon".

Characters

JOHN MANNERS, *a Royalist*
SIR GEORGE VERNON, *of Haddon Hall*
LADY VERNON, *his wife*
DOROTHY VERNON, *their daughter*
RUPERT VERNON, *her cousin, a Roundhead*
THE MCCRANKIE, *a Roundhead*
DORCAS, *Dorothy's maid*
OSWALD, *Manners' servant*
CHORUS OF SIMPLES, GENTLES, RETAINERS

Historically, the marriage of John Manners and Dorothy Vernon took place in 1561. The author, for dramatic reasons, has placed the action of Haddon Hall in the year 1648.

ACT I

The Lovers

The scene of Act One is the terrace at Haddon Hall on a lovely morning in May. The household is assembled to welcome Rupert Vernon, who is to be betrothed to the daughter of the house, his cousin, Lady Dorothy Vernon. Her father, Sir George, and her mother, Lady Vernon, are present and all join in a madrigal in praise of Spring:

Sir George Vernon is a Royalist. But in spite of this he intends to marry his daughter to her cousin, Rupert, who is a Roundhead. There are two reasons for this: fear of Parliament, which, Sir George says, loves him none too well, and the fact that Rupert is laying claim to the Haddon estates and a lawsuit is threatening. "This marriage puts an end to doubts and questions that have troubled me," urges Sir George. But Dorothy, eager as she is to please her father, will not even consider marriage to her Roundhead cousin, for she is in love with John Manners, a younger son of the Duke of Rutland and a proscribed Royalist. Through the good offices of Manners' servant, Oswald, and Dorothy's maid, Dorcas, the lovers manage to correspond and they also manage some stolen meetings.

Later, Rupert Vernon arrives at Haddon Hall with a posse of Puritans, who rejoice in such names as Kill-joy Candlemas, Barnabas Bellows-to-mend and Nicodemus Knock-knee. They are a solemn collection of gloom-mongers, out to abolish every kind of fun, with "all life is sack-cloth and ashes" as their motto. Rupert, however, is a far gayer character and is always making fun of the Puritans. "After a life spent in mortifying the flesh," he tells them, "it would be a crowning mortification if it turned out that the flesh was not meant to be mortified." And he sings:

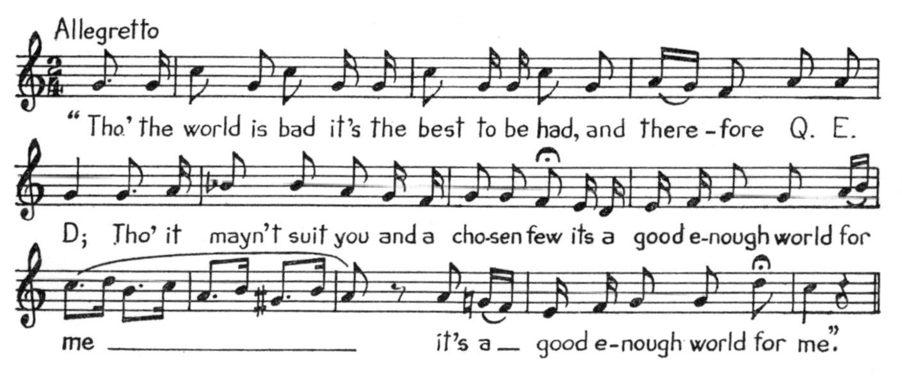

The arrival of Rupert and the long-faced Puritans has a discouraging effect on the company at Haddon Hall, though Rupert begs them not to be influenced by first impressions. He is warmly welcomed by Sir George and asks formally for Dorothy's hand. Sir George assures him that his daughter will obey his wishes, but Dorothy openly refuses and declares that she would rather die than wed him. She will be true to her own heart. Sir George is furious at Dorothy's rebellion. "I ask not words of duty, I ask deeds," he says, and orders her up to her chamber.

ACT II

The Elopement

SCENE 1. The first scene of Act Two takes place outside Haddon Hall. Near one of the side entrances Rupert and his Puritans are sheltering from a storm of rain. Though in Haddon Hall Sir George is giving a ball in his cousin's honour, the Puritans are cooling their heels in a particularly moist and unpleasant situation, simply because their conscientious scruples will not permit them to countenance "carnal junkettings". Rupert is expecting the arrival of the McCrankie, "a Puritan above proof", who is joining them from the Isle of Rum on the west coast of Scotland. Presently there is heard the distant skirl of bag-pipes and the McCrankie appears in a kilt singing:

My name it is McCrankie,
I'm lean an' lang and lanky,
I'm a Moody an' a Sankey
Wound up o' a Scottish reel.

A comedy scene follows the arrival of the McCrankie. He and Rupert get rid of the other Puritans, who withdraw reluctantly, and settle down to a wee drappie or two or three or more. They also boast in a song of what they will do "If we but have our way":

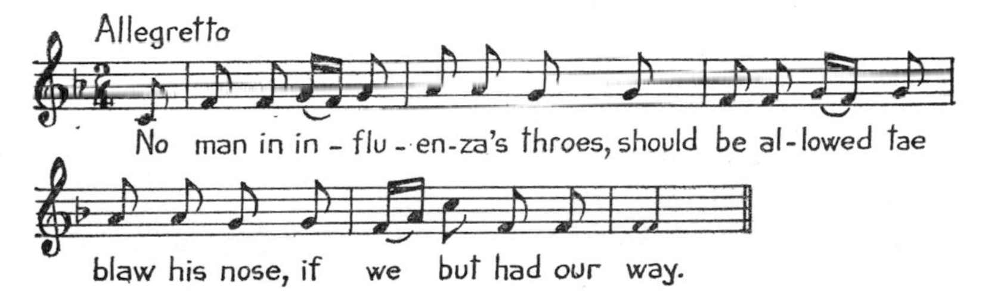

As they are talking Dorcas comes out of the side door, followed by Dorothy. They are joined by John Manners and Oswald, and Manners, taking Dorothy's arm, leads her to where horses, ready saddled, are waiting. They make their escape and Dorothy elopes with her lover.

SCENE 2. While outside the storm rages and Dorothy and John Manners are busy eloping, in the Long Gallery of Haddon Hall Sir George is entertaining his guests. He has just proposed their health when Rupert and the Puritans rush in, dragging Dorcas with them. Rupert reports the elopement and accuses Dorcas of aiding and abetting the lovers' escape. With a furious cry of "To horse, the fugitives pursue," Sir George sets off on a vain pursuit.

ACT III

The Return

At the opening of Act Three, which takes place in the ante-chamber of Haddon Hall, Sir George receives bad news. Parliament has substantiated Rupert's claim to the Haddon estates and Sir George must prepare to leave his ancestral home. But in the nick of time news comes that General Monk has proclaimed Charles II king. John Manners gallops up to Haddon Hall and hands Sir George a warrant from the King, reinstating him as Lord of Haddon, and then proudly leads his wife up to her father. Sir George clasps Dorothy in his arms, and all is forgiven.

The Chieftain

An Original Comic Opera in Two Acts

Written by F. C. BURNAND

Music by ARTHUR SULLIVAN

First produced on 12th December, 1894, at the Savoy Theatre, London, with Courtice Pounds as "Count Vasquez", Walter Passmore as "Peter Adolphus Grigg", Rosina Brandram as "Inez de Roxas" and Florence St. John as "Rita".

The Chieftain *is an extended version of* The Contrabandista *by the same author and composer, first produced on 18th December, 1867, by T. German Reed at St. George's Hall, Langham Place, London. It was written, composed and produced in* sixteen *days.*

CHARACTERS

COUNT VASQUEZ DE GONZAGO

PETER ADOLPHUS GRIGG, *a British tourist in search of the picturesque*

INEZ DE ROXAS, *Chieftainess of the Ladrones*

FERDINAND DE ROXAS, *Chieftain of the Ladrones, disguised as Pietro Slivinsky, a Polish courier*

DOLLY, *Peter Grigg's wife*

RITA, *an English lady engaged to Count Vasquez and in Act Two married to him*

ACT I

The scene of Act One is a rocky mountain pass between Compostello and Seville. Mr. Peter Adolphus Grigg, having concluded the business that brought him to Spain, has begun a pleasure trip with his camera into the mountains, in order to take back to his wife a few pictorial impressions of his trip. On a rocky pass in a wild mountainous region he loses his way and bewails his ill-fortune:

While he is taking a photograph, with his head hidden under a black camera-cloth, Grigg is taken prisoner by a band of brigands, whose Chieftain has disappeared. The law of these *Ladrones* (or brigands) is that, if the Chieftain does not return within a year and a day, the first stranger to arrive in their midst is to be elected their Chieftain and must become the affianced husband of their Chieftainess. Should he refuse these honours, he is to be shot. Under the pressure of carbine, dagger and pistol, Grigg is forced to accept the situation. He is enthroned as husband of Inez de Roxas, deserted wife or possibly widow, and he becomes Chieftain of the *Ladrones*. His accession is welcomed with song and dance (a bolero) though Grigg himself is far from sanguine.

In the meantime, Count Vasquez, a friend of Grigg's, has ventured, disguised as a shepherd, into the mountains to rescue Rita, a young Englishwoman to whom he is engaged and who has recently been taken prisoner by the *Ladrones*. They celebrate their reunion with an ecstatic love-duet:

Rita has been captured merely as a matter of business for the sake of a ransom. Count Vasquez sends for the agreed sum of two thousand pesetas, and while he is waiting for the money to arrive, the Chieftainess of the *Ladrones*, Inez de Roxas, asks him if it is not true that he and his men were in pursuit of her vanished husband, the Chieftain Ferdinand de Roxas. Count Vasquez assures her that that was so but that they never caught him, and he promises that if he gets any news of him he will let her know. Eventually the ransom money is brought by a goatherd, Pedrillo, followed by a detachment of soldiers, whose appearance greatly intimidates the brigands, although the real reason for their presence is merely to provide an effective Finale to Act One. Count Vasquez orders the soldiers to lay down their arms, and then hands over the ransom money to Inez, who presses Vasquez and Rita to remain for her wedding to Grigg and to join in the festivities. A photograph is taken of the wedding ceremony and is duly signed by all present, though Grigg is greatly dismayed at this record of his bigamy. Finally, Count Vasquez and Rita depart (leaving behind the disconsolate Grigg) to the martial strains of:

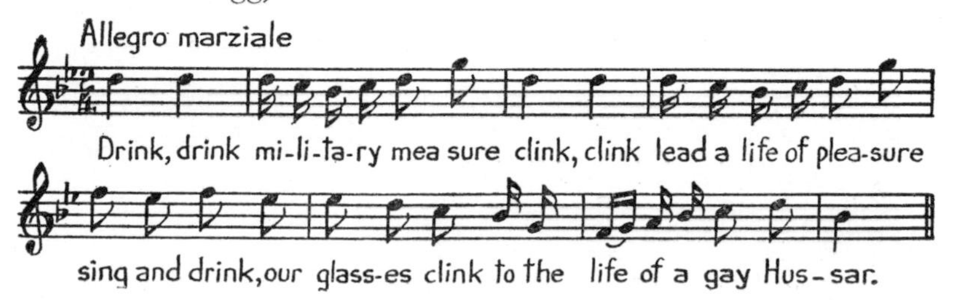

ACT II

At a *posada*, "The Pielade Oro", in the picturesque village of Dehesas on the river Sil, Count Vasquez and Rita, now married, are spending their honeymoon. They are blissfully happy and recall their meeting when Rita was at school at the Convent des Oiseaux in Paris, and how although he was Spanish and she was English, they spoke French, and how they fell in love and eloped.

When Count Vasquez reached Compostello after his departure from the brigands, he sent his secretary with money for Grigg's ransom, and Grigg has now been released on parole on condition that he will return when summoned by the Chieftainess. In the meantime Inez de Roxas and the leading *Ladrones* have disguised themselves and gone in search of their missing Chieftain, Ferdinand, who has made off with the brigands' funds and has vainly attempted to leave Spain. Photographs of the Chieftain are posted up everywhere, and Ferdinand, to avoid the police, has disguised himself as a courier. In this capacity he has fallen in with Mrs. Grigg, who has come to Spain in search of her husband. The Count's secretary accompanies the liberated Grigg and they meet Mrs. Grigg and the courier at Compostello. Here they find that, with the exception of one suitcase, all Grigg's luggage has been taken on by Count Vasquez and Rita to Dehesas. Grigg, therefore, has to join them there to recover his luggage. So, with Mrs. Grigg and accompanied by the courier, he arrives at Dehesas. The courier (i.e. the real Chieftain, Ferdinand de Roxas) intends to stick to the travellers and to return with them to England. Poor Grigg, encumbered with a Spanish wife, or at least an affianced bride, in the person of Inez de Roxas, dares not tell the true story of his adventures to Mrs. Grigg. When he arrives at Dehesas, therefore, he begs Count Vasquez and Rita to help him concoct a convincing story of what befell him in the mountains. He feels that he will never persuade his wife to believe that he has been a Bandit Chieftain and the temporary consort of a Brigand Queen. The Count and Rita duly help him out of his difficulty and Mrs. Grigg is induced to believe that her husband, at the risk of his life, rescued them from the brigands by a daring ride to fetch the police and set the captives free. "Oh, Peter, you are a hero," says Mrs. Grigg. "And I never knew you could ride." "Nor did I," admits Grigg. "It was a painful experience. After that desperate equestrian performance I was quite a Rider Haggard!!"

Inez and the *Ladrones*, all in disguise and in search of the lost chief, now appear on the scene to a gay Spanish tune:

Inez makes the acquaintance of Mrs. Grigg, passing herself off as the Duchess de Roxas and, as such, Mrs. Grigg introduces her to the unfortunate Grigg. The brigands then proceed to threaten him with exposure, and though Grigg intends to deny the story, witnesses are present and there is the damning evidence of the photograph of Grigg and Inez in a decidedly compromising attitude. Grigg purchases the silence of the *Ladrones* and his own freedom with a hundred pounds (advanced by the Count), and Mrs. Grigg never learns the true story of his escapade. But the Chieftain, Ferdinand, by recklessly singing the bandit song by which the Chieftain of the *Ladrones* is known to his followers, is unmasked. He is stripped of his disguise, his weapons are taken from him, he is embraced by his loving wife and welcomed back to the band of brigands, who hope to recover the funds with which Ferdinand absconded. Peter and Mrs. Grigg decide to return to England, where their family anxiously await them, and, bidding good-bye to all their Spanish friends, they depart.

The Beauty Stone

An Original Romantic Musical Drama in Three Acts

Written by ARTHUR W. PINERO

Lyrics by J. COMYNS CARR

Music by ARTHUR SULLIVAN

First produced on 28th May, 1898, at the Savoy Theatre, London, with George Devoll as "Philip, Lord of Mirlemont", Henry A. Lytton as "Simon", Walter Passmore as "The Devil", Ruth Vincent as "Laine", and Rosina Brandram as "Joan".

CHARACTERS

PHILIP, LORD OF MIRLEMONT
GUNTRAM OF BEAUGRANT
SIMON LIMAL, *a weaver*
NICHOLAS DIRCKS, *Burgomaster of Mirlemont*
PEPPIN, *a dwarf*
THE DEVIL
LAINE, *the weaver's daughter*
JOAN, *the weaver's wife*
JACQUELINE
SAIDA
A SENESCHAL
CHORUS OF KNIGHTS, DAMES, PAGES, ALDERMEN, SOLDIERS, TOWNS-
FOLK, COUNTRYFOLK, DANCERS, LUTE-PLAYERS, ETC.

The authors of The Beauty Stone *have supposed that Philip of Mirlemont was, as a youth, one of the goodly company of Lords and Knights who took part with John of Nevers in the battle of Necopolis and subsequently shared exile with their leader. During his stay at Cephalonia, Philip found solace with the Lady Saida. And since the world, it would seem, was no better at the beginning of the fifteenth century than it is in our present day and age, upon the ransom of the captives, Saida and the young Lord of Mirlemont sailed homeward together. The Devil is introduced into the story somewhat in the spirit of the old Mystery and Miracle plays, as a grotesque personage.*

ACT I

SCENE I. The scene is a room in the sombre, wretched dwelling of the weaver, Simon Limal, and the time is the beginning of the fifteenth century. Simon and his wife, Joan, are a prematurely aged, poverty-stricken pair. On the day the curtain rises Mirlemont is *en fête*, for Philip, Lord of Mirlemont, has ordered a Beauty Competition to be held in the town, the winning maiden to be awarded a wreath of rose-buds and a silver girdle. Simon and Joan have a daughter, Laine, uncomely and crippled, who hobbles through life on a crutch. She has just taken the pitcher to fetch water from a well, and on her return has been set upon by a rabble of youths and girls who plague and tease her, breaking her pitcher and pursuing her to her doorstep. Particularly impudent in his behaviour is the dwarf, Peppin. In her distress Laine finds a champion in Jacqueline, a stout-hearted termagant, who puts the mob to flight and belabours the dwarf. When the rabble have dispersed, Simon and Joan, carrying a pitcher, go out to fetch the water, leaving Laine alone after warning her not to open the door to any stranger. When they have gone, Laine ponders on the Beauty Competition, her crooked unsightliness and her longing to be loved, and standing before a poor shrine containing an image of the Virgin she prays:

As her song finishes there is a knocking at the door. A voice utters: "*Pax huic Domui et omnibus habitantibus ea*," and on the threshold stands a Holy Friar, begging for a cup of water. Laine admits him to the house, but tells him that there will be no water till her father and mother return from the well, and she shows him her broken, bottomless pitcher. He puts the pitcher to his lips, takes a deep draught and then turns the mouth downwards, when a stream of water gushes from it. Convinced by this miracle that he must indeed be a very holy man, Laine confides to him her longing for love and beauty. By this time the weaver and his wife have returned and watch open-mouthed as the Friar produces the Beauty Stone, a little pebble which, if laid bare upon the breast of man or maid, has power to change the ugliest form and features into a miracle of beauty. Now it is the Devil in the guise of a Holy Friar whom Laine has, all unwittingly, admitted to the house. Unable to resist the temptation of the Beauty Stone, she seizes it and hobbles away to her chamber to open her bodice and lay it on her breast, and presently she returns and stands before her parents, erect and wondrously beautiful. And upon her arm she carries her useless crutch as though she were bearing a lily.

SCENE 2. In the market-place of Mirlemont the townsfolk are awaiting the arrival of the Lord Philip and the Lady Saida to open the Beauty Contest, when through the crowd comes Peppin, the dwarf, flying in terror from Jacqueline, who pursues him with blows and curses. The Burgomaster chides her, and she answers him: "I have but made the manikin pay the price for trying to buss Laine Limal, the weaver's crippled daughter, an hour gone." Guntram of Beaugrant, the sturdy old warrior and right hand of Philip, then arrives, and the Burgomaster asks if the Lord of Mirlemont is on his way. Guntram says disgustedly that he left him card-playing with the Lady Saida and her demoiselles, and it becomes apparent that Guntram resents the Eastern lady whom Philip brought home from Cephalonia and who is keeping him from marching with John of Nevers, Duke of Burgundy, to the assistance of John of Bavaria, Prince Bishop of Liège, who is besieged by the Lords of Pieruels in the town of Maestricht.

The Devil is also present, masquerading this time as Antonio, Count of Foscano in Lombardy, and when Philip and Saida arrive and take their places he seats himself near by. The Beauty Contest begins, and in front of Lord Philip parade Loyse from St. Denis, Isabeau from far Florennes, Barbe from Bovigny, Gabrielle from St. Hubert and Colinette from Lenalède. But as each maiden appears the Devil utters a disparaging comment on her looks, greatly to the approval of the Lady Saida, until Philip stops the contest, telling the Burgomaster that the Flanders girls seem richer in virtue than in beauty. The Burgomaster is greatly put out, for the townsfolk will now be cheated of their entertainment. But the Devil suggests a solution: that as beauty has failed, ugliness should be given a chance. He proposes that the uncomeliest maid in Mirlemont be brought out and publicly betrothed to the misbegotten dwarf, Peppin. Philip agrees to this grisly form of humour, and the cry goes up: "Bring forth the weaver's daughter." And presently into the market-place comes Laine, transcendently beautiful. Philip is lost in wonder and admiration, and in spite of Lady Saida's jealous urging, "Oh, turn thine eyes away, let not her lure thee on," he crowns Laine with the wreath of rosebuds and clasps the silver girdle around her waist as the curtain falls.

ACT II

SCENE 1. The scene is a hall in Castle Mirlemont. Seated at the head of the table, Philip is playing cards with a party of knights and ladies, and the Devil stands at his side, advising on the conduct of the game. By the window sits Saida, jealous in heart, for her beauty is waning with the years and she is filled with a burning fear lest this lovely creature, whom Philip has had brought to the castle, should work on him her magic spell. While Laine is being made beautiful for her appearance before Philip, Saida dances with her ladies for his pleasure and sings a ballad recalling the days of their early love in Cephalonia:

Gradually Philip is half-recaptured by the lure of the song. His eyes dwell upon Saida tenderly, and at last he rises and is about to embrace her when the Seneschal announces: "The demoiselle Laine Limal." Philip turns as Laine enters and stands in the centre of the hall in all her beauty, and then, entranced, he moves towards her and Saida falls back in rage and despair. In spite of her lowly state Laine is as much in love with Philip as he is with her.

But the Devil is in league with Saida against Laine. When the weaver and his wife arrive at the castle, Laine begs Philip to give her parents fitting raiment and to allow them to dwell with her under his roof. But the Devil, pretending to carry out Philip's commands, leads them away; and later Saida calls Laine to the window and forces her to watch her father and mother being driven from the castle with blows, hissing in her ear: "Yea, they are sent forth with blows. Now thou know'st thyself, know'st what thou hast become, fool, to expect aught else from thy Lord, *thy* Lord, forsooth." Heartbroken and disillusioned, Laine seeks to regain her freedom.

SCENE 2. Back in her home Laine tears open her rich dress and removes the Beauty Stone from around her neck; then, casting it upon the ground at her parents' feet, she rushes distraught into her bed-chamber. Simon picks up the stone and hands it to his wife. "Joan, take thou the stone and let me see again the buxom lass I courted years ago at Zolden." But Joan answers: "Nay, rather let me see the comely lad who would walk out from Freyden o' Sundays with a bunch of flowers in his hand." She persuades him and adjusts the cord about Simon's neck so that the stone falls upon his bare breast. There is a flash of lightning followed by a roll of thunder, and Simon stands there, his face handsome, fresh-coloured and beardless, his hair dark and thick, his body erect and lissom, while poor Laine enters, once again pinched and sickly, her shoulder humped, hobbling on her crutch.

Presently the Devil and Saida appear at the weaver's cottage in search of the Beauty Stone which Saida covets. It is quite obvious from Simon's bearing that he has possession of the stone, and Saida, determined to coax him into giving it up, sets out to ensnare him with her beauty. She entices him away to the castle and, as Joan and Laine attempt to follow, the Devil bars their way and closes the door in their faces.

SCENE 3. Outside the castle the Devil and Saida are in conversation. Saida complains that she has so far failed to persuade Simon to yield up the Beauty Stone, for he argues that were he to do so he would be in danger of losing the very gift that has procured him her favour. "Take him to the castle," the Devil counsels her. "Give him further appetite for your kisses, yet starve him by persistent denial. And ere a week has sped—well, I have oft heard what women can do in my country."

From the castle now sounds a prolonged blast of trumpets, and Guntram, decked for war, appears to announce that Philip, desperate in his love and despised by his friends for his wasted life, is marching at the head of his army to Maestricht to do battle for the Prince Bishop. "Aye," the Devil whispers to Saida, "and when he returns, warm with victory, 'tis thy beauty, freshened by the magic charm the weaver shall yield ye, will draw him to thee again." But Philip bids her a cold farewell as, to cries of "Philip of Mirlemont, the Lion of Flanders", the army moves off. Saida, beckoning Simon to follow her, turns towards the castle, followed by the maledictions of Joan.

ACT III

The scene is set on a terrace of the castle looking down on to the town. From a distance comes the sound of Laine's voice singing a song of a lady who waited at the castle gate for her lover to come back. With her wiles Saida succeeds in persuading Simon to give her the Beauty Stone, and when he turns once more into a feeble, broken old man she turns on him with: "Presume no more, thou vile old man," and the Devil hurries Simon away. There is a commotion now in the town and the seneschal reports the return of the victorious army. Saida, beautiful in white, with all her fresh youth and loveliness restored by the Beauty Stone, awaits the return of her lord. But when he appears there is a bandage over his eyes and he leans upon Guntram. Saida rushes to him with the cry: "Strip the cloth from thine eyes. Look at me!" "I cannot, I am blind," he tells her. With a cry of horror she watches him turn from her and bid them lead him to the weaver's daughter. Though his eyes will not see her twisted, crippled form, yet he can see into her soul. For only the blind can see so deep.

"In truth I am not blind. At last, at last
I see thee truly, know thee as thou art.
Though Heaven hath set a veil upon these eyes
It doth but blacken out the ruined past.
And love's star that lights my sunless skies
Shows clear the way that leads me to thy heart."

The Emerald Isle

or

The Caves of Carrig-Cleena

A Comic Opera in Two Acts

By Basil Hood

Music by Arthur Sullivan *and* Edward German

First produced on 27th April, 1901, at the Savoy Theatre, London, with Robert Evett as "Terence", Isabel Jay as "Rosie" and Walter Passmore as "Professor Bunn".

Characters

EARL OF NEWTOWN, K.P., *Lord Lieutenant of Ireland*
TERENCE O'BRIEN, *a young rebel*
PROFESSOR BUNN, *Shakespearian reciter, character impersonator, etc.*
"BLIND" MURPHY, *a fiddler*
SERGEANT PINCHER, *of H.M. 11th Regiment of Foot*
THE COUNTESS OF NEWTOWN
LADY ROSIE PIPPIN, *her daughter*
MOLLY O'GRADY, *a peasant girl*
CHORUS OF IRISH PEASANTS AND SOLDIERS OF 11TH REGIMENT OF FOOT

ACT I

The scene is set outside the park gates of the Lord Lieutenant's country residence in Ireland: the time is the beginning of the nineteenth century. The Irish peasants greatly resent the methods and behaviour of the English Lord Lieutenant, and their champion is Terence O'Brien, rebel and patriot. Unfortunately for his cause Terence does not speak with a trace of a brogue, for his parents, "tempted by the grasping Government of England", sold their dilapidated estate as a summer residence for the Viceroy and retired to England. Terence is therefore a product of Eton and Oxford. The Lord Lieutenant is perpetually attempting to eliminate all Irish brogue and manners, and Terence, descendant of the Borus, Kings of Erin, is equally emphatic in his determination to restore them to the peasantry. To achieve this he hires the services of Professor Bunn,

"Mesmerist, Ventriloquist, Humorist, Illusionist, Shakespearian Reciter, Character Impersonator and Professor of Elocution". In this infectious Sullivan song the Professor expatiates on the qualities of the typical Irishman, who habitually brandishes a cudgel, suggesting that he should at the same time duck his head:

As the Professor has learnt their secrets, Terence insists that he must become a member of the Clan-na-Gael as the only way to insure his life, and he bids the Professor attend their midnight meeting at the haunted Caves of Carrig-Cleena for the ceremony of initiation and branding. Professor Bunn is left in the charge of "Blind" Murphy, a fiddler. When they are alone Murphy strikes a bargain with the Professor. Although he earns his living as a blind fiddler he can really see perfectly, and he has fallen in love with Molly, an attractive colleen, and is anxious to be "cured" so that he can make love to her properly. For, he asks: "How can I tell her she's sweet and pretty when I'm blind?" The Professor agrees to help him.

Now, Terence is secretly engaged to the Lord Lieutenant's daughter, Lady Rosie Pippin. She has discovered that her father has received an anonymous letter giving information that Terence is in hiding in the Caves of Carrig-Cleena, and she hurries to warn her lover of his danger. All are concerned to discover who is the traitor that wrote the anonymous letter. Molly is convinced that it is "Blind" Murphy, for he has accepted the job of piping the Lord Lieutenant's soldiery on the march against Terence and the rebels. Terence believes Professor Bunn to be the traitor, but though Molly disagrees, she will not voice her own suspicion. Molly now conceives a plan to frighten away the soldiers, who are simple, superstitious men of a Devonshire regiment, by telling them that the caves are haunted by the Fairy Cleena. She is supposed to lure men to her cave and keep them there as prisoners for fifty years. Molly proposes to hoax the soldiers by herself impersonating the Fairy Cleena, and Professor Bunn agrees to support her by dressing up as an octogenarian victim of the Fairy. The plot succeeds triumphantly and the soldiers are properly scared by the appearance of Professor Bunn, looking like Rip van Winkel. The result of the ruse is that the soldiers refuse point-blank to march to the caves, in spite of both threats and cajolery on the part of the Lord Lieutenant. The climax to the scene is reached when Molly's voice is heard in the distance singing eerily:

Panic-stricken, the soldiers turn tail and run, and the curtain descends on an empty stage.

ACT II

The scene is the exterior of the Caves of Carrig-Cleena, a romantic spot in the mountains. It is moonlight. The rebels with Terence are assembled and are congratulating themselves on having got rid of the soldiers, when they are warned by some breathless village girls that the soldiers have pulled themselves together and are marching to the caves. The rebels blame the Professor for this failure to rid them of the soldiers, though when he appears he is given one more chance to redeem his failure and frighten them away. This he now proposes to do by means of an illusion known as "Professor Bunn's apparitions". Molly agrees once again to impersonate the Fairy Cleena, and the Professor enters the caves to rig up his apparatus. Presently there is heard approaching the sound of bagpipes, and "Blind" Murphy arrives. He has come to the cave in order to pretend that he has been "cured" of his blindness by the Fairy Cleena. On instructions from the Professor, Murphy looks into the cave and, to his terror, observes the reflection of Molly, which he takes to be the figure of the dreaded Fairy. He falls senseless to the ground, and the Professor's plan to dispatch Murphy to frighten off the soldiers with an eye-witness account of his experience has failed. When Murphy is discovered by the rebels he is accused of being a traitor, of writing the anonymous letter to the Viceroy and coming to the caves as a spy. Murphy pleads that a blind man cannot be a spy, but it comes out at his trial that he has never been blind, and for this deception he is condemned to banishment. He sings a tender farewell:

But he is greatly comforted when Molly tells him that in spite of everything she loves him, and they go off together.

Day is breaking as the soldiers arrive, and they are immediately accosted by peasant girls, who try to attract their attention away from the rebels. The Sergeant and his men proceed to tell them about their girls in Devon:

When the Lord Lieutenant arrives with his wife, she announces her intention of rewarding every soldier in the ranks with a kiss for bravery. Professor Bunn rescues the Sergeant from having to suffer this indignity by whispering to him to pretend he is bewitched. In this way the Lord Lieutenant is convinced that the caves are occupied not by rebels but by fairies. He produces the anonymous letter, which he now assumes must have been a hoax, and offers a thousand guineas for information that will lead to the discovery of the writer. The Professor promptly claims the reward and confesses that he was the writer. He is paid the thousand guineas, but is also immediately arrested as a rebel to be shot. Then Murphy and the other rebels are discovered, and they also are arrested and ordered to be shot. Finally Terence appears and, claiming responsibility for the rebels, receives the same treatment. Rosie pleads for her lover's life, but the Lord Lieutenant tells her that she must look higher for a husband than a rebel, for American blood runs in her veins. On hearing this the Professor declares that if they had only known that, no one would have thought of rebelling. America, he says, is the friend of Ireland. "You are an English nobleman," he tells the Lord Lieutenant. "Therefore you are nowadays more than half American. Therefore you are our friend, and we are no longer rebels. It would be absurd to shoot us." This explanation is accepted by the Lord Lieutenant and, coupled with the fact of Terence's royal descent, which makes his union with Rosie a highly desirable one, there is now no barrier to a happy ending.

Merrie England

A Comic Opera in Two Acts

Written by BASIL HOOD

Music by EDWARD GERMAN

First produced on 2nd April, 1902, at the Savoy Theatre, London, with Agnes Fraser as "Bessie", Rosina Brandram as "Queen Elizabeth", Henry A. Lytton as "The Earl of Essex" and Walter Passmore as "Walter Wilkins".

CHARACTERS

THE EARL OF ESSEX
SIR WALTER RALEIGH
WALTER WILKINS, *a player in Will Shakespeare's company*
QUEEN ELIZABETH
BESSIE THROCKMORTON, *Lady-in-Waiting*
JILL-ALL-ALONE
THE MAY QUEEN
LONG TOM, BIG BEN } *Royal Foresters*
THE QUEEN'S FOOL
CHORUS OF LORDS, LADIES, TOWNSFOLK, SOLDIERS, HERALDS, ETC.

ACT I

On the banks of the Thames at Windsor, the townsfolk are opening their May-day revels by crowning the May Queen. During the ceremony Sir Walter Raleigh passes by and, joining the revellers, treats them all to a drink. His thoughts are full of love, for, in spite of being the favourite of Queen Elizabeth I, his true heart belongs to one of her Ladies-in-Waiting, Bessie Throckmorton. With the assistance of Wilkins, a strolling player in Will Shakespeare's company, the May Queen, and two others, Sir Walter launches into a quintet on the subject of love:

Soon after this Bessie Throckmorton enters and starts to gather flowers. She has lost a letter from her love, Sir Walter Raleigh, and she tells him that she is fearful lest it be found and brought to the Queen, adding "And then the air of Court would be bad for both of us". But their fears are soon forgotten in their overwhelming love for each other.

Among the May-day revellers is a girl known as "Jill-All-Alone". Strange, wild and something of a simpleton, Jill is denounced as a witch by the May Queen, who incites the superstitious townsfolk to seize Jill and bind her arms. A young forester, Long Tom, champions Jill and demands a fair trial on her behalf. "By what right do you speak for her?" asks the May Queen, and Tom answers, "The right of a free man." The Earl of Essex, who happens to be passing by, hears and applauds his words and action and orders that Jill be set free. Addressing Long Tom he tells him "The Queen loves the courage of thy stock, the yeomen of England. She says they built her Throne". And he sings the well-known song:

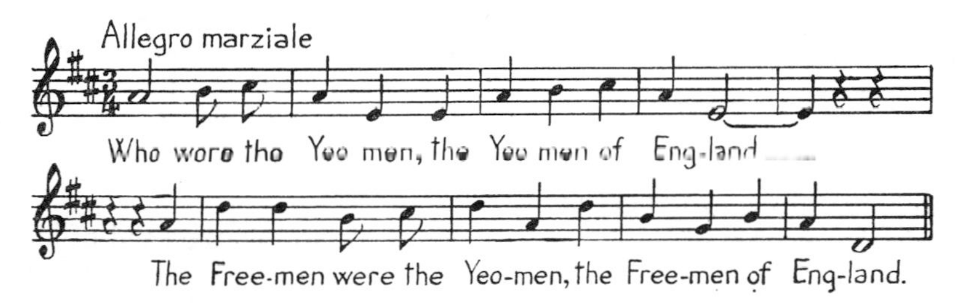

Essex asks Jill why she ventures thither when they are hunting her as a witch. " 'Twas to carry this letter to a lady of the Court, whom I saw drop it in the forest," she replies. The letter is, of course, Sir Walter's love-letter to Bessie Throckmorton, and Essex, taking it, promises to return it. Now, there is intense rivalry between Essex and Raleigh for the Queen's favour, and Essex proposes to use the letter in his possession as a weapon to rouse the Queen's jealousy and further his own cause. He tells Long Tom to keep Jill in his charge and to ask the Queen to judge her.

The royal barge now approaches. Queen Elizabeth is loyally greeted, lands from the barge and sings her song in praise of England:

The May-day games are held in the presence of the Queen, and during a lull Long Tom leads in Jill-All-Alone and begs the Queen to defend her against the accusation of witchcraft. Four citizens of Windsor and the May Queen are her accusers, the jealous May Queen declaring that Jill can draw to herself by magic the love of faithful lovers. Essex now intervenes and hands the Queen Raleigh's love-letter, which he declares was in Jill's possession and may be "a love-charm, a thing of evil purpose". The letter is in the form of an acrostic and the initial letters make the name of "Bessie". Recognising the writing, the Queen believes the love-letter to be intended for herself. But Raleigh, taking it, hands it to Bessie Throckmorton, to whom he wrote it. The Queen, in terrible anger, commands that Jill be burnt as a witch, that Bessie be imprisoned in the castle and Sir Walter Raleigh banished from Court. Then the furious Queen walks to her barge, and the song and dance of the Morris Dancers are heard as the curtain falls.

ACT II

The scene is a glade in Windsor Forest. A prominent feature of the set is the haunted Oak of Herne the Hunter. Jill-All-Alone has managed to avoid capture and is hiding in the forest. She has also contrived Bessie's escape through her knowledge of a secret passage from the castle leading by a trap out of Herne's Oak. In the meantime, Queen Elizabeth has arranged a secret meeting in the forest with an apothecary to whom she offers a hundred crowns for a death-dealing drug with which she proposes to poison Bessie. Sir Walter Raleigh, who has shaved off his beard and is disguised as a forester, overhears the Queen's transaction and when she has departed he accosts the apothecary, who turns out to be the Queen's Fool in disguise. The Fool promises to befriend Raleigh and assures him that his sweetheart shall come to no harm through any fault of his.

Raleigh, unaware of Bessie's escape, now seeks to join the band of Morris Dancers who are due to appear before the Queen and so to enter the castle and attempt to rescue his sweetheart. To this end he approaches the May Queen and begs her to admit him to her troupe of dancers, paying her fulsome compliments and comparing her to the sweetest flower in Dan Cupid's garden—the English Rose:

Raleigh gets his way and is enrolled as a Morris Dancer. When the crowd have withdrawn, Jill leads Bessie out of her hiding-place in Herne's Oak and, telling her to wait, goes off in search of Raleigh, who arrives closely followed by Essex. Essex, realising that his favour with the Queen will be increased if Raleigh marries Bessie, tells Raleigh that they are now friends by circumstance and evolves a plot by which Jill, Bessie and Raleigh shall all obtain the Queen's pardon. According to legend, Herne the Hunter appears only when the reigning Sovereign is about to commit a crime. Essex arranges with Long Tom to disguise himself as Herne, hide in the haunted Oak and appear on an arranged cue.

He then escorts the Queen to the oak to witness a masque performed by the Morris Dancers, who include Raleigh and Bessie. During the masque a distant hunting-horn is heard, and then, to the Queen's dismay, Herne the Hunter comes out of the haunted oak and stands motionless against the red sunset. Horrified, the Queen points to the figure of Herne, while Essex pretends that he sees nothing. So, when the escape of Bessie and Jill is reported, the Queen commands: "Let them go. They are pardoned." Essex offers his arm to the Queen and escorts her back to Windsor Castle, while the Morris Dancers, including Raleigh and Bessie, dance "Robin Hood's Wedding" as the curtain falls.

A Princess of Kensington

A Comic Opera in Two Acts

Written by BASIL HOOD

Music by EDWARD GERMAN

First produced on 22nd January, 1903, at the Savoy Theatre, London, with Walter Passmore as "Puck", H. A. Lytton as "William Jelf", Agnes Fraser as "Kenna" and Louie Pounds as "Joy".

CHARACTERS

SIR JAMES JELLICOE, *a rich banker*
BROOK GREEN, *his junior clerk*
PUCK, *The Imp of Mischief*
WILLIAM JELF, BILL BLAKE, WILL WEATHERLY, JEM JOHNSON — *sailors from H.M.S.* Albion
UNCLE BEN
JAMES DOUBLEDAY, *fisherman*
RECRUITING SERGEANT, *Royal Marines*
OBERON, *King of the Fairies*
AZURIEL, *a Mountain Spirit*
JOY, *Sir James Jellicoe's daughter*
KENNA, *Oberon's daughter*
NELL REDDISH, *niece of the proprietor of "The Jolly Tar"*
CHORUS OF FAIRIES, FISHERGIRLS, FISHERMEN AND TRADESMEN

ACT I

The scene is Kensington Gardens in the early morning of Midsummer Day, where the fairies have been bidden to Oberon's Midsummer Court, this being the one day of the year during which they can disguise themselves as mortals. It is at this Court that the jealous Mountain Spirit, Azuriel, orders his betrothed Kenna, the Princess of Kensington, Oberon's daughter, to produce the mortal, Prince Albion, who once fell in love with her. She must not only find him but prove that he is married to another mortal. Only then will he, Azuriel, no longer distrust her or be jealous of her mortal lover. Kenna and her father, Oberon, beg Puck to find Albion and get him married to a mortal that very day so that all may be well with Azuriel and Kenna. Puck asks Oberon if the other fairies may help in the search, and this request is granted. When the fairies have adopted their various mortal disguises Kenna sings:

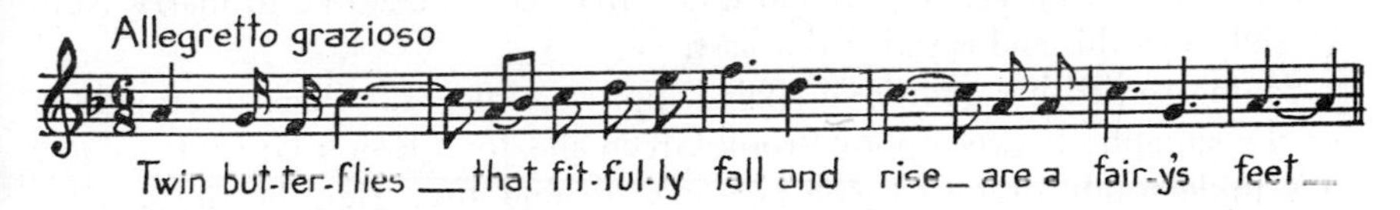

To Kenna's dismay, Puck declares that Albion died many years ago and that the only solution is to find a false Albion and get him married, so that Azuriel may be satisfied. Puck picks on one of four sailors on leave from H.M.S. *Albion*, for he thinks that having the name Albion written on his hat will convince Azuriel that the sailor is indeed the Prince Albion he is so jealous of; and four rather bewildered A.B.'s find themselves, for no reason that they can think of, in Kensington Gardens, where they sing this quartette:

In his search for a girl to be married to the Prince Albion of his creation, Puck assumes the guise of Sir James Jellicoe, a rich banker, who has a daughter Joy and Joy is amazed and disgusted when her father, who had shortly before given his consent to her marriage with his clerk Brook Green, suddenly denies all knowledge of this and insists that she marry a sailor, one William Jelf. The sailor is naturally delighted when Puck, in the shape of Sir James, offers him the hand of his lovely daughter. The only complication is that Jelf's Uncle Ben has arranged for him to marry Nell, the niece of the proprietor of "The Jolly Tar" at Winklemouth. Joy resigns herself to the fact that if she marries against her father's wishes he will cut her off with a shilling, so she decides to accept Jelf. But just as Puck and Kenna bring Azuriel to witness the betrothal of Jelf and Joy, Jelf is confronted with the two marriages arranged for him and decides that he will not wed either girl, but will remain a bachelor. So the fairies' plot has miscarried and the mortals are quite bewildered, as Puck hastily dons the disguise of a Judge and tells Jelf he may marry both ladies if he can find a clergyman willing to perform the ceremony.

ACT II

Act Two takes place outside "The Jolly Tar" at Winklemouth, where Jelf's Uncle Ben is dozing in the sun when the fairies, disguised as fisherfolk, appear. It is an hour before sunset, and Princess Kenna has not yet satisfied the Mountain Spirit Azuriel that Prince Albion is married and therefore no longer interested in her. A Recruiting Sergeant comes to "The Jolly Tar" looking for likely young men, and Sir James' daughter Joy appears from the inn dressed as a servant. She finds it necessary to explain to the Sergeant that she is not an ordinary servant, but that when Mistress Nell marries Jelf she will act as housekeeper, and thus learn household duties so that she will be able to marry the man she loves, poor though he be. Kenna and Puck manage to convince Jelf that his name is Prince Albion and under that name he agrees to marry Nell. Azuriel hears this and is satisfied at last.

Having settled her own love affair happily, Kenna asks Puck to straighten out the situation between poor Brook Green and Joy. Brook Green has come to Winklemouth, disguised as a boatman, to find Joy. Here he sings of his longing for her:

But although Joy is pleased to see Brook, she teases him and they have a quarrel. In despair Brook finds the Recruiting Sergeant and joins the Marines. Joy is dreadfully upset when she hears this, but when Sir James Jellicoe himself appears he rectifies matters by explaining that Brook Green is in his employ and may not enlist without his permission. So Joy's lover is restored to her. Nell decides to marry Uncle Ben and that is the happy end to the Midsummer Day.

Tom Jones

A Comic Opera in Three Acts

By ALEXANDER M. THOMPSON *and* ROBERT COURTNEIDGE

Based on FIELDING'S *novel*

Music by EDWARD GERMAN

First produced in Manchester on 30th March, 1907, at the Princes Theatre and in London on 17th April, 1907, at the Apollo Theatre, with Hayden Coffin as "Tom Jones" and Ruth Vincent as "Sophia".

CHARACTERS

TOM JONES, *a foundling*
MR. ALLWORTHY, *a Somerset magistrate*
BLIFIL, *his nephew*
BENJAMIN PARTRIDGE, *a village barber*
SQUIRE WESTERN
SOPHIA, *his daughter*
HONOUR, *her maid*
SQUIRE WESTERN'S SISTER
LADY BELLASTON
CHORUS OF GUESTS, HUNTSMEN, YOKELS, SOLDIERS, SERVING-MAIDS, ETC.

ACT I

Act One takes place in Squire Western's garden, where a party is being given for the Squire's guest, Tom Jones, who a month earlier had broken his arm saving the life of the Squire's only child, Sophia. Tom Jones has spent the month with the household recuperating. Now Squire Western is determined that Sophia shall marry well and has chosen as bridegroom the rich Blifil, nephew of Mr. Allworthy, a Somersetshire Magistrate into whose family Tom Jones has been supposedly adopted. Unknown to her father, Sophia and Tom have been falling in love in the past weeks, and although the Squire's prim sister suspects what is happening, the Squire takes it for granted that Tom Jones knows his place better than to aim at marrying *his* daughter. Everyone is delighted to see Tom as he enters, dragged on by the ladies, and he is prevailed upon to make a speech and to sing "West Country Lad":

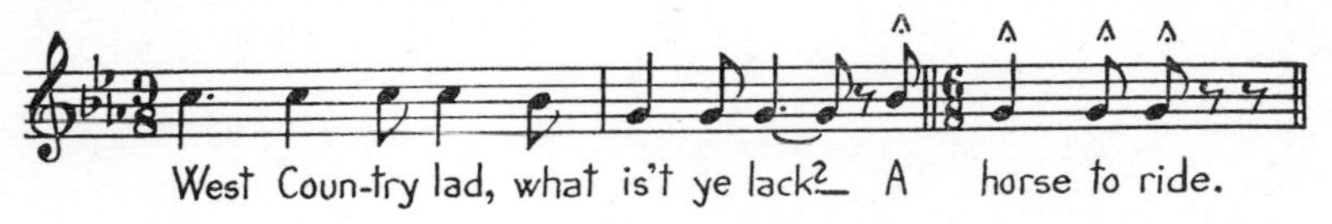

He has not yet declared himself to Sophia, and, left alone in the garden she plaintively wonders just how much he does care for her:

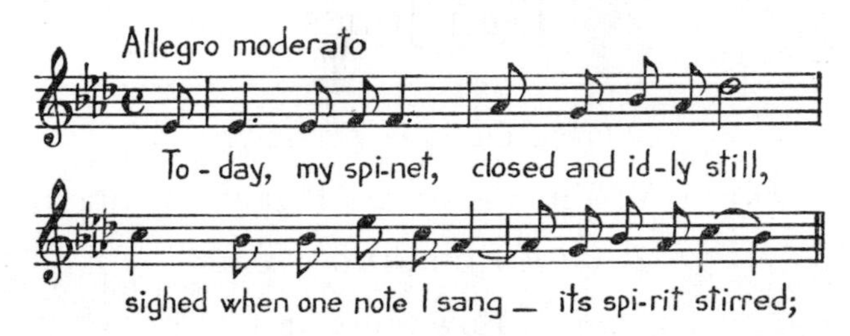

To Sophia's great distress she learns that her father has settled her engagement to Blifil and signed the marriage contract. She pleads with the Squire, telling him that she heartily detests the odious Blifil, but he dismisses this as nonsense and says he is determined on the match. When Tom discovers poor Sophia in tears he is by her side in a moment and tenderly tells her of his love. Blifil, however, comes upon the couple and is extremely offensive to Tom, who knocks him down. Everyone is involved in the ensuing Finale, during which Western disowns Sophia, Tom pleads for help to Allworthy, only to be cast off by him, and the curtain falls on the lovers' hopeless situation.

ACT II

The scene is set in an inn at Upton. Sophia and Tom have run away separately, but by coincidence they have taken the same road. Sophia with her maid Honour is on her way to her cousin Lady Bellaston: Tom has decided to join the army. Squire Western, accompanied by Blifil is pursuing his daughter and has been laid up at this very inn with an attack of gout. His temper is so dreadful that as a last resort the hostess of the inn calls in the village factotum, one Benjamin Partridge, in order that he may practise a "cure" on the Squire. He only succeeds, however, in making the Squire's rage worse. Sophia has sent her maid to find a horse doctor, as her mare has gone lame. Honour, having learned from Partridge that Squire Western is at the inn, returns to her mistress and tells her that to run away is useless, that it is only a wild-goose chase and that she might as well marry Blifil, as there is very little difference between one man and another. Sophia replies with this charming song about "Dream O'Day Jill":

Soon after this Lady Bellaston is carried, half fainting, into the inn, having been attacked by a highwayman and rescued from him by Tom Jones. Much to his embarrassment, she is greatly attracted to him, and goes so far as to let the inn servants think that he is her husband when she takes him off to have breakfast. Partridge, who is hanging round hoping for some business one way or another, overhears the name "Tom Jones". Apparently he knew Squire Western and Allworthy many years ago and is aware of the true story of Tom Jones' birth, which he decides to reveal after first telling Squire Western that both Sophia and Tom are at the inn. All does not go according to plan, however, as Western bursts in upon Tom and Lady Bellaston; Sophia jumps to the conclusion that Tom is fickle and worthless, and leaves a note to that effect; and Tom again decides to take the King's shilling. In the end, persuaded by Partridge that everything can be straightened out in London, Tom accepts Lady Bellaston's offer of her coach and they set off as the curtain falls.

ACT III

The scene opens in Ranelagh Gardens with the company dancing a Gavotte:

Squire Western, having by now heard that Tom is not a penniless orphan, but Blifil's elder brother, has rushed up to London after Sophia to tell her that she can marry Tom Jones. In the meantime, Sophia has had a great social success in London under Lady Bellaston's wing, and makes a grand appearance to sing the well-known waltz song:

At the sight of her Tom summons up his courage and explains everything to Sophia's satisfaction, and the Squire appears in time to bless them both.

Fallen Fairies
or
The Wicked World

An Entirely Original Opera in Two Acts

Written by W. S. Gilbert

Music by Edward German

First produced on 15th December, 1909, at the Savoy Theatre, London, with C. Herbert Workman as "Lutin", Claude Flemming as "Sir Ethais", Leo Sheffield as "Sir Phyllon", Nancy McIntosh as "Selene" and Maidie Hope as "Darine".

Characters

Fairies

THE FAIRY ETHAIS
THE FAIRY PHYLLON
SELENE, *the Fairy Queen*
DARINE, ZAYDA, LOCRINE — *Fairies*
LUTIN, *a serving Fairy*

Mortals

SIR ETHAIS, SIR PHYLLON — *two Hunnish Knights*
LUTIN, *Sir Ethais' henchman*

ACT I

The scene is Fairyland, which for the purposes of the play is supposed to be situated on the upper side of a cloud which floats over the earth. It represents a landscape of ideal beauty, with fountains, trees, waterfalls, etc. On the left is the Fairy Queen's bower. When the curtain rises, the Fairy Locrine is standing on an eminence, peering down through a gap in the cloud and bewailing the wickedness of the Mortal world. Her singing attracts others of the Fairies, who voice their opinion that Mortals must be

> "Wild, barbaric shapes
> All head and tail,
> Some like red, raving apes,
> Some clad in scales
> . . . . .
> All of them foul without and foul within."

But two male Fairies, Ethais and Phyllon, disillusion the girls, telling them that Mortals are formed just as Fairies are formed and that every soul on earth has his Fairy counterpart.

Selene, Queen of the Fairies, now approaches with news of the return from earth of Lutin, the serving Fairy. Presently Lutin appears rising through the gap in the cloud. Eagerly the Fairies question him about life and conditions on the earth below. Lutin embarks on a fascinating tale of a Knight of Portugee, who pursued with love a Moorish maid. But just as he is getting to the exciting part he breaks off, declaring, to the girls' chagrin, that the story is quite unfit for decent ears. Lutin then informs Ethais and Phyllon that the King of the Fairies demands their presence on earth, for he has a priceless gift to bestow on the Fairy world and they are to bear his bounty home. Ethais and Phyllon take their leave and disappear earthwards through the gap in the cloud, while the Fairies speculate excitedly as to what boon the King can possibly give them that they do not already possess. Then Queen Selene tells them of the Mortals' most precious possession. With all their misery, with all their sin, they have the priceless gift of love:

The Fairies, fascinated, crowd round the Queen. "What have we in all our Fairyland to bear comparison with such a gift?" asks Darine. "And may we never love as Mortals love?" asks Zayda. But the Queen tells them that they do not need love in their perfect land, and anyway only a Mortal can inspire such love, and a Mortal may never set foot in Fairyland. Zayda, however, quotes a Fairy law which says that when a Fairy quits his home to visit earth, those whom he leaves behind may summon from the world that Fairy's counterpart, and that Mortal counterpart may stay in Fairyland and fill the Fairy's place till he returns. The younger Fairies, determined to experience the joys of love, urge that if Mortal Man be such a wicked being, Fairy influence could improve his moral welfare. "There is some truth in this," reflects the

Queen; and she finally allows herself to be persuaded into summoning the Mortal counterparts of Ethais and Phyllon. Two roses are cast down to earth through the gap in the cloud, and as each falls Ethais and Phyllon are commanded to appear. Then, to hurried music, Sir Ethais and Sir Phyllon rise through the gap in the cloud, as though violently impelled from below. They are two handsome, barbaric Hunnish Knights, clad in picturesque skins and rude armour, but, though they bear a strong facial resemblance to their Fairy counterparts, they present as strong a contrast as possible in their costumes and demeanour. Their swords are drawn, for the Knights have been interrupted in a duel. The Fairies, half-concealed, watch the combat with great interest. Finally Ethais is severely wounded in the arm, a truce is called and he begs the ladies to bind up his wound. The Knights inquire why they have been summoned. And the Queen tells them:

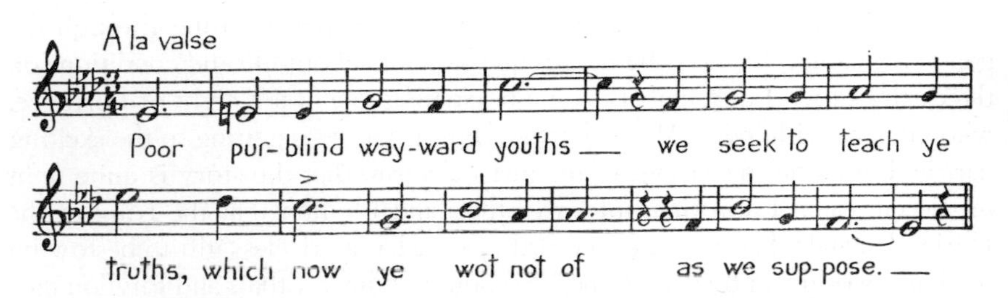

The female Fairies are all enchanted with the two Knights, who begin to flirt with them openly. Queen Selene demands a demonstration of their loyalty to her by a formal gesture, and Ethais promptly kisses her, while Phyllon embraces Darine. Presently Ethais, weak from loss of blood and faint from the pain of his wound, tells the Fairies that he would like to have his henchman, Lutin, with him to administer a certain healing draught. At that moment Fairy Lutin enters, and Ethais, mistaking him for his Mortal counterpart, calls to him to bring the draught. Lutin is appalled at the presence of Mortals in Fairyland and begs the Queen to be warned in time and send them away. "Don't you see," he tells her, "that in each word they speak they breathe of love, and love's the germ of every sin that stalks upon the earth." But Darine turns to the Queen "Send Lutin to earth—then we can summon here his Mortal counterpart. No doubt he, too, stands in need of guidance." So Lutin is dispatched to earth, and as the curtain falls the Queen embraces Sir Ethais; Darine, Zayda, and Locrine hang on Sir Phyllon's neck; while the remaining Fairies group themselves in attitudes of entreaty at the feet of the two Knights.

ACT II

Act Two is the same scene by moonlight. The Fairies, all but Selene and Darine, are discontentedly watching the entrance to Selene's bower. They complain that for six long hours she has been closeted alone with Sir Ethais. "Was it for this that we proposed to her to bring these erring Mortals to our land?" asks Zayda indignantly. "Is this the way to teach a sinful man the moral beauties of a spotless life?" And when Selene emerges from her bower she is accorded a spiteful and mocking reception. "Thou hast done wisely to keep us out of sight," they tell her. "Cage thy bird or he may fly to fairer homes than thine." But Selene can see no wrong in her love for Sir Ethais. Her maternal instinct is aroused by his wounded condition, and she is prepared to give up for his sake all she possesses—riches, honour, life, her very Fairyhood. She gives Sir Ethais a ring and bids him wear it "until thy love fades from thy soul". He assures her that there is no fear of that. Among Mortals it is women who are false: man's love is invariably pure. Selene then leads Sir Ethais back into her bower, watched by the envious Darine. For Darine, too, has fallen for Sir Ethais. "What is this unknown fury that rages in my heart?" she asks aloud. "Jealousy," answers Sir Phyllon, who has overheard her. "And have I done aught to cause this jealousy?" he demands. "Dost thou love me?" Darine asks eagerly, and he tells her: "I love all pretty girls on principle." "But is thy love an all-possessing love? Mad, reckless, unrestrained, infuriate?" she asks impetuously. "That sort of thing," he answers airily. Then she tells him that her love is not for him, but for Sir Ethais, and is disappointed at his calm reception of her news. "What would you have me do about it?" he asks. "Hurl thyself to yonder earth and end at once a life of agony," says Darine intensely. Sir Phyllon is greatly amused and in a duet points out that if all lovers behaved accordingly, the world within a week would be depopulated. Selene now hurries out of her bower, and Darine approaches her, hypocritically sweet. Sir Ethais' wound is not healing, Selene says: what should she do? Darine suggests summoning the Mortal counterpart of Lutin, Sir Ethais' henchman. Selene embraces her. "Thou has saved my Ethais for me," she tells her. "No, not for thee, good sister—for myself," murmurs Darine.

The Mortal Lutin now arrives in Fairyland, and all the girls crowd round him with affectionate curiosity. Zayda sends the other Fairies away to bring refreshment for their guest and, alone with Lutin, makes it her business to warn him against the other Fairies—Locrine is greedy, Darine is vain, Maia's a shrew. "I only am worthy of esteem," Zayda tells him. "If thou wilt love me, I will dower thee with wealth untold, long years and happy life." And she kisses him on the tip of the nose. "You don't take long in coming to the point," is his comment. When the Fairies return with fruit and wine, they question Lutin about himself. He tells them that he has a wife, Darine, and at that moment Fairy Darine enters. Lutin, of course, mistakes her for his wife and starts explaining away how it is that he is surrounded by all these pretty girls. "Be merciful and hear me before you strike," he begs. But Darine wants only one thing from him—the draught to heal Sir Ethais' wound. "Give it to me without delay," she urges. "But tell me first," he demands," how cam'st thou up here, and above all why dost thou want to heal his wound thyself?" Then Darine confesses her love for Sir Ethais. Lutin is shattered. "Oh, Darine, my beloved wife, do not forsake me," he cries, throwing himself at her feet. "I, thy wife?" she asks, astonished. Then she suddenly realises that she must be the Fairy prototype of Lutin's wife and explains the situation. "Then I'm permitted to disport myself with all these fair maids," he exults. Embracing Darine and giving her the phial, he bursts into the joyous song of a husband who:

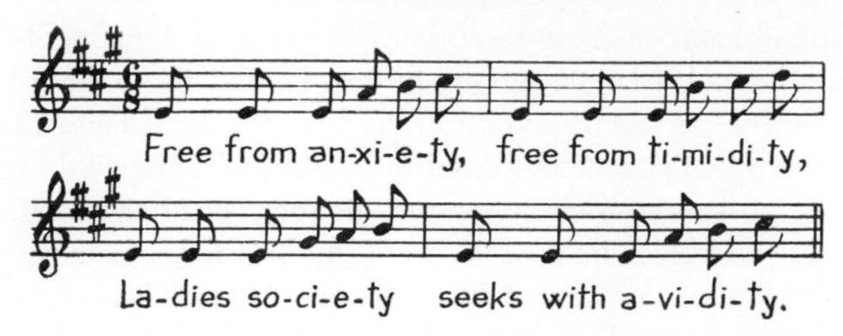

Darine hurries away with the phial to Selene's bower and there she encounters Sir Ethais alone. He is still sick and faint from pain. Craftily Darine says to him: "If Sir Phyllon's words be true, thy wound is but a scratch. He says thou fearest to renew the fight because thou art a coward." Immediately Sir Ethais is up in arms. "Were Lutin here!" he cries. "He is here. I have obtained this precious charm from him," Darine tells him and hands him the phial, demanding in exchange Selene's ring. He swallows the contents and is at once restored to health and vigour. There follows a great argument between the Knights, but eventually Sir Phyllon is able to convince Sir Ethias that he never accused him of cowardice. Sir Ethias turns to Darine. "Didst thou not tell me he had said these things?" he asks, and she replies: " 'Twas but an artifice to gain thy love." He turns on her: "Thou shameless woman, I have done with thee." He begs Sir Phyllon's pardon and the two Knights retire. Queen Selene now appears and the Fairies one and all turn against her, accusing her with cruel words of abusing her royal powers. "Away," they cry. "Thou art no Queen of ours." They take off her crown and put it on Darine. But Selene proudly tells them: "I have a kingdom yet in Ethais' heart." But Darine claims Ethais as hers, showing Selene the ring and Selene, as Ethais appears, notices that her ring is no longer on his finger. He tells her he sold it in exchange for the draught which would enable him to fight Sir Phyllon in defence of his honour—"dearer to my heart than any love of woman." But now the Fairies, Ethais, Phyllon and Lutin, are seen approaching and the Mortals must depart. Desperately Selene tries to detain Sir Ethais. "I'll cling to thee and thou shalt take me to that world of thine," she urges. But he turns on her with the parting words: "Take thee to earth? I love the world too well to curse it with another termagant." He throws off Selene, who falls senseless, and leaps through the cloud in the wake of Phyllon and Lutin as the three Fairies, Ethais, Phyllon and Lutin, return from earth. "Sisters all, we bear the promise of a precious gift. It is that we may love as mortals love," they joyfully cry. But Selene's answer is: "No, no, not that. Such love is for mankind, not us. We will not have this love." The curtain falls as the Fairies kneel in adoration at Selene's feet.

Dorothy

A Pastoral Comedy-Opera

By B. C. STEVENSON

Based on The City Heiress, *a comedy by* APHRA BEHN

Music by ALFRED CELLIER

First produced on 25th September, 1886, at the Gaiety Theatre, London, with Marion Hood (later replaced by Marie Tempest) as "Dorothy", Hayden Coffin as "Harry Sherwood", Redfern Hollins (later replaced by Ben Davies) as "Geoffrey Wilder" and Arthur Williams as "Lurcher".

CHARACTERS

SIR JOHN BANTAM, *the Squire of Chanticleer Hall*
GEOFFREY WILDER, *his nephew*
HARRY SHERWOOD, *Wilder's friend*
JOHN TUPPIT, *landlord of the "Hop-Pole"*
PHYLLIS, *his daughter*
WILLIAM LURCHER, *a sheriff's officer*
DOROTHY BANTAM, *Sir John's daughter*
LYDIA HAWTHORNE, *her cousin*
CHORUS OF VILLAGERS, GUESTS AND GREAT-GRANDMOTHERS

ACT I

Outside the "Hop-Pole" inn in a Kentish village one October day in 1740 the countryfolk on the estate of Sir John Bantam are celebrating the finish of the hop-picking with a rousing Harvest Home. Enjoying the fun are two girls, Dorothy Bantam, Sir John's daughter, and his niece, Lydia Hawthorne. They have dressed up as village girls and greet Phyllis Tuppit, the landlord's daughter, who has become engaged to a young farmer, Tom Strutt. Dorothy and Lydia have decided that they will never marry, and they try to warn Phyllis off marriage also, but without success. Dorothy's antipathy to marriage is the result of her father's arbitrary settlement of her wedded future. If she marries anybody, it must be her cousin, Geoffrey Wilder, Sir John Bantam's nephew and heir. The old man has set his heart on the match. Dorothy has never seen her cousin, who has been living a gay life in London. But this very day Geoffrey has decided, under great financial pressure, to throw in his hand and agree to marry, though unwillingly, his cousin Dorothy on condition that his uncle pays his debts.

En route for Sir John's house, Chanticleer Hall, Geoffrey Wilder and his friend, Harry Sherwood, pull up at the "Hop-Pole" to inquire the way, to refresh themselves and to water and rest their horses. They have made all speed from London since a sheriff's officer, Lurcher by name, has been close on their heels the whole way. When the two young men meet Dorothy and Lydia, who are passing themselves off as the landlord's daughters, Dorcas and Abigail, they are bowled over by their beauty, and Geoffrey decides that, even at the risk of arrest for debt, he will no longer submit to his uncle's demand that he marry his cousin, Dorothy. Dorcas is the only girl for him, and Harry Sherwood feels the same about Abigail. Lurcher then arrives, threatening immediate arrest, but Geoffrey manages to stave it off by saving Lurcher from being ducked in a pond by infuriated villagers after he has served a writ on an unfortunate old woman of the neighbourhood. The subdued and docile Lurcher then agrees to assist Geoffrey in carrying out a scheme which he has concocted to extract money from his uncle without having to marry his cousin, Dorothy, and he promises to accompany the two young men to Chanticleer Hall that evening. Meanwhile the two girls find themselves immensely attracted to the two young men—Dorothy to Geoffrey Wilder and Lydia to Harry Sherwood. To prove their love, Dorothy gives her ring to Geoffrey and Lydia hers to Harry, each making her young man promise never to part with this token.

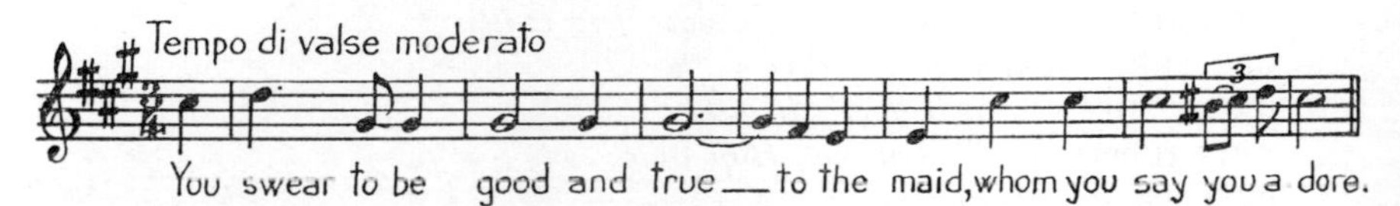

The act finishes with the departure of Geoffrey, Harry Sherwood and Lurcher for Chanticleer Hall.

ACT II

The scene is the hall of Sir John Bantam's country house, Chanticleer Hall. Two staircases lead up to a gallery dominated by a stained-glass heraldic window; suits of armour stand against the walls on which hang ancestral portraits, and a prominent feature of the set is an oaken strong-box. It is night-time, and Sir John Bantam is giving a ball. A stranger is announced, who turns out to be Lurcher in the role of secretary to "His Grace, the Duke of Berkshire". He craves hospitality for "His Grace" and his friend, "Lord Crinkletop", whose carriage has broken down at the gates of Chanticleer Hall. Sir John readily agrees to entertain them, and in come Geoffrey Wilder and Harry Sherwood putting into action their plan of campaign. They do not recognise Dorothy and Lydia as Dorcas and Abigail, and this time it is Harry Sherwood who falls for Dorothy, while Geoffrey is fascinated by Lydia Hawthorne.

When bedtime comes, candles are put out and the guests retire to rest, bidding each other good night in a charming ensemble:

Before the girls retire they manage to charm the young men into presenting them with the rings they received as love tokens from Dorcas and Abigail and, very pleased with themselves and anticipating much fun on the morrow, they go off to bed. Then, alone in the baronial hall in darkness save for a red glow from the fire, Harry Sherwood sings Dorothy a serenade—Hayden Coffin's famous song, "Queen of my Heart":

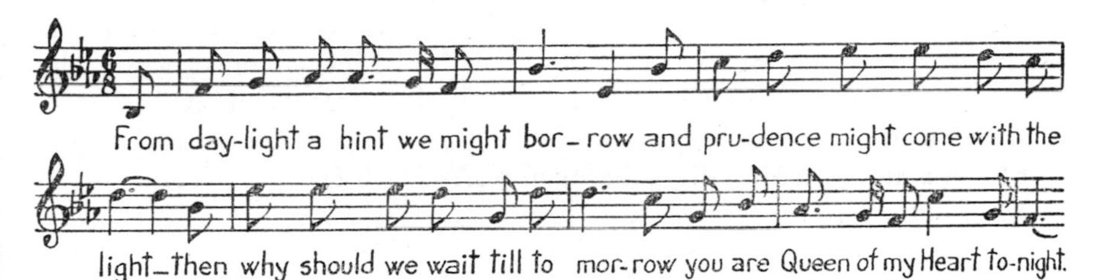

As soon as the house is silent, Geoffrey and Harry, assisted by Lurcher, proceed to put into action Geoffrey's scheme. First of all Harry ties up Geoffrey with a rope. They then both start shouting at the top of their voices, which rouses the household and brings Sir John Bantam down the stairs. He is instantly seized by Harry, who is cloaked and masked, and securely pinioned. When the guests appear it is discovered that the "robbers" have taken none of Sir John's money, but that "the Duke of Berkshire" has not been so fortunate. His cash-box is empty. Sir John inquires how much he has lost, and "the Duke", after some hesitation, quotes the figure of eighty-four pounds—exactly the sum that Geoffrey Wilder owes Lurcher. Sir John insists on making good the sum "His Grace" has lost, and "the Duke" consents to accept a hundred guineas as a loan.

It is now morning and the sound of a hunting-horn is heard. The front door is opened, and there, assembled in the drive, is the huntsman with two "whips" and a pack of hounds. Dorothy and Lydia appear in riding-habits and, escorted by Geoffrey, Harry and Sir John, the Hunt moves off as the curtain falls.

ACT III

Next morning at the Round Coppice, a forest glade in the neighbourhood of Chanticleer Hall, Phyllis Tuppit with her father, the landlord of the "Hop-Pole", and an escort of rustic wedding guests, passes by on her way to church to be married to Tom Strutt. With the coming of daylight Geoffrey and Harry have returned to their senses and to Dorcas and Abigail, and have already written to Dorothy and Lydia breaking off their engagements of the previous night. In reply to their letters they receive a challenge calling upon them to account for their conduct. It comes, apparently, from two young men and summons them to fight a duel at the Round Coppice. The young men turn out to be Dorothy and Lydia, who, dressed in male clothing, wait at the Round Coppice to discover whether their lovers will prefer to fight a duel or to give them up. The two girls, both gun-shy, have loaded their pistols with powder, but when their adversaries arrive they find they have to use the pistols which they have brought and which contain real bullets. They are delighted, however, to find that the young men decline to marry Dorothy and Lydia and are prepared to risk their lives for Dorcas and Abigail. However, faced with the prospect of being forced to fight a real duel, the girls take refuge in flight.

Sir John now turns up at the Round Coppice, where Phyllis and Tom, now married, come to ask his blessing. Lurcher has in the meantime given away the plot, but Sir John is prepared to forgive everything if Geoffrey will marry Dorothy, and eventually he has his way. Dorothy marries her cousin and Lydia marries Harry Sherwood, and the embarrassing circumstances under which Dorothy's ring found its way on to Lydia's finger and Lydia's on to Dorothy's are overlooked. For each of the girls treasures the knowledge that her lover was prepared to die rather than marry her friend.

The Mountebanks

A Comic Opera in Two Acts
Written by W. S. GILBERT
Music by ALFRED CELLIER

First produced on 4th January, 1892, at the Lyric Theatre, London, with J. Robertson as "Alfredo", Cecil Burt as "Risotto", Geraldine Ulmar as "Teresa" and Eva Moore as "Minestra".

CHARACTERS

ARROSTINO ANNEGATO, *Captain of the Tamorras, a secret society*
RISOTTO, *one of the Tamorras*
MINESTRA, *his bride*
ALFREDO, *a young peasant, loved by Ultrice, but in love with Teresa*
TERESA
ULTRICE
THE ALCHEMIST
PIETRO, *proprietor of a troupe of Mountebanks*
BARTOLO, *his clown*
NITA, *a dancing-girl*
ELVINO DE PASTRA, *an innkeeper*
CHORUS OF TAMORRAS, MONKS, VILLAGERS

ACT I

The scene is the exterior of Elvino's mountain inn on a picturesque Sicilian pass. In the distance is a range of mountains, with Etna clearly visible, and a prominent feature of the landscape is a monastery on a steep, rocky elevation. It is a sunny morning one summer day in the early nineteenth century. As the curtain rises a procession of monks winds down the pass, singing, and disappears from view. As they go off a sinister figure appears and watches their departure, and as soon as the coast is clear he makes a sign. Then enter the members of the Tamorra Secret Society, a band of brigands, who today are celebrating the marriage of one of their members, Risotto, to a local girl, Minestra. During the wedding celebrations Arrostino, head of the brigands, announces that the Duke and Duchess of Pallavicini will be passing through the village that evening on their way to Palermo and he proposes to capture them. His plan is for the brigands to seize the monastery, and then, having imprisoned the monks, to don their habits and, by impersonating them, to secure the Duke and Duchess. Minestra is to play an important part in the plot. Disguised as an old woman, she will pretend to have fallen down a rocky ravine by the roadside and lure the Duke and Duchess to her aid by her cries. She will then beg them to take her to the monastery and so lead them into the arms of the waiting brigands. Arrostino explains his plan in a rousing song:

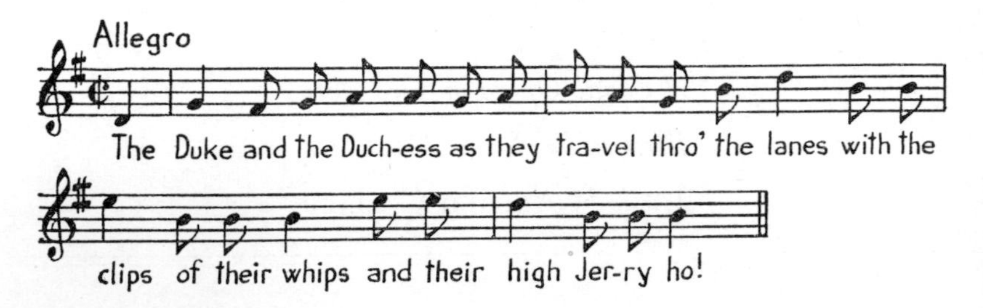

There is another romance afoot in the village between Alfredo, a young peasant, and a girl called Teresa. Now Teresa is fond of exasperating her young man, and eventually Alfredo, tired of Teresa's tantrums, transfers his affections to Ultrice, another girl who has been in love with him and who has been awaiting her chance. Teresa now regrets pretending that she did not love him, and when she sees him making up to Ultrice she feigns madness.

The innkeeper, Elvino, now enters in a state of agitation. Word has come that the Duke and Duchess of Pallavicini intend to stay the night at the inn, and the best bedroom is occupied by an Alchemist in search of the Philosopher's Stone. The Alchemist has hitherto paid for his board and lodging in halfpence, with a written undertaking to turn them all into gold as soon as his discovery is completed. The innkeeper is in awe of the Duke, who has a reputation of being a stickler for etiquette, and he suggests to Alfredo and Ultrice that they should help him with a little rehearsal. Both of them are agreeable to pretending to be the Duke and Duchess, though Teresa makes some caustic comments on their performances.

In the meantime, news of the arrival of the Duke and Duchess has attracted to the village three mountebanks: Pietro, the boss, Bartolo, a clown, and Nita, a dancer. The star turn of their show is the exhibition of two life-size automaton dolls. But these are held up by the customs at the frontier and so, to enable the show to go on, Bartolo and Nita, a devoted pair of lovers, pretend to be the two clockwork dolls, and give their entertainment to the village. But now a dreadful event occurs: the Alchemist, with a terrific explosion, blows himself up. "And this," says the disgruntled landlord, producing a few halfpence, "is all I've been paid for six weeks' board and lodging." It appears that all the Alchemist possessed in the world was a bottle of medicine with a label on it which reads: "This liquid, which should be freely diluted, has the effect of making everyone who drinks it exactly what he pretends to be." This gives

W. S. Gilbert

Mander & Mitchenson

Arthur Sullivan

Hayden Coffin as "Harry Sherwood" in Act Two of *Dorothy*

Agnes Huntington in the title role of Planquette's comic opera *Paul Jones*

Mander & Mitchenson

Gertie Millar as "Mary Gibbs" in the song "Moonstruck" from *Our Miss Gibbs*

Noël Coward and Yvonne Printemps in *Conversation Piece*

Mander & Mitchenson

Mander & Mitchenson

Ivor Novello as "Anthony Allen" and Mary Ellis as "Militza" in the Gipsy Wedding scene from *Glamorous Night*

Pietro an idea: if Nita and Bartolo were to drink the potion they would not only look like clockwork figures, they would actually *be* the two figures. He pours the potion into a wine-skin. Later Alfredo, in his rehearsed role of the Duke, invites the whole company to take wine with him. In spite of Pietro's warning, Alfredo dispenses the potion from the wine-skin in goblets, and all raise the cups to their lips as the curtain falls.

ACT II

The scene is the exterior of the monastery at night. Conditions have entirely changed since the company drank the Alchemist's potion. Minestra, who was pretending to be an old woman in order to entice the Duke and Duchess, now really is an old woman. Alfredo and Ultrice are convinced that they are the genuine Duke and Duchess. Teresa is afflicted with real madness. Nita and Bartolo have become actual clockwork dolls, their insides a mass of ratchets and cogwheels, and the brigands, who were pretending to be monks in order to capture the Duke and Duchess, are now as pious as they can be and incapable of dishonesty. Pietro, however, holds the antidote to correct these abnormal conditions and restore everyone to his or her original state. For on the label of the Alchemist's medicine bottle are the additional words: "If the charm has been misapplied, matters can be restored to their original condition by burning this label." But when he is called upon to produce the antidote, Pietro discovers that the label is missing and declares that he has been robbed. The one who is most affected by this situation is Teresa, and in her madness she seeks to take her life by throwing herself over a parapet into the river. It is the sight of her distress that compels Ultrice to confess that it was she, driven by jealous hatred of Teresa, who stole the label. She then produces it, the antidote is applied, and everybody is restored to his or her original condition.

Erminie

A Comic Opera in Three Acts

By Harry *and* Edward Paulton

Based on the play L'Auberge des Edrets *by* Robert Macaire

Music by Edward Jacobowski

First produced on 9th November, 1885, at the Royal Comedy Theatre, London, with Florence St. John, Frank Wyatt and Harry Paulton.

Characters

THE MARQUIS
ERMINIE, *his daughter*
JAVOTTE, *a maid*
THE CHEVALIER DE BRABAZON
CERISE MARCEL, *Erminie's companion*
EUGÈNE MARCEL, *her brother*
RAVENNES, CADEAU } *two escaped convicts*
ERNEST, VICOMTE DE BRISSAC
CAPTAIN DELAUNAY
PRINCESSE DE GRAMPONEAUX
CHORUS OF VILLAGERS, SOLDIERS, GUESTS

ACT I

The Arrest

The curtain rises to disclose the village of Pontvert *en fête*. A fair is being held and the village green is gay with tents, booths, stalls and bunting. Outside the inn, the "Lion d'Or", the villagers are dancing and making merry. They all stop to crowd round Javotte, a maid from the big house of the village, the Château Pontvert, as she enters to tell them that the party from the Château is en route for the fair. It consists of the Marquis, his daughter Erminie, her companion, Cerise Marcel, Cerise's brother Eugène, who is secretary to the Marquis, and a distinguished guest, the Chevalier de Brabazon. Cerise and Eugène were orphaned and left with ruined estates and prospects, and the Marquis, a distant relation of their mother's, has befriended them, taken them into his household and given them employment. The party from the Château arrive and the old Chevalier is enchanted with the pretty village girls, but Erminie tells him laughingly that love is for the young and impulsive. Erminie and Eugène are secretly in love, but Eugène has not yet plucked up courage to ask the Marquis for her hand. It comes therefore as a terrible shock when the Marquis announces that he has arranged for Erminie to marry the Vicomte de Brissac and that the Vicomte is expected to arrive that day by the diligence. Erminie protests vigorously against having her life organised for her so arbitrarily, but the Marquis tells her firmly that the duty of a soldier's daughter is to obey. Cerise confides to Erminie that she knows Ernest, the younger brother of this Vicomte de Brissac, and that there was formerly a tenderness between them till he was suddenly called home. Then came their family misfortunes, and Cerise has not seen him since.

Now it so happens that this Ernest has succeeded to the title of the Vicomte de Brissac, his elder brother having died. En route for the Château Pontvert he has been attacked by two escaped convicts, Ravennes and Cadeau, who have broken out of Toulon Gaol and are on the run. They have stolen Ernest's credentials and his money and have left him tied to a tree ("Bark to bark" is their description, and it is characteristic of the period comedy). Ravennes and Cadeau duly arrive at Pontvert and order lunch at the "Lion d'Or". Ravennes is both resourceful and presentable, but his companion Cadeau (the comedian of the piece) is drunken, disreputable and eccentric with a parrot cry of "I can prove a halibi". While they are eating their lunch, they overhear through the open french windows of the dining-room a conversation between the Marquis and the Chevalier. From it they learn (*a*) that the Vicomte de Brissac is to be married to Erminie; (*b*) that he is not known to any of the family by sight, the Marquis having fixed up the marriage with his father; and (*c*) that the Vicomte was expected by the diligence but has not turned up. Immediately the resourceful Ravennes steps out through the french windows and, presenting Ernest's credentials, introduces himself as "the Vicomte de Brissac" and Cadeau as "Baron Bonny". He tells a graphic story of how he and his companion, "the Baron", after being set down by the diligence, were attacked by thieves, dragged into the woods, stripped of their valuables and were fortunate to escape with their lives and the rags of their despoilers. The Marquis sympathises with their tale of misfortune, which fully explains their shabby appearance. He introduces "the Vicomte" to Erminie, who receives him coldly. But she is not a girl to give up hope easily, and she confides to Cerise that last night in a dream a tiny bird appeared and told her in a song that all would come right for her and Eugène:

There follows a formal presentation of Erminie's future husband to the villagers by the Marquis. As he is making a speech a company of soldiers march on, singing a stirring song:

Their C.O., Captain Delaunay, announces that they are searching for two convicts who have escaped from Toulon Prison and whom they have traced to Pontvert. At this moment, unfortunately for him, Ernest, who has managed to free himself from his bonds, arrives. Ravennes, in his role of Vicomte de Brissac, immediately denounces Ernest as the robber who attacked him and "the Baron", and poor Ernest is seized by the military and removed to prison.

ACT II

The Betrothal

The scene is the ballroom of the Château Pontvert, where the Marquis is giving a ball. Poor Eugène is greatly depressed and inveighs to his sister, Cerise, at the idea of giving up his beloved Erminie to the loud, bombastic Vicomte. She comforts him with the reflection that it's always darkest before the dawn.

Among the guests at the Château is the elderly Princesse de Gramponeaux. She is enchanted with "Baron Bonny". "His tricks are wonderful," she tells the Marquis. "He charmed the bracelet off my very wrist and declares I shall find it in my jewel-case when I return to Paris; and when a gold necklace and a purse of money were placed under a handkerchief he changed them at a word to a pair of old gloves and a bunch of grapes." Cadeau, who is rather drunk, is having a wonderful time, but Ravennes is concerned lest his vulgar excesses and his petty pilfering may prejudice their safety, and he angrily urges Cadeau to pull himself together and sober up. A sergeant now arrives at the Château, bearing a letter from the Mayor to the Marquis and a written statement by the prisoner (Ernest) for Captain Delaunay. The letter reads: "I have fixed tomorrow for the examination of the prisoner, if convenient for you to be present with the Vicomte de Brissac and his friend." But the Marquis remembers that the notaries are coming to sign Erminie's betrothal contract. This is desperate news to Erminie. She begs her father to postpone the betrothal, but he declares he would do nothing to interfere with her happiness. "I have had experience in suffering," he tells her; "your poor dear mother's loss." "Ah, if I now had her guidance and support," murmurs Erminie. "In fancy I see her tender face and hear her low sweet voice in the dear old lullaby of my childhood days:

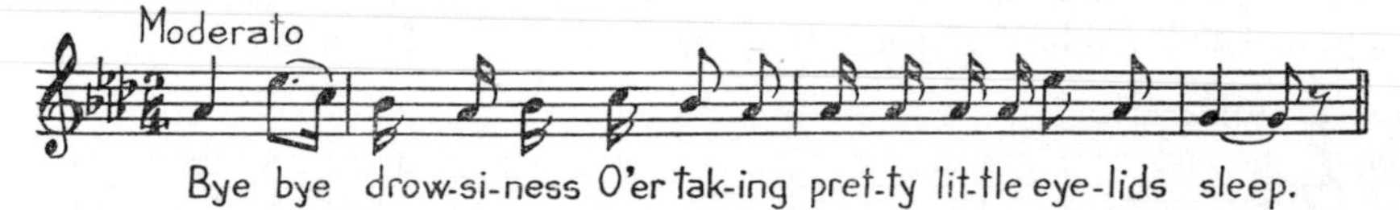

Ravennes now realises that if the papers containing Ernest's defence reach Captain Delaunay and he believes the contents, all is lost so far as he and Cadeau are concerned. So when Erminie comes to him and begs him to release her to marry Eugène and to refuse to sign the betrothal contract, he bargains with her to get possession of the papers. As Captain Delaunay is about to read out Ernest's defence, Erminie takes the papers away from him with the words: "No, no! Captain, business tomorrow. Tonight is devoted to pleasure." Ravennes, when taking the papers from Erminie, whispers that he has a plan to help her and Eugène, and that if she will meet him in the corridor after supper he will explain it to her. After this, dancing is resumed and the curtain falls on a stately gavotte.

ACT III

The Elopement

The scene is a corridor of the Château. Three rooms open out of it—the Princesse's bedroom, the Chevalier's bedroom and Erminie's dressing-room, and from it a staircase ascends to the upper floor. When the curtain rises Ravennes and Cadeau are holding a conference. They plan to make a get-away. Ravennes proposes that Erminie be persuaded to elope in a carriage with Eugène, and that he and Cadeau will then undertake to transport her luggage to the carriage. Part of the plot is to secure her diamonds, for "No female ever eloped without her jewellery," he tells Cadeau. Having carried her baggage to the waiting carriage, their plan is to escape themselves in the conveyance. Ravennes now finds Erminie. He pretends that he has tackled the Marquis, who will not hear of his withdrawing from his engagement to marry Erminie, and that the only course is for her and Eugène to elope. "I will arrange the details, see you safely off and remain to bear the brunt of the Marquis' anger," he promises. He tells her to order a carriage and to go and pack, not forgetting to take her jewellery, which can always be changed into money if necessary. Instructing her to leave her baggage in her dressing-room, he says that he and "the Baron" will carry it to the chaise and then come for her. "This is my dressing-room," Erminie tells him, pointing to the door. "How shall we find it again in the dark?" asks Ravennes. "The doors in the corridor are so alike." "We will drag this suit of armour, which belonged to my great-uncle René, to the right side of the door," she replies. The voices of the guests are now heard approaching as the party breaks up. The Marquis escorts the Princesse to her bedroom. "Where is the dear Baron?" she asks. "He has taken my watch to regulate." Ravennes replies: "He is making an important astronomical observation, taking the altitude of a star." "How accomplished! Just like my poor dear Gramponeaux," sighs the Princesse, quite satisfied. The guests then say good night in a charming part song:

When all is quiet Erminie warns Eugène to meet her in the garden at three in the morning. He is startled, but promises to be there and, hearing the Marquis calling, goes off to see what he wants. Erminie and Cerise now drag the suit of armour into place to mark the door of her dressing-room and they then retire to her bedroom to wait the hour of elopement. Ravennes steals down the staircase and vanishes through the door of Erminie's dressing-room. Presently Cadeau appears and crashes into the suit of armour. He remembers that it marks the position of Erminie's dressing-room but cannot recall whether the room is on the right or on the left. "Right can't be wrong," he says cheerfully and walks straight into the Princesse's bedroom. She screams loudly. Cadeau dashes out of the room and vanishes up the staircase. At that moment the Chevalier walks past on his way to bed, and the Princesse angrily accuses him of trying to "intrude upon the privacy of my apartment". The Marquis and Eugène then appear, and the Marquis, having calmed her down, notices that the suit of armour has been moved and tells Eugène to shift it back to its original place. "Here is your room on the right-hand side of the suit of armour," he tells the Chevalier. Everyone now retires and there is silence till Ravennes appears, looking for Cadeau. Just at that moment the Chevalier comes out of his room, his light having gone out, and in the dark Ravennes mistakes him for Cadeau. He hands the Chevalier a bundle containing valuables belonging to Erminie, including her diamonds, and tells him roughly: "Take it to the bottom of the stairs. Go on and make no mistakes or I'll strangle you." The Chevalier realises that there are burglars in the house, but is too terrified to refuse and goes down the stairs with the bundle. Cadeau now appears and again crashes into the suit of armour, pushing it back to its position to the right of Erminie's door and to the left of the Princesse's room. He denies that he ever took the bundle from Ravennes, and Ravennes, assuming that Cadeau is drunker than he thought, takes him down the stairs to look for the bundle. The Chevalier, having deposited the bundle at the bottom of the stairs, now seeks the safety of his bedroom. "The Marquis told me my door was to the right of the suit of armour," he remembers, and walks straight into the Princesse's bedroom. Her screams rouse the household and lights are brought. She angrily accuses the Chevalier of having designs upon her virtue, but he declares that he is innocent and that there are burglars in the house. Erminie and Cerise then enter in travelling clothes and Erminie confesses that she was going to elope with Eugène. Eugène is dumbfounded, and Erminie tells her indignant father: "Oh! he knew nothing about it. I was going to carry him off. The Vicomte was to help us." In the middle of all this Captain Delaunay appears. He tells the Marquis that the pretended Vicomte is the notorious thief, Ravennes, and the so-called Baron is the escaped convict, Cadeau. Then he introduces Ernest, the genuine Vicomte de Brissac. Eugène and Cerise are delighted to see their old friend, and from Ernest's affectionate attitude to Cerise it is obvious to the Marquis that there is no hope for Erminie in that direction. So with a generous smile he leads Eugène over to Erminie with the words: "Take her, my boy, with my blessing."

Rip Van Winkle

(A Romance of Sleepy Hollow)

Opéra Comique in Three Acts

Libretto by H. MEILHAC, PHILIPPE GILLE *and* H. B. FARNIE

Music by ROBERT PLANQUETTE

First produced on 14th October, 1882, at the Royal Comedy Theatre, London, with Fred Leslie as "Rip Van Winkle", Violet Cameron as "Gretchen" and W. S. Penley as "Derrick".

CHARACTERS

RIP VAN WINKLE, *a village good-for-nothing*
DERRICK VAN SLOUS, *the village lawyer and Rip's rival*
DIEDRICH KNICKERBOCKER, *the village schoolmaster*
CAPTAIN ROWLEY, *of the British Army*
HANS VAN SLOUS, *Derrick's son*
GRETCHEN VAN WINKLE, *Rip's wife*
ALICE, *their daughter*
CAPTAIN HENDRIK HUDSON, *a phantom*
THE RHINE FAY, *a phantom dancer*
CHORUS OF DUTCH SETTLERS, PHANTOMS, NEW YORK LADIES, VILLAGERS

ACT I

The scene is the Dutch settlement of Sleepy Hollow on the banks of the river Hudson near New York. The British rule of George III is openly disputed by the French, and more secretly by the republican party which is springing up in the settlement. When the curtain rises the villagers are celebrating the birthday of the King, whose portrait adorns the signboard of the village inn. Enthusiastically they sing:

"Though he rules from o'er the sea
Faithful colonists are we.
It almost is a shame we're thinking
To make him thus preside o'er drinking."

Soon afterwards a detachment of British soldiers arrives under the command of Captain Rowley to survey a piece of land in a strategic position, which the Government proposes to purchase. The site in question belongs to the village ne'er-do-well, Rip Van Winkle. Rip, who spends his life roaming the Katskill Mountains and poaching salmon in the Hudson river, has a young wife, Gretchen, whom he adores. Sadly she chides Rip with his long absences from home, while Rip regrets that she will never join him on his expeditions. Rip's land, which the Government wants to buy, has been mortgaged to a rascally lawyer, Derrick van Slous, who already sees himself a rich man if Rip cannot discharge his debt. Derrick's son, little Hans, and Rip's daughter, Alice, are childhood sweethearts who intend to marry when they grow up.

Now Rip Van Winkle is by no means the good-for-nothing that everyone supposes. He has made a careful study of the folk-lore and legends of the country-side concerning buccaneers and buried treasure. His explorations are finally successful and he digs up a chest of gold. With part of this treasure he pays off Derrick and redeems his land. The lawyer, however, notices that he has been paid in French coin. This fact, combined with Rip's well-known radical tendencies and long absences in the mountains, gives him the idea of getting even with Rip by accusing him of high treason; and he hurries away to summon Captain Rowley's soldiers to arrest Rip Van Winkle. The villagers urge Rip to fly for safety. As he kisses Gretchen good-bye he assures her that the soldiers will never follow him to his hiding-place. But Gretchen hates the haunted Katskill Mountains and begs him to take care:

Derrick returns with the soldiers, who level their muskets at Rip. But Gretchen shields him with her body and he escapes across a rustic bridge.

ACT II

Rip Van Winkle has made good his escape to the Katskill Mountains. He is followed by a company of villagers, whose ostensible purpose is to capture him, but their real reason is to hamper the soldiers in their pursuit and so assist Rip's escape. The girls of Sleepy Hollow, armed with lanterns, also accompany Gretchen in the search. As night falls and darkness descends the villagers lose heart and urge a return home, but Gretchen, staunch and faithful, refuses to give up, and prays steadfastly for her husband's safety. Gretchen's persistence is rewarded when she meets her husband, but before long they are tracked down by the rascally Derrick. To shield Rip, Gretchen pretends to be in love with Derrick and manages to lure him away, leaving Rip alone in the haunted mountains. He sings a song to cheer himself up, but his voice echoes eerily from the rocks, and he resumes his search for buried treasure. He is energetically plying his pick and shovel in the moonlight when he finds himself surrounded by a sinister company of phantoms: he has strayed into the Glen of Falling Waters, haunted by the ghosts of Hendrik Hudson and his phantom crew. They menace him with diabolical laughter, and when in terror he begs them to tell him who they are, Captain Hudson replies that he and his mariners are forever seeking their way back to their native Netherlands, but are fated not to find it. Rip's supernatural experiences include a Dutch orgy of pipes and schnapps and a game of ninepins. During the drinking he is lured by a water nymph to taste a glass of wine, and this potion combined with the phantoms' spell causes him to fall into the Sleep of Twenty Years. As he loses consciousness, with Gretchen's name on his lips, the phantoms sing:

ACT III

The first scene is the Glen of Falling Waters twenty years later. When the curtain rises Rip Van Winkle is discovered still sleeping in the bracken, while voices of wood-cutters sound from a distance. Rip awakes from his long sleep, now an old man. He descends to the village, and the second scene takes place in Wideawakeville, formerly Sleepy Hollow, which is in the throes of a closely contested election to Congress. Girls are distributing yellow and blue rosettes to Whig and Tory voters, and the candidates are Derrick van Slous, now a wealthy man of property, and Knickerbocker, formerly village schoolmaster. Gretchen is dead, and her daughter, Alice, the same age as her mother was in Act One and exactly like her to look at, has been adopted by the Burgomaster as his housekeeper. Alice is engaged to Derrick's son, Hans, her childhood sweetheart, now a Lieutenant in the American Navy (at war with England). To her joy she receives a letter from him announcing his return home, and happily she sings:

Into the life and bustle of Wideawakeville comes old Rip Van Winkle. No one recognises him and, when he tries to prove his identity, even his own children believe him to be some stray old madman. Little by little he does succeed in recalling himself to their memory, and to his joy Alice and Hans remember the song he used to sing to them as children and join in the refrain:

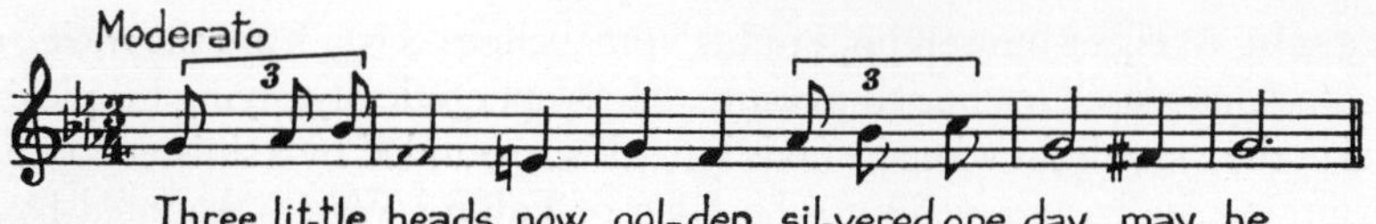

Finally he succeeds in establishing his identity, and Derrick, who has become wealthy through Rip's long absence, is compelled to hand over his wealth and property to the victim he wronged. Thus Rip secures the happiness of Alice and unites her to Hans.

The Old Guard

Opéra Comique in Three Acts

Written by H. B. Farnie

Music by Robert Planquette

First performance on 26th October, 1887, at the Avenue Theatre, London, with Arthur Roberts, Marion Edgecumb (Marion Mackenzie), Fanny Wentworth and Alec Marsh.

Characters

POLYDORE POUPART, *Mayor of the village of Macon*
MONSIEUR DE VOLTEFACE, *envoy of Napoleon*
GASTON DE LA ROCHENOIRE
CAPTAIN MARCEL
SERGEANT CARAMEL
THE MARQUIS D'ARTEMARE
FRAISETTE
MURIELLE
FOLLOW-THE-DRUM, *a vivandière*
CHORUS OF PEASANTS, CONSCRIPTS, LOUIS XVI CI-DEVANTS, COMPANY OF THE OLD GUARD

ACT I

The scene is the village of Vaudrez-les-Vignes near Macon in Burgundy, and prominent features of the set are the *hôtel de ville* and the village inn. It is the first year of the First Empire, when it was the policy of Napoleon I to promote marriages between the daughters of the Legitimist houses and the officers of his army. In this way he sought to conciliate the Faubourg St. Germain. The Emperor is anxious to marry off the daughter of the Marquis D'Artemare to one of his officers, Captain Marcel of the Old Guard. To this end the Marquis is summoned back from England by the Imperial envoy, Monsieur de Volteface, and Mademoiselle D'Artemare is at the same time ordered to return home from Paris. For safety's sake she makes the journey disguised as a peasant. But en route the stage-coach in which she is travelling is attacked by highwaymen and her life is saved by an officer of the Imperial Guard. Though she does not learn his name, Murielle romantically recalls the episode in waltz time:

The village inn is kept by a certain Polydore Poupart, who was formerly valet to the Marquis. Though a Legitimist, he was allowed to stay on after the terror and is now Mayor of the village. Polydore has a waitress called Fraisette, daughter of an old servant of the Marquis, and Polydore remembers that there was at one time a tenderness between her mother, Jaqueline, and the Marquis. The Marquis also recalls that Jaqueline married a certain Corporal Paff, and that when his own wife, the Marquise, died it was Jaqueline who nursed his daughter along with her own. It now appears that Jaqueline went with her husband to Italy in the first campaign, leaving their little daughter, Fraisette, in the care of Polydore Poupart. The Marquis is greatly attracted to Fraisette and is talking to her of her mother when de Volteface enters and salutes Fraisette as the disguised daughter of the Marquis. His error is not corrected and Monsieur de Volteface goes on to announce the Emperor's purpose, which is to marry Mademoiselle Murielle D'Artemare to Captain Marcel, who, in command of a detachment of the Old Guard, is due to pass through the village that night en route for the frontier to repel an Austrian advance. This is most unwelcome news, and the Marquis and his ex-valet, Polydore, put their heads together to contrive a plan to evade the consequences of Napoleon's command. Their plan, born of Monsieur de Volteface's error, is to marry the orphan Fraisette to this Captain Marcel and to invite all the *ci-devant* aristocrats living in the neighbourhood to enjoy the joke at the marriage ceremony, which is fixed to take place at the Château D'Artemare that night. Fraisette is made to believe that she really is the daughter of the Marquis, and Murielle is quite ready to play the part of her maid in the comedy. But though Fraisette consents to be a party to the Marquis' plan of revenge on Napoleon, her heart is really given to a young peasant, Gaston, and the two are deeply in love.

As night falls the Old Guard arrives in the village under the command of Captain Marcel. Among the recruits from the village is the peasant Gaston, and Captain Marcel immediately recognises him as Comte Gaston de la Rochenoire in hiding after the Revolution. The first act curtain descends on a tremendous welcome to the Old Guard:

ACT II

In the hall of the Château D'Artemare that night the guests are assembled for the wedding. All the *ci-devant* aristocrats of the neighbourhood with their wives and daughters have accepted the invitation with relish, and the Marquis and Polydore look forward delightedly to their revenge. But matters do not proceed as smoothly as the Marquis had hoped. For one thing, Captain Marcel recognises in the Maid-in-Waiting (Murielle) the peasant girl whose life he saved in the attack on the stage-coach. For another, Fraisette makes up her mind not to give up Gaston, and in a duet she and Captain Marcel discover that each loves someone else:

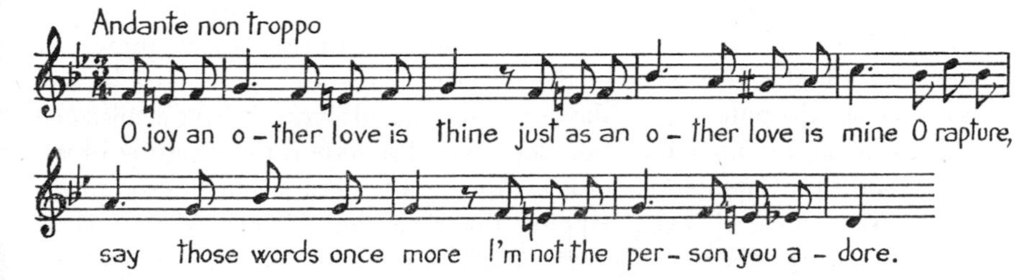

The wedding festivities now begin, and the "heiress of D'Artemare" (Fraisette) is presented to the guests with impatient asides from the Marquis—"Don't bob about like that" . . . "Say something civil"—and acid comments from the noble guests. Up to now Polydore has been hugging himself with malicious pleasure at so successfully scoring off the Corsican. But he receives a sudden shock when he is approached by a senior Sergeant of the Old Guard who informs him that Corporal Paff, before he was killed in Italy, had entrusted him with family papers to be handed over to the Mayor of Vaudrez-les-Vignes. The papers contain startling news. Jaqueline, to revenge herself on her old lover, had changed the two children, and instead of his own child the Marquis has been bringing up the daughter of his servant. Polydore is shattered. He dare not stop the ceremony in the presence of the Imperial Envoy, and if it goes on and the Marquis finds out the deception Polydore blenches at the very thought of his fury. But at the moment when the Mayor is stepping forward to perform the civil marriage ceremony there is a burst of cannon-fire: the enemy have attacked at the very gates of the castle. The situation is saved, for "When the trumpets sound, the bride must wait". Polydore seizes the opportunity to make himself scarce by enlisting, and to the roll of guns and the flash of bayonets the Old Guard marches to battle.

ACT III

Three days after the skirmish with the enemy the troops are still bivouacking in the park of the Château D'Artemare, and both the Marquis and Monsieur de Volteface, seeing no further excuse for delay, insist that the postponed marriage take place. There is only one difficulty. The Mayor is missing. Polydore has decided to leave the country and, as the easiest way to cross the frontier, has disguised himself and enlisted in the Old Guard, which on the next day is due to march into Austria. Captain Marcel now takes his courage in both hands and informs the Marquis of his love for his (supposed) servant, Murielle. The Marquis, however, takes umbrage at what he considers Marcel's presumption and abuses him for trying to evade his honourable marriage engagement. Marcel coldly replies by declaring that he has never been accused of dishonourable conduct since the day he left the roof of the Comte de la Rochenoire. At the mention of this name the Marquis starts. His daughter, as a child, had been betrothed to the son of his friend the Comte. But the coming of the Revolution had separated them, though the Marquis has lately heard that his friend's son, Gaston, is alive and serving under an assumed name in the Old Guard. The impetuous Marquis immediately assumes that Marcel is no other than the young Comte Gaston and without more ado and to the surprise of the happy pair Marcel and Murielle are married by the village Curé in the chapel of the Château. It is only when the unfortunate Mayor is detected and arrested that the mistaken identities are cleared up and it is disclosed that Fraisette *is* the daughter of the Marquis and that Captain Marcel is *not* the Comte Gaston but the son of his father's coachman. All ends happily, for Fraisette, the *real* Mademoiselle D'Artemare, marries her Gaston, while Murielle is happily united to Marcel, the man of her choice. As for Polydore Poupart, he is united to a pretty *vivandière*, "Follow-the-Drum", whose light-hearted amours supply the material of the sub-plot. Polydore has found his spiritual home in the army. As Arthur Roberts sang in his song "The Dashing Militaire":

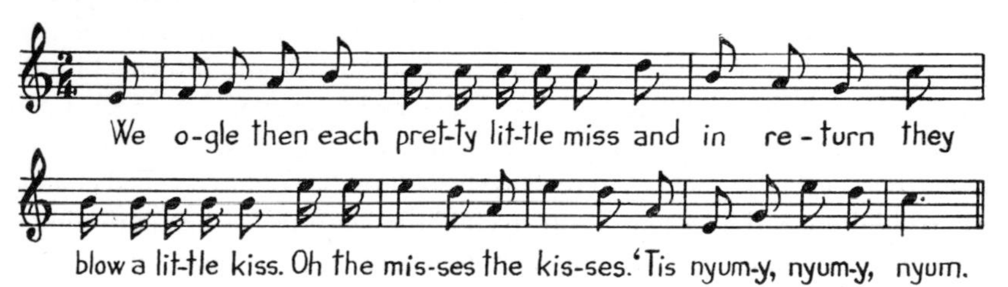

Paul Jones

Opéra Comique in Three Acts

Written by H. B. FARNIE

Music by ROBERT PLANQUETTE

First performed on 12th January, 1889, at the Prince of Wales Theatre, London, with Miss Agnes Huntingdon as "Paul Jones" and Miss Wadman as "Yvonne".

CHARACTERS

PAUL JONES
RUFINO DE MARTINEZ, *a Spanish naval officer*
BICOQUET, *a St. Malo chandler*
DON TROCADERO, *Spanish governor of the island of Estrella*
BOUILLABAISSE, *a smuggler*
PETIT PIERRE, *a fisher lad*
YVONNE, *niece of Bicoquet*
CHOPINETTE, *wife of Bouillabaisse*
MALAGUENA, *niece of Don Trocadero*
CAPTAIN KESTREL, *skipper of a Yankee privateer*
CHORUS OF FISHERMEN, PRIVATEERSMEN, SPANISH AND AMERICAN MAN-O'-WARSMEN, LASSIES OF ST. MALO, LADIES OF THE CHÂTEAU, SPANISH OFFICERS, PAGES, CREOLES, ETC.

ACT I

The scene is the harbour of St. Malo. Outside an inn, "The Cod's Head", Breton fishermen are drinking and trying to persuade the landlady, Chopinette, to give them credit. But Chopinette tartly refuses, telling them that they are no better than her ne'er-do-well husband, Bouillabaisse, for whom she gave up a first-class job as housemaid to the wealthy local chandler, Monsieur Bicoquet. When they are convinced they will get no credit the fishermen depart, and Chopinette retires to the inn. No sooner has she disappeared than Bouillabaisse, a typical old salt, and his apprentice, Petit Pierre, arrive in a boat. Bouillabaisse, ostensibly a fisherman but actually a smuggler, is looking round nervously to see if his wife is about, when he is joined by Paul Jones, a handsome young man apprenticed to the ship's chandler, Monsieur Bicoquet. Paul Jones, the hero of our story, is in love with Monsieur Bicoquet's niece, Yvonne, who returns his love. He has been to sea with Bouillabaisse and Petit Pierre on a smuggling sortie and, safely returned, they sing this charming Barcarolle:

The three then discuss the morning's haul and laugh over an incident which took place while they were "lifting" some casks of contraband liquor from a hide-out known as "The Merman's Cave". They had been interrupted by a bevy of chattering girls celebrating the Feast of St. Yvonne, who, in accordance with the legend, had come to look down the hole in the cave to see their future husbands in the water. Bouillabaisse and Petit Pierre had managed to escape, but Paul had decided to stay and be seen by Yvonne, hoping that she would fancy she had seen in him her future husband. As Bouillabaisse and Petit Pierre are talking they spot the Customs launch approaching and hurry away to shift their boat-load of contraband. Paul Jones is now joined by Monsieur Bicoquet in a very bad temper. He rebukes Paul for absenting himself and finally discharges him, at the same time announcing the unwelcome news that Yvonne has become engaged to Senor Rufino de Martinez, formerly Paul's fellow clerk and now about to be commissioned as an officer in the Spanish Navy. Paul goes sadly away, determined to pack up all his possessions and leave St. Malo.

A bevy of St. Malo girls, among them Yvonne, now appears. They try to persuade Yvonne to tell them the name of the young man whose face she saw in the water of "The Merman's Cave", but she is not to be drawn. As they continue to question her, Senor Rufino appears and declares that he is the lucky man. But all he gets for his pains is a snub from Yvonne, and as the girls depart Chopinette descends on him with a lengthy bill. The next arrival is Captain Kestrel, skipper of a Yankee privateer. He has brought Rufino's sister, Senora Malaguena, niece of Don Trocadero, Governor of Estrella, to St. Malo in his ship. Kestrel is seeking a crew and calls for volunteers to man his ship, the "Flying Cloud". Paul, seeing his opportunity to get away from St. Malo and hoping to earn a fortune and then return and claim Yvonne, signs on—and so do Bouillabaisse and Petit Pierre. In a tender love scene Paul tells Yvonne of his departure. Yvonne tells him that it was his face that she saw in the water of "The Merman's Cave" on the Feast of St. Yvonne and that she is convinced they will be happy in the end. This leads to the big duet of Act One with it's romantic refrain:

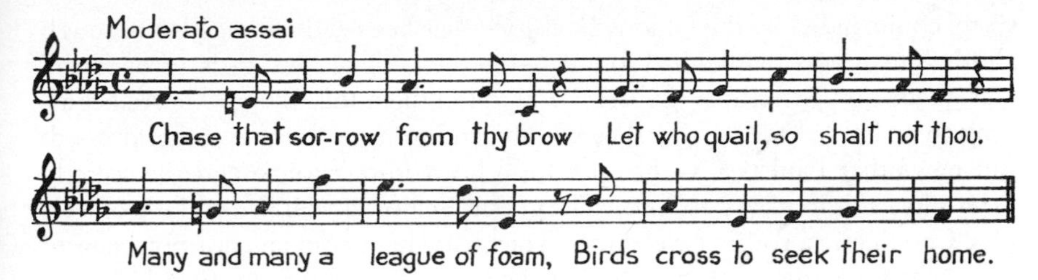

As they are saying good-bye, they are interrupted by Rufino, for whose benefit Yvonne throws both her arms round Paul's neck and kisses him passionately before he goes on board the "Flying Cloud". Rufino retires in fury to prepare for his journey. He is to escort his sister to Madrid, where he is to receive his naval commission and Malaguena is to be married to an old Admiral Mincio. Monsieur Bicoquet, who is greatly attracted by Malaguena, asks her why she wants to marry an old wreck minus one arm, one leg, one ear, one eye and the top of his head. She replies, philosophically, that if the marriage is not a success it won't last long and marks down Bicoquet as a second string to her bow. In the extended finale to the act, Paul persuades Bicoquet to allow Yvonne to postpone her marriage to Rufino for three years: by that time, if he is alive, he hopes to return with a fortune and claim her hand.

ACT II

Act Two takes place on the lawn of the Château Kerbignac, overlooking the Bay of St. Malo. In the distance is a Spanish frigate at anchor. Dawn is breaking as a company of Spanish officers and cadets in cloaks and hats arrive on the scene. They have come with good wishes for Captain Rufino on the day of his betrothal to Yvonne, for three years have now elapsed and Paul Jones has not come back to claim his bride. Gathering beneath Yvonne's window, the Spaniards serenade her:

Rufino thanks them for their good wishes and remarks what a lucky day it was for him when Paul Jones' ship was sunk in the Gulf of Mexico; and he leads his friends off to drink the health of the dear departed and to meet his sister, Malaguena, now Madame Bicoquet. After breakfast Bicoquet settles himself on a garden seat in the sunshine, while Yvonne reads to him from the newspaper. Suddenly a paragraph catches her eye, which reads: "An American armed vessel commanded by the famous Paul Jones has been sighted off Flamborough Head. The report that he had foundered in the Gulf of Mexico is erroneous." Malaguena now interrupts the *tête-à-tête* to tell them that the guests are beginning to arrive for the betrothal ceremony, and to urge Yvonne to get dressed. But news that Paul is alive has put fresh heart into Yvonne and she secretly determines not to marry Rufino. The guests are now assembled and the officers give Chopinette a rousing welcome. They tease her about an enormous pair of *sabots* she is wearing and this provides a cue for the *sabot* song, founded on an old Breton folk-tune:

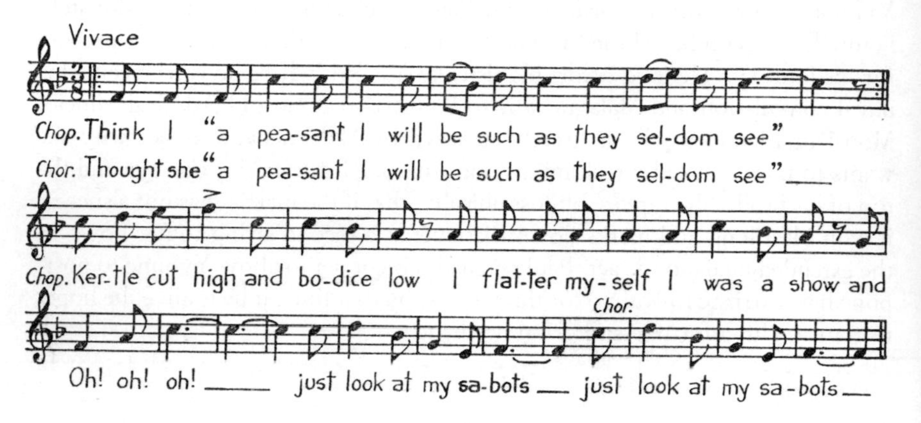

The guests are now assembled, but before the commencement of the betrothal ceremony Monsieur Bicoquet rises to his feet and addresses them: "My friends, before proceeding to the contract of marriage between my niece and Captain Rufino de Martinez, I think it is only right to refer to an engagement, made three years ago with my sanction, by which a certain Paul Jones pledged himself to claim, with a sufficient fortune, the hand of my niece, Yvonne, within three years. This term expires today at 11.45 a.m. It is now 11.40 In five minutes my niece will be free, for this Paul Jones has failed to keep his engagement." "No! He is here," rings out the reply, and to everyone's amazement Paul Jones stands before them. Bicoquet, dumbfounded, demands to see the stipulated fortune, and Bouillabaisse and Petit Pierre stagger in with sacks containing pieces of eight to the tune of half a million francs and Paul produces Bills of Exchange on Paris for another half million. The reunion between Paul and Yvonne is, of course, rapturous, but that between Paul and Captain Rufino is less so. Rufino challenges Paul to a duel, a challenge which Paul accepts. But the duel never takes place. On the following day Malaguena is setting sail for Estrella with her husband and Rufino to introduce Bicoquet to her uncle, Don Trocadero, the Governor. She now arranges with Rufino's Spaniards that when Paul Jones arrives for the duel he and his men will be trapped and carried as prisoners on board the frigate to Estrella. The plan is successful as far as Paul Jones is concerned, but two of his men, Bouillabaisse and Petit Pierre, manage to escape. The act finishes with Paul a captive in irons on board the Spanish frigate, which sails away to this rousing ensemble:

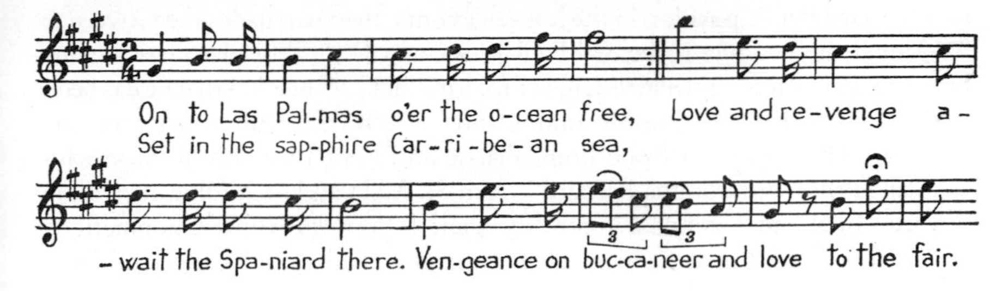

ACT III

Act Three takes place in Government House, Estrella. The Governor, Don Trocadero, uncle to Malaguena and Rufino, is expecting them and his niece's new husband to arrive that day from St. Malo. The Governor has a particularly virulent hatred of Paul Jones, whose piratical sorties have made him the curse of Estrella. He complains that Paul Jones has formed an alliance with the neighbouring King of the Mosquitos, who gives Jones' ship, the "Bonhomme Richard", anchorage. Don Trocadero is exceedingly pompous and conceited and prefaces most of his remarks with: "I don't like to speak of myself, but——". His latest idea is to bribe the King of the Mosquitos with unlimited rum and a paleface squaw to form an alliance with Spain so that next time Paul Jones arrives on the Mosquito shore the Spaniards will be there to trap him. When the party from St. Malo arrive, Don Trocadero is thrilled to learn that his hated enemy Paul Jones is a prisoner on board their frigate. But his joy is turned to fury when Rufino arrives from the harbour with the news that the prisoner has escaped. Paul, determined to see Yvonne and with the courage born of true love, then boldly enters the Governor's house. The first person he encounters is Malaguena, who is about to call the guard and have him arrested when a chance turn in the conversation reveals that it was Paul Jones who was responsible for the death of her first husband. She is immediately all smiles and gratitude to the man who did her such a good turn. She promises to bring him and Yvonne together and in her enthusiasm rapturously embraces him. At this moment Don Trocadero enters, and naturally assumes that Paul must be his niece's new husband, Monsieur Bicoquet, so for the moment Paul is safe. His subsequent reunion with Yvonne leads to a romantic duet:

To safeguard Paul's position in the house, Yvonne then persuades the Governor that Monsieur Bicoquet is the real Paul Jones, and Don Trocadero has the unfortunate man placed under arrest, never for a moment suspecting that he has been deceived. The King of the Mosquitos and his son, the Prince, are now announced. They turn out to be Bouillabaisse and Petit Pierre in disguise who have sailed the "Bonhomme Richard" from St. Malo and are biding their time to rescue Paul and Yvonne. A comedy scene follows in which Chopinette is presented to the King as his new paleface squaw, and Bouillabaisse and Petit Pierre sing a burlesque Indian song, all on one note:

Eventually, when Don Trocadero boasts that he has arrested Paul Jones and proudly displays his captive to Rufino, the deception becomes apparent, and there is nothing for it now but a free fight between Paul and his men and the Spaniards, in which Paul engages Rufino and Bouillabaisse the Governor. The Spaniards are beaten, and Paul hurries on board the "Bonhomme Richard" with Yvonne, followed by Bicoquet and Malaguena, who have had quite enough of Don Trocadero; and as the curtain falls the good ship sails back to St. Malo.

The Nautch Girl

or

The Rajah of Chutneypore

A Comic Opera in Two Acts

Book by GEORGE DANCE

Lyrics by GEORGE DANCE *and* FRANK DESPREZ

Music by EDWARD SOLOMON

First produced on 30th June, 1891, at the Savoy Theatre, London, with Rutland Barrington as "The Rajah Punka", Courtice Pounds as "Indru" and Jessie Bond as "Chinna Loofa".

CHARACTERS

PUNKA, *the Rajah of Chutneypore*
INDRU, *his son*
CHINNA LOOFA, SULLEE, CHEETAH — *his poor relations*
PYJAMA, *the Grand Vizier*
HOLLEE BEEBEE, *a Nautch girl*
BABOO CURRIE, *proprietor of a Nautch troupe*
BUMBO, *an idol*
CHORUS OF NAUTCH GIRLS, LADIES OF THE COURT, SOLDIERS, PRIESTS, COOLIES

ACT I

The scene is described as "A street in the outskirts of Chutneypore". Chutneypore is an imaginary province of India, and its ruler, the Rajah Punka, is in character a combination of autocratic extrovert, of an "off-with-his-head" variety, and a sentimentalist with a phobia for consanguinity. This latter takes the form of filling all the salaried positions in the Government with his poor relations. The most odious, his fifty-fifth cousin, Pyjama by name, holds the post of Grand Vizier. The Rajah's son, Indru, in contrast to his father, is a convinced democrat. Early on in the opera he voices his opinion that

> "The year, the day, the hour is past
> When men should serve the despot caste."

Indru's democratic convictions are the result of his falling in love with a beautiful Nautch girl, the dancer Hollee Beebee. He sings of how he first fell in love with her voice, in this romantic song:

Indru is a Brahmin of the highest caste, and Beebee, too, was formerly descended from high caste, which was lost through a misfortune which occurred to her father, a respected Brahmin, forty years before. He was crossing a river when his boat capsized. A man on the bank threw him a rope and hauled him ashore, but though his life was saved his caste was lost. For the man on the bank was a pariah, and the court held that the taint of dishonour was communicated to him down the rope. He appealed against the decision and the case has been pending ever since. It was to pay Counsel's fees that Beebee took an engagement as a Nautch dancer, but she despairs of the case ever being settled. "Never mind," Indru tells her. "We will be married all the same. If you cannot come up to my level, I must come down to yours." And they swear fidelity to one another.

The Rajah now arrives, heralded with plenty of pomp and an entrance song. This is a cumulative song, built on the pattern of "The House that Jack Built" with the refrain:

The Rajah tries to forbid the match between Indru and Beebee by threatening Baboo Currie, the proprietor of the troupe of Nautch girls, with the forfeiture of his licence, although he is greatly taken with Beebee when he sees her. The Rajah is also seriously worried over the theft of a magnificent diamond, which constitutes the left eye of the sacred Idol, Bumba. The Rajah knows Pyjama to be the thief, but because of the soft spot he has in his heart for his poor relations he feels he cannot denounce him. "What could I do?" he complains. "He fell on his knees and said 'Am I not your fifty-fifth cousin?'"

Indru by now despairs of Beebee ever winning her law-suit and thus regaining caste. He therefore resorts to the desperate measure of appearing in the public bazaar and eating a small plate of potted cow, thus renouncing his caste. He fancies he has now removed every obstacle to his marriage with Beebee. But news arrives that the law-suit has been decided in Beebee's favour. Thus she is promoted in caste at the moment that Indru is degraded and their marriage is as far off as ever. Baboo Currie offers to save the situation by getting them both on the next boat to Europe for a dancing tour with his girls. But the unspeakable Pyjama, as Grand Vizier, remembers an Act of Parliament to the effect that "When a Brahmin marries one of lower caste, together they shall die a traitor's death". He summons the police, and although Beebee manages to escape on board the ship, Indru is arrested and thrown into prison.

ACT II

Act Two takes place in the courtyard of Rajah Punka's palace. A prominent feature of the set is a cell with a grated window, in which Indru is confined after receiving a sentence of six months' imprisonment to be followed by death. The prison sentence is nearly up and Indru is to die on the morrow. Pyjama is chuckling at the success of the first part of his plan. It is the first step towards his ambition to be made Rajah. He has already communicated the facts about Indru in an anonymous letter to the holy Idol, Bumba, which he has laid on his shrine. Pyjama is convinced that when the Idol learns that Punka is the father of a condemned outcast he will certainly sentence *him* to death also. Chortling, Pyjama boasts of his luck, claiming that the secret of his good fortune lies in his subservience to superstition—he never cuts his nails on Friday, nor passes anyone on the stairs, nor looks at the new moon through glass.

Now Indru has a friend in Chinna Loofa, one of the Rajah's other poor relations. She is keen to get married and is always seeking her "affinity". She has already had a go at the Rajah and failed, and now determines to try her charms on Indru. To this end she manages to smuggle into his cell a metal saw. Indru duly escapes, but, grateful as he is to his rescuer, he makes it quite clear to her that his heart still belongs to the absent Beebee. He is hardly out of sight, when Pyjama appears with staggering news: the holy Idol, Bumba, has come to life. Presently Bumba is carried into the courtyard by priests, in a sedan chair. He then informs the Rajah that he has violated the sanctity of the throne. His son has been sentenced to death for attempting to marry out of caste and a felon's father cannot reign over Chutneypore. So Pyjama is appointed Rajah, and Punka, and his son, if he can be found, and all his poor relations are sentenced to be thrown to the sacred crocodiles. Punka has persuaded Bumba to include all his relations in the sentence, hoping thereby to get rid of Pyjama. Chinna Loofa, however, is to be spared, for she has made herself immensely agreeable to Bumba, hoping once more that, in the Idol, she has found her affinity. Bumba is greatly taken with Chinna Loofa and joins her in a rollicking duet with the refrain:

While Indru is skulking about the city, evading recapture, to his joy and amazement he runs into Beebee. She is back from England, together with a marvellous jewel which was given to her there. This turns out to be the missing diamond—Bumba's left eye, in fact. The Idol is entirely appeased by its return. Pyjama's dastardly theft of the diamond is revealed by Punka and Pyjama is duly thrown to the crocodiles. Indru is allowed to marry Beebee, and Chinna Loofa joyfully consents to become the Idol's bride—even though it means being turned to wood. Philosophically she tells herself: "Anybody's bride will do!"

The Vicar of Bray

An Original English Comic Opera in Two Acts

Written by SYDNEY GRUNDY

Music by EDWARD SOLOMON

First produced on 28th January, 1892, at the Savoy Theatre, London, with Rutland Barrington as "The Vicar", Courtice Pounds as "Rev. Henry Sandford" and Rosina Brandram as "Mrs. Merton".

Note. The plot is suggested by the allegory of the song "The Vicar of Bray", and the principal characters are modelled on and named after those in Thomas Day's eighteenth-century children's book Sandford and Merton.

CHARACTERS

REV. WILLIAM BARLOW, *Vicar of Bray*
REV. HENRY SANDFORD, *his curate and pupil*
THOMAS MERTON, *of Bray Manor, another pupil*
MR. BEDFORD ROWE, *a confidential family solicitor*
MRS. MERTON, *a widow*
NELLY BLY, *a première danseuse*
WINIFRED, *the Vicar's daughter*
CHORUS OF STUDENTS, HUNTSMEN, LADY TEACHERS AND LADIES OF THE BALLET

ACT I

"Low Church"

The scene is the village green at Bray and it is the day of the annual school holiday. A rather despondent group of female teachers is gathered together, discussing the dearth of eligible bachelors in the village. Only the Vicar's daughter, Winifred, has a young man. He is her father's Curate, Henry Sandford, but he is such a backward lover that one of the teachers remarks: "When men persist in being maiden-like, the only resource for maidens is to be man-like." Winifred agrees and sings with them:

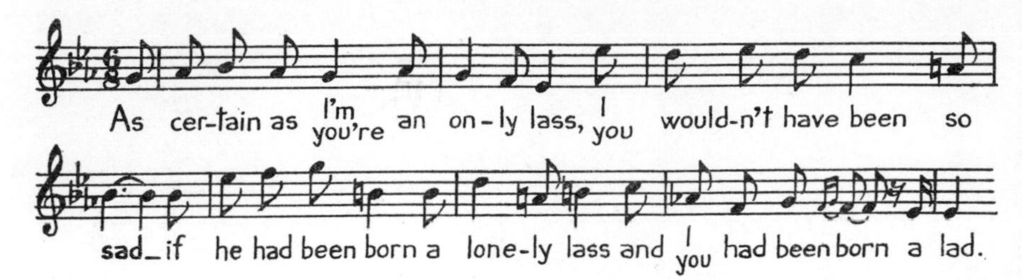

Presently the Vicar, the Reverend William Barlow, appears on the green. He receives a May Day ovation from the villagers and replies with a song, telling them how he became the Vicar of Bray. After the song his curate, the Reverend Henry Sandford, accosts the Vicar and asks first for a rise, which he refers to as "an augmentation of my stipend", and then for Winifred's hand in marriage. The Vicar turns down both requests without the slightest hesitation. He has every intention of marrying off Winifred to the well-to-do young Thomas Merton, only son of his wealthy patron, Mrs. Merton. Sandford is deeply wounded and annoyed and talks of seeing his solicitor. "As if a man of fifty pounds a year could possibly afford a solicitor!" comments the Vicar. At that moment his own solicitor, Mr. Bedford Rowe, appears and the Vicar hastens to consult him on two points. Firstly, the Vicar is considering a proposal of marriage to his wealthy patron, Mrs. Merton, a widow. "What I want to know is this," he asks Rowe. "Does or does not Mrs. Merton's property revert to her late husband's estate on re-marriage?" Rowe tells him it does not. "Secondly," say the Vicar, "I wish to marry my daughter, Winifred, to Tommy Merton. Unfortunately Tommy has set his affections on the *première danseuse* of the *Corps de Ballet* at the Theatre Royal, a notorious person called Miss Nelly Bly. To make matters worse, Winifred has taken it into her head to fall in love with my curate, Sandford. How am I to get rid of him?" "Simplest thing in the world," says Rowe. "Sandford is a conscientious prig." ("You have a happy knack of calling a spade a spade," interjects the Vicar.) "Sandford is Low Church, but you are a time-server." ("You have an offensive way of calling a spade a spade," complains the Vicar.) "I speak as between attorney and client. Turn High Church," he finishes, "and Sandford will of his own accord resign the curacy." The Vicar is greatly taken with his solicitor's suggestion and presently the two men are joined by Mrs. Merton. Mrs. Merton is just as anxious as is the Vicar to see Thomas and Winifred married. But how is it to be accomplished? "Simplest thing in the world," says the solicitor to Mrs. Merton. "You have a general power of appointment over your late husband's estate. Threaten to disinherit Tom." And Mrs. Merton eagerly adopts his suggestion. Then, when they are alone, the Vicar proposes to Mrs. Merton in a duet. She is delighted and, after a token refusal, accepts him.

Sandford has to tell Winifred that her father refuses to sanction their engagement, but he re-affirms his intention to marry her; upon which Winifred, deeply touched, embraces him warmly. But Sandford, the complete prig, rebukes her in shocked tones: "I cannot conscientiously permit demonstrations of affection which have not received the sanction of a civil and religious ceremony. The most I can permit you, Winifred, is to join me in a duet, which I have desired the composer to arrange in such a fashion that I shall appear to greater advantage than you." And he sings:

A sound of galloping hooves is now heard and a company of young men ride on to the scene. They are most unsuitably attired for the first of May, in hunting pink, though they admit it is only done to impress the girls. At the moment there are no girls in sight, but Tom Merton announces that the *Corps de Ballet* of the Theatre Royal, horror-struck by the schisms and dissensions of the Church, have formed themselves into a Co-operative Clerical Reform Association and are coming to interview the Vicar. Presently they arrive on the village green in a terpsichorean flutter. The Vicar peers at the dancers short-sightedly. "Surely I know some of these young ladies," he says. And, indeed, among their number are several of his former Sunday School teachers, who, despairing of ever getting husbands, have gone on the stage to improve their chances. Miss Nelly Bly now invites the Vicar to a tea-party which the ladies of the ballet are giving to the clergy of the surrounding parishes. "There will be cake and buns after which we shall address you," she finishes. "You will address the clergy?" asks the startled Vicar. "Why not?" replies Miss Bly. "You're always trying to improve us, so why shouldn't we try to improve you? I come to hear you preach twice a week, but you never come to see me dance." The Vicar has to agree to the truth of this. But Sandford, arriving with his divinity students, demands the removal of these undesirable young persons. This is the cue for the Vicar to explode his bomb, and he accordingly announces his intention of deserting his Low Church allegiance and allying himself to the High Church. Sandford is appalled at the Vicar's backsliding and forthwith resigns his Curacy, as the solicitor anticipated he would, and declares his intention of serving abroad as a missionary.

"I, rather than infringe the law,
To foreign climes will go;
The Cassowary and Choctaw
Shall cheer me in my woe."

He bids Winifred a tearful farewell and takes his departure.

ACT II

"High Church"

The scene is the Vicarage grounds. The Vicar's secession to High Church principles, in which he is followed by all the divinity students, entails, however, the accompanying frustration of celibacy. The lady Sunday School teachers have in consequence transferred their allegiance from the students to the hunting fraternity. The Vicar confesses that when he "became a pervert" he did not foresee all the consequences. However, there are advantages. Sandford has been disposed of, and nothing has been heard of him since the discovery of his hymn-book among the remains of a cannabalistic festival. Secondly, the Vicar fancies himself no end in his new vestments. And thirdly, he now attends the theatre regularly and takes tea with the ladies of the *Corps de Ballet*. Incidentally, the ladies from the ballet have deserted the hunting fraternity for the Church. Winifred, bereft of her Sandford and believing him to have been devoured, has reluctantly consented to marry Tom Merton. But the Vicar has to break it to Mrs. Merton that owing to his High Church outlook he can no longer marry her, and Mrs. Merton sinks weeping to the ground.

Poor Winifred is very low at the prospect of marrying Tom Merton, to whom she is not in the least attracted. Her thoughts are ever with Sandford, and when she hears his voice again she cannot believe her ears. But Sandford has indeed returned safe and sound. In fact, though he went out to convert the Cassowaries, they, far from eating him, have converted *him*—to common sense and the abandonment of his priggishness. Of course Winifred has now no intention of marrying Tom Merton, and Tom is quite agreeable to handing her over to Sandford. But the Vicar is determined on Winifred's marriage to Tom and is furious at Sandford's reappearance. And he is even more upset when Bedford Rowe, his solicitor, tells him that in view of his ritualistic practices the Court of Arches has deprived him of his benefice and has appointed the Reverend Henry Sandford, in consideration of his missionary labours, to be Vicar of Bray. However, the Vicar is able to strike a bargain. If Sandford will resign his claim to the living of Bray, the Vicar will consent to his marriage with Winifred. "On one condition," says Sandford. "That you will be Low once more." And the Vicar promises: "I will be lower than ever."

The Shop Girl

A Musical Farce

Written by H. W. J. DAM

Music by IVAN CARYLL

Additional numbers by ADRIAN ROSS *and* LIONEL MONCKTON

First produced on 24th November, 1894, at the Gaiety Theatre, London, with Ada Reeve, Seymour Hicks, George Grossmith Jr. and Edmund Payne. Revived, with additional music by Herman Darewski, at the same theatre on 25th March, 1920, with Evelyn Laye in the lead.

CHARACTERS

MR. HOOLEY, *proprietor of the Royal Stores*
CHARLES APPLEBY, *a medical student*
BERTIE BOYD, *one of the boys*
JOHN BROWN, *a millionaire*
MR. MIGGLES, *shop-walker at the Royal Stores*
ADA SMITH, *an apprentice at the Royal Stores*
BESSIE BRENT, *the shop-girl*

ACT I: The Royal Stores
ACT II: Fancy Bazaar in Kensington

A millionaire, Mr. John Brown, has advertised for the missing daughter of a pal of his of the mining camps in Colorado, to whom a fortune of four million pounds is due. Mr. Hooley, the proprietor of the Royal Stores, after making inquiries, believes he has discovered the missing girl to be an apprentice named Ada Smith, who has on her left shoulder the birthmark described in the advertisement. Hooley proposes to Ada and she accepts him, in spite of the fact that she is already engaged to Miggles, the shop-walker of the establishment. (Miggles was played by that great comedian, Edmund Payne, who convulsed Victorian audiences with his trick of picking bits of fluff off the clothes of people to whom he was talking and his way of adjusting the sleeves of the shop assistants. In the second act, by the ingenuity of the author, he appeared as an ancient Roman, in the inky garb of Hamlet, and in the dress of a Pierrot with irresistibly comic effect.) In the end it turns out that the real heiress is Miss Bessie Brent, the prettiest girl in the stores, who is engaged to Charles Appleby, a young but impecunious medical student of good family. The discovery sets matters straight and satisfies everybody, including Appleby's relations.

The Shop Girl is generally recognised to be the first Musical Comedy. It was a new departure in musical show business, for whereas in its predecessor, burlesque, there had been no story at all, *The Shop Girl* presented a perfectly coherent plot. The biggest hit of the score was "Her golden hair was hanging down her back", a number imported from America and sung by Seymour Hicks in his role of Charles Appleby.

The Circus Girl

A Musical Play

By J. T. TANNER *and* ADRIAN ROSS

Lyrics by HARRY GREENBANK *and* ADRIAN ROSS

Music by IVAN CARYLL

With additional numbers by LIONEL MONCKTON

First produced on 5th December, 1896, at the Gaiety Theatre, London, with Seymour Hicks, Ellaline Terriss and Edmund Payne.

CHARACTERS

SIR TITUS WEMYSS
DICK CAPEL
DRIVELLI, *proprietor of a circus*
HON. REGINALD GOWER
COMMISSAIRE OF POLICE
TOOTHPICK PASHA, *the Terrible Turk*
RUDOLPH, *the Cannon King*
BIGGS, *an American bar-tender*
LUCILLE, *a slack-wire walker*
LA FAVORITA, *a bareback rider*
MADAME DRIVELLI
LADY DIANA WEMYSS
DORA WEMYSS

ACT I On the Boulevards, outside the Café de la Régence, Paris
ACT II: Scene 1: In the Ring, at Drivelli's circus
Scene 2: Bureau of the Commissaire of Police
Scene 3: The Artists' Ball
TIME: The Feast of Mi Carême

Dora Wemyss, daughter of Sir Titus and Lady Diana Wemyss, has fallen in love with Dick Capel, a good-looking young man, whom she believes to be none other than Rudolph, the Cannon King of the Circus Drivelli. Dick on one occasion at Dijon deputised for the celebrated performer, and Dora, seeing him in the ring, became infatuated with him. Dora is so obsessed by the glamour of the circus, that Dick dare not confess to her the truth that he is well-connected and rich. Her parents, however, have arranged for her to marry the Hon. Reginald Gower, who is under the spell of a pretty bare-back rider, La Favorita, also a member of Drivelli's circus. Sir Titus, elderly and impressionable, is also fond of going behind the scenes of the circus, and this provides an excuse for the appearance there of various principals of the cast. On one occasion Gower escorts Lady Wemyss and Dora to the circus. They pop down from their box to the stables corridor at intervals, and Lady Diana nearly catches Sir Titus flirting with some Serpentine dancers. He hides in an enormous cannon, from which he is shot into the air, without being injured; and he then attempts to escape unrecognised in a hat and cloak belonging to La Favorita. However, he, Dick and the American bar-tender, Biggs, are arrested and taken before a fussy little French Commissaire. This scene was described in a contemporary theatrical journal as "full of farcical business of the most screaming character". They are finally released and allowed to proceed to the Artists' Ball of the last act, where Dick manages to conciliate Sir Titus, and all ends happily for the lovers.

The comedy of *The Circus Girl* is broad and was greatly to the taste of the public of the nineties. Much of it centres round Biggs, the little bar-tender, who wants to marry Lucille, a slack-wire walker. To obtain the necessary funds he challenges Toothpick Pasha, "The Terrible Turk" of Drivelli's circus, to a wrestling match. The Turk seems likely to make mincemeat of the poor little barman, but Biggs manages to intoxicate his opponent by treating him to champagne, and thus gains the victory. Another comedy character is Madame Drivelli, who has grown too fat to be a circus performer. She is bossed about by her husband, though on occasions he has some difficulty in repressing her. Connie Ediss sang this song, in which Madame Drivelli made fun of herself and her husband's neglect:

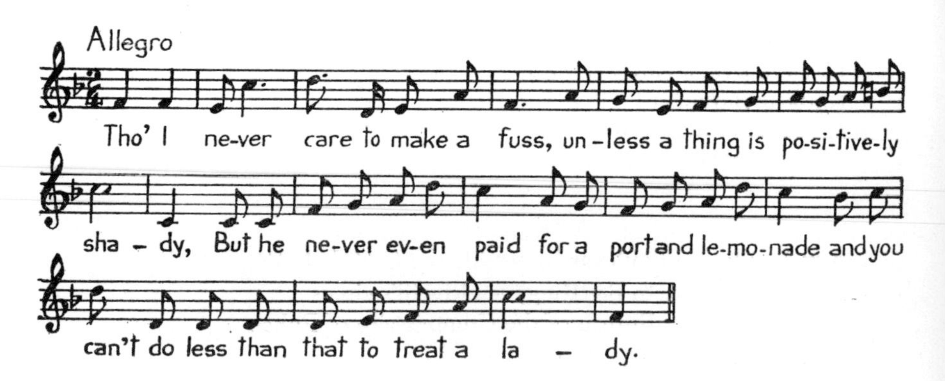

Ellaline Terriss as "Dora" made a big hit with "A simple little string".

A Runaway Girl

A Musical Play

By Seymour Hicks *and* Harry Nicholls

Lyrics by Aubrey Hopwood *and* Harry Greenbank

Music by Lionel Monckton *and* Ivan Caryll

First produced on 21st May, 1898, at the Gaiety Theatre, London, with Ellaline Terriss, Rosie Boote, Louis Bradfield, Edmund Payne and John Coates.

Characters

BROTHER TAMARIND, *a lay brother of St. Pierre*
GUY STANLEY, *Lord Coodle's nephew*
LORD COODLE
SIGNOR PALONI, *Consul at Corsica*
FLIPPER, *a jockey*
CARMINETA, *a musician*
ALICE, *Lady Coodle's maid*
LADY COODLE
DOROTHY, *Stanley's sister*
MARIETTA, *a flower-girl*
WINIFRED GRAY, *an orphan*

Act I: Corsica
Scene 1: A Wood near St. Pierre
Scene 2: Ajaccio
Act II: Venice

In some woods close to the Convent of St. Pierre in the Corsican country-side the girls from the Convent School are picnicking. Among them is Winifred Gray, an orphan and ward of Lord and Lady Coodle. Winifred is being forced to marry a young man she has never seen and, to avoid this distasteful union, she determines to escape from the Convent. To achieve this she joins a troop of wandering musicians, and Brother Tamarind, a lay brother of the Convent, after taking one look at Carmineta, a member of the troupe, decides to accompany her. On arrival at Ajaccio the wandering minstrels encounter a party of Cook's tourists, among whom are Lord and Lady Coodle, Guy Stanley, their nephew, and his sister Dorothy. Now Guy Stanley is the very man whom Winifred is supposed to marry. Though neither is aware of the other's identity it is a case of love at first sight, and Guy is enchanted with "The Minstrel Queen". But the wandering musicians are determined to exploit this love affair to their advantage, and as the price of being allowed to make love to Winifred, Guy has to join a secret society and agree to pay a considerable sum of money. A little jockey, named Flipper, acts as his guarantor. Flipper has got a job as courier to Lord and Lady Coodle through his sweetheart Alice, Lady Coodle's maid. Guy, however, fails to raise the cash, and escapes with Winifred to Venice, accompanied by Flipper and Alice.

Brother Tamarind is greatly concerned at Winifred's flight and, feeling responsible for her welfare, decides to follow her to Venice with his beloved Carmineta. Their flight infuriates the wandering musicians, who have been cheated out of the money they expected to get from Guy Stanley, and now in addition have lost the services of Carmineta and Winifred. They follow the defaulters to Venice and order Flipper, as his guarantor, to kill Guy Stanley. In order to avoid doing this, Flipper and Alice disguise themselves as negroes. Sir William Hake, one of the party of Cook's tourists and a friend of Lord Coodle, recognises Tamarind as the lay brother from Corsica and therefore assumes that Carmineta is the runaway Winifred, and she is accordingly presented to Guy as his future wife and heiress to Lord Coodle. Guy realises that there is a mistake somewhere, and a reward is offered by Lord Coodle for the recovery of Winifred. At the appropriate moment Winifred appears, and is overjoyed to find that Guy is the husband provided for her by her relations, while Guy is equally enchanted to discover that Winifred is the same girl as his Minstrel Queen.

The music of *A Runaway Girl*, apart from opening choruses and finales, has virtually nothing to do with the plot. The most famous number in the score—indeed one of the most famous numbers in all musical comedy—is "Soldiers in the Park", sung by Grace Palotta as one of the Cook's tourists:

Ellaline Terriss had a success with:

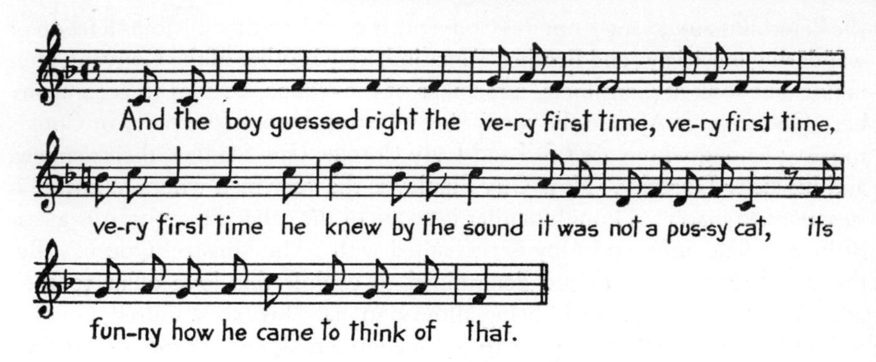

Other popular numbers were Connie Ediss' comedy number "Oh, I Love Society" and the ensemble "The Man from Cook's".

The Messenger Boy

A Musical Play in Two Acts

By James T. Tanner *and* Alfred Murray

Lyrics by Adrian Ross *and* Percy Greenbank

Music by Ivan Caryll *and* Lionel Monckton

First produced on 3rd February, 1900, at the Gaiety Theatre, London, with Lionel Mackinder, Violet Lloyd, Edmund Payne, Rosie Boote, Connie Ediss and Mabel Hobson. The part of "Nora" first played by Violet Lloyd was subsequently played by Marie Studholme.

Characters

CLIVE RADNOR, *a Queen's Messenger*
MR. TUDOR PYKE, *a financier*
LORD PUNCHESTOWN, *Governor of El Barra*
LADY PUNCHESTOWN, *a leader of London Society*
TOMMY BANG, *a district messenger boy*
NORA, *Lady Punchestown's step-daughter*
CHORUS

Act I: Scene 1: Hotel de Luxe, Thames Embankment
Scene 2: Brindisi
Act II: Scene 1: Cairo
Scene 2: Paris Exhibition Gardens

Nora, step-daughter of Lady Punchestown, whose husband Lord Punchestown, Governor of El Barra, is away in Egypt, is in love with Clive Radnor, a young and impecunious Queen's Messenger. She has also attracted the attention of Mr. Tudor Pyke, a financier. He has bought a bill backed by Clive and has also secured several heavy accounts of Lady Punchestown's, which her Ladyship owes to her dressmaker. By threatening to inform his Lordship of her extravagance, Pyke extorts from Lady Punchestown her consent to his proposal for Nora's hand. In order to spoil the chances of Clive, who is going out to Lord Punchestown in Egypt, Pyke proposes to send his Lordship the "Kite" (i.e. the bill which Clive has backed). To this end the financier summons a district messenger boy named Tommy Bang, who is dispatched to El Barra with the strictest injunctions to let nothing—not even a wire from his employers—arrest his progress. Away goes Tommy, and just after his departure Pyke, to his consternation, discovers that he has sent Lord Punchestown his wife's dress-maker's bill instead of the bill which Clive Radnor has backed. He determines to stop Tommy at all costs. Tommy, however, is equally determined to get out to Lord Punchestown. In fact, all the principal characters go out to Egypt. Nora disguises herself as a messenger boy; and Tommy Bang appears in a succession of disguises—as a dancing Dervish and as a mummy—and the machinations of Pyke are again and again defeated. Lord Punchestown is about to open the envelope containing Lady Punchestown's bills when Nora takes it from him and passes it to her mother, thus saving the situation splendidly and bringing the piece to the requisite happy ending.

The big hit number of *The Messenger Boy* was sung by Rosie Boote and was called "Maisie":

Edmund Payne as Tommy Bang sang the title number:

The Orchid

A Musical Play in Two Acts

By JAMES T. TANNER

Lyrics by ADRIAN ROSS *and* PERCY GREENBANK

Music by IVAN CARYLL *and* LIONEL MONCKTON

First produced on 26th October, 1903, at the Gaiety Theatre, London, with Gertie Millar, Ethel Sydney, Gabrielle Ray, Connie Ediss, George Grossmith, Jr., and Edmund Payne.

Note. The Orchid *opened at the new Gaiety Theatre and the first night was attended by Their Majesties King Edward VII and Queen Alexandra.*

CHARACTERS

THE HON. VIOLET ANSTRUTHER, *principal pupil at the Horticultural College*
CAROLINE TWINING, *of a matrimonial turn*
ZELIE RUMBERT, *an adventuress*
JOSEPHINE ZACCARY, *pupil-teacher at the Horticultural College*
MR. AUBREY CHESTERTON, *Minister of Commerce*
THE HON. GUY SCRYMGEOUR, *his nephew*
DR. RONALD FAUSSET, *a country practitioner*
ZACCARY, *a professional orchid-hunter*
COMTE RAOUL DE CASSIGNAT
REGISTRAR
MEAKIN, *gardener at the Horticultural College*

ACT I: The greenhouse at the Countess of Berwick's Horticultural College

ACT II: Scene 1: Place Masséna
Scene 2: Promenade des Anglais
Scene 3: Interior of the Opera House, Nice

An orchid-hunter named Zaccary brings back from Peru to the Minister of Commerce, Mr. Aubrey Chesterton, an orchid worth two thousand pounds, which on the voyage is stolen from him by a seductive adventuress, Zelie Rumbert. Zaccary, however, swindles Meakin, a gardener at the Horticultural College, out of an equally valuable plant, which the Minister gives his nephew, Guy Scrymgeour, to take to Nice. Meakin follows in pursuit of the plant and recovers it by accident: he also has to fight a duel with Comte Raoul de Cassignat of the Quai d'Orsay. A theatrical journal of the period, describing the fight, observed that "Edmund Payne after several absurd experiments with rapier and pistols took up a gigantic two-handed sword and cleared the stage of friend and foe, whereupon the audience became almost hysterical". Incidental to the story are the marriages of two pairs of young people, Ronald and Violet, and Josephine and Guy, who, owing to a mistake of the Registrar, are mixed up. Another feature of the plot is an *amour* between Meakin and Caroline Twining, a lady of ample proportions, to whom he becomes engaged by means of a matrimonial advertisement.

Gertie Millar, as "Violet", had a song about "Little Mary", a euphemism for the stomach recently coined by J. M. Barrie. In 1903 it was still "not done" to mention that part of the anatomy, and many people were grateful to Barrie for breaking the ice.

George Grossmith as "Guy" had an interpolated number from America by Jean Schwarz, to which he wrote his own words. He sang it at the fancy-dress ball in the Opera House, Nice, dressed as a Regency buck. This white scene became the talk of the town. The song was called "Bedelia":

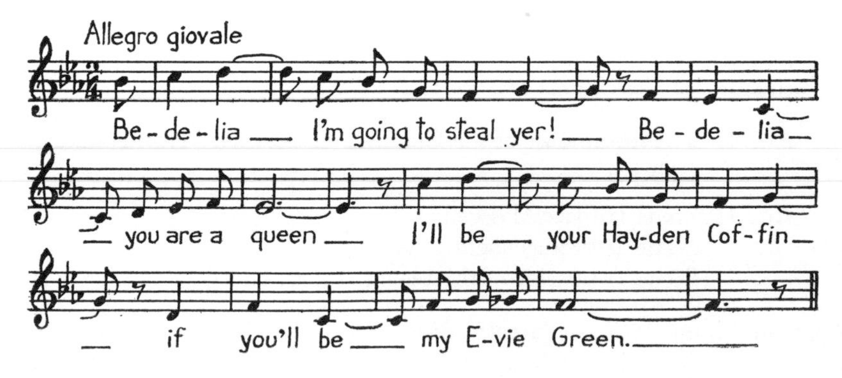

The Toreador

A Musical Play in Two Acts

By JAMES T. TANNER *and* HARRY NICHOLLS

Lyrics by ADRIAN ROSS *and* PERCY GREENBANK

Music by IVAN CARYLL *and* LIONEL MONCKTON

First produced on the 17th June, 1901, at the Gaiety Theatre, London, with Lionel Mackinder, George Grossmith Jnr., Herbert Clayton, Edmund Payne, Marie Studholme, Queenie Leighton, Claire Romaine (later Connie Ediss), Gertie Millar and Florence Collingbourne (later Ethel Sydney).

CHARACTERS

AUGUSTUS TRAILL, *of the British Consulate at Villaya*
PETTIFER, *a dealer in wild animals*
SIR ARCHIBALD SLACKITT, BART., *Lieutenant Welsh Guards*
CARAJOLA, *a toreador*
MORENO, *his friend*
SAMMY GIGG, *a "Tiger"*
DORA SELBY, *a ward-in-chancery*
SUSAN, *proprietress of the "Magasin des Fleurs", Grand Hotel, Biarritz*
MRS. MALTON HOPPINGS, *a widow*
DOÑA TERESA
CORA BELLAMY, *a bridesmaid*
NANCY STAUNTON, *a friend of Dora Selby*
CHORUS OF VISITORS AND BRIDESMAIDS

ACT I: Interior of Susan's flower-shop, Biarritz
ACT II: Market Square, Villaya

Mrs. Malton Hoppings, a wealthy widow, is about to marry a superb-looking Spanish toreador named Carajola. Soon after the rise of the curtain Mrs.

Hoppings arrives with her bridesmaids to inspect the wedding bouquets in Susan's flower-shop. Carajola joins them there. He has come to give his bride the passports with visas for Villaya, in Spain, where they are to spend their honeymoon. But the wedding is delayed by the non-appearance of one of the bridesmaids, Nancy Staunton, who has encountered her dearest friend and school chum, Dora Selby. Carajola is visited at the shop by his friend, Moreno. He tells Carajola that there is to be a Carlist rising in Spain which he is expected to lead, and he also breaks the news that an old flame of Carajola's, Doña Teresa, is on her way to the shop. This means trouble, for Mrs. Hoppings is quite unaware that Carajola was engaged to Teresa when he proposed to her. Another arrival at the flower-shop is Pettifer, an old admirer of Mrs. Hoppings. He is a dealer in wild animals who has put an advertisement in the paper for a tiger. He has also contracted to supply the bulls for the bull-fight in Villaya in which Carajola is to take part. Heralded by a cheerful quartet, "A ride in the puff-puff", Nancy and Dora arrive somewhat late. Dora is a ward-in-chancery, very rich and consequently pursued by fortune-hunters. Among her admirers is Augustus Traill, her guardian's nephew. Dora, wearied by the importunities of the fortune-hunters and believing that Augustus Traill is about to be forced on her as a husband, persuades her friend Nancy Staunton to assume male attire and impersonate an imaginary husband. The two pose as "Mr. and Mrs. Robinson". Dora Selby is sought for by Augustus Traill and Nancy Staunton by Sir Archibald Slackitt.

In Biarritz there is also a pathetic character, Sammy Gigg, a "Tiger" (i.e. a small-sized groom who sat on the boxes of carriages, especially dog-carts and phaetons, wearing a high cockaded hat, livery and top boots). Sammy has come to Biarritz in answer to Pettifer's advertisement. But Pettifer is of course in search of a real tiger. Disappointed in his hopes of a situation, Sammy is at a loose end and very hard up. Doña Teresa now arrives, and soon learns that Carajola is to be married to Mrs. Hoppings. Unfortunately Mrs. Hoppings in company with Pettifer catches Carajola embracing Teresa. In a rage she hands them the passports, and Teresa, taking them, induces the despondent Sammy Gigg to accompany her to Villaya in the character of the toreador. Sammy is delighted with the enthusiastically friendly reception he receives at Villaya, little realising that he will be expected to enter the arena and there meet a particularly vicious bull which has been trained for the ring by Pettifer. He also becomes involved in the Carlist rising, which Carajola was supposed to lead. Bombs are handed to him by a conspirator, with the information that they are time bombs, but he does not know at what hour they are timed to go off. In the end Carajola arrives and matters are straightened out, Carajola relieving Sammy of his bull-fighting and political embarrassments. He claims Teresa, while Mrs. Hoppings accepts Pettifer. "The Robinsons" are exposed, Augustus marries Dora Selby and Sir Archibald Slackitt pairs off with Nancy Staunton.

The score of *The Toreador* is packed with good tunes, headed by a *tour de force* in Pettifer's song with the chorus, "When I marry Amelia" (at St. Paul's):

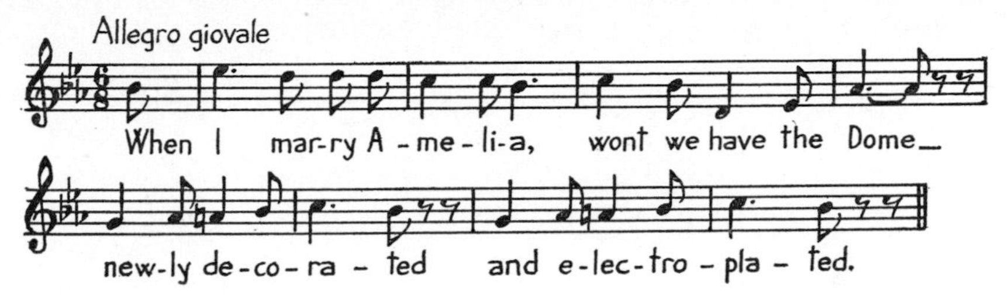

Carajola had a showy toreador's song:

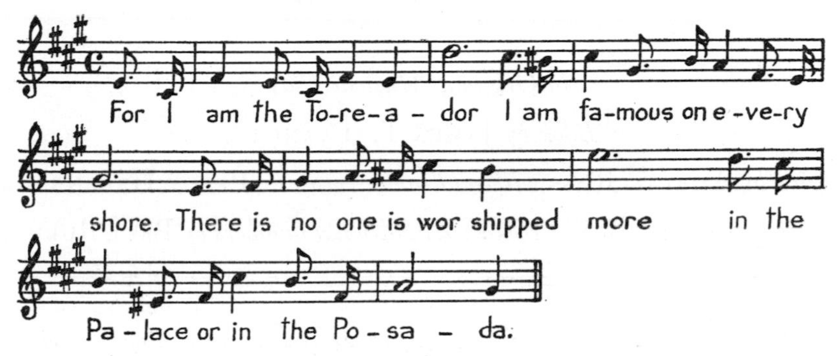

Finally Gertie Millar, on her first appearance at the Gaiety, sang Lionel Monckton's "Keep off the Grass":

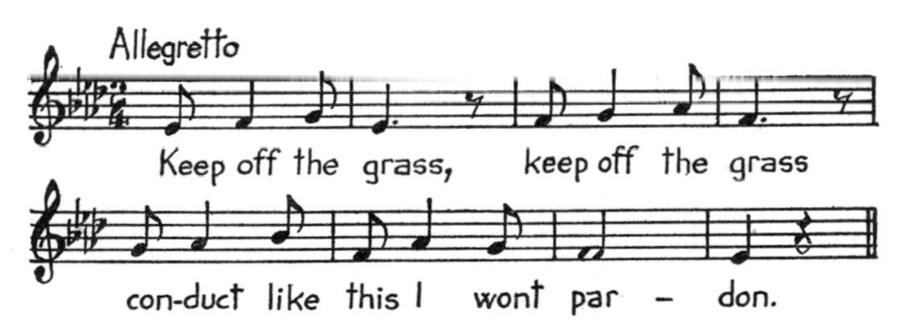

A Country Girl

An Original Musical Play

Book by James T. Tanner

Lyrics by Adrian Ross *with additional lyrics by* Percy Greenbank

Music by Lionel Monckton *with additional numbers by* Paul Rubens

First produced on 1st January, 1894, at Daly's Theatre, London, with Lilian Eldée as "Marjorie", Evie Greene as "Nan", Hayden Coffin as "Geoffrey" and Huntley Wright as "Barry".

Characters

GEOFFREY CHALLONER, R.N.
BARRY, *his valet*
SIR GEORGE VERITY
DOUGLAS VERITY, *his son*
MRS. QUENTIN RAIKES
THE RAJAH OF BHONG, *an Englishman elected Rajah*
PRINCESS MEHELANEH OF BHONG
MADAME SOPHIE, *a dressmaker*
MARJORIE JOY
NAN
LORD GRASSMERE
LORD ANCHESTER
CHORUS OF COUNTRYMEN, MAIDS, SOLDIERS, GUESTS, SERVANTS

ACT I

The scene represents the outskirts of a picturesque Devonshire village. Prominent features of the set are a rose-covered cottage with a garden in front, and the lodge gates of the entrance to the Manor. In the distance is a partly-cut cornfield and the characteristic landscape of the county. It is an afternoon in September, and harvesters and gleaners with sheaves of corn sing the opening chorus. The most prominent resident of the village is Sir George Verity, Deputy Steward of the Borough, who has rented the Manor House from the young Squire, Commander Geoffrey Challoner, R.N., who is abroad. The countryside is in the throes of a Parliamentary election, and Sir George's son, Douglas, is standing as a candidate. Sir George is assiduously making up to Mrs. Quentin Raikes, an influential Society hostess, who he hopes will influence the voting in his son's favour. He proposes marriage to her, but she dodges the issue by declaring that she does not know whether her husband, who was lost in the Himalayas, is alive or dead. Mrs. Quentin Raikes has a great scheme for Douglas Verity's election campaign, which is that the gentry dress up as rustics, canvass the villagers and win their good-will by this display of democratic behaviour. Douglas is greatly attracted to Nan, a Devonshire girl with plenty of character. But Nan has little use for men. "Like flies, all buzz," is her description of them. Nevertheless, Geoffrey Challoner, the absent young Squire, is able to make her heart beat faster.

In the middle of all the election excitement Geoffrey Challoner arrives from abroad, accompanied by his man Barry. Barry, the principal comedian of the piece, is a resourceful character, a brilliant salesman and an arrant flirt. Hearing about the election, Barry insists on his master putting up as a candidate. Geoffrey is perturbed at the prospect, for he has no money, but he is as clay in the hands of Barry, who undertakes to raise the necessary funds. Geoffrey has always been in love with Marjorie Joy, an orphan, brought up on the Squire's estate by her nurse. After Geoffrey went abroad Marjorie moved to London and, unknown to the village, has become a successful singer and actress, under the name of "Miss Montague". Today she, too, has returned to the village. Hearing that Geoffrey is home, she sings the song they used to sing together as children:

Geoffrey hears her singing, and when they meet they find that they are just as much in love as ever.

Fellow passengers of Geoffrey and Barry on board the ship in which they returned to England were the White Rajah of Bhong and his fiancée, Princess Mehelaneh. To Geoffrey's surprise they turn up at the village:

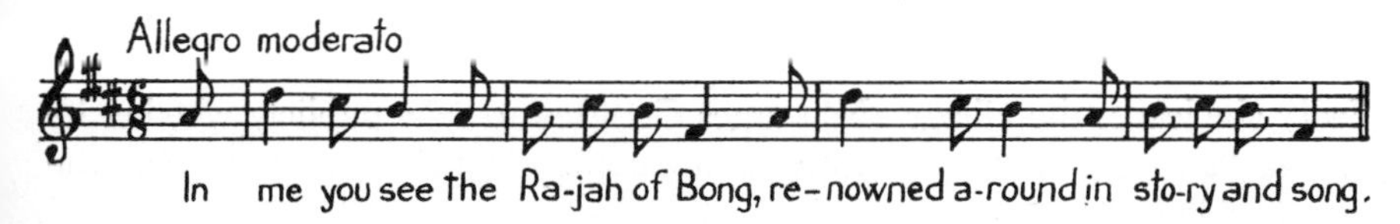

The Rajah is really Quentin Raikes, the husband of Mrs. Quentin Raikes, missing, presumed dead. The Princess does not care two straws for the elderly Rajah, but she has fallen in a big way for handsome Geoffrey Challoner. Barry has hopes of extracting Geoffrey's election funds from the Princess, and to this end he persuades Sir George Verity to offer her and the Rajah hospitality at the Manor. Standing on a cider cask, he addresses the electors, telling them that if they return Geoffrey to Parliament he will marry a Princess with tons of money, give up going to sea and settle down. Geoffrey is furious at Nan's account of Barry's speech and assures her that he loves Marjorie more than ever. "Then why don't you marry her?" asks Nan. "I can't till I have paid my father's debts," is his reply. Just as he is giving her an affectionate, brotherly kiss, Marjorie opens the window of her cottage and watches them disapprovingly. So Nan pushes the embarrassed Geoffrey into the cottage to make it up, and for the moment Marjorie is mollified.

Barry then has another brilliant idea for raising money for Geoffrey's election expenses. Sir George Verity has confided to him that he is doubtful of his son's chances at the poll. Barry, the brilliant salesman, tells him that his young master has a tin-mine to dispose of. He suggests that Sir George buy it, run it and tell the electors that the hours will be short and the wages long. This will ensure his son's election. Sir George falls for this sales talk and buys a useless tin mine for eight thousand pounds. In the village also lives Madame Sophie, a dressmaker with social aspirations, who has made all the rustic dresses for Mrs. Quentin Raikes' election campaign. When that lady cannot pay the bill, however, Sophie blackmails her to introduce the dressmaker into Society. Barry, who in the old days had cast a roving eye in her direction, now comes across Sophie posing as a landscape painter. He eventually recognises his own little Sophie and they recall the days when they were a couple of country chicks.

At the end of Act One Geoffrey is elected to Parliament, but in his hour of triumph his manifold troubles prevent him from savouring his success. For one thing, the Princess is making a dead set at him: she is determined to marry him and take him back to her own country. "There we shall be happy together," she tells him, "under the Deodar":

Geoffrey tells her courteously but firmly that he loves Marjorie and, to soften the blow, gallantly kisses her hand. Unfortunately Marjorie appears at the psychological moment. Seeing Geoffrey kissing yet another girl she decides:

"He loves me not and I
Have but to say Good-bye."

Sadly she leaves the village. Nan urges Geoffrey to state publicly whether he choose "a royal reign" or Marjorie, and Geoffrey makes his declaration as the curtain falls:

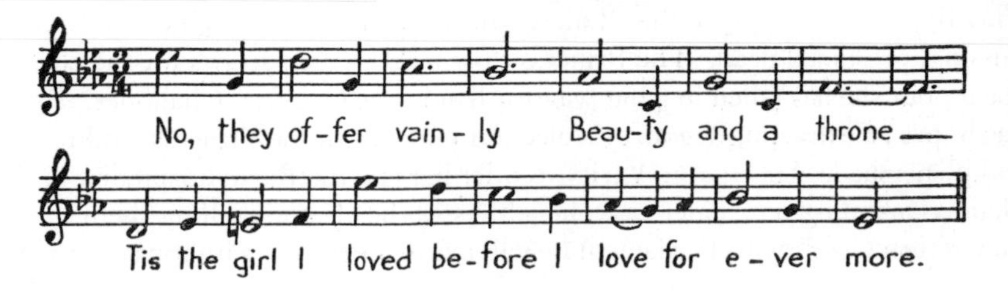

ACT II

At the Ministry of Fine Arts the Minister, Lord Anchester, is giving a ball—a *Bal à la Directoire*—and the guests are in the appropriate period dresses. Marjorie is there, as "Miss Montague", and also Nan, the Quentin Raikeses, and Geoffrey Challoner. Douglas introduces Nan, who is looking magnificent in her *Directoire* dress, to his father. Sir George does not recognise the Devon maid and is very impressed. Barry comes to the ball to keep a jealous eye on Sophie's behaviour with Lord Grassmere. He is disguised as an old dowager and kisses all the girls with relish. Nan instantly recognises that Marjorie and Miss Montague are one and the same person and she tells Marjorie that Geoffrey is at the ball. "With the Princess, I suppose," says Marjorie coldly. Then Nan tells her that Geoffrey is just as much in love with her as ever. "If you want to find out for yourself," she tells her, "meet him as a stranger, as Miss Montague the singer." So when Geoffrey appears and greets her warmly, Marjorie behaves as Miss Montague, a complete stranger. Struck with the great resemblance she bears to his simple little country girl and encouraged by "Miss Montague", Geoffrey pours out his heart to her with fervour, telling of his love for Marjorie:

As far as Marjorie is concerned Geoffrey passes this test with honours. Nan promises to marry Douglas if and when Marjorie and Geoffrey are reunited. Barry, still disguised as a dowager, is posing as a lady of enormous wealth, to whom Sir George Verity promptly proposes marriage, to be sadly disillusioned. Geoffrey has a difficult time restraining the Princess, who is willing to lay everything she possesses at his feet. At long last Geoffrey identifies Marjorie when Lord Anchester asks "Miss Montague" to sing and she obliges with their childhood song: "Hark to the sound of Coo." Then Geoffrey's eyes are opened. He breaks away from Nan, who has managed to restrain him during the song, and, rushing to Marjorie, clasps her in his arms.

The Cingalee

A Musical Play in Two Acts

Book by JAMES T. TANNER

Lyrics by ADRIAN ROSS *and* PERCY GREENBANK

Music by LIONEL MONCKTON *with additional numbers by* PAUL RUBENS

First produced on 5th March, 1904, at Daly's Theatre, London, with Hayder Coffin, Rutland Barrington, Sybil Arundale, Huntley Wright and Isabel Jay.

CHARACTERS

HON. HARRY VEREKER, *a tea-planter*
BOOBHAMA CHETTUR BHOY, *a noble of Kandy*
SIR PETER LOFTUS, *High Commissioner and Judge, Ceylon*
CHAMBHUDDY RAM, *a Baboo lawyer*
NANOYA, *a Cingalese girl*
PEGGY SABINE
LADY PATRICIA VEREKER

ACT I: Vereker's tea plantation, "Karagama", Ceylon
ACT II: Boobhama's palace by the lake of Kandy

Nanoya, a Cingalese girl, is united by a juvenile engagement to the proud and pompous Boobhama Chettur Bhoy, a Kandy nobleman. She runs away from him, however, and at the opening of the play she is working as a tea-girl on her own plantation, which has been fraudulently leased by a crooked Baboo lawyer, Chambhuddy Ram, to handsome Harry Vereker. Nanoya falls in love with Harry Vereker, but Bhoy appeals to British justice in the person of the High Commissioner, Sir Peter Loftus, who decides in Bhoy's favour. Sir Peter, in his capacity as Judge, is hot on the track of Chambhuddy Ram, to charge him with stealing a valuable black pearl. The pearl eventually comes into the hands of Harry, who has obtained it from Peggy Sabine, a teacher of smart Society calisthenics, and he presents the pearl to Nanoya, whom he loves. So the unscrupulous Chambhuddy Ram when accused of its theft is able to lay the blame on Nanoya, and to Harry's despair she is carried off to Boobhama's palace. But while preparations are being made for Nanoya's wedding Harry disguises himself as a rickshaw runner and, with the aid of Peggy Sabine, Chambhuddy Ram and Lady Patricia, manages to rescue her to the fury of Boobhama. So the lovers are united and virtue is triumphant.

Contemporary critics described Sybil Arundale's performance of "My Cinammon Tree" as "Full of simple tenderness":

Huntley Wright played the educated Baboo lawyer, the sleek and artful Chambhuddy Ram, and his malapropisms were received with roars of laughter. He scored a success with "The Wonderful English Pot":

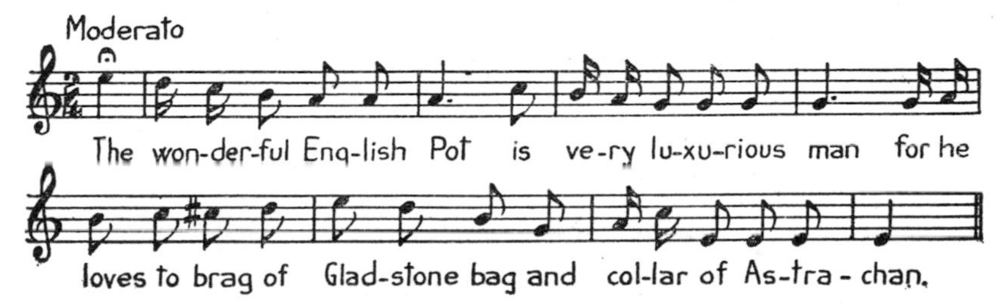

Hayden Coffin as Harry Vereker had two popular numbers:

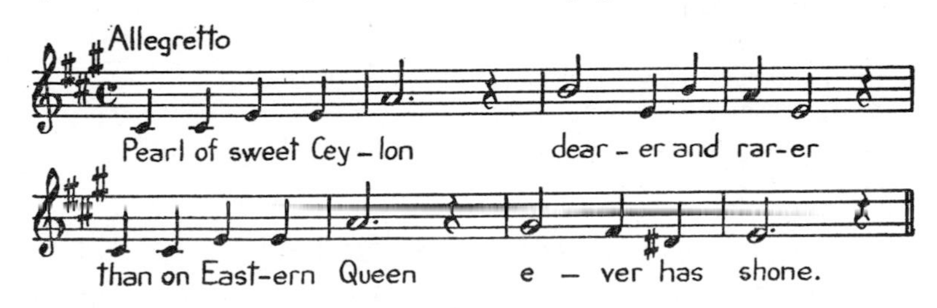

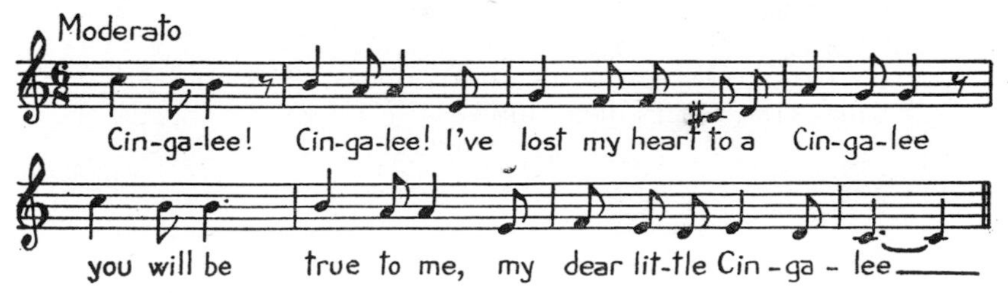

Our Miss Gibbs

Musical Play in Two Acts

Book by "CHRYPTOS"

Constructed by JAMES TANNER

Lyrics by ADRIAN ROSS *and* PERCY GREENBANK

Music by IVAN CARYLL *and* LIONEL MONCKTON

First produced on 23rd January, 1909, at the Gaiety Theatre, London, with Gertie Millar as "Mary", George Grossmith, Jr. as "Hughie" and Edmund Payne as "Tim".

CHARACTERS

THE HON. HUGHIE PIERREPOINT, *an amateur criminal*
THE EARL OF ST. IVES
LORD EYNSFORD, *his son*
LADY ELIZABETH THANET, *engaged to Lord Eynsford*
THE DUCHESS OF MINSTER, *her mother*
MR. TOPLADY, *manager of Garrod's Stores*
MR. BEAVIS, *The Earl's family solicitor*
SLITHERS, *a professional crook*
MRS. FARQUHAR, *an impecunious woman of fashion*
MADAME JEANNE, *modiste at Garrod's*
TIMOTHY GIBBS, *Mary's Yorkshire cousin*
MARY GIBBS
CHORUS OF GIRLS AT GARROD'S STORE, DUDES, IRISH COLLEENS AT THE WHITE CITY, LADIES OF FASHION

ACT I

The scene is the vestibule with general entrance to Garrod's Department Stores. When the curtain rises on a Saturday morning in July 1909 the stage is full of colour and bustle: shop assistants are serving customers, mannequins parading, shop-walkers answering inquiries. The prop of Garrod's Stores and the apple of Mr. Toplady, the manager's, eye is Mary Gibbs, a Yorkshire girl, who runs the flower department. She is enormously popular with the dudes—a 1909 expression describing a young man-about-town. But she has her head screwed on tight as she explains in this song:

Mary's most devoted admirer is Lord Eynsford, who, in the guise of a bank clerk and calling himself Harry Lancaster, visits her at the stores. Lord Eynsford is officially engaged to Lady Betty Thanet, daughter of the Duchess of Minster, but he is really in love with Mary Gibbs, while Betty has given her heart to the Hon. Hughie Pierrepoint. Hughie's ambition is to become an amateur criminal, a kind of "Raffles", which Betty finds very romantic. "It recalls the age of chivalry," she tells her fiancé. "Well, burgling people's places in fun is certainly a knightly amusement," he agrees.

During the day Mary has a visit from her cousin Timothy Gibbs, a simple soul up from Yorkshire. At the stores Tim makes the acquaintance of Hughie Pierrepoint. Hughie has been pursuing his burglarious activities under the tuition of a professional crook, Slithers, and has succeeded in stealing the Ascot Gold Cup from the country house of the Earl of St. Ives, Lord Eynsford's father. He has the cup in a suit-case, which unfortunately proves to be the double of Timothy Gibbs' bag. When Hughie departs he goes off by mistake with Tim's suit-case and, when later Tim has occasion to open his bag, he is amazed to discover the Gold Cup and a collection of burglar's tools. As he is examining the cup Slithers enters. The professional burglar immediately assumes that Tim is another crook and advises him to put the bag in the store's safe deposit. As the two of them go off, Hughie returns. Over his arm are articles of clothing he has "lifted" from the shop. But Mary, who is aware of his activities, intercepts him, asking sweetly: "Shall we charge these to you, Mr. Pierrepoint, or will you pay cash?" Hughie is crestfallen, but Mary is looking such a picture of prettiness that he cheers up and tells her: "You know you're almost my style. I could almost give you a kiss." Mary answers: "And I could almost let you—but not quite." And together they sing:

Tim and Slithers have put the bag containing the cup in the safe deposit and Slithers artfully keeps the key, explaining to Tim: "Now *you've* got the number —50403—and *I've* got the key; one's no good without the other." And the guileless Tim replies: "So we must be together to get it out again. But look here, how shall I find you when I want you?" Slithers tells him: "I shall be in the stores. Blow your euphonium (Tim is a member of the "Bess's o' the Barn" Brass Band) and I'll come the moment I hear it." And with that Slithers disappears.

Betty now breaks off her engagement to Lord Eynsford. But the Duchess has learned of His Lordship's tenderness for Mary Gibbs and has no intention of allowing an entanglement with a shop-girl to stand in the way of his marrying Betty. She therefore commissions the Earl of St. Ives' solicitor, Mr. Beavis, to interview Mary with a view to inducing her to give up Eynsford. "You may tell His Lordship it's just a poor bank clerk I mean to marry and no other," she assures the solicitor. But in the finale of Act One Mary discovers that her Harry Lancaster and Lord Eynsford are one and the same person and is affronted at his deceit. "I never want to see you again," she tells him. What with Mary's troubles and the failure of Hughie and Tim to recover the Gold Cup—for Slithers has disappeared with the key of the safe deposit and fails to answer the summons of the euphonium—the curtain falls on a situation fraught with gloom.

ACT II

For Act Two we are at the Court of Honour in the Franco-British Exhibition, held at the White City, Shepherd's Bush, London. It is late afternoon of the same day. Mr. Amalfi, Director-General, is holding a reception, and the Earl of St. Ives has been invited to receive the guests, conduct them to the stadium to see the finish of the Marathon race (Windsor to London) and to entertain them afterwards to dinner at the Garden Club. Mary Gibbs is visiting the Exhibition. She has left Garrod's Stores and is the guest of a Mrs. Farquhar, who has taken Mary under her wing. Mary is enjoying the experience of mixing in Society.

Her only qualm is the possibility of running into Lord Eynsford. But she is determined to make a good impression and behave like a London girl. During the course of the afternoon Mary and Tim are introduced to Lord St. Ives, who tells them of the loss of the Gold Cup. He declares vehemently that he will not rest until he has seen the thief caught and convicted. This terrifies Tim, who immediately goes in search of Slithers and the key of the safe deposit. In the meantime, Lord Eynsford is mooning about the Exhibition in despair at losing Mary. Hughie does manage to cheer him up slightly by telling him that with girls it is better to leave them alone and they'll come round. Hughie's optimism is infectious, and it was in this scene that George Grossmith sang his tremendous hit "Yip-iaddy-i-ay".

When Tim finds Slithers, Slithers is reading a newspaper which reports that "the police have discovered an important clue to the perpetrator of the burglary at the home of the Earl of St. Ives. The culprit is described as a short man in the disguise of a countryman." To evade arrest Tim now disguises himself as a Marathon sprinter. He is mistaken by the crowd for the winner and carried shoulder high, but when the mistake is discovered he is thrown into the lake, from which he crawls out disconsolately just as Mary passes by. She comforts him and reminds him of the time when, as children, they both fell in the duck-pond of their Yorkshire farm. It is Hughie Pierrepoint who eventually recovers the cup from Slithers—on payment of five hundred pounds, which Slithers splits with the delighted Tim, who feels that his trip to London has not been such a failure after all.

As night falls Mr. Amalfi stages an entertainment for the guests of the Garden Club. It was in this scene that Gertie Millar, as "Mary" in the original production, appeared in the moonlight as a pierrot with eight girls and sang the song "Moonstruck":

In the last scene the Duchess of Minster complains to Lord St. Ives that he is entertaining "the girl from the stores" while she was under the impression that his party was in honour of her daughter, Lady Betty Thanet. Mary admits to the Earl: "I am Mary Gibbs of Garrod's Stores, whom your son has insulted." Proudly the Earl protests: "My son is a gentleman, a man of honour. You accuse him of dishonourable conduct—but read that letter, written to me a fortnight ago." And Mary takes the letter and reads: "I cannot and will not marry Lady Betty. There is only one woman I love and can ever marry—Mary." So Mary and Lord Eynsford are reconciled and everything ends happily, as every Gaiety musical comedy must.

The Arcadians

A Fantastic Musical Play in Three Acts

Book by MARK AMBIENT, A. M. THOMPSON *and* ROBERT COURTNEIDGE

Music by LIONEL MONCKTON *and* HOWARD TALBOT

First produced on 28th April, 1909, at the Shaftesbury Theatre, London, with Florence Smithson as "Sombra", Phyllis Dare as "Eileen", Harry Welchman as "Jack", Dan Rolyat as "Simplicitas" and Alfred Lester as "Doody".

CHARACTERS

JAMES SMITH ("SIMPLICITAS"), *of Smith & Co., Caterers, London*
PETER DOODY, *a jockey*
JACK MEADOWS
SIR GEORGE PADDOCK
FATHER TIME
MRS. SMITH
EILEEN CAVANAGH
CHRYSEA, ASTROPHEL, STREPHON, SOMBRA — *Arcadians*
CHORUS OF ARCADIANS, RACEGOERS, DINERS, ETC.

ACT I

In a remote, secluded corner of the globe lies the land of Arcady. Here in paradisaical conditions the inhabitants live the lives of lotus-eaters. Mundane evils such as lying and jealousy and, indeed, all the seven deadly sins are quite unknown. Time, for the Arcadians, has stood still—as Father Time himself confesses when he pays Arcadia a surprise visit:

The Arcadians have heard from the Sea Serpent tales of another land, a land of strife and turmoil peopled by savages, ugly monsters called the English, who crowd together in a place called London and live in cages of brick and stone. The Arcadians beg Father Time to show them such a monster. He promises to see what he can send them and, remarking that Time must fly, departs.

Soon after he has gone there appears in the sky what looks like a huge bird. Approaching with a mighty roaring, it seems to be about to swoop on the terrified Arcadians, who scatter for shelter. It is in fact a flying machine with an aviator clinging to it. As it sails across the proscenium he releases his grip and rolls down-stage, while the machine continues its flight. The aviator is James Smith, proprietor of Smith & Co., Leviathan Caterers of London. An irrepressible hedonist, Smith is soon on the best of terms with the Arcadians. He quickly takes to the free-and-easy life of Arcadia, especially to a certain Arcadian girl, Sombra. In answer to his inquiry as to who owns the country, Sombra informs him that their master is Pan; and this is the cue for, perhaps, the best known song in the score, "The Pipes of Pan":

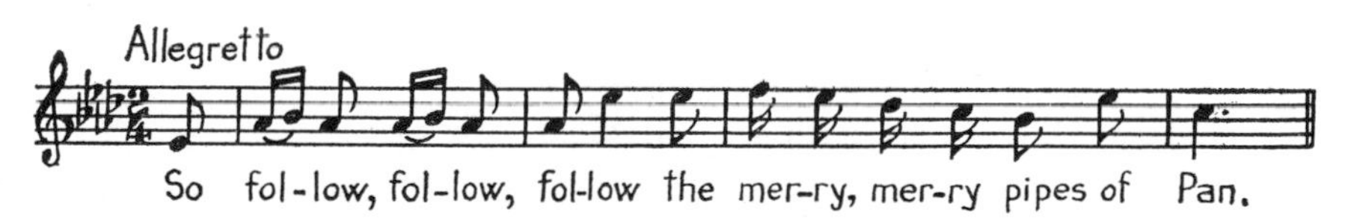

But trouble soon arises. Sombra is loved by a young man, Astrophel. But Astrophel, being an Arcadian, loves all girls. This enables Smith to introduce the subject of jealousy, which he defines as "the friendship one woman has for another". Though jealousy has hitherto been unknown in Arcadia, the emotion is now aroused in Sombra's breast by the sight of Astrophel with another girl, Chrysea, coupled with some lying suggestions by Smith. Astrophel is challenged, but is able to prove that Smith has told a lie (and a lie has also hitherto been unknown in Arcadia).

It is then decided that if Smith is to be an Arcadian, he must be washed in the Well of Truth, and he is accordingly seized and rammed down the well. Having given Smith sufficient time to find Truth at the bottom of the well, they haul him out, very indignant and minus his trousers. For he is now disguised as an Arcadian with bare knees, no whiskers and the name of Simplicitas. In reply to Sombra's question: "Are they all as wicked in London as you were?" Simplicitas tells her: "You were shocked at my little *pâté de faux pas*, but if you heard them in Throgmorton Street you'd have a fit." So the Arcadians decide to go to this place called London and convert the other Monsters there to the simple life.

Sped on their way by Father Time, Sombra, Chrysea and Simplicitas set off on their goodwill mission as the curtain falls.

ACT II

The scene is the race-course at Askwood. Two prominent owners who have horses entered for the Corinthian Stakes are young Jack Meadows and Sir George Paddock. Jack, already in debt, is staking all his fortune on his horse "The Deuce", a savage beast. It has already thrown him, breaking his wrist, and thus prevented him from acting as his own jockey. Jack is in love with Eileen Cavanagh, the niece of Mrs. Smith, who is the wife of our Arcadian caterer. Jack wants to marry her, and his future happiness depends on "The Deuce's" success in the forthcoming race. Sir George Paddock is also anxious to marry Eileen, and his suit is greatly favoured by Mrs. Smith on account of his wealth. Eileen's Irish brogue is one of the charms which so attracts the two ardent men —and what an effect Phyllis Dare created with her song "The Girl with a Brogue":

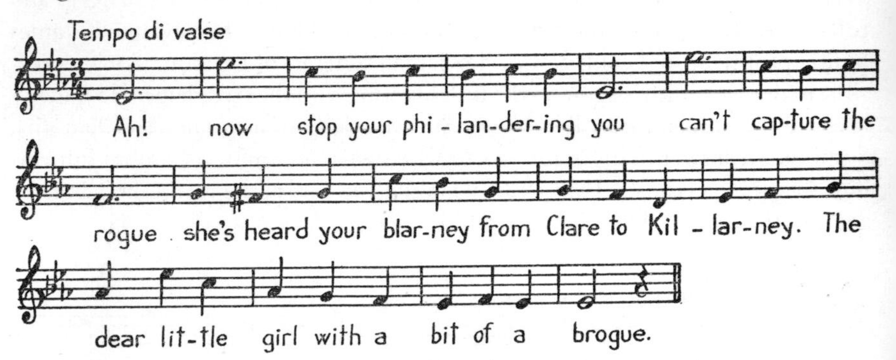

Peter Doody, the jockey who is to ride "the Deuce", now comes on. He is a confirmed pessimist and an old flame of Mrs. Smith, to whom he complains: "Since Jim Smith came down to our village and plucked the rose-bud of my affections from under my nose, life's been a cheap thing to me." As they are talking the sky gradually grows dark. Suddenly there is a flash of lightning which reveals the figures of Sombra, Chrysea and Simplicitas, who have been magically transported by Father Time to Askwood race-course. The race-goers crowd excitedly round them. In answer to eager inquiries of: "Where did they come from?" "Did they drop from the sky?" "Did they spring from the ground?" "Is it a new Salvation dodge?" Chrysea tells the crowd: "We are Arcadians", and Sombra sings them her well-known song in praise of Arcady:

The Arcadian girls score an instantaneous success, and are soon all the rage and fairly mobbed by the smart set. This makes Eileen Cavanagh a little jealous, but the devoted attention of Jack Meadows is sufficient compensation. Jack then receives some serious news. "The Deuce" has savaged Doody and he cannot ride. Jack is bitterly acknowledging defeat when Sombra comes to his rescue, promising to find him a rider. "If you can do this for me," he declares, "I don't know how I can ever thank you." "Why, that is easy," she tells him. "Just kiss me as Astrophel kisses me." Impetuously he kisses Sombra, but unfortunately the kiss is observed by Eileen and very naturally misconstrued by her. Simplicitas is the jockey selected by Sombra to ride "The Deuce". At first he is very dubious at the assignment, but Sombra among her Arcadian accomplishments has the power to speak with animals. She assures him that "The Deuce" has promised to carry him safely. In a thrilling race scene, Simplicitas romps home and the curtain falls on excited cries from the crowd of: "'The Deuce' wins!"

ACT III

Act Three takes place in the Restaurant Arcadia run by Simplicitas on Arcadian lines. Its novelty has created a vogue and business is booming. But the private lives of the various characters concerned in the story are less harmonious. Sombra, for one, is depressed at the lack of success of her efforts to convert Londoners to the simple life. Mrs. Smith feels strangely drawn to Simplicitas while failing completely to recognise in him her husband, James Smith. Simplicitas has embarked on a course of backsliding. He is having the time of his life as a social lion and has no eyes for Mrs. Smith. His only trouble is that Sombra and Chrysea are beginning to suspect the genuiness of his moral behaviour and are always asking awkward questions. Simplicitas therefore gets Jack Meadows to speak for him. So next time Sombra complains that people are saying that Simplicitas does not tell the truth, Jack is ready to vouch for Simplicitas' good conduct, and Sombra tells Jack: "I trust and believe you, Jack, as I trust and believe my brother, Astrophel." As she says it she lifts her face to him and he bends down and gives her a comforting kiss. As ill-luck will have it, Eileen enters the restaurant at this moment and once more sees Jack kissing Sombra. Though Jack had begun to live down the former kiss, this time Eileen is really angry, and in desperation Jack whispers to Simplicitas: "Now it's your turn to help me." Then aloud he says: "Now, Simplicitas, didn't I specially ask that girl *not* to kiss me?" Simplicitas, however, answers: "Certainly not. I cannot tell a lie," and Eileen flounces out, pursued by the unfortunate Jack. Soon after this Peter Doody sings his well-known song "I've gotter motter", which made Alfred Lester famous. With the voice of funereal gloom he used to deliver the cue: "I'm too merry and bright. . . . I must really settle down and try to become more serious." And then he would sing:

In the end Jack and Eileen are reconciled by the intervention of Sombra, who reads them a lecture on the evils of jealousy. Sombra is also the cause of Mrs.

Smith being able to identify Simplicitas as her husband, James Smith, when she describes his arrival in an aeroplane. When he is taxed with his true identity, Simplicitas temporises. "Madam, do you know who you are talking to?" Mrs. Smith, undeterred, replies: "No, but you talk just like my Jim, when he told us that someone pushed him down a well and stole his whiskers." "But I never had any whiskers," urges Simplicitas. Then, with a despairing cry of "Oh, I've told a lie", he falls backwards down the Well of Truth, a prominent feature of the Restaurant Arcadia. He is soon hauled out, however, and reconciled to Mrs. Smith. And Sombra finalises the situation: "He has come back to his people. Let us go back to ours. Come, Chrysea, the pipes of Pan are calling! Our mission to England has failed."

The Quaker Girl

A Musical Play in Three Acts

Book by JAMES T. TANNER

Lyrics by ADRIAN ROSS *and* PERCY GREENBANK

Music by LIONEL MONCKTON

First produced on 5th November, 1910, at the Adelphi Theatre, London, with Gertie Millar as "Prudence", Joseph Coyne as "Tony", Hayden Coffin as "Captain Charteris" and James Blakeley as "Jeremiah".

CHARACTERS

CAPTAIN CHARTERIS, *King's Messenger*
JEREMIAH, NATHANIEL PYM, RACHEL PYM, PRUDENCE — *Quakers*
MONSIEUR DUHAMEL, *Minister of State*
PRINCE CARLO
MONSIEUR LAROSE, *Chief of Police, Paris*
TONY CHUTE, *Naval Attaché at the American Embassy, Paris*
PRINCESS MATHILDE, *an exiled Bonapartist Princess*
PHOEBE, *her maid*
DIANE, *a Parisian actress*
MADAME BLUM, *of the "Maison Blum", Paris*
MRS. LUKYN, *landlady of "The Chequers"*
CHORUS OF QUAKERS, VILLAGERS, CUSTOMERS, EMPLOYEES AND MANNEQUINS

ACT I

It is a June morning and the scene is the village green of a charming, picturesque, typically old-world English village. On the left is a prosperous Elizabethan inn, "The Chequers", and across a foot-bridge in the background stands the Quaker Meeting-House. The tranquil atmosphere of village life has been agitated and excited by news of the arrival at "The Chequers" of a French lady of distinguished antecedents. She is Princess Mathilde. Exiled from France, she has come to England to be married to Captain Charteris, a King's Messenger, who is due to arrive at any moment. There is a strong Quaker element in the village, presided over by two elders, Rachel and Nathaniel Pym. They have a niece, Prudence Pym, an enchantingly pretty girl, to whom Princess Mathilde has taken a great fancy. Prudence longs for fun and a gay life, but is rigorously suppressed by the austere faculty with their hymn-singing.

Captain Charteris duly arrives from Paris, armed with a special licence, and his meeting with his Princess is rapturous. He has brought with him an old friend of hers, Madame Blum, famous Parisian dressmaker of the "Maison Blum", and Tony Chute of the American Embassy in Paris, his best man. Tony is enchanted with the village, and particularly with Prudence, whom he discovers sitting under a tree, and just in the mood to hear someone say to her:

The attraction is mutual and it is an attraction of opposites, as both realise, for they sing in duet:

Acquaintance with Tony is the beginning of the little Quaker girl's backsliding, and when Princess Mathilde asks: "You are coming to the church to see me married?" Prudence answers: "Oh! what would the Friends say?" But she does go, escorted by Tony.

Another backslider among the Quakers is a young man called Jeremiah. He blames his conduct on his parents and pleads: "I'm only a Quaker on Mother's side, and Father will out sometimes." As he complains to his girl-friend Phoebe:

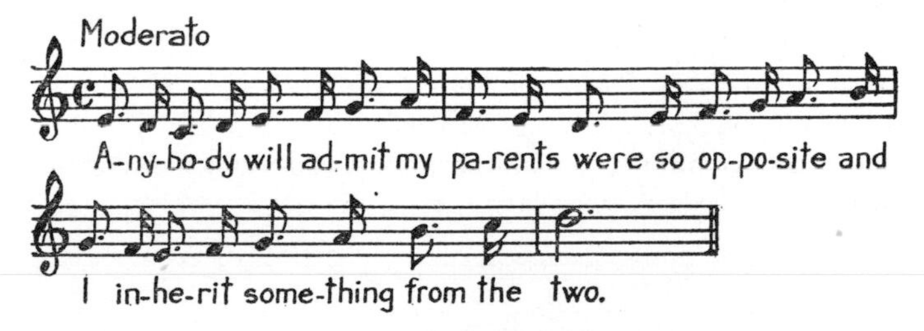

When the marriage service is over, the wedding party return from church for the wedding breakfast at "The Chequers". Princess Mathilde presses Prudence to come to the reception, and she eagerly accepts, remarking: "I suppose I'll have to do penance afterwards." She enjoys herself enormously, and is even tempted by Tony to take a sip of champagne. Unfortunately at the moment the glass is at her lips, Nathaniel, Rachel and the other Quakers appear on the scene. Sternly they order Prudence to leave these sinful people and follow them. But Prudence, backed up by Madame Blum, refuses. Madame Blum, with a keen eye to business, sees possibilities in the attractive simplicity of the Quaker dress. She will make it the new mode in Paris, and she invites Prudence to come to Paris and model it. This is too much for the Quakers, and with threats of the wrath to come and gestures of scornful disapproval they cast off their erring sister. But Prudence, who has plenty of spirit, is undismayed. "You bid me go," she says. "Then be it so, whatever life may give, at least I'll live":

ACT II

Act Two takes place in the "Maison Blum", Madame Blum's dressmaking establishment in Paris. Madame Blum has carried out her idea of introducing the Quaker dress to Paris and it has become the rage. Prudence is working as a mannequin, modelling the Quaker dress, and she is as popular with the men as her dress is with the women. Two of her warmest admirers are Monsieur Duhamel, a distinguished Minister of State, and Prince Carlo. In spite of Madame Blum's warning that the Prince is both dangerous and dissolute, Prudence enjoys herself as his guest, and she particularly enjoys a visit to the races at Chantilly. On the return from Chantilly, the Prince invites her to a ball he is giving that evening, and Prudence accepts with delight. Prince Carlo's invitation constitutes the most popular number of the score:

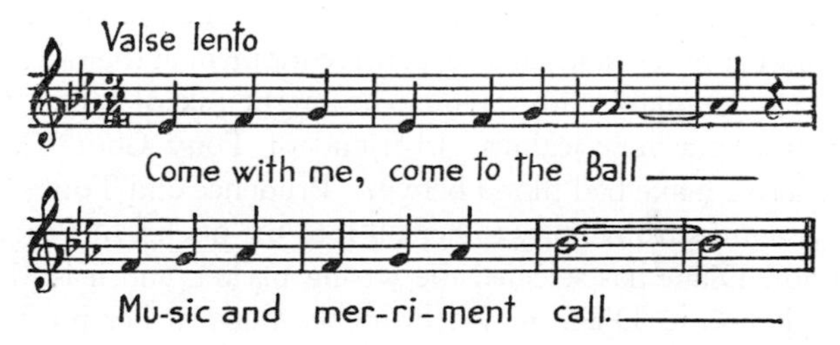

Tony Chute, who is by now madly in love with Prudence and who knows Prince Carlo's character, begs Prudence not to go to the ball or, if she must go, to promise not to dance with anyone but himself. "No, I cannot promise that, friend Tony," says Prudence, "because I do not know how to dance, even with thee." Tony proceeds to give her a dancing lesson. Prudence proves an apt pupil:

In spite of the dancing lesson, Tony begs Prudence not to go to Prince Carlo's ball and, wondering at his serious manner, Prudence promises. But she is unwittingly compelled to break her promise. It so happens that Princess Mathilde has secretly returned to France and is masquerading as a mannequin in Madame Blum's salon. But the police get wind of the exiled Princess's presence in France, and the resourceful Chief of Police, Monsieur Larose, turns up at the most inconvenient moments and in a variety of disguises. Fortunately for the Princess's safety, nature has endowed him with a physical disability and he is always given away by an obvious and extremely comical limp. The recognition by the police of Princess Mathilde, however, is turned by the blackguardly Prince Carlo to his own advantage. He has seen the Princess among the mannequins at Madame Blum's, and he now threatens Prudence that he will disclose the Princess's whereabouts to the police unless she consents to come to his dance that evening. So, for the sake of Princess Mathilde, Prudence reluctantly breaks her promise to Tony.

ACT III

Act Three takes place in the Pré Catalan, a fashionable restaurant in the Bois de Boulogne. Here Prince Carlo is giving his ball. Among the guests are Prudence, Princess Mathilde and her husband. The police are still on the Princess's track and she is horrified when she sees Monsieur Larose enter the ballroom. Her only chance of escaping banishment from France is to obtain an amnesty from Monsieur Duhamel, Minister of State, whose influence is sufficiently powerful to ensure this and who is also present at the ball. The Minister is one of Prudence's warmest admirers and, in an expansive moment at the races at Chantilly, has promised to grant her any favour she might ask of him. Prudence has been the victim of a very jealous girl-friend of Tony Chute's called Diane. Diane, in order to make bad blood between Prudence and Tony, has slipped a packet of love-letters from Tony to herself into the pocket of Prudence's dress. As it turns out, Diane has selected the wrong packet, and it is Monsieur Duhamel's love-letters to Diane which Prudence finds in her pocket. She now tackles the Minister and, reminding him of his promise to grant her any favour she might ask of him, begs him to allow Princess Mathilde to remain in France. Monsieur Duhamel regretfully refuses, and then Prudence, remembering the incriminating letters, returns them to him. He is so touched that Prudence does not attempt to use them as a lever to force him to do her will, that he tells her warmly that he will grant her request. The Princess may stay. The rest of the plot is concerned with explaining to the aggrieved Tony that Prudence's presence at the ball was a bribe to Prince Carlo to prevent his giving away the Princess to the police. So all ends happily and Prudence gets the man she loves:

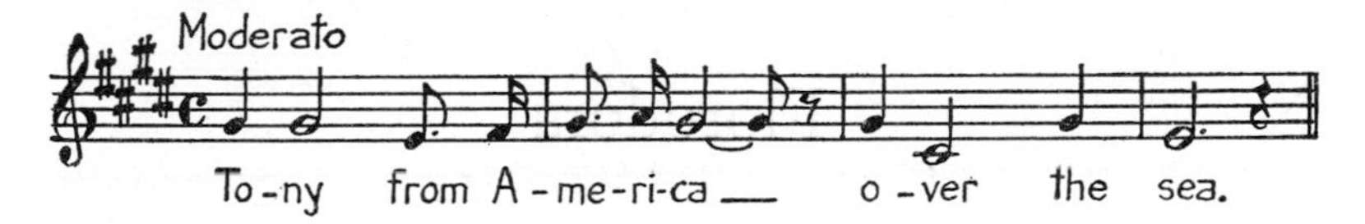

Florodora

A Musical Comedy in Two Acts

Book by OWEN HALL

Lyrics by E. BOYD-JONES *and* PAUL RUBENS

Music by LESLIE STUART

First produced on 11th November, 1899, at the Lyric Theatre, London, with Willie Edouin, Evie Greene, Kate Cutler and Ada Reeve.

CHARACTERS

CYRUS W. GILFAIN, *proprietor of the perfume and of the island of Florodora*
FRANK ABERCOED, *manager for Cyrus Gilfain*
CAPTAIN ARTHUR DONEGAL, *4th Royal Life Guards, Lady Holyrood's brother*
ANTHONY TWEEDLEPUNCH, *a showman, hypnotist, phrenologist and palmist*
DOLORES
ANGELA GILFAIN
LADY HOLYROOD
CHORUS OF FLORODORIAN FARMERS, LABOURERS, FLOWER-GIRLS, WELSH PEASANTS, ETC.

ACT I: Florodora, a small island in the Philippines
ACT II: Abercoed Castle, Wales

The first act is set in Florodora, an island in the Philippines, where the flowers grow, as Lady Teazle wished they would, "under one's feet". The island is owned by a wealthy American, Cyrus W. Gilfain, who exercises a patriarchal rule over the labourers, male and female, in the factory where the famous perfume called "Florodora" is manufactured from a secret recipe. Cyrus W. Gilfain is a rascal who has taken illegal possession of the island. It really belongs to Dolores, the daughter of the late proprietor. Gilfain has brought her up as one of his work-girls and is only seeking an excuse to marry her. A phrenologist named Anthony Tweedlepunch has an inkling of the fraud which has been practised and lands on the flowery shore with the intention of discovering and vindicating the orphan heiress. Gilfain, who is socially ambitious, is anxious that his daughter, Angela, shall marry Frank Abercoed, his manager, who has just come into a title on the death of a relative. So the proprietor of "Florodora" bribes Tweedlepunch to declare on the strength of his phrenological examinations that he, Gilfain, is "made" for Dolores and that Angela is just the wife for Frank Abercoed. But Frank is in love with Dolores, who returns his love, and he refuses to accept the phrenologist's verdict. He leaves for England, promising to return later for his sweetheart.

The second act takes place at Abercoed in Wales, where Gilfain has bought the castle from its impoverished owners. Here he has set up house with his daughter Angela, a certain Lady Holyrood, and a bevy of fashionable beauties whom he entertains in lavish style. Gilfain has come to England in pursuit of Dolores, for Tweedlepunch, having discovered her identity, left the island taking her with him. To the castle come Tweedlepunch and Dolores disguised as wandering musicians, and Frank obtains admission to the castle disguised as an old harpist. Together they succeed in frightening Gilfain into a confession of his rascality by impersonating the ghost of a former occupant of the castle, while Frank, in the harper's disguise, threatens Gilfain with supernatural punishment. The terrified scent proprietor falls on all-fours and promises to make amends by restoring the island to its rightful owner. Dolores as proprietor of "Florodora" is then united to Frank, Angela Gilfain is allowed to marry her own true love, Captain Arthur Donegal, and Gilfain pairs off with the smart little mondaine, Lady Holyrood.

In Act One Dolores has a waltz song called "Silver Star of Love" which became very popular:

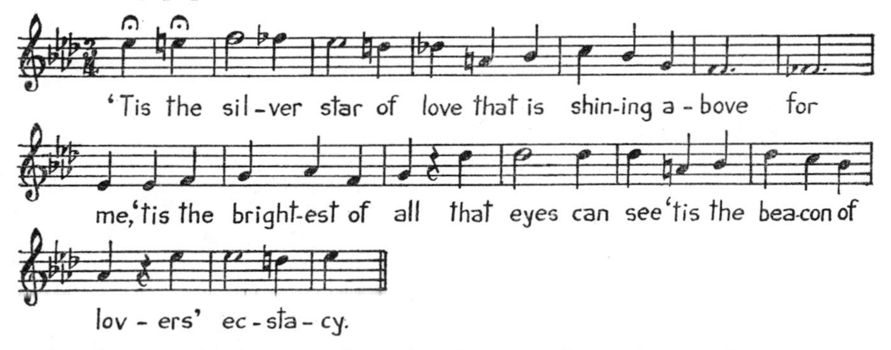

Another popular favourite from Act One was Frank Abercoed's love-song, "The Shade of the Palm":

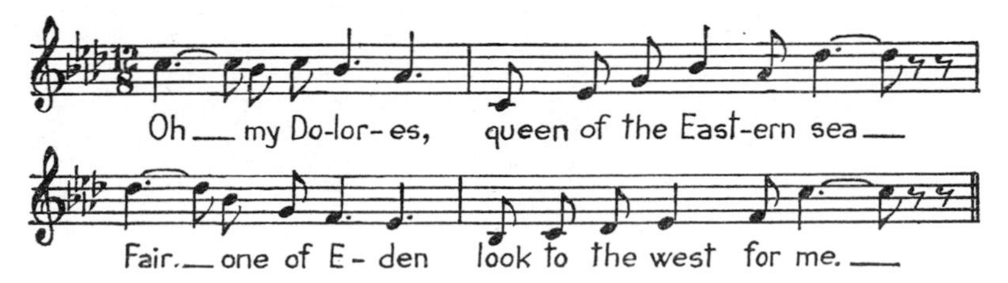

The most famous number in the score, and a classic of musical comedy, is a number in the second act sung by English girls and Gilfain's clerks:

The Geisha

A Musical Play in Two Acts

Book by OWEN HALL

Lyrics by HARRY GREENBANK

Music by SIDNEY JONES

First produced on 25th April, 1896, at Daly's Theatre, London, with Marie Tempest as "O Mimosa San", Hayden Coffin as "Fairfax" and Huntley Wright as "Wun Hi".

CHARACTERS

LADY CONSTANCE WYNNE, *an English visitor*
O MIMOSA SAN, *Chief Geisha*
JULIETTE DIAMANT, *a French girl*
MISS MOLLY SEAMORE
REGINALD FAIRFAX, *a naval officer*
LIEUTENANT KATANA, *of the Governor's Guard*
WUN HI, *proprietor of a tea-house*
THE MARQUIS IMARI, *Governor of the province*
CHORUS OF COOLIES, ATTENDANTS, MOUSMÉS, GUARDS

ACT I

The action of this play takes place in Japan outside the treaty limits, and the scene is the garden of "The Tea-House of Ten Thousand Joys". The curtain rises on a busy scene. Tea-girls are bustling round serving guests, while the Geishas, or singing-girls, accompany themselves on samisens. Wun Hi, the proprietor of the tea-house, a Chinaman, is on the crest of the wave. Business is brisk, and his Geisha girls, especially his principal attraction, the beautiful O Mimosa San, are making plenty of money for him. The tea-house is a favourite resort of some British naval officers from H.M.S. *Turtle*. Prominent among the younger officers is Lieutenant Reginald Fairfax, who regularly visits O Mimosa San, to their mutual delight, although he is more or less engaged to Molly Seamore, an English girl. But the Marquis Imari, Chief of

Japanese Police and Governor of the province, is also an admirer of O Mimosa San. He arrives at the Tea-House while she is entertaining Lieutenant Fairfax and informs Wun Hi that he proposes to marry her on the morrow. Meanwhile O Mimosa San is to see no foreigners unless Wun Hi wants his tea-house licence revoked. Wun Hi is shattered at the thought of losing his most attractive Geisha and begs Juliette, a French girl who acts as interpreter, to "be velly nice to Marquis. Perhaps Marquis like French girlee—leavee Mimosa San—makee much more money for me." Juliette is quite attracted by the idea and has visions of queening it in Paris as a Japanese Marquise, and she and Imari leave the Tea-House together. In the scene that follows O Mimosa San sings to Fairfax one of the best-known songs in the score, "The Amorous Goldfish", with its plaintive refrain:

As the song finishes Fairfax looks up to encounter the disapproving gaze of Lady Constance Wynne, strait-laced leader of the English colony. She tartly reminds him that he is engaged to Molly Seamore. But Fairfax is undeterred, and when she has gone he continues his education of O Mimosa San by introducing the Japanese girl, with a practical demonstration, to the delights of kissing. This upsets O Mimosa San's fiancé, Lieutenant Katana, but she manages to calm his jealousy by pleading that although a Geisha has to be pleasant to everyone who pays for her song, she does not give her love and, renewing her promise to marry him when her two years' apprenticeship is over, she sends him away and re-joins Fairfax.

The Marquis Imari now returns to the tea-house to give Wun Hi his final instructions for the arrangements of his wedding to O Mimosa San. He is furious at finding her with Fairfax, and when Fairfax refers to him as a "fat old Jap", the Marquis loses his temper, tells Wun Hi that one of his guests has insulted him, that his Tea-House licence will be revoked and his Geisha girls put up for auction. As he sweeps out, Geisha girls and tea-girls break into a chorus of lamentation and the British officers discuss plans to combat Imari's intentions. Molly Seamore is the next arrival. She is exceptionally high-spirited and unconventional, and her arrival is characteristic—between the shafts of a rickshaw with the coolie inside. She tells Fairfax that she has come to see what he is up to with the Japanese girls and manages to get O Mimosa San alone. Molly confides to her that she believes her fiancé has fallen in love with a

Japanese girl and sighs: "Why wasn't I born a Japanese girl?" O Mimosa San replies: "Well, then, let me make you a Japanese girl." This is exactly the sort of thing to appeal to Molly Seamore. "A Geisha!" she cries. "Hooray! I'll give Master Reggie Geisha! I think a Japanese Geisha must have the most delightful life in the world." And she rushes away to don her disguise.

Left alone, O Mimosa San ruefully sings "A Geisha's Life" with its rather ironic refrain:

But O Mimosa San is not so simple as she seems. Her object in getting Molly disguised as a Geisha is that at the auction Imari shall purchase her in the belief that he is buying O Mimosa San. The following scene contains the rousing nautical number with which Hayden Coffin nightly brought down the house:

After this the sale of the tea-house begins and the girls are put up to auction. O Mimosa San is the first lot. To Imari's annoyance, Lady Constance Wynne is a bidder. Juliette has put the idea of "getting the girl away from the English officers" into Lady Constance's head in order to have the field to herself to become Marquise Imari. So O Mimosa San is knocked down to Lady Constance, and Imari, fuming, turns his attention to Lot Two. Lot Two is Roli-Poli San, described as "a great singer and dancer but without much experience". This is, of course, Molly in disguise. She urges Fairfax on with "English boy buy Roli-Poli?" but he replies with: "No, thanks! I got tired of roly-poly when I was at school." Imari is interested, but as Roli-Poli is a stranger to him he demands an audition. Molly obliges with "Chon Kina". Imari takes a great fancy to Roli-Poli San, and in spite of Juliette's despairing protests that she is "not good enough for you, Extraordinary Marquis", he buys her for one hundred dollars. "Well, I'm a bargain," is Molly's comment. The act finishes with a brilliant finale ending with an exhortation to the foreigners to leave, as no one is allowed beyond the Treaty limits after sundown. And as the curtain falls, Imari pulls Molly (Roli-Poli San) down on her knees.

ACT II

In the gardens of his palace the Marquis Imari is giving a Chrysanthemum Fête to celebrate his marriage to Roli-Poli San, and at the rise of the curtain the bridal attendants are assembled. Roli-Poli San, however, who is really Molly Seamore in a kimono, has not the slightest intention of marrying Imari. With true bull-dog courage she resists all his advances, even to smacking his face, but she has to admit to herself that she is in a jam and as stuck as a toy monkey on a stick. As Letty Lind used to sing:

By now there is consternation among the English colony at Molly Seamore's continued absence, and headed by Lady Constance Wynne, they arrive at the palace to make inquiries. From Juliette they learn of Molly's escapade and of how she is to be married to Imari at any moment, and they all go off, in different directions and great agitation, to find Imari. The stage being cleared, O Mimosa San enters and for no logical reason sings one of Marie Tempest's most popular successes:

After the song O Mimosa San exits, and there follows a very funny scene between Fairfax and Wun Hi, which culminates in Wun Hi undertaking to produce Molly for a bribe of five hundred pounds. Left alone, Fairfax sings perhaps the most famous song in the score, "Star of my Soul":

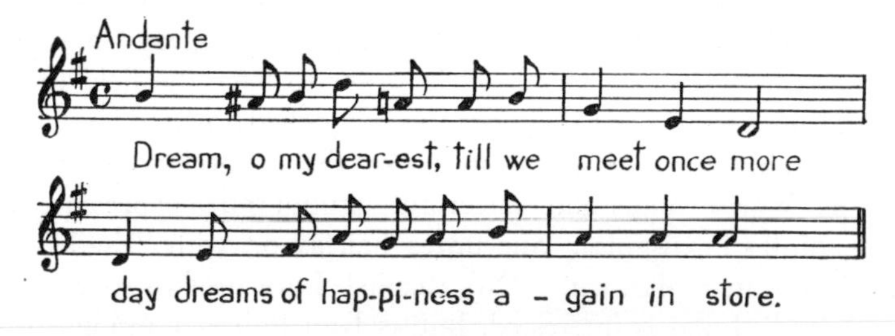

O Mimosa San then returns, and she and Juliette work out a plan to rescue Molly. This necessitates the appearance of O Mimosa San at Imari's wedding, and Wun Hi, who is in charge of the entertainments, approaches Lady Constance with the request "Watchee Mimosa to make sing-song at most noble Marquis' wedding". When she hears the details of the plan, Lady Constance consents and shortly afterwards the wedding festivities begin. After the formal entrance of the Geisha, Wun Hi sings his famous song:

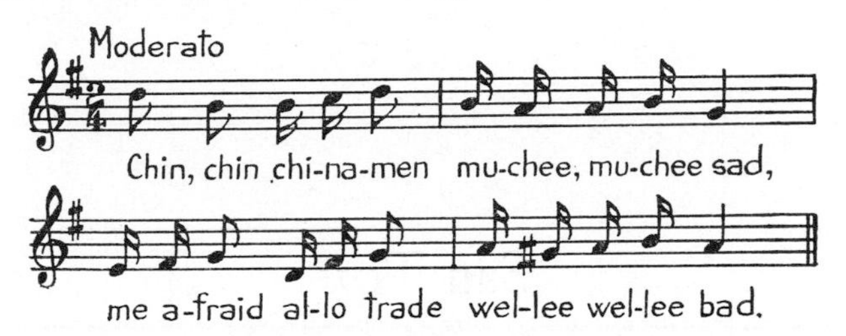

A fortune-teller is now announced, and O Mimosa San enters in disguise, carrying a small box—Oyuki's Box of Fate. Imari draws a lot from the box and is warned against a future of disgrace, dishonour, anguish and doom. Only if he is loved by a young bride will this fate be turned to a life of delight. Imari is shattered by the prophecy and asks if the fortune-teller can do anything for him. Mimosa craftily tells him that she has a love-spell which she can cast over his bride to make her love him. "Good," says Imari. "Go to her at once; cast your spell over her, and make her love me." Mimosa is led out to join Molly and Juliette, who follows her, is substituted for the English girl. Thus it is that Imari, without knowing it, is married to Juliette, and Juliette achieves her ambition to call herself Madame la Marquise. Mimosa is joined to her Japanese soldier, Lieutenant Katana, and Fairfax clasps madcap Molly in his arms as the curtain falls.

San Toy
or
The Emperor's Own

A Musical Play in Two Acts

Book by EDWARD MORTON

Lyrics by HARRY GREENBANK *and* ADRIAN ROSS

Music by SIDNEY JONES

First produced on 21st October, 1899, at Daly's Theatre, London, with Marie Tempest, Hayden Coffin, Rutland Barrington and Huntley Wright.

CHARACTERS

CAPTAIN BOBBIE PRESTON, *son of the British Consul at Pynka Pong*
YEN HOW, *a Mandarin*
LIEUTENANT HARRY TUCKER
FO HOP, *a Chinese student*
POPPY, *Bobbie Preston's sister*
DUDLEY, *her maid*
SAN TOY, *daughter of Yen How*
THE EMPEROR
LI, *a courier*

ACT I: A street in Pynka Pong
ACT II: Hall in the Emperor's palace at Pekin

The Emperor of China has given orders for the enlistment of a bodyguard of female soldiers. This greatly exercises the mind of the Mandarin, Yen How, who is deeply attached to his daughter, San Toy; and to evade the Emperor's command that she enlist in this Amazon corps he makes her conceal her sex by dressing up in boy's clothes. During the Mandarin's absences, Bobbie Preston, son of Sir Bingo Preston, British Consul at Pynka Pong, contrives to meet San Toy, and the two fall in love during the English lessons that he gives her.

Lieutenant Harry Tucker is in love with Bobbie's sister, Poppy, and he watches jealously a close friendship developing between her and this "boy", San Toy. But the Chinese girl has confided her secret to Poppy, who is well aware that San Toy is a girl and knows all about her love for Bobbie.

Yen How has arranged a marriage between San Toy and a Chinese student called Fo Hop. His intention is that after their marriage the bride and bridegroom shall leave their native city of Pynka Pong and that in this way San Toy will be able to evade the Emperor's command to enlist in his Amazon bodyguard. But San Toy, rather than marry the disagreeable and unattractive Fo Hop, decides to resume her sex and enlist in "The Emperor's Own". So one night, during the revels which accompany "the Feast of the Full Moon", she departs with Bobbie, whose father has dispatched him to Pekin on important business. When Fo Hop discovers San Toy's flight with Bobbie he flies into a great rage, discloses the fact publicly that San Toy is a girl and threatens to expose the whole plot to the Emperor. Shortly after this, to Yen How's dismay a letter arrives for him. It is from the Emperor, and informs the Mandarin that the deception has been discovered. The letter further commands Yen How to appear at the palace with San Toy. Yen How is terrified. But when San Toy eventually presents herself at Court to enlist in "the Emperor's Own", the Emperor is enchanted by her grace and charm and treats her slightest wish as law. Unfortunately San Toy has arrived in Pekin before Li, Yen How's courier, who now delivers to the Emperor a letter declaring that he is sending his *son*, San Toy, to the Emperor. Li's tale does not, of course, tally with the facts of the case, and Yen How's arrival is too late to save the courier from arrest. Li is, however, eventually saved from prison. Dudley, Poppy Preston's maid, who has a soft spot for Li, dresses him up as one of the Emperor's female bodyguard and thus effects his rescue, one of Yen How's wives being also dressed up in San Toy's clothes. In the end, San Toy's English education and tastes unfit her to be a wife to the Emperor, and as the disagreeable Fo Hop renounces his claim to her, she is happily united to Bobbie Preston.

In spite of its rather stereotyped, dated libretto, *San Toy* is full of good tunes:

1. Yen How's number with a chorus of his six wives.

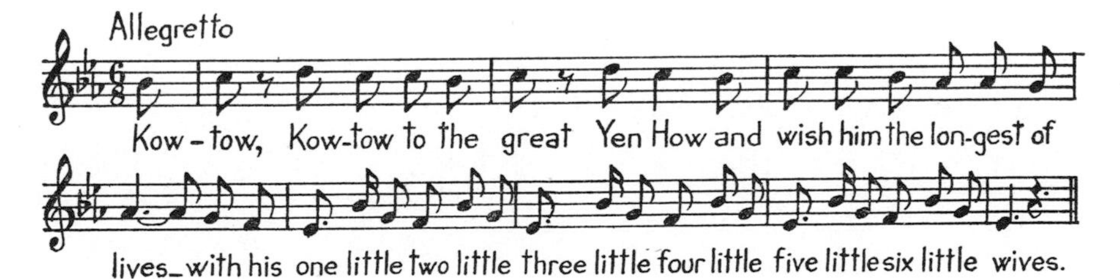

2. San Toy's delicate song "The Petals of the Plum Tree".
3. Dudley's song about Rhoda and her Pagoda tea-shop.

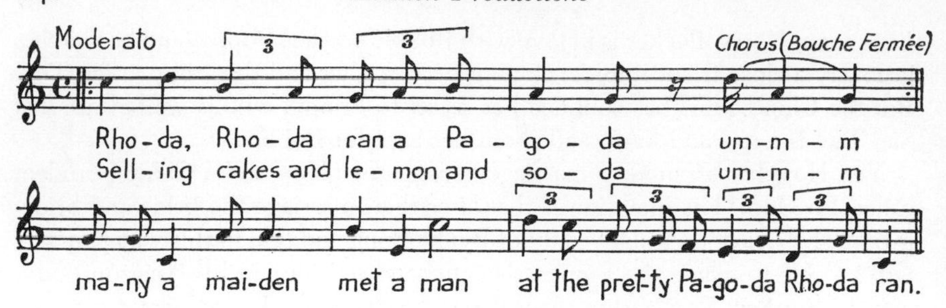

4. San Toy and Bobbie's romantic duet "The little China Maid".

5. Bobbie's love-song "One in the World".
6. Li's admirably characterised Chinese song in pidgeon-English.

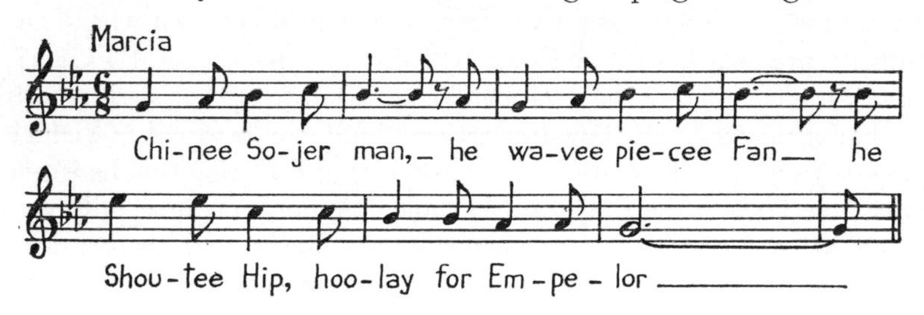

Amasis

An Egyptian Princess

A Comic Opera in Two Acts

By FREDERIC FENN

Music by PHILIP MICHAEL FARADAY

First produced on 9th August, 1906, at the New Theatre, London, with Ruth Vincent as "Amasis", Roland Cunningham as "Prince Anhotep" and Rutland Barrington as "Pharaoh".

CHARACTERS

PHARAOH, *King of Egypt*
PRINCE ANHOTEP, *ruler of Philae*
CHEIRO, *a scribe*
PTOLEMY, *Royal Embalmer*
NEBENCHARI, *the High Priest*
PRINCESS AMASIS, *daughter of Pharaoh*
CHORUS OF MUMMY GUARDS, PRIESTS, AND CITIZENS

ACT I

In the courtyard of the palace of Amasis IX, Pharaoh of Egypt, at Memphis, preparations for a state wedding are in progress. Princess Amasis, daughter of the reigning Pharaoh, is to be married to Prince Anhotep of Philae, young, wealthy and good-looking. It is a love match, and the young couple are blissfully happy. But the atmosphere of joyful celebration is turned to grief and gloom when the Royal Embalmer, Ptolemy, makes the dreadful announcement that one of the Sacred Cats is missing, believed killed. The wedding must be postponed, for, by the law of the land, when a Sacred Cat is killed, until the murderer is discovered, all are equally guilty. Though there is no absolute proof that the animal is dead, traces of blood and fragments of fur have been discovered on a doormat in the Cattery in the palace basement. Death is the penalty for such a crime, and the royal couple are in despair, for Prince Anhotep confides to the Princess that he himself is responsible for the cat's untimely end.

In the early hours of the morning he was writing a love sonnet when he was disturbed by the yowling of a cat. He heaved a brick at it and "Then there came a quick cessation of the row." He subsequently hid the cat's body and believes himself to be free of suspicion. But the sharp eyes of the Royal Embalmer have noticed on Prince Anhotep's dress stains of blood and strands of fur. When he is directly questioned the Prince admits his guilt, and on the eve of his wedding, calling down curses on the Sacred Cattery, he is removed to prison and execution.

ACT II

It is early dawn in the courtyard of the palace, and a few stars shine in the cold blue sky. In the temple voices of priests can be heard intoning a dirge to the dead cat. Out of the palace comes the disconsolate Princess Amasis, bewailing the absence of her lover:

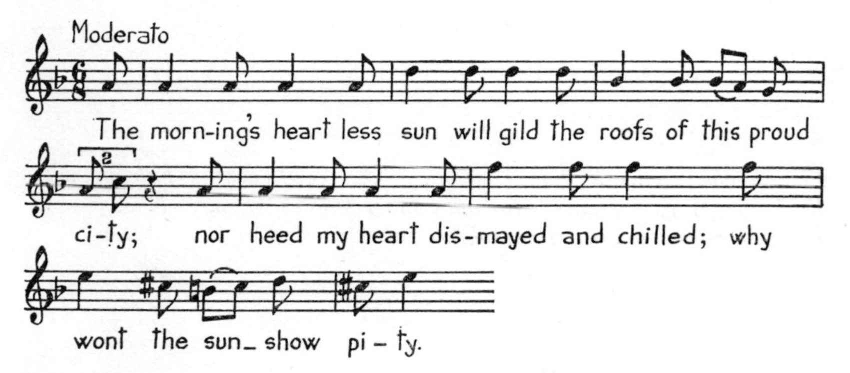

Prince Anhotep has a friend in a poor scribe called Cheiro, who has been engaged to place on record an account of the royal wedding. He is himself deeply in love with the Princess, but realises that his infatuation is a hopeless one. For love of the beautiful Amasis, Cheiro performs a noble act of self-sacrifice and declares that it was he who killed the Sacred Cat. Now since both Prince Anhotep and Cheiro have confessed to killing the cat and neither has produced a body, it would seem that both must die. But Cheiro is determined to save Prince Anhotep's life and, with considerable resource, produces the carcase of a cat. It is accepted as being authentic and Anhotep is released, while Ptolemy removes the dead cat to embalm it, murmuring gleefully: "What a magnificent opportunity to try out my new process." Things look black for poor Cheiro, though he is resigned and declares: "Death is a game that I can play better than life." But at the eleventh hour Amasis comes to his rescue. She has discovered in the penal code an ancient law that any man led forth to die should be reprieved at the request of a pure and kindly maid, and Amasis claims the privilege. Since no one can dispute Amasis' right, Cheiro is released. But the High Priest insists that the law clearly states that when a Sacred Cat is killed someone must die, although, as Pharaoh points out, the difficulty seems to be who that someone shall be. As they are arguing, the problem is solved when news comes that Ptolemy is dead. He had shut the lamented Sacred Cat in his new patent embalming chamber, and when he rashly entered it himself to remove the mummy the dread vapours instantly did their work. "How very droll," is Pharaoh's comment. "Mummified! Ah, well, he was always too clever." And Cheiro records: "The great Princess on this her wedding day performed a crowning act of grace in that she saved the life of one Cheiro, condemned to death for killing one of the Sacred Cats, his real crime, known only to himself, being that he loved the beautiful Amasis."

Miss Hook of Holland

A Dutch Musical Incident in Two Acts

Book by Paul Rubens *and* Austen Hurgon

Lyrics and Music by Paul Rubens

First produced on 31st January, 1907, at the Prince of Wales Theatre, London, with G. P. Huntley as "Mr. Hook" and Isabel Jay as "Sally".

Characters

MR. HOOK, *widower and wealthy liqueur distiller*
SALLY, *his daughter*
CAPTAIN ADRIAN PAAP
BANDMASTER VAN VUYT
LUDWIG SCHNAPPS, *foreman of the distillery*
SIMON SLINKS, *a loafer*
FREDA VOOS
MINA, *maid to the Hooks*
CHORUS OF MARKET-FOLK, SOLDIERS, CHEESE-MERCHANTS, ETC.

ACT I

The scene is the cheese-market of Arndyk, a village on the borders of the Zyder Zee. The curtain rises on the fifty-eighth birthday of Mr. Hook, the local squire and wealthy proprietor of a liqueur distillery. Mr. Hook's daughter, Sally, has made the fortune of her father's firm by inventing a famous liqueur called "Cream of the Sky". During his birthday celebrations Mr. Hook loses the precious recipe of Sally's liqueur. It is found by a lazy loafer, Slinks, who, realising its value, puts it carefully away in view of a possible future reward. Among Mr. Hook's birthday well-wishers is a party of orphans. They appear with a collection of kites which they proceed to fly, assisted by Sally. Sally has lost her heart to a handsome young composer called Van Vuyt, who is bandmaster of a regiment stationed at Arndyk. He has composed a march song which appeals to Sally and especially to Mr. Hook. It has a refrain which goes:

The two young people manage to snatch some stolen moments alone, and one of their favourite meeting-places is "by the side of the sleepy canal".

Van Vuyt's commanding officer, Captain Paap, is also in love with Sally. But he gets very little encouragement from her and is wondering how to improve his chances when he is approached by the lazy loafer, Slinks. Slinks knows all about the Captain's attachment and offers to sell him the recipe of the liqueur, "Cream of the Sky", which he has found. His idea is that when Mr. Hook discovers his loss Captain Paap shall undertake to find the recipe, and so win the gratitude of Sally's father.

Mr. Hook's distillery is at Amsterdam. The foreman there, Ludwig Schnapps, is engaged to Mr. Hook's maid, Mina, and is such a flighty character that in a song she compares him to the Flying Dutchman:

During a visit to Arndyk, Schnapps engages Slinks as an employee of the distillery. But the lazy loafer, permanently work-shy, is only too glad to sell his job to Van Vuyt for two hundred guilders. An anniversary fête to celebrate the invention of Sally's liqueur is to be held on the following day at the distillery, and Van Vuyt is determined to go to Amsterdam, forestall Captain Paap and win the hand of his beloved Sally. The curtain comes down on a rousing send-off as Sally and her father leave for Amsterdam.

ACT II

Act Two takes place in Mr. Hook's liqueur distillery in Amsterdam. The staff are greatly looking forward to the anniversary fête to celebrate Sally Hook's invention of "Cream of the Sky" to be held that evening. Schnapps, the foreman of the distillery, has a penchant for pretty girls, and his fiancée, Mina, who arrives from Arndyk for the fête, discovers his flirtation with an attractive girl called Gretchen. Between the two girls Schnapps has a difficult time, and to pacify Mina he makes her a present of a petticoat, which is the subject of one of Paul Rubens' well-known songs:

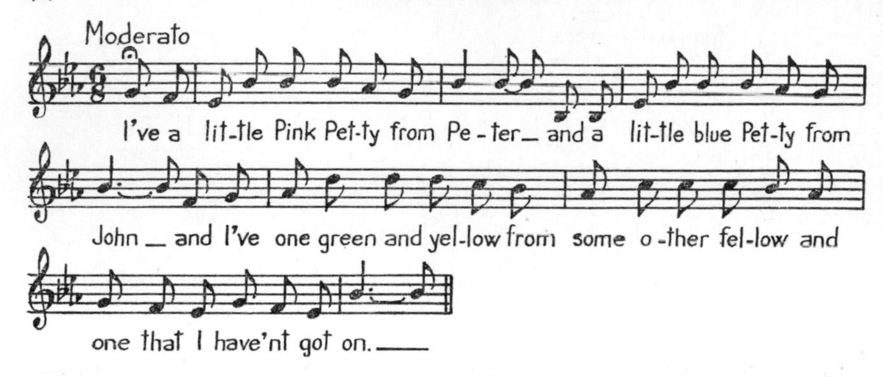

Captain Paap arrives at the distillery with the intention of returning the lost recipe to Mr. Hook. But he learns from Freda Voos, one of the kite-flying orphans seen in the first act and now an employee of the distillery, that Mr. Hook has threatened to have the man arrested who finds the recipe. So the Captain decides to get rid of the recipe and, putting it in an envelope, hands it to one of the workmen to give to Mr. Hook. He fails to recognise in the workman his Bandmaster Van Vuyt, who has duly taken the place of the lazy loafer, Slinks, and is working in the distillery to be near his beloved Sally. Sally and all the girls are, like the men, impatient for the hooter to sound and release them from work to make themselves beautiful for the fête. They are particularly looking forward to discarding their clogs, and Sally sings:

When Van Vuyt hands Captain Paap's envelope containing the recipe to Mr Hook, Mr. Hook flies into a rage and orders Schnapps to send for the police to arrest the scoundrel who has stolen the precious recipe. Van Vuyt is in trouble all round, for Captain Paap, who had forbidden his bandmaster to visit Amsterdam for the fête, has now spotted him in his disguise as an employee of the distillery. However, Sally saves the day. She discovers that Captain Paap has transferred his affections to Freda Voos, and having soundly rated him for his fickleness, makes him promise to forgive Van Vuyt and not to punish him. Finally Sally persuades her father to consent to her marriage to Van Vuyt. Mina marries Schnapps and Captain Paap marries Freda. Such a happy end must, one can only assume, be due entirely to the efficacious effects of that unrivelled liqueur, "Cream of the Sky".

The Mountaineers

A Romantic Comic Opera in Three Acts

Book by GUY EDEN *and* REGINALD SOMERVILLE

Lyrics by GUY EDEN

Music by REGINALD SOMERVILLE

First produced in London on 29th September, 1909, at the Savoy Theatre, with C. H. Workman as "Pierre" and Elsie Spain as "Clarice".

CHARACTERS

PIERRE, *Chief Customs Officer*
CLARICE, *his daughter*
JEAN TINELLI, *her admirer*
CONRAD
GUSTAVE, *a Customs officer*
ANNETTE, *his fiancée*
MISS SPINIFEX, *a spinster*
SERGEANT FREDERICO, *of the Reserve*
CHORUS OF VILLAGERS, SOLDIERS, PARTY GUESTS, ETC.

ACT I

The scene is an Alpine village. On the left of the village square stands an inn built in the style of a chalet, on the right the Customs house; and in the centre a lych-gate leads to the church with its pointed spire. There is a magnificent view over the valley to the snow-capped mountains in the distance. Village life revolves round the Customs house, for this is a frontier village, and the diligence stops here daily for the passengers' baggage to be checked for contraband. The doyen of the Douane, so to speak, is Pierre, elderly and good-natured but also pompous and facetious. He has a daughter, Clarice, who is the heroine of the story. The curtain rises on her birthday, and she is warmly greeted by the villagers. In return she invites them all to a dance which her father is giving that evening. There is some speculation as to whether Jean Tinelli, Clarice's admirer, will be there, and the village girls tease Clarice about Conrad, the handsome young man who has been staying at the inn for the past three weeks. It is common knowledge that he has payed open court to Clarice and has given her a valuable necklace for her birthday. When the villagers have gone, Conrad appears. He has learned of Clarice's lover, Jean, and is extremely jealous. "Why will you not listen to my tender pleadings?" he urges. But Clarice tells him that there is something fascinating about Jean's fiery, stormy violence, and in a duet she explains:

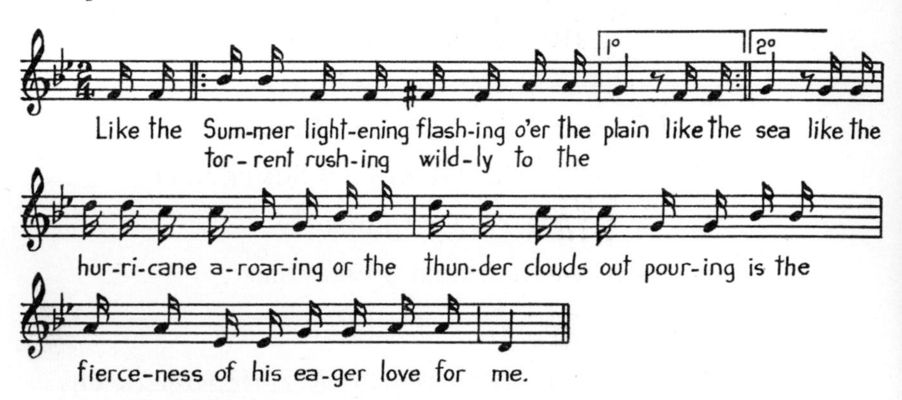

At this point Pierre arrives with his Customs officers. He urges them to watch carefully for the possibility of confiscating any of the passengers' goods, as there are certain articles which he, as a representative of the State, could do with. He particularly mentions neckties and number seventeen collars. The diligence now drives into the village square with a jingling of harness and cracking of whips and draws up at the inn. Among the passengers is an elderly English spinster, Miss Spinifex, and her maid. Miss Spinifex has a penchant for the gentlemen and is enchanted with Pierre's uniform and manly chest; and Pierre, having gone thoroughly through her baggage and noted some valuable jewellery, is equally interested in getting to know her better.

We now meet Jean Tinelli, who has come down from the mountains with a birthday present for Clarice—a gold chain. He is just going to put it round her neck when he notices Conrad's necklace and demands: "Who has given you this?" Before Clarice can reply, Conrad answers, and a painful scene follows. To Clarice's embarrassment, the villagers are beginning to collect and her father comes out of the inn. To pacify the two men and to play for time, Clarice tells them that the man who wishes to win her must propose according to the custom of the village. "And what is that?" asks Conrad. "Why," says Clarice, "don't you know that no right-minded girl in our village will listen to a man's suit until he has shown his pluck by bringing her a sprig of edelweiss from the highest peak yonder?" And she sings them "The Legend of the Edelweiss", the story of a maiden who put her two lovers to this test, of how they perished in a snowstorm and never came back and the maiden died of remorse and a broken heart. Both the lovers accept Clarice's challenge, though Jean tells her bitterly that he seeks the edelweiss "with one thought only and no other, to cast it at the feet of him, thy new-found lover". In spite of the black clouds that are gathering over the mountains and the prayers of all present that they should not go, both men set off, leaving poor Clarice the victim of bitter remorse and terror.

ACT II

Act Two takes place in a room in Pierre's chalet. Clarice's birthday dance is in full swing and the brightly lit room is crowded with a throng of young and energetic dancers. Pierre has invited Miss Spinifex and is improving the acquaintance every moment, until she meets Gustave, one of his staff. The wayward fancy of Miss Spinifex is immediately captured by this new excitement, and to the fury of both Pierre and Gustave's fiancée, Annette, the two go off together. Clarice then comes in alone and depressed. Snow is falling and she is worrying about the two men on the mountain, when there comes a knock on the front door. She opens it, and in the snow stands an old organ-grinder who begs for shelter. Clarice brings him in to the fireside, and during their conversation he offers to tell her fortune in a duet with an attractive waltz refrain:

Clarice goes off to get the organ-grinder some refreshment, and the old man, left alone, notices the necklace which Conrad gave Clarice lying on the table. He picks it up, and at this moment Pierre enters and accuses the old man of theft. Throwing off his disguise, the organ-grinder proves to be Jean, who has concealed his identity to try to find out whether Clarice really loves him. Pierre tells him that if he wants proof of this he should go off to the mountains and bring back Conrad, who is probably by now half-buried in the snow. Then, if Clarice will take him, he can have her. "On the other hand," says Pierre unkindly, "if she takes Conrad, I shall have a rich son-in-law." So, with a friendly farewell, Jean goes out into the night.

Shortly after this there is another knock at the front door, and this time it is a recruiting sergeant, Frederico by name, at the head of a troop of soldiers. The Sergeant brings news of the threat of war with the neighbouring state and warns all reservists to stand by, pending a call-up. Pierre, whose name is on the reserve, immediately begins to make excuses explaining how impossible it will be for him to join up, and to his relief is told that he is far too decrepit to be of any use in the army. Annette is greatly taken with the Sergeant's uniform and manly charms and, flirting outrageously with him, manages to lure Gustave away from Miss Spinifex. Having got him back, she proceeds to tell him what she expects from a husband; for instance

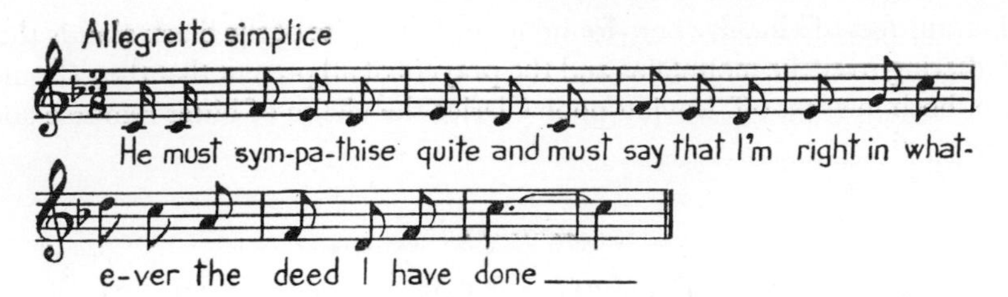

Pierre now attacks Gustave for daring to raise his eyes to Miss Spinifex, and the Sergeant, seeing the chance of a bit of fun, insists that honour can only be satisfied by blood. A comedy scene follows in which both men are exposed for the cowards they are, Gustave hiding in a convenient cupboard and Pierre disappearing up the chimney to avoid a duel. Finally the Sergeant and his troop depart, speeded on their way by the whole village. Clarice, left alone, sinks into a chair and falls asleep, and in a dream sees a wintry scene on the mountain top. Before a shrine Conrad is lying insensible in the snow. Jean enters. Seeing Conrad, he gives a gesture of scorn and prepares to pass him by. But the shrine arrests his attention. Taking off his hat, he makes the sign of the cross and then, impetuously approaching Conrad, raises him in his arms. Drawing a flask of brandy from his pocket he puts it to Conrad's lips. As Conrad shows signs of returning consciousness, Jean takes him in his arms and sets out to carry him to the valley below. Clarice awakens to the sound of distant yodelling. In the finale Jean arrives back with his burden, and Clarice, in gratitude for Conrad's safety, begs Jean to let all be as before between them. But Jean is still smarting from the fact that Clarice found it necessary to put his love to the test. Although in his heart of hearts his love is still unchanged, he repulses Clarice's plea as the curtain falls.

ACT III

In the interval between the acts Jean and Clarice have made it up, and Act Three opens on their wedding day. This happy event encourages Pierre to propose to Miss Spinifex, and when she archly claims the right to be wooed according to the custom of the village, Pierre proudly produces the edelweiss and describes a purely fictitious climb to get it:

At this point there is a sound of bugles and marching feet and Sergeant Frederico is back with his soldiers. War has broken out, and the Sergeant tells his old friend, Conrad, that E Division, which includes Jean, is to be called up and must leave immediately for the front. Conrad is horrified that the man who saved his life should be torn from the arms of his bride on his wedding day. He tries to bribe the Sergeant, but Frederico tells him coldly that the country cannot spare soldiers at such a time. The wedding party now passes by on the way to church and the Sergeant apologetically halts them. He makes his official announcement that war has been declared, that E Division is to be called up and reads out the list of names on the reserve, which includes Jean Tinelli. Pierre angrily protests and Clarice bursts into tears. But Sergeant Frederico is adamant. And now Conrad pays his debt to Jean for saving his life. Addressing the Sergeant, Conrad says: "Sergeant, I understand that if Jean Tinelli can find a substitute he will be exempted from service." The Sergeant confirms that this is so. "Then I will be his substitute," declares Conrad. And bidding them all farewell, he takes his place in the ranks and a rifle is handed to him. As the curtain falls the soldiers march away singing:

Mirette

Opera in Three Acts

Dialogue by HARRY GREENBANK

Founded on the French of MICHAEL CARRÉ

Lyrics by FREDERIC WEATHERLY *and* ADRIAN ROSS

Music by ANDRÉ MESSAGER

First produced on 3rd July, 1894, at the Savoy Theatre, London, with Florence St. John as "Mirette", Courtice Pounds as "Picorin" and Walter Passmore as "Bobinet".

CHARACTERS

FRANCAL, BOBINET, PICORIN, MIRETTE — *gipsies*
BARON VAN DEN BERG, GERARD DE MONTIGNY — *landed gentry*
BIANCA, *Gerard's fiancée*
THE MARQUISE DE MONTIGNY, *Gerard's aunt*
CHORUS OF GIPSIES, VILLAGERS, GUESTS, ETC.

ACT I

In a forest glade in Flanders a band of gipsies are disporting themselves round a large fire. Some are drinking, others playing dice. Just as their leader, Francal, is declaring that gipsies are the only true philosophers, Bobinet enters. He is in a terrible state, having fallen into a pond while trying to steal a duck from a nearby farm. Francal suggests that they all follow Bobinet's example of theft, and the gipsies are preparing to go foraging when Mirette enters. Her story is a strange one. Sixteen years ago Francal had found a woman dying in the frozen roadway with a lovely girl child in her arms. The gipsy band adopted her, called her Mirette and chose her to be their Queen. They care for her tenderly and treat her reverently. Now Francal says it is time she chose a husband from among them. But although Mirette is very fond of Picorin, one of the gipsies, she has been day-dreaming of rich men and princes, and she will not commit herself. The fact that this is the part of the country where she was found makes her long to find out the history of her parentage.

The gipsies then go off to steal what they want from the village, and leave Mirette in the care of Picorin and Bobinet. Picorin confesses his love for her, in spite of Bobinet's intrusions. The camp-fire needs more kindling, and when Mirette retires to a tent to sleep, Picorin goes off to fetch it from the dark forest, leaving Bobinet on guard alone. He is rather unnerved at being left, so he sings a gay little little song to cheer himself up:

The song does not have the desired effect, and, on hearing voices approaching the camp Bobinet puts down his gun and climbs up a tree. The voices belong to two noblemen who are disputing, in a friendly way, the boundaries to their adjoining estates. The gentlemen are the Baron van den Berg and Gerard de Montigny, the latter being engaged to the former's daughter. In the middle of their discussion they come upon Bobinet's gun. In no time they have him down from the tree and realise that the gipsies are trespassing on one or the other's property. The Baron marches Bobinet off, intending to fetch a squad of soldiers to arrest the remaining gipsies, leaving Gerard to take Mirette to his aunt, the Marquise de Montigny, who is in need of a maid. Mirette's beauty entrances Gerard, and she naturally finds him attractive and begs him to fly when she hears the rest of the gipsies returning. On his return Picorin jealously taunts her about her fine gentleman, and Mirette flounces off into the woods, followed by a remorseful Picorin. They are both picked up by the Baron's soldiers, who arrest all the other gipsies and march them off to gaol. Mirette and Picorin, however, are reprieved in order to work as servants for the Marquise de Montigny.

ACT II

A month has passed, and the curtain rises on Mirette singing an old ballad for the Marquise's entertainment:

By this time Gerard is quite infatuated with Mirette and behaves very sullenly with his charming fiancée, Bianca, who has been released from a convent on her betrothal. Mirette has persuaded the Marquise to obtain the release of the gipsies from prison, and Bobinet comes to thank the Marquise. They arrange that the gipsy band shall play and sing for the guests at the betrothal party that evening, and during it Mirette sings of a noble Spaniard and a gipsy girl:

Her performance so enflames Gerard that before all the guests he declares that he will sacrifice everything for Mirette, and he joins the gipsies.

ACT III

On a village green near the château of the Marquise the gipsies are working the village fair. After three weeks of gipsy life Gerard is thoroughly sick of it and Mirette is beginning to see through her "Fairy Prince", and when Bianca, who is truly in love with Gerard, comes searching for him, Mirette makes the somewhat empty gesture of giving him up. Gerard is crestfallen, but delighted and relieved that Bianca will have him back. And the gipsies are overjoyed that Mirette will wed Picorin and remain their Queen after all.

Monsieur Beaucaire

A Romantic Opera in a Prologue and Three Acts

Book by FREDERICK LONSDALE

Founded on BOOTH TARKINGTON'S *novel of the same name*

Lyrics by ADRIAN ROSS

Music by ANDRÉ MESSAGER

First produced on 7th April, 1919, at the Prince of Wales Theatre, Birmingham. First London production on 19th April, 1919, at the Princes Theatre, with Maggie Teyte as "Lady Mary", Marion Green as "Monsieur Beaucaire" and Robert Parker as "The Duke of Winterset".

CHARACTERS

MONSIEUR BEAUCAIRE
PHILIP MOLYNEUX
FREDERIC BANTISON
RAKELL
TOWNBRAKE
FRANÇOIS, *Beaucaire's valet*
THE DUKE OF WINTERSET
BEAU NASH
CAPTAIN BADGER
MARQUIS DE MIREPOIX, *French Ambassador*
LUCY
COUNTESS OF GREENBURY
LADY MARY CARLISLE
CHORUS OF LADIES, COURTIERS, SOLDIERS AND BEAUX

PROLOGUE

It is early in the eighteenth century, when Beau Nash reigned supreme as king of Bath and the Assembly Rooms were the meeting-place of high society. To Bath comes Monsieur Beaucaire, a gentleman of distinguished bearing and French nationality. He is something of a mystery, and in the prologue, which is set in his lodgings, we learn in a conversation between his valet and a friend,

Philip Molyneux, that he is, in fact, the Duke of Orleans escaped from France after being imprisoned by Louis XV. It appears that he had refused to marry the lady of the King's choice and that, after a term in the prison of Vincennes, he escaped through the good offices of the French Ambassador to the Court of St. James, travelling in his suite as his barber. When Beaucaire arrives it also transpires that he is in love with the beautiful and wealthy Lady Mary Carlisle and intends to be present that night at Lady Rellerton's ball, which he knows she is attending. Beaucaire has learned that the unscrupulous Duke of Winterset plans to marry Lady Mary to save himself from financial ruin, and he is anxious to interfere. Molyneux protests that it is courting disaster for him to attend Lady Rellerton's ball. Only a few days earlier the Duke of Winterset had publicly denounced Beaucaire as a barber and had him expelled from the Pump Room. Tonight he is bound to be recognised. But Beaucaire is bent on going to see his lovely Mary, whom he likens to a red rose:

At this point three man, Rakell, Bantison and Townbrake, are shown in, and they are shortly joined by His Grace the Duke of Winterset. Now, although Winterset and his friends have such aristocratic scruples socially, they are not above visiting the rooms of this lackey barber to gamble with dice and cards, for the humble barber appears to have plenty of money and is not afraid to lose it. But Beaucaire has a deeper motive than mere gambling with aristocrats, and when the others have left, with the aid of his friend Molyneux, he sets a trap to catch the arrogant Winterset cheating; a trap into which he falls, for he is caught red-handed with several cards concealed in his sleeve. As the price of silence Winterset is compelled to introduce Beaucaire once again into the society from which he has so recently been expelled. The occasion is to be that very night at Lady Rellerton's ball. As Beaucaire explains: "I'm going to assassinate my poor moustache, and with my hair done *à la mode*, no one will know me. Whom shall I be? Out of compliment to Monsieur, I too will be a Duke. Le Duc de Chateaurien. *Voilà!*"

ACT I

The scene is Lady Rellerton's ballroom. Beaucaire is duly presented to Lady Mary in his role of the Duc de Chateaurien, and she is greatly attracted to the distinguished Frenchman, who pays such graceful and melodious compliments:

Beaucaire makes the most of his opportunities at the ball, especially with Lady Mary, who feels herself increasingly drawn to the aristocratic stranger. She even promises to give him the rose she is wearing in her hair on condition that he performs a service—the simple service of escorting her old friend, Lady Greenbury, to supper. When he consents, they discuss the presentation of the rose in this graceful duet:

"Any time within half an hour will do," are Lady Mary's instructions, and Beaucaire promises: "I pledge my word, Lady Greenbury shall be in the supper room in half an hour." But before he is able to earn his reward he is involved in a duel with Captain Badger, a skilled and swaggering swordsman, bribed to insult and fight Beaucaire by the Duke of Winterset. In an extremely effective scene the duel takes place off stage in the garden, while on stage the guests are dancing an elegant minuet:

Suddenly the cool and stately dance is interrupted by an alarm. Rakell and Molyneux rush in and announce that Captain Badger has succumbed to the greater skill of Beaucaire and lies wounded on the grass. Even as they are speaking, Beaucaire appears at the head of the staircase with old Lady Greenbury on his arm. Advancing to Lady Mary he tells her:

"I did the task you chose
Now may I have my rose?"

Lady Mary takes a rose from her hair and gives it to him, and as the curtain falls he kneels to take it and kisses her hand.

ACT II

Three weeks later Mr. Bantison is giving a garden party near Bath. Many distinguished guests are present, including the great Beau Nash, and the gentlemen one and all are in a ferment of jealousy at the social successes of the Duc de Chateaurien, especially with Lady Mary, whose side, they complain, he never leaves. Incidentally, this scene contains the best-known song in the opera, an admirable example of Messager's sensitive and graceful talent. It is sung by Lady Mary and the chorus.

But of all the gentlemen, the hardest hit by de Chateaurien's success is the Duke of Winterset. His financial position makes it imperative that he marry Lady Mary without further delay, and he is getting desperate. There is only one thing for it—the Duc de Chateaurien must be liquidated. To this end he breaks his promise and divulges to six of his friends that the Duc de Chateaurien is no other than the barber, Beaucaire, who was ignominiously expelled from the Pump Room. As a result, they all attack Beaucaire in d'Artagnan-like combat and each in turn is disarmed, until he is seized from behind by Winterset's lackeys and only rescued in the nick of time, though badly wounded, by his faithful valet. It so happens that at this moment Lady Mary passes in her coach on her way home. She has seen enough of the affair to realise Winterset's villainy, but undeterred he declares that de Chateaurien is no Duke, but a low-born barber, and his six friends swear to Beaucaire's identity. Humiliated in the eyes of Lady Mary, Beaucaire appeals to her not to condemn him unheard, but she is mortified by such evidence of apparent deception, and she turns coldly away, leaving him, broken and bleeding, to fall into the arms of the faithful Molyneux.

ACT III

A week later the Pump Room is filled with a fashionable gathering to welcome the French Ambassador, His Excellency the Marquis de Mirepoix. The men are all agog, as there is a rumour that Beaucaire has declared his intention of being present as a loyal Frenchman to pay his respects to the Ambassador of France. We also learn that, in gratitude to the Duke of Winterset for having saved her from Beaucaire, Lady Mary has promised to become his wife. Among the guests is Philip Molyneux and his fiancée Lucy, whose little romance constitutes the sub-plot of the opera. Lucy is furious with Molyneux for his friendship with the discredited Beaucaire, and at this point they sing an entertaining duet, "We are not speaking now". Lucy is even more upset when Molyneux informs her that Beaucaire is with him. Presently Beaucaire manages to see Lady Mary alone. Her heart soon tells her that whatever the cost, her place is by his side, and she tells him so. At this moment Winterset and a half-dozen of his friends burst into the room and make for Beaucaire, who defends himself with a chair. Winterset turns to Lady Mary, saying: "Madam, this is no place for you," but going to Beaucaire, she replies: "There is only one place for me—beside the man I love." Further proceedings are interrupted by the ceremonial entrance of the French Ambassador, who goes straight to Beaucaire and, bowing low, kisses his hand with the words: "Monseigneur, mon Prince." The Ambassador then tells Beaucaire that he need wear his incognito no more. Thereby absolved from his promise, Beaucaire denounces Winterset as a liar, a cheat and a coward, and when Winterset demands the name of the man who dares to bring such a charge, it is the Ambassador who replies: "Permit me to have the honour of presenting you to His Highness, the Duke of Orleans, Duke of Chartres, Duc de Nemours, Count of Beaujolais and cousin of His Most Christian Majesty, the King of France."

Chu Chin Chow

A Musical Tale of the East

Told by OSCAR ASCHE *and set to music by* FREDERIC NORTON

First produced on 31st August, 1916, at His Majesty's Theatre, London, with Oscar Asche as "Abu Hasan", Lily Brayton as "Zahrat Al-Kulub", and Courtice Pounds as "Ali Baba".

CHARACTERS

ABU HASAN, *a robber chief*
KASIM BABA, *a wealthy merchant*
ALCOLOM, *his wife*
MARJANAH } *his slaves*
ZAHRAT AL-KULUB } *his slaves*
ALI BABA, *his brother*
NUR AL-HUDA, *Marjanah's lover*
A COBBLER
ABDULLAH, *major-domo to Kasim Baba*
CHORUS OF ROBBERS, SLAVES, WEDDING GUESTS, ETC.

ACT I

In Kasim Baba's palace a feast is being prepared for the entertainment that night of a wealthy Chinese merchant, Chu Chin Chow. Watching the preparations are three women: Alcolom, Kasim Baba's wife, and two of his slaves, Marjanah and Zahrat Al-Kulub. All three express their detestation of their Lord, Kasim Baba, praying to Allah that he may lose every dinar of his ill-gotten wealth, for all of them are anxious to escape from his clutches. "There is one coming to the feast tonight with power to grant thy prayers," Zahrat Al-Kulub tells the others. After swearing them to secrecy, she confesses that she is the slave of this very Chu Chin Chow, "even as I was the slave of the Wazir of Sharazynar and of the Hebrew Damascene, Yaccub, and of the Royal Grecian Prince Constantine. For all four be but one and the same man." She reminds them how, after the visit of each of these notabilities, Kasim Baba has been mysteriously robbed or plundered. She winds up by telling them that the true name of the robber of many aliases is Abu Hasan of Khorasan—the Sheik whom all men fear. Zahrat Al-Kulub, acting as his spy, has sent him warning of a sale of slaves to be held by Kasim Baba at sunrise—a sale which will include Marjanah and Zahrat Al-Kulub. She suggests to Marjanah that she bide her time, gain speech with Chu Chin Chow and, under threat of exposure, persuade him to set her (Marjanah) free by purchasing her at the sale, and to release Alcolom by later murdering Kasim Baba. "As for me, my time will come for freedom and revenge. 'Tis written in the sand, his fate and mine," she finishes.

A gong now sounds and Chu Chin Chow enters with his retinue:

Marjanah quickly seizes her opportunity to accost Chu Chin Chow. She bargains with him, and he agrees to purchase her freedom at the sale and to arrange that Alcolom speedily find herself a widow. "If thy mistress will but aid me to rob the comb, she shall remain Queen Bee," he promises. But Abu Hasan realises at the same time that Zahrat Al-Kulub must have betrayed his identity, and he makes her a sinister promise to reward her by restoring her to her lover and arranging for them to live in the midst of unlimited wealth until their death. Kasim Baba now enters and greets his honoured guest, presenting his brother Ali Baba as a "poor half-witted babbler of Baghdad". They sit down to the feast and an entertainment provided by Javanese dancers. Abu Hasan seizes this moment to offer Kasim Baba a price for Marjanah, but Ali Baba, who is tipsy, spoils the negotiations by bidding wildly himself and undertaking to double any offer made by Chu Chin Chow. Later that night Marjanah meets her lover, Nur Al-Huda, son of Ali Baba, who has by his drunken foolishness ruined Marjanah's plan to gain her freedom and marry Nur Al-Huda. There is only one solution—flight. The lovers agree to meet at sunrise near the Turquoise God in the cactus grove, where Marjanah will be gathering fuel with Ali Baba. They will then hasten with all speed from Baghdad. The lovers say good night and Nur Al-Huda sings a tender lullaby:

Next morning the lovers meet in the cactus grove. They rebuke Ali Baba, who has a fearful "hangover", for his drunken behaviour of the previous night, and are about to depart on their journey when the call of the Muezzin is heard. Removing their shoes, they kneel, touching the ground with their foreheads. At that moment out of the bowels of the earth sounds a voice crying:

"Open, Sesame," and to their terror the rocky ground opens. They have just time to hide before Abu Hasan and his robber band appear from an underground cave, singing:

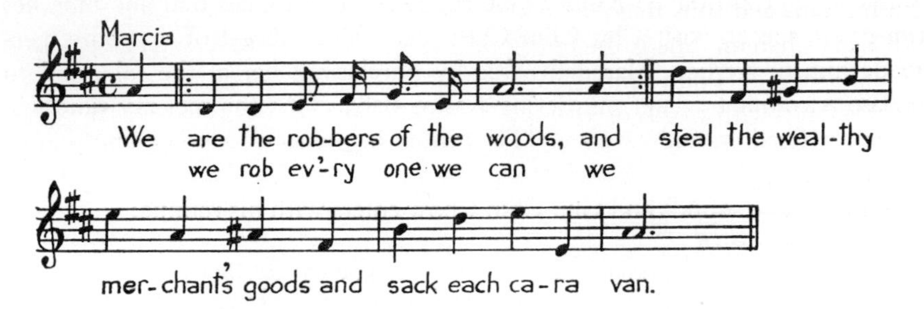

When all the robbers are out Abu Hasan cries: "Shut, Sesame," and the rock closes. They then depart to plunder Kasim Baba at his palace.

Marjanah, Ali Baba and Nur Al-Huda now investigate the cave, and find it full to overflowing with sacks of gold and precious stones. They collect a substantial sum and depart for Kasim Baba's palace to pay the forty thousand pieces of gold which Ali Baba had bid the previous night for Marjanah's freedom. It is vital to Abu Hasan's plan to rob Kasim Baba that Kasim Baba himself should not be present at the sale of slaves. To this end Abu Hasan has given Zahrat Al-Kulub a phial and instructed her to drug her master's cup so that he will be absent from the sale and Alcolom take his place. When he arrives at the palace, Abu Hasan has an interview with Alcolom, and comes to an understanding with her that, provided he undertakes to liquidate Kasim Baba, she will agree to any demands he may make during the sale. When the sale begins and the buyers are assembled, the slaves are paraded and the bidding begins. Various bids are made until Abu Hasan declares: "Put all the lots together and I will bid against thee all." The merchants protest that it is against all law and custom, but Alcolom strikes a gong and commands: "I speak for Kasim Baba. Do as Chu Chin Chow asketh." Later, when Abu Hasan has outbid the others and is asked to put his money down, he answers: "Nay, I give my bond." His bond is accepted by Alcolom, though all other buyers are expected to put down their money. The result of this favouritism is that the slaves are knocked down to Abu Hasan for the sum of 297,201 dinars. He sends immediately for Zahrat Al-Kulub, and tells her that as a reward for her treachery in revealing his identity she and her lover shall live chained in his cave "midst wealth uncountable" till the end of their days. Then Zahrat Al-Kulub, turning on him, tells the other buyers that it is no Chinese merchant with whom they have been bartering, but that Chu Chin Chow is the robber Sheik, Abu Hasan of Khorosan. "Seize him," she urges them. "He is but one." "And forty more," says Abu Hasan, as his robber band march on. Abu Hasan addresses the merchants. "Place all your bags of good Persian gold here on this mat." Groaning, they comply as his attendants collect the spoil. Then with a final command, "Bring Zahrat Al-Kulub to the cave. The Peace upon ye all," he takes his leave.

ACT II

When the curtain rises Abu Hasan has still not kept his promise to dispose of Kasim Baba and thus free Alcolom, whose chief desire is to become Queen of Ali Baba's harem. She is the light of Ali Baba's eyes, and he showers her with compliments—"Thou timid giraffe, who swayest with an elephant roll"—and she responds with words of love:

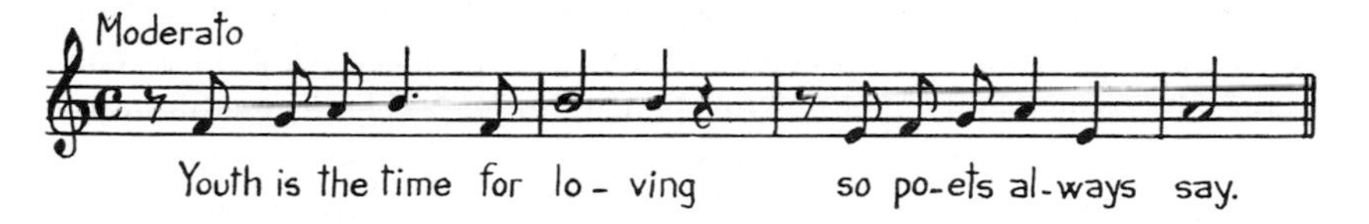

In the meantime, Kasim Baba has jealously marked his brother Ali Baba's improved financial circumstances, and he is determined to discover the source of his wealth. He accordingly questions him, and Ali Baba tells him quite openly the secret of the cave, promising to take him there in the morning. But greed and envy compel Kasim Baba to steal a march on his brother, and that night he sets out for the cave with half a score of mules. Nur Al-Huda and Marjanah, however, divine his purpose and reach the cave first. Here they find Zahrat Al-Kulub gagged and bound to a stake, a prisoner. They cannot release her from her shackels, having no implements, but they promise, on Kasim Baba's arrival, to borrow two of his mules and fetch help from the city. Kasim duly arrives at the cave, but he has forgotten the magic words. Marjanah in concealment speaks them, and as Kasim enters the cave she and Nur Al-Huda slip out, close the door and ride away to Baghdad. Kasim, amazed at the sight of so much treasure, greedily pulls out some sacks of gold. As he is doing so there is a thunder of galloping hooves overhead, and he has just time to hide before Abu Hasan and his robbers are in the cave. Kasim's presence is quickly detected and he screams for mercy, but Abu Hasan draws his "short, sharp scimitar" and to this bloodthirsty song Kasim is swiftly dispatched and his body neatly quartered:

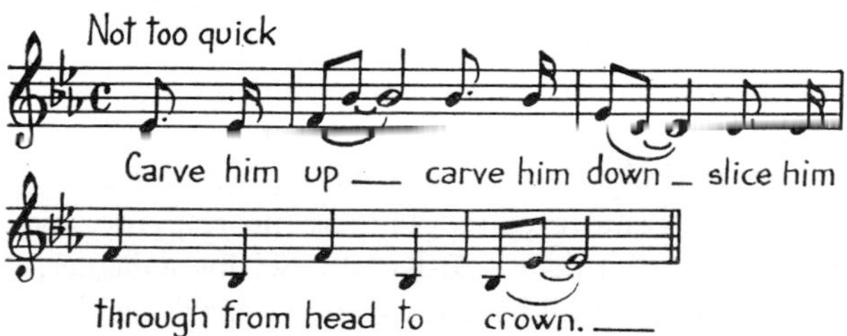

Next day, disguised as a water-carrier, Abu Hasan wanders through the streets of Baghdad. He is greatly worried. Zahrat Al-Kulub has been released from the cave and Kasim Baba's body has been removed. Who can have done this? Seated outside his shop sits a cobbler, singing as he works:

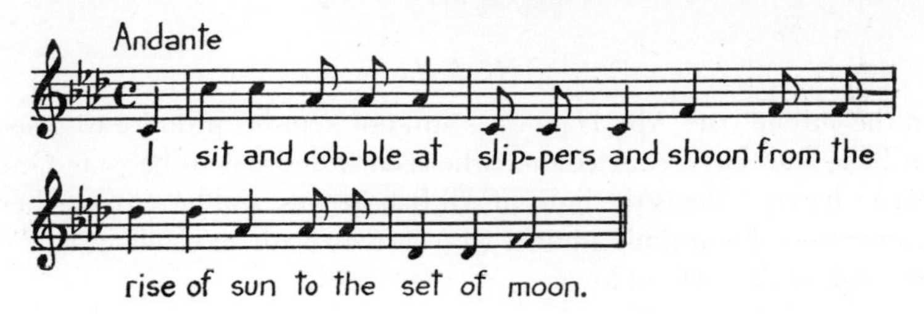

This cobbler unfolds to Abu Hasan a strange tale of how he was led blindfolded to a house by a woman, who bribed him with four pieces of gold to cobble together the dismembered quarters of a human body. "Where was this house?" asks Abu Hasan, and the cobbler answers: "I turned to the left and turned to the right, and yet to the right and once to the left. As I was led into the street after my cobbling was finished, I put my hand behind my back and drew a cross with blue chalk upon the door." Abu Hasan recognises the hand of Zahrat Al-Kulub in all this, but she proves too clever for him, for when he seeks to find the house it is only to discover that every door in the street carries a cross of blue chalk. Later Zahrat Al-Kulub brazenly accosts Abu Hasan, and offers to reveal to him the name of him who holds the secret of the cave if he will set free her lover, whom Abu Hasan still holds as hostage. She tells him that tomorrow night the wedding of Nur Al-Huda and Marjanah is to be held at Kasim Baba's house. "Come thou at moonrise robed as an oil merchant from Jerusalem, with all thy forty followers each hidden in a jar. Obtain permission to store them in the palace till dawn. Then, when all the guests are gathered for the dance, sing thou 'The Song of the Scimitar'. Then, joining in the chorus, ye cut your way out and slay." Abu Hasan is delighted with her plan and duly arrives with his jars. Zahrat Al-Kulub now enlists the help of Abdullah, the major-domo of Kasim Baba's palace. She tells him that in each jar a man is concealed, that the oil merchant is the robber Sheik, Abu Hasan, and of the contemplated attack. They go down the line of jars. As they rap on each one a voice says: "Is it time, O Sheik?" and Zahrat Al-Kulub answers in a gruff voice: "Not yet." She then instructs Abdullah to summon his staff and pour boiling oil into each jar. "And as thou pourest in the oil, sing all of ye to drown their cries." This is duly accomplished.

Later, at the marriage feast, Abu Hasan claims the privilege of a stranger guest to greet the bride and bridegroom with song—"the like of which none here will ever hear again." He then breaks into "The Song of the Scimitar", the cue for his robber band to enter. There is no response, and Abu Hasan, scenting treachery, turns on Zahrat Al-Kulub. Seizing a dagger, she stabs him to the heart, and he falls. "Allah! what hast thou done?" cry the guests, aghast. "I have slain the enemy of man, Abu Hasan of Khorasan, the robber Sheik," she tells them. The body is carried out, the wedding festivities are resumed and the curtain falls to the sound of joy-bells.

Young England

A Light Opera in a Prologue and Three Acts

Book and Lyrics by BASIL HOOD

Music by G. H. CLUTSAM *and* HUBERT BATH

First produced on 23rd December, 1916, at Daly's Theatre, London, with Clara Butterworth as "Betty", Harry Dearth as "Drake", Walter Passmore as "Tom Moon" and Hayden Coffin as "Oxenham".

CHARACTERS

FRANCIS DRAKE
JOHN OXENHAM, *Drake's lieutenant*
SIR GEORGE SYDENHAM
BETTY SYDENHAM, *his daughter*
HARRY SYDENHAM, *his son*
JOAN, *Betty Sydenham's maid*
TOM MOON, *Drake's drummer*
SAM BEST, *his mess-mate*
JOHN DOUGHTY
WILLIAM COURTENAY
QUEEN ELIZABETH I
CHORUS OF DRAKE'S MEN, TOWNSPEOPLE AND THE QUEEN'S COURT

PROLOGUE

The Prologue is a panegyric of "Young, fresh England", and ends with the words:

"Now—now ye rouse to a dead admiral's drums;
And young fresh England hath stood up awake
To spend her youth by following after Drake."

It is followed by a Prelude Picture; a small scene showing the stern of a ship with the coast of Southern Ireland in the background. It is Drake's ship homeward bound, and the steersman and a crew of hearty sailors sing:

At the finish of the song the scene dissolves into:

ACT I

This scene represents Sunday morning in a part of old Plymouth. On the right of the stage is an inn and on the left a church. It is almost time for matins, and the congregation are beginning to arrive. Some small boys are playing "Spanish and English" so noisily that the beadle lays hold of the ringleader for brawling at the church door and asks his name. The boy answers that he is the son of Sir George Sydenham, and shortly after Sir George arrives and removes his son to church. Sir George also has a daughter, Betty, whom he intends to marry off to young William Courtenay. But when Betty and her maid, Joan, arrive we learn from their conversation that Betty is in love with Drake, and Joan with Drake's drummer, Tom Moon.

No sooner have the two girls gone into church than the sound of a gun is heard from the sea, and distant cheering. *The Golden Hind* has docked and the word soon goes round that Drake and his men are back from their voyage round the world. The congregation stream out of the church, as sailors begin to arrive. Drake then enters and receives an ovation from the crowd. He is warmly greeted by Sir George Sydenham, but he has eyes for no one but Betty. Oxenham, his lieutenant, also recalls that he has known Betty since she was a child and she bids them both welcome back to England; the cue for a charming octette in which Joan and Tom Moon join:

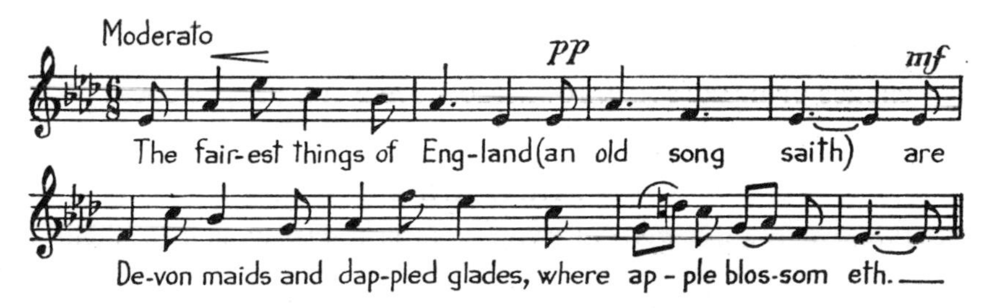

After this Drake manages for a moment to get Betty to himself. They arrange to meet in London, where Betty is to go on the morrow to the Court of Queen Elizabeth, and Drake tells her that he will formally ask her father for her hand in marriage. He offers to show her over *The Golden Hind*, and they are about to go on board when Drake is stopped by a sour-faced man, one John Doughty.

It appears that this Doughty had a brother who sailed with Drake and was caught inciting the crew to mutiny. He was found guilty and condemned to be hanged from the yard-arm. "Rest his soul!" says Drake. "I have no quarrel with his memory nor with thee." But Doughty with a scowl replies: "I call thee butcher. There is no peace between me and thee, hangman." He stalks away, followed by jeers and insults from Drake's sailors, and presently twelve o'clock strikes the hour for the departure of *The Golden Hind.* As Sir George is bidding Drake farewell, young Harry Sydenham, Betty's brother, comes breathlessly up to her. He has been down to the shore to see *The Golden Hind* and by chance has overheard a conversation between the sour-faced Doughty and another. "They spoke of Drake. They will follow him to London, to work him ill. Doughty and the other will meet this day sennight at Deptford, where Drake goes, at the 'Duck and Goose' Tavern, to talk further to some vile purpose. Shall I run to the ship and warn Master Drake?" Betty tells him the ship by this time would be under way, but that Drake in any case would not listen, but would laugh at the danger. "Nay," she says to her brother, "I'll borrow doublet and hose and go myself to Deptford." "I'll go search for some things for thee to wear," he says, and as the curtain falls, the distant voices of Drake's sailors are heard:

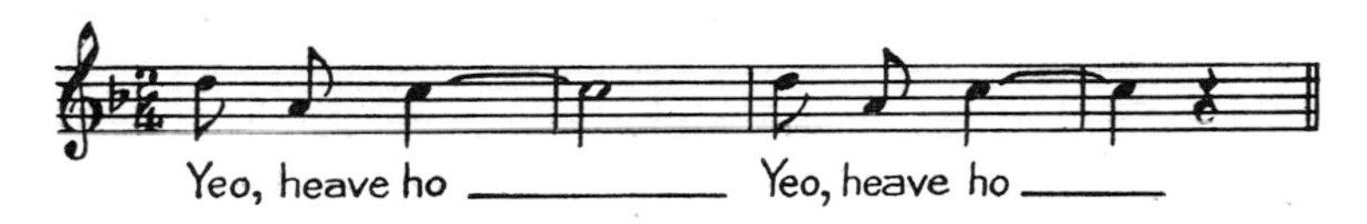

ACT II

Act Two takes place on board Drake's ship *The Golden Hind* at Deptford. When Betty decided to go to Deptford, disguised as a boy, to warn Drake of his danger at the hands of Doughty, her faithful maid Joan insisted on accompanying her similarly clad. Betty has discovered further details of Doughty's plot to injure Drake. Doughty's plan is to drive Drake to rebel against the Queen by persuading her to insist on Betty's immediate marriage to William Courtenay, whom she does not love. If this plan fails, Doughty's men will kidnap Drake, and Doughty will try him for his life, behind closed doors—as he accuses Drake of having tried his brother. All this Betty pours out into Oxenham's ear and, although he is well aware of her identity, Oxenham allows her to appear before Drake in the guise of her brother, Harry. When Drake appears he is delighted to see, as he thinks, Betty's young brother, particularly when the lad informs him that his sister is in the neighbourhood and that a written message will fetch her on board within the quarter of an hour. Drake places his cabin at the lad's disposal, and his companion (the faithful Joan) stands by to help in the composition of the letter.

But though Drake has been deceived over Betty's identity, John Doughty has not. He is aware of her presence on board *The Golden Hind*, and he now arrives bringing Drake news of the Queen's decision to pay a surprise visit to his ship. Courtenay tells Drake of the Queen's anger against Betty, who was commanded to attend Court and is absent. Shortly after this four Westminster school-boys arrive with a poem of welcome in Latin and English to Captain Drake from the Headmaster. One of the boys proudly introduces himself as Harry Sydenham, Betty's brother, and Drake is greatly puzzled. The riddle is solved by Betty emerging from the cabin, looking ravishing in a most becoming dress. Directly she hears of the prospective visit of the Queen, Betty exclaims: "She is enraged with me, she'll not hear reason. I'll away," and she returns to Drake's cabin. Her appearance, however, has been observed by Doughty. A moment later Queen Elizabeth arrives on board. Her first act is to compliment Drake on his wonderful achievement of voyaging round the world, and she inquires how he chose the brave men who went with him. Drake and his mariners make answer in this rousing song:

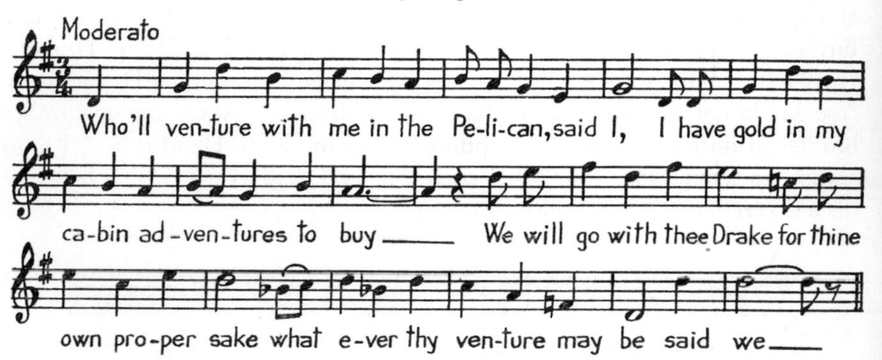

Then the Queen turns to William Courtenay and takes from him a sword. With the command "Kneel, Captain Drake", she gives him the accolade and the order "Rise, Sir Francis Drake". Wild cheering follows, and Queen Elizabeth sings her stirring song, "For England's Sake":

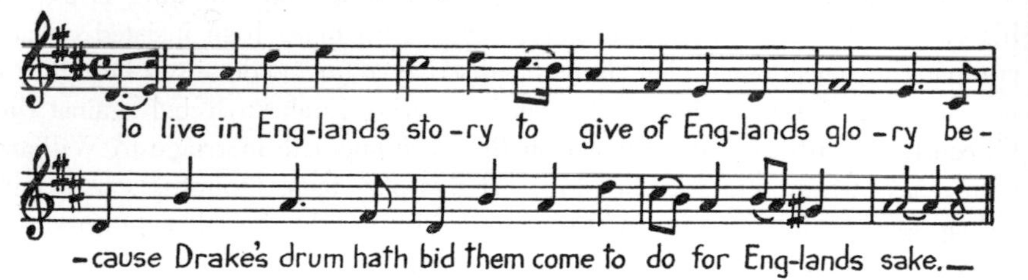

The Queen then demands to be shown the charts of the voyage. Drake tells her they are in his cabin and that he will fetch them, but the Queen declares her intention of visiting his cabin. This, in view of Betty's presence, must be prevented at all costs, and a variety of diversions are devised to distract the Queen. First Lieutenant Oxenham is presented, then leave is sought to present the Westminster scholars with their poem. All this the Queen tolerates with growing impatience. But when leave is sought for the crew to present a Mermaid Masque, the Queen's patience is exhausted. With an irritable "I'll to your cabin, Sir Francis, without more ado", she advances. As she reaches the door it is opened from within and on the threshold stands Betty facing the Queen. With a furious "Thou!" the Queen summons Sir George Sydenham and orders that Betty be immediately disposed of in marriage to Courtenay. Turning to Drake, she tells him to choose between the continued advantage of her royal favour and patronage and Betty's love, and without waiting for his answer leaves the ship. But the two lovers are only strengthened in their decision to hold together.

ACT III

The last act takes place outside a village church in Devon, where a crowd waits for the arrival of the bride, Betty, who is to be married today to William Courtenay. So far there is no sign of the bride or of the Bishop of Kew, whom the Queen has commanded to perform the ceremony. The bridegroom and his best man, Doughty, are impatiently waiting. Doughty still fears trouble from Drake, but Courtenay tells him that Drake has put to sea in *The Golden Hind* and is far away. Doughty, however, is unconvinced and to curb his impatience goes to look out for the Bishop's coming. Left alone, Courtenay sings a romantic love-song "The April of My Heart":

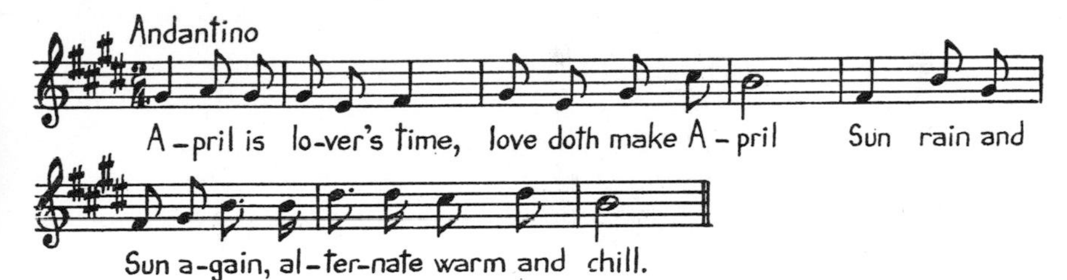

Courtenay then goes into the church.

Drake's drummer, Tom Moon, and a fellow mess-mate, Sam, now arrive, and from their conversation it appears that Drake is sailing the ship hither and that Oxenham is waiting in the inn disguised as the Bishop of Kew. Soon there is a cry of "Here comes the bride", and Betty enters on her father's arm. Shortly afterwards Oxenham appears in his disguise as the Bishop of Kew, attended by two of Drake's men dressed as clergy. But Doughty's sharp eyes have recognised Oxenham beneath the Bishop's robes and, drawing his sword, he stands guard over him. Convinced now that Drake intends an attack, Doughty declares that he has twenty stout farm-hands on the beach to hold him and his boat's crew when they land. But Sam scornfully tells him that the twenty were Drake's own men. "And there," he says, "be one of Drake's guns." In a moment comes a shout of "He's ashore", and Oxenham, throwing off his Bishop's robes, sings—perhaps rather unsuitably at this moment of high excitement—the patriotic "Who Sings of England":

When Drake arrives Courtenay and Doughty are forcibly removed by Drake's men, and though Sir George Sydenham cannot bring himself to give his blessing to the union, Betty is in no doubt. As Oxenham tells Drake: "There's not one here would not follow thee to perdition," and Drake replies, with a glance at Betty: "I'm on the highway to Heaven, Jack." And the happy couple enter the church with the bells chiming.

The Maid of The Mountains

A Musical Play in Three Acts

Book by FREDERICK LONSDALE

Lyrics by HARRY GRAHAM

Music by HAROLD FRASER-SIMSON

With additional numbers by JAMES W. TATE

First produced on 23rd December, 1916, at the Princes Theatre, Manchester. First London production on 10th February, 1917, at Daly's Theatre, with José Collins as "Teresa", Arthur Wontner as "Baldasarre" and Lauri de Freece as "Antonio".

CHARACTERS

BALDASARRE, *chief of a band of brigands*
BEPPO, ANTONIO, CARLO, ANDREA — *brigands*
GENERAL MALONA, *retiring Governor of Santo*
ANGELA, *his daughter*
VITTORIA, *her companion*
CRUMPET, *aide de camp to General Malona*
LIEUTENANT RUGINI, *officer in charge of Devil's Island*
TERESA, *the Maid of the Mountains*
CHORUS OF BRIGANDS, TOWNSFOLK, ISLANDERS, ETC.

ACT I

The scene is the "hide-out" of a band of brigands on a mountain-side. On the left of the stage is a cave and on the right a path leading up the mountain pass. As the curtain rises the brigands are busy storing bundles of loot in the cave. A general air of depression hangs over them, for their chief, Baldasarre, has wearied of a bandit's life and is breaking up the business. To cheer up his comrades, Beppo, in a ringing baritone, sings "Live for today", with its comforting philosophy:

Teresa, the Maid of the Mountains, enters. She is a great favourite with the boys, cooking for them, darning their socks and generally taking care of them. They beg her to use her influence to persuade the chief to stay on, but Teresa protests that Baldasarre is no longer interested in her. "He couldn't tell you whether I was dark or fair," she tells them. When Baldasarre eventually appears he is quite relentless in his determination to break up the band and orders the brigands: "Pack your things: we leave tonight." Grumbling, they retire to the cave, and Baldasarre left alone with Teresa, tells her that she must leave at once. When she protests he points down the ravine, saying: "They've found our hiding-place. We're surrounded. Look!" He continues: "They've no idea there's a woman among us. If you're stopped on the pass, you can say you're a woman from the village. Andrea will take you a little way." Teresa pleads with him to let her stay, but he is adamant. Then she tells him: "You've changed. You used to like me. But lately you've avoided me." Embarrassed by her mood, Baldasarre asks what she will do with her future, and Teresa replies: "I may marry." He asks if there is someone she loves and looking him straight in the eyes she answers: "More than my life." So they say good-bye, and Teresa with tears in her voice sings:

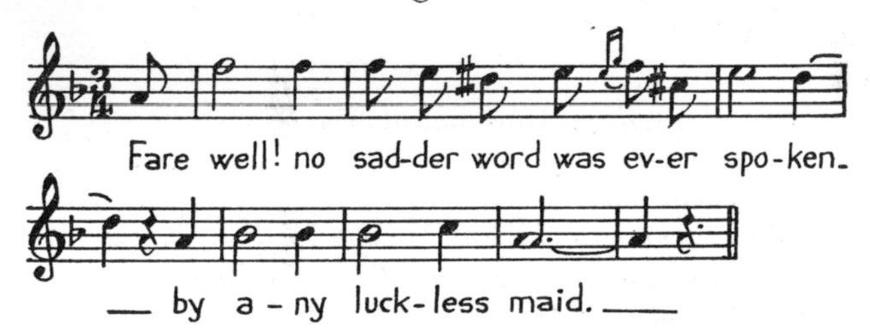

When Teresa and Andrea have left, the brigands are settling down to a grand division of the spoils, when there comes a loud knocking at the gate. Baldasarre tells them in a low voice that the place is surrounded. "We'll make a dash for it," he says. "Carlo, when I give the word, open the gate. Are you ready? Open." Carlo opens the gate, and to their amazement an elegant young woman stands watching them with ironic amusement. It is Angela, the daughter of the Governor of Santo, with her companion, Vittoria. She tells Baldasarre that her father's governorship expires next day and that she and Vittoria have been to the town to buy decorations to welcome the new Governor. On their return they lost their way in the fog and happened to see a light. In a comedy scene that follows, during which Vittoria evinces signs of the utmost terror, there is talk of the notorious robber Baldasarre and his band, the scourge of the neighbourhood, and Angela refers to him as a thief and a cur. After a little refreshment the two women decide, in spite of the fog, to continue on their way. As they are saying good-bye, suddenly Angela stops, her eyes riveted on the lapel of Baldasarre's jacket. "Where did you get that brooch?" she asks, and he replies: "From a girl in a coach." "So you *are* Baldasarre," she accuses, and Baldasarre admits his identity. Angela then tells him exactly what she thinks of him and demands that he open the gate and allow her to leave with Vittoria. Baldasarre, admiring her pluck, detains her long enough to learn that the new Governor will shortly be passing that way in his coach, and then he allows her to leave. She is hardly out of sight when a distracted Andrea arrives with the news that Teresa has been captured and taken to Santo. He has been sent back with a message that if Baldasarre will give himself up, Teresa will be set free. As he is pondering the situation, Baldasarre observes a coach slowly making its way through the ravine. "There goes the new Governor on his way to Santo," he tells the brigands. "The people have never seen him. We must hold up the coach, take his clothes and papers and go to Santo in his place. Come on, boys, follow me." And the curtain falls to a reprise of "Sing hey! sing ho! take no thought for the morrow."

ACT II

The scene is the courtyard of the Governor's palace at Santo. The household is assembled to greet the new Governor, who is to take over that day. While they are awaiting his arrival, the retiring Governor, General Malona, announces the capture of a member of the brigand's band, a girl. With the information which he will extract from her, the General is confident Baldasarre will be in their hands by sundown. But his interview with Teresa is not as successful as he anticipates. She refuses to betray Baldasarre and, reminding him of the saying "There's honour among thieves", she sings:

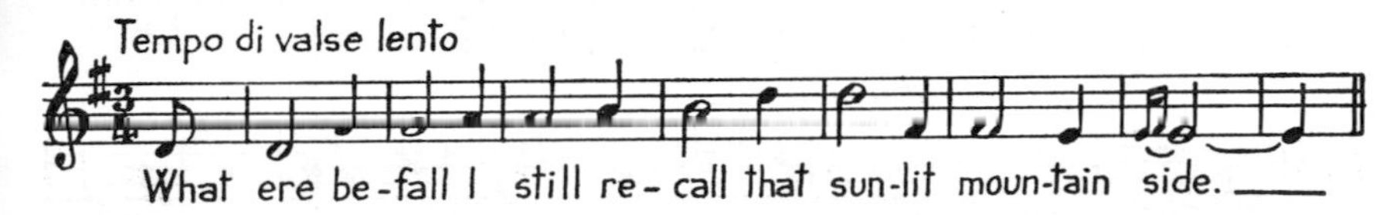

At the end of the song Teresa advances to the General and, after contemptuously snapping her fingers in his face, walks away.

The cry is now raised of "Long live the new Governor", and Baldasarre, Carlo, Beppo and Antonio enter, immaculate in uniform. Baldasarre presents his staff and his credentials as new Governor to General Malona. The General presents his daughter, Angela, who does not recognise Baldasarre in his Governor's uniform and is extremely friendly. When Baldasarre is informed of the capture of a brigand girl, he asks to see her alone. Teresa at first fails to recognise him and is obstinately loyal, but when he reveals his identity she is delighted to see him. He tells her that the real Governor and his staff are safely tied up and are being guarded by Andrea; and that in his role as new Governor he will inform General Malona that Teresa will lead him to Baldasarre's "hide-out" and the two of them will escape with Carlo, Beppo and Antonio. He tells Teresa to be ready to leave at any moment and dismisses her.

These dramatic scenes are interspersed with some broad comedy between Vittoria, Angela's companion, and Antonio. They are husband and wife. Vittoria believed he had been drowned at sea five years before, and is amazed to see him again. For the time being both preserve their incognito, but General Malona, who has his eye on Vittoria, is madly jealous. One of the charming numbers she sings with Antonio is "Husbands and Wives":

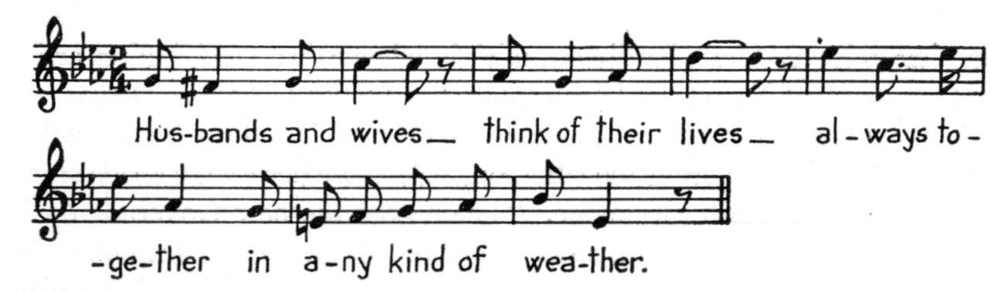

The plot now develops a new twist: a flirtation between Baldasarre and Angela, who are mutually attracted. To such an extent is this so on Baldasarre's side that when Angela begs him to put off his departure to capture the brigands till next day, Baldasarre consents and tells Carlo that they will not be leaving at present. The brigands are most upset at this new situation, and Beppo tells Teresa of Baldasarre's infatuation for Angela and insists that she get him away. Teresa refuses to believe Beppo's story and re-affirms her love for Baldasarre. The scene ends with the well-known duet, "A Paradise for Two":

There follows some further comedy between Vittoria and Antonio and another well-known number for Beppo—"A Bachelor Gay":

In the meantime Baldasarre has made it clear to Teresa that he intends to postpone his departure till the following day, and this rouses her to savage jealousy. After an episode in which Angela laughingly throws him a flower, Teresa's primitive passions are unleashed and she threatens that unless Baldasarre leaves at once with her she will expose him; and in a dramatic musical finale she does so. The act finishes with the arrest of Baldasarre, Carlo, Beppo and Antonio and General Malona's threat of their deportation to Devil's Island, and as the curtain comes down the remorseful Teresa falls fainting to the ground.

ACT III

Act Three takes place on Devil's Island. The scene is a bay with a rocky coastline running out to sea in the distance. A pathway leads up to the village on a hill-top and steep steps cut in the rocks lead down to a sandy beach. As the curtain rises fisherfolk mending their nets are singing as they work. General Malona and his aide-de-camp, Crumpet, arrive in a boat and hold some conversation with the officer in charge of Devil's Island, Lieutenant Rugini. In Act Two Rugini had been posted to Devil's Island as a punishment for daring to raise his eyes to Angela. Rugini now informs the General that the prisoner Baldasarre refuses to divulge the hiding-place of the loot accumulated by his robberies in Santo except to the General himself, and then only on condition that his companions are instantly released. The General goes off to think the matter over and Vittoria sidles up to Lieutenant Rugini and attempts to bribe him to allow her husband, Antonio, to escape. Her efforts, however, are quite unsuccessful. Next, Teresa waylays General Malona and, exerting all her charm, gets so far as to make him admit that he likes her enough to give her anything she wants. She immediately demands: "Give me Baldasarre." Nevertheless, Teresa does not get her way so easily and has to bide her time. Meanwhile, Vittoria and Antonio have decided to let bygones be bygones and join up together once more. He manages to restrain her from giving away all her money to General Malona as a bribe for their liberty. As he points out: "We should still be very happy, darling, but not so comfortable." They cement their reunion in this duet:

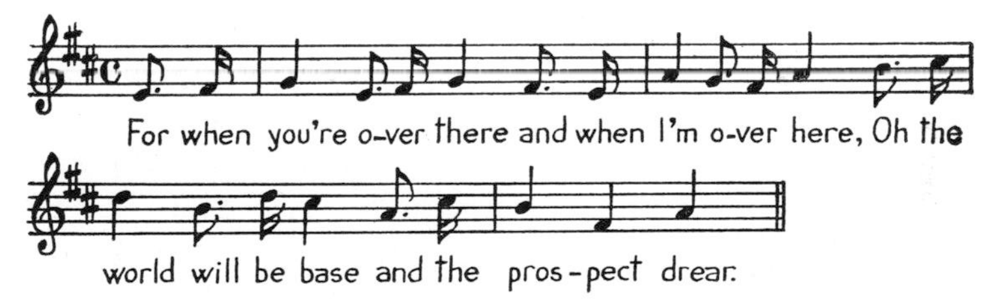

A scene now ensues between Baldasarre and Lieutenant Rugini. The officer is entirely disillusioned in regard to Angela, who had made no effort to prevent his banishment, and he now asks Baldasarre why he did not take his chance of escape in Santo. Baldasarre confesses to his mad infatuation for Angela, and Rugini tells him: "I can't understand why, for a girl like Angela, you gave up Teresa." When he tells Baldasarre that Teresa would give her life to undo the wrong she did him, Baldasarre cynically replies: "If the same conditions arose tomorrow, she'd do it again." "Very well, then," argues Rugini. "Test her. Here is the key to your cell. If she releases you, believing you still care for Angela, I shall be right about her and incidentally get a bit of my own back on old Malona."

The story is almost over. Rugini, sick of Devil's Island and General Malona, assists everybody's escape, he himself leaving in a boat with Vittoria and Tonio, whom he has disguised as the General. Of course Rugini is right about Teresa, who unselfishly urges Baldasarre to take a boat and escape to Angela. However, his eyes now open to her sterling worth, he tells her that his happiest days were those he spent with his Maid of the Mountains; and as the curtain falls they go off happily to the strains of:

The Rebel Maid

A Romantic Light Opera in Three Acts

Book by ALEXANDER M. THOMPSON

Lyrics by GERALD DALTON

Music by MONTAGUE PHILLIPS

First produced on 12th March, 1921, at the Empire Theatre, London, with Clara Butterworth as "Lady Mary", Thorpe Bates as "Derek" and Walter Passmore as "Solomon".

CHARACTERS

LORD MILVERTON, *Lord Lieutenant of the County of Devon*
THE HON. DEREK LANSCOMBE, *his son*
SIR STEPHEN CRESPIGNY, *Royal Commissioner for King James II*
PERCY JEROME, *his Lieutenant*
SOLOMON HOOKER, *Derek's servant*
LADY MARY TREFUSIS, *known as "Snow Bunting, the rebel maid"*
BUNKLE, *a landlord*
SERGEANT, CHORUS OF GUESTS, SERVING MAIDS, VILLAGERS, SOLDIERS, FISHERMEN

ACT I

In the grounds of his house in Devonshire, Lord Milverton is giving a garden party. It is the year 1688 and there are rumours of rebellion and a scare of invasion by the Dutch Prince, William of Orange. Lord Milverton introduces to his guests his nephew, Sir Stephen Crespigny, whom King James has appointed to be his Royal Commissioner in order that the rebellion may be put down with a firm hand. He has come to Devonshire because of reports that there is solid support for the rebellion among Devonshire fishermen; and because he has heard that arms and men are being landed on the coast and that persons of substance are secretly concerned in the plot. Their leader is reputed to be a lady of quality, known as "Snow Bunting". Lord Milverton's son Derek arrives during the garden party and is warmly welcomed by his father. He announces that his visit will be a brief one, as he has some business to dispatch and his cutter, the *Curlew*, is lying in the Channel. Lord Milverton assures Derek that he will be in no hurry to go when he sees his guest, the lovely Lady Mary Trefusis. And on she comes to sing:

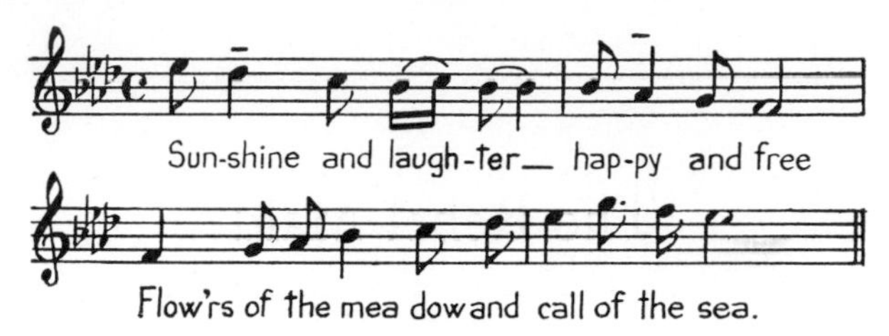

Mary and Derek had been childhood playmates and are now immediately attracted to one another, to the annoyance of Sir Stephen Crespigny, who has fallen in love with Mary.

Now, Derek is an emissary of William of Orange and has come to England to prepare for his landing. Sir Stephen strongly suspects this, and he also suspects that Mary is the rebel maid, "Snow Bunting", secretly engaged in obtaining the support of the local fishermen. His suspicions are confirmed when he intercepts a letter addressed to "Snow Bunting" from Commander of the cutter *Curlew*. It reads: "If coast is clear, show green light on Thursday at ten. If there's danger, show red signal." "On Thursday my redcoats shall be on the spot," says Sir Stephen to his Lieutenant, Percy Jerome. "My information is that the spot is in the neighbourhood of Lady Mary's house at Torbay." As it happens, although both Lady Mary and Derek are staunch supporters of the rebel cause, neither of them is aware of the other's political sympathies. So when Mary asks him what is the business that requires his sudden absence, Derek is unable to confide in her and Mary is unable to say what calls her back so urgently to Torbay. This lack of confidence between the two of them occasions a certain constraint in their relationship, especially as Mary assumes that Derek's departure is to visit another woman. Derek promises that, when he is free to speak, she will be the first in whom he will confide. "And will you tell me the name of the woman you love?" she asks. "That, dear Mary, will be the first thing I shall tell you," he promises. The first act ends with the departure of Sir Stephen and Percy Jerome for Torbay to deal with the rebel landing, accompanied by Lord Milverton as Lord Lieutenant of the county, while guests and villagers cheer them on their way.

ACT II

The scene is "The Jolly Fisherman" inn two days later. The inn stands on the summit of Berry Bay opposite Torbay. Sir Stephen questions various local inhabitants—Bunkle, the landlord, and Solomon Hooker, Derek's servant, who is heavily disguised. He asks them if they have ever seen any person signalling to the rebel ships or whether they have ever set eyes on the mysterious "Snow Bunting", and he offers a reward of two hundred pounds for her capture. But Sir Stephen is met at every turn by well-simulated rustic taciturnity or stupidity.

During the day Lady Mary has a convenient fall from her horse outside "The Jolly Fisherman" which ensures her having to pass the night at the inn. At ten that night, learning that Sir Stephen has placed his soldiers round the inn, Mary, assisted by her maid Abigail, sets the warning signal at red for danger. But Sir Stephen is leaving nothing to chance, and he orders Bunkle, the landlord, to change the red light to a green one, and thus lure the unsuspecting invaders into the trap he has prepared. The rebels duly land, and in the desperate fight that follows Derek, who is in command, takes refuge in the inn. Here he finds Mary. She learns that he is the Commander of the *Curlew* and he learns that she loves him. Then on Derek's cue ("Then let the Devil and all his legions come, Sweetheart, I stay") they sing a love duet:

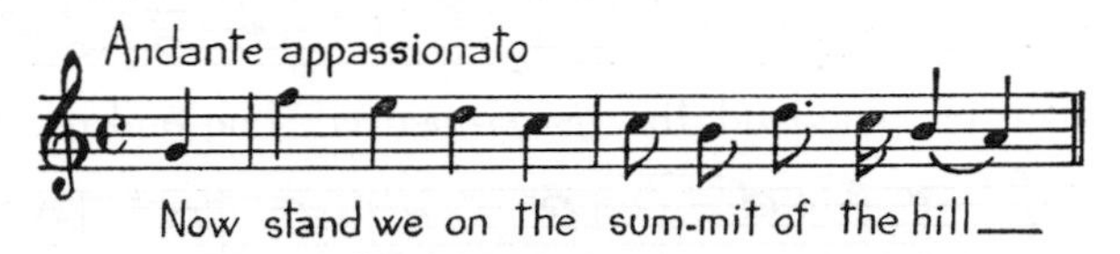

As the duet finishes there is a loud knocking and shouts of: "Open the door in the King's name." Mary urges Derek to escape and shows him a secret passage of which she knows, the inn having been formerly a boating pavilion belonging to her father. But it is too late. Derek has just time to don the landlord's coat and wig which are hanging up, when a Sergeant and five soldiers enter. They are searching for a rebel who was seen to enter the house. Mary calls quickly to Solomon, Derek's servant: "There are rebels here. Help the landlord and these men to search." In a moment the room is full of fishermen, every one of them with rebel sympathies. In an attempt to engineer Derek's escape, Mary calls to him: "Landlord, draw some cider for these men." Derek is leaving the room, when in the doorway he encounters Sir Stephen, and it looks as though the game were up. But the situation is saved by the fishermen. Suddenly they snatch their guns from the soldiers and his sword from the Sergeant. Sir Stephen, too, is disarmed. Abigail opens the entrance to the secret passage and Derek's escape to freedom is assured.

ACT III

Act Three takes place next day on the village green outside "The Jolly Fisherman". Derek has made good his escape, but Sir Stephen Crespigny is relying on the fact that while Lady Mary remains he is certain to return. He gives orders that if Derek is found he is to be shot at sight. Lord Milverton pleads for his only son, but Sir Stephen is adamant. He tells Lord Milverton that it was Lady Mary who engineered Derek's escape, and he makes it quite clear that her only chance of safety is to marry himself. "So that you may secure her estate," sneers the old Lord. "The choice I offer her is between safety and trial for high treason," answers Sir Stephen coldly.

In the meantime, Derek has put out to sea in the *Curlew* to seek the Prince of Orange's fleet and bring it safely to port. But when he lands Derek goes straight to Mary's side and falls into the hands of Sir Stephen's soldiers. News has come that the Prince of Orange has landed at Torbay, and Sir Stephen declares: "Then there is no time to be lost. Let him be shot at once." This disaster, however, is averted by the timely arrival of Prince William. Mary, the rebel maid, surrenders to Derek, and the curtain falls on Derek's well-known song in praise of the fishermen of England, who not only saved his life but, by bringing Prince William's ships safely to port, have saved the liberties of England.

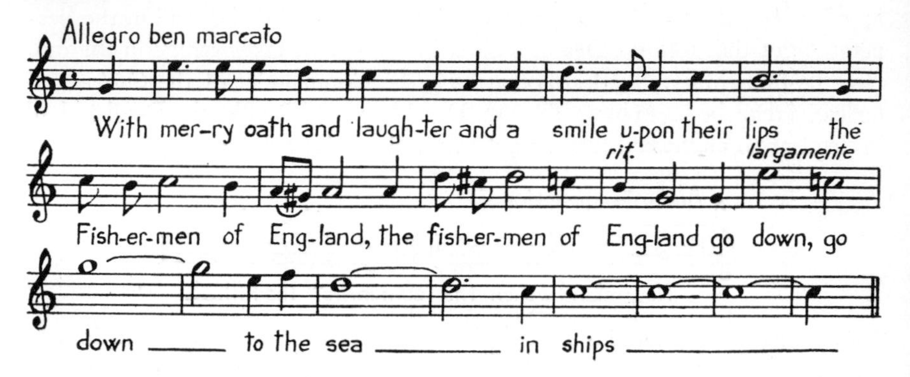

Bitter Sweet

Operetta in Three Acts

By NOEL COWARD

First produced on 18th July, 1929, at His Majesty's Theatre, London, with Peggy Wood as "Sarah", George Metaxa as "Carl" and Ivy St. Helier as "Manon".

CHARACTERS

SARAH MILLICK, (*who appears in the first and last scenes as the Marchioness of Shayne*)
HUGH DEVON, *her fiancé*
MRS. MILLICK, *her mother*
CARL LINDEN, *a music teacher*
HERR SCHLICK, *proprietor of a café in Vienna*
CAPTAIN LUTTE, *an officer in the Austrian Army*
LIEUTENANT TRANISCH
THE MARQUIS OF SHAYNE
DOLLY CHAMBERLAIN
HENRY JEKYLL, *her fiancé*
VINCENT HOWARD, *a band-leader*
FOUR DANCE HOSTESSES
MANON LA CREVETTE, *a diseuse*
CHORUS OF GUESTS, OFFICERS, DEBUTANTES, LADIES OF THE TOWN, ETC.

ACT I

SCENE I. The year is 1929 and the scene is a dance at the house of the Marchioness of Shayne in Grosvenor Square. When the curtain rises a jazz-band is just finishing a dance-tune, and the supper interval follows. The guests disperse to the supper-room and the musicians retire, with the exception of the band-leader, Vincent Howard, who remains at the piano, playing softly to himself. Into the empty ballroom then come a young couple, Dolly Chamberlain and Henry Jekyll. Although they are engaged and are shortly to be married they are not getting on very well, and Dolly is trying her best to pick a quarrel. Eventually she succeeds, and Henry stamps off alone to supper. Left alone, Dolly and Vincent Howard have a conversation from which it is clear that they have come to the end of a rather tawdry love affair. This is to be good-bye, and they are locked in each other's arms in a farewell embrace when Lady Shayne enters the ballroom and stands watching them. They spring guiltily apart and Dolly says defiantly: "Lady Shayne, I love Vincent and he loves me." "Are you sure he loves you?" Lady Shayne asks. They are interrupted at this point by the returning dancers, and the band strikes up a Charleston, but the episode of Dolly and the dance-band leader has upset Lady Shayne, for it has brought back to her with a sense of shock her own past. Unable to bear the raucous jazz tune any longer, she calls to the band to stop; then turns on the younger generation, telling them that they care for nothing but noise and speed, that their dreams of romance are nightmares, their conception of life grotesque. "Come with me a little," she begs them. "I'll show you, listen—listen——" and she sings:

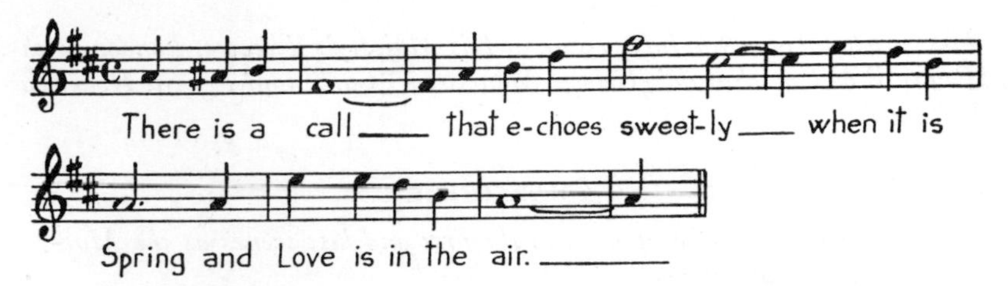

As she finishes singing the lights fade and the story goes back in time to the year 1875, when Lady Shayne was a young girl called Sarah Millick.

SCENE 2. In the music-room of the Millicks' house in Belgrave Square, Sarah is having her final singing-lesson before her marriage to a rather pompous but eminently suitable young man called Hugh Devon. Her singing-teacher is an Austrian, Carl Linden, handsome and romantic-looking, and he and Sarah are obviously attracted to each other. He tells her: "This is the last time we shall be alone together. Although I am playing for the dance tonight, there will be many other people there." Then, pulling himself together with an effort, he commands: "Once more now, your exercises," and they sing the well-known duet:

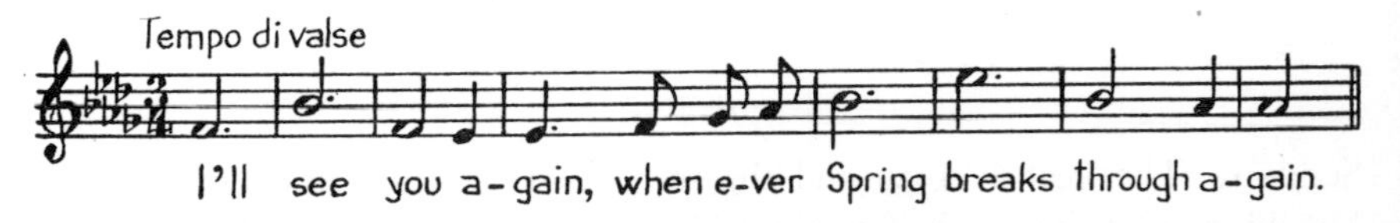

Mrs. Millick and Hugh now enter, and Carl Linden is dismissed. He bids Sarah a formal good-bye and, as he walks out of the room, Sarah, to her mother and her fiancé's utter amazement, collapses sobbing on the sofa and the curtain falls.

SCENE 3. That evening the ballroom of the Millicks' house presents a lively and elegant scene. The band, led by Carl Linden, has just finished a polka, when

Hugh Devon comes out of the supper-room and tells Mrs. Millick that Sarah is behaving very strangely. It appears that at supper she upset a glass of claret over old Sir Arthur Fenchurch, and then merely laughed. Later Sarah appears, flushed and petulant. When Hugh tries to remonstrate she rounds on him, telling him to leave her alone, then she orders the band to play something gay and waltzes round the room by herself. At the end of the evening she apologises to Hugh, but he is still offended and they part on a formal note. When the guests have all gone and only Sarah and her girl-friends remain, Mrs. Millick goes up to bed, and the girls decide to play Blind-man's-buff. After a charming musical version of the elimination test, "Eeny Meeny Miny Mo", Sarah is made "he" and duly blindfolded. As she is groping her way about the room Carl Linden happens to come back to collect some music from the piano. Sarah bumps into him and to steady herself clasps him round the neck. The girls all laugh, but Carl, staggered for a moment, suddenly loses all restraint. Dropping his music, he kisses Sarah full on the mouth, and she, tearing off her bandage, whispers: "It's you I love—now and always." "Come with me now, tonight," he urges. "I'll take care of you, live for you, die for you." "I love Carl. I'm going with him. This is my whole life," she tells the girls and, before their startled eyes Sarah and Carl elope into the night.

ACT II

SCENE 1. Five years later in Vienna, Carl and Sarah (now calling herself Sari) are happily married and employed at Herr Schlick's café. Carl leads the orchestra and Sarah is one of the dance hostesses whose job it is to dance with the customers and get them to spend their money. Sarah's background and upbringing make it difficult for her to unbend sufficiently and unselfconsciously enough to make a success of this job, and she is known to her colleagues as "The Snow Queen". When the curtain rises it is mid-day in the café. Carl is rehearsing the orchestra and cleaners and waiters are busily working. Four of the dance hostesses are gossiping about their rich clients. They discuss Sarah and one declares that "Whenever an officer asks her to dance she goes into a decline". They decide that love is bad for business and sing:

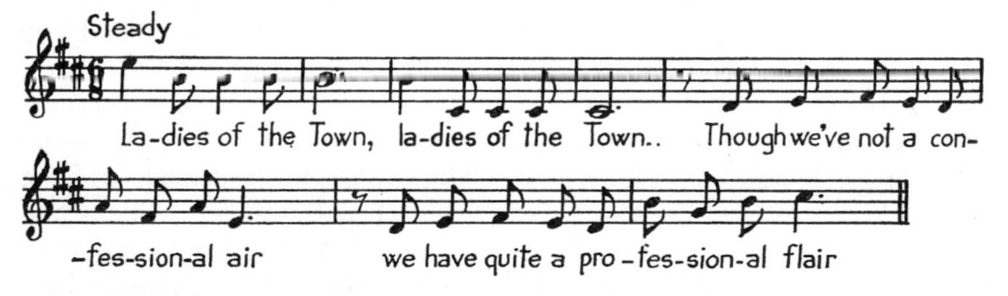

As they leave the café Manon La Crevette enters, a *diseuse* employed as entertainer, getting on in years and losing her looks. She is in love with Carl, with whom, before his marriage, she had had an affair. Manon is jealous of Sarah.

Later an Austrian officer enters the café and asks arrogantly to see Herr Schlick. He wishes to complain about Sarah. She has consistently refused to dance or to sup with him and he insists that Herr Schlick arrange for him to sup with Sarah that evening in a private room. As they are talking Sarah herself comes in, and the officer, Captain Lutte, accosts her and invites her to sup with him. Sarah coldly tells him that she has another appointment. The Captain, with a threatening "We shall see", stalks out of the café, and Herr Schlick tells her furiously: "It may interest you to know that you are losing me one of my most valuable customers." Sarah then learns from Manon that Herr Schlick has arranged for her to sup that evening with Captain Lutte in a private room. Terrified and furious, she seeks out Carl and begs him to take her away. Carl soothes her, promising to take her away on the morrow. They will go to Budapest and start their own little café; Carl has a little money saved and his friend Fritz will help him. Excitedly they discuss the new venture:

Scene 2. At 2 a.m. Herr Schlick's café is doing brisk business. The clientèle consists principally of army officers fraternising with the dance hostesses and other ladies of the town. Lieutenant Tranisch, the possessor of a ringing baritone voice, renders, with chorus of officers, a stirring song in praise of Tokay:

But dark clouds threaten Sarah's horizon. Captain Lutte again complains of her attitude to him, and this time Herr Schlick loses his temper and tells Sarah that both she and her husband Carl may consider their engagements at an end as from tomorrow; and furthermore that, unless she dances willingly and agreeably with Captain Lutte or any other officer who asks her, neither she nor Carl will receive a penny of the week's salary that will be owing to them on their departure. Sarah is shattered but powerless. Later, as Carl and his orchestra are playing a waltz, Captain Lutte asks Sarah to dance. She surrenders herself to the Captain's arms and they begin to waltz. As they dance the Captain becomes more and more aggressively amorous and finally, bending Sarah back, kisses her passionately. In a flash Carl leaps down off his dais on the bandstand, strides up to the Captain and, calling him a filthy, ill-mannered, drunken swine, strikes him in the face. A duel quickly follows. Swords are produced and Carl and the Captain start fencing. But the outcome is a foregone conclusion. Captain Lutte is a brilliant swordsman and is obviously merely playing with Carl, who is quite inexperienced. Finally the Captain knocks Carl's sword out of his hand and runs him through. There is a general outcry and Carl falls. As everyone crowds forward, Sarah takes him in her arms and, murmuring "Sari, my sweet, sweet Sari", Carl dies.

ACT III

Scene 1. The scene is set in the house of the Marquess of Shayne in Grosvenor Square. The year is 1895, fifteen years after the tragic death of Carl. Tonight the Marquess is giving a party to introduce the famous Hungarian singer, Madame Sari Linden. Lord Shayne has fallen in love with Sarah in Vienna and he is very proud of her. When she arrives he introduces her with the words: "My dear, I think you know everyone here." And indeed all the friends who were there the night Sarah eloped with Carl are present and greet her excitedly —even her ex-fiancé, Hugh Devon. As Lord Shayne escorts Sarah to supper four exquisite young men arrive, apologetically declaring: "It's entirely Vernon's fault that we are so entrancingly late." They wear green carnations and sing:

After supper Lord Shayne manages to get Sarah to himself and, telling her that she has refused him in every capital in Europe, proposes yet again. Sarah tells him kindly that after Carl she can never love again, but he urges: "I think I could make you happy—anyhow happier," and she promises to think over his proposal. Then Lord Shayne asks her to sing and she obliges with a song of Carl's about a lovely German Princess who fell in love with a gipsy—a Zigeuner:

As she finishes singing the lights fade and time moves forward once more to the year 1929.

Scene 2. Lady Shayne, once more an old woman, is singing to a lot of young people sprawling on the floor. As she finishes "I'll see you again", Vincent Howard begins to play it as a fox-trot, and Dolly Chamberlain stands motionless by the piano, lost in thought, as the curtain falls.

Conversation Piece

A Romantic Comedy with Music in Three Acts

By Noel Coward

First produced on the 16th February, 1934, at His Majesty's Theatre, London, with Noel Coward and Yvonne Printemps.

Characters

SOPHIE OTFORD
MARTHA JAMES
MRS. DRAGON
PAUL, DUC DE CHANCIGNY-VARENNES
MELANIE
ROSE, *her maid*
THE MARQUIS OF SHEERE
THE DUKE OF BENEDEN } *his parents*
THE DUCHESS OF BENEDEN }
LORD ST. MARYS
LADY JULIA CHARTERIS
CHORUS OF SOLDIERS, GUESTS, MILLINERS, LADIES OF THE TOWN, VISITORS AND CHILDREN

The whole action of the play occurs at Brighton in the year 1811.

ACT I

Paul, Duc de Chancigny-Varennes, a middle-aged French aristocrat, is on the verge of bankruptcy. He has come to Brighton as a last resort and proposes to risk his whole future prosperity on a gamble. With him is a young girl, Melanie, whom he gives out to be an orphan and his ward, the daughter of his old friend, the Marquis de Tramont. Melanie is, in point of fact, a girl he found singing in a café. Impressed by her looks and personality he took her under his wing, had her educated to take her place in society and has brought her to Brighton, the resort of rank and fashion. Paul's plan is to arrange a rich marriage for Melanie and take a commission on the marriage settlement for himself. On the morning that the curtain rises one of Melanie's beaux, the young Marquis of Sheere, is to call upon her. When he arrives at her house he is received not by Melanie but by her guardian, of whose existence he was quite unaware. Paul suavely assumes that the Marquis has come to ask for Melanie's hand and to the young man's dismay declares his intention of calling upon his parents. Left alone with Melanie, Edward tells her quite simply that though he is in love with her it does not blind him to the fact that her guardian is trying to trap him into marrying her. He then asks Melanie to marry him. She looks at him wonderingly and sends him away, telling him to think his offer over seriously and return. As she watches him go she sings very softly:

Later that afternoon Melanie is receiving three rather common friends of hers: Sophie Otford, Martha James and Mrs. Dragon. Her guardian greatly regrets her association with them. She is showing them the latest additions to her wardrobe when the Duke and Duchess of Beneden are announced. The Duchess comes straight to the point. Melanie is acquainted with her son, the Marquis of Sheere. The acquaintance must cease. "Things may be different in France," she tells Melanie, "but here in England there are still two distinct worlds. You belong to one, and my son belongs to the other." She finishes with a bribe of a thousand pounds and a warning that if Edward marries without his parents' consent he will not have a penny. The Duke and Duchess then depart. When her guardian, Paul, returns Melanie describes her encounter with the Duchess and tells him she is sick of the whole scheme. He reminds her that it is a business arrangement and as they are arguing there is a knock at the door. Looking out of the window, they see that the old Duke of Beneden has returned. "Go into the bedroom," says Melanie to Paul. "Listen at the door and do not come out until I say: 'The sea is so pretty'." Paul vanishes and the old Duke is shown in. He has had a brilliant idea—to make Melanie his mistress, and thus get her away from his son. He proceeds to acquaint her with his proposal. He offers her a "dear little house in London, nicely furnished and near Berkeley Square" and three hundred pounds on the first of every month. But Melanie tells him she prefers Brighton to London. As he takes her in his arms she says loudly: "The sea is so pretty," and Paul is in the room. He orders Melanie to withdraw and addresses the embarrassed Duke. "You are the father of the Marquis of Sheere? I see. Good-bye, Monsieur. I will call upon the Duchess later when I have decided what course to take." The old man goes off covered with confusion, while, shaking with silent laughter, Paul and Melanie at the window watch his departure. Later in the Public Gardens Melanie is approached by Lord St. Marys with an invitation from His Royal Highness to sup at the Pavilion. But Paul refuses the invitation on her behalf peremptorily. "Madamoiselle de Tramont has not yet had the honour of being presented to His Royal Highness."

ACT II

The Duc de Chancigny-Varennes renews acquaintance at Brighton with an old flame of his, Lady Julia Charteris, who now decides it would be a good thing if she and Paul got married. Irked by the presence of Melanie, whom she assumes is Paul's mistress, she is extremely offensive to her and the two women have a heated argument. Later Julia learns from Paul that Melanie is not his mistress, but that he is attempting to marry her off to the Marquis of Sheere. When she hears this, Julia is only too anxious to futher Paul's plan. If Paul will give a little supper party, she suggests, she will arrange that the Duke and Duchess of Beneden, Lord Sheere and, say, Lord St. Marys, will be present. The supper party duly takes place, and all the selected guests turn up. The Duchess of Beneden is still slightly dubious about Melanie and recalls "those dreadful women trying on hats" when she called. But Julie assures her that she has known the Chancigny-Varennes family all her life and blames Melanie's lack of knowledge of English people for the company she keeps. Everything is going splendidly and the aristocrats are being as gracious as can be when the door is flung open and the butler announces: "Mrs. James, Mrs. Otford and Mrs. Dragon." There is a moment's horrified silence, and Paul says: "Melanie! Did you invite them?" "*Pourquoi pas?*" she replies. "They are my friends." The party is ruined and the Duchess and the other ladies withdraw haughtily. Melanie is entirely puzzled until Martha James explains: "We never like meeting those sort of women. Most of them are the wives of our gentlemen. It is very awkward." In an attempt to tide over the unpleasantness, Melanie insists on singing. Edward, the Duke of Beneden and Lord St. Marys seat themselves beside the Mesdames Otford, James and Dragon, while Paul sits with Julia. Melanie's accompanist comes in, and she starts to sing. First she sings to Edward with genuine sweetness; then to the old Duke of Beneden, her words tinged with gentle malice; and then she sings to Lord St. Marys with smiling mockery. Last of all she turns to Paul. To him she sings in French an unmistakable love-song. Paul is horrified, for her whole heart is in her voice:

When the guests have left there are bitter recriminations. Paul accuses her of being false to their agreement, and Melanie complains that he has never at any time considered her feelings. Besides, she could not help falling in love with him. She tells him she knows that deep down inside him he too is in love with her. "*Vous allez essayer de m'échapper—cela aussi je le sais—mais vous ne le pourrez pas,*" she cries, and sinks sobbing into a chair.

ACT III

Julia is determined to marry Paul and reasons with him that, now his business agreement with Melanie is at an end, it would be better to send her back to Paris. Julia will supply her with enough money to keep her in comfort until she finds herself a nice husband. Paul is inclined to think Julia is right, but will not commit himself. Then Edward comes to call on Melanie. He realises that she loves Paul and that there is no chance for him, but before he leaves he takes her in his arms for the last time. As he is kissing her, Paul comes in. "Lord Sheere, I congratulate you," he remarks. "It is so pretty to see youth in love." When Edward has gone, Paul asks her: "Are you going to marry him?" She answers: "Yes, Paul, soon—very soon." "I will see you have everything you want," he promises and she replies: "That is very kind of Lady Julia." He tells her he is going away to London. "Come once more to see me before you go," she begs. "Come this evening to a little supper—I will invite Edward, my fiancé, and Lady Julia—it will be to celebrate that we are all so happy." But that evening Edward and Julia, who are the first to arrive for supper, are handed farewell notes from Melanie by the maid, Rose. She has left for France. To Julia's rage, Rose tells them that the Duc de Chaucigny-Varennes went with her. "They was very gay—both of them." Sadly Edward and Julia depart. Soon after, Paul hurries into the house. "Where is mademoiselle?" he asks Rose. "She's gone to France, sir. She left a note for you—here it is." He reads it with a face of utter despair and murmurs distractedly: "She doesn't give any address—she doesn't say where I can find her." He crosses to the window and looks out to sea, and then, resting his head on his arms, breaks down completely. Presently Melanie comes into the room. She tip-toes up to him and, sinking to the floor behind him, takes his hand which is hanging down by his side and tenderly kisses it. He turns slowly and she proffers him a paper bag. "*Mon cher amour.* Would you like a oomboog?" she asks as the curtain falls.

Tantivy Towers

A Light Opera in Three Acts

By A. P. HERBERT

Music by THOMAS F. DUNHILL

First produced on 16th January, 1931, at the Lyric Theatre, Hammersmith, with Olive Evers as "Jenny", Trefor Jones as "Hugh" and Dennis Arundell as "Charles".

Note. In this opera there is no dialogue. The music is continuous.

CHARACTERS

HUGH HEATHER, *a professional singer*
JENNY JAY, *his girl-friend*
CHARLES, VISCOUNT HARKAWAY
LADY ANN GALLOP
THE EARL OF TANTIVY } *their parents*
THE COUNTESS }
CAPTAIN BAREBACK, *M.F.H., engaged to Ann*
CHORUS OF GUESTS, MEMBERS OF THE HUNT, ETC.

The action takes place in Hugh Heather's Chelsea studio and at Tantivy Towers.

ACT I

The scene is the studio in Chelsea of Hugh Heather, a professional singer, where Hugh's birthday is being celebrated by a party. The guests are in fancy dress or "Bohemian" costumes. There are a good many velvet jackets, Russian shawls, pyjamas and red beards. The life and soul of the party is Jenny Jay, Hugh's girl-friend and a dabbler in the pictorial arts, some of whose extremely "modern" pictures decorate the studio.

"It's her belief that art is
An excuse for jolly parties."

Two other guests are Charles, Viscount Harkaway, and his sister, Lady Ann Gallop. Charles, immaculate in a white waistcoat, definitely disassociates himself from the Chelsea crowd:

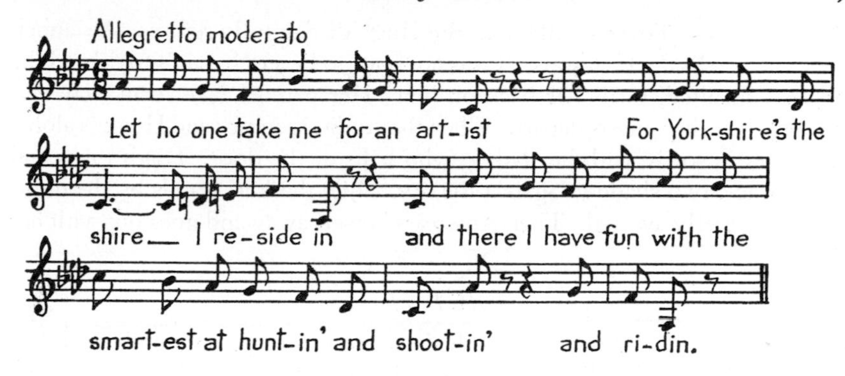

Charles makes no effort to conceal his contempt for art and criticises adversely a female "nude" by Jenny Jay, telling her:

> "I do not believe
> That the daughters of Eve
> Have such very triangular thighs."

Hugh Heather overhears his remarks and is annoyed. Calling to his guests to charge their glasses, he proposes the toast of "The Arts". After the toast has been drunk the ladies all gather round Hugh with birthday kisses, which does not at all please jealous Jenny. Hugh comforts her lightheartedly:

> "Ah, call me not inconstant, who
> Am constantly in love with two!
>
> . . . . .
>
> I could not love thee dear, so well
> Had I not first loved Isobel."

Charles warns his sister that their parents, the Earl and Countess of Tantivy, are on their way to the studio to pick her up and take her home to the country. Ann is very resentful. She likes the freedom of life in Chelsea and is enjoying the party. Noticing Hugh gazing at her ardently she asks Charles who he is:

> *Ann:* Who is that gentleman with eyes aflame?
> *Charles:* He is our host. I do not know his name.

Hugh is enchanted with Ann and tells her so. After this the Earl and Countess arrive at the studio. The Countess inspects Bohemia while the Earl discusses it. His views are even more downright than those of his son, Charles:

> "Let Dagoes paint and write and sing
> But Art is *not* an English Thing."

In spite of their surface disapproval, both the Earl and Countess are intrigued with the Chelsea atmosphere. The Earl is greatly taken with Jenny and invites her down to Tantivy Towers to paint his favourite horse. The Countess, slightly jealous, retaliates by inviting Hugh to stay and sing for them. Jenny urges Hugh to accept and launches into a romantic description of how she imagines Tantivy Towers will look. But Hugh disdainfully refuses. A staunch democrat, he tells the Countess: "I was not born to be a rich man's toy," and the Countess, insulted, turns her back on him. Her parents take Ann away and gradually the other guests depart. When the studio is empty and Hugh is alone, Ann comes in softly with her father, who halts at the door. Hugh turns and they embrace, two shadows against the sky, while the Earl stands by the door, his eyes discreetly averted. Then Ann tears herself away and goes out with her father.

ACT II

In the great hall of Tantivy Towers the Earl and Countess and family party are enjoying their port after dinner and before the Hunt Ball. The scene is a colourful one, with the men in hunting pink. The guests include Jenny Jay and Captain Bareback, Ann's fiancé, and Master of the local Hunt. The Earl proposes the toast of the engaged couple, and the gallant Captain replies in a song with the burden: "Ride straight, ride hard, and be a white man." Charles gives a graphic description of the morning's run and there follows a musical entertainment. After a long and rather boring 'cello solo, Hugh Heather enters, unrecognised. Gazing at Ann he sings:

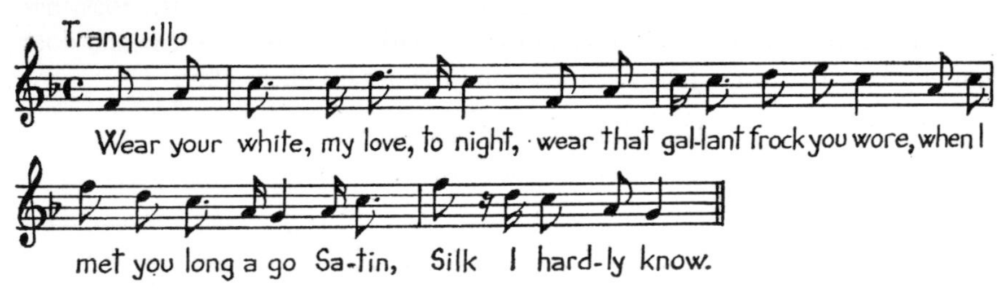

Jenny spots Hugh and, after his song, slips out and catches him. He confesses that he is in love with Ann and that is why he took the engagement. Jenny tells Hugh that Ann is betrothed to Captain Bareback. She does not really love him, but they are united by their mutual passion for fox-hunting. If Hugh would win her love he must take to fox-hunting. As Ann appears, Hugh conceals himself. The guests have gone to powder their noses preparatory to the Hunt Ball and the great hall is empty. Ann, alone, puts a record on the gramophone. It is one of Hugh Heather's popular ballads. She listens, and after a few bars Hugh starts to sing softly with the record. Ann stops the gramophone, Hugh's song continues and she turns and sees him. At the end of the song he kneels and kisses her hand just as Captain Bareback enters and glowers at them jealously. Ann introduces the two men and an argument follows on the subject of blood sports in which, to the Captain's fury, Ann takes Hugh's side. The Captain then appeals to the Earl in these words:

> "Lord Tantivy, I must insist
> on horse-whipping this vocalist."

But the Countess vetoes this proposal and makes the two men shake hands. Ann now enters dressed for the Hunt Ball, wearing the white dress she wore for

Hugh's Chelsea party. It is entirely unsuitable for a Hunt Ball and Captain Bareback tells her so, only to be tartly told to "shut up" by Ann. She asks Hugh to sing, and when he asks: "What shall I sing?" Captain Bareback replies: "John Peel." Hugh duly obliges, and the Captain is so delighted at Hugh's performance that he invites him to go hunting with his hounds on the morrow, promising to lend him a mount. Hugh, however, refuses. There are horrified murmurs of "The Yellow Streak", and Ann, surprised, asks tenderly: "You will come out with me?" "No, no—not even with you," says Hugh and launches into an attack on the cruelty of hunting the fox. The guests listen to him for a little, then they begin to laugh and to sing "John Peel". Finally their voices drown out Hugh, who, seeing himself in a minority of one, retires. The guests break into a gallop as the curtain falls.

ACT III

Act Three takes place in a glade at the edge of Tantivy wood. Hounds are meeting, but the Master, Captain Bareback is dejected, for he has been jilted by Ann. After the Hunt has moved off, Hugh appears, alone and dispirited, and presently down the glade comes a shooting party consisting of the Earl and Countess, Charles and Jenny. Ann joins them, and her father reproaches her with her treatment of Captain Bareback. He asks her:

"Pray child, what is exactly the position?
You don't propose to marry a musician?"

But in spite of the Earl's remonstrances, Ann goes off with Hugh. Charles has been giving Jenny a shooting lesson; but though they have been getting along famously and have decided to get engaged, Jenny's ignorance of country ways is beginning to exasperate Charles. Lunch, consisting of *paté-de-foie gras*, caviare and champagne, restores everyone's spirits, even Hugh's. Suddenly a horn is heard and all leap to their feet. The Hunt is approaching and the fox runs along the fields at the edge of the wood. Ann, the thrill of the chase in her blood, cries: "Hooray, the Hunt! brave Percy." But Hugh is horrified and is only concerned to put the fox out of its misery. He snatches a gun from a clergyman who is standing near, and as the fox passes he shoots it. "Brute!" cries Ann and slaps his face. Captain Bareback, livid with rage, enters carrying the dead fox and strides up to Hugh:

"You, Sir, first you take my wife
Then you take a fox's life,
Now take that——"

and he sets about Hugh with a hunting-crop. Jenny, her loyalty to Hugh aroused, runs to his defence. The two outcasts go slowly off together, while Ann and Captain Bareback, reunited, sing:

"And side by side
Away we'll ride
With Cupid at the saddle-bow."

Derby Day

A Comic Opera in Three Acts

Words by A. P. HERBERT

Music by ALFRED REYNOLDS

First produced on 24th February, 1932, at the Lyric Theatre, Hammersmith, with Leslie French as "Bert", Tessa Deane as "Rose", Scott Russell as "John Bitter" and Frederic Austin as "Sir Horace Waters".

CHARACTERS

SIR HORACE WATERS, J.P.
LADY WATERS
EDDY, *their son*
JOHN BITTER, *a publican*
ROSE, *a barmaid*
MRS. BONES
BERT BONES, *her son, a racing tipster*
CHORUS OF COSTERS, JOCKEYS, RACE-GOERS, ETC.

ACT I

Act One takes place in the garden of "The Old Black Horse" on the day before the Derby. Already a party of costers has arrived, dressed in "pearlies". They are singing the praises of Rose, the barmaid, who is "sweet" on Mr. Eddy, son of Sir Horace and Lady Waters. Mr. Bitter, the landlord, is listening to the troubles of Mrs. Bones when her son, Bert Bones, enters. Bert is a rough diamond with a heart of gold and, by profession, a racing tipster. He immediately gets to work.

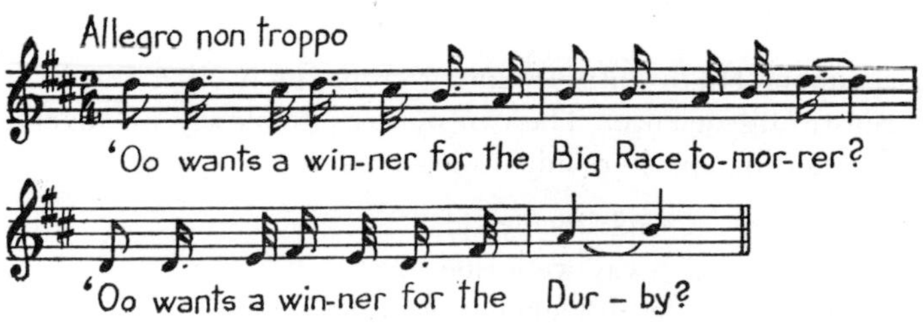

Mr. Bitter puts a stop to this. Apart from the fact that it might lose him his licence, he disapproves of betting as "trying to get something for nothing". He is over-ruled, however, and carried indoors by a friendly but ironical crowd of Cockneys. Rose, left to clear up the tables, wistfully dreams of being a lady and, when she is approached by Bert, who adores her, she holds back and hints that she would like to "better" herself. Bert, suffering from a Cockney's inability to treat love tenderly, does his best:

Rose nearly relents, but at that moment Eddy Waters appears, and immediately she has eyes for no one but him. Unlike Bert, Eddy pays her fluent and insincere compliments which completely take her in, and then, to Bert's dismay she allows herself to be embraced by Eddy, who is simply carrying on a clandestine flirtation. But Eddy is horrified when Rose broaches the question of their marriage. He hastily points out to her that he is still at the University and has not a penny to his name, and that although his father, Sir Horace, is the owner of race-horses he forbids Eddy the stables and keeps him too short of money to enable him to bet. Rose thinks that if only they had enough money to back Sir Horace's horse, Pericles, tipped by Bert Bones as the winner, Eddy could take her away from all this. Eddy tries to dampen these romantic flights of fancy, but he has to conceal himself when his father's jockey, Nick Noddle, appears. Rose is kind to all the little jockeys, and in return they give her the "inside" opinion that Pericles will win the Derby. When the jockeys have gone, Rose goes indoors for a moment and then rushes out and presses a hundred pounds in notes into Eddy's hand, telling him to put it on Pericles and they will go halves with the winnings.

While Eddy is hesitating, Sir Horace and Lady Waters bear down upon "The Old Black Horse". At Lady Waters' instigation, Sir Horace has come to break the news to Mr. Bitter that his licence will not be renewed at the next sessions. Sir Horace is very reluctant to do this, as he really finds no harm in the inn—until he sees his jockey Nick Noddle dance out gaily into the garden. Sir Horace is then transfixed with horror. The fact that he has discovered Eddy, his son, at the inn matters not at all, but that his jockey should be corrupted on the eve of the Derby is too much—the licence will certainly not be renewed. When they have gone Mr. Bitter is in despair, for he has always run his house well and honestly. Then Bert has the brilliant idea of "nobbling" Sir Horace's horse to get their own back, and the idea is taken up at once by the patrons. As the toast is drunk to "The Old Black Horse" it is Rose's turn to despair as she thinks of the hundred pounds she has handed to Eddy to put on the fated Pericles.

ACT II

SCENE I. Act Two opens on a traffic jam on the road to Epsom on the morning of Derby Day. In the foreground are Sir Horace and Lady Waters with Eddy in a Rolls-Royce; just behind them is a battered taxi in which are Mr. Bitter, Mrs. Bones and Bert. Rose, having taken the day off without permission, is with a party of "pearlies" who have stopped at the side of the road for a beer. She sees Eddy and tries to tell him not to back Pericles, but Eddy, lest his parents see him talking to her, pretends not to know her. As she retreats from the Rolls-Royce she is seen and recognised by Mrs. Bones and Bitter, who sacks her on the spot. Rose, now overwrought and rather hysterical, tells Mr. Bitter that she is finished with drawing beer, that she's got a packet on the winner:

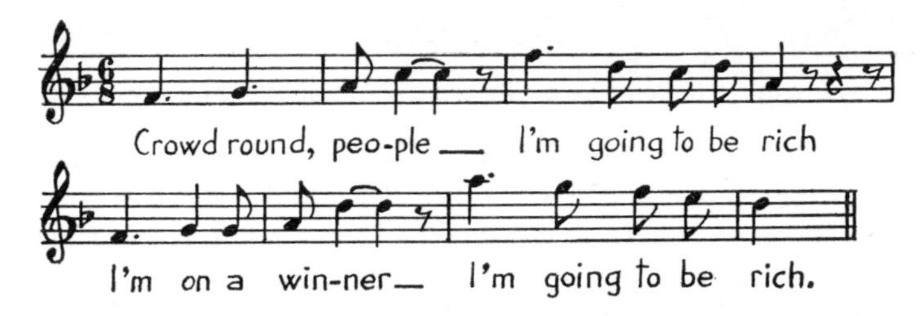

SCENE 2. Scene Two is the paddock outside the stalls in which the horses wait. Pericles—his head wrapped in a hood—peers out of his stall while the fashionable crowd walk up and down, eyeing the favourite. It is evident that this highly strung animal resents even the smallest criticism. Sir Horace pleads eloquently with the horse to concentrate and win the race, and Pericles is touched and inspired by his owner's solemn appeal. As soon as the Waters have left, Mr. Bitter and Bert Bones stealthily approach the horse-box and quietly sing a depressing dirge in which they insult the noble animal and succeed in thoroughly upsetting him. They stand back to view their handiwork when Rose comes warily up to the horse and wistfully sings:

Rose's charm restores the horse's well-being and he becomes a noble animal once more. Bitter and Bert cannot leave matters like this, so they start their minor dirge again, and then Sir Horace returns to resume his appeal. All this is too much for the highly strung thoroughbred, and as the curtain falls—the favourite faints!

SCENE 3. Scene Three is on the rails. In the crowd can be seen the Waters family lunching on top of an aristocratic coach. The bookmakers, Bert among them, are roaring out the odds. Gipsies are begging and the "pearlies" are clustered at the rails. Rose is terribly distressed to find Bert now tipping Love-Lies-Bleeding as the winner—as indeed he proves to be. After the race a very disappointed Sir Horace crosses to his car, followed by Eddy, who, when Rose tentatively puts out her hand to him, roughly brushes her aside. Bert sees all this, and quietly tells Rose that it is all right, as he has won a packet. But Rose in her distress will have nothing to do with him, and she sits moaning to herself: "A hundred pounds! Oh, what shall I do?"

ACT III

Back again in the garden of "The Old Black Horse", on the evening of the day after the Derby, the "regulars" are coming in from their day's work. Mr. Bitter finds time to unburden his heart to Mrs. Bones and asks her to become Mrs. Bitter. Through Mrs. Bones' benign intervention, Rose is now accepted back into Mr. Bitter's employment in time to hear Eddy warn them that his parents intend to make a surprise visit to "The Old Black Horse" this evening, accompanied by the entire bench of Justices, in spite of the fact that half of them will have to come in bath-chairs. Mr. Bitter panics, but Bert takes the whole matter in hand, arranging the men at Halma and chess-tables, and giving all the girls needlework or poetry books. There is a strong protest at this arrangement from Mrs. Bones: "What, read a book at my age?" Mr. Bitter's nerves get the better of him, so Bert gives him his wallet containing his yesterday's winnings and sends him indoors to put it in the safe. The Justices then arrive and are agreeably impressed with the decorum displayed. Unfortunately the charming scene is disrupted by Mr. Bitter bursting out of the house in a fury, accusing Rose of stealing a hundred pounds from his safe. From the look on Eddy's face Bert realises what happened and steps forward to take the blame, but Rose tells them the whole truth, and the tide of opinion turns against Sir Horace and Lady Waters when it is proved that horses drove the poor girl to steal, whereas honest Britons are bred on beer. Of course, the pub is saved, and Sir Horace and the Justices are provided with tankards of beer. Bert gets a moment to tell Rose that he loves her, but he runs out of words again and helplessly asks her: "What's a bloke to say?" Sweetly Rose tells him that this is what he should say:

The Pride of the Regiment
or
Cashiered for His Country

Comic Opera

Book by V. C. Clinton-Baddeley *and* Scobie Mackenzie

Lyrics by V. C. Clinton-Baddeley

Music by Walter Leigh

First produced on 19th September, 1931, at Midhurst and subsequently at the Festival Theatre, Cambridge, on 13th June, 1932. First London production on 6th July, 1932, at the St. Martin's Theatre, with Kathleen Hilliard, Trefor Jones and Gavin Gordon

Characters

GENERAL SIR JOSHUA BLAZES
MILLICENT, *his daughter*
MISS AGATHA } *two elderly spinsters*
MISS ADELAIDE }
THE PRIME MINISTER
CAPTAIN DE VAVASOUR
LIEUTENANT LAUNCELOT BROWN
CHORUS OF LADIES, VILLAGERS, SOLDIERS, ETC.

ACT I

The scene is the drawing-room of General Sir Joshua Blazes' house in Berkeley Square in the autumn of 1854. A Dorcas party is in progress and the assembled ladies include Millicent, the General's daughter, and two elderly spinsters, Miss Agatha and Miss Adelaide. All are busy sewing and knitting cummerbunds, Balaclava helmets and shakos for the gallant soldiers fighting in the Crimea. As they knit they sing:

Conversation is all of the war. Miss Adelaide regales them with the latest titbits of news from the Prime Minister: how he reckons that Sebastopol cannot possibly withstand the assaults of the British for many days, and how the Russians are very cowardly and would have achieved no success at all but for the inclemency of the weather and their very unfair system of spying upon the plans of gallant British Generals. As they are talking there is the sound of cheering and up to the front door drives a barouche. The General and the Prime Minister have arrived for a secret conference and with them are Captain de Vavasour and Lieutenant Brown. The ladies are squired into the garden by the Captain, and the General introduces Launcelot Brown to the Prime Minister. The General is his guardian and has picked the Lieutenant to stop an outbreak of spying and dog the footsteps of the Russian master spy, "Shotoff, the Unknown Terror". Lieutenant Brown then retires and the Prime Minister hands over to the General some secret papers, copies of orders sent to Headquarters, which the General proposes to lock in a drawer in his desk. The Prime Minister, however, tells him: "You soldiers have no finesse, no *savoir-faire*. The first place a spy looks is in your drawer." The Prime Minister himself then conceals the papers in an aspidistra, commenting: "Now I ask you—would you think of looking for them in there?" But the whole episode has been watched by the villainous Captain de Vavasour, and when the General and the Prime Minister have departed he is about to steal the papers when he is interrupted by the entrance of the General's daughter. Millicent is looking very attractive and the venal Vavasour is soon making violent love to her. Though she screams for help, he clasps her in his arms. "Ha! ha! My pretty charmer. Gad! I like a bit of spirit in a woman." Launcelot Brown, Millicent's true love, hears her screams and comes to her rescue, and there is a fight in which Lieutenant Brown gets the worst of it. At Millicent's pleading the Captain drops the fight, declaring: "For your sake, dear lady, I will forgive. Not so easily shall I forget. Good-bye." Alone together Launcelot Brown tells his beloved Millicent that he is leaving for the front. He asks her to wait for him and they sing a duet:

During the duet Captain de Vavasour creeps into the room and removes the secret papers from their hiding-place and sneaks out. When Millicent has departed, Lieutenant Brown busies himself about the room looking for spies, but he is interrupted by the return of the General and the Prime Minister and hides behind a screen. They have returned to check up some references in the secret papers. To the General's dismay he finds they have disappeared. What is more, Lieutenant Brown is discovered hiding behind the screen and is asked to explain his presence. Unwilling to divulge that he was with Millicent he gives a very lame explanation. The General, convinced that he has stolen the secret papers, orders him to produce them, and at that moment the vile de Vavasour enters and, handing the General the papers, claims that he found them hidden under the Lieutenant's bed. On his word, Lieutenant Brown is dismissed the Regiment and the house, and the curtain falls on his disgrace.

ACT II

One afternoon in the early summer of 1856 a company of ladies in gala dress, including Millicent, Miss Adelaide and Miss Agatha, are collected in the garden of the General's country house. The war is over and the troops are expected home from the Crimea. As the General and the Prime Minister come out into the garden, Miss Adelaide and Miss Agatha send the younger ladies into the house. The elderly gentlemen stroll down the yew walk, talking. The General declares that he is giving Millicent to Captain de Vavasour and says how lonely he will be without her. "You should marry," says the Prime Minister. "I am thinking of marrying myself." An unfortunate contretemps follows. "How beautiful the garden is!" remarks the General. "Yes, but what a curious smell!" replies the Prime Minister. "Is it yew?" "Is it me?" protests the General. "Really, Prime Minister, this is a very serious charge." "Excuse me, I said it was yew—YEW". "Oh! *Yew!* Then why didn't you say so before?" finishes the General. At the end of the walk they meet the Misses Adelaide and Agatha, who lure them into two arbours for a conversation tête-à-tête. They discuss the beauties of the garden. "Such a lovely scent!" comment the ladies. "Yes, I am very fond of yew," answer the old gentlemen. Quick as a flash Miss Adelaide and Miss Agatha exclaim: "This is so sudden"—and the General and the Prime Minister are trapped by the scheming old ladies. When the elderly couples have gone, Captain de Vavasour emerges from the hedge. In a soliloquy straight out of melodrama he boasts of his triumphs as "Shotoff, the Unknown Terror", determines to break Millicent's proud spirit and confesses that by "secretly mentioning my name in false dispatches I have gained honour and glory and, I hope, a number of medals. The Queen and everyone else, drat 'em all, honour my name." He then sings a splendid song: "The children's voices guileless sing their welcome to de Vavasour." With florid, Handelian coloratura it continues:

In the meantime, Millicent is in despair· her lover is disgraced, and she is promised to a man she does not love. Roaming alone in the garden she encounters a gipsy who has come through a gap in the hedge, and asks him to tell her fortune. Looking at the palm of her hand he tells her: "There is one that you love. You think him far away, but he is ever close to you. It may be that he will find you here once more before it is too late." The gipsy departs and a burst of cheering announces the arrival of the troops, who march on to a royal welcome from the crowds. The General and Prime Minister both welcome the gallant soldiers and make patriotic speeches. Captain de Vavasour, on the strength of his forged dispatches, is personally decorated. The General formally announces de Vavasour's engagement to Millicent; and Miss Adelaide, Miss Agatha, the General and the Prime Minister sing an ecstatic quartette:

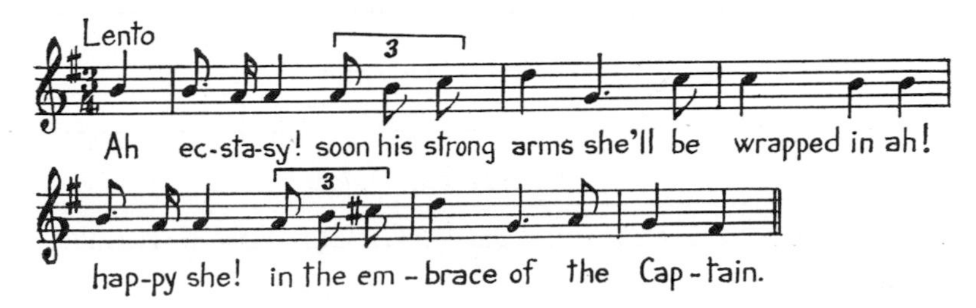

But these ecstasies suffer a dramatic interruption when the gipsy enters and forbids the banns. He explains to the amazed company that he is Lieutenant Brown and how, after his disgrace and dismissal, he went to Russia, determined to track down the "Terror". He recounts how he got on his trail and continues:

"When to land on England's shore
The Terror duly tried,
I dogged him here and dogged him there,
For ever at his side.
I dogged him to this very door
The Terror is de Vavasour."

Advancing on de Vavasour, Launcelot Brown tears open his cloak: it proves to be lined with secret papers of incalculable value, such as "The Smoke Abatement Bill" and "The Foot and Mouth" regulations. De Vavasour is condemned out of hand by the General and led away to be shot. Lieutenant Brown is then decorated with a profusion of medals and the General shakes his hand, telling him: "Lieutenant, you have been cashiered for your country and have now become the Pride of the Regiment. England is proud of you." At this moment two shots are heard. Saluting, the General proclaims: "So perish all traitors. And now on with the dance, let joy be unconfined."

Jolly Roger
or
The Admiral's Daughter

Comic Opera in Three Acts

Book by Scobie Mackenzie *and* V. C. Clinton-Baddeley

Lyrics by V. C. Clinton-Baddeley

Music by Walter Leigh

First produced on 1st March, 1933, at the Savoy Theatre, London, with George Robey, Percy Heming, Muriel Angelus, Victor Orsini and Gavin Gordon.

Characters

SIR RODERICK VENOM, *Governor of Jamaica*
ADMIRAL SIR WILLIAM ROWLOCKS
AMELIA, *his daughter*
MISS POTT, *her companion*
PRUDENCE, *Amelia's maid*
JOLLY ROGER, *a planter*
BEN BLISTER, *his faithful companion*
CHORUS OF LONGSHOREMEN, LADIES, PIRATES, ETC.

ACT I

The action of the opera takes place in and about the town of Kingston, Jamaica, in the year 1690. The scene of Act One is the private landing stage of Government House one Saturday afternoon. Longshoremen are lounging about the quay taking their siesta, and by a small booth sit the orange-women. As the curtain rises they are singing a sea-shanty. A young longshoreman reports that the Governor, Sir Roderick Venom, has captured the "Bloody Pirate". This news is received with unbelief and derision, for the Governor is hated and despised as a cruel tyrant and is believed to be in league with the pirates himself. A hope is expressed that Admiral Sir William Rowlocks, who arrived from England a week ago with his daughter and her companion, has been sent out to put a stop to his tyranny; and the crowd cheer half-heartedly as a boat puts alongside and from it lands the Governor, followed by a young man, Jolly Roger, guarded by two sailors. Jolly Roger is a planter, an honest man, whose father was murdered in a recent rebellion. The Governor has falsely accused Roger of piracy and has had him arrested to quell rumours that he himself is in league with the pirates. Roger is about to be removed to imprisonment in the Coalhole when his departure is stopped by a company of excited girls, who demand to see the "Bloody Pirate". The Governor is offering to have Roger publicly flogged "till the blood spurts out of him", when Admiral Sir William Rowlocks, his daughter Amelia, and her companion Miss Pott, arrive on the scene. The Admiral rebukes the Governor and stops the punishment. Amelia is greatly attracted to Jolly Roger and is convinced that one so fair and young must be innocent, and determines to aid him.

After Roger has been removed to the Coalhole, the Governor has an assignation with the authentic "Bloody Pirate", and confides his suspicions that the Admiral has come to Jamaica armed with a commission from the new Government to overset him. The Governor's intention is to liquidate the Admiral and marry his daughter. He then discloses his plan. He will give a party in the Admiral's honour. All the beauties of the town will be there and he will suggest that the Admiral invite the ladies to visit the King's ship that lies in the bay. "When the Fair Cargo arrives on the quay they will embark in your boats," he tells the pirates. "Then off to the pirate ship and we've got 'em. Admiral thrown to the sharks and a lady for every man down to your Bos'un. Then on with murder, rapine, arson and barratry!" And with a pirate chorus, the Governor launches into a lusty song with the refrain:

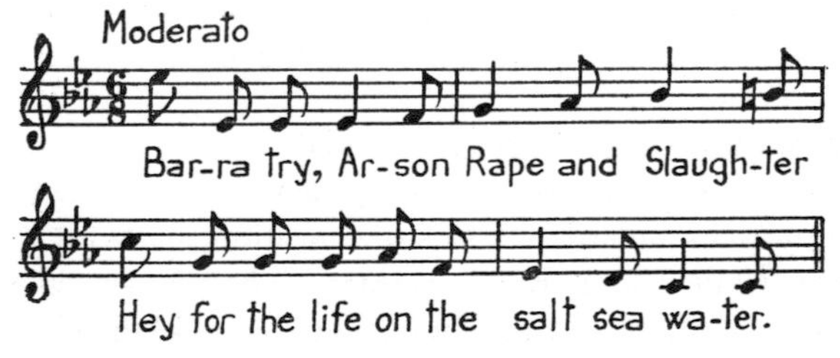

When the Governor and the pirates have departed, a seafaring man, Ben Blister, late of the Royal Navy, peers over the wall. He is Jolly Roger's faithful companion and is searching for him. He gets into conversation with Amelia, the Admiral's daughter, and her maid, Prudence. Prudence has discovered that Roger is buried in a heap of coal with only his head sticking out. Ben Blister, who vouches for Roger's honesty, promises to rescue him. He succeeds with the help of a coal shovel, and Roger is almost surprised, while escaping, by the Governor. But he gets away and encounters Amelia. He is delighted to learn that she now believes in his integrity, and they join in a love duet:

The Governor's plan works perfectly, and the hospitable Admiral jovially invites the ladies on a boating excursion to see his ship. "I have promised some of these girls a private view of my poop," he tells Miss Pott. The ladies and the Admiral then enter the boats and put off. At that moment Roger, concealed behind a barrel, overhears the Governor's instructions to one of the pirates: "Fling Admiral to the sharks tomorrow and then sing ho for Lust and Lechery." Roger leaps on to the wall, where he is attacked by the longshoremen, who believe him to be the "Bloody Pirate"; but with Ben Blister's help he knocks them all down, and both dive into the sea as the curtain falls.

ACT II

Act Two takes place aboard the pirate ship. It is Sunday morning, and, when the curtain rises, the ladies with Amelia and Prudence are discovered lined up in ranks, where, conducted by Miss Pott, they are singing a hymn. As they are singing the pirates come on deck. Amorously inflamed by the sight of so much female beauty, the pirates advance gloatingly on the girls. ("I were ever one for the joys of the flesh," declares pirate Tom.) The ladies shrink back in delighted dismay as the pirates sing:

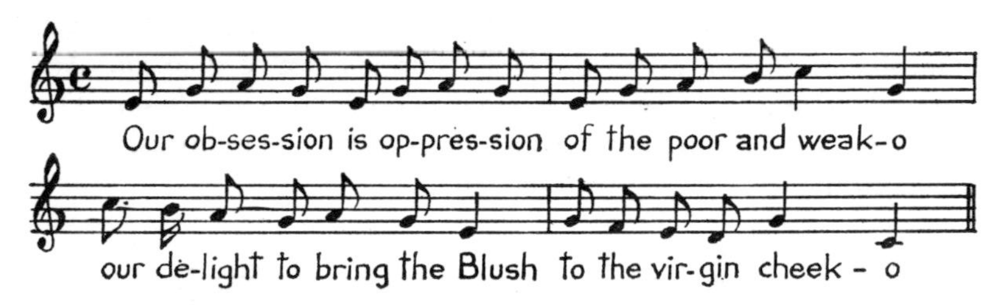

The pirates are about to grab a girl apiece and drag them down below when the Admiral intervenes. He addresses them eloquently on the way to treat a lady, deploring their moral standards and lack of education, and with the assistance of Miss Pott he distributes some religious tracts. The pirates are greatly moved by the Admiral's strictures on their moral conduct and begin to feel the prickings of their nonconformist consciences. The Governor, however, is dismayed at this wave of moral rectitude, realising that if he is not careful these lily-livered pirates will jeopardise his plan to murder the Admiral and marry his daughter. The surest way to restore shaken morale is a double ration of rum, so the order is given to "Grog the men" and the pirates strike up a shanty. During the singing the watch reports a sail to starboard. A boat comes alongside and two ferocious-looking pirates climb aboard. They are Dago Dick and Portuguese Pete, two terrors of the Spanish Main. They are cordially welcomed by everyone except the Governor, who seems to doubt their authenticity—a doubt which is completely justified, for the two newcomers prove to be none other than Jolly Roger and Ben Blister in disguise, bent on rescuing the captives. With difficulty they make contact with Amelia and Prudence, who are delighted to see them. Roger and Amelia's reunion is a tender one, but unfortunately they are taken unawares by the Governor. He gives the alarm and Roger and Ben are arrested, as well as the Admiral and Miss Pott. Two planks are thrust out over the side of the ship, and the first to walk the plank are the Admiral and Miss Pott, who vanish overboard with a mighty splash. They are to be quickly followed by Roger and Ben when Amelia flings herself on her knees before the Governor and begs him to spare their lives. The cunning Governor bargains with her. He agrees to spare their lives if Amelia will promise to marry him; and Amelia promises. The ladies are then driven below, and when they are out of sight the Governor orders:

"Quick, pitch 'em in the sea,
All undeterred
By promised word,
Sing ho! for treachery!"

And for the second time the curtain falls on Roger and Ben in the sea.

ACT III

Two nights later the Governor is giving a ball to celebrate his coming marriage to Amelia. The scene is the terrace of Government House. Amelia is in despair, bereft with one blow of her father and her lover. But help is at hand. Roger and Ben bear charmed lives and, cast up from the sea like Jonah from the belly of the whale, they appear on the terrace during the ball and manage to find Amelia and Prudence. Ben describes how, when they were slung into the sea, the pirates were "so busy a-singing and a-roaring" that they forgot all about the jolly-boat moored alongside. So they were able to board her and get away. Making for land, they espied a splashing in the water, "as might be a couple of porpoises", and were lucky enough to pick up the Admiral and Miss Pott. Once again Roger and Ben are apprehended by the startled Governor and this time he proposes to put out their eyes with a red-hot poker. But the Admiral rushes in waving a Royal Decree from Their Gracious Majesties, William and Mary. Sir Roderick Venom is deprived of his office and Roger is appointed Governor of Jamaica in his stead. The Admiral instructs him to sentence the criminals, but this duty Roger delegates to the less squeamish Ben, who condemns them to be "beaten with bludgeons, sawn in half, boiled in oil and after that flung from the end of the jetty with round shot tied to their feet, so that they die horribly by drowning". The ex-Governor and the pirates are dragged off to execution, and Ben issues his final decree: "That Miss Amelia here, Sir William Rowlocks' daughter, be joined in holy matrimony to Mr. Roger upon that selfsame day as shall her father wed Miss Flora Pott and Prudence honest me."

Glamorous Night

A Romantic Play with Music in Three Acts

By IVOR NOVELLO

Lyrics by CHRISTOPHER HASSALL

First produced on 2nd May, 1935, at the Theatre Royal, Drury Lane, London, with Ivor Novello as "Anthony Allen", Mary Ellis as "Militza Hajos" and Lyn Harding as "Lydeff".

CHARACTERS

H.M. KING STEFAN VIII OF KRASNIA
MILITZA HAJOS, *a Prima Donna*
LORENTI, *a tenor*
LYDEFF, *Prime Minister*
ANTHONY ALLEN, *a young Englishman*
MISS CLEO WELLINGTON, *a coloured stowaway*
CHORUS OF SOLDIERS, MEMBERS OF THE *GLAMOROUS NIGHT* COMPANY, GIPSIES, ETC.

ACT I

SCENE I. The first scene is the exterior of the Militza palace in the capital city of the little kingdom of Krasnia, ruled over by his Majesty King Stefan VIII. When the curtain rises a party of tourists on a pleasure cruise are watching the famous Militza Guards parade. This fine body of men, the guide explains, were named by the King as a tribute to the talent and beauty of the Prima Donna of the Krasnian State Opera House, Madame Militza.

SCENE 2. In the palace Madame Militza is rehearsing with the tenor Lorenti for a new operetta, *Glamorous Night*. The title number would make an attractive solo for any prima donna:

During the rehearsal the King pays Militza a visit, and after the tenor's departure we learn from their conversation that the political situation in Krasnia is both dangerous and explosive. The Prime Minister, Lydeff, is believed to be plotting a revolution to overthrow the monarchy and bring about a dictatorship with himself at the helm. Lydeff loathes Militza and there is open war between them, for Lydeff realises that Militza, as the King's mistress, is the power behind the throne. If she could be got rid of, the weak King could be easily forced to abdicate. Without her influence he would be as putty in the hands of the Prime Minister.

SCENE 3. In the Opera House some days later an expectant audience is attending the première of the new operetta *Glamorous Night*, starring Militza Hajos and the tenor Lorenti. He scores a great success with his big number:

and another hit is their duet:

Just as Militza and Lorenti are singing the last line of the operetta, a man in Krasnian national dress appears running down the aisle of the auditorium. He has a revolver in his hand and is about to shoot at Militza when a young man who is sitting in the stalls realises what is about to happen. He grapples with the man and tries to wrest the gun from him. He is too late to stop him firing, but manages to knock up his arm so that the shot is harmless. Attendants appear from all sides and hustle the two men out of the theatre, while Militza, with great presence of mind, calms the excited buzz of chatter in a little speech with a humorous reference to the "poor man who didn't like my singing". The finale is resumed and the curtain falls to deafening applause.

ACT II

SCENE 1. Next morning Militza desires to see the man who so courageously saved her life, and he is brought to her palace. He turns out to be a young Englishman, Anthony Allen by name, and by profession an inventor in need of capital to finance his invention of a new system of television. When Militza thanks him prettily and as a tangible proof of her gratitude offers him a photograph, he replies: "I'd rather have a cheque." It appears that he had applied to the television company for five thousand pounds to develop his invention but they would only give him five hundred. Wanting desperately to see the world, he has used the five hundred pounds to pay for the luxury suite on board s.s. *Silver Star*, which is making a pleasure cruise. Militza, intrigued and amused by this unconventional young man, assures him that she rates her life at quite a high price and writes him out a cheque for one thousand pounds. Anthony goes happily away, and Militza's next visitor is Lydeff. The Prime Minister has come to present Militza with her passport, "on instructions from the King" he tells her. It is endorsed for every country except re-entry into Krasnia. Militza must leave the country at once. Even as they are talking an angry mob yelling a revolutionary song is heard approaching the palace. Defiantly Militza steps out on to the balcony and replies with the Krasnian national anthem to the accompaniment of hooting and cat-calls. Only when Lydeff assures the crowd that Madame Militza is amenable to reason and will soon have taken her departure do they disperse to their homes. Militza teasingly informs Lydeff that she is taking a short cruise on the s.s. *Silver Star*, as sea air is always beneficial to her voice, and that she expects to see him in his usual box on Thursday week at the next performance of *Glamorous Night*.

SCENE 2. When Militza and her maid arrive on board the s.s. *Silver Star* she arrogantly demands the luxury suite as her right. The purser goes off to arrange matters, but returns, embarrassed, to tell her that the suite has been engaged by a young Englishman who point blank refuses to vacate it. "Oh, an Englishman!" says Militza. "I'll settle this." So Militza and Anthony meet once more. She confesses that she has been turned out of the capital and confides her hope of reaching her home province, Borovidnik, to raise an armed force and march against Lydeff. Their conversation on deck in the moonlight takes place to the liner's orchestra playing a Krasnian gipsy melody.

That evening there is a ship's concert, and a stowaway who has been detected on board, a coloured girl called Miss Cleo Wellington, sings this attractive number, with which Elizabeth Welch always brought down the house:

After the concert, at which Militza sings a song from *Glamorous Night*, Anthony tells her that he has decided that she must leave the ship that night. One or two things he has noticed—continuous light signals from shore and a suspicious foreign gentleman who spends much of his time in the engine-room —have convinced him that another attempt on Militza's life is contemplated. He arranges with the Captain for the use of his launch to land Militza and himself, and they are both about to embark when there is a deafening explosion. Sirens blow, the ship heels over, excited orders are given to put on lifebelts and not panic, and as the lights fade and the curtain falls the ship slowly starts to sink.

ACT III

Scenes 1 and 2. On a mountain-side Militza and Anthony present a dishevelled spectacle. When Lydeff's agent blew up the s.s. *Silver Star*, the ship did not sink but came to rest on a convenient mud-bank, and they managed to escape. Militza, however, has sprained her ankle and is irritable and tearful. Anthony soothes and encourages her with assurances that they must by now be in Borovidnik. They have fallen desperately in love, and Anthony is only restrained from declaring himself by the recollection that Militza is the King's mistress. But when Militza asssures him that she and the King have not been lovers for five years, Anthony takes her in his arms. Soon after this they reach a gipsy encampment, and here they are married according to gipsy laws—by exchanging their life-blood.

Scene 3. Back in the palace at Krasnia, Lydeff has got the whip-hand over the King, who, deprived of the strength and support of Militza's character and personality, is not strong enough to stand up to the Prime Minister. One morning Lydeff produces an instrument of abdication and is about to force the King, at the point of a revolver, to sign it. Lydeff gives His Majesty until he has counted ten to sign and is just about to fire when a shot rings out and Lydeff falls dead. Once again Anthony has come to the rescue of the Royal House of Krasnia. Militza, who succeeded in raising an army of loyal Borovidniks, has marched on Krasnia and defeated Lydeff's revolutionaries. But Stefan's difficulties have given Militza indisputable proof that he needs her presence and her support, and when he urges her to share with him the throne of Krasnia she accepts, sacrificing her love for her country. The King in gratitude to Anthony promises him all the financial aid he needs, on condition that Militza's shall be the first picture to be transmitted on Anthony's new television system. So the lovers are separated, and Anthony watches Militza walk out of the throne-room and out of his life for ever.

The Dancing Years

A Musical Play

By Ivor Novello

Lyrics by Christopher Hassall

First produced on 23rd March, 1939, at the Theatre Royal, Drury Lane, with Ivor Novello, Mary Ellis, Olive Gilbert, Roma Beaumont.

Characters

GRETE SCHONE
RUDI KLEBER, *a composer*
MARIA ZEIGLER, *an operetta star*
PRINCE CHARLES METTERLING
CÄCILIE KURT, *a singing teacher*
HATTIE WATNEY
FRANZL, *an officer*
CHORUS OF OFFICERS, WAITERS, LADIES AND GENTLEMEN-ABOUT-TOWN

ACT I

It is the summer of 1911, and the scene is the garden of an inn outside Vienna. Tables are set under the trees and an unusual feature is a boudoir grand piano standing immediately in front of the inn. As the curtain rises it is not yet daylight. Two young people, Grete Schone, a girl of fifteen, and Rudi Kleber, a budding composer, arrive back from a nocturnal excursion to the mountains. Rudi Kleber is a lodger at the inn, and he learns with dismay from the waitress, Hattie, that the landlady is turning him out and threatening to sell his piano to meet his bill. An early morning party of officers escorting the operetta star, Maria Zeigler, arrive at the inn for breakfast. Rudi Kleber is persuaded to play the piano, and Maria Zeigler, who is rehearsing a new operetta, is enchanted with his compositions, and buys one of his waltz songs for a thousand kronen. Ecstatically she sings to his accompaniment:

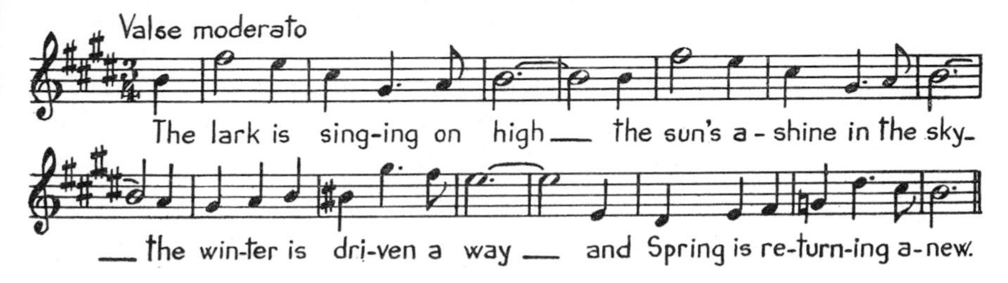

Maria Zeigler has an aristocratic admirer, Prince Charles Metterling. He is anxious to marry her and is deeply in love. But both his devotion and his patience are sorely tried when Maria, who has fallen for Rudi Kleber, tells Rudi that Prince Charles will be only too happy to accommodate him and his piano in a studio in his palace. Maria and Prince Charles depart, and Rudi, politely, goes to see them off. Grete, who has observed that Rudi is smitten by the famous operetta star, is, in spite of her fifteen years, dreadfully jealous. She believes that Rudi has gone off without even saying good-bye to her. But Rudi has not forgotten her and Grete throws herself emotionally into his arms. She tells him that she knows she is at present only a child and makes him promise that he will never ask Maria Zeigler or anyone else to marry him until she is grown up. "I may grow up awful," she tells him, "and if I do you can just say 'I can't, you're awful now, you used not to be'—but give me a chance." And Rudi promises.

Some months later Maria is having a singing lesson from her teacher, Cäcilie Kurt, an ex-operatic star. Frau Kurt taxes Maria with being in love, and Maria confesses openly that so strong is her love for Rudi that she would willingly give up the stage to marry him. When Rudi Kleber arrives they rehearse his duet "The Wings of Sleep", a number from the new operetta, *Lorelei*, which he has written for Maria. Frau Kurt takes the contralto part, and Rudi is so entranced with her singing that he persuades her to accept an engagement to sing it with Maria in the show:

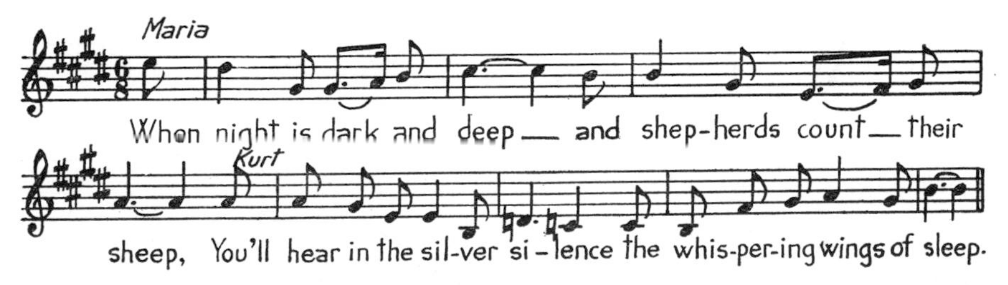

A fortnight later the première of *Lorelei* takes place. The first act has gone excellently, and a large audience, which includes Prince Charles Metterling, is enthusiastic. In the first act interval there is some gossip among the smart set of Maria Zeigler's reputed attachment to the handsome composer, Rudi Kleber, and some of the ladies tease Prince Charles, who assures them that Maria is supping with him after the show. But as the warning bell for Act Two rings an attendant delivers a message from Maria asking Charles to excuse her. "She says she's very tired and she's sure you'll understand," the message ends, and poor Charles is sad at heart.

After the show Maria and Rudi sup tête-à-tête in her apartment. *Lorelei* has been a big success and the two of them are on the crest of the wave and are already deeply in love. Emotionally Maria sings to him:

But Rudi Kleber, to make quite sure, questions Maria about her feeling for Prince Charles, and Maria assures him that their love affair finished before ever she and Rudi met. She tells him to relax and brings him a dressing-gown to put on while he removes his collar and tie. But presently the door opens and Charles comes in. In his whole bearing and conversation he acts the part of Maria's accepted lover. He taunts Rudi with wearing his dressing-gown and offers to lend him a collar and tie, telling him that there are plenty of his in Maria's apartment. Sadly disillusioned Rudi leaves them, while Maria calls after him. "He won't come back," Charles tells her. But Charles is wrong. Rudi does come back and the curtain falls on the lovers in each other's arms.

ACT II

The first scene is a chalet in the Tyrol, and the time is the spring of 1914. Here Maria and Rudi are living in bliss, though, as old Hattie Watney, Maria's English maid, hints to Rudi, Maria's cup would be full if only he would ask her to marry him. Rudi then tells Hattie of the vow he made to Grete to stop her child's heart from breaking. Grete has been studying dancing in England, where she has made a name for herself, and is due home today. Rudi is busy arranging a gala performance for charity and he has written a new number for Maria, who is to sing it:

Rudi has just played the song to Maria and she has her arms around him, when Grete Schone, newly back from England, comes into the room. Rudi greets the now grown-up and sophisticated-looking young woman very affectionately and Maria is distinctly jealous. There is actually no ground for her jealousy, as a handsome young officer, Franzl, has taken Grete under his wing and monopolises her completely. But Maria's jealousy persists and is the cause of a quarrel between herself and Rudi. As a result of it, she writes a note to Prince Charles, who is across the lake at Waldsee, asking him to come and see her. When he arrives she confides to him that as a result of her association with Rudi she is going to have a child. Charles tells her that of course Rudi must now marry her and gently conveys to her that should anything go wrong, his offer of marriage still holds good in spite of everything. Deeply touched by his devotion she goes to see him off and on her return finds Rudi the centre of an admiring crowd, which includes Grete. She tells him that she must speak to him alone: it is important. "Well, give me five minutes then, and when you hear me play this (he plays a few bars of "My Dearest Dear") you'll know I'm free and you'll come down." After this Rudi and Grete are left alone. He tells her of his love for and intention of marrying Maria and playfully she reminds him of his vow to propose to her first. "You needn't have any fear about my answer," she assures him and then asks teasingly: "What would you say if you did care?" As they are talking Maria comes out of her room and from the top of the stairs listens to their conversation. She is just in time to hear Rudi make his mock proposal of marriage to Grete and with a look of suffering hurriedly returns to her room. Rudi and Grete say good night, and when Grete has gone he plays the opening phrase of "My Dearest Dear" on the piano. But Maria does not appear. He dashes up the stairs and into her bedroom, to find it empty. Realising that she must have overheard his proposal to Grete and taken it seriously, he calls distractedly "Maria, Maria".

ACT III

On the following day the gala performance takes place at Belvedere and one of the items on the programme is Grete Schone and the *Corps de Ballet* of the Theater an der Wien in "The Leap Year Waltz". Rudi is greatly exercised at Maria's absence. He is longing to see her and explain the misunderstanding of the previous evening. When they do meet and he tries to convince her that his proposal to Grete was only make-believe, she tells him that she married Prince Metterling that morning for security and faithfulness. Rudi is shattered.

Twelve years later in a restaurant in Vienna Rudi and Maria meet again. All the rancour of their parting is forgotten and they are both as much in love as ever. Maria confesses her unhappiness and Rudi begs her to leave Charles and come to him. But Maria refuses to commit herself and they decide to meet a week later and come to a decision. A week later they meet again where they met for the first time in the garden outside the inn. Maria has brought Rudi's son, Carl, with her—a fine, good-looking boy. Rudi still begs her to come to him, but Maria points out to him the disruption of their son's life that this would mean. He believes himself to be Charles' son and it would be kinder to let well alone. Rudi, sad but resigned, begs her to "talk to him of me sometimes, play some of my music, perhaps—then, if we ever meet, we shan't be quite strangers. I shan't even be unhappy, now that I know we've something we can share." And so the two of them part.

The last scene takes place in a room in a former royal palace in Vienna. The year is 1938. The *anschluss* has taken place and Vienna is under Nazi domination. Rudi Kleber has been arrested for bribing German officials to allow Austrian suspects to leave the country. As he is being interrogated by a Nazi officer Maria arrives and demands to see Rudi. As Princess Metterling she has sufficient influence to effect his release. Before they part he asks her: "Our son, Carl, does he think as they do?" and she assures him: "Oh, no, he thinks as we do." "Oh, thank God," he tells her, "now I shall never feel my life has been completely wasted." Tenderly she asks: "Wasted? How could it be wasted? You know what they'll say of you—they'll say—he made the whole world dance."

King's Rhapsody

A Musical Romance in Three Acts

Devised, written and composed by Ivor Novello

Lyrics by Christopher Hassall

First produced on the 15th September, 1949, at the Palace Theatre, London, with Vanessa Lee, Zena Dare, Phyllis Dare, Olive Gilbert and Ivor Novello.

Characters

PRINCESS CHRISTIANE
HULDA, KIRSTEN } *her sisters*
KING PETER OF NORSELAND, *her father*
QUEEN ELENA OF MURANIA, *the Queen Mother*
COUNTESS VERA LEMMKAINEN
COUNTESS OLGA VARSOV
VANESCU, *Prime Minister of Murania*
NIKKI
MARTA KARILLOS, *an actress*
COUNT EGON STANIEFF
JULES, *a valet*
CHORUS OF VILLAGERS, MURANIANS, MANNEQUINS, SERENADERS, GUESTS, OFFICERS, FLUNKEYS, SERVANTS, GIPSIES, TARTARS AND DANCERS

ACT I

Scene 1. The first scene is a sitting-room in the summer palace of the royal family of Norseland. It is Princess Christiane's eighteenth birthday, and when she comes in from a skiing expedition she receives birthday greetings from her father, King Peter, and her two small sisters, and some lovely presents. The loyal villagers greet her with song and dance and they too bear gifts. After they have gone, the little Princesses, Kirsten and Hulda, tease their sister about her nickname, "the Snow Princess". Has she a cold heart? "I don't know," says Christiane. "It may be cold—it may be just asleep." And she sings:

After the song King Peter sends the little girls away and, alone with Christiane, he tells her that he has arranged a marriage between her and the King of Murania. The old King has died, and Nikki, his son, who has been in exile for twenty years—some say on account of his excessively democratic ideas and others because of a scandalous love-affair—is to succeed him. Nervous of her reaction to his news, the King looks anxiously at his daughter. But Christiane assures him that his news is thrilling. Ever since her school-girl days she has cherished a passion for Nikki and has kept every picture and newspaper cutting about him that she could lay her hands on. The King could not have chosen a husband more to her taste.

SCENE 2. Into a private sitting-room in a small hotel in Paris, one morning some days earlier, walks Elena, the Queen Mother of Murania. She commands her son's valet, Jules, to "be good enough to announce our arrival to Monsieur . . . . What name does he go by here?" "Monsieur Dubois," he answers respectfully and hurries away. Nikki appears in a dressing-gown and kisses his mother affectionately. She brings news of his father's death and an urgent plea to him to return to Murania and succeed to the throne. She also tells him that she has the ideal Queen for him in Princess Christiane of Norseland. For an heir to the throne is essential. After much objection on his part and energetic persuasion on hers, he agrees both to mount his father's throne and marry his mother's choice. Queen Elena then asks after Marta Karillos, an actress and Nikki's mistress, and Nikki stresses the fact that no marriage of convenience that he may make will prejudice his association with her. Soon after this Madame Karillos pays a call on Nikki. The Queen Mother greets her amicably and then takes her departure. Nikki's news that he is to succeed to the throne is a shock to Marta. But Nikki swears to her that although he is compelled to take an official wife to act as Queen and bear him a son, no one will ever replace her in his heart.

SCENE 3. Outside the royal palace at Bledz, the capital city of Murania, a loyal crowd is lining the street. They welcome Princess Christiane, their future Queen, with fervent cheers and singing of the national anthem.

SCENE 4. In a boudoir in the palace, which has been prepared as Christiane's private sitting-room, Queen Elena with her Lady-in-Waiting, Countess Olga Varsov, is awaiting the arrival of her daughter-in-law to be. Christiane arrives with her companion, Countess Vera Lemmkainen. After greetings the Queen Mother apologises for Nikki's absence. He has been called away from the capital to quieten unrest in the Eastern province. Christiane's feminine intuition tells her that the Queen Mother is lying, and she is distressed that Nikki is not present to receive his bride on her arrival. For a moment she panics and cries to Countess Lemmkainen to take her home. Vera, to soothe her, sings Christiane a lullaby of her childhood.

SCENE 5. Late one evening a week later Christiane and Vera are seated conversing in the boudoir. Nikki has still not visited his future Queen, and Christiane asks Vera: "Why is he humiliating me thus?" Vera, unable to contain herself, answers: "Marta Karillos is here in Murania. He is with her now." "So that's the reason for it all. I'm beaten before I start," says Christiane sadly. Vera urges her to decide whether she will remain in Murania or go home, and Christiane tells her: "I must think it out alone," and bids Vera good night. Alone, Christiane crosses to the piano and, sitting down at it, begins to sing. During her song Nikki comes into the room. He listens fascinated, unaware who Christiane is. He has had quite enough to drink and is entirely uninhibited. Christiane realises his state and that he has not recognised her and leads him to suppose that she is the Princess' confidential maid, Astrid. Nikki is enchanted by her. They open a bottle of Imperial Tokay and are soon on the best of terms. Christiane draws him out and Nikki inveighs against his forthcoming marriage and speaks bitterly of Christiane. "But why this hatred?" she aks. "You don't even know her." "I know her signature on a shameful, arrogant scrap of paper: 'If Madame Karillos is expelled from Murania'." That, Nikki complains, was Christiane's condition of marriage. Presently under the influence of the Tokay he mellows and asks "Astrid" to sing, and Christiane obliges:

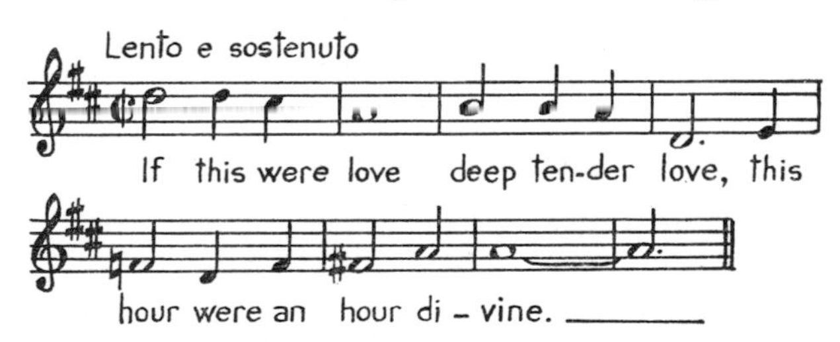

As she finishes singing Nikki catches her in his arms. He pulls her down on to his knee and Christiane melts in his arms.

SCENE 6. Outside the palace under the boudoir window a quartet of gipsy singers and instrumentalists are collected to serenade the Princess. There is a light in the window and the curtains are open. Presently a hand appears and draws the curtains across the window.

SCENE 7. In the palace ballroom a waltz is being danced. The Queen Mother, chatting to the Prime Minister of Murania, is waiting for Nikki to appear. Suddenly, to her horror, she hears the Court Chamberlain announce: "Madame Marta Karillos." The Queen Mother is furious, though outwardly calm. Madame Karillos tells her she was deeply touched to receive an invitation, and also surprised. She promises to leave "after I have paid my respects to Her Royal Highness. I think His Majesty will expect this." When Nikki arrives he categorically denies sending Marta Karillos an invitation to the reception. The Queen Mother is arguing the point when Christiane makes her entrance. The Queen Mother leads her up to Nikki, who immediately recognises her as "Astrid", the pretty maid, to whom he made love only last night. He is bewildered and angry, while Christiane thoroughly enjoys the situation. She asks Nikki to present Madame Karillos to her, as they share a love of music and are both singers. "I am sure Madame Karillos could teach me so much," she tells Nikki. "I think, Your Royal Highness, that I can teach you nothing," says Marta. "Not even endurance?" Christiane finishes. So furious is Nikki that, when the Prime Minister informs him that it is time for him to open the ball, he deliberately ignores Christiane, crosses over to Marta Karillos and asks her to dance with him. Christiane confesses that it was she who sent Madame Karillos the invitation. "My child, you were foolish to invite her, but you acted with great dignity," the Queen Mother tells her, and as Christiane dances with young Count Stanieff he confides to her: "There's not a man in this room that wouldn't run him through the heart for that insult to you."

ACT II

SCENE 1. The first scene is the drawing-room of Marta Karillos' villa on the outskirts of Bledz. It is evening, about nine months after the last scene. Marta is giving a party and Nikki is present, irrespective of the fact that at any moment Christiane's first child is due to be born. "How many guns for a boy?" he asks, and is told twenty-one and eighteen for a girl. He asks Marta to sing. "There's an attractive song I hear everywhere—even in the streets. It sounds like the Mayor of—some, some French name." It is "The Mayor of Perpignan"—a political lampoon against the King. Marta tries to get out of singing it, but Nikki insists:

The point of the song is that the Mayor is *not* a popular figure. Nikki, however, deliberately refuses to see the application. Presently the sound of guns is heard. Twenty-one salutes confirm that Nikki is father of a son and heir. He insists on a reprise of "The Mayor of Perpignan", and during the singing the doors burst open and on the threshold stands the Queen Mother. There is an awkward silence, and Nikki begs the guests to withdraw. Only Marta Karillos remains. "I thought you had an influence—in some ways quite a good one—and yet the night his child is born you lure him to your house," the Queen Mother rebukes her. Nikki is very bitter. "I have a strong desire to see my son, that small piece of humanity who has been designed to push his father off the throne." But he accompanies his mother back to the palace to show himself on the balcony with the little Prince. He bids Marta an affectionate good night, but as he goes she wonders how much longer she can hold him and she weeps quietly.

Scene 2. In the drawing-room of Marta's villa one afternoon six weeks later Christiane, Vera and Count Egon Stanieff are calling on Marta. She is out, and while they await her return they sing a trio which they find upon her piano:

Their singing is interrupted by Nikki's entrance. He asks to be left alone with Christiane. She tells him categorically that Marta Karillos' presence in Murania is no longer to be tolerated, and Nikki retorts that if Marta leaves the country, he goes with her. Christiane begs him to stay and in her pleading he detects a new, a warmer attitude to himself. "Is it possible you are, after all, human?" he asks her. "I thought you ambitious, scheming. You trapped me once," he reminds her, referring to Christiane's impersonation of "Astrid". "It was my only way," she bursts out, and Nikki suddenly realises that Christiane is telling him that she loves him. Their conversation is interrupted when Marta is brought into the room in a half-fainting condition. She has had a terrible experience. Her carriage has been attacked by peasants, armed with sticks and stones and shouting abuse. Even as she is telling her story sounds of an approaching crowd are heard. Nikki has just sent Christiane and Marta out of the room when three roughs enter through the french windows. They are not the least put out by the presence of the King, and when he tells them: "This is a private house," they retort: "We know, the harlot's house. Hand her over, we'll deal with her. Karillos! We spit on her. You and your Karillos are breaking the Queen's heart." "Funny, she never told me. I must ask her about it," Nikki tells them and calls Christiane into the room. Standing loyally by Nikki she tells the roughs: "Madame Karillos is a valued and faithful friend and if I could persuade her to stay in Murania I would do so." Puzzled, the roughs accept the Queen's assurance and go to their homes. In the love scene between Nikki and Christiane which follows there is no possible doubt that they have together found the happiness which has so long escaped them.

ACT III

Scene 1. In the garden of the summer palace at Kalacz, a year later, Nikki is expatiating on the democratic principles of government which he intends to institute. He has Christiane's warmest support, but the Queen Mother is scandalised by his proposals and his plan for the people's rights. He proposes to force this Bill through the Assembly, and if it is rejected he will abdicate.

Scene 2. The same evening in the palace gardens, in spite of the Queen Mother's horrified protests of "Peasants in the castle!", gipsy dancers present a Muranian ballet for the King and Queen's pleasure.

Scene 3. An ante-room in the palace. Nikki's Bill on the people's rights has been turned down by the Assembly, and the Prime Minister calls to demand the King's abdication. He has already prepared the instrument of abdication, and Nikki, after deleting the name of the Queen Mother as regent and substituting Christiane's, signs the document. Then he kisses Christiane. "This isn't good-bye," he tells her. "You'll come to me whenever you can get away—secretly, of course—and that will make it more exciting. And now—head up, fearless eyes, that's how I shall remember you with love and deep, deep gratitude."

Scene 4. In a box at the Paris Opera ten years later Nikki and Marta Karillos are watching the performance. In the interval Vanescu, the Prime Minister of Murania, visits the box. He has come to find out whether or not Nikki is coming to his son's coronation. In spite of veiled threats, Nikki refuses to give any promise not to be there.

Scene 5. The coronation in the Cathedral of Bledz, Murania. Concealed in the shadows Nikki watches the ceremony of the crowning of his son. After all the dignitaries have paid homage to the boy-King the ceremony finishes. Christiane, as she leaves, drops a rose on the altar steps. When the cathedral is empty Nikki comes out of the shadows. He picks up the rose and, moving to the altar, he kneels and prays for the safety of the young King.

Balalaika

A Musical Play in Three Acts (Ten Scenes)

Book and Lyrics by ERIC MASCHWITZ

Music by GEORGE POSFORD *and* BERNARD GRUN

First produced on 22nd December, 1936, at the Adelphi Theatre, London, and on 6th February, 1937, at His Majesty's Theatre, with Clifford Mollison, Muriel Angelus and Roger Treville.

CHARACTERS

ALEXEY VASSILYEVITCH, *Captain of Cossacks*
NICKI
MASHA
LYDIA MARAKOVA, *a dancer*
MARAKOV, *her father, a revolutionary*
MADAME PETROVA, *Ballet Mistress*
COUNT PETER KARAGIN
PRINCE KARAGIN, *his father*
COLONEL BALAKIREV
DENIKOV, *Police Commissar*
MR. AND MRS. RANDALL P. MORRISON
CHORUS OF TOURISTS, GIPSIES, COSSACK OFFICERS, SOLDIERS, REVOLUTIONARIES, GUESTS, WAITERS, ETC.

ACT I

SCENE 1. The scene is a crowded street outside the "Balalaika", a night club in Montmarte, Paris, in the year 1924. At the entrance to the night club stands the doorman, Alexey Vassilyevitch, ex-Captain of Cossacks, and nearby a street singer is singing a Russian song. He is an elderly, shabby man, ex-Colonel Balakirev, and is accompanied by a balalaika player, beside whom sits a dog with a tin mug attached to its collar. The singer's song is full of nostalgic melancholy:

It is the anniversary of the Russian New Year, and the doorman calls over to the singer to remind him that when the night club closes the proprietor, Nicki, is giving a New Year's party for the staff and Russian refugees, and that he will be expected. An American couple address the doorman, Alexey, and ask whether it is true that the waiters in the "Balalaika" are all dukes and princes. Alexey explains that many of the Russians who work in Montmartre did have titles in the old days before the Revolution. As the Americans pass wonderingly into the night club, the lights dim and the scene changes to the year 1914.

SCENE 2. In a rehearsal room of the Marinsky Theatre, St. Petersburg, one evening in July 1914, Madame Petrova, the Ballet Mistress, is taking a rehearsal. She is complaining of the absence of one of her most talented dancers, Lydia Marakova, when Lydia enters full of apologies. The girls are teasing her about a bunch of roses delivered daily to her from an unknown admirer, when into the room march a detachment of Cossacks in their red uniforms, led by Lieutenant Alexey Vassilyevitch, singing a rousing song:

Madame Petrova, outraged at the interruption, sends for the Manager, and his assistant, Nicki, appears. He is quite unable to quell the Cossacks, who crack their whips round his ankles to make him dance. Suddenly their commanding officer, Count Peter Karagin, arrives and orders the Cossacks back to barracks. They retire, followed by the dancers, and Peter and Lydia are left alone. It soon becomes apparent from their conversation that they are old acquaintances. In fact, last time they met Lydia smacked his face. But Peter is in love with her and it is he who sends her roses every day. Before he goes he invites her to a party that night at a little restaurant on the island. "There'll be balalaika music and nightingales," he tells her. "But I shan't be there," she assures him. "We'll see," he says and leaves her. Later Peter's father, Prince Karagin, visits Madame Petrova, who remembers him from the old days. "You used to call for Tamara Voikovsky my best friend, Your Highness." The

Prince has heard of his son's infatuation for Lydia and trusts Madame Petrova to put an end to the affair. As they are talking Lydia rushes into the rehearsal room in search of her roses. As she sees the Prince she stops abashed, and he bends and kisses her hand, saying meaningly: "Enchanted, Mademoiselle."

SCENE 3. At the "Balalaika" restaurant on the island Count Karagin's party is in full swing. His guests are mostly ballet dancers and Cossack officers. Suddenly, to his surprise, Lydia Marakova arrives. She confesses that she has come against her father's wishes because she wanted to see him again and they sing an affectionate duet:

Later Peter's father, Prince Karagin, turns up at the party. He is determined to break up the romance between Peter and Lydia. As they are talking, Lydia's father, Marakov, arrives. He, too, disapproves of Lydia's association with Peter. He is an ardent socialist and despises the aristocracy. "I am perfectly aware," he tells Prince Karagin, "that the most despicable actions are considered harmless, even admirable, when performed by a Prince, a Count or a Lieutenant. But my daughter is young. I cannot risk her being mauled by any Don Juan who finds it amusing." But Lydia refuses to give up Peter, and the two fathers withdraw discomfited. Directly they have gone, Peter publicly announces his engagement to marry Lydia and the happy couple are toasted in champagne to the accompaniment of gipsy music. In the excitement no one notices the entrance of an orderly, who hands Peter an envelope. Peter reads the contents and, jumping up, cries excitedly: "Stop! Stop! Listen to this. 'Imperial cavalry Headquarters, St. Petersburg. From General Commanding the Don Cossack Brigade—to all officers. At midnight tonight His Majesty declared war on Austro-Hungary. All officers are to report to barracks immediately and prepare to entrain at dawn for destination unspecified.'" In a flash the restaurant is the scene of general farewells. "Don't come back till you've beaten them," says Lydia to Peter. "Remember it's Russia first, now." Springing on to a table, Peter gives his guests the toast of "Russia", and all stand to sing the patriotic hymn "Hail to thee, Russia, the land we adore" as the curtain falls.

ACT II

SCENE 1. The regimental headquarters of the Don Cossack Brigade are in a castle in Gallicia and the scene is a salon. Shellfire has smashed a once-lovely room to pieces. Through a gash in the wall can be seen the night sky and snow falling. It is Christmas night 1916 and the Cossack officers are seated round a table on which are *samovar*, bottle of vodka and a tiny lighted Christmas tree. They are recounting reminiscences of home, and Peter recalls Lydia and their engagement party:

Presently Colonel Balakirev calls Peter over. There is serious news from home. Social unrest is rife. The people are desperate, they will do anything to end the war and they are organised. Their leaders are looking for a scapegoat and the Government fear an attempt on the Emperor's life. Headquarters want someone to be with the Emperor night and day—a personal bodyguard—someone brave enough to sacrifice himself if necessary. The choice has fallen on Peter. Accompanied by Nicki, the mild little assistant manager of the Marinsky Theatre, who has acted as his batman throughout the campaign, Peter leaves for home, seen off by his envious brother officers. As the curtain falls distant voices are heard in the Austrian trenches singing their Christmas hymn "*Stille Nacht, heilige Nacht*".

SCENE 2. Scene Two is a corridor backstage in the Marinsky Theatre. The call-boy is calling "First Ballet—five minutes, please" while Masha, the dresser, pulled this way and that by desperate dancers in every stage of undress, declares that she will be a "corpse de ballet" before the evening's through. Tonight is a gala performance in the presence of the Emperor, but a shadow is cast over proceedings when Police Commissar Denikov comes backstage to warn the staff that the police have information that an attempt may be made to assassinate His Imperial Highness during the evening. Lydia is dancing in the second ballet of the evening, Madame Petrova's new creation, "Reflections". As she is waiting in her dressing-room the door opens and Peter stands there. In a moment they are in each other's arms. But already Lydia's ballet is being called and a Cossack officer informs Peter: "His Majesty has arrived, Count Karagin. You should be with him in the box."

SCENE 3. On stage the ballet is well under way when there is the sound of a shattering explosion. Someone has thrown a bomb into the Emperor's box. Thanks to the prompt action of his bodyguard, Peter, in dragging him out of range of the missile, the Emperor is unhurt, but the assassin has escaped in the darkness. An official announces that the Emperor is coming back-stage to thank Count Karagin personally, and as all the dancers curtsy, Prince Karagin announces "His Majesty, the Emperor".

SCENE 4. In a room in a house in St. Petersburg three revolutionaries are waiting on tenterhooks. "He ought to have been here hours ago," one of them complains. Presently Marakov bursts in. "Well—is he?" asks the leading revolutionary. "No, not dead," answers Marakov. "The bomb exploded all right. It hit the ledge of the box, but some young fool of an officer threw him aside. I had to fight to get out. We must clear out of this. There's a train for Odessa at one o'clock." The four men hurry out of the room as the voices of Peter and Lydia are heard on the stairs. They have come to ask for the consent of Lydia's father to their engagement and of course neither of them is aware of Marakov's part in the night's outrage. As they are talking Marakov enters. His fury is aroused at the sight of the man who saved the Emperor's life, and he is about to shoot down Peter when the police rush in and pinion his arms. Lydia learns that it was her father who threw the bomb. But, when Police Commissar Denikov tells Peter that it was through a miniature of Lydia that Marakov dropped while escaping that they traced him and congratulate Peter on beating them to it, Lydia assumes that Peter's interest in her was merely to facilitate his chances of spying on her father. Rounding on him, she cries: "I never want to see you again—never—never!"

SCENE 5. In his palace Prince Karagin is giving a ball and a mazurka has just finished. There is much talk of serious unrest in the city. Presently there are sounds of firing in the streets. The people are armed and are shooting down the guards. Marakov and other prisoners have been released. Suddenly the doors of the ballroom are burst open and a crowd of revolutionaries enter. A spokesman declares: "The house is occupied by order of the Council of Soldiers, Workers and Peasants." Then Marakov enters, calm and dignified. He addresses the Prince. "You remember me, Comrade Karagin. The thing you thought impossible has come to pass. Russia has been taken by the people. Tonight your world finishes. Their world begins." His head high, the Prince walks slowly through the doors followed by Marakov.

ACT III

SCENE 1. The scene is the same as the opening of Act One—Russian New Year's Eve, outside the "Balalaika" night club, Montmartre, Paris. The American couple, Mr. and Mrs. Randall P. Morrison of Cincinnati, have decided to explore the *boîte* and discover if it is really true that the waiters are all dukes and princes. Mrs. Morrison is regrettably and noisily "high". Peter Karagin, now gigolo at the "Balalaika", arrives and greets Alexey, the doorman. Peter is very depressed, and Alexey tries to cheer him up. "It's an up-and-down world," he tells Peter. "We go down and up come Nicki and Masha." For the mild little ex-assistant-manager of the Marinsky theatre, and Peter's ex-batman, has married Masha the dresser, and they now own the "Balalaika". But Peter refuses to be comforted. "I can't go on. I pack up and leave tomorrow," he tells Alexey as he passes into the club.

SCENE 2. The interior of the "Balalaika" is a large room decorated in an exaggeratedly Russian style. The floor is set with supper-tables and on the stage a balalaika orchestra is playing. Nicki and Masha contribute a cabaret number—a gay duet with the refrain "Nichevo":

During the evening Mrs. Randall P. Morrison of Cincinnati has been getting steadily drunker and drunker. She demands to dance with Peter Karagin, and pointedly and offensively pays him in advance. But Peter's low spirits irritate her and she shouts at him: "What's the matter with you, frigidaire? Can't you look as if you were enjoying yourself? You're just a gigolo, and if the customers want to buy you for a party, you gotta do your stuff." Peter calmly hands the furious woman her money back, and this precipitates a violent row which ends in the noisy exit of the Randall P. Morrisons. Soon after the other guests follow suit and the club is emptied. "Now," says Nicki, "we can have a party of our own." In a moment the room is full of ex-Cossack officers and ballet dancers. Only one face is missing—Lydia's. Presently the door opens. It *is* Lydia. Peter does not see her as she stands shyly in the entrance. Ex-Colonel Balakirev is the first to speak. "You should not have come here, Mam'selle—you, the daughter of the Soviet Ambassador." "I'm glad I am," she tells him, "because it has brought me to Paris at last. I could not come before. I was a prisoner." Then they all take Lydia to their hearts. Peter, who still has not observed Lydia, wishes everyone good night. But before he is allowed to go, Nicki insists that he look in the mirror, where according to superstition everyone on New Year's Eve will see the reflection of the one he is to marry. Tiptoeing forward, Lydia stands beside Peter and looks over his shoulder as he gazes in the mirror. He turns in amazement and the lovers are reunited.

The Lisbon Story

A Play with Music

Book and Lyrics by HAROLD PURCELL

Music by HARRY PARR DAVIES

First produced on 17th June, 1943, at the London Hippodrome, with Patricia Burke as "Gabrielle Girard (Gay)" and Albert Lieven as "Karl von Schriner".

CHARACTERS

GABRIELLE GIRARD (GAY), *a singing star of the Parisian theatre*
DAVID WARREN, *of the British Foreign Office*
GONZALEZ, *a fruit vendor*
KARL VON SCHRINER, *of the Berlin Cultural Department*
MICHAEL O'ROURKE
PIERRE SARGON, *a French scientist*
LISETTE SARGON, *his daughter*
LOUISE PANACHE, *Gay's secretary*
STEPHEN GORELLE, *Gay's musical director*
PREFECT OF POLICE
CHORUS OF FISHERMEN, MEMBERS OF THE *LA COMTESSE* COMPANY, ETC.

ACT I

SCENE I. The scene is Paris and the year 1938. In a studio lives Gabrielle Girard, a singing star of the theatre. She is engaged to David Warren of the British Foreign Office and the two young people are deeply in love. On the eve of the production of her new musical, Gay (Gabrielle) sings him the hit number of the show:

The words are prophetic, for David now receives instructions from the Foreign Office posting him to Washington. He begs Gay to join him there directly her show finishes, but she tells him that their love-affair has always been a dream from which they must now awaken and that it is good-bye.

SCENE 2. It is five years later and the scene is Lisbon in 1943—Lisbon, a city of whispers, of strange echoes to secret thought, a city of plots and intrigues. Here in a house on the quayside Gay is living. She quitted Paris when the Nazis occupied France and has made neutral Lisbon her home. One evening she hears a beautiful tenor voice singing outside her house on the quayside:

The singer is a fruit vendor, Gonzalez. Coming out of her house Gay compliments him on his singing and joins in his song. At this moment two German secret agents pass by. One of them is Karl von Schriner, of the Berlin Cultural Department. Part of his job is to persuade distinguished artists to return to their own, Nazi-occupied, countries. He recognises in Gay the famous Parisian singing star Gabrielle Girard. Addressing her, Herr von Schriner proposes that she return to Paris to appear for a season at her own Mogodor Theatre under the Nazi banner. Gay coldly refuses and von Schriner, begging her to think over his proposal, assures her that he will try again. When he has gone and Gay has returned to her house David Warren arrives on the scene. With him is an Irishman, Michael O'Rourke (Mike), and a girl called Lisette Sargon. David and Mike discuss the problem of finding a bed for Lisette for the night. As they are sitting outside a café debating the situation, Gay comes out of her house. Determined not to lose control of her emotions, she greets David calmly, and he begs her help. He tells her that he is concerned with the rescue of a famous French scientist, Pierre Sargon, the inventor of Selumine, a light alloy used in aircraft construction. When France fell Sargon was ordered to hand everything over to the Germans, but he blew up his laboratory and escaped with all his secrets—secrets the Germans would have given anything to possess. "We've found this man and we've got him out of France," David tells her, "and one of our people got his daughter—Lisette here—over the Franco-Spanish border last night. Please, Gay, will you look after her?" Gay promises to do so, and they go on to discuss how to smuggle Pierre Sargon into Lisbon under the noses of the German secret agents. Gay proposes a plan to bring Sargon to Lisbon by boat under cover of the Festival of Blessing the Nets, to be held on the morrow, at which she has promised to sing. Her plan is enthusiastically adopted and Gay takes Lisette into her house.

SCENE 3. Next morning an excited crowd of fishermen with their wives, children and girl-friends are collected on the quayside for the Festival of Blessing the Nets, and together they sing a joyful song:

This is followed by the ceremonial blessing of the nets, performed outside the church doors by a priest. At the conclusion there is a Festival dance, and after that the happy, laughing crowd disperse, leaving David, Gay and Lisette alone. They are on tenterhooks of expectation, as Pierre Sargon's arrival by boat is expected at any moment, but to their dismay Karl von Schriner hangs around and they fear he may be suspicious. However, eventually he departs and Mike appears, escorting a tall, thin man. Lisette hurries forward to greet him but recoils with a cry of "That is not my father". Then the stranger makes his confession and tells his story. "I was hiding with Sargon in Marseilles," he tells them. "We were trying to get a boat to Dakar. But he was waiting for his daughter to join him and always hung back. Time and again he ruined our chances and at last it happened. The Gestapo raided the house. I hid on the roof, but he was taken. I let them think I was Sargon. I had his papers. Sargon was sent to a concentration camp under the name of 'Mariot'." Lisette in despair declares her intention of returning to France to rescue her father. Gay comforts her, but David begs her not to hold out false hopes. Gay persists. "There *is* a way," she declares. At that moment she sees von Schriner looking at them. Walking over to him, she takes his arm in a gesture of friendliness, signifying that she accepts his proposition that she return to Paris.

ACT II

Gay, with her secretary, Louise Panache, her musical director, Stephen Gorelle, and Lisette Sargon all leave for Paris, escorted by Karl von Schriner. At a frontier railway station Gay gets a glimpse of David, who has come to wish her godspeed and to send Mike, disguised as a priest, to assist in the rescue of Pierre Sargon. Arrived in Paris, rehearsals begin for the revival of Gay's well-known musical *La Comtesse*. But nothing is to Gay's taste. The dancing-girls supplied by the Nazi Ministry of Culture cannot dance. Stephen Gorelle agitates for more strings in the orchestra, and worst of all the scenic designs by a German artist are declared by Gay to be impossible. She demands the services of her former designer, Pierre Mariot, now in a concentration camp. Herr von Schriner is anxious to placate Gay in every way. Unaware, of course, that this Mariot is in fact the scientist Pierre Sargon, von Schriner orders him to be traced and brought to Paris. This is duly done, and one morning Gay is invited to the Prefecture of Police to identify her scenic designer. Sargon is led into the room at the Prefecture and fortunately recognises in Gay the famous Gabrielle Girard. Gay has taken the precaution of bringing with her a bracelet made of selumine, belonging to Lisette. It was the first piece that Sargon manufactured and he had it made up into a bracelet for his daughter. During her interview with Sargon, Gay tells him that she is reviving *La Comtesse*. "I can't do it without you. You must help me," she urges. "But I don't understand," he falters. Despairing of ever making him see that her real intention is to effect his escape, Gay pretends to drop the bracelet off her wrist. The Prefect rushes forward to pick it up and fastens it on her wrist. He remarks on the beauty of the platinum. "It isn't platinum; it's another metal very like it—selumine," says Gay meaningly. Then turning to Sargon she urges: "Come with me and go on with your work"—and then at last Sargon understands her intention and agrees to go with her. On von Schriner's instructions "Mariot" is released, and Gay takes him away with her to her studio in the rue Brissot, where there is a blissful reunion between father and daughter. Some days later von Schriner pays a call at the studio. In honeyed tones he proposes that Gay move to the Hotel Crillon. He indicates that he is madly in love with her and that he has been very patient—so far. He also informs her that inquiries have been made and that he is aware that "Mariot" is in reality Pierre Sargon. He bargains with her that if she will become his mistress he will not let the authorities know about Sargon. "I presume you're not going to do anything foolish, like trying to get him out of the country. And now, dear Gay, I hope I've made it clear where your best chance lies. Good night." And von Schriner goes out.

Mike now arrives with news. A plane is being sent the following night at 9.30 p.m. to fly Sargon, Lisette and Gay to England. Mike has taken the party emblem from one of von Schriner's cars, which means that the German sentries will allow their car to leave Paris. He tells Gay that she must be off the stage not a moment later than 9.30. No curtain calls. She must say she is feeling ill and go up to her dressing-room. Mike will look after Pierre Sargon, and Gay is to bring Lisette to the waiting car. The following night the show is running late and everything does not go according to plan.

The final item is the Ballet of Innocence, personified by a girl (played by Lisette) growing up to maturity, while Piety and Evil struggle for the possession of her soul. Piety is eventually overthrown and Innocence enters into a marriage contract with Evil. But the show is running a quarter of an hour late, and Gay realises that at 9.30 p.m., when they should be leaving the theatre, Lisette will still be on the stage. To her dismay she sees von Schriner in the wings watching Lisette, and remembers that she will never be out of his sight except when she goes off the stage to change into her wedding veil. Gay acts quickly. She slips into a white ballet skirt, and when Lisette comes off, it is Gay wearing the wedding veil, who returns to the stage to finish the ballet, while Lisette is hurried away to the waiting car and freedom. The curtain descends to the applause and shouts of *Heil* and Gay stands alone in the centre of the stage. But von Schriner has realised that all is not well. He rushes on to the stage shouting: "Where's Lisette? Where's Sargon, you bitch?" Gay slaps his face and walks through the curtains to address the audience. "Ladies and gentlemen," she says. "You came to see a revival of my old play, but tonight there was a new finale—borrowed from that greater drama that is being played all over

France. If I appear to have collaborated with your Karl von Schriner, my old friends will believe me when I say that I have never, that I could never collaborate with any of you. True, you hold the stage of France for a while, but time has a trick of writing new epilogues to old plays and France will speak your epilogue when once again she finds her voice to . . ." There is a crack of a pistol and Gay falls dead, shot through the heart by a bullet from von Schriner's revolver. Pandemonium breaks out in the auditorium. Gorelle and one of the company go through the curtains and carry Gay's body back-stage. At that moment the sound of aeroplanes is heard. The "crump" of bombs follows. Cries of "Clear the stage", "Take shelter", are raised. But the company ignore them and begin to sing "The Marseillaise". Starting softly, the triumphant anthem swells to drown the noise of the bombs as the curtain falls.

Bless The Bride

Light Opera in Two Acts

Book and Lyrics by A. P. HERBERT

Music by VIVIAN ELLIS

First produced on 26th April, 1947, at the Adelphi Theatre, London, with Lizbeth Webb as "Lucy", Georges Guétary as "Pierre" and Brian Reece as "Thomas Trout".

CHARACTERS

LUCY VERACITY WILLOW
HON. THOMAS TROUT, *her fiancé*
SUZANNE VALOIS } *French actors*
PIERRE FONTAINE }
LUCY'S FATHER
HER MOTHER
HER FIVE SISTERS
HER NANNY
CHORUS OF RELATIONS, CLIENTÈLE OF THE CAFÉ DES POMMES, ETC.

ACT I

SCENE 1. The scene is The Grange, Mayfield, Sussex, and the year is 1870. Here lives the heroine of our story, Lucy Veracity Willow, with her parents and grandparents. She is one of a family of six girls and is to be married on the morrow to the Honourable Thomas Trout. But Lucy is not at all looking forward to marrying Thomas. She has found him to be untruthful, and Cousin George suggests that he has no money and is not even of noble birth. When the curtain rises on the lawn of The Grange garden, a number of ladies and gentlemen are playing croquet. Thomas Trout finds croquet slow and suggests to Lucy that he introduce some friends of his who are staying at the inn. They are French actors and have an exciting new game called tennis. Lucy reluctantly agrees, and Thomas goes off to fetch his friends. They duly appear, and consist of Mademoiselle Suzanne Valois, a strong-minded young woman, and Monsieur Pierre Fontaine, a fascinating Frenchman. A tennis net is rigged up and a game of tennis is started. It involves a deal of unseemly leaping about and exposing of ladies' legs, and when Lucy's parents appear they are affronted at the wild athletics. To Lucy's mortification, Thomas introduces his friends as Monsieur et Madame Fontaine of the French Embassy. Lucy's father civilly invites the French couple to attend a party that night to celebrate Lucy's grandparents' golden wedding, and croquet is resumed in place of tennis. During the game Lucy croquets Pierre into the shrubbery, and this brings them together alone among the laurels. Pierre has already fallen for Lucy and he suddenly seizes her in his arms and kisses her. She struggles—though not excessively—and reminds him that he is married. He denies that Suzanne is his wife and urges Lucy not to believe a word that Thomas says, warning her also that he is broke and is always borrowing money. She is greatly attracted to the handsome Frenchman and sings ecstatically:

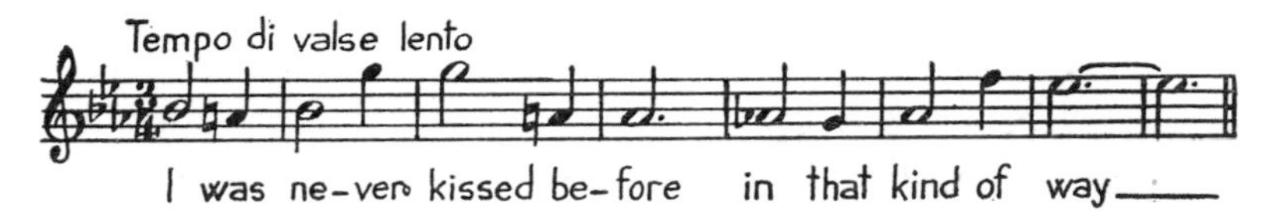

That night the party in celebration of the golden wedding of Lucy's grandparents takes place. Pierre and Suzanne are present, and Pierre, now madly in love with Lucy, begs her in a whispered conversation to give up Thomas and come away with him; but she takes fright and refuses. Suzanne, however, has overheard the conversation and her heart is filled with jealousy. Pierre is invited by Lucy's mother to sing a song of his country and obliges with "Ma Belle Marguerite":

The evening closes with a presentation to the old couple of presents from the family, with musical honours.

SCENE 2. Next morning in the nursery of her childhood Lucy is being dressed for her wedding to Thomas Trout by her old Nanny. A bouquet of flowers arrives for her. It is from Pierre, and a note accompanies it which reads "Look out for the doctor", which greatly puzzles Lucy. She confesses to Nanny that she is not the least in love with Thomas, and she would obviously do anything to get out of having to marry him.

SCENE 3. Lucy's mother and her sisters have left for the church, while her father remains behind to escort his daughter to her wedding. But as the fatal moment approaches Lucy becomes increasingly apprehensive and nervous. As she is getting hysterical a mysterious doctor appears with a black bag. This is of course, Pierre in disguise. Lucy's father is astonished at his presence but thankful to have a medical man to cope with his distracted daughter. Lucy is overjoyed to see Pierre and needs no persuading to consent to elope with him. Disguised in the suit belonging to her father's coloured page-boy, she slips away with Pierre, and the page, attired in her wedding dress, his face veiled, is laid out on a sofa. A message is dispatched to the church to the effect that Lucy has been taken ill and the wedding must be postponed. When the family arrive back the true facts come quickly to light, and Thomas and Lucy's parents decide to leave for France, track down the eloping couple and bring back the erring Lucy.

ACT II

Scene 1. At Eauville-sur-mer Pierre and Lucy are leading a blissful life with only one snag. Suzanne has tracked them down and jealously insists on chaperoning Lucy. It is a lovely morning on the plage and the lovers are enjoying a blissful tête-à-tête. Suzanne is immobilised in a bathing-machine, Lucy having thoughtfully taken the precaution of removing her bathing-dress. When she eventually appears she warns them that she has observed a big man with a telescope who bears a striking resemblance to Lucy's father. She urges Pierre and Lucy to make the most of their time together, for there is news in the paper. War between France and Germany is imminent and Pierre is in the army reserve.

Scene 2. The man with the telescope whom Suzanne has seen is in truth Lucy's father, for he, with Lucy's mother, Thomas and Cousin George have all crossed to France in pursuit of the runaway pair. The men are disguised in pseudo-French beards and wear ulsters and shooting caps. They have been some hours in Eauville making inquiries and are exhausted. In search of a meal they are directed to the Café des Pommes.

Scene 3. In the Café des Pommes, Lucy and Pierre are at a table, but so engrossed in each other that Lucy does not observe the entrance of her family, who sit down at a table and with difficulty order a meal. In order to appear French they order champagne, though Thomas would much prefer a light ale. Pierre and Lucy have still not noticed the family invasion. Looking only at each other, they sing:

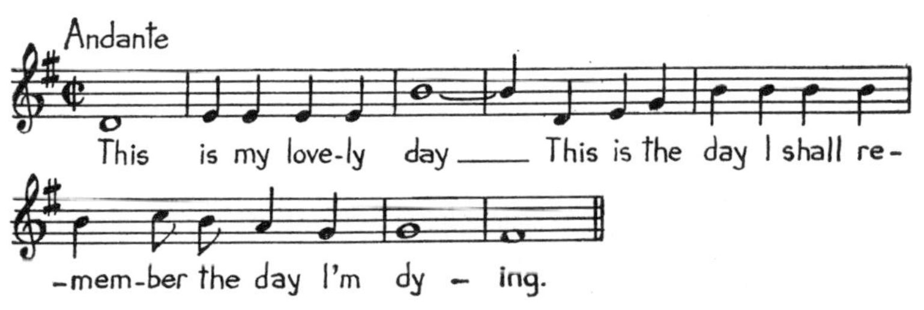

The English family have by now attracted the attention of the police. War is imminent and there is the usual spy scare. Lucy's father's telescope is an object of suspicion and he has been seen on the shore obviously examining forts and defences. There are ugly whispers of "Espions Allemands", and the climax is reached when Thomas' false beard falls into the consommé. As the police are closing in to arrest them Lucy sees them and rushes to their rescue. Suzanne, too, vouches for their nationality and integrity, and the police are satisfied and withdraw. Her parents are full of gratitude to Lucy for coming to their aid and tell her to prepare to return home with them. But Lucy informs them that she is remaining in France and intends to marry Pierre. This infuriates Thomas. He advances menacingly upon Pierre, who now comes in wearing the uniform of a Reservist officer. Thomas challenges Pierre to a duel with cries of "*Epées ou pistolets*", and as they are arguing a man enters the café with a newspaper. War with Germany has been declared and Pierre must leave for the front. After an emotional farewell, Lucy breaks down and is led away by her parents, bound for England.

Scenes 4 and 5. Lucy is back at her home in Sussex. It is her twenty-first birthday, but her heart is heavy. News has come from Suzanne that Pierre has been killed in battle. Ever since his death she has, according to Nanny, been forever telling the cards, worrying her head about the future, dark men and France. Always France. "Ever since the young gentleman was killed she's been the same." One day Thomas Trout arrives to see Lucy. He has bought an engagement ring and tactfully tells her that he still loves her. Lucy tells him frankly that after Pierre she can never love any other man, but she is touched and, retaining his ring, asks him to wait for her. Her sisters appear with the birthday cake, and then another visitor enters. It is Suzanne. Going up to Lucy she says: "It is your birthday? *Alors* I have a little present for you"—and there stands Pierre, alive and well. In her jealousy and desiring Pierre for herself, Suzanne has lied about Pierre's death, but she has regretted it and wishes to make amends. Pierre is about to embrace Lucy when he notices her engagement ring and releases her. Thomas steps forward. Gently he removes his ring from Lucy's finger and hands it to Pierre with the words: "Pierre, I salute you. I salute France, and I have a present for you also." Then taking Lucy's hand he puts it into Pierre's, and the lovers, reunited at last, embrace.

And So To Bed

A Comedy

By J. B. Fagan

Lyrics and Music by Vivian Ellis

First produced on 17th October, 1951, at the New Theatre, London, with Leslie Henson as "Samuel Pepys" and Betty Paul as "Mistress Pepys".

Characters

SAMUEL PEPYS, *Secretary of the Royal Navy*
MISTRESS PEPYS
MISTRESS KNIGHT
PELHAM HUMPHREY
KING CHARLES II
MISTRESS PIERCE
MISTRESS KNEPP
PRODGER, *groom of the bedchamber*
PELLING

ACT I

The first act opens in the living-room of Pepys' house in the year 1669, just after the last entry in the famous Pepys Diary. While the servants are tidying up, a thief attacks a woman outside the house. In the ensuing brawl Pepys throws a pot out of the window, which luckily hits the thief. Seeing that the victim is a pretty woman he rushes outside and brings her, half fainting, into the room. She is Mistress Knight, a well-known actress and a mistress of King Charles. When she learns that her rescuer writes music she sings one of his compositions for him, and they make a rendezvous for that night at her rooms, when Pepys promises to show her some more music. As she leaves, some of Pepys' friends arrive, bringing with them a Frenchified dandy, Pelham Humphrey, who infuriates Mr. Pepys with his airs and his French songs. To prove how fine English voices and songs are Pepys gathers his household together to sing the lilting "Gaze not on swans":

On Mistress Pepys' return from a trip to see her father she finds her husband entertaining among his guests two actresses of very doubtful reputation. Never at a loss, she immediately gets her own back by flirting with the Frenchified Humphrey, who is delighted at receiving the attentions of his hostess. When the guests have left Pepys chides his wife for her behaviour, but she turns the whole thing against him, and having coaxed a new gown from him goes happily to change out of her travelling clothes. During this time Pepys has a gay flirtation with the prettiest maid. Unfortunately his wife enters as they kiss, and her rage has not yet abated when he says he has to go out that evening on business. She has heard that tale many times, and when he returns dressed in all his finery she knows that he is going to see a woman, and the curtain comes down on her vowing to catch him red-handed.

ACT II

Act Two takes place in Mistress Knight's lodgings in Lincoln Inn Fields. Pepys duly arrives, and in order to side step his advances Mistress Knight sings while he accompanies her on the flageolet:

Before they have time to do more than renew their acquaintance it is announced that His Majesty King Charles has decided to call on Mistress Knight. In the momentary panic His Majesty's Secretary of the Navy finds himself pushed into a large chest. A second later King Charles arrives with the request for some entertainment that will put State business out of his mind for a while. Mistress Knight sings to him:

Before they can embrace an agitated Mistress Pepys can be heard demanding to see Mistress Knight, and King Charles just has time to slip behind a curtain before she bursts into the room, where Mistress Knight now has two lovers concealed. In her search for her husband Mistress Pepys discovers the King and is quite overawed at being in his presence. He finds this very charming, and as he now knows that her husband *is* there he deliberately sits Mistress Pepys on the chest in which Pepys is hidden and flirts outrageously with her. She thinks the King is wonderful and tells him all the trouble she has with her errant husband, who will never leave a pretty woman alone. The King, kicking the chest hard, says he thinks it will be better in the future. When she has gone the King opens the chest to reveal the forlorn figure of Pepys, who explains a little nervously that he merely came to make music with Mistress Knight and slipped into the chest in case his presence in her rooms was misconstrued by His Majesty. King Charles roars with laughter, which is cut short by Pepys making an impassioned plea on behalf of the Navy. He is dismissed by a coldly furious King, who has not come to Mistress Knight's to talk State business and who turns to woo her once again as the curtain falls.

ACT III

Later that night in Pepys' house a gay party is going on around a miserable and unhappy Mistress Pepys. It is late and her husband has not yet returned and some of the guests cannot resist making sly remarks about it. When Pepys does return he puts on a brave face and entertains the company with "Bartholomew Fair". At the finish it is more than Mistress Pepys can stand and she runs crying from the room. Pepys is not quite sure what has reduced her to this state, but he bids the guests good night. However, when he is alone and waiting for the storm his wife quietly comes to say she is sorry for flying out like that and asks his forgiveness. They have a charming little scene, at the end of which she solemnly swears that she will never doubt her husband again. Unfortunately at this moment King Charles' Groom of the Bedchamber arrives. Pepys in the previous act had left his flageolet on the settee in Mistress Knight's room, where it was discovered by King Charles, who now sends it rather pointedly to Mistress Pepys. She then realises that Pepys was somewhere in those rooms all the time. Finally she extracts the truth from her husband, who tries, unsuccessfully, to accuse her of being faithless with King Charles. This she puts aside and the curtain falls on Pepys solemnly swearing never to be unfaithful again. At least, not until the next time.

Salad Days

Book and Lyrics by DOROTHY REYNOLDS *and* JULIAN SLADE
Music by JULIAN SLADE

First performance on 1st June, 1954, at the Theatre Royal, Bristol. First London production on 5th August, 1954, at the Vaudeville Theatre, with John Warner as "Timothy", Eleanor Drew as "Jane" and Newton Blick as "The Tramp".

CHARACTERS

TIMOTHY
JANE
THE TRAMP
POLICE-CONSTABLE BOOT
TROPPO
NIGEL DANVERS
FIONA
MINISTER OF PASTIMES AND PLEASURES

ACT I

The scene opens on graduation day at a University. Jane and Timothy are saying Good-bye. They are obviously very attracted to each other and longing to meet again when they both return to their homes in London. Neither of them wishes to look too eager to meet the other, so they casually arrange a rendezvous in the park, not far from the Serpentine. But both fear that their families will have made plans for them and that their lives will not be their own any more. As they recall the good times they have had they realise that at this moment of their lives it is vital to look forward and not back, and they make a pact:

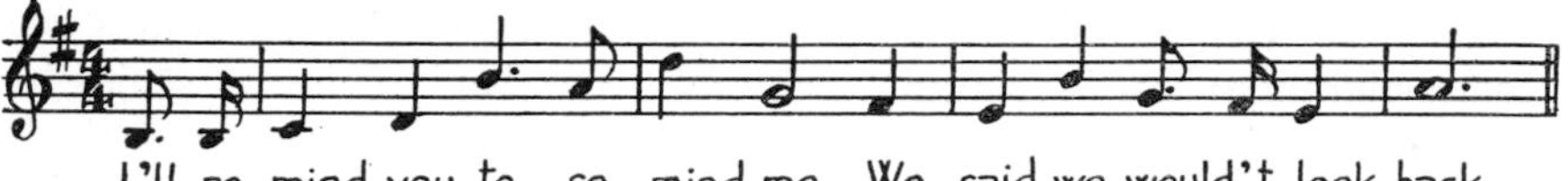

Timothy has a lot of influential uncles, and his parents are determined that he shall get something to do through one uncle or another. He manages to give his family the slip one day in order to meet Jane, who has been waiting for him:

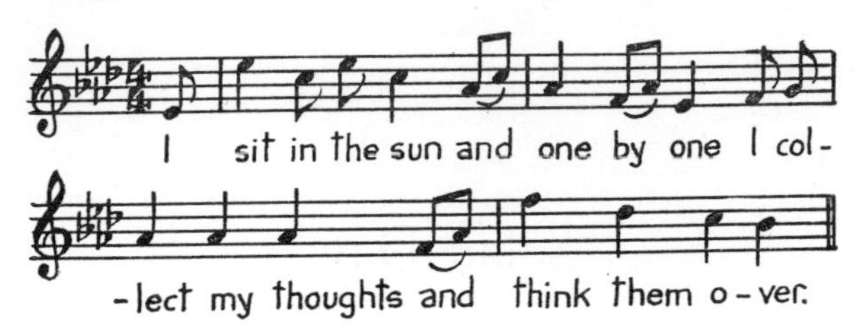

They have a charming scene which ends in their deciding to get married for convenience—as a sure way to stop their families making plans for them—though they are both in love without realising that it is mutual. They have no money, nowhere to live and plan to continue living with their respective parents for the time being. While they have been talking an old tramp has pushed his street piano into the park and has sat down to have his sandwich and bottle of beer. When he has finished he starts to play the piano. This has an extraordinary effect on Timothy and Jane. They simply can't keep still, they find they must dance to the music of the piano:

they sing in amazement. When the tramp stops playing, they are exhausted and beg him to tell them about this fascinating piano. "Her name is Minnie," he tells them, and offers them the job of looking after her for a month, at seven pounds a week payable in advance and any takings from the collections. Timothy and Jane are enchanted with the idea. Soon Timothy is playing the magic piano and everyone in the park is dancing hilariously, including Police-Constable Boot, who has come to see what is causing the disturbance. During the following days reports of these extraordinary happenings in the park reach the ears of the miserable Minister of Pastimes and Pleasures, who determines that all this hilarity must be stopped and the piano suppressed. An odd, dumb character called Troppo has become very attached to "Minnie" and looks after her at night when Jane and Timothy have to return to their homes. He warns them both that the Minister of Pastimes and Pleasures is so furious that he, personally, is taking part in the search for this extraordinary piano.

ACT II

In a night club Jane, with the help of a friend Nigel Danvers, hopes to get a compromising photograph of the Minister of Pastimes and Pleasures who comes nightly to hear the singer "Asphyxia"—not that he appears to enjoy her singing. But Jane and Nigel are unsuccessful and unable to photograph the Minister. After their evening together they run into Timothy, who tries rather unsuccessfully to look as if he did not mind who Jane went out with. Realising by Timothy's jealousy that he does indeed love her, Jane delightedly explains to Nigel their complex marriage arrangement.

The next day in the park the Minister runs into Jane and Timothy and their friends. Troppo rushes "Minnie" away to safety, leaving the others to put the Minister off the track. In the course of the day Troppo loses "Minnie", and the young people go off in a desperate search for her. The month is up and she is due to be handed over to the tramp today. During the search Jane meets the tramp and tells him she is sorry about "Minnie", but that they will certainly find her, for "Minnie" has brought to Jane the happiest days of her life:

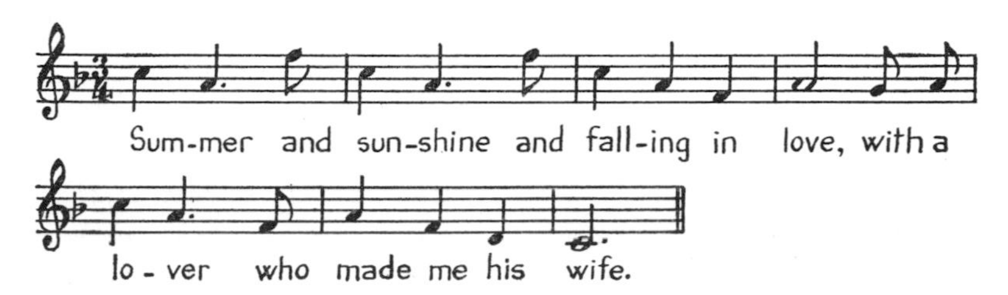

With the help of a flying saucer "Minnie" is found and returned to the tramp, who kindly offers the job of looking after her to Nigel Danvers and his girl-friend, Fiona. The Minister of Pastimes is restrained by his sister, who is Timothy's mother; the parents are reconciled to the young people's marriage, and the curtain falls on them all dancing to the irresistible "Minnie".

AMERICAN MUSICAL COMEDIES AND PLAYS

by David Ewen

INTRODUCTION

It took many years for the American musical theatre to acquire its own identity. The first musical production in the Colonies was *Flora*, a performance that took place in a court room in Charleston, South Carolina, on 8th February, 1735. *Flora* was a ballad opera imported from England. The English ballad opera remained popular in the Colonies for several decades. After the Colonies had become a nation, a new kind of stage production began to attract interest: the burlesque. At that time, burlesque consisted of travesties on or parodies of famous plays, performers or dancers—in song, dance, pantomime and dialogue. One of the earliest was *Hamlet* in 1828, in which John Poole starred; one of the best, *La Mosquita* in or about 1838, satirised the celebrated Viennese dancer, Fanny Elssler, in her performance in *Tarantella*. Burlesques were also for the most part foreign importations; and so were the extravaganzas and spectacles that crowded the New York stage just before and immediately after the Civil War. The accent on female pulchritude (usually in flimsy attire), so important an element in later American musical productions, dates from one of these foreign importations: *Ixion*, in 1869, in which Lydia Thompson and her English blondes shocked New York by having girls appear in skin-coloured tights. The sensational extravaganza, *The Black Crook*, produced in New York on 12th September, 1866—and the most successful theatrical production put on in America up to that time—was, it is true, written by Americans. It is also true that *The Black Crook* introduced some of the ritual subsequently identifying American musical comedy: chorus girls, ornate production numbers, elaborate costuming, songs provocative with sex innuendos, large dance numbers and so forth. Nevertheless, *The Black Crook* came from a foreign matrix. It was a frank imitation of the European extravaganzas which had been visiting the United States for a number of years, beginning with *Novelty, with the Laying of the Atlantic Cable*, produced in New York in 1857 by the Ronzani troupe, a European ballet company. After the middle 1860s, and for the rest of that century, the American stage was literally flooded with foreign operettas: the opera-bouffes of Offenbach and Lecocq among others; the operettas of Suppé and Johann Strauss II; the comic operas of Gilbert and Sullivan. American composers and librettos were, for a long time, driven by the success of these productions to unashamed imitation. The first successful American-written operetta—Willard Spencer's *The Little Tycoon* in 1886—would not have been written if *The Mikado* had not been so successful in America before then; the same holds true for *Wang*, in 1891. The Austrian and German models were uppermost in their minds when Reginald de Koven wrote *Robin Hood*, and after that Victor Herbert, Friml and Romberg wrote those operettas which brightened the corners of the American theatre for several decades beginning with 1894.

Yet all the while that the European influence on the American musical theatre was pronounced and inescapable, tentative efforts were being made to achieve a musical entertainment basically American in style, spirit and format. The minstrel show, first crystallised in 1843, represented such an attempt through the exploitation of the humour, dance and song of the American Negro. But the minstrel show had no plot, characterisations or settings. The first American musical to do so, and at the same time concentrate on American experiences, was *The Brook* in 1879, book and lyrics by Nate Salesbury. The plot was slight, built around mishaps attending a number of Americans during a picnic; the humour was obvious; the songs were just adaptations of familiar tunes. But, all the same, *The Brook* was a pioneer effort to achieve some measure of unity among plot, dialogue and characters within an essentially American play.

A pronounced American personality was introduced into the burlesque-extravaganzas produced and written by Ed Harrigan and Tony Hart (who were also the stars), known as the "Mulligan Guard" series. The format was the European burlesque and extravaganza, but the material was completely American. These Mulligan farces presented a caricature of life in New York with such racial or national groups as the Irish, Germans and Negroes. Their individual speech patterns, behaviour and mannerisms contributed to these plays most of their merriment. These city types were placed within such everyday situations as a picnic, a ball, a chowder, a silver-wedding celebration, an election. Songs by David Braham added to the local flavour. These Harrigan and Hart burlesques first became successful in 1879 with the *Mulligan Guard's Ball* and dominated the New York stage until the partnership of Harrigan and Hart broke up in 1885.

The American musical comedy, however, did not emerge with its familiar panoply until after the turn of the twentieth century. Its parent was George M. Cohan—librettist, lyricist, composer. Ingenuous though were Cohan's methods and techniques, naïve though much of his material was, he was nevertheless a powerful influence in creating an indigenous musical production. Not only were the settings and characters of Cohan's musicals thoroughly American, but his dialogue, lyrics and melody were colloquial and native. The spirit of brashness, cocksureness, energy and chauvinism that pervaded the Cohan musicals were unmistakably American. Cohan also established some of the procedures henceforth governing musical-comedy writing. Any plot, however far-fetched and improbable, was serviceable just so long as it could be the frame for songs, dances, routines and humorous episodes. Not the play was the thing, but the elements within the play. And for many years American musical comedy was governed by this principle.

In those years a musical comedy rarely came into being because a text was found lending itself for musical treatment. The more usual practice was for a producer to have a star, or a group of stars, under contract and then concoct some kind of a play which would highlight the special gifts of performer or performers. The important thing in musical comedy was the kind of business that was assigned to the stars, and it did not matter at all if much of this business was irrelevant to the story. A pattern was evolved which for a long time was adhered to inflexibly, beginning with the rise of the curtain on a line or two of fetching chorus girls chanting an opening number; mammoth production sequences had to end each of the acts. The girl always captured the boy, and the villain always met his just due. Within such a rigid formula, however, some creative figures were able to bring some distinction and personality of style: composers like Friml, Romberg, Herbert and Jerome Kern; lyricists and librettists like P. G. Wodehouse, Guy Bolton, Otto Harbach and Oscar Hammerstein II; performances by stars like Anna Held, Marilyn Miller, Vernon and Irene Castle and many others.

From time to time efforts were made to break loose from the bonds of rigid formula. In the 1920s the Princess Theatre Shows—texts by Guy Bolton, lyrics by P. G. Wodehouse and music by Jerome Kern—represented for the times a radical departure from the kind of musicals then popular on Broadway. The Princess Theatre Shows dispensed with a large apparatus to concentrate on intimate and informal entertainment with small casts and no stars. In place of production numbers, humorous skits and chorus-girl lines, these musicals concentrated on sophistication, witty dialogue, amusing incidents that rose naturally from the context of the play, charming music and a distinctly American personality of plot and characters.

The tendency away from routine was followed with even greater courage in the 1920s by Rodgers and Hart, with Herbert Fields as their librettist. Material long considered tabu in musical comedy was tapped by these inventive and courageous writers: dream psychology, American history, American literature. These men had no hesitancy in abandoning long-accepted procedures of musical comedy when their texts demanded this; and there was always a willingness on their part to endow their writing with a breadth and scope not often encountered in the musical theatre of that day. Rodgers and Hart lifted musical comedy out of the nursery and carried it to adult maturity.

The greatest revolution in the American musical theatre up to that time came in 1927 with *Show Boat*, by Oscar Hammerstein II and Jerome Kern. Here we come to a completely new *genre*—the musical play as distinguished from musical comedy. Now, at long last, the play was the thing, and everything else was subservient to that play. Now, at last, came complete integration of song, humour and production numbers into a single and inextricable artistic entity. Here, finally, was a musical with a consistent and credible story line, authentic atmosphere and three-dimensional characters.

The musical play made further forward strides with *Of Thee I Sing!*, the brilliant political satire by George S. Kaufman, Morrie Ryskind and Ira and George Gershwin; with two more musicals by Jerome Kern, *Cat and the Fiddle* and *Music in the Air*; with several more musicals by Rodgers and Hart, most notably *On Your Toes* and *Pal Joey*; and most of all with the first of the Rodgers and Hammerstein masterworks, *Oklahoma!*, with which the musical play finally became a significant American art form.

After *Oklahoma!*, Rodgers and Hammerstein were the most important contributors to the musical-play form—with such masterworks as *Carousel*, *The King and I* and *South Pacific*. The examples they set in creating vital plays, often rich with social thought, provided the necessary encouragement for other gifted writers to create musical plays of their own, men like Lerner and Loewe, Frank Loesser and Leonard Bernstein among others.

But while the musical play was thus being solidly established as a basic form of the American musical theatre, the musical comedy had not fallen by the wayside. On the contrary—through the years musical comedy, dedicated to escapism and entertainment, grew increasingly sophisticated, subtle, imaginative even while pursuing long-established patterns of behaviour. With musical comedies like *Guys and Dolls*, *Wonderful Town*, *The Pajama Game* and *How to Succeed in Business Without Really Trying*, musical comedy became entertainment *in excelsis*, drawing to itself the best talent the American theatre has to offer in every department.

The musical play and musical comedy are today the two major branches of the American musical theatre. Each is a thriving institution, artistically and commercially, because each has its own place and purpose, and each continues year by year to give promise of a still richer and more eventful future.

Robin Hood

Book and Lyrics by HARRY B. SMITH

Music by REGINALD DE KOVEN

First produced at the Chicago Opera House, Chicago, on 9th June, 1890, with Edwin Hoff as "Robin Hood", Eugene Cowles as "Will Scarlet" and Jessie Bartlett Davis as "Alan-a-Dale".

PRINCIPAL CHARACTERS

ROBIN HOOD
MAID MARIAN
THE SHERIFF OF NOTTINGHAM
LITTLE JOHN
WILL SCARLET
FRIAR TUCK
GUY OF GISBORNE
ALAN-A-DALE

This operetta is based on the legendary exploits of Robin Hood, who, during the reign of Richard the First, was despoiled of his lands and earldom, to become a notorious outlaw. The town of Nottingham is celebrating May Day ("'Tis the Morning of the Fair"). The arrival of Robin Hood and his men is greeted with joy, for to these villagers Robin Hood is a hero. But to the Sheriff of Nottingham he is both an outlaw and an arch-enemy. The Sheriff is planning a marriage between his ward, Guy of Gisborne, and lovely Maid Marian. But as soon as Robin Hood espies her he falls in love and is determined to thwart the Sheriff's designs. It is not long before Marian is also strongly attracted to Robin Hood, and before they express their sentiments to each other in a tender duet, "Though It Was Within This Hour We Met". The Sheriff now comes upon the scene ("I Am the Sheriff of Nottingham"). Robin Hood confronts him with the demand that his confiscated lands and lost title be restored to him. The Sheriff turns Robin Hood down, and Robin Hood expresses his determination to pursue the life of an outlaw ("An Outlaw's Life, the Life for Me").

In Sherwood Forest Robin Hood and his men sing lustily of the good outdoor life ("Oh, Cheerily Soundeth the Hunter's Horn"). Will Scarlet amuses them with a light ditty ("The Tailor and the Crow"), and Little John with a vigorous drinking song ("Brown October Ale"). Maid Marian has come into the forest to seek out Robin Hood, determined never to leave his side ("Forest Song"). Robin Hood responds with no less ardour ("A Troubadour Sang to his Love"). But this idyll is soon interrupted by the precipitous arrival of the Sheriff and his men, who capture some of Robin Hood's followers. But Robin Hood manages to escape.

Marian is now compelled by the Sheriff to marry Guy. At the wedding ceremonies Alan-a-Dale sings a hymn to eternal love "Oh, Promise Me". But the wedding is never consummated. Robin Hood breaks in to save and claim Marian. He is no longer an outlaw. Having received royal pardon from King Richard, he is once again an earl and a member of the landed gentry.

Robin Hood is not only De Koven's most famous of his twenty or so operettas. It is also the most important American operetta preceding Victor Herbert, and the only one of the pre-Herbert era that is still occasionally revived in the United States. Whatever interest this work may have for a contemporary audience arises solely from a single song, "Oh, Promise Me", a number with which its composer is most often identified, and which is today often sung at American weddings.

In view of the uncommon success and popularity of this song, it is interesting to remark that it was not originally written for *Robin Hood.* De Koven, and the lyricist Clement Scott, had written it some years earlier and issued it as a separate publication. During the rehearsals of *Robin Hood*, the need was felt for a third-act sentimental song. De Koven suggested using "Oh, Promise Me", but Jessie Bartlett Davis, who played Alan-a-Dale—and for whom the sentimental number was required—rejected it vigorously. But she could not forget the melody once having heard it. One day in her dressing-room she hummed it to herself—but an octave lower than written. The producer happened to overhear her and convinced her that "if you ever sing that song as you're singing it now on the low octave, it will make your reputation". "Oh, Promise Me" carried Jessie Bartlett Davis to one of the greatest triumphs of her career besides assuring a degree of permanence to *Robin Hood.*

El Capitan

Book by Charles Klein

Lyrics by Tom Frost *and* John Philip Sousa

Music by John Philip Sousa

Staged by H. A. Crips

First produced at the Broadway Theatre on 20th April, 1896, with De Wolf Hopper as "Don Errico" and Edna Wallace Hopper as "Estrelida".

Principal Characters

DON ERRICO MEDIGUA
POZZO
ESTRELIDA

The play is set in sixteenth-century Peru. Don Errico Medigua is a weak Viceroy who is compelled to allow his Chamberlain, Pozzo, to transact all the State business. An insurgent movement has threatened to overthrow the Viceroy; its leader, the redoubtable El Capitan, is dead, though nobody but the Viceroy is aware of this fact. The Viceroy decides to assume the identity of El Capitan, enter the camp of the conspirators and take over as their leader in the insurrection against himself. As El Capitan he meets and falls in love with Estrelida. After he manages to engineer the collapse of the revolt and reveals himself as the Viceroy he must give up Estrelida, since he is already married. Estrelida returns to the soldier she had loved before El Capitan had come into her life.

The principal musical number appears in the second act, a stirring male chorus, "Behold, El Capitan!", which Sousa subsequently adapted into *El Capitan*, one of his famous marches. The first act boasts an eloquent paean to Peru in "From Peru's Majestic Mountains", while the musical highlights of the third act include a beautiful duet, "Sweetheart I'm Waiting" and a lively topical song, "A Typical Tune of Zanzibar".

It may come as a surprise to many that Sousa, who achieved world fame as a "march king", should also have been a composer of operettas. Actually, his first operetta—*The Smugglers* in 1879—antedated his first march by several years. Sousa wrote about a dozen operettas between 1879 and *Victory* in 1915, but only *El Capitan* is remembered, if only for its brilliant second-act chorus, "Behold, El Capitan!".

The Belle of New York

Book and Lyrics by HUGH MORTON
Music by GUSTAVE KERKER
Staged by GEORGE W. LEDERER

First produced at the Casino Theatre on 28th September, 1897, with Edna May as "Violet Gray" and Harry Davenport as "Harry Bronson".

PRINCIPAL CHARACTERS

VIOLET GRAY
HARRY BRONSON

The action takes place in New York in the late 1890s. Harry Bronson, son of the President of the crusading Young Men's Rescue League, is a playboy whose morals leave much to be desired. His father—a staunch public foe of vice—is at his wit's end on how to keep his son from getting continually embroiled in escapades of all kinds. During one of his rounds about town, Harry comes upon a demure and highly attractive Salvation lass, Violet Gray. She is not unaware of her charms, as she openly confesses in her opening number, "They All Follow Me", and later on, in the production's big hit song, "I'm the Belle of New York". She works her charms upon Harry, wins him over completely and effects his complete reform, much to the delight of Harry's father.

Besides Violet's two hit songs, the score includes three other attractive numbers: "When I Was Born the Stars Stood Still", "Teach Me How to Kiss" and "The Purity Brigade".

Edna May, in the role of Violet, became an overnight sensation in New York when, the evening after the première performance, she was suddenly called in to substitute for the ailing star of the show. She brought down the house; the role remained hers even after the star, originally cast for the part, had returned to full health. In London—where *The Belle of New York* amassed the impressive run of 697 performances at the Shaftesbury Theatre—Edna May became the toast of the town.

The Fortune Teller

Book and Lyrics by HARRY B. SMITH
Music by VICTOR HERBERT
Staged by JULIAN MITCHELL

First produced at the Grand Opera House, Toronto, Canada, on 14th September, 1898, with Alice Neilsen in the dual part of "Irma and Musette", Eugene Cowles as "Sandor", Joseph Herbert as "Count Berezowski" and Frank Rushworth as "Captain Ladislas".

PRINCIPAL CHARACTERS

MUSETTE
IRMA
COUNT BEREZOWSKI
SANDOR
CAPTAIN LADISLAS

Irma, a ballet-student at the Budapest Opera, pursues her career diligently without being aware that she is a lost heiress. Her innocence as well as charm are revealed in her song, "Always Be As People Say You Should". Count Berezowski, an impoverished Polish nobleman-musician, has learned of Irma's inheritance and plans to win her as wife so that he might gain possession of the fortune. Irma, however, is in love with the dashing Hungarian hussar, Captain Ladislas, who now makes his entrance in the company of some of his fellow soldiers ("Hungary's Hussars!"). When Irma realises she cannot elude the persistent Count she devises a plan to thwart him. Musette, a gipsy fortune-teller, bears a striking resemblance to her, as becomes self-evident as soon as she makes an appearance with her gipsy friends ("Romany Life" and "Czardas"). What Irma has contrived behind the scenes was to have Musette take her place.

Musette and her gipsies come to the Count's estate, where the Count becomes convinced that she is Irma in disguise. He claims her as his bride and orders that the wedding take place without delay. But Sandor, a gipsy musician, intervenes, insisting that Musette is his betrothed. Indeed, he forthwith expresses his love for the fortune teller in a passionate serenade, "Gypsy Love Song". To complicate matters still further, Irma arrives to take over for Musette. By now everybody is confused as to who is Irma and who Musette, even Captain Ladislas ("Speak, Irma, I Implore You"). But once the Count's real motives for marriage are uncovered and his matrimonial plans are shattered, each of the girl's true identities can be disclosed, and each can return to the arms of the man she loves.

Victor Herbert, America's first significant composer for the stage and one of its foremost composers of operettas, made his operetta bow with *Prince Ananias* in 1894, which passed unnoticed. His first minor successes came in 1895, with *The Wizard of the Nile*, and in 1897, with *The Serenade*. His first masterwork was *The Fortune Teller* in 1898.

The Fortune Teller was written for Alice Neilsen, a Herbert discovery who had become a star in *The Serenade*. In the dual character of Irma and Musette—tailor-made for her special vocal and histrionic gifts, as well as for her piquant personality—Alice Neilsen soared to still greater heights of popularity in the American musical theatre.

One of the most impressive things about this Herbert score is the way in which this Irish-born, German-trained American composer succeeded in writing Hungarian-gipsy music with authentic dash. Unquestionably, the best musical excerpts are those in which the Hungarian-gipsy element is most pronounced.

Babes in Toyland

Book and Lyrics by GLEN MACDONOUGH
Music by VICTOR HERBERT
Staged by JULIAN MITCHELL

First produced at the Grand Opera House, Chicago, on 17th June, 1903, with William Norris as "Alan", Mabel Barrison as "Jane", George W. Denham as "Uncle Barnaby" and Bessie Wynn as "Tom Tom".

PRINCIPAL CHARACTERS

ALAN
JANE
UNCLE BARNABY
THE WIDOW PIPER
CONTRARY MARY
TOM TOM
JILL
BO-PEEP
RED RIDING HOOD
CURLY LOCKS
MISS MUFFET
SIMPLE SIMON
PETER
TOMMY TUCKER
BOY BLUE
THE MASTER TOYMAKER

On 21st January, 1903, there was produced on Broadway *The Wizard of Oz*, a musical fantasy for children. In *Babes in Toyland*, Victor Herbert and his librettist made a studied attempt to write another *The Wizard of Oz* and capitalise on its giant success. Thus they hit on the happy idea of using Toyland as a setting. Though imitations are usually faded carbon copies of the original, soon forgotten, *Babes in Toyland* turned out to be a triumph in its own right, and a childhood classic in the company of *Peter Pan*.

Since it was planned as a huge spectacle with a formidable cast and lavish sets and scenes, the authors of *Babes in Toyland* were not overly concerned with their story. Loosely constructed and, indeed, often confused—with numerous scenes that often have no relevance within the story—the plot serves primarily as an excuse to present characters from fairy tales, children's story books and nursery rhymes in spectacular style; also to piece together a rich and varied succession of musical episodes and interludes.

The play opens with a prologue outside Uncle Barnaby's house. He is a miserly old man who has seized Mother Hubbard's cottage because she has failed to pay her mortgage. He is also cruel to his nephew, Alan, and niece, Jane, who live with him. Within the house, the children are lulled to sleep to the strains of a poignant lullaby ("Go to Sleep"). Later on, Jane and the children are heard singing "I Can't Do the Sum", as they tap their pieces of chalk on their slates to accentuate the rhythm. The story line is advanced when Alan and Jane, threatened by Uncle Barnaby with murder, escape from his house. They survive a storm at sea and a shipwreck, and finally come to the garden of Contrary Mary. There they witness a Butterfly Ballet and come into contact with characters from Mother Goose. After that they visit Toyland, a country dominated by the despot Toymaker. Before the bewildered eyes of Alan and Jane an elaborate Christmas presentation unfolds ("Christmas Tree Grove") and after that a spectacular pageant ("The Legend of the Castle"). With a strange incantation, Toymaker brings his toys to life ("March of the Toys"). They sing a hymn to Toyland ("Toyland"), then band together to kill Toymaker.

The scene shifts to the Palace of Justice in Toyland. Alan is falsely accused of having murdered the Toymaker and, being found guilty, must die by hanging. But at zero hour his innocence is proved. With Jane he now returns home. Uncle Barnaby plots to poison them, but comes to his own doom instead by drinking the poison accidentally. The children are now free to live in peace and enjoy their life for ever more.

The impact *Babes in Toyland* had upon the mature as well as the very young in 1903 is perhaps best revealed by the reaction of one of America's most trenchant music and drama critics, James Gibbons Huneker. He wrote in the *Sun*: "The songs, the dances, the processions, the fairies, the toys, the spiders, and the bears! Think of them all, set in the midst of really amazing scenery, ingenious and brilliant, surrounded with light effects with counterfeit all sorts of things from simple lightning to the spinning of a great spider's web, with costumes rich and dazzling as well as tasteful, and all accompanied with music a hundred times better than is customary in shows of this sort. What more could the spirit of mortal desire?"

Mlle Modiste

Books and Lyrics by HENRY BLOSSOM
Music by VICTOR HERBERT
Staged by FRED G. LATHAM

First produced at the Taylor Opera House, Trenton, New Jersey, 7th October, 1905, with Fritzi Scheff as "Fifi", Walter Percival as "Captain Étienne de Bouvray" and William Pruette as "Count Henri de Bouvray".

PRINCIPAL CHARACTERS

COUNT HENRI DE BOUVRAY
CAPTAIN ÉTIENNE DE BOUVRAY
HIRAM BENT
MME CÉCILE
FIFI

Fifi is a modiste employed by Mme Cécile in a Parisian millinery shop. She harbours the ambition of becoming a great singer. But she also wants to marry the dashing young officer and nobleman, Captain Étienne de Bouvray. The young Captain laments his incapacity to find the right girl, the right place and the right time all together at the same time ("The Time and the Place and the Girl"). But in his heart he knows at least where one of these elements lie—the girl is Fifi. But Fifi appears to be thwarted in both her ambitions. Her marriage to Étienne has been vigorously vetoed by his father, the Count, who wants his son to choose someone from his own social sphere. Besides, her proprietress, Mme Cécile, insists she marry her own son, Gaston, and for Fifi to flout these wishes would mean losing her job. And as for her future as a singer, she does not have the money to develop her career. Nevertheless, she is confident of her talent. She demonstrates her versatility by performing "If I Were On the Stage", an extended routine in which she parodies different song styles: as a country maid she sings a gavotte, as a high-born French lady a polonaise, and so forth. The climax of this number comes with a waltz, "Kiss Me Again", undoubtedly the musical *tour de force* of the entire operetta.

Fifi, however, soon succeeds in interesting Hiram Bent, an American millionaire, to finance her vocal studies. After a year, under the name of Mme Bellini, she goes on to become a celebrated prima donna. As Mme Bellini she is invited to perform at a party given by Count de Bouvray at his estate in St. Mar. That the Count is a crotchety old man is proved by his song, "I Want What I Want When I Want It". When Fifi arrives at his estate in the company of several French officers ("The Mascot of the Troop") the Count recognises her and orders her to leave. Her patron, Hiram Bent, who is also a guest at the party, not only manages to smuggle her back into the house but also to have her appear on the concert programme with the waltz, "The Nightingale and the Star". Her voice wins over the Count so completely that he is now willing to permit his nephew, Étienne, to marry her.

Victor Herbert wrote *Mlle Modiste* for Fritzi Scheff, an opera singer whom he had encouraged to leave the Metropolitan Opera in 1903 to star in his operetta, *Babette*. *Babette* had been a dismal failure. Herbert promised to make amends by writing a new operetta for Fritzi Scheff in which she could shine. As Fifi, Fritzi Scheff proved a sensation, setting into motion a new career in the popular musical theatre even more lustrous than that she had previously enjoyed in opera.

Her rendition of "Kiss Me Again" was, of course, the big moment of the whole operetta. "Kiss Me Again" had not actually been originally intended for *Mlle Modiste*. Herbert wrote the waltz in 1903. Unable to find a place for it, he put it aside. When Fifi's routine, "If I Were on the Stage", called for the parody of a waltz, Herbert remembered "Kiss Me Again" and decided to use it. But on opening night "Kiss Me Again" stopped the show. Herbert wisely decided to revamp his melody from a parody into a dreamy, sentimental melody, and to use it as the operetta's principal love song.

The Red Mill

Book and Lyrics by HENRY BLOSSOM
Music by VICTOR HERBERT
Staged by FRED G. LATHAM

First produced at the Star Theatre, Buffalo, N.Y., on 3rd September, 1906, with Fred Stone as "Con Kidder", David Montgomery as "Kid Conner" and Augusta Greenleaf as "Gretchen".

PRINCIPAL CHARACTERS

CON KIDDER
KID CONNER
JAN VAN BORKEM
WILLEM
CAPTAIN DORIS VAN DAMM
GOVERNOR OF ZEELAND
GRETCHEN

The impact on Victor Herbert of the successful extravaganza, *The Wizard of Oz* in 1903 apparently was profound. Herbert first paid it the flattery of imitation by writing *Babes in Toyland* in 1905. And one year after that he wrote another operetta, *The Red Mill*, in order to set off the comic gifts of Fred Stone and David Montgomery, who had been the stars in *The Wizard of Oz*. In *The Red Mill*, Stone and Montgomery were cast as two Americans, Con Kidder and Kid Conner, stranded penniless in the inn, "The Sign of the Red Mill", in the little Dutch port town of Katwyk-aan-Zee. Unable to pay their bill, these two Americans try to sneak through a window out of the inn, but are caught by Jan Van Borkem, the town Burgomaster, and put in gaol. Willem, the Innkeeper, takes pity on them and offers to let each work off his debt by working for him — Con as an interpreter and Kid as a waiter. Both the Innkeeper and the Burgomaster have problems with their respective daughters, since neither girl is interested in the man selected for her ("You Never Can Tell About a Woman"). Gretchen, the daughter of the Burgomaster, for example, is in love with Captain

Doris Van Damm, but the man her father wants her to marry is the Governor of Zeeland. Gretchen and Doris, in exchanging tender sentiments, plot to flee to some distant isle where they can be together for evermore ("The Isle of Our Dreams"). But the plot of the lovers is overheard by Willem, who passes on the information to the Burgomaster. Gretchen is locked up in the mill for safe-keeping, where she finds enough time to pine away for her loved one and to lose herself in romantic dreams ("Moonbeams"). Con Kidder and Kid Conner come to her rescue. They help her through a window in the mill and lead her to safety on a revolving arm of the windmill.

Wedding preparations for the marriage of Gretchen and the Governor enter high gear in the great hall of the Burgomaster's house. The Governor is anticipating his imminent marriage with lovely Gretchen with considerable relish ("Every Day is Lady's Day With Me"). But, to the consternation of all, the wedding is without a bride, Gretchen having fled. Further attempts are now made by Con and Kid to break up the ceremony by intermittent appearances in various disguises—now as an Italian organ grinder ("Good-a-bye, John"); now as Sherlock Holmes and Dr. Watson. Then the wedding guests are startled with the news that Captain Doris is the heir to an immense fortune. The resistance of the Burgomaster collapses, to the delight of the lovers, who can now marry each other, and of their two American friends, who can now go home ("In Old New York").

Naughty Marietta

Book and Lyrics by RIDA JOHNSON
Music by VICTOR HERBERT
Directed by JACQUES COINI

First produced in Syracuse, New York, on 24th October, 1910, with Emma Trentini as "Marietta" and Orville Harrold as "Captain Richard Warrington".

PRINCIPAL CHARACTERS

ÉTIENNE GRANDET
LIEUTENANT GOVERNOR GRANDET
MARIETTA D'ALTENA
ADAH
CAPTAIN RICHARD WARRINGTON (CAPTAIN DICK)

The curtain rises on Place d'Armes, a square in New Orleans of 1780. Captain Richard Warrington, known as Captain Dick, has come to the city with his men to capture Bras-Pique, a notorious pirate ("Tramp, Tramp, Tramp"). There he meets and becomes a friend of lovely Marietta d'Altena, but he is convinced his interest in her is solely platonic. Marietta had left Naples to avoid an undesirable marriage and joined up with a group of French casquette girls, sent to New Orleans by the King of France to marry Louisiana planters. In her first principal song, Marietta reveals herself to be a mischievous, fun-loving girl who can at turns be very good and very bad ("Naughty Marietta"). Adah now comes on the scene. She is the quadroon slave of Étienne Grandet, son of the Lieutenant Governor. Deeply in love with Étienne, she reveals in a sombre song that she knows her love can never find fulfilment ("'Neath the Southern Moon"). Now Marietta nostalgically recalls her home in Naples ("Italian Street Song").

A monster ball is taking place at the Jeunesse Dorée Club, to which the entire town has come. Étienne is now convinced he loves Marietta and wants to marry her. He decides to get rid of his quadroon slave and auctions her off. Captain Dick gives the highest price, but only to give Adah her freedom. Mistaking

Captain Dick's motives in buying Adah, Marietta is determined to avenge herself on Dick by agreeing to marry Étienne. Meanwhile Captain Dick has come to the full realisation that his one-time friendship has blossomed into love ("I'm Falling in Love With Someone"). Thus he is determined to stop the marriage of Étienne and Marietta. Adah helps him out by revealing that Étienne is really the pirate Bras Pique. Since the Lieutenant Governor refuses to arrest his own son, Étienne makes his escape. Now Captain Dick protests to Marietta how much he really loves her ("Ah, Sweet Mystery of Life"), while Marietta confesses in return that she has loved him all the time.

Sweetheart

Book by Harry B. Smith *and* Fred de Gresac
Lyrics by Robert B. Smith
Music by Victor Herbert
Staged by Fred G. Latham

First produced at the Academy of Music, Baltimore, Maryland, on 24th March, 1913, with Christine MacDonald as "Sylvia", and Thomas Conkey as "Prince Franz".

Principal Characters

SYLVIA
DAME PAULA
PRINCE FRANZ
LIEUTENANT KARL

The programme took special pains to explain that though *Sweethearts* was a "romantic opera" it was based on historic fact. "The story of the opera," says the programme, "is founded on the adventures of Princess Jeanne, daughter of King René of Naples, who reigned in the 15th century. Time has been changed to the present, the locale to the ancient city of Bruges, to which the little princess is carried for safety in time of war and is given the name of Sylvia."

Dame Paula, proprietress of a laundry in Bruges, comes upon an abandoned infant girl. Though her house is full of daughters of her own, she adopts the foundling, names her Sylvia, and raises her. She becomes an extremely attractive and gracious young lady, ripe for romance ("Sweethearts"). Prince Franz of Zilania, travelling incognito, comes upon her and instantly falls in love with her. Franz is about to ascend the throne of Zilania. He does not know that Sylvia in reality is the long-lost crown princess who has first rights to rule that kingdom. After Sylvia and Franz meet, she is reluctant to give him her hand and heart, since she is interested in Lieutenant Karl. After Prince Franz comes upon her at prayer ("The Angelus") he tells her of his love. Slowly, inevitably he wins her over.

After spending a year in a convent, Sylvia comes to Zilania as the fiancée of Prince Franz. The people are awaiting her eagerly ("Waiting for the Bride"). When she arrives, Sylvia explains that convent life had not been too dismal ("In the Convent They Never Taught Me That"). Sylvia is finally identified as the lost princess, but she is only too happy to yield the throne to her future husband.

While *Sweethearts* does not contain that normal quota of outstanding songs that are encountered in other famous Victor Herbert operettas, it is one of the composer's most ambitious scores, and the one that leans closest to opera. The entr'acte between the two acts, built from first-act material, has symphonic breadth; and the extended second-act finale—constructed from recitatives, choral episodes and orchestral interludes—has the structural spaciousness as well as the richness of material that we associate with grand opera. As a distinguished music critic, Herbert F. Peyser, wrote when *Sweethearts* was introduced: "From first to last this music is utterly free from any suggestions of triviality. The abundant melodic flow is invariably marked by distinction, individuality, and a quality of superlative charm. The scoring, exquisite in its piquancy, finesse and deftness, fairly glows in its varied colors. Only a specialist, however, can appreciate to the fullest the very subtle touches of beauty and humor with which Mr. Herbert's instrumentation is replete."

Eileen

Book and Lyrics by Henry Blossom
Music by Victor Herbert
Staged by Fred G. Latham

First produced at the Colonial Theatre, Cleveland, Ohio, on 1st January, 1917, with Grace Breen as "Eileen" and Walter Scanlan as "Captain Barry O'Day".

Principal Characters

CAPTAIN BARRY O'DAY
COLONEL LESTER
LADY MAUDE ESTABROOKE
EILEEN MULVANEY

The action takes place on the west coast of Ireland during the Rebellion of 1798. Captain Barry O'Day returns from France to help his stricken countrymen and to set the stage for French assistance ("When Shall I Again See Ireland?"). When Colonel Lester, an Englishman, learns of O'Day's return he places a price on his head. But O'Day finds a powerful friend in Lady Maude Estabrooke, and a sweetheart in her lovely niece, Eileen.

At her castle, Lady Maude prevails on her niece to sing a French pavane. Eileen complies with "Too-re-loo-re". As a visitor to the castle, O'Day muses over Eileen's beauty and the depth of his feelings for her ("Eileen"). Later the same evening, while strolling in the castle gardens, he comes upon her. They now give voice to their mutual love in the operetta's principal song and one of Herbert's most radiant and most successful melodies, "Thine Alone".

Colonel Lester comes to the castle, finds O'Day there and arrests him. He informs the young Irish rebel that the French fleet had been routed before it could land on Irish soil, and that the chief Irish rebel leader had been seized and imprisoned. When things seem blackest for O'Day the news comes from Dublin that a new government there has granted amnesty to all rebels. Eileen and O'Day are now at liberty to pursue their romance without outside interference. And the Irish rebels raise their voices in a hymn in which they face the future with optimism and hope ("When Ireland Stands Among the Nations of the World").

The libretto of *Eileen* is one of the strongest and most credible of those used by Herbert, and his score is one of his best. He had expended more time and care upon this music than upon any other for the popular theatre; he was continually making alterations; he was more fastidious than heretofore about details of orchestrations and harmonization. Being Irish himself, he responded sensitively to his text by writing many melodies with a delightful Irish brogue. He gave his orchestra greater freedom than ever to emphasise the dramatic scenes, and wrote for it with uncommon skill. And as in the earlier *Sweethearts*, he frequently brought operatic dimension to his writing: in the extended first-act finale, in which chorus, orchestra and individual voices are used with extraordinary effect; in the polyphonic texture of the round which opens the second act; in the extended atmospheric passage preceding the third act. Convinced as he was that here was some of the best music of his career, Herbert was heartbroken that *Eileen* never enjoyed the success he felt it deserved. And this is a sorrow that he carried deep in his heart for the rest of his life.

The Wizard of Oz

Book and Lyrics by L. Frank Baum *adapted from Baum's novel*
Music by A. Baldwin Sloane *and* Paul Tiejens
Staged by Julian Mitchell

First produced at the Majestic Theatre on 21st January, 1903, with Fred Stone as "Scarecrow" and David Montgomery as "Tim Woodman".

Principal Characters

DOROTHY DALE
WITCH OF OZ
SCARECROW
TIM WOODMAN
WIZARD OF OZ

The Wizard of Oz, one of the most successful American extravaganzas of the early twentieth century, has become a stage classic for children old and young. It is repeatedly revived; it has been made into an outstanding motion picture; more recently it received a bountiful production over television in the United States. Made up of a train of eye-filling stage pictures, production numbers and stage effects—and calling for the fullest resources and imagination of the art of scenic designer and costumer—*The Wizard of Oz* never fails to create an impact. There is about it the magic and the wonder of a child's world of fantasy.

A cyclone lifts little Dorothy Dale and her pet cow, Imogene, from their farm in Kansas to Oz, a fairy garden. When the Kansas farmhouse crashes from the sky it kills the cruel witch who for so many years has ruled so despotically over the Munchkins—inhabitants of Oz. The Munchkins are now free. In gratitude the good witch of Oz presents Dorothy with a ring which has the power to grant two wishes. To test the ring, Dorothy wastes her first wish on a trifle. But she has saved her second wish to bring Scarecrow back to life. The latter complains that he has lost his brains, that the only person able to restore them to him is the Wizard of Oz. And so, Dorothy and the Scarecrow go off in search of the Wizard. On the way they meet and are joined by Tim Woodman.

Tim is on the hunt for his heart, which was lost when he fell in love with Cynthia. The three go through various episodes and adventures, but in the end they *do* manage to find the Wizard. Thus Scarecrow gets back his brains, and Tim his heart—much to the delight of little Dorothy.

The musical score was shared by Sloane and Tiejens. Among the best songs contributed by Sloane were "Niccolo's Piccolo" and "The Medley of Nations", while the best of Tiejens included "When You Love, Love, Love" and "I've Waited for you in Loveland". During the long initial Broadway run, and on its subsequent nation-wide tour, various songs by other composers were interpolated from time to time. Two of these became major successes—indeed, they are the leading song hits of the entire show: "Sammy" by James O'Dea and Edward Hutchinson, and "Hurrah for Baffin's Bay" by Vincent Bryan and Charles Zimmerman.

Mention should be made that when the excellent motion-picture adaptation was filmed, starring Judy Garland, and released in 1939, none of the songs from the original stage score were used. Harold Arlen wrote a completely new score that included "Over the Rainbow", which won the Academy Award as the best song to come from the screen that season, and which from then on served as Judy Garland's theme song.

The Prince of Pilsen

Book and Lyrics by FRANK PIXLEY

Music by GUSTAV LUDERS

Staged by GEORGE W. MARION

First produced at the Broadway Theatre on 17th March, 1903, with John W. Ransome as "Hans", Lillian Coleman as "Nellie", and Albert Paar as "Tom".

PRINCIPAL CHARACTERS

HANS WAGNER
NELLIE WAGNER
TOM WAGNER
PRINCE KARL OTTO
MRS. MADISON CROCKER

Hans Wagner, a wealthy brewer from Cincinnati, has come to Europe with his daughter Nellie to visit his son, Tom, an American sailor stationed near Nice, France. When Hans comes to Nice's luxury hotel he is mistaken for Prince Karl Otto, who is also being expected at the time. The more Hans protests that he is not the Prince, the more the belief gains credence that he is, indeed, royalty travelling incognito. Forthwith, Hans is showered with attention and favours and is invited to the leading receptions on the Riviera. He is enjoying himself thoroughly, and for that matter so does the Prince, who finds his sudden obscurity highly delightful, since it permits him to flirt with Nellie without interference. Hans, too, has found romance, in the form of Mrs. Madison Crocker, a rich American widow. All, then, goes well with the principals until Hans happens to come into the possession of a map of secret fortifications. When it is found on his person he is forthwith accused of being a spy. This unforeseen development compels the Prince to step out of his anonymity to identify himself and to clear Hans. It also gives him an opportunity to reveal that since he and Nellie have fallen in love they have decided to get married.

The Prince of Pilsen was one of the most successful American operettas produced between 1900 and 1910. For five consecutive seasons it played to capacity houses on the road; and after its initially successful run in New York it returned to Broadway three times in those five seasons. After that it was given numerous revivals both in and out of New York. Indeed, Jess Dandy—who inherited the role of Hans Wagner from John W. Ransome—appeared in this operetta over five thousand times.

The hit song of the operetta was "The Message of the Violet", a duet of Tom and his girl friend, Edith. Two stirring choruses ("The Heidelberg Stein Song" and "The Tale of the Seashell") and a duet of Prince Karl Otto and Nellie ("Pictures in the Smoke") were also musical highlights.

Little Johnny Jones

Book, Lyrics and Music by George M. Cohan
Staged by George M. Cohan

First produced at the Liberty Theatre on 7th November, 1904, with George M. Cohan as "Johnny" and Ethel Levey as "Goldie".

Principal Characters

JOHNNY JONES
ANTHONY ANSTEY
GOLDIE GATES
THE UNKNOWN

Johnny Jones is an American jockey come to London at the turn of the present century to ride in the Derby ("Yankee Doodle Dandy"). An American gambler, Anthony Anstey—who runs an illicit Chinese gambling combine in San Francisco—tries to bribe Johnny, and failing, becomes determined to destroy him. When Johnny actually loses the Derby Anthony spreads the word that Johnny had not run an honest race. An angry mob follows Johnny to Southampton, where he has come to bid his friends farewell before they sail back to America ("Give My Regards to Broadway"). Johnny is staying behind to prove his innocence. For this purpose he has hired a detective, The Unknown, to sail aboard the same ship upon which Anthony is going home. Johnny has prearranged a signal with The Unknown to send up fireworks if evidence is uncovered to clear him. As he stands at the pier watching the boat gliding into the distance, Johnny sees the fireworks leaping to the sky. Now having proved his honesty, Johnny can go home, win Goldie Gates, the girl he loves and uncover Anthony's nefarious dealings.

George M. Cohan was a one-man monopoly of the American musical theatre. He wrote his own texts, lyrics and music. He also usually appeared in the starring role, served as his own stage director, and even as a producer. *Little Johnny Jones* was his first successful musical comedy. Despite its clichés and ingenuousness in virtually every department, it marked a new day for the American musical theatre. It was an American-made product—in its brashness, breeziness, informality, exuberance and swift pace—a radical departure from the operettas and comic operas which, though written by Americans, were frank imitations of European models. Indeed, it is not too much to say that *Little Johnny Jones* is actually America's first musical comedy with the formats and routines by which musical comedy would be identified for the next two decades.

In *Little Johnny Jones*, Cohan also introduced some of those stage mannerisms which he made famous: dancing with a halting kangaroo step; singing out of the corner of his mouth with a peculiar nasal twang; strutting up and down the stage with a derby or straw hat cocked over one eye, and a bamboo cane in his hand; gesturing to the audience with a forceful forefinger; and introducing a sentimental sermon in verse, in this instance "Life's a Funny Proposition".

Forty-Five Minutes from Broadway

Book, Lyrics and Music by GEORGE M. COHAN

Staged by GEORGE M. COHAN

First produced at the New Amsterdam Theatre on 1st January, 1906, with Fay Templeton as "Mary Jane", Victor Moore as "Kid Burns" and Donald Brian as "Tom".

PRINCIPAL CHARACTERS

MARY JANE JENKINS
TOM BENNETT
FLORA DORA DEAN
MRS. DAVID DEAN
KID BURNS

The town that is "forty-five minutes from Broadway"—and the setting of this musical comedy—is the New York City suburb of New Rochelle. Its citizens are convinced that Mary Jane Jenkins is about to inherit the wealth of her recently-deceased employer whom she had served as a devoted housemaid. But since no will can be found, the fortune is legally bequeathed to the old man's only living relative, Tom Bennett. He comes to New Rochelle to claim the fortune. With him are his sweetheart, Flora Dora Dean, her nagging mother and his secretary, Kid Burns. Burns is a one-time gambler and horse player who is always getting into trouble with his bad manners and insulting candour. He succeeds in provoking a quarrel between Tom and his sweetheart. Meanwhile, Kid Burns falls in love with Mary Jane. He comes upon an old suit in one of whose pockets reposes the will that names Mary Jane. When Kid Burns refuses to marry her, now that she is an heiress while he is penniless, Mary Jane tears up the will rather than give up the man she has come to love.

The two principal songs were both inspired by the heroine: "Mary's a Grand Old Name" and "So Long Mary". Among the other numbers, the most important are the title song, "Stand Up and Fight Like H——", and "I Want to be a Popular Millionaire".

In *Forty-Five Minutes from Broadway* two musical comedy stars who would dominate the stage for the next quarter of a century made their Broadway bow: Fay Templeton and Victor Moore, both of them graduates from burlesque and vaudeville.

The Firefly

Book and Lyrics by OTTO HAUERBACH (HARBACH)
Music by RUDOLF FRIML
Staged by FRED G. LATHAM

First produced 2nd December, 1912.

PRINCIPAL CHARACTERS

NINA
JACK TRAVERS
MRS. VANDARE
PIETRO

The principal character is Nina, a little Italian street singer in New York. She meets and falls in love with the wealthy Jack Travers. When she learns that Jack is a guest on Mrs. Vandare's yacht bound for Bermuda with a group of society folk, Nina disguises herself as a boy, Tony. As "Tony" she ingratiates herself so completely with Mrs. Vandare, that the lady gives her permanent employment aboard the yacht. There "Tony" is falsely accused of being a notorious pickpocket sought by the police. After being cleared, and returning to her original identity as Nina, she is adopted by Pietro, Jack's valet. Nina now pursues her lifelong ambition to become a singer. She develops into a celebrated prima donna who is invited to perform at a gala party at Mrs. Vandare's house. Jack soon discovers this famous singer to be none other than Nina, alias Tony. He also becomes aware of the fact that he has been in love with this girl all his life, and asks her to be his wife.

Since *The Firefly* was written as a frame for the personality and voice of Emma Trentini, the prima donna who had scored so decisively in Victor Herbert's *Naughty Marietta* in 1910, the principal songs in the score are all assigned to her. These include "Giannina Mia" (Friml's studied attempt to write another "Italian Street Song", in the style of the one Herbert had written for Mme Trentini in *Naughty Marietta*), which makes an effective first-act finale; "Love Is Like a Firefly"; "The Dawn of Love"; and "When a Maid Comes Knocking at Your Heart". The only other important song is the duet "Sympathy" for two lesser characters.

There is still one more number associated with *The Firefly*: "Donkey Serenade", without which no revival of this operetta is now complete. This song was not in Friml's original stage score. He wrote it in 1937 in collaboration with Herbert Stothart for the motion-picture adaptation of *The Firefly*; the melody came from a piano piece, *Chansonette*, Friml had written many years earlier.

The Firefly was Friml's first operetta; indeed, it was his first assignment in the theatre of any manner, shape or form. Before *The Firefly*, Friml had written some pieces for the piano and some concert songs, which were highly regarded by his publisher, G. Schirmer, for their charm and personal lyricism. Friml had no ambitions in the popular musical theatre, but was content to remain a piano virtuoso, piano teacher and creator of modest concert music. Then the assignment to write the music for *The Firefly* fell into his lap and changed his destiny overnight.

What happened was that Victor Herbert had been contracted to write *The Firefly* for Mme Trentini as a follow-up to *Naughty Marietta*. During the run of *Naughty Marietta*, Herbert and Mme Trentini became embroiled in a bitter quarrel in which each refused to communicate with the other. Herbert now simply refused to write any more music for her, and she refused to appear in anything Herbert wrote. Since *The Firefly* was scheduled for early production, Arthur Hammerstein, the producer, had to find another composer. G. Schirmer, Friml's publisher, suggested to Hammerstein he take a chance on the young and untried Friml. Speed was essential. With no experienced composer available, Hammerstein yielded to the suggestion. Hammerstein was rewarded for his gamble on a novice with one of the most remarkable operetta scores of that period: the melodies all fresh and expressive and beautifully designed for the voice; the orchestration continually colourful and inventive. On his part, Friml was rewarded for invading a new world by progressing in a single step from inexperience and obscurity to immediate recognition.

Rose Marie

Book and Lyrics by OTTO HARBACH *and* OSCAR HAMMERSTEIN II
Music by RUDOLF FRIML *and* HERBERT STOTHART
Staged by PAUL DICKEY
Dances arranged by DAVID BENNETT

First produced at the Imperial Theatre on 2nd September, 1924, with Mary Ellis as "Rose Marie" and Dennis King as "Jim Kenyon".

PRINCIPAL CHARACTERS

SERGEANT MALONE
JIM KENYON
WANDA
ROSE MARIE LA FLAMME
ED HAWLEY

Rose Marie has for its setting the Canadian Rockies—and thereby hangs a tale. Arthur Hammerstein, the producer, was mulling one day over all the fascinating and exotic places used as backgrounds for operettas. The thought then came to him that no operetta had as yet exploited the colourful region of the Canadian Rockies; then the corollary thought sprang to mind that the heroic figures of the Canadian Mounted Police were ideal operetta characters. Hammerstein called upon Harbach to devise a play with the setting and characters he had in mind, and Harbach enlisted the co-operation of Oscar Hammerstein II for text and lyrics, and Rudolf Friml and Herbert Stothart for the music. And that is how *Rose Marie* came to be written.

If this setting is most unusual for an operetta—and to this day *Rose Marie* is the only successful operetta with the Canadian Rockies as its locale—the story line follows all-too familiar patterns. Rose Marie La Flamme is a singer at Lady Jane's hotel in Saskatchewan, Canada. She is a favourite with both the Mounties and the fur trappers who frequent the place. Though pursued by the wealthy Ed Hawley, she is in love with one man alone: Jim Kenyon, come to Canada to make his fortune. When Wanda, an Indian maid in love with Ed, kills Black Eagle, Hawley contrives to make it appear as if Kenyon is the murderer. Since he has the evidence to clear Jim, Rose Marie comes offering herself to Ed in exchange for Jim's life and freedom. Meanwhile, the Canadian Mounted Police, headed by Sergeant Malone, uncover the facts to incriminate Wanda. Jim and Rose Marie can now pursue their romance unhindered.

The initial success of *Rose Marie* (557 performances on Broadway, and four road companies on tour); its frequent revivals since 1924; its adaptation on two different occasions for the motion-picture screen—all this comes not from the appeal of story, locale or characters, but from its wonderful score. A note in the original programme made the following comment about this music: "The musical numbers of this play are such an integral part of the action that we do not think we should list them as separate episodes." Nevertheless, the best numbers stand sharply apart from the rest of the music: "Indian Love Call", a duet of Jim and Rose Marie; the title number, a duet of Jim and Sergeant Malone; "The Mounties", a stirring male chorus with which the Royal Mounted Police make their first entrance; "The Door of My Dreams", a haunting ballad sung by Rose Marie and chorus just before the end of the play; and "Totem Tom Tom", a colourful musical episode, effectively staged by having girls costumed to resemble totem poles.

The Vagabond King

Book and Lyrics by BRIAN HOOKER *and* W. H. POST *based on J. H. McCarthy's romance,* If I Were King

Music by RUDOLF FRIML

Staged by MAX FIGMAN

First produced at the Casino Theatre on 21st September, 1925, with Dennis King as "François Villon" and Carolyn Thomson as "Katherine de Vaucelles".

PRINCIPAL CHARACTERS

FRANÇOIS VILLON
KATHERINE DE VAUCELLES
HUGUETTE
LADY ANNE

The hero of *The Vagabond King* is the celebrated vagabond French poet of the fifteenth century, François Villon. In an effort to humble the pride of beautiful Katherine de Vaucelles, Louis XI makes Villon "king for a day". During that time he must make love to Katherine. That one day proves unusually eventful, for besides making love, Villon must also head a vagabond army to save Paris, and the throne of Louis XI, from the attacking Burgundians. In the heat of battle, Villon's life is endangered, but he is saved by Huguette, his peasant sweetheart, who sacrifices her own life so that Villon may live. In the end Villon finds solace at court with Lady Anne, who becomes his wife by royal decree.

A swashbuckling play with a picaresque character for its hero, *The Vagabond King* reaches its musical peak with the stirring chorus "Song of the Vagabonds". In a more romantic or sentimental vein are "Only a Rose", "Some Day" and "Huguette Waltz".

The Vagabond King was made into a Hollywood motion picture on three different occasions, most recently in 1956, starring Kathryn Grayson and Oreste.

Madame Sherry

Book and Lyrics by Otto Hauerbach (Harbach) *adapted from a French vaudeville by Hugo Felix*

Music by Karl Hoschna

Staged by George W. Lederer

First produced at the New Amsterdam Theatre on 30th August, 1910, with Lina Abarbanell as "Yvonne", Elizabeth Murray as "Catherine" and Ralph Herz as "Theophilus".

Principal Characters

UNCLE THEOPHILUS
EDWARD SHERRY
CATHERINE (MADAME SHERRY)
LULU
YVONNE SHERRY

Edward Sherry, a gay blade, tries to dupe his eccentric millionaire uncle, Theophilus, by passing off his landlady, Catherine, as his wife Madame Sherry, and Lulu and her dancing pupils as their children. The main action of the operetta highlights the antics of Catherine, trying to pass herself off as a socialite, and the efforts of Theophilus to uncover his nephew's deception through skilful detective work. When the uncle discovers the truth he forgives his wayward nephew, who, by this time, has found romantic interest in his cousin, Yvonne, whom he is eager to marry.

Karl Hoschna's score—described by *Theater Magazine* at the time as the best New York has heard since Victor Herbert's *Mlle Modiste*—boasted a resounding song hit in a suggestive number, "Every Little Movement Has a Meaning All Its Own". The waltzes "Girl of My Dreams" and "The Birth of Passion"; an amusing ditty delivered by Theophilus in an inebriated state, "I'm All Right"; and a rhythmic number described in the programme as "Afro-American" and entitled "Mr. Johnson, Good Night"—all these made a further significant contribution to one of the most successful operettas of its day.

The Pink Lady

Book and Lyrics by C. M. S. McLELLAN (HARRY MORTON) *adapted from* Le Satyre, *a French farce by* GEORGES BERR *and* MARCEL GUILLEMAND

Music by IVAN CARYLL

Staged by HERBERT GRESHAM

Musical numbers staged by JULIAN MITCHELL

First produced at the New Amsterdam Theatre on 13th March, 1911, with Hazel Dawn as the "Pink Lady", Alice Dovey as "Angèle" and William Elliott as "Lucien".

PRINCIPAL CHARACTERS

LUCIEN
CLAUDINE (*the Pink Lady*)
ANGÈLE

The slight plot is merely the frame for a succession of handsomely mounted sets and several infectious tunes. It can be summarised briefly. Lucien, a wealthy Parisian playboy in the early 1900s, takes Claudine, the Pink Lady, to a fashionable restaurant; she is his former girl friend. There they come upon Lucien's current fiancée, Angèle. Lucien hastily introduces the Pink Lady to Angèle as Mme Dondider, wife of a furniture dealer. For the rest of the play Lucien must continually extricate himself from the difficulties in which his lie placed him.

The Pink Lady proved to be a delectable *bon bon.* Philip Hale, the distinguished American music and drama critic, said: "Here we have a musical comedy that does not depend upon the antics of an acrobatic comedian, or the independent display of brazen-faced show girls." "Everyone should see *The Pink Lady,*" remarked Earl Derr Biggers—and practically everybody did. New attendance records were established by it at the New Amsterdam Theatre, while one of the most successful national tours enjoyed by any production up to that time managed to smash many old ones in several cities. It was due to the popularity of this play that the colour pink became fashionable in women's clothes that season.

Caryll's delightful score included two waltzes, both sung by the Pink Lady: "My Beautiful Lady", in which she appeared to be accompanying herself on the violin, and "Kiss Waltz", where she tried to teach males the art of kissing. The best comic number was "Donny Did, Donny Don't" sung by the cast as it filed down a majestic stairway.

The impressive staging included eye-filling scenes at the Compiègne forest, in a furniture shop in Rue St. Honoré and during the Ball of Nymphs and Satyrs.

Maytime

Book and Lyrics by Rida Johnson Young *and* Cyrus Wood
Music by Sigmund Romberg
Staged by Edward F. Temple, Allen K. Foster *and* J. J. Shubert

First produced at the Shubert Theatre on 16th August, 1917, with Peggy Wood as "Otillie" and Charles Purcell as "Richard".

Principal Characters

COLONEL VAN ZANDT
OTILLIE VAN ZANDT
RICHARD WAYNE
CLAUDE

The Van Zandts and the Waynes are carried over a period of some sixty years, from about 1840 to the turn of the new century. In Washington Square, in New York, Otillie van Zandt and Richard Wayne are in love. Richard's father is the owner of a mansion whose deed has been turned over to Otillie's father in payment of a long-standing debt. One day, Otillie and Richard come upon that deed. They decide to bury it in the garden in a box in which they also placed their rings as a token of eternal love. Thus Richard's father can keep possession of his home. But the love affair of Otillie and Richard has less happy results. Otillie's father compels her to marry Claude, a distant relative. He is a chronic gambler, who is continually in debt; upon his death he leaves Otillie penniless. Her house has to be put up for auction. Richard, still in love with her, though by now married to somebody else, buys the house and deeds it to Otillie without her even discovering who her benefactor is. Many years then pass: Otillie is dead. Her grand-daughter, also named Otillie, now runs a dressmaking establishment in her grandmother's house. Here Richard's grandson comes, sees Otillie and falls in love with her on sight. The happiness denied the grandparents is finally visited on the third generation.

The most famous musical number is the waltz "Will You Remember?", which occurs initially in the first act as the love song of Otillie and Richard, and recurs several times throughout the play as a kind of leading motive. It returns in the last act as the love song of Otillie's and Richard's grandchildren. Several other numbers, while less popular, are equally pleasing for their Continental-type lyricism and charm. These include "The Road to Paradise" and "Dancing Will Keep You Young".

Romberg had written many scores for the Broadway theatre before *Maytime*: for revues, extravaganzas, musical comedies and in 1915 for the operetta *The Blue Paradise*. *Maytime* was his greatest box-office triumph up to that time. So great was the demand for tickets that—for the first time in Broadway history—a second New York company was formed within a year of the première to play in a nearby auditorium (the 44th Street Theatre).

Blossom Time

Book and Lyrics by DOROTHY DONNELLY *based on the German operetta* Das Dreimaedlerhaus, *by* HEINRICH BERTÉ

Music by SIGMUND ROMBERG *based on the composition of* FRANZ SCHUBERT

First produced at the Ambassador Theatre on 29th September, 1921, with Bertram Peacock as "Schubert" and Olga Cook as "Mitzi".

PRINCIPAL CHARACTERS

FRANZ SCHUBERT
MITZI
FRANZ VON SCHOBER

In 1916 there was produced at the Raimund Theatre in Vienna a delightful operetta by Heinrich Berté called *Das Dreimaedlerhaus* based on the life and music of Franz Schubert. It proved such a success that it was soon seen throughout Europe; in England it was given in 1922 in English under the title, *Lilac Time.* The American producers, the Shuberts, who had bought the American rights, decided to have it completely rewritten to suit American tastes. Dorothy Donnelly was recruited for the libretto and lyrics, and Sigmund Romberg for the music. Both of them proceeded to forget the original, and went on to write new material of their own for an operetta now named *Blossom Time.* Thus, though the programme of *Blossom Time* carries the legend that it was adapted from *Das Dreimaedlerhaus*, the similarity between the two operettas is not even skin deep.

In *Blossom Time*—as in *Das Dreimaedlerhaus*—no attempt was made to stick to biographical facts. In the Romberg operetta Franz Schubert is deeply in love with Mitzi. As an expression of his feelings he writes a love song to her, "The Song of Love". Too timid and shy to let Mitzi know he loves her, or even to deliver his song to her, he recruits his dearest friend, Franz von Schober, to be his emissary by singing his song to her. Mitzi thinks the song is Schober's, and is touched by it to the point that she falls in love with him. Thus Schubert has lost Mitzi to his best friend. Heartbroken, he loses the will to live and to create;

the symphony upon which he has been working must be left unfinished. When it is being performed, Schubert is too ill to attend the concert. But he finds enough strength to write his immortal religious hymn, "Ave Maria", with virtually his last breath.

"The Song of Love", the principal number in the score—and one of Romberg's greatest song hits—is, of course, based on the main melody from the first movement of Schubert's *Unfinished Symphony*. In the same way Romberg used other Schubert melodies within the popular-song framework. "Tell Me Daisy" came from the main subject of the second movement of the *Unfinished Symphony*; "Three Little Maids", from the ballet music from *Rosamunde*; "Serenade", from the immortal Lied, *Staendchen*. It is perhaps amusing or ironic to remark that while all that Franz Schubert earned from his entire musical output during a lifetime was about $500, Romberg's royalties through the years from his adaptation of Schubert's music in *Blossom Time* amounted to close to a million dollars.

With an initial two-year run on Broadway, and American tours by four companies, *Blossom Time* became one of the most successful American operettas of all time; and through its repeated revivals in different parts of the United States, it has become a classic of the American musical theatre.

The Student Prince

Book and Lyrics by DOROTHY DONNELLY
Music by SIGMUND ROMBERG
Staged by J. C. HUFFMAN

First produced at the Jolson Theatre on 2nd December, 1924, with Ilse Marvenga as "Kathie" and Howard Marsh as "Prince Karl Franz".

PRINCIPAL CHARACTERS

PRINCE KARL FRANZ
DOCTOR ENGEL
KATHIE
PRINCESS MARGARET

The operetta opens in the palace of the mythical kingdom of Karlsberg. It is 1860. Prince Karl Franz, heir to the throne, is bored with royal life in his native land. With his tutor, Doctor Engel, he plans a visit to the old German University town of Heidelberg. Engel recalls nostalgically his own youth in Heidelberg, as the Prince looks forward with considerable anticipation to his future freedom in that delightful city ("Golden Days"). When they arrive in Heidelberg it is spring, and the world is in bloom. The Prince, now incognito, joins his new comrades in a student's song ("Students' Marching Song"), after which they parade to the "Golden Apple Inn". There the students raise their Steins of beer in a robust toast to drink and romance ("Drinking Song"). They call for Kathie, the lovely young daughter of the innkeeper. She addresses the students with considerable warmth of feeling, after which she comes to the Prince's table and dedicates to him a sentimental song about Heidelberg ("In Heidelberg Fair"). The students respond with a vigorous rendition of the age-old student hymn, "*Gaudeamus Igitur*". Before long, Kathie and the Prince are strongly attracted to each other. In the ensuing weeks their friendship ripens into love ("Deep in My Heart"); one beautiful evening the Prince is inspired to sing a serenade under her window ("Serenade"). But their love idyll is doomed. The news arrives from Karlsberg that the king is dead, and Prince Karl Franz must return to ascend the throne. More than that, he must, for reasons of State, marry Princess Margaret. Realising that their life together is over, they bid each other a sentimental farewell.

But back in Karlsberg, the new king cannot forget Heidelberg or Kathie. As he sits in his royal suite, visions arise of the place where he had been so happy, and the girl with whom he had so been in love. Unable to contain himself any longer, he leaves Karlsberg to revisit Heidelberg. When the lovers meet again they are deeply moved, but they also know that a permanent union is an impossibility. They say farewell for a last time, with a pledge to keep at least their memories of each other alive as long as they live.

The original New York run of *The Student Prince* (608 performances) represented the longest of any Sigmund Romberg operetta. The operetta is now a classic of the American theatre, repeatedly revived.

The Desert Song

Book and Lyrics by OTTO HARBACH, OSCAR HAMMERSTEIN II *and* FRANK MANDEL

Music by SIGMUND ROMBERG

Directed by ARTHUR HURLEY

Musical numbers staged by ROBERT CONNOLLY

First produced at the Casino Theatre on 30th November, 1926, with Vivienne Segal as "Margot" and Robert Halliday as "Pierre".

PRINCIPAL CHARACTERS

MARGOT BONVALET
GENERAL BIRABEAU
PIERRE BIRABEAU
ALI BEN ALI

The Desert Song is set in North Africa in or about 1925. It opens in the retreat of the famous bandit chief, Red Shadow, whom the French have been unsuccessfully trying to capture. The Red Shadow and his men enter to the stirring strains of "Ho", or "Song of the Riffs". One of his men informs him that Margot Bonvalet, with whom the bandit is in love, is about to marry Pierre, son of the Governor of the province. He exacts the promise from his men that they are not to harm her, but he himself is determined to prevent the marriage at all costs. The scene changes to the home of the Governor, General Birabeau, where a bevy of girls questions the wisdom of having married soldiers ("Why Did We Marry Soldiers?"). Margot is then introduced ("French Marching Song"); after that she joins the soldiers' wives in a haunting refrain, "Romance". Suddenly the Red Shadow and his associates appear. The bandit addresses Margot passionately ("The Desert Song", sometimes also known as "Blue Heaven"), then abducts her.

He takes her to the palace of Ali Ben Ali, where he tries to win her love. But she repulses him, saying she can love one man alone—Pierre. Gallantly, the Red Shadow promises to bring Pierre to Margot. While the Red Shadow is gone, Pierre appears; but to her amazement, Margot finds she can no longer respond to him warmly, now that she has met the virile and glamorous bandit. Dismayed, Pierre takes his leave. Upon the return of the Red Bandit, he redoubles his ardent attempt to win Margot's love, by recalling the strains of "The Desert Song". He suddenly finds her responsive. But at this point General Birabeau and his men have come to rescue Margot. When the General rushes towards the bandit with drawn sword the latter refuses to defend himself. His men, considering him a coward, abandon the Red Shadow, and send him off to exile, where he spends his time pining for Margot ("One Alone"). The strange behaviour by the bandit in refusing to fight the General in self-defence is soon explained. When the Red Shadow is captured and brought before the General the discovery is made that he is the General's son, Pierre, in disguise. Pierre is restored to the good graces of the French, and he finds the arms of Margot awaiting him.

Irving Berlin

Dolores Gray as "Annie" and Bill Johnson in *Annie Get Your Gun*

Jerome Kern

Mander & Mitchenson

George Gershwin

Herbert Fields, Richard Rodgers
and Lorenz Hart

A.P

"The Surrey
with the Fringe
on Top"
from *Oklahoma*

Vanda[illegible]

Gertrude Lawrence as "Anna Leonowens" and Yul Brynner as "The King of Siam" in *The King and I*

The New Moon

Book and Lyrics by Oscar Hammerstein II, Frank Mandel *and* Laurence Schwab

Music by Sigmund Romberg

Musical numbers staged by Bobby Connolly

First produced at the Imperial Theatre on 19th September, 1928, with Evelyn Herbert as "Marianne" and Robert Halliday as "Robert".

Principal Characters

MONSIEUR BEAUNOIR
CAPTAIN PAUL DUVAL
VICOMTE RIBAUD
ROBERT
MARIANNE

The New Moon is freely based on the career of Robert Mission, a French aristocrat of the eighteenth century. The opening scene takes place in New Orleans in 1788. Monsieur Beaunoir, a wealthy shipowner, has several French bondservants. One of them is Robert, who has fallen in love with his master's daughter, Marianne. The ship, "The New Moon", arrives from France bringing Captain Paul Duval with orders from the king to arrest an escaped French nobleman accused of revolutionary activities; his name is Chevalier Robert Mission. The Captain suspects that Robert Mission is assuming the identity of a bondservant, but when Beaunoir lines his men up for the Captain's inspection Robert skilfully eludes detection. He stays in hiding, but none the less succeeds in penetrating the Beaunoir household during a gala ball to meet Marianne secretly and steal from her a kiss ("One Kiss"). Vicomte Ribaud, a spy, uncovers Robert's identity and effects his arrest. Marianne and Robert part, vowing to remain true to each other ("Wanting You").

Robert is taken aboard "The New Moon" to be shipped back to France. Back in New Orleans, Marianne dreams of the time when her lover will return to her—in one of the most beautiful melodies Romberg ever wrote and the musical high-point of the entire operetta, "Lover, Come Back to Me". On the ship a successful mutiny liberates Robert and his fellow bondsmen. They set up camp on a small island off the coast of Florida. The news suddenly arrives from France that it has just become a Republic. No longer a political refugee, Robert, now reunited with Marianne, can set up a new government as part of the French Republic.

Besides the musical numbers singled out in the above synopsis, this excellent Romberg score includes two other memorable melodies, both in the first act: "Softly, as in a Morning Sunrise", sung by Robert's friend, Philippe; and the robust song of Robert and his bondsmen, "Stout-Hearted Men".

When tried out-of-town before the New York première, *The New Moon* gave every indication of being a failure. Audiences were indifferent, and the critics were hostile. Extensive revisions followed, with such fruitful consequences that when the operetta reached New York, St. John Ervine, writing in the *New York World*, could now call it "the most charming and fragrant entertainment of its sort that I have seen in a long time". It stayed on at the Imperial Theatre for almost two years, had several companies on the road and commanded from Hollywood the highest price thus far paid for a Broadway musical.

Very Good, Eddie

Book by PHILIP BARTHOLOMAE *and* GUY BOLTON *based on* Over Night *by* BARTHOLOMAE

Lyrics by SCHUYLER GREEN

Music by JEROME KERN

First produced at the Princess Theatre on 23rd December, 1915, with Ernest Truex as "Eddie", Alice Dovey as "Elsie" and Helen Raymond as "Georgina".

PRINCIPAL CHARACTERS

EDDIE KETTLE
GEORGINA
PERCY DARLING
ELSIE

Two honeymoon couples meet at a New York pier as they are about to board a dayline boat sailing up the Hudson River. The men, Eddie and Percy, have been friends of long standing and are delighted to meet each other so unexpectedly. Eddie introduces his wife, Georgina, to Percy, and in turn is introduced to Percy's bride, Elsie. They engage in happy small talk and are enjoying each other's company when, somehow, the women get separated from their respective husbands. When the boat sails, Eddie finds he is aboard with Percy's wife, while his own wife and Percy have been left behind on the pier. For the rest of the trip Eddie and Elsie must carry on the fiction that they are really married to each other to avoid gossip. The pretence, of course, is accompanied by all kinds of mirth-provoking embarrassments and difficulties. When the voyage is over, they come to the Rip Van Winkle Inn, where Percy and Georgina catch up with them. The girls finally return to their respective husbands to pursue the normal honeymoon thus far denied them.

Very Good, Eddie was a "Princess Theatre Show", a genre of the American musical theatre that got its name from the auditorium in which it was presented. The Princess Theatre was a small house with only 299 seats. An enterprising theatre manager and agent conceived the idea of presenting intimate, inexpensive and informal little musicals there with small casts, no stars and very little scenery. What started out as sheer commercial expediency, ended up as a revolution in the American theatre. This was a welcome departure from the lavish productions then enjoyed by Americans, where the main interest was on stars, production numbers and sets. In *Very Good, Eddie*, however, the emphasis lay on smart dialogue, wit, sophisticated songs and American characters and situations. The success of the "Princess Theatre Shows" was the needed stimulus for other imaginative writers and composers—men, for example, like Rodgers and Hart—to write similarly fresh and imaginative musicals.

Kern's scores for these shows were invariably the element that gave them their greatest distinction. In *Very Good, Eddie* Kern's fresh and ingratiating lyricism was found in numbers like "Babes in the Woods" and "Nodding Roses", while his happy comic touch was present in "When You Wore a Thirteen Collar".

Oh Boy!

Book by Guy Bolton
Lyrics by P. G. Wodehouse
Music by Jerome Kern
Staged by Edward Royce

First produced at the Princess Theatre on 20th February, 1917, with Tom Powers as "George" and Anna Wheaton as "Jackie".

Principal Characters

LOU ELLEN
GEORGE BUDD
JACKIE SAMPSON

The setting is a small American college town. George Budd and Lou Ellen have just been married when Lou Ellen is suddenly summoned out of town to visit her sick mother. Dejected at being left alone so soon after his marriage, George goes to a party at the local college inn. One of the guests there is a seductive little girl, Jackie Sampson, who becomes involved in a general rumpus. When the police are summoned Tom hides Jackie in his own apartment to save her from arrest. As various people come to visit Tom, the young lady dons various disguises and goes through sundry impersonations to explain her presence in the young man's apartment while his wife is away. But Lou Ellen, who makes a sudden return from her mother's house, is not easily convinced that everything is on the up and up with her husband. Only when her own father confesses that, on the sly, he had been Jackie's escort at the party and that Tom had acted only to save his reputation, is Lou Ellen placated.

Oh Boy! was the most successful of the "Princess Theatre Shows" which had introduced a new sophistication, simplicity and Americanism into the Broadway musical stage with *Very Good, Eddie*. The Kern score was outstanding for two unforgettable ballads: "Till the Clouds Roll By" (a title later used for Jerome Kern's screen biography) and "An Old Fashioned Wife". The best comedy number was "Nesting Time", a parody on a sentimental song then extremely popular in America, "Apple Blossom Time", but using for its locale the Flatbush section of Brooklyn.

Leave It to Jane

Book by Guy Bolton *based on* The College Widow, *a play by* George Ade

Lyrics by P. G. Wodehouse

Music by Jerome Kern

Staged by Edward Royce

First produced at the Longacre Theatre on 28th August, 1917, with Edith Hallor as "Jane" and Robert G. Pitkin as "Billy".

Principal Characters

PETER WITHERSPOON
JANE WITHERSPOON
BILLY BOLTON
HIRAM BOLTON
FLORA WIGGINS

Leave It to Jane was one of two musical comedies by Jerome Kern produced in 1917 with a college-town setting, the other being *Oh Boy!*

Jane is the daughter of Peter Witherspoon, president of Atwater College in Indiana. By her own admission she is a girl well able to get what she wants ("Leave It to Jane") and mainly through her powers as a siren ("The Siren's Song"). When the star full-back, Billy Bolton, threatens to bolt Atwater for a rival college, Bingham, of which his father Hiram is the benefactor, Jane goes to work on him; for to lose Billy would mean to lose the big game of the year. In the process of getting him to stay at Atwater, Jane falls in love with him.

Besides the two principal songs of Jane—the title number and "The Siren's Song"—the Jerome Kern score includes an excellent comedy item in "Cleopatterer", sung by Flo, a vigorous and brusque waitress; "The Sun Shines Brighter"; and "Wait Till Tomorrow".

In 1959 *Leave It to Jane* was revived in New York in an off-Broadway production that proved so successful it stayed on for several years, before going on a nation-wide tour. It was Kern's music that made *Leave It to Jane* almost as much a delight in 1959 as it had been in 1917. As Richard Watts, Jr., noted in his criticism of the revival: "I have remembered the Kern score with delight, recalling five of the songs in particular. And, hearing them again last night, I was happy to find that, not only was the score as a whole as charming and freshly tuneful as memory has made it, but my quintet came off easily the best of a gloriously melodious lot. . . . *Leave It to Jane* must stand on its unforgettable melodies."

Sally

Book by Guy Bolton

Lyrics by Clifford Grey *and* Buddy de Sylva

Music by Jerome Kern, *with additional music by* Victor Herbert

Staged by Edward Royce

First produced at the New Amsterdam Theatre on 12th December, 1920, with Marilyn Miller as "Sally", Leon Errol as "Connie" and Walter Catlett as "Otis Hooper".

Principal Characters

CONNIE
SALLY
BLAIR FARQUAR
OTIS HOOPER

Sally is a dishwashing waif at the Elm Tree Inn. Connie—a former Balkan duke thrown out of his country during a revolution—is one of the waiters there, and becomes Sally's friend and protector. He contrives to get Sally to a garden party on a millionaire's estate in Long Island. Disguised as a Russian ballerina, Sally wins the hearts of all the guests with her dancing, and particularly that of wealthy young Blair Farquar. Sally goes on to pursue a dancing career. She becomes a star of the Ziegfeld *Follies* and gains Blair as a husband.

Sally was the meeting ground for an incomparable star and an immortal song. The star was Marilyn Miller, who gave to both the title role and the musical comedy "a curious enchantment which no reproduction in other lands or other mediums captured", as Guy Bolton and P. G. Wodehouse recalled. One of the high moments in her performance came when, as a dirty-faced waif looking hopefully into the future, she sang one of Kern's most famous ballads, "Look for the Silver Lining". The other memorable songs in the Kern score were "Whip-poor-will" and "The Little Church Around the Corner".

Florenz Ziegfeld gave *Sally* a lavish production. One of the most bountifully staged sequences was "The Butterfly Ballet", for which Victor Herbert wrote the music.

Show Boat

Book and Lyrics by OSCAR HAMMERSTEIN II *based on the novel by* EDNA FERBER

Music by JEROME KERN

Staged by JEROME KERN *and* OSCAR HAMMERSTEIN II

Dances by SAMMY LEE

First produced at the Ziegfeld Theatre on 27th December, 1927, with Norma Terris as "Magnolia", Howard Marsh as "Gaylord" and Helen Morgan as "Julie".

PRINCIPAL CHARACTERS

CAP'N ANDY
JULIE
GAYLORD RAVENAL
MAGNOLIA
JOE
KIM

"Cotton Blossom", a show boat travelling up and down the Mississippi River in or about 1890, has come to Natchez. Stevedores are hard at work on the levee, while the gay crowds have come to welcome the arrival of the show folks ("Cotton Blossom"). Gaylord Ravenal, a dashing young man who is also an irresponsible gambler, meets Magnolia aboard ship. She is the daughter of Cap'n Andy, owner of "Cotton Blossom". She soon reveals to Gaylord that, since she is most at ease in the world of make believe, she would like to become an actress. Gaylord counters by inquiring why the two of them cannot make believe that they know each other well ("Only Make Believe"). After Gaylord leaves, Magnolia asks Joe what he thinks of Gaylord. Joe prefers to be evasive: he advises Magnolia to direct her question to the Mississippi, which knows all the answers ("Ol' Man River").

A half hour later, in the kitchen pantry of "Cotton Blossom", Magnolia confesses to Julie—star of the Show Boat—that she has just fallen in love. Julie warns Magnolia to be careful about falling in love, that love is a treacherous thing, that a girl must be sure that the man she loves is worthy of her ("Can't Help Lovin' Dat Man").

A sheriff then comes to the boat to warn Cap'n Andy that under no circumstances are Julie, and her husband Steve, to be permitted to appear in the Show Boat performance that evening. Julie is a Negress, and her husband is half white; local laws forbid miscegenation. Julie and Steve make their leave of their good friends on "Cotton Blossom". Their parts in the show are hurriedly assumed by Magnolia and Ravenal. After the performance that night, on the boat's deck Magnolia and Gaylord confess to each other how much they are in love ("You are Love"), and Gaylord asks Magnolia to marry him.

Several years elapse. Magnolia and Gaylord are married and have a daughter, Kim. Cap'n Andy comes to visit them at the Midway Plaisance of the Chicago World's Fair. Julie reveals to her father that Gaylord is irresponsible, that his changing fortunes as a gambler have poisoned their lives; but none the less she loves him still. But before long, Gaylord deserts his wife and child. To earn a living, Magnolia applies for a singing job at the Trocadero. The singing star there is none other than Julie, who entertains her audience with a poignant rendition of the ballad "Bill". When Julie discovers that Magnolia is out of work, she precipitously gives up her own job at the Trocadero so that Magnolia might take over. Magnolia does—and becomes a huge success. Then Cap'n Andy comes to the Trocadero to take her and Kim back to "Cotton Blossom". There a repentant Gaylord is waiting for his wife and daughter.

With *Show Boat* a new art form emerged in the American musical theatre for the first time: the musical play as distinguished from musical comedy. Here was a rich, colourful, nostalgic chapter from the American past filled with humour, gentle pathos, tenderness and high drama. It bewitched the eye, ear and heart. It was a revelation; and it was a revolution. Here was something unique for the musical stage of that day: an American musical comedy with dramatic truth; a plot with a logical, believable line; a love story that rang true. Here were three-dimensional characters in place of the cardboard images previously populating the musical stage. Here were authenticity of background and atmosphere. Here were dialogue and lyrics that were supple, fresh and imaginative—capable of soaring to poetic heights without abandoning the vernacular and the idiomatic. And, finally, here was a musical score which was an extravagant outpouring of the most wonderful melodies. Though it was a pioneer in creating a new genre in the musical theatre—and though many remarkable productions since 1927 have developed the musical play into a genuine art form—*Show Boat* still remains one of the best of the species. In its frequent revivals, whether on stage or screen, *Show Boat* still never fails to cast a spell on audiences.

It was for a revival of *Show Boat* on Broadway, in 1946, that Kern wrote the last song of his rich career, "No One But Me". Before that revival could reach the stage, Kern suffered a cerebral haemorrhage that proved fatal. He died in New York City on 11th November, 1945. The revival of *Show Boat*, for which Kern had come to New York, opened at the Ziegfeld Theatre on 5th January, 1946, to begin a run of 418 performances.

The Cat and the Fiddle

Book and Lyrics by Otto Harbach
Music by Jerome Kern
Staged by Jose Ruben

First produced at the Globe Theatre on 15th October, 1931, with Bettina Hall as "Shirley" and Georges Metaxa as "Victor".

Principal Characters

VICTOR FLORESCU
SHIRLEY SHERIDAN
DAUDET

The setting is present-day Brussels. Shirley Sheridan, an American girl crazy about popular music, lives near the studio of a serious Rumanian composer, Victor Florescu, who is writing an opera, *The Passionate Pilgrim.* Neither has much respect for the other's musical tastes. Daudet, a producer, visits Florescu's studio one day to listen to his opera score. From Shirley's apartment come the strains of an American popular tune. Daudet points out to Florescu that such a song might very well make the opera a success. Florescu writes that tune, and his opera is a success. Meanwhile, the two young people have overcome their musical prejudices to appreciate the other's musical preferences and to embark on a fruitful romance.

The Cat and the Fiddle was a highly unconventional musical comedy for its time. It dispensed with chorus girls completely and sidestepped both big production numbers and comedy routines. The emphasis was on the story line and the characterisations, and all the music had to be basic to the plot. The best numbers included the canzonetta that ran through the play, "The Night Was Made for Love", together with "She Didn't Say Yes", "Poor Pierrot", "The Breeze That Kissed Your Hair" and "One Moment Alone". Each helped to carry along the action of the play.

Music in the Air

Book and Lyrics by OSCAR HAMMERSTEIN II
Music by JEROME KERN
Staged by OSCAR HAMMERSTEIN II *and* JEROME KERN

First produced at the Alvin Theatre on 8th November, 1932, with Walter Slezak as "Karl Reder", Katherine Carrington as "Sieglinde" and Tullio Carminati as "Bruno Mahler".

PRINCIPAL CHARACTERS

KARL REDER
SIEGLINDE LESSING
DR. WALTER LESSING
FRIEDA HATZFELD
BRUNO MAHLER

In the small Bavarian mountain town of Edendorff Dr. Walter Lessing is the town music teacher and conductor of the local choral society ("Melodies of May"). Karl Reder, the local schoolteacher, is in love with Dr. Lessing's daughter, Sieglinde. Dr. Lessing has written a beautiful melody to Karl's lyrics ("I've Told Every Little Star"), which the latter hopes to get published. For this purpose, Karl and Sieglinde make the trip to Munich by foot. There Karl meets the famous operetta star, Frieda Hatzfeld, who begins a mild flirtation with him. Sieglinde now becomes a friend of Bruno Mahler, a librettist. Mahler finds Sieglinde most appealing ("The Song Is You") and would like her to star in his new operetta, *Tingle Tangle.* Their new separate romantic interests cause a rift between Karl and Sieglinde. But Sieglinde proves a failure on the stage, and before long Frieda is bored with Karl. Sieglinde recalls nostalgically her little Bavarian town where she had been so happy with Karl; and Karl recognises that Sieglinde is the only girl he has ever really loved ("We Belong Together"). The couple, therefore, return to Edendorff, happy to forget the big city, and ready to resume their romance.

Beyond the melodic distinction of its two principal songs ("I've Told Every Little Star" and "The Song Is You"), Jerome Kern's score is memorable for choral numbers (such as "Melodies of May") and folk-like tunes, like "Egern on the Tegern See", which contribute a welcome touch of atmospheric authenticity.

Roberta

Book and Lyrics by OTTO HARBACH *based on the novel of* ALICE DUER MILLER

Music by JEROME KERN

Staged by HASSARD SHORT

Dances by JOHN LONERGAN

First produced at the New Amsterdam Theatre on 18th November, 1933, with Tamara as "Stephanie", Raymond E. (Ray) Middleton as "John Kent" and Bob Hope as "Huckleberry Haines".

PRINCIPAL CHARACTERS

JOHN KENT
AUNTIE MINNIE ("ROBERTA")
STEPHANIE
LADISLAW
HUCKLEBERRY HAINES

The curtain rises on a fraternity house at Haverhill College, where we learn that John Kent, football half-back, jilted by his girl, decides to go off to Paris with his friend Huckleberry Haines. John plans to visit his aunt Minnie, who as "Roberta" is the proprietress of a fashionable modiste shop. There John meets Stephanie, the firm's principal designer, who is involved with a young man named Ladislaw. But after John takes over the management of the shop he wins Stephanie's love. Stephanie turns out to be a Russian princess.

The love interest, story line, characters and even the comedy involving Huckleberry are all incidental here to the lavish display of female fashions during the fashion show in the first act. But not incidental by any means—indeed, it was the main reason for the success of *Roberta*—was Jerome Kern's music. Two haunting ballads are among Kern's greatest: the poignant "Yesterdays", where Roberta nostalgically recalls her past, and "Smoke Gets In Your Eyes", with which Tamara, in the role of Stephanie, nightly stopped the show. Other distinguished numbers in this memorable score are "The Touch of Your Hand", "Something Had to Happen" and "Armful of You".

In the title role Fay Templeton—star of burlesque and musical comedy for almost half a century—made her farewell stage appearance. As if in compensation, a new stage star arose in the same production—Bob Hope playing the part of Huckleberry Haines.

No, No, Nanette

Book by Otto Harbach *and* Frank Mandel
Lyrics by Irving Caesar
Music by Vincent Youmans
Staged by H. H. Frazee

First produced in America at the Globe Theatre on 16th September, 1925, with Louise Groody as "Nanette", Wellington Cross as "Billy Early" and Charles Winniger as "Jimmy Smith".

Principal Characters

BILLY EARLY
NANETTE
SUE
JIMMY SMITH
BETTY
FLORA
WINNIE

Nanette is the vivacious, fun-loving daughter of Billy Early, wealthy publisher of Bibles. Her fiancée, Tom, looks askance at her frivolous diversions, but is ready to wait patiently until she is ready to settle down and marry him ("I'll Be Waiting for You"). Nanette's father also has a weakness for good times—and girls. When the Early family comes to Atlantic City, in New Jersey, for a holiday, Billy takes three winsome girls under his protective wing: Betty from Boston, Flora from San Francisco and Winnie from Washington. This happy trio has no difficulty getting Billy to open up his pocket-book, as well as his heart. Meanwhile, Billy's lawyer, Jimmy Smith—though married—enjoys a mild flirtation with Nanette ("I Want to Be Happy"). Tom now becomes increasingly concerned over Nanette's flippant ways, especially when she stays out all night from home without giving an explanation for her absence. But when pressed Tom promises to trust Nanette and believe in her ("Tea for Two"). With Billy's wife, Sue, on the warpath against her philandering husband, Jimmy

Smith arranges to pay the girls off handsomely for keeping quiet. And Sue, who is nobody's fool, informs Billy that since he seems to enjoy spending money on girls, she has every intention of keeping him happy for the rest of his life with her extravagance.

The run of 321 performances that *No, No, Nanette* enjoyed on Broadway gives no clue to its immense global success in the 1920s. In London, where it had opened six months before coming to Broadway, it achieved the formidable engagement of 665 performances. After its stay on Broadway seventeen companies were formed to present it in Europe, South America, New Zealand, the Philippines and China, bringing in a profit of well over two million dollars.

Hit the Deck

Book by HERBERT FIELDS *based on* Shore Leave, *a play by* HUBERT OSBORNE

Lyrics by LEO ROBIN *and* CLIFFORD GREY

Music by VINCENT YOUMANS

Staged by LEW FIELDS *and* ALEXANDER LEFTWICH

Dances by SEYMOUR FELIX

First produced at the Belasco Theatre on 25th April, 1927, with Louise Groody as "Loulou" and Charles King as "Bilge".

PRINCIPAL CHARACTERS

LOULOU
BILGE

In Newport, Rhode Island, Loulou is the owner of a successful coffee shop frequented by sailors. One of them is Bilge, a likeable young fellow with whom Loulou is in love. When Bilge gets his orders to set sail for foreign ports Loulou shuts up shop to follow him. She goes wherever Bilge's ship carries him. All the while she is trying to convince him to marry her. Apparently, all that is holding Bilge back is his conscience: he does not like the idea of marrying a woman with money when he is penniless. Loulou solves the problem neatly by signing away all her money to their first-born child.

Two of Youmans' song classics are found here. Strange to say, neither one had been written directly for this production. One is a rousing sailors' chorus, "Hallelujah". This was a melody written by Youmans almost a decade earlier when he had served in the United States Navy during the First World War; at that time the melody became extremely popular with Navy bands. The other song is "Sometimes I'm Happy". Youmans first wrote this tune in 1923 for the musical, *Mary Jane McKane*, but it was never used there. After that, with a new set of lyrics, it appeared in *A Night Out* without attracting much interest. In *Hit the Deck*—with yet another set of lyrics—it became the hit of the show.

Lady be Good

Book by GUY BOLTON *and* FRED THOMPSON
Lyrics by IRA GERSHWIN
Music by GEORGE GERSHWIN

First produced at the Liberty Theatre on 18th December, 1924, with Fred Astaire as "Dick Trevor" and Adele Astaire as "Susie Trevor".

PRINCIPAL CHARACTERS

DICK TREVOR
SUSIE TREVOR
J. WATTERSON WATKINS

Dick and Susie Trevor are a brother-and-sister dance team. Engagements in vaudeville and the musical-comedy stage have grown so meagre that they are reduced to accepting jobs entertaining at the homes of friends. At one of these parties Dick meets a rich girl, who falls in love with him. When he shows little interest in her, she decides to punish him by evicting him from his apartment, since she is the landlord. Here comes one of the finest scenes in the musical. Dispossessed, the Trevors find all their furniture in the street outside the house. Susie, the practical homemaker, tries to make the new setting as attractive as possible by neatly arranging the furniture around the corner lamp-post and hanging on it the sign "God Bless Our Home". Broke and homeless, Dick decides that it might be wise, after all, to demonstrate some interest in the rich girl. Matters are then allowed to drift to the point where Dick finds himself on the threshold of matrimony. To save her brother from marrying a girl he does not love, Susie contrives with J. Watterson Watkins, an unscrupulous lawyer, to pose as a Mexican widow for the purpose of getting an inheritance, and thus relieve Dick of his financial problems. This fraud is exposed, and the fortune does not materialise. But by now Dick has managed to extricate himself from the clutches of his bride-to-be.

Lady Be Good was Gershwin's first successful musical comedy. Of even greater importance: it was here that, for the first time, he collaborated with his brother, Ira, on the lyrics for an entire show. From this point on, Ira would be George's lyricist for his most significant Broadway musicals.

In this score George Gershwin achieved full maturity as a popular composer, bringing an altogether new stature to the popular music of his day. His tricky metres and rhythms in "Fascinating Rhythm", the personal lyricism of the title song and "So Am I" and the distinct harmonic colorations of "The Half Of It Dearie Blues" sounded a completely new note for the American musical stage.

George Gershwin also wrote for *Lady Be Good* what many consider his greatest song, "The Man I Love". But during out-of-town tryouts of *Lady Be Good* it was deleted because it slowed up the action. A few years later, Gershwin tried to find a place for the song in another musical, the first version of *Strike Up the Band!* and once again it had to be discarded. After that it was released as an individual number and first became successful in London before catching on in New York.

Oh Kay!

Book by Guy Bolton *and* P. G. Wodehouse
Lyrics by Ira Gershwin
Music by George Gershwin
Staged by John Harwood *and* Sammy Lee

First produced at the Imperial Theatre on 8th November, 1926, with Gertrude Lawrence as "Kay", Oscar Shaw as "Jimmy" and Victor Moore as "Shorty".

Principal Characters

KAY
JIMMY WINTERS
SHORTY MCGEE

Kay and her brother, a duke, come to America from England. Having fallen into financial difficulties, they rent out their yacht to rum-runners, this being the period of Prohibition in the United States. When the yacht is pursued by prohibition agents, and Kay and her brother are suspected of rum-running, they find refuge in the estate of the Long Island playboy, Jimmy Winters. The rum-runners conceal their illicit cache of liquor in the basement of the estate and get one of their men, Shorty McGee, to take on the job of butler so that he can keep a watchful eye on the precious cargo. A little man with a broken voice and timid manner, Shorty moves about in a befuddled state in a profession his nature had never intended him to pursue. Once Kay and Jimmy meet they fall in love, but before they can get married, Kay must free herself of the false charge of smuggling, and Jimmy must extricate himself from the girls who are continually pursuing him.

Though Gertrude Lawrence had previously made a Broadway appearance with *Charlot's Revue*, a production imported from London in 1924, *Oh Kay!* was her bow in American musical comedy. As Kay, she brought to the stage an unforgettable touch of enchantment, especially in the presentation of two remarkable Gershwin songs: "Someone to Watch Over Me" and "Do, Do,

Do". This was the first of a memorable series of characterisations that she was destined to bring to Broadway. Victor Moore, as the hapless butler, also realised in this musical-comedy one of his triumphant performances.

The Gershwin score was a veritable cornucopia of riches. Besides the two numbers already mentioned, it included "Clap Yo' Hands" and "Fidgety Feet", in Gershwin's most robust rhythmic vein, and "Maybe", in a more lyrical manner.

Girl Crazy

Book by Guy Bolton *and* John McGowan
Lyrics by Ira Gershwin
Music by George Gershwin
Staged by Alexander Leftwich
Dances staged by George Hale

First produced at the Alvin Theatre on 14th October, 1930, with Ethel Merman as "Kate", Ginger Rogers as "Molly", Allen Kearns as "Danny" and Willie Howard as "Gieber".

Principal Characters

DANNY CHURCHILL
GIEBER GOLDFARB
MOLLY GRAY
KATE FOTHERGILL

Danny Churchill, a New York playboy, is interested only in wine, women and song—much to the despair of his father, a business tycoon. Feeling that Danny might perhaps be cured of his irresponsible ways if separated from the fleshpots of the big city, his father sends him off to Custerville, Arizona, where women and temptations are few and far between. Danny makes the long trip west in Gieber Goldfarb's taxicab. Once in Custerville, he proceeds to transform the one-horse town into a Great White Way. He opens a dude ranch with Broadway chorus girls and a gambling room. Things are humming in Custerville, and Danny is pretty much in his element. But then he meets and falls in love with Molly Gray, the pretty postmistress of the town. Molly finally effects the cure for Danny which his father had been hoping for.

Girl Crazy was the musical in which Ethel Merman, queen of American musical comedy, made her Broadway debut. She appeared as Kate Fothergill, wife of the man running the gambling establishment. Upon her first appearance in this musical—dressed in a tight black satin skirt slit to the knee and a low-cut red blouse—she sang "Sam and Delilah". Her tones, like the piercing sounds of a trumpet, pierced through the theatre and held the audience spellbound; her personality charged the atmosphere with electric sparks. After that she sang "I Got Rhythm"—in which she held a high C sixteen bars while the orchestra went on with the melody—and "Boy What Love Has Done To Me". There was no question in anybody's mind at that première that a star was born. And for the next quarter of a century and more that star shone over Broadway with incomparable lustre.

It took a good deal of brilliance on the part of the other elements in this production not to be completely obscured by Miss Merman's sensational debut. That other elements withstood this competition and survived speaks volumes for their intrinsic significance. There were, first and foremost, several other songs by George Gershwin besides those which Ethel Merman made so memorable: the haunting ballad "Embraceable You", the love song of Danny and Molly; a second poignant ballad, "But Not for Me", also one of Molly's songs; a delightful take off on hillbilly music, "Bidin' My Time", sung by a quartet of rubes who drifted in and out of the production during scene changes. Apart and beyond the Gershwin music, *Girl Crazy* boasted the incomparable comedy of Willie Howard in one of his strongest musical-comedy performances; Ginger Rogers, as an ingenue, in her first important Broadway appearance; and an orchestra in the pit that numbered several men destined for greatness in jazz, including Benny Goodman, Glenn Miller, Red Nichols and Gene Krupa.

Of Thee I Sing!

Book by Morrie Ryskind *and* George S. Kaufman
Lyrics by Ira Gershwin
Music by George Gershwin
Staged by George S. Kaufman
Dances staged by George Hale

First produced at the Music Box Theatre on 26th December, 1931, with William Gaxton as "Wintergreen", Victor Moore as "Throttlebottom" and Lois Moran as "Mary Turner".

Principal Characters

JOHN P. WINTERGREEN
ALEXANDER THROTTLEBOTTOM
DIANA DEVEREUX
MARY TURNER
THE CHIEF JUSTICE
THE FRENCH AMBASSADOR

A Presidential campaign is being waged in the United States. The opening scene is a five-minute torchlight parade to further the campaign of John P. Wintergreen. The illuminated signs read: "A Vote for Wintergreen is a Vote for Wintergreen" and "Even Your Dog Loves Wintergreen". The politicians sing Wintergreen's praises ("Wintergreen for President").

In a dingy hotel room the politicians gather to discuss and arrive at a campaign issue. During the course of the conversation it is apparent that none of them know whom they had nominated to be Wintergreen's running mate, since Vice-Presidents have long been the forgotten men in American politics. Indeed, when the Vice-Presidential candidate arrives in the form of meek and timid little Alexander Throttlebottom, nobody recognises him. When he finally identifies himself, Throttlebottom reveals that he has come to bow out of the race, since he doesn't want his mother to find out that he is running for

Vice-President. The politicians assure him that his mother can never possibly uncover this dark secret, and thereby they allay his fears. This matter out of the way, the politicians settle down to the main business of the day. In a moment of inspiration they decide that the best campaign issue for Wintergreen is "love". A beauty contest in Atlantic City will determine who will be "Miss White House" and the First Lady of the Land.

In Atlantic City speculation is rife as to who will win the beauty contest ("Who Is the Lucky Girl to Be?"). The choice of the judges finally falls on a delectable southern belle by the name of Diana Devereux. But Wintergreen announces he has no intention of marrying her. Having met Mary Turner, a campaign secretary—a simple girl who has a particular talent for making the best corn muffins in the world—there is only one girl in the world for him. The judges sample Mary Turner's muffins, agree with his choice and designate her as "Miss White House".

The loving couple campaign throughout the country on a "love ticket". At a huge political rally at Madison Square Garden the politicians are jubilant over the effect of their campaign issue ("Love Is Sweeping the Country"). The audience is entertained with a wrestling match. While all this is going on, Wintergreen proposes to Mary and is accepted. Jubilant, he ascends the platform to sing the campaign song ("Of Thee I Sing").

Wintergreen and Throttlebottom are elected on the "love ticket" by a landslide. In Washington, in front of the Capitol, the nine Supreme Court judges enter singing. President Wintergreen promises to uphold the Constitution; he also bids farewell to his bachelor days ("Here's a Kiss for Cinderella"). Hardly had these ceremonies ended, when Diana Devereux storms in to accuse Wintergreen of breach of promise. She insists she is the one who was selected as "Miss White House" and she plans to sue. Notwithstanding this disagreeable interlude, President Wintergreen and Mary get married and settle down in the White House. In his office, Wintergreen is attending to matters of State. He is also being interviewed by reporters about the slight to Diana Devereux. The French Ambassador appears ("*Garçon, s'il vous plaît*") to lodge a protest for his country. Diana Devereux happens to be of French extraction ("She's the Illegitimate Daughter"). Confusion reigns. A demand is sounded for the President's resignation. Some even suggest impeachment. But Wintergreen is calm, since all he is interested in is—Mary ("Who Cares?")

The subject of the President's impeachment reaches the Senate floor, pushed by the Southern bloc. But some other business must first be transacted. One of the Senators brings up the long overdue problem of Paul Revere's horse, Jenny; it seems that the Government had forgotten to bestow on her a pension. The entire Senate rises in silent homage, and with bowed head, to Jenny. But the question of the President's impeachment can no longer be delayed. As the Vice-President calls the roll, it seems that impeachment is inevitable. Just then Mary bursts in with the news that the President is "in a delicate condition" ("I'm About to Become a Mother"). Throttlebottom echoes the sentiment of the entire Senate when he remarks that the United States has never yet impeached an expectant father. The Senate rallies to Wintergreen's defence. The

Supreme Court is hurriedly summoned, for it must decide the sex of the baby. With a fanfare, it reaches the decision: a boy. But there soon comes a second fanfare. The Supreme Court now brings in the decision of "a girl", for Mary is the proud mother of twins. Everyone is in a jubilant mood, except the French Ambassador, who feels strongly that the children rightfully belong to France. But Wintergreen comes up with a solution that meets with the full approval of the Ambassador. Since the Constitution clearly specifies that the Vice-President must take over for the President when the latter cannot fulfil his duties, Throttlebottom must marry Diana Devereux. The general rejoicing is climaxed with the appearance of Mary on a gold-canopied bed, bearing a child in each arm.

On 2nd May, 1932, *Of Thee I Sing!* became the first musical comedy to win the Pulitzer Prize in drama. "This award may seem unusual," read the citation, "but the play is unusual. . . . Its effect on the stage promises to be very considerable, because musical plays are always popular, and by injecting satire and point into them, a very large public is reached."

Of Thee I Sing! was a sharp departure from anything the Broadway musical theatre had witnessed up to that time. It sidestepped the old formulas and clichés to present a devastating satire (almost in the vein of Gilbert and Sullivan) on the political scene in Washington, D.C. Dialogue, lyrics, humour and music were consistently fresh and sparkling. George Gershwin's music opened new dimensions both for the musical theatre and for himself by including extended sequences combining solo numbers, recitatives and choruses, and by introducing innumerable subtleties translating nuances of text and lyrics into their musical equivalents.

Dearest Enemy

Book by Herbert Fields
Lyrics by Lorenz Hart
Music by Richard Rodgers
Staged by John Murray Anderson
Dances by Carl Hemmer

First produced at the Knickerbocker Theatre on 18th September, 1925, with Helen Ford as "Betsy" and Charles Purcell as "Captain Sir John".

Principal Characters

MRS. ROBERT MURRAY
JANE MURRAY
CAPTAIN HENRY TRYON
GENERAL HENRY CLINTON
GENERAL SIR WILLIAM HOWE
GENERAL JOHN TRYON
CAPTAIN SIR JOHN COPELAND
BETSY BURKE

Dearest Enemy is a page from American history. During the Revolutionary War Mrs. Robert Murray receives an urgent message from General Washington: She is to detain British officers at her Murray Hill residence "by every means at your discretion"—long enough to enable the Continental Army to make a strategic withdrawal. Mrs. Murray and the other Continental ladies are philosophical about their mission, as they explain "War Is War". The British general staff, and the other red-coats, find the Continental ladies most endearing and fall a ready victim to this manoeuvre. General Tryon discovers he is "Old Enough to Love"; Mrs. Murray's daughter, Jane, attracts Captain Henry Tryon. The principal love interest involves Betsy Burke and Captain Sir John Copeland, as they reveal in the hit song, "Here In My Arms".

The settings, costuming—and an intermission curtain depicting a map of old

New York—presented such an "endlessly lovely picture" to the critic, Alexander Woollcott, that he insisted that they alone were "worth the price of admission". But there was a good deal more to recommend *Dearest Enemy* than its attractive trappings. Fresh in subject matter, spontaneous in its treatment, full of a gaiety that was at times discreetly spiced with salaciousness, *Dearest Enemy* was (as its programme took pains to point out) an "American musical play" rather than a "musical comedy". The Rodgers score was not only studded with fine songs but also with duets, trios and choral numbers. The spirit of the eighteenth century was evoked in a gavotte which opened the second act; a martial note was injected in a stirring number for Sir John and his soldiers in "Cheerio". The music was good enough and important enough to tempt Percy Hammond to describe the production as "a baby grand opera". General Washington makes only a single brief appearance—in the stirring patriotic finale which closes the play.

Peggy-Ann

Book by HERBERT FIELDS *based on* Tillie's Nightmare, *by* EDGAR SMITH

Lyrics by LORENZ HART

Music by RICHARD RODGERS

Directed by LEW FIELDS

Dances by SEYMOUR FELIX

First produced at the Vanderbilt Theatre on 27th December, 1926, with Helen Ford as "Peggy-Ann" and Lester Cole as "Guy".

PRINCIPAL CHARACTERS

PEGGY-ANN
MRS. FROST
GUY PENDELTON

Peggy-Ann was the first successful American musical-comedy to make extensive use of dream psychology. The daughter of Mrs. Frost, a boarding-house proprietress in Glens Falls, New York, Peggy-Ann has for three years been engaged to a humdrum and prosaic local boy, Guy Pendelton. Life for Peggy-Ann is just a succession of boring episodes from which her future marriage with Guy promises no release. Peggy-Ann therefore succumbs to dreams and fantasies. In her dream she sees herself going to New York. As she makes the trip, accompanied by a chorus of girls, the scene shifts from Glens Falls to the big city, while the girls change from country to city dress in full view of the audience. The impenetrable maze of New York traffic suddenly becomes unravelled as the police go off quietly for lunch. What follows in New York acquires a kind of surrealistic quality in which the absurd becomes the rule. Peggy-Ann's ruthless sister appears as a devil with red horns; pills assume the size of golf balls; fish speak with an English accent; policemen sport pink moustaches; Cuban race-horses are interviewed. When Peggy-Ann goes off with a young millionaire for a love idyll on his yacht, the cruise becomes a scene of mutiny when the crew learns to its horror that the pair is not married. When Peggy-Ann finally does get married she attends her wedding dressed only in step-ins, while during the ceremony a telephone book is used instead of a Bible. All the while, disordered dances and undisciplined lights contribute to the planned chaos. Awakening from the dream, Peggy-Ann reconciles herself to the grim reality that dictates she must marry Guy and stay in Glens Falls. The end of the play takes place on a darkened stage, and consists only of a slow comedy dance.

Years before the invasion of dream psychology into Broadway and Hollywood—fourteen years before Moss Hart's psycho-analytic musical comedy *Lady In the Dark*—*Peggy-Ann* was a Freudian musical. It had a Debussy-like, Impressionistic quality in which fantasy became confused with reality; where the absurd, outlandish and the impossible frequently became plausible.

The authors had a field day in their freedom from accepted musical-comedy procedures. There is no opening chorus; actually there is no singing or dancing whatsoever for the first fifteen minutes. The dances are not typical musical-comedy routines but ballets, a forewarning of the bold directions Rodgers and Hart would later take. Rodgers' music was also at times unconventional, though it did contain such good tunes as "A Tree in the Park", "Where's That Rainbow?" and "Maybe It's Me". He achieved fantasy by means of nebulous chords that follow Peggy-Ann in her dreams. Through delicate harmonisations (particularly in the verse), "A Tree in the Park" becomes a rhapsody of love. "Havana" has a rich dash of Spanish colour in its rhythms.

A Connecticut Yankee

Book by HERBERT FIELDS *based on* MARK TWAIN'S A Connecticut Yankee in King Arthur's Court

Lyrics by LORENZ HART

Music by RICHARD RODGERS

Staged by ALEXANDER LEFTWICH

Dances by BUSBY BERKELEY

First produced at the Vanderbilt Theatre on 3rd November, 1927, with William Gaxton as "Martin" and "The Yankee", Constance Carpenter as "Alice" and "Alisande" and June Cochrane as "Evelyn".

PRINCIPAL CHARACTERS

MARTIN
ALICE CARTER
THE YANKEE
THE DEMOISELLE ALISANDE LE CARTELOISE
KING ARTHUR
SIR LANCELOT
SIR GALAHAD
MERLIN
MISTRESS EVELYN LA BELLE-ANS
QUEEN MORGAN LE FAY

The prologue takes place at the present time in the United States. Martin and his fiancée, Alice Carter, are guests at a party. When Martin begins to flirt with another girl Alice hits him over the head with a champagne bottle. Losing consciousness, Martin enters a dream world in which he is a Yankee back in old Camelot. Taken prisoner, he is brought to King Arthur's Court, where he is sentenced to burn at the stake. The Yankee suddenly remembers that an eclipse of the sun is due. He tells the Court he is a magician able to make the sun go black. When the eclipse takes place King Arthur is so impressed with the

Yankee's powers that he has him appointed Sir Boss. The Yankee now takes over the management of Camelot on a commission basis. He introduces the advances of twentieth-century science and big business, in short order transforming Camelot into a modern-day city with radio, billboard, telephones and efficiency experts. King Arthur begins to talk like Calvin Coolidge (America's President in 1927); Merlin talks in American slang.

Fresh, witty, spontaneous and satirical—in dialogue, lyrics and music—*A Connecticut Yankee* found a good deal of merriment in Camelot and with the Knights of the Round Table more than a half century before Lerner and Loewe wrote *Camelot*. *A Connecticut Yankee* was a more consistently unified work than *Camelot*, emphasising laughter and mockery without digression, where *Camelot* often allowed itself to lapse into the glamour, romance and spectacle of operetta.

Richard Rodgers' score boasted one of his greatest song hits of his career with Hart in "My Heart Stood Still". Rodgers and Hart had previously written this number for a London revue, *One Damn Thing After Another*, but bought it back for this musical comedy. Other musical delights included "Thou Swell", "On a Desert Island With Thee" and "I Feel at Home With You".

When *A Connecticut Yankee* was revived on Broadway in 1943—with an updated text—four new musical numbers were included, one of which was "To Keep My Love Alive".

On Your Toes

Book by Richard Rodgers, Lorenz Hart *and* George Abbott

Lyrics by Lorenz Hart

Music by Richard Rodgers

Staged by Worthington Miner

Choreography by George Balanchine

First produced at the Imperial Theatre on 11th April, 1936, with Ray Bolger as "Phil Dolan III", Tamara Geva as "Vera Barnova" and Doris Carson as "Frankie Frayne".

Principal Characters

PHIL DOLAN II
LIL DOLAN
PHIL DOLAN III
FRANKIE FRAYNE
SIDNEY COHN
VERA BARNOVA

Phil Dolan II and Lil are a pair of vaudevillians ("Two-a-day for Keith") who have high aspirations for their son, Phil Dolan III. They want him to forget all about the stage and find a future in a more cultural pursuit. Young Phil becomes a music instructor, interested only in great music ("The Three B's") and in the more serious aspects of the dance. In Frankie Frayne, a young student who writes songs, he finds a kindred spirit ("There's a Small Hotel"), but he is actually in love with a ballerina, Vera Barnova, a member of the Russian ballet. To be near the woman he loves, Phil joins the ballet and becomes a participant in the performance of a grandiose ballet along classic designs based on the Scheherazade theme, *Princess Zenobia*. The performance is a fiasco, and the company hovers dangerously on the brink of financial ruin. Meanwhile, Sidney Cohn has submitted to Phil a bizarre modern ballet called *Slaughter on Tenth Avenue*, which he has repeatedly tried to get the Russian Ballet to perform without success. When the backer of the company, Peggy Porterfield, threatens to withdraw her financial support the company decides, as a last desperate measure, to mount *Slaughter on Tenth Avenue.* When Vera's dancing partner is completely incapable of performing the modern routines Phil takes over the part and helps make the ballet a formidable success. After that he discovers that it is Frankie and not Vera with whom he is really in love.

On Your Toes was Broadway's first successful musical comedy to tap the world of the ballet both for the subject-matter of text and for its main production numbers. Of the latter the most significant is *Slaughter on Tenth Avenue*, with which the musical comes to a climax. A modern ballet, treated with the utmost seriousness of artistic purpose, it is actually a satire on gangster stories. A hoofer and his girl, fleeing from murderous gangsters, take refuge in a Tenth Avenue café, where the gangsters catch up with him and shoot the girl. The hoofer himself is finally saved by the police. For his music to *Slaughter on Tenth Avenue*, Rodgers borrowed none of his own material previously used in the play, but created an extended and sustained score, rich in melodic invention and symphonic in dimension. Though "There's a Small Hotel" became one of the leading song hits of 1936, it was *Slaughter on Tenth Avenue* that won accolades from audiences and critics. Almost twenty years after it was first seen, Richard Watts, Jr., could still say of it: "A sizable number of jazz ballets have passed this way since it first appeared, but it still is something of a classic in its field, and the music Mr. Rodgers wrote for it continues to seem one of the major achievements of his career."

Pal Joey

Book by John O'Hara *based on his own stories*
Lyrics by Lorenz Hart
Music by Richard Rodgers
Staged by George Abbott
Dances by Robert Alton

First produced at the Ethel Barrymore Theatre on 25th December, 1940, with Gene Kelly as "Joey", Vivienne Segal as "Vera" and Leila Ernst as "Linda".

Principal Characters

JOEY
LINDA ENGLISH
VERA SIMPSON

Joey is a master of ceremonies in a dingy night-club in Chicago's South Side. He is hard-boiled, cynical, double-dealing, but also a fellow of considerable charm. He meets lovely Linda outside a pet shop and proceeds at once to reveal to her that she might prove an inspiration to him ("I Could Write a Book"). He invites Linda to his night-club where he impresses her with his songs and entertainment. Another guest that evening is Vera Simpson of the Chicago Social Register. She is considerably taken with Joey and invites him to her table. There Joey proves so brash and impudent that Vera leaves the night-club agitatedly; but Joey, with his usual self-confidence, is certain she will be back. He is, of course, right. Nobody has had the nerve to treat Vera the way Joey did, and for this reason Vera is fascinated by him. She fits him out with handsome clothes and is ready to pamper and pet him because, as she confesses freely, she has gone wild over him ("Bewitched, Bothered and Bewildered"). Vera proves excessively generous. She sets him up in a magnificent apartment ("In Our Little Den of Iniquity"), then buys him a night-club of his own, the Chez Joey.

After the club has opened and has become a success, Linda visits Vera to warn her of a plot she had overheard. An agent and a singer at the club plan to blackmail her: to reveal to Vera's husband her affair with Joey if she is not ready to pay a handsome price for silence. Vera asks Linda if she has come to her with this warning out of her interest in Joey. Linda shrugs her shoulders and insists she has no use for the cad ("Take Him"). When one of the blackmailers arrives for his money he finds that Vera has summoned the police, and makes a hasty and undignified retreat. At this point Vera informs Joey she has grown tired of him and sends him on his way. Having lost not only Vera but also Linda, Joey decides sadly to leave town for good.

Pal Joey was a forceful and uncompromising presentation of unpleasant characters and situations; and it offered a seamy side of life in a disreputable neighbourhood. This was strong medicine for American theatre audiences in 1940, so long accustomed to only sweetness and light in their musicals. They rejected it. "How can you draw sweet water from a foul well?" inquired the critic, Brooks Atkinson, reflecting the general reaction to this unusual production. But when *Pal Joey* was revived on Broadway in 1952 it found both critics and audiences more ready to accept an unorthodox musical that avoided the hackneyed and was willing to treat its audiences as adults. Richard Watts, Jr., and Robert Coleman both described the musical as a masterwork. *Pal Joey* now achieved the longest run of any revival of a musical in the history of the Broadway theatre. In addition, it received the New York Drama Critics Award as the best musical of the season and became the first musical ever to gather as many as eleven Donaldson Awards.

Oklahoma!

Book and Lyrics by Oscar Hammerstein II *based on* Green Grow the Lilacs, *a play by* Lynn Riggs

Music by Richard Rodgers

Directed by Rouben Mamoulian

Choreography by Agnes De Mille

First produced at the St. James Theatre on 31st March, 1943, with Alfred Drake as "Curly", Joan Roberts as "Laurey" and Celeste Holm as "Ado Annie".

Principal Characters

CURLY
LAUREY
JUD FRY
WILL PARKER
ADO ANNIE CARNES
AUNT ELLER
JUDGE ANDREW CARNES

The setting is the Indian territory now known as the State of Oklahoma; the time, soon after the turn of the present century. Aunt Eller is churning butter outside her farmhouse as from offstage come the strains of "Oh, What a Beautiful Mornin'". The singer is Curly, come to invite Aunt Eller's niece, Laurey, to a box-social that evening. When Laurey appears she feigns indifference to Curly so he presses his invitation by describing to her the surrey in which he will take her to the party ("Surrey with the Fringe on Top"). But he is finally compelled to confess that the surrey is only a figment of his imagination, a fact that sends Laurey off in anger. Will Parker now appears with a description of his recent experiences at a fair in Kansas City ("Kansas City"), where he won fifty dollars in a steer-roping contest. That fifty dollars is highly important to him: he wants to marry Ado Annie and her father, Judge Andrew Carnes, had specified that he will not give his consent until Will can manage to accumulate such a sum.

In spite of her assumed diffidence towards and anger at Curly, Laurey is really in love with him. To arouse his jealousy she decides to go to the box-social with the hired-hand, a despicable character. When Laurey discovers that Curly intends going to the affair with another girl she tosses her head indifferently ("Many a New Day"). Meanwhile, Ado Annie has let it be known that her partner would be the Persian peddler, Ali Hakim; at the same time she reveals that she is the kind of a girl who cannot refuse a man anything ("I Can't Say No").

The flirtatious overtures that Akim has been making to Ado Annie make her father insist that the peddler marry the girl. Will is out of the running: he has extravagantly spent his fifty dollars on presents.

When Curly and Laurey again meet they decide to go to the social together, after all; but for the sake of the neighbours they will be discreet about their behaviour or be misunderstood in their intentions towards each other ("People Will Say We're in Love"). There is now the business of informing Jud he has lost his partner for the evening. Curly visits him at his dismal and shabby room in the smokehouse, and at first gets Jud into a good humour by telling him that though the people appear unfriendly they really think well of him and would mourn his death no end ("Pore Jud!"). Then having delivered his message, he leaves Jud wallowing in self-pity ("Lonely Room").

In a dream which becomes an elaborate dance sequence, Laurey imagines how it would be to marry Curly. She further sees Jud breaking up the marriage, beating up her lover and forcing her to get off with him. She is rudely awakened from this dream by Jud's appearance. He has come to insist she go with him to the party. When, a moment later, Curly appears for the same purpose, Laurey—fearful that her dream had been an ominous warning of things to come—suddenly decides to go with Jud instead of Curly, much to the latter's confusion and bewilderment.

The box-social, with which the second act opens, proves to be a gay affair. Farmers and cowmen speak of their mutual rivalry with good humour ("The Farmer and the Cowman"). Then the auction of food boxes takes place, the men bidding for the boxes of the girls of their choice. A spirited contest ensues for Laurey's box between Jud and Curly. Determined to be the winner, Curly sells everything he owns and gets the box for the exorbitant price of $42.31. Meanwhile, Akim pays Will fifty dollars for all his presents. Having no intention of marrying Ado, Akim would very much like to see Will get the girl. Now Will and Ado are in a position to talk about their future together ("All or Nothin'").

Three weeks later, the marriage of Curly and Laurey takes place. Jud, drunk, breaks into the festivities and threatens Curly with a knife. In the ensuing brawl Jud falls on the blade and dies. A makeshift trial is hurriedly improvised by Judge Carnes so as not to delay the young couple. Curly is acquitted of murder, and he is free to go off with his bride on their honeymoon ("Oklahoma!").

The saga of the trials and tribulations of *Oklahoma!* before it reached its première performance in New York to become one of the surpassing triumphs of the American theatre is by now a twice-told tale. Virtually everybody connected with the production was convinced he was involved in a box-office disaster. Here was a musical without stars; without "gags" and humour; without the routines and production numbers so traditional with musical comedy; without the sex appeal of chorus girls in flimsy attire. Here was a musical that strayed into realism and grim tragedy, with Jud as one of its main characters, and his death as a climax of the story. Here, finally, was a musical which for the first time in Broadway history leaned heavily upon American folk-ballet—the choreography by Agnes De Mille, one of America's foremost choreographers and ballet dancers. *Oklahoma!* might be fine art, was the general consensus of opinion before première time, but it was poison at the box-office. The effort to get the necessary financial backing proved a back-breaking operation, successfully consummated only because the Theatre Guild, which had undertaken the production, had many friends and allies. But there was hardly an investor anywhere who did not think he was throwing his money down a sewer.

When *Oklahoma!* opened out of town scouts sent back to New York the succinct message: "No Girls, No Gags, No Chance." After the New York opening, the line was revised to read: "No Girls, No Gags, No Tickets." For at that première performance the surpassing beauty, the freshness, the imagination and the magic of this musical play held the audience spellbound from the opening curtain on. There was a vociferous ovation at the end. The next day the critics vied with each other in the expression of superlatives. One of them, Lewis Nichols, did not hesitate to describe it as a "folk opera".

But *Oklahoma!* not only opened new vistas for the American musical theatre with its new and unorthodox approaches, and with the vitality and inspiration of Hammerstein's text and lyrics and Rodgers' music. It created box-office history. It ran on Broadway for five years and nine months (2,248 performances), breaking all of the then existing records both for length of run and for box-office receipts. A national company toured the United States for ten years, performing in about 250 cities before an audience exceeding ten million. In addition, when the New York engagement ended the original company went on a tour of seventy-one cities. Companies were formed to produce the play in Europe, South Africa, Scandinavia, Australia and for the armed forces in all the theatres of war during the last years of the Second World War. In London its run proved the longest in the three-hundred year history of the Drury Lane Theatre.

Carousel

Book and Lyrics by OSCAR HAMMERSTEIN II *based on* Liliom, *a play by* FERENC MOLNAR *as adapted by* BENJAMIN F. GLAZER

Music by RICHARD RODGERS

Staged by ROUBEN MAMOULIAN

Dances by AGNES DE MILLE

First produced at the Majestic Theatre on 19th April, 1945, with John Raitt as "Billy" and Jan Clayton as "Julie".

PRINCIPAL CHARACTERS

JULIE JORDAN
MRS. MULLIN
BILLY BIGELOW
CARRIE PIPPERIDGE
ENOCH SNOW

To the strains of the "Carousel Waltz" the curtain rises upon an amusement park in a New England town in 1873. Fishermen, sailors, mill girls and children are enjoying the sights and sounds of a carnival atmosphere. Two mill girls, Carrie Pipperidge and Julie Jordan, are having a good time until Mrs. Mullin, proprietress of the carousel, insults them. When her handsome, strapping barker, Billy Bigelow, jumps to the defence of the girls, Mrs. Mullin summarily fires him. Billy, being a happy-go-lucky fellow, does not take this dismissal to heart; on the contrary, he invites Julie to have a beer with him. While he is off to get his belongings, Carrie asks her friend Julie whether she finds Billy attractive, but Julie is singularly evasive ("You're a Queer One, Julie Jordan"). Carrie thereupon confides to Julie that she has a fellow of her own, the fisherman Enoch Snow, whom she plans to marry ("When I Marry Mr. Snow"). When Billy returns and is left alone with Julie they begin to talk about love, and the kind of person each would be attracted to. When Billy inquires if Julie could ever marry a person such as he is, Julie replies that she would—*if* she loved him ("If I Loved You"). The romance soon takes wing: Julie and Billy get married.

Making preparations for the first clam-bake of the year, the fishermen, mill girls, sailors and children are ebullient over the vernal season ("June Is Bustin' Out All Over"). Carrie and Enoch Snow dream about their future together as man and wife ("When the Children Are Asleep"). At this point Billy learns that Julie is pregnant. Though up to now completely irresponsible and incapable of meeting the emotional and domestic demands made upon him by marriage, Billy is suddenly filled with a sense of parental pride and with an overwhelming feeling of tenderness for both his wife and his unborn child ("Soliloquy"). He is determined to get money for them to assure their future.

The clam-bake proves a gay affair ("This Was a Real Nice Clam Bake"), alive with good humour, rowdy spirits and song. Julie, however, is touched with sadness, knowing as she does that her husband is volatile in his moods and undependable in his behaviour; yet she loves him deeply, and for this reason there is no point in her wondering if he is good or bad ("What's the Use of Wond'rin'"). But that there is much bad in Billy becomes evident when he gets involved in a hold-up. Caught by the police, he commits suicide to elude arrest. Overwhelmed by her grief, Julie tries to find solace in the comforting words of her friend, Nettie ("You'll Never Walk Alone").

Billy arrives in Heaven, where he defiantly tells two of its police that he does not regret his actions on Earth. For this he is doomed to spend fifteen years in Purgatory. At the end of that period the Starkeeper in Heaven permits him to return to Earth for a single day to gain redemption for his soul. Snatching a star from the firmament, which he intends as a gift to his daughter, Billy comes back to Earth. He finds that she is an unhappy child who is incapable of receiving his gift. As a reflex action in his disappointment, Billy slaps her face, but the slap is given in love, and not in hate, and so the girl feels no pain. Through his understanding and tenderness, Billy is able to lift his daughter out of her misery and to fill her with hope and courage. He now watches the ceremony during which Julie is graduating from school, happy to see that her head is now high, happy too that he has found redemption.

As the immediate successor to *Oklahoma!*—the musical play with which Rodgers and Hammerstein made stage history—*Carousel* takes the American musical play another impressive step forward. From many points of view, it is better than *Oklahoma!*, though its performance history is less spectacular. The text has greater depths of feeling, a more encompassing humanity and greater universality—with tragic overtones not often encountered on the musical stage. The fusion of music and the text is even more sensitive here than in *Oklahoma!*. Song flows into speech and speech into song; melody and text become one. Extended sequences combine prose, verse and speech, or recitative and melody. The orchestra often becomes an eloquent commentator on what has just happened or is about to happen. And Rodgers' artistic horizon is extended. Here he is much more than the shaper of fresh, original and beautiful melody; he is a musical dramatist. For the orchestra he now writes with symphonic breadth. The form and style of his windswept melodies and his expansive musical scenes, now unhampered by structural limitations, were dictated by the requirements of the text without concern for convention or tradition. His dramatic expressiveness succeeds time and again to penetrate to the very core of a character or situation.

South Pacific

Book by Oscar Hammerstein II *and* Joshua Logan *based on* Tales of South Pacific, *by* James A. Michener

Lyrics by Oscar Hammerstein II

Music by Richard Rodgers

Staged by Joshua Logan

First produced at the Majestic Theatre on 7th April, 1949, with Ezio Pinza as "Emile de Becque", Mary Martin as "Nellie" and Juanita Hall as "Bloody Mary".

Principal Characters

ENSIGN NELLIE FORBUSH
EMILE DE BECQUE
BLOODY MARY
LT. JOSEPH CABLE
LIAT

The curtain rises on an island in the Pacific during the Second World War. At the home of the wealthy, middle-aged French planter, Emile de Becque, two Eurasian children are performing an impromptu minuet and chanting a French ditty ("Dites-moi"). Emile, who had settled on this island some years before the outbreak of the war, is host at dinner to the charming American nurse, Ensign Nellie Forbush. She reveals to him some facets of her personality ("Cockeyed Optimist"). The two are strongly attracted to each other, and it does not take them long to realise that they are in love ("Some Enchanted Evening"). Before Nellie leaves, Emile asks her to consider becoming his wife.

In another part of the island a group of American sailors, Seabees and Marines are singing the praises of Bloody Mary, a Tonkinese ("Bloody Mary is the Girl I Love"). Bloody Mary excites the interest of the Americans in the mysterious nearby island of Bali Ha'i, declared off-limits to them; the Americans suspect that the French planters have secreted there all their womenfolk as protection from the Americans. All this talk reminds the Americans that they have everything on this island that they could possibly want except—dames. They lament the lack in no uncertain terms ("There Is Nothing Like a Dame"). When the handsome Lieutenant Cable appears, Bloody Mary instantly sees in him a prospect as husband for her lovely daughter, Liat. Mary now begins to stimulate also Cable's interest in Bali Ha'i ("Bali Ha'i"). While his curiosity in the place is aroused, there are for the moment more important things on Cable's mind: he is to establish a coast watch on a nearby Japanese-held island. Since Emile de Becque knows this terrain well, Cable wants to induce him to join him on this dangerous mission. The commanding officers, consequently, call on Nellie's help by asking her to find out as much as she can about Emile. Meanwhile, Nellie has come to the conclusion that marriage with Emile might very well be a mistake, considering the differences in their age and background ("I'm Gonna Wash That Man Right Outa My Hair"). But Emile succeeds, at last, in convincing her that all her fears are groundless. There is no longer any question with Nellie that she loves Emile more than any man she has ever met ("I'm in Love with a Wonderful Guy").

Having found the woman of his dreams, Emile has no intention of endangering his life by helping Cable; and no arguments can persuade him to change his mind. The mission temporarily delayed, Cable can now devote a few days for recreation. He makes for Bali Ha'i, where Mary brings him to Liat, a sensitive Tonkinese girl of seventeen. Though she speaks only French, and Cable only English, they fall helplessly in love. Cable takes Liat in his arms and tells her of his feelings in song ("Younger than Springtime").

Back at Emile's plantation, Nellie discovers for the first time that he is the father of two Eurasian children, having formerly lived with a Polynesian girl. This news so upsets Nellie that she leaves Emile, determined never again to see him.

Bloody Mary brings Liat from Bali Ha'i to convince Cable to marry her. She describes the happy life he would have with the girl, a life full of the most beautiful things ("Happy Talk"). Bloody Mary is even willing to turn over to Cable all the money she has saved. Cable is so deeply moved by all this that he presents Liat with a gift of a man's gold watch which he had inherited from his grandfather. Tenderly, pathetically, Cable tries to explain to Mary that he can never marry Liat. In a fit of temper, Bloody Mary smashes the watch on the ground, drags Liat away and mumbles that she will arrange to have Liat marry somebody else.

Emile now comes to Nellie to plead with her not to allow his Eurasian children to come between them. Nellie insists that it is not the children that is bothering her, but their mother; the thought of Emile having loved a Polynesian is too much for her to bear. Cable, a witness to this conversation—and who instantly recognizes that he too rejected love because of racial prejudice—comments softly that hate is not born in man, as Nellie is tempted to believe, that it happens *after* birth; that a man has to be taught to hate and fear ("Carefully Taught"). He then tells Emile that should he survive this war he, too, would like to make his permanent home on this island. But the island has suddenly lost all its appeal for Emile, now that he has lost the woman he loved and with her his paradise ("This Nearly Was Mine"). In fact, since he has no use for life any longer, he is ready to accompany Cable on their dangerous war mission.

They penetrate the Japanese island, whence they relay back information which makes it possible for the American forces to destroy twenty Japanese surface craft and pave the way for a successful invasion of fourteen Japanese-held islands. In the performance of his duties Cable is killed. But Emile survives. When he returns to his plantation he finds Nellie waiting for him—playing with and feeding his children.

With *South Pacific*, Rodgers and Hammerstein rose to new towering heights of success, both commercially and artistically, following their triumph with *Oklahoma!* and *Carousel.* There was hardly any question in anybody's mind at the première performance of *South Pacific* that this was a classic of the musical theatre of the stature of *Oklahoma!* and *Carousel.* The veteran producer Arthur Hammerstein called it the greatest musical show Broadway had ever seen, perfect in every respect. The critic Richard Watts, Jr., described it as "a thrilling and exultant musical play, an utterly captivating work of theatrical art". The response at the box-office was as exultant as that of critics and veteran theatre-goers. *South Pacific* ran five years on Broadway (1,925 performances), earning nine million dollars. The tour of the national company over a period of several years earned several more millions. The motion-picture adaptation grossed domestically more than sixteen million dollars, the sixth highest in the history of talking pictures in America. *South Pacific* played two and a half years in London, after which the company went on a tour that lasted another year and a half. It was also given in foreign translations in many other leading European capitals. The sheet music of its songs sold two million copies, and the long-playing recording of the score two million discs. The name "South Pacific" was licensed for cosmetics, dresses and lingerie. In addition to all this, *South Pacific* received most of the coveted awards, including the Pulitzer Prize for Drama, the New York Drama Critics Award as the season's best musical, seven Antoinette Perry and nine Donaldson Awards.

The King and I

Book and Lyrics by OSCAR HAMMERSTEIN II *based on* MARGARET LANDON'S *novel*, Anna and the King of Siam

Music by RICHARD RODGERS

Staged by JOHN VAN DRUTEN

Choreography by JEROME ROBBINS

First produced at the St. James Theatre on 29th March, 1951, with Gertrude Lawrence as "Anna" and Yul Brynner as the "King".

PRINCIPAL CHARACTERS

ANNA LEONOWENS
LOUIS LEONOWENS
THE KING
TUPTIM
LADY THIANG
LUN THA

In the 1860s the King of Siam—in his attempt to bring Western culture to his country—engaged Anna Leonowens, an attractive English schoolteacher, to teach his royal princes and princesses. On arriving in Siam with her son, Louis, she tries to allay her own fears and those of her son by whistling a tune ("I Whistle a Happy Tune"). Once in the palace, Anna is shocked to learn that she and her son will not get a house of their own as had been promised her by the King. She is also witness to the arrival of Tuptim, brought from Burma by Lun Tha, as a gift to the King of Siam. The King is pleased with Tuptim, and turns a deaf ear to Anna's complaints about having to live in the palace. He then summons his sixty-seven princes to meet Anna. They file in in an impressive procession ("March of Royal Siamese Children"). After they leave, Lady Thiang arouses Anna's sympathy for Tuptim by explaining that Tuptim and Lun Tha are deeply in love, and that once Lun Tha returns to Burma they will never again see each other. Anna can be duly sympathetic, for she can never forget how much she had loved her husband Tom, now dead ("Hello, Young Lovers").

In the palace grounds the King confesses that he is not sure of anything at all, that he does not know how much his children should be taught, and what is right or wrong ("A Puzzlement"). But Anna has no such qualms. After she and the children become acquainted with each other ("Getting to Know You") a unique bond of sympathy and affection develops between teacher and pupils. Nevertheless, Anna is unhappy, still determined to live with her son, not in the palace like a menial, but in a house of their own. She confides her feelings to the King in no uncertain terms, and the King just as forcefully reminds her that she is just a servant and must behave like one. This exchange so upsets Anna that she leaves the King in a huff. In her bedroom she gives vent to her rage ("Shall I Tell You What I Think of You?"). Meanwhile, Tuptim and Lun Tha meet secretly in the darkness of the palace gardens to exchange love vows ("We Kiss in a Shadow").

A crisis is developing in Siam. An agent in Singapore has discovered letters to the British describing the King of Siam as a barbarian and suggesting that Siam be made a protectorate. This information upsets Anna no end, for despite her differences with the King, she has come to admire him and cannot tolerate his being called a barbarian ("This Is a Man"). She comes to the King's study to apologise to him for having lost her temper. When the King tells her of his political difficulties, and advises her that Sir Edward Ramsey and other high-ranking English men and women are coming to visit Siam and judge for themselves, Anna suggests that they be entertained in grand style, but with a European dinner and ball, and with all the Siamese princes and princesses wearing European dress. In another part of the palace, while this is going on, Lun Tha and Tuptim are making plans to run away together ("I Have Dreamed").

The visiting English are entertained with a monster ball and with a ballet, "The Small House of Uncle Thomas", in which *Uncle Tom's Cabin* is translated in terms of the Siamese dance. The visit is a huge success: Sir Edward needs no further proof that he is dealing here with cultured and sensitive people and not with barbarians. Both Anna and the King are exhilarated by the success of their efforts, which encourages Anna to describe to the King some other European customs, such as social dancing ("Shall We Dance?"). Suddenly Tuptim is brought to the King. She has been caught red-handed trying to escape. The King orders that she be whipped, but Anna fiercely takes her part and prevents the King from carrying out this order. Lun Tha, however, has been killed.

By now Anna feels that she can stay in Siam no longer, and makes preparations to return to England. But before she can leave, the King falls seriously ill. On his death-bed the King implores her to stay on in Siam, promising to meet any conditions she might impose. When the royal children join in this entreaty Anna cannot find it in her heart to leave a country, a people and, most of all, the pupils she has come to love.

It took considerable courage for Rodgers and Hammerstein to adapt Margaret Landon's novel for the musical stage. Here was a story in which no love interest involved the two leading characters, and which ends with the death of the hero. Here, too, was a story with mostly Oriental characters—except for four Anglo-Saxons, none of whom were Americans. The authors met their challenge without equivocation. They created a picture of the East with dignity, and without resorting to any of the clichés so long identifying the Orient and Orientals in musical comedy. Lyrics, dialogue, music, settings, costumes and ballet were all beautifully integrated into a single artistic creation which represented to one critic (Danton Walker) "a flowering of all the arts of the theater". In *The King and I*, as Richard Watts, Jr., pointed out, we see "an East of frank and unashamed romance, seen through the eyes of . . . theatrical artists of rare taste and creative power".

Flower-Drum Song

Book and Lyrics by OSCAR HAMMERSTEIN II *based on a novel by* C. Y. LEE

Music by RICHARD RODGERS

Directed by GENE KELLY

Choreography by CAROL HANEY

First produced at the St. James Theatre on 1st December, 1958, with Pat Suzuki as "Linda Low", Miyoshi Umeki as "Mei Li" and Larry Blydon as "Sammy Fong".

PRINCIPAL CHARACTERS

WANG TA
WANG CHI YANG
SAMMY FONG
DR. LI
MEI LI
LINDA LOW
FRANKIE
HELEN CHAI

The setting is San Francisco's Chinatown; the characters are Chinese; the basic theme is the struggle between Eastern and Western traditions, between the old and the new.

Wang Ta, elder son of Wang Chi Yang, has fallen in love with Linda Low, owner of a night spot, Thunderbird. But Sammy Fong, who is both completely Westernised and Americanised, has come to Wang Chi Yang to propose a match between Ta and Mei Li, a girl from the East, a "picture bride". Indeed, he has brought her with him. She is a sweet, diffident young girl of whom Wang approves wholeheartedly. He is further impressed by her when she sings for him an ancient Chinese song ("A Hundred Million Miracles"). Sammy thrusts a marriage contract into Wang's hands, hoping to consummate the deal quickly. But Dr. Li, the girl's father, objects, since the original contract had specified that the girl was to marry Sammy.

Ta is having a date with Linda. She is indeed very much of a female, as she elaborates in a song ("I Enjoy Being a Girl"). She is aggressive and forward, just as Ta is shy and withdrawn. When Ta offers to marry Linda she shows some interest, knowing how rich his father is; but she also insists that she must first get the permission of her brother, Frankie, a sailor.

Preparations are now being made in the Wang household for the forthcoming marriage of Ta and the "picture bride", even though the two have not yet met. When they do, Mei falls instantly in love with him. But Ta is very little impressed by this plainly dressed, retiring little girl. But when she dresses up in a glamorous gown presented her by her future father-in-law and stands resplendent before Ta he begins to take notice of her.

That night a party is taking place in the garden of Wang's house. Among the guests are Linda Low and her brother Frankie. With a prod from his sister, Frankie informs Wang that he has been seriously considering Ta's request for Linda's hand and has given his consent. Linda embraces Wang warmly and calls him "father". All this has caught Wang completely unawares. He sternly informs his son that such a marriage cannot be accepted. With Ta still determined to marry Linda, Sammy Fong is placed in the terrible predicament of having to marry Mei Li himself, a most undesirable prospect, since he has known Linda a long time and has more than a passing interest in her. He does his best to discourage Mei from having any interest in him ("Don't Marry Me"). Wily Sammy must now devise some way of changing this sorry situation. He invites Wang and his family to the Thunderbird night-club to witness Linda's act, the climax of which is a tantalising strip-tease. Wang, shocked, leaves in a huff. He is more determined than ever that his son will never marry a girl like this. Sammy is highly pleased with himself at this development. Linda is upset to the point of throwing a champagne bucket on Sammy's head. And Ta finds refuge at the home of Helen Chai, a seamstress, where he spends the night on a couch. Mei Li comes there the following morning to get Wang's jacket mended. Noticing Ta's dinner jacket, she jumps to conclusions, and leaves the apartment in horror. But there is nothing between Ta and Helen, whose only feeling for Ta is that of tenderness. When Ta leaves, she expresses her sense of loneliness in a poignant ballad, "Love, Look Away".

By now, Ta is convinced that Linda is not for him. He comes back home to admit to his father that the old man was right, that Mei Li was the girl he should marry. But it is now Mei Li who refuses to consider marriage, or to have any further associations with Ta. Such a complicated turn of affairs can be discussed and straightened only at a meeting of the Three Family Association. Sammy Fong comes there with the news that he and Linda have decided to get married and settle down to domesticity. This does not please the Association at all. Having examined a contract previously drawn up between Sammy and Mei Li, the Association decrees that nobody but Mei shall become Sammy's wife. In vain does Sammy try to convince Linda that nothing has been changed between them, that even if he is "framed" into marrying Mei he will continue to love Linda.

Wedding plans are now being crystallised. Ta comes to Mei Li to bring her a wedding gift of an old family clock. When he gives her a fraternal kiss of congratulations he cannot hide the fact that he is deeply in love with her. But it is apparently too late. The wedding procession takes place on one of San Francisco's streets. The bride, heavily veiled, is carried on a sedan chair to her future husband, Sammy. As dictated by custom, Sammy drinks from a wedding goblet, then offers the goblet to his new wife. But when the bride removes her veil she turns out to be not Mei but Linda. It is then that Mei Li announces that since she has entered the United States illegally, all marriage contracts and decisions by the Family Association are null and void. This development leaves Mei Li free to marry Ta.

The Sound of Music

Book by Howard Lindsay *and* Russel Crouse *suggested by* The Trapp Family Singers, *by* Maria Augusta Trapp

Lyrics by Oscar Hammerstein II

Music by Richard Rodgers

Directed by Vincent J. Donehue

Musical numbers staged by Joe Layton

First produced at the Lunt-Fontanne Theatre on 16th November, 1959, with Mary Martin as "Maria", Theodore Bikel as "Captain von Trapp" and Patricia Neway as the "Mother Abbess".

Principal Characters

MARIA RAINER
THE MOTHER ABBESS
CAPTAIN GEORG VON TRAPP
LIESL
ROLF GRUBER
ELSA SCHRAEDER

The main characters of *The Sound of Music* are members of an actual family, the Trapps, who successfully toured the world of music in choral concerts.

The first scene takes place at the Nonnberg Abbey in Austria in 1938. The nuns are pursuing their respective tasks, but the postulant Maria is not with them, for she is lying in a hammock on the mountain-top enjoying the beauty of Nature ("The Sound of Music"). The nuns, and the Mother Abbess particularly, are considerably disturbed about her, since they are convinced she is not ready to enter upon a life dedicated solely to religion ("Maria"). The Mother Abbess confesses that there are many pleasures in life which she shares with Maria ("My Favourite Things"), but for Maria's sake she decides to send the postulant away to serve as temporary governess for the seven children of Captain Georg von Trapp, a retired Austrian Naval officer, and a widower.

Maria comes to this household and completely wins over the children's affection, particularly after she entertains them and allays their fears during a thunderstorm ("The Lonely Goatherd"). She teaches the children to love music, and especially to sing ("Do, Re, Mi"). And she can be uniquely sympathetic to the oldest of the children, Liesl, when she gets involved in her first love affair, with the village boy, Rolf Gruber ("Sixteen Going on Seventeen").

The Captain brings from Vienna Elsa Schraeder, his fiancée, who prevails on him to give a huge party. After the children bid the guests good night ("So Long, Farewell"), Maria becomes suddenly aware that she has fallen in love with her employer. Horrified, she flees from the villa back to the Abbey, where the Mother Abbess encourages her to overcome any obstacle that may lie in the way of her happiness ("Climb Every Mountain"). Returning to the villa, she finds that the Captain and his fiancée have separated following a quarrel over Nazism. The romance of Maria and the Captain now develops rapidly. They get married in a festive ceremony at the Abbey. After returning from their honeymoon, the Nazis—who by now have invaded Austria—summon the Captain back to naval duty. An avowed anti-Fascist, the Captain resolutely refuses to do so. He arranges to flee from the villa with his wife and children. With the Nazis in pursuit, the Trapps hide in the garden of the Abbey, and after that make their way to freedom by foot over the mountains.

With *The Sound of Music* the epoch-making collaboration of Rodgers and Hammerstein came to an end: Oscar Hammerstein II died on 23rd August, 1960. Happily, this partnership, which changed the destiny of the American musical theatre, ended on a note of triumph. *The Sound of Music* is the most beautiful and glowing musical Rodgers and Hammerstein had written since *The King and I*, and their greatest box-office triumph since that time. Before coming to New York it had accumulated the largest advance sale in the history of the Broadway theatre—about three million dollars—and during its first two years in New York there was never an empty seat in the house.

Good News

Book by LAURENCE SCHWAB *and* BUDDY DE SYLVA
Lyrics by BUDDY DE SYLVA *and* LEW BROWN
Music by RAY HENDERSON
Staged by EDGAR MACGREGOR

First produced at the 46th Street Theatre on 6th September, 1927, with Mary Lawlor as "Constance", John Price Jones as "Tom" and Zelma O'Neal as "Flo".

PRINCIPAL CHARACTERS

TOM MARLOWE
CONSTANCE LANE
BOBBY RANDALL
FLO

Good News is a musical comedy with a college setting and a football game as the pivot on which the plot rotates. When first produced, the college rah-rah spirit was early injected into the performance. The ushers were dressed in the then traditional college uniform of jersey shirts; just before the beginning of the overture the men in the orchestra let loose several loud "Rah-Rah-Rahs". The curtain rises on Tait College, where football is king. Tom Marlowe, captain of the team, is in danger of not being able to play in the year's big game with Colton College, because he cannot pass his grades. Constance Lane, however, has coached him into passing the necessary examinations. In this process, love interest is sparked. At the big game Tom almost becomes the goat when he fumbles the ball. But Bobby Randall recovers it and is instrumental in winning the game. Tom is still the college football hero, and as such he completes his conquest of Constance.

The college spirit pervades the score, particularly in numbers like "The Girls of Pi Beta Phi", sung by a girls' chorus, and the dynamic "Varsity Drag", sung by Zelma O'Neal as Flo, a performance that helped make her a star. The principal love song of Connie and Tom is "The Best Things in Life are Free", a title used many years later for the screen biography of De Sylva, Brown and Henderson, the authors of *Good News*.

Anything Goes

Book by Guy Bolton, P. G. Wodehouse, Howard Lindsay *and* Russel Crouse

Lyrics and Music by Cole Porter

Choreography by Robert Alton

Directed by Howard Lindsay

First produced at the Alvin Theatre on 21st November, 1934, with William Gaxton as "Billy", Ethel Merman as "Reno" and Victor Moore as "Moon".

Principal Characters

BILLY CROCKER
RENO SWEENEY
REVEREND DR. MOON
HOPE HARCOURT
SIR EVELYN OAKLEIGH

The main action takes place on a luxury liner sailing from New York to Southampton. But first we come to a preliminary scene in a smart New York bar. Reno Sweeney, a night-club entertainer, on the eve of leaving for Europe, expresses her sentiments for Billy Crocker in "I Get a Kick Out of You".

Once she boards the liner she discovers to her delight that Billy is also a passenger, though an unlisted one. He had come to bid Reno "*bon voyage*" when he comes upon his one-time fiancée, Hope Harcourt, *en route* to England to marry Sir Evelyn Oakleigh. His former love for Hope suddenly revived, Billy impetuously decides to stay on the ship when it sets sail, even though he possesses neither a passport nor a ticket. He manages to get both from a pathetic-looking, broken-voiced little man who is Public Enemy No. 13 fleeing from the police disguised as a clergyman, Reverend Dr. Moon. One of Moon's confederates had failed to show up at sailing time, and Billy can use his ticket and passport if he is willing to travel in disguise. Once the ship leaves harbour, Billy is able from time to time to emerge from his disguise—once to be romantic with Hope ("All Through the Night"); another time to exchange saucy compliments with Reno ("You're the Top"). When Moon's real identity is revealed he is confined to the brig by the ship's captain. The latter is suddenly inspired to hold an improvised revival meeting with Moon as his main penitent. After Moon inspires some of the passengers to confess their sins Reno carries the revival meeting to a stirring climax with "Blow, Gabriel, Blow".

All the principals come to Oakleigh's home in England, where Hope and Sir Evelyn are to get married. The prospect of marriage pleases neither of them, since their union had been an arrangement of convenience to save Bailey Products, a floundering business establishment. But Hope and Sir Evelyn soon learn that Bailey Products is not bankrupt at all; that, indeed, a buyer stands ready to purchase it for several million dollars. Thus Hope and Evelyn are free to go their separate ways. Hope returns to Billy, while Sir Evelyn and Reno discover each other. Meanwhile, word has come from Washington, D.C., that "Moon" is free to go as he pleases: the police are not interested in him at all, since he is as harmless as a cream-puff. The sudden loss of status upsets the little man no end. "Sometimes," he whines, "I just can't understand *this* administration in Washington!"

When *Anything Goes* was first projected the text was the work of Bolton and Wodehouse exclusively. Their story concerned a shipwreck, and its impact on some off-beat characters. But before *Anything Goes* could go into rehearsal, a major sea disaster actually took place off the coast of New Jersey: the burning of the *Morro Castle*, in which 134 people lost their lives. Shipwrecks consequently had suddenly become a highly sensitive area for the exploitation of song and humour. Vinton Freedley, the producer, prevailed upon Howard Lindsay and Russel Crouse to revise the libretto completely. This was the first time that Lindsay and Crouse worked together, initiating a playwriting partnership that was destined to become one of the most successful in the American theatre, and built on the solid foundation of one of the outstanding musical comedies of the 1930s.

Mexican Hayride

Book by HERBERT *and* DOROTHY FIELDS

Lyrics and Music by COLE PORTER

Staged by HASSARD SHORT

Choreography by PAUL HAAKON

First produced at the Winter Garden on 28th January, 1944, with Bobby Clark as "Joe Bascom", June Havoc as "Montana" and Wilbur Evans as "David Winthrop".

PRINCIPAL CHARACTERS

JOE BASCOM, *alias* HUMPHREY FISH
MONTANA
DAVID WINTHROP
LOMBO CAMPOS

The Plaza de Toros, in Mexico City, is crowded with Mexicans and visiting Americans loudly cheering the success of Montana, the celebrated American lady bullfighter. Custom dictates that Montana throw the ear of the bull at someone in the stands, and thus give him the honour of being for one week the "Amigo Americano". Montana plans to throw the ear at David Winthrop, the handsome young American *chargé d'affaires* with whom she is in love. But when she catches a glimpse of her cousin, Joe Bascom, alias Humphrey Fish—an American fugitive from justice, and Montana's cousin—she becomes so furious that she forgets herself and throws the ear at him. Thus Joe willy-nilly becomes "Amigo Americano". But Joe does not relish the honour, since the resultant publicity might reveal his true identity. He tries to escape from his hotel room, but is constantly frustrated by the arrival of beautiful senoritas come to do him honour. He decides, at last, to make the most of the situation. He now becomes acquainted with Lombo Campos, a speculator and "con" man, and with him conceives the idea of starting a private lottery. The venture proves so successful that the Government steps in to nail down the operators. Joe is thus exposed, and David Winthrop, suspecting Montana of being her cousin's partner in this shady deal, breaks off with her.

The second act opens in Xochimilco. The gardens are crowded with holiday visitors, and Joe and Campos, having escaped from prison, appear disguised as marachi players. David and Montana, now reconciled, are also here, searching for the escaped criminals. When they come upon Joe he once again makes a strategic retreat. We next find him with his shady business partner in Taxco, this time assuming the dress of tortila vendors. They are finally apprehended. Brought back to Mexico City, they are turned over to the American authorities. There is a final outburst of celebration in the streets of Mexico City for "Amigo Americano Week", while Montana and David are more convinced than ever of their mutual love.

The main love song, "I Love You", is assigned to the hero. Montana has two delightful comic numbers in Cole Porter's most winning sophisticated manner: "There Must Be Some One For Me" and "Count Your Blessings". "Sing to Me Guitar" provides some local Mexican flavour.

Kiss Me Kate

Book by BELLA *and* SAN SPEWACK
Lyrics and Music by COLE PORTER
Staged by JOHN C. WILSON
Dances by HANYA HOLM

First produced at the New Century Theatre on 30th December, 1948, with Alfred Drake as "Fred", Lisa Kirk as "Lois" and Patricia Morison as "Lilli".

PRINCIPAL CHARACTERS

FRED GRAHAM
LILLI VANESSI
LOIS LANE
BILL CALHOUN

A present-day theatrical troupe is presenting Shakespeare's *The Taming of the Shrew* in Baltimore, Maryland. The cast includes Fred Graham and his former wife, Lilli; also Bill Calhoun, an irresponsible gambler, and the girl in whom he is interested, Lois Lane. Bill breaks down and confesses to Lois that he is involved with gangsters, who have his I.O.U. for $10,000 from a crap game. This is not the first time Lois has had to tolerate Bill's escapades, and she inquires poignantly why he cannot behave himself ("Why Can't You Behave?"). Meanwhile Fred and his ex-wife—though divorced—begin to realise that their one-time tender feelings for each other have not completely died out. They start to reminisce about the shows in which they had appeared—including an old-fashioned Viennese operetta ("Wunderbar"). Just before the opening night of *The Taming of the Shrew*, Fred sends his star, Lola, flowers. By mistake they come to Lilli's dressing room—further proof to her that Fred still loves her. She now openly reveals that that love is reciprocated ("So In Love").

On stage, the performance of *The Taming of the Shrew* is taking place ("We Open in Venice"). As a play within a play, we learn that Bianca cannot get married until her older sister, Katharine, has found a husband ("Tom, Dick and Harry"). When Petruchio arrives in Padua to seek out a rich wife ("I've Come to Wive it Wealthily in Padua") he is chosen for Katharine. The latter, a shrew, makes no attempt to conceal her feelings about men ("I Hate Men"), while Petruchio knows that Katharine is not the woman of his dreams ("Were Thine That Special Face"). Nevertheless, he agrees to marry her.

We are now transferred from Shakespeare's Padua back to the intrigues within the theatrical company. Having learned that Fred's flowers were meant for Lola, Lilli bursts into a fit of temper, and announces hotly that she is leaving the company for good. Her departure, however, is delayed by the arrival of gangsters come to collect from Bill the $10,000 for his I.O.U.

In the second act we return to *The Taming of the Shrew*. Petruchio and Katharine are now man and wife. Since her violent tempers and caprices are complicating Petruchio's life no end, he begins to recall nostalgically his single-blessedness ("Where Is the Life that Late I Led?"). Back stage, when Bill reprimands Lois for flirting with one of the actors, she makes light of her tendency to be fickle ("Always True to You In My Fashion"). But, for all his troubles with Lois, Bill has good cause for cheer. There has been a violent shake-up in the gangster world, as a result of which Bill's I.O.U. is no longer valid. Bill and Lois are now reconciled, and Katharine and Fred return to each other.

Kiss Me Kate is the high ground of Cole Porter's long and fruitful career as a composer for the musical theatre. It is the only one of his musicals to exceed a thousand performances on Broadway (1,077). It is also the only one given half-way around the world in over a dozen translations. In Poland *Kiss Me Kate* was the first American musical comedy ever seen there; and at the Volksoper in Vienna it proved the greatest box-office attraction in the sixty-odd-year history of that theatre. The strongest suit of this production is, of course, Cole Porter's music. Never before, or since, has he been so rich and varied in his invention. At turns he is satiric, witty, nostalgic, sensual. Walter F. Kerr did not overstate the case when in his review he remarked that this score is "one of the loveliest and most lyrical yet composed for the contemporary stage".

Can-Can

Book by ABE BURROWS
Lyrics and Music by COLE PORTER
Staged by ABE BURROWS
Dances by MICHAEL KIDD

First produced at the Shubert Theatre on 7th May, 1953, with Lilo as "La Mome Pistache", Peter Cookson as "Aristide" and Gwen Verdon as "Claudine".

PRINCIPAL CHARACTERS

JUDGE ARISTIDE FORESTIER
CLAUDINE
HILAIRE JUSSAC
BORIS ADZINIDZINADZE
LA MOME PISTACHE

In the Montmartre district of Paris in 1893 the can-can is all the rage, though forbidden by the authorities. La Mome Pistache is the owner of a café where this dance is being surreptitiously performed, and for this reason the authorities decide to clamp down on the place. Aristide Forestier, a judge, is sent there to investigate the situation. He finds the café to be a delightful place, and its owner even more delectable ("C'est magnifique"). Pistache works her wiles on the hapless judge to get him to close his eyes to the goings-on in her cabaret ("Live and Let Live"). Aware that he has fallen in love with Pistache ("I Am in Love"), Aristide now summons all his legal skill and judicial influence to clear the good name of the cabaret and its owner. His ultimate success in getting Pistache out of her legal complications leads her to sing a hymn of praise to the beautiful city on the Seine ("I Love Paris"), permits the can-can to flourish in the full light of day and brings the venerable judge and Pistache to each other's arms. While all this goes on, a subsidiary love plot involves Claudine, a soubrette, with two men: Boris, a Bulgarian sculptor, and Hilaire, an art critic. One of the most amusing episodes comes at the beginning of the second act with a broad caricature of artist and art critic ("Never, Never Be an Artist"). The principal dance sequence comes in the first act with a comic ballet set in the Garden of Eden.

It might well be said that it is the city of Paris, more than Pistache, who is the heroine in *Can-Can*: the Paris of Toulouse-Lautrec, the Moulin Rouge and the can-can. Paris is evoked nostalgically not only in the best song in the score, "I Love Paris", but also in the beautiful settings and the opening curtain depicting the city by Jo Mielziner; in the broad travesty of an apache dance conceived by Michael Kidd; and in the climactic can-can which brings the musical comedy to an exciting conclusion.

Johnny Johnson

Book and Lyrics by PAUL GREEN

Music by KURT WEILL

Directed by LEE STRASBERG

First produced at the 44th Street Theatre on 1st November, 1936, with Russell Collins as "Johnny" and Phoebe Brand as "Minny Belle".

PRINCIPAL CHARACTERS

JOHNNY JOHNSON
MINNY BELLE TOMPKINS
ANGUISH HOWINGTON

A crowd had gathered in the village square of a small American town in 1917. A monument to peace, designed by Johnny Johnson, is being dedicated. During the ceremonies the Mayor makes a fiery speech about the necessity of keeping America out of the European War. These festivities are abruptly interrupted by the announcement that America has just declared war on Germany. The monument is completely forgotten; the atmosphere changes radically. Now the Mayor exhorts his young men to put on uniforms, and the crowd is yelling for the blood of the "Huns". This sudden transformation with his friends and neighbours startles Johnny Johnson. He becomes even more mystified when his girl friend, Minny Belle Tompkins, insists he enlist in the Army. Johnny answers that he has no cause for which to give up his life. When the crowd disperses and Johnny is left to himself he unveils his monument. One word stands out large and clear on the base: PEACE.

It is not long before Johnny finds a good reason for going to war: This is a conflict to end all conflicts, he has been told, a conflict not against the German people but their militaristic leaders. Now he, too, is fired with the war spirit, much to the delight of his proud girl friend ("Oh, Heart of Love").

As a recruit, Johnny is given an intelligence test which he answers with such sophistication and wisdom that he is suspected of being insane. Aroused by this accusation, he fells his accuser with one blow. This exhibition leads the recruiting officer to accept him eagerly into the Army.

And now Johnny, in uniform, is sailing out of New York for overseas duty. As the ship sails quietly out of the harbour and past the Statue of Liberty, Johnny makes a poetic pledge never to disgrace either the girl he loves or his country. As he moves away from the rail, the Statue of Liberty comes to life and vows to avenge anybody who is unfaithful to her ("Song of the Goddess").

In the second act Johnny is somewhere in France behind the lines. French soldiers are expressing their war-weariness ("Song of the Wounded Frenchmen"); the English and Irish can only think nostalgically of tea ("The Tea Song"); an American cowboy recalls his life on the range ("Rio Grande"). Assigned to a dangerous mission, Johnny dreams of Minny Belle ("Johnny's Dream"), with the roar of cannon serving as his lullaby. His mission is to capture an enemy sniper. Johnny creeps "over the top", a bread knife as his only weapon. He finds his victim hiding petrified in a churchyard. The German boy —his name is Johann—tells Johnny that neither he nor any other German wants to engage in this war. Suddenly, in a moment of humanity, Johnny decides to let this German go free, sending him back to his own country with some speeches of President Wilson to help promote the cause of peace.

While crawling back to his own lines, Johnny is wounded and sent to an army hospital. There he learns about a plan by the Allies to launch a major battle. Eager to stop all this bloodshed, Johnny effects his escape from the hospital by stealing a cylinder of laughing gas and spraying it on the doctors and nurses. He now bursts in upon a conference of the Allied High Command. Johnny begs them to call off their new offensive, but they only laugh at him. Johnny now turns upon them his laughing gas, which has such an effect on them that they call off the battle and appoint Johnny a general. But the effect of the gas soon wears off. Battle orders go out anew, and Johnny is arrested. Effecting his escape from an army prison, Johnny makes his way into the heat of battle. There he finds the German soldier, Johann, dead. Tenderly he cradles the dead boy in his arms. Accused of treason, Johnny is once again arrested.

Sent to a psychiatrist ("Psychiatry Song"), Johnny is consigned to an insane asylum. There the inmates create a miniature League of World Republics whose aim is to evolve the machinery for world peace ("Hymn to Peace").

Eventually, Johnny is released from the asylum and sent home. He finds that Minny Belle has married the town's rich man, Anguish Howington. To earn a living, Johnny becomes a pedlar of toys. A boy scout comes to buy a toy soldier, but Johnny tells him angrily that he never sells toy soldiers, only toy animals. The boy nevertheless reimburses Johnny with a five-cent piece; he also reveals he is the son of Anguish and Minny Belle. Johnny goes his way—singing of his unshaken faith in humanity ("Johnny's Song").

Johnny Johnson was Kurt Weill's first American production. He had left Germany upon the rise of the Nazi regime in 1933, after having become the country's most successful creator of "popular" operas by virtue of *The Rise and Fall of the City of Mahogany* and *The Three-Penny Opera*. He was brought to the United States by Max Reinhardt, the eminent producer, who was projecting an ambitious stage pageant of Jewish history, text by Franz Werfel, for which he wanted Weill to write the score. This pageant, *The Eternal Road*, suffered numerous delays, and was not produced until 1937. Meanwhile, Weill was commissioned by the Group Theatre in New York to write songs for Paul Green's *Johnny Johnson.* Consequently, it was with this play that Weill made his American debut. This bitter tirade against war—combining, as Brooks Atkinson said of it, "caricature, satire, musical comedy, melodrama, social polemics and parable"—was the kind of text which had made him so famous in Germany; the kind of text with pronounced social and political colorations which Bertolt Brecht used to prepare for him. Weill's score for *Johnny Johnson* was still very much in the *Zeitkunst* style he had developed for Brecht's plays: a sophisticated and skilful amalgamation of sound musical values with music-hall tunes and popular idioms of all sorts. There is very little American identity in these songs, except for "Rio Grande". That American identity, however, was not slow in coming, making its appearance in Weill with *Knickerbocker Holiday* in 1938.

Knickerbocker Holiday

Book and Lyrics by MAXWELL ANDERSON
Music by KURT WEILL
Staged by JOSHUA LOGAN
Dances by CARL RANDALL *and* EDWIN DENBY

First produced at the Ethel Barrymore Theatre on 19th October, 1938, with Walter Huston as "Peter Stuyvesant", Ray Middleton as "Washington Irving", Richard Kollmar as "Brom" and Jeanne Madden as "Tina".

PRINCIPAL CHARACTERS

PETER STUYVESANT
MYNHEER TIENHOVEN
TINA TIENHOVEN
BROM BROECK
WASHINGTON IRVING

In a brief prologue, Washington Irving decides to write a satire on the early Dutch settlers of Manhattan. Suddenly Manhattan island of 1647 comes into view. A group of elders—the town council—headed by Mynheer Tienhoven, come to discuss their new governor, Peter Stuyvesant, soon due from Holland. After that Washington Irving comes to introduce his hero—Brom Broeck, a penniless young man with a gift for disobeying orders and getting into trouble. Brom would like to marry Tienhoven's daughter, Tina, and for her sake he promises to behave in a more conventional manner ("It Never Was You"). Brom is seized by the council members for failing to get a permit for sharpening knives—a business which Brom had recently undertaken. They even plan to hang him: This is Hanging Day and not another suitable candidate is in sight. But Brom points out that his crime is not punishable by death, that any of the elders might do nicely for the hanging, since all of them are guilty of selling brandy and firearms to the Indians. The council members counter by declaring that since Brom has made an accusation against such an august body he has, indeed, committed a crime deserving hanging. Brom now has only one request to make, to which the council accedes: he wants to be hanged not by the neck but by his belly, a newer method being adopted, he says, by the more civilised communities.

As Brom is suspended from his stomach, Peter Stuyvesant arrives. He orders Brom's release, since he feels that anybody clever enough to have saved his life by devising such a method of punishment deserves to live. This disposed of, Stuyvesant proceeds to promulgate the new laws governing the island. After the crowd disperses, Stuyvesant informs his council that he plans taking over all illicit operations, for which purpose he appoints Tienhoven as pay-off man. Tienhoven now strategically decides to have Tina marry the Governor, and convinces her that in time she will get used to the idea ("Young People Think About Love"). Stuyvesant is enthusiastic. When Tina begs for a reasonable postponement of their wedding, Stuyvesant insists it take place immediately, since he is no longer a young man ("September Song").

Brom comes to Stuyvesant to complain about some of the new laws. The Governor has him arrested. When the council expresses objections to some of Stuyvesant's high-handed methods he has soldiers point their guns at them. This action convinces the council that discretion is the better part of valour, and so they raise their voices loud in praise of the "New Freedom" ("All Hail, the Political Honeymoon").

With Brom in prison, Washington Irving remarks wryly that in times like these good men are in gaol and criminals are free. Tina visits Brom and conspires to escape with him. But her father, overhearing the plot, points out the serious consequences for all concerned if Tina does not marry the Governor. To these developments, Washington Irving proves most sympathetic ("There's Nowhere to Go but Up").

Convinced that a nation at peace is a stagnant nation, Stuyvesant leads an army in a war, though for the time being he can find no enemy ("To War"). He also changes the economy so that the Government can forthwith take over all free enterprise. This meets with further disapproval on the part of the council ("Our Ancient Liberties").

And now the wedding of Tina and Stuyvesant is about to take place. Before the marriage can be consummated, the festivities are interrupted by an attack by Indians. Brom, having by now escaped from gaol, joins Stuyvesant and others in challenging the Indians and beating them back into the woods. In this battle Brom's friend, Tenpin, is killed ("Dirge for a Soldier"). Though he has thus proved his heroism, and by the same token has saved his town and its governor from disaster, Brom must still stand trial. Brom now openly accuses Stuyvesant of having engaged in the illicit business of selling brandy and firearms to the Indians. Enraged, Stuyvesant orders Brom's immediate death by hanging. But the council members, now weary of Stuyvesant's tyranny, refuse to follow orders. Stuyvesant now commands his soldiers to shoot Brom down. At this point Washington Irving intervenes to remind Stuyvesant that he must mend his ways if he is to be remembered well by posterity. Apparently, Stuyvesant is convinced. He frees Brom, and allows him to marry Tina.

The author of libretto and lyrics of *Knickerbocker Holiday* was Maxwell

Anderson, making his debut as a writer for the musical-comedy stage. Despite his eminence as one of America's foremost playwrights, Maxwell Anderson did not make the most important contribution to the success of this musical comedy. That contribution came from Walter Huston's performance as Peter Stuyvesant, and Weill's songs, of which "September Song" is probably one of the most famous he ever wrote. As Brooks Atkinson said in his review: "It is the composer Weill with his delightful music and actor Huston, gaily spinning about on his peg leg, who provide the holiday."

Lady in the Dark

Book by Moss Hart
Lyrics by Ira Gershwin
Music by Kurt Weill
Directed by Hassard Short *and* Moss Hart
Choreography by Albertina Rasch

First produced at the Alvin Theatre on 23rd January, 1941, with Gertrude Lawrence as "Liza", Victor Mature as "Randy" and Danny Kaye as "Russell".

Principal Characters

LIZA ELLIOTT
KENDALL NESBITT
CHARLES JOHNSON
RUSSELL PAXTON
RANDY CURTIS
DR. BROOKS

Lady in the Dark was not the first musical comedy to make extensive use of psychoanalysis and dream psychology. That distinction belongs to an early musical by Rodgers and Hart, *Peggy-Ann*, produced in 1926. But *Peggy-Ann* had been far ahead of its times: Americans were not yet overly concerned with their psyches, frustrations and inhibitions. By 1941, however, America had become fully Freudian-conscious. Moss Hart—himself a graduate of psychoanalytic treatment—sensed the time was now ripe for a musical on that subject. Much of the subsequent vogue for psychiatric or psycho-analytic subjects on the stage and screen can be said to have started with *Lady in the Dark*.

Liza Elliott, editor of the fashion magazine *Allure*, has come to consult Dr. Brooks, a psychiatrist. She insists she is physically well and normal in both her love and business behaviour. But she *has* been suffering from seizures of depression and fatigue, and on the counsel of her own physician she has decided to seek out the cause. Asked by Dr. Brooks to describe anything that may come to mind, however insignificant, Liza mentions a song learned in childhood, which now haunts her continually in moments of terror. She begins to hum that tune, and as she hums the stage darkens and we are carried for the first time into Liza's dream world. Twelve men in evening clothes are serenading her ("Oh, Fabulous One in Your Ivory Tower"). She is not the conservatively dressed and prim editor we first encountered, but a radiant, red-haired, beautifully attired siren. Her chauffeur (who, in real life, is actually Russell Paxton, photographer of *Allure*) brings her to Columbus Circle, where she mounts a soap box to expound her personal philosophy ("One Life to Live"). After that she visits an exclusive night-club, where she is greeted by the head waiter (actually none other than Kendall Nesbitt, the publisher of *Allure*, and Liza's lover). The crowd expresses its adulation of Liza. The music grows intense and frantic. The scene melts away, and we are back at Dr. Brooks' office. The physician points out that in this dream Liza sees herself as a woman of allure, whereas in real life she prefers to be unprepossessing. Another contradiction is that whereas Liza tells other women how to be beautiful in her magazine, she herself does not take advantage of this advice.

In Liza's office a cowboy screen star, Randy Curtis, has come to be photographed for the magazine. After he leaves, Kendall Nesbitt arrives to inform Liza that his wife has finally agreed to divorce him and that he will soon be free to marry Liza. This news does not have the exhilarating effect on Liza that might be expected. On the contrary—she feels depressed and faint. Dismissing Kendall abruptly, she locks the door of her office, and falls wearily on a couch. Suddenly she begins to hum a fragment of the child's tune, and drifts into a dream world in which Kendall and she have gone into a jeweller's shop to purchase a wedding ring. Instead of a ring the salesman offers them a golden dagger. Now Randy, the movie star, appears and makes violent love to Liza ("This Is New"), but six ravishing girls lure Randy away. Left to herself, Liza soliloquises about a princess, wooed by two suitors, neither of whom can win her, since they are unable to solve a riddle posed them by the king. But a minstrel gives the correct answer, and thus gets the princess's hand ("The Princess of Pure Delight"). The scene shifts suddenly to a church where Kendall and Liza are about to be married. A chorus insists she does not love Kendall. Frantically, Liza expostulates that she does. The dream degenerates into a nightmare.

At her next session with Dr. Brooks Liza reveals that her interest in simple, unostentatious clothes dates from her early childhood. She also informs the psychiatrist that she has a dinner date with Randy she intends breaking. Dr. Brooks points out that her fetish for plainness is a refusal to compete with other women; and that her dread of marriage comes from the fear of having Kendall all to herself. These revelations so upset Liza that she rushes impetuously out of the office.

The next morning Liza comes late to her office, where a new issue of *Allure* is going to press. When Kendall enters, she tells him firmly she no longer loves him. She is also abrupt with one of her editorial associates, Charley Johnson, who resents having a female boss and wants to go off to another magazine. Later on she dresses elegantly to await the arrival of Randy, come to take her to dinner.

The second act takes place first in Liza's office the following afternoon, where she must decide on a cover design for the Easter issue. Charley Johnson suggests a circus scene. Magically, that scene comes to life ("Dance of the Tumblers") with Russell Paxton as ringmaster. The main event is the trial of Liza for her inability to make up her mind; Charley is the prosecutor and Randy the defence lawyer. To the accompaniment of "The Best Years of His Life" Russell Paxton denounces Liza for having deprived Kendall of his finest years, and then refusing to marry him. The music impresses Russell, who, upon discovering that the melody is by Tchaikovsky, proceeds to rattle off the names of every Russian composer he can think of ("Tchaikovsky"). That ended, Liza takes the stand in her own defence ("Saga of Jenny"). When the jury decides in Liza's favour the dream sequence is over.

That evening, Liza tells Dr. Brooks that in this dream she experienced once again the hurt and humiliation of her childhood. As she talks, Liza is carried back to the time when, as a child, she was jealous of her mother's beauty, a disagreeable emotion, of which she rids herself only with her mother's death. Time after time, Liza loses the boy she likes to a more appealing girl. To one lad, whom she favours above others, she sings a haunting melody ("My Ship"), which is actually the tune that so long had been tormenting Liza the woman. Dr. Brooks emphasises that as a child Liza, having lost a succession of boyfriends, sought refuge in being plain; that as a woman she is rebelling against this form of feminine escape.

One week later, at the office, Randy urges Liza to marry him. She has the strength he needs, he confesses, since he himself is actually weak. Liza asks for time in which to think this proposal over, when Charley bursts in, full of plans for the new issue. For the first time Liza recognises a salient truth that has so long been eluding her: it is Charley, a strong man, that she loves and wants to lean upon for the rest of her life. They begin to chant the strains of "My Ship" as an earnest of their future happiness together.

Of the many salient elements that went into making *Lady in the Dark*, one of the most remarkable musical productions of the 1940s—Moss Hart's text, Weill's extraordinary effective music so sensitively attuned to the dream sequences, Ira Gershwin's nimble lyrics—one element above all others stood out in bold relief. This was Gertrude Lawrence as Liza, a virtuoso performance of the first order. In the comparatively lesser role of Russell Paxton, Danny Kaye demonstrated for the first time in a Broadway theatre his immense potential as a comedian, and his skill with a glib song lyric demanding rapid-fire delivery.

One Touch of Venus

Book by S. J. PERELMAN *and* OGDEN NASH *based on* The Tinted Venus, *a short story by* F. ANSTEY

Lyrics by OGDEN NASH

Music by KURT WEILL

Directed by ELIA KAZAN

Choreography by AGNES DE MILLE

First produced at the Imperial Theatre on 7th October, 1943, with Mary Martin as "Venus", Kenny Baker as "Rodney" and Ruth Bond as "Gloria".

PRINCIPAL CHARACTERS

VENUS
RODNEY HATCH
WHITELAW SAVORY
MOLLY GRANT
GLORIA KRAMER
MRS. KRAMER

A statue of Venus has come to the Whitelaw Savory Foundation of Modern Art. Molly Grant, Savory's secretary, explains that such a work of art is not incongruous in a modern gallery, since anyone who has what Venus has is never out of place. Rodney Hatch, Savory's barber, admires Venus, but is convinced his girl friend, Gloria, is much more beautiful. Then he slips on Venus's finger the engagement ring he has bought for Gloria. There is a roll of thunder, a blast of wind and momentary darkness. Venus comes to life—and she is in love with Rodney. When he tries to flee from her she runs after him into his apartment, where he reaffirms his great love for Gloria ("How Much I Love You"). Since Venus continues to dog his steps, he decides it is necessary to clothe her somewhat more respectably than does the thin gauze which separates her from nudity. They go to Rockefeller Plaza at the noon-day hour. (The midday commotion at Rockefeller Plaza is interpreted in an extended dance sequence.)

Venus wonders why Rodney appears so immune to her charms. Can it be, she wonders, that during her long slumber through the centuries, love has gone out of style? ("I'm a Stranger Here Myself"). Then she walks through a store window and proceeds to remove the clothes from a dummy with which she dresses herself. The police seize her, but she is saved by Whitelaw Savory. Savory falls in love with her at sight ("West Wind"), but Venus insists she can love only one man—Rodney ("Foolish Heart").

Meanwhile Gloria has come to town with her mother from New Jersey ("Way Out West in Jersey"). When Gloria asks for her engagement ring Rodney confesses it had been stolen by—a statue! Gloria and her mother are convinced Rodney is leading some sort of double life. Venus, recognising Gloria as her rival for Rodney's heart, arranges to have her transported to the North Pole. Then Venus comforts Rodney for losing Gloria ("Speak Low"). By now Rodney becomes fully aware that he is being suspected by the police of having stolen the statue of Venus that has disappeared so mysteriously from the Whitelaw Savory Foundation. He decides to go to the museum and explain matters to Savory. There, at a costume ball, Savory refuses to believe Rodney. Worse still, he accuses Rodney and Venus of having murdered Gloria. Rodney and Venus are then dragged off to gaol.

In prison, Venus reiterates her love for Rodney, then uses her magical powers to throw open the prison doors. They go off to a hotel room, where Rodney finally succumbs to Venus's charms. Rodney then dreams of what it would be like to be married to Venus and live with her in a suburban development. This is an ambitious ballet episode which ends with Venus's return to her own land.

The idyllic affair between Venus and Rodney is over. She returns to her place in the museum. Gloria, back from the North Pole, is so enraged at Rodney she refuses to have any further communication with him. In the museum, Rodney looks longingly at the statue he has recently loved as a woman. A young girl, who bears a striking resemblance to Venus, enters the museum and seeks some information from Rodney. He looks at her, smiles, takes her hand and walks out of the museum with her.

Choreographed by Agnes De Mille (her first Broadway assignment since her success with *Oklahoma!*), *One Touch of Venus* places a considerable emphasis on ballet, with two major sequences—"Forty Minutes for Lunch" and "Venus in Ozone Heights". The latter is important in the plot development, since it provides the first indication that Venus has every intention of returning to her inanimate state.

Lost in the Stars

Book and Lyrics by MAXWELL ANDERSON, *based on* ALAN PATON'S *novel,* Cry, the Beloved Country

Music by KURT WEILL

Staged by ROUBEN MAMOULIAN

First produced at the Music Box Theatre on 20th October, 1949, with Todd Duncan as "Stephen Kumalo", Inez Matthews as "Irina" and Julian Mayfield as "Absalom".

PRINCIPAL CHARACTERS

STEPHEN KUMALO
ABSALOM
LINDA
IRINA
ARTHUR JARVIS

Alan Paton's moving novel of racial conflicts in South Africa, *Cry, the Beloved Country*, was the source of *Lost in the Stars*. At the hands of Maxwell Anderson and Kurt Weill, the musical play became a work not only of surpassing compassion and humanity and a promise of man's brotherhood but also a work of such impressive artistic dimension that there have been some American critics who prefer to identify it not as a "musical play" but as an opera. Indeed, on several occasions *Lost in the Stars* has been successfully performed by American opera companies. Weill consigned some of the most eloquent music of his score to the chorus, which occasionally occupies a unique role as a kind of commentator-interpreter.

The play opens in the little South African hill village of Ndotsheni, where Reverend Stephen Kumalo, a humble Negro preacher, looks after his people. He is pining for his son Absalom, who has long since left home to earn money for his future education and from whom Kumalo has not heard a word for a year. Absalom's mother is convinced that either the boy is in trouble or has deserted them, but the father reassures her that true love can never separate people, however great the distance, however long the time of separation, however impenetrable the silence ("Thousands of Miles"). In spite of this encouragement, Stephen allows himself to be persuaded by his wife to use their live's savings for a visit to the city of Johannesburg in search of their son. But the preacher fails to find his son there.

Meanwhile, Absalom is in a honky-tonk in Johannesburg, listening to Linda sing a provocative ditty ("Who'll Buy?"). Absalom is now in love with Irina, who is about to bear him a child. In an effort to get some badly needed money for his girl and unborn child, Absalom joins a gang in a robbery. Irina is upset to see him thus get involved in crime ("Trouble Man"), and heartbroken when she discovers he has killed a white man. A chorus is now heard to comment upon the terror striking everybody in South Africa: the terror of the masses for the powerful few, and the terror of the powerful few for the masses ("Fear").

Reverend Kumalo visits his son in prison with the vain hope of being of some help. In his immense sorrow, Kumalo cannot help wondering if God had not deserted him and his flock ("Lost in the Stars"). Nevertheless, he prays to God for guidance and help ("O Tixo, O Tixo, Help Me").

At the trial, Absalom's accomplices manage to get acquitted by lying, but Absalom is found guilty and must die by hanging. At this point the chorus returns, this time to lament the loss of a good son and the waste of a good man ("Cry, the Beloved Country").

In the hills of Ndotsheni, Kumalo gathers his flock. They raise their voices in a poignant chant about the life of man who is born in darkness and who in darkness must die ("Bird of Passage"). Just before Absalom is executed, the father of the murdered man comes to visit Kumalo. Instead of bringing hate in his heart, he comes with pity and human understanding: he realises that their mutual sorrow and loss has made them brothers, even though one is white, and the other black.

Lost in the Stars was Weill's last Broadway musical play: he died in New York City less than a year after its première, on 3rd April, 1950. With *Lost in the Stars* Weill's career in the theatre had come to full circle. He had begun his career in Germany by making opera into popular music; and he had ended his career in America by succeeding in making popular music into opera.

Cabin in the Sky

Book by Lynn Root

Lyrics by John La Touche

Music by Vernon Duke

Staged by George Balanchine

First produced at the Martin Beck Theatre on 25th October, 1940, with Ethel Waters as "Petunia", Todd Duncan as "Lawd's General" and Katherine Dunham as "Georgia Brown".

Principal Characters

LUCIFER, JR.
LAWD'S GENERAL
LITTLE JOE
PETUNIA
GEORGIA BROWN

The Lawd's General and Lucifer, Jr., are fighting for the possession of the soul of a humble Negro, Little Joe. Joe is a simple sort, who is always getting into trouble, and who succumbs to the seductive wiles of Georgia Brown. Petunia, in love with Joe, is his ally in his struggle between good and evil. Evil conquers; Joe shoots Petunia in a dance hall. But Petunia is understanding and forgiving, and for this reason Little Joe is given admission to Heaven, and the Lawd's General in turn proves triumphant over Lucifer, Jr.

Though *Cabin in the Sky* had an unspectacular performance history—its Broadway run consisted of only 156 performances—it is one of the glories of the Broadway musical theatre. As a sensitive portrait of Negro life and psychology—presented with dignity, simplicity and authenticity—it has rarely been equalled. The musical play was all of one piece—music, text, dialogue, lyrics and choreography emphasising the folk element, and never degenerating into caricature or spectacle. Vernon Duke's score—the best of his career on Broadway—included several stand-outs: "Takin' a Chance on Love", with which Ethel Waters inspired an ovation every performance; the title number; and "Honey in the Honeycomb".

Carmen Jones

Book and Lyrics by OSCAR HAMMERSTEIN II, *based on the libretto for the opera* Carmen *by* HENRI MEILHAC *and* LUDOVIC HALÉVY

Music by GEORGES BIZET

Staged by HASSARD SHORT

Choreography by EUGENE LORING

First produced at the Broadway Theatre on 2nd December, 1943, with Muriel Smith and Muriel Rahn alternating as "Carmen Jones", Luther Saxon and Napoleon Reed alternating as "Joe", Carlotta Franzell and Elton J. Warren alternating as "Cindy Lou" and Glenn Bryant as "Husky Miller".

PRINCIPAL CHARACTERS

CINDY LOU
SERGEANT BROWN
JOE
CARMEN JONES
HUSKY MILLER

Carmen Jones is one of the most interesting experiments in the American musical theatre. Oscar Hammerstein II, a long-time admirer of Bizet's opera *Carmen*, conceived the idea of translating the story of *Carmen* into modern American terms and with modern American characters. At the same time, he borrowed virtually the entire Bizet score, making no alterations or additions whatsoever, and only minor deletions. The result was no mere stunt, but theatre of the most compelling force, a "memorable milestone in the upward and onward course of the great American showshop", as the critic Robert Garland reported.

Hammerstein transferred his setting from nineteenth-century Seville to an American southern town and Chicago, during the Second World War. Workers in a southern parachute factory are idling about; children are parading in mock military formation. Carmen Jones, a seductive factory worker, is making flirtatious overtures to Corporal Joe, a soldier stationed in town ("Dat's Love" —the *Habanera*). Plucking a rose from her hair, she throws it at him, then rushes into the factory. As Joe is thinking about Carmen, Cindy Lou, his childhood sweetheart, has come to him with a message from his mother. After she leaves, Joe is hastily summoned into the factory to arrest Carmen, who has just choked a girl in a rowdy brawl.

En route to the guardhouse, Joe and Carmen stop off at a roadside inn. She tries to induce him to let her go free and escape to a hot spot run by her friend Billy Pastor ("Dere's a Café in de Corner"—the *Seguidille*). Carmen's wiles and seductive ways are too much for Joe, who, in spite of his better judgement, lets her go. For such dereliction of duty he is taken into custody by Sergeant Brown.

Released from gaol three weeks later, Joe makes for Billy Pastor's café to meet Carmen. The place is alive with jazz; the habitués are noisy and in good spirits. Husky Miller, the famous prize-fighter, is greeted enthusiastically as he makes his appearance with a circle of admirers. After he has boasted about his powers in the ring ("Stan' Up and Fight"—the *Toreador Song*), Carmen is so attracted to him that she listens with more than passing interest when he suggests she go off with him to Chicago.

Meanwhile Joe has come to the café, a box of candy for Carmen in hand. He showers her with love, becomes sentimental over the flower she had tossed to him and which he has since kept as a tender memento ("Dis Flower"—the *Flower Song*). Carmen makes a pretence of doubting him. She insists he must prove his love for her by going away without official leave from the Army and taking her to Chicago. Failing to convince him, she provokes a fight between Sergeant Brown and Joe. Having struck a superior officer, in consequence of which he is threatened by a prison sentence, Joe decides to run off with Carmen after all.

The second act opens in a fashionable country club in Chicago, where Husky Miller is entertaining Carmen and her friends. Joe slinks in, looking for Carmen; when he finds her, she brushes him away rudely. Crestfallen, Joe has now come to realise that all the sacrifices he has made for Carmen have been in vain. Carmen returns to her friends, who are playing cards. Seizing a deck, Carmen cuts it in half, then goes pale as she turns up a nine of spades—a card prophesying death. But her dark mood is instantly dissipated as Husky announces a gala dinner party for all, with plenty of drinks, girls and entertainment. Just then, Cindy Lou slips in timidly looking for Joe, having come to bring him the sad news that his mother is dying. When Husky inquires from Cindy just what it is she sees in Joe to love, she describes his many virtues ("My Joe"—*Micaëla's Air*).

The scene shifts to the street outside the Stadium where Husky is to engage in a championship bout. The boxer arrives with Carmen, dressed in finery and jewels, under his arm. After Husky enters the arena Carmen is stopped by Joe. Shabby and worn, he begs her to return to him. When Carmen mocks him savagely he plunges a knife in her breast, then falls sobbing on her prostrate body. Within the stadium the cheers are ringing loud and clear for Husky Miller.

An excellent motion picture, released in 1954, was made of *Carmen Jones* with an all-Negro cast starring Harry Belafonte and Dorothy Dandridge, produced by Otto Preminger.

Song of Norway

Book by Milton Lazarus, *based on a play by* Homer Curran

Music and Lyrics by Robert Wright *and* George "Chet" Forrest, *music adapted from the works of* Edvard Grieg

Staged by Charles K. Freeman

Choreography by George Balanchine

First produced at the Imperial Theatre on 21st August, 1944, with Lawrence Brooks as "Grieg", Irra Petina as "Louisa Giovanni" and Helena Bliss as "Nina Hagerup".

Principal Characters

EDVARD GRIEG
RIKARD NORDRAAK
NINA HAGERUP
LOUISA GIOVANNI

Though the old-world operetta was a dying form in the American theatre by 1944, it still had enough vitality to produce a major success. Built around the life and music of Edvard Grieg, *Song of Norway* enjoyed one of the longest initial Broadway runs of any operetta (860 performances), and has since that time been frequently revived in different parts of the United States.

The play opens in Bergen, Norway, during the Midsummer Eve Festival of St. John. The townspeople are preparing for a holiday commemorating their patron saint. To the strains of Grieg's Piano Concerto, Rikard Nordraak—eminent young Norwegian poet and composer—predicts the imminent emergence of a man who will combine within himself music and history. "Norway waits for the song of one man," Nordraak says enthusiastically, "and then she'll find her voice and sing again." That man is Nordraak's friend, young Edvard Grieg, who promises to write his country's songs and give his country a new artistic stature. Engaged to his childhood sweetheart, Nina Hagerup, Grieg looks forward with confidence to his future as musician and man. But the smooth surface of his personal life and career are disturbed with the presence of

Louisa Giovanni, a glamorous prima-donna, who intends to win Grieg for herself. Swept off his feet by her beauty and worldly ways, Grieg runs off with her to Rome. But there he grows restive as he begins to yearn for Nina, whom he truly loves, and for his mission of producing Norway's music. When he learns that his young friend, Nordraak, is dead he finds the courage to break from Louisa, and return to Norway, and to his beloved.

The principal song of this score, "Strange Music", is a popular version of Grieg's *Wedding Day in Troldhaugen* from his *Lyric Pieces* for piano; the love song of Grieg and Nina, "I Love You", is an adaptation of Grieg's Lied, "*Ich liebe Dich*", which Grieg had actually written for Nina. Musical episodes from the G major Violin Sonata, *Peer Gynt*, *Norwegian Dance No. 2*, the Piano Concerto and other *Lyric Pieces* provided further material for songs and background music for ballets.

On the Town

Book and Lyrics by BETTY COMDEN *and* ADOLPH GREEN, *based on an idea by* JEROME ROBBINS

Music by LEONARD BERNSTEIN

Staged by GEORGE ABBOTT

Choreography by JEROME ROBBINS

First produced at the Adelphi Theatre on 28th December, 1944, with Sono Osato as "Ivy", Betty Comden as "Claire", Adolph Green as "Ozzie" and Nancy Walker as "Hildy".

PRINCIPAL CHARACTERS

CHIP
OZZIE
GABEY
IVY SMITH
CLAIRE
HILDY

Three American sailors come to Manhattan on a short shore-leave. They are Chip, Ozzie and Gabey. New York is a wonderful town ("New York, New York"), and the three sailors are hell-bent for a good time. But each has his own idea of fun, since Chip is serious-minded, Ozzie is happy-go-lucky and Gabey an incurable romantic. They argue about what to do and where to go, and finally agree to begin their adventures by taking the subway. There Gabey sees a photograph of Ivy Smith, selected that month as subway's "Miss Turnstiles". Gabey insists that this is the girl he wants to date. When Chip and Ozzie realise they cannot dissuade Gabey they help him hunt out the girl. Each sets out in a different direction to find her. During the search, Chip meets a woman taxi-driver who is a victim of excessive enthusiasms ("I Get Carried Away"), and whose enthusiasm of the moment is Chip. Ozzie proceeds to the Museum of Natural History, where he comes upon Hildy, an anthropology student, and a girl of many talents ("I Can Cook, Too"). Gabey, during his wanderings about town, comes to Carnegie Hall. There, in one of the studios, he finds Ivy, taking singing lessons.

On the Town was a musical-comedy extension of *Fancy Free*, a ballet with choreography by Jerome Robbins and music by Leonard Bernstein, successfully introduced in New York on 18th April, 1944. "One of the freshest musicals to come into town in a long time," as Lewis Nichols of the *New York Times* described it, *On the Town* had freshness, exuberance and youth. Its breathless pace and feeling of excitement was maintained from opening curtain to the finale by George Abbott's skilful directorial hand. But its value as entertainment, great though this was, is not all that has made this musical comedy such an important event in the American theatre. As Leonard Bernstein's first Broadway score, and Jerome Robbins' first assignment as choreographer in musical comedy, *On the Town* helped introduced two creative figures to the American musical theatre who would henceforth make to it a formidable contribution.

Wonderful Town

Book by Joseph Fields *and* Jerome Chodorov, *based upon the play* My Sister Eileen *by* Fields *and* Chodorov *and the stories by* Ruth McKenney

Lyrics by Betty Comden *and* Adolph Green

Music by Leonard Bernstein

Staged by George Abbott

Dances and musical numbers staged by Donald Saddler

First produced at the Winter Garden on 25th February, 1953, with Rosalind Russell as "Ruth", Edith Adams as "Eileen" and George Gaines as "Robert Baker".

Principal Characters

APPOPOLOUS
WRECK
VALENTI
EILEEN
RUTH
ROBERT BAKER
FRANK LIPPENCOTT
CHICK CLARK

The action takes place in New York's Greenwich Village; the time is the 1930s. A guide is taking some tourists through the Village, pointing out not only its quaintness and charm but also some of its more picturesque inhabitants ("Christopher Street"). Ruth and Eileen, two girls from Ohio, now appear, having come to the big city to find their respective fortunes—Ruth as a writer and Eileen as an actress. They come upon Appopolous, a landlord whose sideline is painting modern canvases, and who rents them a basement room. The place has all the possible inconveniences of a slum apartment, including some not generally found there—such as the continual blasting that goes on underneath the place in the construction of a new subway. The girls, appalled at their new surroundings, give way to nostalgia for home ("O-H-I-O"). Their discomfort grows when they notice the oddball characters who drift in and out of their place as if it were a public place. One is the ex-football star Wreck, who entreats the girls to put him up for a few nights. It seems that the girl with whom he is living in a nearby apartment is being visited by her parents. A second visitor to the apartment of Ruth and Eileen is Valenti, the owner of a Greenwich Village night-club, who promises to give Eileen a chance if only she can manage to get herself known. Then there is Frank Lippencott, manager of a drug store, who has taken a fancy to baby-faced Eileen. Ruth, the older of the two sisters, proves less fortunate with romance, as she laments in a ditty explaining her formula for losing a man ("One Hundred Easy Ways"). Notwithstanding her poor score in the matter of love, she does not lose heart, since she is far more interested in getting ahead as a writer. She invades the office of *Manhatter*, gets an interview with its associate editor, Robert Baker, and leaves him with a bundle of manuscripts.

Wreck, meanwhile, takes over the management of the girls' household, does their menial work, takes messages. He helps them arrange a gala dinner to which Robert Baker is invited, and with him a young journalist, Chick, who says he will do everything he can to get Ruth an assignment with his paper. During the course of the dinner, Baker tells Ruth that she shows creative talent but that she should confine herself to subjects with which she is familiar. Upset to have her work thus criticised, Ruth leaves in a huff. Baker, meanwhile, soliloquises about his ideal of a woman, with Ruth uppermost on his mind ("A Quiet Girl"). Just then, Ruth receives a message from Chick's newspaper to go out on an assignment: to interview a group of millionaire Brazilian naval cadets just arrived in Brooklyn, New York. When she gets to the Navy Yard she fells the entire Brazilian Navy in one swoop with her charm and vitality, especially when she joins them in dancing a Conga. They are so enthralled by this girl that they follow her all the way back to the Greenwich Village, where they proceed at once to make a play for Eileen. As Eileen tries to elude them, pandemonium is let loose, the police arrive and Eileen is arrested. In prison she manages to win the hearts of the police, one of whom serenades her with an Irish ballad ("Darlin' Eileen"). Because of her arrest, Eileen has received so much publicity that Valenti is now more than willing to give her a chance in his night-club show. Ruth gets a newspaper job. The girls have made good in the wonderful town, and, in addition, they have also found true love. A celebration at Valenti's night-club is definitely called for. The dynamic Ruth leads the customers in a frenetic rag-tag dance ("Wrong Note Rag").

Like the proverbial cat, the saga of Ruth and Eileen in Greenwich Village has had nine lives. It started out as a series of short stories by Ruth McKenney in *The New Yorker*. Joseph Fields and Jerome Chodorov dramatised it into a highly successful non-musical Broadway comedy. After that a musical-comedy version seemed preordained. Fields and Chodorov made the adaptation, enlisting Comden and Green for the lyrics, and Leonard Bernstein for the music. (This was young Leonard Bernstein's second score for the Broadway stage. The first had been *On the Town* in 1944.) *Wonderful Town* became one of the leading successes of the season. Sparked by the vibrant, briskly paced direction of George Abbott, the dynamic performance of Rosalind Russell as Ruth, and the extremely effective and varied songs of Bernstein, *Wonderful Town*, as Robert Coleman reported, "roared into the Winter Garden like a hurricane". It stayed there two years, receiving the Drama Critics Award as the best musical of the year, and earning for Bernstein the Antoinette Perry and Donaldson Awards for the best Broadway score of the season. It toured the United States in a national company, was broadcast in 1958 over a nationwide television network and was successfully produced in several European capitals.

West Side Story

Book by ARTHUR LAURENTS *based on a conception by* JEROME ROBBINS

Lyrics by STEPHEN SONDHEIM

Music by LEONARD BERNSTEIN

Directed and choreographed by JEROME ROBBINS

First produced at the Winter Garden on 26th September, 1957, with Carol Lawrence as "Maria", Larry Kert as "Tony" and Chita Rivera as "Anita".

PRINCIPAL CHARACTERS

TONY
MARIA
ANITA
RIFF
BERNARDO
DOC

West Side Story transfers Shakespeare's *Romeo and Juliet* to present-day New York. The love story of Romeo and Juliet becomes that of Maria and Tony. The feud between the houses of the Capulets and the Montagues is re-created in one involving two teen-age gangs, the Jets and the Sharks. The famous balcony scene of the Shakespeare drama transpires on a fire-escape of an ugly New York tenement.

The curtain rises on a bleak scene representing a warehouse. For the next five minutes not a word is spoken. Instead we get an extended dance sequence by the two gangs, the mood is sinister. This establishes not only the emotional climate for the play that follows but also provides a warning of some of the impending action. One of these gangs is the Jets, who are determined to prevent the invasion into their territory by any Puerto Rican. The rival gang, the Sharks, is made up entirely of Puerto Ricans. Both gangs arrange a meeting at a dance held in the neighbourhood gymnasium for the purpose of arranging the time, place and weapons for a major gang fight, or "rumble". A climactic point is here reached with an exciting mambo dance. At this dance Maria, sister of Riff, leader of the Sharks, meets and falls in love with Tony, a member of the rival Jets. Belonging as they do to enemy camps, Tony and Maria must henceforth carry on their love idyll in greatest secrecy. In the song and dance-sequence, "Somewhere", they escape from the squalor and grimness of reality into a fanciful dream world. In "Maria" Tony gives voice to his feelings about the girl he has come to love, and in "I Feel Pretty" Maria describes her own reactions to the miracle of love. Their love blossoms out in a poignant scene on the tenement fire-escape and in the best ballad of the score, "Tonight". They eventually go through a mock marriage—which they themselves take most seriously—in a bridal shop where Maria is employed and where the dress dummies serve as their guests. This episode finds interpretation in dance in "One Hand, One Heart". But the hatred that separates the Jets and the Sharks also spells doom for their ill-fated romance. Then the "Rumble" erupts—a dramatic incident that once again finds its equivalent in dance movements—Tony kills Maria's brother. She is ready to forgive Tony, even to elope with him. But before this can happen, Tony is killed by an avenging Shark.

Such dramatic material, realistic, grim and alive with social problems, is undoubtedly better suited for the opera house than the Broadway stage. Truth to tell, *West Side Story* is more of an opera than a musical play. Dance has been elevated to new importance in the theatre by being required to carry on much of the dramatic action in a way never before attempted on Broadway. As John Martin, the dance editor of the *New York Times*, pointed out, the drama of *West Side Story* lies not so much in "talked plot but in moving bodies. The muscles of trained dancers are tensed and untensed and tensed again, stimulated by emotional tensions stimulating them still further in return. These tensions are transferred automatically across the footlights and into the musculature of every spectator in the house, willy nilly. The cast acts and reacts in terms of movement, and that is the most direct medium that exists for the conveying of inner shades of meaning."

If Bernstein's score has decidedly popular overtones in songs like "Tonight" and "I Feel Pretty" it also boasts operatic dimensions in the grimly realistic overture and in the atmospheric backgrounds for the ballet sequences. Within the music—as within the various ballet episodes—are caught much of the ugliness, agony and neuroticism of slum life in New York; but also, some of the beauty and poetry which sometimes touches the lives of these tortured adolescents. Contrast can also be found in several satirical numbers in which a welcome tone of mockery is introduced: notably, in "America", an amusing interpretation of the United States from the point of view of a Puerto Rican, and "Gee, Officer Krupke", an ironic commentary on the attempt by psychologists and social workers to cope with juvenile delinquency.

An artistic triumph of the first magnitude, *West Side Story* also prospered at the box-office. A three-year run on Broadway was followed by an extended national tour and a return engagement on Broadway; the total number of performances in New York was only twenty-seven short of the magic "one thousand mark". On 12th December, 1958, *West Side Story* received unqualified acclaim in London at its première there. In 1961 a tour of Israel, Africa and the Near East brought new accolades to this production. In the same year a momentous motion picture adapted from the stage play was successfully released in the United States.

Annie Get Your Gun

Book by HERBERT *and* DOROTHY FIELDS

Lyrics and Music by IRVING BERLIN

Directed by JOSHUA LOGAN

Dances by HELEN TAMIRIS

First produced at the Imperial Theatre on 16th May, 1946, with Ethel Merman as "Annie" and Ray Middleton as "Frank".

PRINCIPAL CHARACTERS

FRANK BUTLER
ANNIE OAKLEY
COL. WILLIAM F. CODY, "BUFFALO BILL"

The heroine is a rough and tumble backwoods girl who is the star of Buffalo Bill's Wild West Show and handy with a rifle. We first meet up with her at Wilson House, a summer hotel on the outskirts of Cincinnati, Ohio. She betrays that she is an uncultivated female who only knows to do that which comes naturally to her ("Doin' What Comes Natur'lly"). She soon meets up with Frank Butler of Pawnee Bill's Show. He is a big, sentimental fellow who is attracted only to sweet and demure girls ("The Girl That I Marry"). Annie finds Frank appealing, but she lacks the gift of getting men to become interested in her ("You Can't Get a Man With a Gun"). But they have one thing in common, show business, and with Buffalo Bill they proceed to sing its praises ("There's No Business Like Show Business").

Six weeks have passed. The scene shifts to a Pullman car of an Overland train speeding to Minneapolis. By now Frank and Annie have begun to manifest an interest in this thing called love ("They Say It's Wonderful"). At the Arena Frank confesses that he has begun to succumb to Annie's vigorous charms ("My Defences Are Down").

A Wild West Show then takes place within the Arena. The programme includes a Drum Dance, a Ceremonial Chant and Annie appearing as an Indian squaw ("I'm an Indian, Too").

The romance of Annie and Frank, however, encounters difficulties by virtue of the fact that they are rivals, each being a member of a different Wild West company. Annie bemoans the fact that she has been weak enough to fall for Frank ("I Got Lost in His Arms"), and tries finding consolation in the fact that she has a good many things to be happy over, even if love is denied her ("I Got the Sun in the Morning"). But their problem finds a neat resolution when the two Wild West Shows merge into a single outfit, and Frank and Annie become members of the same company. There is still a good deal of competition between them ("Anything You Can Do"), but the competition is now good-natured.

Annie Get Your Gun was the greatest box-office triumph of Irving Berlin's rich Broadway career; it is his only musical to achieve a run of more than one thousand performances. The score is his best and most varied for the theatre, yielding as it does at least half a dozen substantial song hits. (One of these, "Show Business", has since become the unofficial anthem of the American theatre.) But brilliant and inventive though were Berlin's melodies and lyrics, his was by no means the only salient contribution to a remarkable production. Mention should also be made of Ethel Merman's compelling and irresistible performance as Annie; Joshua Logan's imaginative staging; and the colourful choreography of Helen Tamiris.

Call Me Madam

Book by RUSSEL CROUSE *and* HOWARD LINDSAY
Lyrics and Music by IRVING BERLIN
Staged by GEORGE ABBOTT
Dances by JEROME ROBBINS

First produced at the Imperial Theatre on 12th October, 1950, with Ethel Merman as "Sally", Paul Lukas as "Cosmo" and Russell Nype as "Kenneth".

PRINCIPAL CHARACTERS

SALLY ADAMS
KENNETH GIBSON
COSMO CONSTANTINE
PRINCESS MARIA

The programme contained the following information: "The play is laid in two mythical countries. One is called Lichtenburg, the other is the United States of America."

The curtain rises in Washington, D.C., where Sally Adams is being sworn in as the new Ambassador to Lichtenburg. ("Where the hell is Lichtenburg?" she inquires with her customary directness, when the swearing-in ceremony is over.) She has appointed young Kenneth Gibson, a serious student of economics and international affairs, to her embassy staff. When Kenneth tries to sound out Sally's views on Lichtenburg's economy, and discovers she is completely innocent of any information, he inquires how she came to be an Ambassador. With no less candour, Sally tells him ("I'm the Hostess with the Mostes' on the Ball"). Sally then arranges a gala farewell party for her many friends in both political parties ("Washington Square Dance").

In a public square in Lichtenburg the townspeople have been waiting for hours for their new Ambassador. But, apparently, she has lost her way *en route* to the duchy. When she finally arrives she is given a royal welcome and introduced to Lichtenburg's striking Prime Minister, Cosmo Constantine. Taken with him, Sally immediately inquires if Lichtenburg needs any money from the United States and is taken aback to learn from the Prime Minister that he considers any loan from Washington unthinkable for his government.

A few weeks later Cosmo escorts Sally to the lively Lichtenburg Fair (paid for out of Sally's personal funds). The place is alive with gaiety and activity ("The Ocarina"). Here Kenneth meets the lovely Princess Maria of Lichtenburg for the first time, and impresses her with his immense fund of information about her country. He is at once completely captivated by her beauty and charm ("It's a Lovely Day Today").

As time passes, Sally proceeds to create consternation in Lichtenburg. She is brash, unconventional, uninhibited, and her actions and speech have created shock. Cosmo, however, is more than ever delighted with her, to Sally's immense satisfaction ("The Best Thing for You Would Be Me").

But word has come back to Washington about Sally's undiplomatic behaviour, and three Congressmen are sent to investigate. They appear at a lavish Embassy Ball, where they are flabbergasted to learn that Lichtenburg is one place that refuses to consider a loan from the United States. The Congressmen also take time out to do a bit of politicking of their own by maintaining that they have found a candidate for the United States Presidential election of 1952 ("They Like Ike"). While all this is going on, Kenneth is oblivious to anything and everything except his growing love for the Princess ("You're Just in Love").

Sally is finally recalled to Washington; but Kenneth stays behind in Lichtenburg to help build there a hydro-electric plant and to marry the Princess. Cosmo comes to Washington to get a decoration, and when Sally and he meet again they finally recognise that they, too, are in love.

Finian's Rainbow

Book by E. Y. HARBURG *and* FRED SAIDY
Lyrics by E. Y. HARBURG
Music by BURTON LANE
Staged by BRETAIGNE WINDUST
Choreography by MICHAEL KIDD

First produced at the 46th Street Theatre on 10th January, 1947, with Ella Logan as "Sharon", Donald Richards as "Woody" and David Wayne as "Og".

PRINCIPAL CHARACTERS

FINIAN MCLONERGAN
SHARON
OG
WOODY MAHONEY
SUSAN MAHONEY
SENATOR BILLBOARD RAWKINS

The setting of this social-conscious fantasy is the mythical town of Rainbow Valley, in the State of Missitucky, in southern United States. Finian McLonergan and his daughter Sharon arrive here from their Irish homeland ("How Are Things in Glocca Morra?"), bearing a crock of gold which they stole from the leprechaun, Og. They want to bury the gold in ground adjoining Fort Knox (where the United States has its gold reserves) in the mistaken belief that this is fertile ground for money to grow fruitfully. (Otherwise, they argue, why should the United States want to bury its gold there?) Finian purchases a tract of land from the local sharecroppers in a community where most of the property is owned by Negroes. When Rainbow Valley prospers, a rabble-rousing, Negro-hating Senator from Missitucky, Billboard Rawkins, schemes to snatch the land from its rightful owners. The sharecroppers, headed by Woody Mahoney, join forces to fight the Senator. Finian's golden crock has the power to fulfil three wishes. Finian first uses these magic properties to transform the

Senator into a Negro evangelist, so that he might know what it is like to live as a coloured man. The second wish is taken over by Og, the leprechaun. Og, who has fallen in love with Woody's sister, Susan—a deaf-mute able to communicate with people only by dancing—wants speech and hearing restored to her. The third and last wish is reserved to bring Sharon happiness. With the land safe in the hands of the sharecroppers, and with fulfilment through love coming to Sharon and Woody and Susan and Og, the fantasy comes to a jubilant end with "That Great Come and Get It Day".

American social and economic problems are prominently stressed throughout the progress of this fantasy. Subjects like the poll tax, sharecropping, the greed for gold, race prejudice and left-wing Socialism are attacked with stinging satirical barbs not only in text and lyrics but also in such winning numbers, outstanding for their scintillating lyrics, as "The Begat", "Necessity" and "When the Idle Poor Become the Idle Rich". However, the enchantment of fantasy-theatre is not sacrificed. The romantic element in the play is pronounced in several beautiful ballads, including "Look to the Rainbow" and "If This Isn't Love". To Og, who has a forgivable weakness for the opposite sex, the score has assigned two sprightly humorous tunes, as notable for their lyrics as for their melodies, in "Something Sort of Grandish" and "When I'm Not Near the Girl I Love".

Brigadoon

Book and Lyrics by ALAN JAY LERNER
Music by FREDERICK LOEWE
Staged by ROBERT LEWIS
Choreography by AGNES DE MILLE

First produced at the Ziegfeld Theatre on 13th March, 1947, with David Brooks as "Tommy", George Keane as "Jeff" and Marion Belle as "Fiona".

PRINCIPAL CHARACTERS

TOMMY ALBRIGHT
JEFF DOUGLAS
HARRY BEATON
ANDREW MACLAREN
FIONA MACLAREN
JEAN MACLAREN
MEG BROCKIE
CHARLIE DALRYMPLE
MR. LUNDIE
JANE ASHTON

Described by its authors as "a whimsical musical fantasy", *Brigadoon* is set in a magic Scottish village which comes out of the Highland mists once every hundred years, only to disappear after one day. Two American tourists—Tommy Albright and Jeff Douglas—on a visit to Scotland get lost in a forest. They hear distant voices ("Brigadoon"), then see a village come hazily into view. Entering it, they come to MacConnachy Square, in Brigadoon, where a gay fair is taking place. Andrew MacLaren has come there with his two daughters, Fiona and Jean; the latter is soon to be married to Charlie Dalrymple, much to the displeasure of Harry Beaton, who wants to marry her himself. Meg Brockie, a brash young woman, expresses surprise that Fiona is not jealous of her sister, since becoming a bride is quite an event and achievement in Brigadoon. Fiona explains by giving Meg a clue to her personal philosophy ("Waitin' for My Dearie"). When Jeff and Tommy are observed all the activities in the square stop short, for they are not only strangers but strangers from a distant land. Tommy is immediately attracted to Fiona. When the latter announces she is going to gather heather for her sister's wedding, Tommy insists he be allowed to accompany her. At first Fiona declines, but she grows more amenable after Tommy has sung a plaintive tune to her ("Heather on the Hill"). They now go off, hand in hand.

Later, in the MacLaren home, Jean is preparing to pack in preparation for her imminent wedding. The bridegroom, Charlie, comes to inscribe his name in the MacLaren family album, after which he sings of his intense longing for his bride ("Come to Me, Bend to Me"). Then Fiona and Tommy return from their expedition, late and happy. When Jeff appears, Tommy confides his feelings for Fiona ("Almost Like Being in Love"). Jeff and Tommy come upon the family album. Glancing through it, they remark the peculiar coincidence that a hundred years ago, on this very day, a Fiona MacLaren was married to a Charlie Dalrymple. It is their first clue that something eerie is happening around them. Fiona refuses to enlighten them, so they seek out one of the venerable citizens of Brigadoon, Mr. Lundie, and learn from him of the strange history of this town that lives one day every hundred years.

The wedding ceremony now takes place, with the festive townspeople enjoying songs and dances. Suddenly Harry Beaton arrives, determined to prevent the marriage from taking place. He lunges at the bridegroom with his knife, but, fortunately, Tommy arrests his hand. As Harry flees, Jeff trips him; Harry falls on his head and is instantly killed.

When the wedding is over Tommy confesses to Fiona he loves her dearly ("There But for You Go I"). Because of Fiona he is determined to stay in Brigadoon, come what may. But Jeff convinces him that it is impossible for Tommy to live in a dream, that reality dictates Tommy must return home to New York and marry his fiancée, Jane Ashton. Sadly, Tommy realises the wisdom of Jeff's words. He bids Fiona a tender farewell ("From This Day On") and leaves Brigadoon with Jeff.

Back in New York, Jane Ashton upbraids Tommy for having failed to "come to me" as soon as he had returned from Europe. The words "come to me" strike a responsive chord with Tommy. In a mist he sees Fiona before him in Brigadoon. This vision convinces him that he must break with Jane Ashton once and for all. It also convinces him that he must return to Scotland. With Jeff once again as his companion Tommy is back in the forest outside Brigadoon. Somewhere in the mist, whispers Tommy, there is a girl he desperately wants but knows he will never get. Jeff inquires if this is the reason Tommy has made the long journey back to Scotland. Tommy now reveals he simply had to convince himself that Fiona and Brigadoon belong not to the real but to the dream world. Suddenly Tommy hears voices in the distance, and sees Mr. Lundie approaching him. He takes Tommy by the hand to lead him back to Brigadoon. "You see," explains Mr. Lundie, "love can do anything—*even* miracles." Waving farewell to Jeff, Tommy follows Mr. Lundie into the Highland mists.

Brigadoon was a red-letter day for the American theatre, if only because it was the first major Broadway success by Lerner and Loewe, the words-and-music duo that later created the history-making *My Fair Lady.* But even if *My Fair Lady* had never been written, *Brigadoon* would still have earned for its authors an honoured place in the American musical theatre. The Drama Critics Circle singled it out as the best play of the season, the first time a musical had been thus honoured. And there was sound reason for this choice. *Brigadoon* is one of the most delightful fantasies the American musical stage has known—fresh and inventive in its characterisations, dialogue and lyrics; utterly enchanting in its melodies. As Brooks Atkinson said of it: "The incantation is complete and easy."

My Fair Lady

Book and Lyrics by ALAN JAY LERNER, *based on* BERNARD SHAW'S Pygmalion

Music by FREDERICK LOEWE

Staged by MOSS HART

Choreography by HANYA HOLM

First produced at the Mark Hellinger Theatre on 15th March, 1956, with Rex Harrison as "Higgins", Julie Andrews as "Liza" and Stanley Holloway as "Doolittle".

PRINCIPAL CHARACTERS

ELIZA DOOLITTLE
FREDDY EYNSFORD-HILL
MRS. EYNSFORD-HILL
COLONEL PICKERING
HENRY HIGGINS
ALFRED P. DOOLITTLE
MRS. HIGGINS

The place is London; the time, 1912. It is a blustery March evening outside Covent Garden, where street-entertainers are performing for the arrival of opera patrons. Flower girls are selling bouquets. Dapper young Freddy Eynsford-Hill upsets the flowers of Eliza Doolittle, a cockney flower merchant. As she protests volubly, and later as she tries to sell some flowers to Colonel Pickering, Professor Henry Higgins from a distance is painstakingly writing down her speech in a little notebook, for he is a distinguished phonetician interested in all kinds of dialects. Liza at first suspects he is a policeman, but Higgins manages to convince her otherwise. By her dialect he can recognise the place of her origin, since, as he insists, he can place any Englishman within six miles of his home by the quality of his speech. This leads him to lament that of all nationalities, the English are the ones incapable of speaking their own language correctly ("Why Can't the English?"). Spurred on by a wager with Colonel Pickering, Higgins decides to transform Liza in speech, manner and dress into a duchess.

But Liza has her own ideas of what constitutes the good life ("Wouldn't It Be Loverly").

In a slum area in Tottenham Court Road, Liza's father, Doolittle, and his pals have been drinking. Doolittle, having exhausted his funds, prevails on Liza to give him some money, after which he jubilantly gives voice to his general philosophy on life ("With a Little Bit of Luck").

Liza has now come to live with Professor Higgins, who devotes himself painstakingly to teaching her how to act like a grand lady. Higgins convinces both her and her father that, beyond this experiment, he has no further interest in her. Indeed, he is a confirmed bachelor who never allows himself to get involved with a woman ("I'm an Ordinary Man"). At long last Liza responds to Higgins' instruction and manages to drop her cockney accent ("The Rains in Spain"), much to the delight of Higgins and Pickering, who proceed to express their joy in an uninhibited fandango.

At Ascot Pickering informs Mrs. Higgins that her son will soon make his appearance with the transformed Liza. Within the enclosure, elegant gentlemen and ladies are watching the races—their reactions reflected in the ballet, "Ascot Gavotte". Eliza now appears under Higgins' arm. Beautifully gowned, and very much the lady, she instantly captures the heart of young Freddy Eynsford-Hill. Smitten, Freddy later haunts Higgins' house for a sight of Liza ("On the Street Where You Live").

The night of the Embassy Waltz has arrived. It is here that Liza is to meet her final test. Exquisitely attired, and in every sense the well-groomed lady, Liza carries herself with the utmost poise, as she dances a waltz with Higgins ("Embassy Waltz"). Her triumph is complete: She is taken for a Hungarian of royal blood. Later the same night, back at Higgins' place, Pickering is exuberant over Liza's triumph, while Liza herself nostalgically recalls the pleasures of that evening ("I Could Have Danced All Night"). But before long she turns angrily upon Higgins for not having left well enough alone by allowing her to remain a flower salesgirl. For, now that she is a lady, what will become of her? Higgins suggests she marry some nice young man. This serves only to arouse Liza further. Packing her things, she storms out of Higgins' house to stumble outside into Freddy. He protests that he is in love with her, but Liza is sceptical ("Show Me") and brushes him off. In an attempt to find her true identity she returns to the flower mart outside Covent Garden, where she is not recognised, even by her own father. When he does he gives her the cheerful news that he is about to get married ("Get Me to the Church on Time").

Meanwhile, Higgins is upset to discover Liza has left him and is led to wonder why women behave the way they do ("A Hymn to Him"). When next he does see Liza, it is at his mother's house, where Liza has come for a brief visit. He would like her to come back to him, but when Liza informs him that Freddy has asked to marry her he loses his temper and calls her a fool. Liza retorts that she can marry anybody she wishes, that, as a matter of fact, she can get along in life very well without Mr. Higgins ("Without You").

At his home, at dusk, Higgins recalls Liza and realises how much she has come to mean to him ("I've Grown Accustomed to Her Face"). Without her, he is lost and lonely. Liza slips silently in as he is thus musing. When he finally notices her he barks: "Liza! Where the devil are my slippers!"

In adapting Bernard Shaw's *Pygmalion* for the musical-comedy stage the highest standards were applied to every aspect of the musical theatre—text, lyrics, music, choreography, direction, Cecil Beaton's costuming and Oliver Smith's sets—to create as near perfect a production as human ingenuity and imagination could contrive. The result was, as the critic William Hawkins said, "a legendary evening", or, in the words of Brooks Atkinson, "one of the best musicals of the century . . . close to the genius of creation". With these and similar critical accolades as a springboard, *My Fair Lady* went on to become the greatest commercial triumph the American theatre has known. On 13th June, 1961, it became the longest-running production in Broadway history, outdistancing the Rodgers and Hammerstein musical play, *Oklahoma!*, which had held that record up to then. By that time it had been seen by over three million patrons, and had earned almost forty million dollars; the long-playing recording by the original cast sold over three million discs at a price of fifteen million dollars; the motion-picture rights were sold for over five million dollars. The national tour of a second company begun on 18th March, 1957, stayed on the road several years, breaking box-office precedents in city after city. Numerous companies were formed to present it throughout the civilised world, including the Soviet Union in 1960.

Camelot

Book and Lyrics by ALAN JAY LERNER, *based on* The Once and Future King *by* T. H. WHITE

Music by FREDERICK LOEWE

Staged by MOSS HART

Choreography by HANYA HOLM

First produced at the Majestic Theatre on 3rd December, 1960, with Richard Burton as "Arthur", Julie Andrews as "Guenevere" and Robert Goulet as "Lancelot".

PRINCIPAL CHARACTERS

ARTHUR
GUENEVERE
MERLYN
LANCELOT
MORDRED
MORGAN LE FEY

Camelot is a setting of the legend of King Arthur and his Knights of the Round Table. The play opens with the arrival of Guenevere in Camelot. Come to marry Arthur, she is greeted festively by the Court. Arthur himself, who is both shy and nervous, is not present. He is hiding in the nearby woods ("I Wonder What the King Is Doing Tonight?"). Guenevere has come to the woods, having slipped away from the ceremony. She is uncertain about herself and her future ("Simple Joys of Maidenhood"). She stumbles into Arthur without knowing he is her future husband. After telling her about life in Camelot ("Camelot"), Arthur discloses his identity. Since they are both immediately charmed with the other, they are delighted at the thought of becoming husband and wife.

In his palace in Camelot Arthur learns from Merlyn the wisdom of peace and brotherhood, and thus is inspired to establish the Round Table. The news of this reaches young Lancelot in France, who is determined to come to Camelot and join Arthur's knights ("*C'est moi*"). After he arrives, a gala outing takes place on the castle grounds ("The Lusty Month of May"), where Arthur introduces his wife to Lancelot. Guenevere takes an instant dislike to this cocky young fellow and instigates him to engage three knights of the Round Table in a jousting match ("Then You May Take Me to the Fair"). In vain does Arthur try to dissuade Guenevere from taking sides against Lancelot, and failing to do so, is completely at a loss to understand a woman's way ("How to Handle a Woman").

In the jousting match Lancelot handily defeats all three knights, to the amazement of his onlookers, and to the growing admiration of Guenevere. Lancelot meanwhile has fallen in love with the Queen. Torn by inner conflict between this love and his devotion to Arthur, he asks permission to leave Camelot for foreign conquests. He comes back to Camelot two years later, and in an impressive ceremony Arthur now makes him a Knight of the Round Table. Arthur is not unaware that Lancelot is still in love with Guenevere, nor has he failed to notice that by now his queen is strongly attracted to the young, handsome knight. Yet he must remain silent, for not to do so would be to disturb the tranquillity of Camelot. Meanwhile, Lancelot reveals to Guenevere his tender feelings for her ("If Ever I Would Leave You"). Guenevere is responsive. Nevertheless, she remains faithful to Arthur, and is his helpmate in carrying on the affairs of State ("What Do Simple Folks Do").

Mordred, Arthur's illegitimate son, now comes to Camelot to dishonour the King and thus gain the throne for himself. He prevails on his sorceress-aunt, Morgan le Fey, to trap Arthur in a forest one night. While Arthur is gone, Lancelot visits Guenevere in her chambers, where she breaks down and tells Lancelot how much she loves him ("I Loved You Once in Silence"). Mordred bursts into the room with some of the Knights of the Round Table to accuse Lancelot of treachery and to imprison him. Lancelot succeeds in escaping from prison, but Guenevere is sentenced to burn. At the zero hour, however, she is saved by Lancelot, who takes her off with him to France.

For the sake of his own honour and that of Camelot, Arthur must now wage war on France. Just before the final battle he meets Lancelot and Guenevere, and forgives them both. But the war must go on. In camp, Arthur meets a young stowaway who wants to join the Round Table. Arthur knights him on the field of battle and sends him back to England to grow up there and carry on for another generation the ideals of Camelot.

As the immediate successor of *My Fair Lady*—and with so many of the collaborators who had made *My Fair Lady* an unforgettable stage experience—a good deal was expected of *Camelot* when it arrived on Broadway. It achieved the unprecedented advance sale of three and a half million dollars, and forthwith was sold to the motion pictures for three million dollars more. But while *Camelot* was no *My Fair Lady*—and thus aroused a good measure of disappointment among the critics—it was nevertheless a musical play with many moments of enchantment and with some of the most handsomely mounted sets Broadway had seen in many a year.

Camelot was director Moss Hart's farewell to the theatre. He died of a heart attack in Palm Springs, California, early in 1962.

Guys and Dolls

Book by Jo Swerling *and* Abe Burrows, *based on* The Idylls of Sarah Brown *by* Damon Runyon *and characters from other* Runyon *stories*

Lyrics and Music by Frank Loesser

Staged by George S. Kaufman

Choreography by Michael Kidd

First produced at the 46th Street Theatre on 24th November, 1950, with Robert Alda as "Sky", Isabel Bigley as "Sarah" and Vivian Blaine as "Adelaide".

Principal Characters

NICELY-NICELY JOHNSON
RUSTY CHARLIE
BENNY SOUTHSTREET
SARAH BROWN
ARVIDE ABERNATHY
NATHAN DETROIT
MISS ADELAIDE
SKY MASTERSON

The world of Damon Runyon's stories was circumscribed: New York's fabulous Gay White Way, Broadway. This world is populated by a motley crew of eccentrics, non-conformists, Salvation Army do-gooders, or just plain irresponsibles: gamblers, night-club entertainers, and various categories of "jerks". It is this world, and these people, that are found in *Guys and Dolls*, a musical comedy described in the programme as a "fable of Broadway".

The curtain rises on Broadway—the restless movement of its varied personalities and its feverish atmosphere beautifully captured in George S. Kaufman's direction. Three gamblers—Nicely-Nicely, Benny and Rusty Charlie—are soon found poring over the day's racing form in a studied effort to pick the day's winners ("Fugue for Tinhorns"). Near by is the Save-a-Soul Mission of the Salvation Army, directed by Arvide Abernathy ("Follow the Fold"). Here Sky Masterson, a happy-go-lucky sort of fellow, meets the Salvation Army lass.

Sarah Brown. He finds her fair game for his romantic sport. But Sarah tells him in no uncertain terms that he is not her kind of man, and that when such a man comes along she will know ("I'll Know").

At the Hot Spot night-club chorus girls are going through one of their routines ("A Bushel and a Peck"). One of these entertainers, Adelaide, laments that she is addicted to psychosomatic colds ("Adelaide's Lament"). The cause —Nathan Detroit. She has been keeping company with him fourteen years. But since he is a chronic gambler, there is always some game of chance to come between them just as they are about to get married. At that very moment Nathan is involved in trying to find a place to house a floating crap game for some high players just come to town; and so, once again matrimony is farthest from his mind. His fellow gamblers, Nicely-Nicely and Benny, sympathise with him, for they have only contempt for anybody who allows himself to get deeply involved with a girl ("Guys and Dolls").

Meanwhile, Sky Masterson is pursuing Sarah. Stimulated by a bet, he decides to invite her to Havana. Her better judgement notwithstanding, Sarah goes off with Sky. In Havana she comes face to face with the glaring truth that she has fallen in love with him ("If I Were a Bell"). For his part, Sky has also come to realise that his game has become deadly serious; that he, too, was knee-deep in love ("I've Never Been in Love Before").

But after they return to Broadway, Sarah discovers that not love, but a bet, had been Sky's motive in taking her to Havana. She refuses to have anything more to do with him. Her troubles are compounded with the news that the Mission is in danger of closing down because not enough people take advantage of its services. With Sky's help, the Mission is saved: with his wide circle of friends on and near Broadway he can see to it that the Mission is crowded. Sarah's romantic interest in him is thereby revived. Her love affair with Sky achieves a happy resolution in marriage; and so, at long last, does that of Nathan and Adelaide.

Romance, however, is incidental in *Guys and Dolls* to the colourful picture provided of New York life, to the insight into the strange impulses and unique motivations governing the lives of some of the city's more picturesque characters.

Guys and Dolls was one of the greatest successes that the Broadway theatre has known. Its run of 1,200 performances netted more than twelve million dollars. Samuel Goldwyn then purchased the motion-picture rights for a million dollars plus a percentage, and cast Marlon Brando, Frank Sinatra and Jean Simmons in the leading roles.

The Most Happy Fella

Book, Lyrics and Music by FRANK LOESSER, *based on* They Knew What They Wanted *by* SIDNEY HOWARD

Staged by JOSEPH ANTHONY

Choreography by DANIA KRUPSKA

First produced at the Imperial Theatre on 3rd May, 1956, with Robert Weede as "Tony", Jo Sullivan as "Rosabella" and Art Lund as "Joe".

PRINCIPAL CHARACTERS

CLEO
ROSABELLA
TONY
HERMAN
JOE

The first scene takes place in a middle-class French restaurant in San Francisco, where Cleo and Rosabella are waitresses. The latter has received a note from one of the patrons, Antonio Esposito of Napa, California, who begs her to correspond with him.

When the scene shifts to Tony's ranch in Napa he has been corresponding with Rosabella for several weeks. After receiving her photograph, he feels he is in love with her and wants to marry her ("I'm a Most Happy Fella"). Rosabella has asked him in exchange, for one of his pictures, but being middle-aged and not too attractive, he is afraid to send it for fear of losing her.

On the Main Street, four young men—including Herman, one of Tony's hired hands—are remarking that Tony, having found a girl to love, should really be a happy man. As far as they are concerned, all they can do is to stare at girls from a street corner ("Standing on the Corner").

Back at the ranch, Joe—Tony's foreman—tells his employer that he is growing restless and is thinking of quitting his job. Tony asks Joe for his photograph as a memento. Later on, in his desperate attempt to win Rosabella's love, Tony sends her Joe's photograph as his own.

This photograph achieves its mission. Rosabella is coming to Napa to marry

Tony. The place is festive and the townspeople are celebrating. Rosabella arrives, valise in hand, timid and self-conscious. Seeing Joe, she recognises him from the photograph, and thus believes he is her future husband. But Joe soon disenchants her and reveals to her Tony's deception. Upset, Rosabella insists she is going back to San Francisco without even seeing Tony. Just then an uproar is heard. Tony, *en route* to meet Rosabella at the bus depot, had suffered a serious accident and is now being brought home on a stretcher. When Tony sees Rosabella his face glows with happiness, and he addresses her with such tenderness that Rosabella cannot summon the courage to tell him she is leaving.

And so, after a period of convalescence, Tony marries Rosabella. Soon after the wedding ceremony Rosabella rushes outside the house. She is weeping—unhappy at the fate that has tied her to an old, sick man. Joe—now compelled by circumstances to stay on as Tony's foreman—consoles her. It is not long before they are in each other's arms.

After several weeks have elapsed, Tony—fearful that Rosabella might become bored and lonesome in Napa—sends for Cleo to come and live with them ("Happy to Make Your Acquaintance"). When she arrives Herman greets her ("Big D"); they become interested in each other at once. Rosabella describes to Cleo how tender, solicitous and generous Tony has been to her, and how she has come really to love him. Later on, Rosabella confides her feelings to Tony himself. This inspires such delight in Tony that he decides to throw a mammoth party. At its height Rosabella is seen, valise in hand, dressed for a journey. She is leaving Napa and Tony for good, having learned that she is pregnant with Joe's baby. When she breaks down and confesses the truth to Tony he is seized by such a fit of rage that he raises his cane to strike her and to shout warnings that he will kill Joe at sight.

Rosabella and Cleo have come to the bus depot at Napa to leave for San Francisco. But they are followed by Tony, come to take Rosabella back with him. He loves her too much not to forgive. Besides, he is overjoyed at the thought that she will give birth to a child who will become "Tony's bambino".

Though there are several outstanding songs in Loesser's score, it is much more than just a collection of fine tunes. For *The Most Happy Fella*, Loesser created a music of almost operatic dimensions. Almost three-quarters of the play is set to music. As Don Walker, the play's orchestrator, pointed out, "we pass into dialogue only for those developments that are not emotional in content, such as exposition". Within his expansive frame, Loesser has placed arias, recitatives, duets, canons, choral numbers dances, instrumental interludes, parodies and folk hymns. "He has told " said Brooks Atkinson, "everything of vital importance in terms of dramatic music."

The Most Happy Fella had a run of about two years on Broadway (678 performances) before going on tour. The New York Drama Critics Circle selected it as the best musical of the season.

How to Succeed in Business Without Really Trying

Book by ABE BURROWS, JACK WEINSTOCK *and* WILLIE GILBERT, *based on* How to Succeed in Business Without Really Trying *by* SHEPHERD MEAD

Lyrics and Music by FRANK LOESSER

Directed by ABE BURROWS

Musical staging by BOB FOSSE

Choreography by HUGH LAMBERT

First produced at the 46th Street Theatre on 14th October, 1961, with Rudy Vallee as "Biggley" and Robert Morse as "Finch".

PRINCIPAL CHARACTERS

FINCH
J. B. BIGGLEY
ROSEMARY
FRUMP
MR. TWIMBLE
HEDY
WOMPER

As the curtain rises, Finch, a window-cleaner, is diligently studying *How to Succeed in Business.* He is a brash, self-confident, but endearing young man determined to follow the rules of the book and confident of the goal to which it will lead him. The book's first rule is to get a job in a large firm, and Finch easily contrives to find a place for himself in the mail room of World Wide Wickets. This is a typical big-business establishment with a plethora of departments, department heads, secretaries and intrigues. The girls file to their desks at opening time, remove the covers from their typewriters and forthwith leave for their "coffee break". This morning there happens to be no coffee, a situation that causes general panic ("Coffee Break"). One of the secretaries is lovely Rosemary who, at first glance, finds much in Finch that is appealing, and who forthwith informs us of her ideal of a man ("Happy to Keep his Dinner Warm").

In the mail room Finch's immediate boss, Frump (the company president's nephew), is ambitious to get ahead, and continually telephones his mother to further his interests in the firm. Mr. Twimble, the head of the mail room, is about to be elevated to a new post; Frump has every hope and intention of getting Twimble's job. But after Twimble has amplified on the methods that had made him successful in the mail room for a quarter of a century ("The Company Way"), he announces that his successor is Finch. Finch's "Bible"—*How to Succeed*—had specially warned him, first that he will get a job in the mail room, and second, that to get ahead his energies must be concentrated on the problem of getting *out* of the mail room. Finch turns down Twimble's job in favour of Frump—"for the sake of the team", he explains. This gesture does not pass unnoticed by the higher-ups in the firm, including the president himself, J. B. Biggley. After that Finch is never at a loss for the proper manoeuvre, word of cajolery, successful intrigue or correct gesture by which to gain continual promotions in the firm. All the while Rosemary has become more determined than ever to capture Finch, and though he is much too busy with getting ahead to think of romance, he is finally manoeuvred into taking her out for dinner ("Been A Long Day").

Finch's secretary complicates his romance for a while. She is Hedy, a flaming sex-pot who is Biggley's personal property, and for that reason brought into the establishment. She proceeds to create havoc among the male workers, who are reminded (in one of the show's finest production sequences) that "A Secretary is Not a Toy". Finch uses her to good advantage to eliminate one of the higher-ups and thus get his job. Hedy, however, has eyes only for Finch, even succeeds at one point in enticing him into her arms for a passionate kiss. This kiss fills the atmosphere with music as far as Finch is concerned; his emotions are stirred for the first time—but with love not for Hedy but for Rosemary.

Finch keeps on working his way up the ladder in World Wide Wickets. He finally endears himself even to Biggley, the president, by allowing himself to be caught at his work desk after appearing to have spent the whole night dedicated to his job; by permitting Biggley to discover that he, Finch, is a graduate of Biggley's Alma Mater ("Grand Old Ivy"); and finally by dropping a hint that he, like Biggley, finds relaxation in knitting. Recognising him as a brother-under-the-skin, Biggley is finally tempted into appointing Finch vice-president in charge of advertising. In this office Finch conceives a treasure-hunt television programme to advertise World Wide Wickets, with Hedy as the star. The idea proves a fiasco; for the first time it seems that Finch has come to the end of the road. But he wins the sympathy of Womper, chairman of the Board of Directors, when the latter discovers that Finch had been a window cleaner; Womper himself had started out in business the same way. Finch uses his good influence to convince Womper to be merciful to his dealings with the employees, since all men are brothers ("Brotherhood of Man"). It does not take long for Hedy to attract Womper's interest once she sets her mind to it. After Womper marries her he decides to devote all his time and energies to her. He resigns his post at World Wide Wickets and selects Finch to succeed him. As for Rosemary, whether Finch is just a window cleaner or the chairman of the Board, she still loves him ("I Believe in You").

Wish You Were Here

Book by ARTHUR KOBER *and* JOSHUA LOGAN, *based on* KOBER'S *play*, Having Wonderful Time

Lyrics and Music by HAROLD ROME

Staged and choreographed by JOSHUA LOGAN

First produced at the Imperial Theatre on 25th June, 1952, with Patricia Morand as "Teddy Stern", Jack Cassidy as "Chick Miller" and Sheila Bond as "Fay Fromkin".

PRINCIPAL CHARACTERS

TEDDY STERN
CHICK MILLER
FAY FROMKIN
ITCHY FLEXNER
PINKY HARRIS
LOU KANDEL
HERMAN FABRICANT

One of the phenomena of social life in America is the summer adult camp in the mountains where young city folk come for one week or two to play by day and enjoy romance by night. Arthur Kober wrote a delightful comedy with the setting of an adult camp called *Having Wonderful Time*, successfully produced on Broadway in 1937. Fifteen years later he collaborated with Joshua Logan in transforming it into an equally successful musical comedy, *Wish You Were Here.*

The entire action takes place at Camp Karefree, described as a "typical Catskill Mountains resort in which the lure is not peace and quiet but the enormous and noisy battle of 'activities'". The staff is serenading a busload of new arrivals ("Camp Karefree Song"). Among these guests are Teddy Stern, a pretty young girl, and her fiancé, Herman Fabricant, a middle-aged business man. Herman has come just for the day to see Teddy get settled. Teddy rooms with an outgoing and exuberant blonde from the Bronx, Fay Fromkin, who introduces the newcomer to Lou Kandel, owner of the camp, and Itchy Flexner, the social director. Itchy gives the girls some idea of the nature of his unusual profession ("Social Director"). After that Teddy attracts the interest of the camp Romeo,

Pinky Harris, but Fay advises her that the wisest policy for a girl is not to concentrate on any one man but to play the field ("Shop Around"). Just then the supper bell summons the guests to the dining-room.

Later that evening, outside the social hall, Teddy meets Chick Miller, a young law student who is employed as camp waiter during the summer to earn tuition money. Since it is the duty of all waiters to double by night as gigolos and dance with the girls, Chick seizes Teddy—when Lou Kandel is watching him—and waltzes with her around the porch.

Having thus become acquainted, Teddy and Chick soon find themselves more than passingly interested in each other. As they walk along the wooded path they hear from a distance the camp band playing "Wish You Were Here", a song which, as Chick explains to Teddy, is all about a boy and girl meeting in a summer camp. Then Chick confides that his ambition is to become a lawyer, and for this reason it is ever so important for him not to get seriously involved with a girl until he makes his mark. Teddy also maintains that she would prefer not getting emotionally involved just yet. They draw up a pact to spend a good deal of time with each other having fun in camp.

Despite this understanding, they do manage to fall in love. At Eagle Rock Chick begins to talk to Teddy dreamily of marriage, and the wonderful life they could have together. Teddy then breaks down and confesses she is already engaged. The news upsets Chick, but he becomes even more aroused when Teddy discloses that under no circumstances can she give up her fiancé. Stalking off angrily, Chick tries to find consolation with one of the other girls at camp, much to Teddy's grief.

At a moonlight frankfurter roast Pinky notices how depressed Teddy is, and to raise her spirits he sings a comical serenade, "Don José of Far Rockaway". When Teddy notices Chick with another girl she suddenly feigns interest in Pinky, even to the point of eagerly accepting his invitation to visit him at his cabin. There she has several drinks, and dances with Pinky around the room, when Chick suddenly bursts in. He is contemptuous at finding a "bride-to-be" in the arms of the leading "wolf" of the Catskills. In rebuttal, Teddy shouts at him to keep out of her life, that she has no obligations to him whatsoever. When Chick has left the drinks begin to work havoc with Teddy, who falls into Pinky's bed in the sleep of the dead. Much to Pinky's disgust, she remains in such a hopeless condition for the rest of the night.

The following morning, Herman Fabricant has come for a brief visit to see how Teddy is faring. It is certainly an inauspicious moment for such a visit, since Teddy is not in her cabin, and has obviously not been there all night. Herman, only too ready to make the all too obvious inference, is willing to forgive and forget—but only if Teddy pack up her valises at once and returns home with him. As Teddy is about to depart, she decides to give Chick a sisterly kiss of farewell, which, in spite of her better judgement, turns out to be a most passionate embrace. Nobody need tell Herman now what the score really is as far as Teddy is concerned. Magnanimously, he thrusts into Chick's hand the engagement ring he had previously given to Teddy, and Chick places it tenderly on Teddy's finger.

Fanny

Book by S. N. Behrman *and* Joshua Logan, *based on a trilogy of plays by* Marcel Pagnol

Lyrics and Music by Harold Rome

Staged by Joshua Logan

Dances by Helen Tamiris

First produced at the Majestic Theatre on 4th November, 1954, with Ezio Pinza as "César", Florence Henderson as "Fanny", William Tabbert as "Marius" and Walter Slezak as "Panisse".

Principal Characters

MARIUS
FANNY
PANISSE
CÉSAR
CÉSARIO

Marius is the son of César, who operates a little café at the Marseille water-front, *Bar de la Marine*. He is in love with the sea, dreams of the time when he can go off to exotic lands in the square rigger, the *Malaise*, about to set off on a five-year scientific expedition. But he knows his father would never give his consent, for César has set his heart on having Marius take over the bar. Besides, he is stirred by Fanny, who in turn is deeply in love with him. Panisse, a wealthy sailmaker and a widower, comes into the bar and confides to Marius that he plans some day to get married again ("Never Too Late for Love"). Actually the person he has in mind is Fanny. He invites Fanny to a drink and haltingly confesses to her his hopes and dreams. As he tries to caress her, Marius storms at him in outrage, indicating to the delighted Fanny that there is a streak of jealousy in Marius that might very well be a token of budding love. In trying to win Marius' love, Fanny finds an ally in César, who would like his son to settle down. He berates Marius for not being more considerate of Fanny's feelings, and tries to convince him that one of the best things about going away is coming home again ("Welcome Home"). When Marius starts to close down the bar for the night Fanny slips in timidly, obviously overwrought emotionally. She has come to confess to Marius how deeply she really loves him ("I Have Come to Tell You"). Marius insists that Fanny means much to him ("Fanny"). But he urges her to forget him, since he is booked to sail the following morning on the *Malaise*, to be gone for five years. When Fanny bravely decides not to stand in Marius' way and his destiny the young lad breaks down and takes her in his arms, in an irresistible surge of passion.

Marius sails away the following day. César refuses to forgive his son, nevertheless he keeps hounding the postman for a letter that might bring him some news. At last a letter comes. César has Fanny read it to him, so that both might share the news together. They learn Marius is well, happy and fascinated by his work; he also inquires after Fanny. But he has no way of knowing that Fanny is pregnant with his child; and that, to give her child a name, she has decided to marry Panisse.

Old Panisse is beside himself with joy when he learns from Fanny she will marry him, and his delight remains undiminished, even when she confesses she is about to have Marius' baby. Panisse insists that he has always dreamed of having a son, and that it is now being given to him as a blessed gift for his old age. Already he is making plans to change the sign on his establishment to read "Panisse and Son" ("Panisse and Son").

The wedding is festive. Fanny, dressed in her beautiful wedding gown, dances gaily with her husband. Suddenly she grows faint. In a kind of mist she sees herself dancing not with Panisse but with Marius, who is soon smothering her with kisses. But the vision fades, and Fanny once again is in Panisse's arms.

When, a few months later, Fanny gives birth to her son, Panisse's happiness knows no bounds. As soon as he gets the news, he proceeds to hang up his new sign on the front of his sailmaker's shop—"Panisse and Son".

The second act opens with a gala party celebrating the first birthday of Césario, Fanny's son. After the guests go, Panisse makes preparations to leave for Paris to transact some business. His baby's birthday, and his first separation from Fanny, makes him unduly sentimental. He sings a poignant hymn of praise to his wife ("To My Wife"). After kissing Fanny farewell, he departs. Left alone, Fanny starts to do some knitting, when she senses that somebody has entered her room through the window. It is Marius, temporarily back in Marseille. At first, Fanny and Marius are self-conscious, guarded in their exchange of greetings. But when Marius manages to discover that Fanny's child is also his he unbends completely and confesses how the thought of Fanny had always been uppermost in his mind while he was away ("The Thought of You"). His tenderness undermines Fanny's resistance completely. They rush into each other's arms. Suddenly César appears and tears them apart. He reminds Fanny that she is a married woman. When Marius angrily takes his father to task for having concealed from him the fact that he was the father of Fanny's child, César reminds him firmly that the baby's father is the one who loves him, not the one who gave him life only to desert him ("Love Is a Very Light

Thing"). Marius, now realising he can never claim either Fanny or Césario, leaves suddenly.

The years pass. Panisse, Fanny and Césario now live in a house outside Marseille. The boy is twelve years old; for his birthday, a circus has been hired to give a performance on the lawn. The boy expresses curiosity about Marius, about whom he has continually heard a good deal, and whose wanderings on the seven seas are a source of considerable fascination for him. But nobody is willing to say anything about the young man. When Césario learns that Marius is working in a garage in Toulon, near Marseille, he slips away to visit him. There he confides to Marius that he, too, wants to go to sea and begs Marius to take him along on his next voyage. Marius not only convinces the boy that his place is with his parents but takes him back home. There Panisse, now seriously ill, dictates a letter asking Marius to marry Fanny. "She will be free soon," he adds. "I will rest easier knowing she has someone to care for her, especially if it's the one she has always loved."

Marcel Pagnol's trilogy about Marius and Fanny—entitled *Marius*, *Fanny* and *César*—was for a long time a classic of the French stage and screen before it became an American musical comedy. Even Hollywood made a picture of it more than a quarter of a century ago, *The Port of Seven Seas*. The three plays were adapted for the musical stage by S. N. Behrman and Joshua Logan; for the former, one of America's most distinguished playwrights, this was his debut as a writer of musical-comedy librettos. For a text filled with compassion and humanity, and rich with penetrating insight into character, Harold Rome created his most ambitious score. His songs searched deeply into the hearts of the principal characters; his background music skilfully underscored the changing moods of the play.

In the strange way in which Hollywood sometimes operates, when it transferred *Fanny* to the screen in 1960 in a lavish production, all the songs were deleted, and a smattering of Rome's score was used merely as a background.

The Pajama Game

Book by GEORGE ABBOTT *and* RICHARD BISSELL, *based on the novel* 7½ Cents *by* RICHARD BISSELL

Music and Lyrics by RICHARD ADLER *and* JERRY ROSS

Directed by GEORGE ABBOTT

Choreography by BOB FOSSE

First produced at the St. James Theatre on 13th May, 1954, with Eddie Foy, Jr., as "Hines", Carol Haney as "Gladys", John Raitt as "Sid Sorokin" and Janis Paige as "Babe Williams".

PRINCIPAL CHARACTERS

HINES
GLADYS
SID SOROKIN
BABE WILLIAMS
HASLER

A strike is imminent in a pajama factory in Cedar Rapids, Iowa: The Union is seeking a wage raise of seven and a half cents an hour. Hines, the factory manager, keeps the girls on their toes by timing their production with a stop-watch and the girls respond by working at white heat in a race with the clock ("Hurry Up, Hurry Up, Hurry Up"). When Babe Williams, head of the Union grievance committee, comes to the plant's new superintendent, Sid Sorokin, to state the Union's case she finds herself attracted to him, even though she realises he is in the enemy camp. Sid also finds Babe highly appealing. When he tries to make a date with her she rejects him, reminding him that he is the superintendent of the plant and she of the Grievance Committee. When she leaves the office Sid flips on his dictaphone and confides to it his feelings about Babe ("Hey, There").

At a gay picnic for the factory workers Sid encounters Babe and complains that he, too, has a grievance: He has been trying to be a good fellow to a girl who is indifferent. Babe lightly explains that, perhaps, the girl is hard-boiled, that perhaps if he came to know her he would not care for her at all. But Sid remains unconvinced by her suppositions. The first opportunity he finds, he seizes Babe and kisses her ardently. Babe, caught unawares, offers little resistance. All around them, the picnic goes into high gear, with everyone in high spirits ("Once a Year Day").

A few days later, Sid visits Babe at her home. When he once again tries to kiss her she pushes him away. The more he tries to make some advances, the more she insists upon indulging in small talk to deflect him. Finally, she explains that what is really separating them is "seven and a half cents". She insists she intends to fight as hard as she can for the Union, regardless of how she feels about Sid personally. In the hallway of the Union headquarters word is being circulated that the boss, Hasler, is asking to see the Union officials; the feeling grows that the Union is about to score a victory. As far as Sid and Babe are concerned, their main interest now is in each other—as they take pains to explain when the Union members leave them to themselves ("There Once Was a Man"). Back in the shop, the Union members are glum: Hasler has given them a runaround. In defiance, the Union leaders order the works to return to their jobs, but to "slow down" on their operations. Sid belligerently demands from the help an "honest day's work" and threatens to fire anybody who is a slacker. This so outrages Babe that she kicks her foot into the machinery and causes a general breakdown. Without a second thought, Sid fires her; Babe storms angrily out of the factory.

The second act opens in Eagle Hall, where the Union is conducting a meeting. But first there is a bit of entertainment for the members, including an engaging little routine entitled "Steam Heat" performed by Gladys and two other union members, all dressed in tight-fitting men's black suits and derby hats.

Meanwhile, Sid tries in vain to contact Babe in order to square himself with her. He finally corners her at her home, where he begs her to understand and sympathise with his position. But Babe turns a deaf ear, rushes away from him and bursts into tears in the privacy of her bedroom. This turn in his personal affairs makes Sid determined to find some way to effect peace between management and labour. He suspects that the key to this problem is the one that opens the actual lock with which the company ledgers are kept securely sealed. In an effort to get that key from Gladys, the book-keeper, he invites her to a hot spot, Hernando's Hideaway ("Hernando's Hideaway"). She accepts eagerly, enjoys several drinks with him and then, being inebriated, all too willingly turns over the key to Sid. As he had suspected, the ledgers reveal that Hasler had long been adding the seven and a half cents raise demanded by the workers to the factory cost of his product. Thus caught red-handed, Hasler is compelled to yield to the Union's demands.

At the Union headquarters the members are figuring out that though seven and a half cents an hour raise is not much, over a period of years it can amount to a good deal ("Seven and a Half Cents"). Just then Sid arrives with the joyous news that the Union has won out. A celebration erupts in which even Hasler joins. Sid and Babe are particularly jubilant, for the obstacle to their romance has been removed. They, too, celebrate—at Hernando's Hideaway.

The Pajama Game was mainly the work of fresh, untried talent. The composer-lyricists—Richard Adler and Jerry Ross, whose collaboration involved both the music and the lyrics—here wrote their first complete musical-comedy score. Also new to the Broadway stage were the producers, the choreographer and Carol Haney, one of the stars. But these young people had the courage of their inexperience—for they were tackling a subject long regarded as taboo for the popular musical stage: labour problems involving factory workers, with a strike as a pivot of the plot; a musical comedy without fancy costumes and with comparatively little sex appeal. Yet, with the cards apparently stacked against it, *The Pajama Game* went on to become one of the greatest successes in the history of the Broadway theatre: it was the eighth musical to achieve a run in excess of a thousand performances. After that it was made into a highly successful motion picture starring Doris Day, but otherwise utilising most of the members of the original stage cast.

Damn Yankees

Book by DOUGLASS WALLOP *and* GEORGE ABBOTT, *based on* The Year the Yankees Lost the Pennant *by* WALLOP

Lyrics and Music by RICHARD ADLER *and* JERRY ROSS

Directed by GEORGE ABBOTT

Dances staged by BOB FOSSE

First produced at the 46th Street Theatre on 5th May, 1955, with Stephen Douglass as "Joe", Gwen Verdon as "Lola" and Ray Walston as "Applegate".

PRINCIPAL CHARACTERS

MEG HARDY
APPLEGATE
JOE HARDY
VAN BUREN
LOLA

Damn Yankees is the only successful musical comedy built around the American national pastime of baseball—the baseball story neatly combined with the age-old Faust theme. Joe Hardy is a middle-aged, happily married baseball fan. He is found in his living-room watching a game over television. Joe is in the depths of despond, for his favourite team, the Washington Senators, seems incapable of getting a winning stride. Suddenly the devil, in the person of Applegate, visits him with a proposition: Would Joe be willing to trade his soul if the Senators won not only the pennant but also the World Series? Joe is more than willing; he has never put much stock in his soul in the first place. Suddenly Joe sheds years. More than that, he has magically acquired singular powers as a baseball player. Meanwhile, Van Buren, manager of the Senators, tries to build up his team's morale ("Heart"). It is a hopeless job, for the Senators can hardly expect that their new rookie, Joe Hardy, could be of any use in lifting them from their habitual doldrums. But Joe proves the spark plug necessary to send the team flying at full speed to victory after victory.

Things may be rosy for the team, but Joe is in black despair. He misses his wife, Meg, sorely. His conscience also bothers him: he has disappeared from home without leaving a clue to his whereabouts. He tries to lift his spirits by renting a room in her house just to be near her. But this only tantalises him further, since he is unable to tell Meg that he is really her husband, alive and well.

Applegate, alias the devil, once again steps into the picture. In an effort to win Joe completely away from his wife, Applegate enlists the services of Lola, a beautiful witch, to capture Joe's heart. Lola coquettishly tells Joe that she is in the habit of getting anything she goes after ("Whatever Lola Wants"). She then performs a seductive mambo ("Who's Got the Pain?").

The Washington Senators, with Joe as star, come out on top in their league. The World Series is at hand. Despite the team's success, and despite Lola's wiles, Joe still misses his wife and wants to get back to her. Suddenly he realises that if he does not play in the World Series the Senators cannot win; and if the Senators cannot win the World Series his bargain with the devil is broken. Thus Joe manages to keep his soul, lose Lola, return once again to his wife and once again assume the unexciting identity of a middle-aged baseball fan.

Damn Yankees was the second and last of the two musical comedies in which Richard Adler and Jerry Ross collaborated on music and lyrics, the first having been *The Pajama Game*. Like its eminent predecessor, *Damn Yankees* stayed on Broadway for over a thousand performances, the ninth musical to join this select circle. With two such resounding triumphs coming in rapid succession, Adler and Ross became one of the most promising song-and-words team to hit Broadway since Rodgers and Hart. Tragically, this fruitful partnership was destined to come to an abrupt end when Jerry Ross died in 1955 of chronic bronchiectasis at the age of twenty-nine.

Plain and Fancy

Book by JOSEPH STEIN *and* WILLIAM GLICKMAN, *suggested by an original play by* MARION WEAVER

Lyrics by ARNOLD B. HORWITT

Music by ALBERT HAGUE

Directed by MORTON DA COSTA

Dances by HELEN TAMIRIS

First produced at the Mark Hellinger Theatre on 27th January, 1955, with Richard Derr as "Dan", Shirl Conway as "Ruth" and Gloria Marlowe as "Katie".

PRINCIPAL CHARACTERS

DAN KING
RUTH WINTERS
PAPA YODER
KATIE YODER
EZRA REBER
PETER REBER

The setting is the little town of Bird in Hand, in Lancaster County, Pennsylvania, the home of the Amish sect, which adheres tenaciously to its old customs, dress, speech and codes of morality and ethics. Here come Ruth and Dan to inspect and sell a farm Dan had recently inherited. They meet and become fascinated by the quaint life and manners of the Amish people. One of them is Papa Yoder, whose daughter, Katie, is on the eve of marrying the farmer, Ezra Reber. Preparations for the wedding are keeping the Yoder household feverishly active. Ezra's brother, Peter, who has been away from home for two years, suddenly makes his reappearance. He is an irresponsible and restless lad who is the despair of his good father. It soon becomes apparent that Peter and Katie had once been in love and that neither has quite forgotten the other. With great nostalgia they recall the delights of their youth in the production's principal song, "Young and Foolish". Katie then confesses that she does not love

Ezra at all, that it is a marriage of convenience to which she submits to please her father; and in time Ezra breaks down and lets it be known that he is not at all happy to make Katie his wife ("Why Not Katie?") Dan now becomes involved in this family problem by inquiring from Papa Yoder why he insists upon a marriage in which neither party is in love with the other. Papa Yoder's answer is to say that the Amish are simple people whose aim is a good and moral life in which love is only a minor consideration ("Plain We Live"). When Papa Yoder's farm burns down the old man is certain that his son, Peter, has brought a curse on the family. Peter, apparently, thinks so too, for he is now determined to leave his family for good, and entreats Katie to go off with him ("Follow Your Heart"). But when Dan sells his farm to Peter, so that he can live a respectable and productive life among his own people, the young man decides to stay. With Peter now a man of property, Papa Yoder gives his consent for his marriage to Katie.

Bells Are Ringing

Book and Lyrics by BETTY COMDEN *and* ADOLPH GREEN
Music by JULE STYNE
Directed and choreographed by JEROME ROBBINS

First produced at the Shubert Theatre on 29th November, 1956, with Judy Holliday as "Ella" and Sydney Chaplin as "Jeff".

PRINCIPAL CHARACTERS

ELLA PETERSON
SUE
SANDOR
JEFF MOSS

"Susanswerphone" is a telephone-answering service in Manhattan run by Sue with the assistance of her cousin, Ella Peterson. Ella is the kind of girl who puts on lipstick before answering the phone, and who gets personally involved in the private affairs of her clients. One of them is a playwright, Jeff Moss, with whom Ella falls in love, even though she has never met him, a relationship she regards as perfect ("It's a Perfect Relationship"). Since Jeff is having trouble getting started on his new play, Ella is determined to help him out. Meanwhile Sue allows her boy friend Sandor, the head of Titanic Records, to set up a branch office in her telephone-answering establishment; actually his record business is a blind for a bookmaker establishment, the musical compositions and their opus numbers serving as a code for making bets ("It's a Simple Little System"). The police suspect that Sandor's operations are just a front for a vice ring.

At long last Ella meets Jeff by invading his apartment in order to encourage him to start working on his play. She convinces him that people are friendly everywhere ("Hello, Hello There"), and in time even arouses his friendliness towards her ("Long Before I Knew You"). Meeting her later in Central Park, he confesses, at last, that he is in love with her ("Just in Time"). He then takes her to a party, where, at a loss for proper conversation, Ella tries to impress the guests by rattling off the names of famous people ("Drop That Name"). Aware that she did not fit in this company, that she was even unworthy of Jeff, she steals away from the party ("The Party's Over").

At a night-club Jeff meets some other clients of "Susanswerphone" whose careers have been helped by Ella. They decide to go and look for her. By now, Ella is determined to leave the big city and go home for good ("I'm Goin' Back"). But the arrival of Jeff quickly convinces her to change her mind, especially after he takes her in his arms.

In *Bells are Ringing* Judy Holliday—veteran of stage and screen—made her musical-comedy debut. Singing, dancing, clowning and miming, she stole the show.

Gypsy

Book by ARTHUR LAURENTS, *based on the autobiography of* GYPSY ROSE LEE

Lyrics by STEPHEN SONDHEIM

Music by JULE STYNE

Staged and Choreography by JEROME ROBBINS

First produced at the Broadway Theatre on 21st May, 1959, with Ethel Merman as "Rose", Jack Klugman as "Herbie" and Sandra Church as "Louise".

PRINCIPAL CHARACTERS

BABY LOUISE
BABY JUNE
ROSE
HERBIE
LOUISE
JUNE
TULSA
MR. GOLDSTONE
KRINGELEIN

Gypsy was the musical-comedy adaptation of *Gypsy: A Memoir*, the autobiography of Gypsy Rose Lee, who has become famous in burlesque as a strip-tease artist. With her sister, June (the distinguished motion-picture star, June Havoc), she had had a rich career in the theatre, always driven on to ever-greater successes by an over-ambitious and persevering mother.

The play opens in a little vaudeville house where several child acts are being rehearsed for a contest. The team of Baby Louise and Baby June are one of the attractions; their mother, Rose, seated in the back of the house, continually thunders out bits of advice to her children. When the three return home Rose prevails on her husband to provide funds with which to build a vaudeville act around June. That act "Baby June and Her Newsboys" tours the vaudeville circuit for a number of years.

We next encounter the girls and their mother backstage in Baton Rouge, Louisiana. Herbie, a salesman, saunters in. Now he gives the theatre manager advice to put a motion-picture into his show; now he urges Rose to allow her kids to grow up in a normal home under the normal guidance of parents. Something about Herbie impresses Rose that he has the makings of a good agent. She suggests that they team up to further June's career ("Small World"). Now the act reaches Akron, Ohio. It is Louise's birthday, and a celebration is taking place in the family's dingy hotel room. They eat chow mein and egg rolls; Louise gathers her gifts, one of which is a live pet lamb; and the talk is all about a new farm act Mama Rose has in mind for June. When Herbie appears, he brings with him Mr. Goldstone, who represents the Orpheum vaudeville circuit. His influence and connections are tapped.

When the act arrives in New York they contact T. T. Grantziger, a producer. In their hotel room Herbie tries to convince Rose to marry him, give up show business and relax the control she has over her daughters. But Rose has a single mind and a single purpose, and will permit nothing to deflect her. She promises Herbie she will marry him, but only when June's name finally goes up in lights on Broadway.

Grantziger signs the act for a week in one of his downtown theatres. He is convinced June can be a star, but only if she is willing to go through an intensive period of study and preparation, and break off the ties that bind her mother to her. Mother Rose, of course, would have nothing of this preposterous idea. June also lacks interest, but only because by now she has come to hate the stage, the act and the kind of life she has been forced to lead.

When the act comes to Buffalo one of its boys, Tulsa, confides to Louise his ambition to devise a song-and-dance routine of his own with some female partner and to tour cabarets and night-clubs. He improvises a few steps to demonstrate what he has in mind, using a broom as partner; then he tosses the broom away and dances with Louise ("All I Need is the Girl"). By the time the act arrives in Topeka it begins to fall apart. The boys are demanding more money. Worse still, June has deserted, having eloped with Tulsa. Mother Rose may be beaten, but she is surely not defeated. She will devise a *new* act, this time around Louise. And as she begins to make plans, she can hardly contain her excitement ("Everything's Coming up Roses").

The new act is not much better than the old one, nor is it much more successful. It goes from town to town playing in musty old theatres; even so, bookings are not plentiful. To endow a bit more sex appeal to the routine, Louise comes up with the idea of having the girls appear as peroxide blondes. Billed as "Rose Louise and Her Hollywood Blondes", the act is booked for a burlesque house in Wichita, Kansas, though the company is deluded into believing it is a legitimate theatre. When Rose discovers the truth she is determined to take her act away, but Louise reminds her that they have no place to go, and no money. Besides, Louise has no qualms whatsoever about appearing in burlesque. She now assumes the name of Gypsy Rose Lee, is taught a few burlesque routines by Tessie, a veteran, and goes on the stage as a strip-tease artist. The audience loves her. Louise becomes a burlesque star.

By now, Herbie is convinced that Rose will never marry him, or loosen her hold on Louise. He decides at last to go his own way, and bids Rose a permanent farewell. But Rose can think of only one thing: her daughter is a star; she has been signed as the stellar attraction for Minsky's Burlesque in New York. There, sensing her newly found power, Louise decides to break with her mother once and for all. Henceforth, as Louise tells her mother firmly, she, and she alone, will handle her own career in her own way without parental guidance; she suggests to her mother she find a new interest, like running a school for children. Rose is at first defiant, insisting she knows more about show business than anybody in the world. She mocks her daughter for being a burlesque queen and even taunts her by imitating some of her routines. But when the storm blows over Rose realises that Louise is right, after all. They part as friends; but as partners in show business they are through for good.

The Music Man

Books, Lyrics and Music by MEREDITH WILLSON, *based on a story by* MEREDITH WILLSON *and* FRANKLIN LACEY

Staged by MORTON DA COSTA

Choreography by OONA WHITE

First presented at the Majestic Theatre on 19th December, 1957, with Robert Preston as "Harold Hill" and Barbara Cook as "Marian".

PRINCIPAL CHARACTERS

HAROLD HILL
MARCELLUS WASHBURN
MARIAN PAROO
MRS. PAROO
MAYOR SHINN

The play is set mainly in the little town of River City, Iowa, in 1912, but the opening scene is on a moving train in which the dialogue of travelling salesmen and the musical background beautifully simulate the bouncy rhythm of the jogging train. Aboard this train the salesmen are discussing the selling powers of one Harold Hill, without realising that he is also one of the passengers. Harold Hill gets off at River City and comes to the centre of the town. There an old crony, Marcellus Washburn, tells him he will never be able to work his racket in this town: Harold Hill's racket is to go from town to town and influence its citizens to start a boys' band; then to abscond with the money the townspeople give him for the purchase of instruments and uniforms. Marcellus further informs Harold that the main obstacle in River City is the town librarian–music teacher, Marian Paroo, a "stuck up" sort of girl, who can be counted upon to see right through Harold's chicanery. Undaunted, Harold Hill proceeds to arouse the town's enthusiasm for starting a boy's band by pointing out the corrupt influence on their children of the local pool parlour ("Trouble"). When Marian Paroo appears Harold tries to win her over with his charm, but she brushes him off rudely. But Marian is a soft and sentimental girl, as she reveals by speaking to the stars ("Goodnight, My Someone").

Inside the gymnasium of Madison High School a patriotic tableau is being given; Mayor Shinn follows with an address. Harold Hill demands the attention of the audience and starts once again to expound his ideas about a boys' band until the kids become infected with his enthusiasm ("Seventy-Six Trombones"). Later the same evening, Harold Hill goes to the library to win Marian over to his cause. He tries to impress her by telling her he is a "professor" of music, a graduate of the Gary, Indiana University, in the gold medal class of 1905. But Marian tells him in no uncertain terms that he cannot mesmerise or hoodwink her the way he had done the rest of the townspeople. Thus brushed off unceremoniously, Harold consoles himself with the idea that, after all, he has no possible interest in a girl as prim and as conventional as Marian ("The Sadder But Wiser Girl"). Nevertheless, he makes another effort to win over Marian, by sneaking up to her desk at the library and trying to convince her that he is infatuated with her ("Marian the Librarian").

But all the while, Harold keeps alive the enthusiasm for his band project, and goes about town signing applicants. Cuttingly, Marian asks him why he does not use his gift to greater advantage at a carnival. She knows he is a fraud, and thus will have no traffic with him, even though she is not the kind of a girl who waits for a knight in shining armour ("My White Knight"). The reason Marian knows he is a fraud is because she has consulted the *Indiana State Educational Journal* and has discovered that Gary, Indiana University, had not even been founded in 1905. She is about to bring this information to the leading citizens of the town when Wells Fargo arrives with the musical instruments and uniforms, creating so much enthusiasm and excitement among her neighbours that she simply does not have the heart to disillusion them about Harold Hill. Indeed, now that Harold has, indeed, delivered the instruments and uniforms without absconding with the money she is much more sympathetic to him; and there is no question in her mind that he is a man of considerable charm. Her resistance to him is finally broken: She comes to tell Harold she is in love with him ("Till There Was You"). Now Harold Hill gives himself up completely to making a success of the boys' band. In a stirring finale the boys appear in full regalia and sound their first raucous notes as members of the town band.

Unsinkable Molly Brown

Book by RICHARD MORRIS
Music and Lyrics by MEREDITH WILLSON
Staged by DORE SCHARY
Choreography by PETER GENNARO

First produced at the Winter Garden on 3rd November, 1960, with Tammy Grimes as "Molly" and Harve Presnell as "Johnny Brown".

PRINCIPAL CHARACTERS

MOLLY TOBIN
JOHNNY (LEADVILLE) BROWN
PRINCE DE LONG

In the opening scene Molly Tobin and her brothers are indulging in a rough-and-tumble game in front of their shack in Hannibal, Missouri; the time is the beginning of the present century. Molly is a wild, uninhibited, backwoods girl, who immediately reveals that what she lacks in culture or polish she more than makes up for with spunk and vitality ("I Ain't Down Yet"). Some day, she announces confidently, she will be powerful and rich. In search of such a future, she goes on foot to Leadville, Colorado, and gets a job singing in the Saddle Rock saloon ("Belly Up to the Bar, Boys"). There she meets and falls in love with Johnny Brown, who before long proposes marriage to her ("I've Already Started"). On their wedding night Johnny mysteriously deserts his bride for a week, but when he returns he showers a fortune on her: $300,000 which he had received from the sale of a claim. When all this money is accidentally burned Johnny is only temporarily taken aback. He promises Molly he will find another claim and once again make her rich. He is as good as his word: Setting off for Colorado, he becomes one of the wealthiest miners there. At an elegant social event, to which Jimmy and Molly are invited, Molly introduces herself with her customary boisterousness ("Beautiful People of Denver"), but finds herself snubbed by her social peers. Undaunted, she announces a huge party in her own house. When nobody shows up, Molly decides to brush the dust of Colorado off her shoes and set off with Johnny for Europe.

A few years later, in one of Paris's salons, Molly is the darling of royalty. But, unable to forget how she had been snubbed in Colorado, she is determined to avenge herself. She invites all her highborn friends to come home with her, where Molly throws another gala party. This time the cream of Colorado society shows up and is impressed by the distinguished foreign visitors. But some of the less-desirable elements in Colorado break in on Molly's party, with the result that a rowdy free-for-all ensues. The party disintegrates into a fiasco, Molly decides to go back to Europe in the company of Prince de Long. Johnny, however, insists on staying home, where, after the passage of time, he begins to miss her sorely ("Soliloquy").

In Monte Carlo Prince de Long begs Molly to divorce Johnny and marry him ("*Dolce far niente*"). Molly hesitates, because she has not forgotten Johnny ("I May Never Fall in Love with You"). The memory of Johnny sends her back home. She books passage on the *Titanic* on its maiden voyage. When the *Titanic* collides with an iceberg on 14th April, 1912, sending almost fifteen hundred passengers to their death, the hardy Molly manages to survive, being one of the seven hundred carried to safety in lifeboats. Back in Colorado, she finds Johnny waiting for her, and her friends ready to salute her courage with the rousing refrain of her own song, "I Ain't Down Yet".

Fiorello !

Book by Jerome Weidman *and* George Abbott
Lyrics by Sheldon Harnick
Music by Jerry Bock
Staged by George Abbott
Choreography by Peter Gennaro

First produced at the Broadhurst Theatre on 23rd November, 1959, with Tom Bosley as "Fiorello", Patricia Wilson as "Marie", Howard da Silva as "Ben" and Ellen Hanley as "Thea".

Principal Characters

FIORELLO
NEIL
MARIE
BEN
THEA

The central character is one of the most colourful political figures in the history of New York City: Fiorello H. La Guardia. After being for many years a crusading lawyer dedicated to the underprivileged and the underdog, he became in 1932 New York's Mayor on a Fusion ticket. As Mayor he fought crime and corruption with the vigour and fearlessness that had characterised him previously as a lawyer and a Congressman. A rambunctious little man with unconventional ways and a spirited temper, La Guardia had a particular gift for stirring a hornet's nest. Colourful, dramatic, iconoclastic and very much of an individualist, La Guardia was a choice subject for stage treatment. The wonder is that it took the theatre so long to discover it.

Fiorello ! traces La Guardia's career only to the point where he reaches City Hall. It concentrates on his early years of law practice in Greenwich Village, his election to Congress, his service in the First World War and his two marriages. The prologue is the only place we encounter La Guardia as Mayor. He is reading the comic strips to children over the city radio station because a newspaper strike has deprived them of their comics.

Then the clock is turned back several decades. We are now in La Guardia's two-room law office in Greenwich Village just before the Second World War. Some shabbily dressed people are waiting to talk to him. Neil, his law clerk, laments that he never seems to find the time for clients able to pay their bills. Fiorello bursts into his office like a typhoon. With whirlwind energy he disposes of many items of business, including interviewing the clients come for his help. Suddenly he announces his intention of visiting Ben Marino, Republican leader of the 14th Congressional district, in order to try to get the nomination for Congress. His secretary, Marie, is taken completely by surprise, since she knows full well that no Republican has ever been elected to Congress in that district.

Fiorello and his secretary Marie come to Ben's political clubroom, where he is playing poker with some of his cronies. As they play, they discuss in song the similarity between the game of poker and that of politics ("Politics and Poker"). Fiorello interrupts them to suggest they nominate him for Congress. Ben—a level-headed realist who knows that no Republican can win the election—asks wearily, "Why not?"

Fiorello leaves Ben to join the striking workers of Nifty Shirtwaist picketing the factory. La Guardia convinces the working girls to leave the picket line and join him in a meeting at their headquarters. There he rallies them with a lecture about the oppressed working class, sweat shops and ruthless employers. He promises to bail them out if they get arrested, and to fight their cases in court. He also manages to extract a dinner date from one of the working girls, Thea.

Fiorello's campaign now gains momentum. His clerk, Neil, speaks for his candidacy on a street corner, and so does Thea. Fiorello goes now to one district, now to another, tackling local political problems and attacking Tammany Hall—now speaking in the Italian language, now in Yiddish.

La Guardia is elected. The scene shifts to his office in Washington, D.C. America is at war and Congressman La Guardia is a strong advocate of the Draft Act, since he feels this is the only democratic way to get Americans into uniform. Ben and Marie come down to try to convince him to change his mind about this act, since many constituents in New York are opposed to it. But Fiorello tells them with considerable heat that he represents *all* America, not just a corner of New York. After the Draft Act has been passed, La Guardia announces he has enlisted in the Army. A party is given in his honour at Ben's club room, where the guests dance to the strains of a nostalgic waltz ("Till Tomorrow").

A rapid series of montages, some staged, others shown through motion-pictures, carry La Guardia through the war.

When the second-act curtain rises ten years have elapsed. Fiorello is married to Thea. At his apartment we learn that Thea is not well; also that Fiorello is running for Mayor against James J. Walker. Fiorello tells Ben he is determined to crack down on all crooks, gamblers and political operators. Some of these disreputable characters meet at a party to discuss ways and means of getting rid of this uncontrollable candidate. They conceive a plan. They will have a thug turn in a false fire alarm and create so much havoc and confusion that nobody will notice that a load of paving rocks will be dumped from the roof on Fiorello as he makes a street speech. La Guardia gets wind of the plan. He stations Neil near the fire alarm, and posts the police on the roof. Neil abandons his fire-alarm post upon receiving word that Thea has just died. Thus the thugs are free to pull the alarm. But while the rocks are thrown at Fiorello, he miraculously goes unharmed.

Fiorello does not win the election from Walker. Undaunted, he sets himself the mission of defeating corrupt politicians in court, if he cannot do so in City Hall. He sets into motion the legal machinery whereby Tammany Hall is investigated by Judge Seabury. Ben Marino and his boys chortle with delight at this development, for their political rivals are thus being discredited. In their club they gleefully go through the motions of a travesty on the investigation, with Ben impersonating the various witnesses ("Little Tin Box").

The play now ends abruptly with a rapid forecast of what lies in the future for Fiorello. He runs for Mayor, this time on a Fusion ticket, and wins. He also finds personal happiness again through marriage with his faithful secretary, Marie.

Fiorello! was one of the top musical-comedy successes not only of the season but also of the decade. During its two-year run on Broadway it captured virtually every prize in sight, including the Pulitzer Prize, the Drama Critics Award and numerous Antoinette Perry and Donaldson Awards.

Bye Bye Birdie

Book by MICHAEL STEWART

Lyrics by LEE ADAMS

Music by CHARLES STROUSE

Staging and Choreography by GOWER CHAMPION

First produced at the Martin Beck Theatre on 14th April, 1960, with Dick Gautier as "Conrad Birdie", Dick Van Dyke as "Albert Peterson", Chita Rivera as "Rose Grant" and Paul Lynde as "Mr. MacAfee".

PRINCIPAL CHARACTERS

ALBERT PETERSON
ROSE GRANT
KIM MACAFEE
MR. MACAFEE
CONRAD BIRDIE

Bye Bye Birdie has found a good deal of not so innocent merriment in the younger generation, in the craze for Rock 'N' Roll, and in that apostle of Rock 'N' Roll music, Elvis Presley.

The play opens with a motion-picture montage of Conrad Birdie, singing idol of teenagers, whose resemblance to Elvis Presley cannot be regarded as accidental.

We are suddenly shifted to the office of the Almaelou Music Company in New York. Albert Peterson, its director, has just had the disconcerting news that his valuable property, Conrad Birdie, is about to be drafted into the Army. Peterson's secretary, Rose, is not sympathetic. She is convinced that this is the best thing that could happen to her employer, who can now give up the music racket, go back to college, become an English teacher and perhaps settle down with her in a little apartment. In spite of this argument, Rose has found a way to save Peterson, and pick up a good deal of publicity for Birdie. A name is picked at random from the Birdie Fan Club: Kim MacAfee, aged fifteen, sophomore at the Sweet Apple High. The gimmick is to have little Kim give Birdie his last kiss as a civilian.

In Sweet Apple, Ohio, we get a rapid look at teenagers monopolising telephones in seemingly endless and inconsequential conversations. In her home, teenager Kim confides in song how wonderful it would be to be a full-grown woman ("How Lovely to Be a Woman")—even while putting on an outrageously unfeminine attire of blue jeans, thick sweater and baseball cap. A telephone call now informs her she is the chosen of the select: Conrad Birdie is coming to Sweet Apple to get her good-bye kiss.

When Birdie arrives, he is, of course, welcomed by a crowd of cheering, hysterical, adulating kids. The crowd dissolves when Birdie is conducted to City Hall. Kim is left behind with Hugo, her boy friend. The latter is upset because his girl is about to kiss somebody else. Kim does everything she can to assure him that Hugo is the boy in her life ("One Boy"). At City Hall the Mayor gives a welcoming speech to Birdie, to the accompaniment of shrieks from the young fry. In return, Birdie gives his recipe for success ("Honestly Sincere").

The following morning the breakfast table in the MacAfee household is elaborately set in honour of their distinguished guest. When he appears he ignores all the food to partake of a can of beer. Then he quietly announces he is going back to sleep until lunchtime. Though at first considerably upset by this scene, Mr. MacAfee gets into the spirit of the whole thing when Albert Peterson tells him that Birdie and the whole MacAfee family will appear on the Ed Sullivan television show, where the historic kiss from Kim is to take place. That telecast brings the first act to a riotous conclusion. When Kim steps up to kiss Birdie an unrehearsed sequence breaks up this sentimental episode. Hugo rushes in front of the camera, denounces Birdie as a love thief and knocks him out with a well-aimed punch.

The second act, like the first, opens with a motion-picture montage. This one portrays all the possible means of disseminating news, from jungle drums to Wall Street tape.

Rose, in Kim's bedroom, is in a sentimental mood over Albert. All the same, she wonders what it is she has seen in him so long ("What Did I Ever See in Him?"). Then Rose announces that she is leaving Albert for good; at the same time little Kim decides to run away from home. As if all this were not enough to create havoc and confusion, Birdie now becomes temperamental. He is tired of the whole publicity stunt, will have nothing more to do with it and plans to step out on the town and meet some "chicks" ("A Lot of Livin' To Do"). Outside the house he meets Kim with valise in hand. He seizes her, insisting there are places for them to go and things for them to do; what he has in mind, specifically, is a quiet rendezvous in an ice-house. When Mr. MacAfee discovers that Kim has gone with Birdie he expresses both indignation over and puzzlement at the younger generation ("Kids").

Hugo and Rose have come to the town bar to forget their respective woes. Albert reaches her there by phone, pleading for her to listen to him ("Baby, Talk to Me"). Rose is stubborn, hangs up angrily and storms into an adjoining room, where a meeting of the Shriners, a fraternal organisation, is taking place.

She not only breaks up their discussions with her abandoned dancing, but also sends the members scurrying for cover under the tables. In short order, Albert appears looking for Rose, and Mr. and Mrs. MacAfee for their daughter, Kim. When they all learn that Kim and Birdie are in the ice house they proceed there —only to discover that each of the two youngsters is bored stiff with the other and trying to find a way of getting away. Thus, at long last Kim and Hugo reach reconciliation. So do Albert and Rose, who plan to get married in the town of Pumpkin Falls, Iowa, and settle down to small-town life. As for Birdie, after the developments of the preceding days, army life will surely seem like a vacation.

When *Bye Bye Birdie* slipped rather unobtrusively into New York it gave little promise of becoming a hit. The cast boasted no one who could be described as having box-office appeal. Dick Gautier, in the leading role, was making his first Broadway appearance, and Dick Van Dyke, another leading performer, had never before appeared in a musical comedy. The producer was unknown. So were the librettist, lyricist and composer, all of whom were here writing their first full-length musical. And though Gower Champion was famous as dancer and choreographer, he had never before served as a stage director. As John Chapman remarked in his review: "One of the best things about it is that practically *nobody* is connected with it." Yet, *Bye Bye Birdie* proved a smash success. It was riotously funny; it had considerable bounce and zest; it had some wonderfully imaginative dance routines; it had some good songs; and, most of all, it had the freshness, sparkle and impudence of youth. As Mr. Chapman said further: "It is the funniest, most captivating and most expert musical comedy one could hope to see in several seasons of showgoing."

APPENDIX

LONDON PRODUCTIONS OF AMERICAN MUSICALS

Robin Hood	Prince of Wales Theatre, 5 February 1891 (under the title *Maid Marian*)
El Capitan	Lyric Theatre, 10 July 1899
The Belle of New York	Shaftesbury Theatre, 12 April 1898
The Fortune Teller	Shaftesbury Theatre, 9 April 1901
The Red Mill	Palace Theatre, 1 May 1947
The Prince of Pilsen	Shaftesbury Theatre, 14 May 1904
Rose Marie	Drury Lane Theatre, 20 March 1925
The Vagabond King	Winter Garden Theatre, 19 April 1927
The Pink Lady	Globe Theatre, 11 April 1912
The Student Prince	His Majesty's Theatre, 3 February 1926
The Desert Song	Drury Lane Theatre, 7 April 1927
The New Moon	Drury Lane Theatre, 4 April 1929
Very Good, Eddie	Palace Theatre, 18 May 1918
Oh Boy!	Kingsway Theatre, 27 January 1919 (under the title *Oh Joy!*)
Sally	Winter Garden Theatre, 10 September 1921
Show Boat	Drury Lane Theatre, 3 May 1928
The Cat and the Fiddle	Palace Theatre, 4 March 1932
Music in the Air	His Majesty's Theatre, 19 May 1933
No, No, Nanette	Palace Theatre, 11 May 1925
Hit the Deck	London Hippodrome Theatre, 3 November 1927
Lady Be Good	Empire Theatre, 14 April 1926
Oh Kay!	His Majesty's Theatre, 21 September 1927
Peggy-Ann	Daly's Theatre, 27 July 1927
On Your Toes	Palace Theatre, 5 February 1937
Pal Joey	Prince's Theatre, 31 March 1954
Oklahoma!	Drury Lane Theatre, 30 April 1947
Carousel	Drury Lane Theatre, 7 June 1950
South Pacific	Drury Lane Theatre, 1 November 1951
The King and I	Drury Lane Theatre, 8 October 1953
Flower-Drum Song	Palace Theatre, 24 March 1960
The Sound of Music	Palace Theatre, 18 May 1961
Good News	Carlton Theatre, 15 August 1928
Anything Goes	Palace Theatre, 14 June 1935

Kiss Me Kate	Coliseum Theatre, 8 May 1951
Can-Can	Coliseum Theatre, 14 October 1954
Song of Norway	Palace Theatre, 7 March 1946
Wonderful Town	Prince's Theatre, 24 February 1955
West Side Story	Her Majesty's Theatre, 12 December 1958
Annie Get Your Gun	Coliseum Theatre, 7 June, 1947
Call Me Madam	Coliseum Theatre, 15 March 1952
Finian's Rainbow	Palace Theatre, 21 October 1947
Brigadoon	His Majesty's Theatre, 14 April 1949
My Fair Lady	Drury Lane Theatre, 30 April 1958
Guys and Dolls	Coliseum Theatre, 28 May 1953
The Most Happy Fella	Coliseum Theatre, 21 April 1961
Wish You Were Here	Casino Theatre, 10 October 1953
Fanny	Drury Lane Theatre, 15 November 1956
The Pajama Game	Coliseum Theatre, 13 October 1955
Damn Yankees	Coliseum Theatre, 28 March 1957
Plain and Fancy	Drury Lane Theatre, 25 January 1956
Bells Are Ringing	Coliseum Theatre, 14 November 1957
The Music Man	Adelphi Theatre, 16 March 1961
Bye Bye Birdie	Her Majesty's Theatre, 15 June 1961

INDEX

C

D

S

T

U

V

W